Shooter's Bible

NO. 93, 2002 EDITION

ARTICLES EDITOR
William S. Jarrett

SPECIFICATIONS EDITOR
Wayne van Zwoll

DESIGN & PRODUCTION DIRECTOR
Dominick S. Sorrentino

PRODUCTION & DESIGN
Lesley A. Notorangelo/D.S.S.

ELECTRONIC IMAGING
Lesley A. Notorangelo/D.S.S.

FIREARMS CONSULTANTS
Bill Meade, Frank Zito

COVER PHOTOGRAPHER
Ray and Matt Wells

PUBLISHER
Stephen McKelvain

PRESIDENT
Jeffrey K. Reh

VICE PRESIDENT & GENERAL MANAGER
Stephen Otway

PRODUCT MANAGER, FIREARMS
Joe Troiani

DIRECTOR OF BRAND MARKETING & COMMUNICATIONS
Stephen McKelvain

DIRECTOR OF SALES & STRATEGIC MARKETING
Jack T. Muety

ABOUT OUR COVER

The gun pictured on the front cover is a Bertuzzi Sidelock Over and Under shotgun in 20 gauge commissioned by New England Arms Corp. of Kittery Point, ME. The Bertuzzi Brothers make approximately twenty-five guns per year in the time-honored, handmade fashion. This gun has 28-inch barrels and is equipped with a hand-filled solid rib and double triggers. It is stocked in exhibition grade Turkish walnut with a hand-rubbed oil finish. The stock is fitted with a skeleton buttplate engraved with small gold flowers highlighting the exquisite craftsmanship by master engraver M. Dassa. The engraving is comprised of beautifully detailed bulino game scenes bordered by a semi-relief ornamental pattern highlighted with gold flowers and leaves. This elegant work blends both traditional scroll with gentle highlights in gold to create a masterwork in metal that breaks new ground in artistic gunmaking.

STOEGER PUBLICATIONS

New for 2001

LABRADOR RETRIEVERS, An Owner's Companion

by Anthony W. Jury

In this book, Anthony Jury briefly explores the history of the breed and interprets the breed standards before going on to consider all the practical aspects of owning a Labrador Retriever, from choosing a puppy, training and diet, to general management, health care and specific ailments, breeding, pregnancy and whelping. Fully illustrated with black and white photographs and line drawings, this book will prove to be invaluable, not only to the new owner but to all Labrador Retriever enthusiasts. A comprehensive yet accessible guide to a most remarkable breed.

GUN TRADER'S GUIDE
Twenty-fourth Edition

The Gun Trader's Guide has been the standard reference for collectors, dealers, shooters and gun enthusiasts since 1953. This 592 page edition provides complete updated specifications, dates of manufacture and current market average values for over 6,000 handguns, rifles and shotguns, both foreign and domestic. A complete index is provided for easy reference to all guns plus handy thumb tabs help readers find, identify and price firearms with ease.

HUNTING AMERICA'S WILD TURKEY

by Toby Bridges

Author of The Complete Book of Whitetail Hunting, Advanced Muzzle Loader's Guide and over 1,000 articles, Toby Bridges enlists the aid of several experts in the field of wild turkey hunting, each one offering his experience and techniques on luring these big birds within shotgun range. The author begins by introducing the major subspecies of wild turkeys, then leads his readers toward time-tested methods for bringing down these elusive gobblers. The National Wild Turkey Federation plays a major role throughout, along with "must have" information on scouting, shotgun loads, weather, clothing and the all-important turkey calls.

COWBOY ACTION SHOOTING

by Ron Harris

Author Ron "El Escritor" Harris tells the fascinating story of the Single Action Shooting Society (SASS), the fastest growing organization of its kind, with more than 30,000 members. Heavily illustrated - including many photos in full color - this book tells how these modern "cowboys and girls" have re-created the Old West, right down to the original (or reproduction) handguns, rifles and shotguns, with separate and colorful chapters on costumes, mounted action shooting, stages, gunleather, ammunition and just plain fun and festivities.

SPANISH HANDGUNS
The History of Spanish Pistols & Revolvers

by Gene Gangarosa, Jr.

Firearms expert Gene Gangarosa, Jr., has written the definitive work on the development of Spanish handguns from the late 19th century to 2001. His 320-page, heavily illustrated book features the story of the Basque people of northern Spain, whose skilled arms makers produced the famed Astra, Ruby (Llama) and Jo-Lo-Ar (Star) pistols. Serial numbers, slide markings, disassembly procedures, ammunition and much more are included.

HECKLER & KOCH
Armorers Of The Free World

by Gene Gangarosa, Jr.

In this, his 8th book (all published by Stoeger Publishing), author Gangarosa focuses on the role played by Heckler & Koch in arming the world's police and military forces. Embellished by more than 500 illustrations, this book provides brief histories and important developments of the major military handguns and rifles used throughout the world, plus machine guns, submachine guns and sporting rifles. A specifications table lists the length, weight, capacity, width and height of each entry. Among the more notable examples are the P9 series handgun, HK940 sporting rifle and FAL military rifle.

STOEGER PUBLICATIONS

Other Fine Publications From Stoeger

ADVANCED BLACK POWDER HUNTING *by Toby Bridges*
ADVANCED BOWHUNTING *by Roger Maynard*
AMERICA'S GREAT GUNMAKERS *by Wayne van Zwoll*
ANTIQUE GUNS: THE COLLECTOR'S GUIDE, *2nd Edition, by John Traister*
THE BEST OF HARLEY DAVIDSON
BOOK OF THE 22: THE ALL-AMERICAN CALIBER *by Sam Fadala*
A CENTURY OF HARLEY DAVIDSON *by Peter Henshaw*
CLASSIC BIKES *by Peter Henshaw*
COMPLETE BOOK OF FLYFLISHING *by Arthur Oglesby*
COMPLETE BOOK OF TROUT FLYFISHING *by Goran Cederberg,*
Steen Ulnito & Gunnar Johnson
THE COMPLETE FISH COOKBOOK *by Dan & Inez Morris*
COMPLETE GUIDE TO CLASSIC RIFLES *by Gene Gangarosa Jr.*
COMPLETE GUIDE TO COMPACT HANDGUNS *by Gene Gangarosa Jr.*
COMPLETE GUIDE TO MODERN RIFLES *by Gene Gangarosa Jr.*
COMPLETE GUIDE TO SERVICE HANDGUNS *by Gene Gangarosa Jr.*
COMPLETE BOOK OF WHITETAIL HUNTING *by Toby Bridges*
COMPLETE RELOADING GUIDE *by John & Bob Traister*
DECEIVING TROUT *by John Parsons*
DRESS 'EM OUT *by Captain James A. Smith*
FIBERGLASS ROD MAKING *by Dale P. Clemens*
FIREARMS DISASSEMBLY WITH EXPLODED VIEWS *by John Karns & John Traister*
FISH & SHELLFISH CARE & COOKERY *by Ken Oberrecht*
THE FLYTIER'S COMPANION *by Mike Dawes*

SPORTING COLLECTIBLES
by R. Stephen Irwin, M.D.

A "must-have" book for collectors of rare sporting treasures, from classic rifles and shotguns to books and posters, duck decoys, fish decoys, knives and more. In all, author/editor Irwin has included 14 different subjects, all illustrated with nearly 300 photos, many of them "one-of-a-kind."

THE WORKING FOLDING KNIFE
by Steven Dick

Steven Dick, the author, has worked with practically every form of folding knife currently available. If you need a handy little pocketknife, check out the chapter on "slipjointed folders under 4 inches closed". From the Classic American Barlow to exotic folders, *The Working Folding Knife* has it all.

THE FLYTIER'S MANUAL *by Mike Dawes*
FLYTYERS MASTERCLASS *by Oliver Edwards*
FN BROWNING: ARMORER TO THE WORLD *by Gene Gangarosa Jr.*
4X4 VEHICLES *by John Caroli*
GAME COOKBOOK, *New Revised Edition, by Geraldine Steindler*
GREAT SHOOTERS OF THE WORLD *by Sam Fadala*
GREAT TRUCKS *by David Hodges*
GUNSMITHING AT HOME: LOCK, STOCK & BARREL *by John E. Traister*
GUN TRADER'S GUIDE *24th Edition*
THE HANDBOOK OF FLYTYING *by Peter Gathercole*
HANDLOADER'S GUIDE *by Stanley W. Trzoniec*
HANDLOADER'S MANUAL OF CARTRIDGE CONVERSION *by John J. Donnelly*
HOW TO BUY AND SELL USED GUNS *by John Traister*
HUNTING AND SHOOTING WITH THE MODERN BOW *by Roger Maynard*
LEGENDARY SPORTING RIFLES *by Sam Fadala*
MODERN BERETTA FIREARMS *by Gene Gangarosa, Jr.*
MODERN SPORTING RIFLE CARTRIDGES *by Wayne van Zwoll*
P-38 AUTOMATIC PISTOL *by Gene Gangarosa, Jr.*
PETER DEANE'S GUIDE TO FLYTYING
RIFLE GUIDE *by Sam Fadala*
SHOOTER'S BIBLE 1940 REPRODUCTION
TAXIDERMY GUIDE, *3rd Edition, by Russell Tinsley*
TO RISE A TROUT *by John Roberts*
THE WALTHER HANDGUN STORY *by Gene Gangarosa Jr.*
THE WORKING FOLDING KNIFE *by Steven Dick*

STOEGER PUBLISHING COMPANY

Every effort has been made to record specifications and descriptions of guns, ammunition and accessories accurately, but the Publisher can take no responsibility for errors or omissions. The prices shown for guns, ammunition and accessories are manufacturers' suggested retail prices (unless otherwise noted) and are furnished for information only. These were in effect at press time and are subject to change without notice. Purchasers of this book have complete freedom of choice in pricing for resale.

Published by Stoeger Publishing Company
17603 Indian Head Highway, Suite 200
Accokeek, Maryland 20607

Library of Congress Catalog Card No.: 63-6200
International Standard Book No.: 0-88317-224-0

Manufactured in the United States of America

In the United States:
Distributed to the book trade and to the sporting goods trade by
Stoeger Industries
17603 Indian Head Highway, Suite 200
Accokeek, Maryland 20607
Tel: 301-283-6300 Fax: 301-283-6986

Contents

FORWARD

Shooter's Bible 2002

FEATURE ARTICLES

For the most part, humor has been an infrequent guest in our annual mix of topics on these pages. It's about time we corrected any impressions among our readers that we're a humorless bunch. Take a look, for example, at our lead piece—*Elk Hunting for Turkeys*—by our Specifications Editor and longtime contributor, Wayne van Zwoll. You'll be rolling in the aisles over Wayne's description of his first wild turkey hunt. You'll also learn a thing or two about how to hunt these elusive birds.

Next Sam Fadala, sets his sights on those little lumps of metal up front. In *Sights of Iron*, he traces the history of iron sights right up to the present. As Sam concludes, iron sights are still with us for one big reason—they work! We've also called on Ken Horowitz to bring us up to speed on the subject of metallic shooting. His article explains the do's and don'ts of competing with those elusive steel targets using pistols and revolvers instead of rifles.

The next article addresses a lapse on our part: a piece by and about women. Marcia Murdock jumped at the opportunity to describe how, why and where the modern woman hunts big game in her own fashion. More and more hunters on the distaff side have been encouraged to join the men on hunting expeditions—and doing it with great success, thank you.

In the previous edition of Shooter's Bible, we introduced Joseph Greenfield, Jr., whose humorous article on training and hunting with bird dogs caused many readers to chuckle. In *Why Hunt Birds?*, Dr. Greenfield, a prominent heart surgeon at Duke University Medical Center, continues his friendly assault on those obstreperous hounds who seem bent on making his life miserable. Anyone who's ever chased a quail will identify with the doctor's good-natured musings on the subject.

Next in our lineup of stars is Stan Trzoniec, a 25-year veteran outdoor writer and photographer. In *Hunting the Wily Woodchuck*, he describes the various "perfect" loads and rifles he has used in hunting woodchucks and other small game. As Stan points out, varmint hunters have it made, not only in their choice of rifles, but cartridges and optics as well.

Last—but definitely not least—is Toby Bridges, another steady contributor, who introduces the next generation of muzzleloaders personified by the new Savage Model 10ML. This in-line ignition muzzleloader has become the first production muzzleloader ever designed, engineered and built to shoot modern smokeless propellants. Toby explains how it all works.

In *Guns On The Net* Wilf Pyle, our good friend north of the border, brings us up-to-date on modern technology in the world of hunting, loading and all manner of outdoor gear. He truly believes the Internet has changed our lives and will continue to do so. It behooves us all to hear what Wilf has to say about this sometimes difficult but essential topic. He also supplies a list of firearms manufacturers on the Net, from Armlite to Wilson Combat. Many other "www" listings can be found in the Directory of Manufacturers and Suppliers, beginning on p. 557. Immediately following Wilf Pyles' piece is our Manufacturers' Showcase. We invite all firearms-related readers to browse through its pages.

SPECIFICATIONS

You'd think that after more than a century of producing lever-action rifles, single-action handguns and pump-action shotguns, American armsmakers would go on to something new. It's a credit to Walter Hunt, Sam Colt and John Browning that these mechanisms remain popular. Truly, there *has* been progress.

Just turn these pages. Modern rifles and shotguns may have the look and feel of guns built decades ago, but they're made of sterner stuff, and most can be counted on to deliver better accuracy. Fit, finish and function? Well, the old-timers knew how to make a slick revolver and smooth-shucking pump and lever guns. Unfortunately, the care to detail lavished on utilitarian guns in bygone days is prohibitively expensive now. You won't get the warm feel for an entry-level synthetic-stocked rifle like the new Remington 710 that you might have had from a Remington 721 fifty years ago. On the other hand, the 710 shoots well, and its stock is darned near indestructible.

You'll find more horsepower in these pages than appeared in *Shooter's Bible* when I was a youngster. Remington continues to expand its Ultra Mag line, adding a 7mm and a .375 to its brawny .300 and .338 cartridges. Winchester has followed John Lazzeroni's lead in announcing a stubby rimless round with magnum zip. Imagine revving over 3000 feet per second from a 180-grain .308 bullet in a short action! Capitalizing on its hugely popular .45-70 Guide Gun, Marlin announced a .450 Magnum cartridge for its ported, short-barreled Model 1895. And Weatherby has chambered its lightweight Mark V for the potent .338-06.

You'll find more muscle in handgun rounds too, with Ruger's new .480. And shotshells shorter than 3 inches seem undernourished these days. Turkey and goose loads in 3?-inch hulls are no longer oddities. Heavy loads of hard lead and tungsten-iron shot launched at 1400 fps are sure to get your shoulder's attention! But Federal's buffered Power Pattern System, with a layer of steel shot over tungsten-iron, is even tougher on the birds. Recoil-shy? New lighter target loads break clays without wrecking your clavicle. The venerable Western brand has appeared again on affordable shotgun ammo from Winchester.

Our 2002 *Shooter's Bible* announces what's new in loading components too, like the Swift Scirocco hunting bullets that combine a sleek shape with deep penetration after upset. You'll find complete bullet lists for Barnes, Berger, Nosler, Hornady, Sierra, Speer—even Woodleigh. The powders that drive 'em are here as well, with the latest in handloading equipment from Dillon, Hornady, Lyman, Redding and RCBS. For those who buy ammunition over the counter, we offer a ballistics section the likes of which you won't find anywhere else. Here in one easy-to-read list are all the commercial loads for your favorite rifle cartridge—with data on bullet speed, energy and drop.

Shooter's Bible also features iron sights and scopes. You'll find new rangefinding reticles from Burris and a new LPS scope from Leupold. Stateside companies are getting a vigorous challenge from overseas. Scopes made in Japan are much better than they used to be: sturdier, brighter, with finer resolution. In fact, some lenses used by American and European optics firms come from the Far East. Austria's Kahles brand has charged ahead with its new Kahles 2-7x36, which may be the best bargain in a practical big game scope to come along this year. Zeiss has fielded a more affordable line of variable scopes, while Aimpoint's 7000 offers the latest in Red Dot technology.

All told, lots of new products appear in this year's Shooter's Bible, plus an expanded custom gun section so you can see what's happening outside the factories. As always, it's been a pleasure bringing you this annual compendium of shooting equipment. We hope you enjoy it!

– *William S. Jarrett, Articles Editor*
– *Wayne van Zwoll, Specifications Editor*

Articles

Elk Hunting
For Turkeys

By Wayne van Zwoll

"A tom turkey can see you blink when he's not lookin' and you're not blinkin'," said the round-bellied farmer in the faded coveralls. He rocked back on his heels, scratched chalk whiskers and squinted from beneath a seed corn hat. "Breathe hard, and he's gone."

It was the same message I'd gotten from everyone. You couldn't move at all. To kill a turkey you had to make like a stump. In fact, the more you became like a stump, the better. If the ants went to work on you, the thing to do was act stumplike and let them.

"I don't like to sit still for more than 20 minutes or so," I said tentatively, quadrupling my all-time record for staying in one spot. Twenty minutes could seem like the Pleistocene. Longer, if you had to sit in rain or cold wind.

"Twenty minutes?" The farmer sounded impressed.

"Well, yes," I answered modestly. "But I wasn't always so patient."

The silence that followed could have been mistaken for reverence. But then somebody in the back of the cabin snickered. There was high wheeze, as if a balloon had been stretched too tight. "Lawsy, did you hear that? Twenty minutes!" Suppressed cackling, then breathless shrieks. I saw a man go down, holding his side as if shot. Another doubled over in his wicker chair. Tears came to his eyes as he tried to get a breath. "Haw!" yelped another. Then he too prostrated himself on the table, scattering a so-so hand of poker, "Tw-twenty!" he gasped. "Oh my goodness! Tw-tw-twen- Haw!" and he buried his head in his hands and shook. Two men were on their backs now, kicking like

FULL CAMO MAY NOT BE ENOUGH WHEN THER'ES NO COVER. A BLIND WOULD HELP CONCEAL GUN MOVEMENT.

WORKING THE SLATE. THE SIMMONS SCOPE ON THIS MOSSBERG TURKEY GUN HELPS CENTER THE PATTERN.

beetles, while another pair stumbled for the door. They appeared to be choking.

My initial reaction had been to dial 911 and hail the paramedics pronto. But I'd learned on my first trip to Texas that customs were different down here. I wasn't sure I had a handle on this yet. Not that I was new to hunting camps–I'd seen such strange behavior before. But usually there was a reason. I'd have to sort it out.

Later one of the men came up to my bunk and apologized for his outburst. "No, no, no. It wasn't anything you said," he assured me. "It's my hearing. Too much shotgunning. I thought you said," and suddenly he bent double again, straining to hold it back. "I thought you said…." He was hyperventilating now, so I put down the book I'd been reading. But he waved me away from the phone, howling, "Twen- twen- twenty minutes! Ha!" Tears

streamed down his red cheeks as he pushed himself to his feet and tottered off, shaking his head. "I thought you said, twen- twenty….Oh mercy! mercy!"

The hunters at turkey camp near Uvalde last spring were less demonstrative, probably because I let it slip that there was nothing I'd rather do than sit with Mother Texas for an ice age waiting for a turkey to walk into shotgun range. I don't lie very effectively, though, and I noticed some concern. Steve Packer, who'd hosted lots of turkey hunters, said I would get a good spot. His Rocky Top Outfitters crew would help me shoot my first turkey.

In the woods well before dawn next morning, my guide, a quiet, wiry man in his thirties, gently told me we might have to "set awhile." He watched me as might a physician administering a potent new drug. When there was no reaction, he got bolder. "We might have to set for a piece." That's

DECOYS ARE ANOTHER TOOL FOR TURKEY HUNTERS PATIENT ENOUGH TO "SET A PIECE."

Texan for Pleistocene. The words have a common root, "piece" coming on late in the Pleistocene era, when Texans began hunting turkeys and couldn't abide words requiring lip movement in the blind. I could see this young man was probably cursing himself for having drawn the short straw and getting the greenhorn. I didn't want to make life difficult for him by letting on that I had no intention of waiting a "piece" or a Pleistocene for a turkey.

In new country you can sit still longer because there are things you haven't seen before. You wait on dawn, watching black become shades of gray, listening to sounds you haven't heard, smelling different smells, vigilant for movement that's unlike movement you're used to. After five minutes, you realize that you have been there a long time.

I was determined to show some measure of professionalism. After all, I too had guided hunters —mainly to elk. How much more elusive could a turkey be? Slowly, I shoveled a few handfuls of dry leaves up around my white cotton socks, which I now realized would gleam like semaphores when the sun came up.

My outfit was first-class: Realtree Advantage camouflage from head to—well, pant cuffs. I did not own a pair of camouflage boots. In warm weather, I seldom wore anything but jogging shoes and crew socks, even in the Rockies. As a couple of distant gobblers opened up, however, it came

to me that boots might be a better plan. When the chiggers reached my ankles, boots began to make even more sense. Larry Weishuhn had told me their local name: "Red bugs." I was soon coming up with some of my own.

But then a turkey gobbled close by, on the south side of a great dry wash that we faced from the north. At 150 yards the bird strutted into view. I forgot about time, then, and watched. He gobbled back when my amigo expertly worked the call. But he did not come closer. Many minutes later he was still strutting, still gobbling. Meanwhile, sunshine had swept in under the trees, and the day was heating up. We would not have long to wait.

REALTREE ADVANTAGE CAMOUFLAGE HELPS THIS HUNTER AND HIS SHOTGUN REMAIN UNDETECTED.

THE GUN IS ONLY USEFUL WHEN IT'S POINTED AT A TURKEY. BE READY TO SHOOT BEFORE A GOBBLER COMES IN!

The turkey eventually wandered back the way it had come, into heavy timber. My bladder was about to burst and I suggested with universal hand signals that I didn't want that to happen and would have to stand up. He obliged me, as any guide would, by urinating too, doing so with subtle but well-rehearsed reticence. The unspoken message: "I could easily have sat here until the end of geologic time, but since you, Greenhorn client, can't sit still for more than *twenty minutes*, I might as well join you."

By this time the turkey was climbing in thicker timber. Foliage hid our quarry, which meant there was foliage hiding us. What were we doing standing here? The first few yards of our sneek were uncomfortable because this was definitely poor form. Keeping one thick cedar between us and the gobbler, we managed to tip-toe across the riverbed. Then we hunkered behind the cedar, the last of our

A REST FOR A SHOTGUN? YOU BET! A TREE STEADIES YOUR NERVES TOO, AND OFFERS CONCEALMENT.

cover. Working the call, my friend could not bring the bird closer. The last time he clucked, there was no response.

Though it is a textbook sin, sometimes you just have to look. At least, that's what I do when the elk get quiet. So I peeked around the cedar, certain that the turkey knew something was up, and certain too that the bird was at the edge of my range. I didn't want to shoot over 40 yards.

The turkey saw me about when I saw the turkey, and I hissed something urgent to my companion. A precocious chap, he gobbled immediately, and the bird stopped cold in the middle of a long stride. I had the crosswire of my Simmons scope "where pretty meets ugly," as Larry had advised, and a 2-ounce bucket of number 5's from Federal's $3^{1}/_{2}$-inch Premium turkey load suddenly drove the bird to the ground. He did a lot of flopping, which apparently is normal. It was my first turkey ever. And a record for sitting still.

"We paced it at 39 yards," I said at the interrogation. It had been the only bird killed that morning. Of course it was a gift. I didn't point out that moving in on the bird had a lot to do with getting the shot.

That same afternoon other, more experienced hunters called in turkeys. The next morning brought more birds to bag. I got the details on that episode: how the evening before two hunters had located a roost, then engineered a dawn ambush and executed it so perfectly that the pair got two toms from one

TEXAS OFFERS PLENTY OF HUNTING FOR RIO GRANDE TURKEYS. UVALDE COUNTY YIELDED THIS GOBBLER.

SMALL SPRING-TIME STREAMS CAN FLOOD LATER IN THE YEAR. IN APRIL THESE BOTTOMS HAVE TURKEYS!

HUNTING IN PAIRS—ONE HUNTER CALLING, ONE SHOOTING—CAN PAY OFF IN ANY TURKEY COUNTRY.

group of birds and could have had three. That was how it should be done.

My second morning brought no action. I went out with another hunter, and we waited a long, long time without seeing a turkey. Then I told him I wanted to still hunt back to the camp. He looked at me in a queer way, then shrugged and ambled off to his rendezvous with the guide in a pickup.

I walked as if I were hunting elk: slowly. I didn't glass because the brush was quite thick, and the birds nearby were the ones I needed to see. Only a few yards along a Jeep track, I spotted a young tom easing through some weeds. Another turkey followed. I let them vanish, then sprinted 10 steps to get within 40 yards. Two bigger toms crossed

the track slowly. I followed them with my scope, not wanting to fill my last tag with a long shot. Easing up to the weed patch, I spied a bright red turkey's head as it periscoped up to have a look at me. The bird did not like its options, and it sprinted downhill, taking wing as it cleared the weeds. Two more toms chose that way out. I never saw the fourth.

Later I sneaked to within 20 yards of a lone hen, returning to camp with only stories. But I'd had fun still hunting, and the next morning tried it again, poking along a sand track, watching the graceful flight of whitetails as they bounded off, flags waving crazily. In mid-morning, coming around a bend in the trail, I glimpsed through a

small opening the form of a turkey's head. It hadn't been much of a look – really not a look at all. But big game hunting had taught me the value of noting tiny details out of place, of believing yourself when you sense something's amiss.

So I stopped and stayed very still. A couple of deer sailed past. I did not move. Then, slowly, I raised the Mossberg and very, *very* slowly peeked around a bush. I found myself looking squarely into the beak of a red-headed tom. I didn't dare move the muzzle even the few inches needed to center him in the scope. He eyed me for a milli-

SIMMONS SCOPE, MOSSBERG SHOTGUN, FEDERAL 3.5-INCH MAGNUM 5S—A DEADLY COMBINATION.

LARRY WEISHUHN USED A MOSSBERG SHOTGUN AND FEDERAL MAGNUM LOADS TO DOWN THIS GOBBLER.

second, decided he didn't like what he saw and disappeared. As he did so, I eased the crosswire to where he'd been and waited, hoping he – or another turkey – would fill the spot.

Again, I was lucky. Another tom poked his head around the bush to give his companion a second opinion. The load of 5s hurled him to the ground.

Back at camp, I asked why more hunters didn't still hunt when the gobblers refused to cooperate. Here, on the tail of the mating season, only expert callers had brought toms in, and we were still several birds from a perfect score.

"It's not safe," was the consensus. "You stalk a gobble, and it may be another hunter."

"Surely you must see the turkey to shoot it," I argued. "In fact, you have to sex it, and a lot of hunters want to see beard. You can't very well shoot a hunter if you tick through that checklist."

My mentors shrugged. "Not every turkey hunter is so patient. Even some who sit for a long time on stand can jump to conclusions when they hear

JIM NIEMIEC SHOT THIS OUTSTANDING RIO GRANDE GOBBLER NEAR ELKTON, OREGON WITH AN ITHACA PUMP.

brush rustle, especially if they've coaxed a gobble from that direction. It ain't the way we think sportsmen *should* act; nobody *should* shoot unless they have the bead on an honest-to-gosh tom." Unfortunately, they concluded, the risk of an accident rises when hunters are prowling about the woods instead of sitting still.

This explanation left me a bit deflated. I'd thought sneaking up on a bird that in its sleep could see you bat an eye behind a tree made for a fine job of still hunting. Now it seemed improper form. My kills lost some of their luster. Perhaps to acknowledge my first-day Pleistocene vigil, one veteran winked and said that "anybody what can sneak on a turkey's got a sneak like a weasel." It sounded complimentary.

A lot of turkey guides will discourage you from moving to a tom. Even on a private ranch, where you know about the other hunters, sitting is still correct form. So I wasn't surprised later, in a turkey camp in Oregon's Coast Range, to hear another guide cackle when I proposed still hunting. But then he added: "You can't sneak on a turkey."

Now, "can't" is a strong word. If he'd said I can't sit more than five minutes without fidgeting or can't work a slate call without flushing turkeys half

THIS TEXAS GOBBLER FELL TO A 39-YARD SHOT AFTER WAYNE SNEAKED 100 YARDS ACROSS OPEN GROUND.

a section away, I would have conceded the point. But can't still hunt? Land sakes, I'd be a sorry hunter indeed if I couldn't slip to within 40 steps of an Oregon turkey! The more I thought about it, the less I wanted to have a tom called into my lap. The challenge of cat-footing my way to a shot became suddenly more compelling when I was told that it couldn't be done.

So on the second evening, when we spotted a couple of toms and a hen in a small hillside meadow below timber, it was all I could do to keep from bounding after them. That wouldn't do, however. I had to think about the broader picture. This guide had tried hard to bring a turkey to me and had

THE AUTHOR USED A BENELLI SHOTGUN WITH FEDERAL 3-INCH MAGNUM 5X TO TAKE THIS OREGON BIRD.

been a fine companion in the woods. Jim Niemiec had invited me to share his turkey hunt here. The Big K Ranch, west of Roseburg near Elkton, was a spectacular place, spilling from the hills into a remote crook of the Umpqua River and surrounded by patchwork timber alive with turkeys. Proper etiquette was to do what the locals suggested. That would also give me the best odds. Still, those turkeys had looked approachable.

"Want to swing up into the forest?" asked Bwana. "We have about an hour left." I grinned

FULLY OUTFITTED IN REALTREE ADVANTAGE CAMOUFLAGE, THIS HUNTER WENT UNNOTICED UNTIL TOO LATE!

my consent. And that is how, as dusk was finishing behind thick clouds, we found ourselves on the back side of the hill where we'd seen those turkeys. He looked at me and read my mind. "You want to give 'em a try?" I was already stuffing 12-bore shells into the Benelli.

They wouldn't be an easy project, even if they were still in the meadow. The only cover I had was the curve of the hill, which meant the turkeys could see me before I spotted them. I eased forward, hoping the sun, wherever it was above the sky's gray belly, would hang around a few more minutes.

It was just good luck that I spied the tom before he saw me. Sixty yards, I guessed. I waited until the hill would give me another few steps, then closed the range to 50. That's when I saw the hen. She was in the open below me; the toms, now hidden, would likely keep climbing. Light was fading fast. I decided to let the hen spot me. Perhaps she'd leave without detonating the birds I was after.

When she pegged me, she putted and sprinted hard for the timber. I scrambled upslope, hoping to take advantage of a moment of confusion. I spied red heads over the curve of the hill, eased to one knee and brought the lightweight autoloader to my shoulder. Then I crept forward to a bush and eased upright, half expecting the birds to be gone. But there they were, at attention, 35 steps away. They had spotted me; there wasn't much time. Alas, they were so close together that a shot would have hit both! I waited. Short seconds later the right-hand bird decided to split, and I triggered a 3-inch load of Federal 5s into the other.

"Well, you showed me." He didn't say I had been lucky (I had). Or that I couldn't do it tomorrow (probably not). Or that the bird was a big jake, not a tom (you can't tell when you see only the head against the sky). He could have told me that Realtree Advantage must be darned effective camo to mask a moving hunter (it is), but that to become a genuine turkey addict I'd have to learn to sit still and call the birds. He could have reminded me to forego white socks next time out—and yes, to put on that face mask! He didn't say any of those things, because he was a gentleman.

Or maybe because he knew a hopeless case when he saw one. **SB**

Sights Of Iron

By Sam Fadala

A LITTLE LUMP of metal up front, centered on the barrel, nothing to line up with—that was the early "iron sight." It was about as precise as reading tea leaves to tell the future. Still, it was a beginning. Better were certain crossbow sights of an earlier era, including apertures; but crude aiming devices matched the smoothbore military muskets at the time, which was nothing to shout about. The ancient longbow could put a dozen matched arrows into a fist-sized group at 50 paces, something easily provable today with a shooting machine. Meanwhile, haphazard loading techniques and the absence of uniform projectiles translated into bucket-sized patterns at the same distance for the musket. As accuracy escalated, the need for a better way to direct bullets to the target grew exponentially. Arrows were directed from bows *reflexively*, through hand-eye coordination, but aiming a gun the same way was a disaster. Despite what some believed to be true snap-shooting, the marksman simply concentrated his view on the target.

A gun firing a single projectile must put that one bullet on a path dictated by sights, no matter how crude those sights may be. There's the parabola to consider: the arched path traced by a bullet from muzzle to target. Through experience alone, some shooters learned how much "Arkansas elevation" to take at longer ranges, as well as "Kentucky windage" to correct for those bullets that strayed left or right of the mark. Those old-timers who said, "I never look at my sights; I just up and shoot," were definitely looking at their sights. Call it second nature. Meanwhile, rank and file warfare made for big targets—not a lone soldier, but a whole line of men.

Even so, the Brown Bess musket, with its lame excuse for sights, cost the British Red Coats innumerable defeats because their guns lacked a repeat-able aiming device. The British military discovered that when their soldiers faced American sharpshooters in Louisiana. There, at the Battle of New Orleans, some 10,000 British troops under General Pakenham took on General Jackson, who led half that many men. The colonists were not hiding behind trees and rocks, as some have proposed. Both sides fought in the rank and file style. It was later reported that "as they [the British] advanced to the charge they were killed by the hundreds, yet did not falter. When within 200 yards of the American line, the Kentucky and Tennessee riflemen, deadly shots, four ranks deep, fired line by line. The slaughter was terrible, but the British pressed on to the very parapets."

In that battle, the British lost 700 killed, 1,400 wounded and 500 prisoners. The Americans suffered only eight dead and 13 wounded. It was straight-shooting that did it—accurate rifles *with* good sights.

THIS SEMI-BUCKHORN REAR SIGHT ON A LYMAN PLAINS RIFLE INDICATES A COMPLETELY "CLEAN" NOTCH THAT IS RECTANGULAR IN SHAPE AND HIGHLY VISIBLE. MATCHED WITH A BLADE FRONT SIGHT, THE SIGHT PICTURE IS QUITE EFFECTIVE.

Alignment is the operative word with regard to open iron sights. The eye accommodates three planes: front sight, rear sight, and target. Not as popular nowadays as in the past, proper *fixed* iron sights are still capable of amazingly close bullet clustering. Early fixed types were admittedly crude, little more than a blip of metal up front, plus a lump and a slit at the rear. Fixed sights for Ken-tucky/Pennsylvania long guns and pistols, however, were quite a different story. I own a Roy-land Southgate flintlock with fixed sights (*fixed* meaning no built-in device to affect adjustment, such as a ladder under a moveable rear sight). The front sight is dovetailed directly into the top barrel flat about an inch behind the muzzle. The rear, a plain metal fixture with a V-slit, is attached dove-tail-style about eight inches in front of the pan. Lying very low on the barrel, these seemingly archaic sights provide an extremely clear picture. The gunsmith who made my flintlock set the sights so that a .42 caliber round ball would strike dead center at 75 yards when driven by a nominal powder charge.

Most fixed iron sights found on old-time long guns actually were not "fixed." One or both were set in a dovetail notch to allow for windage, with the front sight filed *down* or replaced with a taller one for changes in elevation. The rear sight was

THIS REAR SIGHT IS SET IN A DOVETAIL NOTCH TO FACILITATE MOVEMENT LEFT OR RIGHT IN ORDER TO CHANGE WINDAGE (LEFT-RIGHT POINT OF IMPACT ON THE TARGET). THE SIGHT CANNOT, HOWEVER, BE MOVED UP OR DOWN TO ALTER THE VERTICAL POINT OF IMPACT ON THE TARGET.

drifted to the left to make the next bullet strike left, or it moved to the right to change the point of impact in that direction. The front sight was filed down to bring the group higher on the target, or a higher sight installed to lower point of impact. Meanwhile, fixed irons found on cap 'n' ball revolvers, such as the still-popular (as a replica) Model 1858 Remington, provided far less adjustment cap-ability. The front sight of this revolver is integral to the barrel. There's no dovetail notch in

THIS WILLIAMS REAR SIGHT ENCOMPASSES BOTH WINDAGE AND ELEVATION ADJUSTMENTS.

which to slide the sight. True, it can be filed down, but making it taller requires more metal, not replacement. Bending left or right is also possible— left to direct bullets to the right, and right to move the group left. There is no rear sight, but rather a long groove in the top strap that serves as one, more or less. Colt revolvers of the same era utilized a similar front sight, but with a notch cut into the hammer nose acting as a rear sight with the hammer cocked.

The *tube sight* continues to confuse shooters in this new century because it resembles a scope without lenses. It's a true iron sight, exactly what the name infers: a metal tube. One of its main purposes was to act as a shade, denying direct sunlight on the metal sights within the tube itself. Logic suggest that the tube sight (and sometimes barrel length) was a forerunner of the scope. Instead of iron

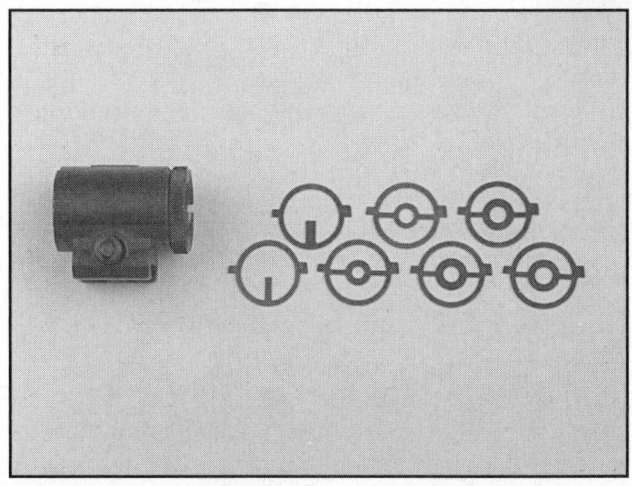

A HOODED FROM SIGHT INCLUDES REPLACEABLE INSERTS THAT PROVIDE SEVERAL DIFFERENT CONFIGURATIONS.

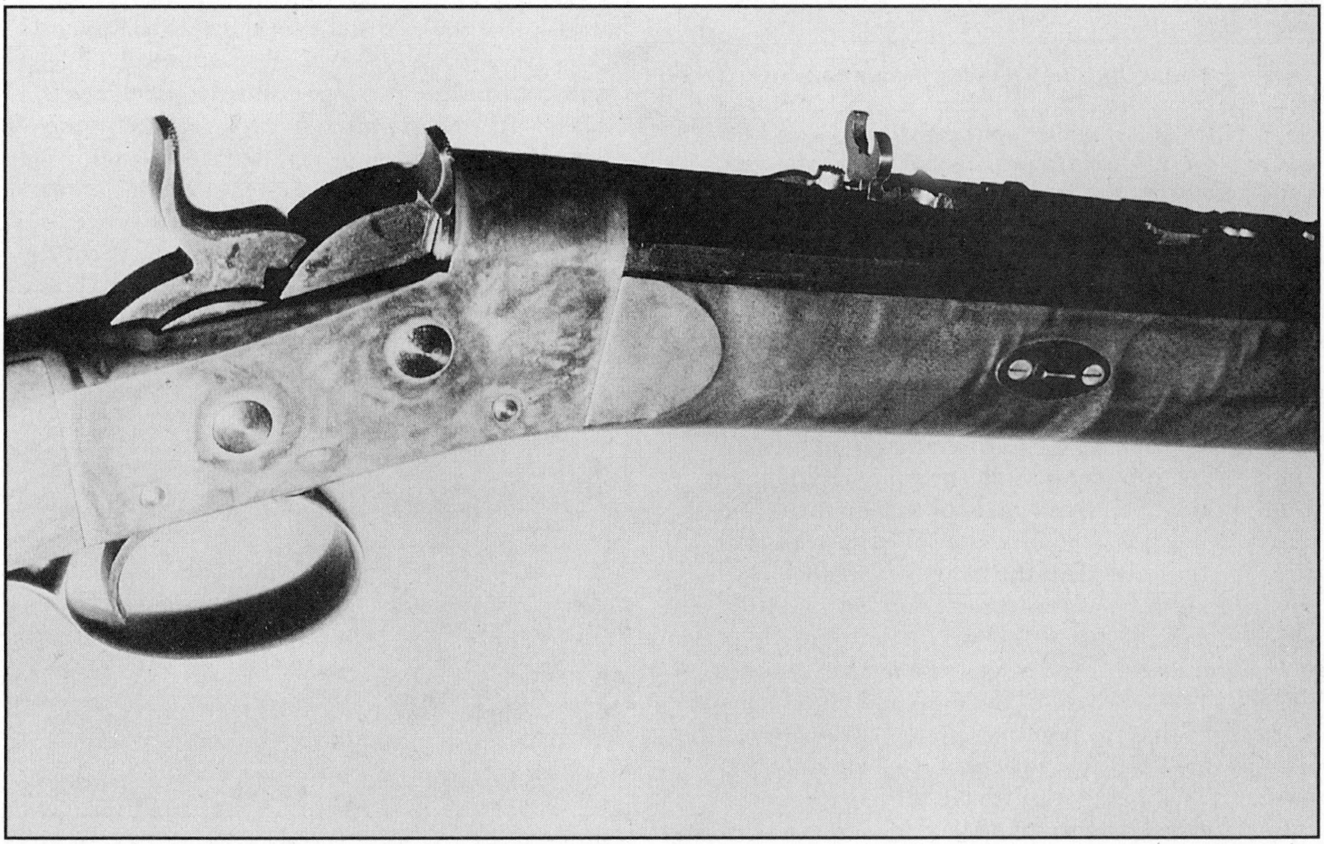

FOR THE SHOOTER, THIS BUCKHORN STYLE REAR SIGHT APPEARS AS TWO HORNS. THE PROJECTIONS ARE ACCUSED OF HIDING THE TARGET AND ADDING NOTHING TO THE SIGHT PICTURE ITSELF; BUT IN FACT BUCKHORN SIGHTS HAVE BEEN USED EFFECTIVELY FOR A LONG TIME AND REMAIN VIABLE.

THIS VERNIER TANG REAR SIGHT INCORPORATES SEVERAL PEEP HOLES. SHOOTERS CAN SELECT THE ONES THEY CONSIDER CORRECT FOR WINDAGE AND ELEVATION CHANGES. THE LOWER HOLES ARE FOR LONGER SHOTS, THE LEFT AND RIGHT HOLES FOR WINDAGE CORRECTIONS.

sights, why not install in the tube the right number of lenses in the correct order? Voilá! A scope was born. Logical, yes, but probably hogwash. Terrestrial telescopes long predated tube sights. It follows that someone had the idea of mounting an existing scope on a firearm, rather than putting lenses into a tube sight. Still, the tube sight remains a link in the iron sight's chain of development. Not only was it adjustable, it isolated the shooter's view so as to concentrate on the target while blocking superfluous light waves. An eye cup with a little hole—a peep, if you will—was one option. Up front, you might install a globe, a simple round metal ball on a pedestal. The peep and globe were so effective that the combination remains with us, witness those black powder shoots where heavy target rifles graced with metallic tube sights create surprisingly stingy groups.

Variations in iron sights number in the hundreds, but the next reasonably defined option, following the fixed open iron, is the modern

adjustable open iron. Normally, its front sight is stationary, although it often is moveable in a dovetail notch, with the rear *fully* adjustable (for both windage and elevation). The adjustable iron can be accomplished in a number of ways. A notched piece of metal, called a ladder, can be used to move the rear sight up or down. Or the rear sight may be hinged, allowing the entire unit to lift off the barrel. Another possibility is a series of leaf sights, with each little plate set at a different height for different ranges. Almost a standard now is the *folding rear sight* with a faceplate that's adjustable up or down, left or right, and often moveable via screws. Good as it is, this modern open iron sight holds no advantages over those found on well-designed muzzleloaders of the past two centuries.

One reason for producing such splendid groups with the venerable "long rifles" of the past hinges on a simple optical fact: using a rifle with a long barrel, place the rear sight several inches forward of the eye with the front sight at a considerable distance from the rear sight and the picture will clear up. As the eyes grow older, visual accommodation—the eye focusing on the three planes simultaneously—become more difficult. With the rear sight mounted several inches up-barrel, however, mature eyes get a big break. The distance between

FOR LONG-RANGE SHOOTING—IN THIS CASE, BLACK POWDER CARTRIDGE SILHOUETTE AT DISTANCES UP TO 900 YARDS—THE VERNIER TANG REAR SIGHT IS HIGHLY EFFECTIVE.

THIS WINCHESTER MODEL 1894 RIFLE CAME
EQUIPPED WITH A TANG SIGHT ADJUSTABLE FOR
LONG-RANGE SHOTS.

front and rear sights is known as "sight radius." Long-barreled muzzleloaders naturally have a longer sight radius. That's why over-50 marksmen are often seen shooting respectable off-hand groups on paper targets 25, 50, 100 yards and even farther. Add to this the fact that the lengthy barrels of the elderly gentlemen's black powder rifles "hang" well; i.e., the rifle's up-front weight promotes steady holding.

Receiver sights are also known as peep or aperture, especially when coupled with muzzleloaders that have no receiver. The name itself is accurate, though, because it infers a sight mounted close to the eye. Regardless, the function is identical, featuring a disc or metal ring with a hole in it for a rear sight. The front sight can be one of many types, including a globe, normally hooded for shade and protection against breakage, a blade, bead, or the venerable Patridge. The last-named was not named for the bird in the pear tree, but for E.E. Patridge, one-time president of the U.S. Revolver Association. In 1892 he developed his sight for handguns, but it works as well on rifles. It's flat-sided, often thick, and appears as a rectangle or square-top, whether resting optically in a rear sight notch or

standing on its own (as viewed through a peep). The blade sight is quite similar to the Patridge but is usually thinner.

Modern shooters have trouble with aperture sights usually because they try too hard and fail to understand the concept, which is quite simple. Trying to center the front sight in the circle of light created by the peep is the wrong approach. It retains the three-plane image, which is exactly what the peep sight gets rid of. Rather, the shooter simply looks through the peep hole, ignoring it completely after that. Because the eye focuses dead center on the highest concentration of light, there's no need to observe the aperture itself. The marksman concentrates on only two, instead of three, planes: the front sight and the target. The rest is automatic. With peep sights providing a clean picture of aim point and target, the shooter has only to "paste" the front sight on the target and maintain that picture while squeezing off a round. Front sights that appear square, such as blade or Patridge (not globe or bead), work well with the six-o'clock hold, where the target "sits," optically speaking, on the front sight. In other words, the target looks as though it's resting on top of the front sight.

A FINE MICROMETER PEEP SIGHT, FULLY
ADJUSTABLE FOR WINDAGE AND ELEVATION, IS
MOUNTED ON A WINCHESTER MODEL 75 .22 RIM-
FIRE RIFLE.

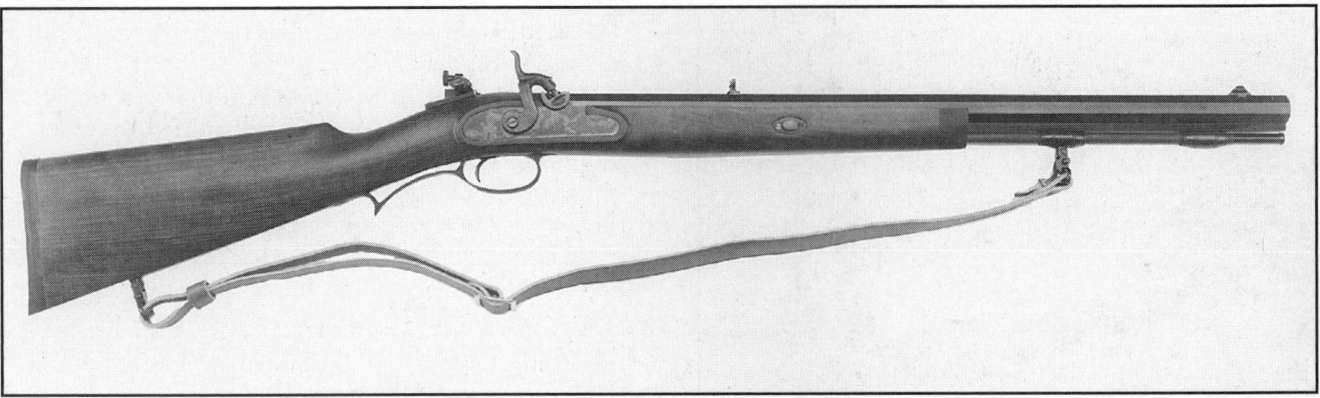

LYMAN'S DEERSTALKER HUNTING RIFLE IS EQUIPPED WITH AN APERTURE SIGHT MADE BY THE SAME COMPANY.

Peep sights are terrific because they require only two instead of three focusing planes. They are laudable on account of adjustment. A micrometer peep's refined "clicks" have a specific point-of-impact value at given distances. Practiced sharpshooters who are aware of a given range go up or down so many clicks in order to change point of impact on the target. The rifle may be sighted—for example, three inches high at 100 yards—putting its shots about four inches high at 200. That's not a problem, since group size alone encompasses the difference of a mere inch. Should a rifleman wish to fire at 300 yards, he can elevate a specific number of clicks. That way, he doesn't have to apply "Arkansas elevation," guessing at where to hold. Simply put, he holds right on target. If the shot is only 75 yards away, he may click down a specific

number so the sight picture is once again right on the money, with no hold-under required. Not all aperture sights are micrometer-adjusted, however, but each has some means of altering point of bullet impact.

The *tang peep* sight got its name because it was bolted down to the upper tang of the rifle. It was also hinged so that it could be put into battery (shooting position) or folded down to protect it from damage—or, in addition, allow the use of an open iron sight. Two distinctly different types of tang sights are available. On some sporting rifles, the tang is used only for long-range shooting. Open iron sights do the rest. On others, the tang peep was the only sight, enjoying high status with long-range target shooters. The aperture was very close to the eye, not always a grand idea on hunting

OUT OF PLACE ON AN AIR RIFLE? HARDLY. THIS DAISY ADULT PRECISION MODEL 753 TARGET RIFLE INCLUDES A HIGH-GRADE APERTURE SIGHT WITH MATCHING FRONT SIGHT.

rifles. One lady sportsperson learned the hard way when a tang sight reared back into her eye as she was aiming at a big game animal.

The *vernier tang* was especially ideal for target work, thanks to its fine-adjustment capability for both windage and elevation, sometimes with a combined spirit level to indicate cant (tilting) of the rifle. The sight was named for Pierre Vernier (1580-1637), a mathematician who invented a short graduated scale that slid in contrast to a longer graduated scale designed for more precise measurements, as in the vernier caliper, which allows micro-measurements in length, width, thickness, and depth. The very name signifies fine adjustment.

Open iron sights do not enjoy micrometer or vernier peep sight level of control, but the good ones still produce remarkably close groups. The open irons on my custom .54 caliber muzzleloader provide a super sight picture with a "fine bead" or

WHILE THIS STAINLESS IN-LINE MUZZLELOADER (TOP) COMES WITH SCOPE MOUNTS (ABOVE), IT ALSO HAS AN ADJUSTABLE OPEN REAR SIGHT.

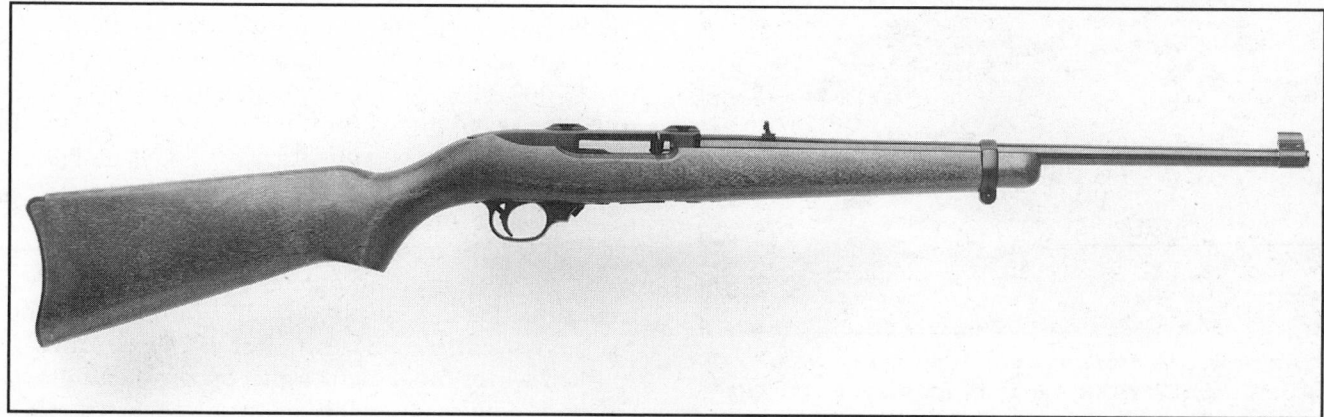

FAR FROM DEFUNCT, THE OPEN IRON SIGHT IS OFTEN THE ONE THAT COMES ON FACTORY RIFLES, SUCH AS THE RUGER MODEL 10/22 RIMFIRE SHOWN.

"coarse bead." The rear sight of my custom muzzle-loader is double-notched. The first notch, halfway up the sight, is for the fine bead. The coarse bead hold puts the front sight exactly on line with the extreme top of the rear sight notch. When loaded for big game, the fine bead is used for shots up to 75 yards, the coarse bead for shots up to the maximum range of the .54 caliber round ball, and up to 125 yards for deer-sized or smaller game. Beyond that distance, the 230-grain round ball loses too much energy to be reliable.

A major problem with open irons is proper sight picture. Often, the match between the front and rear sight is incorrect, mainly because the front sight, optically speaking, fills the rear sight notch, leaving no frame of reference. Rather, there should be light on both sides of the front sight as it nestles, visually, into the rear sight notch. That way, the front sight relates to the rear sight the same with every shot. Without light on both sides of the front sight, the shooter can't tell if the front sight is truly centered in the notch of the rear sight. There's no reference point. Light on both sides of the front sight, however, provides a reference point that can be relied on time and again. This problem does not, of course, reside with the peep sight, which has light all around the bead or blade.

FIBER OPTIC SIGHTS ON THIS MUZZLELOADER PROVIDE TWO BRIGHT GREEN DOTS ON THE REAR SIGHT, HIGHLY VISIBLE EVEN IN LOW LIGHT.

Telescopic sights are, of course, best for extremely close bullet grouping. There isn't a benchrest rifle in the world that isn't scoped with a high magnification glass. The single-plane view, plus an enlarged target, puts scopes at the top of the hill—but iron sights are far from obsolete. There's a ranch in my home state of Wyoming that thrives in whitetail deer. Due to their high population, hunters are allowed—in fact, encouraged—to fill three tags, one antlered and two antlerless. Since the venture is mainly for protein, I carry my 9x56mm Mannlicher carbine into the tangle of abundant creek bed thickets. This rifle wears a unique receiver sight, different because it pivots out of the way as the bolt is worked. It's not a micrometer, but I've fiddled with adjustment until it's well sighted in.

Up jumps the deer, one second allowed to assess buck, doe, or fawn. Flip the safety latch left, cock the set trigger, aim, fire. One more for the pot. Would a scope have worked here? Of course, but I am content with the Mannlicher's peep, just as it was placed on the rifle in 1921 when it left the factory (I have records to prove it). I'm also happy with the open irons on my .54 caliber round ball muzzleloader, as well as a few .22 rimfires I've come to know well. It's amazing what can be accomplished with simple metal sights on these and other rifles, no matter how far back in time we travel. Iron sights are still with us for one big reason—they work! **SB**

THE ORIGINAL "FIXED" OPEN IRON SIGHT WAS MUCH BETTER THAN APPEARANCES SUGGEST. THE FLAT TOP WITH ITS SMALL NOTCH, COUPLED WITH A FINE BLADE FRONT SIGHT, PROVIDES A CLEAN SIGHT PICTURE.

Metallic Silhouette Shooting– With Handguns

By Ken Horowitz

DAWN'S EARLY GLOW had long since yielded to the brightness of a clear morning as I steadied my sights on the belly of a beast 200 yards down-range. With pounding heart, my finger slid the trigger beyond its breaking point, and the dropping hammer sent a 150 grain bullet on it way. A half-second of eternity passed before the ram toppled where it had stood.

Had I been one of a select few to win a western state lottery for bighorn sheep? Perhaps this was the sweetness of a pleasant dream? It was neither of these. I had entered the exhilarating world of shooting metallic silhouettes with a handgun, and the ram was a 55-pound tempered steel target, one of ten identical metal siblings shot in the farthest relay of a competition entry. The doors of this challenging handgun target sport had swung wide open for me in a sport where shooter classifications and entry categories allow newcomers to shoot alongside veteran champions. Scores are measured only against shooters of like ability using similar equipment. More important, independent of one's score, the shooting is fun. For the beginner, only a few toppled targets are needed to be drawn into the game for good.

Until a few years ago, I had heard only references to handgun metallic shooting. I didn't realize how readily accessible and widespread the matches were. While some variations of the sport exist, the leading sanctioning body today is the International Handgun Metallic Silhouette Association (IHMSA). Over the years it has made this an "easy entry" sport,

with enough categories to guarantee qualification. The matches themselves follow standard rules, enabling a shooter to travel to different ranges with no frustrating surprises.

One important key to the popularity of these matches is their simplicity. Each match entry consists of 40 targets—10 each of chickens, pigs, turkeys and rams—set at ever increasing distances.

A SHOOTER FIRES AT BIG BORE PIGS FROM THE STANDING POSITION WHILE A SPOTTER LETS THE SHOOTER KNOW WHERE THE BULLETS ARE IMPACTING THE TARGETS.

Scoring is straightforward. Either a target is toppled or it isn't. A ringer, which occurs when a target is hit but doesn't fall, is the same as a miss. For each target that's toppled, the shooter receives one point. A perfect score is 40, and to settle ties among the more proficient shooters, 10 smaller shoot-off targets are added. Members of IHMSA keep a personal classification card for measuring shooters according to their abilities. There are more rules, of course, but first let's look at the origins of the sport and its modern rebirth.

During the early part of the 20th century, myth and reality formed a romantic blend in northern Mexico. More precisely, it was about the time the rest of the world was preoccupied with World War I. Names like Pancho Villa, Carranza and others still conjure up historic memories of turmoil during a period of revolution, wars involving the United States, and just plain banditry. Even for those who lacked the social graces of diplomacy, feats and celebrations abounded wherein large crowds of local supporters joined the festivities calling for large quantities of meat. This was an opportunity not to be missed by those who professed skill at arms. As for the animals, rather than undergoing traditional slaughter, they were tethered at various distances and promptly dispatched by the very same arms used in battle.

Without doubt, practicality called for the use of the firearms at hand, including the rifles and pistols that typified the hodgepodge of Mexican Revolutionary arms of the day. Since good times know no borders, it's likely this practice may have occurred elsewhere in southwestern U.S. Sometime later, the practice evolved as a sport only, although it's doubtful that any edible meat went to waste. Eventually, whether by political correctness or economic expediency, the sport grew into metallic silhouette targets, much the same way that shotgun sports graduated from live birds to clays.

A SHOOTER TAKES AIM AT BIG BORE CHICKENS, WITH PIGS AND RAMS IN THE BACKGROUND (THE BIG BORE TURKEYS ARE NOT VISIBLE IN THIS PHOTO). THE BLACK TARGETS TO THE LEFT ARE SMALL BORE AND FIELD PISTOL TURKEYS AND RAMS.

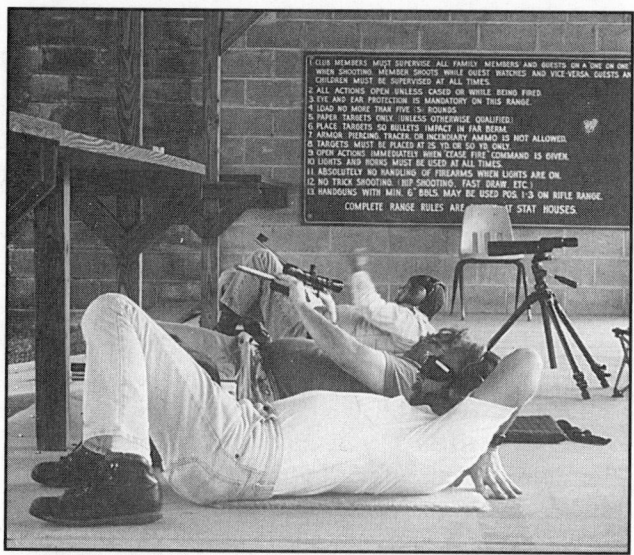

WHEN SHOOTING AT SMALL BORE CHICKENS AND PIGS, SHOOTERS ASSUME THE CREEDMORE POSITION.

Over the next half-century or so, shooting metallic silhouette targets certainly took place, but it wasn't until the 1970's that IHMSA, under the leadership of Elgin Gates, turned it into the internationally standardized sport it has since become. While IHMSA did not invent silhouetting, it did breathe new life into a dormant and unregulated pastime. Other organizations have their silhouette regulations, of course, including shooting with rifles, but when it comes to sanctioning handguns for the dispatching of steel targets, IHMSA emerged as the recognized leader.

Three primary types of competition exist: Big Bore, Small Bore and Field Pistol. These entries are broadly circumscribed by the size and distance of the targets, ammunition and the type of gun used. Each is further broken down into categories of competition based upon variations in the type of handgun and shooting position used. It's easiest to address basic rules by competition type, as follows:

BIG BORE

The Big Bore chickens are set at 50 meters, pigs at 100 meters, turkeys at 150 meters and rams at 200 meters. The rams can also be set at 200 yards, providing this alternative is announced at the beginning of a match, enabling ranges with existing berms at 200 yards to accommodate a sanctioned match.

All targets have standard dimensions and weights, including specifications regarding footing, by which shooters may travel among the ranges under the same conditions. Each competitor starts with the chickens and has two minutes to shoot at five targets—left to right—moving to the next target regardless of whether or not there's been a hit or a miss. When the two minutes are up, the firing line is made safe and the targets are reset. Prior to shooting at this first bank of five targets, each one is freshly sprayed with paint. Now is a good time to look at the bullet marks on the fallen targets and make fine adjustments to your sights. When time is called, another two minutes are allotted for shooting at the next bank of five chickens, thereby completing shots at ten such targets. After that, the targets are given another fresh spray coat of paint so the next shooter can begin his or her round of targets with no marks.

Next comes the first bank of five pigs, while a new shooter moves in on the chickens. At the same time, whoever was shooting at the pigs has moved on to the turkeys, and so on. Once finished with the turkeys, the final shots are aimed at the rams. Thus, each contestant rotates through the stations of the relay, firing ten shots at each animal, or 40 shots in all. Thirty seconds for loading and making

WHILE IN THE CREEDMORE POSITION, THIS SHOOTER USES HIS LEG AS A REST WHILE SUPPORTING HIS HEAD WITH HIS OFFSIDE HAND. SAFETY CONSIDERATIONS REQUIRE THAT THE MUZZLE BE WELL IN FRONT OF THE SHOOTER.

A TARGET SETTER SPRAYS BIG BORE CHICKENS BETWEEN RELAYS. DEPENDING ON THE BACKGROUND, TARGETS, WHICH ARE USUALLY PAINTED BLACK, MAY BE PAINTED OTHER COLORS, USUALLY WHITE.

adjustments are allowed prior to each two-minute firing segment, plus whatever time it takes to reset the targets and make the range safe. In all, it takes about an hour to complete the entire entry. Time permitting, a contestant can shoot as many entries per match as desired, spending a whole leisurely day at the match, or firing a quick entry and then going about his business.

Almost any centerfire rifle or pistol cartridge is suitable for Big Bore, subject only to safety and target damage rules. Some weight limitations apply on certain guns, but they are quite liberal, with few firearms disqualified. Early in the development of the modern version of handgun silhouetting, it was declared unfair to compare performances among firearms straight-from-the-box as opposed to those that have been enhanced, such as extra-long barrels and varying types of sights. Rather than restricting the type of firearm, it was decided to form different categories that would preclude hardware from gaining undue advantages for one shooter over another. Special efforts were made to prevent silhouette

shooting from becoming a money game, with expensive hardware playing a dominant role in determining match results. The outcome has been the establishment of categories based on production guns and unlimited guns, further modified by whether they wear open iron sights or are optically enhanced.

Production handguns are limited to barrels measuring 10?" or less, with their weight not to exceed four pounds. Replacement stocks, for example, are acceptable. The same applies to drop-in, readily available parts as opposed to custom enhancements. Unlimited guns add half a pound to their allowable weight and barrels may be up to 15" in length (an additional pound added for optical sights and mounts.) Obviously, the production gun rule is not overly restrictive and is, in fact, quite liberal in terms of the guns that are allowed to compete. Unlimited guns raise the ceiling so high that few guns are disqualified from shooting in Big Bore events.

The second major category determinant is shooting position, whether standing or all-inclusive freestyle, which allows shooters great latitude (but not the use of artificial rests). The most popular freestyle position is known as Creedmoor, in which shooters lie down on their backs, their feet toward the targets and knees drawn up, using a lower leg as a kind of shooting rest. Given a choice of gun type and shooting position, there's enough variation to accommodate a spread between novice and expert.

SMALL BORE

Small Bore is shot with 22 Long Rifle cartridges only. The targets for this event are 3/8 scale and are set at the following distances: 25 yards (chickens); 50 yards (pigs); 75 yards (turkeys); and 100 yards (rams). Because the scale is less than the reduction in the distances at which Big Bore targets are shot, the sight picture of the Small Bore variety is a bit worse than that of larger targets. Coupled with the sensitivity to wind inherent in light 22 caliber bullets, many shooters find Small Bore to be the most challenging of the major IHMSA fields of fire, exceeded in difficulty only by the newest (but not yet universal) sub-discipline of Big Bore Half-Scale. In that case, half-scale targets are set at Big Bore distances, with all the rules and restrictions of Big Bore, including guns and cartridges, in force.

Rules involving barrel length and weight, which designate firearms as production or unlimited types, are about the same as those for Big Bore, with a few minor differences. For example, Small Bore has separate production classes for semi-automatics, single shot pistols and revolvers. This reflects the wide availability of good .22 Long Rifle pistols in a wide variety of action types.

The number of targets is the same and the course of fire is identical to Big Bore: first the chickens, five in a bank, left to right, proceeding through the banks in the same order, finishing with the last bank of rams (40 targets altogether, either knocked onto the ground or counted as a miss). In fact, the range commands for all courses of fire are the same. Once the shooters are called to the line, they must get into position but without handling their firearms. Upon the command to load, they have 30 seconds to make any final adjustments, then load and await the command to fire. If for any reason a gun is discharged before the command to fire is given, that shot will not count as a hit and is considered lost; i.e., only four rounds are allowed on that bank, starting with the second target and moving rightwards. Upon the command to fire, each shooter has two minutes to take all five shots. Actually, this is more than ample time. After all guns have been fired, the final command for a cease-fire is given, whereupon all shooters must

make their firearms safe and retreat from the firing line. Once the range commander is satisfied that the line is safe, the target setters may go downrange to reset the target and, assuming both banks of animals have been completed, repaint all targets.

FIELD PISTOL

No category captures the essence of handgun silhouetting as well as the Field Pistol. Only two categories—Production and Production Any Sights—are involved, and each is fired from the standing position (no freestyle positions are permitted as in Big Bore and Small Bore). Designed primarily for plain out-of-the-box pistols, this event harkens back to the days when a shooter's prowess was measured by the ability to shoot those firearms that are carried in the normal course of events. Over the years, some expansion of permissible Field Pistol cartridges has led to such specialized cartridges as the 22 Hornet, 270 REN, 32-20 and, most recently, the 25-20. Basic Field Pistol cartridges—i.e., .22 LR and .22 WMR—are straight-wall, centerfire pistol cartridges. This brings out all those 38 Special, 9mm and other handguns shooters carry for general use. As long as a shooter brings to the range some inherent accuracy, a set of adjustable sights and steadiness of hand, this segment of handgun silhouetting may be the most comfortable for new shooters when testing the waters of steel target shooting. Field Pistol targets are

IN THE FOREGROUND ARE BIG BORE CHICKENS; BEHIND ARE THE BIG BORE PIGS, PARTLY OBSCURED BY THE TARGET SETTERS. FURTHER TO THE RIGHT ARE THE BIG BORE TURKEYS; AND IN THE FAR DISTANCE, BARELY VISIBLE, ARE THE BIG BORE RAMS AND SHOOTOFF TARGETS. THE BLACK TARGETS TO THE LEFT ARE SMALL BORE AND FIELD PISTOL TURKEYS AND RAMS. OUT OF SIGHT TO THE LEFT ARE THE CHICKENS AND PIGS FOR THESE EVENTS.

half-Big Bore scale (in meters) set at the same distances as the Small Bore targets (in yards); hence they offer the largest sight picture when set at less than half the distances (approximately 45%) as Big Bore.

I prefer a handgun that takes advantage of the upper limits of permissible firearms eligible for Field Pistol. There's no question that a longer barrel provides a better sight radius, which is especially helpful in long distance shooting. Good adjustable sights are a plus, as well. However, if my only gun was one that met the eligibility specifications of a Field Pistol but was less than ideal, I'd use it anyway. For example, a four- to six-inch barreled .357 Magnum with open sights would qualify. Since there is relatively little drop out to 100 yards, a shooter who applied good "Kentucky windage" might do quite well at Field Pistol.

Like most pastimes, there are always nice accessories to have once you're thoroughly involved. But other than basic safety equipment, such as good hearing and sight protection, everything else can wait. When choosing a freestyle position, a shooting mat is called for, usually a carpet remnant. A spotting scope is certainly handy, but it can wait; meanwhile, you can use someone else's. Although I bring a spotting scope to every match, I find that other shooters use it more than I do (in fact, I know several regulars who've never bothered to get one). Other minor accessories include blast shields, which protect a shooter's leg from the cylinder blast of a revolver should he or she choose to shoot Creedmore.

Handgun silhouetters, like many shooters in general, are very much into reloading, but it's not absolutely essential. Much depends upon one's cartridge preferences. Some handloaders may be attracted to silhouetting simply because it offers so many unique opportunities for cartridge optimization, especially the Big Bore silhouette loads. That's probably something to note for the future, not for purposes of entering the game.

GETTING STARTED

Even though the opportunity was right under my nose, it took many years of general target shooting before I found handgun silhouetting. As a popular sport, it eschews the race for expensive firearms in favor of guns that are already owned. It also provides unlimited gun categories that take into account reasonable changes a shooter may want to make. Prizes and awards are restricted in the interest of keeping the sport purely one of enjoyment, without turning it into a huge financial enterprise as so many other shooting sports have become. As an extension of this low-profile ap-proach, handgun metallic silhouette shooting is not generally advertised or underwritten by the same benefactors who support spectator shooting events boasting a large advertising customer base. Nonetheless, the endurance of the silhouetting sport has been tenacious, with matches held all over the country each week.

While many of these matches are held at private clubs, free entry is open to the general public for sanctioning purposes. You can even do a trial run in a local match before becoming an IHMSA member, just to see what it's like. If you like what you see, you'll need to join IHMSA to get a classification card prior to competing on a regular basis. Once you've paid a nominal membership fee, the doors are open to shoot at sanctioned matches at one of several clubs where you may otherwise not have been able to gain entry.

Until I began shooting silhouettes, I had read a few things about the sport and somehow formed the mistaken impression that it was only practiced far from my home. I couldn't have been more wrong. To my surprise, I discovered more matches were being shot within reasonable driving distance from where I live than perhaps anywhere in the country. Since then, I've encountered no other sport where so many shooters are ready and willing to help one another. Your fellow shooters will eagerly spot for you, adjust your gun, recommend loads, and do whatever is required to keep the sport user friendly. When you do show up for your first match, just let the match director know you'd appreciate a little help. You'll be amazed at how accommodating everyone is. **SB**

For more information on membership in IHMSA and any matches that may be held in your area, contact IHMSA, Inc., P.O. Box 368, Burlington, IO 52601-0368, or visit the website at http://ihmsa.org.

Women Hunters: Who Are We?

By Marcia Murdock

IN WRITING THIS article, I figured it would be easy to talk to several serious, experienced women hunters and get their collective opinions about who we are and how we differ from our male counterparts. There was only one problem—it was hunting season. Everybody was too busy. Finally, I did manage to catch up with several women hunters between my hunts and theirs. What I had hoped would be an interesting project for me was an understatement. When they found out what I was working on, some of my male hunting friends expressed their own ideas. The women I contacted talked with their own hunting friends, and so my database grew. When I was done soliciting the opinions and ideas of perhaps three dozen women and men, I found that we women have a lot in common with each other—*and* with our male counterparts. While there may be some real differences between the genders in terms of when and where we hunt, the women I heard from ran the gamut from hard-core, intense hunters to vacationers, meat hunters and trophy hunters. They come from all kinds of backgrounds and occupations, but they all share a common love of the outdoors that began during childhood. The truth is, if someone tried to pick us out of a crowd, it would be no easy task.

I have always believed there were more of us out there than most people expected. Maybe it's because, in part, we always had to make do with men's clothing and equipment, there being no decent stuff available for us. We have blended in because of "gender camouflage." I suspect this even more strongly because of an encounter with another woman hunter this past elk season. I had stepped out of

dark timber into a pullout on a forest road just as a pickup full of hunters drove by. The person in the passenger window returned my wave half-heartedly until she realized I was a woman. Then she smiled brightly, waved eagerly, and turned to get a better look. I'll admit that, until she smiled, I didn't recog-

BRONITA'S FIRST DEER WAS TAKEN WITH A BLACK POWDER RIFLE, BUT HER .25-06 DID A NICE JOB ON THIS COLORADO MULE DEER BUCK. (PHOTO BY BUD JOHNSON)

BEFORE ERIN HUNTED ELK, SHE TRIED HER HAND AT
PRONGHORN. (PHOTO COURTESY OF ERIN BOGNAR)

WHAT MAKES US TICK?

It's true, there are a lot of casual hunters out there—both male and female—and among the women I polled, including myself, hunting is not just a hobby, it's a lifestyle. Many of the most important life decisions I've made centered around protecting my time for hunting, and I'm not alone. My selection of a spouse was critical—only a hunter can truly understand another hunter—and my job had to offer enough sflexibility in its scheduling for the fall hunting season. My vacation time is invariably devoted to scouting and hunting trips, causing a good friend of mine to call me "the most dedicated hunter I know."

In my study of women hunters, I found we had many things in common, including our backgrounds and basic lifestyles. Most of us were raised around

nize her as a woman, either. We shared a special moment of recognition and kinship, though we never spoke a word.

Several years ago, I encountered another female hunter as I was returning from one of my forays into the "back-of-beyond." I never saw human tracks save my own, so the look of surprise on a fellow hunter's face was understandable as he saw me pull up over a ridgeline. His look turned to amazement as I saw him say to himself, "It's a woman!" By then he was close enough to see my long hair and curved figure under the heavy wool garb. From a distance, he had clearly assumed I was another guy.

Because the women I've talked to are capable, confident and self-sufficient, they've never needed "rescuing." As a result, the brief biographies that follow produced no such material of the "tough -guy-bailed-out-the-lucky-little-lady" variety. On the contrary, a few of us swapped stories about bailing out some guys on occasion. The fact is, most of us hunt solo, care for our own game, pack out our own meat, and do all the messy butchering after a hunt. As you might imagine, we all stay in pretty good shape, boast of well-honed hunting skills, and are proficient at survival skills as well.

SHIRLEY WAS READY FOR THIS NICE WEST TEXAS
MULE DEER WHEN HE CAME HER WAY. PLENTY OF
PRACTICE ON WHITE-TAILED DEER PAID OFF.
(PHOTO BY A. FRANK CMAJDALKA)

HAVING GOTTEN A CHANCE TO HUNT MORE EXOTIC GAME A FEW YEARS AGO, JANET MADE A DIFFICULT STALK ON THIS CARIBOU BULL. HER PET RECURVE BOW AND WELL-TUNED INSTINCTIVE SHOOTING DID THE JOB NICELY WHEN THE SHOT CAME. (PHOTO COURTESY OF JANET GEORGE)

firearms and were exposed to hunting in our youth. We generally got our hunting licenses as soon as we turned legal age. Outdoorswomen since childhood, we remain confident in our abilities to cope and to meet whatever challenges come our way head-on. Most of us pursue other outdoor activities as well, including fishing, camping, hiking, boating and photography. We are, as a rule, independent, pragmatic and capable. But our real passion lies in the enjoyment of the outdoors—soaking in all the smells, sounds and colors, absorbing every detail of what's happening around us. While we are primarily big game hunters, we occasionally hunt waterfowl and small game when "serious" hunting doesn't take precedence. No matter what, we can't *imagine* giving up our hunting lifestyles.

Interestingly, most of us prefer to hunt alone. We like the feeling of confidence—that we can handle whatever comes up—and we enjoy those opportunities that remind ourselves of those feelings. We prefer to make our own decisions and our own mistakes. Hunting alone also seems to relieve the

pressure to shoot (real or imagined) because of someone else's compulsion rather than our own. Simply put, we feel we can hunt more effectively by ourselves. Almost to a woman, we actively mentor others. We love to teach our children, grandchildren and friends. We volunteer at "Becoming an Outdoors Woman" workshops, share our knowledge with scouts, teach hunter and firearms safety courses, and generally try to draw others to the wonders of outdoor life.

In an attempt to define how we hunt, and what is ultimately important to us, I asked several of the women in this study to share their favorite hunting stories. Although only a few of their stories appear below, lots more contributed their thoughts and ideas. Perhaps these stories will best illustrate our differences from men.

JACKIE

Jackie began her big game hunting career at 14 on an outing with her father. A longtime horsewoman, she is comfortable alone and well-prepared for the outdoors. When I asked Jackie about her most memorable hunt, she described with a lingering excitement the day she took her daughter Kelly on her first successful elk hunt. As she was guiding

THE AUTHOR HAD JUST GUIDED HER FRIEND BILL TO THIS PRONGHORN BUCK WHEN GAY, WHO'D BEEN BOWHUNTING FOR ELK ON ANOTHER PART OF HER RANCH, HAPPENED BY. (PHOTO BY BILL O'CONNOR)

THE AUTHOR, HAVING DECIDED TO MAKE A RECENT PRONGHORN HUNT MORE OF A CHALLENGE, BOUGHT THIS USED, OPEN-SIGHTED MARLIN .30-30 AND GOT WITHIN 41 PACES FOR THE SHOT. (PHOTO BY MARCIA MURDOCK)

Kelly to a place where she knew a fair-sized elk herd had been sighted, Jackie encountered five spike bulls in a small meadow. Kelly had a bull tag in her pocket, but at 200 yards she wasn't comfortable taking a shot, so Jackie encouraged her to wait. After the bulls had wandered away, the two hunters walked through a bunch of cows and calves, who slowly got up from their beds and left, filling the air with elk talk. As Jackie and Kelly climbed upwind, they caught up with three of the cows and followed then, keeping a distance of 20 yards until the wind tattled on them. The hunters both had a great laugh as the cows "nearly turned themselves inside out" leaving the premises.

Suddenly, Jackie spotted antler tips—a bull was approaching! She and Kelly scurried behind a tree and waited as the bull walked along, its head bobbing as he strolled up the elk path. Jackie, who earlier had coached Kelly on shot placement, watched the bull's head-on approach in anticipation. Kelly waited, her left-handed rifle resting against the tree. All was silent. When the bull lifted his chin, the way was clear for the shot. Boom! The three-point bull went down like a ton of bricks at 17 paces.

JANET

Janet is a bowhunter, and a darned good one. Well known locally, her advice as a wildlife biologist is sought out by hunters of all ages and backgrounds. Although Janet as a child would often tag along with her pheasant-hunting father, she never actually hunted until she was 18. Once she was eligible and experienced enough to hunt big game alone, she chose as her first venture an archery hunt for elk! Nothing like starting the hard way.

It wasn't until she drew her third archery sheep tag that Janet finally caught up to a bighorn ram— the hunt of her dreams. She hunts with a rifle now and then, but the bow is her passion. As an instinctive shooter (no sights), her effective range is limited to distances that riflemen would consider paltry; however, this ability puts her in close proximity to her target—just the way she likes it. Because she limited herself to a bow, she experienced some trying times in her attempts to fill the first two tags without connecting. After 41 days afield in her third season, she finally got her third tag—but not before the ram she had watched all summer bolted after the fickle wind in an alpine basin had betrayed her.

Undeterred, Janet kept at it, finally spotting a nice ram at daylight. She waited until the ram bedded, then spent half a day working in on him. When

KATHY COLLECTED THIS BULL ELK WITH HER WEATHERBY IN .300 WIN. MAG., HER FAVORITE RIFLE. MOST WOMEN CHOOSE SMALLER CALIBERS, BUT SEVERAL WOMEN HUNTERS INTERVIEWED USE LARGER CALIBERS WHEN APPROPRIATE. (PHOTO COURTESY OF KATHY PABST)

she reached what she thought was the right ledge, she suddenly realized she was one too high. Taking off her boots, she slowly descended the last 150 yards across crunching lichens until she launched the fatal arrow some 40 feet from above the ram between her sock-footed toes. Lulled into thinking the tiny crunches of Janet's footsteps were the sounds of numerous chipmunks, the ram had kept on dozing.

BRONITA

Bronita had her first hunting experience ten years ago, after her husband had retired. They had always fished together and enjoyed other outdoor activities, but with the children grown and with more time to themselves, the couple wanted to do more things together. Bronita had become quite familiar with firearms, but she hadn't tried hunting before. That gap in her resume was filled one afternoon while she was hunting with her husband. They had just skirted some heavy timber when something caught her attention. Bronita wasn't sure if it was the movement of an antler or the twitch of an ear, when suddenly two large antlers materialized in the gloom. There he was, bedded in the shade to escape the heat of the day. Bronita shot and the buck lay still. Her husband, however, spotted a buck running off and thought she had missed. But Bronita could still see her deer and insisted it was dead. As the couple approached the fallen buck, they realized there had, in fact, been two bucks lying close together, and one of them had escaped. It all made for a happy memory for two hunters working together in an attempt to take some meat home.

ERIN

Erin had been an outdoorswoman and a serious fish hunter since she was a child, but she didn't start hunting until she married a hunter. The first year she and Paul were married, she invited herself along on her husband's elk hunt. He was delighted, and they have hunted as a team now for 17 years. But Erin's favorite hunt actually involved her friend, Mike, and his first elk. Erin had taken her cow on opening day and talked Mike into using her favorite ambush spot the following morning. After he left, she relaxed in camp and awaited the day's developments. Not long after daylight, Mike returned to

THE AUTHOR'S THREE-WEEK BIGHORN HUNT WAS HARD-WON. SHE AND HER HUSBAND RON SPENT SEVERAL WEEKS IN THE COLORADO HIGH COUNTRY TO EARN THEIR RAMS. (PHOTO BY BARRY SMITH)

camp looking for help. He had shot the elk and was overwhelmed by the sheer size of the bull. With Erin's help, the field dressing process was completed in due time, and they had begun quartering. Erin was standing near the head, running the knife, as the two hunters worked on one shoulder. Mike, his back to the elk's tail, was holding the leg and following her directions when suddenly Erin spotted a red fox trotting fearlessly through the woods straight towards them. The cheeky little fellow stepped right up to an exposed haunch not two feet from Mike and grabbed hold. Erin waved her knife in the air and yelled, "You can't have that!" Mike spun around, dumbfounded to find this impudent scavenger trying to make off with part of his prize bull. The fox backed off and sat down next to a tree not 20 feet away, watching as Erin and Mike continued the quartering. The persistent thief tried another pass but was unable to snatch a hindquarter. Finally, Erin cut loose a shank and tossed it to the fox. He grabbed it and scampered off with his prize.

THE AUTHOR WAS ALONE WHEN SHE SHOT HER
FIRST PRONGHORN, THEN LOADED HIM WHOLE INTO
HER JEEP FOR THE TRIP HOME.

GAY

Gay is a typical rancher; as capable and independent as they come. As a ranch kid, she was quite familiar with firearms. When they were youngsters, she and her older sisters hunted prairie dogs and sage grouse with their .22s, but Gay couldn't hunt big game until she turned 14. When the time came, her father took her on her first deer hunt and produced her first buck—but not before learning a new lessons she'll never forget.

Considering her locale, it's natural that Gay should have collected some nice pronghorn, mule deer and elk over the years; but the one animal she couldn't hunt at home was the wild sheep. She had been saving up for a stone sheep hunt for some time, but when she finally arrived for the long-anticipated hunt, the sheep had somehow vanished. What had been a normally good hunting area now held only a few sheep—and no legal rams.

Gay and her guide covered a lot of country looking for legal rams, but found none. Near the end of her time, fortunately, they discovered two rams and spent the next three days trying to get close to them.

But the rams were unapproachable until finally, in desperation, the guide volunteered to circle around and spook them back toward Gay. A risky strategy, but it was the last day. The guide left her with some advice: "Before you shoot, be sure it's legal."

Leaving Gay standing alone in a field of boulders, the guide took off. Although she's a reasonably good marksman, Gay dislikes shooting offhand, nor does she like shooting at running game. Still, she waited in tense anticipation. Finally, after a tough eleven days, she filled her tag with a beautiful ram. Happy and relieved, Gay later described how she and the guide had packed the fallen ram back up the scree field on their hands and knees. Memories made, never to be forgotten

MARCIA (IN HER OWN WORDS)

My father occasionally hunted small game, and I didn't know anyone who hunted deer. At 14, I was the only girl in my hunter education course (the first of its kind offered in our area). After buying a small

PERSISTENCE PAID OFF FOR THE AUTHOR WHEN
SHE CONNECTED ON HER FIRST BULL ELK. SHE HAD
RETURNED TO THE ROUGH WYOMING OUTBACK FOR
A SECOND GO AND BROUGHT HOME THE SAME BULL
THAT HAD SLIPPED AWAY EARLIER. (PHOTO BY RON
MURDOCK)

AN UPHILL SPRINT FOLLOWED BY A PATIENT WAIT BROUGHT THIS BLACK HILLS BULL TO BAG.

game license, I persuaded my father to take me hunting—even though I desperately wanted to hunt deer. Immediately following my 18th birthday, I bought my first rifle and, later on, two deer licenses—one in New York and the other in Vermont. On my first deer hunt, I never saw a deer, but I did push one from its bed. I was hooked, and haven't missed a big game season since then.

Living in the west, I've had the opportunity to hunt a number of species which, in my early years, were only exotic dreams. With luck I'll eventually add most of North America's big game species to my lifetime bag. There are a few, such as brown or grizzly bears, that I have no desire to kill. Others, like the rocky mountain goat, I'll probably hunt only once; but deer and elk will probably keep me coming back until my knees have failed completely. True preying animals, with their keen senses and highly developed instincts for evasion, will forever hold my fascination. Like Janet, I prefer to get close to my game. I study their behavior intensely, look for chinks in their defensive strategies, then try to employ what I've learned in one-on-one contests with my quarry.

In addition to my self-guided bighorn hunt and a few other memorable incidents over the years, one of my most satisfying hunts came when I filled a cow elk tag in Colorado. It began one morning when an elderly gentleman I knew shot a nice fat cow from a

small herd. Since it looked like he didn't need help in field dressing the cow, I asked if I could follow up on the elk herd. He probably thought I was nuts, but wished me luck. At first, I could see from the running tracks in the snow that the elk herd was moving rapidly, but then slowed down gradually. Evidently my quarry had forgotten their recent fright and were letting their guard down. I eased forward a few steps at a time, wincing as the snow crunched audibly under my feet. Then I caught a glimpse of that distinctive yellowish color of an elk's rump patch in the forest ahead. As I continued to ease forward, more elk shapes materialized in the dark timber. Most of them were lined up with their backs to me, but finally one cow turned to quarter. Instantly, the shot from my favorite 7mm Rem. Mag. Broke the silence. The calf closest to me had been only about 12 paces away when I pulled the trigger.

To me, that is the epitome of a great hunt—to get close, well within the flight range, and then before you're discovered, make a clean one-shot kill. I've always enjoyed the proximity of other wildlife, as I did on that day when the gray jays flew in to pilfer my kill. Inspired to share my loot, I left several large chunks of elk suet in the forks of trees where the birds could reach and the coyotes could not. The song-dogs and pine martins would have their own share of the boned-out carcass when I was done packing meat.

THE DIFFERENCES BETWEEN WOMEN AND MEN HUNTERS

Are women really any different from guys who are also serious hunters? I've asked my contributors to this article that question and, collectively, we think we're not that different. Most of us are out there for the same reasons. We love the outdoors, the solitude, the wildlife, the feeling of independence and self-sufficiency. We're in search of fresh meat, trophies, a break from stress-filled lives, and the companionship of other hunters who understand our pursuit. You never hear about most of us, because we go about our hunting in a matter-of-fact fashion. We are nearly invisible and unremarkable in our hunting attire, and most of us avoid the limelight. Generally, as with most hunters, we appreciate

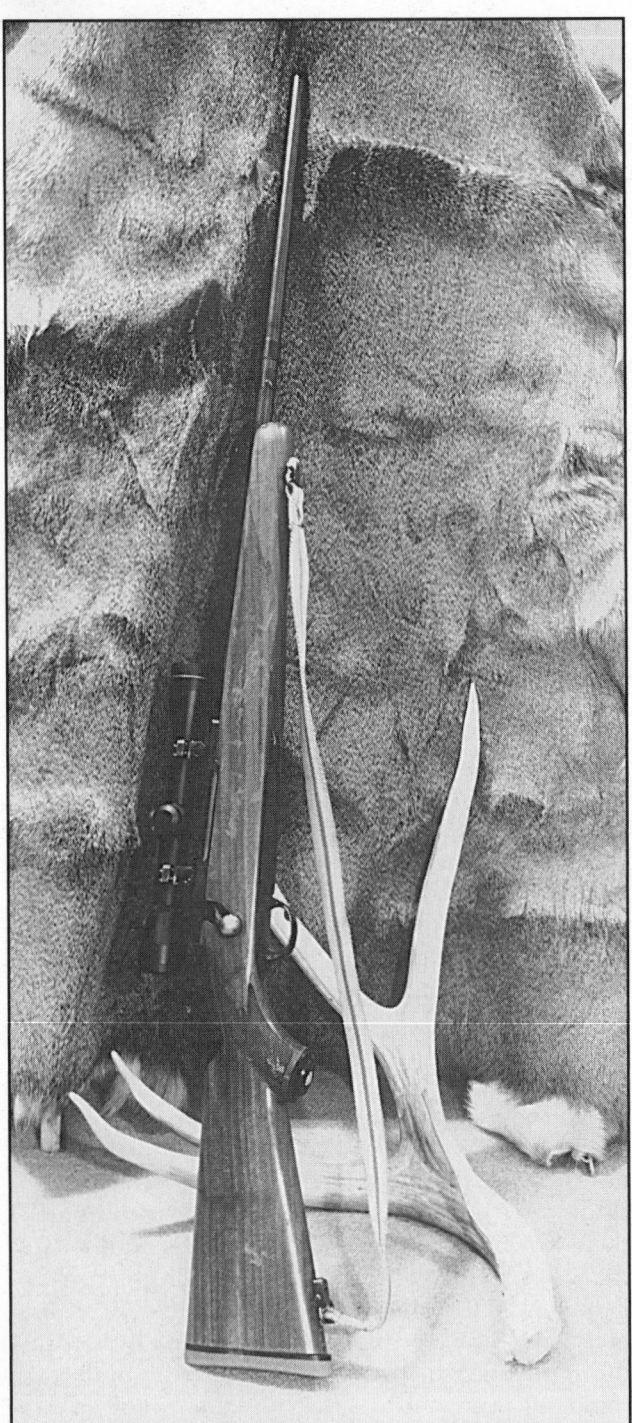

THE AUTHOR'S FAVORITE RIFLE, A BEAT-UP, CUT-DOWN RUGER M77 IN 7MM REM. MAG. TOPPED WITH A FIXED 4X LEUPOLD SCOPE, IT HAS DONE A FINE JOB OF COLLECTING MANY DIFFERENT SPECIES OF GAME.

a chance at bringing down a really impressive trophy animal, but we're willing to settle for a really good *hunt*. We've demonstrated that point by the stories we've recited here. Not one of them includes a score, a size, or a grand point count. It isn't that we're un-interested in trophies; it's that we're more interested in the experiences of the hunt.

One difference we feel may be accurate is that women apparently avoid what are considered "iffy" shots. None of us will take shots we don't like. The size of the trophy, or how badly we want to shoot the animal, won't force us to take what we consider bad shots. We'll simply pass up a shot we don't like, and we'll work to get a better one. We're very patient about waiting for a shot to set up, and we're deliber-ate in choosing what we want. We're not hoping for a good hit—we want to *know* it's one. Therein lies what may be a difference we have with men. They tend to take riskier shots, seemingly in direct pro-portion to the size of the trophy, whereas our great-est concern is a quick, clean kill.

There are as many hunting styles among women as among men. One apparent difference we've found is based on societal/cultural differences that result in men who feel pressured to perform well in the hunt-ing arena. We women haven't had to handle the pressure of expectations placed on us; in fact, no one ever really *expected* us to hunt. Men in general appear to their female counterparts as more goal-driven in shooting game and feel more pressured by their peers to *succeed*. There are, of course, excep-tions to these observations on both sides of the gender divide.

With one exception, the women I interviewed for this article didn't mention ballistics. Most didn't mention what caliber rifle they normally use either, but the most common were .243, .270, 7mm-08 and .25-06. Some women use different calibers for different-sized game, with sizes ranging upwards through .30-06, 7mm Rem. Mag., .338 Win. Mag., and .300 Win. Mag. Some of us own more than one rifle, but for many one rifle does it all. Scopes and other gadgets were never even mentioned, nor were makes or models, bullet weights or loads. To most of us, rifles are simply tools to get the job done. As long as a rifle fits, and it puts game down the way we want, we'll remain true to that rifle—except for Janet, whose bow does the job. **SB**

Why Hunt Birds?

By Joseph C. Greenfield, Jr., M.D.

FOR MORE THAN 50 years, especially after arriving back home with the seat of my pants ripped open by a barbed wire fence, my body lacerated from an encounter with cat-claw briars, and covered with mud and slime after falling into a well-disguised bog, I've asked myself, "Why hunt birds?" Even when everything has gone well, there remain questions in my mind about the sanity of this avocation.

Why hunt birds—specifically, bob-white quail? I have no ready answer, although some may cite healthy exercise and putting meat on the table as motivating factors. Certainly they haven't the slightest bearing on why I hunt birds. Although the sport does require considerable walking, a more vigorous and less time-consuming method of exercising can be achieved with an exercise bicycle. Certainly the mental strain and loss of voice that results from dealing with obstreperous pointers cannot be considered healthy. As for the concept of bird hunting as a source of cheap table fare, it is nothing short of ludicrous. My cost for one year usually runs around $80 per bird—hardly qualifying it as inexpensive food. Granted that quail may taste great to many, but the fact is others (including me) prefer chicken!

In addition to the hunter himself, bird hunting requires three components: birds, bird dogs, and shotguns. The lure of bird hunting is perhaps best explained by examining the following groups of people who are generally regarded as bird hunters: 1) General Outdoorsmen; 2) Shooters; 3) Field Trial Fraternity; 4) Dog Owners: 5) Gun Collectors; and 6) True Bird Hunters.

General outdoorsmen view bird hunting as only one component in a long list of sporting activities, including hunting upland game, waterfowl, and big game. Big game hunting also provides opportunities

for collecting trophies. General outdoorsmen enjoy the camaraderie of a variety of sports, especially drinking and bragging, with bird hunting playing only a minor role in the total sporting experience. They are unlikely to concern themselves with high quality dog work or owning fine shotguns.

The second group—shooters—have a built-in need to kill a large quantity of game. They are, by nature, very competitive and consider bird hunting a sport in which the person who kills the most birds is declared the winner. Shooters can be readily identified by the first question they invariably ask regarding a hunt: "How many birds did you get?" Most bird hunters I've met in recent years fall into this category. They are often good shots, but they won't hesitate to empty a five-shot automatic each time a covey rises. The current plethora of bird hunting preserves depends on these individuals for clients,

ANNE, POINTING QUAIL AT J&R OUTFITTERS NEAR INDIANTOWN, FL. 1991

MISSY'S LITTER, AGE SIX WEEKS, POSES NEAR DURHAM, NC. EVEN AT THAT YOUNG AGE, THESE DOGS WERE VERY IMPRESSIVE. 1996

who may spend $400 or $500 for a day's work. Shooters will expound on how pleased they are about the performance of the high quality of dogs provided for them. But when asked for particulars, prior to or during the covey rise, it becomes clear they had no idea whether the dogs were even in the same county. Shooters regard a shotgun as a useful tool, never as a work of art.

Members of the third group—the field trial community—enjoy the competition of field trails and watching bird dogs perform. They vary between people of wealth who find enjoyment in paying a trainer a lot of money to oversee a dog they own but hardly know, to sportsmen who train and handle their own dogs. Professional and amateur trainers alike are often dedicated, knowledgeable individuals who expend enormous amounts of energy developing dogs with the skills needed to win field trials. But here's the rub: the same characteristics in a dog that result in win-

ning field trials do not necessarily define an excellent bird-hunting dog. I have purchased several pointers who competed successfully in "Shoot-to-Retrieve" trials but were incompetent when it came to finding and pointing wild birds. One very positive aspect of field trails, however, is that dogs bred to perform in major open competition have generally maintained the style and hunting drive of the English pointer. Hat's off to the breeders and trainers responsible.

The fourth category—dog owners—are mostly interested in exercising their dogs. Hunting is not part of their makeup. They have either purchased or been given bird dogs—often a Brittany, Irish setter, or some other fuzzy breed—and become quite attached to them. Having read a description of their dogs provided by the American Kennel Club, these owners have concluded they should be hunters. And so they tramp through the woods, exercising their pets and helping them maintain

healthy bowel habits. Fine shotguns are not part of this scenario.

Gun collectors comprise the fifth category. They avidly seek and acquire fine shotguns anz are enthralled by the feel of a custom double. And while they will occasionally try out their treasures in a hunting venue, their interest in bird hunting and bird dogs is remote at best. Owning the shotgun is what counts, not hunting with it.

The final group, the true bird hunters, consider their addictive avocation nothing less than a key to the enjoyment of life. From late November until early March, the everyday problems of life become unimportant: *Quail season is open!* All the components of bird hunting—birds, dogs, shotguns—combine to paint a beautiful canvas indeed. Unless he's physically disabled, the true bird hunter will choose to hunt wild quail. This endeavor can entail either many hours of fruitless searching, or else taking part in an extraordinarily expensive endeavor. Many shooting preserves make considerable efforts to simulate wild bird hunting by releasing birds as a substitute for the real thing. But for dyed-in-the-wool bird hunters, wild quail in their natural habitat are prerequisites.

A love of bird dogs—the second component in the triad—is essential. In the deep South, the pointer is the overwhelming choice. The dedicated bird hunter insists on high quality dog work and isn't satisfied unless the dogs perform to an extremely high standard. And last, true bird hunters admire fine shotguns. It goes without saying that their choice has to be a double barrel. What kind? Well, if God believed an over-under was superior to a side-by-side, He would have placed our eyes in a different configuration. I will grudgingly admit, though, that using an over-under does not automatically disqualify a person from being a true bird hunter.

Why hunt birds? The simple answer is this: nothing—absolutely nothing—beats watching a pair of pointers cover a picturesque piece of ground in a workmanlike manner before slamming on their brakes to a stylish point. What's even better is admiring them as they handle a running covey with amazing precision. This tableau, followed immediately by the feel of a fine double shotgun brought into play, all accompanied by the thunderous sound of a covey flushing, is an experience without equal.

SHOOTING QUAIL—A PRIMER

Early in life I was taught to believe that a side-by-side double barrel shotgun was the only appropriate weapon with which to hunt birds. I've never questioned the wisdom of this premise, nor have I tried an alternative. Numerous articles and books have been written by notable experts about the proper choice of a shotgun, and I cannot question their sagacity. It all boils down to this: if the only goal is to kill quail, any shotgun that fits should be adequate. I began hunting with a 20-gauge Parker that belonged to my grandfather, and I became reasonably proficient with it. About the time I turned 40, I began wounding too many birds, but it took several years for me to realize that I needed a denser pattern and more shot. I've used a 12-gauge ever since. The 12-gauge shells I now hunt with have either 1 or 11/8 ounces of shot. The recent trend to increase the number of shot in a 20-gauge shell has essentially turned the 20 into a 12. However, the "souped-up"

THE AUTHOR AND LUKE. PHOTO TAKEN JUST AS A COVEY OF BIRDS LEFT THE GROUND. HOBE SOUND, FL. 1993

POPPY, POINTING IN AN OPEN FIELD. INDIANTOWN, FL. 1996

20 won't pattern as well as the 12 because the shot string is longer. Contrary to the opinion of many outdoor sports mavens, it is *not* more sporting to use a 20-gauge. Any shotgun used for upland gunning should also be fairly light. Mine weighs six pounds, four ounces, which is just right for me and not much heavier than most 20-gauge shotguns. Professionals who make their living shooting in international skeet, sporting clays and trap competition, or who are on the live pigeon circuit, generally prefer a heavy gun. No doubt such well-trained athletes do quite well killing quail with a 7 1/2-pound or heavier shotgun. They have the speed and strength to point and shoot a heavier gun quickly, even in thick cover. But, as one grows older and reflexes slow down, a lighter gun makes a better choice. It's true that a lighter gun will produce more recoil, but then most bird hunters shoot far less than those who expend two to three hundred shells a day in competition. What about the choke? It's hard to beat improved cylinder.

In my opinion, the primary secret to successful bird shooting *is to become thoroughly familiar with your shotgun.* Pointing and shooting should become second nature. How much time should be spent practicing in order to excel? Rather than learning by actually hunting, and where opportunities are limit-

ed, I recommend buying or borrowing a hand trap or another device that throws skeet. Once you can break 90 percent of the skeet thrown at all angles, you'll be sufficiently skilled to kill birds.

Your choice of shotgun shells isn't too critical, but avoid the cheapest ones on the market. They contain soft shot that is easily deformed, resulting in poor patterns and poor penetration. Shells with hard shot are recommended. Although quail can be killed with shot sizes ranging from six to nine, I've settled on 7?.

The next lesson is simple: *concentrate on killing the quail.* Along with many dedicated bird hunters, I find this advice incredibly difficult to follow. I am so entranced watching the dogs point and enjoying the entire spectacle that my mind drifts away from the task at hand. On many occasions, birds have flown off in all directions without any presence of mind on my part to shoot. So if your only goal is to kill birds, paying attention to other aspects of the hunting experience can be a real hindrance.

Following are a few more observations that might help place you in the best possible situation to kill birds. First, be sure to consider quail as having the

LIB II, POINTING WITH BIRD IN MOUTH. JOEY O'BANNON LOOKS IMPRESSED. 1993

CODY, POINTING SAGE GROUSE NEAR FARSON, WY. 1997

attributes of a gentleman who is an unwilling participant in the sport. These birds deserve every courtesy, including that of a clean kill. It goes without saying that quail must be shot *only* while on the wing. Ground shooting is the moral equivalent of stealing money from the church collection plate.

Next, successful shooting begins with a correct approach to the pointing dogs. They should be approached in a way that avoids shooting directly over them when the covey flushes. Despite opinions to the contrary, quail cannot be driven in any predetermined direction. They fly wherever they want, usually to their favorite cover where they have an uncanny ability to interpose a bush or sapling between themselves and the hunter as they make their escape. The hunter therefore needs to survey the terrain, identify the most likely escape route, then try to position himself for an unobstructed shot after the flush. The hunter should walk to the pointing dogs at a reasonably brisk gait, keeping his eyes focused in front of the dog, not on the ground (a bird seen on the ground, when flushed, will invariably be missed). When the covey flushes, the hunter should be well-balanced and positioned to shoot. If right-handed, the left foot should be slightly in front, the body weight shifted forward for an easy pivot in either direction. The hunter should approach the covey

with short, quick steps to facilitate good balance and allow him to assume the correct shooting position.

The gun should be carried with the butt below the armpit and, according to common practice, with the muzzle pointing up approximately 45 degrees. Actually, you'll get better accuracy with the muzzle pointed in a downward direction, Then, as it's brought up to point, the gun's momentum will follow in the same direction as the rising bird. Conversely, with the muzzle pointing up, the momentum carries the gun in precisely the wrong direction. Also, most birds flying directly away from the hunter are missed by undershooting., hence another argument in favor of carrying the shotgun with the muzzle pointed down. The only problem is that, with the muzzle down, the hunter might inadvertently discharge the weapon and blow his dog's head off.

When, after moving 20 to 30 feet in front of the pointing dogs, nothing has happened, stop and order the dogs to relocate and point. If the birds are running, both hunter and dogs must follow in a hurry. The goal is to move the dogs fast enough so the birds can't escape, but without flushing them.

THE AUTHOR CARRIES A SAGE GROUSE WHILE FAITH POINTS ANOTHER. 1997

THE SWAMP BUGGY, LOADED WITH ALL SORTS OF PARAPHERNALIA, IS READY FOR A DAY'S HUNT.

When the covey flushes, try to kill the first bird off the ground. If it doesn't fall, shoot again. But if the bird goes down and the hunter feels compelled to shoot again, there's plenty of time to pick out a second target. Good hunters avoid shooting into the middle of a covey; instead, they pick out birds on the periphery. The scarcity of wild quail makes it mandatory not to "covey shoot" and risk wounding several birds.

The appropriate time to shoot after the birds have flushed has been dealt with by numerous writers, including the late, great Nash Buckingham, an accomplished athlete who shot thousands of quail. In his book, *Mark Right*, he admonished hunters not to shoot so fast as to miss or disintegrate the bird. Buckingham's "repression technique" taught hunters to wait for the covey to get airborne *before* picking out a bird and shouldering the shotgun. That advice is well and good if your reflexes happen to be as fast

as his. Mine aren't. Under normal circumstances, by the time I can point and squeeze the trigger, the bird should be within killing distance. I may have disintegrated a few birds at close range using this approach but at least I've avoided wounding even more birds at 30 or 35 yards.

The best way to determine the proper time to shoot after the birds have flushed is by judging your own capabilities correctly. For me, the hardest bird to hit is one that flies straight away. I often undershoot because I failed to account for the fact that the bird is rising. A rising bird must be covered by the muzzle when the shot is taken. A flushed bird that flies directly over the hunter is difficult to hit. Usually the hunter must turn around and find the bird again before shooting. For right-handed shooters, the easiest bird to hit is one that flies to his left, because it stays in range for a longer time. Also, the right-to-left movement of the shotgun is a natural

one. Birds flying from left to right, however, are harder to kill. When the hunter swings his gun to the right, he often drops (rainbows) the muzzle of the gun and undershoots. But whether the bird flies to the left or right, the hunter should move the muzzle along the plane of the bird's flight, with the shot taken just as the muzzle passes the bird. Frankly, when I'm functioning correctly, I'm totally unaware of everything except pointing the gun and watching the bird fall.

As soon as the gun is empty, reload and be ready to shoot again (this is not uncommon when a covey flushes and one or two birds sit and flush late). Often in close cover, once the gun has been fired, a hunter can't tell if a bird has been hit. Even when he thinks he's missed, the dogs should be sent in the direction the birds flew. I'm amazed by the number of times a dog has found a dead bird 100 yards or more from the point of flush. The key to killing birds from a covey rise is to pick out just one bird—then make sure you've killed it. Strangely, most hunters shoot with less success on coveys than on singles, in part due to all the excitement generated by the covey rise and the difficulty in picking out one bird among many. On the other hand, a hunter who has lost the thrill of a covey rise should probably switch to bungee jumping or skydiving.

In a case where flushed birds have taken off over a pond or thick marsh where it will be impossible to

HORATIO (SON) AND MISSY (MOTHER) POINTING. INDIANTOWN, FL. 1999

AN ENTIRE CONTINGENT OF BIRD DOGS ON THE "CHAIN GANG" WAITING TO BE FED. IN FARSON, WY. 1998

retrieve them, it's best not to shoot. Should the hunter follow this advice, but his dog expects a reward for his efforts no matter what, my advice is to discharge the gun and mutter a favorite profanity. That's the best way I've learned to communicate a *miss* to a dog. Frequently a bird with only a broken wing will dive to the ground and appear quite dead. Unless you're certain the bird has been killed outright, let the dog "hunt dead" immediately. That way, the bird won't have time to run off.

On a given day, how many birds from a covey should be killed? My personal limit is one per covey rise and one single. A covey can thus be hunted two or three times without being decimated.

When hunting released birds, especially those that have been in the field for only a short period of time, the sport *changes markedly*. For example, because their feathers lack oil, released quail become waterlogged—especially early in the morning—and have a hard time getting airborne. An instinctive bird shooter will hesitate, then delay too long. By the time he fires, the birds will be out of range. Newly released birds know nothing about cover and will fly willy-nilly in any direction. Trying to figure their escape route is a waste of time. Rather than fly through bushes and other obstructions, as do wild quail, the released birds fly over them. Also, when

pen-raised birds flush they frequently alight after traveling only a few yards. This is danger time for bird dogs in the vicinity can easily be shot. One of my favorite bird dogs—Fanny—was killed by an overzealous bird hunter trying to bring down a short-flighted bird. A quick-witted bird dog can actually catch slow-flying released birds in the air. This makes it mandatory when pulling the trigger that the only living thing in a pattern is the bird.

All this advice is predicated on the notion that the reader hunts by himself or herself. For me, hunting with someone else generally detracts from the enjoyment of quail hunting, which probably puts me in a minority. Obviously, if two dedicated bird hunters are compatible and enjoy hunting together, that's fine. But two should be the limit. Unless you are thoroughly

THE AUTHOR POSES IN THE GUN ROOM HOLDING A 12 GAUGE PURDY PRESENTED BY HIS COLLEAGUES IN 1995 ON THE OCCASION OF HIS RETIREMENT AS CHAIRMAN OF THE DEPARTMENT OF MEDICINE AT DUKE MEDICAL CENTER, NC.

familiar with the hunting habits of a companion, you run the risk of having some portion of your anatomy rearranged by a trigger-happy partner.

When two hunters go into the field, rules must be established and adhered to. It should be made crystal clear who will shoot at which bird, and that no shot will ever be taken in the direction of the other hunter. The hunter on the right who is approaching the pointing dogs must shoot only those birds that fly to the right, while his partner shoots those moving to the left. Occasionally both hunters may double on the same bird as it flies directly ahead, but it's not acceptable to crossfire into the other hunter's territory. The truth is, quail hunting for the uninitiated can be quite dangerous. In that regard, it's vital to know at all times where your partner is. For some reason, a novice frequently assumes he must stalk the pointing dogs, moving toward them very slowly, as if emulating Daniel Boone. He will invariably fall behind until suddenly the back of his partner's head becomes an excellent target for a load of shot. If, despite repeated requests to keep up, your partner continues to lag, fall on the ground and feign a seizure. It may save your life. And don't believe him when he swears, "I won't shoot unless a bird flies my way." When a covey flushes, a novice hunter may be seized by temporary in-sanity and do things he'll vehemently deny later on. Unfortunately, his hunting partner, if dead, will not be in a position to refute his version. Especially dangerous is shooting at singles the dog hasn't pointed. For example, a bird flushing between two hunters and flying to the rear is always best left for another day.

Should your partner ever shoot at a bird flying over your head, DEPART. Leave the scene. Don't even wait for your momentary deafness to recede. Your companion is a trigger-happy madman intent on adding you to his trophy collection.

I hope these musings will not only help readers in their efforts to improve marksmanship when hunting quail, but provide as well a framework for participating safely in this great sport. SB

Dr. Greenfield's further adventures with quail hunting and dog training will be published in book form, under the title **A Quail Hunter's Odyssey,** *by Amwell Press, P.O. Box 5385, Clinton, NC 08809-0385.*

Hunting The Wily Woodchuck: Finding The Perfect Load

By Stan Trzoniec

AS FAR BACK as I can remember, there never seemed to be a year that I did not pursue the wily woodchuck. Starting at the tender age of eight, my uncle's farm in New York State was a heaven on earth for this young hunter. During the summer months, I roamed the fields stalking chucks with nothing more than an old Winchester single-shot .22 rifle and a pocket of green apples. It was this rich experience that helped me in later years to hone the skills I needed for hunting larger game on the North American continent.

But while I was new to the sport a half-century ago, men had already been hunting woodchucks for decades. Even in the days when propellants, rifles and optical sights had yet to reach their peak, it was a great pastime. Anyone could enjoy this outdoor activity at a modest cost; moreover, the woodchuck was found in most states, not to mention the vast rolling plains of Canada. These animals love rich, green fields loaded with clover, especially in the summer months. When you got right down to it, hunting woodchucks was at best a massive freelance effort to control a species that populated quickly at a time when natural predators were relatively scarce.

I can remember while riding our tractor on the side fender how the chucks would pop up and down, running from one hole to the other, or just lying lazily on fieldstone walls. Often they would overrun the fields, causing farmers to seek out an expert chuck hunter in the area. And that's how I became one popular kid! Landowners where I lived and beyond were happy to rid their fields of these pests. It certainly was cheaper and much easier to supply a lad like myself with a box of .22 long rifle cartridges than it was to sacrifice a heifer to the but-cher because of a broken leg or hip caused by a chuck hole.

To me, that was the golden age for both varmint rifles and cartridges. Looking back, I recall hunters from town setting up their heavy barreled target rifles, complete with Unertl scopes, chambered in

THE AUTHOR SCOUTS THE FIELDS FOR SIGNS OF A WOODCHUCK ON A HOT DAY IN JULY.

THE AUTHOR PREFERS TO ACTIVELY HUNT WOOD-
CHUCKS, RATHER THAN SIT STILL AND SNIPE AT THEM
AS THEY APPEAR. BLENDING IN BEHIND A FARM
TRACTOR (AS SHOWN) IS ONE SUCCESSFUL TECH-
NIQUE FOR SURPRISING THOSE PESKY VARMINTS.

the .219 Donaldson Wasp or .220 Swift. Both
cartridges have always fascinated me, but for some
reason that .219 Donaldson was the most popular
among the fellows in and around Portlandville
and Cooperstown, New York. The mystique of
that particular cartridge stayed with me over the
years; in fact, not long ago I had a Ruger Number
1 chambered in the .219 Donaldson. I've since
put it to good use on a regular basis around the
shorter hedgerows of the local farmland.

While I was still popping chucks at 50 to 60
yards with my time-worn Winchester, the chuck
hunters I knew had the luxury of shooting custom
rifles chambered in the .22 Hornet, .22 Niedner
Magnum or the .22 Savage High Power, which, by
the way, used the same 25-35 case necked down to
.22 caliber. Still later, as I moved into my teens and
took more of an interest in guns and cartridges, I
can remember the .218 Bee, .219 Zipper, .220 Swift

and .257 Roberts. There was also some mention of
a new cartridge, called the "Varminter," that was
getting lots of attention. Actually, it was nothing
more than the .250/3000 Savage case necked down
to .22 caliber. Later, it would be publicly commer-
cialized as the .22/250 Remington and remains one
of the best-selling factory varmint cartridges around.

But these represented only the tip of the iceberg.
Forgotten now are such classic cartridges as the .228
Ackley Magnum, .22 Gibson High Power, .22 HP
Lovell, .22 Streamline and the Mashburn Zipper.
Some varmint hunters went to even greater lengths.
For example, John G. Schnerring took a 7mm case,
necked it down to .22 caliber, and came up with
the .22/4000, claiming he got 3,999 fps with a 45
grain bullet with 42 grains of 3031 powder (later,
he recorded 4059 fps).

THE TELLTALE SIGN OF A CHUCK IS USUALLY A
TALL MOUND OF DIRT AROUND AN ENTRANCE HOLE;
THE ESCAPE HOLE, HOWEVER, IS ACTUALLY LESS
NOTICEABLE AND FURTHER AWAY.

Rifles tailored to the needs of the small game aficionado started to take on a different look as well. We began to see more and more custom rifles chambered for these so-called wildcat cartridges. Since the major arms manufacturers were not interested in wildcats, this was the only way to go for those who preferred shooting these experimental and mostly untested cartridges. Winchester High Wall rifles became especially popular because woodchuck hunting, being such a leisurely sport, really didn't need repeating rifles. Equipped with high combs, short forends and fancy wood, they were both pretty to look at and surprisingly accurate. Later, some hunters utilized the likes of Remington-Hepburn, Sharps-Bochardt and Stevens single-shot actions as the basis for their homegrown varmint rigs.

For the traditionalist, Mauser-styled actions were always in demand. Really good woodchuck rifles were made from the Remington Model 720 or 30-S bolt action. Winchester's fine Model 54 was chambered for both the .22 Hornet and .220 Swift, followed by the Model 70. Vintage National Match

AFTER FIRING HIS WEATHERBY RIFLE IN .224 WEATHERBY MAGNUM, THE AUTHOR SHOWS OFF A CHUCK MOMENTS AFTER IT WAS TAKING A NAP ON A STONE WALL SOME 325 YARDS DOWN RANGE. USING A BIPOD IS ESSENTIAL FOR SUCH SHOTS, ESPECIALLY WHERE NATURAL RESTS ARE NOT AVAILABLE.

NEXT TIME, TRY SITTING DOWN, USING ANY REST THAT'S HANDY WHEN DISPATCHING CHUCKS AT RANGES UP TO 300 YARDS.

ALL KINDS OF RIFLES ARE USED EFFECTIVELY IN THE SPORT OF WOODCHUCKING. AT AROUND 200 YARDS, THE AUTHOR USED A BROWNING SINGLE-SHOT LEVER RIFLE CHAMBERED IN .22/250 REMINGTON. NOTE THE CLOVER-RICH FIELD IN WHICH THE AUTHOR FOUND HIS WOODCHUCK.

Springfields were chambered for varmint cartridges despite their longer actions. Recently, a varmint hunter told me that if you didn't have a Springfield with the nickel steel bolt it simply wasn't worth the trouble of making the conversion. According to him, this was the best of the best and well-suited for most wildcatting activities.

Rifle scopes 25 years ago were more than adequate for field use. Binoculars and cameras had paved the way for scopes from Belding and Mull, Lyman, Fecker and Unertl, among others. The Lyman 8X and 10X, plus the Unertl 10X, were the most widely used in my neck of the woods. The Unertl was by far the most exotic, complete

with a recoil spring that ran the length of the scope tube. It helped to take the brunt of recoil forces, enabling hunters to keep a constant zero on distant targets. Apparently it worked, because I can recall seeing plenty of Unertl scopes atop various rifles.

While that may all be great for hunters out west, chuck hunting has gotten more restrictive in the east. Urban sprawl has made most of the farmers I know sell out to the developers. Now, with increasingly less land available woodchucks are becoming harder and harder to find. Where I live, small cartridges are called for, but in the western part of New York, medium and even larger bore rifles with lighter bullets are used for targets at longer ranges. Actually, using a big game rifle for woodchucks is a good way to become familiar with one of these rifles before embarking on an expensive hunt further west.

Varmint hunters today have it made—not only in their choice of rifles, but in their cartridges and optics too. Every year, something new or exciting comes on the market. Whether you choose to shoot with commercial or wildcat cartridges, the choices never seem to end. For practical woodchuck hunting. I stick to calibers .24 and below. While larger cartridges can reach out further (depending upon bullet weight and velocity), they can, when fired all day long, become heavy and tiresome. Simply put, it becomes a matter of physics: small calibers equal less recoil, better accuracy and more fun. And speaking of accuracy, if your rifle doesn't shoot one-inch groups at 100 yards or less, you'd better get another one.

FOR LONG RANGE SHOOTING, A SCOPE WITH A PARALLAX ADJUSTMENT IS ADVISABLE. WITH IT, YOU'LL BE DEAD ON WITH BOTH SHOT AND FOCUS ON DISTANCE SHOTS.

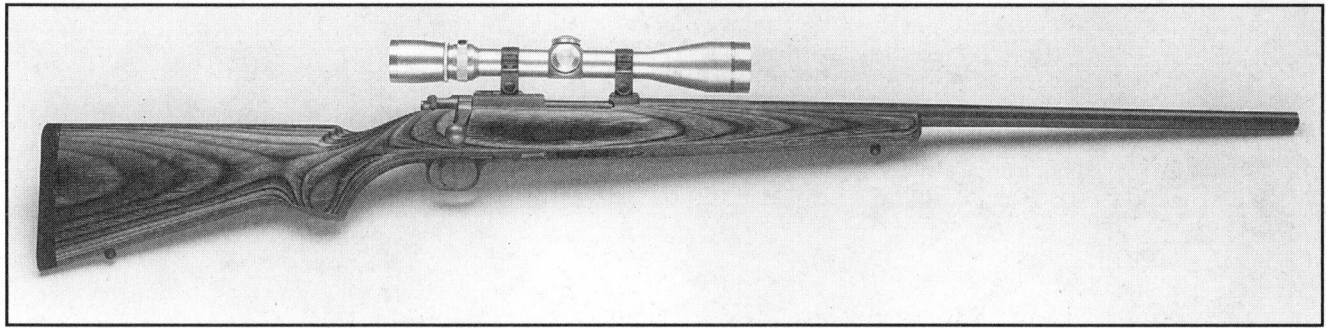

FOR HUNTING IN ALL KINDS OF WEATHER, TAKE A LOOK AT THIS SPORTER RIFLE COMPLETE WITH LAMINATED STOCK: A PERFECT EXAMPLE OF A RUGER RIFLE COMPLETE WITH A LEUPOLD 3-9 SCOPE.

Fortunately good and inexpensive rifles abound. Whether your choice is bolt action, lever, single shot or semiautomatic, there's plenty to choose from. My own preference leans toward sporter-type rifles that I can carry all day, as opposed to "heavy-barrel" guns that limit travel because of their weight. Remington has seemingly covered the field in both rifles and cartridges from .17 Remington to the .243 Winchester or .25/06 Remington. With rifles available in both right- and left-hand actions, the choice is not limited to wood stocks or blued actions. Synthetic stocks, longer barrels and stainless actions are now available, and there are even special rifles tailored to your size and build, not to mention your cartridge preference and financial situation. A few years back, Remington's Custom Shop made a tack driver for me in .222 Remington (with a custom rifle you have more control over the final product). In my case, the shop honored my request for a sporter rifle complete with a stock of slightly fuller proportions, especially in the forearm, so I could "benchrest" the gun in the field. Remington came

through exactly as I had envisioned the final product, complete with a target-type trigger. With a Bausch and Lomb target scope, this rifle can shoot half-inch groups all day with hand loads.

Browning also offers an extensive line for varmint hunters, including sporter- and varmint-styled A-Bolt rifles. A special model—called the *Micro Hunter*—is chambered in the .22 Hornet. It checks in at six pounds (plus a few ounces) making it a good companion for all-day hunting. Browning's line of single shot rifles has grown over the years, one of my all-time favorites being the Model 1885 Low Wall chambered in .22 Hornet, along with such perennial favorites as the .223 Remington and .243 Winchester.

Sturm, Ruger has certainly made a name for itself in contemporary gun designs, offering several good choices for woodchuck hunters. At the top of my list is Ruger's Number 1, which can be had ready-made in .218 Bee Hornet, and even the .220 Swift. I often use the Ruger action as the basis for my wildcats, including the .219 Donaldson and the new .225 Winchester. The Ruger M-77 bolt action series

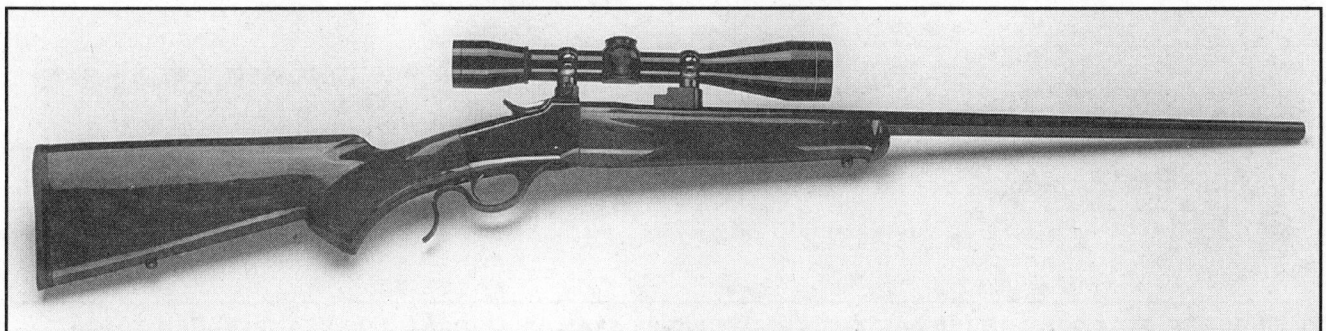

THIS BROWNING LOW WALL IN .22 HORNET IS THE PERFECT CHOICE FOR CLOSE-IN SHOTS (WITHIN 100 YARDS OR SO). TOPPED OFF WITH A LEUPOLD 6X SCOPE, IT'S HIGHLY ACCURATE—ESPECIALLY WITH HANDLOADS.

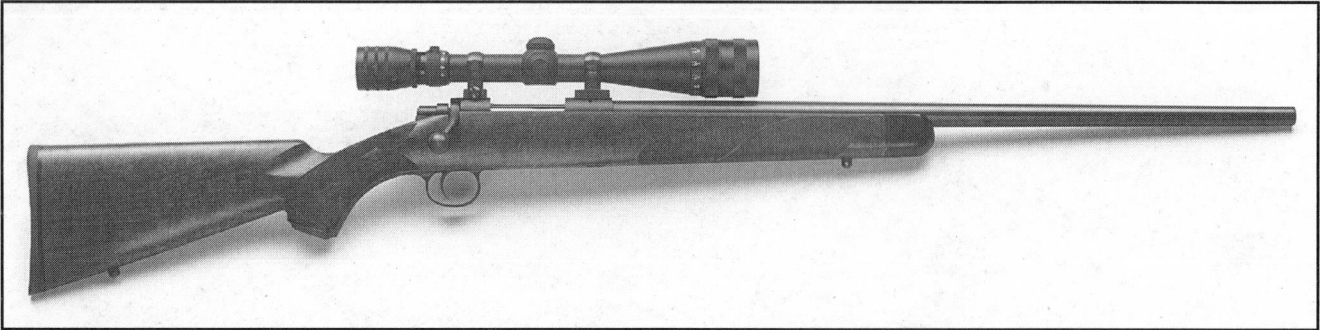

FOR HUNTING WOODCHUCKS, YOU CAN'T BEAT A FINE CUSTOM RIFLE—ESPECIALLY WHEN YOU CAN'T FIND THE CARTRIDGE YOU'VE BEEN LUSTING AFTER. WHEN THE AUTHOR WANTED A RIFLE IN THE .221 REMINGTON FIREBALL, HE TURNED TO COOPER ARMS. THE END RESULT WAS THIS GREAT RIFLE CAPABLE OF LESS THAN HALF-INCH GROUPS WITH SELECTED HANDLOADS.

comes in the usual .22 cartridge assortment, including the Swift. For folks who want a lighter piece, the new line of Model 77/44's are chambered in .22 Long Rifle, .22 Magnum or .22 Hornet.

Weatherby brings an interesting heritage into the world of varmint rifles and I'm privileged to have samples of the very best. One is the "Varmint-Master," a trim, nicely stocked, short action rifle chambered for the .224 Weatherby Magnum and .22/250 Remington. Armed with an original Weatherby scope and chambered in the company's proprietary .224 Weatherby, I've gunned down more than my share of chucks at ranges surpassing 300 yards. Sadly, this rifle is not available on a production basis (although you can still find it on the secondary market). But there's a more high-tech version, called the "Super VarmintMaster," which has taken the VarmintMaster's place. With a slightly

longer, heavier barrel fluted to dissipate heat, all wrapped up in a synthetic stock and chambered in the .22/250 Remington, it is field-ready and extremely accurate.

Winchester, of course, has its own line of varmint rifles, all of which I've used at one time or another. Available in both wood and synthetic stocked versions, these newly designed Model 70 rifles have brought the heritage and class of a famous company to hunters in the field. Along with its revamped line of Tikka rifles, Sako offers a neat line of varmint rigs and sporting rifles. Cooper Arms in Montana built me a "production-custom" rifle in .221 Remington Fireball that has become one of the most accurate rifles in my rack. H-S Precision makes tack drivers in a choice of calibers (on an "order only" basis), while Savage and the new Mossberg SSi promise to yield some unique shooting experiences.

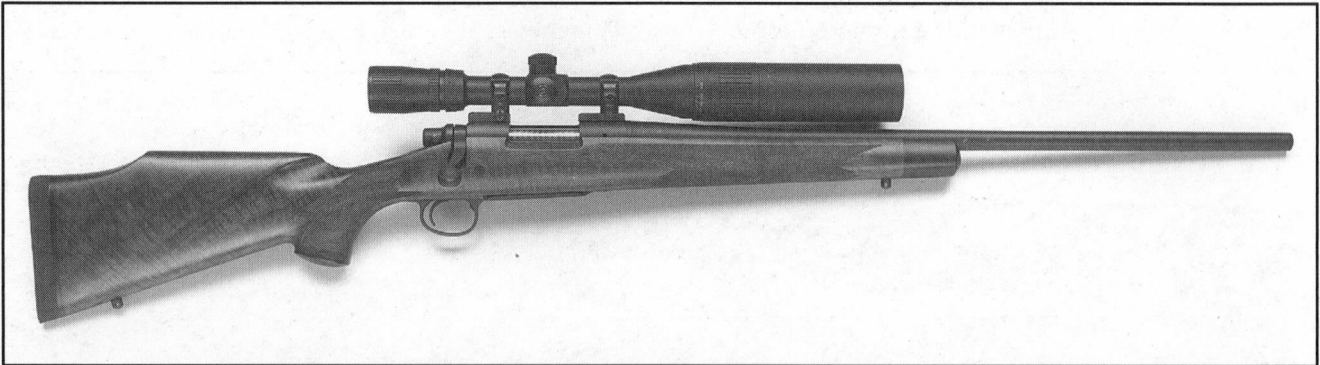

IT'S HARD TO BEAT SOME OF THE FACTORY CUSTOM SHOPS AVAILABLE TODAY. FOR EXAMPLE, REMINGTON BUILT THIS RIFLE FOR THE AUTHOR WITH A LENGTHENED FOREARM AND HEFTIER PROPORTIONS ALL CHAMBERED IN THE TACK-DRIVING .222 REMINGTON.

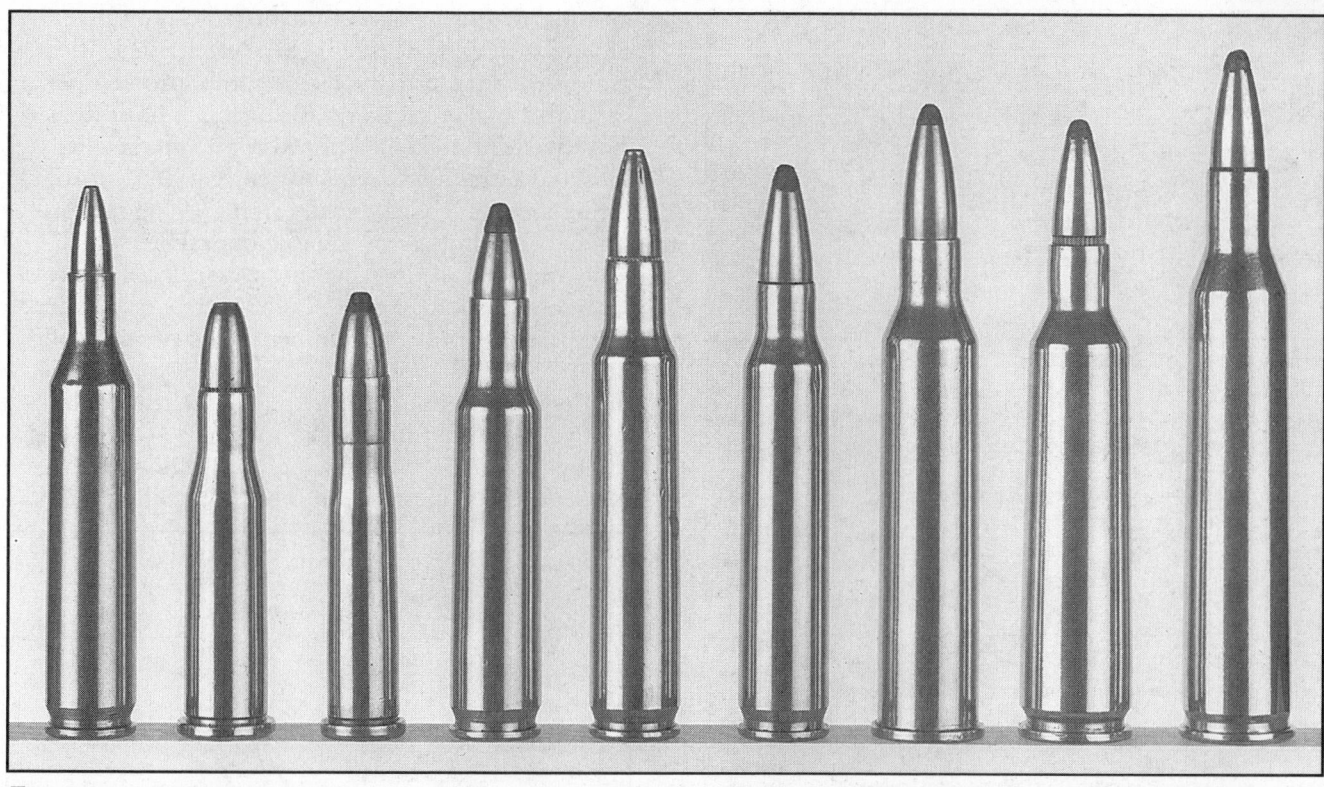

FOR MOST VARMINT HUNTING SITUATIONS, THIS LINEUP OF .22 CALIBER CARTRIDGES WILL DO THE JOB IN MOST AREAS. FROM LEFT TO RIGHT: 17 REMINGTON, .218 BEE, .22 HORNET, .222 REMINGTON, .222 REM. MAG., .223 REMINGTON, .225 WINCHESTER, .22/250 REMINGTON, .220 SWIFT.

Modern, efficient cartridges like the ones mentioned above have helped make woodchuck hunting a pleasure—and over the years I've used almost every one of them. On the lower end of the scales, I like the .218 Bee, .219 Zipper, .22 Horner and .22 K-Hornet (which can be fire-formed from common .22 Hornet brass right there in the chamber of a new rifle). The .221 Remington Fireball (now discontinued) in the older Remington XP-100 pistol is a great round in any rifle, matching favorably with the .22 PPC. The same applies to the more common .222, .223 and .22/250 Remington cartridges. I also like the .224 Weatherby Magnum and the .220 Swift. Most, if not all, of the more common .22 caliber cartridges can be counted on to deliver at least 3,500 to 4,000 fps without much effort on the shooter's part.

Moving up the woodchuck scale, there are the .243 Winchester, .257 Roberts, .25/06 Remington, or even the .257 Weatherby with lighter bullets for greater velocity and taut string trajectories. Recoil may prove too strong for some folks, but most hunters, especially out west, can prove their mettle on small game like the woodchuck even when the distances start to hit the 300-mark.

Handloading and wildcatting go hand in hand, of course, with some cartridges becoming what I call "no-sweat" wildcats. They can all be formed easily be means of die sets or by fire-forming within a rifle chamber, adding a new dimension in varmint hunting possibilities. Cartridges like the .22 Remington BR, .22 PPC, .22 K-Hornet, .225 Winchester, or even the .219 Donaldson Wasp, can be whipped up in short order. Obviously, you'll need a gun to go along with these "no-sweat" wildcats, but a custom barrel maker can turn the job around in a hurry so you can return to the hunt without missing a beat.

Even without getting into wildcat cartridges, all commercial ones can be tailored to a specific rifle simply by trying as many brands as your wallet

FOR THOSE WHO LIKE TO SPEND LONG AFTERNOONS IN THE FIELD, AND WHERE COST IS A FACTOR, HANDLOADING IS THE WAY TO GO. ALL COMPONENTS SHOWN ARE READILY AVAILABLE; AND DON'T FORGET, LOADING MANUALS SHOULD ALWAYS BE USED FOR ACCURATE LOADS AND INFORMATION.

allows. Like handloading, the more rounds you shoot, the better chance of finding the perfect load for your rifle. By way of illustration, I was shooting a Weatherby Vanguard in .22/250 Remington a few years ago and had purchased enough for varmint hunting only. After trying a dozen or more factory loads, the last one—Winchester's sampling of the same cartridge—shrunk group sizes down to within a half-inch at the century mark. I took note of the

lot number on the flap of the box and promptly ordered a case. That rifle is still shooting half-inch groups with the original factory ammunition.

In this high-tech world, woodchuck hunting is still what you make it. For those who are new to the game, after a few years, when that first cutting comes around, you'll actually start looking forward to it. Your mind will wonder about taking some time off, maybe splurging on a new rifle, or another set of dies, or maybe some bullets, brass or powder. On these early days of summer, I find myself scouting the fields for both chucks and their fresh hole diggings. Sure enough those guys are already hard at work preparing for another summer of frolicking. It all takes me back to my good old childhood days. Now all I need are some of those green apples! **SB**

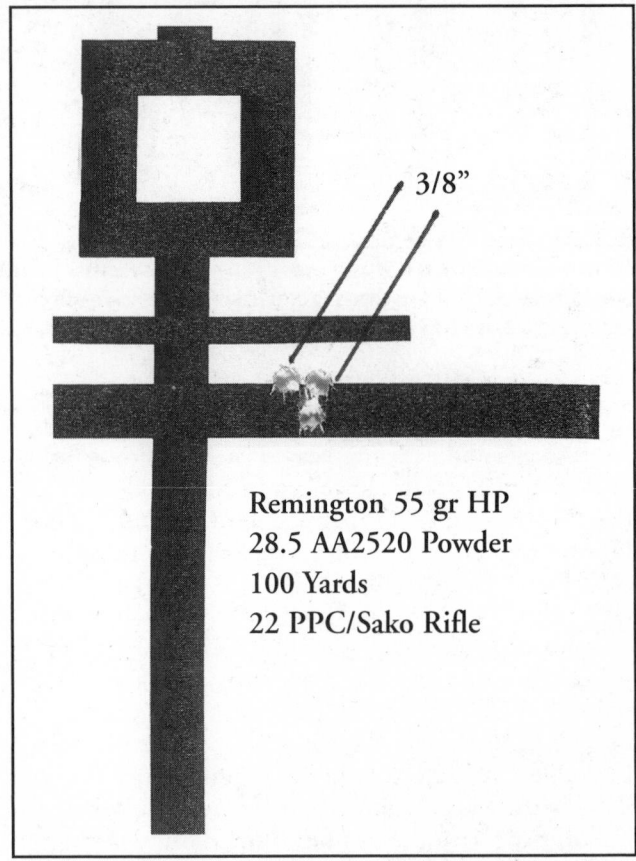

3/8"

Remington 55 gr HP
28.5 AA2520 Powder
100 Yards
22 PPC/Sako Rifle

THIS DRAWING REPRESENTS A PRIME EXAMPLE OF A GREAT VARMINT COMBINATION. HUNTING CHUCKS WITH THE .22 PPC CARTRIDGE, THE AUTHOR SQUEEZED OUT GROUPS AS SMALL AS THIS ONE AT 100 YARDS. PERFECT!

Guns On The Net

BY WILF E. PYLE

TO STATE THE obvious, electronic technology of the chip variety surrounds us and has become part of our everyday lives. You can't go shooting or hunting these days without seeing a cell phone, a palm pilot or a notebook computer somewhere near the shooting hand of a hunter. Indeed, Stoeger's *Shooter's Bible* was among the first firearm publications to bring the world of shooting software to the attention of its readers with a full review (by this author) of shooter-oriented software in a 1989 article called "Computer Software for Today's Shooters." Now, it is the Internet's turn. Who would have guessed, only a few years ago, that this too would blossom into the world's grandest interactive catalog—at least, for the time being. For most shooters, it's difficult to grasp that what started out as a military tool with restricted applications, or an academic curiosity that linked university mathematicians and theoreticians, would end up downloaded onto the desks and benches of shooters right next to their loading tools and other assorted outdoor gear.

Briefly, the Internet story began in 1973 when the U.S. Defense Advanced Research Projects Agency investigated ways of interlinking the various types of packet networks existing at that time. The idea was to develop what computer geeks call "communication protocols," which are really codes that let computers talk to each other once they are hooked up across many networks. They called this the *Interneting Project*, and the system of networks that emerged from its research became known as the "Internet."

By 1986, the U.S. National Science Foundation had begun its development of the NSFNET, which now provides a major communication service for the Internet. The National Aeronautics and Space Administration (NASA) and the U.S. Department of Energy both contributed additional resources, called NSINET and ESNET. In Europe, major international backbones, such as NORDUNET and others, provided connections to more than 100,000 computers on a large number of networks.

THE AUTHOR FOUND THIS BANDOLEER ON THE INTERNET USING DOGPILE. IT MAKES A NICE MATCH FOR THE .30-30 MODEL 94 WINCHESTER (SHOWN ABOVE) HE CARRIED IN HIS YOUTH.

THE INTERNET ALLOWS USERS TO SORT OUT DIFFERENT MODELS AND CLASSES OF FIREARMS. THE AUTHOR UNCOVERED SOME BASIC INFORMATION ABOUT THE UNIQUE MODEL 24 DOUBLE BARREL WINCHESTER SHOTGUN (ABOVE) AND THE UNCOMMON STEVENS MODEL 58 REPEATING BOLT ACTION SHOTGUN (BELOW) WITH ITS 3-SHOT MAGAZINE.

Much early support for the Internet community came from the U.S. federal government. During the late 1980s, Internet users and network sites grew internationally and soon began to include commercial facilities. Indeed, the bulk of the Internet system today is made up of private networking facilities in educational and research institutions, businesses and government organizations throughout the world. Today, more than 300 million websites on the World Wide Web are in use. Pick a favorite aspect of shooting or firearms, and you'll find a website touting its goods and services or providing advice on nearly every technical feature of interest to technophiles and users everywhere. One particularly interesting aspect of the Net is the extensive use of "chat rooms," where questions, information and general old-fashioned storytelling are available for surfers to thread into. This communication form was unknown until the web blossomed. In the past, magazine editors hired whole stables of writers who banged out technical answers to distant questions on manual typewriters. Jack O'Connor alone received about 2,000 questions a months. Now, with realtime Net services, an answer is often only moments away. This has made information truly available to the masses. Marshall McLuhan was probably right when he said, "The medium is the message."

Recently, major firearms companies have begun cataloging and showcasing their products on the net. Up to then, they were slow in jumping on the Net bandwagon because they had always felt that too few shooters or gun buffs were all that interested in keyboarding. But as new shooters have entered the market place, things have changed. Those same companies now seek information in a form and substance with which they're comfortable and familiar. As for older shooters, the truth is that many .30-06 shooters

are dying to have their own computers and high-speed Internet connections. Those who are not directly related—so-called edge players—comprise the shooting and hunting marketplace: mould makers, bullet casters, reloading supply makers, cases, safes, gun locks and related items. All of these adjuncts were quick to see the benefits of the world-wide Net and its ability to get into the workplaces or home offices of small businesses and independent entrepreneurs.

The Net is also a kind of techno-tool that has achieved prominence at the right time. Office workers have found themselves chained to a computer terminal for years—giving new meaning to the word "linked"—in search of information concerning their daily routines. Small wonder that computer skills have been transferred to special interests, such as guns and shooting. Not many people today work outdoors where computers have not yet captured the work environment fully. Also, many of those people who now work at home are linked through the Net to their regular jobs.

Another important issue is the relatively low cost at which computer hardware and accessories (called

peripherals) are obtained. The first desktop computer I ever used was a Wang 2000 magnetic reader. It cost several thousand dollars in 1970 and had just enough capacity to determine simple statistics and produce strange-looking reports on green cash register tape that only a dedicated computer nerd could interpret. Today, for the cost of a couple boxes of cartridges, you can have access to the Internet and a month's use of highspeed lines, plus a printer that can output every color of the rainbow.

Book publishers were among the first to appreciate the web as an amazing marketing opportunity, witness the recent rash of books about the Internet. Commercial interests of all kinds have now repositioned the Internet beyond the sole domain of the research and educational communities. For shooters, the ease with which outdoor books can be bought through the Net from booksellers or direct from the publishers represents a major advantage, enabling shooters to obtain the kind of information we need. This whole notion of empowering an individual with quick and easy availability of information is the foundation for the Internet's growing success. Most people today have access to a computer and some form of

SCOPE MANUFACTURERS ARE WELL REPRESENTED ON THE INTERNET. CHECK OUT THESE SITES, MANY OF WHICH ARE IN THE DIRECTORY (BEGINNING ON P. 557) FOR THE LATEST PRODUCT INFORMATION.

the Internet, ranging anywhere from dial-up to highspeed lines. The technology has been much improved, with many complex electronic actions having taken place unseen by users. In computer talk, this process is referred to as "transparent procession." These improved technologies, taken together, have provided an information tool transcending all ages, economic classes and interests.

Armed with on-line knowledge, the firearms hobbyist can now participate in making decisions, both large and small, concerning relevant products, general information, background history and detailed technical specifications. The entire firearms industry and its related products are now easily located on the web, making it easier for enthusiasts in remote locations to find products and obtain information. In the past, firearms companies and associated suppliers counted heavily on costly trade shows, expensive catalogues, a taciturn firearms press and active advertising campaigns to get their messages to the gun-buying public. The Net has changed all this. Firearms enthusiasts can turn to innumerable websites in search of product information prior to making decisions to buy.

WHAT'S A WEBSITE ANYWAY?

A good website contains content relevant to the user—whether educational or entertaining—and features up-to-date information. A good site should contain all the information a potential buyer needs when making decisions or acquiring more information. The best websites offer visitors a feeling of community—that they are talking and exchanging information with friends, or at least people of similar

mind. Where direct payment by credit card is accepted, sites must be secure.

One unique aspect of electronic cataloging is the way in which web pages are designed so as to enhance a company's services. A well-designed web page is more than electronic brochures; rather, it represents the company and acts in such a way that viewers may interact with the company. A web page gives readers access to the company in a way that is unavailable in any other medium. Net surfers can ask questions, receive customized product information by E-mail, select products designed for their needs, or scroll through the products, much like turning the pages on a big television catalog.

Those who seek additional information or direct contact with the company, E-mail capability is unbeatable. Firearms enthusiasts are encouraged to use this facility often. Some argue that E-mail is the single most useful capability available to Net users. It lets you talk directly to product suppliers and to express your opinions with some assurance that a quick response is forthcoming. A shooter in need of bullet information a few days before a big game hunt can expect a quick E-mail response by a major bullet manufacturer. E-mail is also a good way to let manufacturers know about the performance of their products in the field. Most companies invite direct contact.

One complaint about the Internet from beginners is finding sites that are related to their interests in a timely manner. This is true especially with firearm-related sites whose names are product or company specific. On the other hand, many companies offer

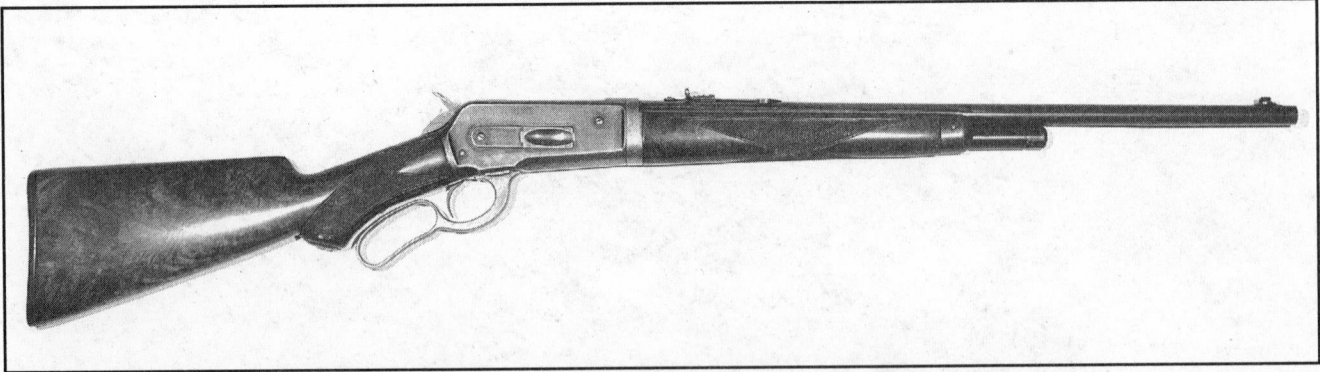

THIS RUGER SINGLE SHOT IS REPRESENTATIVE OF RUGER FIREARMS. A VISIT TO THIS SITE WILL INDICATE HOW RUGER HAS GROWN WELL BEYOND THE MANUFACTURE OF FIREARMS AND IS NOW ADDRESSING MANY OF THE LEGAL ISSUES FACING THE SHOOTING COMMUNITY.

HARD-TO-FIND ITEMS, SUCH AS IRON RIFLE SITES, ARE EASILY LOCATED USING COMMON SEARCH ENGINES. A QUICK SEARCH FOR THIS RARE LYMAN RECEIVER SIGHT TURNED UP SEVERAL HITS.

products that are not related to firearms; and there is also a large import community which brings into the U.S. and Canada a mix of firearms related and non-related to hunting and shooting.

Following is a brief guide for expanding an arsenal of search tools so that readers may receive firearm information in the most direct and broadest way possible. Of the various search tools available, we shall consider three: the *search* engine, the *meta-search* engine, and the directory. To build lists of specific products or interest, use the bookmark capability of your browser. If one source doesn't have what you're looking for, move on to the next. The easiest way to go is with the search engine, which uses other software to troll the World Wide Web in a methodical way. It then creates a record of everything it finds and places the contents into a large database. One way to use a search engine is to seek out a clearly named organization—for example, **Winchester**. Your search should result in dozens of sites that include the word *Winchester*. The user must then winnow through the results, finding whatever Winchester data that are of interest. Most likely you'll find many geographical

and place names in the search results. Another way to search is to use a more inclusive term, such as the word "firearms." This method will return hundreds of sites with the word "firearm" used in dozens of ways. The user must then pore through hundreds of web pages to find what he or she is looking for.

Following are a few common search engines and the results of entering the word "firearm" as part of a search for guns and related equipment:

- **Google** is located at http://www.google.com. This engine outlines search results based on matching search phrases and on how many sites link to a page. This search engine contains over 1,247,340,000 web pages, or about one-third of all web pages on the net.
- **Altavista** is found at http://www.altavista.com. This engine enables users to look for documents in a specific foreign language. For the search on the world "firearm," some 70,690 sites were found.
- **Northern Light** is found at http://www.northern-light.com. It claims to have one of the largest web indexes available (516,457 hits for the "firearm" query).
- **Lycos** is located at http://www.lycos.com. It's a large search engine founded in 1995 and is part of the Lycos network, one of the most visited hubs on the Internet, reaching nearly half of all web users in the U.S. For the word "firearm," 194,175 websites were found in the search box.
- **Excite**, located at http://www.excite.com, is a popular search engine featuring a software product that combines search-and-retrieval with automatic hypertext linking, subject-grouping and automatic abstracting. When the world "firearm" is entered into this search engine, 13,645 postings resulted.
- **Meta-Search Engines** are web search sites that take a query and send it out to several other search tools —a kind of search engine within a search engine. The first few answers are retrieved from each search engine and offered on-line in the form of a list. The search engine indicates what's available within each engine should a user wish to continue working with a particular search engine. Meta-search engines work best with simple queries, a major advantage for those who seek information on firearm sites and related products.

These search tools work best at the beginning of a search, giving users a quick feel for the kind of information that's available in the electronic world. They also prove useful at the end of a search, i.e., as a way

of discovering any web pages that may have been missed. A good example is the word "bullet," which involves several different manufacturers producing similar but slightly different bullets. Once a bullet style has been searched, a meta-search may turn up additional manufacturers or types. In short, it's a good way to double-check whether you have all the information that might be relevant.

Following are some of the more interesting meta-search engines out there in electronic land:

• **Dogpile** at http://www.dogpile.com has access to 26 search sites but only searches three at a time. It then moves on to the next set of three search engines. A large number of responses are possible. Dogpile, by the way, uses the term "fetch" to ignite a search. A search on the word "bullet" produced over 500,000 hits from 12 different search engines.

• **Mamma** is found at http://www.mamma.com. It performs searches of the major search engines and presents the results with a "related searches" category. This is particularly useful in the shooting sports category, since many web pages feature geographic names or company names, while others use shooting and hunting terms in their names but have nothing to do with the actual pursuit of shooting or hunting. This engine can help sort some of this out.

• **Metacrawler** is situated at http://www.meta-crawler.com/index.html. It offers searches of major search engines and combines the results onto one list. For the word "firearm," several search engines were listed as having been visited, including Alta-Vista, DirectHit, Excite, Google, GoTo, Infoseek, LockSmart, Internet Keywords, Thunderstone, WebCrawler and FindWhat.

Directories can also help beginning surfers obtain useful contacts in the firearms world quickly and accurately. A directory usually employs a staff to cull sites that meet specific criteria, then places these sites in easily navigated categories and subcategories. An important difference between an electronic directory and a search engine is the role played by judgment in studying the information. For those with search engines, it's up to each individual to sort through the various sites resulting from a query. With a directory, much pre-sorting has taken place with the user relying on the judgment of others in advising which sites to visit. Keep this in mind when looking at the following directories.

• **Yahoo** (http://yahoo.com) is one of the most popu-

lar directories on the web, allowing users to drill down from 14 main categories. Use the "Recreation and Sports" category to click down on hunting resources, shooting and related product opportunities. The site does provide access to some interesting and different firearm products that will eventually evolve into mainstream products for shooters and hunters. It was through this site that http://www.-chambersafe.com/install.cfm was accessed to provide the latest information on this interesting firearm safety device.

• **Librarians Index to the Internet** (http://www.lii.org) contains over 6,000 Internet resources chosen by various librarians for their usefulness. For gun interests, this site provides many links into the shooting and hunting world; but many of the specifics which more advanced firearm aficionados will be looking for are not so easily found. Spending your time with search engines while seeking details on bullets, trajectory, rifling and other more advanced topics may prove more satisfactory.

• **Looksmart** (http://www.looksmart.com), with 18,000 subjects from the web, lays claim to being the global leader in search infrastructure. As such, it offers quality search solutions to leading portals, media companies and an international Internet service provider. Shooters and hunters must go in under the heading of "sports" and drill down for whatever information is needed. It's best to follow the outdoor recreation pick and then click on "hunting" or "firearms" picks to get where you want to go.

• **Open Directory Project** (http://www.dmoz.org) is an extremely comprehensive directory providing access to over a million websites. Subjects such as reloading, retailers, competition shooting, black powder, ammunition, collectables and shooting are all available under the recreation pick. With only a quick review of this site, a beginning surfer can quickly gain access to many shooting-type sites.

A thumbnail review of some top gun sites on the web follows, along with comments on the value or quality of the information each site contains. This is not an exhaustive list, but it is offered as a starting point for long-time firearms users who may be just starting to surf the World Wide Web. An interesting website to begin with is http://www.shooters.com, which outlines most information available on the net. For shooters, the page featuring a list of directories is

a good place to start. It shows everything from firearms manufacturers, writers and publishers to guides and outfitters.

One of the better firearm websites is the Ruger site at http://www.ruger-firearms.com . It features a Ruger news pick and provides an up-to-the-minute update on Ruger's latest series of legal challenges. The product menu button provides a colorful and immediate listing of all Ruger products. Another important website is http://www.marlinfirearms.com . Here you'll learn that Marlin's "Bullseye" trademark has been used since 1922 on all Marlin walnut buttstocks. Interestingly, this site does not provide E-mail and chat room services. Some companies obviously will have to come dragging and kicking into the new millennium.

For a listing of products available from the Winchester/U.S. Repeating Arms site, check out http://www.winchester-guns.com . An interesting item on this site is the number of rifles listed in the .444 Marlin cartridge. The company claims this may be the most ideal rifle ever made for hunting big deer and bear in heavy brush and dark timber conditions. The modified Model '94 is called the Timber Carbine, built on the slab-sided Big Bore action and chambered in 444 Marlin. The barrel is 18" long and is ported to keep recoil under control for fast follow-up shots.

The next choice is http://www.weatherby.com, site of the world-famous Weatherby guns long associated with high terminal velocities and striking power at intermediate to long range. This site explains, among other things, how Weatherby's high velocity success is achieved; i.e., by offering rifles with an 11-degree parabolic target crown for even gas displacement during firing.

Next, visit the Mossberg site at http://www.jerice-co.com, where the history of this venerable company is detailed. One of the more interesting items to learn from this site concerns changes made in the Mossberg product line over the last few years. At one time, the company favored the .22 rimfire as its preeminent model, whereas today the company's shotguns receive the most attention.

The Ithaca gun company is located at http://www-.ithacagun.com/ . Here the reader learns that for three generations prior to 1958, this company had been primarily a shotgun manufacturer. This tradition began to change with the public announcement in 1958 of a new .22 caliber semiautomatic, called the Ithaca X-5 Lightning. The new gun, commonly referred to as the X-5C, was a clip-fed rifle equipped with a 7- or 10-shot clip.

Those in search of Savage Arms need look no farther than the site found at http://www.savagearms.com. It features a useful rate-of-twist chart for all rifle barrels made by Savage. It doesn't take much searching to note that the Model 99 lever action has disappeared from the company's list, but still survives under the designation Model 24F-20.

As for the Remington firearms site located at http://www.remington.com, it takes only moments to discover that more than 19 versions of the Model 700 bolt action Remington rifle still exist. The site also provides an invaluable list of contacts at virtually all of the firearms companies. In addition, Remington provides a comprehensive list of production dates for each model it has built.

The site http://www.browning.com offers Browning's lineup of firearms along with an e-line of items —caps, shirts, jackets, to name a few—of interest to users of Browning products. The company's history begins with a time-line that starts with the birth of John Moses Browning in 1855 and continuing to 1995 with the introduction of the Browning Gold series of shotguns. There's also a complete serial number listing of firearms produced by the company.

Checking out guns on the web can be fun as well as informative. If the Net still baffles you, try searching for http://www.netlingoo.com, then click on "Getting to Know the Internet." It's all there, believe me.

[A comprehensive listing of firearms manufacturers on the Net follows. In addition, readers may check the Directory, which begins on p. 557, for many more websites of interest, from Accurate Arms to Z-Hat Custom Dies.]

- **Armalite** – firearms manufacturer http://www.armalite.com
- **Autauga Arms** – pistol manufacturer http://www.autaugaarms.com
- **American Derringer Corp.** – firearms manufacturer http://www.amderringer.com/
- **AR-7 Industries** – firearms manufacturer http://www.ar-7.com/
- **Barrett Firearms Manufacturing Inc.** - .50 caliber rifle manufacturer http://www.barrettrifles.com
- **Beeman Precision Airguns** – air rifles and pistols http://www.beeman.com

- **Benelli USA Corp.** – firearms manufacturer
  http://www.benelliusa.com/
- **Benjamin Sheridan** – air rifles and pistols
  http://www.crosman.com/
- **Beretta USA Corporation** – firearms manufacturer
  http://www.beretta.it/
- **Bond Arms** – derringer type firearms manufacturer
  http://www.bondarms.com/
- **Browning** – firearms, clothing, archery and acces-sory manufacturer http://www.-browning.com/
- **Bushmaster Firearms** – firearms manufacturer
  http://www.bushmaster.com/
- **Casull Arms Corporation** – firearms manufacturer
  http://www.casullarms.com/
- **Christensen Arms** – specialty rifle manufacturer
  http://www.christensenarms.com/
- **Clark Custom Guns** – custom pistols and accessories http://www.clarkcustomguns.com/
- **Cogswell & Harrison** – London gunmaker
  http://www.cogswell.co.uk/
- **Colt Manufacturing Company** - firearms manufacturer http://www.colt.com/colt/
- **Connecticut Valley Arms (CVA)** – firearms manufacturer http://www.cva.com/
- **Ceska Zbrojavka (CZ)** – firearms manufacturer
  http://www.czub.cz/
- **Crosman Corporation** – air rifles and pistols manufacturer http://www.crosman.com/
- **Daisy Manufacturing Company, Inc.** – air rifles and pistols http://www.crosman.com/
- **Dakota Arms** – firearms manufacturer
  http://www.dakotaarms.com/
- **Dixie Gun Works, Inc.** – antique guns, parts and accessories http://www.dixiegunworks.com
- **DS Arms** – rifle manufacturer and importer
  http://www.dsarms.com/
- **Freedom Arms** – firearms manufacturer
  http://www.fredomarms.com/
- **Fulton Armory** – U.S. military rifles, gunsmithing services and the M1 Garand Information Place
  http://www.fulton-armory.com/
- **Glock Firearms** – firearms manufacturer
  http://glock.com/
- **Hammerli** – firearms manufacturer
  http://www.hammerli.com/
- **H&R 1871, Inc.** –firearms manufacturer
  http://www.gzanders.com/manu/hr.html

- **Interarms** – firearms and accessory importer
  http://www.interarms.com/
- **Ithaca Gun Company** – firearms manufacturer
  http://www.ithacagun.com/
- **Kimber Rifles** – firearms manufacturer
  http://www.kimberamerica.com/
- **Magnum Research, Inc.** – firearms manufacturer
  http://www.magnumresearch.com/
- **Marlin Firearms Company** – firearms manufacturer
  http://marlin-guns.com/
- **October Country Muzzleloading** – muzzleloading and muzzleloading accessories http://www.oct-country.com/
- **O.F. Mossberg & Sons, Inc.** – firearms manufacturer http://www.mossberg.com/
- **Navy Arms** – firearms manufacturer
  http://www.navyarms.com/
- **North American Arms** – firearms manufacturer http://www.naaminis.com/
- **Olympic Arms** –0 firearms manufacturer
  http://www.olyarms.com/
- **Para Ordnance Mfg., Inc.** – firearms manufacturer http://www.paraord.com/
- **Remington Arms Company, Inc.** – firearms and accessory manufacturer
  http://www.remington.com/
- **Rossi Arms** – http://www.rossiusa.com/
- **Sig Arms** – firearms manufacture
  http://www.sigarms.com/
- **SKB Shotguns** – firearms manufacturer
  http://www.skbshotguns.com/
- **Smith & Wesson** – firearms and accessory manufacturer http://www.smith-wesson.com/
- **Springfield Armory** – firearms and accessory manufacturer http://www.springfield-armory.com/
- **Sturm, Ruger & Company, Inc.** – firearms manufacturer http://www.ruger-firearms.com/index.html
- **Taurus** – firearms manufacturer
  http://www.taurususa.com/
- **Thompson-Center Arms Company, Inc.** – firearms manufacturer http://www.tcarms.com/
- **U.S. Repeating Arms Company (Winchester)** – firearms manufacturer
  http://www.winchester-guns.com/
- **Lothar Walther** – firearms manufacturer
  http://www.lothar-walther.com/
- **Wilson Combat** – firearms and accessorymanufacturer http://www.wilsoncombat.com/ **SB**

TIMELESS

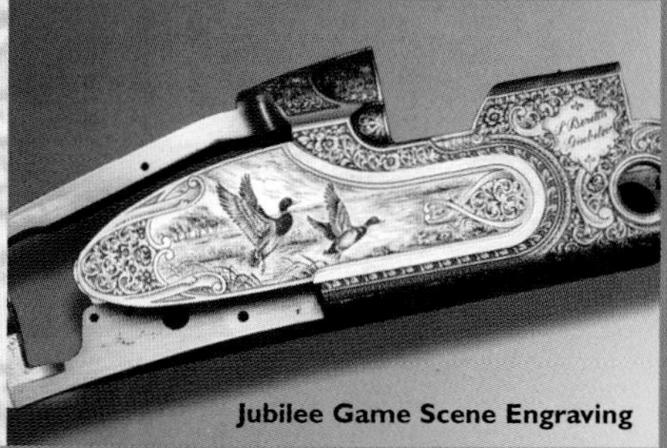

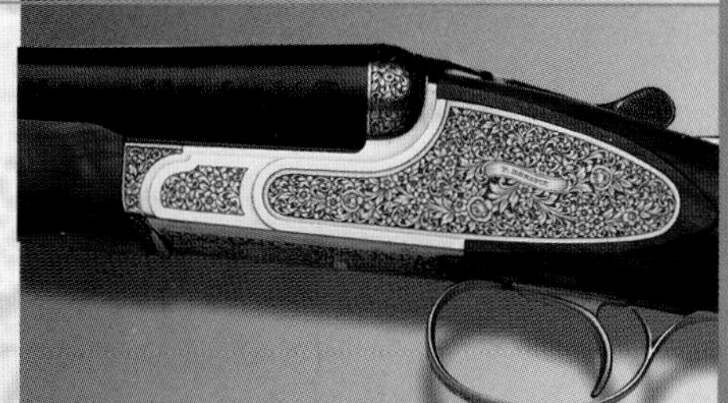

Muzzleloading: It'll Never Be The Same

By Toby Bridges

IT'S TRUE. MUZZLELOADING has changed—drastically. Since the mid-1980, this 700-year-old shooting sport has been constantly modernized. Today's in-line ignition muzzleloaders, firing plastic saboted jacketed bullets and pushed along by pelletized powder charges, are a far cry from the long-barreled frontloaders and fodder carried into the wilderness by the likes of Daniel Boone and Jim Bridger. And yet, with all these new developments in muzzleloading, the sport will surely be subject to change one more time. During the summer of 2000, Savage Arms (Westfield, MA) dared to invade territory where no other muzzleloader manufacturer has ever trespassed: it tooled up and began producing the first production muzzleloaders ever designed, engineered and built to shoot modern smokeless propellants.

Niotrocellulose-based smokeless powders have always been strictly taboo when used in anything loaded from the front. These powders, which are used to load ammunition for modern centerfire rifles, handguns and shotguns, produce pressures far too excessive for conventional in-line ignition muzzleloaders. Thanks to a revolutionary new concept in muzzleloader ignition systems, Savage Arms has harnessed the energy and user friendliness of modern smokeless powders without placing shooters in danger.

Since early 1977, I've been privileged to have an opportunity to shoot and hunt with this futuristic muzzleloading system. I first learned of the concept while compiling information for a new muzzleloading book, called *Advanced Black Powder Hunting* (Stoeger Publishing Co., Accokeek, MD). After only a few hundred rounds I knew I was given the rare opportunity to experience more than a sneak peek at the future of muzzleloading. The concept around which the new Savage Model 10ML was built is the brainchild of custom riflesmith Henry Ball of Greensboro, North Carolina. The heart of this system is its modern centerfire bolt action receiver.

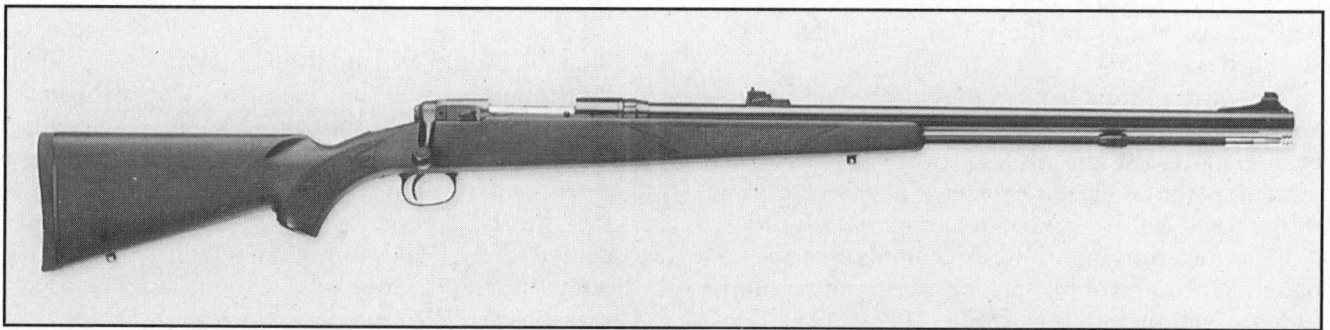

TAKE AWAY THE RAMROD AND THE NEW SAVAGE MODEL 10ML LOOKS EXACTLY LIKE THE WELL-ESTABLISHED MODEL 110 CENTERFIRE RIFLE.

CUSTOM RIFLE MAKER HENRY BALL UTILIZED A HOWA ACTION TO CREATE THIS FINE CUSTOM SMOKELESS POWDER MUZZLELOADER. THE NEW SAVAGE MODEL 10ML, HOWEVER, DELIVERS THE SAME PERFORMANCE FOR ABOUT ONE-SIXTH THE COST.

Ball's original "smokeless pole" featured a short Interarms Max-X action, to which he installed a turn-in-28 inches twist .50 caliber barrel. Like all in-line ignition muzzleloaders, Ball's features a breech plug at the rear end of the barrel. But instead of a nipple, the breech plug on this new frontloader has a chamber that accepts a reusable stainless steel percussion ignition module utilizing a hot No. 209 shotshell primer.

To constrict the fire from the primer, and to prevent granules of powder from filtering back into the chamber area—all the while keeping the pressures created by the smokeless powder load from escaping to the rear—Ball's patented design relies on a tiny .030" orifice running from the chamber into the barrel. When one of his stainless steel ignition modules are chambered in this rifle, 100% of the fire from a No. 209 primer passes through the orifice and into the barrel for guaranteed ignition. The

extremely precise fit of the module in the chamber also makes this system exceptionally weatherproof.

Before Henry Ball built one of his custom smokeless powder muzzleloaders for me, I had an opportunity to fire several thousand rounds through his original Mark-X rifle, along with others built with Sako, Howa and Remington actions. I've also seen several of Ball's rifles using Remington rolling block and Martini dropping block single-shot actions (another was built purportedly on a Ruger No. 1 action). But the most interesting Henry Ball muzzleloader I've ever shot was built with a receiver for a Winchester Model 94 lever action rifle.

My initial experience with this system recommended using loads from Henry Ball. Now, I've been writing books and articles about muzzleloaders since the early 1970s, always with the warning: **"NEVER SHOOT SMOKELESS POWDER."** So it was with great reservation that I loaded Ball's

THE REUSABLE STAINLESS STEEL PERCUSSION IGNI-
TION MODULE SITS IN THE RECEIVER OF A BALL-
BUILT CUSTOM SMOKELESS POWDER MUZZLELOADER.

Mark-X actioned muzzleloader with 33 grains of Alliant 2400 behind a saboted 260 grain .451" Speer jacketed hollow-point, took aim at a 100-yard target, and touched off a shot. I was amazed at the low recoil, the speed at which the bullet sped down-range, and, most of all, its accuracy. My first three shots printed into a 1 1/2-inch cluster at 100 yards. My second group was even better. Best of all, there was no need to wipe fouling from the bore between shots, or to tear down the rifle and scrub fouling from the bore and other metal parts.

It was during the last half of 1999 that Savage Arms first caught wind of Ball's unique muzzleloading system. The company had been eyeing the muzzleloader market for some time, but with superb bolt-action designs like the Remington Model 700ML and the Ruger Model 77/50 already available, Savage felt there wasn't enough demand for another in-line ignition muzzleloader, at least not one that offered muzzleloading hunters anything better than existing rifles designed to shoot black powder or Pyrodex. But after shooting a .50 caliber

rifle Ball had built for a Savage Model 110FP Tactical rifle, Savage's C.E.O. Ron Coburn and his staff immediately realized that this was truly a design that was anything but muzzleloading as usual.

For the 7 3/4-pound .50 caliber Model 10 ML, Savage elected to use a modified version of the short Model 12 single-shot varmint/target action, incorporating barrel and receiver threads (unique to this rifle). The difference between this and other Savage center-fire actions is the "single shot" aspect. There's also an ejector on the bolt, or a cut-out in the bottom of the receiver for a magazine. The stainless steel ignition module has to be pushed into the chamber (with a finger or thumb) and the bolt closed behind it. When the bolt is opened, however, the module is extracted from the chamber and sits at the face of the bolt until it's removed by the shooter. The elimination of the ejector prevents the action from tossing the module out of the receiver when the bolt is pulled to the rear.

Each Model 10ML comes with a special breech plug wrench and decapping tool. The ignition modules can be primed simply by pushing a standard No. 209 shotshell primer into the primer pocket, using nothing more than thumb pressure. To remove a fired primer, the decapping pin is slipped into the cone-shaped end of the module and the pin is tapped against a hard surface (a screwdriver handle,

THE SLIGHTLY REDESIGNED SAVAGE PERCUSSION
IGNITION MODULES CAN BE REUSED FOR 250 OR
MORE SHOTS. THE AUTHOR RELIED ON WINCHESTER
NO. 209 PRIMERS FOR MOST OF HIS SHOOTING.

THE AUTHOR HAS DISCOVERED THAT MEDIUM BURN RATE POWDERS, SUCH AS ACCURATE ARMS XMP-5744 AND IMR-4227, PRODUCE OPTIMUM PERFORMANCE OUT OF THE SAVAGE MODEL 10ML.

coated liberally with synthetic grease to make certain the plug remains "removable." I have found anti-seize compounds (available from most automotive parts stores) to be ideal.

Another patented feature of the Model 10ML is its removable and replaceable vent liner in front of the breech plug. With a standard in-line rifle, the nipple of the ignition system is the replaceable "wear" part. After 300 or so shots, the orifice that runs through even the best of nipples begins to erode. The result is increasing blowback as the tiny hole grows larger. The vent liner on the Model 10ML breech plug serves the same purpose. With the hotter smokeless charges that make this rifle perform, erosion of the orifice becomes noticeable after 150 or so shots. For only a couple of dollars, however, the liner is easily replaced. As with the breech plug, the threads of the vent liner must also be lubricated with a synthetic grease or anti-seize compound.

Thanks to the noncorrosive nature of nitrocellulose-based smokeless powders, maintenance and

a small hammer, or a small block of wood), knocking out the spent primer. I've performed wear tests on these modules and have found that, on average, they have a life span of between 250 and 350 uses.

The module's cone-shaped nose is what makes contact with the internal shape of the chamber, creating the gas seal, which is essential. New out-of-the-box modules generally require that the shooter use about 15 to 20 pounds of downward pressure on the bolt handle in order to seat the module in the chamber. Once a precise fit of the softer module and hardened breech plug has been established, subsequent use of the module requires only 5 to 10 pounds of pressure on the bolt handle to chamber the primed module.

Savage makes its wrenches long enough so that the breech plug can be removed without banging the rear end of a mounted scope. In fact, the larger end of the decapping pin fits precisely into a side opening at the rear of the wrench, providing leverage for loosening a tight-fitting plug. According to Savage, it's important that the threads of the breech plug be

FOR MOST HUNTING LOADS, THE AUTHOR FOUND THE SIMPLE PLASTIC DIPPERS OF THE LEE PRECISION'S POWDER MEASURE KIT TO BE A RELIABLE AND EASY WAY TO MEASURE RELATIVELY PRECISE POWDER CHARGES LIKE VIHTAVOURI'S N110 (SHOWN) FOR THE MODEL 10ML.

cleanup of the Model 10ML is a cinch, requiring little more care than most centerfire bolt action rifles. Between April and December 2000, I fired more than 3,800 rounds through a prototype Model 10ML, checking out powders, saboted bullets and shotshell primers. On most days, I'd shoot 40 to 50 rounds, and at the end of the shooting session I'd merely pull out the breech plug, remove the vent liner, run a few dampened patches through the bore, re-lube the threads of the bent liner and breech plug and reinstall them. After wiping down the outside with an oily cloth, I could forget about the rifle until it was time to shoot again. Total time spent cleaning: usually five to ten minutes.

A muzzleloader requiring little cleaning and maintenance has long been a dream for most hunters. Too often, muzzleloading big game hunters who are successful during the last few hours of an afternoon hunt are faced with taking care of the game downed, removing it out of the field to a check station that same evening, and on to the meat pole or processing plant. All this must be done before time can be devoted to caring for the rifle that was used to harvest the game. When shooting and hunting with loads comprised of either black powder or the substitute Pyrodex, close attention to the rifle is mandatory. The fouling or residue left behind by either of these propellants is extremely corrosive. Under certain high humidity or damp weather conditions, fouling left in the bore over-night can totally ruin a high quality muzzleloader. Cleaning a dirty muzzleloader has, in fact, always been a major concern, in some case severe enough to keep many modern day shooters from even becoming involved in the sport. The Savage Model 10ML has all but eliminated the mess and fuss associated with shooting a frontloading rifle. Following a successful day in the deer woods chasing elk or stalking other big game animals, this rifle can be left a day or even a month, without having to scrub the bore or worry about ruining the rifle.

For several years, Knight Rifles, Thompson/ Center Arms and a few other muzzleloader manufacturers have heavily promoted the use of three 50 grain Pyrodex Pellets (150 grain powder charge) behind modern saboted bullets for "magnum" big game-taking performance. Thompson/Center claims that with only three compressed 50 grain pellets, its

Encore 209x50 Magnum can propel a saboted 240 grain bullet out of the muzzle at slightly more than 2,200 f.p.s., with muzzle energy equivalent to a 7mm Remington Magnum. What the manufacturers don't tell you is that with three 50 grain pellet powder charges your rifle will rear back with the kick of a Missouri mule!

Savage's new Model 10ML, with its eight lands and grooves, one turn-in-24 inches rate of twist and 24-inch barrel, can be loaded and fired with traditional black powder or Pyrodex—even the magnum three pellet loads, which are the maximum for most other contemporary in-line ignition muzzleloaders. On the other hand, this .50 caliber muzzleloading rifle can be loaded with cleaner burning, better performing smokeless powders. Three such powders that tend to perform extremely well in this system are IMR-4227 (or Hodgdon H-4227), Accurate

MODEL 10ML MUZZLELOADER DESIGNER HENRY BALL DUMPS IN A PRE-MEASURED CHARGE OF SMOKELESS POWDER WHILE WRINGING OUT AN EARLY PRODUCTION RUN RIFLE.

Arms XMP-5744 and Vihtavouri N110. All three are short cut extruded powders of the medium burn rate variety—i.e., a little slower than Alliant 2400, but faster than Alliant Reloader 7. Of the three, IMR-4227—the first powder I shot through the Savage 10ML prototype—is the slowest burning. When the prototype arrived from Savage for testing, I pulled a 2.8 10x Simmons ATEC scope off a custom rifle Henry Ball had built for me and mounted it on the receiver with a set of Weaver-style bases (the Millett rings were already on the scope). Before loading the rifle, I ran several dry patches through the bore to wipe excess oil from the barrel, then fired a fouling shot to burn any lube that may have been missed.

My first shot on paper printed three inches high and three inches right of the quarter-sized black target dot. Instead of making an immediate sight change, I fired a group, shooting 45 grains of IMR-4227 behind a 300 grain .452" Hornady XTP jacketed hollow point loaded with a black sabot (from Muzzleload Magnum Products). My next two shots printed an inch inside the first test firing. In all, those first three shots from the Model 10ML prototype punched out a sub-one-inch in the target paper at 100 yards.

That revamped high-pressure sabot made by Muzzleload Magnum Products was developed to withstand the pressures of three 50 grain Pyrodex Pellet loads, which had become popular with hunters looking for maximum knockdown power. Using my custom .50 caliber Ball smokeless muzzleloader, 45 grains was the maximum charge of IMR-4227 I could shoot behind MMP's standard sabots without blowing the skirt of the plastic base. Before my first day of test-firing the Model 10ML, I had

SOUTHPAW HENRY BALL PREPARES TO TOUCH OFF A SHOT WITH THE ORIGINAL PROTOTYPE OF THE MODEL 10ML HE BUILT FOR SAVAGE ARMS.

THE UNIQUE FLUTED DEVEL "RADIALLY DYNAMIC" BULLET (FROM LEVED CARTRIDGE LTD.) PROVED EXCEPTIONALLY ACCURATE WHEN FIRED FROM THE SAVAGE MODEL 10ML.

loader. A 45 grain charge of XMP-5744 pushes this light bullet from the muzzle of Savage's muzzleloader at almost 2,350 f.p.s., with many 100-yard three-shot groups punching out little more than one ragged hole. My best 100-yard group shot with this load produced literally one oblong hole measuring three-eighths of an inch center to center.

I was so intrigued with the design and accuracy of this bullet that I jumped at the opportunity to head for south Texas, where I joined Charlie Kelsey, owner of Leved Cartridge Ltd., in wringing out the Savage Model 10ML and DEVEL bullet on some wild hogs. Despite 100-plus degree temperatures, I was able to dump nine wild porkers with Savage's prototype frontload. That first victim was the first head of game ever taken with the new muzzleloader. Both rifle and bullet preformed flawlessly. Every one

worked up to 48 grains of IMR-4227, pushing the saboted 300 grain Hornady XTP at around 2,175 f.p.s. A switch to the 250 grain .451" XTP hollow-point bullet, along with the same high-pressure sabot, brought muzzle velocity close to 2,250 f.p.s. Moreover, there was much less recoil when shooting the same bullet and sabot with three 50 grain Pyrodex Pellets. Groups continued to average between one and 1? inches across at 100 yards. This superb whitetail load generates around 3,000 ft. lbs. of energy at the muzzle, and at 150 yards it delivers a 250 grain Hornady XTP hollow point with more energy left over than any standard in-line ignition rifle develops at the muzzle using the same saboted bullet and 100 grains of Pyrodex.

At the same time I was testing the Model 10ML with XMP-5744, a new saboted muzzleloading projectile with a unique shape—the DEVEL "Radially Dynamic" bullet (from Leved Cartridge Ltd., Georgetown, TX)—arrived. This non-expanding projectile made from a copper/tin composite produced results in a light 175 grain .45 caliber bullet nearly as long as the 300 grain Hornady XTP. Instead of expansion, the DEVEL bullet relies on five distinct flutes that run from a star-shaped nose back along the ogive to create a hydraulic shock wave upon impact. The bullet worked perfectly with MMP's high pressure sabots and proved one of the most accurate bullets I've ever shot with a muzzle-

WITH MOST SMOKELESS POWDER LOADS, THE SAVAGE MODEL 10ML WILL PRODUCE HIGHER VELOCITIES, HARDER-HITTING PERFORMANCE, AND FAR LESS RECOIL THAN IS POSSIBLE WITH THREE 50 GRAIN PYRODEX PELLET LOADS.

THE AUTHOR FOUND THE NEW SAVAGE MUZZLE-
LOADER CAPABLE OF ASTOUNDING 100-YARD ACCU-
RACY. GROUPS LIKE THIS SUB ONE-INCH THREE-
SHOT CLUSTER ARE FAIRLY COMMON.

of the wild hogs, ranging in weight from around 100 to 125 pounds, dropped where they stood at the sound of the shot. It didn't matter if the hog was at 30 yards or 130 yards.

During the heat of late summer, though, I discovered one thing about those hot, smokeless loads fired from a Savage muzzleloader. Once the temperatures climbed into the upper 80s or 90s, accuracy with near maximum loads begins to suffer. The high pressure MMP sabots, which perform best out of the Savage Model 10ML, were actually developed for loads comprised of three 50 grain Pyrodex Pellets. Depending on the bullet weight, these loads develop approximately 16,000 to 18,000 p.s.i. inside the barrel. The smokeless powder loads fired from the Model 10ML develop barrel pressures that range between mid-30,000 to low 40,000 p.s.i., enough to destroy any other muzzleloader.

These pressures are comparable to those produced by cartridge rifles chambered for such calibers as the old .30/30 Winchester. .35 Remington or .444 Marlin. In the world of centerfire cartridges, the pressures and velocities produced by the Model 10ML would be considered on the low side. But in the world of muzzleloading rifles, these pressures and velocities are definitely on the high side. However, the design of the Model 10ML makes it the strongest muzzleloader ever made for commercial use; in fact, Savage conducted tests to determine the 10ML's destruct point and was unable to damage the rifle, even when the remote fired test gun was loaded with three powder charges (90 grains of a hot smokeless powder) and three projectiles. The saboted 300 grain bullets were loaded one on top of another so as to produce enough pressure to blow the barrel or ignition system. The load failed —not the rifle.

That doesn't mean a shooter can add as much powder as he pleases. The weak link lies with the small plastic sabot separating the powder charge from the bullet. Once pressures reach the upper 40,000 p.s.i. range, the sabot simply falls apart, with excess pressure escaping around the bullet and out the muzzle. And when the sabot blows, both accuracy and velocity suffer.

The hottest powder for accuracy using the Model 10ML while still producing impressive velocities is IMR-SR 4756. Shooting only 28 grains of this powder, the 175 grain DEVEL bullet leaves the muzzle at about 2,375 f.p.s. Groups fired with this load average about 1 1/2 inches across—and that's with outside temperatures in the upper 70s. But when shooting slightly slower burning powders—i.e., Hodgdon HS-6 or Alliant Blue Dot—a charge of only 20 grains completely destroyed the plastic sabot. The higher outside temperatures rise, the more easily a plastic sabot will blow. Smokeless powder loads fired from this rifle heat up the barrel; so when it's 90 degrees outside, a barrel won't cool down quickly, if at all. During hot weather, the plastic material sabots are made of becomes much softer and more pliable than during cooler months. When a saboted bullet is rammed down the bore of a hot barrel and left to sit there for several minutes before it's shot, it becomes even softer and more pliable. And when it's hit with 30,000 to 40,000 pounds of push, the pres-

sure is more than the thin skirt can withstand. During hot weather months, the Savage Model 10ML continues to shoot with amazing accuracy with loads that leave the barrel at 2,000-2,100 f.p.s. But when things begin to cool off in the fall, this rifle can be stocked up for truly "MAGNUM" muzzleloader performance on big game. The best accuracy at the highest velocities, I've found, are achieved when temperatures drop into the 40s and 30s.

Just before the fall of 2000 hunting season, I began shooting with Vihtavouri N110, a powder that has become an exceptional performer out of the Model 10ML. Physically, granule-size is perfect, and the burning rate is exactly where it needs to be, in the middle of the medium burn rate—hotter than IMR-4227, but cooler than Alliant 2400. Weighing each and every powder charge meticulously on a balance beam scale is time-consuming, but up until

recently I'd been doing just that. Then one day I borrowed a Precision Powder Measure Kit (made by Lee Precision) of 15 small plastic dippers ranging in volume from .3cc to 4.3cc. The kit also contains a comprehensive slide rule that lists the charges each dipper size measures for 95 popular powders, each one different from the other.

On my first try at measuring Vihtavouri N110 with the Lee dippers, I got lucky. I chose the 3.7cc dipper, which measure 44.4 grains of this particular powder. Loading the powder behind a saboted 250 grain Hornady .45 XTP, I soon discovered that the Model 10ML prototype and an early production-run rifle I owned both shot quite well with this powder and bullet combination. Firing either rifle, groups at 100 yards were generally well inside 1 1/2-inches, and a few were right at one inch across. When fired across the screens of a Shooting CHRONY

CUSTOM RIFLESMITH HENRY BALL TURNS THE OUTSIDE BARREL CONTOURS FOR ONE OF HIS UNIQUE CUSTOM "SMOKELESS" POLES. SAVAGE HAS BASED ITS NEW MODEL 10ML ON BALL'S PATENTED DESIGN.

"Beta Model" chronograph, the load produced an average velocity of 2,359 f.p.s. Equally impressive was an average deviation of only 5 f.p.s.!

Before that fall hunting season ended, I took several nice bucks and a few does with the Savage rifle and load. Every deer I hit with the speedy 250 grain Hornady XTP hollow point was anchored right on the spot. One big ten-pointer was easily the largest whitetail buck I've ever taken. It was standing at 80 yards when I touched off the shot. I had purposely held high on the shoulder in order to drop the deer where he stood. The bullet impacted exactly where I'd been holding, first angling down through the chest cavity, then ending up against the inside of the skin on the opposite shoulder. That 350-pound on-the-hoof whitetail dropped in his tracks—and with 3000 ft. lbs. (approx.) of energy at the muzzle, I can't say I was surprised.

The 44.4 grain charge of N110 also performs well with the 300 grain Hornady XTP. Average velocity with the heavier bullet averaged 2,240 f.p.s., which translates into 3,350 ft. lbs. of knockdown power. Accuracy with both the standard 300 grain XTP and the newer, heavier jacketed 300 grain XTP-MAG was exceptional. As with the lighter 250 grain version, most groups were well inside 1 1/2 inches, with one remarkable 3/4-inch group fired with the standard jacket version of the 300 grain XTP. So, if you're tired of hitting game as big as elk with something that doesn't do the job, this combination of rifle, powder and bullet is for you.

Since I first began shooting this system more than four years ago, I've been amazed at the negativity this technology has encountered—not from the consumer, but from the muzzleloading industry itself. We've seen it all before, though. The modern in-line percussion rifle was met with the same opposition, as were the plastic saboted handgun bullets used on big game. To understand how much innovation forces change, take a look at what the vast

HORNADY'S .45 CALIBER XTP JACKETED HOLLOW-POINT BULLETS HAVE PROVEN TO BE EXCEPTIONALLY ACCURATE AND HARD-HITTING BIG GAME BULLETS OUT OF THE SAVAGE MODEL 10ML. SHOWN IS THE 300 GRAIN .452" XTP WITH THE MUZZLELOAD MAGNUM PRODUCTS HIGH-PRESSURE SABOT.

PYRODEX IS LEGALLY AND TECHNICALLY CLASSIFIED AS "SMOKELESS PROPELLANT." IN FACT, THE WARNING LABEL ON A CAN OF PYRODEX IS EXACTLY THE SAME AS THAT FOUND ON A CAN OF HODGDON H-4227 (SHOWN). THE SAVAGE MODEL 10ML IS THE ONLY MUZZLELOADER BUILT TO HANDLE THE HIGHER PRESSURES OF MODERN SMOKELESS POWDERS LIKE H-4227.

majority of muzzleloading hunters are shooting today. The only real concern I've heard from consumers is the fear that such advanced technology will have a negative impact on the special muzzleloading seasons we now enjoy. Let's face it, muzzleloading has become a performance-driven hunting sport. The Savage Model 10ML is simply a better tool for harvesting game cleanly. The rifle is more user friendly, delivering a hard-hitting projectile with the punch needed for clean, on-the-spot kills. It is NOT a long range centerfire that loads from the muzzle. Bear in mind that Knight Rifles and Thompson/Center Arms are already claiming 200-yard killing power with their in-line rifles and Pyrodex Pellet loads.

Doubtless, there will be legislation in an attempt to ban this rifle and/or smokeless powder loads during the special muzzleloader seasons. However,

each and every container of Pyrodex is clearly marked "Smokeless Propellant," and easily more than 80 percent of all muzzleloading shooters and hunters now use this powder over black powder. It will be difficult indeed for a game department to ban the use of one smokeless powder while allowing the use of another.

Simply put, the great thing about the Model 10ML is its ability to be loaded and shot with Pyrodex or Pyrodex Pellets for the hunting seasons, while still allowing shooters to enjoy shooting their muzzleloaders with smokeless powder loads through the off season—and without all the hassles of cleaning. Once the Model 10ML has been fired with Pyrodex, though, the rifle must be cleaned immediately after shooting, as with any other muzzleloader. Thankfully, this versatile rifle offers the shooter a choice. **SB**

FORREST INC. OFFERS RIFLE/PISTOL MAGAZINES

Whether you're looking for a few spare magazines for that obsolete 22 rifle or pistol, or wish to replace a 10-shot with the higher-capacity pre-ban original, all are available from FORREST INC. With one of the largest selections of magazines, they offer competitive pricing especially for dealers who buy in quantity.

FORREST INC. also stocks parts and accessories for the Colt 1911 45 Auto Pistol, the SKS and MAK-90 rifles, and many U.S. military rifles. One of their specialty parts is firing pins for obsolete weapons.

Call or write for more information and a **FREE** brochure, **DEALERS WELCOME! HIGH CAPS OUR SPECIALTY!**

FORREST INC.
P.O. Box 326, Lakeside, CA 92040
Tel: 619-561-5800 *Fax:* 1-888-GUNCLIP
Web: www.GUNMAGS.com

MODEL G9729 COMBO LATHE MILL

Specifications:
- Swing over bed: 16½"
- Swing over cross slide: 11½"
- Distance between centers: 31"
- Spindle: 4-bolt intrinsic
- Spindle nose taper: MT#4
- Speeds: 7 lathe/ 16 mill/drill
- Speed Range: 120-1300 RPM
- Spindle taper(drill): MT#3
- Spindle travel(drill): 4⁵⁄₁₆"

- Motor: ¾ HP, Single Phase, 220V
- Approx. ship. weight: 525 lbs.

Includes:
- 5" 3-jaw chuck
- ½" drill chuck
- MT#3 drill chuck arbor ⅜" x 16 TPI
- Steady rest • Follow rest
- 6" backplate
- Two dead centers

The **G9729** is **$1,395.00** and shipped in the lower 48 states for **$115.00**.

Please check current pricing before ordering!

3 LOCATIONS
Bellingham, WA / Williamsport, PA / Springfield, MO

grizzly.com   Visit their Web site!

350301658

TEL: 1-800-523-4777 • FAX: 1-800-438-5901

MEDIA CODE
92C

MANUFACTURERS' SHOWCASE

THE CENTURY 2000 DEFENDER "C2K"
FROM BOND ARMS, INC.

The Century 200 Defender ("C2K") is the ultimate in self-defense. With its 3.5" double barrel, the C2K chambers the 3" .410 00 Buck Shot with five pellets. It also features a rebounding hammer, retracting firing pins, crossbolt safety, cammed locking lever, spring-loaded extractor and interchangeable barrels. Choice of caliber includes .410 with 3" chambers and .410/45LC with 2.5" chambers.

For further information, contact:

BOND ARMS, INC.
P.O. Box 1296 • Granbury, TX 76048
Tel: (817) 573-4445 • *Fax:* (817) 573-5636

Model ST1

TRIUS
"Setting the Standard for 45 Years"

The TRIUS 1-STEP (shown) is almost effortless to use: (1) Set arm and place target on arm. (2) Step on pedal to put tension on arm and release target in one motion.

Birdshooter: quality at a budget price–now with high-angle retainer. *Model 92R:* the original "foot trap" *TrapMaster:* sit-down comfort plus pivoting action.

Trius traps are adjustable without tools; feature lay-on loading: singles, doubles, plus piggy-back doubles–offer unparalleled variety.

TRIUS PRODUCTS INC.
P.O. Box 25, Cleves, OH 45002
Tel: 513-941-5682
Web Site: www.trius.com

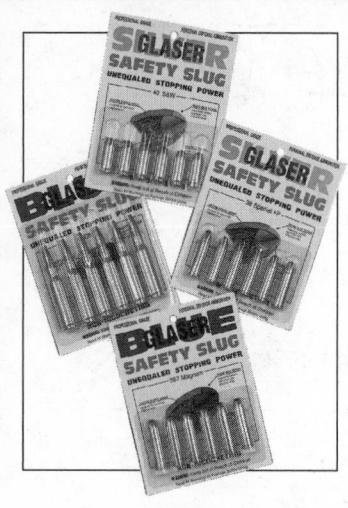

MANUFACTURERS' SHOWCASE

BENCH ⊕ MASTER® RIFLE REST

The Bench Master Rifle Rest is a rugged, compact and highly adjustable rifle-shooting accessory—one that offers precision line-up and recoil reduction when sighting in a rifle, testing ammunition or shooting varmints. It features three course positions totaling 5.5", with 1.5" fine adjustment in each course position, plus leveling and shoulder height adjustments for maximum control and comfort. Because of its unique design, the Bench Master can easily double as a rifle vise for scope mounting, bore sighting and cleaning. It comes with a LIFETIME Warranty and a list price of only $124.95. For a free brochure, call or write:

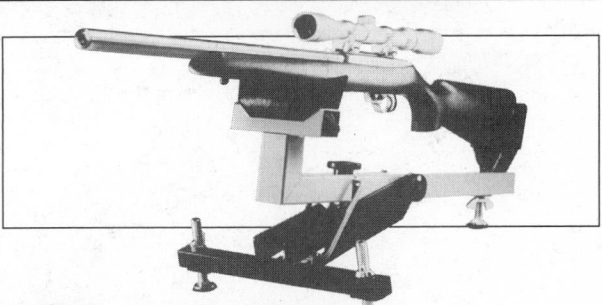

DESERT MOUNTAIN MFG.
2001 W. Fourth Plain • Vancouver, WA 98660
Tel: 360-693-5835 *Fax:* 360-693-7916

CNC MACHINED TRIGGER GUARD

This is a complete CNC machined trigger guard eqipped with precision EDM parts. It features an internal pretravel adjustment that is set at the factory in order to greatly reduce pretravel. This new match trigger guard is CNC machined from a solid billet of high strength aircraft aluminum. The hammer is a precision ground 440C stainless steel. The sear and disconnector are EDM manufactured parts. The trigger is black anodized and equipped with an overtravel adjustment screw. The trigger is reset internally. An automatic bolt release and an extended magazine release are also included.

VOLQUARTSEN CUSTOM LTD.
24276 240th Street • P.O. Box 397 • Carroll, IA 51401
Telephone: 712-792-4238 *Fax:* 712-792-2542
E-mail: vcl@netins.net • *Web Site:* www.volquartsen.com

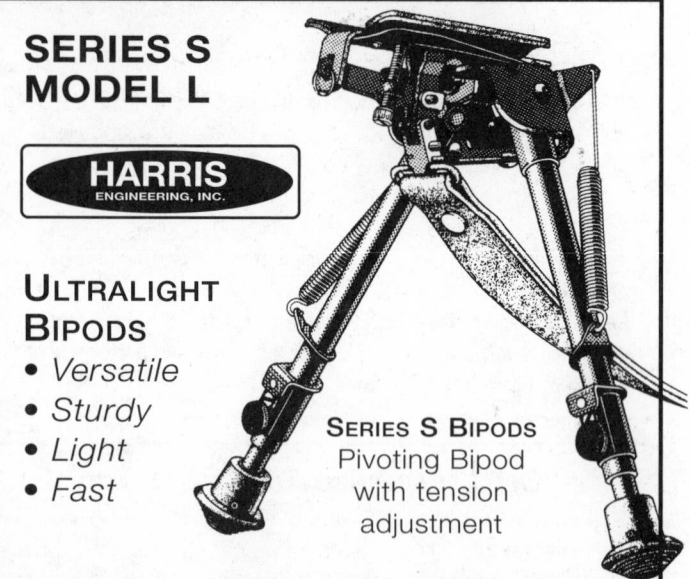

This section of Shooter's Bible will feature custom guns from the most prestigious of the world's small shops. Mass production of interchangeable parts and the factory manufacture of small arms didn't come about until the 19th century. Until then, all guns were essentially unique unto themselves, though basic mechanisms and styles were shared among many makers. The custom gun survives because connoisseurs of firearms want something better than can be had from factory assembly lines, and they're willing to pay for the hand labor.

In its true sense, "custom" means built to order, with the customer dictating the gun's features and dimensions. There are practical limits to custom orders, of course. Few shops will offer an action to the buyer's specifications. They are constrained by the costs of designing and building actions (as well as by patents and the fact that most of the best actions are already in production) to use what is already available from major arms suppliers. To say that a rifle is not really a custom rifle because it employs a Remington 700 action is being too severe.

The gunmakers featured in this section are not the only competent craftsmen in the field. Indeed, there are gunmakers, stockers, metalsmiths and engravers practicing today whose work is the best of its kind ever seen. Quality standards (and prices) continue to climb. In future editions of Shooter's Bible, you'll find the best of the best in custom guns.

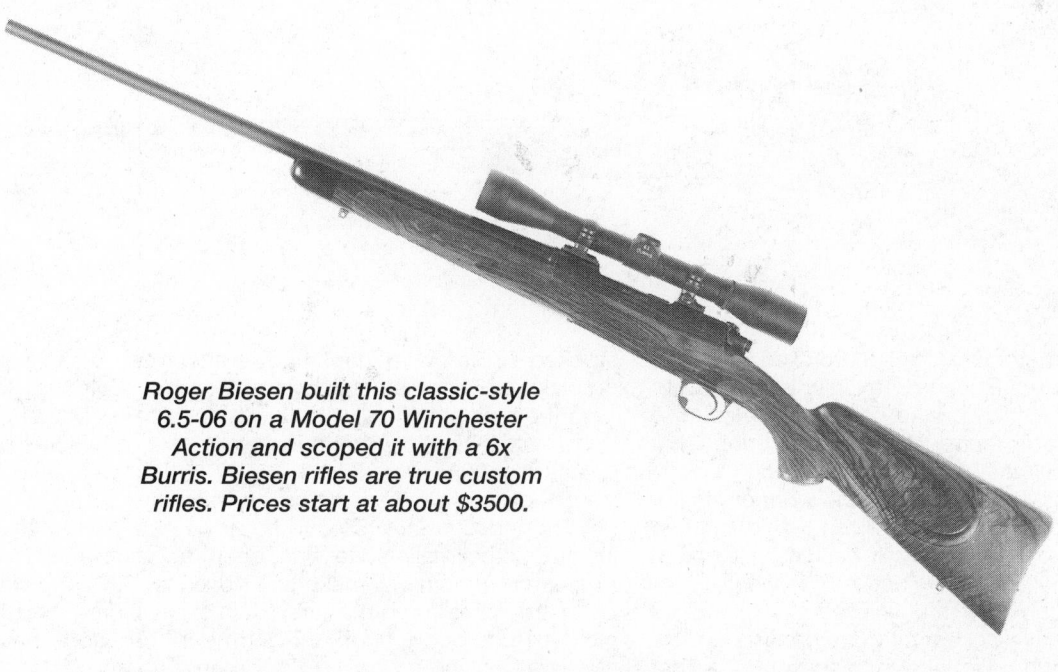

Roger Biesen built this classic-style 6.5-06 on a Model 70 Winchester Action and scoped it with a 6x Burris. Biesen rifles are true custom rifles. Prices start at about $3500.

Custom Gunmakers

*For addresses and phone/fax numbers of manufacturers and distributors included in this section, please turn to **DIRECTORY OF MANUFACTURERS AND SUPPLIERS** on page 557.*

KENT BOWERLY

Gunmaker

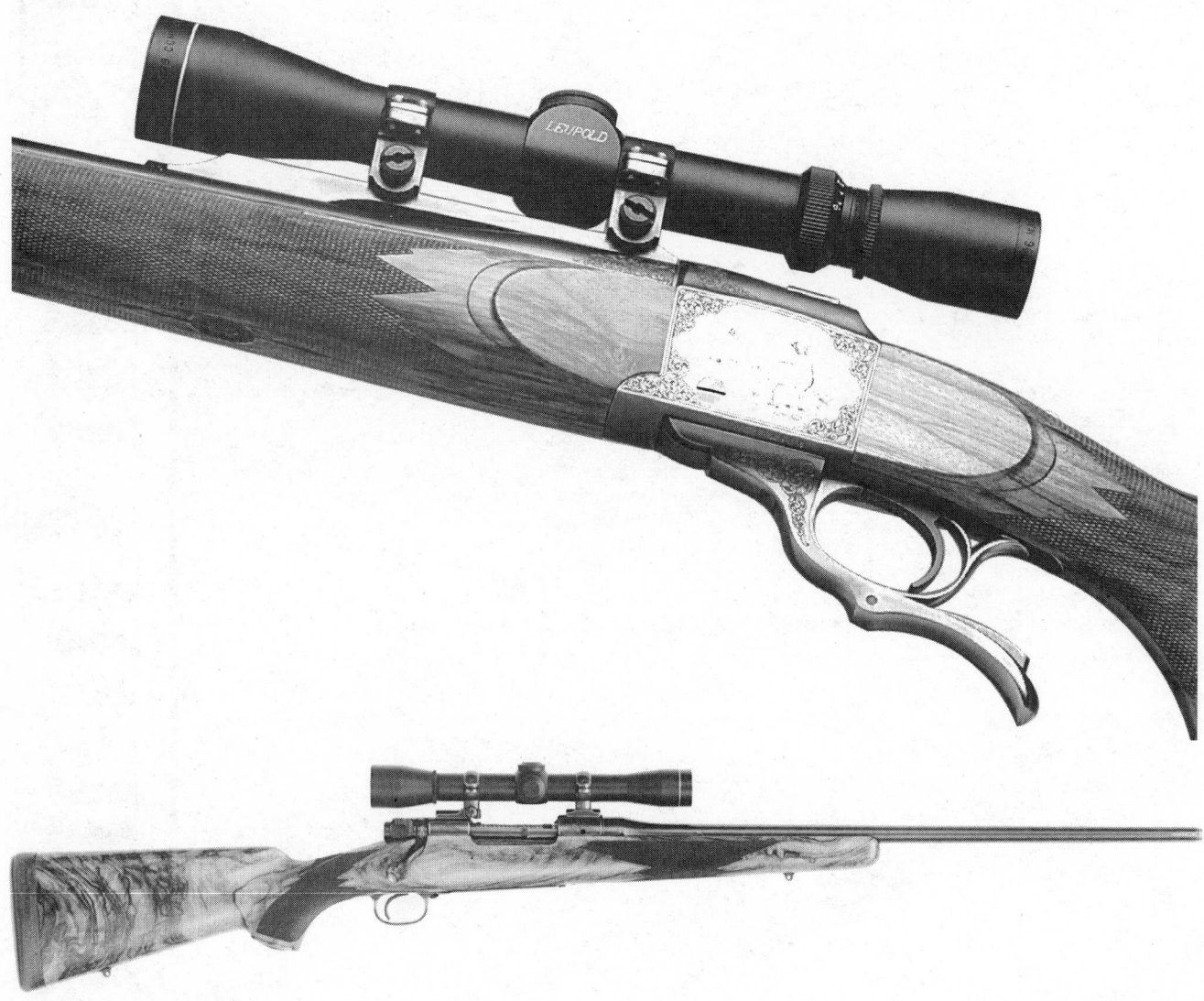

Kent Bowerly began stockmaking in 1958, converting a Springfield 03-A3 with a Roberts semi-inletted stock. His work was admired by friends who offered to pay him to do similar stockwork for them. Thus began a hobby that developed into a legitimate part-time avocation.

In the mid-60's, Kent was exposed to the work of master stockmakers, Al Biesen and Earl Milliron. This inspired him to concentrate on classic stock designs. Although basically self-taught, Kent credits Earl Milliron with coaching him on tools, techniques, and finishes.

A serious hunter, Kent places a strong emphasis on rifle accuracy and function. He works on the premise that a firearm first must be intrinsically accurate, but also be stocked so its owner can shoot it accurately under field conditions. Kent stocks both rifles and shotguns but says the majority of his work is with the Pre-64 Model 70 Winchester, Dakota 76, and Ruger #1. He also works on a variety of Mausers.

Kent took early retirement as an executive in the boat building industry in 1985 and has since been busy as a full-time stockmaker. He has been a member of the American Custom Gunmakers Guild since 1987 and was Guild treasurer for five years. Kent's rifles produced in his well-equipped shop in Redmond, Oregon, have appeared on the cover of RIFLE magazine and in Nikon optics catalogs.

Jim Coffin's interest in guns dates to the second world war. In the late forties he bought surplus 1917 Enfields, and followed up with a Springfield in 1954. That year he also bought his first new rifle, a .30-06 Model 70 Winchester, and a new model 21 Winchester shotgun. During a 22-year career as a Marine pilot, Jim kept his interest in firearms, and was able to hunt near duty stations from Ontario to India. But it wasn't until after retirement that he became intrigued with building his own custom rifles. In 1984 Jim became a member of the American Custom Gunmakers Guild and has since continued to improve and refine his work.

Jim's main interest is in "working guns" - not decorative pieces. He learned to checker and finish a stock long before turning professional, because he reworked many stocks to better their fit. He knows that intrinsic rifle accuracy is of little account if the stock does not help the shooter to aim and execute a shot. He encourages his customers to outline what they want, and to let him serve as an advisor. Jim counts himself fortunate to have attracted some discriminating shooters - and to have made good friends in the process. One rifle job led to a moose hunt down the Copper River in Alaska!

Like many of his colleagues, Jim considers stockmaking an avocation, not a living. His work shows a high level of care because he does care about it. It is his signature. Some of Jim's favorite rifles are built on Mauser and Winchester Model 70 actions. He lives and works in the Willamette River town of Corvallis, Oregon.

**"LEGEND" DANGEROUS
GAME VERSION**

D'Arcy Echols, a riflemaker in Utah, is well known in the custom gun fraternity where he has been active for the past 20 years. In 1997 a customer suggested that D'Arcy build a commercial rifle that functioned and shot as well as his custom rifles but that was a bit less expensive. The result is D'Arcy's "Legend" rifle, with the heart of a Winchester Model 70 Classic action and the metalsmithing that has made Echols custom rifles a hallmark of dependability. A McMillan synthetic stock, designed especially for this rifle, adds durability and trims cost. D'Arcy offers three versions of the "Legend."

The standard model comes in 7mm Remington, 300 Winchester, 300 Weatherby, 338 Winchester Magnum chamberings. Cryogenically-treated Krieger chrome-moly barrels complement the M70 action, which D'Arcy modifies to hold four rounds in the magazine instead of the usual three. He also lengthens the loading port for easy access. When fitting the barrel, he remachines then laps the recoil lug seats and lugs, and squares up the receiver face and bolt face. He repins the trigger and bolt stop and grinds sear surfaces for a crisp, consistent 3 1/4-pound trigger pull. The scope base holes are enlarged to accept 8-40 screws, and he installs his own Weaver-style bases.

D'Arcy pillar-beds the actions in the McMillan stocks, which feature a high, straight comb and cheekpiece, functional checkering, an open grip and a cast-off butt to put the shooter's eye right behind the scope. Length of pull is to order. All steel gets a matte blue finish. D'Arcy shoots each rifle a minimum of 40 times to confirm feeding, safety and accuracy.

The Dangerous Game rifle, available in 375 H&H and 416 Remington Magnums, as well as .458 Lott, has a barrel-mounted front swivel and additional action work to ensure flawless feeding with big roundnose bullets. Otherwise it is like the standard model. Iron sights can be ordered.

The Long Range rifle, available in 300 Weatherby Magnum only, has a 26-inch fluted Krieger barrel of slightly heavier dimensions (.750 at the muzzle). Barrel lengths on other Legend rifles depend on chambering and customer special requests.

Prices:

LEGEND **$4,500.00**
DANGEROUS GAME *(illustrated above)* **4,750.00**
LONG RANGE **4,600.00**
D'Arcy Echols still builds a limited number of walnut-stocked
    custom rifles *(illustrated, below)* . . . . **Prices on request**

CUSTOM RIFLE

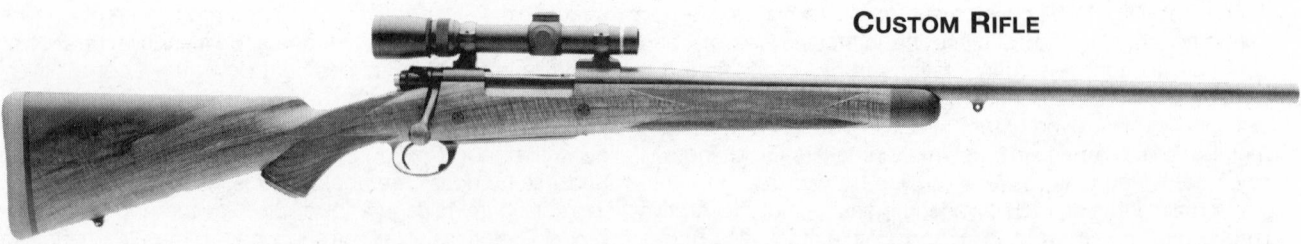

**PRE-64 WINCHESTER
M70 .30-06**

RUGER #1 .375 H&H ENGRAVING BY TIM GEORGE OF LYNCHBURG, VA

Chuck Grace has had a life-long interest in firearms. Growing up in northern Michigan, he was exposed to hunting and most outdoor sports. He attended Trinidad St. Jr. College's gunsmithing program in 1971 so he could turn his "tinkering" hobby into a profession. He has specialized in fine custom stocks and rifles since about 1980. Chuck has been a member of the American Custom Gunmakers Guild since its inception in 1983 and was chosen as the stockmaker on the #16 annual project - a pre-64 Model 70 Winchester in 7x57 recently raffled off at the ACGG annual exhibition in Reno, Nevada. Chuck keeps busy making stocks, doing custom checkering and building complete custom rifles at his small shop in Trinidad, Colorado. He also works on other jobs such as barrel chambering and restoration projects. His stocks start at **$3500** and complete rifles at around **$5000**.

DARWIN HENSLEY

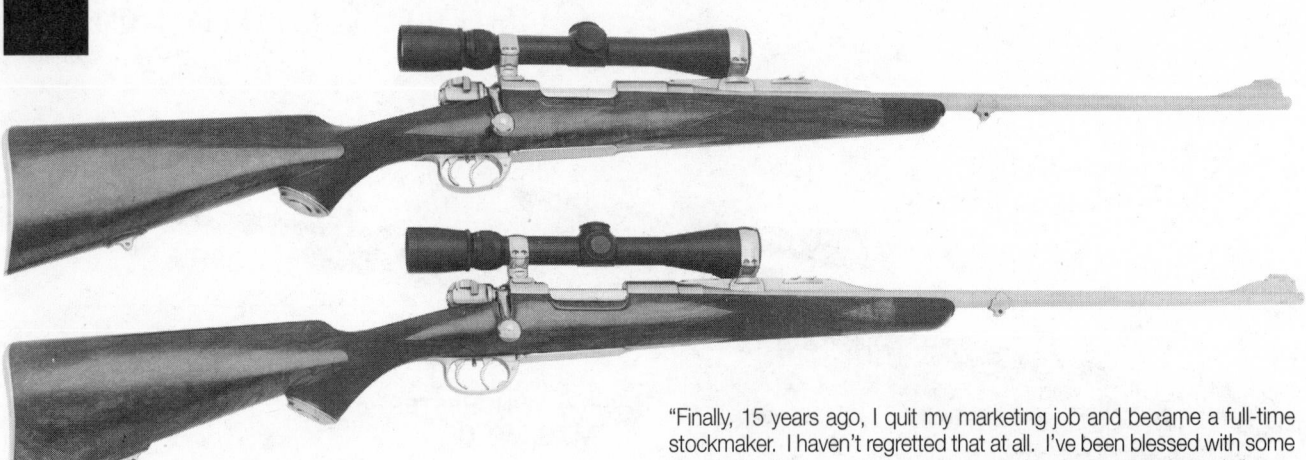

Darwin Hensley was born in 1942 on an Iowa farm. "Life in those times was simple," he says. "if you were bored, you had to fix things or build things to entertain yourself. There was no TV or computer to bombard you with entertainment." Darwin amused himself with a pocket knife, carving and whittling. "We moved to town when I was 10, but I kept that knife busy," he recalls. Darwin spent summers with grandparents on their farm. "Grandpa's 1890 Winchester .22 pump gave me a break from whittling. I still have that rifle."

After graduating from high school, Darwin earned B.A. and B.S. degrees. His favorite field was woodworking, in which he excelled. "I taught art for two years following," Darwin says, "but then I decided there just wasn't enough money in it for my family. I went into marketing and stayed there 25 years. My wife and I raised our two children during that time."

Indulging his fascination with guns, Darwin bought and sold high-grade firearms and did stock work on the side. "But there was never enough time for that," he declares.

"Finally, 15 years ago, I quit my marketing job and became a full-time stockmaker. I haven't regretted that at all. I've been blessed with some wonderful clients, and I wake up every day eager to go to work."

Darwin is a versatile stockmaker, a master of trim profiling as these photos show. "It's important that a rifle shoot and handle well; but beyond that, its design should show a harmony of parts. I mean, the lines, components, engraving, checkering, fit and finish should work together to achieve an overall effect. It's wrong for one of the rifle's parts to draw attention from the whole. I'm very careful to fit a rifle to its owner, physically and in less tangible ways. I like to include subtle details that can only be discovered after careful inspection."

Among the most stunning single-shot rifles displayed at the last Custom Gun Guild show was a Darwin Hensley miniature Gibbs Farquharson (bottom). Chambered in .17 Hornet, it has the slender, classic lines of the two rifles above it – a miniature Jeffery Farquharson in 2R-Lovell (middle) and a miniature Alex Henry in .218 Bee (top). The two bolt rifles above are matched Kurz Mausers, in .22-250 and 7mm-08. Metal work on four of these rifles is by Steve Heilmann. Engraving on the single-shots is by Terry Wallace. The Bee features metalwork by Darwin, who says he sometimes just has to put down that pocket knife to machine a little metal!

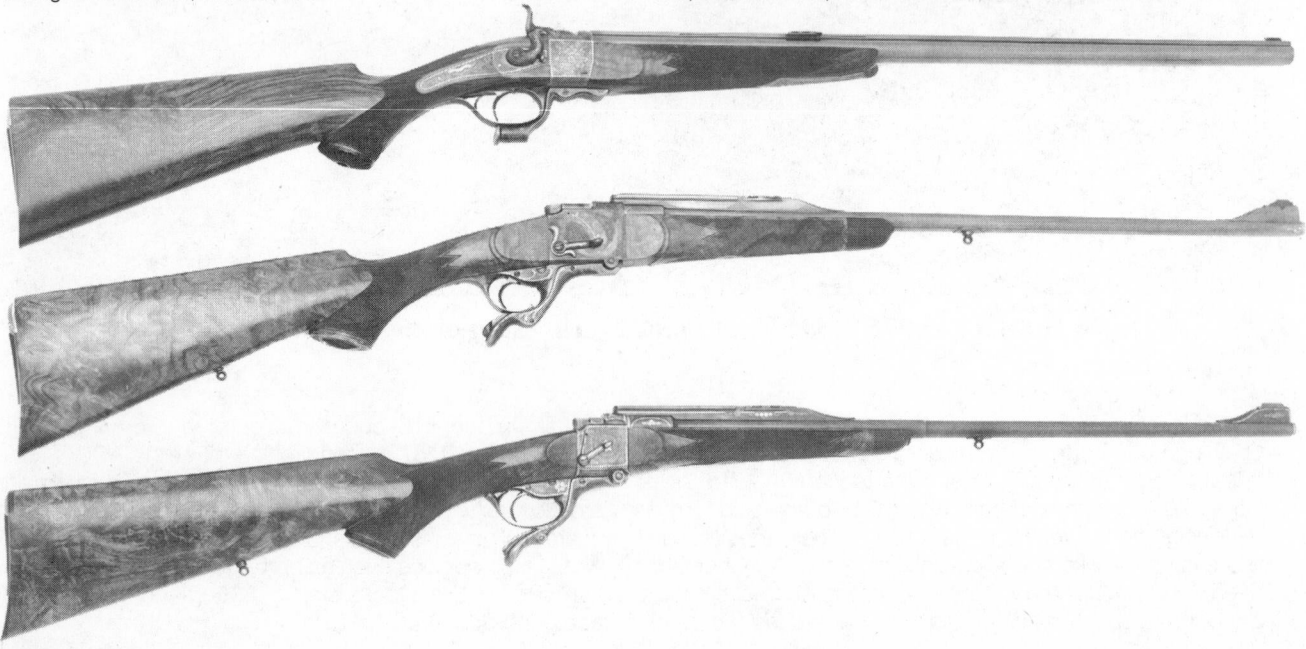

Custom Gunmaker

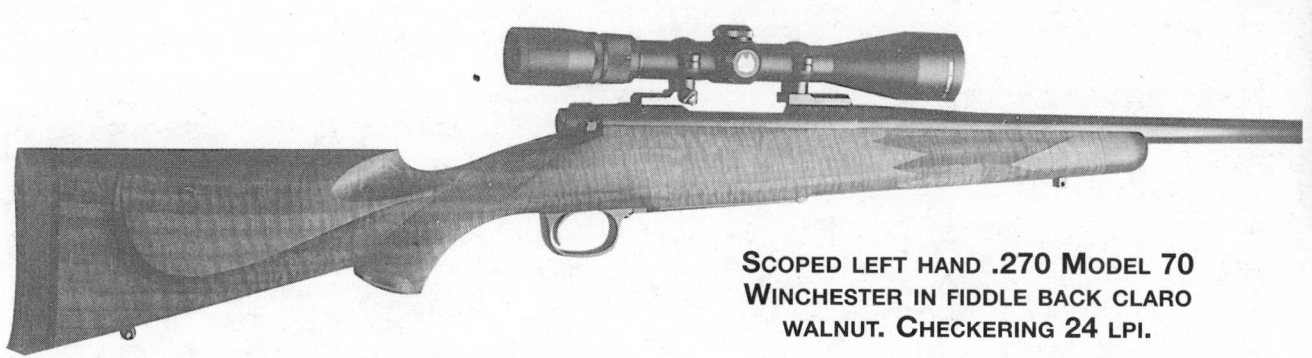

SCOPED LEFT HAND .270 MODEL 70
WINCHESTER IN FIDDLE BACK CLARO
WALNUT. CHECKERING 24 LPI.

BERETTA 20 GA CONVERTED TO AN
ENGLISH STYLE STOCK IN ENGLISH
WALNUT. CHECKERING 26 LPI.

SCOPED LAMINATED
"SHARPSHOOTER" IN .300
WEATHERBY. FLUTED 26"
SCHNEIDER BARREL.

Bob Hisserich is relatively new to gunmaking, having built stocks since 1985. But his talent and diligence are obvious in these examples of his work.

"Its tough to build a rifle that looks as good as it shoots, but I try. I make my rifles one at a time. Accuracy is an easy thing to achieve. Barrels are better than ever and as long as the barrel is installed correctly and the action is trued, the rifle basically has no choice but to shoot accurately. Getting the rifle to look good at the same time is the difficult part. A custom gun shouldn't look like a junior high school shop project."

You can have both attributes here. Accuracy and good looks. I own a Honig/Rodman duplicator capable of duplicating to within .0001." I believe in only one style of stock: Classic. No thumbhole stocks. I do make several crossover stocks each year. These stocks are designed for left-eye dominant shooters to shoot right handed. This also allows someone who has lost the sight in his right eye to continue shooting right handed by leaning his head over the stock and using his left eye to aim." Bob works from his shop in Mesa, Arizona.
Price: **$1,895.00**

PATRICK HOLEHAN

Gunmaker

Patrick Holehan Classic Hunter and Safari Hunter show the clean, graceful lines of the entire Hunter Series.

Arizona gunmaker Patrick Holehan is an exuberant young man with a wide smile and a firm handshake. He is also a serious student of classic hunting rifles and a craftsman with an eye for perfection. His tenure in the gunmaking business is not long; but his work reflects the skills of a true professional. Patrick has an artist's sense of proportion. His stocks show grace and elegance in slender contours that stop just short of racy. He is keen to do his best work always, a requisite in what has become a very competitive industry. Patrick Holehan's checkering shows the attention to detail that distinguishes accomplished craftsmen from people who want to become famous building rifles.

While Holehan rifles are custom projects, Patrick offers several basic variations of what he calls the Hunter Series. All are based on Classic Winchester Model 70 actions, and all come with either hand-made walnut or fiberglass stocks that are pillar bedded and reinforced. Patrick trues barrel seating surfaces, laps the locking lugs, hones and polishes the feed ramp and bolt race. He builds up the receiver ring and bridge to a "double square bridge" configuration that accepts quick-release scope rings. Patrick likes cryogenically-treated barrels and uses only those of highest quality. Barrel lengths and contours, like magazine style and capacity, vary with model. Customers can order from a long list of options. The standard Classic Hunter retails for $3350 with a fiberglass stock, $4050 with a wood stock. The Long Range Hunter is in the same price range, as is the Light Weight Hunter with standard magazine. The Light Weight Hunter with blind magazine costs about $300 less. The Safari Hunter retails for $3800 and $4550 with fiberglass and wood stocks. Patrick Holehan also offers both wood and fiberglass stocks as an interchangeable set with all rifle models. Additional cost varies. Holehan rifles are available in any standard chambering and wildcats that will fit the Model 70 action.

STEVEN DODD HUGHES

Gunmaker

After three years of gunsmithing school, Steven Dodd Hughes started working as a full-time professional custom gunmaker in 1978. For more than a decade, his focus was building muzzleloading firearms from patterns of the 18th and 19th century. Hughes now speciaizes in early cartridge guns creating one-of-a-kind single-shot rifles, double-barrel shotguns and a few high-grade lever action rifes. Current projects include a Winchester Model 1873 .44-40 in a Deluxe 1 of 1000 style, sidelock SXS shotguns based on European metalwork and custom Dakota single-shot rifles with a 1920's London flair. Other projects include fancy Marlin lever guns, boxlock "game gun" shotguns and Winchester High Wall and Low Wall custom rifles from .22 to .45-70. Delivery time usuallly runs from 1 1/2 to 2 years and Hughes's base price is about $10,000. He does no bolt-action rifle work of any kind. Hughes has also written numerous magazine articles about the custom gun trade and contributes the *"Fine Gunmaking"* column for Shooting Sportsman Magazine. His book *Fine Gunmaking: Double Shotguns* was published by Krause Pub. in 1998. A new book, Custom rifles in Black & White, was released recently by Fandango Press.

Hughes designed this custom Winchester High Wall as if it had been created in a London gunshop Circa 1920. It has a 24" octagon barrel with integral quarter-rib and front sight base and weighs 7-1/4 lbs. Stocked in English Walnut, everything is new except the original Winchester action.

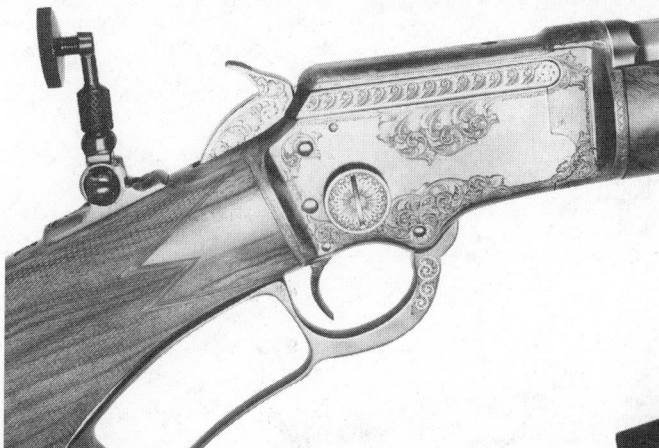

A completely custom M-39A by Hughes follows the theme of the 1897 Deluxe Marlin rimfire rifles. The stock is English Walnut with the distinctive Marlin "S" curve grip profile.

Custom Dakota #10 IN .280 by Steven Dodd Hughes with a new trigger guard, trigger and other metalwork. Hughes stocked the rifle in a style similar to 1920's British single-shots. William Gamradt engraved the rifle with scroll and border work.

DAVID MILLER

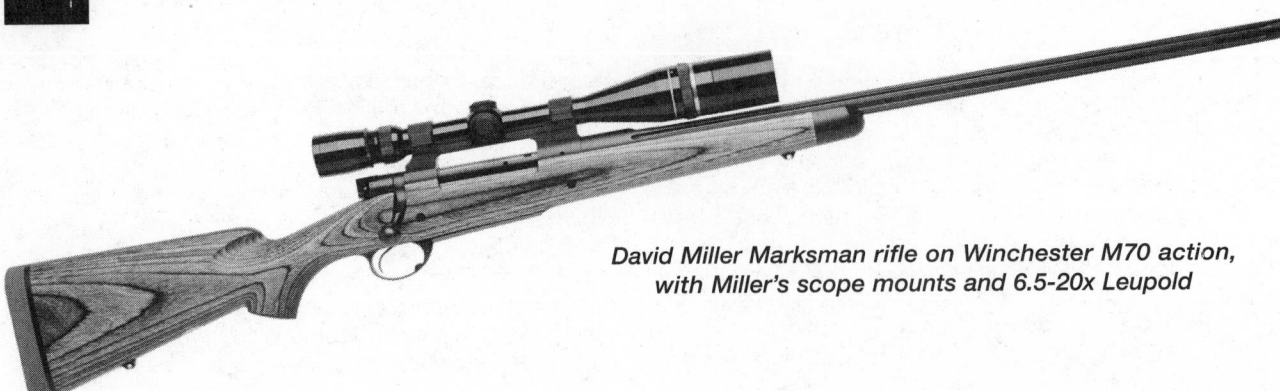

David Miller Marksman rifle on Winchester M70 action, with Miller's scope mounts and 6.5-20x Leupold

A fine example of custom rifle building is David Miller's work, shown here. The Tucson, Arizona craftsman has been making rifles for most of his adult life. Until recently, he was best known for his fine rendering of hand-fashioned classic-style bolt rifles. Several were highlights at annual conventions of Safari Club International. A few years ago he put together a rifle for his own special type of hunting Coues deer at long range in the desert hinterlands south of his Tucson shop. The rifle featured a laminated stock, not the exquisite English walnut his customers were used to seeing. It had a Winchester Model 70 action, pillar bedded for accuracy, and a long fluted barrel chambered in .300 Weatherby Magnum. David used his own scope mounts to attach a 6.5-20x Leupold scope with special range-finding reticle. Fellow hunters saw and shot the rifle and wanted a copy. Now David and partner Curt Crum are busy building both the full-custom Classic rifle and the new Marksman. A stickler for rifles that shoot well, David puts the best components and workmanship into both rifles. The Marksman lacks only the options, detailing and fine walnut of the custom Classic. David routinely shoots deer at ranges beyond the capability of most hunters. He insists that with practice and the right rifle (a Marksman!), long-distance shooting can put more venison on the table. His collection of records-class Coues deer show that his Marksman gets lots of use. Base price for this rifle is **$9,000**.

TONY SCHUELKE

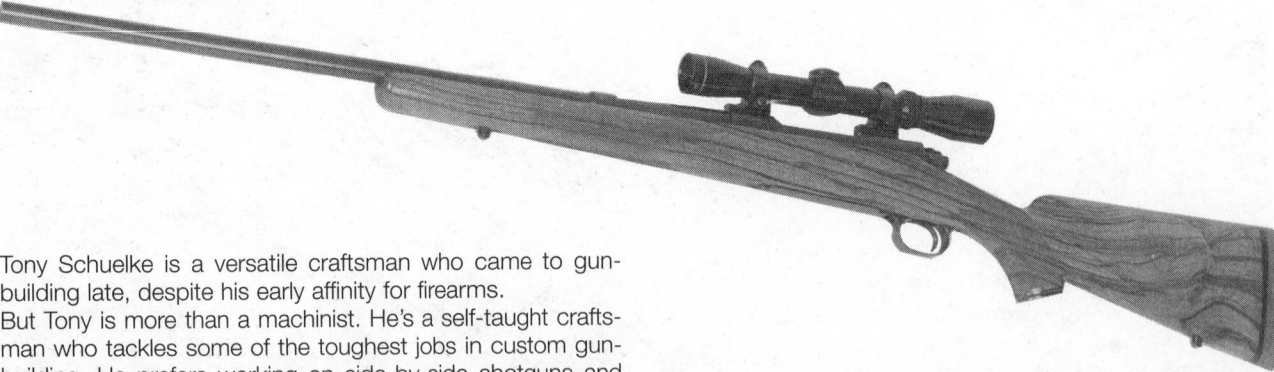

Tony Schuelke is a versatile craftsman who came to gun-building late, despite his early affinity for firearms.

But Tony is more than a machinist. He's a self-taught crafts-man who tackles some of the toughest jobs in custom gun-building. He prefers working on side-by-side shotguns and looks for ways to be creative - especially in checkering. Tony is an accomplished man with a file, checkering not only stocks but bolt handles. He's also proud of the skeleton grip caps he fabricates in his shop. While he doesn't imitate anyone, Tony takes every opportunity to study the work that he admires.

A good listener when clients approach him with their ideas, he'd rather respond than recommend, pointing out that custom guns - especially side-by-sides - are more like art than implements. Individuality is important to some people, and little details that have no bearing on performance can matter a great deal. Tony keeps shop in Glencoe, Minnesota.

Riflemaker

Gene Simillion Premier Rifle, .270 on a Winchester Model 70 action with Leupold 2-7x scope.

Coloradan Gene Simillion has been building custom sporting rifles for nearly 20 years. He grew up near renowned stockmaker Keith Stegall and says he got the inspiration to craft rifle stocks from Keith. Later, Gene honed his wood- and metal-working skills in college, graduating with a teaching degree in industrial arts.

"That wasn't too smart," Gene says with a frown. "I should have figured out beforehand that teachers work during hunting season." Gene started building rifles full-time, then spent a year in Kalispell under the tutelage of crack stockmaker Jerry Fisher. Gene also credits Montanan Tom Burgess with teaching him a lot about custom metal-smithing. "I'm a student of good workmanship," he says. "So I've paid attention to the likes of Monte Mandarino, D'Arcy Echols and Don Klein."

Gene Simillion notes that little has changed in the stye of his work since the early days. "The clean, classic look is as popular as ever–maybe even more so. I like to think I'm better at the job now." On any project, Gene's aim is to produce a rifle with "accuracy, flawless function, and elegant beauty." He says the main difference between custom rifles and the best factory-built guns is in the detailing.

Two grades of rifles come from Gene's Gunnison, Colorado shop. The Premier Rifle is a true custom effort, built to each customer's exact specifications. Gene prefers to use new Model 70 Winchester Classic actions but will substitute pre-64 Model 70s, Mauser 98s, Remington 700s and others on request. Gene installs his own scope bases. A hand-checkered bolt knob and screwless sling swivel studs are standard. Magnum rifles get a second recoil lug and a crossbolt, a custom magazine box and follower. Extended magazines are an option–so too quarter ribs and iron sights. Stocks are of the finest walnut, hand-checkered in point or fleur-de-lis patterns..

SIMILLION PREMIER RIFLE $7,500.00
  MAGNUMS 8,000.00

A less costly custom rifle is Gene's Classic Hunter. Built only on the new Winchester 70 Classic action, it also features new bottom metal and a top-quality, cut-rifled barrel hand-bedded in a high-grade checkered walnut stock with screwless swivel bases. The Classic Hunter shows less detailing than the Premier, and the customer has fewer options. Gene came up with this rifle a couple of years ago to bridge the gap between true custom rifles and the semi-custom factory-built rifles like those produced by Dakota.

STANDARD CLASSIC HUNTER. $5,400.00
  MAGNUMS 6,000.00
  HEAVY MAGNUMS (.375 H&H and up) 6,500.00

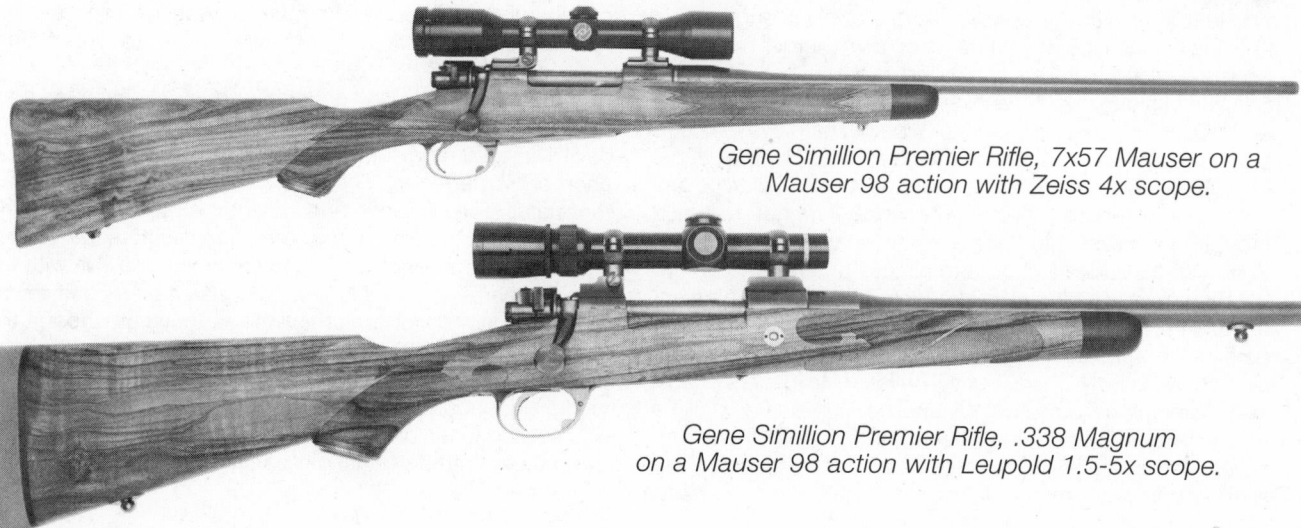

Gene Simillion Premier Rifle, 7x57 Mauser on a Mauser 98 action with Zeiss 4x scope.

Gene Simillion Premier Rifle, .338 Magnum on a Mauser 98 action with Leupold 1.5-5x scope.

CHARLIE SISK

Riflemaker

About 45 minutes northeast of Houston, in the smaller Texas town of Crosby, 34-year-old gunmaker Charlie Sisk is on the phone talking with customers. It's one of his strengths, this keeping in close touch with the people who order his super-accurate rifles. But it's not the only talent. Charlie built his first gun in high-school machine shop - a .257 Roberts on a 98 Mauser action - and has been working hard ever since to build a reputation in a competitive industry. He specializes in synthetic-stocked bolt rifles that shoot very well. "I'd say they can all shoot half-inch, because I've got half-inch groups," he says. "But I'm not a half-inch shooter.'

Such candor endears Charlie to his customers, who are for the most part a pretty critical lot. Charlie's rifle's don't wear handsome wood. They're not engraved. They're meant to be shot. And beauty is only as beauty does. Charlie works almost exclusively on bolt-action rifles. He prefers Model 700 Remingtons but says Winchester 70s come in close behind. He likes Hart barrels becaued he's found them consistently accurate. Still, he takes nothing for granted. "Hart specifies groove-diameter tolerance of .0005-inch," Charlie

says. "But mine are air-gauged and don't vary more than .0001. I also inspect each barrel with a bore-scope. And my chambering is done with match-grade live-pilot reamers to ensure concentricity "My rifles have to shoot tight groups."

But bench accuracy isn't enough for hunters who must control lightweight rifles under field conditions. Charlie adds Jewell triggers and takes care that his synthetic stocks fit each client perfectly. They are also meticulously mated to the metal. Rifle balance and weight matter to Charlie, who prides himself in doing all the work on a rifle personally. That includes "blueprinting" actions to square up the bolt with the bore. Charlie makes his own muzzle brakes. He thinks most rifles will shoot about as well as they can shoot if the forend tip puts a little pressure on the barrel. However, he will free-float barrels on request. Charlie Sisk commonly works up loads for his customers. He likes the chance to add service to his product, get to know the customer better - and prove that his hunting rifles are indeed as accurate as any around!

"I'm one of those lucky people who knew right away what they want in the way of a career," says Dale Storey. After high school, Dale enrolled in the Colorado School of Trades, perhaps the best-known of American institutions for turning out skilled gunmakers. He started working on guns soon after graduating CST in 1962, but didn't commit to the trade full-time until 1981. "Uncle Sam used some of my talents for awhile," he says. After military service and two degrees from Montana State University, Dale taught at a high school and post-secondary schools for 11 years - "to bankroll my gunshop." Since turning professional, he has worked on a variety of rifles, from the black-powder muzzleloaders that were his early love, to modern bolt guns.

One of Dale's favorite projects is a half-stock plains rifle, true in line and feature to its ancestors. A new interest is Alex Henry rifles. He built one recently, and it is indeed a most elegant black-powder arm. Dale traces his interest in muz-

zleloaders to mentor V.M. Starr, who taught him much about their history and how they should be built. Starr was instrumental in bringing shotgun shooting to the annual black-powder rendezvous at Friendship, Indiana.

Dale Storey now works mainly on modern rifles, emphasizing that the heart of every fine hunting rifle is perfect balance. "No one thing should dominate a rifle, in form or function," he says. "A rifle must point quickly and shoot accurately from hunting positions." He points out that high-quality parts are essential but adds that putting them together is what distinguishes an able craftsman from an assembler. Dale says he can do "almost everything" in building a rifle. He leaves the engraving and inlay work to others, however. Liz Dolbare did that part of the Alex Henry project.

A hunter and shooter, Dale is pleased to call Wyoming home. He works in Casper.

MARK STRATTON

Custom Gunmaker

The photo above is a 1909 Argentine Mauser in 7mm-08. The photo was taken by Leupold and was the centerfold in its 1998 catalog. (Photo is courtesy of Leupold.) This rifle has a 22" octagon Shilen barrel, 1 in 9. It has a Timney trigger, Chapman two-position safety. Mark Stratton built the scope bases. The stock is English walnut with an ebony forearm tip, and point pattern 24-lines-per-inch checkering. The scope is a Leupold 3 x 9 Compact. Engraving by Darrel Nelson.

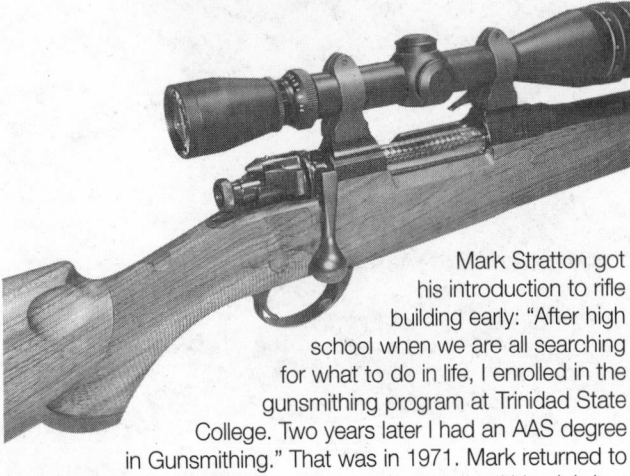

This 1910 Mexican small ring Mauser in 6mm Remington has a 1936 cocking piece. 1-in-10 twist Shilen barrel has been recontoured by Mark Stratton. The scope is a Leupold 4 x 12 Vari X II with Warne rings. Mark Stratton built the scope bases. There is a Timney trigger and a swing safety by Glen Chapman. An English walnut stock with a fleu-de-lis and ribbons, has 22 lines-per-inch checkering. Precise Metalsmithing made the magazine and trigger guard.

Mark Stratton got his introduction to rifle building early: "After high school when we are all searching for what to do in life, I enrolled in the gunsmithing program at Trinidad State College. Two years later I had an AAS degree in Gunsmithing." That was in 1971. Mark returned to Southern California and got a part-time gunsmithing job in a warranty repair gun shop in Orange County. He soon found that gunsmithing was not the shortcut to fast cars.

He went to work for an electronics company as a machinist, and in the off hours put together barreled actions. He stocked them at home. Mark sold his first rifle in 1974 to a friend for the cost of the parts. For the next several years he built rifles for friends for the experience. In 1978 he moved to the Seattle area and went to work for another electronics company. He was making models and prototypes of new products - and again using off hours for custom rifle building. He was getting good at the craft, but didn't feel confident enough to hang out a shingle.

In 1988 Mark attended the American Custom Gunmakers Guild show in Reno. The level of work at the Gunmakers Guild show was much higher than he'd seen before, and it subsequently raised the level of his work. Competent as a machinist, Mark struggled to become a better stockmaker.

"In 1991 one of the Guild members was talking about making an octagon barrel," Mark continued, "but was unsure about how to go about it. I had developed the tooling for octagons back in the 70's. I hadn't written anything since college but agreed to put my technique on paper. The article went well and so far I've written 15 technical tips articles on machine setups and tooling. In 1998 I was asked to become associate editor of the *gunmaker* for metalsmithing technical tips. I now have a column in almost every edition. At this point I wasn't a regular member of the guild. I decided not to become a regular member because I wasn't a full-time gunmaker."

In 1994 Mark started advertising his work at trade shows. It was very well received. So well, in fact, that he now has his own shop and is building custom firearms full-time. In 2001 Mark became a member of the Gunmakers Guild.

"In 1995 I was asked to put on a week-long seminar in both metalsmithing and stockmaking at Trinidad State College. I'm now teaching metalsmithing and a tooling seminar every year at Trinidad and I will teach this seminar for the first time Montgomery Community College in Trop, North Carolina this year." Sharing his love of the craft - and its secrets - is an unexpected bonus for this talented gunmaker, who now resides in Lynnwood, Washington.

Rifles

*For addresses and phone/fax numbers of manufacturers and distributors included in this section, please turn to **DIRECTORY OF MANUFACTURERS AND SUPPLIERS** on page 557.*

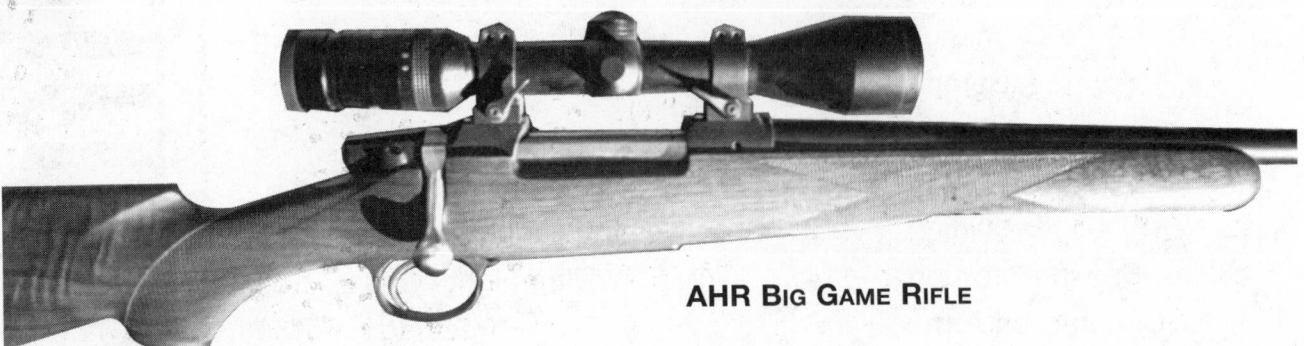

AHR BIG GAME RIFLE

The foundation of every AHR rifle is the strong, beautifully finished CZ 550 action. Its smooth and dependable controlled-round CZ 550 complements a rugged adjustable trigger. This classic action wears your choice of a English walnut or all-weather synthetic stock. The classic design in both the walnut and the all-weather stocks is by master stockmaker Jerry Fisher.

The 25-inch American Hunting Rifles barrel - chrome moly or stainless steel - is rifled with the rate of twist best suited to the premium hunting bullets loaded in each specific cartridge. The outstanding accuracy of these barrels often surpasses that of other production rifles that cost much more.

AHR rifles are available in the standard .270 Winchester and .30-06 Springfield, as well as a wide variety of our own proprietary cartridges from a .220 to a .411. All of our cartridges are based on original designs by Ken Howell, noted writer and author of the popular book, *Designing and Forming Custom Cartridges*.

Hunters will quickly find that the 12 Howell cartridges, designed specifically for hunting varmints and big game, offer more case capacity–and power–than comparable standard rounds.

Howell cartridges are designed for efficiency and long barrel life. These new cartridges confirm experienced hunters' opinion that belted magnum cases aren't necessary for game-killing power.

A Family of Cartridges With Classic Roots

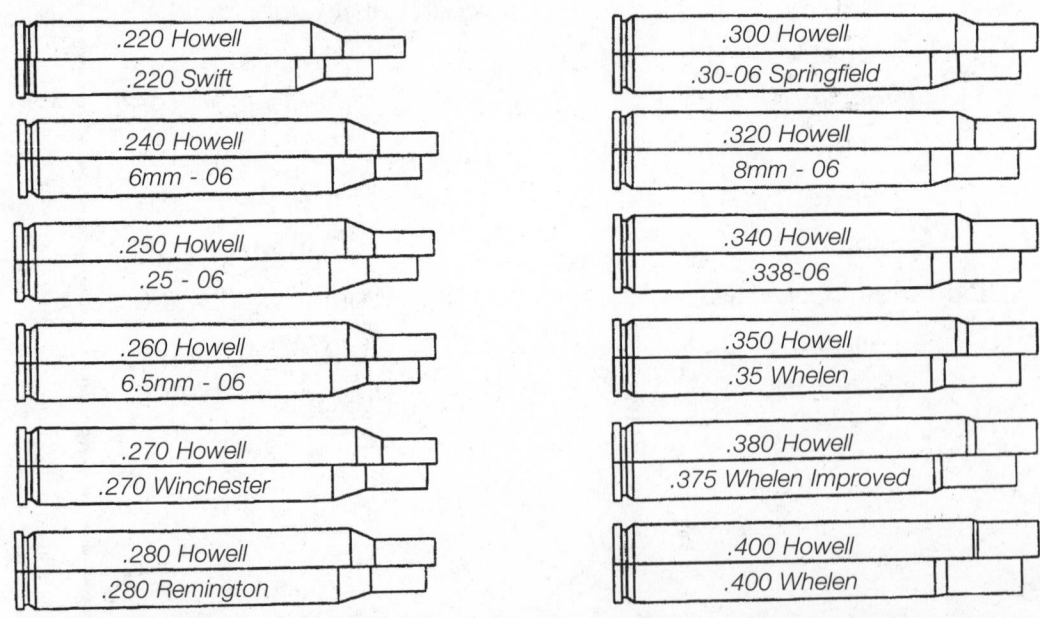

.220 Howell	.300 Howell
.220 Swift	.30-06 Springfield
.240 Howell	.320 Howell
6mm - 06	8mm - 06
.250 Howell	.340 Howell
.25 - 06	.338-06
.260 Howell	.350 Howell
6.5mm - 06	.35 Whelen
.270 Howell	.380 Howell
.270 Winchester	.375 Whelen Improved
.280 Howell	.400 Howell
.280 Remington	.400 Whelen

Head size is .473 (same as .30-06). Shoulder angle is sharper, at 25 degrees. Case length: 2.60"

**MODEL 2013
SUPER MATCH**

Julius Gottfried Anschutz, son of a German gunsmith, founded J.G. Anschutz in 1856 to build pocket pistols, shotguns and rifles. In 1896 the firm moved out of its small workshop into a factory. Five years later Julius Anschutz died, and his sons, Fritz and Otto, assumed control of the business. By 1911 there were 200 people working at the Anschutz plant. When Otto died shortly after the first world war, Fritz and his sons, Rudolf and Max, continued to build the enterprise.

Growth came to an abrupt halt in 1945, when the factory was shut down pursuant to Germany's surrender in World War II. But five years later J.G. Anschutz GmbH was founded to make air pistols and repair firearms. Soon it turned to target rifles and even resumed manufacture of the Flobert-type guns that had been among the firm's original products. Anschutz target rifles began to build a reputation among the world's elite shooters, and the company grew to 250 employees.

In 1968 Dieter Anschutz, a fourth-generation member of the family, became chief executive, as the Anschutz name became more and more prominent in Olympic competition. In 1992 his son, Jochen, became company president. Jochen and Dieter now manage J.G. Anschutz together. An ultramodern plant in Ulm, Germany, produces what has become recognized world-wide as the standard against which all rimfire target rifles and pistols are judged. Anschutz rifles captured all of the gold medals, and all but two of the silver medals in the Barcelona Olympic Games. The company's competition air rifles and pistols have done almost as well as the firearms.

MODEL 2013 "SUPER MATCH"

Since the 1960s, the Model 54 rimfire action has set the standard in competitive three-position and smallbore prone shooting. The current version, with a heavy, rectangular receiver, attaches to the stock with four action screws. This action is the heart of the Model 2013 Super Match Special — and of the 2013 Benchrest, the 2007, 2012, 1907, 1912, and 1913 rifles. It is also featured in the 1808 D-RT Running Target, 54.18 MS Metallic Silhouette and 1808 MS-R Silhouette rifles. Its fine trigger mechanism, close tolerances and extremely fast lock time make it a logical choice for competitive marksmen. Anschutz .22 rimfire barrels, noted for one-hole accuracy, complement the 54 action.

The 2013 Super Match is the latest and most sophisticated in a long line of Super Match rifles for freestyle shooting events. Available in both right- and left-hand versions, it comes with adjustable two-stage match trigger (with safety). The trigger-piece can be moved longitudinally and tilted up to 15 degrees. There's a forearm accessory rail with hand stop and palm rest fitted to the thumbhole stock. A fully adjustable cheekpiece complements a hook butt assembly adjustable for cant, pitch, length and drop. A host of accessories, including match sights and counter-weights is available.

Barrel length: 27.1 inches.
Rifle weight: 14.3 pounds.
Price: w/palm rest $2,250.00
       left-hand 2,280.00

ANSCHUTZ RIFLES

MODEL 1907

Match 54 action in an economical rifle, with adjustable cheekpiece and butt assembly.
Barrel Length: 25.9 inches *Rifle Weight:* 10.5 pounds
Price:. **$1,385.00**
   left-hand **1,455.00**
   with 2213 metal stock **1,985.00**

MODEL 1912 "SPORT RIFLE"

Match 54 action in a lightweight international-style rifle engineered to stay under the 6.5kg weight limit. The walnut stock has a forend raiser block, fully adjustable hook buttplate and cheekpiece, and forward hand stop and swivel.
Barrel Length: 25.9 inches.
Rifle Weight: 11.4 pounds.
Price:. **$1,665.00**
   left-hand **1,725.00**

MODEL 1808 D-RT "RUNNING TARGET"

A fully adjustable trigger, as per the Model 2013 "Super Match" and lightning-quick lock time help competitors excel on the moving-target range. A removable barrel extension improves smoothness of swing. The stock is specially configured for off-hand shooting, with adjustable cheekpiece and butt assembly.
Barrel Length: 32.6 inches.
Rifle Weight: 9.0 pounds.
Price:. **$1,699.00**

MODEL 54.18 MS R "SILHOUETTE"

Designed expressly for metallic silhouette shooting, this rifle weighs only 8.1 pounds. The adjustable two-stage trigger is set at 4.4 ounces. The Match 54 action has been modified to accept a 5-shot magazine. A rubber buttpad is standard.
Barrel Length: 22.4 inches
Price: $1,280.00

RIFLES

MODEL 1827 "FORTNER"

This rifle is built for biathlon competition, an Olympic event that combines skiing and marksmanship. Competitors must shoot twice at the 10-km point, four times at 20 km into the race and twice at a relay point of 7.5 km. Each station requires five shots prone and five standing. The Anschutz 1827 has a straight-pull repeating action to increase speed of fire. It weighs 8.8 pounds and is equipped with magazine holders. The walnut stock features adjustable cheekpiece and butt assembly. A special front sight hood protects the sight and bore from snow.
Barrel Length: 21.6 inches.
Price: $1,810.00
   left-hand 1,850.00

MODEL 1903

A competitive rifle for riflemen on a budget, the 1903 has a M64-type action with two-stage adjustable trigger. The hardwood stock features a forward accessory rail and an adjustable cheekpiece. The buttplate is vertically adjustable; length of pull can be changed by adding or deleting spacers.
Price: $670.00
   left-hand 710.00

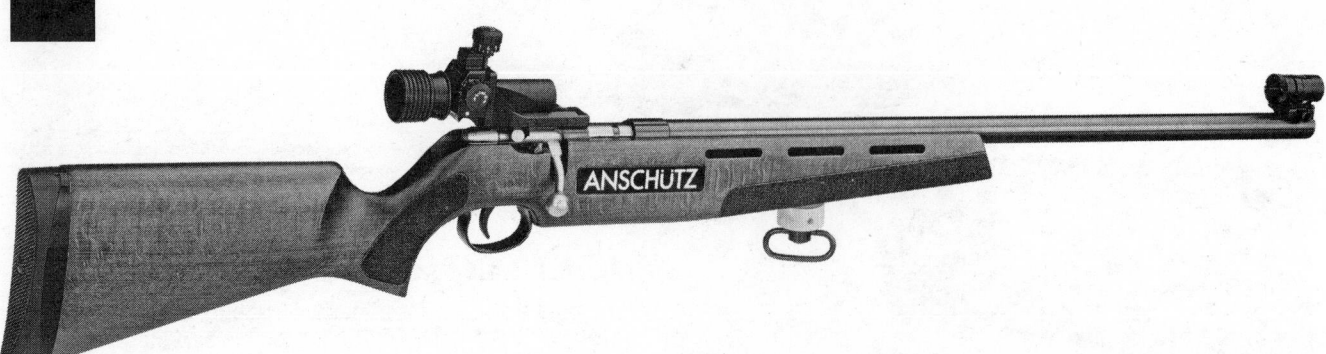

MODEL 1451 (not shown)

An affordable rifle with target-rifle potential, this 5-pound repeater has a trim action, checkered hardwood stock and iron sights on a 21-inch sporter-weight barrel. The receiver is grooved for a scope.
Price: **$335.00**
 (threaded barrel or tangent rear sight $10 extra each)

MODEL 1700 SERIES SPORTERS (not shown)

Both the Anschutz 1700 custom & classic series are bolt action repeaters with a 54 sporter action and detachable magazine. Features include dual locking lugs, claw extractor, recessed bolt face and independent bolt release, wing safety, single stage trigger. Barrel is free floated, drilled and tapped with a target-crowned muzzle. Available with a monte carlo stock or Meister grade.
Prices: CUSTOM SERIES
1710D MC stock 22LR. **$905.00**
 Meister Grade 1,057.00
1720D MC stock 22WMR 920.00
 Meister Grade 1,072.00
1730D Sporting Rifle 22 Hornet 1,004.00
 Meister Grade 1,156.00

MODEL 1451 R SPORT TARGET

This modestly-priced target rifle has the same action as the 1451 sporter but with a heavier 20-inch barrel adapted to target sights, and a target-style stock with aluminum slide rail and vertically adjustable butt. The two-stage trigger and fast lock time help boost scores. **Weight:** 6.5 pounds.
Price: **$380.00**
 *(target sights **$282** extra)*

1740D Sporting Rifle 222 Rem **1,040.00**
 Meister Grade **1,156.00**
CLASSIC SERIES
1710D Heavy Barrel 22LR **$843.00**
 Meister Grade 994.00
1720D Sporting Rifle 22WMR. 857.00
 with heavy barrel 857.00
 Meister Grade 939.00
1730D Sporting Rifle 22 Hornet 939.00
 with heavy barrel 995.00
 Meister Grade **1,090.00**
1740D Sporting Rifle 222 Rem 939.00
Also Available: NEW! Model 1448 Claybird
 (smooth bore bolt rifle .22) 295.00

MODEL 2013 "BENCHREST" BR-50

Barreled action: Compact connection between barreled action and stock, heavy rectangular receiver attached with 4 action screws. The accuracy of the barreled action and the extremely short locktime within a range of milliseconds offer best conditions for success. **Barrel:** Cylindrical match barrel **Stock:** Non-stained stock with wide, flat, forend, especially developed for benchrest shooting **Caliber:** .22 LR **Barrel length:** 50 cm/19.6" **Rifling:** 50 cm/16.6" **Total length:** 97 cm/38.1" **Weight appr.:** 4,7 kg/10.3 lbs **Version:** Single loader
Price: **$1,575.00**

Arnold Arms designed and builds its own Apollo action with a clever extractor that helps ensure positive function. In its center position, the 3-position safety allows the action to be cycled for loading and unloading without fear of discharge. Squaring and truing operations usually reserved for custom rifles are standard on every Apollo. Lugs are lapped and the action glass bedded for accuracy. The Apollo action is optional on some Arnold rifles.

Most Arnold rifles are built on other actions, in a variety of configurations to satisfy every hunter and target shooter. Match-grade barrels and McMillan synthetic stocks are used throughout, though walnut stocks are available by special order. Rifles are available in chamberings from 223 to 458, including Arnold's own line of high-performance cartridges. Some examples of big game rifles:

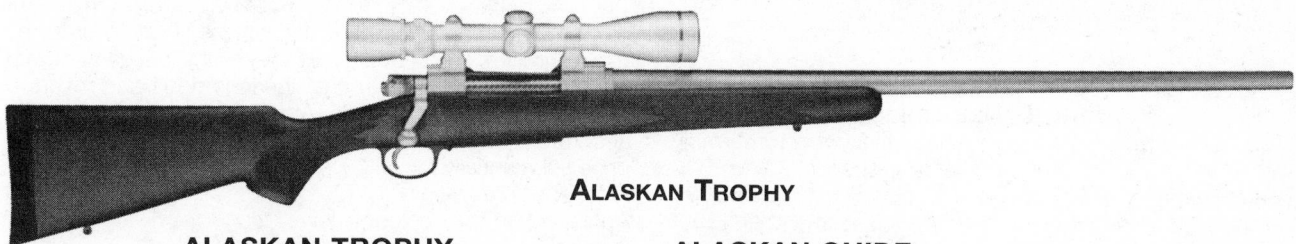

ALASKAN TROPHY

ALASKAN TROPHY

Each rifle features a fully accurized and trued action in stainless steel with a stainless steel match grade sporting contour barrel and choice of McMillan black or camo stock. Barrel lengths available are 22"-24" for non-magnums and 24"-26" for magnums. Chamberings are available in all popular cartridges plus most wildcats and the Arnold line of cartridges.

Prices: Remington 700 action rifle start at **$2,695.00**
Winchester M70 action rifle **2,695.00**

ALASKAN GUIDE

These rifes come with the same components as the "Alaskan Trophy" but have Express sights and a barrel band for the front sling swivel installed as standard equipment. Available in .338 magnum to .458 magnum.

Prices:
Remington 700 SS action built rifle, upgraded with three-.
position safety and Ssko style extractor. **$3,799.00**
Winchester M70 SS action rifle. **3,399.00**

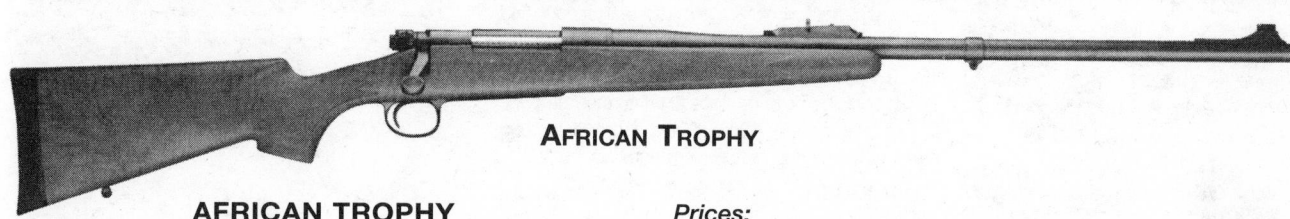

AFRICAN TROPHY

AFRICAN TROPHY

Each rifle features a fully trued and accurized action in chrome-moly matte blued steel with sporting contour match grade barrel and synthetic McMillan stock in either black or camo finish. Each rifle is given the Arnold "Accu*Pro" treatment and is available in .223 to .338 magnum calibers as well as most wildcats and the Arnold lines of cartridges.

Prices:
Remington 700 action rifle start at **$2,695.00**
Winchester M70 action rifle start at **2,595.00**
Same as above but with
walnut stock . . . . **P.O.R.**
Same as above but with black teflon coated
stainless steel barrel . . . . **Add 229.00**

GRAND AFRICAN

GRAND AFRICAN

This line of custom rifles comes with Express sights and barrel band for front sling swivel, and is available in "A" through "AAA" American dark, English walnut, Bastogne, as well as "Exhibition grade. Available in .338 magnum to .458 magnum. Remington 700 action rifles come equipped with a three-position safety and Sako extractor as a standard upgrade.

Prices: With McMillan synthetic stock **$3,995.00**
With walnut Hunter Classic stock. **3,895.00**
With "A" English walnut stock, ebony forend
and steel grip cap. Start at **6,595.00**
Winchester Model 70 action rifles:
With walnut Hunter Classic stock. **3,595.00**
With "A" Engllish walnut stock, ebony forend and
steel grip cap. Start at **6,295.00**

RIFLES

MARK II "NEUTRALIZER"

ARNOLD NEUTRALIZER SERIES RIFLES
Mark II "Neutralizer"

Built on the ApolloTM action, stainless steel or chrome-moly with match grade barrel. Choice of calibers .223 to .300 Winchester magnum. Rifle shown shot 3.5" groups at 1,600 yards daily for two weeks in New Mexico, September 1996. Features include Remington 700 action (choice of chrome-moly blued or stainless steel) with detachable box magazine, match grade barrel (chrome-moly or stainless steel) in Palma to heavy varmint contours. McMillan A2 or A3 tactical stocks available in black, woodland, arctic, desert or urban camo. Adjustable cheekpiece standard. Sako extractor, 3-position safety and thicker recoil lug standard on the Neutraizer rifles,

and triggers are set at choice of 2.5 or 3 pounds. Available in .223, .308 and .300 Winchester magnum. Because Match rifles are typically built to order by shooters who know what they want, prices vary with options. Magnum chamberings don't add much to the cost of a match rifle. An adjustable stock or super-accurate barrel, or a sophisticated trigger can boost price substantially.

Prices:

Apollo action rifle, includes Jewell trigger	**$4,599.00**
Remington 700 action with features outlined above	**3,499.00**
Remington 700 action with DBM and 2-position safety and Remington extractor	**2,999.00**
Winchester Model 70 action	**2,949.00**

Options include Timney, Shilen or Jewell triggers, adjustable buttplate.

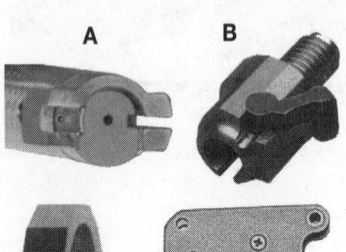

A. CONE HEAD BOLT AND BREECH with new combination bolt face provides both drop-in and controlled-round feed capabilities.

B. 3-POSITION POSITIVE LOCK SAFETY locks both the bolt and firing pin. Intermediate position allows for easy field stripping and cleaning and ejecting live rounds without accidental discharge.

C. TRIGGER is fully adjustable. Each one is hand finished and assembled to precise tolerances and fit.

D. RECOIL LUG has 36,500 pounds shear strength. It is designed & surface ground for precise alignment (perpendicular axis to bore centerline) providing perfect mating of receiver and barrel.

THE APOLLO ACTION

Available for all popular calibers from .222 to .458 including the 6mm, .257, .270, .300, .338 & .458 Arnold Magnums. Finishes include blue, matte black, black teflon or stainless steel.

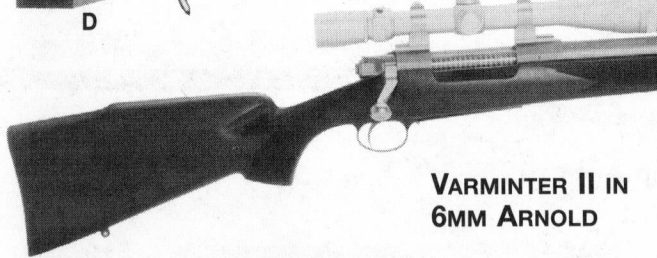

VARMINTER II IN 6MM ARNOLD

VARMINTER II

Fully accurized action with match grade heavy sporter 27" barrel, cryogenically treated, bedded and free-floated in McMillan varminter synthetic stock. Choice of black, woodland, desert or arctic camo. All rifes guaranteed capable of shooting 1/2" groups. Available in all popular varmint cartridges plus many wild-cats and the .244, .257 and 6.5 Arnold Magnums.

Prices:

Remington 70 CM matte blue barreled action	**$2,595.00**
Remington CM blue with detachable box magazine	**2,695.00**
Remington SS barreled action	**2,695.00**
Remington SS with detachable box magazine	**2,695.00**
Winchester M70 CM matte blue barreled action	**2,595.00**
Winchester M70 SS matte barreled action	**2,695.00**
Additional selections include:	
Arnold laminated varmint stock	**Add 199.00**
Teflon coated barreled action	**Add 229.00**

AUTO-ORDNANCE

103

Semi-Automatic Rifles

This veteran design became famous during the "roaring twenties" and World War II.
These replicas are legal autoloaders, not machine guns.

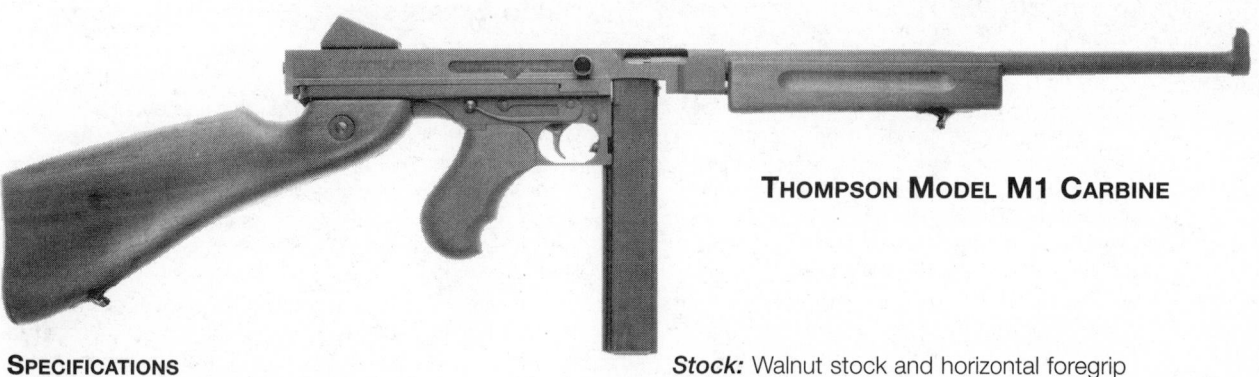

THOMPSON MODEL M1 CARBINE

SPECIFICATIONS
Caliber: 45 ACP *Barrel Length:* 16.5"
Overall Length: 38" *Weight:* 11.5 lbs.
Sights: Blade front; fixed rear

Stock: Walnut stock and horizontal foregrip
Features: Side cocking lever; frame and receiver milled from solid steel
Price: $850.00

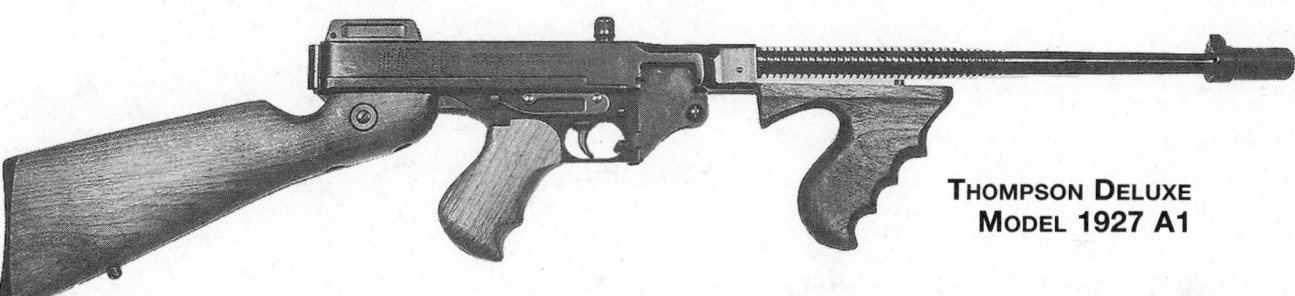

THOMPSON DELUXE MODEL 1927 A1

SPECIFICATIONS
Caliber: 45 ACP
Barrel Length: 16.5"
Overall Length: 41" *Weight:* 13 lbs.
Sights: Blade front; open rear adjustable

Stock: Walnut stock; vertical foregrip
Also available:
THOMPSON 1927A1C LIGHTWEIGHT (45 Cal.). Same as the 1927 A1 model, but weighs only 9.5 lbs.
Price: $950.00

MODEL 1927 A1 COMMANDO

SPECIFICATIONS
Caliber: 45 ACP
Barrel Length: 16.5"
Overall Length: 41"

Weight: 13 lbs.
Sights: Blade front; open rear (adjustable)
Finish: Black (stock and forend)
Price: $950.00

RIFLES

Rifles

www.StoegerIndustries.com

2002 Edition

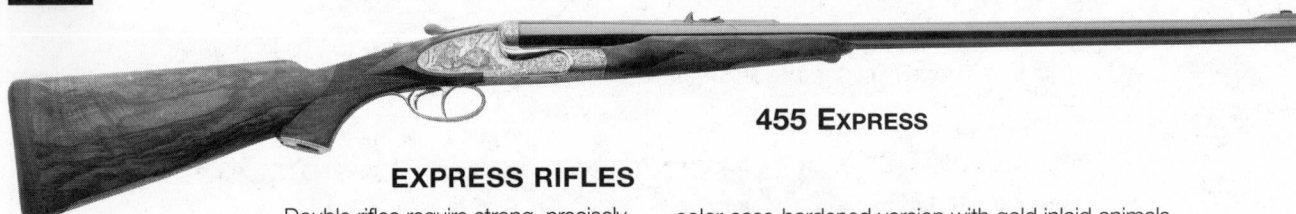

455 EXPRESS

EXPRESS RIFLES

Double rifles require strong, precisely-fitted actions to handle large, high pressure cartridges. Barrels must be joined with absolute precision for optimum convergence. The SS06 and SS06EELL Over-and Under Express Rifles offer rifled barrels of special steel cold-hammered in three calibers: 9.3x74R, .375 H&H Mag. and .458 Win. Mag. An extra set of matching 12 gauge barrels is available. Hand-finished, hand-checkered stocks and forends are made from select walnut or walnut briar. A special trap door compartment for extra cartridges is fitted inside the stock, and a cavity under the pistol-grip cap holds a set of spare front sights. The SS-06 is finished with light engraving on the color case-hardened receiver. The SS06 EELL sports a receiver hand-engraved with game scenes, or a

color case-hardened version with gold inlaid animals.

The 455 Side-by-Side Express Rifle action is made of special high-strength steel and forged with an elongated 60mm plate. This increases the distance between the hinge pin and the three-lug locking system to compensate for stress when shooting. To withstand the pressure of high-powered cartridges, the sealed receiver has reinforced sides, and the top tang extends fully up to the stock comb to strengthen attachment of the stock. An articulated front trigger and automatic blocking device eliminate the possibility of simultaneous discharge. The safety (automatic on request) provides for quick, reliable and positive on/off operation. The Boehler steel barrels are joined with a Demibloc chamber system.

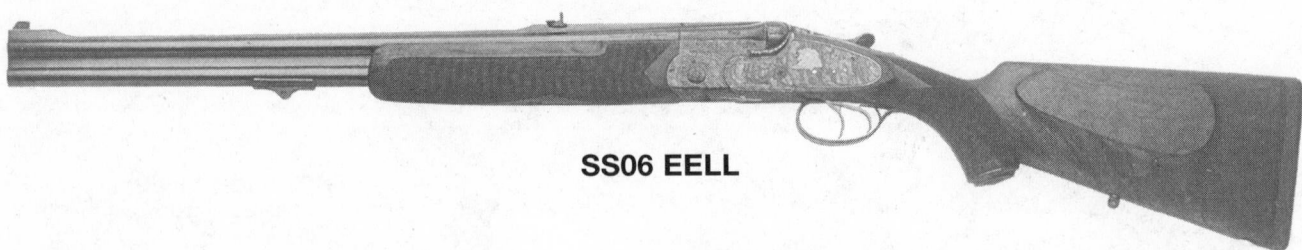

SS06 EELL

SS06 OVER-UNDER EXPRESS RIFLE
SPECIFICATIONS
Calibers: 375 H&H, 458 Win. Mag., 9.3x94R
Barrel length: 24" (12 ga. matching interchangeable barrels available)
Weight: 11 lbs.
Sights: Blade front sight; V-notch rear sight w/folding leaf (claw mounts for Zeiss scope factory fitted and sighted-in at 100 meters)
Price: **$50,000.00**
Note: MODEL SS06 EELL is also available in same calibers and features hand-engraved game scenes on the receiver or color case-hardened w/gold inlaid animals. **$50,000.00**

455 SIDE-BY-SIDE EXPRESS RIFLE
SPECIFICATIONS
Calibers: 375 H&H, 416 Rigby, 458 Win. Mag., 470 N.E., 500 N.E.
Barrel length: 23" - 25"
Weight: 11 lbs.
Sights: Fixed front sight w/folding blade; V-notch rear sight
Price: **$50,000.00**
Note: MODEL 455 EELL is also available (same price and calibers) featuring Bulino-style game scene engraving or intricate scroll work and walnut briar stock and forend.

PREMIUM GRADE EXPRESS RIFLE SPECIFICATIONS

MODEL	9.3x 74R	.375 H&H MAG.	CALIBER* .416 RIGBY	.458 H&H MAG.	.470 N.E.	.500 N.E.	BARREL LENGTH (CM/IN)	AVERAGE WEIGHT (KG/LBS)**
SS06	√	√		√			62/24	5.00/11.0
SS06 EELL	√	√		√			62/24	5.00/11.0
455		√	√	√	√	√	60/23 to 65/25	5.00/11.0
455 EELL		√	√	√	√	√	60/23 to 65/25	5.00/11.0

*SS06 EELL Models are available with interchangeable 12 gauge shotgun barrels upon request.
**Weights are approximate, dependent on wood density and barrel length.

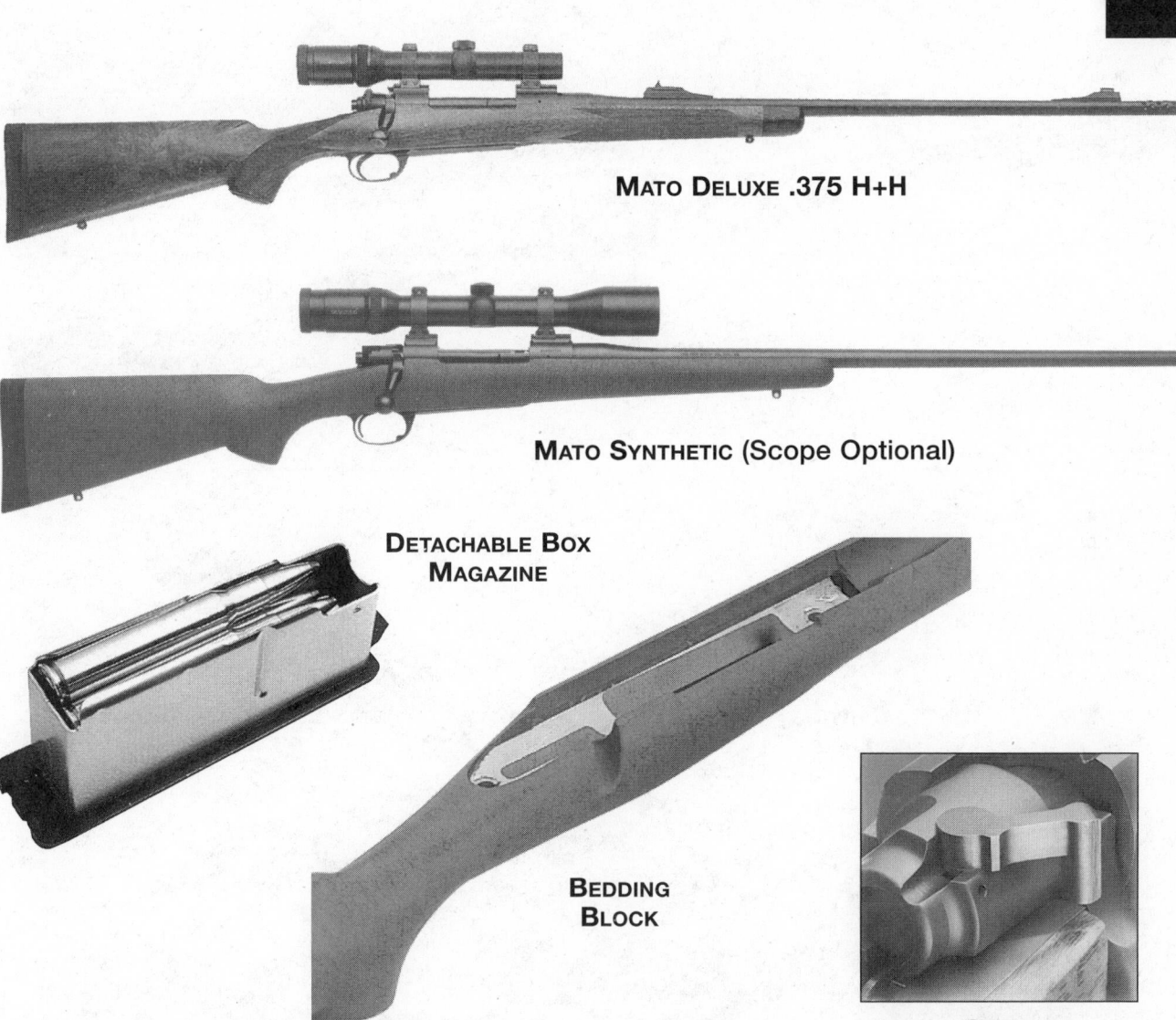

MATO DELUXE .375 H+H

MATO SYNTHETIC (Scope Optional)

DETACHABLE BOX MAGAZINE

BEDDING BLOCK

SAFETY

RIFLES

BERETTA MATO BOLT-ACTION RIFLE

Beretta's Mato was developed with help from Don Allen, whose Dakota rifles have the same clean, appealing lines. ("Mato", incidentally, is the Dakota Indian name for "bear.") This Beretta features controlled-round feed with a Mauser-style extractor that grabs cartridges from a detachable box magazine clipped to a hinged floorplate. The magazine can be top-loaded. A three-position safety allows cycling of the bolt while the striker is locked back. The Mato's sturdy trigger can be adjusted for weight of pull, sear engagement and overtravel. Receivers are machined from bar stock, and the 24-inch barrels are hammer-forged from top-grade chrome-moly steel. Stocks have high, straight combs for quick aim and a classic profile. On the walnut-stocked Deluxe model, wood with exceptional figure is available as an "X-Tra Wood"

option. The Mato is also available with a synthetic stock of Kevlar, fiberglass and graphite. An action-length aluminum bedding block ensures rigidity and perfect fit. All stocks come standard with a solid recoil pad. The Mato in .375 features iron sights and a muzzle brake; its front swivel is on a barrel band. Engraving, fiber-optic sights, a set trigger and other options are available for this rifle, which comes in .270 Win., .280 Rem., 7mm Rem. Mag., .30-06 Sprg., .300 Win. Mag., .338 Win. Mag. and .375 H&H Mag. *Weight:* 8 pounds.

Price: Mato Synthetic $1,117.00
Mato Synthetic .375 . . . . 1,474.00
Mato Deluxe 2,470.00
Mato Deluxe .375 . . . . 2,795.00

Rifles

S689 GOLD SABLE
(Scope Optional)

CARYING CASE

BERETTA SILVER SABLE II AND GOLD SABLE OVER/UNDER RIFLES

Built on Beretta's 20-gauge boxlock frame, these over/under rifles are chambered in .30-06, 9.3x74R and .444 Marlin. They feature double mechanical triggers for reliability.

The front trigger is hinged for greater comfort. The 24" barrels are regulated with iron sights but can also be fitted with hook-type scope rings. Hand-finished walnut stocks feature a European-style cheekpiece, ventilated recoil pad and initial plate. The Silver Sable has a nickel-colored receiver engraved with game scenes; the Gold Sable has a scroll-engraved case-hardened receiver. *Weight:* 7.7 lbs.

Price: Silver Sable II . . . . **NA**
Gold Sable. . . . . **NA**

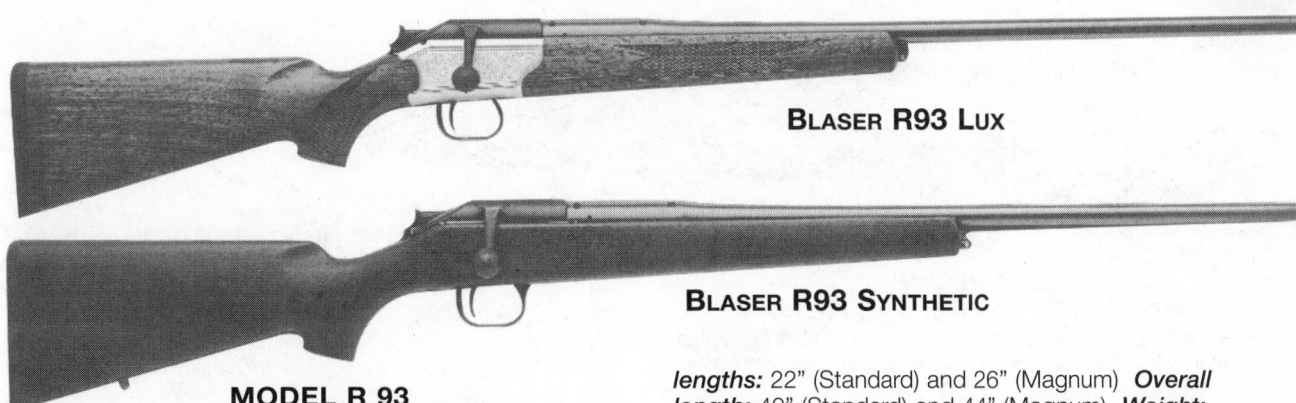

BLASER R93 LUX

BLASER R93 SYNTHETIC

MODEL R 93
BOLT ACTION SERIES
The Blaser straight-pull action is the fastest bolt mechanism on the market. An expanding collar locks the bolt. A finely adjustable trigger and interchangeable barrel option are bonuses.

SPECIFICATIONS (CLASSIC)
Calibers: (interchangeable) *Standard:* .25-06 Rem 6.5x55, 7x57, 7mm/08 Rem, 22-250, 243 Win., 270 Win., 30-06, 308 Win. *Magnum:* 257 Weatherby Mag., 7mm Rem. Mag., 300 Win. Mag., 300 Wby. Mag., 300 Rem U.M., 338 Win. Mag., 375 H&H, 416 Rem. Mag. *Barrel*

lengths: 22" (Standard) and 26" (Magnum) *Overall length:* 40" (Standard) and 44" (Magnum) *Weight:* (w/scope mounts) 6.5 lbs. (Standard) and 7 lbs. (Magnum) *Safety:* Cocking slide *Stock:* Two-piece Custom and Deluxe Walnut recoil pad, hand-cut checkering (18 lines/inch, borderless) *Length of pull:* 13.75"
All BLASER 93 rifles can be ordered left-handed at an additional $155.00.
Prices: CLASSIC $3,865.00
LX 1,990.00
SYNTHETIC. 1,695.00
ATTACHÉ 5,660.00
GRAND LUXE 5,160.00

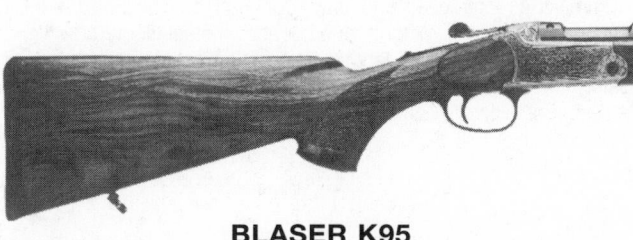

BLASER K95 LUXUS

BLASER K95
The Blaser K95 is a single-shot, break-action rifle available in two styles, the Luxus with hand engraving on the receiver, and the Standard. Both lightweight models can be easily taken down and reassembled without any loss of zero. Select walnut stocks, point-pattern checkering.

SPECIFICATIONS
Calibers: Standard: .243 Win., .270 Win., 30-06 Sprg., 308 Win. *Magnum:* 7mm Rem., 300 Win., .300 Wby. *Barrel lengths:* 23.6" (Standard) and 25.6" (Magnum) *Overall length:* 40.16" (Standard) and 42.13" (Magnum) *Weight:* 5.5 lbs. (Standard) and 5.8 lbs. (Magnum)
Prices: LUXUS. $3,395.00
STANDARD 2,895.00

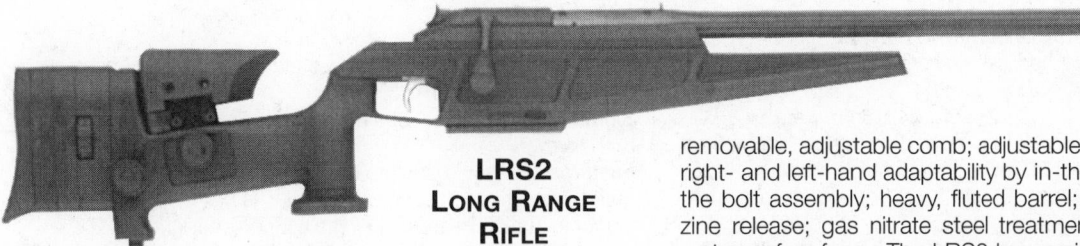

LRS2
LONG RANGE RIFLE

BLASER R93 LONG RANGE SPORTER 2
Features: straight-line bolt pull with a radial locking system; fully adjustable trigger; fore-and-aft-adjustable trigger blade;

removable, adjustable comb; adjustable buttstock (for length); right- and left-hand adaptability by in-the-field replacement of the bolt assembly; heavy, fluted barrel; ambidextrous magazine release; gas nitrate steel treatment to provide a hard, rust-proof surface. The LRS2 has an improved stock and a new 5-shot in-line magazine. Accessories include a folding bipod, muzzle brake and hand rest. Available in .308 Win., .300 Win. Mag. and .338 Lapua.
Price: $2,480.00

Custom Tactical

LIGHT TACTICAL

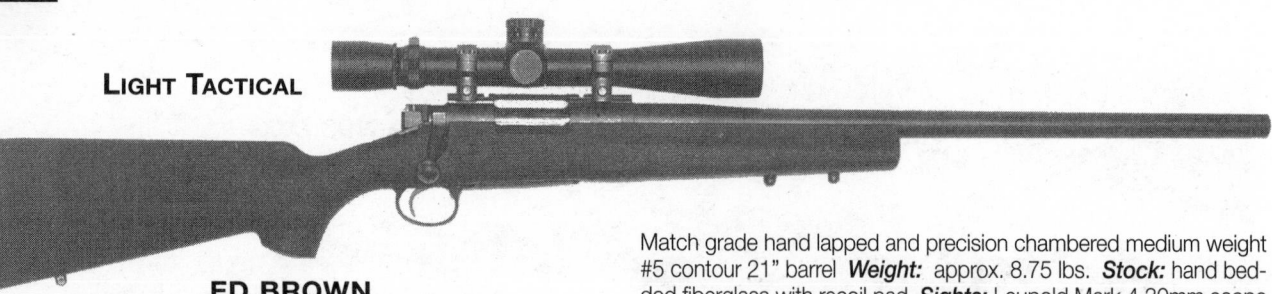

ED BROWN
MODEL 702, LIGHT TACTICAL

A compact, super accurate tactical weapon intended for Military, Law Enforcement and Security forces around the world. Makes a great compact varmint rifle too!

SPECIFICATIONS
Caliber: 223, 22-250, 243, 7mm/08, and 308 (7.62 NATO) *Barrel:*

Match grade hand lapped and precision chambered medium weight #5 contour 21" barrel *Weight:* approx. 8.75 lbs. *Stock:* hand bedded fiberglass with recoil pad *Sights:* Leupold Mark 4 30mm scope mounts utilizing heavy duty 8-40 screws *Features:* Ed Brown Custom short repeater action, aluminum trigger guard and floor plate. Three position safety securely locks bolt closed *Options:* Stock color, stainless steel barrel, different contour barrel, additional calibers, hinged steel floor plate.
Price: from **$2,800.00**

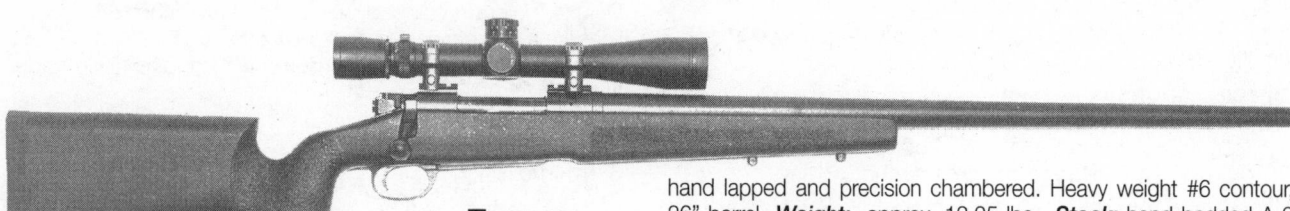

TACTICAL

ED BROWN
MODEL 702, TACTICAL

A heavy-barreled tactical rifle with prone stock. Built for the utmost in accuracy.

SPECIFICATIONS
Caliber: 7.62 NATO (308), 300 Win Mag. *Barrel:* Match grade,

hand lapped and precision chambered. Heavy weight #6 contour, 26" barrel *Weight:* approx. 12.25 lbs. *Stock:* hand bedded A-3 fiberglass tactical stock with recoil pad *Sights:* Leupold Mark 4 30mm scope mounts utilizing heavy duty 8-40 screws *Features:* Ed Brown Custom short or long repeater action, steel trigger guard and hinged floor plate. Action length depends on caliber. Three position safety securely locks bolt closed. *Options:* Stock color, stainless steel barrel, different contour barrel, additional calibers
Price: from **$3,200.00**

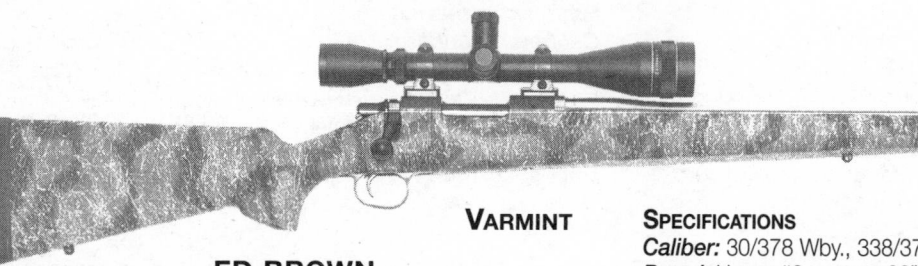

VARMINT

ED BROWN
MODEL 702, VARMINT

A custom varmint rifle with tactical rifle heritage.

SPECIFICATIONS
Caliber: 223, 22-250, 220 Swift, 6BR, 243, 6mm Rem, 308 Win. *Barrel:* Match grade hand lapped and precision chambered. Medium weight #5 contour 26" or heavy weight #17 contour 24" barrel *Weight:* approx. 9 lbs. *Stock:* hand bedded fiberglass with recoil pad *Sights:* Talley scope mounts utilizing heavy duty 8-40 screws *Features:* Ed Brown Custom short single shot action with a steel trigger guard, fully adjustable trigger, and a three position safety *Options:* Stock color, stainless steel barrel, different contour barrel, additional calibers, 2 oz. trigger
Price: from **$2,500.00**

SPECIFICATIONS
Caliber: 30/378 Wby., 338/378 Wby, 338 Laupa, 50 Peacekeeper
Barrel: Heavy #8 contour 26" with muzzle brrake
Weight: approx. 13 lbs.
Stock: hand bedded A-2 fiberglass tactical stock with Pachmayr Decelerator recoil pad
Sights: Leupold Mark 4 30mm scope mounts utilizing heavy duty 8-40 screws
Features: Ed Brown Custom single shot action with a steel trigger guard. Three position safety securely locks bolt closed
Options: The 50 Peacekeeper is a cartridge designed by J.D. Jones for maximum efficiency with the 50 caliber bullet. It is based on the 460 Weatherby case but handles the 50 BMG bullet. This gun only weighs around 13 lbs., but provides 88% of the effectiveness of the full-size 50 BMG round.
Price: from **$3,500.00**

Custom Hunting

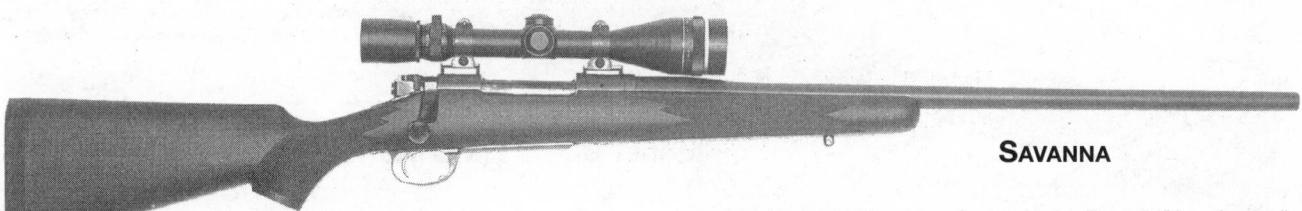

SAVANNA

ED BROWN
MODEL 702, SAVANNA

An accurate hunting rifle with classic-style stock, in most popular chamberings.

SPECIFICATIONS
Long Action Calibers: 25/06, 270 Win., 280 Remington, 280 Ackley Imp., 7mm Rem Magnum, 7STW, 30/06, 300 Win Magnum, 300 Wby, 300 Ultra, 338 Win. Mag. ***Short Action Calibers:*** Same as Ozark ***Barrel:*** Match grade hand lapped and precision chambered. Light weight #3 contour in standard calibers 24" length, medium weight #4 on magnum calibers, 26" length ***Weight:*** approx. 7.5 lbs. ***Stock:*** fiberglass sporter with cheek piece, checkering and recoil pad ***Sights:*** Talley scope mounts utilizing heavy duty 8-40 screws ***Features:*** Ed Brown Custom action with machined steel trigger guard and hinged floor plate. Three position safety securely locks bolt closed. 3.700 magazine box length ***Options:*** Stock color, stainless steel barrel, different contour barrel, additional calibers, detachable box magazine
Price: from $2,800.00

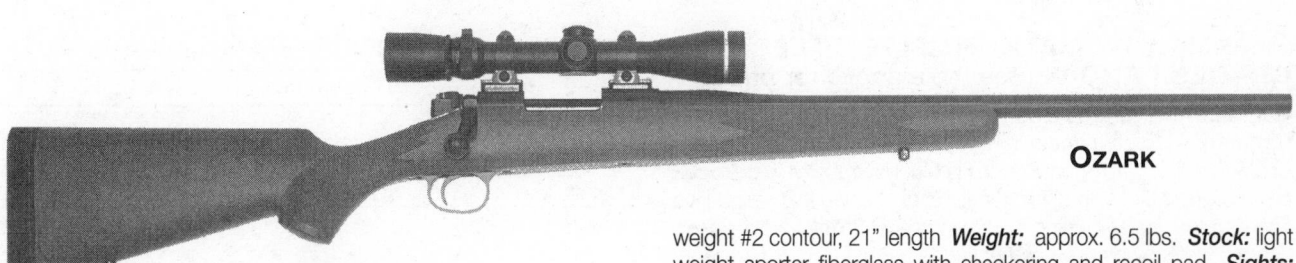

OZARK

ED BROWN
MODEL 702, OZARK

A light-weight hunting rifle, made on a short action with a light stock and short barrel. A modern carbine.

SPECIFICATIONS
Caliber: 223, 22-250, 243, 6mm, 7mm/08, 308, 300 WSM ***Barrel:*** Match grade hand lapped and precision chambered. Extra light weight #2 contour, 21" length ***Weight:*** approx. 6.5 lbs. ***Stock:*** light weight sporter fiberglass with checkering and recoil pad ***Sights:*** Talley scope mounts included utilizing heavy duty 8-40 screws ***Features:*** Ed Brown Custom short repeater action with a blind magazine and steel trigger guard. Three position safety securely locks bolt closed. 2.850 magazine box length ***Options:*** Stock color, stainless steel barrel, different contour barrel, additional calibers, hinged steel floor plate, detachable box magazine
Price: from $2,500.00

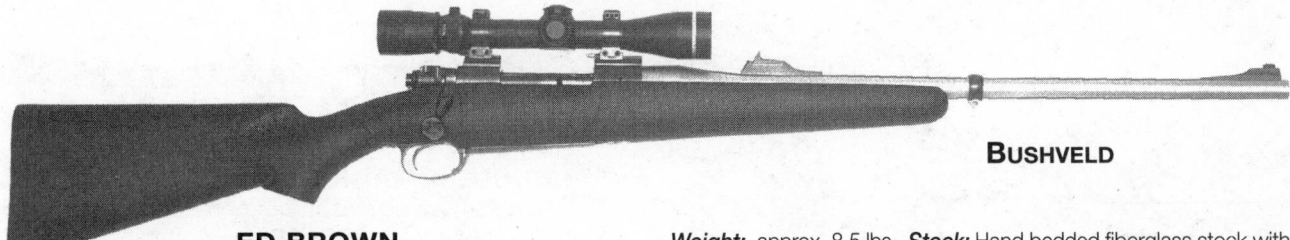

BUSHVELD

ED BROWN
MODEL 702, BUSHVELD

A dependable dangerous game rifle with iron sights and deep magazine.

SPECIFICATIONS
Caliber: 375 H&H, 416 Rem Mag., 458 Win Mag, also any Savanna Caliber ***Barrel:*** Match grade hand lapped and precision chambered. Medium weight, or heavy weight depending on caliber 24" length ***Weight:*** approx. 8.5 lbs. ***Stock:*** Hand bedded fiberglass stock with monte carlo style butt, cheek piece, and recoil pad ***Sights:*** Talley scope mounts utilizing heavy duty 8-40 screws ***Features:*** Ed Brown Custom action, steel trigger guard and floor plate. Three position safety securely locks bolt closed ***Options:*** Stock color, stainless steel barrel, different contour barrel, additional calibers, QD scope rings, iron sights, barrel mounted sling swivel
Price: from $2,900.00

RIFLES

MODEL BL-22 LEVER-ACTION RIFLE

RIMFIRE RIFLE SPECIFICATIONS

MODEL	CALIBER	BARREL LENGTH	SIGHT RADIUS	OVERALL LENGTH	AVERAGE WEIGHT	PRICE
Semi-Auto 22 Grade I	22 LR	19.25"	16.25"	37"	5 lbs. 3 oz.	**$479.00**
Semi-Auto 22 Grade VI*	22 LR	19.25"	16.25"	37"	5 lbs. 3 oz.	**1,028.00**
BL-22 Grade I	22 LR, Long, Short	20"	15.875"	36.75"	5 lbs.	**415.00**
BL-Grade II	22 LR, Long, Short	20"	15.875"	36.75"	5 lbs.	**471.00**

Blued or Grayed

22 SEMI-AUTOMATIC RIMFIRE RIFLES GRADES I AND VI (See table above for prices)

SPECIFICATIONS (See also table above)
Capacity: 11 cartridges in magazine, 1 chamber **Safety:** Cross-bolt type **Trigger:** Grade I is blued; Grade VI is gold colored **Sights:** Gold bead front, adjustable folding leaf ear; drilled and tapped for Browning scope mounts **Stock & Forearm:** Grade I, select walnut with checkering (18 lines/inch); Grade VI, high-grade walnut with checkering (22 lines/inch).

STOCK DIMENSIONS

	SEMI-AUTO	BL-22
Length of Pull	13.75"	13.5"
Drop at Comb	1 3/8"	.625"
Drop at Heel	2.375"	2.25"

SEMI-AUTO RIMFIRE GRADE 1

NEW BUCK MARK SPORTER

BUCK MARK RIFLE SERIES

Built on the same design as the proven Buck Mark pistol's straight blowback action. Offered in a Sporter model with a tapered barrel. Hi-Viz fiber optic sights and an integral rail scope mount. Also offered in a Target model with a heavy barrel with the same integral rail scope mount. All chambers are hand-reamed and muzzle crowns are recessed to protect them from damage that could deteriorate accuracy. **Barrel:** 18" **Overall Length:** 33 5/8"
Price: Sporter or Target $518.00

MODEL 1885 LOW WALL RIFLE

Modeled after the single-shot rifle John Browning designed and later sold to Winchester, these dropping-block single-shots feature the same solid construction and high-quality components. *Calibers:* 22 Hornet, 260 Rem. HIGH WALL: 22-250 Rem., 270 Win., 30-06 Sprg., 7mm Rem. Mag., 45-70 Govt., 454 Casull.
Price: $997.00

MODEL 1885 HIGH WALL BPCR
(BLACK POWDER CARTRIDGE RIFLE)

SPECIFICATIONS
Calibers: 40-65, 45-70 Govt. *Barrel Length:* 30" *Overall Length:* 46.125" *Weight:* 11 lbs. (45-70 Govt.); 11 lbs. 7 oz. (40-65) *Sight Radius:* 34" *Rate of Twist:* 1 in 16" (R.H.)
Price: $1,766.00

RIFLES

A-BOLT HUNTER BOLT-ACTION CENTERFIRE RIFLES

BOSS (Ballistic Optimizing Shooting System) is now optional on all A-Bolt models (except standard). BOSS adjusts barrel vibrations to allow a bullet to leave the rifle muzzle at the most advantageous point in the barrel oscillation, thereby fine-tuning accuracy with any brand of ammunition regardless of caliber.

This hard-working rifle features a practical grade of walnut and low-luster bluing. Includes the standard A-Bolt fast-cycling bolt, crisp trigger, calibrated rear sights and ramp-style front sights. Optional BOSS on a clean, tapered barrel. Receiver is drilled and tapped for a scope mount; HUNTER model has open sights.
Prices: No Sights $620.00
Magnum 646.00
MICRO HUNTER (shorter barrel and length of pull) 614.00

A-BOLT II SPECIFICATIONS (See following page for additional A-Bolt prices)

CALIBER	TWIST (R.H.)	MAGAZINE CAPACITY	HUNTER	WHITE GOLD MEDAL	MEDAL	MICRO HUNTER	STAINLESS STALKER	COMP STALKER	ECLIPSE M-1000	ECLIPSE
375 H&H	1:12"	3	—	—	•	—	•	—	—	—
338 Win. Mag.	1:10"	3	•	—	•	—	•	•	—	—
300 Win. Mag.	1:10"	3	•	•	•	—	•	•	•	•
300 Rem. U Mag.	1:10"	4	—	—	•	—	•	—	—	—
338 Rem. U Mag.	1:10"	4	—	—	•	—	•	—	—	—
7mm Rem. Mag.	1:9.5"	3	•	•	•	—	•	•	—	•
25-06 Rem.	1:10"	4	•	•	•	—	•	•	—	—
270 Win.	1:10"	4	•	•	•	—	•	•	—	•
280 Rem.	1:10"	4	•	—	•	—	•	•	—	—
30-06 Sprg.	1:10"	4	•	•	•	—	•	•	—	•
300 WSM	1:10"	4	•	—	•	—	•	•	—	—
243 Win.	1:10"	4	•	—	•	•	•	•	—	•
308 Win.	1:12"	4	•	—	•	•	•	•	—	•
260 Rem.	1:10"	4	•	—	•	•	•	•	—	•
7mm-08 Rem.	1:9.5"	4	•	—	•	•	•	•	—	—
22-250 Rem.	1:14"	4	•	—	•	•	•	•	—	•
223 Rem.	1:12"	6*	•	—	•	•	•	•	—	—
22 Hornet	1:16"	6*	—	—	—	•	—	—	—	—

• *Magazine capacity of 223 Rem. models is up to 5 rounds on Micro-Hunter (up to 6 on other models).*

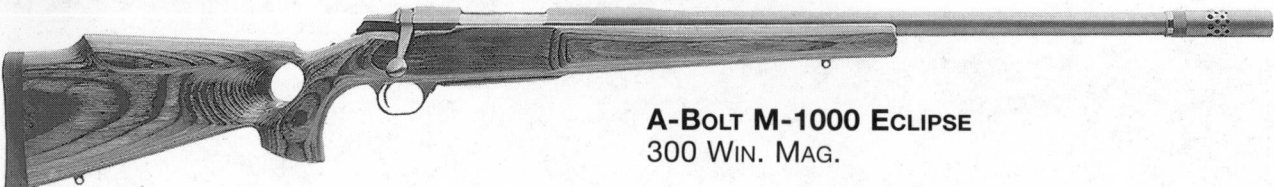

A-BOLT M-1000 ECLIPSE
300 WIN. MAG.

A-BOLT ECLIPSE MODELS WITH THUMBHOLE STOCK

The proven action and barrel of the A-Bolt are included in the A-Bolt Eclipse Series. The thumbhole stock itself is crafted from rugged gray/black, multi-laminated hardwood.

The Eclipse is available in long and short action hunting models with standard A-Bolt barrel, and a short-action varmint version with a heavy barrel. All are BOSS equipped.

A-BOLT SERIES   Prices
MEDALLION no sights standard, BOSS $810.00
MEDALLION standard, no sights 730.00
MEDALLION L.H., no sights, BOSS 838.00-864.00
MEDALLION L.H., no sights. 758.00-784.00
MEDALLION MAGNUM no sights, BOSS 836.00
MEDALLION MAGNUM, no sights 756.00

A-BOLT SERIES   Prices
STAINLESS STALKER no sights, BOSS $893.00-919.00
STAINLESS STALKER no sights 813.00-839.00
STAINLESS STALKER L.H., no sights, BOSS 918.00-944.00
STAINLESS STALKER L.H., no sights 838.00-864.00
COMPOSITE STALKER, no sights, BOSS 716.00-742.00
COMPOSITE STALKER, no sights. 639.00-665.00

ECLIPSE HUNTER, no sights, BOSS . . . **$1,017.00-1,043.00**
ECLIPSE M-1000, w/BOSS. 1,048.00

Also Available:
CARBON FIBER STAINLESS STALKER
With steel-lined carbon fiber barrel for lighter weight.
Chamberings: 22-250 and .300 Win. Mag.
Price: $1,750.00-1,776.00

NEW: 300 WINCHESTER SHORT MAGNUM
Features: 23" barrel, 3-round detachable magazine, lightweight (6 lbs. 9 oz.)
Price: HUNTER $646.00
  COMPOSITE STALKER. 665.00
  MEDALLION 756.00
  STAINLESS STALKER 839.00

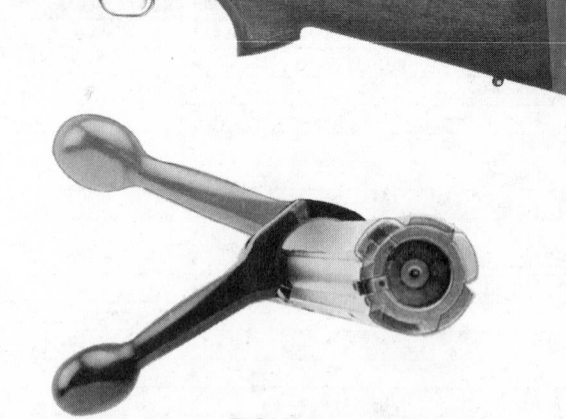

LEFT-HAND A-BOLT MEDALLION
Only a few popular bolt-action rifles have traditionally been built in left-hand versions. Browning joins a growing movement to accommodate lefties with its A-Bolt II, Boss is available.

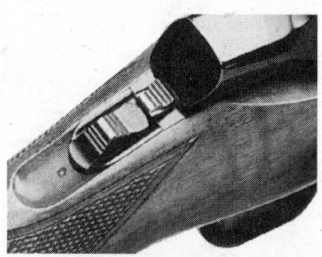

SAFETY
The top-mounted safety is perfectly positioned for easy operation. This location also allows the shooter to see the status at any angle.

BOLT
The short 60° bolt throw allows faster follow-up shots and also permits greater clearance between the bolt handle and scope. The flattened bolt knob itself is canted at a 30° angle to fit the hand more naturally.

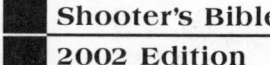

LIGHTNING BLR

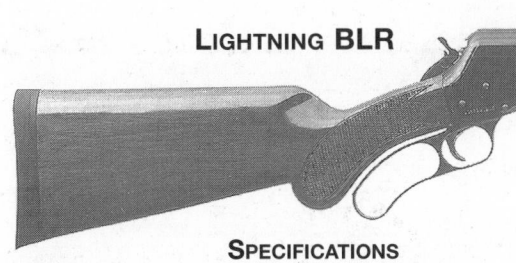

SPECIFICATIONS
Calibers: *Long Action*–270 Win., 30-06 Springfield, 7mm Rem. Mag., 300 Win. Mag. *Short Action*–22-250 Rem., 243 Win., 7mm-08 Rem., 308 Win. **Capacity:** 4 rounds; 3 in magnum calibers

Barrel Length: *Long Action*–22" (24" magnum calibers) *Short Action*–20" **Overall Length:** *Long Action*–42 7/8" (44 7/8" magnum calibers) *Short Action*–39.5" **Approximate Weight:** *Long Action*–7 lbs. 4 oz. (7 lbs. 12 oz. magnum calibers) *Short Action*–6 lbs. 8 oz. **Sight Radius:** 17.75" (19.75" magnum calibers)
Prices: Short Action **$649.00**
Long Action 686.00

NEW BAR STALKER

BAR STALKER SERIES
Composite, short action with open sights (243 + 308 only)
Price: **$809.00**
Composite, open sights (Magnum) 883.00
Composite, Boss (Magnum)

BAR MARK II SAFARI

BAR MARK II SAFARI, LIGHTWEIGHT & STALKER SEMIAUTOMATIC RIFLES

The BAR Mark II features an engraved receiver, a redesigned bolt release, new gas and buffeting systems, and a removable trigger assembly. Crossbolt safety with enlarged head; hinged floorplate, gold trigger; select walnut stock and forearm with cut-checkering and swivel studs;

BAR MARK II SPECIFICATONS
Calibers: Standard–243 Win., 25-06, 270 Win., 308 Win.; Magnum–7mm Rem. Mag., 300 Win. Mag., 338 Win. Mag.; Lightweight–243 Win., 270 Win., 30-06 Springfield; 308 Win. **Capacity:** 4 rounds; 3 in magnum **Barrel Length:** Standard–22"; Magnum–24"; Lightweight–20" **Overall Length:** Standard–43"; Magnum–45"; Lightweight–41" **Average Weight:** Standard–7 lbs. 6 oz.; Magnum–8 lbs. 6 oz.; Lightweight–7 lbs. 2 oz. **Sight Radius:** Standard–17.5"; Magnum–19.5"; Lightweight–15.5"
Prices: BAR Mark II Safari
STANDARD CALIBERS: No sights, BOSS **$891.00**
Open sights, no BOSS 833.00

13.75" length of pull; 2" drop at heel; 1 5/8" drop at comb. The New Lightweight model features alloy receiver and shortened barrel. Features high-grade, gloss walnut stock, gray receivers with engraved scenes (mule + whitetail deer on standard and elk and moose on Magnum).

No sights, no BOSS 815.00
MAGNUM CALIBERS: No sights, BOSS 967.00
Open sights 909.00
No sights, no BOSS 890.00
BAR MARK II LIGHTWEIGHT
Open sights, no BOSS 833.00
Open sights, no BOSS Magnum 909.00
BAR HIGH GRADE
Standard (270 Win or 30-06) 1,820.00
Magnum (7mm Mag or 300 Win Mag) 1,876.00

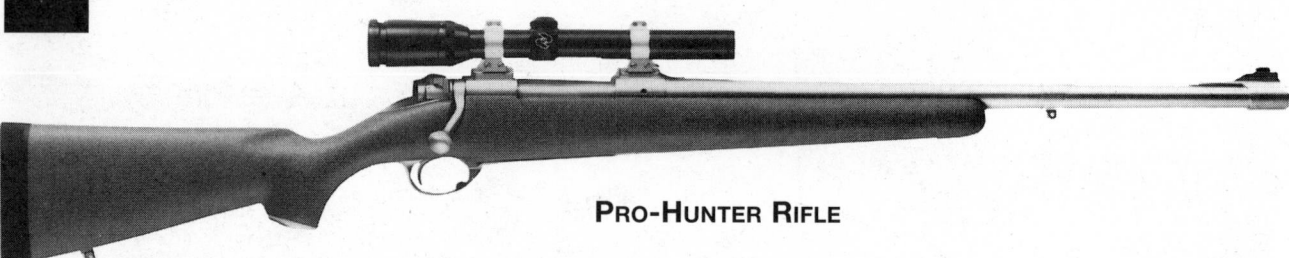

PRO-HUNTER RIFLE

Designed for the serious game hunter or guide, this custom version of Brown Precision's Pro-Hunter rifle begins as a Winchester Model 700 Super Grade action with controlled feed claw extractor. The trigger is tuned to crisp let-off at each customer's specified weight. A Shilen Match Grade stainless-steel barrel is custom crowned and hand fitted to the action.

The Pro-Hunter Elite features choice of express rear sight or custom Dave Talley removable peep sight and banded front ramp sight with European dovetail and replaceable brass bead. An optional flip-up white night sight is also available, as is a set of Dave Talley detachable T.N.T. scope mount rings and bases installed with Brown's Magnum Duty 8X40 screws.

All metal parts are finished in either matte electroless nickel or black Teflon. The barreled action is glass bedded to a custom Brown Precision Alaskan-configuration fiberglass stock, painted according to customer choice and fitted w/premium 1" buttpad and Dave Talley trapdoor grip cap. Weight ranges from 7 to 15 lbs., depending on barrel length, contour and options.

Optional equipment: drop box magazine, KDF or Answer System muzzle brake, Mag-Na-Port, Zeiss, Swarovski or Leupold scope, Americase aluminum hard case.
Prices: **$3,495.00**
Left-hand model **3,695.00**

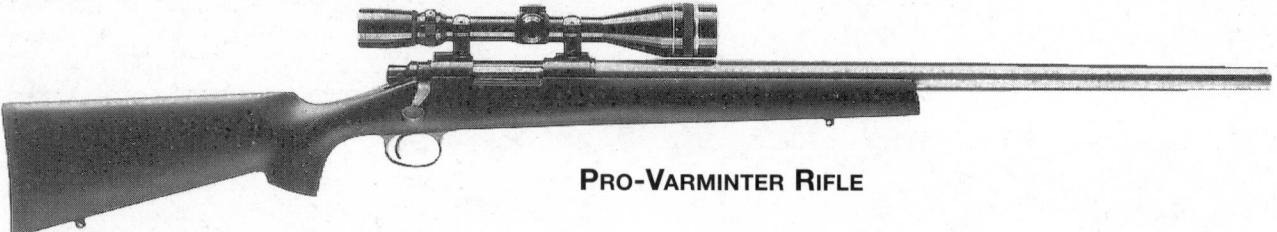

PRO-VARMINTER RIFLE

The standard Pro-Varminter is buillt on the Remington 700 or Rremington 40X action (right or left hand) and features a hand-fitted Shilen Match Grade Heavy Benchrest stainless-steel barrel in bright or bead-blasted finish. The barreled action is custom-bedded in Brown Precision's Varmint Special Hunter Bench or 40X Benchrest-style custom fiberglass, Kevlar or graphite stock.

Options include metal finishes, muzzle brakes, target or varmint scopes, triggers, barrels, stock dimensions
Prices:
Right-hand Model 700 Action **$2,495.00**
For Left-hand Model 700 . . . . **2,695.00**
Model 40-XB (inc. target trigger) **3,195.00**

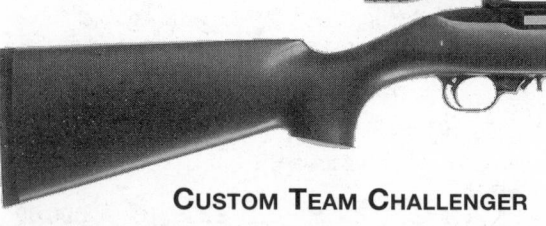

CUSTOM TEAM CHALLENGER

This custom rifle was designed for use in the Chevy Trucks Sportsman's Team Challenge shooting event. It's also used in metallic silhouette competition as well as in the field for small game and varmints. Custom built on the Ruger 10/22 semi-automatic rimfire action, which features an extended magazine release, a simplified bolt release and finely tuned trigger. This rifle is fitted with either a Brown Precision fiberglass or Kevlar stock with custom length of pull up to 15". The stock can be shortened at the butt and later relengthened and repainted to accommodate growing youth shooters. Stock color is also optional. To facilitate shooting with scopes, the lightweight stock has high-comb classic styling. The absence of a cheekpiece accommodates either right- or left-handed shooters, while the stock's flat-bottom, 1 3/4" forearm ensures maximum comfort in both offhand and rest shooting. Barrels are custom-length Shilen Match Grade .920" diameter straight or lightweight tapered.

Prices:
With blued action/barrel. **$1,395.00**
With blued action/stainless barrel **1,495.00**
With silver action/stainless barrel **1,595.00**

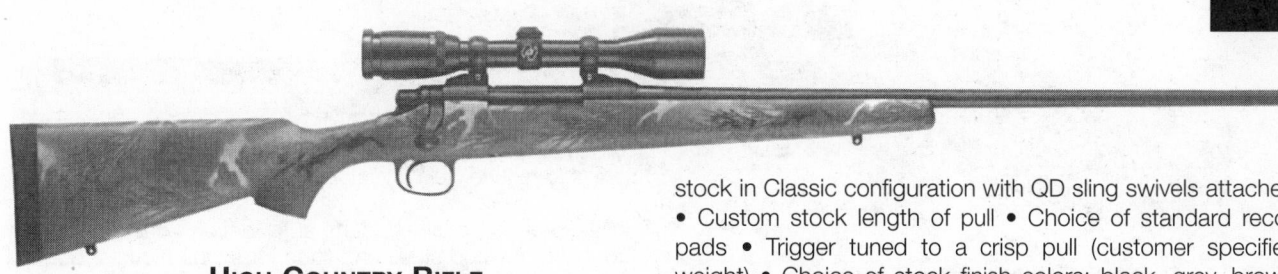

HIGH COUNTRY RIFLE

High Country Rifle Standard Features: • Remington 700 ADL, BDL or Mountain Rifle standard caliber barreled action • Brown Precision Custom Fiberglass, Kevlar or Graphite stock in Classic configuration with QD sling swivels attached • Custom stock length of pull • Choice of standard recoil pads • Trigger tuned to a crisp pull (customer specifies weight) • Choice of stock finish colors: black, grey, brown or green • Weight: 5 lbs. and up depending on stock, barrel length and contour, caliber, options and customer's intended use.

Price: . . . . .from $1,695.00

This custom rifle has all the same features as the standard High Country rifle, but scaled-down to fit the younger or smaller shooter. Based on the Remington Model 7 or Model 700 barreled action, it is available in calibers 223, 243, 7mm-08, 6mm and 308. The rifle features a shortened fiberglass, scopes and accessories.

All Youth Rifles include a deluxe package of shooting, reloading and hunting accessories and information to increase a young shooter's interest.

Price: . . . . from $1,695.00

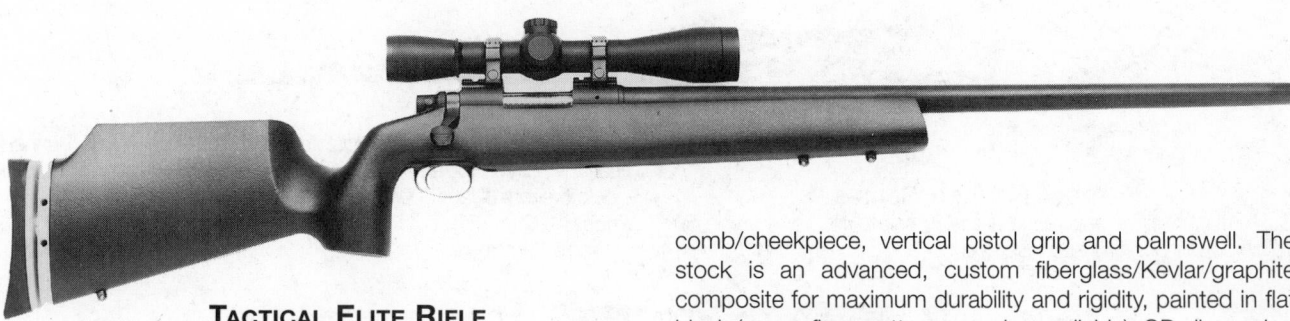

TACTICAL ELITE RIFLE

Brown Precision's Tactical Elite is built on a Remington 700 action and features a bead-blasted Shilen Select Match Grade Heavy Benchrest Stainless Steel barrel custom-chambered for 223 Rem., 308 Win., 300 Win. Mag. (or any standard or wildcat caliber). A nonreflective custom black Teflon metal finish on all metal surfaces ensures smooth bolt operation and 100 percent weatherproofing. The barreled action is bedded in a target-style stock with high rollover comb/cheekpiece, vertical pistol grip and palmswell. The stock is an advanced, custom fiberglass/Kevlar/graphite composite for maximum durability and rigidity, painted in flat black (camouflage patterns are also available). QD sling swivel studs and swivels are standard.

Other standard features include: three-way adjustable buttplate/recoil pad assembly with length of pull, vertical and cant angle adjustments, custom barrel length and contour, and trigger tuned for a crisp pull to customer's specifications. Options include muzzle brakes, Leupold or Kahles police scopes, among others, and are priced accordingly.

Price: $3,195.00

CARBONCHALLENGER THUMBHOLE

Custom ultra-lightweight graphite barreled precision target and small-game rimfire rifle. Up to 20" long match-grade stain-

Christensen Arms pioneered the use of steel-lined carbon-fiber barrels to reduce weight without reducing stiffness.

less steel barrel liner, semi-auto action, custom trigger, synthetic or wood stock and fitted for scope mounts. Bedded with action free floating. **Weight:** 3 to 4.5 pounds **Accuracy:** 3 shots .5" or less at 50 yards.
Price: **$879.00**

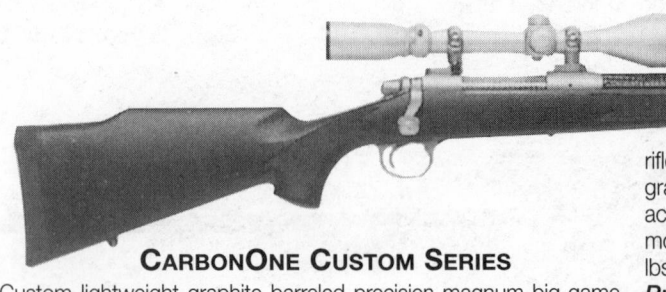

CARBONONE CUSTOM SERIES

Custom lightweight graphite barreled precision magnum big-game

rifle. All popular Magnum calibers available. Up to 28" long match-grade stainless steel barrel liner, head spaced minimum, accurized action, custom trigger, synthetic or wood stock and fitted for scope mounts. Bedded with graphite barrel free floating. **Weight:** 5.5 to 6.5 lbs. **Accuracy:** 3 shots .5" or less at 100 yards.
Price: **$2,299.00**

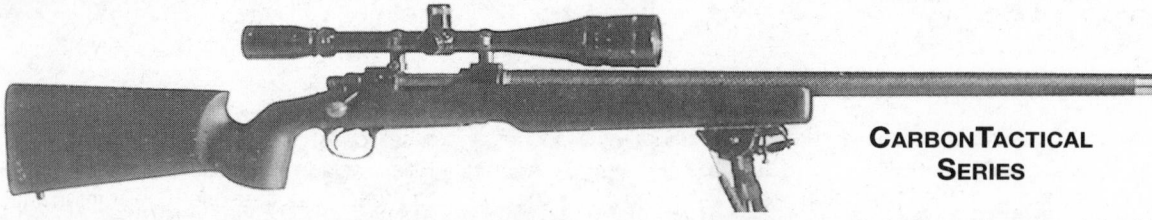

CARBONTACTICAL SERIES

Custom lightweight graphite, barreled precision tactical rifle. All popular calibers available. Up to 28" long match-grade stainless steel barrel liner, head spaced minimum, muzzle break optional, accurized

action, custom trigger, synthetic or wood stock and fitted for scope mounts. Bedded with free-floating graphite barrel. **Weight:** 5 to 8 pounds **Accuracy:** 3 shots .5" or less at 100 yards.

CARBONRANGER SERIES

Custom lightweight long range precision sniper rifle. Available in 50 caliber. Up to 36" long stainless steel barrel liner, chambered to mini-

mum tolerances. E.D.M. precision machined Omni Wind Runner accurized action (or an action of choice), custom trigger, retractable stock. 5 shots 8" at 1000 yards.
Prices: **$4,299.00**
   Single Shot **3,450.00**

CARBON ONE HUNTER

CARBON ONE HUNTER RIFLE SERIES

The Carbon One Hunter Rifle is based on a factory action of your choice (Remington, Browning or Winchester). The rifle is equipped

with the quality Christensen large diameter, high strength, ultra-light, high modulus graphite/epoxy barrel casing applied over a factory grade steel, machined barrel. The barrel is free-floating for accuracy and the trigger is tuned to a crisp 3-3.5 lbs. Total rifle weight is 6.5-7.25 lbs. depending on model.
Price: **$1,199.00**

BILLY DIXON
1874 SHARPS SPORTING RIFLE

It was June 27, 1874 at Adobe Walls on the Canadian River in the Texas panhandle. Billy Dixon and 27 buffalo hunters were surrounded by more than 500 Kiowa and Comanche warriors. The Kiowa medicine man told the war-riors that his medicine made them invisible to the bullets of the white eyes. When Dixon fired his Sharps sporting rifle and reportedly knocked a Kiowa from his horse at 1538 yards (7/8 mile) the Indians departed with haste. Billy Dixon was later awarded the Congres-sional Medal of Honor while acting as scout of the Army under Gen. Nelson Miles and lived a long life as a Texas peace officer.
Barrel: 32" Octagon *Caliber:* .45-.70
Prices:
Retail **$1,295.00**

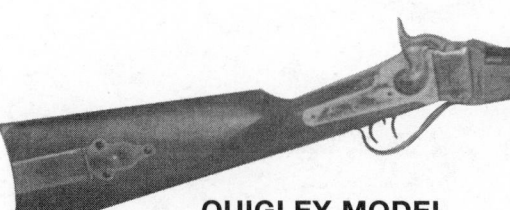

QUIGLEY MODEL
1874 SHARPS SPORTING RIFLE

This single shot rifle is capable of the accuracy depicted in the epic film. The Cimarron Quigley model is a faithful reproduction of that long rifle from down under.
Barrel: 34" Octagon *Caliber:* .45-70, .45-.120
Prices:
Retail: **$1,495.00**

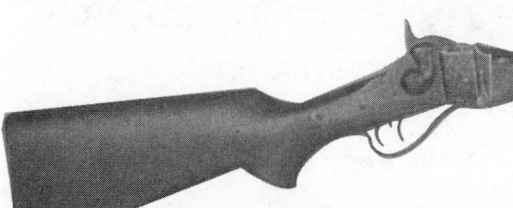

SILHOUETTE MODEL
1874 SHARPS SPORTING RIFLE

The Cimarron Model 1874 Sharps silhouette rifle was created for the shooter who demands a sound, accurate, basic Sharps. The pistol grip stock gives ultimate control for off hand shooting while the shotgun style butt plate provides maximum comfort. The barrel features cut rifling, lapped and polished for maxi-mum accuracy. *Barrel:* 32" Octagon *Caliber:* .45-.70
Prices:
Retail **$1,095.00**

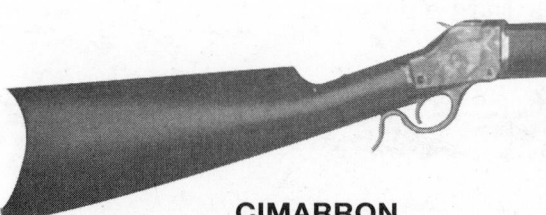

CIMARRON
FIREARMS CO. 1885 HIGH WALL

The Winchester single shot hunting rifle was placed on the market in the early 1880's. It is regarded by many as being the most reliable, strongest, most symetrical and altogether best single shot rifle ever produced. It is doubtless stronger than the Sharps rifle, is better designed, made of better materials and is of better appearance than that famous arm. All these rifles proved very accurate and reliable. Regrettably, the Winchester single shot rifle is no longer available. Cimarron's rendition of this John Browning rifle is every bit as strong and accurate as the original. *Barrel:* 30" Octagon *Caliber:* 45-70, 45-90, 40-65, 38-55
Prices:
Retail. **$995.00**

CIMARRON FIREARMS

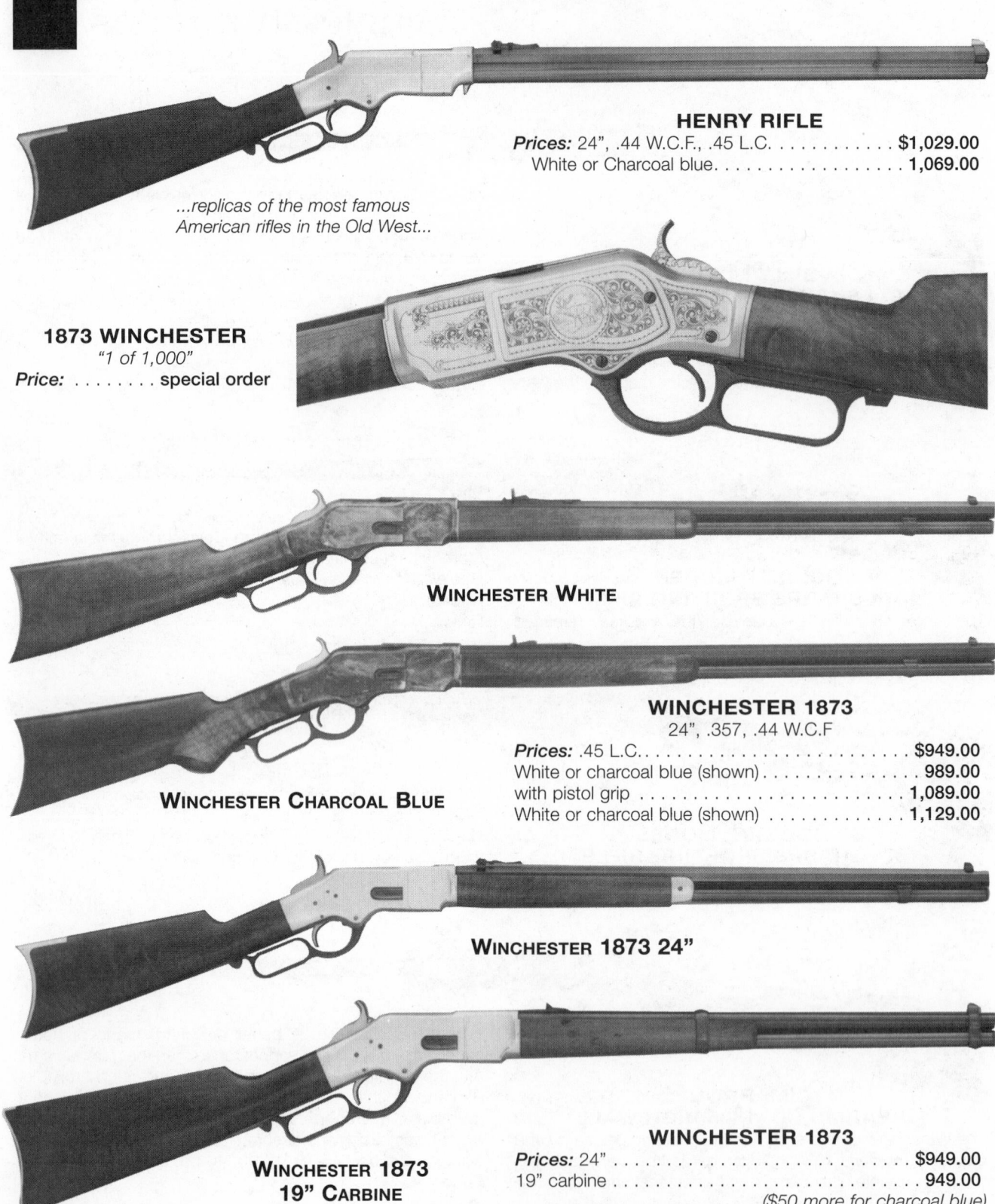

HENRY RIFLE
Prices: 24", .44 W.C.F., .45 L.C. $1,029.00
White or Charcoal blue. **1,069.00**

...replicas of the most famous American rifles in the Old West...

1873 WINCHESTER
"1 of 1,000"
Price: . . . . special order

WINCHESTER WHITE

WINCHESTER 1873
24", .357, .44 W.C.F
Prices: .45 L.C. $949.00
White or charcoal blue (shown) **989.00**
with pistol grip **1,089.00**
White or charcoal blue (shown) **1,129.00**

WINCHESTER CHARCOAL BLUE

WINCHESTER 1873 24"

WINCHESTER 1873
Prices: 24" $949.00
19" carbine **949.00**
($50 more for charcoal blue)

WINCHESTER 1873
19" CARBINE

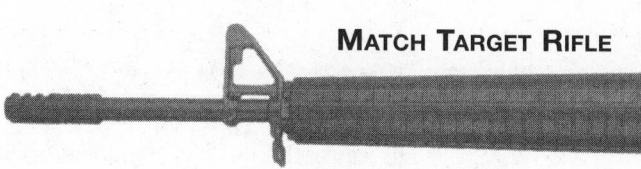

MATCH TARGET RIFLE

MATCH TARGET RIFLES

Features: Improved accuracy; suppressed recoil; accepts optics; ideal for competition; 2-position safety
Price: . . . . **from $1,111.00**
Available: **MT6601:** .223 caliber; matte black finish, 1-7 twist; 8 lbs., 20" barrel, 39" overall length
MT6601C: Same as above, plus compensator; 8.75 lbs., 20" barrel, 39" overall length
MT6551: .223 caliber; matte black finish, 1-7 twist; 8 lbs., 20" barrel, 39" overall length

MT6700: .223 caliber; matte black finish, 1-9 twist; 8.5 lbs., 20" barrel, 39" overall length; heavy barrel with flattop receiver
MT6700C: Same as above, plus compensator; 8.75 lbs., 20" barrel, 39" overall length
MT6731: .223 caliber; matte black finish, 1-9 twist; 7.1 lbs., 16.1" barrel, 34.5" overall length; heavy barrel with flattop receiver

COOPER ARMS RIFLES

Varmint Extreme Series

Cooper Arms was founded in 1990 by a small group of ex-Kimber employees whose goal was to produce the world's most accurate and beautiful rifles and make them 100% in America. The company has since gained a reputation for manufacturing some of the world's most accurate rifles. Cooper Arms produces a series of accurate, single shot and repeating, bolt action rifles in three basic stock designs and a variety of calibers ranging from custom cartridges like the .17 Squirrel to the .25-06 Ackley Improved. Produced in either the Custom Classic design or the Western Classic featuring Doug Turnbull's case color hardening, hand struck octagon barrels, and AAA select Claro walnut. Cooper produces three action sizes to match each cartridge. The new **MODEL 57** is available in .22 Long Rifle and in four configurations.
Prices: . . . . **from $1,095.00 to $2,495.00**

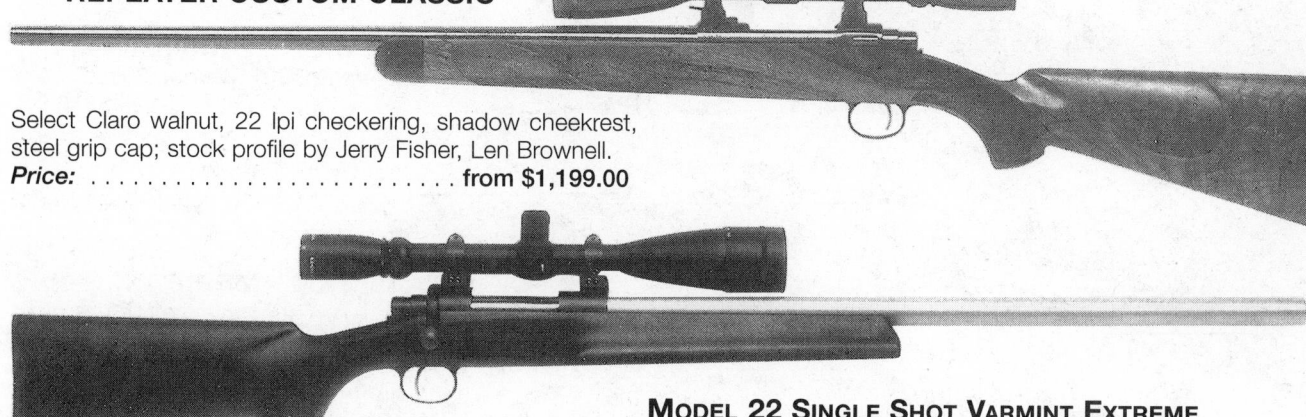

MODEL 22
REPEATER CUSTOM CLASSIC

Select Claro walnut, 22 lpi checkering, shadow cheekrest, steel grip cap; stock profile by Jerry Fisher, Len Brownell.
Price: . . . . **from $1,199.00**

MODEL 22 SINGLE SHOT VARMINT EXTREME

SPECIFICATIONS
Calibers: 22-250, 220 Swift, 243, 25-06, 308, 6mm PPC
Capacity: Single shot *Barrel Length:* 24" *Action:* 3 front locking lugs; glass-bedded *Trigger:* Single-stage Match, fully adjustable; Jewell 2-stage (optional) *Stock:* AAA Claro wal-
nut, hand checkered, oil finished free-floated barrel channel
Prices: MODEL 38 (mini action) $1,795.00
MODEL 21 (short action) 1,795.00
MODEL 22 (medium action) 1,995.00

CZ RIFLES

The rimfire rifles produced by Ceska Zbrojovka Uhersky Brod are ranked among the best of their kind. Quality, long service life, accuracy and safety are the main virtues of these firearms. The CZ 452 - 2E ZKM rimfire rifles offer a compact design with a robust Mauser-type action. The trigger has an adjustable pull. The rifles feature a tangent rear sight adjustable for elevation and windage. The receiver is factory milled for telescopic sight mounts. The CZ 452 - 2E ZKM rifles are supplied with a magazine holding 5 or 10 cartridges.

LUX

CZ 452 - 2E ZMK LUX

Caliber: .22 LR (5/10 cartridges), .22 WMR (5 cartridges)
Overall length: 42.6" *Barrel Length:* 24.8" *Sight Radius:*
20.0" *Weight:* 7 lbs. *Sights tangent rear sight:* 25-200m
Price: 22 LR $351.00
22 mag 378.00

SCOUT YOUTH RIFLE

CZ 452 - 2E ZKM SCOUT YOUTH RIFLE

The CZ 452-2E ZKM Scout rifle is a compact rimfire rifle intended for young shooters. Due to its shortened dimensions, reduced weight and single round loading device it is a perfect first rifle for any boy or girl. 5 and 10 round magazines are available for the Scout rifle. *Caliber:* .22 LR *Magazine Capacity:* 5/10 cartridges *Overall length:* 32.8" *Barrel Length:* 16.2" *Weight:* 4.0 lbs. Hammer forged barrel
Price: $179.00

VARMINT

CZ 452 - 2E ZKM - VARMINT

Caliber: .22 LR *Overall length:* 39" *Weight:* 7 lbs.
Price: $378.00

AMERICAN

CZ 452 - 2E ZKM AMERICAN

CZ 452 - ZKM American - This quality rimfire rifle has been adapted to the requirements governing the USA. The barrel is a 22½" long, and is made without open sights. The top of the receiver is fitted with a 9 mm wide dovetail groove for mounting a scope. *Caliber:* .22 LR, .22 WMR *Overall length:* 40" *Weight:* 6 lbs.
Price: 22 LR $351.00
22 mag 378.00
Also Available in 22 LR w/synthetic
stock & nickel finish 351.00

The CZ 550 series rifles represent a line of elegant, aesthetic and ergonomically designed firearms. The diversified range of CZ 550 models with their characteristics and elegant design solutions meet contemporary requirements for sporting and hunting weapons. The rifles are provided with a compact trigger mechanism featuring a single-set trigger firmly connected to the barrelled action. The trigger can be used as a single stage trigger, while the set-trigger can regulate trigger pull and trigger travel before and after discharge.

The set-trigger can be easily dismantled without impairing its functional properties or adjustment of the single stage trigger mechanism. CZ 550 rifles have a two position noiseless safety which is disengaged in a forward direction as standard. Stocks are fitted with sling-swivels as standard, and quick release swivels can be fitted on request. The CZ 550 rifles with open sights are provided with a bead front sight and rear sight located so as not to interfere with even the biggest rifle scopes.

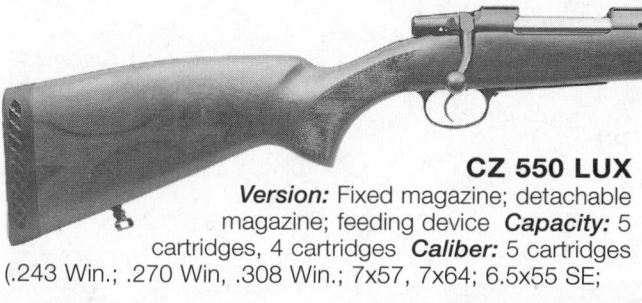

CZ 550 LUX

Version: Fixed magazine; detachable magazine; feeding device *Capacity:* 5 cartridges, 4 cartridges *Caliber:* 5 cartridges (.243 Win.; .270 Win, .308 Win.; 7x57, 7x64; 6.5x55 SE;

30-06 Sprg.; 9.3 x 62 4 cartridges (.243 Win.; .308 Win.; .22-250) *Overall length:* 44.7" *Barrel length:* 23.6" *Weight:* 7.3 lbs.
Price: $540.00
with detachable magazine 560.00
American 540.00-560.00
FS 635.00-655.00

CZ 550 FS

CZ 550 SAFARI MAGNUM (not shown)

The CZ 550 Safari is a true "Magnum" length action, it has all the features of the CZ 550 line and one standing 2 folding express sights, a Turkish walnut Lux stock is standard. This model is intended for heavy or dangerous game.

Calibers 375 H&H Mag., .416 Rigby, 458 Win Mag.
Price: $773.00
Also Available: CZ 550 MEDIUM MAGNUM,
.300 Win. Mag. and 7mm Rem. Mag. 621.00
CZ 550 PRESTIGE, 270 Win. & 30-06
calibers only 621.00
CZ 550 VARMINT, 308 Win only. 589.00

CZ 700 SNIPER M1

CZ 700 SNIPER M1

The CZ 700 Sniper M1 cal. .308 Win. is designed for tactical sniping and long-range hunting.
Features:
1) Match-grade barrel in 7.62 NATO (308)
2) Thumbhole laminated stock with adjustable butt and cheekpiece
3) Oversize, easy-to-reach bolt handle on low-throw bolt

4) Deep-well magazine 5) Bipod/swivel rail
Price: $2,097.00

The CZ 527 is a precision repeating rifle, designed for sport shooting and hunting. The trigger mechanism is of single set design adjustable for both pull and trigger travel. The safety is a two-position rotary lever which locks the trigger mecha- nism, while simultaneously blocking the bolt closed. The top of the receiver has milled grooves to accommodate scope mounts. The stock's surface is finished in a semi-matte polyurethane lacquer.

CZ 527 LUX

CZ 527 Lux with Turkish walnut stock with cheekpiece **Caliber:** .22 Hornet, .222 Rem., .223 Rem. **Magazine Capacity:** 5 cartridges **Overall length:** 42.4" **Barrel length:** 23.6" **Weight:** 6.2 lbs.
Price: **$540.00**
Also Available: CZ 527 M Carbine, Calibers: 7.62x39 Russian and .223 Rem. **540.00**

CZ 527 FS

CZ 527 FS - a classic Bavarian style Mannlicher stock of turkish walnut, cheekpiece **Caliber:** .22 Hornet, .222 Rem., .223 Rem. **Magazine Capacity:** 5 cartridges **Overall length:** 38.5" **Barrel length:** 20.5" **Weight:** 6.0 lbs.
Price: **$621.00**

527 PRESTIGE

Caliber: .22 Hornet, .223 Rem. **Magazine Capacity:** 5 car- tridges **Overall length:** 40.4" **Barrel length:** 21.9" **Weight:** 6.2 lbs.
Price: **$621.00**

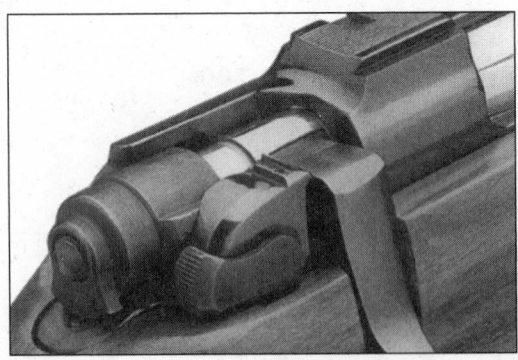

The safety in its off position

DAKOTA 10 SINGLE SHOT

SPECIFICATIONS

Calibers: Most rimmed/rimless commercially loaded types
Barrel Length: 23" **Overall Length:** 39.5" **Weight:** 6 lbs.
Features: Receiver and rear of breech block are solid steel without cuts or holes for maximum lug area (approx. 8 times more bearing area than most bolt rifles); crisp, clean trigger pull; removable trigger plate allows action to adapt to single-set triggers; straight-line coil-spring action and short hammer fall combine for fast lock time; smooth, quiet top

tang safety blocks the striker forward of the main spring; strong, positive extractor and manual ejector adapted to rimmed/rimless cases. XX grade oil-finished English, Bastogne or Claro walnut stock.

Price:	$3,595.00
BARRELED ACTIONS	2,050.00
ACTIONS ONLY	1,675.00
Also Available:	
DAKOTA 10 MAGNUM SINGLE SHOT	$3,595.00
Barreled actions	2,050.00
Actions only	1,675.00

DAKOTA 76 RIFLES
SPECIFICATIONS

Calibers:
SAFARI GRADE: from 257 Roberts to 416 Rem.
CLASSIC GRADE: from 220 Swift to 416 Rem.
AFRICAN GRADE: 404 Jeffery, 416 Dakota, 338 Lapna, 416 Rigby, 450 Dakota
Barrel Lengths: 21" or 23" (Classic); 23" only (Safari); 24" (African) **Weight:** 7.5 lbs. (Classic); 9.5 lbs. (African); 8.5 lbs. (Safari) **Safety:** Three-position striker-blocking safety allows bolt operation with safety on **Sights:** Ramp front sight; standing-leaf rear **Stock:** Choice of X grade oil-finished

DAKOTA 76 AFRICAN GRADE

English, Bastogne or Claro walnut (Classic); choice of XXX grade oil-finished English or Bastogne walnut w/ebony forent tip (Safari)

Prices:	
CLASSIC GRADE	$3,595.00
SAFARI GRADE	4,595.00
AFRICAN GRADE	4,995.00
Barreled Actions: Classic Grade	2,095.00
Safari Grade	2,450.00
African Grade	2,950.00
Actions: Classic Grade	1,850.00
Safari Grade	1,995.00
African Grade	2,500.00

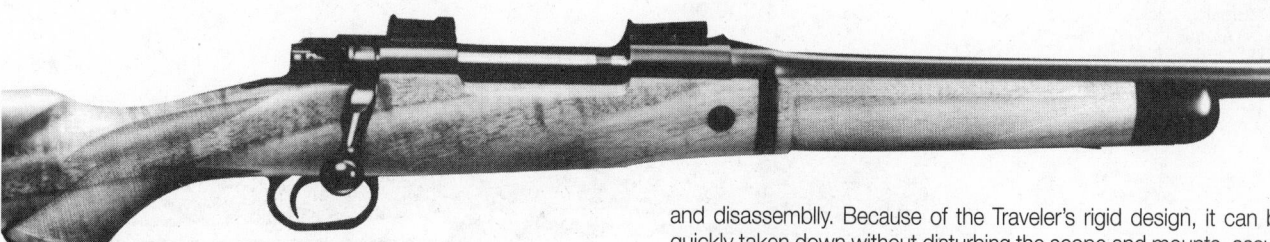

DAKOTA ARMS TRAVELER

The Dakota Traveler rifle can be easily broken down and carried in a small case or conventional suitcase, with the largest portion of the disassembled rifle being the barrel. With additional barrels available in a wide range of calibers, it offers great convenience for the traveling hunter.

The Traveler is based on the long-proven Dakota 76 design, and is stocked in checkered walnut. It features threadless disassembly. There are no threads to wear or stretch, no interrupted cuts and no possibility of headspace increasing even after repeated assembly

and disassemblly. Because of the Traveler's rigid design, it can be quickly taken down without disturbing the scope and mounts, assuring consistent, repeatable accuracy.

Additional barrels/calibers can be fitted on the same action, providing true worldwide hunting capability. Three families of actions are available: standard length, including the .257 Roberts, .25-06, 7x57, .270, .280, .30-06, .338-06 and .35 Whelen; short magnums, including the 7mm Rem. Mag., .300 Win. Mag., .338 Win. Mag., 416 Taylor and .458 Win. Mag.; and Dakota short magnums that include-their proprietary 7mm, .300, .330 and .375 Dakota cartridges.

Prices:	
CLASSIC	$4,495.00
SAFARI	5,495.00

RIFLES

Rifles

DAKOTA ARMS

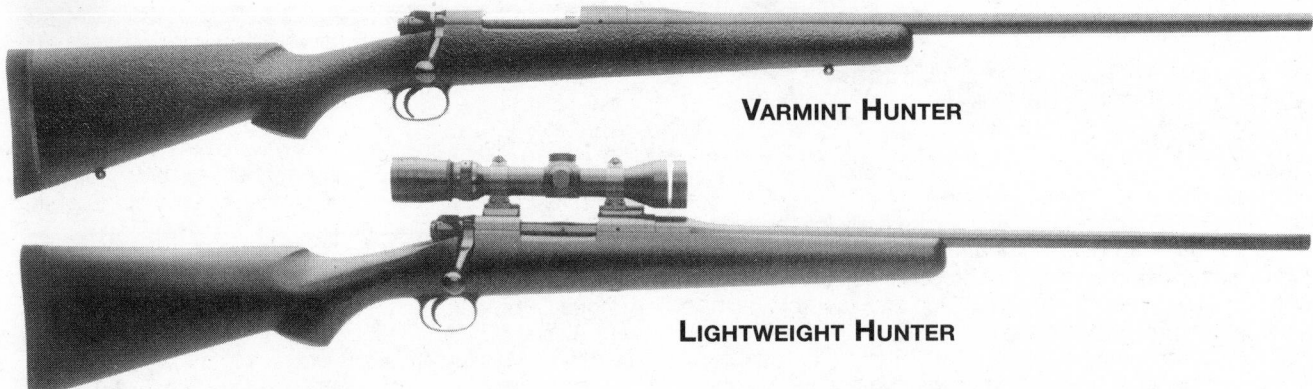

VARMINT HUNTER

LIGHTWEIGHT HUNTER

DAKOTA 97 VARMINT, LONG RANGE & LIGHTWEIGHT HUNTER RIFLES

DAKOTA HUNTER SERIES BOLT ACTION RIFLES (not shown)
97 LONG RANGE HUNTER
Fibergass stock, 2 sling swivel studs, 1" black recoil pad, 13 5/8 length of pull, overall weight 7.7 lbs., overall length 45" to 47", calibers 25-06 through 375 Dakota. RH only.
Price: **$1,995.00**

97 LIGHTWEIGHT HUNTER
Fibergass stock, 2 sling swivel studs, 1" black recoil pad, 12 5/8 length of pull, overall weight approximately 6-6 1/2 lbs., overall length 43", calibers 22-250 through 330, RH only.

97 VARMINT HUNTER
Walnut-stocked round short-action solid-bottom single shot, 24" chrome-moly barrel #4, adjustable trigger, 13 5/8 length of pull, 1/2" black pad, approximate weight 8 lbs, calibers 17 Rem through 22-250, RH only.
Price: w/semi-fancy wood stock **$2,495.00**
w/semi-fancy wood stock, checkering, floor plate **2,995.00**
Barreled action **1,300.00**

LONG BOW TACTICAL E.R. (ENGAGEMENT RIFLE)

SPECIFICATIONS
Caliber: 338 Lapua, 300 Dakota, 330 Dakota
Action: Blind magazine
Barrel Length: 28" stainless steel
Overall Length: 50"-51"
Length Of Pull: 12 $^7/_8$"-14 $^3/_8$"
Weight: 13.7 lbs. (w/o scope)
Stock: McMillan fiberglass (black or olive drab green); matte finish
Features: Adjustable cheekpiece; 3 sling swivel studs; bipod spike in forend; controlled round feeding; claw extraction system; one-piece optical rail; 3-position firing pin block safety; deployment kit; muzzlebrake
Price: **$4,250.00**
Action only **2,500.00**

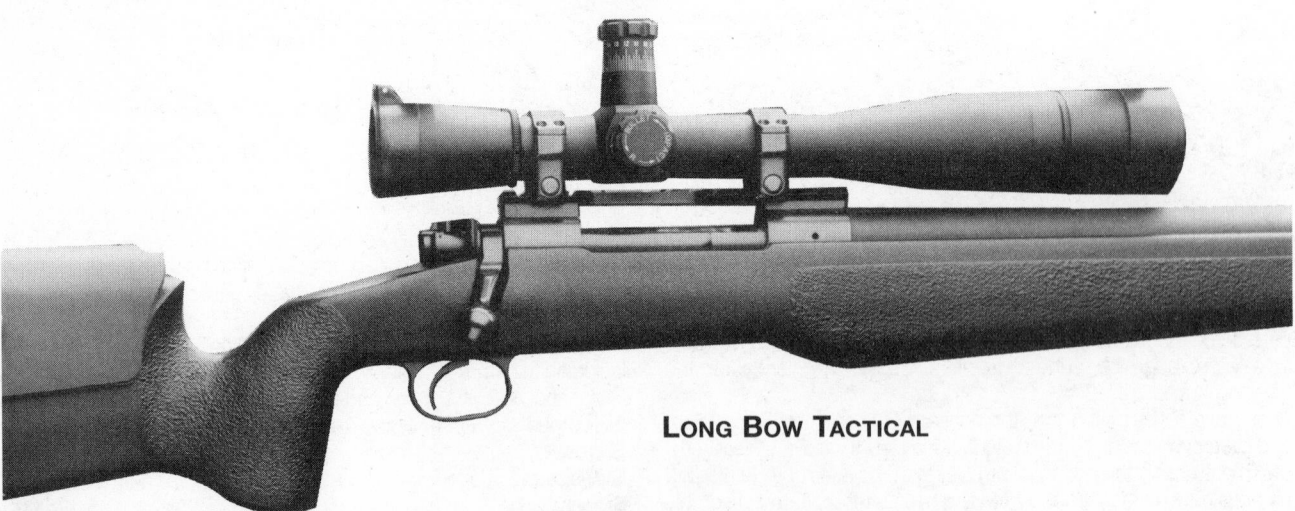

LONG BOW TACTICAL

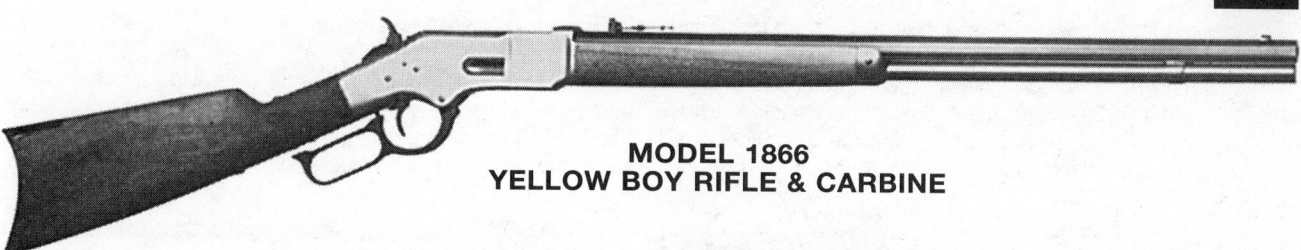

MODEL 1866
YELLOW BOY RIFLE & CARBINE

RIFLES

1860 HENRY RIFLE (not shown)

Calibers: 44-40 and 45 LC **Barrel length:** 24.25";
Overall length: 43.75" **Weight::** 9.25 lbs.
Blued barrel, walnut stock, brass frame
Price: $1,230.00

MODEL 1866 YELLOW BOY RIFLE & CARBINE

Calibers: 45 Long Colt, 38 Special and 44-40. Blued barrel, walnut stock, brass frame.
Prices:
Rifle $920.00
Carbine 900.00

MODEL 1873 SPORTING RIFLE

SPECIFICATIONS
Calibers: 357, 44-40, 45 Long Colt **Barrel length:** 24.25"
octagonal **Overall length:** 43.25" **Weight::** 8.16 lbs.
Features: Magazine tube in blued steel; frame is casehardened steel; stock and forend are walnut
Price $1,150.00

Also available:
MODEL 1873 CARBINE. Same features as
the 1873 Sporting Rifle, except in 45 Long Colt only
with 19" barrel. **Overall length:** 38.25" **Weight:** 7.38 lbs.
Price: $1,130.00

EUROPEAN AMERICAN ARMORY

HW 660 WEIHRAUCH RIMFIRE
TARGET RIFLE (SINGLE SHOT)

SPECIFICATIONS
Caliber: 22 LR **Barrel length:** 26" **Overall length:** 45.33"
Weight: 10.8 lbs. **Finish:** Blue **Stock:** European walnut

w/adjustable black rubber buttplate and comb
Features: Adjustable match trigger; left-handed stock
available; aluminum adjustable sling swivel; adj. vertical
and lateral cheekpiece; rear sight click-adjustable for
windage and elevation; aluminum forend rail; polished
feed ramp; external thumb safety
Price: $999.00
Laminated 1,159.00

FRANCOTTE RIFLES

August Francotte rifles are available in all calibers for which barrels and chambers are made. All guns are custom made to the customer's specifications; there are no standard models. Most bolt-action rifles use commercial Mauser actions; however, the magnum action is produced by Francotte exclusively for its own production. Side-by-side and mountain rifles use either boxlock or sidelock action. Francotte system sidelocks are back-action type. Options include gold and silver inlay, special engraving and exhibition and museum grade wood. Francotte rifles are distributed in the U.S. by Armes de Chasse (see Directory of Manufacturers and Distributors for details).

BOLT-ACTION RIFLE

SPECIFICATIONS
Calibers: 9.3x62, 375 H&H, 416 Rigby, others
Barrel length: To customer's specifications
Weight: 8 to 12 lbs., or to customer's specifications
Stock: A wide selection of wood in all possible styles according to customer preferences; prices listed below do not include engraving or select wood.
Engraving: Per customer specifications
Sights: All types of sights and scope

BOLT-ACTION RIFLES	Prices
Standard Bolt Action 9.3x62	$7,000.00
Magnum Action 375 H&H, 416 Rigby	8,900.00

BOXLOCK SIDE-BY-SIDE DOUBLE RIFLES	Prices
Std. boxlock double rifle (9.3X74R, 8X57JRS, 7X65R, etc.)	$12,700.00
Std. boxlock double (Magnum calibers)	27,500.00

SIDELOCK S/S DOUBLE RIFLES	
Std. sidelock double rifle (9.3X74R, 8X57JRS, 7X65R, etc.)	$17,500.00
Std. sidelock double (Magnum calibers)	27,250.00

MOUNTAIN RIFLES	
Standard boxlock	$12,000.00
Std. boxlock (Mag. & rimless calibers)	Price on request
Standard sidelock (7RM and .243 WM)	36,334.00

HARRINGTON & RICHARDSON

ULTRA HUNTER

ULTRA SINGLE-SHOT RIFLES
SPECIFICATIONS
Calibers: 22 WMR, 223 Rem. & 243 (Varmint), 25-06, 308 Win., 450 Marlin **Action:** Break-open; side lever release; positive ejection **Barrel Length:** 22" (308 Win.); 24" bull barrel (223 Rem., Varmint) 26" (25-06) **Weight:** 7 to 8 lbs. **Sights:** None (scope mount included) **Length Of Pull:** 14.25" **Drop**

At Comb: 1.25" **Drop At Heel:** 1 1/8" **Forend:** Semibeavertail **Stock:** Monte Carlo; hand-checkered cinnamon laminate stock **Features:** Sling swivels on stock and forend; patented transfer bar safety; automatic ejection; hammer extension; rebated muzzle; scope base included
Price:
Ultra Hunter and Varmint $268.95
Also available:
ULTRA COMP in 30-06 and 270 Win. **Barrel Length:** 24".
Weight: 7-8 lbs. Camo laminate stock, muzzle brake scope base included. 303.95

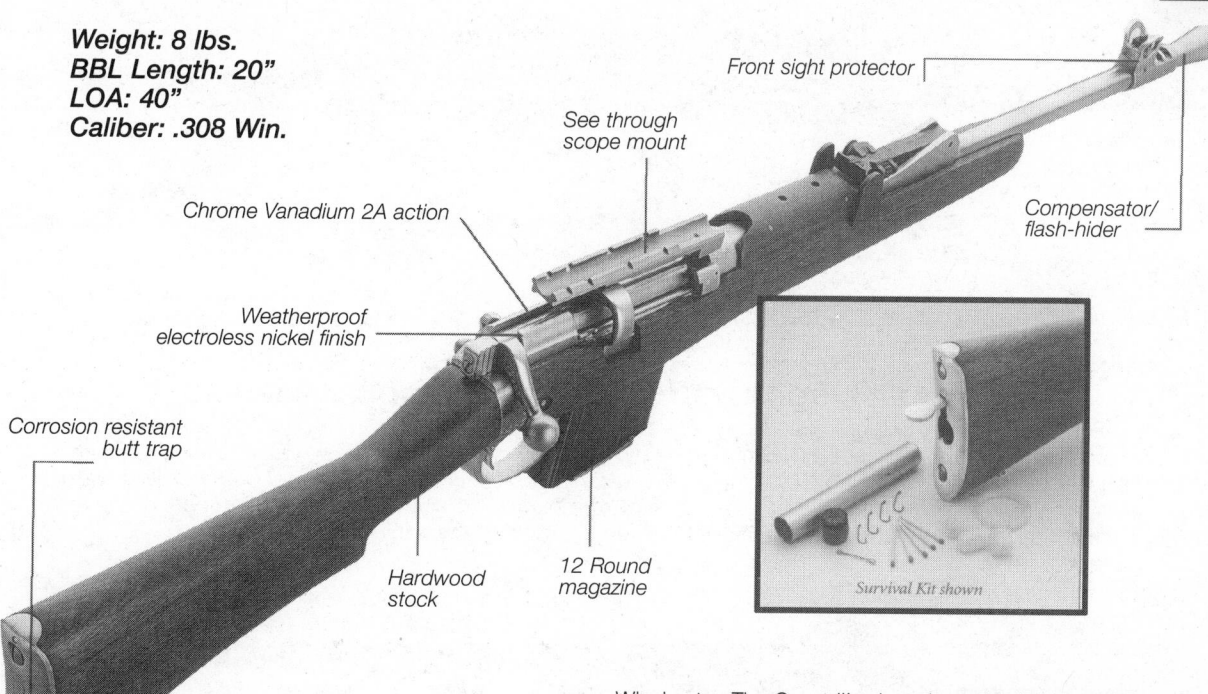

Weight: 8 lbs.
BBL Length: 20"
LOA: 40"
Caliber: .308 Win.

Front sight protector

See through scope mount

Chrome Vanadium 2A action

Compensator/ flash-hider

Weatherproof electroless nickel finish

Corrosion resistant butt trap

Hardwood stock

12 Round magazine

Survival Kit shown

RIFLES

Gibbs Rifle Company's Sport Specialty rifles include the Quest II Extreme Carbine. Like its military cousin, the No. 7 Jungle Carbine, the Quest II is made on a modern 2A Chrome Vanadium steel barreled action and is chambered for the popular, powerful .308

Winchester. The Quest II's electroless nickel finish protects against the elements and is fitted with a unique compensator/flash-hider that tames recoil and reduces muzzle jump. Pre-fitted see-through scope mount allows open sights to be used and accepts Weaver-based optics and accessories. The butt trap houses a no-nonsense survival kit with Brunton liquid filled compass, waterproof matches, fire starter, snare wire, twine and fishing kit. The Quest II Extreme Carbine is lightweight, rugged and hard-hitting, making it perfect for the trail, camp, cabin and hunting vehicle.

M71/84 REFURBISHED
PRODUCT CODE: MSR71R

Gibbs Rifle Company's newest addition to its line of historical remakes is the arsenal reconditioned Mauser M71/84, the first bolt-action repeating rifle ever built by Paul and Wilhelm Mauser. The M71/84 was adopted by Germany in 1871 and upgraded to an 8-round tubular magazine repeater in 1884. It saw combat in the colonial wars of Africa and in World War I. Mauser M71/84's were also

used during countless conflicts worldwide for over 80 years. These guns are truly rare and sought after by collectors.
Gibbs has taken original M71/84 rifles with 100+ years of grime, use and wear and carefully restored them to new condition using both original and reproduction parts. All barreled actions are completely original, with the exception of some small parts and have been arsenal re-finished using the same methods employed in their original manufacture. These barreled actions are then hand-fitted to 1-piece replica stocks that mirror the originals in every way, including all interior and exterior dimensions and inspection marks.
The Gibbs Arsenal Reconditioned M71/84 rifle are available for a limited time only.

**USC CARBINE
BASE MODEL**

HECKLER & KOCH USC .45 ACP AUTOLOADING CARBINE

A combination of advanced polymers, ordnance steel and a simple blow-back action make this a reliable, lightweight autoloading rifle. An optional Picatinny rail mounts easily for attaching a scope or electronic sight. The rear sight is fully adjustable. A bolt catch holds the action open after the last round from the 10-shot polymer magazine. An oversize trigger guard and ambidextrous safety make shooting easier with gloves. The 16-inch hammer-forged barrel and skeleton polymer stock keep weight to only 6 pounds. Sling swivel holes and a rubber cheek rest and recoil pad are standard. *Price:* **$1,199.00**

**SL8-1 RIFLE
BASE MODEL**

HECKLER & KOCH SL8-1 .223 AUTOLOADING RIFLE

Built largely of polymers around a steel frame, this gas-operated autoloader weighs only 8.5 lbs with a 21" free-floating barrel. The mechanism is based on the proven German G36 design. Field-stripping to three modular components can be done in seconds with the removal of two hex screws. The thumbhole stock includes an adjustable butt and hardpoints for mounting a forend rail. A removable, adjustable rear sight complements a Picatinny scope rail that can also be removed. The safety is ambidextrous; so is the bolt cocking lever. A 10-round detachable box magazine is of clear polymer. *Price:* **$1,599.00**

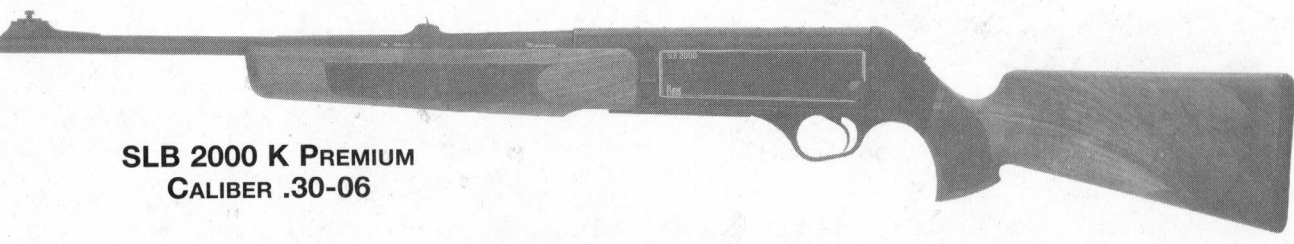

**SLB 2000 K PREMIUM
CALIBER .30-06**

SLB 2000 .30-06 RIFLE

The SLB uses a proven gas operating system that is extremely robust. The same bolt system can handle a wide array of popular international hunting cartridges (.308, .30-06, 7x64mm, 9.3x62mm) when a barrel conversion is made. The exaggerated shape and angle of the pistol grip makes offhand shooting easier. Iron sights are included.
Price: . . . . **NA**

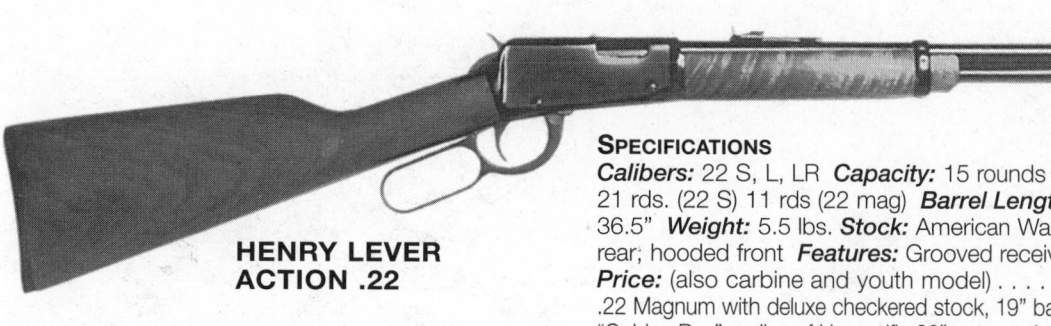

HENRY LEVER ACTION .22

SPECIFICATIONS
Calibers: 22 S, L, LR **Capacity:** 15 rounds (22 LR); 17 rds. (22 L); 21 rds. (22 S) 11 rds (22 mag) **Barrel Length:** 18" **Overall Length:** 36.5" **Weight:** 5.5 lbs. **Stock:** American Walnut **Sights:** Adjustable rear; hooded front **Features:** Grooved receiver for scope mount
Price: (also carbine and youth model) $249.95
.22 Magnum with deluxe checkered stock, 19" barrel 299.95
"Golden Boy" replica of Henry rifle 20" octagon barrel 379.95

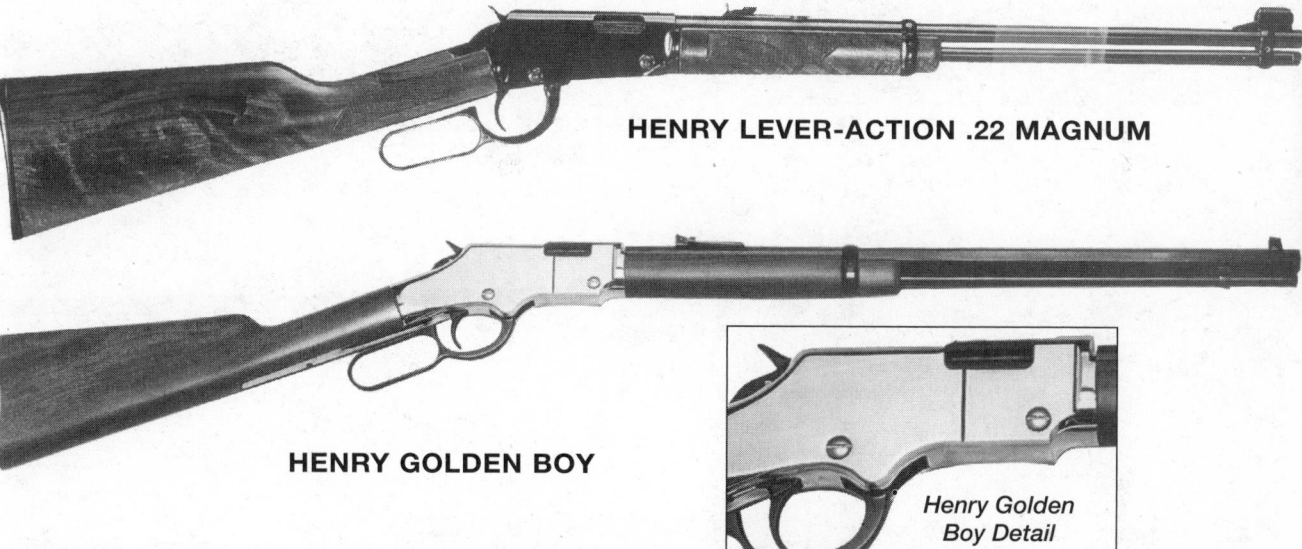

HENRY LEVER-ACTION .22 MAGNUM

HENRY GOLDEN BOY

Henry Golden Boy Detail

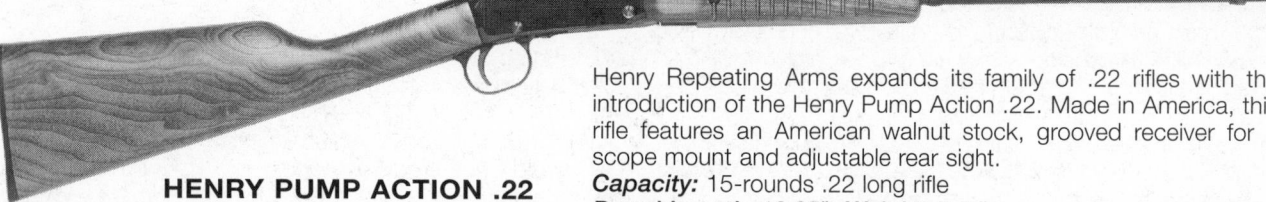

HENRY PUMP ACTION .22

Henry Repeating Arms expands its family of .22 rifles with the introduction of the Henry Pump Action .22. Made in America, this rifle features an American walnut stock, grooved receiver for a scope mount and adjustable rear sight.
Capacity: 15-rounds .22 long rifle
Barrel Length: 18.25" **Weight:** 5.5 lbs.
Price: $249.95

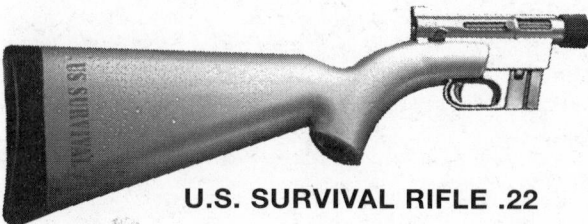

U.S. SURVIVAL RIFLE .22

SPECIFICATIONS
Calibers: 22 long rifle **Capacity:** 9-shot **Barrel Length:** 16.25"
Overall Length: 35.25" **Sights:** Adjustable rear sight **Features:** Barrel and action fit in floating waterproof stock; comes with two 8-round magazines, grooved receiver for scope.
Price: $165.00

RIFLES

**AMERICAN CLASSIC
375 H&H**

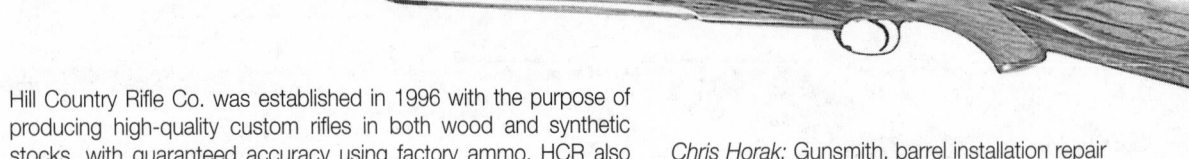

Hill Country Rifle Co. was established in 1996 with the purpose of producing high-quality custom rifles in both wood and synthetic stocks, with guaranteed accuracy using factory ammo. HCR also specializes in accurizing factory rifles and is a complete gunsmithing shop for commercial bolt-action rifles.

Every rifle is tested for accuracy in a 100-yard, underground test range, using factory ammo. HCR does the barrel break-in and scope mounting so the rifle is delivered ready to hunt.

Customers can choose McMillan synthetic stocks or French, English, or Turkish walnut. HCR will also use good Claro and Bastogne Walnuts when requested. Lilja, Hart, and Krieger barrels are standard. All actions are aluminum pillar bedded, with free-floating barrels in both wood- and synthetic-stocked rifles, HCR guarantees 3-shot, 1/2" groups at 100 yards with factory ammo for most calibers.

HCR's includes specialists, no jack-of-all-trades.

David Fuqua: President and Gunsmith, barrel installation and chambering
Hector Herrera: In charge of accurizing and bedding department
Mike Fricks: Gunsmith, builds all wood stocks

Chris Horak: Gunsmith, barrel installation repair
Matt Bettersworth: General Manger, Sales.

AMERICAN CLASSIC 375 H&H
• *Winchester Model 70 Action* • *Custom Extended Extractor* • *Custom Checkered Bolt Handle* • *Custom Checkered Bolt Release* • *Lilja #6, CM, 1:12 Twist 22" Barrel* • *Exhibition English Walnut Stock* • *Ebony Forend Tip w/ Widow's Peak* • *Contoured Cross Bolts* • *Talley European Rear Bridged Stud* • *Barrel Band Sling Stud* • *Barrel Band Front Site* • *Single Leaf Adjustable Rear Site* • *Biesen Steel Butt Plate* • *Fischer Skeleton Grip Cap* • *Sunny Hill Drop Box Bottom Metal* • *HCR Accurizing* • *1" Factory Ammo Guarantee*
Price: **$7,500.00**

Hill Country Rifle Company
5726 Morningside Drive
New Braunfels, TX 78132

In 1978 Tom Houghton bought Atkinson Gun Company and combined it with H-S Engineering to form H-S Precision, Inc., in Prescott, Arizona. Two years later the firm began manufacturing test barrels for Winchester, and two years after that H-S began producing Fiberthane rifle stocks. In 1984 the company came up with an aluminum bedding block, now used on all its Pro-Series stocks, which appeared in 1985. They feature a blend of fiberglass, Kevlar and unidirectional carbon fiber. In 1988 H-S Precision developed a take-down rifle, receiving the patent two years later when the firm moved to Rapid City, South Dakota. There Tom Houghton and his crew updated both engineering and manufacturing with CAD and CNC technology. In 1994 the 15,000-square-foot facility grew with the addition of 10,000 square feet designated for stock production only.

By this time H-S was manufacturing synthetic stocks for both Remington and Winchester. It was also building custom rifles with its own super-accurate cut-rifled barrels. Law enforcement agencies were steady patrons. In 1996 the plant expanded by another 25 percent; the next year the series 2000 single-shot pistol appeared, followed by series 2000 rifles on the company's own actions.

The H-S Precision Pro-Series 2000 action combines many of the best features of the Winchester Model 70 and Remington 700 rifles. Available in two lengths, it is the heart of several H-S Precision semi-custom rifles, including a take-down model. Rifles of 30 caliber and smaller are guaranteed to shoot 1/2-inch groups at 100 yards. Big-bore rifles are guaranteed to shoot into one minute of angle.

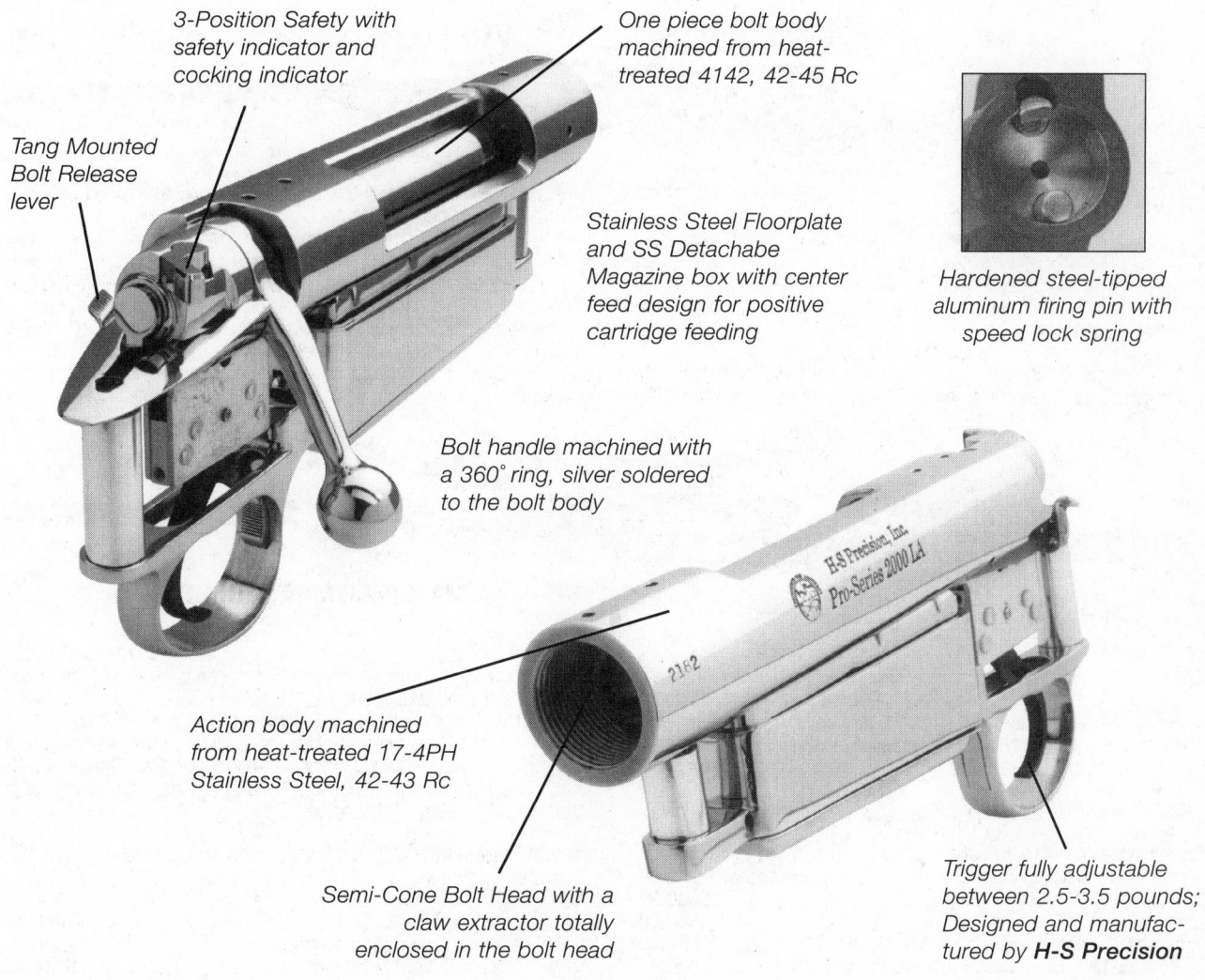

3-Position Safety with safety indicator and cocking indicator

Tang Mounted Bolt Release lever

One piece bolt body machined from heat-treated 4142, 42-45 Rc

Stainless Steel Floorplate and SS Detachabe Magazine box with center feed design for positive cartridge feeding

Hardened steel-tipped aluminum firing pin with speed lock spring

Bolt handle machined with a 360° ring, silver soldered to the bolt body

Action body machined from heat-treated 17-4PH Stainless Steel, 42-43 Rc

Semi-Cone Bolt Head with a claw extractor totally enclosed in the bolt head

Trigger fully adjustable between 2.5-3.5 pounds; Designed and manufactured by *H-S Precision*

Pro-Series 2000

PHR (PROFESSIONAL HUNTER RIFLE)

The Pro-Series 2000 PHR is a slightly heavier version of the Pro-Series 2000 SPR rifle. Because of the larger magnum calibers, available for the Pro-Series 2000 PHR, the increased weight is a necessity. The Pro-Series 2000 PHR is designed to handle the new "super magnums" such as the 300 Rem Ultra Mag or the 338 Lapua.

FEATURES
• *Pro-Series 2000* stainless steel action with detachable magazine • 3 rounds in the magazine box
• *Pro-Series 10X* match grade stainless steel barrel • Fluted (except 416 Rigby) • 24" or 26" magnum contour • Optional muzzle brake • Built in recoil reducer • Choice of color • Metal finish – Teflon® or *Pro-Series* PFTE Matte Black • Weight* – 7.75 - 8.25 pounds • Calibers – 7mm STW, 300 Win Mag, 300 Rem Ulltra Mag, 338 Win Mag, 416 Rem Mag, 375 H&H Mag, 338/300 Ultra Mag, 375/300 Ultra Mag, 338 Lapua, 416 Rigby
• *Pro-Series* synthetic stock with full length bedding block chassis system, sporter style

VTD (VARMINT TAKE-DOWN SYSTEM)

Pro Series 2000 Take-Down rifles are covered by the same 1/2 minute of angle accuracy and repeatability guarantee as all other Pro-Series 2000 rifles (3 shots at 100 yards). Pro-Series 2000 Take-down rifle systems are tested for accuracy and repeatability with factory match ammunition.

FEATURES
• *Pro-Series 2000* stainless steel action, long or short
• *Pro-Series* stainless steel floorplate with detachable magazine • 4 rounds in the magazine box, standard calibers • 3 rounds in the magazine box, magnum calibers
• *Pro-Series 10X* match grade stainless steel barrel • Fluted • 23.5" varmint contour • Optional muzzle brake • PSV29B - long action • Choice of color • Metal finish – Teflon® or *Pro-Series* PFTE Matte Black • Weight* – 8.50 - 9.00 pounds • Calibers – 308 Win, 300 Win Mag • Options • Additional caliber capabillity by adding a second barrel
• *Pro-Series* synthetic stock with ful length bedding block chassis system, varmint style

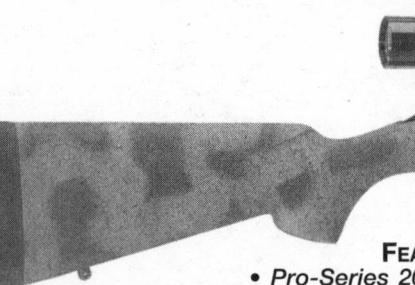

VAR (VARMINT RIFLE)

FEATURES
• *Pro-Series 2000* stainless steel action, long or short
• *Pro-Series* stainless steel floorplate with detachable magazine • 4 rounds in the magazine box, standard calibers • 3 rounds in the magazine box, magnum calibers • 3 rounds in the magazine box, 338 Lapua
• *Pro-Series 10X* match grade stainless steel barrel, heavy barrel • Fluted • 24" heavy contour • Optional muzzle brake
• *Pro-Series* synthetic stock with full length bedding block chassis system, tactical style • PST25 - short action, fully adjustable length of pull and cheek piece • PST26 - long action, fully adjustable length of pull and cheek piece • Choice of color • Metal finish – Teflon® or *Pro-Series* PFTE Matte Black • Weight* – 10.75 - 11.25 pounds • Calibers – 308 Win, 300 Win Mag, 338 Lapua

Prices: Sporter, with 2000 action **$1,850.00**
Sporter, with customer's M70 or M700 action **1,250.00**
Pro-Hunter, with 2000 action **2,000.00**
Varmint, with 2000 action **1,850.00**
Varmint, with customer's M70 or M700 action **1,250.00**
Pro-Hunter Take-Down, with 2000 action and one barrel . **2,200.00**
Varmint Take-Down, with 2000 action and one barrel . . . **2,100.00**

Varmint Take-Down, with 2000 action and two barrels
(same head size) **3,100.00**
Varmint Take-Down, with 2000 action and two barrels
(different head sizes) **3,300.00**
Additional barrels, same head size **1,000.00**
Additional barrels, different head sizes **1,200.00**
Tactical rifles priced on request only.

HOWA LIGHTNING RIFLES

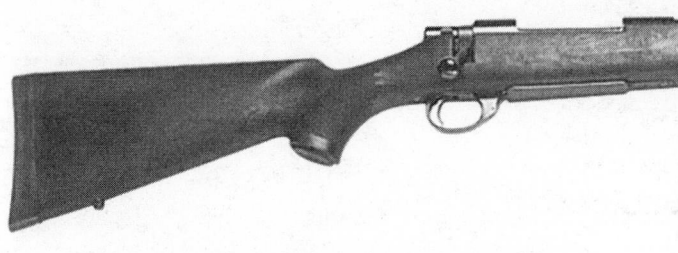

LIGHTNING BOLT-ACTION RIFLE

The rugged mono-bloc receivers on all Howa rifles are machined from a single billet of high carbon steel. The machined steel bolt boasts dual-opposed locking lugs and triple relief gas ports. Actions are fitted with a button-release hinged floorplate for fast reloading. Premium steel sporter-weight barrels are hammer-forged. A silent sliding thumb safety locks the trigger for safe loading or clearing the chamber. The stock is ultra-tough polymer.

SPECIFICATIONS

Calibers: 22-250, 223, 243, 270, 308, 30-06, 300 Win. Mag., 338 Win. Mag., 7mm Rem. Mag. **Capacity:** 5 rounds (3 in Magnum) **Barrel length:** 22" (24" in Magnum) **Overall length:** 42.5" **Weight:** 7.5 lbs. (7.7 lbs. in Magnum) **Finish:** Blue

Price: STANDARD MODEL	**$464.00**
In Magnum calibers	**486.00**
STAINLESS	**549.00**
In Magnum calibers	**571.00**
HUNTER *(hardwood stock, checkered) add*	**22.00**
VARMINT (223, 22-250, 308 Win)	**496.00**
Stainless	**594.00**
hardwood stock add $22.00	
Barreled actions	**$347.00-447.00**

RIFLES

JARRETT CUSTOM RIFLES

STANDARD HUNTING RIFLE

Jarrett's Standard Hunting Rifle incorporates a McMillan stock with Decelerator pad in choice of finishes. #4 match-grade barrel on Remington 700 or Winchester 70 action with Talley scope mounts. Case, sling load data and custom-loaded ammo included. **Finished Weight:** 8.5 lbs.
Price: **$3,550.00**

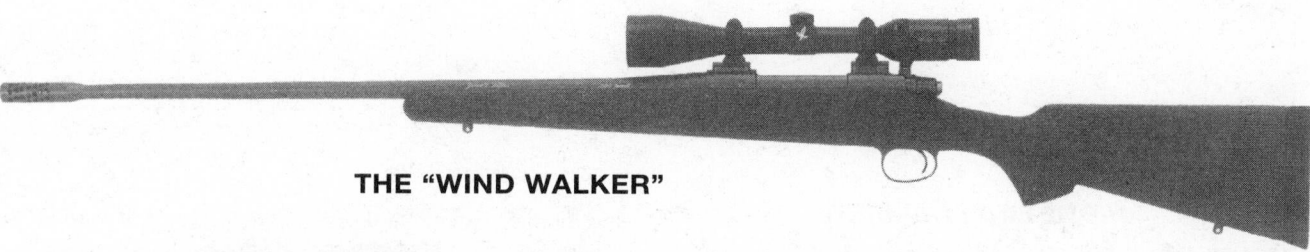

THE "WIND WALKER"

WIND WALKER

Same specifications as the Standard model, but with a Kevlar stock and skeletonized Rem. 700 action for lighter weight (finished, with Swarovski 3-10x 42 A1 scope in Talley mounts, the Windwalker weighs 7.25 lbs.). Muzzle brake, case, sling, load data and custom-loaded ammo included.
Price: **$4,395.00**

THE WALKABOUT

The WalkAbout is a short, handy rifle built on a Remington 700 short action and chambered for your choice of standard or popular wildcat cartridges. The Jarrett barrel is 20" long; the stock is by McMillan and comes in a variety of finishes.

At 7.5 pounds, finished, the WalkAbout includes Talley mounts and rings with the scope you specify. Case, sling, load data and 20 rounds of ammunition are also furnished.
Price: **$3,550.00**

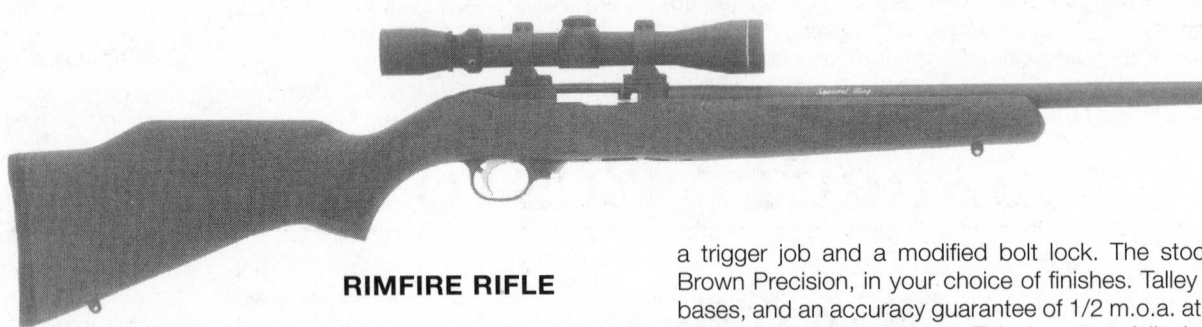

RIMFIRE RIFLE

The Jarrett Rimfire Rifle is built on a Ruger 10/22 receiver. The 18-inch match-grade barrel is available in Target and hunting contours. Action work includes precise barrel fitting,

a trigger job and a modified bolt lock. The stock is from Brown Precision, in your choice of finishes. Talley rings and bases, and an accuracy guarantee of 1/2 m.o.a. at 50 yards, are part of the package. This is a carefully built rimfire designed for one-hole groups.
Price: **$1,800.00**
   Target **1,995.00**

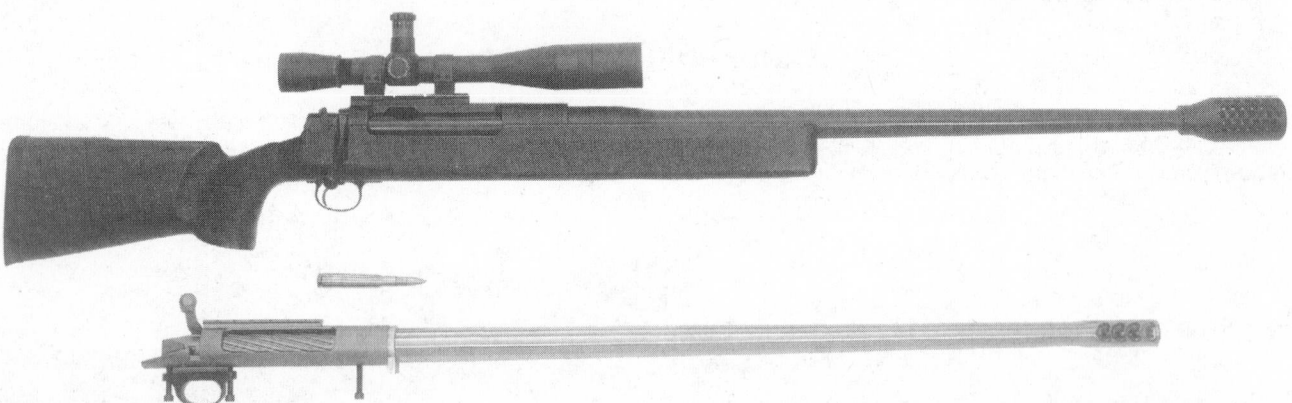

JARRETT 50 CALIBER

The Jarrett 50 is built on a McMillan receiver in either single-shot or magazine configuration. A match-grade KP barrel with compensator, a McMillan stock and military scope mounts bring rifle weight to 28 to 45 pounds depending on your choice of barrel contour and length (30" to 34"). Jarrett

develops an accurate load and supplies 20 rounds of ammunition. Scope of choice: Leupold Ultra 24X.
Not shown: Jarrett special rifles made to order in Tactical, Bench Rest, Youth and Professional Hunter styles.
Price: (single shot) **$6,700.00**
   Repeater **6,950.00**

Three models of this rifle are available - the "Classic Safari", the "Safari" and the "Tradition". The "Classic Safari", is the choice of hunters after African big game. The "Safari" is designed for scope use as well. The "Tradition" is ideal for the globe-trotting big-game hunter. All models are available in several chamberings with standard and custom features, and each rifle is produced individually. A Johannsen Express Rifle represents true custom work.

TRADITION

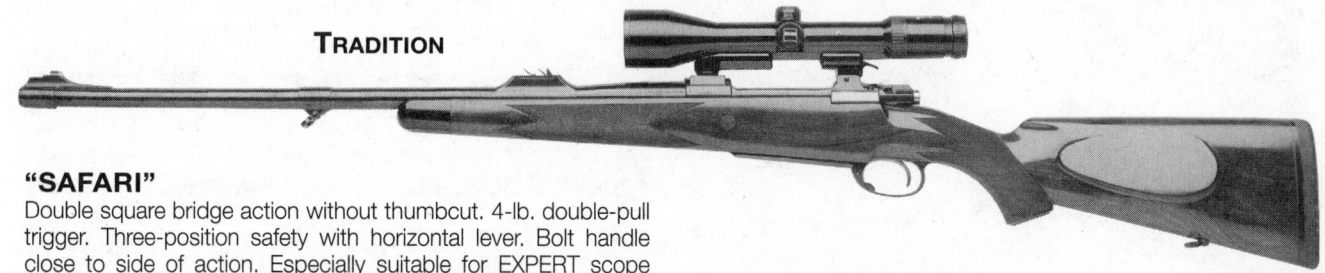

"SAFARI"

Double square bridge action without thumbcut. 4-lb. double-pull trigger. Three-position safety with horizontal lever. Bolt handle close to side of action. Especially suitable for EXPERT scope mount. 2-mm silver bead combined with fold-away 4-mm Holland & Holland-type ivory bead. Express sight with two leaves. Safari-style stock with 1-3/4"/2-1/2" drop. Oil finish. 26" barrel. Length overall 47". Weight from approx. 8 lbs. 6 oz. depending upon caliber. *Standard calibers:* .375 H & H Magnum, 4-shot, or .416 Rigby, 3-shot.
Price:. $10,250.00

Magazine capacities, maximum:

CALIBER	NORMAL FLOORPLATE	RIGBY FLOORPLATE
.300 Weatherby Magnum	4	5
.338-378 Weatherby Magnum	3	4
.375 H & H Magnum	4	5
.416 Rigby	3	4
.450 Dakota	3	4
.500 Jeffery	3	4

Other calibers upon request.

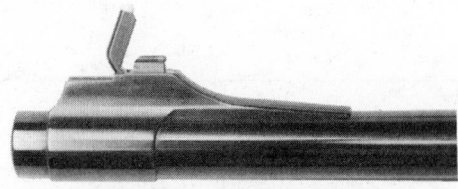

HOLLAND & HOLLAND-TYPE NIGHT SIGHT
The "Classic Safari" and "Safari" models come with a 4-mm ivory bead that can be flipped up to cover the 2-mm silver bead under poor light conditions.

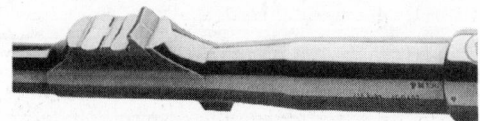

EXPRESS SIGHT
The rear sight with its two leaves fits into a special ring base. The rear sight base extends around the barrel and has the second recoil shoulder on the underside, which is important for large-bore rifles.

"CLASSIC SAFARI"
Single square bridge action with thumbcut. 4-lb. double-pull trigger. Three-position wing safety. Traditional bolt handle. 2-mm silver bead combined with a fold-away 4-mm Holland & Holland-type ivory bead. Express sight with two leaves. Safari-style stock with 1-3/4"/2-1/2" drop. Oil finish. 24" barrel. Length overall 45". Weight from approx. 8 lbs. 3 oz. depending upon caliber. *Standard calibers:* .375 H & H Magnum, 4-shot, or .416 Rigby. 3-shot.
Price:. $9,500.00

"TRADITION"
Double square bridge action without thumbcut. Adjustable-pull single-set trigger. Three-position safety with horizontal lever. Low bolt handle. Especially suitable for EXPERT scope mount. "Masterpiece" front sight base with 2.5-mm fluorescent bead. Express sight with two leaves. Stock with straight comb and 1-3/4"/2" drop. Oil finish. 26" barrel. Length overall 47". Weight from approx. 8 lbs. depending upon caliber. *Standard calibers:* .300 Weatherby Magnum, 4-shot, .375 H & H Magnum, 4-shot.
Price:. $10,550.00

WING SAFETY – The "Classic Safari" features a wing safety with "safe" and "fire" clearly indicated in gold.
PEEP SIGHT – For precision sighting with open sights - or to compensate for less than perfect vision - the peep sight mounted on the cocking piece can be raised into position.

MODEL CDGA 6345 EMPIRE GRADE SEMIAUTOMATIC 22LR

MODEL CDGA 4103 FIELD GRADE BOLT ACTION

STANDARD M-20P SEMIAUTOMATIC

MODEL M-12Y YOUTH BOLT ACTION

KBI/CHARLES DALY RIFLE SPECIFICATIONS

ITEM NO.	CAPACITY	CALIBER	BARREL LENGTH	OVERALL LENGTH	PRICE
FIELD GRADE					
CDGA 4103	6	22LR	22 5/8"	41"	$135.00
CDGA 4164	10	22LR	20 1/4"	40 1/2"	135.00
CDGA 4238	Single Shot	22LR	16 1/4"	32"	155.00
CDGA 4279	6	22LR	17 1/2"	34 3/8"	149.00
SUPERIOR GRADE					
CDGA 5047	6	22LR	22 5/8"	41 1/4"	189.00
CDGA 5159	5	22 MRF	22 5/8"	41 1/4"	209.00
CDGA 5261	5	22 Hornet	22 5/8"	41 1/4"	369.00
CDGA 5302	10	22LR	20 1/4"	40 1/2"	209.00
EMPIRE GRADE					
CDGA 6116	6	22LR	22 5/8"	41 1/4"	349.00
CDGA 6208	5	22 MRF	22 5/8"	41 1/4"	369.00
CDGA 6270	5	22 Hornet	22 5/8"	41 1/4"	479.00
CDGA 6345	10	22LR	20 1/4"	40 1/4"	334.00

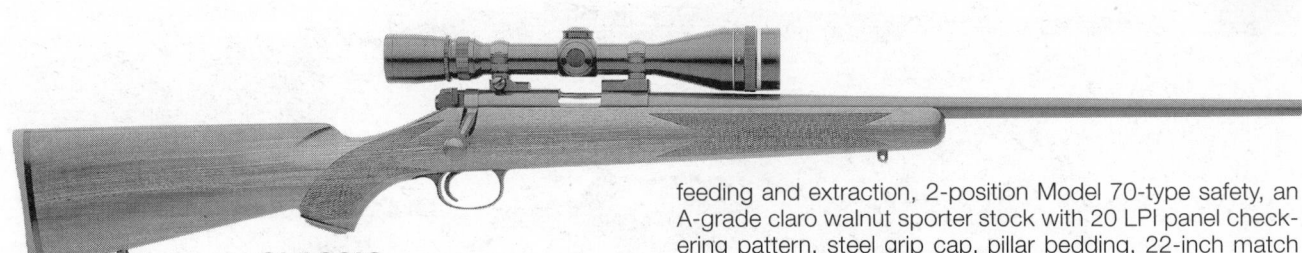

CLASSIC

The Kimber 22 Classic features the new Kimber 22 action with Mauser claw extractor for positive controlled round feeding and extraction, 2-position Model 70-type safety, an A-grade claro walnut sporter stock with 20 LPI panel checkering pattern, steel grip cap, pillar bedding, 22-inch match grade light sporter barrel, match grade chamber and trigger, bead-blasted blue finish and 5 round magazine.
Price: Super America **$1,560.00**

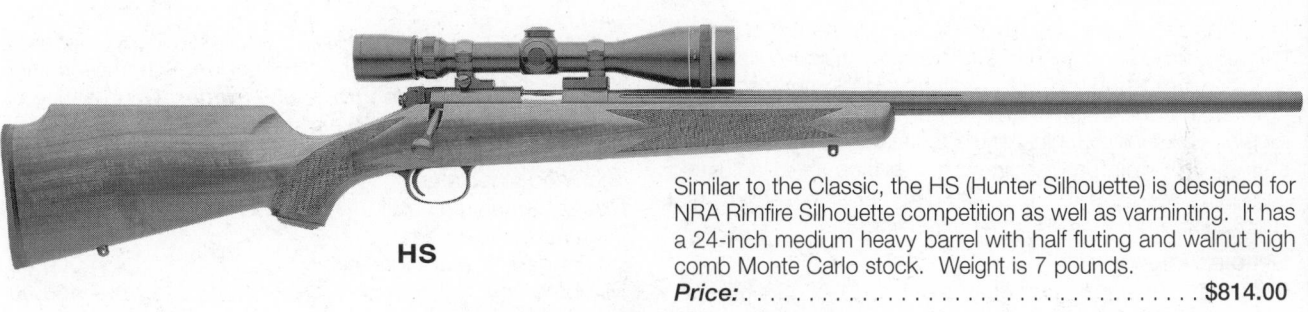

HS

Similar to the Classic, the HS (Hunter Silhouette) is designed for NRA Rimfire Silhouette competition as well as varminting. It has a 24-inch medium heavy barrel with half fluting and walnut high comb Monte Carlo stock. Weight is 7 pounds.
Price: **$814.00**

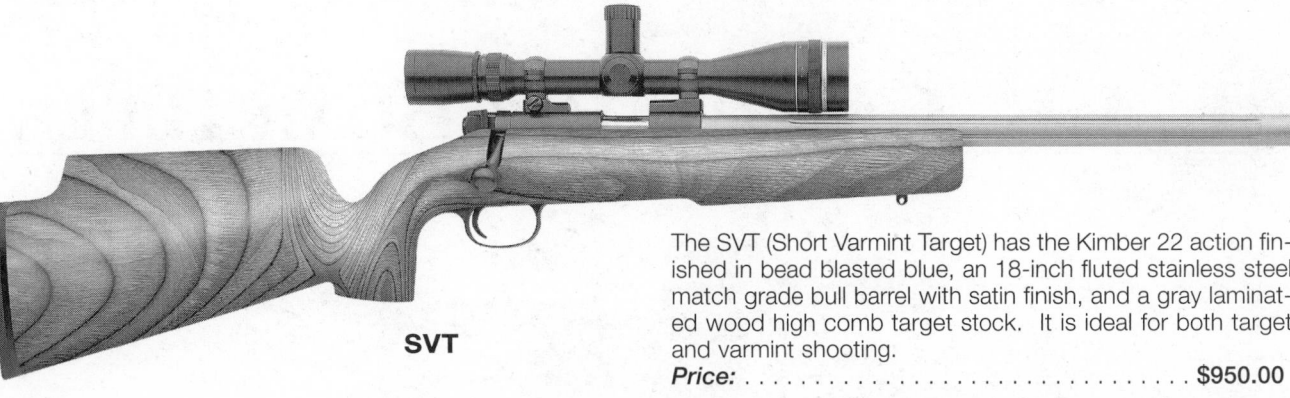

SVT

The SVT (Short Varmint Target) has the Kimber 22 action finished in bead blasted blue, an 18-inch fluted stainless steel match grade bull barrel with satin finish, and a gray laminated wood high comb target stock. It is ideal for both target and varmint shooting.
Price: **$950.00**

84M

The **MODEL 84M** Classic features a lightweight Mauser action with full length claw extractor, two position Model 70-type safety, match grade trigger and five round magazine with sculpted steel floorplate and trigger guard. The 22-inch match grade barrel has a light sporter contour and match grade chamber. The A-grade premium claro walnut stock has 20 LPI side panel checkering and a steel grip cap. Available in .243 Win, .260 Rem., 7 mm-08 Rem. and .308 Win. Weight is approximately 5 pounds, 10 ounces.
Price: **$895.00**
VARMINT MODEL 7 lbs. 5 oz. in 22-250
 w/26" barrel **978.00**

RIFLES

KRIEGHOFF DOUBLE RIFLES

CLASSIC SIDE-BY-SIDE DOUBLE RIFLE

Krieghoff's Classic Side-by-Side offers many standard features, including: Schnable forearm...classic English-style stock with rounded cheekpiece...UAS anti-doubling device...1" quick-detachable sling swivels... Decelerator recoil pad...short opening angle for fast loading ...compact action with reinforced sidewalls...sliding, self-adjusting wedge for secure bolt...automatic hammer safety...horizontal firing-pins...Purdey-style barrel extension.

SPECIFICATIONS
Calibers: Standard—7x65R, 308 Win., 30-06, 30R Blaser, 8x57 JRS, 8X75 JRS, 9.3X74R; *Magnum*—375 H&H Flanged Mag. N.E., 375 H&H Mag., 416 Rigby, 458 Win. Mag., 470 N.E., 500 N.E. *Action:* Thumb-cocking break/action *Barrel length:* 23.5 *Trigger:* Double triggers with steel trigger guard *Weight:* 7.5 to 11 lbs. (depending on caliber and wood density) *Options:* 21.5" barrel; engraved sideplates

Prices: STANDARD $7,850.00
Interchangeable barrels
  (installed, w/extra forearm) 4,500.00
MAGNUM 9,450.00
Interchangeable barrels 5,500.00

L.A.R. GRIZZLY BIG BOAR RIFLE

BIG BOAR COMPETITOR

BIG BOAR COMPETITOR

SPECIFICATIONS
Caliber: 50 BMG
Capacity: Single shot
Action: Bolt action, bull pup, breechloading
Barrel length: 36"
Overall length: 45 1/2" *Weight:* 30.4 lbs.
Safety: Bolt stop safety

Features: All-steel construction; receiver made of 4140 alloy steel, heat-treated to 42 R/C; bolt made of 4340 alloy steel; low recoil (compares to a 12 ga. shotgun)

Prices: $2,570.00
PARKERIZED 2,670.00
NICKEL FRAME 2,820.00
FULL NICKEL 2,920.00

These state-of-the-art rifles feature 17R stainess steel receivers with two massive locking lugs, a match grade 416R stainless steel barrel, fully adjustable benchrest-style trigger, and a Lazzeroni-designed synthetic stock that is hand-bedded using aluminum pillar blocks. Included is a precision-machined floorplate/triggerguard assembly.

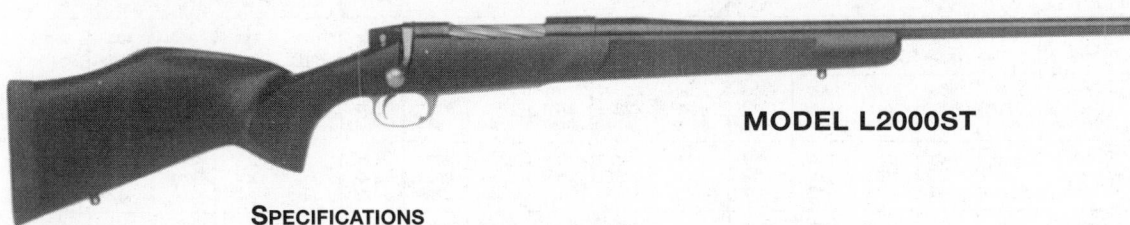

MODEL L2000ST

SPECIFICATIONS
Calibers: 6.53 (.257) Scramjet®; 7.21 (.284) Firebird™; 7.82 (.308) Warbird®; 8.59 (.338) Titan® **Capacity:** 4 rounds (one in chamber) **Barrel Length:** 27" **Overall Length:** 47.5"

Weight: 8.1 lbs. **Stock:** Lazzeroni fiberglass sporter; right or left hand available
Price: L2000ST $4,499.00

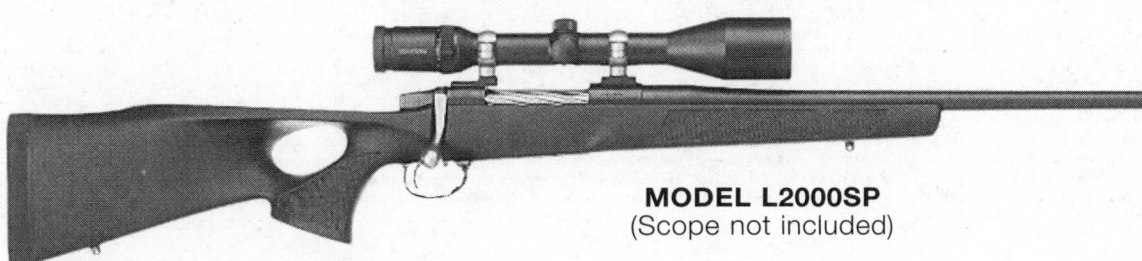

MODEL L2000SP
(Scope not included)

SPECIFICATIONS
Calibers: 6.53 (.257) Scramjet®; 7.21 (.284) Firebird™; 7.82 (.308) Warbird®; 8.59 (.338) Titan® **Capacity:** 4 rounds (one in chamber) **Barrel Length:** 25" **Overall Length:** 45.5"

Weight: 7.8 lbs. **Stock:** Lazzeroni fiberglass thumbhole; right hand only
Price: L2000SP $4,499.00

MODEL L2000DG
(Scope not included)

SPECIFICATIONS
Calibers: 10.57 (.416) Meteor® only **Capacity:** 4 rounds (one in chamber) **Barrel Length:** 24" **Overall Length:** 44.5"
Weight: 9.6 lbs. **Stock:** Lazzeroni fiberglass sporter; right or left hand available.
Price: L2000DG $4,499.00

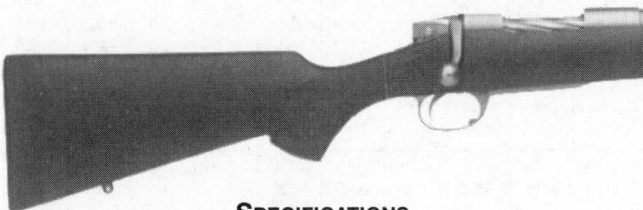

MODEL L2000SA

SPECIFICATIONS
Calibers: 6.17 (.253) Spitfire®; 6.71 (.264) Phantom®; 7.21 (.284) Tomahawk®; 7.82 (.308) Patriot®; 8.59 (.338) Galaxy® **Capacity:** 4 rounds, one in chamber (Tomahawk, Patriot, Galaxy); 5 rounds, 1 in chamber (Spitfire, Phantom)

Barrel Length: 24" (except Galaxy) **Overall Length:** 42.5" **Weight:** 6.8 lbs. **Stock:** Lazzeroni slimline stock; right or left hand avail.
Price: L2000SA $4,499.00

RIFLES

LAZZERONI BALLISTICS

Long Magnum Cartridges

CARTRIDGE	BULLET	VELOCITY in Feet per Second						ENERGY in Foot-Pounds						PATH OF BULLET Above or below line-of-sight of riflescopes mounted 2" above bore				
Cartridge	Weight Grains	Muzzle	100 Yards	200 Yards	300 Yards	400 Yards	500 Yards	Muzzle	100 Yards	200 Yards	300 Yards	400 Yards	500 Yards	100 Yards	200 Yards	300 Yards	400 Yards	500 Yards
6.53 (.257) SCRAMJET®	85	4000	3689	3399	3128	2874	2633	3021	2569	2181	1847	1559	1309	1.3	2.2	0.0	−5.7	−15.7
	100	3750	3501	3266	3044	2833	2631	3123	2722	2370	2058	1782	1537	1.6	2.4	0.0	−6.2	−16.7
	120	3550	3319	3101	2893	2694	2504	3219	2814	2456	2138	1854	1602	1.9	2.8	0.0	−6.9	−18.7
7.21 (.284) FIREBIRD™	120	3950	3698	3461	3237	3024	2821	4158	3645	3193	2792	2437	2121	1.3	2.1	0.0	−5.4	−14.7
	140	3750	3522	3306	3101	2905	2718	4372	3857	3399	2990	2625	2297	1.6	2.4	0.0	−6.0	−16.1
	160	3550	3351	3161	2979	2805	2637	4478	3990	3551	3155	2796	2471	1.9	2.7	0.0	−6.6	−17.6
7.82 (.308) WARBIRD®	130	3975	3697	3438	3193	2962	2742	4562	3948	3412	2944	2533	2172	1.3	2.1	0.0	−5.5	−15.1
	150	3775	3542	3323	3114	2915	2724	4747	4181	3679	3231	2831	2473	1.6	2.4	0.0	−6.0	−16.0
	180	3550	3352	3163	2983	2810	2643	5038	4493	4001	3558	3157	2794	1.9	2.7	0.0	−6.6	−17.6
	200	3350	3162	2983	2810	2644	2484	4985	4442	3952	3509	3106	2742	2.3	3.1	0.0	−7.5	−20.0
8.59 (.338) TITAN®	185	3550	3334	3129	2933	2746	2566	5178	4568	4023	3535	3098	2706	1.9	2.7	0.0	−6.8	−18.2
	200	3450	3230	3020	2820	2629	2445	5287	4633	4051	3533	3070	2656	2.1	2.9	0.0	−7.3	−19.7
	225	3300	3110	2927	2752	2584	2421	5442	4832	4282	3785	3336	2929	2.4	3.2	0.0	−7.8	−20.8
	250	3150	2977	2810	2649	2494	2344	5510	4920	4384	3896	3453	3050	2.7	3.5	0.0	−8.5	−22.6
10.57 (.416) METEOR®	300	3100	2888	2686	2493	2308	2131	6403	5559	4809	4143	3550	3026	3.0	3.9	0.0	−9.5	−25.6
	400	2800	2634	2474	2320	2171	2028	6965	6165	5440	4784	4190	3656	1.5	0.0	−7.2	−20.8	−41.9

*Note: This table was calculated by computer using a standard modern technique to predict trajectories and recoil energies from the best available cartridge data. Figures shown are expected to be reasonably accurate; however, the shooter is cautioned that performance will vary because of variations in rifles, ammunition, atmospheric conditions and altitude. Velocities were determined using 27-inch barrels; shorter barrels will reduce velocity by 30 to 85 fps per inch of barrel removed. Trajectories were computed with the line-of-sight 2 inches above the bore centerline at 3000 ft. elevation. B.C.: Ballistic Coefficient supplied by the bullet manufacturers. An * in the ballistics chart indicates Lazzeroni factory-loaded ammunition.*

Short Magnum Cartridges

CARTRIDGE	BULLET	VELOCITY in Feet per Second						ENERGY in Foot-Pounds						PATH OF BULLET Above or below line-of-sight of riflescopes mounted 2" above bore				
Cartridge	Weight Grains	Muzzle	100 Yards	200 Yards	300 Yards	400 Yards	500 Yards	Muzzle	100 Yards	200 Yards	300 Yards	400 Yards	500 Yards	100 Yards	200 Yards	300 Yards	400 Yards	500 Yards
6.17 (.243) SPITFIRE®	70	3812	3492	3195	2917	2656	2410	2259	1895	1587	1323	1097	903	1.7	2.6	0.0	−6.6	−18.2
	85	3618	3316	3036	2992	2523	2287	2471	2077	1740	1450	1202	987	2.0	2.9	0.0	−7.4	−20.3
	100	3419	3181	2957	2743	2539	2344	2596	2248	1942	1671	1432	1220	2.3	3.1	0.0	−7.7	−20.9
6.71 (.264) PHANTOM®	100	3514	3294	3086	2887	2697	2515	2742	2411	2115	1851	1616	1404	2.0	2.8	0.0	−7.0	−18.8
	120	3312	3117	2930	2751	2579	2414	2923	2589	2289	2018	1773	1553	2.4	3.2	0.0	−7.8	−20.9
	140	3109	2934	2767	2605	2450	2299	3005	2678	2381	2111	1866	1644	2.9	3.7	0.0	−8.8	−23.4
7.21 (.284) TOMAHAWK®	120	3563	3333	3115	2908	2710	2521	3383	2961	2587	2254	1958	1693	1.9	2.8	0.0	−6.9	−18.5
	140	3379	3170	2971	2781	2598	2423	3550	3125	2745	2405	2100	1826	2.3	3.1	0.0	−7.6	−20.4
	160	3152	2970	2796	2629	2467	2311	3530	3136	2779	2456	2163	1899	2.8	3.6	0.0	−8.6	−23.0
7.82 (.308) PATRIOT®	130	3571	3318	3080	2855	2640	2436	3681	3180	2740	2354	2013	1713	2.0	2.8	0.0	−7.1	−19.2
	150	3363	3152	2951	2759	2575	2398	3767	3310	2902	2536	2209	1916	2.3	3.2	0.0	−7.7	−20.7
	180	3184	3000	2825	2656	2493	2336	4052	3600	3191	2821	2485	2182	2.7	3.5	0.0	−8.5	−22.5
	200	3012	2838	2671	2510	2355	2205	3626	3221	2853	2519	2217	1943	3.1	4.0	0.0	−9.5	−25.3
8.59 (.338) GALAXY®	185	3201	3002	2811	2629	2454	2285	4210	3703	3248	2840	2474	2146	2.7	3.6	0.0	−8.6	−23.0
	225	2968	2786	2611	2443	2281	2125	4402	3899	3407	2983	2600	2257	3.3	4.2	0.0	−10.1	−26.8
	250	2761	2594	2433	2277	2128	1984	4232	3736	3287	2881	2515	2186	1.6	0.0	−7.4	−21.6	−43.5
10.57 (.416) MAVERICK®	300	2741	2542	2351	2169	1995	1830	5006	4306	3685	3136	2653	2232	1.7	0.0	−7.9	−23.4	−47.5
	400	2452	2302	2158	2019	1885	1758	5341	4710	4138	3622	3159	2747	2.3	0.0	−9.7	−28.0	−56.1

Note: This table was calculated by computer using a standard modern technique to predict trajectories and recoil energies from the best available cartridge data. Figures shown are expected to be reasonably accurate; however, the shooter is cautioned that performance will vary because of variations in rifles, ammunition, atmospheric conditions and altitude. Velocities were determined using 26-inch barrels; shorter barrels will reduce velocity by 30 to 85 pfs per inch of barrel removed. Trajectories were computed with the line-of-sight 2 inches above the bore centerline at 3000 ft. elevation. B.C.: Ballistic Coefficient supplied by the bullet manufacturers.

Lone Star specializes in rolling block rifles, a design popularized by Remington after the Civil War. Some buffalo hunters used rolling blocks because, like the fabled Sharps, they could handle large, powerful cartridges. Lone Star builds commercial and custom rifles on actions manufactured in house. Styles available include:
• Black Powder Silhouette • Creedmoor • Sporting
• Deluxe Sporting • Buffalo Rifle • Custer Commemorative
• Gove Underlever • Cowboy Action

Standard rifles are available in three configurations and come with round barrels, single trigger, case-colored actions and straight-grained American walnut stocks. The match-grade barrels are the same as those used on custom models. Chamberings for the standard rifles include:
• 40-60 and 45-70 in the Silhouette model
• 30-40 Krag in the Sporting model 32-40, 38-55, 40-65, 45-70 and 45 Long Colt in the Cowboy Action model
Price: standard rifles **$1,495.00**

RIFLES

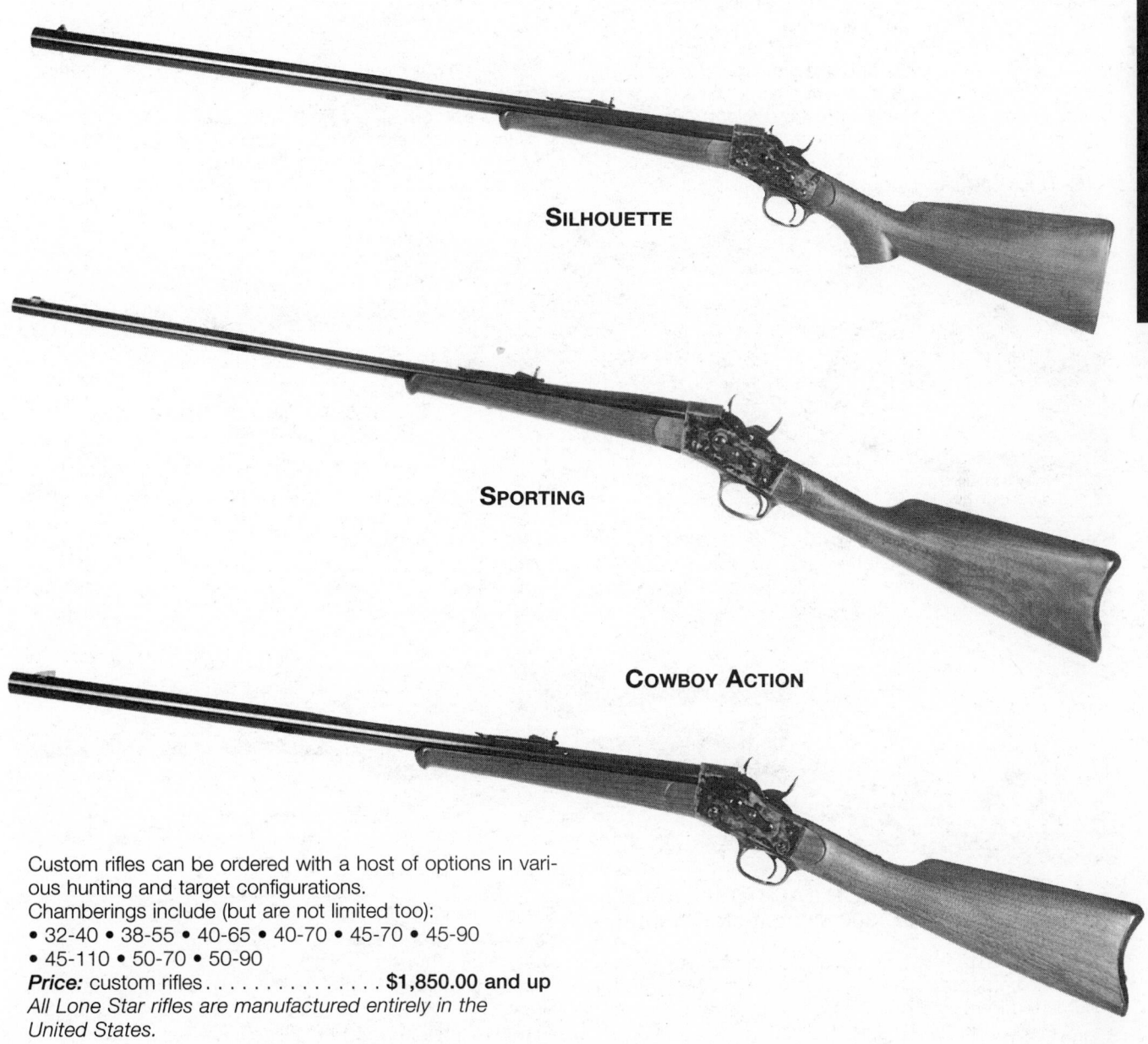

SILHOUETTE

SPORTING

COWBOY ACTION

Custom rifles can be ordered with a host of options in various hunting and target configurations.
Chamberings include (but are not limited too):
• 32-40 • 38-55 • 40-65 • 40-70 • 45-70 • 45-90
• 45-110 • 50-70 • 50-90
Price: custom rifles . . . . **$1,850.00 and up**
All Lone Star rifles are manufactured entirely in the United States.

MAGNUM RESEARCH

MOUNTAIN EAGLE
SPORT BARREL

MOUNTAIN EAGLE
BOLT-ACTION RIFLE

SPECIFICATIONS
Calibers: 270 Win., 280 Rem., 30-06 Springfield, 7mm Mag., 300 Wby. Mag., 300 Win. Mag., 338 Win. Mag., 340 Wby. Mag., 375 H&H Mag., 416 Rem. Mag.
Capacity: 5-shot magazine (long action); 4-shot (Magnum action) *Action:* SAKO-built to MRI specifications
Barrel length: 24" *Overall length:* 44" *Weight:* 7 lb. 13 oz.
Sights: None *Stock:* Fiberglass composite
Length of pull: 13 5/8" *Features:* Adjustable trigger; high comb stock one-piece forged bolt; free-floating, match-

grade, Krieger, benchrest barrel; recoil pad and sling swivel studs; Platform Bedding System for front lug; pillar-bedded rear guard screw; lengthened receiver ring; solid steel hinged floorplate
Price: **$1,499.00**
   Left Hand **1,549.00**
   375 H&H Mag. and 416 Rem. Mag. **1,799.00**
Also available:
VARMINT EDITION. In 222 Rem. and 223 Rem.
   with stainless steel Krieger barrel (26") **$1629.00**
Mountain Eagle rifles are now available in a left-hand version, and with "Magnum Lite" carbon fiber barrels.

BARRACUDA STOCK STYLE

MAGNUM LITE RIMFIRE

The Magnum Research Magnum Lite 10/22 rifle is built on a Ruger action with rotary magazine and blowback, autoloading mechanism. The carbon-fiber barrel is 75 percent lighter than a comparable steel barrel but gives match-quality accuracy. An integral muzzle port

reduces whip. Available in .22 Long Rifle and .22 WMR, the Magnum Lite comes with a Hogue composite stock of traditional design, or a Turner laminated "Barracuda" stock.
Price: w/"Barracuda" stock **$799.00**
w/Hogue composite stock **599.00**
WMR Model w/"Barracuda" **799.00**
WMR Model w/Hogue **999.00**

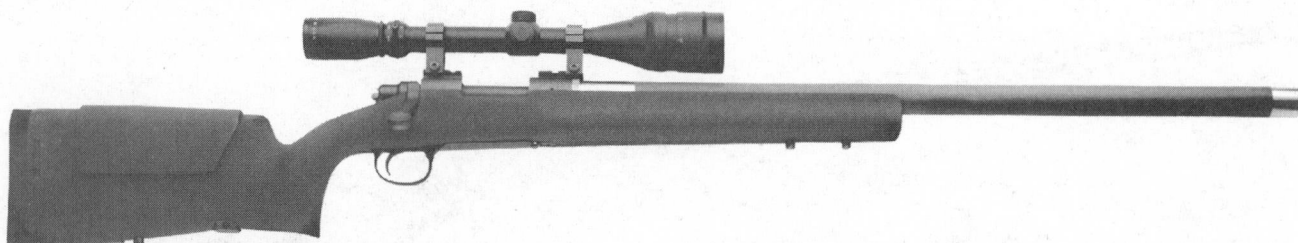

MAGNUM RESEARCH TACTICAL RIFLE
.308 Winchester or .300 Winchester Magnum

- MAGNUM LITE™ graphite barrel (26 inch) Unidirectional graphite composite
- Accurized Remington® 700 action
- H-S Precision™ tactical stock

SPECIFICATIONS
Weight: average 8.3 lbs.
Overall Length: adjustable
Adjustable Trigger: 2.5 to 5 lbs.
Height: adjustable comb
Price: **$2,400.00**
Also Available in .223 Rem and 22-250

MODEL 60

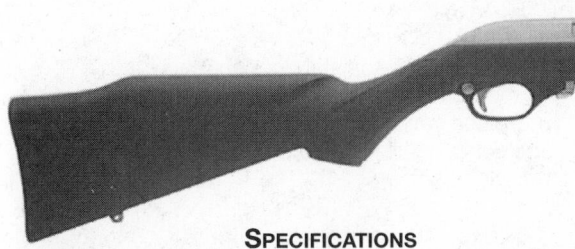

MODEL 60C

SPECIFICATIONS

Caliber: 22 Long Rifle **Capacity:** 14-shot tubular magazine **Barrel Length:** 22" **Overall Length:** 40.5" **Weight:** 5.5 lbs. **Sights:** Ramp front sight with brass bead and Wide-Scan hood; adjustable open rear, receiver grooved for scope mount **Action:** Self-loading; side ejection; man-

ual and automatic "last-shot" hold-open devices; receiver top has serrated, nonglare finish; crossbolt safety **Stock:** One-piece Maine birch Monte Carlo stock, press-checkered, with full pistol grip; Mar-Shield® finish

Price:	$176.00
Stainess 60SB	223.00
Stainess, synthetic stock 60SSK	244.00
Stainess, laminated stock 60SS	281.00
New 60C with blued steel, camo stock	208.00

MODEL 70PSS "PAPOOSE"

Action: Self-loading; side ejection; manual bolt hold-open; crossbolt safety; stainless-steel breech bolt and barrel **Sights:** Screw adjustable open rear; ramp front; receiver grooved for scope mount **Stock:** Black fiberglass-filled synthetic with abbrev. forend, nickel-plated swivel studs
Price: $288.00

SPECIFICATIONS

Caliber: 22 Long Rifle **Capacity:** 7-shot clip **Barrel Length:** 16.25" **Overall Length:** 35.25" **Weight:** 3.25 lbs.

MODEL 7000

SPECIFICATIONS

Caliber: 22 LR **Capacity:** 10 shots **Action:** Self-loading; side ejection **Barrel Length:** 18" heavy target; recessed muzzle (16 grooves) **Overall Length:** 37" **Weight:** 5.25 lbs.

Stock: Monte Carlo black fiberglass-filled synthetic **Sights:** No sights; receiver grooved for scope mount (1" scope ring mounts standard) **Features:** Manual bolt hold-open; crossbolt safety; steel charging handle
Price: $236.00
Also available: MODEL 795. Same as Model 7000 but w/screw-adjustable open rear sight w/brass bead; no scope mount **Weight:** 4.5 lbs. $167.00

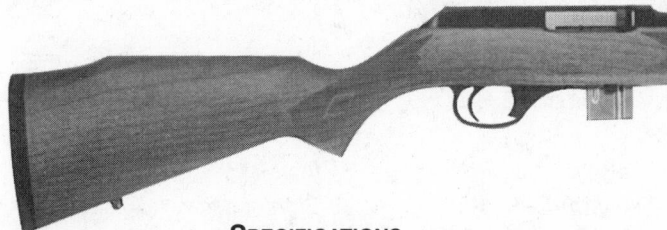

MODEL 922M SELF-LOADER

ramp front sight w/brass bead and removable Wide-Scan™ hood **Stock:** Monte Carlo walnut finished hardwood, checkered w/rubber rifle butt pad and swivel studs **Features:** Garand type safety; magazine safety; receiver sandblasted to prevent glare; manual bolt hold-open; automatic last-shot bolt hold-open
Price: $454.00

SPECIFICATIONS

Caliber: 22 WMRF **Capacity:** 5-shot nickel-plated magazine **Barrel Length:** 20.5" Micro-Groove **Overall Length:** 39.75" **Weight:** 6.5 lbs. **Sights:** Adjustable folding semi-buckhorn rear sight;

RIFLES

MODEL 25NC (shown) AND 25N

A bolt-action, bottom-fed repeater, the 25N holds 7 .22 Long Rifle cartridges. The 22" Micro-Groove barrel ensures fine accuracy. Fitted with open sights, this rifle readily accepts a scope and can be ordered with one. The hardwood stock has a natural finish. Mossy Oak Break-Up camouflage distinguishes the 25NC stock. *Weight:* 5.5 lbs.
Price: 25N $199.00
    with scope 205.00
    25NC................................. 233.00

MODEL 25MN

SPECIFICATIONS
Caliber: 22 WMR (not interchangeable w/other 22 cartridges) *Capacity:* 7-shot clip magazine *Barrel Length:* 22" with Micro-Groove® rifling *Overall Length:* 41"

Weight: 6 lbs. *Sights:* Adjustable open rear; ramp front sight; receiver grooved for scope mount
Stock: One-piece walnut finished press-checkered Maine birch Monte Carlo w/full pistol grip; Mar-Shield® finish; swivel studs
Price: $227.00
    Model 25 MNC with camo stock 263.00

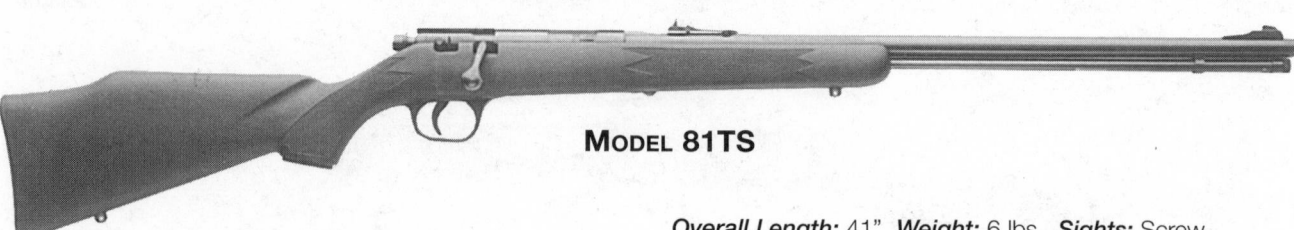

MODEL 81TS

SPECIFICATIONS
Caliber: 22 Short, Long or Long Rifle *Capacity:* Tubular magazine holds 25 Short, 19 Long, 17 Long Rifle cartridges *Barrel Length:* 22" w/Micro-Groove® rifling (16 grooves)

Overall Length: 41" *Weight:* 6 lbs. *Sights:* Screw-adjustable open rear; ramp front *Stock:* Monte Carlo black fiberglass-filled synthetic w/swivel studs and molded-in checkering
Price:................................... $200.00

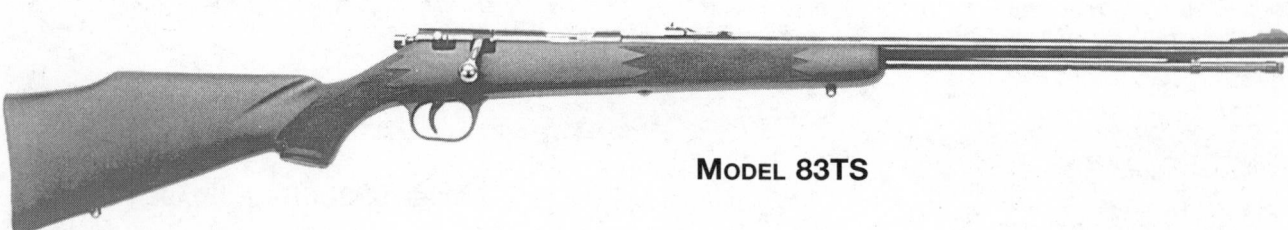

MODEL 83TS

SPECIFICATIONS
Caliber: 22 WMR (not interchangeable with other 22 cartridges) *Capacity:* 12-shot tubular magazine *Action:* Bolt action; positive thumb safety; red cocking indicator *Barrel Length:* 22" with Micro-Groove® rifling (20 grooves) *Overall*

Length: 41" *Weight:* 6 lbs. *Sights:* screw adjustable open rear; ramp front sight; receiver grooved for scope mount *Stock:* Monte Carlo black fiberglass synthetic stock; swivel studs
Price: $244.00

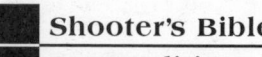

MARLIN 15YN "LITTLE BUCKAROO™"

SINGLE SHOT 22
BEGINNER'S RIFLE

SPECIFICATIONS

Caliber: 22 Short, Long or Long Rifle **Capacity:** Single shot **Action:** Bolt action; easy-load feed throat; thumb safety; red cocking indicator **Barrel Length:** 16.25" (16 grooves) **Overall Length:** 33.25" **Weight:** 4.25 lbs. **Sights:** Adjustable open rear; ramp front sight **Stock:** One-piece walnut-finished press-checkered Maine birch Monte Carlo w/full pistol grip; tough Mar-Shield® finish **Price:** $197.00

MARLIN 7000T WITH SCOPE

This accurate, autoloading .22 has a Micro-Groove target barrel 18" long. The nickel-plated box magazine holds 10 rounds. The red, white and blue laminated birch stock accepts forend accessories on an aluminum tail. A rubber buttplate is adjustable for drop, length of pull and cant. **Length:** 37", **Weight:** 7-1/2 pounds. **Price:** $465.00

RIFLES

Marlin Lever-Action .22 Rifle

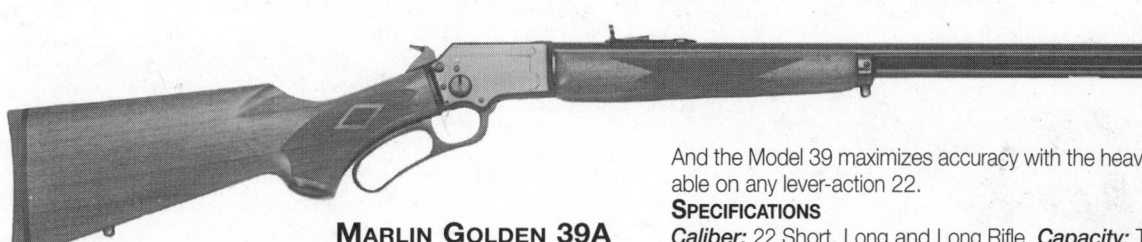

MARLIN GOLDEN 39A

A premier-quality .22 rifle, the 39A features:
SOLID RECEIVER TOP. You can mount a scope on your Marlin 39 by screwing on the machined scope adapter base provided. The screw-on base is a neater, more versatile method of mounting a scope on a 22 sporting rifle. The solid top receiver and scope adapter base provide a maximum in eye relief adjustment. The 39 receiver is clean, flat and sandblasted to prevent glare. Exclusive brass magazine tube **MICRO-GROOVE® BARREL.** Marlin's famous rifling system of multi-grooving has consistently produced fine accuracy because the system grips the bullet more securely, minimizes distortion, and provides a better gas seal.

And the Model 39 maximizes accuracy with the heaviest barrels available on any lever-action 22.

SPECIFICATIONS

Caliber: 22 Short, Long and Long Rifle **Capacity:** Tubular magazine holds 26 Short, 21 Long and 19 LR cartridges
Action: Lever; solid top receiver; side ejection; one-step takedown; deeply blued metal surfaces; receiver top sandblasted to prevent glare; hammer block safety; rebounding hammer **Barrel:** 24" with Micro-Groove® rifling (16 grooves) **Overall Length:** 40" **Weight:** 6.5 lbs. **Sights:** Adjustable folding semibuckhorn rear, ramp front sight with Wide-Scan™ hood; solid top receiver tapped for scope mount or receiver sight; scope adapter base; offset hammer spur for scope use—works right or left **Stock:** Two-piece cut-checkered American black walnut w/fluted comb; full pistol grip and forend; blued-steel forend cap; swivel studs; grip cap; Mar-Shield® finish; rubber buttpad **Price:** $525.00

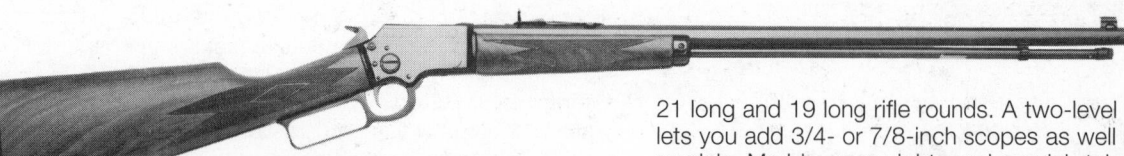

MARLIN 1897 COWBOY

This .22 rimfire with 24" octagon barrel is built on a Model 39 action. The full-length magazine holds 26 short, 21 long and 19 long rifle rounds. A two-level scope adapter lets you add 3/4- or 7/8-inch scopes as well as standard 1" models. Marble open sights and a quick-takedown receiver are standard, as is a checkered, straight-grip walnut stock. **Overall length:** 40", **Weight:** 6-1/2 pounds. **Price:** $708.00

444P OUTFITTER

MARLIN 444P

The 444P "Outfitter" is chambered in .444 Marlin. It features 2/3-length magazines (5-shot capacity), straight-grip walnut stocks with cut checkering, recoil pads and porting at the muzzle to reduce kick. *Length:* 37" (barrel 18.5") *Weight:* 6.75 pounds
Price: (with sights) $612.00

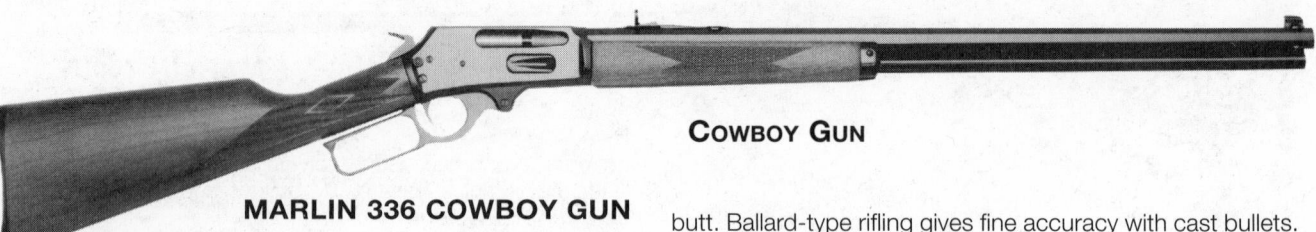

COWBOY GUN

MARLIN 336 COWBOY GUN

Available in 30/30 and 38/55, this rifle has a 24-inch octagon barrel and 6-shot full-length magazine. The checkered, straight-grip walnut stock has a hard-rubber butt. Ballard-type rifling gives fine accuracy with cast bullets. Marble open sights add a traditional touch. *Length:* 42-1/2 inches, *Weight:* 7-1/2 pounds
Price: $697.00

MODEL 336SS in
Stainless Steel with Cut Checkering

30/30 Win. Lever action; 6-shot tubular magazine; approx. wt. 7lbs.; 20" stainless steel Micro-Groove® barrel; hammer block safety; 38.5" o.a. length; genuine American black walnut checkered pistol grip stock with fluted comb and tough Mar-Shield® finish; rubber rifle butt pad; nickel-plated swivel studs; adjustable folding semi-buckhorn rear, ramp front sight with brass bead and removable Wide-Scan™ hood; tapped for receiver sight and scope mount; offset hammer spur for scope use – works right or left. Stainless steel receiver, barrel, lever, trigger guard plate, magazine tube and loading gate. Safety lock included.
Price: $608.00

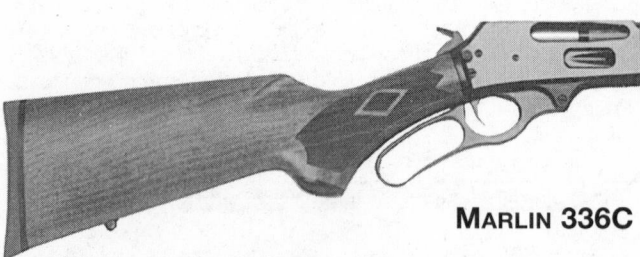

MARLIN 336C

SPECIFICATIONS

Calibers: 30-30 Win., and 35 Rem. *Capacity:* 6-shot tubular magazine *Action:* Lever action w/hammer block safety; deeply blued metal surfaces; receiver top sandblasted to prevent glare *Barrel:* 20" Micro-Groove® barrel

Sights: Adjustable folding semibuckhorn rear; ramp front sight w/brass bead and Wide-Scan™ hood; tapped for receiver sight and scope mount; offset hammer spur for scope use (works right or left) *Overall Length:* 38.5" *Weight:* 7 lbs. *Stock:* Checkered American black walnut pistol-grip stock w/fluted comb and Mar-Shield® finish; rubber rifle buttpad; swivel studs
Price: $502.00
   Model 336 A, 30-30 only, birch stock 429.00
   Model 336 CC, 30-30 only, camo stock 478.00

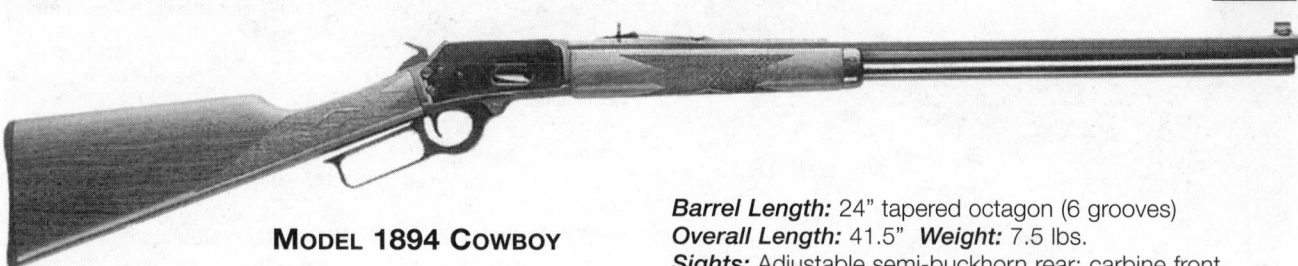

MODEL 1894 COWBOY

SPECIFICATIONS
Calibers: 357 Mag./38 Special, 44 Mag./44 Special, 45 Colt *Action:* Lever action w/squared finger lever
Capacity: 10-shot tubular magazine

Barrel Length: 24" tapered octagon (6 grooves)
Overall Length: 41.5" *Weight:* 7.5 lbs.
Sights: Adjustable semi-buckhorn rear; carbine front
Stock: Straight-grip American black walnut w/cut-checkering and hard rubber buttplate
Features: Mar-Shield™ finish; blued steel forend cap; side ejection; blued metal surfaces; hammer block safety
Price: $775.00

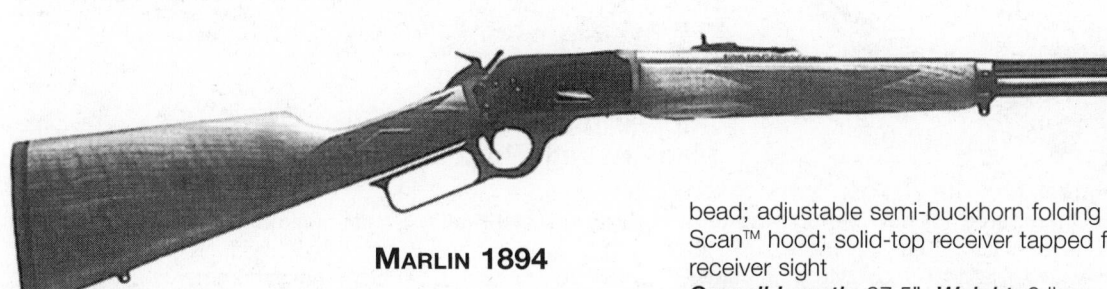

MARLIN 1894

SPECIFICATIONS
Calibers: 44 Rem. Mag./44 Special *Capacity:* 10-shot tubular magazine *Action:* Lever action w/square finger lever; hammer block safety *Barrel Length:* 20" w/deep-cut Ballard-type rifling *Sights:* Ramp front sight w/brass

bead; adjustable semi-buckhorn folding rear and Wide-Scan™ hood; solid-top receiver tapped for scope mount or receiver sight
Overall Length: 37.5" *Weight:* 6 lbs.
Stock: Checkered American black walnut stock w/Mar-Shield® finish; blued steel forend cap; swivel studs
Price: $526.00
Also Available: MODEL 1894C (not shown) similar to 1894 except .357 Magnum, 38 Spec., 18.5" barrel, 9-shot magazine.
Price: $526.00

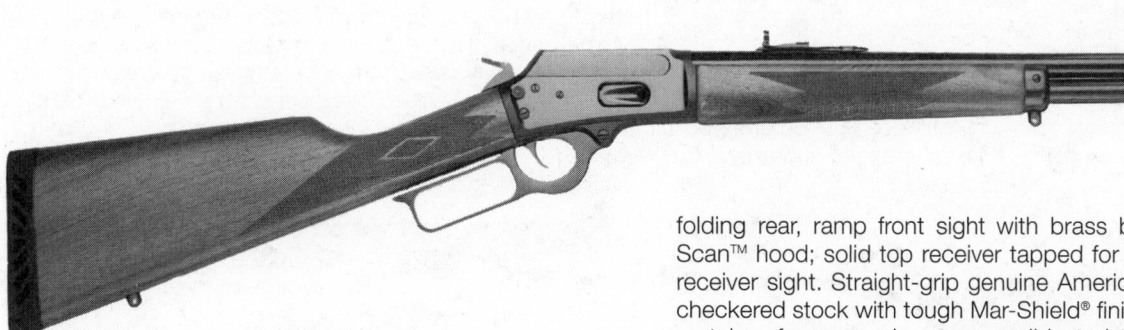

MODEL 1894P
with Ported Barrel

44 Rem. Magnum/44 Special. Lever action; 8-shot tubular magazine; squared finger lever; 16.25" ported barrel with deep-cut Ballard-type rifling; hammer block safety; 33.75" o.a. length; approx. wt. 5.75 lbs.; adjustable semi-buckhorn

folding rear, ramp front sight with brass bead and Wide-Scan™ hood; solid top receiver tapped for scope mount or receiver sight. Straight-grip genuine American black walnut checkered stock with tough Mar-Shield® finish; deeply blued metal surfaces; receiver top sandblasted to prevent glare; ventilated recoil pad; swivel studs; blued steel fore-end cap; offset hammer spur for scope use—works right or left. Safety lock included.
Price: $546.00
Also Available
   MODEL 1894 CP (357 Mag/38 Spec) 546.00

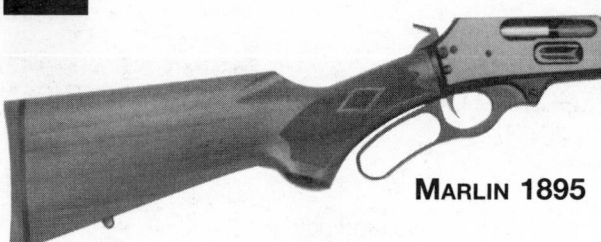

MARLIN 1895

SPECIFICATIONS

Caliber: 45-70 Government **Capacity:** 4-shot tubular magazine **Action:** Lever action; hammer block safety; receiver top sandblasted to prevent glare **Barrel:** 22" w/deep-cut Ballard-type rifling **Sights:** Ramp front sight w/brass bead; adjustable semibuckhorn folding rear and

Wide-Scan™ hood; receiver tapped for scope mount or receiver sight **Overall Length:** 40.5" **Weight:** 7.5 lbs. **Stock:** Checkered American black walnut pistol-grip stock w/rubber rifle buttpad and Mar-Shield® finish; swivel studs
Price: **$599.00**
Also available: MODEL 1895G "GUIDE GUN" WITH PORTED BARREL. Same caliber, capacity, action, sights. Stock has straight grip, ventilated recoil pad. **Barrel Length:** 18.5"
Overall Length: 37" **Weight:** 6.75 lbs.
Price: **$612.00**
   Model 1895 GS in stainless steel. 719.00

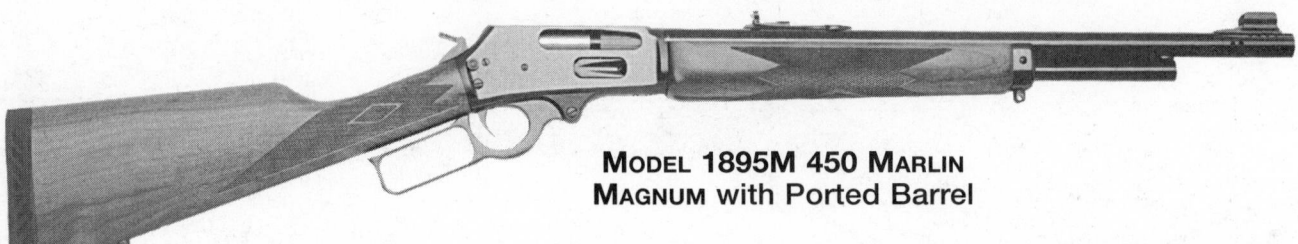

MODEL 1895M 450 MARLIN MAGNUM with Ported Barrel

Chambered for new belted magnum cartridge. Lever action; 4-shot tubular magazine; 18.5" ported barrel with Ballard-type cut rifling; hammer block safety; 37" o.a. length; approx. wt. 6.75 lbs.; genuine American black walnut straight-grip stock with cut checkering; ventiliated recoil pad; tough Mar-Shield® finish; swivel

studs; adjustable folding semi-buckhorn rear, ramp front sight with brass bead and Wide-Scan™ hood; receiver tapped for scope mount or receiver sight; offset hammer spur for scope use – works right or left; deeply blued metal surfaces; receiver top sandblasted to prevent glare. Safety lock included.
Price: **$660.00**

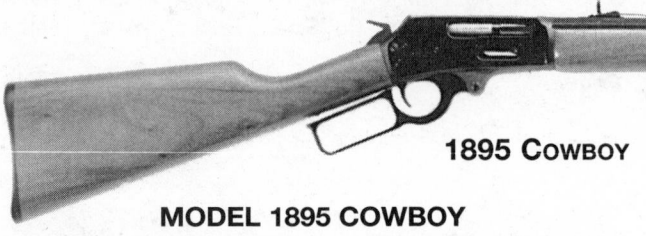

1895 COWBOY

MODEL 1895 COWBOY

45-70 Government. 9-shot tubular magazine; squared finger lever; 26" tapered octagon barrel with deep-cut Ballard-type rifling; hammer block safety; 44.5" o.a. length; approx. wt. 8

lbs.; straight-grip genuine American black walnut stock with hard rubber butt plate and tough Mar-Shield® finish; blued steel fore-end cap; adjustable Marble semi-buckhorn rear, Marble carbine front sight; receiver tapped for scope mount or receiver sight; offset hammer spur for scope use – works right or left; deeply blued metal surfaces; receiver top sandblasted to prevent glare. Safety lock included.
Price: **$775.00**

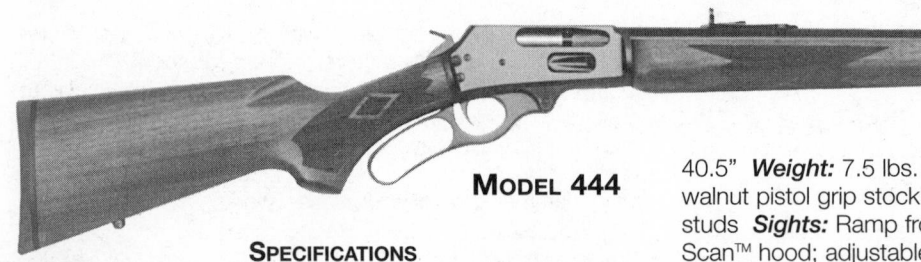

MODEL 444

SPECIFICATIONS

Caliber: 444 Marlin **Capacity:** 5-shot tubular magazine
Barrel: 22" w/deep-cut Ballard-type rifling **Overall Length:**

40.5" **Weight:** 7.5 lbs. **Stock:** Checkered American black walnut pistol grip stock with rubber rifle buttpad; swivel studs **Sights:** Ramp front sight with brass bead and Wide-Scan™ hood; adjustable semibuckhorn folding rear; receiver tapped for scope mount or receiver sight
Price: **$599.00**

MARLIN 22 TARGET RIFLE

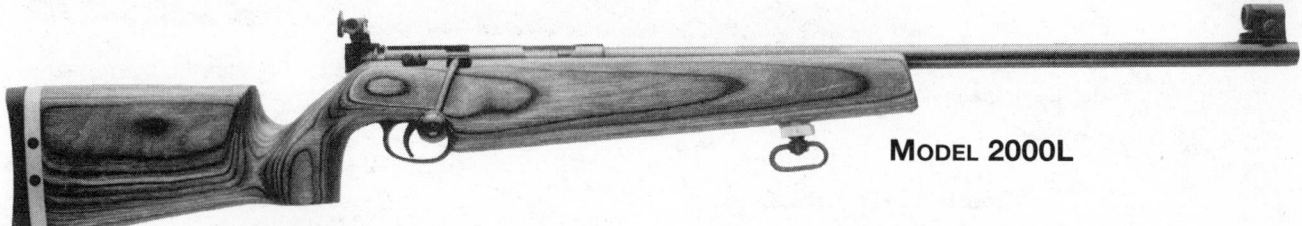

MODEL 2000L

SPECIFICATIONS

Caliber: 22 LR only   *Capacity:* Single shot   *Action:* Bolt action; thumb safety; patented two-stage target trigger; red cocking indicator   *Barrel Length:* 22" heavy, selected Micro-Groove w/match chamber and recessed muzzle   *Overall*

Length: 41"   *Weight:* 8 lbs.   *Sights:* Fully adjustable target rear peep sight; hooded front sight w/10 aperture inserts   *Stock:* Laminated black/grey w/ambidextrous pistol grip; butt plate adjustable for length of pull, height, angle; aluminum forearm
Price: $711.00

MERKEL RIFLES

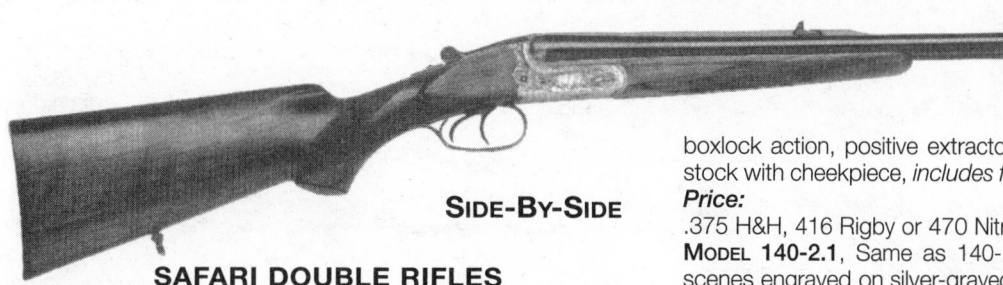

SIDE-BY-SIDE

SAFARI DOUBLE RIFLES

MODEL 140-2, Greener cross bolt with double under barrel locking lugs, scroll engraved silver-grayed receiver, Anson & Deely

boxlock action, positive extractors, double triggers, pistol grip stock with cheekpiece, *includes fine leather fitted luggage case.*
Price:
.375 H&H, 416 Rigby or 470 Nitro Express **$8,995.00**
MODEL 140-2.1, Same as 140-1, but with fine African game scenes engraved on silver-grayed receiver.
Price:
.375 H&H, 416 Rigby or 470 Nitro Express **$9,995.00**

MOSSBERG RIFLES

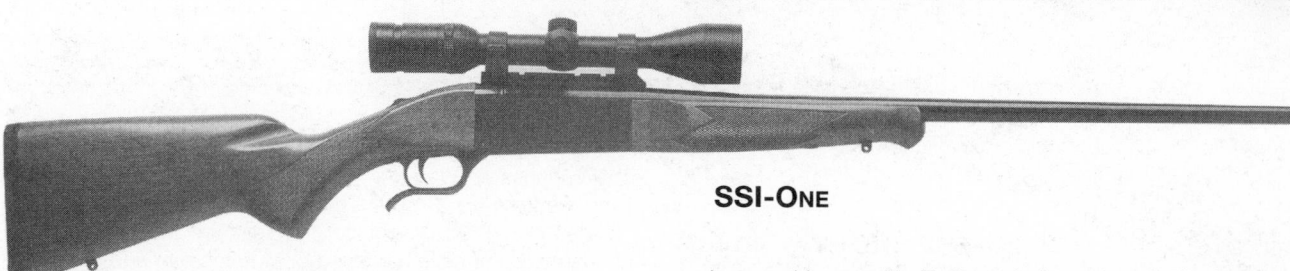

SSI-ONE

MOSSBERG SSI-ONE SINGLE SHOT INTERCHANGEABLE RIFLE & SHOTGUN

The Mossberg SSI is a bold step into the competitive centerfire rifle market for the 80-year-old company. This hammerless single-shot with quick-change barrels offers a choice of six chamberings and is easy for left-handed shooters to use.

SPECIFICATIONS

Calibers, Gauge: .223 Rem., .22-250 Rem., .243 Win., .270 Win., .308 Rem., .30-06 Sprg., 12 Gauge rifled slug

and smoothbore with Turkey choke tube, 3.5" chamber *Finish:* Classic Satin finished stock & forend. Matte blue receiver & barrel   *Length Overall:* 40" Sporter, Varmint, Slug   *Barrel Length:* 24" Sporter, Varmint, Slug   *Action:* Lever-opening, break-action, top tang safety, selective ejector   *Approx. Weight:* 8 lbs. Sporter, Slug 10 lbs. Varmint   *Sights:* Barrel drilled and tapped for scope mounts (scope base included)   *Stock:* Select Walnut
Price: $459.00
   .22-250 w/bull barrel 480.00

1866 SHORT RIFLE

Designed for the Cowboy Action Shooter, this model features a handy 20" octagon barrel with a semi-buckhorn rear sight.

SPECIFICATIONS
Caliber: .38 Special, .44-40 or .45 Colt *Barrel Length:* 20" *Weight:* 7 lbs. 8 oz. *Overall Length:* 39.25"
Sights: Buckhorn rear, blade front
Price: $725.00

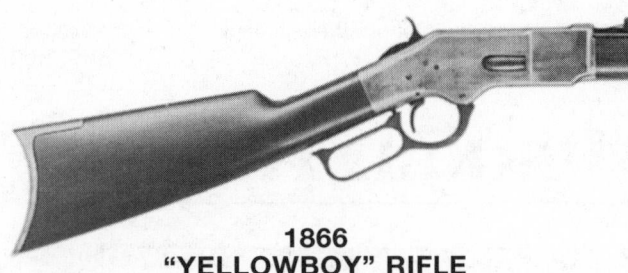

1866 "YELLOWBOY" RIFLE

The 1866 model was Oliver Winchester's improved version of the Henry rifle. Called the "Yellowboy" because of its polished brass receiver, it was popular with Indians, settlers and cattlemen alike.

SPECIFICATIONS
Caliber: 38 Special, 44-40, 45 Colt *Barrel Length:* 24" full octagon *Overall Length:* 42.5" *Weight:* 8.25 lbs.
Sights: Blade front; open ladder rear *Stock:* Walnut
Price: $725.00
Saddle Gun version w/19" barrel 715.00

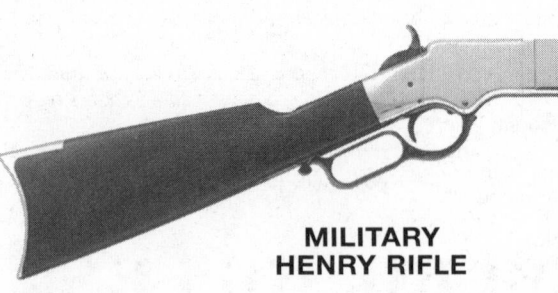

MILITARY HENRY RIFLE

This accurate replica of "that damned Yankee rifle" – The Henry – gave troops unrivaled firepower in its day. Navy Arms redesigned the highly polished brass frame by specially reinforcing it to handle the demands of skirmishing and Cowboy Action Shooting. N-SSA approved. Authentic in every detail, including left-side sling swivel and buttplate trap.
Price: $955.00

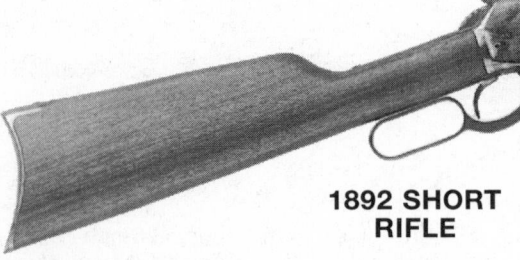

1892 SHORT RIFLE

1892 SHORT RIFLE

The Winchester 92 came with several barrel lengths. Two are available from Navy Arms. The "Short Rifle" is a replica of the "Texas Special" 92 Winchester that featured a 20" full octagonal barrel. Color case hardened or blue receiver and furniture.

SPECIFICATIONS
Calibers: 357 Mag., 44-40 or 45 Colt
Barrel Length: 20" or 24" octagon
Weight: 6.25 lbs. or 7 lbs.
Sights: Blade front; semibuckhorn rear
Stock: American walnut
Price: $525.00
Also Available:
Stainless Steel 565.00

IRON FRAME HENRY
SPECIFICATIONS
Caliber: 44-40 or 45 Colt *Capacity:* 13 rounds
Barrel Length: 24" *Overall Length:* 43"
Weight: 9 lbs. *Stock:* Walnut
Finish: Blued or casehardened *Feature:* Steel frame
Price: $1,005.00

NAVY ARMS REPLICA RIFLES

RIFLES

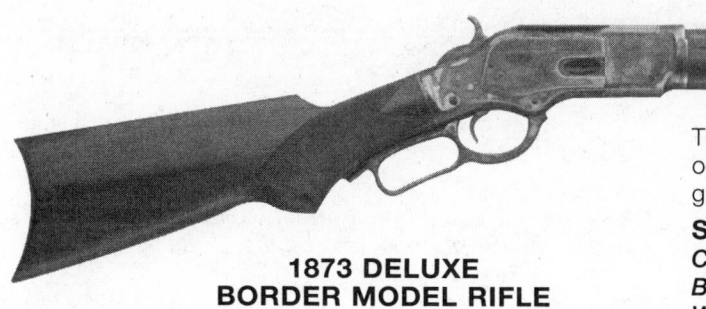

1873 DELUXE
BORDER MODEL RIFLE

This deluxe version of the 1873 Border Model features a 20" octagonal barrel and a walnut stock with checkered pistol grip and forend.

SPECIFICATIONS
Caliber: 357 Mag., 44-40 or .45 Colt
Barrel Length: 20" *Overall Length:* 39.25"
Weight: 7 lbs. 6 oz.
Sights: Blade front, buckhorn rear
Price: $995.00

REPLICA 1873 WINCHESTER RIFLE
(not shown)

Known as "The Gun That Won the West," the 1873 was the most popular lever-action rifle of its time. This fine replica features a case hardened receiver.

SPECIFICATIONS
Caliber: 357 Mag., 44-40 or 45 Colt
Barrel Length: 24" *Overall Length:* 43"

Weight: 8.25 lbs.
Sights: Blade front; open ladder rear
Stock: Walnut
Price: $875.00
Also available: 1873 CARBINE
(19" barrel) 855.00
1873 "BORDER MODEL" RIFLE
(20" Oct. barrel) 875.00

REPLICA 1873
WINCHESTER SPORTING RIFLE

This replica of the elegant Winchester 1873 Sporting Rifle features a checkered pistol grip, buttstock, case hardened receiver and blued octagonal barrel.

SPECIFICATIONS
Caliber: 357 Mag., 44-40 or 45 Colt
Barrel Length: 24"
Overall Length: 43 1/4"
Weight: 8 lbs. 4 oz.
Sights: Blade front; buckhorn rear
Prices:
24" Barrel. $995.00

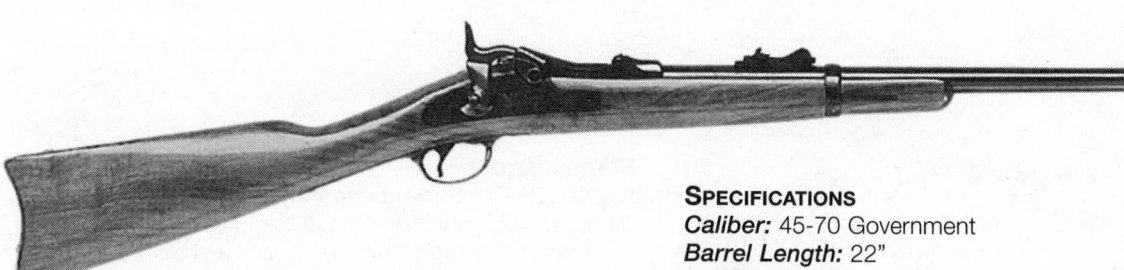

1873 SPRINGFIELD CAVALRY CARBINE

A reproduction of the classic U.S. "Trapdoor" Springfield carbine used by the 7th Cavalry at The Battle of Little Big Horn.

SPECIFICATIONS
Caliber: 45-70 Government
Barrel Length: 22"
Overall Length: 40.5"
Weight: 7 lbs.
Sights: Blade front, military ladder rear
Stock: Walnut *Features:* Saddle bar with ring
Price: $930.00

Rifles

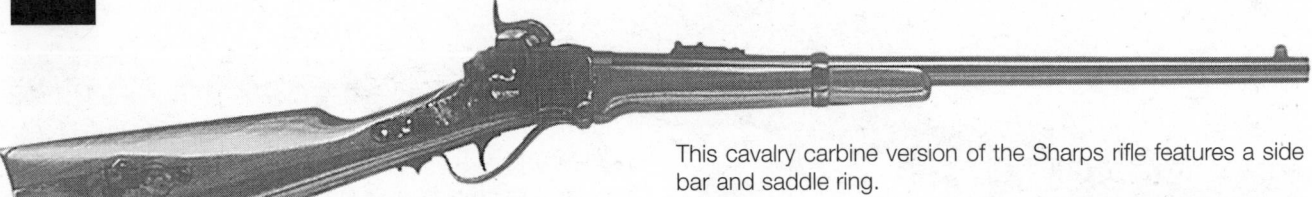

1874 SHARPS CAVALRY CARBINE

This cavalry carbine version of the Sharps rifle features a side bar and saddle ring.

SPECIFICATIONS
Caliber: 45-70 percussion *Barrel Length:* 22" *Overall Length:* 39" *Weight:* 7 ³/₄ lbs. *Sights:* Blade front; military ladder rear *Stock:* Walnut
Price:. $1,000.00

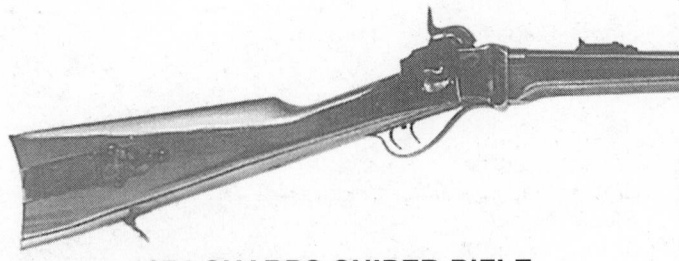

1874 SHARPS SNIPER RIFLE

This 1874 three-band sharpshooter's rifle was a popular target rifle at the Creedmoor military matches and was the issue longarm of the New York State Militia.

SPECIFICATIONS
Caliber: 45-70 *Barrel Length:* 30" *Overall Length:* 46 ³/₄" *Weight:* 8 lbs. 8 oz. *Stock:* Walnut *Features:* Double-set triggers; casehardened receiver; patchbox and furniture
Price:. $1,195.00
Also available:
SINGLE TRIGGER INFANTRY MODEL. **$1,125.00**
PLAINS RIFLE (32" barrel) **1,055.00**

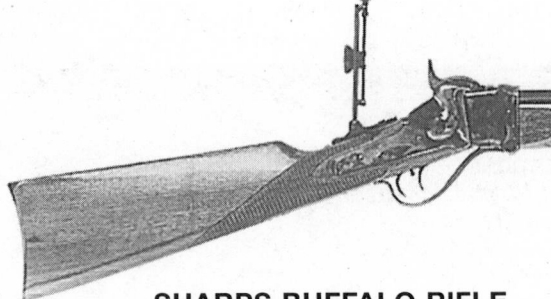

SHARPS BUFFALO RIFLE

This deluxe version of the rifle that came to be known simply as "buffalo gun" was favored by market hunters on the Great Plains after the Civil War.

SPECIFICATIONS
Caliber: 45-70 *Barrel Length:* 28" octagonal
Overall Length: 46" *Weight:* 10 lbs. 10 oz. *Sights:* Blade front, ladder rear (tang sight optional w/set triggers only–**$75.00** *Stock:* Walnut *Features:* Color casehardened receiver and furniture; double-set trigger
Price:. $1,160.00

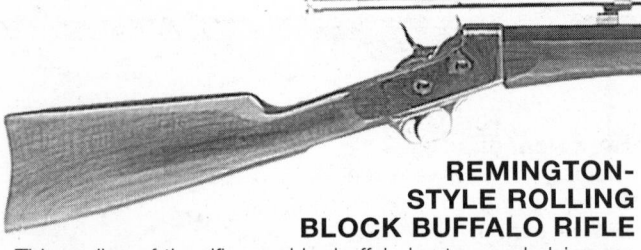

REMINGTON-STYLE ROLLING BLOCK BUFFALO RIFLE

This replica of the rifle used by buffalo hunters and plainsmen of the 1800s features a case hardened receiver, trigger guard and walnut stock and forend. The tang is drilled and tapped to accept the optional Creedmoor sight.

SPECIFICATIONS
Caliber: 45-70 *Barrel Length:* 26" or 30"; full octagon *Sights:* Blade front, open notch rear *Stock:* Walnut stock and forend *Feature:* Shown with optional 32.5" Model 1860 brass telescopic sight **$210.00**; Compact Model (18"): **$200.00**
Price: With casehardened steel **$765.00**
Creedmoor model w/globe front, folding tang sights, checkered pistol grip stock **995.00**

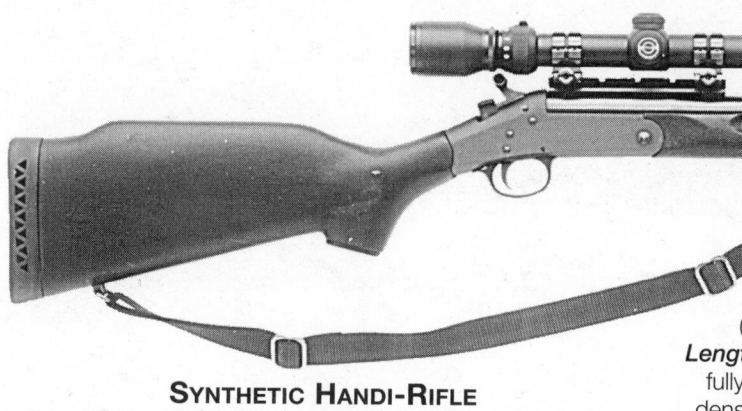

Synthetic Handi-Rifle

New England Firearms® Handi-Rifle now features a black Monte Carlo synthetic stock and forend. This version includes a factory-mounted scope base and an offset hammer extension to ease cocking when a scope is mounted. The rifles all include the patented NEF Transfer Bar System, which virtually eliminates the possibility of accidental discharge.

Specifications

Calibers: 22 Hornet, 223 Rem., 243 Win., 270 Win., 280 Rem., 30-30 Win., 30-06 Springfield; 44 Rem. Mag., 45-70 Gov't **Action:** Break-open; side lever release; automatic ejection **Barrel Length:** 22" (26" in 270 Win.) **Overall Length:** 38" (40" in 270 Win.) **Length Of Pull:** 14.25" **Weight:** 7 lbs. **Sights:** Ramp front; fully adjustable rear; tapped for scope mount **Stock:** High density polymer; black matte finish; sling swivels; recoil pad
Price: **$228.95**
Also available: HANDI-RIFLE with hardwood stock in all chambering plus 308 Win., 7x57, 7x64, .357 Mag. with sights or scope base, depending on chambering and barrel style HANDI-RIFLE YOUTH with hardwood stock, 223 Rem. and 243 Win.. . . . . **227.95**

RIFLES

Handi-Rifle Youth, 223 Rem and 243 Win.

Super Light Youth Handi-Rifle

SUPER LIGHT YOUTH HANDI-RIFLE™

New England Firearms' youth version of its Superlight Handi-Rifle with lightweight synthetic stock and Super Light taper on the barrel. The matte black synthetic stock and forend feature a non-slip finish plus a sling, swivels and recoil pad.

Specifications

Caliber: 22 Hornet, 223 Rem & 243 Win. **Action:** Single shot; break-open; side lever release; automatic ejection **Barrel Length:** 20" **Overall Length:** 33" **Drop At Heel:** 1

¹/₈" **Drop At Comb:** 1 ¹/₈" **Length Of Pull:** 11.75" **Weight:** 5 ¹/₃ lbs. **Sights:** Ramp front; fully adjustable rear; tapped for scope mount **Stock:** High density polymer; black matte finish; sling swivels; recoil pad
Price: **$227.95**
Also available: SUPER LIGHT HANDI-RIFLE in adult configurations SPORTSTER youth or adult in 22 LR and 22 WMR **121.95**
The SURVIVOR is available in 223 and 308. Features include bull barrel, hollow synthetic stock, thumbscrew take down **227.95**

Survivor 223 and 308 Bull Barrel

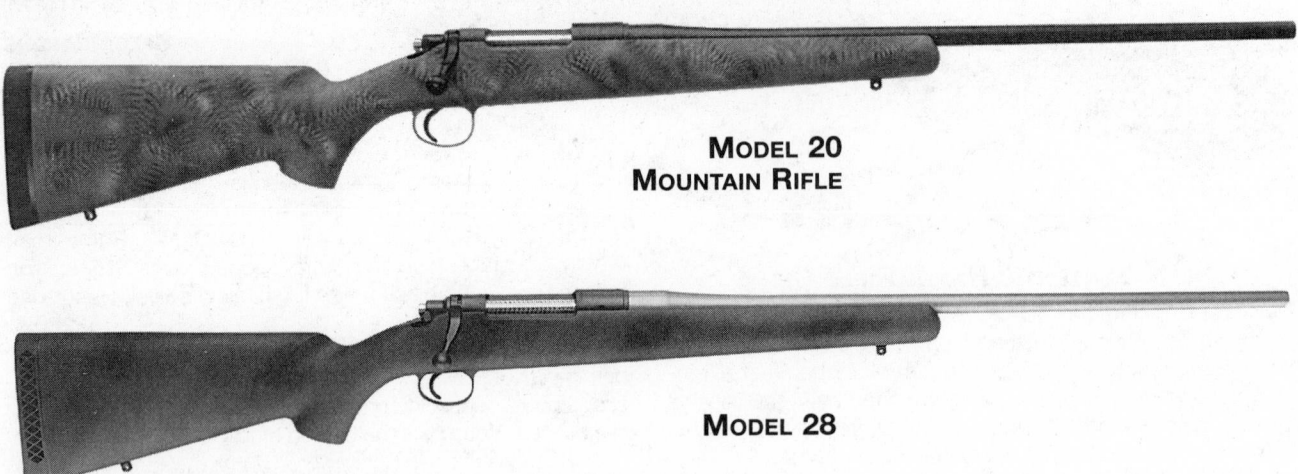

**MODEL 20
MOUNTAIN RIFLE**

MODEL 28

MODEL 20 SERIES

SPECIFICATIONS
Calibers (Short Action): 6mm Rem., 17 Rem., 22 Hornet, 222 Rem., 222 Rem. Mag., 22-250 Rem., 223 Rem., 243 Win., 250-3000 Savage, 257 Roberts, 257 Ackley, 7x57 Mauser, 7X57 Ackley, 7mm-08 Rem., 284 Win., 300 Savage, 308 Win., 358 Win.
Barrel Length: 22" **Weight:** 4.75 lbs.
Safety: Two-position safety allows bolt to open or lock with sear blocked
Stock: Kevlar/Graphite composite; choice of 7 or more colors
Price: $2,500.00
   Left Hand 2,600.00

Also Available:
MODEL 24 SERIES (Long Action) in 270 Win., 30-06, 25-06, 280 Rem., 280 Ackley, 338-06, 35 Whelen **Weight:** 5.25 lbs.
   Barrel Length: 22" $2,600.00
   Same as above in Left-Hand Model 2,700.00
MODEL 28 SERIES (Magnum Action) in 264 Win., 7mm Rem., 300 Win., 338 **Weight:** 5.5 lbs.
   Barrel Length: 24" 2,900.00
   Same as above in Left-Hand Model 3,000.00
MODEL 40 SERIES (Magnum Action) in 300 Wby. and 416 Rigby **Weight:** 6.5 lbs. and up
   Barrel Length: 24" 2,900.00
   Same as above in Left-Hand Model 3,000.00

MODEL 20 RF

SPECIFICATIONS
Caliber: 22 LR
Barrel Length: 22" (Douglas Premium #1 Contour)
Weight: 5.25 lbs.
Sights: None (drilled and tapped for scope)
Stock: Composite
Features: Recoil pad; sling swivels; fully adjustable Timney trigger; 3-function safety; color options
Price:
   Single Shot $800.00
   Repeater 850.00

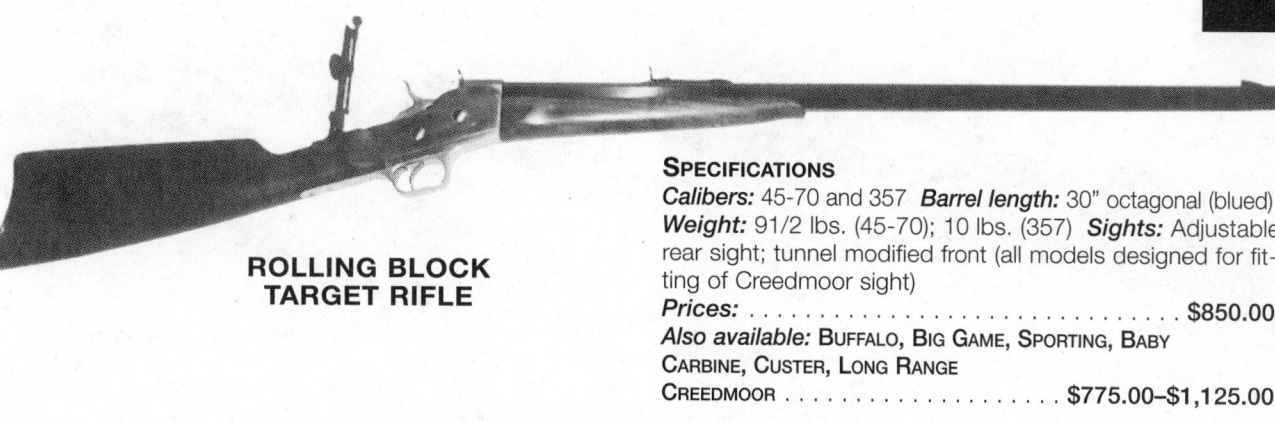

ROLLING BLOCK
TARGET RIFLE

SPECIFICATIONS
Calibers: 45-70 and 357 *Barrel length:* 30" octagonal (blued)
Weight: 9 1/2 lbs. (45-70); 10 lbs. (357) *Sights:* Adjustable
rear sight; tunnel modified front (all models designed for fitting of Creedmoor sight)
Prices: $850.00
Also available: BUFFALO, BIG GAME, SPORTING, BABY
CARBINE, CUSTER, LONG RANGE
CREEDMOOR . . . . $775.00–$1,125.00

RIFLES

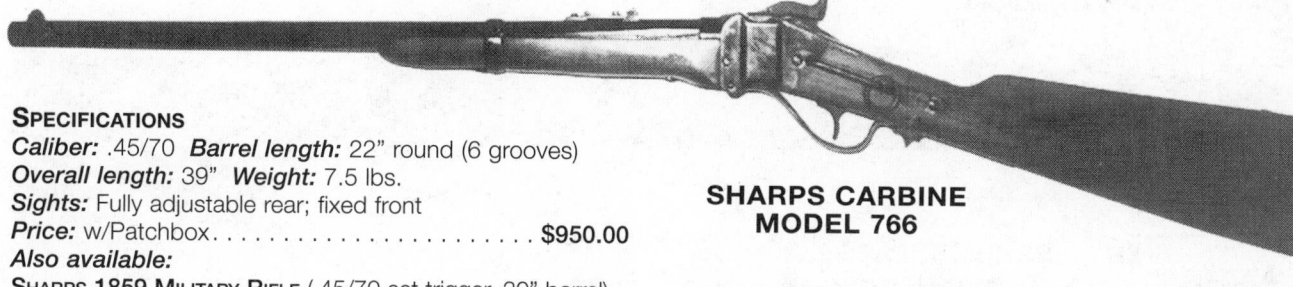

SHARPS CARBINE
MODEL 766

SPECIFICATIONS
Caliber: .45/70 *Barrel length:* 22" round (6 grooves)
Overall length: 39" *Weight:* 7.5 lbs.
Sights: Fully adjustable rear; fixed front
Price: w/Patchbox. $950.00
Also available:
SHARPS 1859 MILITARY RIFLE (.45/70 set trigger, 30" barrel)
Price:. 1,099.00
SHARPS SPORTING RIFLE .40/65 set triggers, 32" oct. barrel
Price:. 1,075.00

SHARPS LONG RANGE TARGET RIFLE (.45/70, .45/90, .45/120,
34" half octagon barrel, target sights)
Price:. $1,425.00

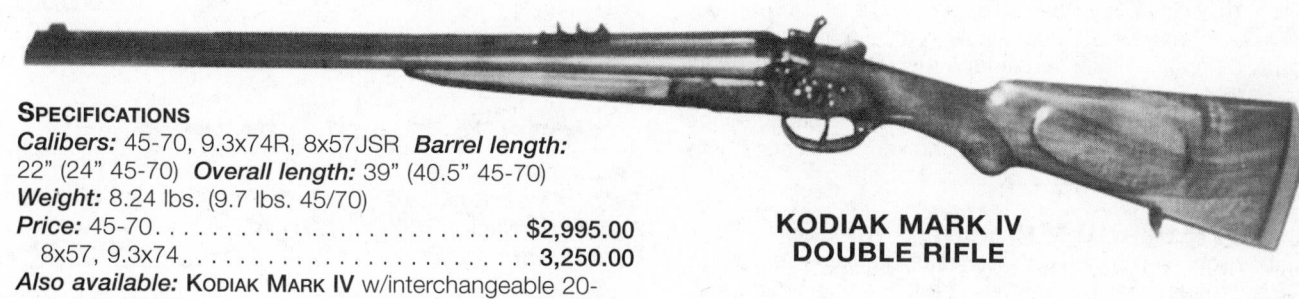

SPECIFICATIONS
Calibers: 45-70, 9.3x74R, 8x57JSR *Barrel length:*
22" (24" 45-70) *Overall length:* 39" (40.5" 45-70)
Weight: 8.24 lbs. (9.7 lbs. 45/70)
Price: 45-70. . . . . $2,995.00
8x57, 9.3x74. . . . . 3,250.00
Also available: KODIAK MARK IV w/interchangeable 20-
gauge barrel *Price:*. $4,250.00

KODIAK MARK IV
DOUBLE RIFLE

MORTIMER
TARGET RIFLE

SPECIFICATIONS
English-style European walnut stock with cheekpiece and
hand checkering; color-case-hardened lock; 54 caliber, 7-
groove barrel (octagon to round) 36" long. *Overall length:*
52" *Weight:* 8.8 pounds
Price: $995.00

PRAIRIE GUN WORKS

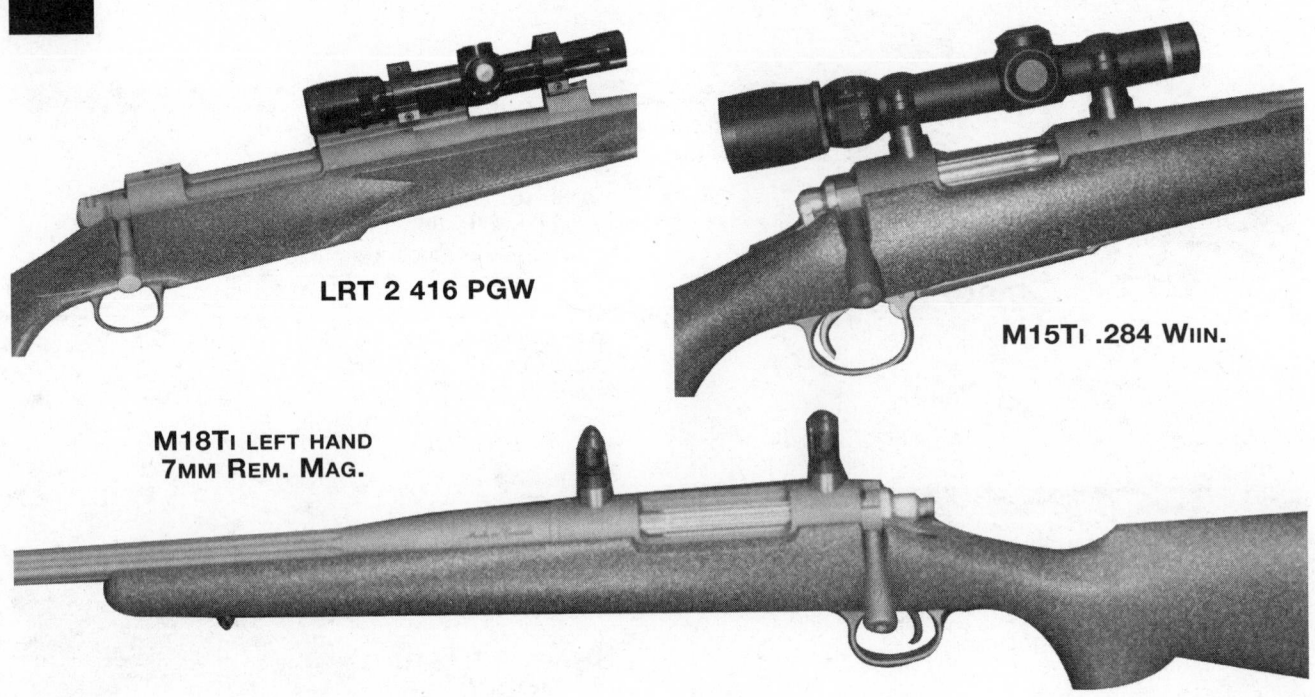

LRT 2 416 PGW

M15Ti .284 Win.

**M18Ti left hand
7mm Rem. Mag.**

LRT-2 SERIES RIFLES

Dangerous game, long range target, and tactical versions are available in this series. The smallest rounds that this action is suitable for is the .378 and Rigby based magnums. These rifles are ideal for large calibers such as the .505 Gibbs (and PGW line of wildcats), and other large rounds like the .585 Nyati. A 4-shot magazine box is available on this rifle. The .408 Cheyenne (.416) is capable of firing a 400-grain bullet at over 3000-fps, making this the flattest shooting and hardest hitting .416 on the market. Stainless pillars and McMillan "Express" or Tactical stocks hold the recoil. These rifles are available with several different scope mount/sight options, plus muzzle brakes. Weights in this series range from 10 to 18 pounds.

M15 AND M18 SERIES RIFLES

Lightweight rifles based on Ti series of Titanium rifle actions. These rifles feature match grade stainless barrels, kevlar/glass stocks, Titanium scope bases, fully adjustable triggers, and customer supplied specifications such as length of pull, barrel length, and twist. The M15Ti rifle (short) is suitable for cartridges up to the size of the .284 Win. and its wildcats. The M18Ti rifle (long) is suitable for cartridges up to the Remington "Ultramag" and its wildcats. These rifles can be built from 4.25 lbs. to 6.25 lbs.

Some of the unique features found on the Ti series rifles: cone breech, 1/4"-28 base/ring screw attachment, wire EDM lugways, one piece bolt, double plunger ejectors, Sako type extraction, left or right hand bolt/port configurations available, aluminum pillar bedding, removablle muzzle brake with cap, barrel flutes X8.

Prices:

M15Ti Ultralight.	$2,800.00
M18Ti Ultralight.	2,800.00
M15Ti Varmint	2,400.00
M15Ti Benchrest.	2,400.00
M15 Tactical stainless	2,900.00
M18 Tactical stainless	2,900.00
LRT-2 PGW/Gibbs	3,900.00
LRT-3.50 single shot	4,200.00

MODEL M-15 ULTRA LITE (not shown)

SPECIFICATIONS

Caliber: Most Short Action calibers
Action: Remington 700 Short Action
Barrel length: 22" Douglas Match Grade
Length of pull: 13.5"
Weight: 4.5-5.25 lbs.
Stock: Fiberglass-Kevlar composite w/integral recoil lug; recoil pad installed *Finish:* Black or grey textured finish
Sights: Custom aircraft-grade aluminum scope mounts
Features: Trigger set and polished for 3 lb. pull; bolt fluted, hollowed and tapped w/Ultra Lite custom firing pin and bolt shroud
Price: $2,800.00
Also available:
MODEL M-18. Same specifications and price as Model M-15, except chambered for long-action calibers (up to 340 Weatherby)
Price: 2,900.00

DOUBLE BARREL RIFLE .577 NITRO

The word "Express" was coined by James Purdey the younger to publicize his rifles. He likened their performance to a railway or "Express" train, which was heavy, travelled with great velocity and had a flat trajectory.

The action blocks for all guns are cut from certified forgings, for consistency of grain throughout, and are so fitted to the barrels as to give an absolute joint.

The actioner then fits the fore-part, the locks, the strikers and the safety work before finally detonating the action.

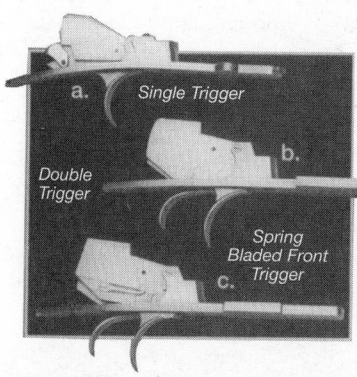

a. Single Trigger

Double Trigger **b.**

Spring Bladed Front Trigger **c.**

Purdey's double-barrel Express rifles are built to customer specifications on actions sized to each particular cartridge. Standard chamberings include .375 H&H Magnum and .470, .577 and .600 Nitro Express. The Purdey side by side action patented in 1880 is still made now with only very minor changes. The action mechanism, designed by Frederick Beesley, retains a portion of the energy in the mainsprings to facilitate the opening of the gun.

The over-under is derived from the Woodward, patented in 1913.

A – Single trigger
The Purdey single trigger works both by inertia and mechanically. It is simple, effective and fast. The firing sequence is fixed, therefore no barrel selection is possible.

B & C – Double Triggers
The standard double triggers (B) can be augmented with an articulated front trigger (C). This device alleviates damage to the back of the trigger finger on discharge.

Purdey "Rail Mount" system with integral recoil bar.

Purdey's own large calibre action

Classic Mauser '98 Action

Purdey makes its own dedicated actions for bolt rifles in the following calibers: .375 H&H, .416/450 Rigby or other, .500 and .505 Gibbs.

The action length is suited to cartridge length in each caliber. Mauser Square Bridge and Mauser '98 actions are available.

RAIL MOUNT SYSTEM
This is Purdey's own system for big bolt rifles. It is very secure and facilitates fast on/off. Rings and mounts are all made with an integral recoil bar from a single piece of steel. This system is recommended for Purdey actions and Mauser Square Bridge actions.

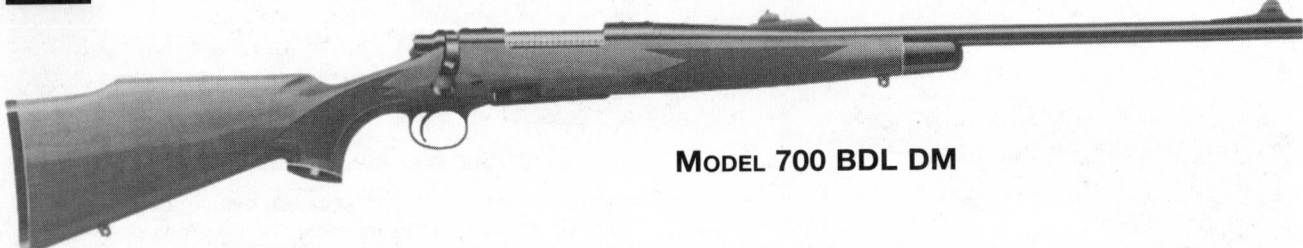

MODEL 700 BDL DM

MODEL 700 BDL DM

The MODEL 700 REMINGTON bolt-action rifle first appeared in 1962. Since then it has become one of the most popular rifles of all time and is now available in myriad configurations and chamberings. MODEL 700 BDL DM rifles feature the standard Remington BDL barrel contour, with 22" barrels on standard-caliber models and 24" barrels on magnum-caliber rifles. The detachable box magazine holds 4 standard rounds, 3 magnums. Chamberings include .270, 30-06, 7mm Rem. Mag., .300 Win. Mag. Stainless version comes in .25-06, .270, .280, 7mm-08, .30-06, 7mm Rem. Mag., .300

Win. Mag. All barrels have a hooded front sight and adjustable rear sight. Additional features include polished blued-metal finish, high-gloss, Monte Carlo-style walnut stock, white line spacers, 20 lines-per-inch checkering, recoil pad and swivel studs. All models feature fine-line engraving on receiver front rings, rear bridges, non-ejection receiver sides and floorplates.

Prices: MODEL 700 BDL DM. $693.00
   Magnum 720.00
   Stainless 767.00-793.00

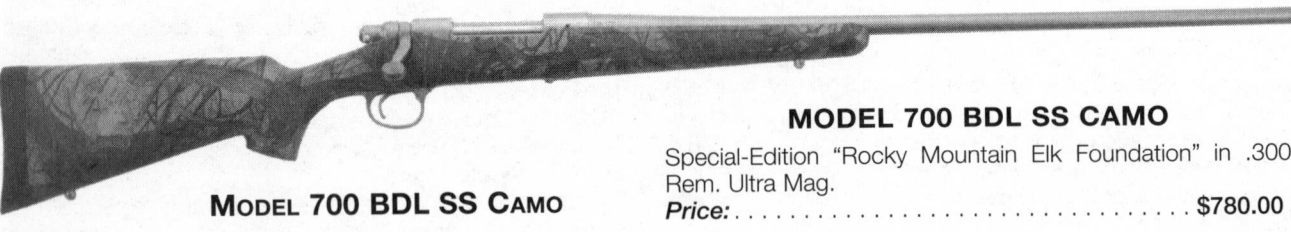

MODEL 700 BDL SS CAMO

MODEL 700 BDL SS CAMO

Special-Edition "Rocky Mountain Elk Foundation" in .300 Rem. Ultra Mag.
Price: $780.00

MODEL 700 BDL SS

MODEL 700 BDL AND BDL SS

This Model 700 features the Monte Carlo American walnut stock finished to a high gloss with fine-cut checkering. Also includes a hinged floorplate, sling swivel studs, hooded ramp front sight and adjustable rear sight. Also available in stainless synthetic version (Model 700 BDL SS) with stainless-steel barrel, receiver and bolt plus synthetic stock for maximum weather resistance.

MODEL 700 BDL

Prices: In 222 Rem., 22-250 Rem., 223 Rem., 243 Win., .280, 25-06 Rem., 270 Win., 30-06, 7mm-08. . . . . **$645.00**
In 17 Rem., 7mm Rem. Mag., 300 Win. Mag., .338 Win. Mag.. . . . . 672.00

Ultra Mags (7mm, 300, 338, 375) **685.00**
Left Hand in 270 Win., 30-06. . . . . **672.00**
Left Hand in 7mm Rem. Mag. **699.00**
Left Hand Ultra Mags. **712.00**
MODEL BDL SS (Stainless Synthetic)
In 270 Win. 30-06.. . . . . **692.00**
In 375 H&H Mag.. . . . . **719.00**
In 7mm Rem. Mag., 300 Win. Mag., .338 Win. Mag., 7mm Rem Ultra Mag., .375 Rem Ultra Mag., .300 Rem. Ultra Mag., .338 Rem. Ultra Mag.. . . . . . **732.00**

MODEL 700 BDL SS DM-B

Available in *Calibers:* 7mm STW, 300 Win. Mag., *Barrel length:* 25.5" (magnum contour barrel). Stainless synthetic detachable magazine with muzzle brake.
Price: $856.00

MODEL 700 VLS
(VARMINT LAMINATED STOCK)

The **MODEL 700 VLS** features a blued, heavy-contour varmint barrel, laminated synthetic stock, hinged magazine floorplate and sling swivel studs. **Barrel length:** 26"

Overall Length: 45.5" **Weight:** 9 lbs. **Length of pull:** 13 ³/₈" **Drop at comb:** ¹/₂" **Drop at heel:** ³/₈" **Chamberings:** .223, .22-250, 6mm Rem., .243, .308

Price:	$688.00
VS with synthetic barrel in .223, .22-250, .308	769.00
Left hand, same calibers	796.00
w/26" fluted barrel in 22-250 Rem., 223 Rem., 220 Swift	927.00

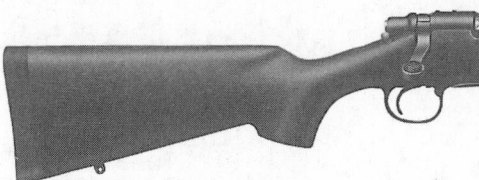

MODEL 700 "SENDERO"

Remington's Sendero rifle combines the accuracy features of the Model 700 Varmint Special with long action and magnum calibers for long-range hunting. The 26-inch barrel has a heavy varmint profile and features a spherical concave crown. For additional specifications, see table on the following page.

Price: .25-06, .270	$769.00
Magnum: 7mm Rem. Mag., .300 Win. Mag.	796.00

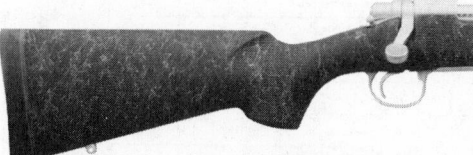

MODEL 700 SENDERO SF
(Stainless Fluted)

This version of the Model 700 Sendero features satin-finished stainless steel receiver and bolt and a 26-inch heavy stainless barrel with six longitudinal flutes designed to improve heat

dissipation and reduce gun weight (8.5 lbs.). A spherical, concave crown protects the muzzle. Other features include a composite synthetic fiberglass stock, graphite reinforced by du Pont Kevlar, and a full-length aluminum bedding block. **Chamberings:** .25-06, 7mm Rem. Mag, 7STW, .300 Win. Mag., .300 Ultra Mag., .338 Ultra Mag., 7mm Rem Ultra Mag

Price:	$927.00
Magnum	953.00
Ultra Magnum	967.00

MODEL 700 ADL

MODEL 700 ADL

Synthetic model has a fiberglass-reinforced synthetic stock, positive checkering, straight comb, raised cheekpiece and black rubber recoil pad. Stock and blued metalwork have a non-reflective black matte finish.

Price:	$543.00
Magnum	569.00
Synthetic	468.00
Synthetic/Magnum	495.00
Youth (1" shorter)	468.00

(See also table on the following page for prices, calibers and additional specifications)

RIFLES

REMINGTON BOLT-ACTION RIFLES

MODEL 700 TITANIUM

At 5 1/2 pounds (long-action) and 5 1/4 pounds (short-action), the new Model 700 Titanium is, as its name implies, an ideal rifle for high-altitude hunts. The key to its feathery feel starts with a titanium receiver (drilled and tapped for mounts). Titanium delivers incredible strength, but at a lighter weight than steel. Complementing the receiver is a bolt featuring spiral-cut flutes and a skeleton handle - both of which further reduce the overall weight. It has a 22" stainless steel barrel and is available in: 260 Rem, 270 Win, 7mm-08 Rem, and 30-06.

Price:. **$1,199.00**

MODEL 700 CENTERFIRE RIFLE SPECIFICATIONS

	17 Rem.	220 Swift	222 Rem.	22-250 Rem.	223 Rem.	6mm Rem.	243 Win.	25-06 Rem.	6.5x55 Swedish	250 savage	257 Roberts	270 Win.	280 Rem.	7mm-08 Rem.	7mm Rem. Mag.	30-06 Springfield	308 Win.	300 Win. Mag.	300 Wby. Mag.	35 Rem.	350 Rem. Mag.	35 Whelen	8mm Rem. Mag.	338 Win. Mag.	375 H&H Mag.	416 Rem. Mag.	458 Win. Mag.
Model Seven Lightweight	•				•	•	•							•			•										
Model Seven Stainless Synthetic					•																						
Model Seven Youth					•																						
Model Seven Custom KS				•										•			•				•	•					
Model Seven Mannlicher			•	•	•	•	•			•	•			•			•				•	•					
Model 700 ADL							•					•				•	•	•									
Model 700 Classic																			•								
Model 700 BDL	•		•	•	•		•	•				•	•	•	•	•	•							•			
Model 700 BDL LH				•			•					•			•	•	•										
Model 700 BDL, DM						•	•	•				•		•		•	•										
Model 700 BDL, DM, LH							•					•			•	•	•										
Model 700 BDL, SS, DM						•	•	•				•	•	•	•	•	•	•						•			
Model 700 Stainless Synthetic												•	•	•	•	•	•	•						•			
Model 700 Varmint Synthetic		•	•	•													•										
Model 700 Varmint Synthetic, Stainless, Fluted		•		•	•												•										
Model 700 VLS			•	•	•	•											•										
Model 700 Mountain Rifle DM							•	•				•	•	•		•	•										
Model 700 Mountain Rifle, Custom KS												•	•	•		•	•	•			•	•		•	•	•	•
Model 700 Mountain Rifle, Custom KS, LH												•	•	•		•	•	•			•	•		•	•		
Model 700 Mountain, Custom KS, Stainless												•	•	•		•	•	•			•	•			•	•	
Model 700 Safari Classic																								•	•	•	•
Model 700 Safari Classic, LH																									•	•	•
Model 700 Safari, Monte Carlo																								•	•	•	•
Model 700 Safari KS																								•	•	•	•
Model 700 Safari KS, LH																								•	•	•	
Model 700 Safari KS Stainless																									•	•	•
Model 700 Alaska Wilderness															•			•	•						•	•	
Model 700 African Plains															•			•							•	•	
Model 700 Sendero										•																	
Model 700 Custom	•	•	•	•	•	•	•	•			•	•	•	•	•	•	•	•			•	•		•	•	•	

MODEL 700 CLASSIC (7mm-08)

Since Remington's series of Model 700 Classics began in 1981, the company has offered this model in a special chambering each year.

The Model 700 Classic features an American walnut, straight-combed stock without a cheekpiece for rapid mounting, better sight alignment and reduced felt recoil. A hinged magazine flloorplate, sling swivel studs and satin wood finish with cut-checkering are standard, along with 24" barrel. Receiver drilled/tapped for scope mounts.
Price: **$645.00**

MODEL 700 MOUNTAIN DM (DETACHABLE MAGAZINE) RIFLE

The Remington Model 700 MTN DM rifle features the traditional mountain rifle-styled stock with a pistol grip pitched lower to position the wrist for a better grip. The cheekpiece is

designed to align the eye for quick, accurate sighting. The American walnut stock has a handrubbed oil finish and comes with a brown recoil pad and deep-cut checkering. The Model 700 MTN DM also features a lean contoured 22" barrel that helps reduce total weight to 6.5 pounds (no sights). All metalwork features a glass bead-blasted, blued-metal finish. **Calibers:** 25-06 Rem., 260 Rem., 270 Win., 280 Rem., 7mm-08 Rem., and 30-06 Springfield.
Price: **$693.00**

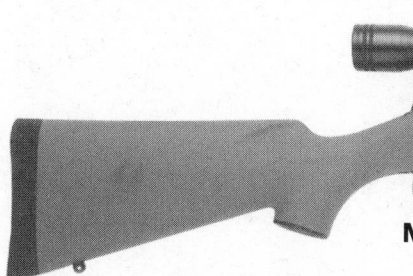

MODEL 710

Features: • New Model 710 bolt design employs three unique locking lugs that lock the bolt inside the barrel rather than the receiver. • Proven Remington cylindrical receiver design features a unique new fiberglass-reinforced, self-lubricating nylon receiver insert, impregnated with both silicon and Teflon, for smooth, reliable bolt operation. • Shorter 60° degree bolt throw (vs. 90° throw on competing rifles) delivers faster follow-up shots. • 22" steel barrel is cold-

forged and button-rifled with 6-groove, right-hand, 1-in-10 twist rifling. Additionally, the barrel is hydraulically pressed to the receiver for permanent attachment and bedded in the stock. • Removable, dual-stack steel magazine box with center feed and four-round capacity. • Dark-gray specially textured synthetic composite stock with raised cheekpiece black recoil pad and sling swivel studs. • 42.5" overall length, 7 1/8 lbs. • Exclusive, key-operated Remington Integrated Security System. • Pre-mounted, bore-sighted 3-9x40 Bushnell Sharpshooter scope with high-grade rings and mounts. • Initially offered in popular .270 Win. and .30-06 Sprg. calibers.
Price: with scope **$425.00**

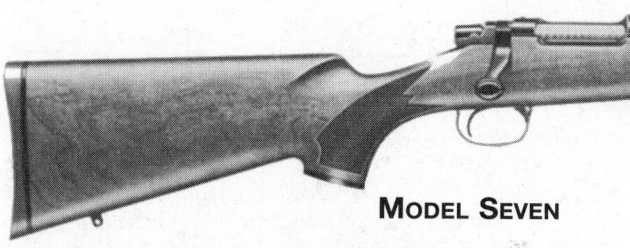

MODEL SEVEN

The short-action **MODEL SEVEN** is built to the accuracy standards of the famous Model 700. Its tapered 20" barrel is free floating out to a single pressure point at the forend

tip. A fully enclosed bolt and extractor system, ramp front and fully adjustable rear sights and sling swivel studs are standard. The Youth Model features a hardwood stock that is 1 inch shorter for easy control. Chambered in 223, 243, 260, 7mm-08 and 308.
Prices: Laminate **$647.00**
Laminate/Stainless 740.00
Youth (hardwood) 531.00
Stainless Synthetic 692.00

REMINGTON BOLT-ACTION RIFLES

Custom Guns

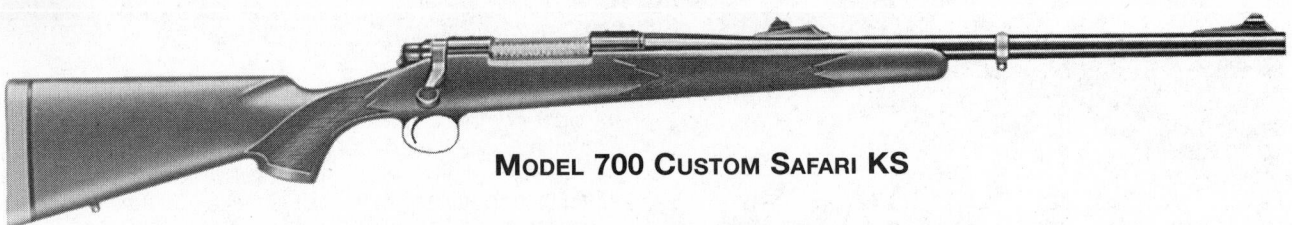

MODEL 700 CUSTOM SAFARI KS

MODEL 700 SAFARI
w/**MONTE CARLO STOCK**

MODEL 700™ SAFARI GRADE bolt-action rifles provide big-game hunters with a choice of either wood or synthetic stock. Model 700 Safari Monte Carlo (with Monte Carlo comb and cheekpiece) and Model 700 Safari Classic (with straight-line classic comb and no cheekpiece) are the satin-finished wood-stock models. Both feature hand-cut checkering and two reinforcing crossbolts covered with rosewood plugs. The Monte Carlo model also has rosewood pistol-grip and forend caps. All models are fitted with sling swivel studs and 22" or 24" barrels. Synthetic stock has simulated wood-grain finish, reinforced with Kevlar® (KS).
Calibers: 8mm Rem. Mag., 375 H&H Magnum, 416 Rem. Mag. and 458 Win. Mag. **Capacity:** 3 rounds. **Avg. Weight:** 9 lbs. **Overall Length:** 44.5" **Rate of Twist:** 10" (8mm Rem. Mag.); 12" (375 H&H Mag.); 14" (416 Rem. Mag., 458 Win. Mag.)
Price:
CUSTOM KS SAFARI $1,453.00
LH CUSTOM KS SAFARI 1,532.00
CUSTOM KS SAFARI STAINLESS. 1,622.00

**MODEL 700 ALASKAN
WILDERNESS RIFLE (AWR)**
This custom-built rifle has the same rate of twist and custom magnum barrel contour as the African Plains Rifle below, but features a Kevlar-reinforced composite stock. **Calibers:** 7mm Rem. Mag., 7mm STW, 7mm Rem Ultra Mag., .300 Rem. Ultra Mag., 300 Win. Mag., 300 Wby. Mag., 338 Win. Mag., .338 Rem. Ultra Mag., 375 H&H Mag., 375 Rem Ultra Mag. **Capacity:** 3 shots **Barrel length:** 24" **Overall Length:** 44.5" **Weight:** 6 lbs. 12 oz.
Price:. $1,524.00

MODEL 700 AFRICAN PLAINS RIFLE (APR)
The custom-built Model 700 APR rifle has a laminated classic wood stock and the following specifications. **Calibers:** 7mm Rem. Mag., 7mm Rem Ultra Mag., 300 Win. Mag., 300 Wby. Mag., 300 Rem. Ultra Mag., 338 Win. Mag., 338 Rem Ultra Mag., 375 H&H Mag., 375 Rem Ultra Mag **Capacity:** 3 shots **Barrel length:** 26" **Overall Length:** 46.5" **Weight:** 7.75 lbs. **Rate Of Twist:** R.H. 1 turn in 9.25" (7mm Rem. Mag.); 10" (300 Win. Mag. and 338 Win. Mag., .338 Rem. Ultra Mag.); 12" (30 Wby. Mag. and 375 H&H Mag.)
Price:. $1,641.00

MODEL 7400 (HIGH GLOSS STOCK)

Calibers: 243 Win., 270 Win., 30-06, 30-06 Carbine, 308 Win. **Capacity:** 5 centerfire cartridges (4 in the magazine, 1 in the chamber); extra 4-shot magazine available **Action:** Gas-operated; receiver drilled and tapped for scope mounts

Barrel Lengths: 22" (18.5" in 30-06 Carbine) **Weight:** 7.5 lbs. (7.25 lbs. in 30-06 Carbine) **Overall Length:** 42" **Sights:** Standard blade ramp front; sliding ramp rear **Stock:** Satin or high-gloss (270 Win. and 30-06 only) walnut stock and forend; curved pistol grip **Length Of Pull:** 13 ³/₈" **Drop At Heel:** 2.25" **Drop At Comb:** 1 ¹³/₁₆"
Price: **$624.00**
  Synthetic **509.00**

MODEL 7600
(HIGH GLOSS STOCK)

The Model 7600 shares nearly the same specifications as the Model 7400 featured above, except the 7600 is pump action. **Drop At Heel:** ¹⁵/₁₆" **Drop At Comb:** ⁹/₁₆"
Price: **$576.00**
  Synthetic **473.00**

RIFLES

MODEL 700 ETRONX
SYSTEM COMPONENTS

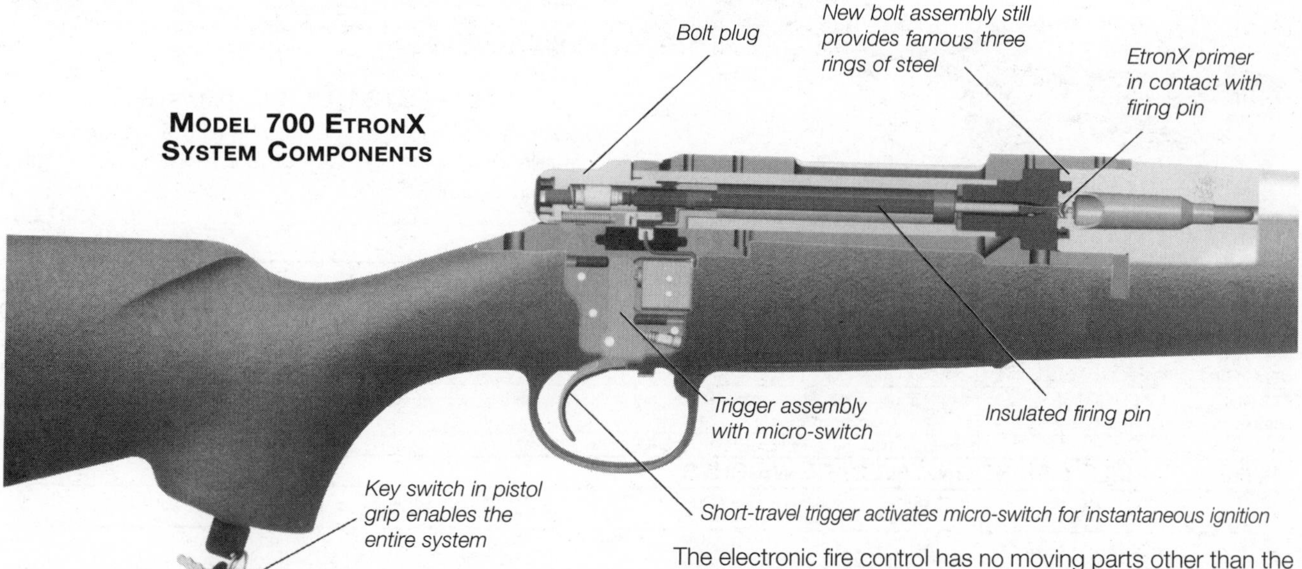

Bolt plug

New bolt assembly still provides famous three rings of steel

EtronX primer in contact with firing pin

Trigger assembly with micro-switch

Insulated firing pin

Key switch in pistol grip enables the entire system

Short-travel trigger activates micro-switch for instantaneous ignition

REMINGTON 700 ETRONX

Remington's ground-breaking EtronX System is claimed to be the most significant advance in rifle and ammunition performance since the development of self-contained cartridges. For the first time, cased centerfire cartridges can be fired by a completely non-mechanical system that ignites primers by means of an electric pulse.

The electronic fire control has no moving parts other than the trigger – no sear to be released or firing pin to move and strike the primer. Instead, an internal electric circuit is completed when the trigger is pulled. This sends an electrical charge through the system to an electrically responsive primer, igniting it instantaneously. The result is the fastest lock time of any rifle on the market.
In outward appearance, the EtronX resembles a 700 VS SF, with its fluted 26" barrel. The EtronX is chambered in .220 Swift, .22-250 and .243.
Price: **$1,999.00**

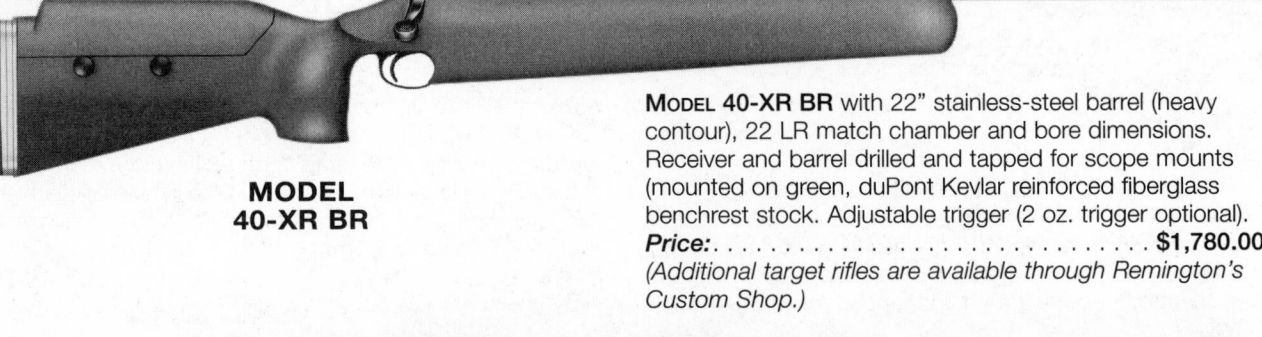

**MODEL
40-XR BR**

MODEL 40-XR BR with 22" stainless-steel barrel (heavy contour), 22 LR match chamber and bore dimensions. Receiver and barrel drilled and tapped for scope mounts (mounted on green, duPont Kevlar reinforced fiberglass benchrest stock. Adjustable trigger (2 oz. trigger optional).
Price: **$1,780.00**
(Additional target rifles are available through Remington's Custom Shop.)

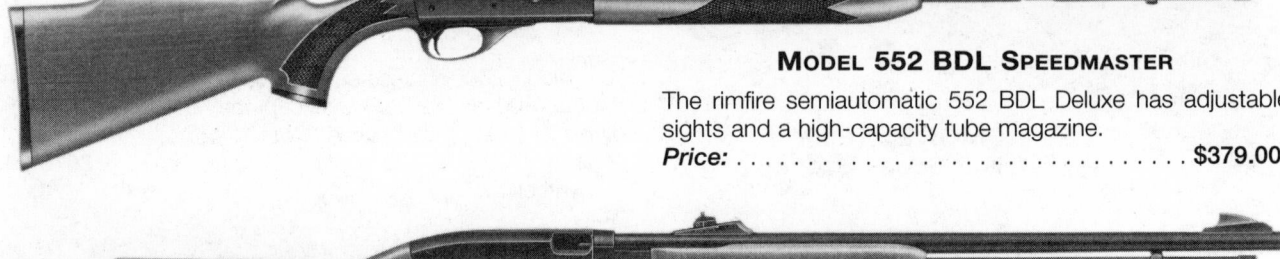

MODEL 552 BDL SPEEDMASTER

The rimfire semiautomatic 552 BDL Deluxe has adjustable sights and a high-capacity tube magazine.
Price: **$379.00**

MODEL 572 BDL FIELDMASTER

The pump-action 572 Fieldmaster has all the features of the 552 autoloader, including high-comb checkered stock, tube magazine, adjustable sights.
Price: **$392.00**

MODEL 572/552 RIFLE DIMENSIONS/AVERAGE WEIGHTS

Model	Action Type	Mag./Clip Capacity	Barrel Length	Overall Length	Avg. Wt. (lbs.)	Order No.	Stock Mat'l	Stock Finish	BBL Mat'l	BBL Finish
552 BDL Deluxe Speedmaster	Autoloading (.22 S, L, LR)	15*	21"	40"	5 3/4	5594	American Walnut	Gloss	Carbon Steel	Polished Blue
572 BDL Deluxe Fieldmaster	Pump (.22 S, L, LR)	15*	21"	40"	5 1/2	5624	American Walnut	Gloss	Carbon Steel	Polished Blue

*Nominal stock dimensions: (552/572): 13 5/8" length of pull, 1 3/8" drop at comb, 2 5/8" drop at heel. *17 .22 shorts.*

MODEL 597 RIFLE DIMENSIONS/AVERAGE WEIGHTS

Model	Action Type	Barrel Length	Overall Length	Avg. Wt. (lbs.)	Order No.	Stock Mat'l	Stock Finish	BBL Mat'l	BBL Finish
597	Autoloading (.22 LR)	20"	40"	5 1/2	6550	Gray Synthetic	Matte	Carbon Steel	Satin Blue
597 LSS	Autoloading (.22 LR)	20"	40"	5 1/2	6556	Brown Laminated	Satin	416 Stainless	Satin Stainless
597 SS	Autoloading (.22 LR)	20"	40"	5 1/2	6565	Gray Synthetic	Matte	416 Stainless	Satin Stainless
597 MAGNUM	Autoloading (.22 WMR)	20"	40"	6	6560	Black Synthetic	Matte	Carbon Steel	Satin Blue
597 MAGNUM LS	Autoloading (.22 WMR)	20"	40"	6	6566	Gray Laminated	Satin	Carbon Steel	Satin Blue
*597 HB	Autoloading (.22 LR)	20"	40"	6	6579	Brown Laminated	Satin	Carbon Steel	Satin Blue
*597 HB MAGNUM	Autoloading (.22 WM)	20"	40"	6	6581	Brown Laminated	Satin	Carbon Steel	Satin Blue

*Nominal stock dimensions: (597): 14" length of pull, 1 1/2" drop at comb, 2 1/4" drop at heel. *New For 2001*

MODEL 597 SERIES

Remington's autoloading rimfire rifles–the Model 597™ Series–are available in 7 versions, offering a choice of carbon or stainless steel barreled actions, synthetic or laminated wood stocks, and chambering for either standard 22 Long Rifle or 22 Magnum ammo. All M597™ rifles feature beaver-tail-style forends rounded with finger grooves for hand-filling control. The top of the receiver blends into the pistol grip, creating a rimfire autoloader that points like a shotgun but aims like a rifle. Features include a bolt guidance system of twin steel rails for smooth bolt travel and functional reliability. The 20-inch barrels are free-floated for consistent accuracy with all types of rimfire ammunition. A new trigger design creates crisp let-off for autoloading rifles. Bolts on the 22 LR versions are nickel-plated. The magnum-version bolt has a special alloy steel to provide controlled, uniform function with magnum cartridges. All receivers are grooved for standard tip-off mounts and are also drilled and tapped for Weaver-type bases. Adjustable open sights and one-piece scope mount rails are standard, as are spare magazines.

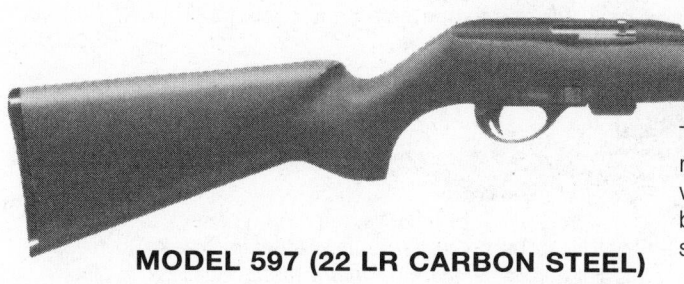

MODEL 597 (22 LR CARBON STEEL)

The M597™ is chambered for 22 Long Rifle ammunition and matches Remington's carbon steel barrel with a strong, light-weight, alloy receiver. All metal has a non-reflective, matte black finish. The rifle is housed in a one-piece, dark gray synthetic stock. *Price:* $163.00
w/stainless barrel 217.00

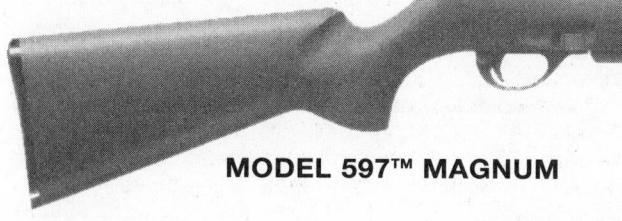

MODEL 597™ LSS

The M597™ LSS (Laminated Stock Stainless) has a satin-finished stainless steel barrel and matching, gray-tone alloy receiver. Chambered for 22 LR cartridges. Its stock is of laminated wood in light and dark brown tones.
Price: $272.00

MODEL 597™ MAGNUM

Chambered for 22 Win. Mag. rimfire cartridges, the M597™ MAGNUM features a carbon steel barrel, alloy receiver and black synthetic stock.
Price: $321.00
w/Laminated Stock. 377.00

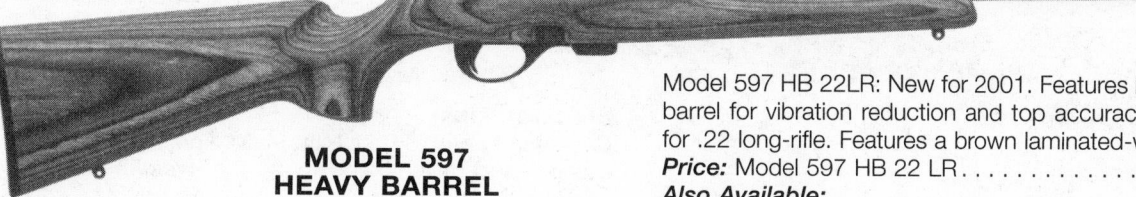

MODEL 597 HEAVY BARREL

Model 597 HB 22LR: New for 2001. Features heavy-contour barrel for vibration reduction and top accuracy. Chambered for .22 long-rifle. Features a brown laminated-wood stock.
Price: Model 597 HB 22 LR $265.00
Also Available:
22 Win Mag. 399.00

RIFLES, INC.

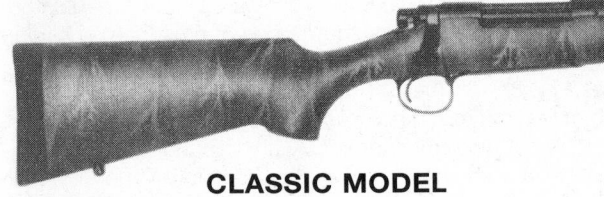

CLASSIC MODEL

SPECIFICATIONS
Calibers: Customized for varmint, target or hunter specifications, up to 375 H&H **Action:** Remington or Winchester stainless steel controlled-round feed with lapped bolt
Barrel Length: 24"-26"; stainless-steel match grade,

lapped **Weight:** 6.5 lbs. **Stock:** Pillar glass bedded; laminated fiberglass, finished with textured epoxy **Features:** Fine-tuned adjustable trigger; hinged floor-plate triggerguard
Price:................................... $2,000.00
   left hand **2,100.00**
Also Available: Signature Series, a long-range rifle on the stainless Remington 700 action, with 27-inch fluted stainless barrel, McMillan synthetic stock, 300 Rem. Ultra Mag only, 1/2 m.o.a, numbered and signed **2,800.00**
   Left-hand **2,950.00**

SAFARI MODEL

SPECIFICATIONS
Action: Winchester Model 70 controlled-round feed; hand lapped and honed bolt; drilled and tapped for 8X40 base screws **Barrel Length:** 23"-25"; stainless-steel match

grade, lapped **Weight:** 9 lbs. **Muzzle Break:** Stainless Quiet Slimbrake **Metal Finish:** Matte stainless or black Teflon **Stock:** Pillar glass bedded; double reinforced laminated fiberglass/graphite; finished with textured epoxy **Features:** Fine-tuned adjustable trigger; hinged floor-plate **Options:** Drop box for additional round; express sights; barrel band; quarter ribs
Price:................................... $2,700.00
   w/Options **3,770.00**

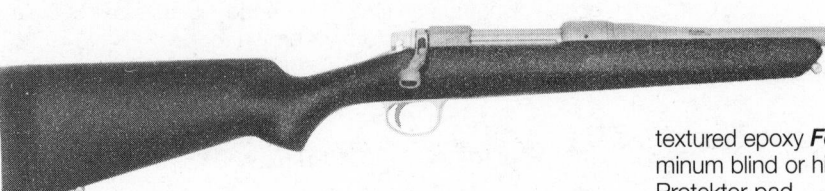

LIGHTWEIGHT STRATA STAINLESS MODEL

SPECIFICATIONS
Calibers: Up to 375 H&H **Action:** Stainless Remington; fluted, tapped and handle-hollowed bolt; aluminum bolt shroud **Barrel Length:** 22"-24" depending on caliber; stainless-steel match grade **Weight:** 4.75 lbs. **Stock:** Pillar glass bedded; laminated Kevlar/Boron/Graphite, finished with

textured epoxy **Features:** Matte stainless metal finish; aluminum blind or hinged floorplate trigger guard; custom Protektor pad
Price:................................... $2,600.00
   left hand **2,750.00**
Also Available: LIGHTWEIGHT 70 in calibers up to 375 H&H.
Barrel Length: 22" to 24" stainless steel match grade.
Weight: 5.75 lbs. **Stock:** laminated Kevlar/Graphite/Boron finished with textured epoxy. Trigger is fine-tuned.
Price:................................... $2,500.00
   left hand **2,650.00**

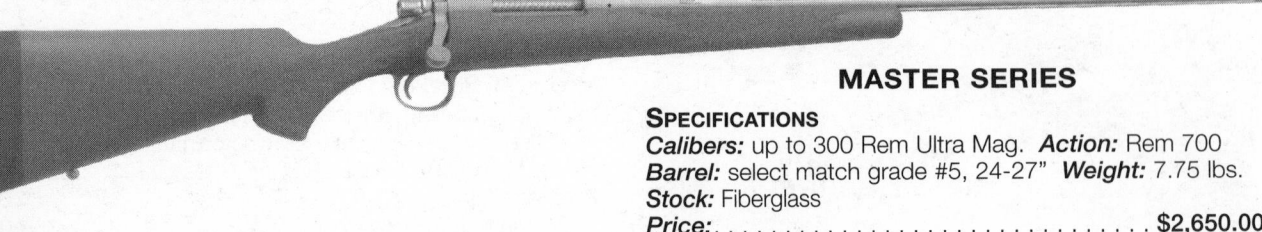

MASTER SERIES

SPECIFICATIONS
Calibers: up to 300 Rem Ultra Mag. **Action:** Rem 700
Barrel: select match grade #5, 24-27" **Weight:** 7.75 lbs.
Stock: Fiberglass
Price:................................... $2,650.00

RUGER CARBINES

167

MODEL 10/22RBM

RUGER 10/22 MAGNUM

This .22 Magnum autoloader uses a heavy bolt in a blowback mechanism that feeds from the proven 10/22 rotary magazine. Integral scope bases augment open sights. The carbine-style walnut stock and 18.5" barrel make this a fast-handling rimfire. *Length:* 37" *Weight:* 6.5 lbs.
Price: $450.00

RIFLES

MODEL PC9

After several years of research, Ruger engineers combined 10/22 and P-series technology to create an autoloading rifle that uses popular pistol cartridges and Ruger pistol magazines. This handy carbine meets the needs of personal defense, sporting use, law enforcement and security agencies. Advanced synthetics and precision investment-casting technologies allow for improved performance and substantially reduced costs. The Ruger Carbine has a chrome-moly steel barrel, receiver, slide and recoil springs, and features a checkered High Impact Synthetic stock with rubber buttplate. Adjustable open sights and patented integral scope mounts are standard. The Ruger Carbine also features a combination firing-pin block and slide lock. Trigger engagement is required for the firing pin to strike the primer. The slide locks to prevent chambering or ejection of a round if the riflle is struck on the buttpad. This safety system is backed up by a manual crossbolt safety located at the rear of the trigger guard. A slide stop locks the slide open for inspection and cleaning.

MODEL PC9 AUTOLOADING CARBINE
SPECIFICATIONS
Caliber: 9mm or 40 auto
Capacity: 10 rounds
Action: Mass impulse delayed blowback
Barrel Length: 16.25" *Overall Length:* 34.75"
Weight: 6 lbs. 4 oz. *Trigger Pull:* Approx. 6 lb.
Rifling: 6 grooves, 1 turn in 10" RH
Stock: du Pont "Zytel" matte black
Finish: Matte black oxide
Sights: Blade front, open rear plus provision for scope mounts (ghost ring version also available)
Sight Radius: 12.65"
Safety: Manual push-button crossbolt safety (locks trigger mechanism) and internal firing-pin block safety
Features: Bolt lock to prevent accidental unloading or chambering of a cartridge; steel barrel, receiver, slide and recoil spring unit w/black composite stock
Price: $575.00
All Ruger long guns come standard with cable lock & keys.

Rifles

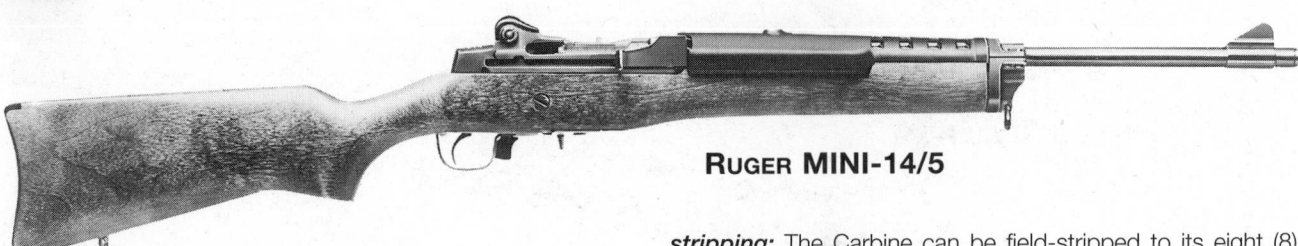

RUGER MINI-14/5

Mechanism: Gas-operated, autoloading. **Materials:** Heat-treated chrome molybdenum and other alloy steels as well as music wire coil springs are used throughout the mechanism to ensure reliability under field-operating conditions. **Safety:** The guard-mounted safety blocks both the hammer and sear. The slide can be cycled when the safety is on. **Firing pin:** The firing pin is retracted mechanically as the bolt unlocks. The rifle can only be fired when the bolt is safely locked. **Stock:** One-piece American hardwood reinforced with steel liner at stressed areas. Sling swivels standard. Handguard and forearm separated by air space from barrel to promote cooling under rapid-fire conditions. **Field**

stripping: The Carbine can be field-stripped to its eight (8) basic sub-assemblies in a matter of seconds and without use of special tools.

RUGER MINI-14
SPECIFICATIONS
Caliber: 223 (5.56mm)
Barrel Length: 18.5"
Overall Length: 37 1/4" **Weight:** 6 lbs. 8 oz.
Magazine: 5-round, detachable box magazine
Sights: Rear adj.for windage/elevation.
Prices: MINI-14/5 Blued $606.00
K-MINI-14/5 Stainless 664.00
K-MINI-14/5P Stainless, synthetic 664.00
(Scope not included)

MINI-14/5R RANCH RIFLE

SPECIFICATIONS
Caliber: 223 (5.56mm) **Barrel Length:** 18.5"
Overall Length: 37 1/4" **Weight:** 6 lbs. 8 oz.
Magazine: 5-round detachable box magazine.

Sights: Fold-down rear sight; 1" scope rings (factory machined scope mount system available on all Ranch models)
Prices: MINI-14/5R Blued $649.00
K-MINI-14/5R Stainless 710.00
K-MINI-14/5RPS Stainless, Synthetic 710.00

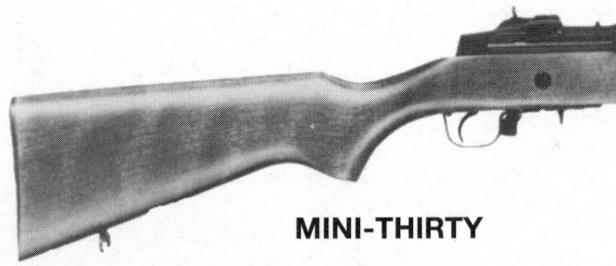

MINI-THIRTY

This modified version of the Ruger Ranch rifle is chambered for the 7.62 x 39mm Soviet service cartridge. Designed for use with telescopic sights, it features low, compact scope-mounting for greater accuracy and carrying case, and a buffer in the receiver. Sling swivels are standard.

SPECIFICATIONS
Caliber: 7.62 x 39mm **Barrel Length:** 18.5" **Overall Length:** 37 1/8" **Weight:** 6 lbs. 14 oz. (empty) **Magazine Capacity:** 5 shots **Rifling:** 6 grooves, R.H. twist, 1:10" **Finish:** Blued or stainless **Stock:** One-piece American hardwood w/steel liners in stressed areas **Sights:** Blade front; peep rear (factory machined scope mount system available on all Ranch models).
Prices: Blued $649.00
Stainless Steel 710.00
Also Available: K-MINI-30P, 7.62x39mm, all-weather, matte stainless 710.00

STANDARD 10/22 CARBINE

MODEL K10/22RP "ALL WEATHER"

MODEL K10/22RBI
INTERNATIONAL CARBINE STAINLESS

MODEL 10/22T TARGET

Introduced in 1964, Ruger's 10/22 is still a best-seller. It follows the Ruger design practice of building a firearm from integrated sub-assemblies. For example, the trigger housing assembly contains the entire ignition system, which employs a high-speed swinging hammer to ensure the shortest possible lock time. The barrel is assembled to the receiver by a unique dual-screw dovetail system that provides unusual rigidity and strength—and accounts, in part, for the exceptional accuracy of the 10/22.

SPECIFICATIONS

Mechanism: Blow-back, semiautomatic. **Caliber:** 22 LR, high-speed or standard-velocity loads. **Magazine:** 10-shot capacity, exclusive Ruger rotary design; fits flush into stock. **Barrel:** 18.5", assembled to the receiver by dual-screw dovetail mounting for added strength and rigidity. **Overall Length:** 37 1/4". **Weight:** 5 lbs. **Sights:** 1/16" brass bead front;

single folding-leaf rear, adjustable for elevation; receiver drilled and tapped for scope blocks or tip-off mount adapter (included). **Trigger:** curved finger surface, 3/8" wide. **Safety:** sliding cross-button type; safety locks both sear and hammer and cannot be put in safe position unless gun is cocked. **Stocks:** Birch, laminated, American walnut or synthetic. **Finish:** blued or anodized or brushed satin.

Prices: MODEL 10/22 RB STANDARD $235.00
MODEL 10/22 DSP DELUXE
   (Hand-checkered American walnut) 299.00
MODEL K10/22 RB STAINLESS 273.00
MODEL K10/22 RBI INTERNATIONAL CARBINE
   w/full-length stock stainless 299.00
   10/22 RBI blue 275.00
MODEL 10/22T TARGET (no sights) Hammer-
   forged 20" barrel, laminated target-style stock . .415.00
   stainless 465.00
MODEL 10/22RP "All Weather" synthetic stock 235.00
   stainless 273.00
MODEL K10/22TNZ TARGET with custom
   laminated stock, stainless 649.00

Ruger's Farguharson-style single-shot rifle first appeared in 1966. These illustrations show the variations currently offered in the Ruger No. 1 Single-Shot Rifle Series. Ruger No. 1 rifles have a Farquharson-type falling-block action and select American walnut stocks. Pistol grip and forearm are hand-checkered to a borderless design. Price for any listed model is **$797.00** (except the No. 1 RSI International Model: **$818.00**). Barreled Actions (blued only): **$575.00**

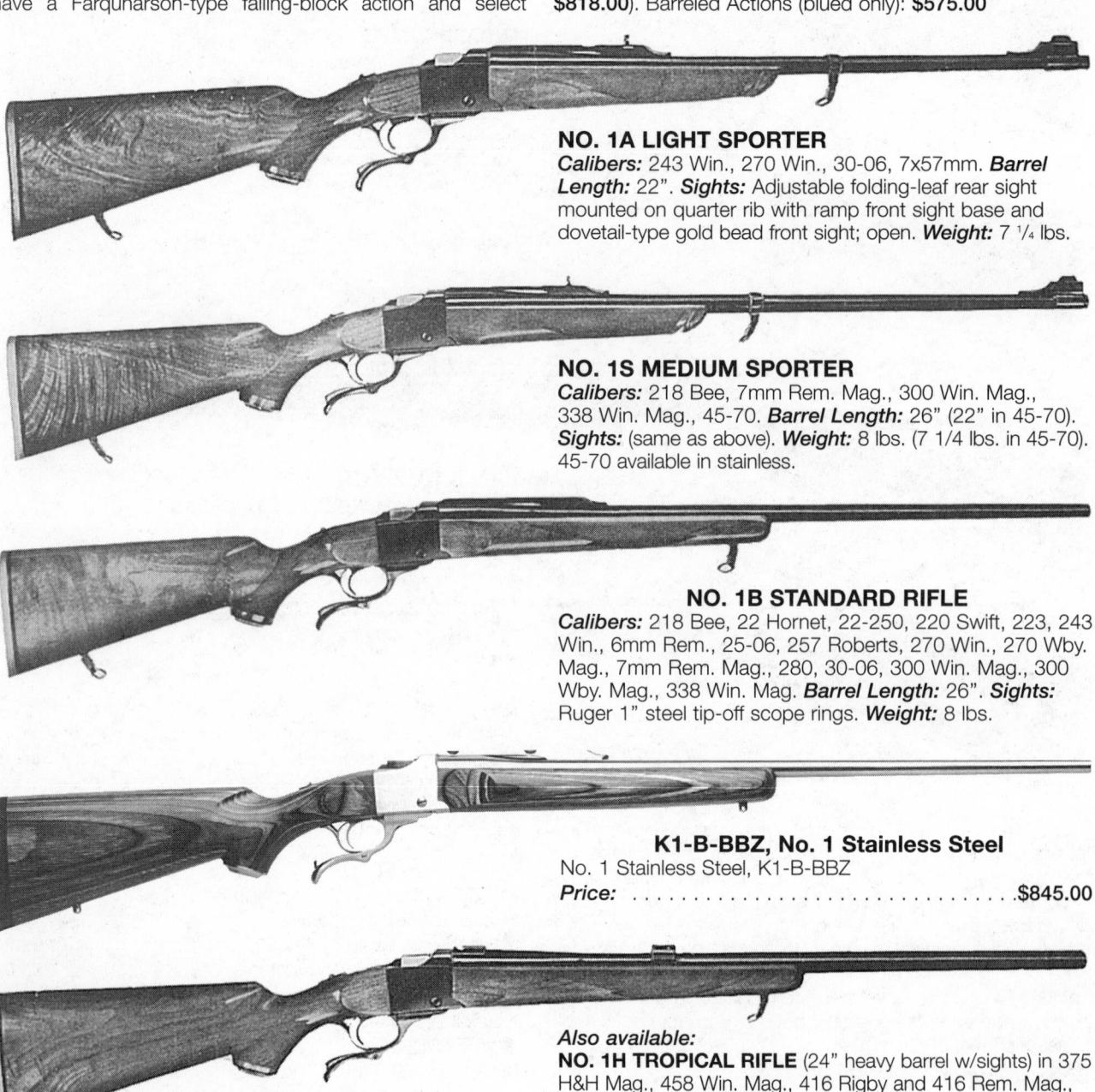

NO. 1A LIGHT SPORTER
Calibers: 243 Win., 270 Win., 30-06, 7x57mm. *Barrel Length:* 22". *Sights:* Adjustable folding-leaf rear sight mounted on quarter rib with ramp front sight base and dovetail-type gold bead front sight; open. *Weight:* 7 1/4 lbs.

NO. 1S MEDIUM SPORTER
Calibers: 218 Bee, 7mm Rem. Mag., 300 Win. Mag., 338 Win. Mag., 45-70. *Barrel Length:* 26" (22" in 45-70). *Sights:* (same as above). *Weight:* 8 lbs. (7 1/4 lbs. in 45-70). 45-70 available in stainless.

NO. 1B STANDARD RIFLE
Calibers: 218 Bee, 22 Hornet, 22-250, 220 Swift, 223, 243 Win., 6mm Rem., 25-06, 257 Roberts, 270 Win., 270 Wby. Mag., 7mm Rem. Mag., 280, 30-06, 300 Win. Mag., 300 Wby. Mag., 338 Win. Mag. *Barrel Length:* 26". *Sights:* Ruger 1" steel tip-off scope rings. *Weight:* 8 lbs.

K1-B-BBZ, No. 1 Stainless Steel
No. 1 Stainless Steel, K1-B-BBZ
Price: $845.00

NO. 1V VARMINTER
Calibers: 22-250, 220 Swift, 223, 25-06, 6mm. *Barrel Length:* 24" (26" in 220 Swift). *Sights:* Ruger target scope blocks, heavy barrel and 1" tip-off scope rings. *Weight:* 9 lbs.

Also available:
NO. 1H TROPICAL RIFLE (24" heavy barrel w/sights) in 375 H&H Mag., 458 Win. Mag., 416 Rigby and 416 Rem. Mag., .375 H&H available in stainless
NO 1. RSI INTERNATIONAL (20" lightweight barrel and full-length stock) in 243 Win., 270 Win., 30-06 and 7x57mm
NO 1. STAINLESS (24" standard or 26" heavy barrel) laminated hardwood stock, in .22-250, .25-06,30-06, 243 WFN, 7mm Rem. Mag., 7mm STW, .300 Wby. Magnum

MODEL 77/22RH HORNET
$555.00 ($575.00 77/22 RSH w/Sights)
The Model 77/22RH is Ruger's first truly compact centerfire bolt-action rifle. It features a 77/22 action crafted from heat-treated alloy steel. Exterior surfaces are blued to match the hammer-forged barrel. The action features a right-hand turning bolt with a 90-degree bolt throw, cocking on opening. Fast lock time (2.7 milliseconds) adds to accuracy. A three-position swing-back safety locks the bolt; in its center position firing is blocked, but bolt operation and safe loading and unloading are permitted. When fully forward, the rifle is ready to fire. The American walnut stock has recoil pad, grip cap and sling swivels installed. One-inch diameter scope rings fit integral bases.

SPECIFICATIONS
Caliber: 22 Hornet
Capacity: 6 rounds (detachable rotary magazine)
Barrel length: 20" *Overall length:* 39.25"
Weight: 6 lbs. (unloaded)
Sights: Single folding-leaf rear; gold bead front
Length of pull: 13 3/4"
Drop at heel: 2 3/4" Drop at comb: 2"
Finish: Polished and blued, matte, nonglare receiver top
Also available: MODEL K77/22VHZ Varmint w/stainless-steel heavy barrel, laminated American hardwood stock.
Price: (w/o sights) $599.00

RIFLES

MODEL 77/44 RS

Chambered in .44 Magnum, the new 77/44 is a short (18.5" barrel), lightweight (6 lbs.) deluxed grade carbine based on the same action used in the 77/22. Action features right-hand turning bolt with 90-degree bolt throw. *Capacity:* 4 rounds
Price: blued $580.00
stainless (K77/44RSP) 580.00

MODEL K77/22BVZ VARMINT

MODEL 77/22 RIMFIRE RIFLE

The Ruger 22-caliber rimfire 77/22 bolt-action rifle has been built especially to function with the patented Ruger 10-Shot Rotary Magazine concept. The magazine throat, retaining lips and ramps that guide the cartridge into the chamber are solid alloy steel that resists bending or deforming.

The 77/22 weighs just under six pounds. Its heavy-duty receiver incorporates the integral scope bases of the patented Ruger Scope Mounting System with 1-inch Ruger scope rings. With the 3-position safety in its "lock" position, a dead bolt is cammed forward, locking the bolt handle down. In this position the action is locked closed and the handle cannot be raised.

All metal surfaces are finished in nonglare deep blue or satin stainless. Stock is select straight-grain American walnut, hand checkered and finished with durable polyurethane.

An All-Weather, all-stainless steel **MODEL K77/22RS** features a stock made of reinforced synthetic glass fiber. *Weight:* Approx. 6 lbs.

SPECIFICATIONS
Calibers: 22 LR and 22 Magnum. *Barrel length:* 20". *Overall length:* 39 1/4". *Weight:* 6 lbs. (w/o scope, magazine empty).
Feed: Detachable 10-Shot Ruger Rotary Magazine.
Prices: 77/22R Blue, w/o sights, 1" Ruger rings . $525.00
77/22RM Blue, walnut stock, plain barrel,
 no sights, 1" Ruger rings, 22 Mag. 525.00
77/22RS Blue, sights included, 1" Ruger rings . . . 535.00
77/22RSM Blue, American walnut, iron sights 535.00
K77/22-RP Synthetic stock, stainless steel, plain
 barrel with 1" Ruger rings 525.00
K77/22-RMP Synthetic stock, stainless steel,
 plain barrel, 1" Ruger rings 525.00
K77/22-RSP Synthetic stock, stainless steel, gold
 bead front sight, folding-leaf rear, Ruger 1"rings . 535.00
K77/22RSMP Synthetic stock, metal sights,
 stainless. 535.00
VARMINT SPECIFICATIONS: *Barrel length:* 24", *Overall Length:* 43.25", *Weight:* 6 7/8 lbs.
K77/22VBZ Varmint Laminated stock, scope
 rings, heavy barrel, stainless 565.00

Mark II Series

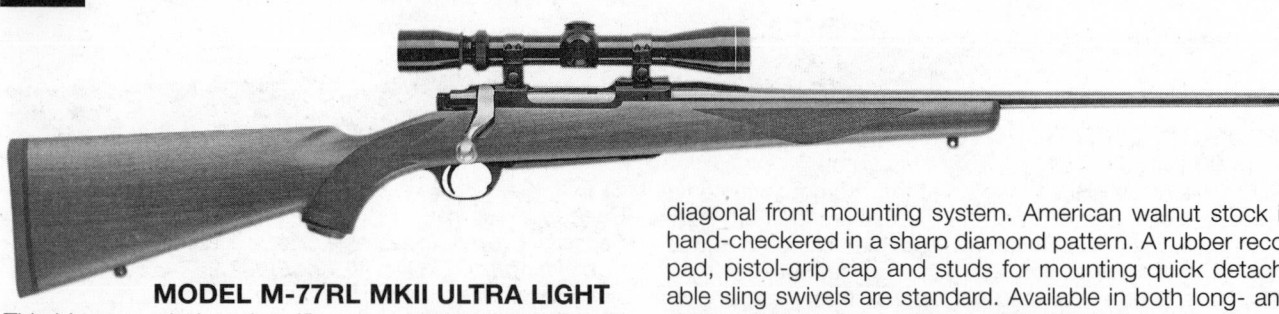

MODEL M-77RL MKII ULTRA LIGHT

This big-game, bolt-action rifle encompasses the traditional features that have made the Ruger M-77 one of the most popular centerfire rifles in the world. It includes a sliding top tang safety, a one-piece bolt with Mauser-type extractor and diagonal front mounting system. American walnut stock is hand-checkered in a sharp diamond pattern. A rubber recoil pad, pistol-grip cap and studs for mounting quick detachable sling swivels are standard. Available in both long- and short-action versions, with Integral Base Receiver and 1" Ruger scope rings. **Calibers:** 223, 243, 257, 270, 30-06, 308. **Barrel length:** 20". **Weight:** Approx. 6 lbs.
Price: **$699.00**

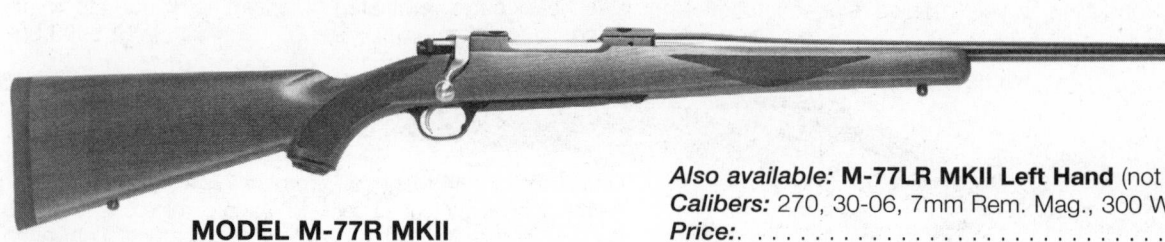

MODEL M-77R MKII

Integral Base Receiver, 1" scope rings. No sights.
Calibers: (Long action) 6mm Rem., 6.5x55mm, 7x57mm, 257 Roberts, 270, 280 Rem., 30-06 (all with 22" barrels); 220 Swift, 25/06, 7mm Rem. Mag., 300 Win. Mag., 338 Win. Mag. (all with 24" barrels); and (Short Stroke action), 22/250, 223, 243, 260 Rem., 308 (22" barrels). **Weight:** Approx. 7 lbs.
Price: **$649.00**

Also available: M-77LR MKII Left Hand (not shown).
Calibers: 270, 30-06, 7mm Rem. Mag., 300 Win. Mag
Price:. **$649.00**

MODEL M-77RS MKII (not shown)

Integral Base Receiver, Ruger steel 1" rings, open sights.
Calibers: 243, 25-06, 270, 7mm Rem. Mag., 30-06, 300 Win. Mag., 308, 338 Win. Mag., 6mm (22" barrel)
Weight: Approx. 7 lbs.
Price: **$735.00**

MODEL K77RSBZ MKII

MODEL KM77RBZ MKII

Stainless steel, laminated stock, scope rings
Calibers: 223, 22-250, 243, 270, 280, 7mm Mag., 308, 30-06, 300 Win. Mag., 338 Win. Mag.
Price: KM77RSBZ. **$699.00**
With sights & rings (243 Win., 7mm Mag., 30/06, .300 Win. Mag., 338 Win Mag) **765.00**

MODEL M-77RSI MKII

MODEL M-77RSI MKII INTERNATIONAL

International full-length stock, Integral Base Receiver, open sights, Ruger 1" steel rings. **Calibers:** 243, 270, 30-06, 308
Barrel Length: 18.5" **Weight:** Approx. 6 lbs.
Price: **$735.00**

Mark II Series (w/Three Position Safety/Fixed Ejectors)

**MODEL M-77VT MK II
HEAVY BARREL TARGET**

MODEL M-77VT MK II
HEAVY-BARREL TARGET

Features Mark II stainless-steel bolt action Target, gray matte finish, two-stage adjustable trigger. No sights.

SPECIFICATIONS
Calibers: 22-250, 220 Swift, 223, 243, 25-06 and 308.
Barrel Length: 26", hammer-forged, free-floating stainless steel. **Weight:** 9 ³/₄ lbs. Stock: Laminated American hardwood with flat forend.
Price: KM-77VT MKII $779.00

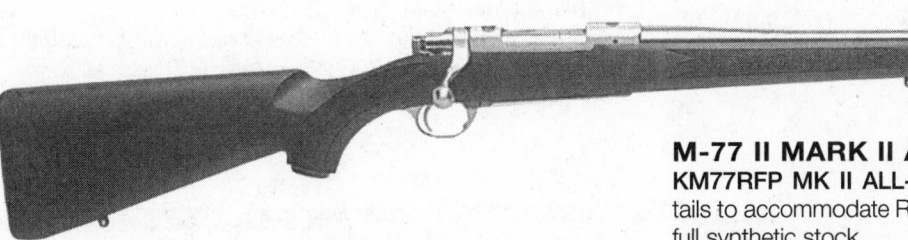

M-77 MARK II ALL-WEATHER

M-77 II MARK II ALL-WEATHER

KM77RFP MK II ALL-WEATHER Receiver w/integral dovetails to accommodate Ruger 1" rings, no sights, stainless steel, full synthetic stock.
Calibers: 223, 22-50, 243, 25-06, 270, 280, 30-06, 7mm Rem. Mag., 300 Win. Mag., 308, 338 Win. Mag. 260 Rem. **$649.00**
MODEL KM77RSFP Receiver w/integral dovetails to accommodate Ruger 1" rings, metal sights, stainless steel, synthetic stock.
Calibers: 243, 270, 7mm Rem. Mag., 30-06, 300 Win. Mag., 338 Win. Mag. *(scope not included)* $725.00

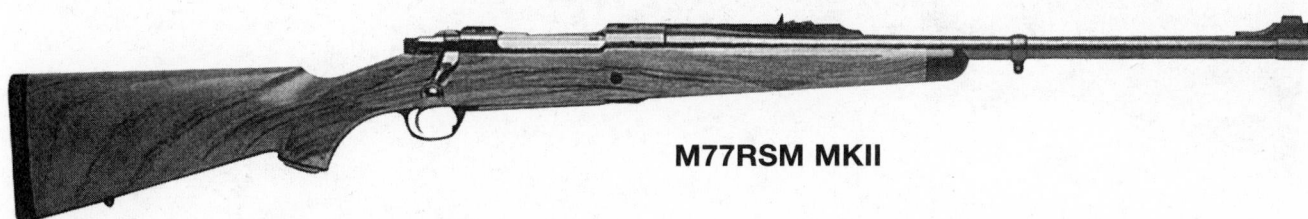

M77RSM MKII

RUGER 77 RSM MK II MAGNUM RIFLE

This "Bond Street"-quality African hunting rifle features a quarter rib machined from a single bar of steel; Circassian walnut stock with black forend tip; steel floorplate and latch; a Ruger Magnum trigger guard with floorplate latch designed flush with the contours of the trigger (to eliminate accidental dumping of cartridges); a three-position safety; Express rear sight and front sight ramp with gold bead sight. Also available in Express Model (long action, no heavy barrel).

SPECIFICATIONS
Calibers: 375 H&H, 416 Rigby. **Capacity:** 4 rounds (375 H&H) and 3 rounds (416 Rigby). **Barrel Length:** 23" **Overall Length:** 44" **Barrel Thread Diameter:** 1¹/₈" **Weight:** 9 ¹/₄ lbs. (375 H&H); 10 ¹/₄ lbs. (416 Rigby), 9.75 lbs. (others)
Price: 375, 416 . . . . $1,695.00
Also available: EXPRESS MODEL, (long action) 270, 7mm, 30-06, 300 Win. Mag., 338 Win. Mag.
Price: EXPRESS $1,625.00

Sako 75 Hunter

The **SAKO 75 HUNTER** is the first rifle to offer an action furnished with both a bolt with three locking lugs and a mechanical ejector. The traditional thumb safety has two positions. Cartridge removal or loading is done by pressing a separate bolt release button in front of the safety. No need to touch the safety to remove a cartridge and then disengage it by mistake under difficult or stressful conditions. The new cold hammer-forged barrel is manufactured in an advanced custom-built robotic cell. The new SAKO features a totally free-floating barrel. Instead of checkering, this all-stainless, all-weather model has soft rubbery grips molded in the stock to provide a firmer, more comfortable hold than with conventional synthetic stocks. The selected moisture stabilized high-grade walnut ensures quality and craftsmanship.

Other features include:
• Five bolt siding guides • 70° Bolt Lift • Totally free-floating cold hammer-forged barrel • Positive safety system with separate bolt release button for safe unloading • Detachable staggered 5-round magazine • Five (5) action sizes for perfect cartridge match • All-Stainless metal parts and All-Weather synthetic stock with special grips • Selected moisture stabilized walnut stock with hand-crafted checkering • Integral scope rails

Prices:

SAKO 75 HUNTER
22"barrel (17 Rem., 222 Rem., 223 Rem., 22-250 Rem., 243 Win., 7mm-08, 308 Win., 25-06 Rem., 270 Win., 280 Rem., 30-06, ... **$1,115.00**
24" barrel (7mm Rem. Mag., 300 Win. Mag., 338 Win. Mag., 375 H&H Mag., 416 Rem. Mag. **1,145.00**
26" barrel (270 Wby. Mag., 7mm STW, 7mm Wby. Mag., 300 Wby. Mag., 340 Wby. Mag., 300 Rem. Ultra Mag . . . **1,145.00**

SAKO 75 STAINLESS SYNTHETIC
22" barrel (22-250 Rem., 243 Win., 308 Win., 7mm-08 25-06 Rem., 270 Win., 30-06) **$1,205.00**
24" barrel (7mm Rem. Mag., 300 Win. Mag., 338 Win. Mag., 375 H&H Mag.) **1,235.00**
26" barrel (7mm STW, .300 Wby. Mag., 300 Rem Ultra Mag.) Hinged floor plate.

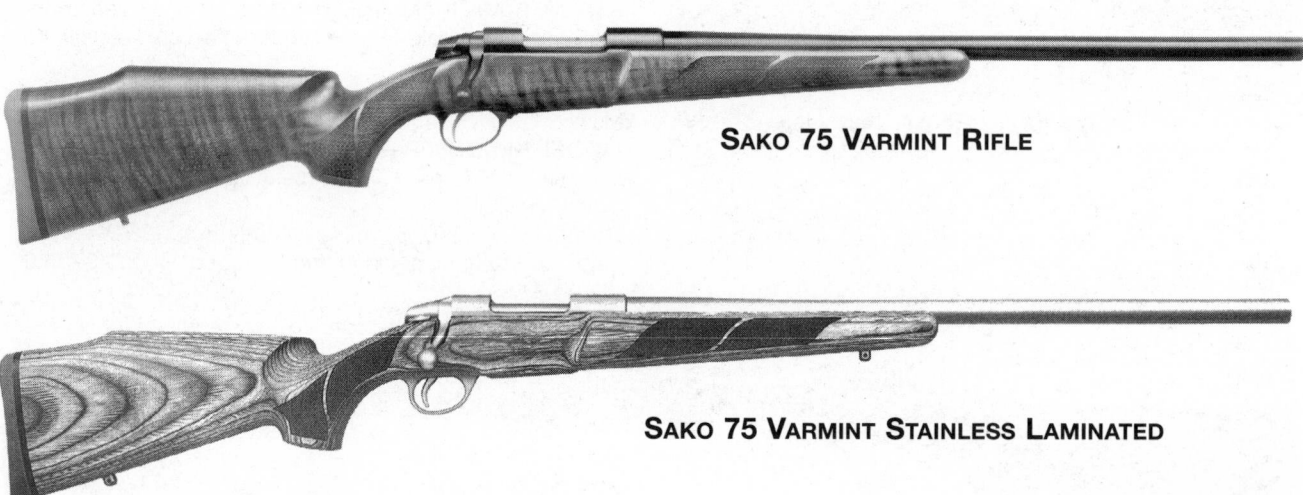

SAKO 75 VARMINT RIFLE

SAKO 75 VARMINT STAINLESS LAMINATED

SAKO 75 VARMINT RIFLE

The SAKO 75 Varmint Rifle uses only the highest grade steel in the construction of the action, bolt, barrel and all internal parts. SAKO cold hammer-forges heavyweight bar stock into one of the truest, most accurate barrels available. The 24" free-floated barrel is matched to the appropriate action size to eliminate excessive weight. The matte lacquered walnut stock features a beavertail forearm for additional stability and support when shooting from sandbags. The SAKO 75 is the first and only rifle with three locking lugs and a mechanical ejector. Other SAKO features include a one-piece forged bolt with five gliding surfaces, a detachable magazine, and a smooth 70 degree bolt lift.

Calibers:
17 Rem., 222 Rem., 223 Rem., 22-250 Rem., 22 PPC, 6mm PPC
Price:. **$1,280.00**
Also Available: 75 VARMINT STAINLESS LAMINATED from 222 Rem. to 6mm PPC. **1,375.00**

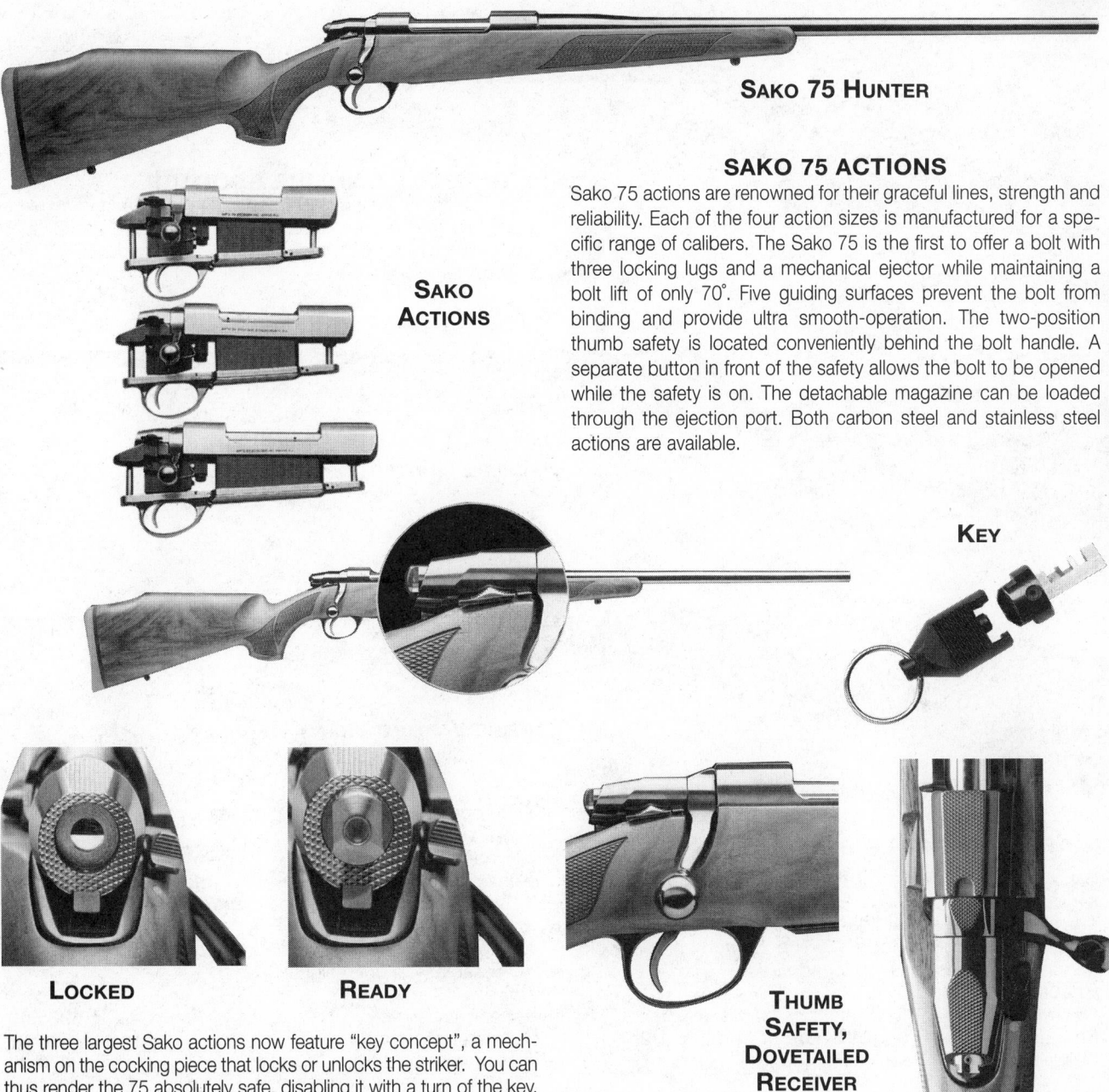

SAKO 75 HUNTER

SAKO ACTIONS

SAKO 75 ACTIONS

Sako 75 actions are renowned for their graceful lines, strength and reliability. Each of the four action sizes is manufactured for a specific range of calibers. The Sako 75 is the first to offer a bolt with three locking lugs and a mechanical ejector while maintaining a bolt lift of only 70°. Five guiding surfaces prevent the bolt from binding and provide ultra smooth-operation. The two-position thumb safety is located conveniently behind the bolt handle. A separate button in front of the safety allows the bolt to be opened while the safety is on. The detachable magazine can be loaded through the ejection port. Both carbon steel and stainless steel actions are available.

KEY

LOCKED

READY

THUMB SAFETY, DOVETAILED RECEIVER

RIFLES

The three largest Sako actions now feature "key concept", a mechanism on the cocking piece that locks or unlocks the striker. You can thus render the 75 absolutely safe, disabling it with a turn of the key. Three keys are provided with each rifle, and others can be ordered by rifle serial number from the 7500 patterns. All Sako Model 75 rifles except those built on the smallest actions will soon come standard with the key concept lock.

"The key blends into the rifle contours when the lock is open and the gun is operational," explained Mr. Paul-Erik Toivo, president of Sako Ltd. "When the key is removed, the lock takes effect and the hunting rifle is completely safe and inoperative."

This revolutionary concept puts complete control of the safety and security of the rifle in the hands of its owner. "When the key is removed, there is no way to operate the gun, even accidentally. Any attempts to pick the lock will render the rifle unusable," said Mr. Tolvo. He also noted that the Sako 75 is considered the very best bolt action rifle in the industry. "The Sako 75 is the best hunting rifle in the world. It is only natural that we wanted to offer it with added security and safety for its owner and society in general. We believe this will become the new standard in gun safety."

FINNFIRE SPORTER

The Sporter has a ergonomical competition stock, adjustable cheekpiece and heel plate. The heavy barrel makes it an ideal gun when unerring accuracy is required. (scope and mount not included)

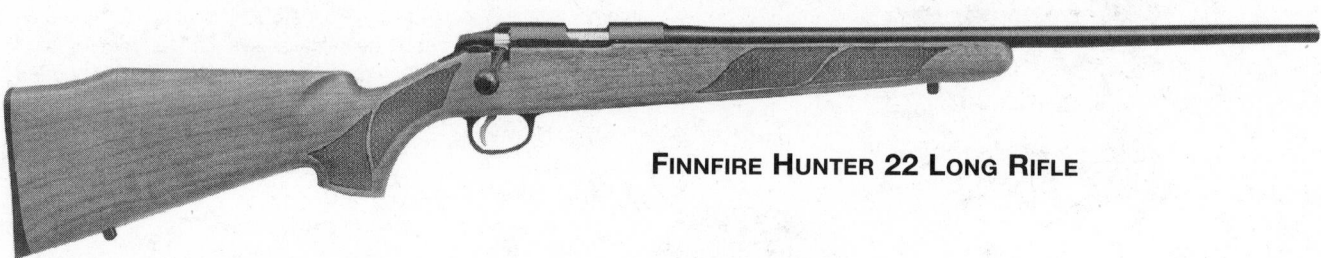

FINNFIRE HUNTER 22 LONG RIFLE

FINNFIRE VARMINT HEAVY BARREL

FINNFIRE 22 LR BOLT-ACTION RIFLE

SAKO of Finland designed the .22 Finnfire to make it as similar to its "big brothers" as possible—just scaled down. The single-stage adjustable trigger is a carbon copy of the trigger found on the Model 75. The 22-inch barrel is cold-hammered to ensure superior accuracy.

SPECIFICATIONS
Overall length: 37 1/2" ***Weight:*** 5 1/4 lbs. (Hunter, Sporter) ; 7 1/2 lbs. (Varmint) ***Rate of twist:*** 16 1/2"
Other outstanding features include:

- European walnut stock with matte lacquer finish
- 50° bolt lift
- Free-floating barrel
- Integral 11mm dovetail for scope mounting
- Two-position safety that locks the bolt
- Cocking indicator
- Five- or 10-shot detachable magazine
- Available with open sights

Price:
SPORTER $925.00
HUNTER 825.00
VARMINT 870.00

SAKO 75 FINNLIGHT (NOT SHOWN)

The new Sako 75 Finnlight is a purpose-built rifle especially suited for long hunts on terrain. It offers pinpoint accuracy, excellent balance, uncompromising strength and reliability in a compact and attractive package.

Sako 75 Finnlight has been built to meet the same demanding requirements as other Sako 75 rifles. The free floating barrel is fluted for rigidity, lightness and faster cooling. Light synthetic stock with soft over-moulded rubber gripping surfaces ensures good grip in all conditions. For a lightweight rifle Sako 75 Finnlight has excellent caliber selection.

Prices: Synthetic/Stainless (243 Win., 7mm-08 Rem., 308 Win., 25-06 Rem., 270 Win., 280 Rem., 30-06, 6.5x55). $1,235.00
Magnums (7mm Rem. Mag., 300 Win. Mag.) . 1,260.00

SAKO 75 DELUXE BOLT-ACTION RIFLE

The fine-touch features you expect of the deluxe grade SAKO are here: **1**-Reliable safety system with a separate bolt release button. **2**-First ever bolt with three locking lugs and a mechanical ejector. Five guiding surfaces prevent bolt binding and provide smooth operation. Four action sizes for perfect cartridge fit. **3**-Totally free-floating cold hammer forged barrel for ultimate accuracy. Test with a slip of paper. **4**-Sako Deluxe 75 Hunting Rifle has stainless steel lined staggered magazine with hinged floorplate and aluminum follower for faultless operation. Positive feeding angle is only 3-5 degrees. **5**-Fancy grade, high-grained walnut. Old-world craftmanship Rosewood pistol grip cap with silver inlay. **6**-Classic detail–Rosewood fore-end tip. The accuracy, reliability and superior field performance for which SAKO is famous are still here too.

DELUXE BOLT-ACTION RIFLE

The scope mounting system on these SAKOS are among the strongest in the world. Instead of using separate bases, a tapered dovetail is milled into the receiver, to which the scope rings are mounted. This sleek system has been proven over 20 years on the field. SAKO Original Scope Mounts and SAKO scope rings are available in low, medium and high in one-inch and 30mm.

Prices: ACTION I
in 17 Rem., 222 Rem. & 223 Rem. **$1,615.00**
ACTION III
In 22-250 Rem., 243 Win., 7mm-08 and 308 Win. **1,615.00**
ACTION IV
In 25-06 Rem., 6.5x55 SE, 270 Win.,
280 Rem., 30-06 . . . . **1,615.00**
ACTION V
In 270 Wby. Mag., 7mm Rem. Mag., 7mm STW, 7mm Wby. Mag., 300 Win. Mag., 300 Wby. Mag., 338 Win. Mag., .340 Wby. Mag., 375 H&H Mag., 416 Rem. Mag. **1,645.00**

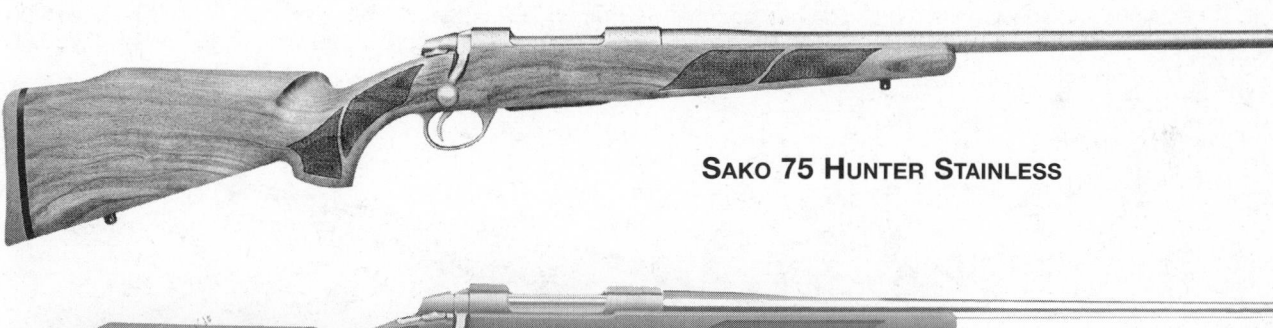

SAKO 75 HUNTER STAINLESS

SAKO 75 STAINLESS SYNTHETIC

SAKO 75 ACTION

SAKO 75 HUNTER STAINLESS

Detachable box magazine, checkered walnut stock, standard and magnum chamberings.
Price:
23", .270 Win., 30-06 . . . . **$1,205.00**
24" 7mm Rem. Mag., 300 Win. Mag.,
338 Win. Mag. **1,235.00**
26" 7mm STW, 300 Wby. **1,235.00**

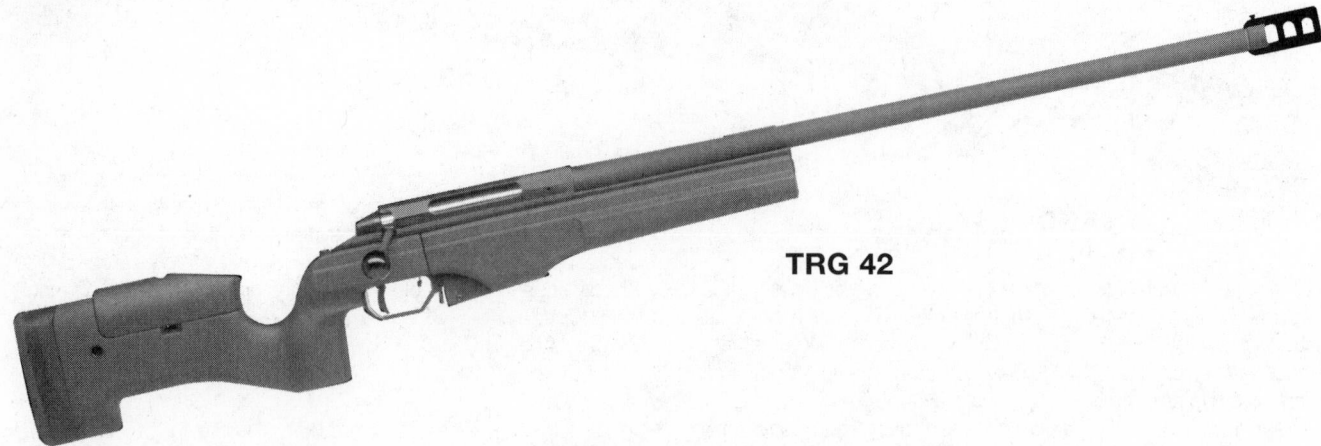

TRG 42

SAKO TRG 22/42

SAKO TRG 22/42 rifles are designed for long-range competition. The TRG 22 in 308 Win.excels in 300-meter UIT standard competition rifle and serves the governments of several nations as their primary sniper rifle.

The TRG 42 in 300 Win. Mag and .338 Lapua Mag. is a true long-range competition rifle. It can also be equipped with various implements to accommodate the tactical sniper.

Both TRG actions and special match grade barrels (chromemoly or stainless) are cold hammer-forged. The sturdy bolt with three locking lugs feeds rounds reliably from the centerline of a detachable staggered magazine. The high-tech constructed aluminum reinforced composite stock can be completely adjusted to match the individual preferences of all shooters. The target trigger is a fully adjustable 2-stage unit. Optilock quickmount allows any target scope to be positioned properly on the action.

Prices: TRG-22 in 308 Win **$2,415.00**
TRG-42 in .338 Lapua or 300 Win Mag **2,760.00**

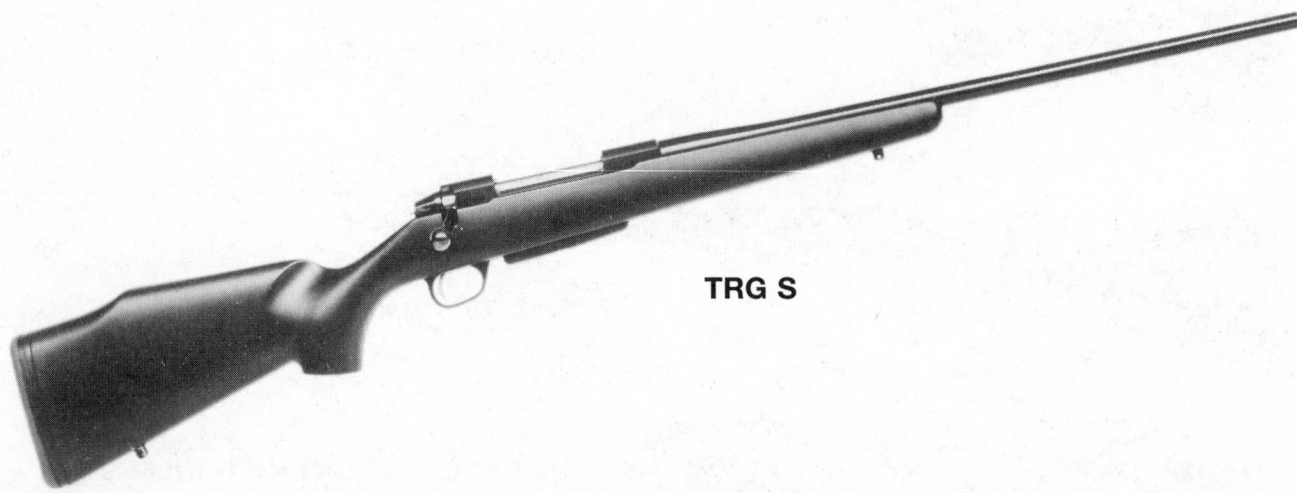

TRG S

SAKO TRG-S

This sophisticated hunting rifle is designed with same principles as Sako's famed competition TRG rifle. Bolt is massive, with 3 symmetrical locking lugs and thus a short 60 degree bolt lift. Detachable magazine feeds reliably from centerline, straight to chamber. Stock is high-tech composite with integrated fiberglass reinforced skeleton for rigidity and accuracy.

Free floating cold hammer-forged barrel, adjustable trigger.
Calibers: .338 Lapua Mag, 30-378 Wby. Mag
Price: **$875.00**

RIFLES

MODEL		Action	Total Length Inches	Barrel Length Inches	Weight lbs (approx.)	Caliber / Rate of Twist	Stock Finish	Sights	Trigger	Magazine Capacity	Stainless / Key
75 HUNTER		I	41 3/4	22	6 3/8	22LR–9.3x62 group	Oiled(+)			6	
		III	42 7/8	22 7/16	7 1/4		Oiled(+)			5	
		IV	43 3/4	22 7/8	7 15/16		Oiled(+)			5	
		V	45 5/8	24 3/8	8 5/8		Oiled(+)			4	
		V	47 1/4	26	8 13/16		Oiled(+)			4	
		V	47 1/4	26	8 13/16		Oiled(+)			4	
75 HUNTER STAINLESS		I	41 3/4	22	6 3/16		Oiled(+)			6	
		III	42 7/8	22 7/16	7		Oiled(+)			5	
		IV	43 3/4	22 7/8	7 3/4		Oiled(+)			5	
		V	45 5/8	24 3/8	8 3/8		Oiled(+)			4	
		V	47 1/4	26	8 5/8		Oiled(+)			4	
75 DELUXE		I	45 3/4	22	6 3/8		Oiled(+)/Lacquered(+)			6	
		III	42 7/8	22 7/16	7 1/4		Oiled(+)/Lacquered(+)			5	
		IV	43 3/4	22 7/8	7 15/16		Oiled(+)/Lacquered(+)			5	
		V	45 5/8	24 3/8	8 5/8		Oiled(+)/Lacquered(+)			4	
		V	47 1/4	26	8 13/16		Oiled(+)/Lacquered(+)			4	
75 BATTUE		IV	40	19 1/4	7 3/4		Oiled(+)			5	
		V	40 1/2	19 1/4	7 15/16		Oiled(+)			4	
75 VARMINT		I	43 1/4	23 5/8	8 1/8		Oiled(+)			6	
		III	44	23 5/8	8 5/8		Oiled(+)			5	
		IV	44 1/2	23 5/8	8 13/16		Oiled(+)			5	
		V	44 7/8	23 5/8	9		Oiled(+)			4	
		V	44 7/8	23 5/8	99		Oiled(+)			4	
		V	47 1/4	26	9 1/4		Oiled(+)			4	
75 VARMINT LAMINATED STAINLESS		I	43 1/4	23 5/8	8 5/8					6	
		III	44	23 5/8	9					5	
75 SYNTHETIC STAINLESS		III	42 7/8	22 7/16	7					5	
		IV	43 3/4	22 7/8	7 3/4					5	
		V	45 3/4	24 3/8	8 3/8					4	
		V	47 1/4	26	8 5/8					4	
		V	47 1/4	26	8 5/8					4	
75 FINNLIGHT		III	40 3/4	20 1/4	6					5	
		IV	41 3/4	20 7/8	6 1/2					5	
		V	43 3/4	22 9/16	7 1/4					5	
TRG-S	M995		47 1/4	26	8 1/8					3	
TRG-22	TRG-22		45 1/4	26	10 1/4					10	+
TRG-42	TRG-42		47 1/4	27 1/8	11 1/4					7	+
FINFIRE MODELS											
HUNTER	P94S		39 1/2	22	5 3/4	22LR				5	
VARMINT	P94S		40 1/2	23	7 1/4	22LR				5	
SPORTER	P94S		40 1/2	23	7 1/2	22LR				10	

Caliber / Rate of Twist column headers (left to right):
22 LR (16.5"), 17 Rem (10"), 222 Rem (14"), 223 Rem (12"), 22 PPC® USA (14"), 6 PPC® USA (12"), 22-250 Rem (14"), 243 Win (10"), 7mm-08 Rem (9.5"), 308 Win (11"), 25-06 Rem (10"), 6.5x55 SE (8"), 270 Win (10"), 7x64 (10"), 280 Rem (10"), 30-06 (11"), 9.3x62 (14"), 270 Wby Mag (10"), 7mm Rem Mag (9.5"), 7mm Wby Mag (9.5"), 7mm STW (9.5"), 300 Win Mag (11"), 300 Wby Mag (11"), 300 Rem Ultra Mag (11"), 338 Win Mag (10"), 340 Wby Mag (10"), 375 H&H Mag (12"), 30-378 Wby Mag (11"), 338 Lapua Mag (12")

Feature column headers: Stock Finish — Oiled, Lacquered, Matte Lacquered, Injection Moulded; Sights — Open Sights, Without Sights; Trigger — Single Stage Trigger, Double Stage Trigger; Magazine — Detachable, Hinged Floorplate, Magazine Capacity; Stainless Steel Barrel, Stainless Steel Action, Key Concept

• = as standard   + = as option   Rifle weight may varie depending on wood density and caliber. The manufacturer reserves the right to modify specifications.

MODEL SHR 970 SYNTHETIC

SIG SHR 970 BOLT ACTION RIFLE

The bolt of this centerfire rifle locks into the barrel, not the receiver, ensuring constant headspace and permitting interchange of barrels. In fact, barrels on the SHR 970 can be switched quickly and easily in the field with no other change if the cartridge head sizes are the same (different-size heads require switching the bolt as well). Hammer-forged barrels conribute to accuracy, as does the bedding block. The 65-degree bolt lift makes followup shots quick and effortless. A three-position safety and detachable box magazine make unloading a snap. Stocks are available in checkered

European walnut or synthetic versions, both with quick-detach swivel studs. Metal is "Ilaflon"coated to prevent rust and corrosion. The SHR 970 rifle is chambered for the .25-06, .270, .280, 7mm Rem. Mag., .308, .30-06 and .300 Win. Mag. The STR tactical or long range rifle comes only in .308 and .300 Win. Mag. **Barrel lengths:** 22" for standard calibers, 24" for magnums and the fluted STR barrels. **Weight:** 7.2 and 7.4 pounds for the SHR, 11.6 for the STR. **Prices:**

SHR synthetic $499.00
SHR walnut 550.00
STR. 899.00

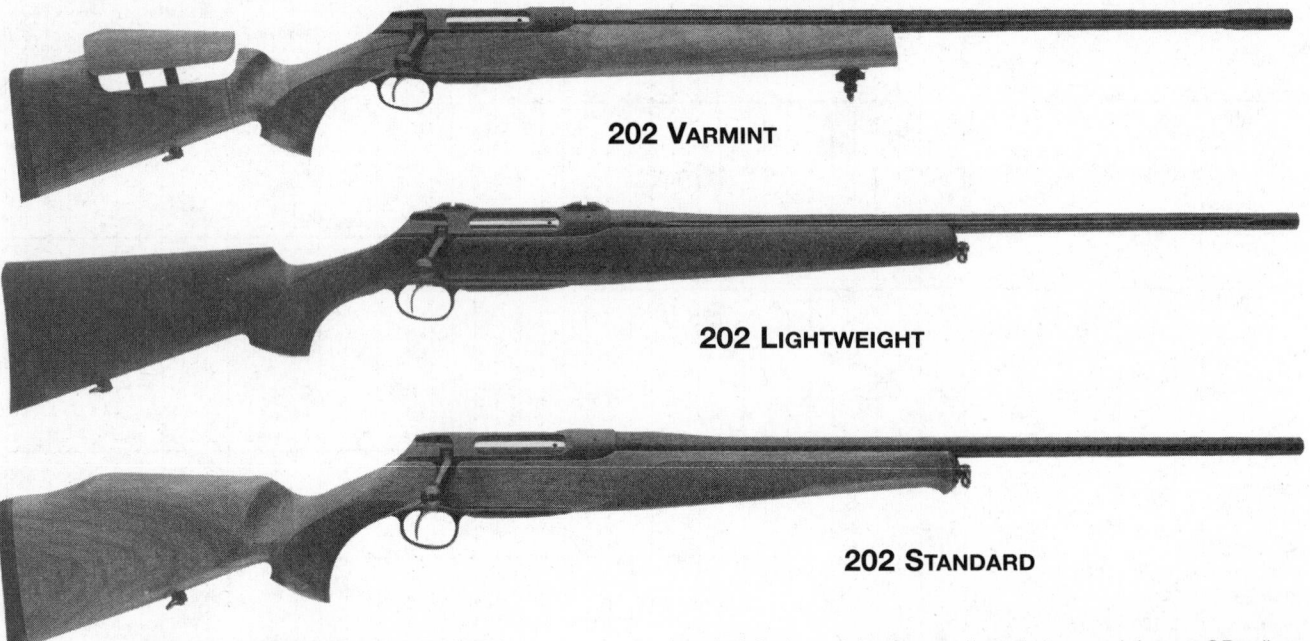

202 VARMINT

202 LIGHTWEIGHT

202 STANDARD

MODEL 202 BOLT ACTION
SPECIFICATIONS

Calibers: 25-06 Rem., 243 Win., 6.5x55, 270 Win., 308, 30-06 S'field; *Supreme Magnum calibers:* 7mm Rem. Mag., 300 Win. Mag., 300 Wby. Mag., 375 Win. Mag. **Action:** Bolt takedown **Capacity:** 3 rounds **Barrel Length:** 23.6"; 26" (Supreme Magnum) **Overall Length:** 44.3"; 46" (Supreme Magnum) **Weight:** 7.7 lbs.; 8.4 lbs. (Supreme Magnum) **Stock:** Select American claro walnut with high-gloss epoxy finish and rosewood forend and grip caps; Monte Carlo comb with cheekpiece; 22 line-per-inch diamond pattern, hand-cut checking **Sights:** Drilled and tapped for sights and scope bases **Features:** Adjustable two-stage trigger; polished and

jeweled bolt; quick-change barrel; tapered bore; QD sling swivel studs; black rubber recoil pad; Wundhammer palm swell; dual release safety; six locking lugs on bolt head; removable box magazine; fully enclosed bolt face; three gas relief holes; firing-pin cocking indicator on bolt rear
Prices:

Standard synthetic $1,259.00
Standard walnut 1,249.00
Also available: Lightweight. $1,395.00
Supreme w/walnut stock 1,385.00
SSG 3000 Tactical Rifle 2,560.00
Varminter. 1,495.00
Left hand (30-06 w/walnut only) 1,395.00

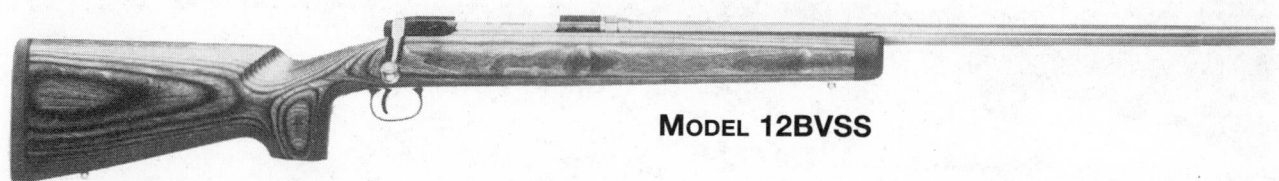

MODEL 12BVSS

MODEL 12BVSS SHORT ACTION VARMINT

SPECIFICATIONS

Calibers: 223 Rem., 22-250 Rem., and 308 Win. Single-shot Model available in 223 Rem. and 22-250 Rem. **Capacity:** 5 + 1 **Barrel Length:** 26" fluted heavy barrel **Overall Length:** 46.75" **Magazine:** Top loading internal **Weight:** 9.5 lbs. **Sights:** None. Drilled and tapped for scope mounts **Stock:** Laminated hard wood with high comb, ambidextrous grip and ebony tip **Finish:** Fluted stainless steel with recessed muzzle **Features:** Short Action precision long range rifle with dual pillar bedding

Price: **$595.00**
Also Available: FVSS with black synthetic stock, 9 lbs. 549.00

RIFLES

MODEL 12VSS
VARMINTER

MODEL 12VSS-SHORT ACTION
SPECIFICATIONS

Calibers: .223 Rem., 22-250 Rem., 308 Win. **Overall Length:** 45.75" **Weight:** 11.25 lbs. **Sights:** Drilled and tapped for scope mounts **Stock:** Choate™ adjustable black synthetic stock. **Barrel:** Heavy fluted stainless steel, recessed target muzzle, button rifled and free floating. **Magazine:** Internal box with (4) round capacity **Features:** Blue/Stainless steel bolt action, *Sharp Shooter* trigger, Choate™ stock. Scopes, rings, bases and bipod not included.

Price: **$869.00**

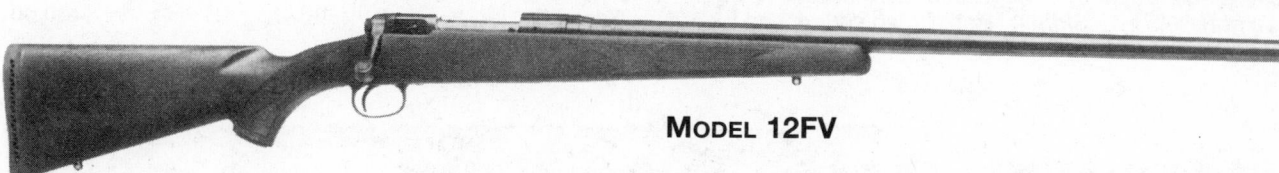

MODEL 12FV

MODEL 12FV SHORT ACTION VARMINT

SPECIFICATIONS

Calibers: 223 Rem., 22-250 Rem., 308 Win.
Capacity: 5
Barrel Length: 26"
Overall Length: 46.75"
Magazine: Top loading internal
Weight: 9 lbs.

Sights: None. Drilled and tapped for scope mounts
Stock: Durable black synthetic with scrolled checkering and dual pillars
Finish: Blued with recessed muzzle
Features: Short-action varmint rifle with 26" button rifled heavy barrel

Price: **$465.00**

SAVAGE ARMS

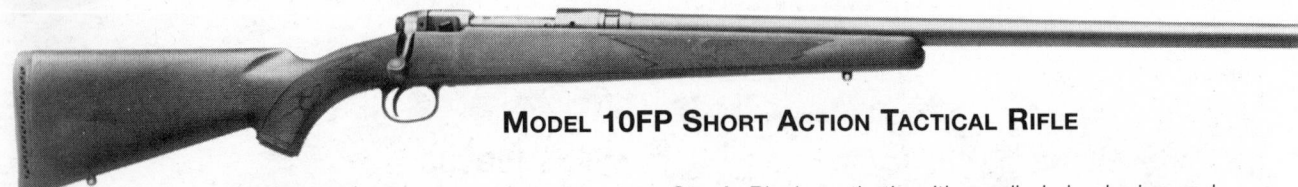

MODEL 10FP SHORT ACTION TACTICAL RIFLE

SPECIFICATIONS

Calibers: 223, 7mm-08, 260, 308 *Capacity:* 5
Barrel Length: 24" heavy barrel *Overall Length:* 43.75"
Magazine: Top loading internal *Weight:* 8 lbs.
Sights: None. Drilled and tapped for scope mounts

Stock: Black synthetic with scrolled checkering and dual pillars
Finish: Black non-reflective with recessed target style muzzle
Features: Short action heavy barrel rifle with twin pillar bedding
Price: **$486.00**

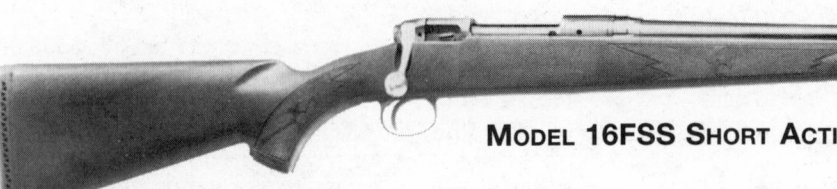

MODEL 16FSS SHORT ACTION WEATHER WARRIOR

SPECIFICATIONS

Calibers: 223, 243, 7mm-08, 308 *Capacity:* 5
Barrel Length: 22" *Overall Length:* 40.75"
Magazine: Top loading internal *Weight:* 6 lbs.
Sights: None. Drilled and tapped for scope mounts

Stock: Durable black synthetic with scrolled checkering and dual pillars *Finish:* Stainless steel
Features: Short action satin finished 400 series stainless steel barreled action
Price: **$484.00**

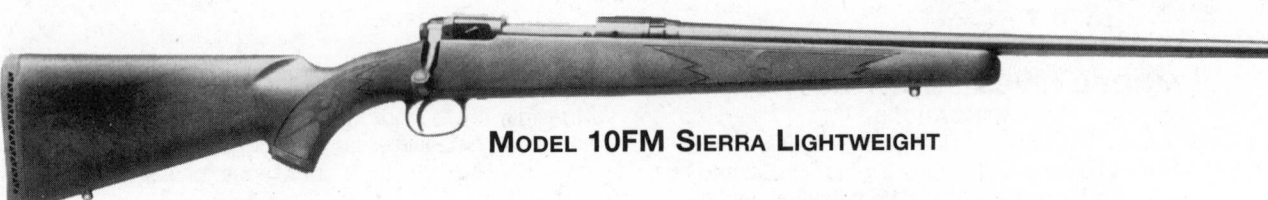

MODEL 10FM SIERRA LIGHTWEIGHT

SPECIFICATIONS

Calibers: 243, 7mm-08, 308
Capacity: 5 + 1 *Barrel Length:* 20"
Overall Length: 41.5" *Magazine:* Top loading internal
Weight: 6.25 lbs. *Sights:* None. Drilled and tapped for

scope mount; bases included
Stock: Lightweight graphite/fiberglass filled composite stock with positive checkering *Finish:* Blued
Features: Blue alloy steel barreled action
Price: **$460.00**

MODEL 110FP TACTICAL

SPECIFICATIONS

Calibers: 25-06 Rem., 30-06 Spfd., 7mm Rem. Mag., 300 Win. Mag. *Capacity:* 5 rounds (1 in chamber) *Barrel Length:* 24" (w/recessed target-style muzzle) *Overall Length:* 45.5"
Weight: 8.5 lbs. *Sights:* None; drilled and tapped for scope

mount; bases included *Features:* Black matte nonreflective finish on metal parts; bolt coated with titanium nitride; stock made of black graphite/fiberglass-filled composite with positive checkering; left-hand model available
Price: **$486.00**

MODEL 11F SHORT ACTION HUNTER

SPECIFICATIONS
Calibers: 223 Rem., 22-250 Rem., 243 Win., 7mm-08 Rem., and 308 Win. *Capacity:* 5 *Barrel Length:* 22" standard weight *Overall Length:* 42.75" *Magazine:* Top loading internal *Weight:* 6.75 lbs. *Sights:* Available in right/left hand. Drilled and tapped for scope mounts *Stock:* Durable black synthetic with scrolled checkering and dual pillars *Finish:* Blued
Features: Short Action with dual pillar bedded stock
Price: $428.00

RIFLES

MODEL 11G SHORT ACTION CLASSIC AMERICAN STYLE HUNTER

SPECIFICATIONS
Calibers: 223 Rem., 22-250 Rem., 243 Win., 7mm-08 Rem., 260 Rem., and 308 Win. *Capacity:* 5 *Barrel Length:* 22" *Overall Length:* 42.75" *Magazine:* Top loading internal *Weight:* 6.75 lbs. *Sights:* Available with or without (11GNS) Available in right/left hand. Drilled and tapped for scope mounts *Stock:* American style walnut finished hardwood with fancy scrolled, diamond point checkering and black recoil pad *Finish:* Blued
Price: $405.00

MODEL 10GY SHORT ACTION LADIES/YOUTH RIFLE

SPECIFICATIONS
Calibers: 223 Rem., 243 Win. and 308 Win.
Capacity: 5
Barrel Length: 22" standard weight
Overall Length: 39.25"
Magazine: Top loading internal
Weight: 6.25 lbs.
Sights: None. Drilled and tapped for scope mounts
Stock: American style walnut finished hardwood with cut checkering
Finish: Blued
Price: $405.00

Long Range And Scout Rifles

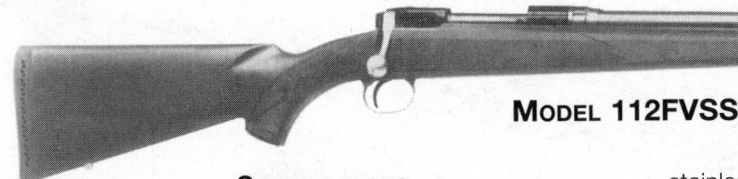

MODEL 112FVSS LONG ACTION

SPECIFICATIONS

Calibers: 25-06 Rem., 30-06, 7mm Rem. Mag., 300 Win. Mag. (single-shot model available in 220 Swift, 300 Win. Mag.) *Capacity:* 4 + 1 *Barrel Length:* 26" fluted,

stainless steel *Overall Length:* 47.5" *Weight:* 10.3 lbs. *Sights:* Graphite/fiberglass-filled composite w/positive checkering
Price: $549.00

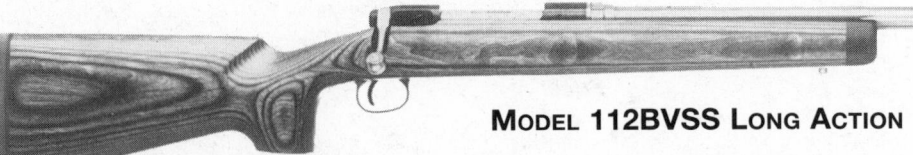

MODEL 112BVSS LONG ACTION

SPECIFICATIONS

Calibers: 25-06, 7mm Rem. Mag., 300 Win Mag., 30-06 Sprgfld., (single-shot model also available in 220 Swift, 300 Win. Mag.) *Capacity:* 4 + 1 *Barrel Length:* 26" fluted

heavy barrel, stainless steel *Overall Length:* 47.5" *Weight:* 10 lbs. (approx.) *Sights:* None; drilled and tapped *Stock:* Laminated hardwood w/high comb; ambidextrous grip
Price: $595.00

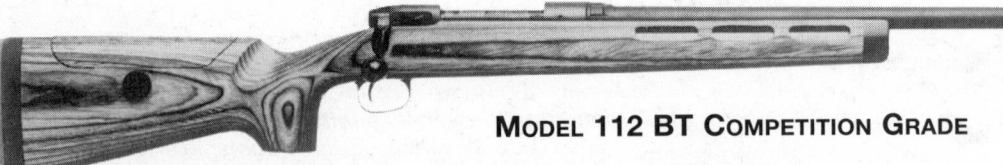

MODEL 112 BT COMPETITION GRADE

SPECIFICATIONS

Calibers: 223 Rem. and 308 Win. Mag. (single-shot available in 300 Win. Mag.)
Capacity: 5 + 1
Barrel Length: 26"; blackened stainless steel w/recessed

target/style muzzle
Overall Length: 47.5"
Weight: 10 7/8 lbs.
Stock: Laminated brown w/straight comb
Price: $1,049.00

SAVAGE "SCOUT" RIFLE-MODEL 10FCM

Ultra-light weight and extremely well balanced, the **10FCM** SAVAGE "SCOUT" is the ideal rifle for any outdoor situation. Weighing approximately 6 pounds and sporting a 20" barrel,

this fast handling carbine is chambered in 7mm-08 and .308. *Features:* Detachable Box Magazine: Capacity four (4) plus one (1) in the chamber; Removabe Ghost Ring Rear Sight with Gold Bead Front Sight; One-piece Scope Mount for long eye relief scope; Large Ball Bolt Handle; Rifleman's Combo Shooting Sling/Carry Strap with Q.D. Swivel Set; "Dual Pillar Bedded" synthetic stock
Price: $540.00

MODEL 116FSS "WEATHER WARRIOR"

Savage Arms combines the strength of a black graphite fiberglass polymer stock and the durability of a stainless-steel barrel and receiver in this bolt-action rifle. Major components are made from stainless steel, honed to a low refllective satin finish. Drilled and tapped for scope mounts. Left-hand model available.

SPECIFICATIONS
Calibers: 270 30-06, 7mm Rem. Mag., 300 Win. Mag., 338 Win. Mag., 7mm STW, 300 Rem Ultra Mag *Capacity:* 2-4 rounds *Barrel Length:* 22"-26" *Overall Length:* 45"-46.5" *Weight:* 6.5-7.75 lbs.
Price: $484.00

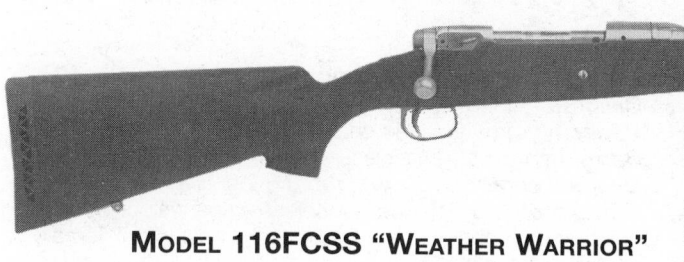

MODEL 116FCSS "WEATHER WARRIOR"

Calibers: 270, 30-06, 7mm Rem. Mag., 300 Win. Mag. This bolt-action rifle has the same quality features as the Model 116FSS plus a removable box magazine with recessed push-button release for ease in loading and unloading. Left-hand model available. *Price:* $532.00
Also Available: MODEL 16FCSS short action in 243, 7mm-08, 308

MODEL 116BSS — LONG ACTION

MODEL 116BSS WEATHER WARRIOR

SPECIFICATIONS
Calibers: 270 Win., 30-06, 7mm Rem. Mag., 300 Win Mag., 300 Rem Ultra Mag. *Barrel Length:* 24" or 26" *Weight:* 7 lbs to 7.75 lbs. *Features:* Laminate stock with cut checkering, stainless steel barrel.
Price: $644.00

MODEL 116FSAK – LONG ACTION
MODEL 116FLSAK – LEFF-HAND

MODEL 116FSAK

SPECIFICATIONS
Calibers: 270 Win., 30-06, 7mm, 300 Win Mag., 338 Win. Mag., 7mm STW, 300 Rem Ultra Mag. *Barrel Length:* 22"-26" *Weight:* 6.75 lbs to 7.75 lbs. *Features:* Synthetic stock, stainless barrel, adjustable muzzle brake. Left-hand available.
Price: $558.00

SAVAGE CENTERFIRE RIFLES

MODEL 111GC CLASSIC HUNTER

SPECIFICATIONS

Calibers: 270 Win., 30-06 Springfield, 7mm Rem. Mag., 300 Win. Mag. **Capacity:** 5 rounds (4 rounds in Magnum calibers) **Barrel Length:** 22" (standard) 24" (Magnum) **Overall Length:** 43.5" (45.5" Magnum calibers)

Weight: 6 ³/₈-7 lbs. **Sights:** Adjustable **Stock:** American-style walnut-finished hardwood; cut checkering **Features:** Detachable staggered box-type magazine; left-hand model available
Price: **$441.00**

MODEL 116SE SAFARI EXPRESS

SPECIFICATIONS

Calibers: 300 Win., 338, .375 H&H, 458 Win. Mag. **Capacity:** 4 rounds (1 in chamber) **Barrel Length:** 24" stainless steel w/AMB **Overall Length:** 45.5" **Weight:** 8.5 lbs. **Sights:** 3-leaf express **Stock:** Classic-style select-grade walnut w/cut checkering; ebony tip; stainless-steel crossbolts; internally vented recoil pad
Price: **$942.00**

MODEL 114U

SPECIFICATIONS

Calibers: 270 Win., 30-06 Spfld (22" bbl.); 7mm STW, 7mm Rem. Mag., 300 Win. Mag. (24" bbl.) **Overall Length:** 43.5" **Weight:** Approx. 7 lbs. **Rifling Twist:** 1 in 10" (270 Win., 30-6 Spfld., 300 Win. Mag.); 1 in 9.5" (7mm Rem. Mag.) **Features:** High gloss American Walnut Stock with ebony tip; Custom checkering on the grip and forend; High luster blued finish on the barrel, receiver, and bolt handle; Precision laser-etched Savage logo on bolt body; Drilled and tapped for scope mounts
Price: **$513.00**

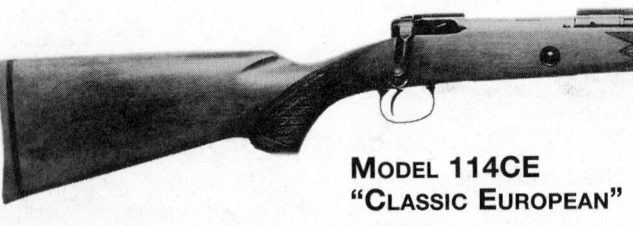

MODEL 114CE "CLASSIC EUROPEAN"

SPECIFICATIONS

Calibers: 270 Win., 30-06 Sprgfld., 7mm Rem. Mag., 7mmx64 Brenneke, 300 Win. Mag. **Capacity:** 3 rounds (magnum); 4 rounds (standard); plus 1 in each chamber

Barrel Length: 22" (standard); 24" (magnum) **Overall Length:** 43.5" (standard); 45.5" (magnum) **Weight:** 7 ¹/₈ lbs. (approx.) **Finish:** Oil-finished walnut stock w/schnabel tip, cheekpiece and French skip-line checkering on grip and forend **Features:** Rubber recoil pad; pistol-grip cap with gold medallion; high-luster blued finish on receiver barrel and bolt handle; side button release; adjustable sights; precision rifled barrel; drilled and tapped
Price: **$554.00**

Rimfire Rifles

MARK I-G SINGLE SHOT

SPECIFICATIONS
Caliber: 22 Short, Long or LR **Capacity:** Single shot
Action: Self-cocking bolt action, thumb-operated rotary
safety **Barrel Length:** 20.75" **Overall Length:** 39.5"

Weight: 5.5 lbs.
Sights: Open bead front; adjustable rear
Stock: One-piece, walnut-finish hardwood, Monte Carlo
buttstock w/full pistol grip; checkered pistol grip and forend
Features: Receiver grooved for scope mounting
Price: $131.00
Also available:
MARK I-G YOUTH (19" barrel). 131.00

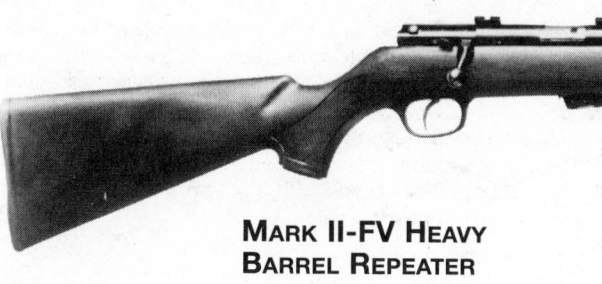

MARK II-FV HEAVY BARREL REPEATER

SPECIFICATIONS
Caliber: 22 LR **Capacity:** 5 rounds **Barrel Length:** 21"
heavy weight **Overall Length:** 39.75" **Magazine:** 5 shot
detachable clip **Weight:** 6 lbs. **Sights:** None. Weaver
style bases included **Stock:** Black synthetic with positive
checkering **Finish:** Blued free floated, button rifled with
recessed target style muzzle **Features:** Heavy barrel with
synthetic stock in 22 LR
Price: $198.00

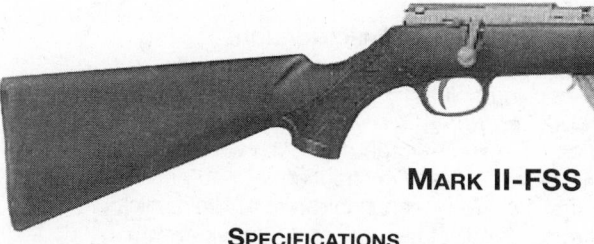

MARK II-FSS

SPECIFICATIONS
Caliber: 22 LR **Capacity:** 10 rounds **Barrel Length:** 21"
(1 in 16" twist) **Overall Length:** 39.5" **Weight:** 5 lbs.
Stock: Synthetic **Sights:** Bead front sight; adjustable open
rear **Features:** Stainless steel barrelled action

Price: $172.00
Also available: MARK II-G w/one-piece walnut-finished
Monte Carlo-style hardwood stock, blued steel bolt-action
receiver, bead front sight $142.00
MARK II-GY LADIES/YOUTH w/19" barrel (37" overall)
  Weight: 5 lbs. 142.00
MARK II-GXP w/4x15mm scope (LH model avail.) . 149.00
MARK II-F synthetic stock. 131.00

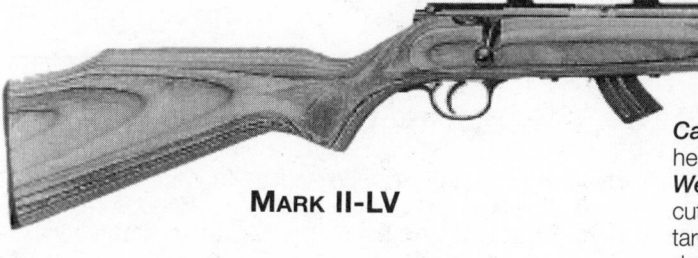

MARK II-LV

SPECIFICATIONS
Caliber: 22 LR **Capacity:** 10 rounds **Barrel Length:** 21"
heavy barrel (1 in 16" twist) **Overall Length:** 39.75"
Weight: 6.5 lbs. **Stock:** Grey laminated hardwood stock;
cut-checkered **Features:** Precision button rifled with recessed
target-style muzzle; machined blued steel barreled action;
dovetailed for scope mounting
Price: $227.00

MODEL 93G MAGNUM

SPECIFICATIONS
Caliber: 22 WMR **Capacity:** 5 rounds **Barrel Length:** 20.75" **Overall Length:** 39.5" **Weight:** 5.75 lbs. **Sights:** Bead front; sporting rear with step elevator **Stock:** cut-checkered walnut stained hardwood. Left hand available
Price: $164.00

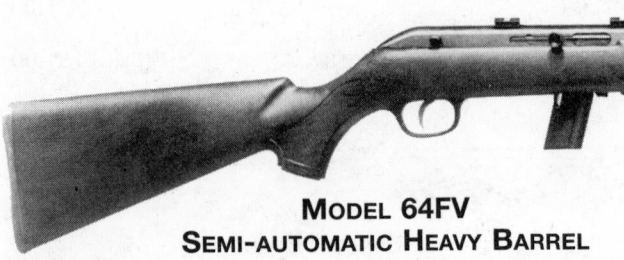

MODEL 64FV
SEMI-AUTOMATIC HEAVY BARREL

SPECIFICATIONS
Caliber: 22 LR **Capacity:** 10 rounds **Barrel Length:** 21" heavy weight **Overall Length:** 40.75" **Magazine:** 10 shot

detachable clip **Weight:** 6 lbs. **Sights:** None. Weaver style bases included **Stock:** Black synthetic with positive checkering **Finish:** Blued, button rifled with recessed target style muzzle **Features:** Semiauto blue alloy steel barreled action
Price: $166.00
Also Available: MODEL 64F standard barrel
with sights 5.5 lbs. 126.00
MODEL 64G standard barrel with sights 5.5 lbs.
and hardwood stock. 136.00

MODEL 900TR
TARGET REPEATER

SPECIFICATIONS
Caliber: 22 Long Rifle **Capacity:** 5 rounds **Action:** Self-cocking bolt action, thumb-operated rotary safety **Overall Length:** 43 $5/8$" **Approx. Weight:** 8 lbs. **Stock:** One-piece, target-type with walnut finish hardwood; comes with shooting rail and hand stop **Sights:** Receiver peep sights with 1/4 min. click micrometer adjustments, target front sight with inserts
Price: $448.00

MODEL 111FXP3

"Package" rifle with internal-box magazine (C version with detachable box), black synthetic stock, 22" barrel, sling, 3-9x32 scope.

Calibers: 223 Rem, 22-250 Rem., 243 Win., 7mm-08 Rem., 308 Win., 25-06 Rem.,270 Win., 30-06 Sprg., 7mm Rem. Mag., 300 Win. Mag., 338 Win. Mag. **Capacity:** 5 rounds (4 in Magnum) **Weight:** 6.5 lbs.
Price: $486.00

RIFLES

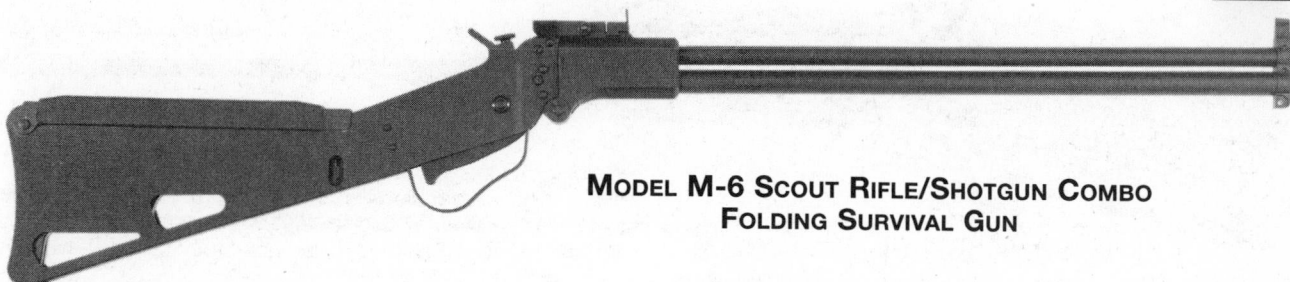

MODEL M-6 SCOUT RIFLE/SHOTGUN COMBO FOLDING SURVIVAL GUN

SPECIFICATIONS
Calibers: 22 LR/.410 and 22 Hornet/.410
Barrel Length: 18.25" (1:15" R.H. twist in 22 LR; 1:13" R.H. twist in 22 Hornet)
Overall Length: 32"
Weight: 4 lbs.

Sight Radius: 16 ¹/₈" *Finish:* Parkerized or stainless steel
Features: .410 shotgun barrel (2.5" or 3" chamber) choked Full; drilled and tapped for scope mount with Weaver base; lockable plastic carry case
Price: $185.00
Stainless Steel. 219.00

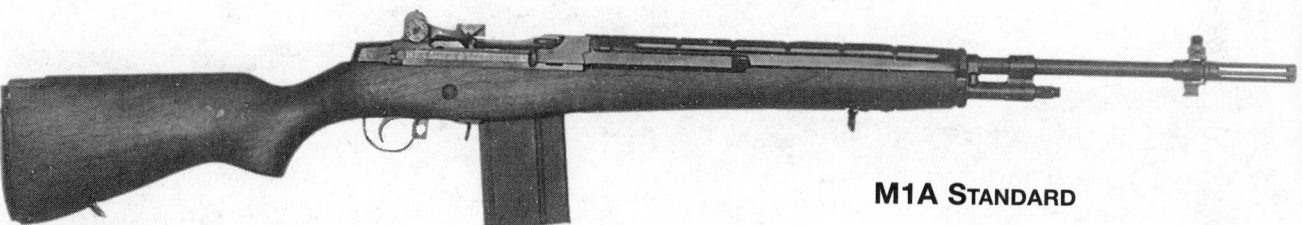

M1A STANDARD

SPECIFICATIONS
Calibers: 308 Win./7.62mm NATO (243 or 7mm-08 optional) *Action:* gas-operated, self-loading
Capacity: 5- or 10-round box magazine
Barrel Length: 22"
Rifling: 6 groove, RH twist, 1 turn in 11"
Overall Length: 44 ¹/₃"
Weight: 9.2 lbs.
Sights: Military square post front; military aperture rear, adjustable for windage and elevation
Sight Radius: 26.75"

Prices:
   Standard w/walnut stock $1,448.00
Also available:
BASIC M1A RIFLE w/painted black fiberglass stock,
   caliber 308/7.62mm only 1,319.00
M1A SCOUT RIFLE w/scope mount and handguard, black
fiberglass stock. 1,529.00
w/walnut stock 1,639.00
National Match (match-grade barrel and trigger) . . . 1,995.00
Super Match (heavy match barrel, special rod
   guide, heavy stock) 2,449.00

M1A-A1 SCOUT RIFLE

SPECIFICATIONS
Calibers: 308 Win./7.62mm
Action: gas-operated, self-loading
Barrel Length: 18" (w/o flash suppressor) *Overall Length:* 40.5" *Weight:* 8.9 lbs. (9 lbs. w/walnut stock)

Sights: Military square post-front, aperture rear with one MOA adjustments *Sight Radius:* 22.75"
Prices:
w/walnut stock. $1,639.00
w/black fiberglass stock. 1,529.00

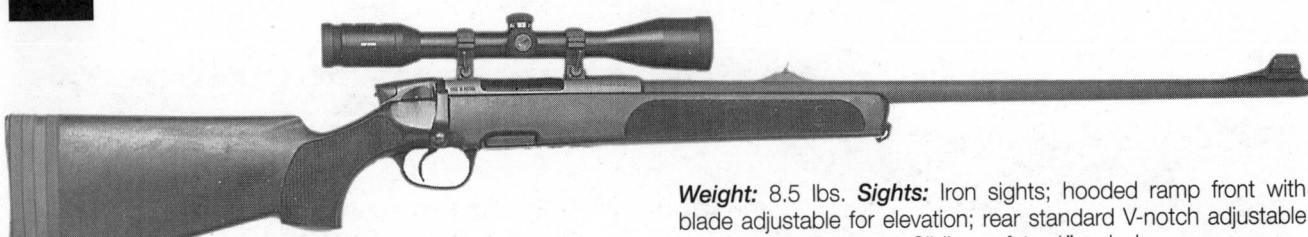

STEYR SSG-PI

The Steyr SSG features a black synthetic Cycolac stock (walnut optional), heavy Parkerized barrel, five-round standard (and optional 10-round) staggered magazine, heavy-duty milled receiver.

SPECIFICATIONS
Calibers: 308 Win. *Barrel Length:* 26" *Overall Length:* 44.5"

Weight: 8.5 lbs. *Sights:* Iron sights; hooded ramp front with blade adjustable for elevation; rear standard V-notch adjustable for windage. *Features:* Sliding safety; 1" swivels.
Prices: MODEL SSG-PI Cycolac half-stock (26" bbl. with sights in 308 Win.). **$1,699.00**
MODEL SSG-PII (without sights) **1,699.00**
MODEL SSG-P-IV in 308 Win. w/16.75", heavy barrel, no sights. **2,659.00**
MODEL SSG-PII McMILLAN 20" or 26" heavy barrel adjustable stock, no sights. **2,299.00**

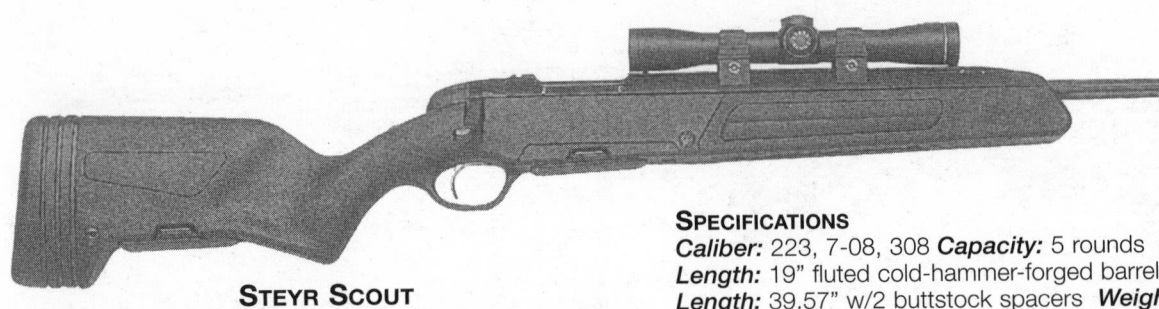

STEYR SCOUT

The Steyr Scout package is equally effective as a sporter, tactical or survival rifle. Among its features are: safe bolt system, roller tang safety and black Zytel stock; integral bipod, flush sling sockets and forward-mounted Leupold 2.5X Scout Scope. Luggage case and two magazines included.

SPECIFICATIONS
Caliber: 223, 7-08, 308 *Capacity:* 5 rounds *Barrel Length:* 19" fluted cold-hammer-forged barrel *Overall Length:* 39.57" w/2 buttstock spacers *Weight:* 7 lbs. (w/scope and mounts) *Sights:* Factory-installed Leupold 2.5 X 28mm IER *Stock:* Zytel w/13.58" length of pull (adjustable, w/spacers)
Price: Package. **$2,699.00**
Rifle only.. . . . . **1,969.00**

SBS (SAFE BOLT SYSTEM) MANNLICHER CLASSIC MODEL

SPECIFICATIONS
Calibers: 243 Win., 25-06, 6.5x55, 308 Win., 270 Win., 7mm-08, Spr 30-06, 7x57, 260 Rem., 280 Rem.
Capacity: 4 rounds (3 rounds in Magnum, Prohunter and Forester); detachable staggered box magazine

Barrel Lengths: 20" *Weight:* 7.5 lbs.
Safety: 3-position roller safety
Trigger: Single adjustable trigger
Sights: Ramp front w/balck adjustment for elevations; rear standard V-notch adjustable for windage; drilled and tapped for mounts
Finish: Blued; hand-checkered fancy European oiled walnut stock
Features: Rotary cold hammer-forged barrel; front locking lug bolt
Prices: **$1,749.00**

Steyr SBS Hunting Rifle Series

PROHUNTER

SBS PROHUNTER-SYNTHETIC STOCK
23.6" barrel, no sights, matte blue finish, 2 removable butt spacers, flush mounted QD swivels, 7.4 lbs., .243, .25-06, .260, 6.5 x 55, .270, 7mm-08, .280, .308, .30-06, accepts optional Hi-Capacity magazine kit
Price: $769.00

Also available: PROHUNTER MAGNUM, .26" barrel in 7 mm Rem Mag, .300 Win Mag **$799.00**
PROHUNTER STAINLESS STEEL 859.00
PROHUNTER STAINLESS STEEL MAGNUM 889.00
PROHUNTER CAMO (Mossy Oak, Camo stock,
  blued steel) 829.00
PROHUNTER CAMO MAGNUM 859.00
PROHUNTER 376 CAMO (in .376 Steyr) 919.00
PROHUNTER SS CAMO 919.00
PROHUNTER SS CAMO MAGNUM 949.00

PROHUNTER SS CAMO

PROHUNTER MOUNTAIN
20" barrel, no sights, matte blue finish, in .243, 25-06, .260, 6.5x55, .270, 7mm-08, .308, .30-06

Price: **$769.00**
PROHUNTER MOUNTAIN STAINLESS STEEL 859.00
PROHUNTER MOUNTAIN CAMO (Mossy Oak, Camo
  stock, blued steel) 829.00
PROHUNTER MOUNTAIN STAINLESS STEEL CAMO 919.00

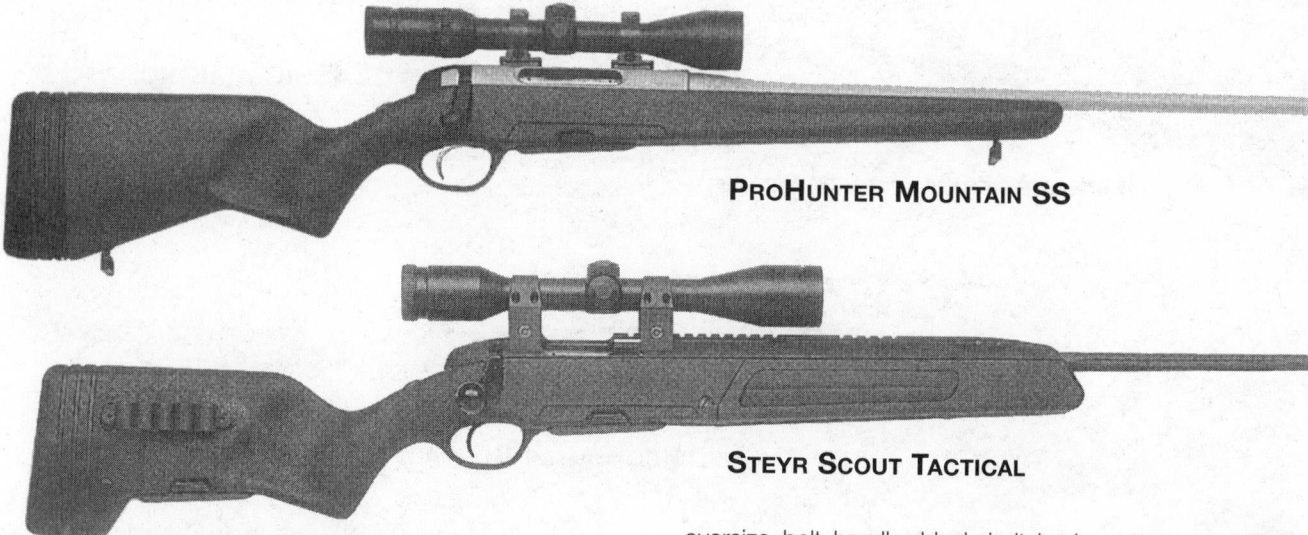

PROHUNTER MOUNTAIN SS

STEYR SCOUT TACTICAL

STEYR SCOUT TACTICAL
Black synthetic stock with removable spacers, 19.25" fluted barrel, full length optic rail (Weaver style), Integral bipod,

oversize bolt handle, black bolt body, emergency "Ghost Ring" sights and two 5 round magazines, .223, .308
Price: $2,069.00
SCOUT TACTICAL STAINLESS STEEL 2,159.00

RIFLES

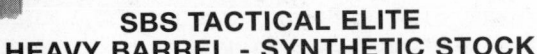

SBS TACTICAL ELITE

SBS TACTICAL ELITE
HEAVY BARREL - SYNTHETIC STOCK

Caliber: 223 Rem or 308 Win 26" heavy barrel, two 5-round detachable magazines (w/spare buttstock storage), no sights, matte blue finish, black bolt body with oversize bolt handle, Zytel stock with adj. cheekpiece and fully adj. buttplate, full-length Picatinney spec mounting rail, forearm mounting rail, 5 QD swivel stations, accepts Hi-Capacity 10 round magazine with adapter

Price: $2,399.00
Stainless 2,499.00
Package (includes ZF optic) 3,499.00

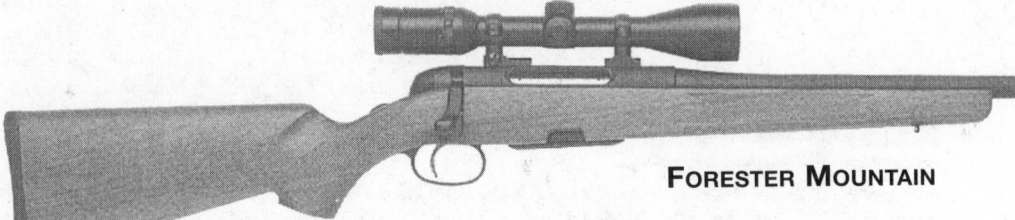

STEYR SBS FORESTER MOUNTAIN

20" sporter barrel, 5-round detachable magazine, adjustable trigger, no sights, satin-finish classic-style walnut stock, 7.2 lbs., in .243, .25-06, .260, 6.5x55, .270, 7mm-08, .308, .30-06

FORESTER MOUNTAIN

Price: $829.00
Also available: Forester with 24" barrel (in .280 Rem too)
7.4 lbs 799.00
Forester Magnum, 26" barrel in 7mm Rem, 300 Win Magnum 829.00

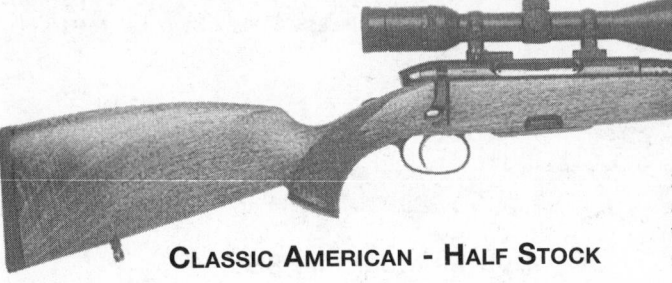

CLASSIC AMERICAN - HALF STOCK

STEYR SBS CLASSIC AMERICAN

24" sporter barrel, 5-round detachable magazines, adjustable trigger, no sights, satin-finish walnut stock with forend tip, 7.2 lbs, in .243, 25-06, .260, 6.5x55, .270, 7mm-08, .280, .308, .30-06

Price: $1,549.00

STEYR SBS
PROHUNTER COMPACT

Synthetic Zytel stock with 2 butt spacers included, special "shock absorbing" recoil pad, 20" barrel with iron sights, flush

PROHUNTER COMPACT

mounted QD swivels, accepts optional Hi-Capacity magazine kit, matte blue finish, 243, .260, 7mm-08, .308, .376 Steyr

Price: $819.00
Also available: PROHUNTER COMPACT STAINLESS STEEL . . 909.00

The Szecsei & Fuchs double-barrel bolt action rifle may be the only one of its kind. Built with great care and much handwork from the finest materials, it follows a design remarkable for its cleverness. And while the rifle is not light-weight, it can be aimed quickly and offers more large-caliber firepower than any competitor. The six-shot magazine feeds two rounds simultaneously, both of which can then be fired by two quick pulls of the trigger. **Chamberings:** .300 Win, 9.3 x 64, .358 Norma, .375 H&H, .404 Jeff, .416 Rem., .458 Win., .416 Rigby, .450 Rigby, .460 Short A-Square, .470 Capstick, .495 A-Square, .500 Jeff **Weight:** 14 lbs. with round barrels, 16 with octagon barrels. **Price:** . . . . **Available on request**

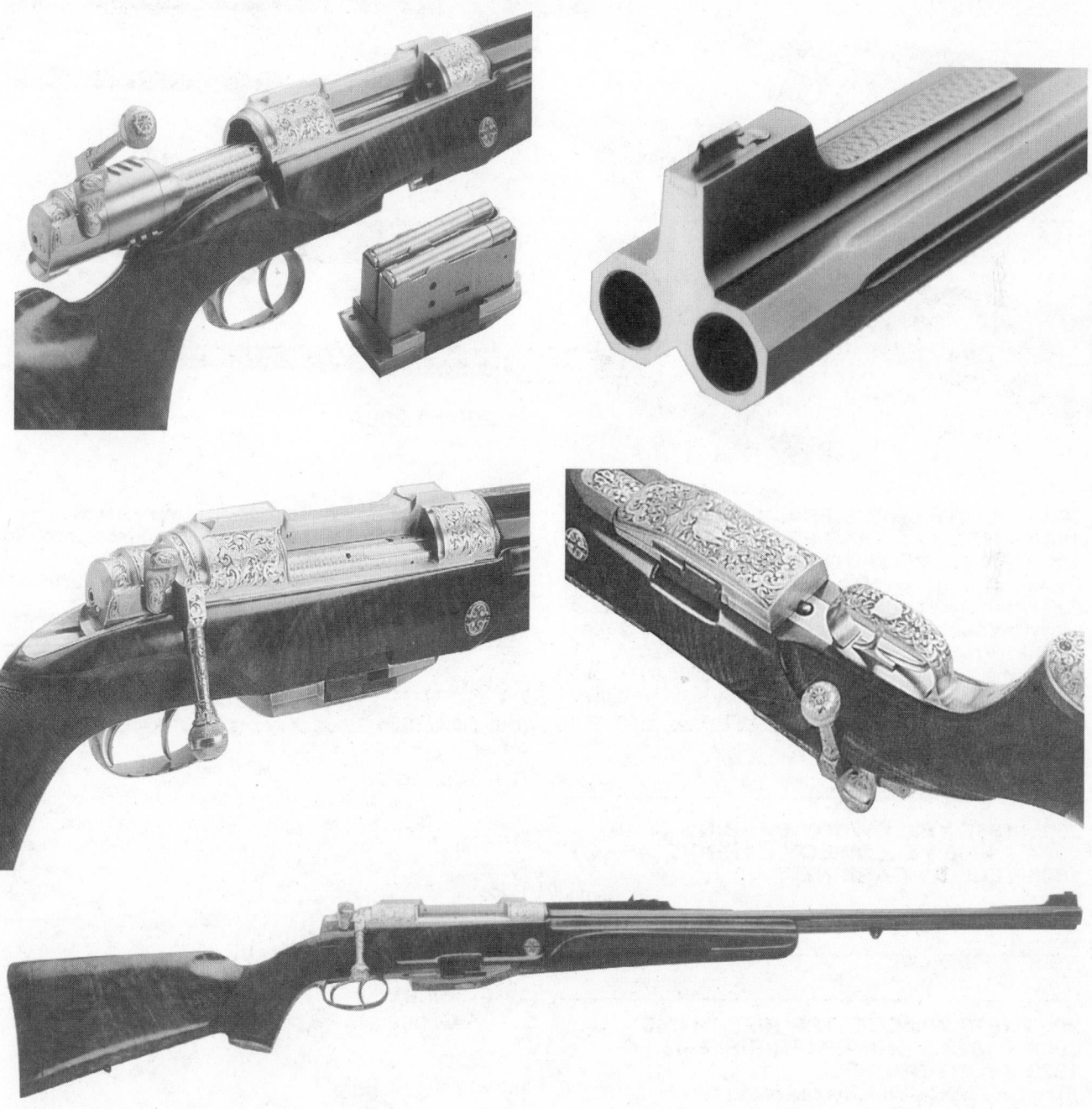

Faithful to the original, this "Henry", required a good deal of skill to reproduce. It was the first lever-action repeating rifle to be both practical and reliable. It derived from the Volcanic carbines of Walter Hunt, and was named after B. Tyler Henry, who refined the rifle. It would become the cornerstone of the Winchester line.

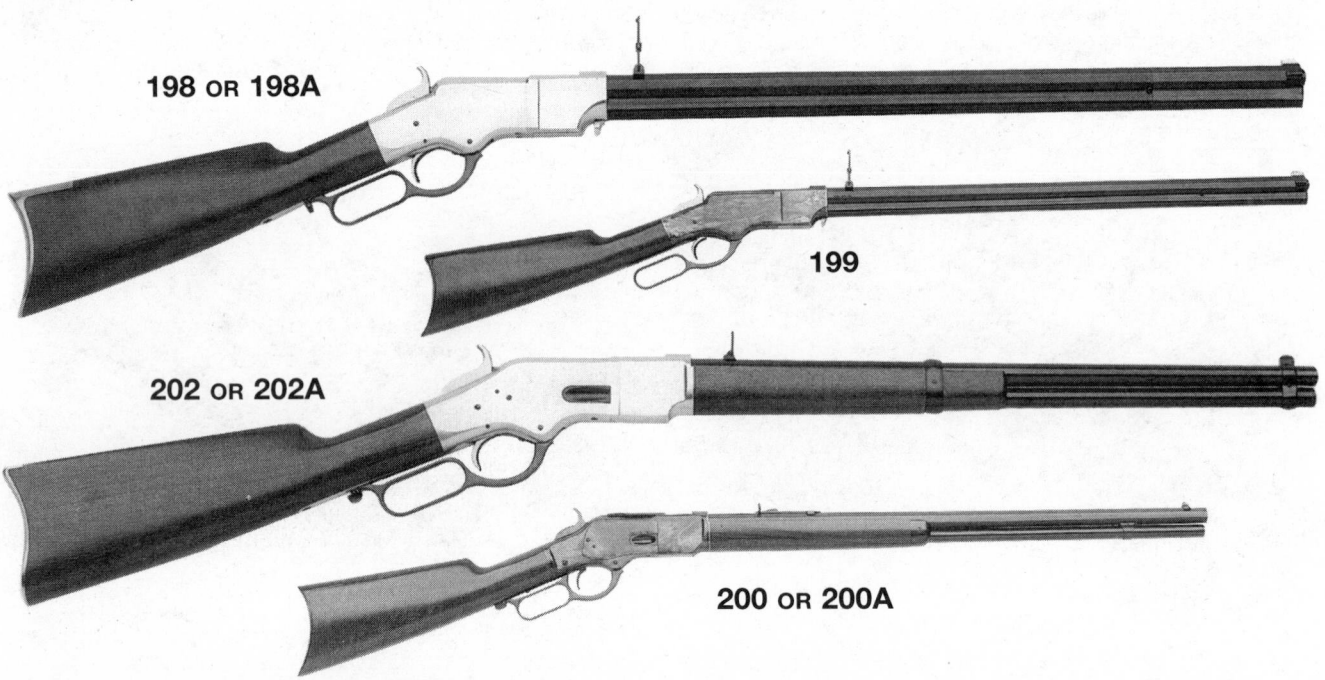

198 OR 198A

199

202 OR 202A

200 OR 200A

198 - HENRY BRASS FRAME 44/40
198A - HENRY BRASS FRAME .45 LC
199-HENRY RIFLE STEEL FRAME 44/40

The first real production of Henry Rifle with the Frame and Butt Plate in Steel. Total production was around 400. The first models had no lever latch. Only a few specimens are available now and they are the most valued by collectors around the world.

Price: wholesale $935.00-975.00

MODEL	CAL.	BBL. LENGTH	OVERALL LENGTH	MAGAZINE CAPACITY
198	44/40	24-1/4"	43-3/4"	13-9 shots
198A	45 LC	24-1/4"	43-3/4"	13-9 shots
199	44/40	24-1/4"	43-3/4"	13-9 shots

202 - 1866 YELLOWBOY CARBINE 44/40
202A - 1866 YELLOWBOY CARBINE .45 LC
1866 YELLOW CARBINE

Price: $735.00

MODEL	CAL.	BBL. LENGTH	OVERALL LENGTH
202	44/40	19"	38 1/4"
202A	45 LC	19"	38 1/4"

200 - 1873 WINCHESTER RIFLE 44/40
200A - 1873 WINCHESTER RIFLE 45 LC
1873 SPORTING RIFLE

The original Winchester 73 had a long life, from 1873-1927. It is probably the only gun to have given its name to a movie. Its steel frame enabled use of the .44/40, a more powerful round than the .44 Henry. Demand quickly pushed production into the hundreds of thousands.

Price: $895.00

MODEL	CAL.	BBL. LENGTH	OVERALL LENGTH
200	44/40	24 1/4"	43 1/4"
200A	45 LC	24 1/4"	43 1/4"

5505-FRONT SIGHT GLOBE, Sight has a 3/8" dovetail.
Price: $22.00

5508-TANG PEEP SIGHT
This tang sight is the famous target and hunting sight of the Old West. This sight has the precision adjustment for windage and elevation. Sight is blue finish and will fit original 1873 Winchester Rifles.
Price: $80.00

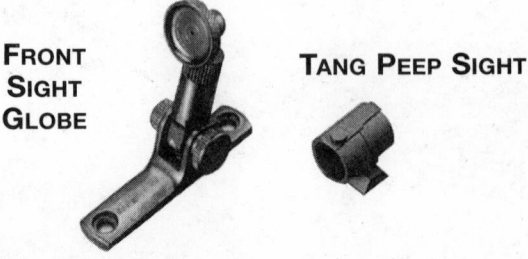

FRONT SIGHT GLOBE　　**TANG PEEP SIGHT**

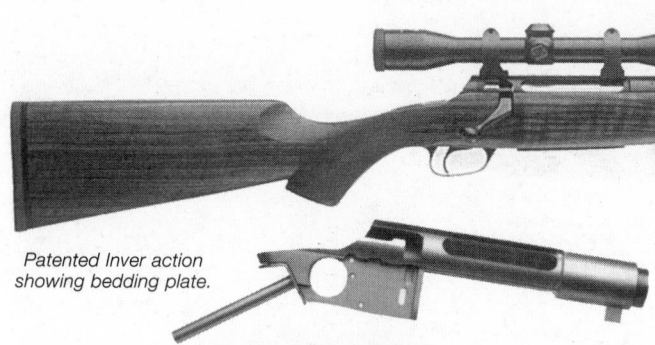

Patented Inver action showing bedding plate.

THE INVER RIFLE

The heart of the rifle is the patented Inver action, designed and developed by Thompson & Campbell. Machined from a single block of high-grade steel, it provides flawless functioning, mechanical simplicity and great strength. A conical triple-lugged bolt head enshrouds and supports the head of the chambered cartridge.

Designed primarily for use with a fine quality telescopic sight supplied on quick-detachable mounts, the Inver rifle also incorporates a unique system of open sights. A detachable foresight and flip-up backsight allow precision shooting with the same sighting axis as the scope, thus maintaining the firer's head position on the carefully-tailored stock. A two-stage trigger system is available as an option.

Action: Patented front lock-in 3 lug bolt action **Magazine:** Detachable 4 round box **Barrel length:** 22 inches **Safeties:** Stalking safe on tang. wing safety on bolt; Firing pin immobiliser on both **Trigger:** Single stage (two stage optional) **Telescopic Sight:** Best quality optics - owner's preferred choice can be fitted **Open Sights:** Flip up rear aperture; Detachable post foresight **Stock:** Walnut, takedown capacity **Weight:** From 8 lbs **Calibers:** All popular sporting calibers **Other Features:** Flush-fitting pop-out sling swivel studs; fitted case **Price:** . . . . **Available on request**

THE CROMIE RIFLE

The deluxe Cromie rifle is the flagship of the Thompson & Campbell range. The Cromie is stocked to the owner's personal fit and style with a stock of exhibition-grade walnut and supplied in a traditional leather carrying case. The action, receiver and detachable scope mounts are hand-engraved with gold inlays. The action and scope-mount steel are blued or colour case-hardened. The latter provides a marbled finish that is protective and wear resistant. The Cromie model also comes with an octagonal barrel, a distinctive and traditional design feature of many fine old sporting rifles now revived by Thompson & Campbell.

Action: Patented front locking 3 lug bolt action **Magazine:** Detachable 4 round box **Barrel length:** 24 inches octagonal profile **Safeties:** Stalking safe on tang. wing safety on bolt; Firing pin immobiliser on both **Trigger:** Single stage (two stage optional) **Telescopic Sight:** Best quality optics - owner's preferred choice can be fitted **Open Sights:** Optional **Stock:** Exhibition grade walnut; takedown capacity **Weight:** 8 lbs **Calibers:** All popular sporting calibers **Other Features:** Flush-fitting pop-out sling swivel studs; fitted case. **Price:** . . . . **Available on request**

THE JURA RIFLE

Fully stocked, with the walnut running right up to the muzzle, the Jura is true to a long-established Continental tradtion. Owing to its full length stock the Jura is not a takedown rifle, and comes in a full-length carrying case. The 17-inch barrel gives the Jura a significantly shorter overall length than the other Thompson & Campbell models.

The Jura's short overall length makes it both fast-handling and easy to carry even in thick cover. When shooting from the confines of a high seat, and when climbing in and out, the Jura is particularly easy to use. Since much woodland and driven rifle shooting is done from a standing or sitting position, rather than prone as on the open hill, the Jura's stock dimensions, pistol grip contours, scope eye-relief and wide angle lens can be subtly but significantly regulated to provide the most comfortable and accurate fit for this kind of sport.

Action: Patented front locking 3 lug bolt action **Magazine:** Detachable 3- and 5-round box **Barrel length:** 17 inches **Safeties:** Stalking safety on tang, wing safety on bolt; Firing pin immobiliser on both **Trigger:** Single stage (two stage optional) **Telescopic Sight:** Best quality optics - owner's preferred choice can be fitted **Open Sights:** Optional **Stock:** Walnut; not takedown **Weight:** from 7.5 lbs **Calibers:** All popular sporting calibers **Other Features:** Flush fitting pop out sling swivel studs; fitted case. **Price:** . . . . **Available on request**

RIFLES

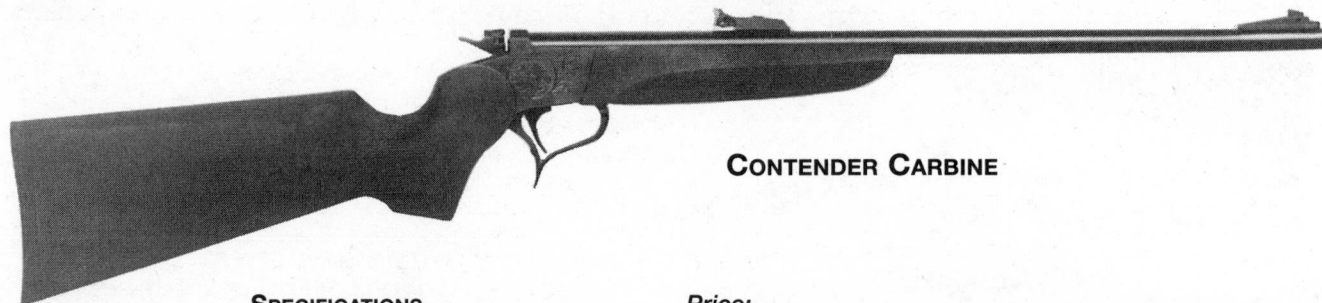

CONTENDER CARBINE

SPECIFICATIONS

Available in 5 *calibers:* 22 LR Match, 22 Hornet, 223 Rem., 7x30 Waters, 30-30 Win. *Barrels:* 21 inches, interchangeable. Adjustable iron sights; tapped and drilled for scope mounts. *Weight:* 5 lbs. 3 oz.

Price:
CONTENDER CARBINE w/standard walnut stock in 22
    Hornet, 223 Rem. 7x30 Waters 30-30 Win. **$571.38**
CONTENDER CARBINE with Match Grade 22
    LR barrel **583.04**

T/C 22LR CLASSIC

SPECIFICATIONS

A blowback autoloading 22, the new Classic featues fiber optic sights, an 8-shot magazine, walnut stock and match-grade 22" barrel threaded to the receiver.
Price: **$335.55**

ENCORE RIFLE

SPECIFICATIONS

Calibers: 22-250 Rem., 22 Hornet, .223 Rem., .243 Win., 25-06 Rem., .270 Win., .7mm-08 Rem., 7mm Rem. Mag., .308 Win., .30-06 Spfd., .300 Win. Mag., 45-70 Govt.
Action: Single-shot, break-open
Barrel lengths: 24" and 26" heavy barrel (.22-250 Rem., 223 Rem., 25-06 Rem., 7mm Rem. Mag., and 300 Win. Mag. only)

Overall length: 38 1/2" (24" barrel); 40 1/2" (26" barrel)
Weight: 6 3/4 lbs. (24"); 7 1/2 lbs. (26")
Trigger: Adjustable for overtravel
Safety: Automatic hammerblock w/bolt interlock
Stock: American walnut with Schnabel forend and Monte Carlo buttstock
Features: Interchangeable barrels, sling swivel studs
Price: with composite walnut **$602.43**
    with composite stock **582.29**
    45-70 Government **597.77**
    Composite walnut. **618.41**
    SST **650.43**

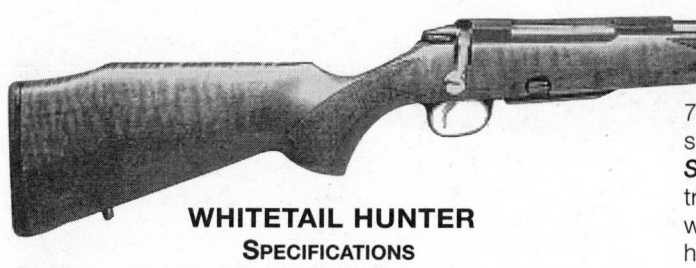

WHITETAIL HUNTER
SPECIFICATIONS

Calibers: 22-250, 223, 243, 7mm-08, 308 (Medium); 25-06, 270, 30-06 (Long); 7mm Mag., 300 Win. Mag., 338 Win. Mag. **Capacity:** 3 rounds (5 rounds optional); detachable magazine **Barrel Lengths:** 22.5" (24.5" Magnum) **Overall Length:** 42" (Medium); 42.5" (Long); 44.5" (Magnum) **Weight:**

7 lbs. (Medium); 7 ¼ lbs. (Long); 7.5 lbs. (Magnum) **Sights:** No sights; integral scope mount rails; drilled and tapped **Safety:** Locks trigger and bolt handle **Features:** Oversized trigger guard; short bolt throw; customized spacer system; walnut stock with palm swell and matte lacquer finish; cold hammer-forged barrel

Price: **$615.00**
    Magnum 645.00
Also Available: Left Hand 680.00
    Left Hand Magnum 710.00
WHITETAIL PRO, identical to Hunter, with adjustable cheekpiece

WHITETAIL BATTUE
SPECIFICATIONS

The Tikka Battue with its open sights is specially designed for snapshooting. Wide V-shaped rear sight is height adjustable. Fast, well balanced shots are easy to master with the Tikka Battue. • Walnut stock, oil finished or matte lacquered • Patented buttplate system. The length of pull

and pitch of the buttplate are easily adjusted with optional spacers. • Adjustable trigger pull from 2-4 lbs without first pull • Short and long action, including Magnum, plunger ejector • Special open sights with height adjustable rear sight • Integral scope mount rails, receiver tapped for universal scope mount blocks • Detachable 3-round clip magazine, 5-round magazine as option • Short, free floating, deeply blued, cold hammer-forged barrel • Called Tikka Whitetail Trapper if delivered without open sights
Price: Magnums . . . . **$624.00-$659.00**

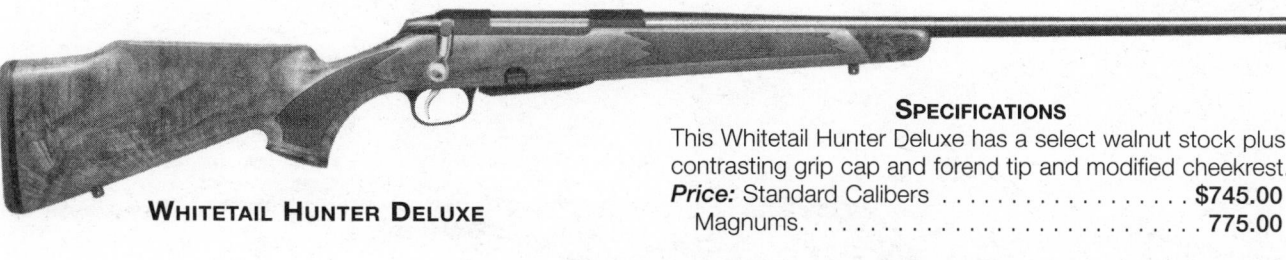

WHITETAIL HUNTER DELUXE

SPECIFICATIONS
This Whitetail Hunter Deluxe has a select walnut stock plus contrasting grip cap and forend tip and modified cheekrest.
Price: Standard Calibers **$745.00**
    Magnums. 775.00

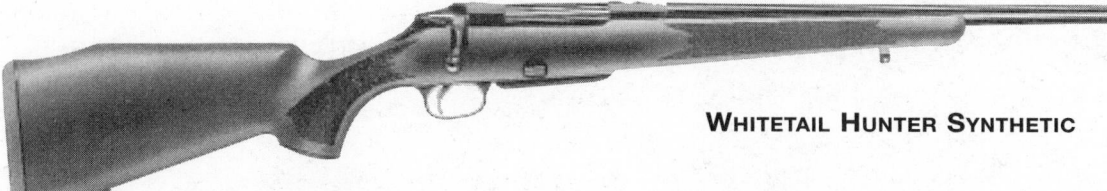

WHITETAIL HUNTER SYNTHETIC

SPECIFICATIONS
Same specifications as the standard Whitetail Hunter, except with All-Weather synthetic stock.
Price: **$615.00**
    Magnum 645.00

Also available:
WHITETAIL HUNTER STAINLESS SYNTHETIC.
Same specifications as above, except with stainless steel receiver, barrel and bolt. **$680.00**
In Magnum calibers 710.00

RIFLES

SPORTER

SPORTER

SPECIFICATIONS
Calibers: 223 Rem., 22-250 Rem., 308 Win.
Barrel Length: 23 3/8"

Blued barrel, adjustable wood stock.
Price: $950.00

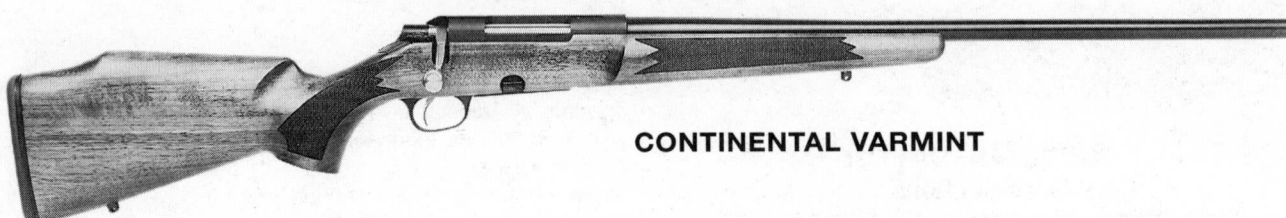

CONTINENTAL VARMINT

SPECIFICATIONS
Calibers: 17 Rem., 22-250, 223, 308
Capacity: 5 rounds
Barrel Length: 26 *Overall Length:* 46"
Weight: 8 lbs. 10 oz.

Finish: Matte lacquer walnut stock w/palm swell
Features: Recoil pad spacer system; quick-release detachable magazine; beavertail forend; cold hammer-forged barrel; integral scope mount rails; adjustable trigger
Price: $720.00

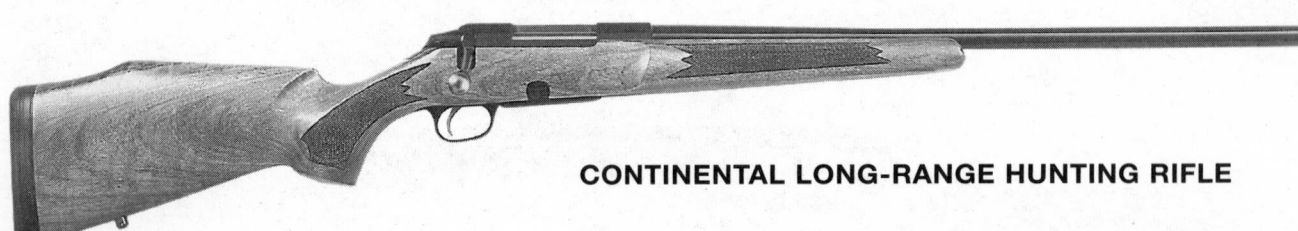

CONTINENTAL LONG-RANGE HUNTING RIFLE

SPECIFICATIONS
Calibers: 25-06 Rem., 270 Win., 7mm Rem. Mag., 300 Win. Mag.
Capacity: 5 rounds in standard calibers, 4 rounds in magnum calibers
Barrel Length: 26" heavy barrel

Overall Length: 46.5"
Weight: 8 lbs. 12 oz.
Finish: Matte lacquer walnut stock w/palm swell
Features: Same as Continental Varmint model
Price: $720.00
    Magnum Calibers. 750.00

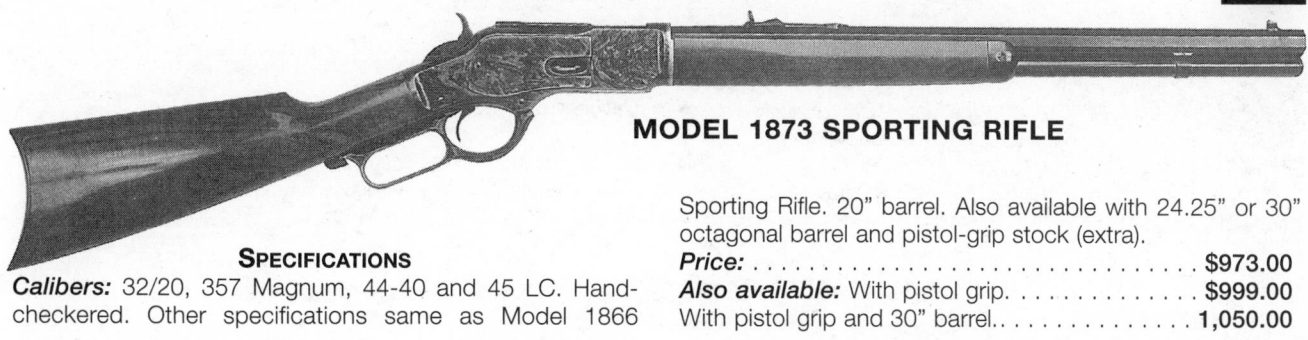

MODEL 1873 SPORTING RIFLE

SPECIFICATIONS
Calibers: 32/20, 357 Magnum, 44-40 and 45 LC. Hand-checkered. Other specifications same as Model 1866

Sporting Rifle. 20" barrel. Also available with 24.25" or 30" octagonal barrel and pistol-grip stock (extra).
Price: $973.00
Also available: With pistol grip. $999.00
With pistol grip and 30" barrel.. .... **1,050.00**

MODEL 1871 ROLLING BLOCK BABY CARBINE

SPECIFICATIONS
Calibers: 22 LR, 22 Hornet, 22 Magnum, 357 Magnum
Barrel Length: 22" **Overall Length:** 35.5" **Weight:** 4.85 lbs. **Stock and forend:** Walnut **Trigger guard:** Brass
Sights: Fully adjustable rear; ramp front **Frame:** Color-case-hardened steel
Price: $590.00

HENRY RIFLE

SPECIFICATIONS
Calibers: 44-40, 45 LC **Barrel Length:** 18.5", 22.25", 24.25" (half-octagon, with tubular magazine) **Overall Length:** 38", 41.5", 43.75" **Weight:** 7.9, 9, 9.26 lbs. **Frame:** Brass **Stock:** Varnished

American walnut
Price: $980.00
Henry Rifle Steel **1,050.00**

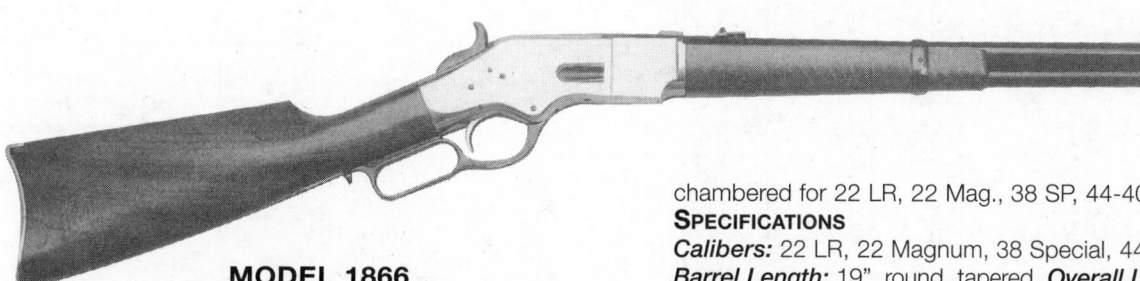

MODEL 1866 YELLOWBOY CARBINE

The frist gun to carry the Winchester name, this model was born as the 44-caliber rimfire cartridge Henry and is now

chambered for 22 LR, 22 Mag., 38 SP, 44-40, and 45 LC.
SPECIFICATIONS
Calibers: 22 LR, 22 Magnum, 38 Special, 44-40, 45 L.C.
Barrel Length: 19", round, tapered **Overall Length:** 38.25"
Weight: 7.380 lbs. **Frame:** Brass **Stock and forend:** Walnut
Sights: Vertically adjustable rear; horizontally adjustable front
Price: $760.00

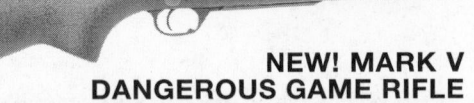

MARK V DELUXE
The Mark V Deluxe stock is made of hand-selected American walnut with skipline checkering, traditional diamond-shaped inlay, rosewood pistol-grip cap and forend tip. Monte Carlo design with raised cheekpiece properly positions the shooter while reducing felt recoil. The action and hammer-forged barrel and hand-bedded for accuracy, then deep blued to a high-luster finish. See also specifications tables below and on the following page.

***Calibers*: 24" Barrel:** 22-250, 243, 240 Wby. Mag., 25-06 Rem, 270, 280, 7mm-08, 30-06, 308 Win. **$1,649.00**
26" Barrel: In 257 Wby. Mag., 270 Wby. Mag., 7mm Wby. Mag., 300 Wby. Mag. and 340 Wby. Mag. **$1,699.00**
28" Barrel: In 416 Wby. Mag., 378 Wby Mag.. . . . **1,999.00**
In 460 Wby. Mag.. . . . . **2,349.00**

NEW! MARK V DANGEROUS GAME RIFLE
The new Mark V Dangerous Game Rifle is designed specifically for the person who makes their living as a professional hunter or the hunter who is serious about their pursuit of dangerous game. It features a hand-laminated, black composite stock (Kevlar and fiberglass) with a CNC-machined aluminum bedding block, combined with a short bolt throw Mark V action and a 24" barrel. An adjustable ramp, shallow gold-filled "V" rear and barrel band hooded front sight with large gold bead provides for immediate sight alignment and target acquistion. A Pachmayr Decelerator recoil pad reduces felt recoil.

Prices: Available in 375 H&H, 375 Wby, 416 Rem., 458 Win.. . . . . **$2,599.00**
378 Wby, 416 Wby, 460 Wby. **2,659.00**

MARK V® RIFLE SPECIFICATIONS

Model	Caliber	Barreled Action	Weight *	Overall Length	Magazine Capacity	Barrel Length/Contour	Rifling	Length of Pull	Drop at Comb	Monte Carlo	Drop at Heel
SVM (Super VarmintMaster) Repeater	.223 Rem.	RH 26"	8 1/2 lbs.	46"	5+1 in chamber	26" #4	1-12" twist	13 5/8"	3/4"	3/8"	1 1/8"
	.22-250 Rem.	RH 26"	8 1/2 lbs.	46"	4+1 in chamber	26" #4	1-14" twist	13 5/8"	3/4"	3/8"	1 1/8"
	.243 Winchester	RH 26"	8 1/2 lbs.	46"	5+1 in chamber	26" #4	1-10" twist	13 5/8"	3/4"	3/8"	1 1/8"
	7mm-08 Rem.	RH 26"	8 1/2 lbs.	46"	5+1 in chamber	26" #4	1-9 1/2" twist	13 5/8"	3/4"	3/8"	1 1/8"
	.308 Winchester	RH 26"	8 1/2 lbs.	46"	5+1 in chamber	26" #4	1-12" twist	13 5/8"	3/4"	3/8"	1 1/8"
SVM (Super VarmintMaster) Single Shot	.223 Rem.	RH 26"	8 1/2 lbs.	46"	5+1 in chamber	26" #4	1-12" twist	13 5/8"	3/4"	3/8"	1 1/8"
	.22-250 Rem.	RH 26"	8 1/2 lbs.	46"	4+1 in chamber	26" #4	1-14" twist	13 5/8"	3/4"	3/8"	1 1/8"
	.220 Swift	RH 26"	8 1/2 lbs.	46"	5+1 in chamber	26" #4	1-14" twist	13 5/8"	3/4"	3/8"	1 1/8"
	.243 Winchester	RH 26"	8 1/2 lbs.	46"	5+1 in chamber	26" #4	1-10" twist	13 5/8"	3/4"	3/8"	1 1/8"
	7mm-08 Rem.	RH 26"	8 1/2 lbs.	46"	5+1 in chamber	26" #4	1-9 1/2" twist	13 5/8"	3/4"	3/8"	1 1/8"
	.308 Winchester	RH 26"	8 1/2 lbs.	46"	5+1 in chamber	26" #4	1-12" twist	13 5/8"	3/4"	3/8"	1 1/8"
SPM (Super PredatorMaster)	.223 Rem.	RH 24"	6 1/4 lbs.	44"	5+1 in chamber	24" #2	1-12" twist	13 5/8"	3/4"	3/8"	1 1/8"
	.22-250 Rem.	RH 24"	6 1/4 lbs.	44"	4+1 in chamber	24" #2	1-14" twist	13 5/8"	3/4"	3/8"	1 1/8"
	.243 Winchester	RH 24"	6 1/4 lbs.	44"	5+1 in chamber	24" #2	1-10" twist	13 5/8"	3/4"	3/8"	1 1/8"
	7mm-08 Rem.	RH 24"	6 1/4 lbs.	44"	5+1 in chamber	24" #2	1-9 1/2" twist	13 5/8"	3/4"	3/8"	1 1/8"
	.308 Winchester	RH 24"	6 1/4 lbs.	44"	5+1 in chamber	24" #2	1-12" twist	13 5/8"	3/4"	3/8"	1 1/8"
Mark V Ultra Lightweight	.243 Winchester	RH 24"	5 3/4 lbs.	44"	5+1 in chamber	24" #1	1-10" twist	13 5/8"	3/4"	3/8"	1 1/8"
	.240 Wby. Mag.	RH 24"	5 3/4 lbs.	44"	5+1 in chamber	24" #1	1-10" twist	13 5/8"	3/4"	3/8"	1 1/8"
	7mm-08 Rem.	RH 24"	5 3/4 lbs.	44"	5+1 in chamber	24" #1	1-9 1/2" twist	13 5/8"	3/4"	3/8"	1 1/8"
	.308 Winchester	RH 24"	5 3/4 lbs.	44"	5+1 in chamber	24" #1	1-12" twist	13 5/8"	3/4"	3/8"	1 1/8"
	.25-06 Rem.	RH 24"	5 3/4 lbs.	44"	5+1 in chamber	24" #1	1-10" twist	13 5/8"	3/4"	3/8"	1 1/8
	.270 Winchester	RH 24"	5 3/4 lbs.	44"	5+1 in chamber	24" #1	1-10" twist	13 5/8"	3/4"	3/8"	1 1/8
	.280 Rem.	RH 24"	5 3/4 lbs.	44"	5+1 in chamber	24" #1	1-10" twist	13 5/8"	3/4"	3/8"	1 1/8
	.30-06 Springfield	RH 24"	5 3/4 lbs.	44"	5+1 in chamber	24" #1	1-10" twist	13 5/8"	3/4"	3/8"	1 1/8
	.257 Wby. Mag.	RH 26"	6 3/4 lbs.	46 5/8"	3+1 in chamber	26" #2 mod.	1-10" twist	13 5/8"	1"	3/8"	1 1/2"
	.270 Wby. Mag.	RH 26"	6 3/4 lbs.	46 5/8"	3+1 in chamber	26" #2 mod.	1-10" twist	13 5/8"	1"	3/8"	1 1/2"
	7mm Rem. Mag.	RH 24"	6 3/4 lbs.	44 5/8"	3+1 in chamber	24" #2 mod.	1-9 1/2" twist	13 5/8"	1"	3/8"	1 1/2"
	7mm Wby. Mag.	RH 26"	6 3/4 lbs.	46 5/8"	3+1 in chamber	26" #2 mod.	1-10" twist	13 5/8"	1"	3/8"	1 1/2"
NEW	.338-06 A-Square	RH 24"	6 lbs.	44"	5+1 in chamber	24" #2	1-10" twist	13 5/8"	3/4"	3/8"	1 1/2"
	.300 Win. Mag.	RH 24"	6 3/4 lbs.	44 5/8"	3+1 in chamber	24" #2 mod.	1-10" twist	13 5/8"	1"	3/8"	1 1/2"
	.300 Wby. Mag.	RH 26"	6 3/4 lbs.	46 5/8"	3+1 in chamber	26" #2 mod.	1-10" twist	13 5/8"	1"	3/8"	1 1/2"
Mark V Ultra Lightweight (left-hand)	.257 Wby. Mag.	LH 26"	6 3/4 lbs.	46 5/8"	3+1 in chamber	26" #2 mod.	1-10" twist	13 5/8"	1"	3/8"	1 1/2"
	.270 Wby. Mag.	LH 26"	6 3/4 lbs.	46 5/8"	3+1 in chamber	26" #2 mod.	1-10" twist	13 5/8"	1"	3/8"	1 1/2"
	7mm Wby. Mag.	LH 24"	6 3/4 lbs.	44 5/8"	3+1 in chamber	24" #2 mod.	1-9 1/2" twist	13 5/8"	1"	3/8"	1 1/2"
	7mm Wby. Mag.	LH 26"	6 3/4 lbs.	46 5/8"	3+1 in chamber	26" #2 mod.	1-10" twist	13 5/8"	1"	3/8"	1 1/2"
	.300 Win. Mag.	LH 24"	6 3/4 lbs.	44 5/8"	3+1 in chamber	24" #2 mod.	1-10" twist	13 5/8"	1"	3/8"	1 1/2"
	.300 Wby. Mag.	LH 26"	6 3/4 lbs.	46 5/8"	3+1 in chamber	26" #2 mod.	1-10" twist	13 5/8"	1"	3/8"	1 1/2"
Mark V Accumark	.223 Rem.	RH 24"	7 lbs.	44"	5+1 in chamber	24" #3	1-12" twist	13 5/8"	3/4"	3/8"	1 1/8"
	.22-250 Rem.	RH 24"	7 lbs.	44"	4+1 in chamber	24" #3	1-14" twist	13 5/8"	3/4"	3/8"	1 1/8"
	.243 Winchester	RH 24"	7 lbs.	44"	5+1 in chamber	24" #3	1-10" twist	13 5/8"	3/4"	3/8"	1 1/8"
	.240 Wby. Mag.	RH 24"	7 lbs.	44"	5+1 in chamber	24" #3	1-10" twist	13 5/8"	3/4"	3/8"	1 1/8"
	7mm-08 Rem.	RH 24"	7 lbs.	44"	5+1 in chamber	24" #3	1-9 1/2" twist	13 5/8"	3/4"	3/8"	1 1/8"
	.308 Winchester	RH 24"	7 lbs.	44"	5+1 in chamber	24" #3	1-12" twist	13 5/8"	3/4"	3/8"	1 1/8"
	.25-06 Rem.	RH 24"	7 lbs.	44"	5+1 in chamber	24" #3	1-10" twist	13 5/8"	3/4"	3/8"	1 1/8
	.270 Winchester	RH 24"	7 lbs.	44"	5+1 in chamber	24" #3	1-10" twist	13 5/8"	3/4"	3/8"	1 1/8"
	.280 Rem.	RH 24"	7 lbs.	44"	5+1 in chamber	24" #3	1-10" twist	13 5/8"	3/4"	3/8"	1 1/8"
	.30-06 Springfield	RH 24"	7 lbs.	44"	5+1 in chamber	24" #3	1-10" twist	13 5/8"	3/4"	3/8"	1 1/8"
Mark V Dangerous Game Rifle™ NEW	.375 H&H	RH 24"	8 3/4 lbs.	44 5/8"	3+1 in chamber	24" #3	1-12" twist	13 5/8"	1"	9/16"	1 1/2"
NEW	.375 Wby. Mag.	RH 24"	8 3/4 lbs.	44 5/8"	3+1 in chamber	24" #3	1-12" twist	13 5/8"	1"	9/16"	1 1/2"
NEW**	.378 Wby. Mag.	***RH 26"	8 3/4 lbs.	***46 5/8"	2+1 in chamber	***26" #3	1-12" twist	13 5/8"	1"	9/16"	1 1/2"
	.416 Rem. Mag.	RH 24"	8 3/4 lbs.	44 5/8"	3+1 in chamber	24" #3	1-14" twist	13 5/8"	1"	9/16"	1 1/2"
NEW	.416 Wby. Mag.	***RH 26"	8 3/4 lbs.	***46 5/8"	2+1 in chamber	***26" #3	1-14" twist	13 5/8"	1"	9/16"	1 1/2"
NEW*	.458 Win. Mag.	RH 24"	8 3/4 lbs.	44 5/8"	3+1 in chamber	24" #4	1-14" twist	13 5/8"	1"	9/16"	1 1/2"
NEW**	.460 Wby. Mag.	***RH 26"	9 1/2 lbs.	***46 5/8"	2+1 in chamber	***26" #4	1-16" twist	13 5/8"	1"	9/16"	1 1/2"
Mark V Deluxe	.22-250 Rem.	RH 24"	6 3/4 lbs.	44"	4+1 in chamber	24" #1	1-14" twist	13 5/8"	3/4"	3/8"	1 1/8"
	.243 Winchester	RH 24"	6 3/4 lbs.	44"	5+1 in chamber	24" #1	1-10" twist	13 5/8"	3/4"	3/8"	1 1/8"
	.240 Wby. Mag.	RH 24"	6 3/4 lbs.	44"	5+1 in chamber	24" #1	1-10" twist	13 5/8"	3/4"	3/8"	1 1/8"
	7mm-08 Rem.	RH 24"	6 3/4 lbs.	44"	5+1 in chamber	24" #1	1-9 1/2" twist	13 5/8"	3/4"	3/8"	1 1/8"
	.308 Winchester	RH 24"	6 3/4 lbs.	44"	5+1 in chamber	24" #1	1-12" twist	13 5/8"	3/4"	3/8"	1 1/8"
	.25-06 Rem.	RH 24"	6 3/4 lbs.	44"	5+1 in chamber	24" #1	1-10" twist	13 5/8"	3/4"	3/8"	1 1/8
	.270 Winchester	RH 24"	6 3/4 lbs.	44"	5+1 in chamber	24" #1	1-10" twist	13 5/8"	3/4"	3/8"	1 1/8"
	.280 Rem.	RH 24"	6 3/4 lbs.	44"	5+1 in chamber	24" #1	1-10" twist	13 5/8"	3/4"	3/8"	1 1/8"
	.30-06 Springfield	RH 24"	6 3/4 lbs.	44"	5+1 in chamber	24" #1	1-10" twist	13 5/8"	3/4"	3/8"	1 1/8"
	.257 Wby. Mag.	RH 26"	8 1/2 lbs.	46 5/8"	3+1 in chamber	26" #2	1-10" twist	13 5/8"	7/8"	3/8"	1 3/8"
	.270 Wby. Mag.	RH 26"	8 1/2 lbs.	46 5/8"	3+1 in chamber	26" #2	1-10" twist	13 5/8"	7/8"	3/8"	1 3/8"
	7mm Wby. Mag.	RH 26"	8 1/2 lbs.	46 5/8"	3+1 in chamber	26" #2	1-10" twist	13 5/8"	7/8"	3/8"	1 3/8"
	.300 Wby. Mag.	RH 26"	8 1/2 lbs.	46 5/8"	3+1 in chamber	26" #2	1-10" twist	13 5/8"	7/8"	3/8"	1 3/8"
	.340 Wby. Mag.	RH 26"	8 1/2 lbs.	46 5/8"	3+1 in chamber	26" #2	1-12" twist	13 5/8"	7/8"	3/8"	1 3/8"
**	.378 Wby. Mag.	***RH 28"	9 1/2 lbs.	48 5/8"	2+1 in chamber	***28" #3	1-12" twist	13 7/8"	7/8"	3/8"	1 3/8"
**	.416 Wby. Mag.	***RH 28"	9 1/2 lbs.	48 5/8"	2+1 in chamber	***28" #3	1-14" twist	13 7/8"	7/8"	3/8"	1 3/8"
**	.460 Wby. Mag.	***RH 28"	10 1/2 lbs.	48 3/4"	2+1 in chamber	***28" #4	1-16" twist	14"	7/8"	3/8"	1 3/8"

Custom rifles are also available. Consult your Weatherby dealer or the Weatherby Custom Shop for specifications. All rifles are drilled and tapped for scope. **Specifications subject to change without notice.** *Weight approximate. Varies due to stock density and bore diameter. **Available with Weatherby Accubrake only. ***Measurement includes Accubrake.

RIFLES

NEW! MARK V SPM

The new SPM (Super Predator-Master) was designed specifically for the "on-the-move" varmint hunter calling in coyote, fox, bobcat or other large predators. Built on the Mark V action for standard cartridges, the SPM is a lightweight 6.25 lbs. and features a 24" Criterion "button-rifled" barrel by Krieger, cryogenically treated to reduce stress and maintain accuracy. The barrel sports longitudinal flutes to dissipate heat and is finished with an accuracy-enhancing 11° target crown. The SPM features a specially-designed ultra lightweight hybrid composite Monte Carlo stock in distinctive tan with black spiderweb patterning. A CNC-machined aluminum bedding block provides a solid, stable platform for the action while a Pachmayr Decelerator pad reduces felt recoil. Available in .223, .22-250, 243, 7mm-08, 308

Price: **$1,459.00**

WEATHERBY SVM VARMINTMASTER BOLT-ACTION RIFLE

Weatherby's new SVM Varmintmaster has a short Mark V action and a 26" cryogenically stress-relieved Krieger button-rifled barrel of stainless steel. A hand-laminated synthetic stock features an aluminum bedding block and wide, flat forend. **Weight:** 8.5 lbs.

Price: **$1,459.00**

EUROMARK

SLS

MARK V EUROMARK

The Euromark features a hand-rubbed oil finish and Monte Carlo stock of American walnut, plus custom grade, hand-cut checkering with an ebony pistol-grip cap and forend tip.
Prices: 26" Barrel In Weatherby Magnum calibers
257, 270, 7mm, 300 and 340 . . . . **$1,749.00**

28" Barrel In .378 Wby Mag. and
416 Wby. Mag. **2,049.00**
24" Barrel In 7mm Rem. Mag., 300 Win. Mag.,
338 Win. Mag. and 375 H&H Mag. **1,749.00**
SLS **1,339.00**

ACCUMARK

MARK V ACCUMARK

This rifle features a specially-designed, hand-laminated raised-comb Monte Carlo synthetic stock (a combination of Kevlar, unidirectional fibers and fiberglass). It also features a molded-in, CNC-machined aluminum bedding plate that stiffens the receiver area of the rifle when the barreled action is secured to the block, providing a stable and rigid platform for the action. To give the Accumark stock a distinctive yet functional look, a matte black gel coat finish is accented with faint grey "spider web" patterning. A cold hammer-forged, heavy contour, 26" (button-rifled 24" for standard calibers) 410 Series stainless steel free-floated barrel features a special longitudinal fluting system. The flutes increase barrel surface to help dissipate heat, while a .705" diamter muzzle (.722 for standard calibers) with recessed field crown is concentrically perfect to assure pinpoint accuracy. Adding to the accuracy potential of this rifle is a Weatherby factory-tuned trigger assembly. Each trigger is fully adjustable with sear engagement preset at between .008 to .014 and a let-off weight of 4 lbs.
Prices: 26" Barrel In 257, 270, 7mm, 7mm STW, 300, 340
Magnum calibers **$1,459.00**
28" Barrel In 30-378 Wby. and 338-378 Magnum
calibers. **1,669.00**
Also available in left hand, additional **1,499.00**
28" barrel, left hand **1,719.00**

ULTRA LIGHTWEIGHT

MARK V ULTRA LIGHTWEIGHT

The Mark V Ultra Lightweight provides everything a custom-built lightweight does at half the price. It tips the scales at 5.75 lbs. (6.75 lbs. on magnum models), making it an ideal choice for packing into mountainous terrain or for all-day hunts.

Based on the Mark V action, it features a chrome moly receiver, with weight-trimming alloy follower and floorplate. Deepened and widened flutes on the bolt reduce weight, along with a "skeletonized" bolt handle and bolt sleeve. Weight-reducing flutes are also employed on the 410 Series stainless steel 24" or 26" (depending on caliber) special-contour barrel, which features an accuracy-enhancing recessed field crown. Rounding out the Ultra Lightweight is

a specially-designed, hand-laminated raised comb Monte Carlo stock, featuring a molded-in, CNC-machined aluminum bedding plate that stiffens the receiver area of the rifle when the barreled action is secured to the block. A Pachmayr Decelerator pad dissipates recoil. Flat shooting. Hard hitting. Ultra lightweight. Also available in a left-hand model. *Overall length:* 44" and 46". *Weight:* about 6 lbs.

Prices:
24" Barrel: 243, 240 Wby., 25-06, .270, 7mm-08,
   .280, .308, .30-06, 338-06 A Square **$1,349.00**
26" Barrel: 257 Wby., 270 Wby., 7mm Rem.,
   7mm Wby., 300 Wby., .300 Win. **1,399.00**
Also Available: Left hand. **1,459.00**

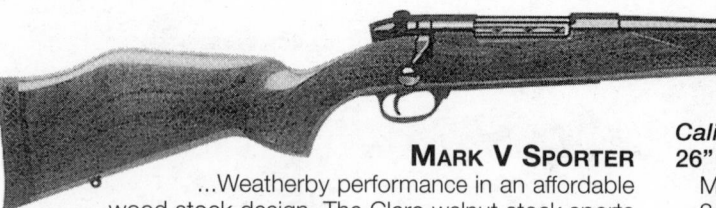

MARK V SPORTER

...Weatherby performance in an affordable wood stock design. The Claro walnut stock sports a satin urethane finish, fineline diamond point checkering and a Pachmayr Decelerator pad. All metalwork is bead blasted matte blued to a low lustre finish for a distinctive and functional look. In magnum or standard cartridges, the Mark V Sporter evokes an element of pride, both in the rack and in the field.

SPECIFICATIONS

Calibers:
26" Barrel: 257 Wby. Mag., 270 Wby.
   Mag., 7mm Wby. Mag., 300 Wby. Mag. and
   340 Wby. Mag. **$1,099.00**
24" Barrel: 7mm Rem. Mag., 300 Win. Mag.,
   338 Win. Mag. and 375 H&H Mag. **$1,099.00**
Also available:
EUROSPORT. Same specifications and prices but with hand-rubbed satin oil finish.

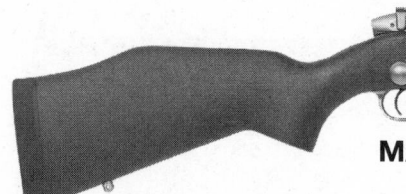

MARK V FIBERMARK STAINLESS

NEW! FIBERMARK COMPOSITE

The Weatherby Fibermark was first introduced in 1983, sporting the industry's first production rifle with a composite stock. This Fibermark is set on a black hybrid composite stock of Kevlar and unidirectional fiberglass. The Monte Carlo stock is pillar-bedded to reduce torque on the action and improve accuracy. Metalwork is bead-blasted matte blue. The rifle is available on both Magnum (26" barrels) or Standard (24" barrels) Mark V actions.

NEW! FIBERMARK STAINLESS

Similar to the new Fibermark, the Fibermark Stainless offers a black hybrid composite stock that is pillar-bedded to reduce action torque and improve accuracy—a feature not found on other production composites. All metalwork is 410 Series stainless steel, bead-blasted to a matte finish. Available in magnum or standard actions.

Prices: **$849.00**
Magnum **899.00**
   30-378 Wby. **1,079.00**
Stainless **1,079.00**
   Magnum **1,129.00**
   30-378 Wby. **1,289.00**

**WEATHERBY
MARK V
LAZERMARK**

LAZERMARK

A custom-carved walnut stock distinguishes this Weatherby. Traditional high-gloss finish.

Prices: **26" Barrel**
In Weatherby Magnum calibers 257, 270, 7mm,
   300 and 340 . . . . **$1,849.00**
28" Barrel, 378 Wby. Mag. + 416 Wby Mag. . . . **2,179.00**
460 Wby. Mag. **2,559.00**

MARK V STAINLESS

MARK V MAGNUM OR STANDARD LIGHTWEIGHT STAINLESS

Features 400 Series stainless steel. The action is hand-bedded to a lightweight, injection-molded synthetic stock.

Prices: **MARK V STAINLESS**
24" Barrel
.22-250, .243, .240 Wby., 25-06, .270, .280,
   7mm-08, .30-06, .308 . . . . **$979.00**
7mm Rem. Mag., 300 Win. Mag., 338 Win.
   Mag. and 375 H&H Mag. **1,029.00**
26" Barrel, Weatherby Magnum calibers 257, 270, 7mm
   Rem. Mag., 300 and 340 . . . . **$1,029.00**
28" Barrel, 30-378 Wby. Mag. **1,189.00**

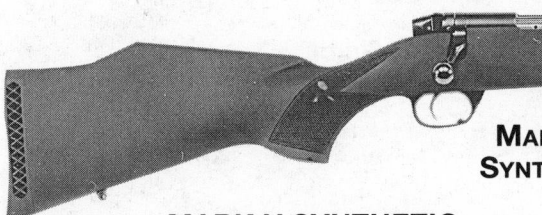

**MARK V
SYNTHETIC**

MARK V SYNTHETIC

Features an injection-molded synthetic stock with dual-tapered checkered forearm. Comes with custom floorplate release/trigger guard assembly and engraved flying "W" monogram.

Prices: **MARK V SYNTHETIC**
24" Barrel: .22-250, .243, .240 Wby, .25-06, .270, 7mm-
   08, .280, .30-06, .308 . . . . **$779.00**
7mm Rem. Mag., 300 Win. Mag., 338 Win.
   Mag. and 375 H&H Mag. **829.00**
26" Barrel, Weatherby Magnum calibers 257, 270,
   7mm, 7mm STW, 300 and 340 . . . . **829.00**
28" Barrel, 30-378 Wby. Mag., 338-378 Wby. **979.00**

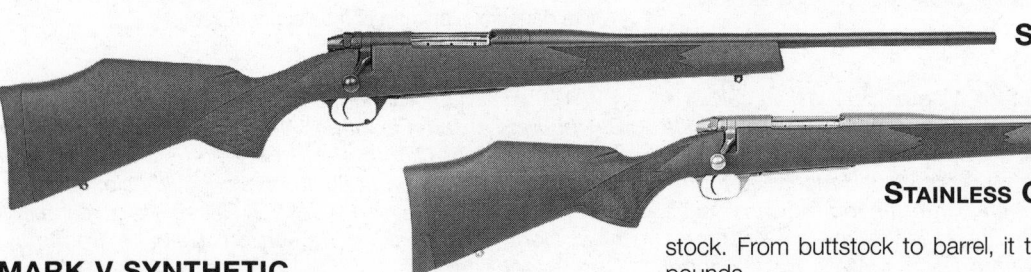

SYNTHETIC CARBINE

STAINLESS CARBINE

MARK V SYNTHETIC & STAINLESS CARBINE

SYNTHETIC. With a lightweight 20" barrel, this is a good choice for the tight confines of a treestand, high in the mountains or as a working ranch rifle. All metalwork is bead-blasted matte blued, bedded to a raised comb, injection-molded synthetic stock. From buttstock to barrel, it tips the scales at just six pounds.
STAINLESS. Has all of the features of the Mark V Stainless and a lightweight 20" barrel.
Prices: **CARBINE MODEL** (20" in 243 Win., 7mm-08
   Rem., 308 Win.) **$779.00**
STAINLESS CARBINE **979.00**

Custom Guns

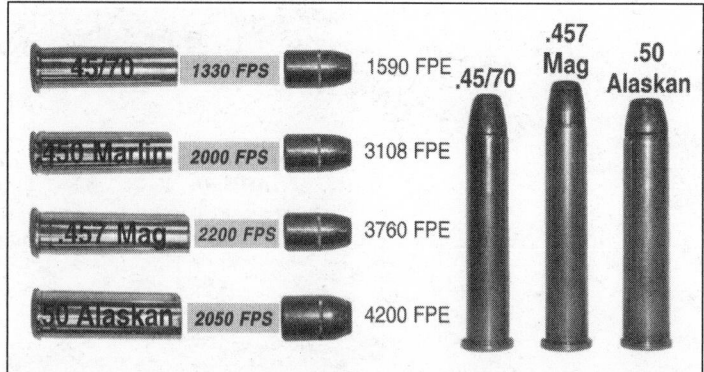

				.457	.50
45/70	1330 FPS		1590 FPE	.45/70 Mag	Alaskan
.450 Marlin	2000 FPS		3108 FPE		
.457 Mag	2200 FPS		3760 FPE		
.50 Alaskan	2050 FPS		4200 FPE		

BIG GUNS FOR BIG STUFF

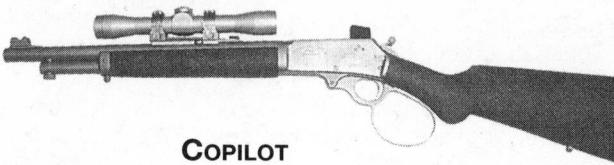

COPILOT

"THE ORIGINAL"

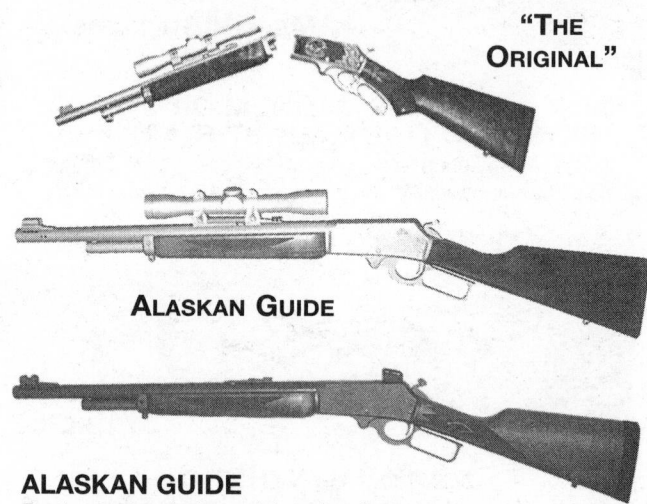

ALASKAN GUIDE

COPILOT .457 MAGNUM

Wild West Gun's Alaskan CoPilot rifle, a big-bore take-down lever-action, has become renowned for its quality, reliability and compactness. Now, there's a new .457 Magnum, which uses a 350 grain bullet at 2200 fps to develop 3700 foot-pounds of muzzle energy.

PARKERIZED COPILOT .50 ALASKAN

Not only does the .50 Alaskan CoPilot fit in a compact carry case, it chambers a 50-caliber cartridge that fires 450-grain bullet at approximately 2050 fps with 4200 foot pounds of muzzle energy. The performance of this will impress anyone looking for serious knockdown power!

ALASKAN COPILOT

Take-Down Rifle • WWG .457 Mag or .50 Alaskan caliber • wood stock cut to your length of pull • Take-Down Rifle Conversion • Trigger pull set at 3-4 pounds • Barrel cut & crowned 16 1/2", 18 1/2" or 20" • Vented magazine tube • Fiber-optic front sight with slotted hood • Carry case (padded canvas) • Action Tuned for reliability • Pachmayr Decelerator Pad • Parkerized finish • WWG recoil control porting system

WWG .457 MAG - 45/70 PACKAGE	$1,649.00
ON A 1895SS RIFLE	1,299.00
.50 ALASKAN PACKAGE	1,799.00
.50 ON A 1895SS RIFLE	1,449.00

ALASKAN GUIDE

For those who don't need the take-down feature, Wild West guns has a standard Marlin in .457 Magnum. This short quick-handling rifle will use standard 45/70 ammunition too. The .50 Alaskan chambered in the Alaskan Guide is capable of stopping any animal on earth. It offers peace of mind if you're hiking where dangerous animals can be encountered.

ALASKAN GUIDE

• WWG .457 Mag or .50 Alaskan Caliber • Trigger pull set at 3-4 pounds • Barrel length 18 1/2" only • Action tuned for reliability • Recoil Control Porting • Wood stock cut to your length of pull • fiber optic front sight with slotted hood • Vented magazine tube • WWG Ghose Ring rear sight • Straight-grip stock • Parkerized finish • Pachmayr Decelerator Pad

WWG .457 MAG - 45/70 PACKAGE	$1,099.00
ON A 1895G RIFLE	749.00
.50 ALASKAN PACKAGE	1,249.00
.50 ON A 1895G RIFLE	899.00
TAKE-DOWN CONVERSION-ADDITIONAL COST	450.00

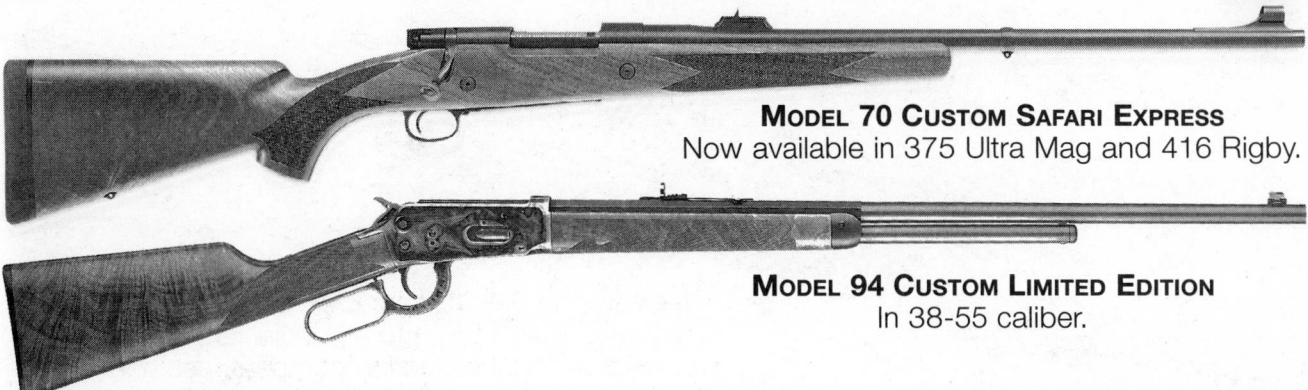

MODEL 70 CUSTOM SAFARI EXPRESS
Now available in 375 Ultra Mag and 416 Rigby.

MODEL 94 CUSTOM LIMITED EDITION
In 38-55 caliber.

RIFLES

CUSTOM GUN SHOP RIFLES

Item No. Right Hand	Item No. Left Hand	Caliber	Magazine Capacity	Barrel Length	Length of Pull	Weight (Lbs.)	Sugg. Retail
Model 70 "Classic" Custom African Express							
535-912138	535-918138	375 H&H Mag.	4	24"	14"	9-1/2	$3,998
535-912139	535-918139	416 Rem Mag	4	24	14	9-1/2	3,998
535-912159	535-918159	416 Rigby	3	24	14	9-1/2	4,435
535-912144	535-918144	458 Win Mag	4	22	14	9-1/4	3,998
535-912154	535-918154	458 Loft	4	22	14	9-1/4	3,998
535-912145	535-918145	470 Capstick	3	24	14	9-1/2	3,998
Model 70 "Classic" Custom Safari Express							
535-911138	535-919138	375 H&H Mag	3	24"	13-3/4"	9-1/4"	$2,790
535-911158	535-919158	375 Ultra Mag	3	24	13-3/4	9-1/4	2,790
535-911139	535-919139	416 Rem Mag	3	24	13-3/4	9-1/4	2,790
535-911159	535-919159	416 Rigby	3	24	13-3/4	9-1/4	3,280
535-911144	535-919144	458 Win Mag	3	22	13-3/4	9	2,790
535-911154	535-919154	458 Lott	3	22	13-3/4	9	2,790
Model 70 "Classic" Custom SA (Short Action)							
535-915212	-	257 Roberts	5	22	13-3/4	7-1/2	$2,385
535-915249	-	260 Rem	5	22	13-3/4	7-1/2	2,385
535-915218	-	7mm-08	5	22	13-3/4	7-1/2	2,385
535-915255	-	300 WSM	3	22	13-3/4	7-1/2	2,385
535-915220	-	308 Win	5	22	13-3/4	7-1/2	2,385
535-915223	-	358 Win	4	22	13-3/4	7-1/2	2,385
535-915260	-	450 Marlin	3	22	13-3/4	8-1/4	2,385
Model 70 "Classic" Custom Take-Down							
535-908231	-	7mm Rem Mag	3	26"	13-1/2	8-1/2	$3,595
535-908253	-	300 Ultra Mag	3	26	13-1/2	8-1/2	3,595
535-908238	-	375 H&H Mag	3	24	13-1/2	9	3,595
535-908239	-	416 Rem Mag	3	24	13-1/2	9	3,595
Model 70 "Classic" Custom Ultimate Classic							
535-900225	535-901225	25-06 Rem	5	24"	13-3/4"	7-1/2	$2,635
535-900219	535-901219	6.5 x 55 Swe	5	24	13-3/4	7-1/2	2,635
535-900229	535-901229	264 Win Mag.	3	26	13-3/4	7-1/2	2,635
535-900226	535-901226	270 Win	5	24	13-3/4	7-1/2	2,635
535-900227	535-901227	280 Rem	5	24	13-3/4	7-1/2	2,635
535-900228	535-901228	30-06 Spfld	5	24	13-3/4	7-1/2	2,635
535-900251	535-901251	338-06	5	24	13-3/4	7-1/2	2,635
535-900247	535-901247	35 Whelen	5	24	13-3/4	7-1/2	2,635
535-900230	535-901230	7mm Rem Mag	3	26	13-3/4	7-3/4	2,635
535-900256	535-901256	7mm Ultra Mag	3	26	13-3/4	7-3/4	2,635
535-900231	535-901231	7mm STW	3	26	13-3/4	7-3/4	2,635
535-900233	535-901233	300 Win Mag	3	26	13-3/4	7-3/4	2,635
535-900234	535-901234	300 Weath Mag	3	26	13-3/4	7-3/4	2,635
535-900253	535-901253	300 Ultra Mag	3	26	13-3/4	7-3/4	2,635
535-900236	535-901236	338 Win Mag	3	26	13-3/4	7-3/4	2,635
535-900257	535-901257	338 Ultra Mag	3	26	13-3/4	7-3/4	2,635
Model 70 "Classic" Custom Extreme Weather							
535-916228	535-917228	30-06 Spfld	5	24	13-3/4	7-1/4	$2,140
535-916230	535-917230	7mm Rem Mag	3	26	13-3/4	7-1/2	2,140
535-916233	535-917233	300 Win Mag	3	26	13-3/4	7-1/2	2,140
535-916253	535-917253	300 Ultra Mag	3	26	13-3/4	7-1/2	2,140
535-916236	535-917236	338 Win Mag	3	26	13-3/4	7-1/2	2,140
535-916261	535-917261	375 H&H Lwt	3	22	13-3/4	7-1/2	2,140
Model 94 "Classic" Custom Limited Edition							
534-040117	-	38-55 Win	5	26"	13-1/2	7-1/4	$2,393

Notes: For additional capacity, add one round in chamber. Drops are measured from center line of bore. Twist is right hand. Scopes, bases and/or rings are not included unless otherwise noted. Suggested retail prices are in U.S. dollars and are subject to change without notice. Note: Model 70 Custom Takedown is available in most SAAMI approved calibers.

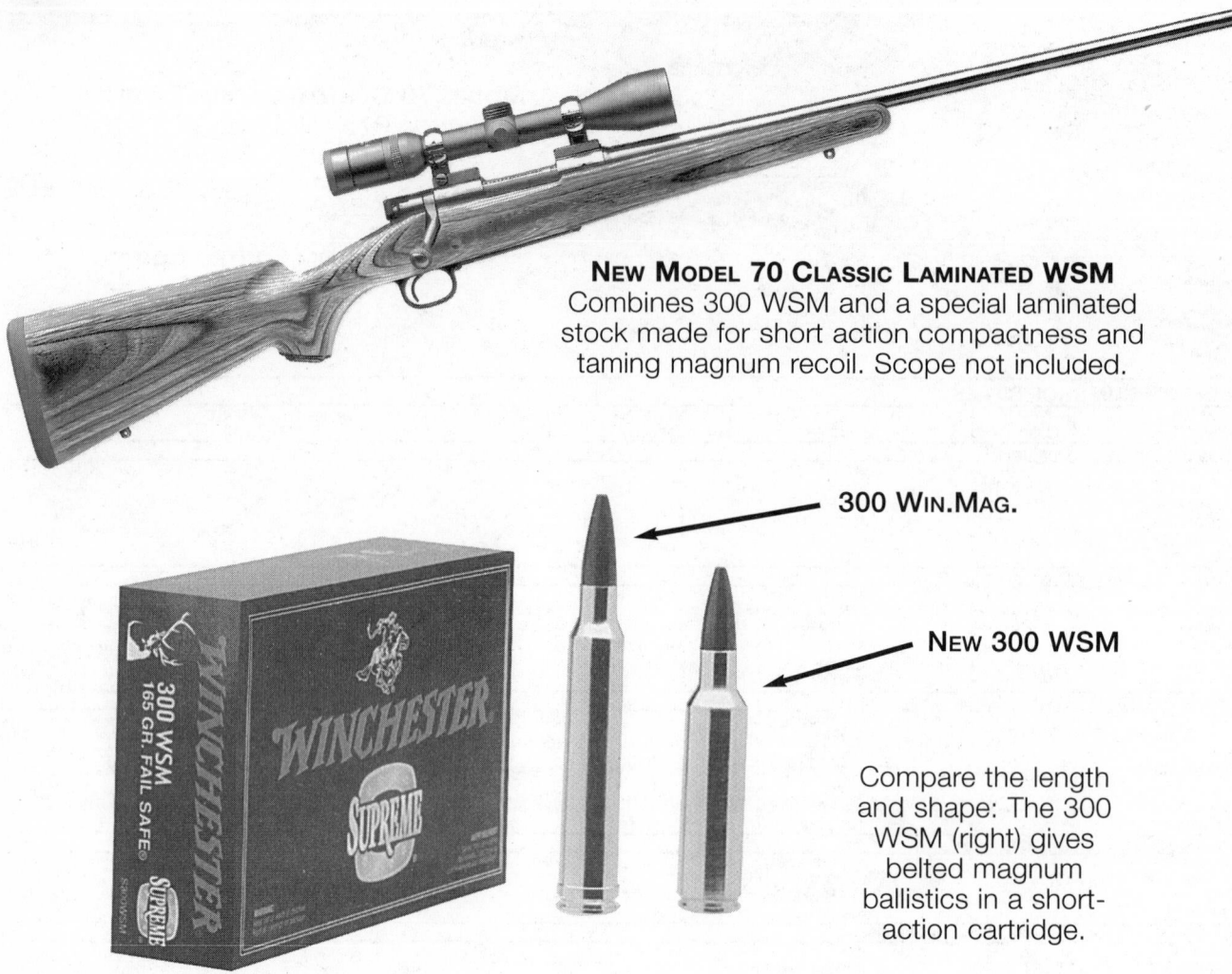

NEW MODEL 70 CLASSIC LAMINATED WSM
Combines 300 WSM and a special laminated stock made for short action compactness and taming magnum recoil. Scope not included.

300 WIN.MAG.

NEW 300 WSM

Compare the length and shape: The 300 WSM (right) gives belted magnum ballistics in a short-action cartridge.

MODEL 70 CLASSIC
NEW FEATHERWEIGHT WSM

The Featherweight WSM features a true short action receiver for compact proportions and a sporter-weight 24" barrel for accuracy. The walnut stock has the Featherweight configuration with Schnabel fore-end, checkering, jeweled bolt, knurled bolt handle and Classic style, claw extractor action.

MODEL 70 CLASSIC
NEW STAINLESS WSM

Sometimes the weather and conditions demand a stainless barrel and action along with a rugged composite stock. They're often the situations in which you need a magnum caliber. The Stainless WSM has a slightly more compact short action combined with a compact stock and 24" sporter barrel for handling ease, all with the knockdown power previously reserved for much heavier, bulkier rifles.

MODEL 70 CLASSIC
NEW LAMINATED WSM

With its special brown laminated stock, short magnum action and sporter-weight barrel, this is the most unique of all the new 300 WSM rifles. The laminated stock forms solid platform for the action. The stock is fitted with a 1" deluxe recoil pad for your comfort. The 24" barrel provides extra compactness and a few ounces less weight. Blued receiver and barrel.

Winchester's Model 70, introduced in 1937, has been called "the rifleman's rifle." Its rugged, adjustable trigger, smooth bolt action, Mauser extractor and three-position safety made it an American legend among hunters and target shooters. A "new model 70" in 1964 reduced production costs but dis-mayed shooters who called for a return to the old model. Now Winchester 70s have the clean lines and high-quality fit and finish that sportsmen want. Available in controlled-feed and push-fed versions with many stock variations, they once again have become the archetypal American rifle.

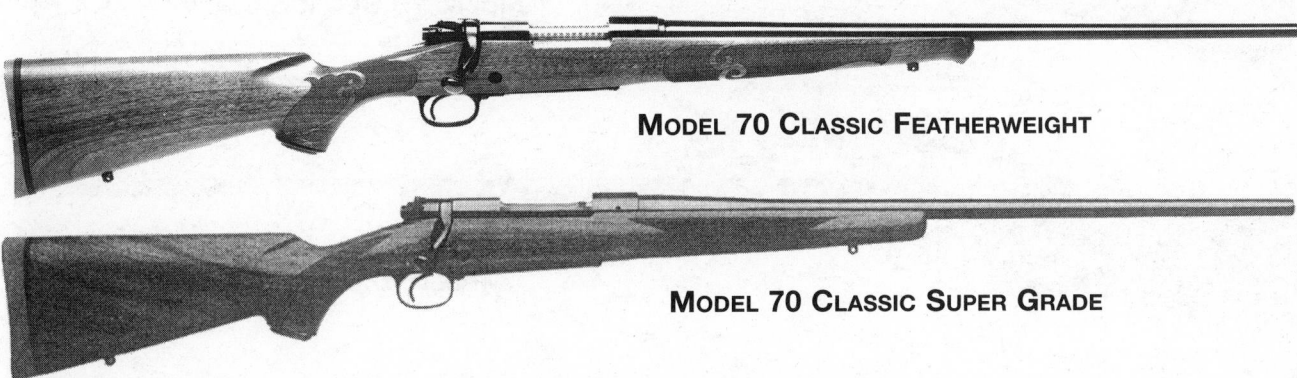

MODEL 70 CLASSIC FEATHERWEIGHT

MODEL 70 CLASSIC SUPER GRADE

RIFLES

MODEL 70 CLASSIC MODELS WITH PRE-'64 TYPE ACTION

Suggested Retail Right Handed	Left Handed	Caliber	Magazine Capacity*	Barrel Length	Nominal Overall Length	Nominal Length of Pull	Nominal Drop at Comb	Nominal Drop at Heel	Nominal Weight (Lbs.)	Rate of Twist I Turn In	Features
CLASSIC FEATHERWEIGHT (BLUED)											
$712	—	22-250 Rem.	5	22"	42"	13-1/2"	9/16"	7/8"	7	14"	Walnut Stock
712	—	243 Win.	5	22	42	13-1/2	9/16	7/8	7	10	Walnut Stock
712	—	6.5 x 55mm Swed.	5	22	42	13-1/2	9/16	7/8	7	8	Walnut Stock
712	—	308 Win.	5	22	42	13-1/2	9/16	7/8	7	12	Walnut Stock
712	—	7mm-08 Rem.	5	22	42	13-1/2	9/16	7/8	7	10	Walnut Stock
712	—	270 Win.	5	22	42-1/2	13-1/2	9/16	7/8	7-1/4	10	Walnut Stock
740	—	300 WSM	3	24	42-1/2	13-1/2	9/16	7/8	7-1/2	10	Walnut Stock
712	—	30-06 Spfld.	5	22	42-1/2	13-1/2	9/16	7/8	7-1/4	10	Walnut Stock

Stainless Models available in 22-250, 243, 308, 270, 30-06.

*For additional capacity, add one round in chamber when ready to fire. Drops are measured from center line of bore. Rate of twist: RH.

SPECIFICATIONS & PRICES: MODEL 70 CLASSIC MODELS

Suggested Retail Right Handed	Left Handed	Caliber	Magazine Capacity*	Barrel Length	Nominal Overall Length	Nominal Length of Pull	Nominal Drop at Comb	Nominal Drop at Heel	Nominal Weight (Lbs.)	Rate of Twist I Turn In	Features
CLASSIC SAFARI EXPRESS											
$1081	$1117	375 H&H Mag.	3	24"	44-3/4"	13-3/4"	9/16"	1 5/16"	8-1/2	12"	Sights, Walnut Stock
1081	—	416 Rem. Mag.	3	24	44-3/4	13-3/4	9/16	1 5/16	8-1/2	14	Sights, Walnut Stock
1081	—	458 Win. Mag.	3	22	42-3/4	13-3/4	9/16	1 5/16	8-1/4	14	Sights, Walnut Stock
CLASSIC SUPER GRADE											
$975	—	25-06 Win.	5"	24"	44-3/4"	13-3/4"	9/16"	13/16"	7-3/4	10"	Walnut Stock
975	—	270 Win.	5	24	44-3/4	13-3/4	9/16	13/16	7-3/4	10	Walnut Stock
975	—	30-06 Spfld.	5	24	44-3/4	13-3/4	9/16	13/16	7-3/4	10	Walnut Stock
1003	—	7mm Rem. Mag.	3	26	46-3/4	13-3/4	9/16	13/16	8	9-1/2	Walnut Stock
1003	—	300 Win. Mag.	3	26	46-3/4	13-3/4	9/16	13/16	8	10	Walnut Stock
1003	—	338 Win. Mag.	3	26	46-3/4	13-3/4	9/16	13/16	8	10	Walnut Stock
CLASSIC SPORTER LT (BLUED)											
$699	—	25-06 Rem.	5	24"	44-3/4"	13-3/4"	9/16"	13/16"	7-3/4	10"	Walnut Stock
699	$733	270 Win.	5	24	44-3/4	13-3/4	9/16	13/16	7-3/4	10	Walnut Stock
669	733	30-06 Spfld.	5	24	44-3/4	13-3/4	9/16	13/16	7-3/4	10	Walnut Stock
727	—	7mm STW	3	26	46-3/4	13-3/4	9/16	13/16	8	9-1/2	Walnut Stock
727	761	7mm Rem. Mag.	3	26	46-3/4	13-3/4	9/16	13/16	8	9-1/2	Walnut Stock
727	761	300 Win. Mag.	3	26	46-3/4	13-3/4	9/16	13/16	8	10	Walnut Stock
727	—	338 Win. Mag.	3	26	46-3/4	13-3/4	9/16	13/16	8	10	Walnut Stock
761	—	300 WSM	3	24	44-3/4	13-3/4	9/16	13/16	7-3/4	10	Laminated Stock

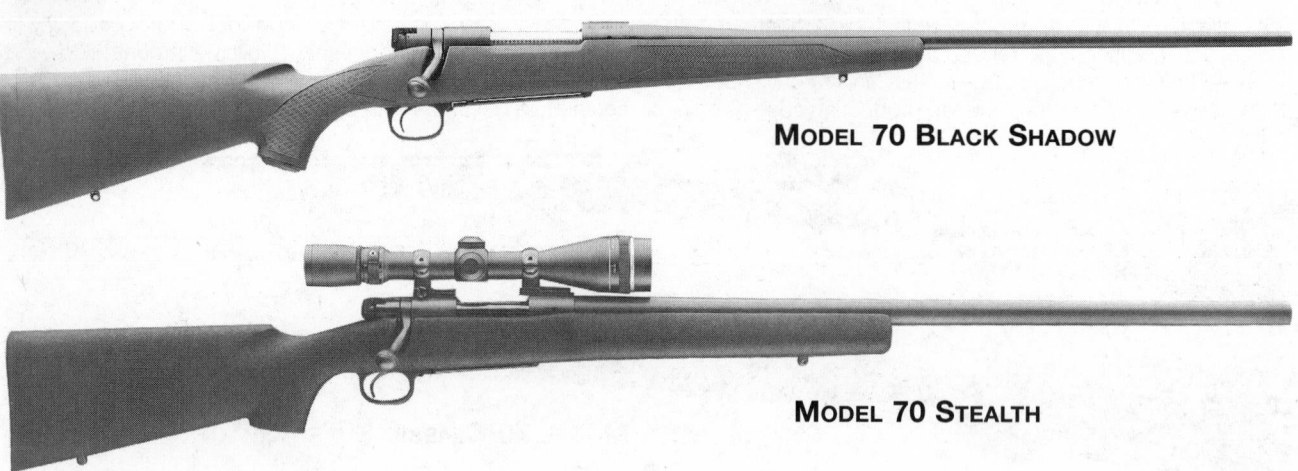

MODEL 70 BLACK SHADOW

MODEL 70 STEALTH

SPECIFICATIONS & PRICES: MODEL 70 CLASSIC MODELS *(Cont.)*

SUGGESTED RETAIL RIGHT HANDED	LEFT HANDED	CALIBER	MAGAZINE CAPACITY*	BARREL LENGTH	NOMINAL OVERALL LENGTH	NOMINAL LENGTH OF PULL	NOMINAL DROP AT COMB	NOMINAL DROP AT HEEL	NOMINAL WEIGHT (LBS.)	RATE OF TWIST I TURN IN	FEATURES
CLASSIC STAINLESS (COMPOSITE)											
$768	—	270 Win.	5	24"	44-3/4"	13-3/4"	9/16"	13/16"	7-1/4	10"	Composite Stock
768	—	30-06 Spfld.	5	24	44-3/4	13-3/4	9/16	13/16	7-1/4	10	Composite Stock
798	—	7mm STW	3	26	46-3/4	13-3/4	9/16	13/16	7-1/2	9-1/2	Composite Stock
798	—	7mm Rem. Mag.	3	26	46-3/4	13-3/4	9/16	13/16	7-1/2	9-1/2	Composite Stock
798	—	300 Win. Mag.	3	26	46-3/4	13-3/4	9/16	13/16	7-1/2	10	Composite Stock
798	—	300 Ultra. Mag.	3	26	46-3/4	13-3/4	9/16	13/16	7-1/2	10	Composite Stock
798	—	300 WSM	3	24	44	13-3/4	9/16	13/16	7-1/4	10	Composite Stock
798	—	338 Win. Mag.	3	26	46-3/4	13-3/4	9/16	13/16	7-1/2	10	Composite Stock
889	—	375 H&H Mag.	3	24	44-3/4	13-3/4	9/16	13/16	7-1/4	12	Sights, Composite Stock
CLASSIC COMPACT											
$712	—	243 Win.	4	20"	39-1/2"	13"	9/16"	3/4"	6-1/2	10"	Walnut Stock
712	—	308 Win.	4	20	39-1/2	13	9/16	3/4	6-1/2	12	Walnut Stock
712	—	7mm-08 Rem.	4	20	39-1/2	13	9/16	3/4	6-1/2	9-1/2	Walnut Stock

MODEL 70 PUSH FEED MODELS

SUGGESTED RETAIL RIGHT HANDED	LEFT HANDED	CALIBER	MAGAZINE CAPACITY*	BARREL LENGTH	NOMINAL OVERALL LENGTH	NOMINAL LENGTH OF PULL	NOMINAL DROP AT COMB	NOMINAL DROP AT HEEL	NOMINAL WEIGHT (LBS.)	RATE OF TWIST I TURN IN	FEATURES
COYOTE											
$679	—	223 Rem.	6	24	44	13-1/2	5/8	3/4	9	9	Laminated Stock
679	—	22-250 Rem.	5	24	44	13-1/2	5/8	3/4	9	14	Laminated Stock
679	—	243 Win.	5	24	44	13-1/2	5/8	3/4	9	10	Laminated Stock
STEALTH											
$768	—	223 Rem.	6	26	46	13-1/2	3/4	1/2	10-3/4	9	Accu Block
768	—	22-250 Rem.	5	26	46	13-1/2	3/4	1/2	10-3/4	14	Accu Block
768	—	308 Win.	5	26	46	13-1/2	3/4	1/2	10-3/4	12	Accu Block
BLACK SHADOW®											
$512	—	270 Win.	5	22"	42-3/4"	13-3/4"	9/16"	13/16"	7-1/4	10"	Composite Stock
512	—	30-06 Spfld.	5	22	42-3/4	13-3/4	9/16	13/16	7-1/4	10	Composite Stock
542	—	7mm Rem. Mag.	3	24	42-3/4	13-3/4	9/16	13/16	7-1/4	9-1/2	Composite Stock
542	—	300 Win. Mag.	3	22	42-3/4	13-3/4	9/16	13/16	7-1/4	10	Composite Stock

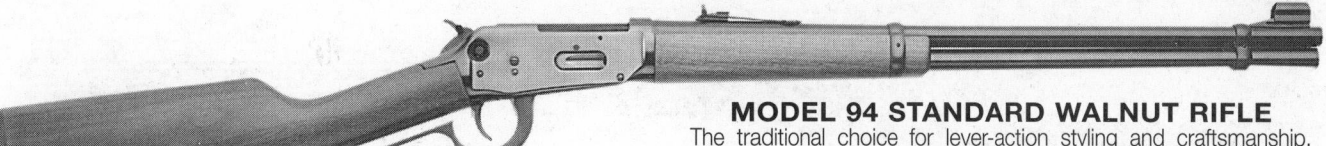

MODEL 94 STANDARD WALNUT RIFLE

The traditional choice for lever-action styling and craftsmanship. America's favorite deer rifle for half a century! Exposed-hammer lever action with angled ejection and crossbolt safety. American walnut stock and forearm have a protective stain finish with precise-cut wraparound checkering. It has a 20-inch barrel with hooded blade front sight and semibuckhorn rear sight.

MODEL 94 WALNUT TRAPPER CARBINE

With 16-inch short-barrel lever action and straight forward styling. Compact and fast handing in dense cover, it has a 5-shot magazine capacity (9 in 45 Colt or 44 Rem. Mag./44 S&W Special). *Calibers:* 30-30 Win., 357 Mag., 45 Colt, and 44 Rem. Mag./44 S&W Special.

RIFLES

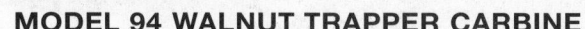

MODEL 94

Suggested Retail	Caliber	Magazine Capacity*	Barrel Length	Overall Length	Nominal Length of Pull	Nominal Drop at Comb	Nominal Drop at Heel	Nominal Weight (Lbs.)	Rate of Twist 1 Turn In	Features
RANGER COMPACT										
$355	30-30 Win.	5	16"	33-1/4"	12-1/2"	1-1/8"	1-3/4"	5-7/8	12"	Rifle Sights, SL
378	357 Mag.	9	16	33-1/4	12-1/2	1-1/8	1-3/4	5-7/8	16	Rifle Sights, SL
LEGACY										
$457	30-30 Win.	7	24	42-1/8	13-1/2	1-1/8	1-7/8	6-3/4	12	PG, Rifle Sights, SL
457	357 Mag.	12	24	42-1/8	13-1/2	1-1/8	1-7/8	6-3/4	16	PG, Rifle Sights, SL
457	45 Colt	12	24	42-1/8	13-1/2	1-1/8	1-7/8	6-3/4	26	PG, Rifle Sights, SL
457	44 Rem. Mag.	12	24	42-1/8	13-1/2	1-1/8	1-7/8	6-3/4	26	PG, Rifle Sights, SL
RANGER										
$355	30-30 Win.	6	20"	38-1/8"	13-1/2"	1-1/8"	1-7/8"	6-1/4	12"	Rifle Sights, SL
TRADITIONAL										
$440	30-30 Win. checkered	6	20"	38-1/8"	13-1/2"	1-1/8"	1-7/8"	6-1/4	12"	Rifle Sights
407	30-30 Win. not checkered	6	20"	38-1/8"	13-1/2"	1-1/8"	1-7/8"	6-1/4	12"	Rifle Sights
463	44 Mag. checkered	6	20"	38-1/8"	13-1/2	1-1/8	1-7/8	6-1/4	26"	Rifle Sights
TRAILS END										
$445	357 Mag.	11	20	38-1/8	13-1/2	1-1/8	1-7/8	6-1/2	16	Rifle Sights, SL
445	44 Rem.	11	20	38-1/8	13-1/2	1-1/8	1-7/8	6-1/2	26	Rifle Sights, SL
445	45 Colt	11	20	38-1/8	13-1/2	1-1/8	1-7/8	6-1/2	26	Rifle Sights, SL
BIG BORE										
$465	444 Marlin	6	20	38-1/8"	13-1/2"	1-1/8"	1-7/8"	6-1/2	38	Rifle Sights, LL
TRAPPER										
$407	30-30 Win.	5	16"	34-1/4"	13-1/2"	1-1/8"	1-7/8"	6	12	Rifle Sights, SL
431	44 Rem.	9	16	34-1/4	13-1/2	1-1/8	1-7/8	6	26	Rifle Sights, SL
431	357 Mag.	9	16	34-1/4	13-1/2	1-1/8	1-7/8	6	16	Rifle Sights, SL
431	45 Colt	9	16	34-1/4	13-1/2	1-1/8	1-7/8	6	26	Rifle Sights, SL
PACK RIFLE										
$496	30-30 Win.	4	18"	36-1/8"	13-1/2"	1-1/8"	1-7/8"	6-1/4	12"	PG, Rifle Sights
505	45 Rem. Mag.	5	18	36-1/8	13-1/2	1-1/8	1-7/8	6-1/4	26	PG, Rifle Sights
TIMBER CARBINE										
$573	444 Marlin	5	17-3/4"	36"	13-1/2"	1-1/8"	1-7/8"	6	12	Rifle Sights

Bushnell 4X32 scope and see-thru mounts available.

MODEL 94 RANGER

MODEL 94 RANGER is an economical version of the Model 94.
Also available: RANGER COMPACT in 30-30 Win. and 357 Mag.
Price: **$355.00**

MODEL 94 PACK RIFLE

18" barrel in 30-30 and .44 Maagnum, fuller pistol grip and forend.
Prices: 30-30 . . . . **$496.00**
44 . . . . **506.00**

MODEL 94 BIG-BORE WALNUT

Improved performance. Available in 444 Marlin in walnut and Black Shadow versions.
Price: **$465.00**

BLACK SHADOW

MODEL 94 TRAILS END

SPECIFICATIONS
Calibers: 357 Mag., 44 Rem. Mag., 45 Colt. *Capacity:* 11 shot magazine. *Barrel length:* 20". *Overall length:* 38 1/8". *Weight:* 6.5 lbs. Standard loop or large loop.
Price: **$445.00**

MODEL 94 LEGACY
Standard Loop Lever

SPECIFICATIONS
Calibers: 30-30 Win., 357 Mag., 44 Rem. Mag., 45 Colt.
Capacity: 6 shots (30-30 Win.); 11 shots (other calibers); add 1 shot for 24" barrel. *Barrel length:* 20" or 24".
Overall length: 42 1/8" w/24" barrel. *Weight:* 6.75 lbs.
Price: **$457.00**

WINCHESTER LEVER-ACTION

.22 Rifles

The 9422 Series is based on an exposed-hammer, side-ejecting lever action noted for its smoothness and reliability. Checkered American walnut stocks and a rich blue add to the appearance. Open sights augment a receiver grooved for scope mounts.

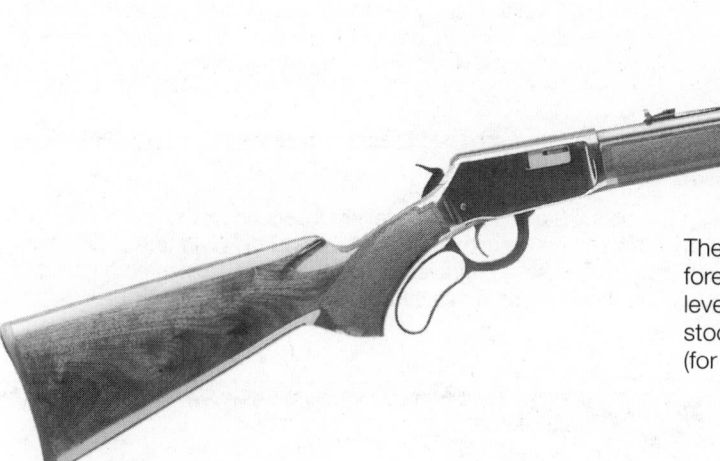

MODEL 9422 LEGACY

The Model 9422 Legacy has a semi-pistol grip stock, long forearm nose, and long 22 ½" barrel. Styled after centerfire levers of a century ago, it features a cut checkered walnut stock and fore-end, adjustable sights. Hammer extension (for use with a scope) included.

RIFLES

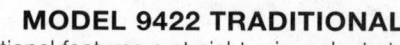

MODEL 9422 TRADITIONAL

The Traditional features a straight grip walnut stock with cut checkering. Modeled after the famous Winchester 94, this rifle has become the standard of comparision for other 22 lever actions. Choose 22 LR or 22 WMR. Hammer extension (for use with a scope) included.

MODEL 9422 RIMFIRE RIFLES

Item Number	Caliber	Magazine Capacity	Barrel Length	Nominal Overall Length	Nominal Length of Pull	Nominal Drop at Comb	Nominal Drop at Heel	Nominal Weight (Lbs.)	Rate of Twist 1 Turn In	U.S. Sugg. Retail
LEGACY										
524-027103	22 Rimfire	15 LR	22-1/2"	39-1/8"	13-1/2"	1-1-8"	1-7/8"	6	16"	$473
524-027104	22 WMR	11	22-1/2	39-1/8	13-1/2	1-1/8	1-7/8	6	16	496
TRADITIONAL										
524-024103	22 Rimfire	15 LR	20-1/2"	37-1/8"	13-1/2"	1-1/8"	1-7/8"	6	16"	$444
524-024104	22 WMR	11	20-1/2	37-1/8	13-1/2	1-1/8	1-7/8	6	16	464

www.StoegerIndustries.com

Rifles
2002 Edition

WINCHESTER RIFLES

Limited Edition And Historic

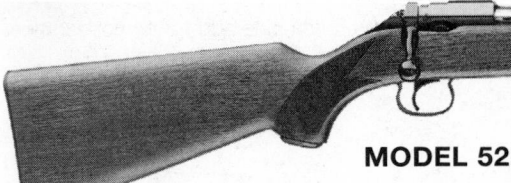

MODEL 52B

The 52 is considered by many the finest bolt action .22 rifle ever made. Features the renowned Micro-Motion trigger system. Match .22 rimfire chamber, smooth bolt operation and 5-shot magazine just like the originals. Produced in small numbers every year.

NEW MODEL 1895 .405 WINCHESTER

This was the gun Teddy Roosevelt described as his "big medicine". He took three of them in .405 caliber on his historic African safari. High grades have engraved elk and whitetail scenes on a polished white receiver. Grade I is blued. (Small quantities available).

MODEL 1885 LOW WALL RIMFIRE

The classic Low Wall Winchester in .22 Long Rifle caliber. Its trim stock, half octagon/half round barrel and special chamber dimensions contribute to accuracy. Drilled and tapped for scope mounts or tang-mounted peep (available separately). Limited to 2,400 Grade I and 1,100 High Grade rifles.

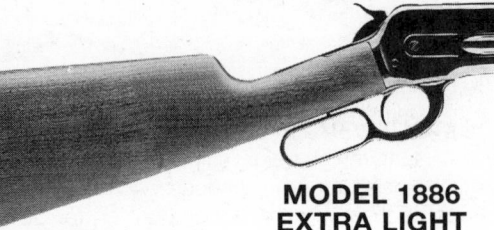

MODEL 1886 EXTRA LIGHT

This rifle has a 22" round tapered barrel, solid frame, shotgun style steel buttplate and half magazine. Its exceptionally strong action is chambered for powerful 45-70. Two grades in limited numbers: High Grade features extra fancy checkered walnut stock and engraved game scenes on a blued receiver.

HISTORIC RIFLES

Model	Caliber	Magazine Capacity *	Barrel Length	Nominal Overall Length	Nominal Length of Pull	Nominal Drop at Comb	Nominal Drop at Heel	Nominal Weight (Lbs.)	Rate of Twist 1 Turn in	U.S. Sugg. Retail
LIMITED EDITIONS										
MODEL 1885 LOW WALL 22 GRADE I	22 Long Rifle	n/a	24-1/2"	41"	13-1/2"	7/8"	1-1/2"	8	16"	$828
MODEL 1885 LOW WALL 22 HIGH GRADE	22 Long Rifle	n/a	24-1/2'	41"	13-1/2"	7/8"	1-1/2"	8	16"	1,180
MODEL 1886 EXTRA LIGHT GRADE I	45-70	4	22"	40-1/2"	13-1/4"	1-1/8"	1-5/8"	7-1/4	22"	1,152
MODEL 1886 EXTRA LIGHT HIGH GRADE	45-70	4	22"	40-1/2"	13-1/4"	1-1/8"	1-5/8"	7-1/4	22"	1,440
CLASSIC TRADITIONS - IN LINE CONTINUING MODELS										
MODEL 52B BOLT ACTION	22 Long Rifle	5	24"	41-3/4"	13-1/2"	1-3/8"	2-5/16"	7	16"	662
MODEL 1895 GRADE I *NEW*	.405 Win.	4	24"	42"	13-1/4"	2-7/8"	3-5/8"	8	10"	1,045
MODEL 1895 HIGH GRADE *NEW*	.405 Win.	4	24"	42"	13-1/4"	2-7/8"	3-5/8"	8	10"	1,532

Shotguns

MODERN BERETTA FIREARMS
by Gene Gangarosa Jr.

Modern Beretta Firearms traces the development of Beretta's famous variations including: Models 92S, 92S-1, 92SB, 92SB-F, 92FSS and many more. Illustrated with hundred of photos, this book is not only informative, but sheer reading pleasure.

THE LEGEND OF HARLEY DAVIDSON
by Peter Henshaw

Examine a proud heritage of iconic motorcycles, charting the evolution of these machines and the lives of the people who rode and raced them throughout the last century. The Harley-Davidson is a motorcycle around which a 'lifestyle' has developed, with its own gatherings, attire, attitudes and passions. This book samples the Harley experience and explores the relationship between man and machine. Photographs from all over the USA and Europe in vivid color illustrate these exceptional machines in all their glory.

*For addresses and phone/fax numbers of manufacturers and distributors included in this section, please turn to **DIRECTORY OF MANUFACTURERS AND SUPPLIERS** on page 557.*

AMERICAN ARMS SHOTGUNS

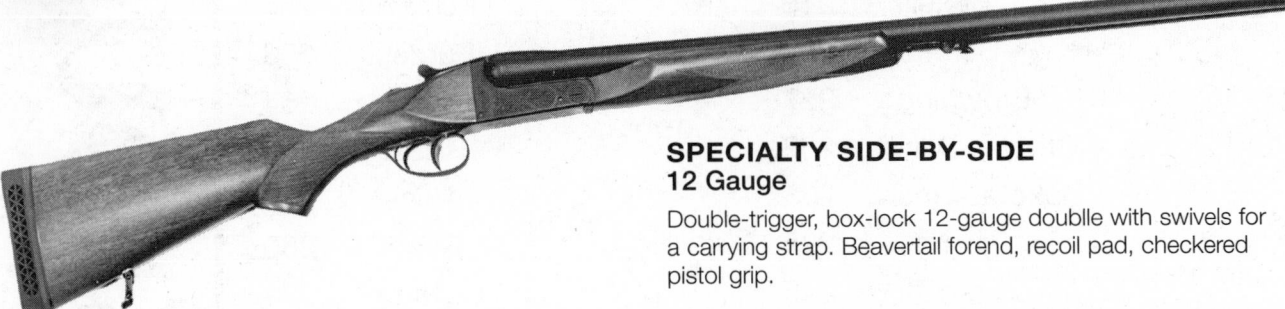

SPECIALTY SIDE-BY-SIDE
12 Gauge

Double-trigger, box-lock 12-gauge doublle with swivels for a carrying strap. Beavertail forend, recoil pad, checkered pistol grip.

SPECIALTY OVER/UNDER
12 Gauge

Boxlock over/under, 10 or 12 gauge, single selective trigger, strap swivels, vent rib, checkered stock.

SPECIALTY CAMO (SILVER WT/OU)
SPECIFICATIONS

Features nonreflective Mossy Oak "Breakup" Camo pattern. Specifications same as WS/OU 12 ga., including auto selective ejectors and AA1 choke tubes (IC-M-F).

SPECIFICATIONS

MODEL	GAUGE	BBL. LENGTH	CHAMBER	CHOKES	AVG. WGT.	PRICES
WT/OU	10	26"	3.5"	CT-2	9 lbs. 10 oz.	$995.00
WS/OU	12	28"	3.5"	CT-3	7 lbs. 2 oz.	799.00
WT/OU Camo	12	26"	3.5"	CT-3	7 lbs.	885.00
TS/SS	12	26"	3.5"	CT-3	7 lbs. 6 oz.	799.00

CT-3 Choke Tubes IC/M/F. CT-2 = Choke tubes F/F. Drop at Comb = 1 1/8"; Drop at Heel = 2 3/8"

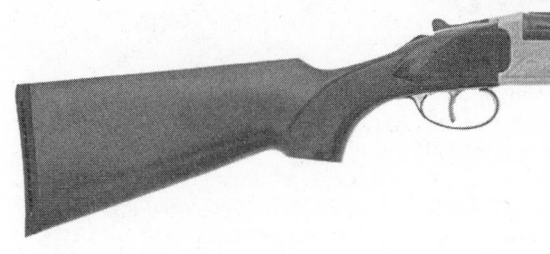

SILVER I OVER AND UNDER
(W/Fixed Chokes & Extractors)

Features polished white frame w/outline engraving; blued trigger guard, top lever and forward latch; radiused rubber recoil pad.

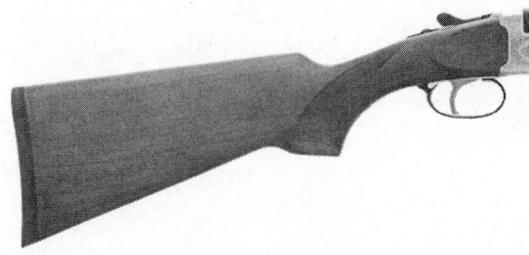

SILVER II
(W/Choke Tubes & Automatic Selective Ejectors)

Same features as Silver I, but with more refined engraving. Models in 16, 20 and .410 gauge have fixed chokes.

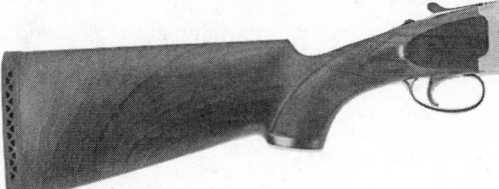

SILVER SPORTING
(Ported, w/Choke Tubes)

SHOTGUNS

SPECIFICATIONS

MODEL	GAUGE	BBL. LENGTH	CHAMBER	CHOKES	AVG. WEIGHT	PRICES
Silver I	12	26" – 28"	3"	IC/M-M/F	6 lbs. 15 oz.	$649.00
	20	26" – 28"	3"	IC/M-M/F	6 lbs. 12 oz.	649.00
	28	26"	2.75"	IC/M	5 lbs. 14 oz.	679.00
	.410	26"	3"	IC/M	6 lbs. 6 oz.	679.00
Silver II*	12	26" – 28"	3"	CT-3	6 lbs. 15 oz.	769.00
	16	26"	2.75"	IC/M	6 lbs. 13 oz.	769.00
	20	26"	3"	CT-3	6 lbs. 12 oz.	769.00
	28	26"	2.75"	IC/M	5 lbs. 14 oz.	815.00
	.410	26"	3"	IC/M	6 lbs. 6 oz.	815.00
Sporting**	12	28" – 30"	2.75"	CTS	7 lbs. 6 oz.	965.00

CT-3 Choke Tubes IC/M/F Cast Off = ³/₈" CTS = SK/SK/IC/M   Silver I and II: Pull = 14 ¹/₈"; Drop at Comb = 1 ³/₈"; Drop at Heel = 2 ³/₈"
Silver I and II: Pull = 14 ¹/₄"; Drop at Comb = 1 ¹/₂"; Drop at Heel = 2 ¹/₂"   * 2 Barrel Set: **$115.00** **Silver Upland Lite (12 and 20 ga.) = *$925.00**

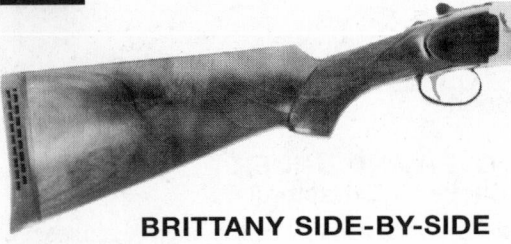

BRITTANY SIDE-BY-SIDE

SPECIFICATIONS
Gauges: 12, 20
Chamber: 3"
Chokes: CT-3

Barrel Length: 26"
Weight: 6 lbs. 7 oz. (20 ga.); 6 lbs. 15 oz. (12 ga.)
Features: Engraved case-colored frame; single selective trigger with top tang selector; automatic selective ejectors; manual safety; hard chrome-lined barrels; walnut English-style straight stock and semi-beavertail forearm w/cut checkering and oil-rubbed finish; ventilated rubber recoil pal; and choke tubes with key
Price: **$885.00**

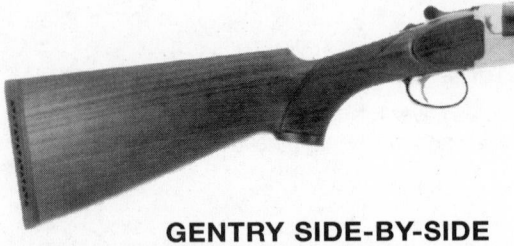

GENTRY SIDE-BY-SIDE

Features boxlocks with engraved English-style scrollwork on side plates; one-piece, steel-forged receiver; chrome barrels; manual thumb safety; independent floating firing pin.

SPECIFICATIONS
Gauges: 12, 20, 28, .410
Chamber: 3" (except 28 gauge, 2.75")

Barrel Lengths: 26", choked IC/M (all gauges; 28", choked M/F (12 and 20 gauges)
Weight: 6 lbs. 15 oz. (12 ga.); 6 lbs. 7 oz. (20 and .410 ga.); 6 lbs. 5 oz. (28 ga.)
Drop At Comb: 1 $^3/_8$"
Drop At Heel: 2 $^3/_8$"
Other Features: Fitted recoil pad; flat matted rib; walnut pistol-grip stock and beavertail forend with hand-checkering; gold front sight bead
Prices:
  12 or 20 ga. **$750.00**
  28 or .410 ga. **795.00**

PHANTOM SYNTHETIC

SPECIFICATIONS
Gauge: 12 *Barrel:* 24"/26"/28", cold hammered forged chrome lined with bright blue finish *Choke:* IC-M-F
Chamber: 3" *Features:* Gas operated semi-automatic shoots 2 3/4" or 3" shells interchangeably. Approved for steel shot, checkered synthetic forend and stock, screw-in choke tubes (3), magazine cut-off for quick unloading and safety, five round magazine.
Price: **$439.00**

PHANTOM HOME PROTECTION

SPECIFICATIONS
Gauge: 12 *Barrel:* 19" threaded barrel for external choketubes (2), and swivel studs *Choke:* SK, M, F
Chamber: 3" *Features:* Same as Phantom Synthetic
Price: **$449.00**

PHANTOM FIELD

SPECIFICATIONS
Gauge: 12 *Barrel:* 24"/26"/28", cold hammered forged chrome lined with bright blue finish *Choke:* IC-M-F
Chamber: 3" *Features:* Same as Phantom Synthetic, except for checkered walnut forend and stock
Price: **$439.00**

AYA SHOTGUNS

Boxlock Shotguns

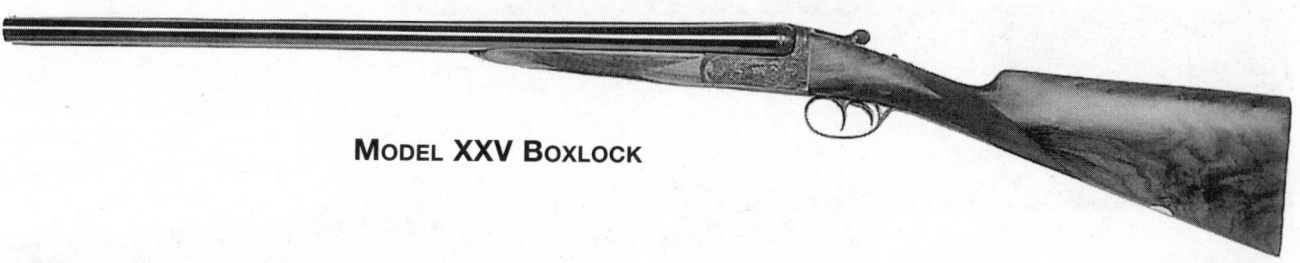

MODEL XXV BOXLOCK

AYA boxlocks use the Anson & Deeley system with double locking lugs, incorporating detachable cross pin and separate plate to allow easy access to the firing mechanism. Barrels are chopper lump, firing pins are bushed, plus automatic safety and ejectors and metal oval for engraving of initials. Other features include disc set strikers, replaceable hinge pin, split bottom plate.
Barrel lengths: 26", 27" and 28"

Weight: 5 to 7 pounds, depending on gauge.

MODEL	Price
MODEL XXV BOXLOCK: 12 and 20 gauge only	$2,635.00
MODEL 4 BOXLOCK: 12, 16, 20, 28, .410 ga.	2,025.00
MODEL 4 DELUXE BOXLOCK: Same gauges as above	2,995.00

Sidelock Shotguns

AYA sidelock shotguns are fitted with London Holland & Holland system sidelocks, double triggers with articulated front trigger, automatic safety and ejectors, cocking indicators, bushed firing pins, replaceable hinge pins and chopper lump barrels. Stocks are of figured walnut with hand-cut checkering and oil finish, complete with a metal oval on the buttstock for engraving of initials. Exhibition grade wood is available as are many special options, including a true left-hand version and self-opener. Available from Armes de Chasse (see Directory of Manufacturers and Suppliers).
Barrell lengths: 26", 27", 28", 29" and 32". *Weight:* 5 to 7 pounds, depending on gauge.

MODEL	Prices
MODEL 1: Sidelock in 12 and 20 ga. w/special engraving and exhibition quality wood	$7,170.00
DELUXE	8,295.00
MODEL 2: Sidelock in 12, 16, 20, 28 ga. and .410 bore	3,375.00
MODEL 53: Sidelock in 12, 16 and 20 ga. with 3 locking lugs and side clips	4,745.00
MODEL 56: Sidelock in 12 ga. only with 3 locking lugs and side clips	7,870.00
MODEL XXV/SL: Sidelock in 12 and 20 ga. only w/Churchill-type rib	3,895.00

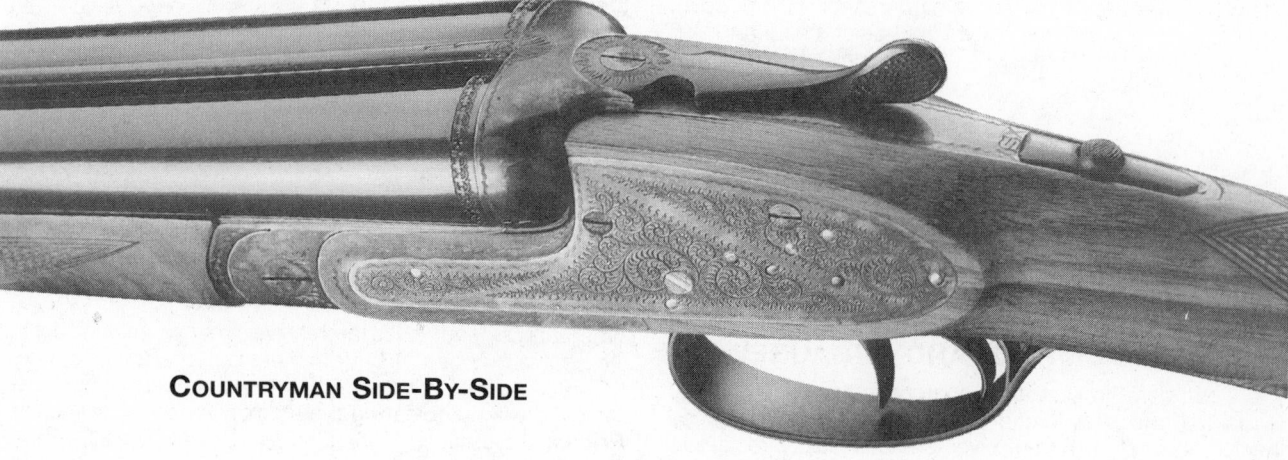

COUNTRYMAN SIDE-BY-SIDE

SHOTGUNS

Shotguns 2002 Edition

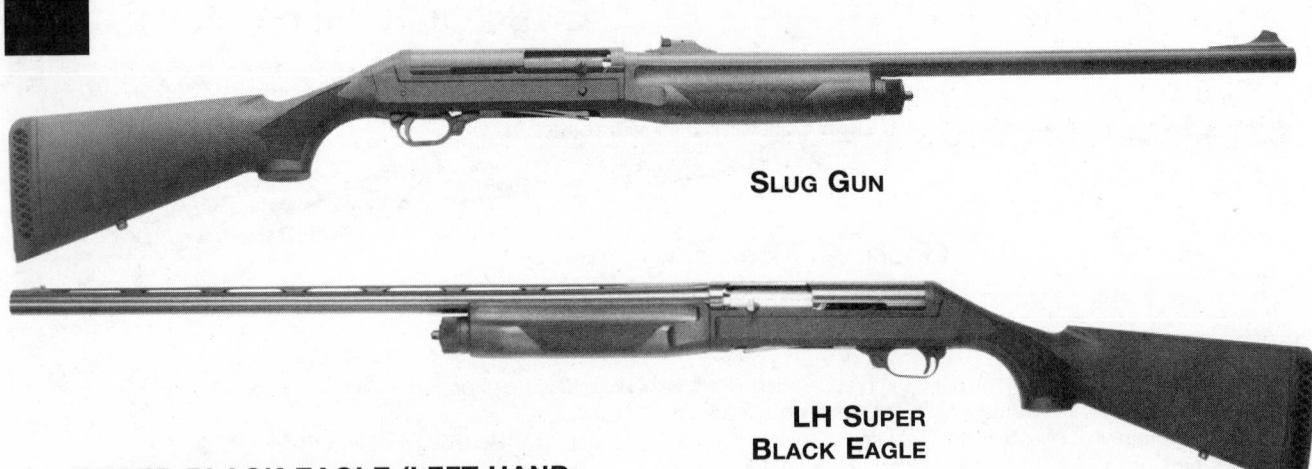

SLUG GUN

LH SUPER
BLACK EAGLE

SUPER BLACK EAGLE (LEFT-HAND VENT RIB AND SLUG GUN SHOWN)

Benelli's Super Black Eagle shotgun fires every type of 12 gauge shell currently available without adjustment.

It also features a specially strengthened steel upper receiver mated to the barrel to endure the toughest shotgunning with magnum loads. The alloy lower receiver keeps overall weight low.

Stock: Satin walnut (28") with drop adjustment kit; high-gloss walnut (26") with drop adjustment kit; or synthetic stock

Finish: Matte black finish on receiver, barrel and bolt (28"); blued finish on receiver and barrel (26") with bolt mirror polished (camo options available)

Features: Montefeltro rotating bolt with dual locking lugs. For additional specifications, see table on following page.

Prices: Wood Satin $1,265.00
Synthetic 1,250.00
Camo 1,345.00
In lefthand, synthetic 1,300.00
LH Camo 1,395.00
Rifled slug, wood 1,330.00
  Synthetic 1,315.00
  Camo 1,430.00

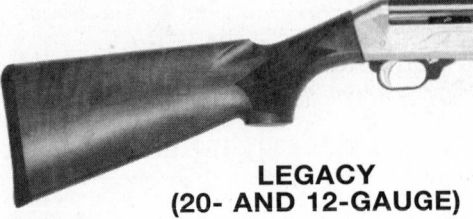

LEGACY (20- AND 12-GAUGE)

Features lower alloy receiver and upper steel receiver cover and interchangeable barrel with mid-point bead and red light-gathering bar front sight. Also Benelli's inertia recoil

12-GAUGE

operating system; cartridge drop lever (to indicate hammer-cocked condition; set of 5 choke tubes for use with lead or steel shot); chambered round removable without emptying the magazine; handles all 2 3/4" and 3" shells within gauge with over 1 1/2 oz. of shot. **Price:** $1,380.00

NOVA PUMP
Realtree® X-tra Brown, available in 12 ga. only

NOVA PUMP (12- AND 20-GAUGE)

The world's first truly modern shotgun is the Benelli NOVA. A molded, steel reinforced glass/polymer matrix replaced the traditional stock and receiver. The bolt locks directly into the barrel and provides all the strength necessary for heavy 3.5" loads. The Nova's fore-arm is finger-grooved for a sure

grasp and extends over the receiver front to prevent pinching as it is pumped. A button in the bottom of the fore-arm activates a shell stop that allows the chambered shell to be removed without releasing the ammunition in the magazine.
Prices: Synthetic $405.00
Camo 470.00
Rifled Slug 575.00

SPORT MODEL

Features 28" barrel, interchangeable ribs, Montefeltro style forearm, adjustable butt pad, oil finish stock, optional shell catcher. Other models have same fast, reliable recoil-operated action but differ in dimensions.

Price: **$1,370.00**

Prices vary by model

BENELLI SHOTGUN SPECIFICATIONS

SUPER BLACK EAGLE – 12 Gauge - 2 3/4", 3" and 3 1/2"

Item Number	Barrel Length	Stock	Magazine Capacity	Choke(s)	Type of Sights	Overall Length	Average Weight	Length of Pull	Drop at Heel	Drop at Comb
SUPER BLACK EAGLE										
10000	28"	Satin walnut	3+1	C,IC,M,IM,F	Red bar	49.63"	7.5 lbs.	14 1/4"	2 1/2"	1 5/8"
10010	26"	Satin walnut	3+1	C,IC,M,IM,F	Red bar	47.63"	7.4 lbs.	14 1/4"	2 1/2"	1 5/8"
10005*	26"	Satin walnut	3+1	C,IC,M,IM,F	Red bar	45.63"	7.3 lbs.	14 1/4"	2 1/2"	1 5/8"
10015	28"	Synthetic	3+1	C,IC,M,IM,F	Red bar	49.63"	7.5 lbs.	14 1/4"	2 1/2"	1 5/8"
10020	26"	Synthetic	3+1	C,IC,M,IM,F	Red bar	47.63"	7.4 lbs.	14 1/4"	2 1/2"	1 5/8"
10025	24"	Synthetic	3+1	C,IC,M,IM,F	Red bar	45.63"	7.3 lbs.	14 1/4"	2 1/2"	1 5/8"
10040	28"	Camo**	3+1	C,IC,M,IM,F	Red bar	49.63"	7.5 lbs.	14 1/4"	2 1/2"	1 5/8"
10045	26"	Camo**	3+1	C,IC,M,IM,F	Red bar	47.63"	7.4 lbs.	14 1/4"	2 1/2"	1 5/8"
10050	24"	Camo**	3+1	C,IC,M,IM,F	Red bar	45.63"	7.3 lbs.	14 1/4"	2 1/2"	1 5/8"
SUPER BLACK EAGLE RIFLED SLUG										
10030	24"	Satin Walnut	3+1	Rifled bore	Open rifle	45.63"	7.6 lbs.	14 1/4"	2 1/2"	1 5/8"
10035	24"	Synthetic	3+1	Rifled bore	Open rifle	45.63"	7.6 lbs.	14 1/4"	2 1/2"	1 5/8"
10095	24"	Camo**	3+1	Rifled bore	Open rifle	45.63"	7.6 lbs.	14 1/4"	2 1/2"	1 5/8"

MONTEFELTRO – 12 Gauge and 20 Gauge - 2 3/4" and 3"

Item Number	Barrel Length	Stock	Magazine Capacity	Choke(s)	Type of Sights	Overall Length	Average Weight	Length of Pull	Drop at Heel	Drop at Comb
MONTEFELTRO - 12 Gauge										
10800	28"	Satin walnut	4+1	C,IC,M,IM,F	Red bar	49.5"	7.1 lbs.	14 3/8"	2 3/8"	1 1/2"
10810	26"	Satin walnut	4+1	C,IC,M,IM,F	Red bar	47.5"	6.9 lbs.	14 3/8"	2 3/8"	1 1/2"
10820	24"	Satin walnut	4+1	C,IC,M,IM,F	Red bar	45.5"	6.8 lbs.	14 3/8"	2 3/8"	1 1/2"
MONTEFELTRO - 20 Gauge										
10830	26"	Satin walnut	4+1	C,IC,M,IM,F	Red bar	47.5"	5.6 lbs.	14 3/8"	2 3/8"	1 1/2"
10835	24"	Satin walnut	4+1	C,IC,M,IM,F	Red bar	45.5"	5.5 lbs.	14 3/8"	2 3/8"	1 1/2"
MONTEFELTRO SHORT STOCK - 20 Gauge										
10831	26"	Satin walnut	4+1	C,IC,M,IM,F	Red bar	45.6"	5.4 lbs.	12 1/2"	2 1/8"	1 1/2"
10836	24"	Satin walnut	4+1	C,IC,M,IM,F	Red bar	43.6"	5.3 lbs.	12 1/2"	2 1/8i"	1 1/2"

LEGACY – 12 Gauge - 2 3/4" and 3"

Item Number	Barrel Length	Stock	Magazine Capacity	Choke(s)	Type of Sights	Overall Length	Average Weight	Length of Pull	Drop at Heel	Drop at Comb
LEGACY - 12 Gauge										
10400	28"	Select Satin walnut	4+1	C,IC,M,IM,F	Red bar*	49.63"	7.5 lbs.	14 1/2"	2 1/4"	1 3/8"
10405	26"	Select Satin walnut	4+1	C,IC,M,IM,F	Red bar*	47.63"	7.4 lbs.	14 1/2"	2 1/4"	1 3/8"
LEGACY - 20 Gauge - 2 3/4" and 3"										
LEGACY - 20 Gauge										
10420	26"	Select Satin walnut	4+1	C,IC,M,IM,F	Red bar*	47.63"	6.0 lbs.	14 1/2"	2 1/4"	1 3/8"
10425	26"	Select Satin walnut	4+1	C,IC,M,IM,F	Red bar*	45.63"	5.8 lbs.	14 1/2"	2 1/4"	1 3/8"

*Red bar front sight and metal bead mid sight.

SPORT – 12 Gauge - 2 3/4" and 3"

Item Number	Barrel Length	Stock	Magazine Capacity	Choke(s)	Type of Sights	Overall Length	Average Weight	Length of Pull	Drop at Heel	Drop at Comb
SPORT - 12 Gauge										
10610	28"	Satin walnut	4+1	C,IC,M,IM,F	Red bar	49.63"	7.1 lbs.	14 3/8"	2 1/4"	1 3/8"
10615	26"	Satin walnut	4+1	C,IC,M,IM,F	Red bar	47.63"	7.0 lbs.	14 3/8"	2 1/4"	1 3/8"

M1 FIELD – 12 Gauge - 2 3/4" and 3"

Item Number	Barrel Length	Stock	Magazine Capacity	Choke(s)	Type of Sights	Overall Length	Average Weight	Length of Pull	Drop at Heel	Drop at Comb
11000	28"	Satin walnut	3+1	C,IC,M,IM,F	Red bar	49.5"	7.4 lbs.	14 3/8"	2 1/4"	1 3/8"
11010	26"	Satin walnut	3+1	C,IC,M,IM,F	Red bar	47.5"	7.3 lbs.	14 3/8"	2 1/4"	1 3/8"
11005	28"	Synthetic	3+1	C,IC,M,IM,F	Red bar	49.5"	7.4 lbs.	14 3/8"	2 1/4"	1 3/8"
11015	26"	Synthetic	3+1	C,IC,M,IM,F	Red bar	47.5"	7.3 lbs.	14 3/8"	2 1/4"	1 3/8"
11020	24"	Synthetic	3+1	C,IC,M,IM,F	Red bar	45.5"	7.2 lbs.	14 3/8"	2 1/4"	1 3/8"
11025	21"	Synthetic	3+1	C,IC,M,IM,F	Red bar	42.5"	7.0 lbs.	14 3/8"	2 1/4"	1 3/8"
11035	28"	Camo*	3+1	C,IC,M,IM,F	Red bar	49.5"	7.4 lbs.	14 3/8"	2 1/4"	1 3/8"
11040	26"	Camo*	3+1	C,IC,M,IM,F	Red bar	47.5"	7.3 lbs.	14 3/8"	2 1/4"	1 3/8"
11045	24"	Camo*	3+1	C,IC,M,IM,F	Red bar	45.5"	7.2 lbs.	14 3/8"	2 1/4"	1 3/8"
11050	21"	Camo*	3+1	C,IC,M,IM,F	Red bar	42.5"	7.0 lbs.	14 3/8"	2 1/4"	1 3/8"
M1 FIELD RIFLED SLUG										
11060	24"	Synthetic	3+1	Rifled bore	Open rifle	45.6"	7.6 lbs.	14 3/8"	2 1/4"	1 3/8"
11065	24"	Camo*	3+1	Rifled bore	Open rifle	45.6"	7.6 lbs.	14 3/8"	2 1/4"	1 3/8"
M1 FIELD – 20 Gauge - 2 3/4" and 3"										
11090	26"	Synthetic	3+1	C,IC,M,IM,F	Red bar	47.3"	5.8 lbs.	14 3/8"	2 1/4"	1 3/8"
11092	24"	Synthetic	3+1	C,IC,M,IM,F	Red bar	45.3"	5.7 lbs.	14 3/8"	2 1/4"	1 3/8"
11094	26"	Timber HD	3+1	C,IC,M,IM,F	Red bar	47.3"	5.8 lbs.	14 3/8"	2 1/4"	1 3/8"
11096	24"	Timber HD	3+1	C,IC,M,IM,F	Red bar	45.3"	5.7 lbs.	14 3/8"	2 1/4"	1 3/8"

SHOTGUNS

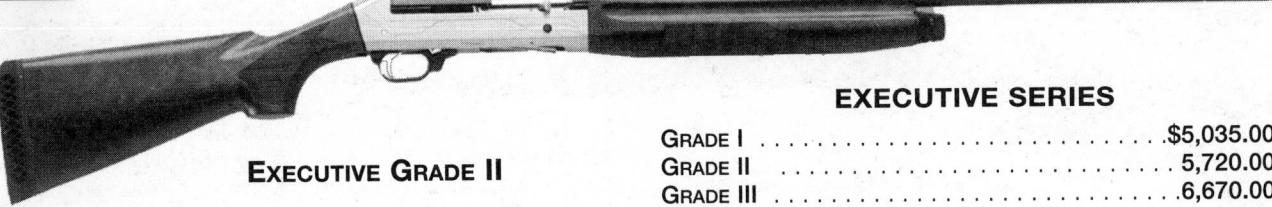

EXECUTIVE SERIES

EXECUTIVE GRADE II

GRADE I	.$5,035.00
GRADE II	.5,720.00
GRADE III	.6,670.00

BENELLI SHOTGUN SPECIFICATIONS *(Continued from previous page)*

EXECUTIVE – 12 Gauge - 2 3/4" and 3"

ITEM NUMBER	BARREL LENGTH	STOCK	MAGAZINE CAPACITY	CHOKE(S)	TYPE OF SIGHTS	OVERALL LENGTH	AVERAGE WEIGHT	LENGTH OF PULL	DROP AT HEEL	DROP AT COMB
EXECUTIVE - Grade I										
11420	28"	Select Satin walnut	4+1	C,IC,M,IM,F	Red bar*	49.63"	7.85 lbs.	14 1/2"	2 1/4"	1 3/8"
11400	26"	Select Satin walnut	4+1	C,IC,M,IM,F	Red bar*	47.63"	7.75 lbs.	14 1/2"	2 1/4"	1 3/8"
EXECUTIVE - Grade II										
11430	28"	Select Satin walnut	4+1	C,IC,M,IM,F	Red bar*	49.63"	7.85 lbs.	14 1/2"	2 1/4"	1 3/8"
11405	26"	Select Satin walnut	4+1	C,IC,M,IM,F	Red bar*	47.63"	7.75 lbs.	14 1/2"	2 1/4"	1 3/8"
EXECUTIVE - Grade III										
11440	28"	Select Satin walnut	4+1	C,IC,M,IM,F	Red bar*	49.63"	7.85 lbs.	14 1/2"	2 1/4"	1 3/8"
11410	26"	Select Satin walnut	4+1	C,IC,M,IM,F	Red bar*	47.63"	7.75 lbs.	14 1/2"	2 1/4"	1 3/8"

*Red bar front sight and metal bead mid sight/.

NOVA PUMP – 12 Gauge - 2 3/4", 3" and 3 1/2"

ITEM NUMBER	BARREL LENGTH	STOCK	MAGAZINE CAPACITY	CHOKE(S)	TYPE OF SIGHTS	OVERALL LENGTH	AVERAGE WEIGHT	LENGTH OF PULL	DROP AT HEEL	DROP AT COMB
NOVA PUMP										
20000	28"	Synthetic	4+1	IC,M,F	Red bar	49.5"	8.0 lbs.	14 1/4"	1 3/4"	1 1/4"
20003	26"	Synthetic	4+1	IC,M,F	Red bar	47.5"	7.9 lbs.	14 1/4"	1 3/4"	1 1/4"
20006	24"	Synthetic	4+1	IC,M,F	Red bar	45.5"	7.8 lbs.	14 1/4"	1 3/4"	1 1/4"
20015	28"	Camo*	4+1	IC,M,F	Red bar	49.5"	8.0 lbs.	14 1/4"	1 3/4"	1 1/4"
20018	26"	Camo*	4+1	IC,M,F	Red bar	47.5"	7.9 lbs.	14 1/4"	1 3/4"	1 1/4"
20021	24"	Camo*	4+1	IC,M,F	Red bar	45.5"	7.8 lbs.	14 1/4"	1 3/4"	1 1/4"
NOVA PUMP RIFLED SLUG**										
20054	24"	Synthetic	4+1	Rifled bore	Open rifle	45.5"	8.1 lbs.	14 1/4"	1 3/4"	1 1/4"
NOVA PUMP SPECIAL PURPOSE										
20050	18.5"	Synthetic	4+1	Cyl. bore	Open rifle	40.5"	7.2 lbs.	14 1/4"	1 3/4"	1 1/4"
20051	18.5"	Synthetic	4+1	Cyl. bore	Ghost-ring	40.5"	7.2 lbs.	14 1/4"	1 3/4"	1 1/4"
NOVA PUMP – 20 Gauge - 2 3/4", 3" and 3 1/2"										
20030	26"	Synthetic	4+1	IC,M,F	Red bar	49.4"	6.6 lbs.	14 1/4"	1 3/4"	1 1/4"
20035	24"	Synthetic	4+1	IC,M,F	Red bar	47.4"	6.5 lbs.	14 1/4"	1 3/4"	1 1/4"
20040	26"	Timber HD	4+1	IC,M,F	Red bar	49.4"	6.6 lbs.	14 1/4"	1 3/4"	1 1/4"
20045	24"	Timber HD	4+1	IC,M,F	Red bar	47.4"	6.5 lbs.	14 1/4"	1 3/4"	1 1/4"

SPECIAL PURPOSE – 12 Gauge - 2 3/4" and 3"

ITEM NUMBER	BARREL LENGTH	STOCK	MAGAZINE CAPACITY	CHOKE(S)	TYPE OF SIGHTS	OVERALL LENGTH	AVERAGE WEIGHT	LENGTH OF PULL	DROP AT HEEL	DROP AT COMB
M1 TACTICAL										
11260	18.5"	Pistol grip	5+1	IC,M,F	Ghost-ring	39.75"	7.0 lbs.	14 3/8"	2 1/4"	n/a
11261	18.5"	Standard	5+1	IC,M,F	Ghost-ring	39.75"	7.0 lbs.	14 3/8"	2 1/4"	1 3/8"
11200	18.5"	Pistol grip	5+1	IC,M,F	Open rifle	39.75"	6.7 lbs.	14 3/8"	2 1/4"	n/a
11201	18.5"	Standard	5+1	IC,M,F	Open rifle	39.75"	6.7 lbs.	14 3/8"	2 1/4"	1 3/8"
M1 ENTRY										
11225	14"	Pistol grip	5+1	Cyl.	Ghost-ring	35.5"	6.7 lbs.	14 3/8"	2 1/4"	n/a
11227	14"	Standard	5+1	Cyl.	Ghost-ring	35.5"	6.7 lbs.	14 3/8"	2 1/4"	1 3/8"
11245	14"	Pistol grip	5+1	Cyl.	Open rifle	35.5"	6.6 lbs.	14 3/8"	2 1/4"	n/a
11247	14"	Standard	5+1	Cyl.	Open rifle	35.5"	6.6 lbs.	14 3/8"	2 1/4"	1 3/8"
M1 PRACTICAL										
11255	26"	Standard	8+1	IC,M,F	Ghost-ring	47.63"	7.6 lbs.	14 3/8"	2 1/4"	1 3/8"
M3 CONVERTIBLE PUMP/AUTO										
11606	19.75"	Pistol grip	5+1	Cyl.	Ghost-ring	41.0"	7.4 lbs.	14 3/8"	2 1/4"	n/a
11605	19.75"	Standard	5+1	Cyl.	Ghost-ring	41.0"	7.4 lbs.	14 3/8"	2 1/4"	1 3/8"
11601	19.75"	Pistol grip	5+1	Cyl.	Open rifle	41.0"	7.2 lbs.	14 3/8"	2 1/4"	n/a
11600	19.75"	Standard	5+1	Cyl.	Open rifle	41.0"	7.2 lbs.	14 3/8"	2 1/4"	1 3/8"
NOVA PUMP SPECIAL PURPOSE										
20050	18.5"	Standard	4+1	IC ,M,F	Open rifle	40.0"	7.2 lbs.	14 1/4"	1 3/4"	1 1/4"
20051	18.5"	Standard	4+1	IC,M,F	Ghost-ring	40.0"	7.2 lbs.	14 1/4"	1 3/4"	1 1/4"

LEFT-HAND MODELS – 12 Gauge

ITEM NUMBER	BARREL LENGTH	STOCK	MAGAZINE CAPACITY	CHOKE(S)	TYPE OF SIGHTS	OVERALL LENGTH	AVERAGE WEIGHT	LENGTH OF PULL	DROP AT HEEL	DROP AT COMB
SUPER BLACK EAGLE – 12 Gauge - 2 3/4", 3" and 3 1/2"										
10075	28"	Synthetic	3+1	C,IC,M,IM,F	Red bar	49.63"	7.5 lbs.	14 1/4"	2 1/2"	1 5/8"
10070	26"	Synthetic	3+1	C,IC,M,IM,F	Red bar	47.63"	7.4 lbs.	14 1/4"	2 1/2"	1 5/8"
10065	24"	Synthetic	3+1	C,IC,M,IM,F	Red bar	45.63"	7.3 lbs.	14 1/4"	2 1/2"	1 5/8"
10090	28"	Camo*	3+1	C,IC,M,IM,F	Red bar	49.63"	7.5 lbs.	14 1/4"	2 1/2"	1 5/8"
10085	26"	Camo*	3+1	C,IC,M,IM,F	Red bar	47.63"	7.4 lbs.	14 1/4"	2 1/2"	1 5/8"
10080	24"	Camo*	3+1	C,IC,M,IM,F	Red bar	45.63"	7.3 lbs.	14 1/4"	2 1/2"	1 5/8"
M1 FIELD – 12 Gauge - 2 3/4" and 3"										
11070	28"	Synthetic	3+1	C,IC,M,IM,F	Red bar	49.5"	7.4 lbs.	14 3/8"	2 1/4"	1 3/8"
11072	26"	Synthetic	3+1	C,IC,M,IM,F	Red bar	47.5"	7.3 lbs.	14 3/8"	2 1/4"	1 3/8"
11074	24"	Synthetic	3+1	C,IC,M,IM,F	Red bar	45.5"	7.2 lbs.	14 3/8"	2 1/4"	1 3/8"
11080	28"	Camo*	3+1	C,IC,M,IM,F	Red bar	49.5"	7.4 lbs.	14 3/8"	2 1/4"	1 3/8"
11082	26"	Camo*	3+1	C,IC,M,IM,F	Red bar	47.5"	7.3 lbs.	14 3/8"	2 1/4"	1 3/8"
11084	24"	Camo*	3+1	C,IC,M,IM,F	Red bar	45.5"	7.2 lbs.	14 3/8"	2 1/4"	1 3/8"
MONTEFELTRO – 12 Gauge - 2 3/4" and 3"										
10805	28"	Satin Walnut	4+1	C,IC,M,IM,F	Red bar	49.5"	7.1 lbs.	14 3/8"	2 3/8"	1 1/2"
10815	26"	Satin Walnut	4+1	C,IC,M,IM,F	Red bar	47.5"	6.9 lbs.	14 3/8"	2 3/8"	1 1/2"

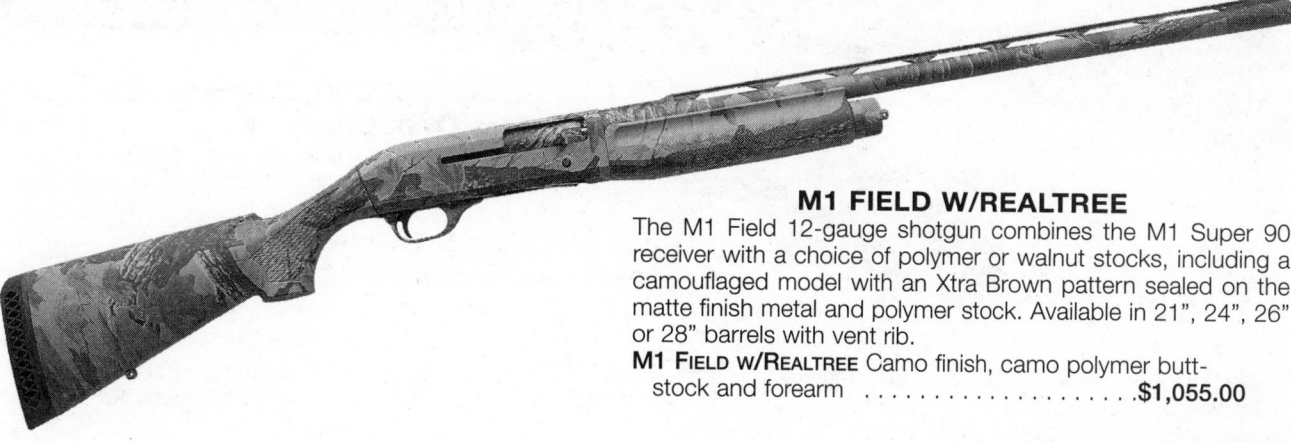

M1 FIELD W/REALTREE

The M1 Field 12-gauge shotgun combines the M1 Super 90 receiver with a choice of polymer or walnut stocks, including a camouflaged model with an Xtra Brown pattern sealed on the matte finish metal and polymer stock. Available in 21", 24", 26" or 28" barrels with vent rib.

M1 FIELD W/REALTREE Camo finish, camo polymer butt-stock and forearm **$1,055.00**

MODEL M1 FIELD

Also available:

MODEL M1 TACTICAL w/18 1/2" bbl. **$930.00**
   With pistol-grip stock, ghost ring sights **1,100.00**
M1 PRACTICAL, 26" barrel, ghost ring sight,
   synthetic stock **1,245.00**
MODEL M1 FIELD (polymer stock)
   w/21", 24", 26", 28" bbl. **960.00**
MODEL M3 PUMP/AUTO SERIES
   Standard stock, 19 3/4" barrel **1,100.00**
   w/Ghost Ring Sight and standard stock **1,145.00**
MODEL M1 FIELD 20 GAUGE W/24" OR 26" BBL.
   Synthetic stock **960.00**
   Timber HD stock **1,055.00**

MONTEFELTRO VENT RIB

Prices:
12 Ga.—24", 26", or 28" Barrel
   (20 ga.—24" or 26" barrel only) **$975.00**
Left Hand w/26" or 28" Barrel. **990.00**
Short Stock (20 ga., 12.5" pull) **1,005.00**

SHOTGUNS

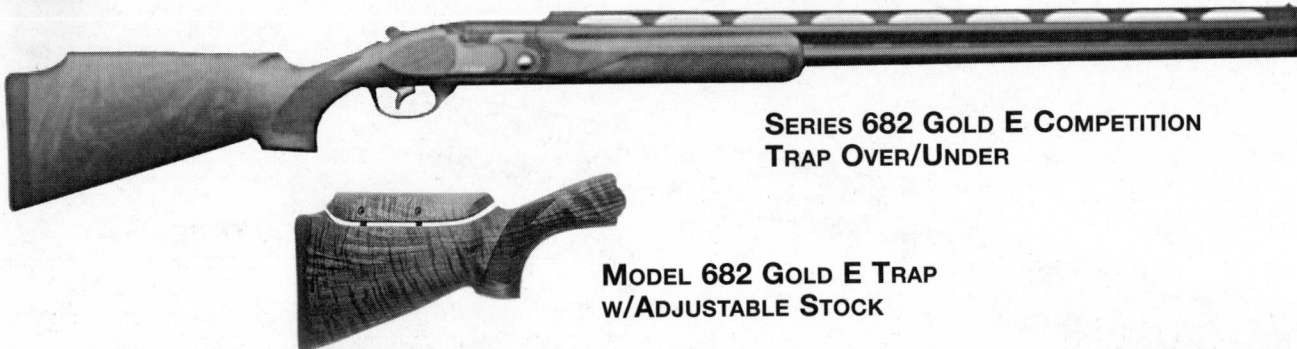

SERIES 682 GOLD E COMPETITION TRAP OVER/UNDER

MODEL 682 GOLD E TRAP w/ADJUSTABLE STOCK

These 12 gauge Model 682 Trap guns feature adjustable gold-plated, single-selective sliding trigger; low-profile improved boxlock action; manual safety w/barrel selector; 2.75" chambers; auto ejector; competition recoil pad buttplate; hand-checkered walnut stock.
Weight: Approx. 8 lbs. **Barrel Lengths/Chokes:** 30 Imp. Mod./Full (Black); 30" or 32" Mobilchoke® (Black); Top

Single 32" or 34" Mobilchoke®; Combo: 30" or 32" Mobilchoke® (Top), 30" IM/F (Top), 32" Mobilchoke® (Mono), 30" or 32" Mobilchoke® ported
Prices:
MODEL 682 GOLD E TRAP
  w/Adjustable Stock $4,320.00
    COMBO TOP 5,305.00

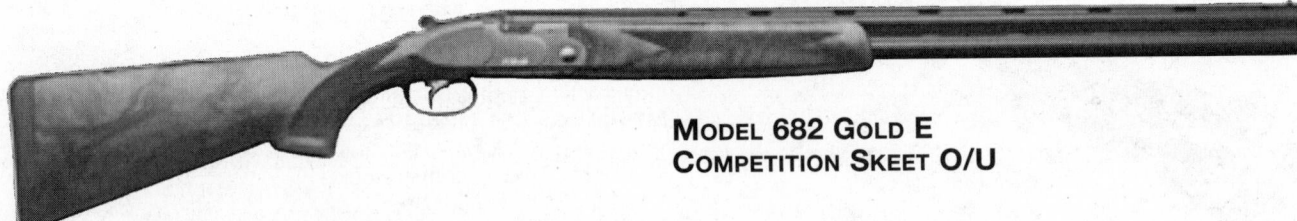

MODEL 682 GOLD E COMPETITION SKEET O/U

This 12-gauge skeet gun sports a hand-checkerd premium walnut stock w/silver oval for initials, forged and hardened receiver w/Greyston finish, manual safety with trigger selector, auto ejector, silver inlaid on trigger guard.
Action: Low-profile hard chrome-plated boxlock **Trigger:**

Single adjustable sliding trigger **Barrels:** 28" or 30" blued barrels with 2.75" chambers **Stock dimensions:** Length of pull 14.75"; drop at comb 1 3/8"; drop at heel 2.25" **Sights:** fluorescent front and metal middle bead **Weight:** Approx. 7.5 lbs.
Price: (incl. fitted case) $4,320.00

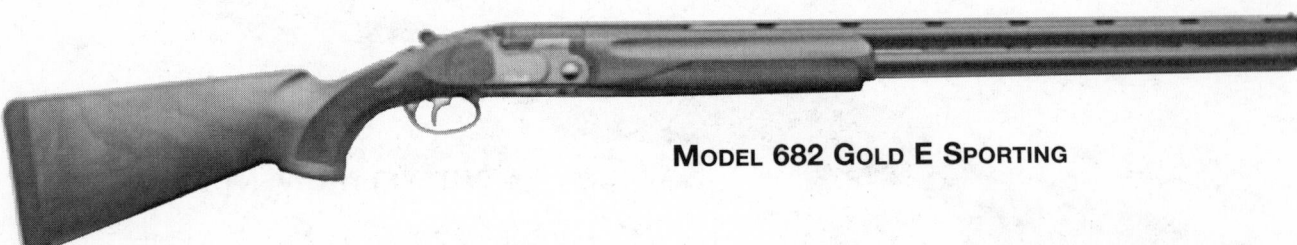

MODEL 682 GOLD E SPORTING

These competition-stye sporting clays guns feature 28" or 30" barrels with four flush-mounted screw-in choke tubes (Full, Modified, Improved Cylinder and Skeet), plus hand-checkered stock and forend of fine walnut, 2.75" or 3" chambers and adjustable trigger. **MODEL 682 GOLD** features Greystone

finish, an ultra-durable finish in gunmetal grey w/gold accents; also available in 32" barrel. **MODEL 686 SILVER PIGEON SPORTING** has coin silver receiver with scroll engraving.
Prices: 682 GOLD E SPORTING $3,850.00
686 SILVER PIGEON SPORTING 1,931.00

MODEL 686 ONYX

SPECIFICATIONS

Gauges: 12, 20 *Chambers:* 3" and 3.5" *Barrel Lengths:* 26""
and 28" *Chokes:* Mobilchoke® screw-in system *Weight:* 6 lbs.

12 oz. (12 ga.); 6.2 lbs. (20 ga.) *Stock:* American walnut with
recoil pad (English stock available) *Features:* Automatic ejectors; matte black finish on barrels and receiver to reduce glare

Price:	**$1,583.00**
Model 686 Onyx Sporting	**1,639.00**
w/x-Tra Wood	**1,778.00**

MODEL 687 SILVER PIGEON SPORTING

This boxlock over/under features enhanced engraving pattern,
schnabel forend and an electroless nickel finished receiver.
Chamber: 3" Mobilchoke® screw-in tube system *Gauges:* 12 & 20

Prices: MODEL 687 SILVER PIGEON SPORTING	**$2,363.00**
MODEL 687 SILVER PIGEON SPORTING COMBO	**3,151.00**
MODEL 687 SILVER PIGEON II, 12 or 20	**2,134.00**
MODEL 687 SILVER PIGEON II SPORTING, 12 ga. only	**2,196.00**

MODEL 687EELL DIAMOND PIGEON (not shown)
MODEL 687EELL COMBO (20 and 28 ga.)

In 12, 20 or 28 ga., this model features the Mobilchoke®
engraved choke system, a special premium walnut stock
and silver receiver with engraved sideplate.

Prices:

MODEL 687 EELL DIAMOND PIGEON	**$5,598.00**
MODEL 687EELL COMBO (20 and 28 ga.)	**6,245.00**
Also available:	
MODEL 687EELL DIAMOND PIGEON SKEET	**4,984.00**
w/adjustable stock	**6,050.00**
DIAMOND PIGEON SPORTING (12 ga.)	**5,737.00**

MODEL 687EL GOLD PIGEON FIELD (not shown)

Features game-scene engraving on receiver with gold highlights. Available in 12, 20 gauge (28 ga. and .410 in small frame).

SPECIFICATIONS

Barrels/Chokes: 26" and 28" with Mobilchoke® *Action:* Low-
profile improved boxlock *Weight:* 6.8 lbs. (12 ga.) *Trigger:*
Single selective with manual safety *Extractors:* Auto ejectors

Prices: MODEL 687EL (12, 20, 26" or 28" bbl.)	**$4,099.00**
MODEL 687EL SMALL FRAME (28 ga./.410)	**4,273.00**
MODEL 687EL SPORTING (12 ga. only)	**4,182.00**
w/sideplate engraving	**4,554.00**
MODEL 687EL GOLD PIGEON II (sideplate engraving)	**4,513.00**

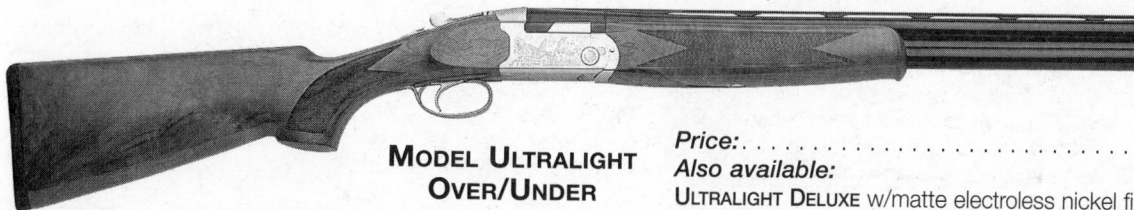

MODEL ULTRALIGHT OVER/UNDER

SPECIFICATIONS

Barrel: 12 ga, 26" or 28" *Stock:* Select walnut *Features:*
Nickel finish receiver w/game scene engraving; black rubber
recoil pad; single selective trigger

Price:	**$1,869.00**

Also available:

ULTRALIGHT DELUXE w/matte electroless nickel finish receiver
w/gold game scene engraving; walnut stock and forend; light
aluminum alloy receiver reinforced w/titanium breech plate

Price:	**$2,070.00**
Ultralight X-Tra wood	**2,022.00**
Ultralight (matte)	**1,931.00**

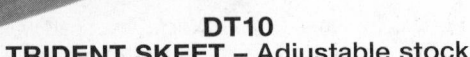

DT10
TRIDENT SKEET – Adjustable stock

Four major developments set the Beretta DT10 Trident competition over-and-unders apart from other competition shotguns: 1) A new internal barrel configuration (Optima-Bore). Available on some models, this improves shot distribution. 2) The new Optima-Choke competition choke-tubes. Longer and slimmer, with an internal profile to make patterns uniform. 3) Specific point of impact. While the models for Olympic Trap, Skeet and Sporting Clays have a common central point of impact, the models designed for American Trap deliver a high point of impact. 4) Correct distribution of mass. This gives the gun a center of mass coaxial with the first (bottom) barrel, eliminating muzzle rise and affording faster target acquisition on the second shot.

The DT10 Trident X-Trap Combo allows the shooter to maintain a steady, unaltered sighting plane and point of impact with both barrels. The initials "DT" in DT10 are an abbreviation of "Detachable Trigger". The trigger position can be adjusted with the screwdriver provided. Top lever design is based on the needs of the top shooters. The gun is simpler to use for left-handers. The safety is shaped to provide the best hold and smoothest working movement. Lightning-fast lock times and an ultra-crisp trigger pull are provided by "V" shaped mainsprings. Trident available in 12 gauge with barrel length ranging from 28" to 34".

Prices:
Trident Trap, Adjustable stock **$9,450.00**
Trident Trap, Combo Top single 11,995.00
Trident Trap, Bottom Single combo 12,270.00
Trident Skeet 9,450.00
Trident Sporting 9,240.00

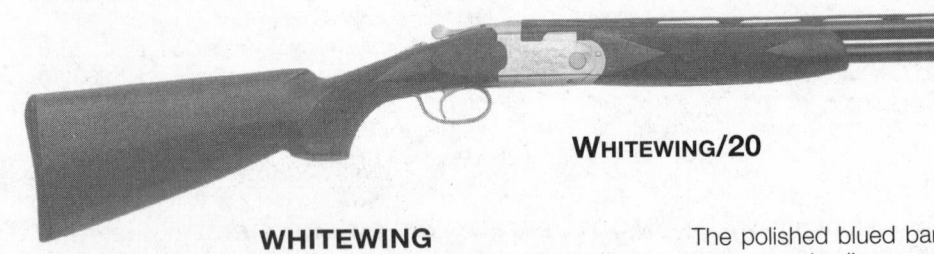

WHITEWING/20

WHITEWING

Practical and functional, the Whitewing is distinguished by a polished finish of the receiver, top lever, trigger plate and trigger guard. The top and hinges have a matte, anti-glare finish, while the trigger is gold-plated. The side panels are lightly engraved with hunting scenes.

The polished blued barrels feature an open side rib design that not only allows more rapid cooling, but also makes for even quicker handling. Special sling swivels can be installed on request. The stock dimensions and fore-end are customized for hunting to afford pointability and balance.
Price: Whitewing (12 or 20 ga.) **$1,295.00**

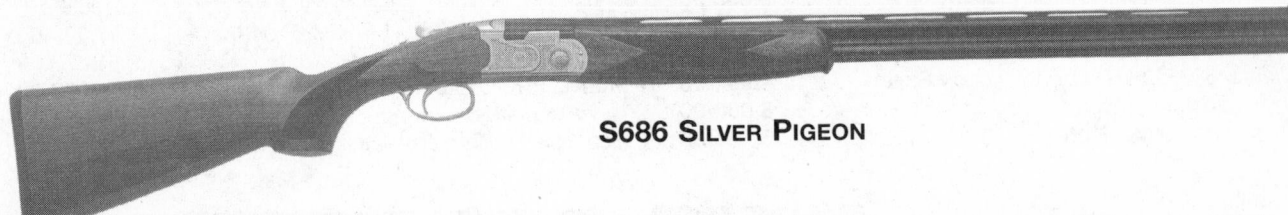

S686 SILVER PIGEON

S686 SILVER PIGEON
BERETTA'S CLASSIC OVER-AND -UNDER

Rich scroll work on the receiver and an elegant nickel finish set the Silver Pigeon apart, as do its superior performances. The stock's fine-cut checkering and the Schnabel fore-end complements the Silver Pigeon's stylish appearance. The Silver Pigeon Combo set includes interchangeable barrels in 20 and 28 gauges, while the High Gloss version features ultra-polished enhancements on the receiver, stock and fore-end. The X-Tra Wood model boasts beautifully grained walnut wood finish. Produced in 12, 20 and 28 gauge models, the Silver Pigeon features Beretta's exclusive universal chamber, which allows

the Silver Pigeon to accommodate all 3" Magnum cartridges (excluding 28 gauge) and improves performance when using 2 3/4" cartridges.
Price: Silver Pigeon **$1,869.00**
  w/ X-tra wood 2,022.00
Silver Pigeon (2 barrel set) 2,587.00
Silver Pigeon Trap Top Mono 1,869.00
Silver Pigeon Sporting 1,931.00
  w/X-tra wood 2,070.00
Also available: 686E Sporting (12 or 20 ga.) *Features:* enhanced styling, carrying case, accessories, 5 choke tubes
Price: 2,008.00

MODEL 470 SILVER HAWK SIDE-BY-SIDE

SPECIFICATIONS
Gauge: 12 and 20 *Chamber:* 3"
Action: Low profile, improved box lock
Choke: IC/IM, M/F *Barrel Length:* 26" and 28" *Weight:* 6.5 lbs. (12 ga.); 5.9 lbs. (20 ga.)
Sights: Metal front bead *Stock:* Select walnut, checkered

Features: Silver satin chrome finish on receiver, trigger guard, forend iron, top lever, trigger, trigger plate and safety/select lever; hand-chased scroll, engraving on receiver, top lever, forend iron and triggerguard; gold inlaid hawk's head on top lever. *Price:* 12 ga. $3,630.00
20 ga. 3,755.00

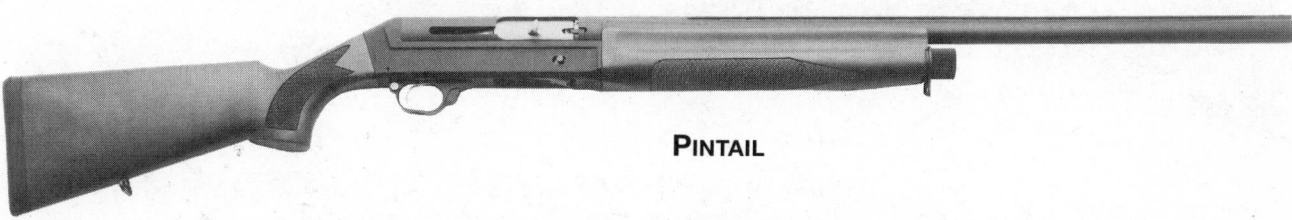

PINTAIL

This 12-gauge semiautomatic shotgun with short-recoil operation is available with 24" or 26" barrels and Mobilchoke®. Finish is nonreflective matte on alll exposed wood and metal surfaces; receiver is aluminum alloy.

SPECIFICATIONS
Barrel Lengths: 24", 26", 28"; 24" Slug
Weight: 7.3 lbs. *Stock:* Checkered selected hardwood or camo *Sights:* Bead front
Price: $757.00
Also Available:
PINTAIL RIFLED SLUG featuring fully rifed barrel w/1 in 28" twist. Upper receiver and barrel permanently joined as one unit.
Price: $899.00
Pintail Rifled Slug Combo 1,047.00

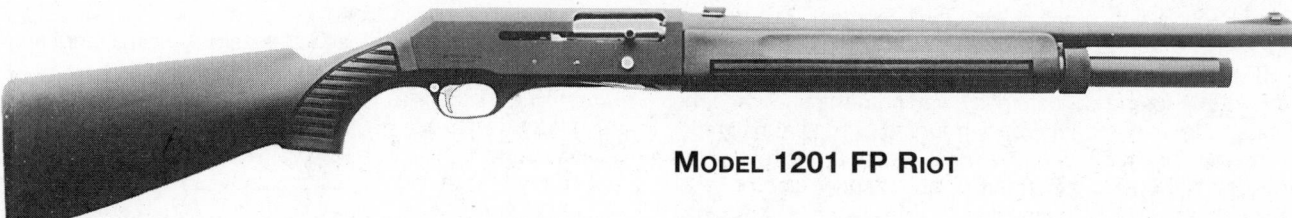

MODEL 1201 FP RIOT

This all-weather semiautomatic shotgun features an adjustable polymer stock and forend with recoil pad. Lightweight, it sports a unique weather-resistant matte black finish to reduce glare, resist corrosion and aid in heat dispersion; short recoil action for light and heavy loads, tritium sights.

SPECIFICATIONS
Gauge: 12 *Chamber:* 3"
Capacity: 6 rounds
Choke: Cylinder (fixed) *Barrel Length:* 18"
Weight: 6.3 lbs. *Sights:* Blade Front; adjustable rear
Price: $890.00

SHOTGUNS

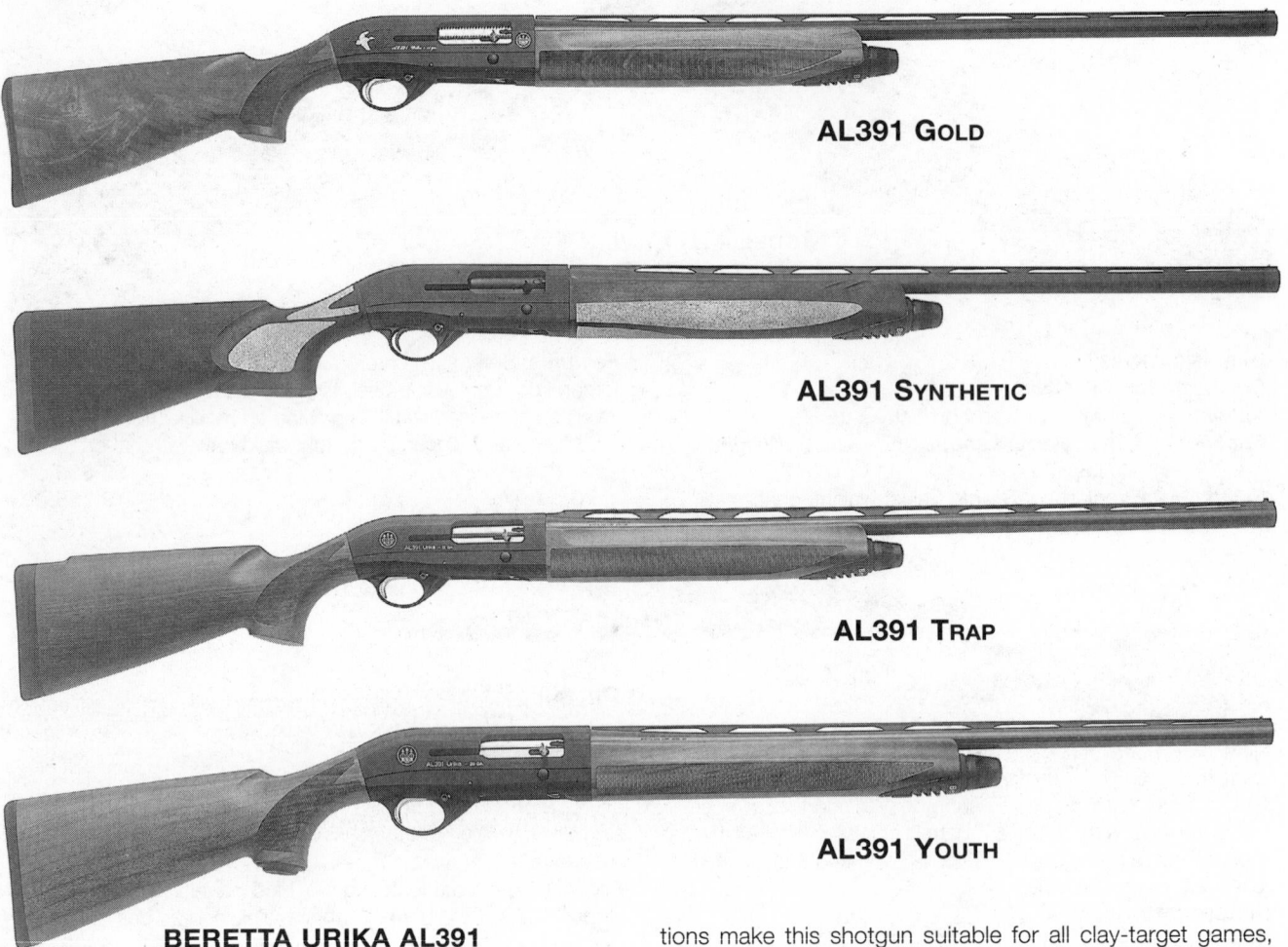

AL391 GOLD

AL391 SYNTHETIC

AL391 TRAP

AL391 YOUTH

BERETTA URIKA AL391 AUTOLOADING SHOTGUN

The Beretta AL391 features a self-compensating gas valve that ensures reliable functioning with a wide range of factory loads, from skeet to heavy waterfowl charges. The valve is housed in a cylinder that stays with the barrel to permit quick and easy removal of the barrel. A gas valve flange on the front of the forend deflects gas away from the shooter. The gas system is compact, keeping forend bulk to a minimum. Recoil has been reduced by a small device at the rear of the receiver that cushions bolt thrust, and a spring and polymer ring inside the forend cap. Beretta considered details when designing this gun, equipping the forend cap with a magnet so the sling swivel does not fall off during disassembly. Both synthetic and walnut stocks adjust for drop and cast via shims. The receiver is of lightweight alloy to limit weight (the lightest 12-bore weighs only 6.6 lbs.) Camouflage versions of the AL391 are available with Advantage, Wetlands and Realtree Hardwoods patterns. Special-purpose configura-

tions make this shotgun suitable for all clay-target games, and there's a youth model with smaller dimensions. All AL 391s, 12- and 20-gauge, are chambered for 2 3/4- and 3-inch shells and come with barrel lengths from 24" to 30". The guns come in a molded lockable case with five interchangeable chokes and wrenches, stock shims and two recoil pads, plus gun oil.

Prices: Urika AL391 . . . .$984.00
   Synthetic 984.00
   Camouflage 1,083.00
   Gold (black receiver) .1,180.00
   Gold Lightwt. 1,217.00
   Youth 984.00
   Sporting 1,027.00
   Gold Sporting (black receiver) 1,224.00
   Gold Sporting (silver receiver) 1,260.00
   Trap 1,027.00
   Gold Trap (black receiver) 1,224.00
   Parallel Target 1,027.00

BROWNING SHOTGUNS

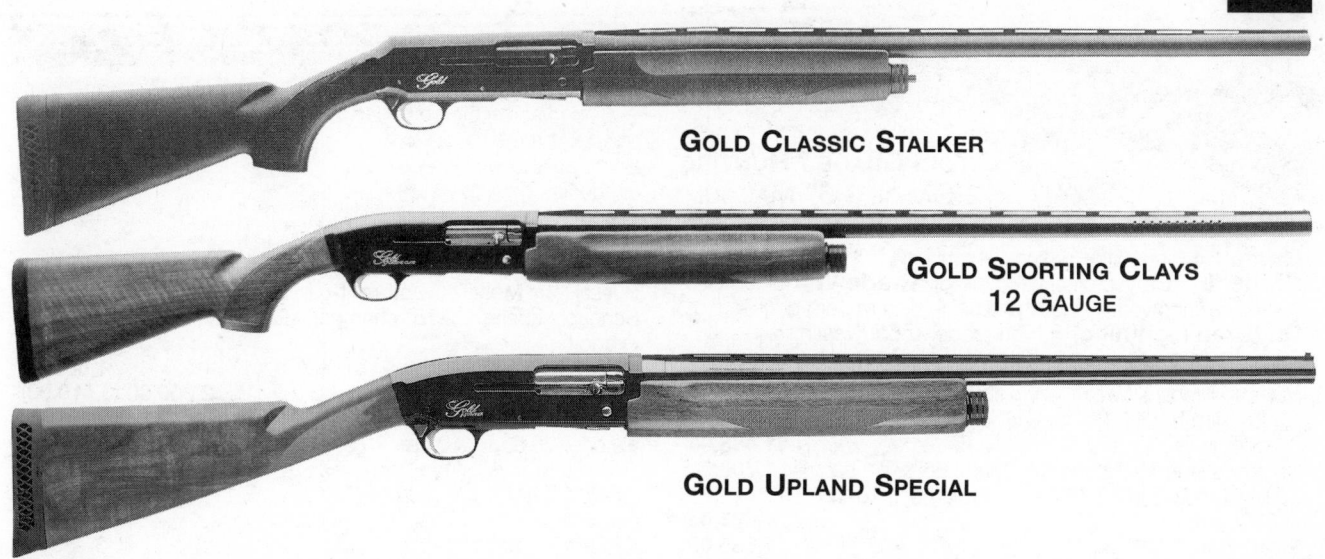

GOLD CLASSIC STALKER

GOLD SPORTING CLAYS 12 GAUGE

GOLD UPLAND SPECIAL

BROWNING GOLD SHOTGUNS have been called the most versatile autoloaders on the market, with a unique gas metering system that shoots light 2.75" shells or heavy loads from 3.5" hulls. An assortment of barrels, stocks and sights adapts this shotgun to all upland game, waterfowl and deer hunting situations. There's also a 10-gauge version. The gun's quick pointing qualities and reliability have already made it a favorite of hunters and clay target shooters–a fitting heir to the now-discontinued **BROWNING AUTO 5**.
Prices: GOLD HUNTER 12 or 20 ga., 3" chamber $894.00
3.5" chamber 1,038.00
GOLD RIFLED DEER HUNTER 20 ga. 987.00

GOLD STALKER 12 ga., 3" 856.00
3.5" 1,002.00
GOLD RIFLED DEER STALKER 948.00
GOLD MOSSY OAK 12 ga., 3" 967.00
3.5" 1,146.00
GOLD RIFLED DEER BREAK-UP 1,046.00
GOLD SPORTING CLAYS 939.00
GOLD GC SPORTING CLAYS 1,457.00
GOLD LADIES SPORTING CLAYS 902.00
GOLD FUSION 902.00
GOLD UPLAND SPECIAL .894.00

SPECIFICATIONS GOLD 12 AND 20

GAUGE	MODEL	BARREL LENGTH	OVERALL LENGTH	AVERAGE WEIGHT	CHOKES AVAILABLE
12	Hunter	30"	51"	7 lbs. 13 oz.	Invector-Plus
12	Hunter	28"	48.5"	7 lbs. 6 oz.	Invector-Plus
12	Hunter	26"	46.5"	7 lbs. 3 oz.	Invector-Plus
20	Hunter	28"	48.25"	6 lbs. 14 oz.	Invector
20	Hunter	26"	46.25"	6 lbs. 12 oz.	Invector

Extra barrels: 24, 26, 28, 30" – 12 gauge 3.5": **$413.00**, Mossy Oak Camo: **$439.00** • 24,26,28, 30" – 12 and 20 gauge 3": **$336.00**, Mossy Oak Camo:**$364.00**

DEER GUN

SPECIFICATIONS GOLD LIGHT 10 BREAKUP ($1,224.00) & STALKER ($1,155.00)

CHAMBER	BARREL LENGTH	OVERALL LENGTH	AVERAGE WEIGHT	CHOKES
3.5	28"	50"	9 lbs. 10 oz.	Standard Invector
3.5	26"	48"	9 lbs. 7 oz.	Standard Invector

SHOTGUNS

CITORI GRADE I HUNTING
12 GAUGE 3.5" MAGNUM

Grade I = Blued steel w/scroll engraving
Grade III = Grayed steel w/light relief **Grade VI =** Blued or grayed w/engraved ringneck pheasants and mallard ducks;
GL (Gran Lightning) = High-grade wood w/satin finish

CITORI PRICES (all Invector-Plus chokes unless noted otherwise)
HUNTING MODELS (w/pistol-grip stock, beavertail forearm, high-gloss finish) 12 & 20 ga. w/3" chamber 26", 28",
30" barrels **$1,486.00**
SPORTING HUNTER 12 ga., 3.5" Mag., 28 & 30" barrels . **1,709.00**
Same as above in 12 & 20 ga. 3" chamber, 26", 28",
30" barrels **1,607.00**
SATIN HUNTER in 12 ga., 3.5" chamber, 26" & 28" barrel . . **1,535.00**
WHITE LIGHTNING 12 & 20 ga., Grade I, 3" chamber . . . **1,583.00**
28 ga., 2.75" chamber **1,654.00**
410 ga., 3" chamber **1,654.00**
LIGHTNING MODELS (w/classic rounded pistol grip, Lightning-style forearm) Grade I, 12 & 20 ga., 3" chamber 26"
& 28" barrels **$1,534.00**
Same as above in Grade GL **2,184.00**
Grade III. **2,300.00**
Grade VI **3,510.00**
MICRO LIGHTNING MODEL (20 Ga.) Grade I,
2.75" chamber, 24" barrel. **1,591.00**
SUPERLIGHT MODELS (w/straight-grip stock, slimmed-down Schnabel forearm; 2.75" chamber, 12 (20 ga.)
Grade I **1,590.00**
28 or 410 . . . . **1,666.00**
Grade III (and VI) . . . . **2,300.00 (3,510.00)**
LIGHTNING MODELS w/Standard Invector chokes (Lightning models only, 28 and .410 ga., 2.75" chamber, 26" & 28" barrels)
Grade I **1,594.00**
Grade GL **2,302.00**
Grade III. **2,570.00**
Grade VI **3,780.00**
Grade I Superlight Feather 12 ga. **1,756.00**
XS 12,20 (28, .410) . . . . **2,266.00 (2,338.00)**
UPLAND SPECIAL (12 & 20 ga.)
Grade I only, 24" barrel. **1,583.00**

CITORI OVER & UNDER FIELD SHOTGUNS

MODEL	GAUGE	BARREL LENGTH	CHAMBER	MODEL	GAUGE	BARREL LENGTH	CHAMBER
HUNTER SERIES				**Gran Lightning**	12	28"	3"
Satin Hunter	12	28"	3 1/2"		12	26"	3"
	12	26"	3 1/2"		20	28"	3"
Hunter	12	30"	3"		20	26"	3"
	12	28"	3"		28	28"	2 3/4"
	12	26"	3"		28	26"	2 3/4"
	20	28"	3"		.410	28'	3"
	20	26"	3"		.410	26"	3"
FEATHER SERIES				**White Lightning**	12	28"	3"
Superlight Feather	12	26"	2 3/4"		12	26"	3"
Lightning Feather	12	28"	3"		20	28"	3"
	12	26"	3"		20	26"	3"
	20	28"	3"		28	28"	2 3/4"
	20	26"	3"		28	26"	2 3/4"
Lightning Feather Combo	20/28	27"	3" & 2 3/4"		.410	28"	3"
LIGHTNING SERIES					.410	26"	3"
Lightning	12	28"	3"	Micro Lightning	20	24"	2 3/4"
	12	26"	3"	**UPLAND SERIES**			
	20	28"	3"	White Upland Special	12	24"	2 3/4"
	20	26"	3"		20	24"	2 3/4"
	28	28'	2 3/4"	Superlight, Grade I	12	28"	2 3/4"
	28	26"	2 3/4"		12	26"	2 3/4"
	.410	28"	3"		20	26"	2 3/4"
	.410	26"	3"		28	26"	2 3/4"
					.40	26"	3"

LIGHT SPORTING MODEL 802ES

Sporting 12 ga. O/U. **Barrel Length:** 28"
Overall Length: 45.5". Invector-Plus stainlless steel choke tubes. **Weight:** 7 lbs. 5 oz.
Price: $2,063.00

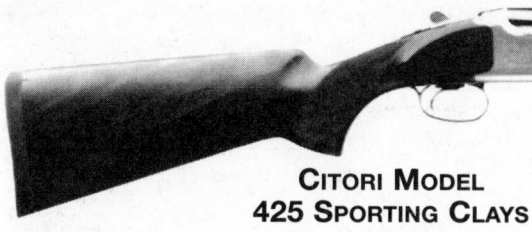

**CITORI MODEL
425 SPORTING CLAYS**

MODEL 425

MODEL 425 (12 & 20 Ga.)
Grade I, 28", 30", 32" bbls. $2,006.00
Grade GC (Golden Clays) 3,977.00

MODEL	GAUGE	BARREL LENGTH	CHAMBER
CITORI OVER AND UNDER TARGET SHOTGUNS			
425 Sporting Clays	12	30"	2 3/4"
	12	28"	2 3/4"
	20	30"	2 3/4"
	20	28"	2 3/4"
Lightning Sporting (high rib)	12	30"	3"
	12	28"	3"
Lightning Sporting (low rib)	12	30"	3"
	12	28"	3"
Sporting Hunter	12	30"	3 1/2"
	12	28"	3 1/2"
	12	30"	3"
	12	28"	3"
	12	26"	3"
	20	28"	3"
	20	26"	3"
FEATHER XS SERIES			
	12	30"	2 3/4"
	12	28"	2 3/4"
	20	30"	2 3/4"
	20	28"	2 3/4"
	28	30"	2 3/4"
	28	28"	2 3/4"
	.410	30"	3"
	.410	28"	3"
ULTRA XS SERIES			
Ultra XS Sporting	12	30"	2 3/4"
	12	28"	2 3/4"
	20	30"	2 3/4"
	20	28"	2 3/4"
	28	30"	2 3/4"
	28	28"	2 3/4"
	.410	30"	3"
	.410	28"	3"

MODEL	GAUGE	BARREL LENGTH	CHAMBER
Ultra XS Skeet	12	30"	2 3/4"
	12	28"	2 3/4"
NEW	20	30"	2 3/4"
NEW	20	28"	2 3/4"
Ultra XS Skeet w/adj. comb	12	30"	2 3/4"
	12	28"	2 3/4"
NEW	20	30"	2 3/4"
NEW	20	28"	2 3/4"
TRAP SHOTGUNS			
CITORI ULTRA XT TRAP			
Conventional Stock	12	32"	2 3/4"
	12	30"	2 3/4"
Adjustable Comb	12	32"	2 3/4"
	12	30"	2 3/4"
BT-100 TRAP			
Monte Carlo Stock	12	34"	2 3/4"
	12	32"	2 3/4"
Adjustable Stock	12	34"	2 3/4"
	12	32"	2 3/4"
BT 100 TRAP, STAINLESS STEEL			
Monte Carlo Stock	12	34"	2 3/4"
	12	32"	2 3/4"
Adjustable Comb	12	34"	2 3/4"
	12	32"	2 3/4"
NEW-BT-99 TRAP			
Conventional Stock	12	34"	2 3/4"
	12	32"	2 3/4"
Adjustable Comb	12	34"	2 3/4"
	12	32"	2 3/4"

SHOTGUNS

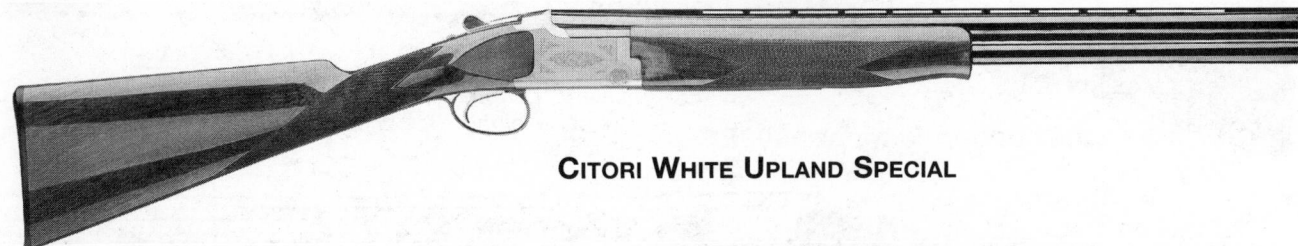

CITORI WHITE UPLAND SPECIAL

CITORI WHITE UPLAND SPECIAL

has a shorter, straight-grip stock Schnabel forend and 24"
barrel, 12 or 20 ga., 2 3/4". Like all Citoris, the White
Upland has backbored barrels and automatic ejectors.
Price:. 1,583.00

NITEX FEATHER XS SERIES (not shown)

Sporting clays shotguns with alloy receivers incorporating
steel breech face.
Prices:
12, 20 ga.. . . . . $2,266.00
28, .410 ga. 2,338.00

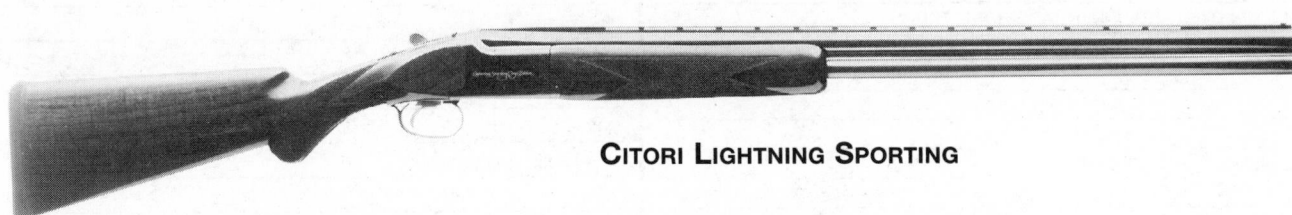

CITORI LIGHTNING SPORTING

CITORI SPORTING HUNTER AND LIGHTNING SPORTING

Many of these lively over/under shotguns are available with
ported barrels, adjustable combs, the option of high or low
ribs. Prices on request to Browning.
Prices: LIGHTNING SPORTING
Grade I, high rib, ported bbl., 3". $1,770.00

Grade I, low rib. 1,691.00
SPORTING HUNTER
Grade I, 3.5" chamber, tapered rib, 12 ga. $1,709.00
Grade I, 3" chamber, 12 & 20 ga.,
    tapered rib 1,607.00

(See previous page for specifications)

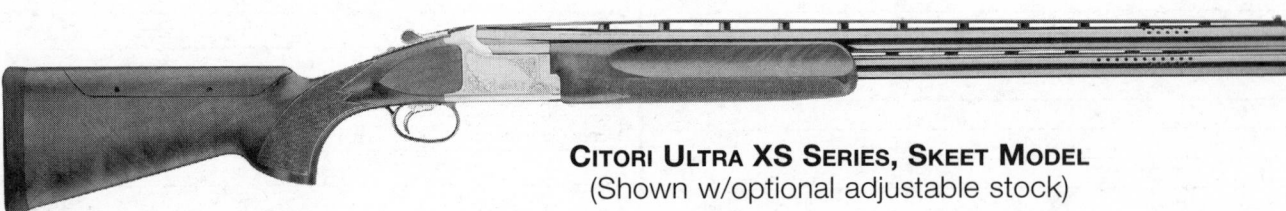

CITORI ULTRA XS SERIES, SKEET MODEL
(Shown w/optional adjustable stock)

ULTRA XT TRAP MODELS

Prices:
12 GAUGE, SILVER NITRIDE RECEIVER,
    PORTED BARRELS, Grade I. $2,022.00
    w/adjustable comb 2,265.00

ULTRA XS SKEET MODELS

Prices:
12 & 20 GAUGE, SILVER NITRIDE, PORTED BARRELS
    Grade I $2,162.00
    w/adjustable comb 2,380.00

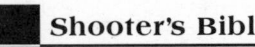

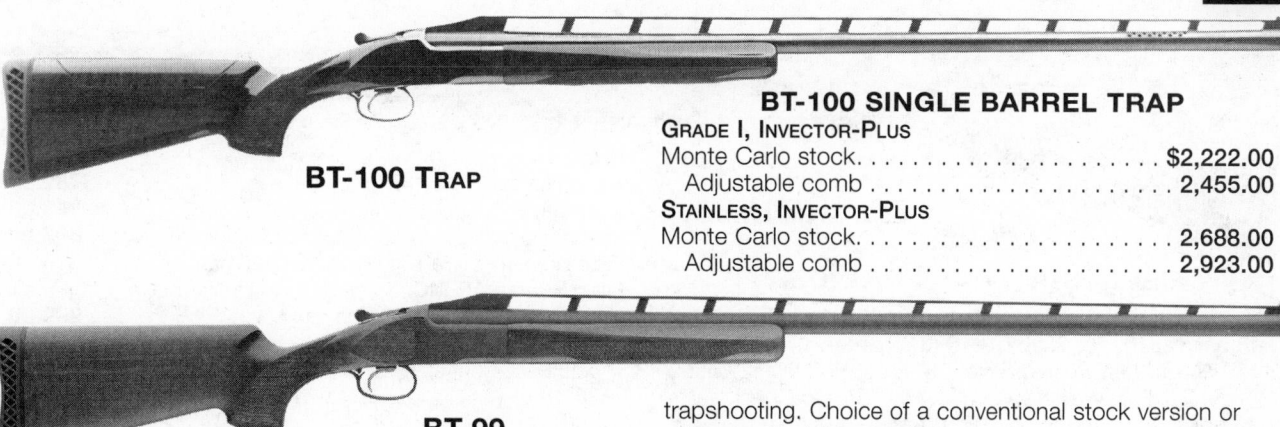

BT-100 TRAP

BT-100 SINGLE BARREL TRAP
GRADE I, INVECTOR-PLUS
Monte Carlo stock $2,222.00
  Adjustable comb 2,455.00
STAINLESS, INVECTOR-PLUS
Monte Carlo stock 2,688.00
  Adjustable comb 2,923.00

BT-99

The BT-99's full beavertail forearm and high-post rib are the basic features that have made the BT-99 a standard in

trapshooting. Choice of a conventional stock version or with an adjustable comb.
Prices:
Conventional stock . . . . $1,216..00
  Adjustable comb 1,449.00

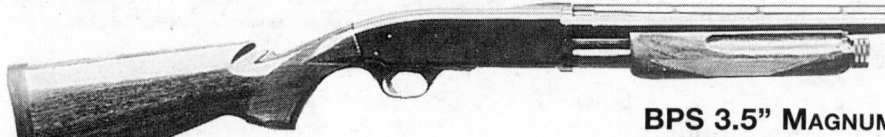

BPS 3.5" MAGNUM
(12 Gauge)

BPS SPECIFICATIONS

GAUGE	MODEL	CHAMBER	CAPACITY[2]	BARREL LENGTH	OVERALL LENGTH	AVERAGE WEIGHT	CHOKES AVAILABLE[1]
10 Mag	Hunter & Stalker	3.5"	4	30, 28, 26, 24" 46-52"		9.25-9.5 lbs.	Invector
12, 3.5" Mag	Hunter	3.5"	4	30, 28, 26, 24" 45-51"		7.5-8.5 lbs.	Invector-Plus
12, 3.5" Mag	Stalker	3.5"	4	30, 28, 26, 24" 45-51"		7.5-8.5 lbs.	Invector-Plus
12	Hunter & Stalker	3"	4	30"	50.75"	7 lbs. 12 oz.	Invector-Plus
12	Hunter & Stalker	3"	4	28"	48.75"	7 lbs. 11 oz.	Invector-Plus
12	Hunter & Stalker	3"	4	26"	46.75"	7 lbs. 10 oz.	Invector-Plus
12	Standard Buck Special	3"	4	24"	44.75"	7 lbs. 10 oz.	Slug/Buckshot
12	Upland Special	3"	4	22"	42.5"	7 lbs. 8 oz.	Invector-Plus
12	Hunter & Stalker	3"	4	22"	42.5"	7 lbs. 7 oz.	Invector-Plus
12	Game Gun Turkey Special	3"	4	20.5"	40 7/8"	7 lbs. 7 oz.	Invector
12	Game Gun Deer Special/Rifled	3"	4	20.5"	40 7/8"	7 lbs. 7 oz.	Fully Rifled Barrel
12	Game Gun Deer Special/Smooth	3"	4	20.5"	40 7/8"	7 lbs. 7 oz.	Special Inv./Rifled
12	Game Gun Cantilever Mount	3"	4	20.5"	40 7/8"	7 lbs. 9 oz.	Fully Rifled
20	Hunter	3"	4	28"	48.75"	7 lbs. 1 oz.	Invector-Plus
20	Hunter	3"	4	26"	46.75"	7 lbs.	Invector-Plus
20	Micro	3"	4	22"	41.75"	6 lbs. 11 oz.	Invector-Plus
20	Upland Special	3"	4	22"	42.75"	6 lbs. 12 oz.	Invector-Plus
28	Hunter	2.75"	4	28"	48.75"	7 lbs. 1 oz.	Invector
28	Hunter	2.75"	4	26"	46.75"	7 lbs.	Invector
.410	Hunter	3"	4	26"	46.75"	6 lbs. 13 oz.	

BPS FIELD MODEL PRICES
SPECIFICATIONS
Prices:
HUNTER 3" chamber 26", 28", 30" barrels $464.00
STALKER, w/synthetic stock 448.00
  Camo 529.00
GAME GUN Deer Special (20.5" barrel) w/5"
  rifled slug choke tube 500.00

w/barrel for sabot slugs 568.00
SMALL GAUGE FIELD (28 gauge, 28" or 26") 495.00
MAGNUM MODELS Hunting & Stalker Grades
  (10 ga. and 12 ga.) w/3.5" Mag. chamber
  (26" and 28" barrels) Hunter 552.00
  Stalker 537.00
  w/Mossy Oak camo finish 617.00

SHOTGUNS

Imported By K.B.I., Inc.

FIELD OVER/UNDER

FIELD HUNTER OVER/UNDER

SPECIFICATIONS
Gauges: 12, 16, 20, 28 and .410 (3" chambers); 28 ga. (2.75") *Barrel Lengths/Chokes:* 28" Mod./Full; 26" IC/Mod.; .410 ga. Full/Full *Weight:* Approx. 7 lb. *Stock:* Checkered walnut pistol-grip and forend *Features:* Blued engraved receiver; chrome-moly steel barrels, gold single-selective trigger, automatic safety, extractors, gold bead front sight

Prices:
FIELD HUNTER - 12, 16 or 20 ga. $789.00
    28 ga. 849.00
    .410 ga. 895.00
FIELD HUNTER - Ultra-Light MC 12 or 20 ga. 899.00
FIELD HUNTER AE-MC. Same as Field Hunter but w/5
    choke tubes (12 and 20 ga. only) 999.00
SUPERIOR HUNTER AE. Gold single-sellective trigger,
    gold bead front sight, silver engraved receiver.
    28 ga. 1,109.00
    .410 ga. 1,155.00
SUPERIOR HUNTER AE-MC. Same as above in 12
    and 20 ga. w/5 choke tubes 1,199.00

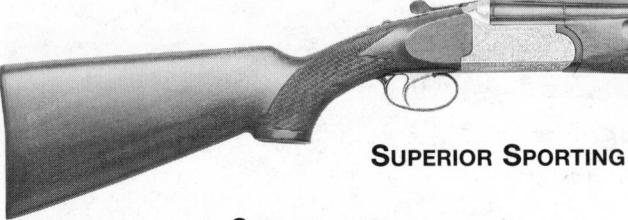

SUPERIOR SPORTING

SPECIFICATIONS
Gauges: 12 (3" chambers) *Barrel Lengths/Chokes:* 28" & 30" with multi-choke (5 tubes) *Weight:* Approx. 7 lb.

Stock: Checkered walnut pistol-grip buttstock w/semi-beavertail forend *Features:* Silver engraved receiver, ported chrome-moly steel barrels, gold single-selective trigger, automatic safety, auto-ejectors, red bead front sight
Prices: SUPERIOR SPORTING $1,279.00
SUPERIOR TRAP-MC. Same as above
    (2.75" chamber) 30" bbl. only 1,325.00

EMPIRE EDL HUNTER

SPECIFICATIONS
Gauges: 12, 20, .410 ga. (3" chambers); 28 ga. (2.75") *Barrel Lengths/Chokes:* 26" & 28"–5 multi-choke tubes in 12 & 20 ga.; 26" IC/M in 28 ga.; 26" Full/Full in .410 ga. *Weight:* Approx. 7 lb. *Sights:* Red bead front; metal bead center *Stock:* Checkered walnut pistol-grip buttstock

w/semibeavertail forend *Features:* Silver engraved receiver, full sideplate, chrome-moly steel barrels, gold single-selective trigger, automatic safety, auto-ejector, recoil pad
Prices: EMPIRE EDL HUNTER
12 or 20 ga. $1,619.00
28 ga. 1,579.00
.410 ga. 1,629.00
EMPIRE SPORTING. 12 only, w/30" and 28" ported barrels,
    no metal bead center sight 1,519.00
EMPIRE TRAP-MC. 12 ga. w/30" bbl. (unported)
    metal bead center sight, recoil pad 1,559.00

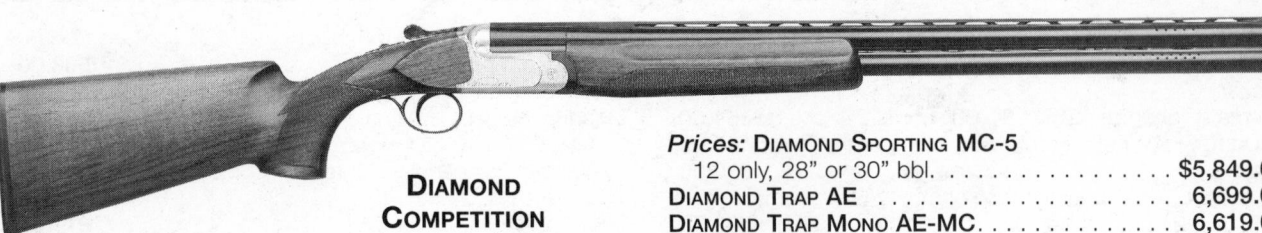

DIAMOND COMPETITION

Prices: DIAMOND SPORTING MC-5
    12 only, 28" or 30" bbl. $5,849.00
DIAMOND TRAP AE 6,699.00
DIAMOND TRAP MONO AE-MC. 6,619.00

CHARLES DALY SHOTGUNS

Imported By K.B.I., Inc.

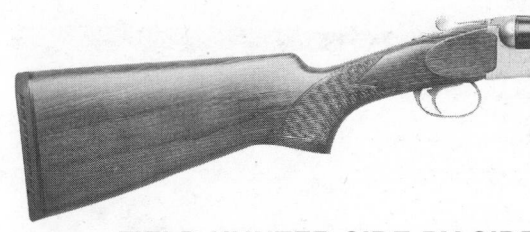

FIELD HUNTER SIDE BY SIDE

SPECIFICATIONS
Gauges: 10, 12, 20 and .410 (3" chambers); 28 ga. (2.75")
Barrel Lengths/Chokes: 32" Mod./Mod.; 30" Mod./Full; 28" Mod./Full; 26" IC/Mod.; .410 ga. Full/Full *Weight:*

Approx. 6 lbs.-11.4 lbs. *Stock:* Checkered walnut pistol-grip and forend *Features:* Silver engraved receiver; gold single-selective trigger in 10, 12 and 20 ga.; double trigger in 28 and 410 ga.; automatic safety, extractors, gold bead front sight. Imported from Spain
Prices:
10 ga.	$789.00
12 or 20 ga.	759.00
28 or .410 ga.	689.00

SUPERIOR GRADE (not shown)

SPECIFICATIONS
Gauges: 12 and 20; 3" chambers
Barrel Lengths/Chokes: 28" Mod./Full; 26" IC/Mod.
Weight: Approx. 7 lb. *Stock:* Checkered walnut pistol-grip buttstock and splinter forend
Features: Silver engraved receiver, chrome-lined steel barrels, gold single trigger, automatic safety, extractors, gold bead front sight
Prices:
SUPERIOR HUNTER (12 and 20)	$1,059.00
28 gauge or 410	1,029.00

EMPIRE HUNTER
Same as above w/hand-checkered stock auto ejectors, game scene engraved receiver	1,349.00

DIAMOND DL HUNTER (not shown)

SPECIFICATIONS
Gauges: 12, 20, .410 ga. (3" chambers; 28 ga. (2.75")
Barrel Lengths/Chokes: 28" Mod./Full; 26" IC/Mod.; 26" Full/Full in .410 ga. *Weight:* Approx. 5-7 lbs.
Stock: Select fancy European walnut, English-styled, beavertail forend, hand-checkered, hand-rubbed oil finish
Features: Fine steel drop-forged action with gas escape valves; fine steel demiblock barrels w/concave rib; selective auto ejectors, hand-detachable double safety sidelocks w/hand-engraved rose and scrollwork; front-hinged trigger, casehardened receiver. Imported from Spain.
Prices:
DIAMOND DL 12 or 20 ga.	$6,999.00
28 or .410 ga.	6,999.00

Rifle/Shotgun Combination Guns

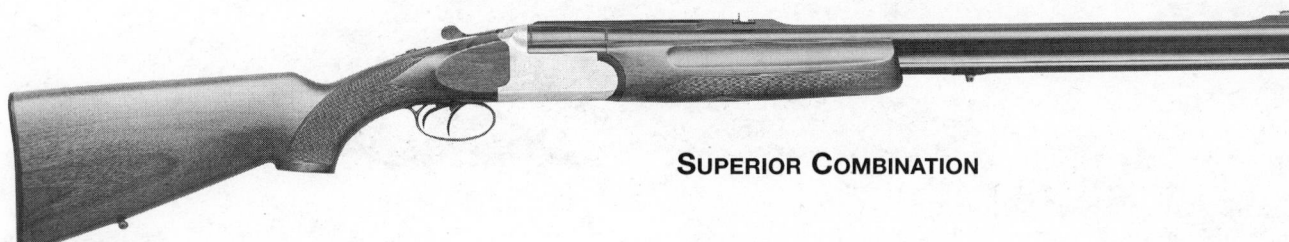

SUPERIOR COMBINATION

SPECIFICATIONS
Gauge/Calibers: 12/22 Hornet, 223 Rem., 30-06 Sprgfld.
Barrel Length/Choke: 23.5", shotgun choke IC
Weight: Approx. 7.5 lbs.
Stock: Checkered walnut pistol-grip buttstock and semi-beavertail forend

Features: Silver engraved receiver forged and milled from a solid block of high-strength steel; chrome-moly steel barrels, double trigger, extractors, sling swivels, gold bead front sight
Prices:
SUPERIOR COMBINATION.	$1,359.00

EMPIRE COMBINATION. Same as above w/deluxe walnut European-style comb/cheekpiece, slim forend . . **1,799.00**

CHARLES DALY SHOTGUNS

Semi-Auto Shotguns

SUPERIOR SPORT

**FIELD HUNTER MM VR –
SEMI-AUTO – MAXI MAG**

SPECIFICATIONS

FIELD GRADE-12 gauge Barrel lengths/chokes: 22"/ CYL, 24"/MC-3, 26"/MC-3, 28"/MC-3, 30"/MC-3. Features: walnut, synthetic or camo stock.

Prices: synthetic stock. $399.00
camo stock 489.00
Also Available: FIELD GRADE MAXI-MAG 3.5"
   synthetic $579.00
   camo. 679.00

SUPERIOR GRADE-Features hand checkered Turkish Walnut stock. Sporting model has a wide 10mm rib and ported barrel and Monte Carlo stock.
Prices:
HUNTER $529.00
SPORT 599.00
TRAP 569.00

Pump Shotguns

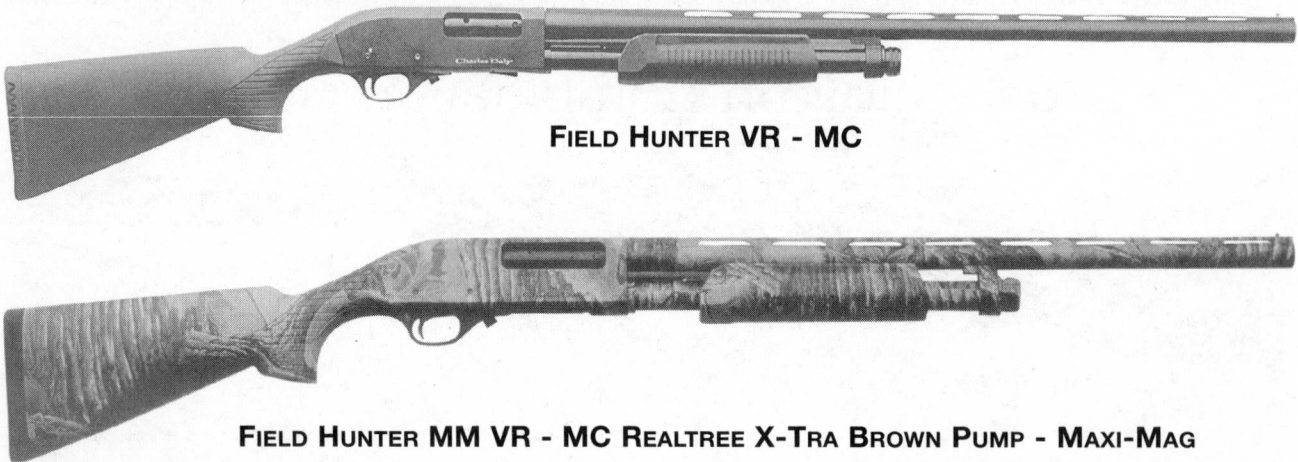

FIELD HUNTER VR - MC

FIELD HUNTER MM VR - MC REALTREE X-TRA BROWN PUMP - MAXI-MAG

SPECIFICATIONS

FIELD GRADE-12 and 20 ga.
Prices:
synthetic stock 12 ga. $269.00
camo 12 ga. 359.00

synthetic 20 ga. 269.00
camo 20 ga. 359.00
Also Available: MAXI-MAG 3.5"
   12 ga. synthetic $329.00
   12 ga. camo 429.00

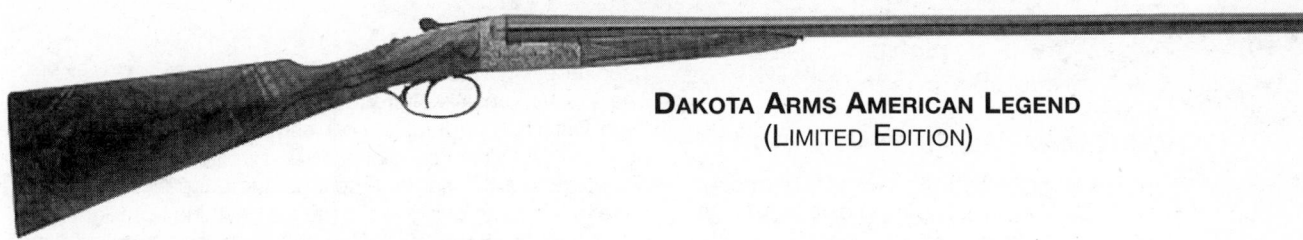

DAKOTA ARMS AMERICAN LEGEND
(LIMITED EDITION)

DAKOTA LEGEND SHOTGUNS

PREMIER GRADE

Exhibition Engllish Walnut wood, French Grey Finish, 50% coverage engraving, straight grip, splinter forend, hand rubbed oil finish, boxlock, ejectors double trigger, 27" barrels, game rib with gold bead, selective ejectors, choice of chokes, and Americase.
Price: (12 or 20 ga) **$13,950.00**
add 10% for 28 or 410 ga.

LEGEND GRADE

Special Selection English Walnut, 27" barrel, game rib, straight grip, splinter forend, double triggers, round aciton, French Grey finish, selective ejectors, checkered butt, stock oval, full coverage scroll engraving, choice of chokes, gold bead, oak and leather case.
Price:(12 or 20 ga) **$18,000.00**
add 10% for 28 or 410 ga.

FOX SHOTGUNS

DE GRADE ENGRAVED SHOTGUN

CUSTOM BOXLOCKS

SPECIFICATIONS

Gauges: 16, 20, 28 and .410 *Barrel:* Any barrel lengths and chokes; rust blued Chromox or Krupp steel barrels *Weight:* 5 /to 6/lbs. *Stock:* Custom stock dimensions including cast; hand-checkered Turkish Circassian walnut stock and forend with hand-rubbed oil finish; straight grip, full pistol grip (with cap), or semi-pistol grip; splinter, schnabel or beavertail forend; traditional pad, hard rubber plate, checkered, or skeleton butt *Features:* Boxlock action with automatic ejectors; scalloped, rebated and color casehardened receiver; double or Fox single selective trigger; hand-finished and hand-engraved. This is the same

gun that was manufactured between 1905 and 1930 by the A.H. Fox Gun Company of Philadelphia, PA, now manufactured in the U.S. by the Connecticut Shotgun Mfg. Co. (New Britain, CT).
*Prices:**

CE GRADE	$11,000.00
XE GRADE	12,500.00
DE GRADE	15,000.00
FE GRADE	20,000.00
EXHIBITION GRADE	30,000.00

**Grades differ in engraving and inlay, grade of wood and amount of hand finishing needed.*

SHOTGUNS

VARIOMAX 912 - 3.5" MAGNUM

The technical prowess of Franchi is exemplified through development of the new Variomax 3 1/2" autoloading 12 ga. shotgun. Based on the proven design principles of the Variopress, this new 3 1/2" version uses the same type of lightweight receiver and a multi-lugged rotary bolt which locks directly to the chrome barrel. The gas system has been redesigned to handle 2 3/4", 3" and even 3 1/2" shells. The 912 Variomax is offered with the new Advantage Timber High Definition camouflage for serious turkey or waterfowl hunters. A non-glare black finish is offered as standard. Regardless of the game, a serious shotgunner will appreciate a gas system designed to handle anything from light field loads to the heaviest 3 1/2" magnum loads, supplied with three standard choke tubes in IC, MOD and FULL.

Price: $940.00
Timber HD Camo 1,035.00

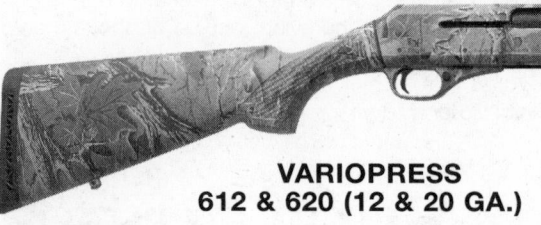

VARIOPRESS
612 & 620 (12 & 20 GA.)

Autoloading shotguns have undergone a great deal of refinement since their inception, and Franchi has moved the arena of development to the next level of sophistication with the Variopress.

A strong and lightweight receiver houses a multi-lugged rotary bolt which locks directly to the barrel. The included three choke tubes IC, MOD and FULL can handle virtually any game a true shotgunner may pursue.

The Variopress uses a patented dual safety system which blocks the sear and removes tension from the hammer spring if the bolt is out of battery.

For the traditionalist, walnut stocks and forends are available but black synthetic is offered as well. The Variopress 612 and 620 are also available in full Advantage camouflage. There is even a defense model of the 612 which has an 18 1/2" barrel with a true CYL bore. It can handle 3" slugs to light bird shot loads. For 2001, a two shot magazine extension is available as an option.

Prices:
(available in 24", 26", or 28" barrel)
12 or 20 ga $710.00
Synthetic (12 ga only) 670.00
Camo (12 or 20 ga) 785.00
612 Defense 635.00
612 Sporting (30" barrel) 1,045.00

612 SPORTING (NOT SHOWN)

Recoil conscious competitors may choose the 612 Sporting Auto. The superior function of this autoloader forms the basis for a uniquely light recoiling competition shotgun. The 30" barrel has a 4" lengthened forcing cone, is ported, and includes extended quick-change choke tubes. This combination of sighting radius, low recoil and excellent patterning make the 612 Sporting deadly on targets.

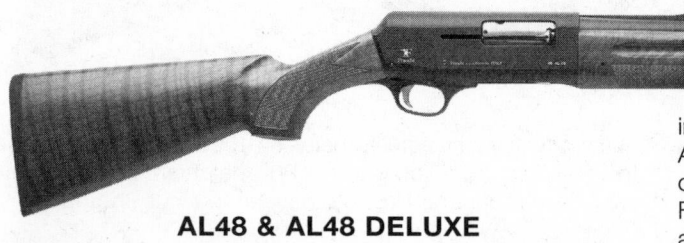

AL48 & AL48 DELUXE

Classic shotguns can still be produced. The Franchi AL 48 represents the ultimate refinement of John Browning's long recoil design for autoloaders. Even though it was the first truly successful autoloading action, time has proven it to be both strong and reliable. Today, the Franchi AL 48 continues to prove just how capable the long recoil design can be.

A standard field grade available in 12, 20 and 28 ga., and a Deluxe grade in 20 and 28 ga. are offered. All models include a steel shot-proofed, chrome-lined barrel. The entire AL 48 series features a ventilated rib and a set of three choke tubes in CYL, IC and MOD for added versatility. The Field grade AL 48 has a walnut stock and forend as well as a matte finish on metal surfaces to minimize reflected light. The Deluxe grade includes a higher grade walnut stock and forend, plus a high polish finish on most metal surfaces.

Prices:
AL48, 12 ga $700.00
20 ga 715.00
28 ga 790.00
AL48 Deluxe, 20 ga 825.00
28 ga 950.00

ALCIONE SPORT – 12 GAUGE

ALCIONE LIGHT FIELD – 20 GAUGE

ALCION SPORT

The Alcione Sport over-under is available in 12 ga. with 30" ported barrels, extended knurled choke tubes and is chambered for 2 3/4" target loads. A 10mm wide rib quickly pulls the eye to targets and builds scores. It uses a manual safety as well as mechanical triggers, which do not require recoil from the first barrel to fire the second barrel due to a bad primer.

The Alcione Sport has removable receiver sideplates. The stock and forend are shaped from high grade walnut and have special dimensions for the serious competitor. The Alcione Sport offers accessory 20 ga. barrel sets, as well as left handed stock dimensions.

The Alcione SX has a high grade walnut stock with fine checkering. The receivers are highly polished and feature delicate etchings.

Price:
Alcione Field $1,185.00
Left Hand 1,200.00
Alcione SX 1,635.00
Alcione Sport 1,565.00
Alcione LF (12 or 20 ga) 1,305.00

SHOTGUNS

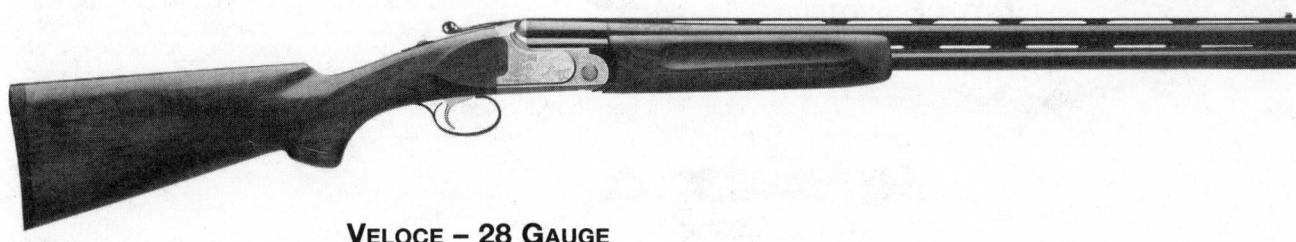

VELOCE – 28 GAUGE

VELOCE

The lightweight Veloce is available in 20 ga. and 28 ga. only, and is built on its own aluminum alloy frame using round through bolts rather than underlugs for locking. This mechanism allows the receiver to be quite shallow, adding to the balance and feel. A steel insert in the breech face adds further strength. The Veloce features engraved sideplates with gold embellished game scenes. The trigger is mechanical for added reliability in the field and barrel selection is accomplished by setting the tang mounted safety lever for the desired firing sequence. Stocks and forends are beautifully figured walnut and expertly checkered. The stock features a round pistol grip for natural pointing and the forend is of a fluted design. The barrels have 3" chambers in 20 ga. and 2 3/4" chambers in 28 ga. They are chrome lined for increased durability and include a set of choke tubes in CYL, IC and MOD. The monoblock is jeweled for both a pleasing appearance and added resistance to wear. "Veloce" means "fast" in Italian, and at only 5 1-2 pounds, this fast-swinging speedster is the perfect companion for a long day's hunt.

Prices:
Veloce, 20 ga. $1,365.00
Veloce, 28 ga. 1,380.00

HARRINGTON & RICHARDSON

Single-Barrel Shotguns

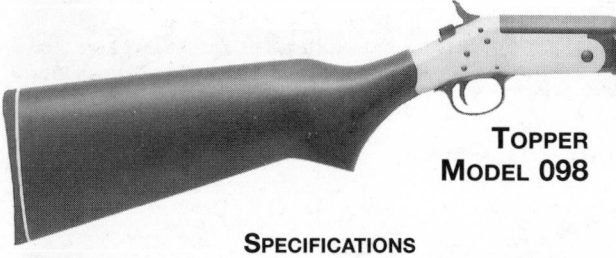

TOPPER MODEL 098

SPECIFICATIONS
Gauges: 12, 20 and .410 (3" chamber); 16 and 28 ga. (2.75" chamber) **Barrel Lengths:** 26" and 28" **Weight:** 5 to 6 lbs. **Action:** Break-open; side lever release; automatic ejection

Stock: Full pistol grip; American hardwood; black finish with white buttplate spacer **Length Of Pull:** 14.5"
Price: **$116.95**
Also Available: TOPPER DELUXE - MODEL 098 12 ga. 28" mod screw in choke 3.5" **136.95**
TOPPER JUNIOR CLASSIC 20, 28, and .410, 22" barrel, hand checkered American black walnut stock and 12.5" pull.
Price: **$150.95**

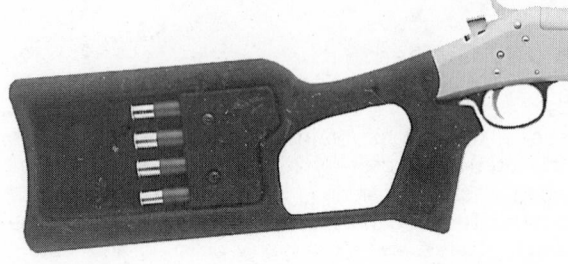

.410 TAMER SHOTGUN

This barreled .410 snake gun features single-shot action, transfer-bar safety and high-impact synthetic stock and forend.

Stock has a thumbhole design that sports a full pistol grip and a recessed open side, containing a holder for storing ammo. Forend is modified beavertail configuration. Other features include a matte, electroless nickel finish. **Weight:** 5-6 lbs. **Barrel Length:** 20" (3" chamber) **Choke:** Full
Price: **$128.95**

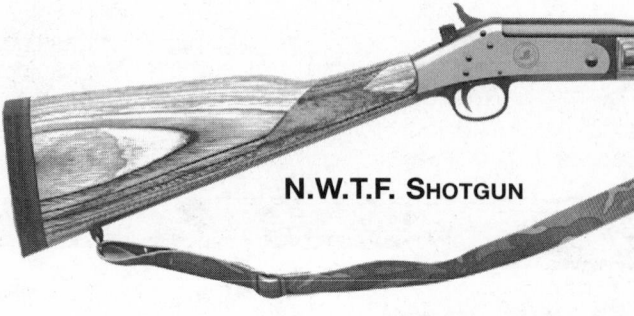

N.W.T.F. SHOTGUN

SPECIFICATIONS
12 gauge with NWTF engraved frame, hand checkered, camo laminate stock and forend, 24" barrel with 3.5" chamber and full choke.
Price: **$176.95**
Also Available: NWTF YOUTH 20 ga., 22" barrel, 3" chamber and Modified choke **Price:** **$169.95**

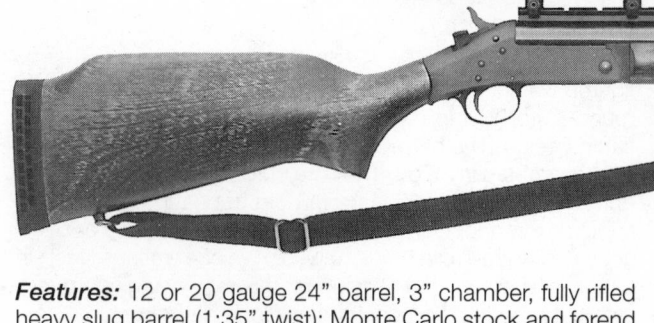

ULTRA SLUG HUNTER

Features: 12 or 20 gauge 24" barrel, 3" chamber, fully rifled heavy slug barrel (1:35" twist); Monte Carlo stock and forend of American hardwood w/dark walnut stain; matte black receiver; transfer-bar system; scope rail, swivels and sling; ventilated recoil pad. **Price:** **$207.95**

Also available: ULTRA YOUTH SLUG HUNTER. Features 12-gauge barrel blank underbored to 20 gauge and shortened to 22"; factory-mounted Weaver-style scope base; reduced Monte Carlo stock of American hardwood with dark walnut stain; vent recoil pad, sling swivels and black nylon sling.
Price: **$207.95**
SLUG HUNTER DELUXE. Features hand checkered camo laminate wood **Price:** **255.95**

HECKLER & KOCH FABARMS SHOTGUNS

Heckler & Koch shotguns have features for top ballistic performance and durability, plus fine handling qualities. Double guns are built on milled steel or alloy monoblocs, with single selective triggers, interchangeable chokes, hand-checkered walnut stocks. They're chambered for 3"shells (turkey and waterfowl models for 3.5-inch magnums). Autoloaders are gas-operated with no parts in the buttstock. They have fixed ejectors and shim-adjustable buttstocks. Camouflage models are available. Pump guns have synthetic stocks, double action bars and Picatinny rails for scopes. Weights vary on all models, depending on gauge and barrel length. Youth and special-purpose shotguns are part of the line.

FABARM'S TRIBORE BARREL SYSTEM

The ported TriBore Barrel System consists of three distinct internal bore profiles. It offers the advantages of back-boring, but with even less recoil. The first or "overbore" region is just in front of the chamber and forcing cone. Its .7401 diameter reduces pressure and kick. A second bore, or "first choke", is in the middle of the barrel and gradually takes inside diameter to .7244 (cylinder bore), allowing the shot to attain its maximum velocity. The third bore consists of standard choking, followed by a cylinder area at the muzzle, allowing charge to exit with no disruption, improving downrange pellet distribution.

GOLD LION MARK II 12 GAUGE
with 28" barrel (26- and 24" models also available)

GOLD LION MARK II SEMIAUTOMATIC

Prices:
GOLD LION MARK II Semiautomatics 12 ga. $849.00
CAMO LION 12 ga. 979.00
SPORTING CLAYS EXTRA 1,249.00

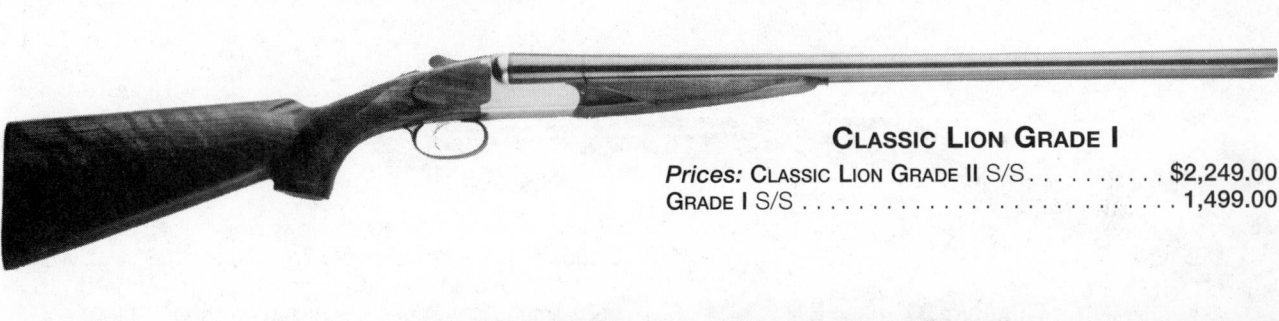

CLASSIC LION GRADE I

Prices: CLASSIC LION GRADE II S/S $2,249.00
GRADE I S/S 1,499.00

SHOTGUNS

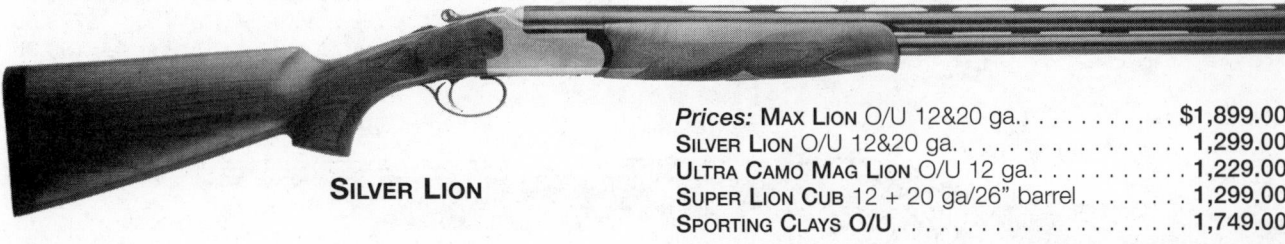

SILVER LION

Prices: MAX LION O/U 12&20 ga. $1,899.00
SILVER LION O/U 12&20 ga. 1,299.00
ULTRA CAMO MAG LION O/U 12 ga. 1,229.00
SUPER LION CUB 12 + 20 ga/26" barrel 1,299.00
SPORTING CLAYS O/U 1,749.00

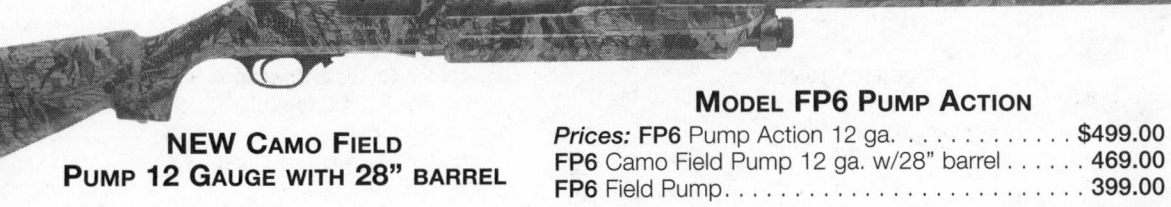

NEW CAMO FIELD
PUMP 12 GAUGE WITH 28" BARREL

MODEL FP6 PUMP ACTION

Prices: FP6 Pump Action 12 ga. $499.00
FP6 Camo Field Pump 12 ga. w/28" barrel 469.00
FP6 Field Pump. 399.00

MODEL 37 DEERSLAYER II 12 GA.

SPECIFICATIONS
Gauges: 12, 16 or 20 (3" chamber) *Barrel Lengths:* 20" or 25" *Choke:* Rifled bore; or smooth bore *Weight:* 7 lbs. *Stock:* Monte Carlo cut-checkered walnut stock and forend
Price: $614.95
Also Available: DEERSLAYER
Rifled Deluxe (12 or 20) 564.95
Smoothbore (12, 20, 16) 564.95

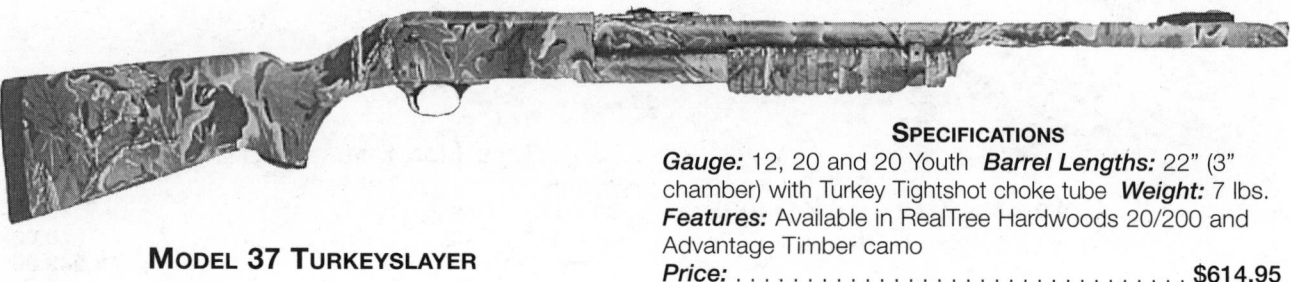

MODEL 37 TURKEYSLAYER

SPECIFICATIONS
Gauge: 12, 20 and 20 Youth *Barrel Lengths:* 22" (3" chamber) with Turkey Tightshot choke tube *Weight:* 7 lbs. *Features:* Available in RealTree Hardwoods 20/200 and Advantage Timber camo
Price: $614.95

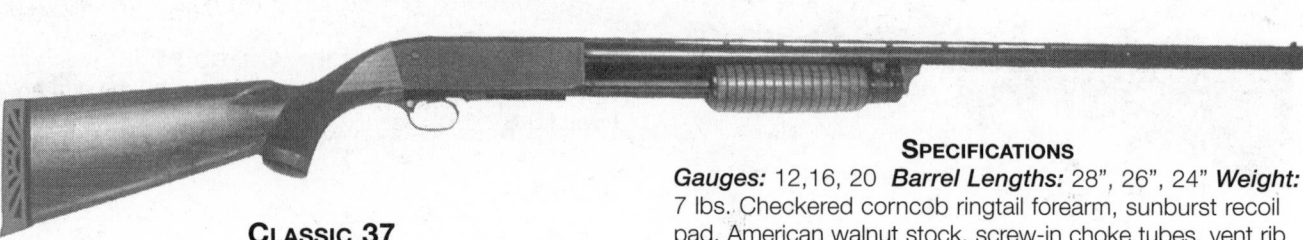

CLASSIC 37

SPECIFICATIONS
Gauges: 12,16, 20 *Barrel Lengths:* 28", 26", 24" *Weight:* 7 lbs. Checkered corncob ringtail forearm, sunburst recoil pad, American walnut stock, screw-in choke tubes, vent rib
Price: $779.95
ULTRALIGHT (20 ga. only) 799.95

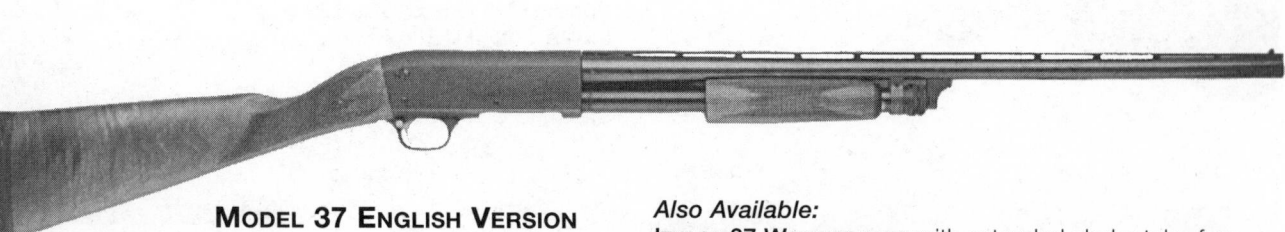

MODEL 37 ENGLISH VERSION

SPECIFICATIONS
Gauge: 12, 16, 20 (3" chamber)
Barrel Lengths: 24", 26", 28" and 30"
Weight: 7 lbs. with slim, checkered straight-grip stock
Price: $599.95

Also Available:
ITHACA 37 WATERFOWLER with extended choke tube for steel shot $679.95
ITHACA 37 CLASSIC TRAP AND SPORTING CLAYS shotguns with special stocks and Briley choke tubes. Adjustable stocks optional 1,395.95
ITHACA 37 FEATHERLIGHT FIELD GUN
12, 20, 16 .... 599.95

KRIEGHOFF SHOTGUNS

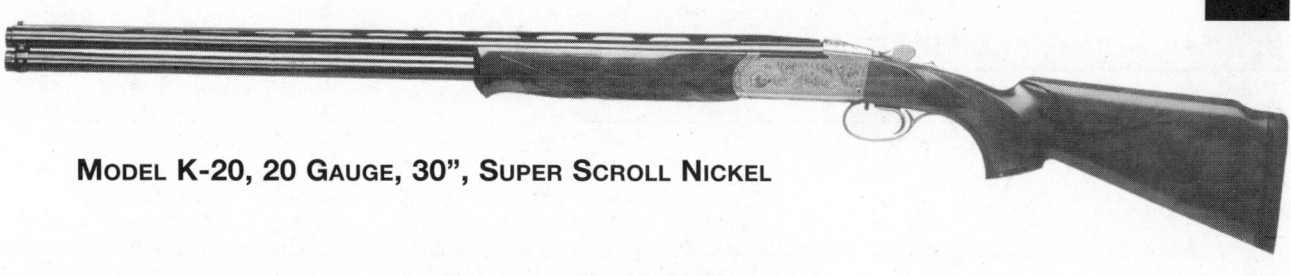

MODEL K-20, 20 GAUGE, 30", SUPER SCROLL NICKEL

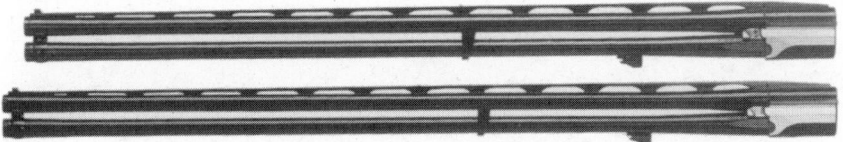

K-20 Extra barrels, 28 Gauge, 28" and 30". Also available in .410

SPECIFICATIONS

Barrels: 20 ga/3" (28" Choke Tubes (5) Tapered flat rib, 11-7, 5 mm); 20 ga/3" (30" Choke Tubes (5) Tapered flat rib, 11-7, 5 mm); 28 ga/3" (28" Choke Tubes (5) Tapered flat rib, 10, 5-7 mm); 28 ga/3" (30" Choke Tubes (5) Tapered flat rib, 10, 5-7 mm); .410/3" (28" Choke Tubes (5) Tapered flar rib, 9,5-6mm); .410/3" (30" Choke Tubes (5) Tapered flar rib, 9,5-6mm)

Chokes: Choke Tubes (CT) bottom and top, 5 included. Available are Cylinder (C), Skeet (S), Improved Cylinder (IC), Modified (M), Improved Modified (IM), Full (F).

Sights: White pearl front bead and metal center bead

Action: Case hardened, nickel plated steel with satin grey finish **Trigger:** Single selective mechanical trigger, adjustable for finger length.

Trigger pull: Approximately 3-1/2 to 4 lbs.

Safety: Top tang push button safety. Can be locked in "off" position.

Stocks: Hand-checkered select European walnut with satin epoxy finish.

Standard stocks are: # 3 Sporting/International Skeet. #9 Skeet/Field.

Forearm Standard: # VII Schnabel.

Grade: Standard is classic scroll engraving, similar to the K-80.

Weight: Approximately 7 1/4 lbs.

Case: All K-20 sporting guns come in a fitted aluminum case holding one, two or three sets of barrels.

Prices: . . . .**Price on request**

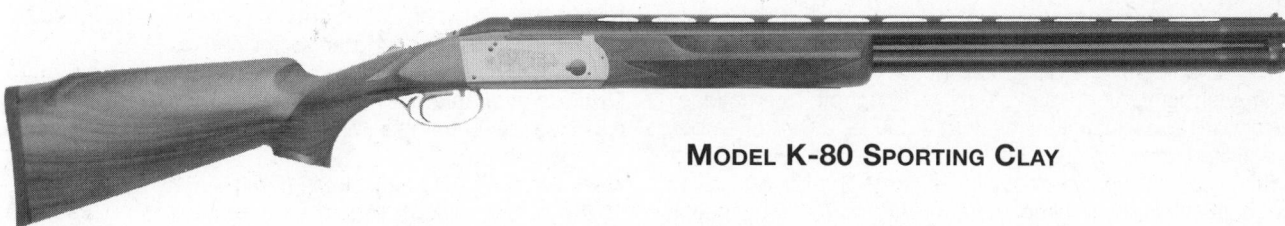

MODEL K-80 SPORTING CLAY

MODEL K-80 TRAP, SKEET, SPORTING CLAY AND LIVE BIRD

Barrels: Made of Boehler steel; free-floating bottom barrel with adjustable point of impact; standard Trap and Live Pigeon ribs are tapered step; standard Skeet, Sporting Clay and International ribs are tapered or parallel flat.

Receivers: Hard satin-nickel finish; casehardened; blue finish available as special order

Triggers: Wide profile, single selective, position adjustable.

Weight: 8 1/2" lbs. (Trap); 8 lbs. (Skeet)

Ejectors: Selective automatic

Sights: White pearl front bead and metal center bead

Stocks: Hand-checkered and epoxy-finished Select European walnut stock and forearm; stocks available in seven different styles and dimensions

Safety: Push button safety located on top tang.

Also available:

SKEET SPECIAL 28" and 30" barrel; tapered flat or 8mm rib; 5 choke tubes.

Price: Standard $7,575.00

SPECIFICATIONS AND PRICES MODEL K-80 *(see also preceding page)*

Model	Description	Bbl. Length	Choke	Standard	Bavaria	Danube	Gold Target	Extra Barrels
TRAP	Over & Under	30"/32"	IMI/F	$7,375.00	$12,525.00	$23,625.00	$27,170.00	$2,900.00
		30"/32"	CT/CT	8,025.00	13,175.00	24,275.00	27,820.00	3,550.00
	Unsingle	32"/34"	Full	7,950.00	13,100.00	24,200.00	27,745.00	3,575.00
	Combo	30" + 34"	IM/F&F	10,475.00	15,625.00	26,725.00	30,270.00	3,575.00
	(unsingle)	32" + 34"	CT/CT&CT	11,550.00	16,700.00	27,800.00	31,345.00	4,000.00

Optional Features:

Screw-in chokes (Unsingle)	$425.00
Single factory release	425.00
Double factory release	750.00

Model	Description	Bbl. Length	Choke	Standard	Bavaria	Danube	Gold Target	Extra Barrels
SKEET	4-Barrel Set	28"/12 ga.	Tula					$2,990.00
		28"/20 ga.	Skeet					2,650.00
		28"/28 ga.	Skeet	$16,950.00	$22,100.00	$33,200.00	$36,745.00	2,650.00
		28"/.410 ga.	Skeet					2,650.00
	2-Barrel Set	28"/12 ga.	Tula	11,840.00	16,990.00	28,090.00	31,635.00	4,150.00
	Lightweight	28" + 30"/12 ga.	Skeet	6,900.00	N/A	N/A	N/A	2,650.00
	1-Barrel Set	28"	Skeet	8,825.00	13,975.00	25,075.00	28,620.00	4,150.00
	International	28"/12 ga.	Tula	7,825.00	12,975.00	24,075.00	27,620.00	2,990.00
	Skeet Special			7,575.00	12,725.00	23,825.00	27,370.00	3,300.00
SPORTING CLAYS	Over/Under w/screw-in tubes (5)	28" + 30" + 32"/ 12 ga.	Tubes	$8,150.00	$13,300.00	$24,400.00	$27,945.00	$3,300.00

Optional engravings: Super Scroll – $1,995.00: Gold Super Scroll – $4,450.00: Parcours – $2,100.00; Parcours Special – $3,950.00

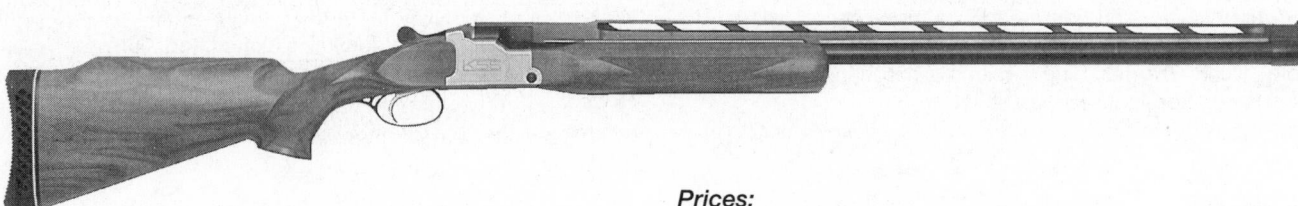

MODEL KS-5

The KS-5 is a single barrel trap gun made by KRIEGHOFF, Ulm/Germany, and marketed by Krieghoff International. Standard specifications include: 12 gauge, 2 3/4" chamber, ventilated tapered step rip, and a casehardened receiver (satin gray finished in electroless nickel). The KS-5 features an adjustable point of impact from 50/50 to 70/30 by means of different optional fronthangers. Screw-in chokes and factory adjustable comb stocks are available options. An adjustable rib (AR) and comb stock (ADJ) are standard features.

The KS-5 is available with pull trigger or optional factory release trigger, adjustable externally for poundage. The KS-5 can be converted to release by the installation of the release parts. To assure consistency and proper functioning, release triggers are installed only by Krieghoff International. Release parts are not available separately. These shotguns are available in Standard grade only. Engraved models can be special ordered.

Prices:

KS-5 32" or 34" barrel, Full choke, case $3,695.00
KS-5 Special 32" or 34" barrel, Full choke, AR ADJ, cased 4,695.00

Options available:

KS-5 Screw-in chokes (M, IM, F), add to base price $425.00
KS-5 Factory ADJ (adjustable comb stock), **add** to base price $395.00

Other Features and Accessories:

KS-5 Regular Barrel	$2,100.00
KS-5 SPECIAL Barrel (F)	2,750.00
KS-5 Screw-In Choke Barrel	2,525.00
KS-5 SPECIAL Screw-In Choke Barrel	3,175.00
KS-5 Factory Adjustable Stock	1,145.00
KS-5 Stock	750.00
KS-5 Forearm	290.00
KS-5 Release Trigger (installed)	295.00
KS-5 Fronthanger	70.00
KL-5 Aluminum Case	425.00
KS-5 Individual Choke Tubes	75.00

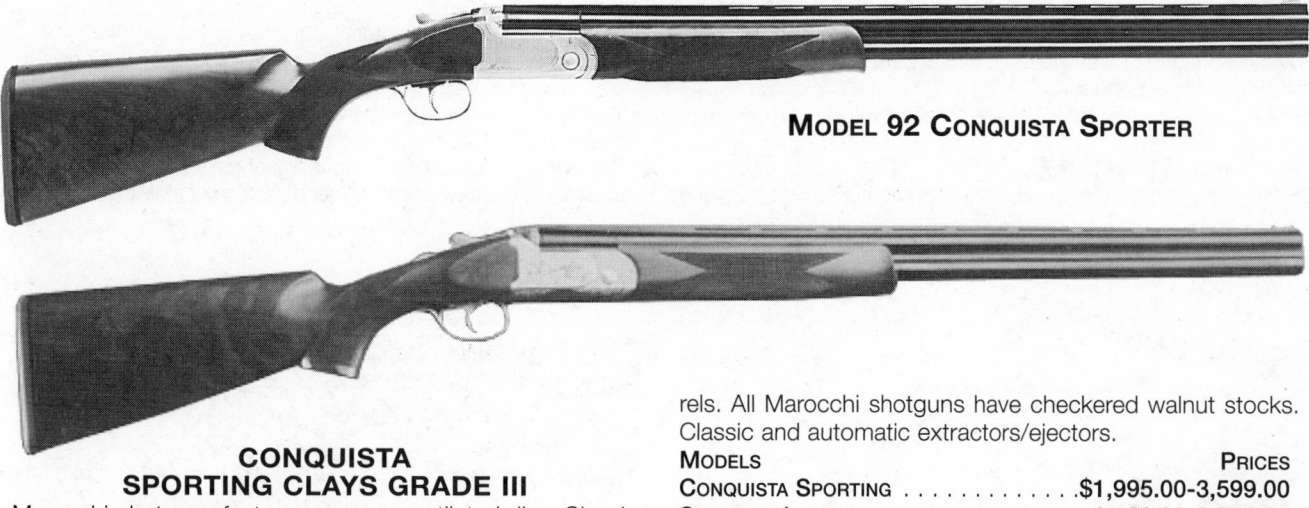

MODEL 92 CONQUISTA SPORTER

CONQUISTA
SPORTING CLAYS GRADE III

Marocchi shotguns feature concave ventilated ribs. Classic middle rib on barrels fitted with chokes. Boxlock action has replaceable hingepins, adjustable selective trigger and automatic ejectors. Magnum Field model is bored for 3" shells. Classic Doubles are 3" guns with back-bored, ported barrels. All Marocchi shotguns have checkered walnut stocks. Classic and automatic extractors/ejectors.

MODELS	PRICES
CONQUISTA SPORTING	$1,995.00-3,599.00
SPORTING LEFT	2,120.00-3,995.00
LADY SPORT	2,120.00-2,300.00
CONQUISTA TRAP	1,995.00-3,599.00
CONQUISTA SKEET	1,995.00-3,599.00
CLASSIC DOUBLES	1,598.00

SPECIFICATIONS CONQUISTA SHOTGUNS (all 12 Gauge)

	CONQUISTA SPORTING	SPORTING LEFT	LADY SPORT	CONQUISTA TRAP	CONQUISTA SKEET	CLASSIC DOUBLES
BARRELS						
Gauge	12	12	12	12	12	12
Chamber	2 3/4"	2 3/4"	2 3/4"	2 3/4"	2 3/4"	2 3/4"
Barrel Length	28",30",32"	28",30",32"	28",30"	29",30"	28	30"
Chokes	Contrechokes	Contrechokes	Contrechokes	Full/Full	Skeet/Skeet	Contre Plus
TRIGGER						
Trigger type	Instajust Selective	Instajust Selective	Instajust Selective	Instajust	Instajust Selective	Instajust Selective
Trigger Pull (Weight)	3.5 - 4.0 lb.s	3.5 - 4.0 lb.s	3.5 - 4.0 lb.s	3.5 - 4.0 lb.s	3.5 - 4.0 lb.s	3.5 - 4.0 lb.s
Trigger Pull (Length)	14 1/2" - 14 7/8"	14 1/2" - 14 7/8"	13 7/8" - 14 1/4"	14 1/2" - 14 7/8"	14 1/2" - 14 7/8"	14 1/4" - 14 5/8"
STOCK						
Drop at comb	1 7/16"	1 7/16"	1 11/32"	1 9/32"	1 1/2"	1 3/8"
Drop at heel	2 3/16"	2 3/16"	2 9/32"	1 11/16"	2 3/16"	2 1/8"
Cast at heel	3/16" Off	3/16" Off	3/16" Off	3/16" Off	3/16" Off	N/A
Cast at toe	3/8" Off	3/8" On	3/8" Off	5/16" Off	3/16" Off	N/A
Stock			Select Walnut			
Checkering	20 lines/inch	20 lines/inch	20 lines/inch	20 lines/inch	20 lines/inch	18 lines/inch
OVERALL						
Length Overall	45" - 45"	45" - 49"	44 3/8"-46 3/8"	47" - 49"	45"	47"
Weight Approx.*	7 7/8 lbs.	7 7/8 lbs.	71/2 lbs.	8 1/4 lbs.	7 3/4 lbs.	8 1/8 lbs.

SHOTGUNS

MERKEL SHOTGUNS

Over/Under Shotguns

Merkel over-and-unders were the first hunting guns with barrels arranged one above the other, and they have since rivalled side-by-sides in popularity.

- Available in 12, 16 and 20 gauge (28 ga. in Model 201E with 26 ³/₄" barrel)
- Lightweight (6.4 to 7.28 lbs.)
- The high, narrow forend protects the shooter's hand from the barrel in hot or cold climates
- The forend is narrow and therefore lies snugly in the hand to permit easy and positive swinging
- The slim barrel line provides an unobstructed field of view and thus permits rapid aiming and shooting
- The over-and-under barrel arrangement gives straight-line recoil, eliminating the torque and lateral deflection of side-by-sides

MODEL 2001EL

**MODEL 303EL
SIDELOCK**

MERKEL OVER/UNDER SHOTGUN

SPECIFICATIONS
Gauges: 12, 16, 20, 28
Barrel Lengths: 26.75" and 28"
Weight: 6.4 to 7.28 lbs.
Stock: English or pistol grip in European walnut
Features: All models include three-piece forearm, automatic ejectors, Kersten double crossbolt lock, Blitz action and single selective or double triggers.
Prices:
MODEL 2001EL
  12, 20, 28 . . . . **$6,895.00**
  2001EL Sporter **6,895.00**

MODEL 2000EL Kersten double cross-bolt lock; scroll engraved silver-grey receiver; modified Anson & Deeley box action; ejectors; single or double triggers, luxury grade wood; pistol grip or English-style stock.
  12 ga., 20 . . . . **$5,495.00**
  2000EL Sporter **5,495.00**
MODEL 2002EL Same features as Model 2000EL but with hunting scenes w/arabesque engraving
  12 ga. 28"; 20 ga. and 28 ga., 26.75" **10,995.00**
SIDELOCKS
MODEL 303EL Double trigger, auto ejectors, straight or pistol grip. 12, 20, 28 . . . . **19,995.00**

MODEL 2002EL

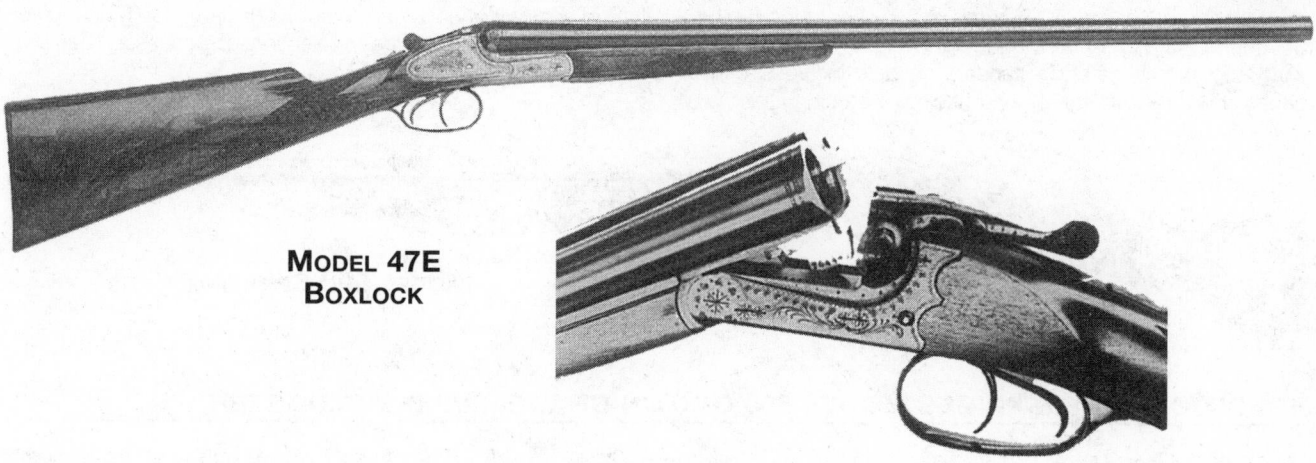

**MODEL 47E
BOXLOCK**

MODEL 47E
Greener cross bolt with double under barrel locking lugs, scroll engraved case hardened receiver, Anson and Deely box-lock action, Holland & Holland ejectors, single selective or double triggers, pistol grip or English style stock., includes fitted luggage case
12 or 16 ga. 28" IC/MOD, MOD/FULL $2,995.00
20 ga. 26 3/4" IC/MOD, MOD/FULL 2,995.00

MODEL 147E
Greener cross bolt with double under barrel locking lugs, fine engraved hunting scenes on silver-grayed receiver, Anson and Deely boxlock grip or English style stock, includes fitted luggage case
12 or 16 ga. 28" IC/MOD, MOD/FULL $3,695.00
20 ga. 26 3/4" or 28" IC/MOD, MOD/FULL 3,695.00
28 ga. 26 3/4" or 28" IC/MOD, MOD/FULL 3,695.00

MODEL 147EL
Greener cross bolt with double under barrel locking lugs, fine engraved hunting scenes on silver-grayed receiver, receiver, Luxury Grade Wood, Anson and Deely boxlock action, Holland & Holland ejectors, single selective or double triggers, pistol grip or English style stock, includes fitted luggage case
12 or 16 ga. 28" IC/MOD, MOD/FULL $4,695.00
20 ga. 26 3/4" or 28" IC/MOD, MOD/FULL 4,695.00
28 ga. 26 3/4" or 28" IC/MOD, MOD/FULL 4,695.00

MODEL 280EL
Greener cross bolt with double under barrel locking lugs, fine hunting scenes on silver-grayed receiver, Anson and Deely boxlock action, Holland & Holland ejectors, double triggers, Luxury Grade Wood, English style stock, includes fitted luggage case.
28 ga. 28" IC/MOD $5,495.00

MODEL 360EL
Greener cross bolt with double under barrel locking lugs, fine hunting scenes on silver-grayed receiver, Anson and Deely boxlock action, Holland & Holland ejectors, double triggers, Luxury Grade Wood, English style stock, includes fitted luggage case
410 ga. 28', MOD/FULL $5,495.00

MODEL 280/360EL TWO BBL SET
Greener cross bolt with double under barrel locking lugs, fine hunting scenes on silver-grayed receiver, Anson and Deely boxlock action, Holland & Holland ejectors, double triggers, Luxury Grade Wood, English style stock, includes fitted luggage case
Price:
28 ga. 28", IC/MOD; extra barrels - 410 ga. 28"
MOD/FULL, ...$7,995.00
Also Available:
S models wih Holland & Holland
sidelock actions .from $5,795.00
147SS model with detachable locks 8,495.00
247 SL and 447 SL models with arabesque engraving (sidelock)
247SL $7,495.00
447SL 9,695.00

CUSTOM STOCKING
(Stock dimensions to customers specs.)
Price: $1,395.00

LEFT HAND STOCKING
(Standard stock dimensions, 4mm cast on)
Price: $895.00

Note: (12, 20 and 410 ga. supplied with 3-inch chambers; 16 and 28 ga. supplied with 2 3/4 inch chambers)

SHOTGUNS

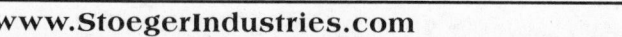

MOSSBERG SHOTGUNS

Model 500 Sporting

All Mossberg Model 500 pump-action shotguns feature 3" chambers, Milspec tough, lightweight alloy receivers with "top thumb safety." Standard models includes 6-shot capacity with 2 3/4" shells, cut-checkered stock, Quiet Carry forend, gold trigger, blued Woodland Camo or Marinecote metal finish and the largest selection of accessory barrels. Ten-year limited warranty.

MODEL 500 SPORTING

SPECIFICATIONS & PRICES MODEL 500 CROWN GRADE (FIELD & SLUGSTER)

Ga.	Stock #	Barrel Length	Barrel Type	Sights	Chokes	Stock	Length O/A	Wt.	Q.D. Studs	Notes	Prices
12	50120	28"	Vent rib, ported	2 Beads	Accu-Choke	Honey Satin	48"	7.2		IC, Mod. & Full Tubes	$301.00
12	Bantam 52132	24"	Vent rib, ported	2 Bead	Accu-Set	Honey Satin	43"	7.0		IC, Mod. & Full Tubes	301.00
12	Slug 50045	24"	Slugster, ported	Rifle	CYL Bore	Honey Satin	44"	7.0			301.00
20	Bantam 54132	22"	Vent Rib, ported	2 Beads	Accu-Choke	Honey Satin	42"	6.9		Mod. Tube Only, Bantam Stock	301.00
20	50136	26"	Vent Rib	2 Beads	Accu-Choke	Honey Satin	46"	7.0		IC, Mod. & Full Tubes	301.00
.410	Bantam 50112	24"	Vent Rib	2 Beads	Full	Honey Satin	43"	6.8		Fixed Choke, Bantam Stock	301.00
.410	50104	24"	Vent Rib	2 Beads	Full	Honey Satin	44"	6.8		Fixed Choke	301.00
12	54232	24"	Trophy Slugster™ Ported	Scope Mount	Rifled Bore	Honey Satin	44"	7.3	Y	Dual-Comb™ Stock	398.00
12	54244	24"	Slugster, ported	Rifle	Rifled Bore	Honey Satin	44"	7.0	Y		367.00
12	54844	24"	Slugster, ported	Rifle	Rifled Bore	Honey Satin	44"	7.0	Y		398.00
20	54233	24"	Trophy Slugster™ Ported	Scope[e Mount	Rifled Bore	Honey Satin	44"	s6.9	Y	Dual-Comb™ Stock	398.00
20	Bantam 58252	24"	Slugster	Rifle	Rifled Bore	Honey Satin	44"	s6.9	Y	Bantam Stock	367.00

SPECIFICATIONS MODEL 500 COMBOS

Ga.	Stock #	Barrel Length	Barrel Type	Sights	Chokes	Stock	Length O/A	Wt.	Q.D. Studs	Notes	Prices
12	54243	28" 24"	Vent rib, ported Trophy Slugster™ ported	2 Beads Scope Mount	Accu-Choke Rifled Bore	Honey Satin	48"	7.2	Y	IC, Mod. & Full Tubes Dual-Comb™ Stock	$457.00
12	54264	24" 24"	Vent rib, ported Slugster, ported	2 Beads Rifle	Accu-Choke Rifled Bore	Honey Satin	48"	7.2	Y	IC, Mod. & Full Tubes	440.00
20	54282	26" 24"	Vent Rib Slugster, ported	2 Beads Rifle	Accu-Choke Rifled Bore	Honey Satin	46"	7.0	Y	IC, Mod. & Full Tubes	422.00
12	54169	28" 18.5"	Vent rib, ported Plain	2 Beads Bead	Accu-Choke Cyl. Bore	Honey Satin	48"	7.2		IC, Mod. & Full Tube Pistol Grip Kit	386.00
20	54188	22" 24"	Vent Rib Slugster, ported	2 Beads Rifle	Accu-Choke Rifled Bore	Honey Satin	42"	7.0		IC, Mod. & Full Tubes Bantam Stock & Forearm	414.00

SPECIFICATIONS 500/590 MARINER & 500 SPECIAL PURPOSE

Gauge	Barrel Length	Sight	Stock #	Finish	Stock	Capacity	Overall Length	Weight	Notes	Price
MODEL 500/590 MARINER™ (CYLINDER BORE BARRELS)										
12	18.5"	Bead	50273	Marinecote™	Synthetic	6	38.5"	6.8	Includes Pistol Grip	$468.00
12	20"	Bead	50299	Marinecote™	Synthetic	9	40"	7.0	Includes Pistol Grip	484.00
MODEL 500 SPECIAL PURPOSE (CYLINDER BORE BARRELS) PERSUADER/CRUISER										
12	18.5"	Bead	50411	Blue	Synthetic	6	38.5"	6.8	Includes Pistol Grip	$329.00
12	18.5"	Bead	50440	Blue	Pistol Grip	6	28"	5.6	Includes Heat Shield	333.00
20	18.5"	Bead	50452	Blue	Synthetic	6	38.5"	6.8	Includes Pistol Grip	329.00
20	18.5"	Bead	50450	Blue	Pistol Grip	6	28"	5.6		322.00
.410	18.5"	Bead	50455	Blue	Pistol Grip	6	28"	5.3		322.00
12	20"	Bead	50579	Blue	Synthetic	8	40"	7.0	Includes Pistol Grip	322.00
12	20"	Bead	50580	Blue	Pistol Grip	8	40"	7.0		322.00

Model 835 Ulti-Mag Pump Shotguns

Mossberg's Model 835 Ulti-Mag pump action shotgun has a 3.5" 12-gauge chamber but can also handle standard 2.75" and 3" shells. Field barrels are over-bored and ported for optimum patterns, reduced muzzle-jump and felt recoil reduction. Cut-check-ered Honey Satin-finished stocks, Quiet Carry™ forearms and gold triggers are standard. Camo models are drilled and tapped for scope and feature detachable swivels and sling. All models include a Cablelock™ and 10-year limited warranty.

MODEL 835 ULTI-MAG

MODEL 835 ULTI-MAG COMBO

SPECIFICATIONS AND PRICES MODEL 835 ULTI-MAG (12 GAUGE, 6 SHOT)

GA	STOCK NO.	BARREL LENGTH	TYPE	SIGHTS	CHOKE	FINISH	STOCK	O.A. LENGTH	W.	STUDS	NOTES	PRICE
ULTI-MAG™ 835 CROWN GRADE												
12	68220	28"	Vent Rib, Ported	2 Beads	Accu-Mag	Blue	Walnut Finish	48.5"	7.7		Mod. Tube Only	$370.00

CAMO							
GA	Stock No.	Barrel Length	Type	Choke	Finish	Stock	Price
12	62447	24"	Vent Rib, Ported, Fiber Optic Sights	Ulti-Full Only	Advantage Timber	Synthetic	$525.00
12	62040-6	24"	Vent Rib, Ported, Fiber Optic Sights	Ulti-Full Only	Rt. X-Tra Brown	Synthetic	525.00
12	62234	24"	Vent Rib, Ported, Fiber Optic Sights	Ulti-Full Only	R.T. Hardwoods	Synthetic	525.00
12	68143-8	24"	Combo, Vent Rib, Ported	Ulti-Full Only	Woodlands	Dual Comb®	524.00
		24"	Integral Scope Base, Ported	Fully Rifled Bore	Woodlands		
12	62445-9	28"	Vent Rib, Ported	Hunter Set	M.O. Shadow Grass	Synthetic	583.00
12	68231-2	24"	Vent Rib, Ported, Fiber Optic Sights	Ulti-Full Only	Woodlands	Synthetic	423.00
12	68235-0	28"	Vent Rib, Ported	Mod Only	Woodlands	Synthetic	407.00
12	68243-5	24"	Combo, VR, Ported, Fiber Optic Sights	Ulti-Full Only	Woodlands	Synthetic	572.00
12		24"	Fiber Optic Rifle Sights, Ported	Fully Rifled Bore	Woodlands		
MODEL 835® SPECIAL HUNTER™							
12	66720-3	28"	Vent Rib, Ported	Mod Only	Parkerized	Synthetic (Black)	$370.00

Model 695 Bolt Action

The 3-inch chambered 12-gauge Model 695 bolt-action shotgun features a 22-inch rifled barrel and rugged synthetic stock. This combination delivers the fast handling and fine balance of a classic sporting rifle. Every Model 695 comes with a two-round detachable magazine and Weaver-style scope bases to give hunters the advantage of today's specialized optics.

Mossberg's fully rifled slug barrels are specially "ported" to help soften the recoil and reduce muzzle jump. Non-rotating dual claw extractors ensure reliable ejection and feeding. Ten-year limited warranty. New fiber-optic sights speed your aim. Also available with Woodland Camo stock.

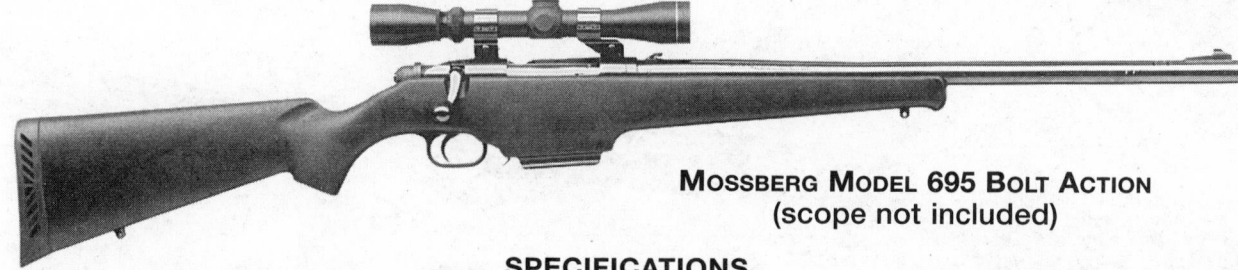

MOSSBERG MODEL 695 BOLT ACTION
(scope not included)

SPECIFICATIONS

GAUGE	MODEL NO.	BARREL LENGTH	BARREL TYPE	SIGHTS	FINISH	STOCK	CHOKE	PRICE
12	59001	22"	Rifled Ported	Iron	Matte	Black Synthetic	Cyl. Bore	$345.00
12	59802	22"	Rifled Ported	Fiber Optic	Matte	Synthetic	Cyl. Bore	367.00
12	59008	22"	Rifled Ported	Fiber Optic	Matte	OFM Camo Synthetic	Cyl. Bore	397.00

SHOTGUNS

NEW ENGLAND ARMS FAIR

(Fabrica Armi Di Isidoro Rizzini)

NEW ENGLAND ARMS FAIR *(Fabrica Armi di Isidoro Rizzini)* shotguns: Boxlock, fullly chrome-lined monoblock barrels with vent ribs, choke tubes standard on 12, 16, 20, 28 gauge guns (fixed chokes on .410), hand-checkered Turkish walnut, single selective triggers, automatic safety and ejectors, straight or semi-pistol grip, custom options available.

Prices: M500 . . . . $2,250.00
M600 . . . . 2,995.00
M702 . . . . 3,995.00
M900 . . . . 3,995.00

MODEL 900

MODEL 702

MODEL 600

MODEL 500

NEW ENGLAND FIREARMS

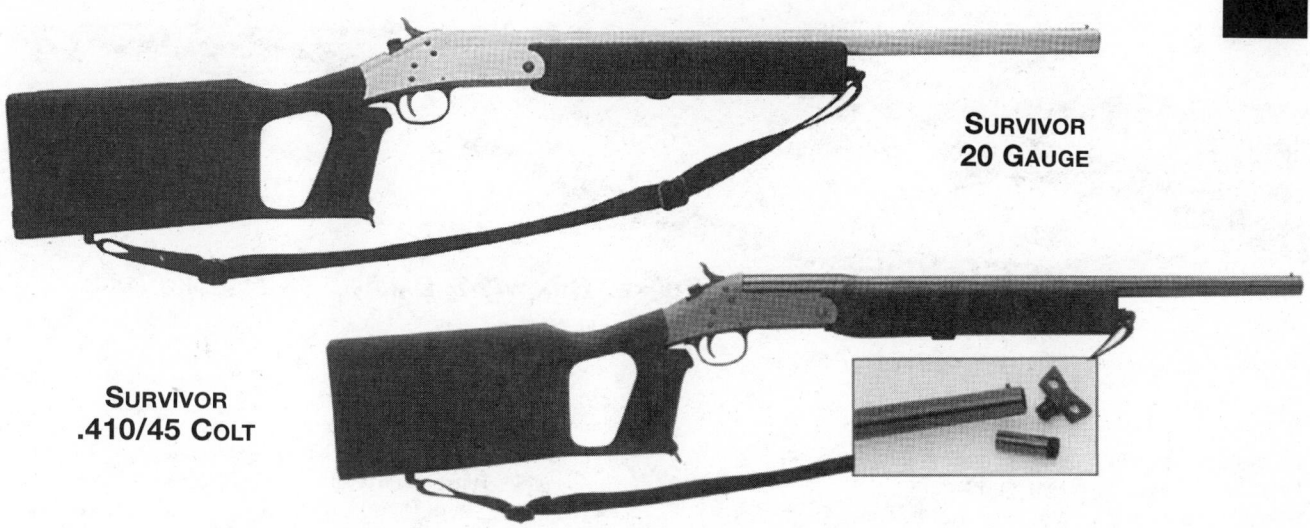

SURVIVOR 20 GAUGE

SURVIVOR .410/45 COLT

SURVIVOR SERIES

This series of survival arms is available in 12 and 20 ga. with either a blued or electroless nickel finish. All shotguns feature the New England Firearms action with a patented transfer bar and high-impact, synthetic stock and forend. The stock is a modified thumbhole design with a full and secure pistol grip. The buttplate is attached at one end with a large thumbscrew for access to a large storage compartment holding a wide variety of survival gear or extra ammunition. The forend, which has a hollow cavity for storing three rounds of ammunition, is accessible by removing a thumbscrew (also used for takedown).

SPECIFICATIONS
Action: Break open, side-lever release, automatic ejection
Guage: 12, 20, .41/45 Colt (Combo) **Barrel Length:** 22"
Choke: Modified **Chamber:** 3" (Combo also available w/2.5" chamber) **Overall Length:** 36" **Weight:** 6 lbs.
Sights: Bead **Stock:** High-density polymer, black matte finish, sling swivels

Prices: Blued finish $129.95
Nickel finish 150.95
.41/45 Colt Combo, blued 164.95
  Nickel 178.95

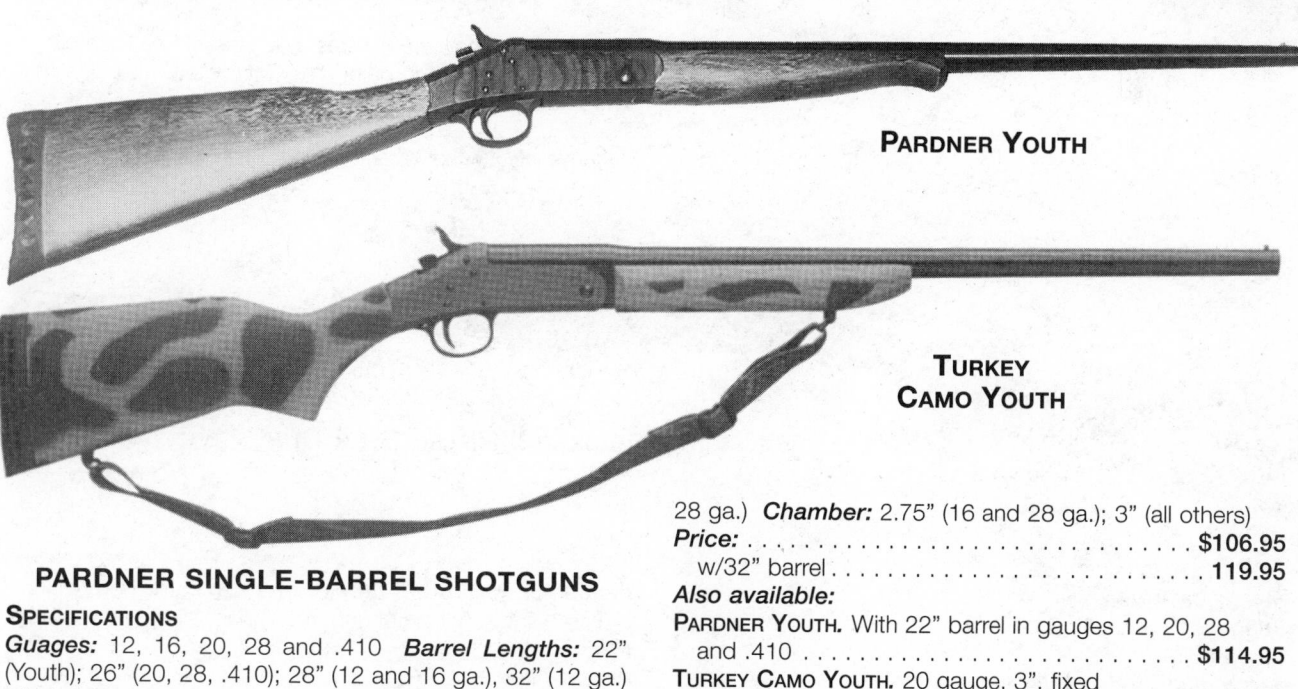

PARDNER YOUTH

TURKEY CAMO YOUTH

PARDNER SINGLE-BARREL SHOTGUNS

SPECIFICATIONS
Guages: 12, 16, 20, 28 and .410 **Barrel Lengths:** 22" (Youth); 26" (20, 28, .410); 28" (12 and 16 ga.), 32" (12 ga.)
Chokes: Full (alll gauges, except 28); Modified (12, 20 and 28 ga.) **Chamber:** 2.75" (16 and 28 ga.); 3" (all others)
Price: $106.95
  w/32" barrel 119.95
Also available:
PARDNER YOUTH. With 22" barrel in gauges 12, 20, 28 and .410 . . . . $114.95
TURKEY CAMO YOUTH. 20 gauge, 3", fixed full choke 128.95

SHOTGUNS

TURKEY GUN w/24" BARREL, TK2 CHOKE TUBE

TURKEY GUN

SPECIFICATIONS
Guage: 12 (3.5" chamber) *Choke:* Full
Barrel Length: 24" *Overall Length:* 44"
Weight: 9.5 lbs. *Sights:* Bead sights
Stock: American hardwood; walnut or camo finish; full
pistol grip; ventilated recoil pad. *Length Of Pull:* 14.5"

Price: with full choke, camo paint,
swivels & sling $128.95
with screw-in choke, black finish 142.95
Also Available: TURKEY GUN. With 24" 10 ga., screw in, choke,
black matte finish, swivels and sling $199.95
with camo paint 205.95

SPECIAL PURPOSE
WATERFOWL SINGLE SHOT (10 ga.)

This sporting shotgun features a 32" barrel, (48" overall),
Modified choke, camo paint finish, swivels and sling.
Weight: 9.5 lbs.
Price: $197.95
Also Available: with 28" barrel, walnut finish stock

TRACKER II RIFLED SLUG GUN

SPECIFICATIONS
Guages: 12 and 20 (3" chamber)
Choke: Rifled bore
Barrel Length: 24" *Overall Length:* 40"
Weight: 6 lbs. *Sights:* Adjustable rifle sights

Length Of Pull: 14.5" *Stock:* American hardwood; walnut
or camo finish; full pistol grip; recoil pad; sling swivel studs
Price: $150.95
Also available:
TRACKER SLUG GUN w/Cylinder Bore, both gauges 142.95

The heart of the Perazzi line is the classic over/under, whose barrels are soldered into a monobloc that holds the shell extractors. At the sides are the two locking lugs that link the barrels to the action, which is machined from a solid block of forged steel. Barrels come with flat, step or raised ventilated rib. The finely checkered walnut forend is available with schnabel, beavertail or English styling, and the walnut stock can be of standard, Monte Carlo, Skeet or English design. Double or single nonselective or selective triggers. Sideplates and receiver are hand engraved.

Over/Under Game Models

GAME MODEL MX20C

GAME MODELS MX8, MX12, MX16, MX20, MX8/20, MX28 & MX410

SPECIFICATIONS
Gauges: 12, 20, 28 & .410
Chambers: 2.75"; also available in 3"
Barrel Lengths: 26" and 27.5"
Weight: 6 lbs. 6 oz. to 7 lbs. 4 oz.
Trigger Group: Nondetachable with coil springs and selective trigger
Stock: Interchangeable and custom; schnabel forend
Prices:

STANDARD GRADE	$9,930.00 - $18,020.00
SC3 GRADE	15,300.00 - 24,270.00
SCO GRADE	26,000.00 - 35,080.00
SCO GOLD GRADES	29,370.00 - 38,350.00

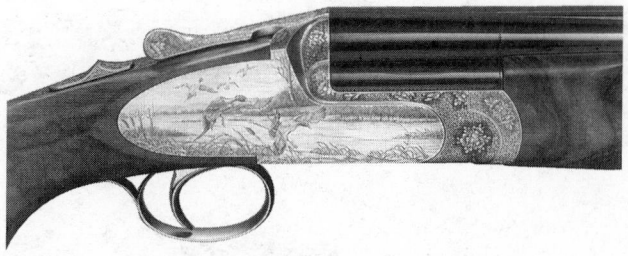

SCO SIDEPLATE ENGRAVING
(applicable to MX8 and MX12 models of any version)

American Trap Single Barrel Models

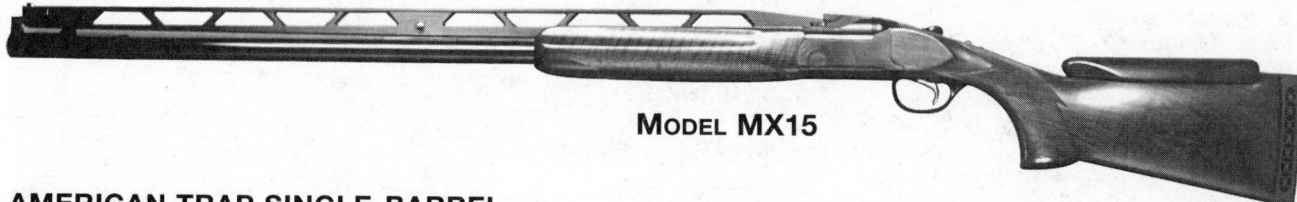

MODEL MX15

AMERICAN TRAP SINGLE-BARREL MODELS MX15, MX15L & MX2000

SPECIFICATIONS
Gauge: 12
Chamber: 2.75"
Barrel Lengths: 32" and 34"
Weight: 8 lbs. 6 oz.
Choke: Full

Trigger Group: Detachable and interchangeable with coil springs
Stock: Interchangeable and custom made
Forend: Beavertail
Prices:

MX15	$7,670.00
MX15L	9,270.00
MX2000	8,830.00

SHOTGUNS

Competition Over/Under Shotguns

Olympic, Double Trap, Skeet, Sporting, Pigeon & Electrocibles

MODEL MX10

MODEL DB81 TRAP

MX8 SPORTING

**MX8 SKEET
SCO GRADE**

SPECIFICATIONS STANDARD GRADE
Gauges: 12 and 20
Barrel Lengths: 27.5", 28 3/8", 29.5", 30.75", 31.5"
Prices: **MX8** 12 ga., removable trigger group
   29.5", 30.75" and 31.5" barrels **$9,010.00**
MX10 12 & 20 ga., w/adj. stock and rib 29.5",
   30.75" and 31.5" bbl.. . . . . **14,980.00**
MX8/20 20 ga. removable trigger group
   26.75", 27.5", 28 3/8", 29.5", 30.75"
   and 31.5" barrels. **9,010.00**
MX8 SPORTING 12 ga. w/external selector
   and 5 chokes; 27.5", 28 3/8", 29.5",
   and 31.5" barrels. **9,980.00**
MX8 CLASSIC 12 ga. **11,380.00**
MX2000 12 ga. **9,930.00**
DB81 w/adjustable trigger 29.5",
   and 31.5" barrels. **9,820.00**

Note: **PIGEON & ELECTROCIBLE MODELS** available in
  MX1B, MX-8B, MX2000 only w/27.5", 28.75",
  29.5" barrels **$9,010.00-18,000.00**
Also Available:
SC3 GRADE (Models MX8, MX820,
  MX8C, MX1B, MX8B **$15,300.00-16,470.00**
SCO GRADE (same models as
  SC3 Grade). **26,000.00-27,230.00**
SCO GOLD GRADE
  (same models as above) **29,370.00-30,540.00**
SCO GRADE SIDEPLATES
  (same models as above) **39,880.00-41,100.00**
SCO GOLD GRADE SIDEPLATES
  (same models above). **46,350.00-47,530.00**

Side By Side Game Gun

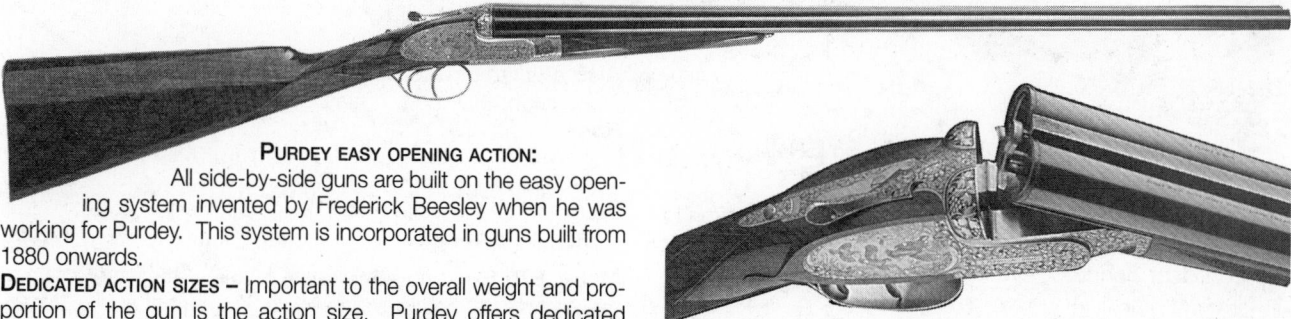

PURDEY EASY OPENING ACTION:

All side-by-side guns are built on the easy opening system invented by Frederick Beesley when he was working for Purdey. This system is incorporated in guns built from 1880 onwards.

DEDICATED ACTION SIZES – Important to the overall weight and proportion of the gun is the action size. Purdey offers dedicated action sizes for each of the bores 10, 12, 20, 28 & .410 in square bar, round bar and ultra bar shapes.

EXTRA BARRELS – Purdey's can supply an extra pair of barrels of a different gauge for their guns, such as 28 gauge on a 20 gauge, and .410 on a 28 gauge. These guns are made with a single forend for both bores.

CHOPPER LUMP BARRELS – All Purdey barrels, both SxS and O/U, are of chopper lump construction.

Each individual tube is hand filled and then "struck up" using striking files. This gives the tube the correct Purdey profile with wall thickness tollerance of .001". Dependant on the final weight of the gun wall thicknesses are recommended at, and made to, .032". Once polished the individual tubes are jointed (joined at the breech) using silver solder. The loop iron is similarly fixed. Once together the rough chokes can be cut and the internal bores finished using a traditional lead lapping technique.

RIBS – always designed to provide the sighting profile the shooter seeks - are hand-filed to suit the barrel contour exactly, and then soft-soldered (using tin) to the barrels, using pine resin as the fluxing agent. Pine resin provides extra water resistance to the surfaces enclosed by the ribs.

Over & Under Gun

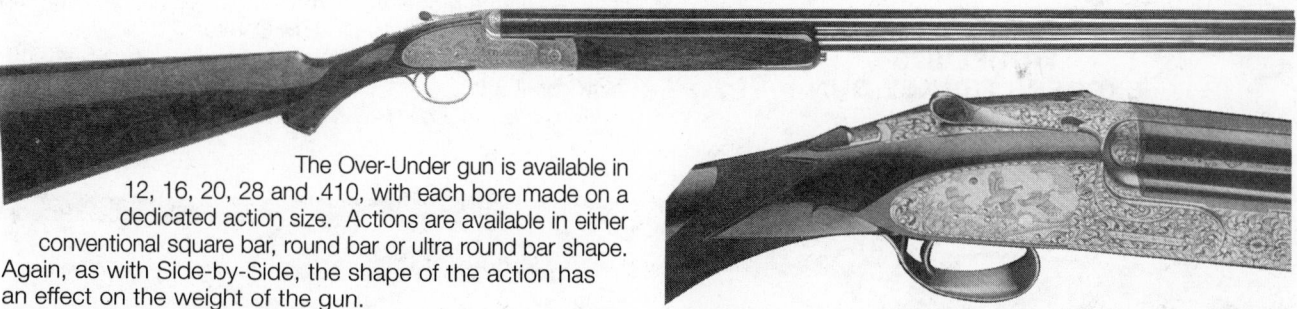

The Over-Under gun is available in 12, 16, 20, 28 and .410, with each bore made on a dedicated action size. Actions are available in either conventional square bar, round bar or ultra round bar shape. Again, as with Side-by-Side, the shape of the action has an effect on the weight of the gun.

FIRING SEQUENCE – Conventionally, the Purdey over-under will shoot the lower barrel first, but can be made to shoot the top barrel first if required. All prices on request.

THE CHOKE SECTION

THE PERCENTAGES OF CHOKE	
Cylinder	45%
Improved Cylinder	50%
1/4 Choke	55%
1/2 Choke	60%
3/4 or Modified Choke	65%
Choke	70%
Full Choke	75%
Skeet (2)	45%
Skeet (1)	40%

The standard for regulating and patterning the shooting of a gun is the percentage of the shot charge, which is evenly concentrated in a circle of 30" diameter at a range of 40 yards. *(Purdey choke restrictions 1/1000 inch.)*

12 Bore 2.75" 1.25 oz No.6	
FULL CHOKE	.038 - .040
CHOKE	.035
.75 (MOD)	.022
.5 CHOKE	.016-.017
.25 CHOKE	.010-.01
IMP CYL	.007-.008
CYL	.003
SKEET	Open Bore

12 Bore 2.5" 1 oz. No. 6	
FULL CHOKE	.038 - .040
CHOKE	.030
.75 (MOD)	.018-.019
.5 CHOKE	.012-.013
.25 CHOKE	.006-.007
IMP CYL	.003
CYL	.002

20 Bore 2.75"	
FULL CHOKE	.038 - .040
CHOKE	.030
.75 (MOD)	.018-.019
.5 CHOKE	.012-.013
.25 CHOKE	.007-.008
IMP CYL	.006
CYL	.003
SKEET	Open Bore

28 Bore 2.75"	
FULL CHOKE	.026
CHOKE	.020
.75 (MOD)	.018
.5 CHOKE	.015
.25 CHOKE	.011
IMP CYL	.007
CYL	.003
SKEET	Open

SHOTGUNS

MODEL 870 WINGMASTER
12 Gauge, Light Contour Barrel

This restyled **870** "**Wingmaster**" pump has cut checkering on its satin-finished American walnut stock and forend for confident handling, even in wet weather. Also available in Hi-Gloss finish. An ivory bead front sight is included on 26", 28" and 30" barrel with REM Choke. The 870 handles 3" and 2 1/2" shells interchangeably.

SPECIFICATIONS
Overall length: 46.5" (26" barrel), 48.5" (28" barrel), 50.5" (30" barrel).
Weight: 7.25 lbs. (w/26" barrel).
Price: $569.00

Also available: MODEL 870 WINGMASTER. 20 Ga. Lightweight (6.5 lbs.), American walnut stock and forend.
Price: $569.00
    28 ga. 649.00
    410 ga. 596.00
WINGMASTER CLASSIC TRAP (12 ga, 30" barrel, 2.75",
    Monte Carlo stock) 775.00

MODEL 870 EXPRESS (NOT SHOWN) features the same action as the Wingmaster and is available with 3" chamber and 26" or 28" vent-rib barrel. It has a hardwood stock with low-luster finish and solid buttpad. Choke is Modified REM Choke tube and wrench.
Overall length: 48.5" (28" barrel). *Weight:* 7.25" lbs (26" barrel).
Prices: 12 & 20 ga. $329.00
Left Hand 12 ga. 356.00
w/Black Synthetic Stock & Forend
    (Right Hand only) 12 ga. 329.00

MODEL 870 EXPRESS TURKEY GUN

The MODEL 870 EXPRESS TURKEY GUN boasts all the same features as the Model 870 Express, except has 21" vent-rib barrel and Turkey Extra-Full REM Choke.
Price: $343.00
Now available:
    w/stock and forend in Realtree Advantage Camo 396.00

MODEL 870 EXPRESS DEER GUN

This 12-gauge, pump action deer gun is for hunters who prefer open sights. Features a 20" barrel, quick-reading iron sights, fixed Imp. Cyl. choke and Monte Carlo stock. Also available with fully rifled barrel.
Price: With Rifle Sights $329.00
    Fully Rifled 363.00

MODEL 870 EXPRESS SUPER MAGNUM
(not shown)

For those who seek the power and range of 12 gauge 3.5" magnum shotshells, the MODEL 870 EXPRESS SUPER MAGNUM represents a good value. In addition to having the strength and reliability of the Model 870 Wingmaster, this model has the added versatility of handling 12 ga. 2 3/4" to 3 1/2" loads. The existing breech bolt and receiver have been designed to accommodate the big shells. Also available is a Turkey Camo shotgun with a 23"

vent rib and 3 1/2" chamber with a synthetic stock and forend, plus checkering and vented recoil pad. Fully camouflaged with Real Tree Advantage. Remington also offers Synthetic and Combo models
Prices: MODEL 870 EXPRESS SUPER MAGNUM $369.00
    TURKEY CAMO 500.00
    Synthetic Model (26" vent rib) 376.00
Combo 20" fully rifled deer barrel and 26" vent rib
    w/wood stock and forend, vented recoil pad . . . 516.00

REMINGTON SHOTGUNS

MODEL 870 EXPRESS "YOUTH" GUN

Designed for youngsters and small adults. It's a 20-gauge lightweight with a 1-inch shorter stock and 21-inch barrel. Complete with REM Choke and ventilated rib barrel, it is also available with a 20" fully rifled, rifle-sighted deer barrel.

SPECIFICATIONS
Barrel length: 21" *Stock Dimensions:* Length of pull 12.5" (including recoil pad); drop at heel; 2.5" drop at comb 1 ⅝"
Overall length: 39" (40.5" w/deer barrel) *Average weight:* 6 lbs.
Choke: REM Choke-Mod. (vent-rib version).
Prices:
20-Gauge Lightweight $329.00
w/Deer Barrel 363.00
w/Real Tree Advantage camo stock and forend 396.00

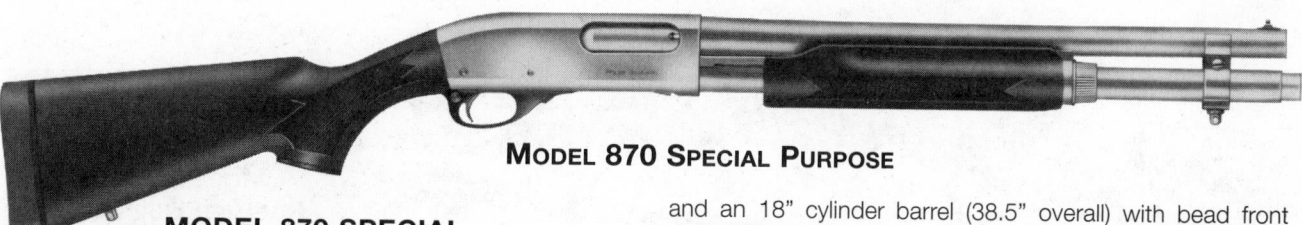

MODEL 870 SPECIAL PURPOSE

MODEL 870 SPECIAL PURPOSE MARINE MAGNUM

Remington's MODEL 870 SPECIAL PURPOSE MARINE MAGNUM is a versatile, multipurpose security gun featuring a rugged synthetic stock and extensive, electroless nickel plating on all metal parts. This shotgun utilizes a standard 12-gauge Model 870 receiver with a 7-round magazine extension tube

and an 18" cylinder barrel (38.5" overall) with bead front sight. The receiver, magazine extension and barrel are protected (inside and out) with heavy-duty, corrosion-resistant nickel plating. The synthetic stock and forend reduce the effects of moisture. The gun is supplied with a black rubber recoil pad, sling swivel studs, and positive checkering on both pistol grip and forend. *Weight:* 7.5 lbs.
Price: $545.00

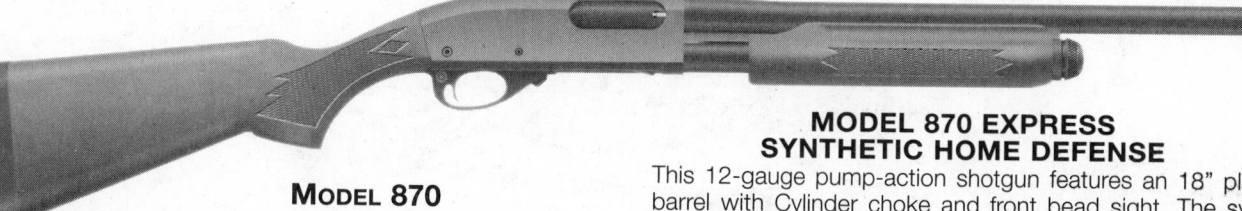

MODEL 870 EXPRESS

MODEL 870 EXPRESS SYNTHETIC HOME DEFENSE

This 12-gauge pump-action shotgun features an 18" plain barrel with Cylinder choke and front bead sight. The synthetic stock and forend have a textured black, nonreflective finish and positive checkering.
Price: $316.00

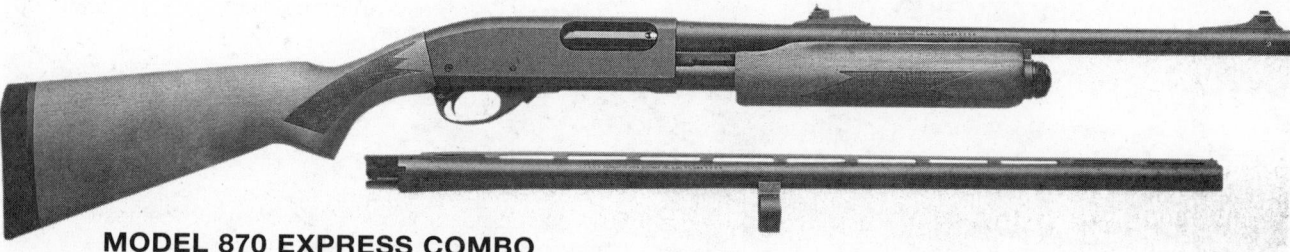

MODEL 870 EXPRESS COMBO

The MODEL 870 EXPRESS in 12 and 20 gauge offers all the features of the standard Model 870, including twin-action bars, quick-change 26" or 28" barrels, REM Choke and vent rib plus low-luster, checkered hardwood stock and no-shine finish on barrel and receiver. The Model 870 Combo is packaged with an

extra 20" deer barrel, fitted with rifle sights. The 3-inch chamber handles all 2 3/4" and 3" shells.
Weight: 7.5 lbs.
Price: $436.00
with Fully rifled barrel with rifle sights 469.00

MODEL 11-87 PREMIER AUTOLOADER

Remington's redesigned 12-gauge MODEL 11-87 PREMIER AUTOLOADER features new, light-contour barrels that reduce both barrel weight and overall weight (more than 8 ounces). The shotgun has a standard 3-inch chamber and handles all 12-gauge shells interchangeably— from 2 3/4" field loads to 3"

Magnums. The gun's interchangeable REM choke system includes Improved Cylinder, Modified and Full chokes. Select American walnut stocks with fine-line, cut-checkering in satin or high gloss finish are standard. Right-hand models are available in 26", 28" and 30" barrels (left-hand models are 28" only).
Prices: Light Contour Barrel $756.00
Left Hand, 28" Barrel 809.00
Also available:
MODEL 11-87 EMBELLISHED RECEIVER 756.00

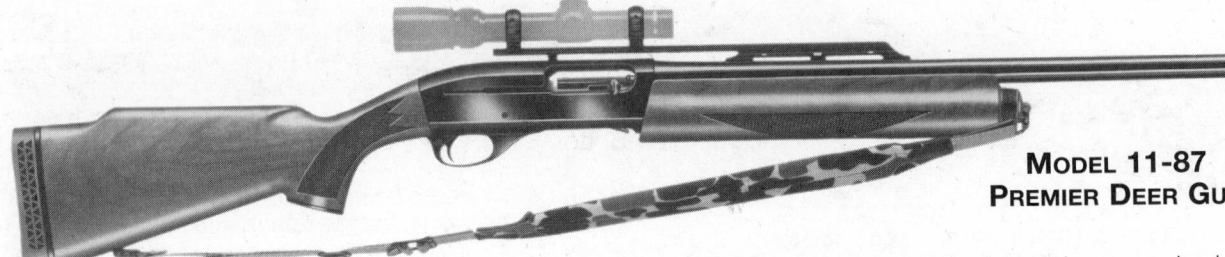

MODEL 11-87 PREMIER DEER GUN

MODEL 11-87 SPS SPECIAL PURPOSE DEER GUN

Features the same finish as other SP models plus a padded, camo-style carrying sling of Cordura nylon with QD sling swivels. Barrel is 21" (41" overall) with rifle sights and rifled and IC choke (handles all 2 3/4" and 3" rifled slug and buckshot

loads as well as high-velocity field and magnum loads (does not function with light 2 3/4" field loads). *Weight:* 8.5 lbs. with black synthetic stock
Price: $789.00
w/fully rifled barrel and cantilevered mount 836.00
Also Available: PREMIER MODEL with Fully Rifled Barrel and cantilevered mount $836.00

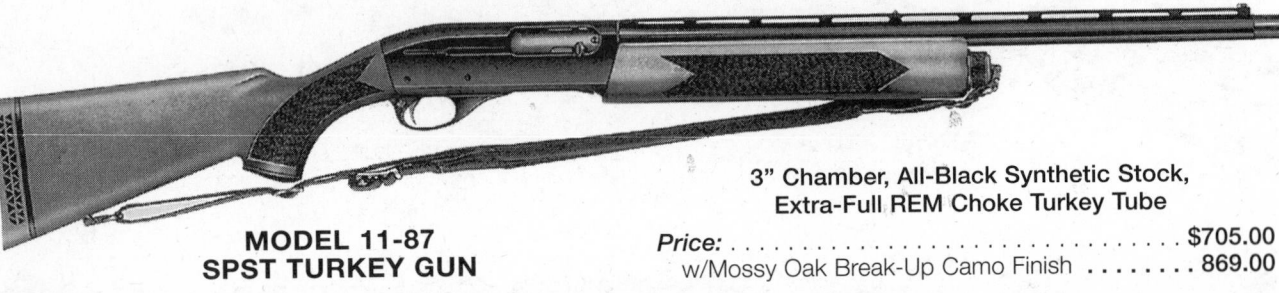

MODEL 11-87 SPST TURKEY GUN

3" Chamber, All-Black Synthetic Stock, Extra-Full REM Choke Turkey Tube
Price: $705.00
w/Mossy Oak Break-Up Camo Finish 869.00

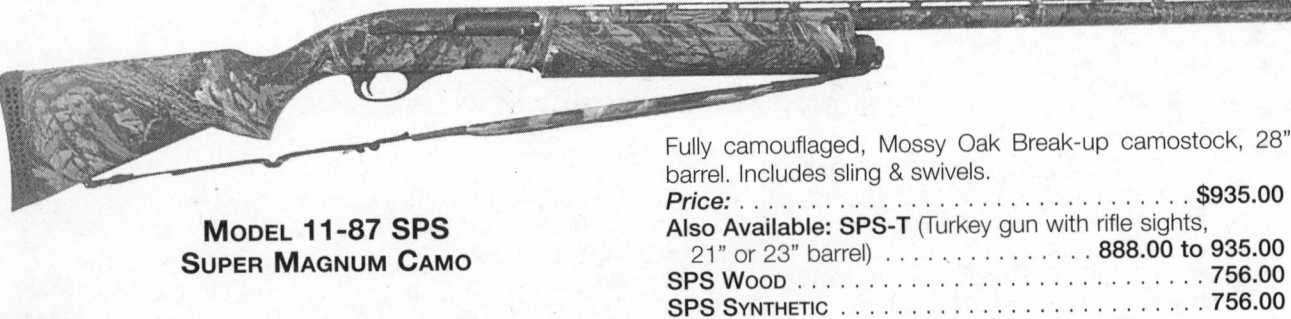

MODEL 11-87 SPS SUPER MAGNUM CAMO

Fully camouflaged, Mossy Oak Break-up camostock, 28" barrel. Includes sling & swivels.
Price: $935.00
Also Available: SPS-T (Turkey gun with rifle sights, 21" or 23" barrel) . . . . 888.00 to 935.00
SPS WOOD 756.00
SPS SYNTHETIC 756.00

SHORT, FAT, AND SASSY.

The shape of things to come in centerfire rifles.

A-Bolt Composite Stalker (pictured), Stainless Stalker, Hunter and Medallion model rifles are available in the new 300 WSM. (Scope not included)

Over the past half-decade, centerfire rifles have experienced a trend toward reduced weight. Lighter and more compact rifles — typically called Ultralight or Mountain rifles — are being shouldered every year, with Browning among those contributing to the trend. Now, in a synergistic partnership with Winchester Ammunition, the leaders in ammunition development, we have created a new cartridge that combines the current generation of lightweight rifles with heretofore unachieved ballistics — the 300 Winchester Short Magnum.

It is the ultimate combination of lightweight, short-action rifles with ballistics rivaling those typically reserved for long-action, belted magnums. Now hunters can access the most remote, rugged country in pursuit of the biggest and most challenging game with a level of confidence that could only come from Browning and Winchester.

Visit your dealer or our website for availability and ballistic information.

300 Win. Mag.

300 WSM

BROWNING®

www.browning.com

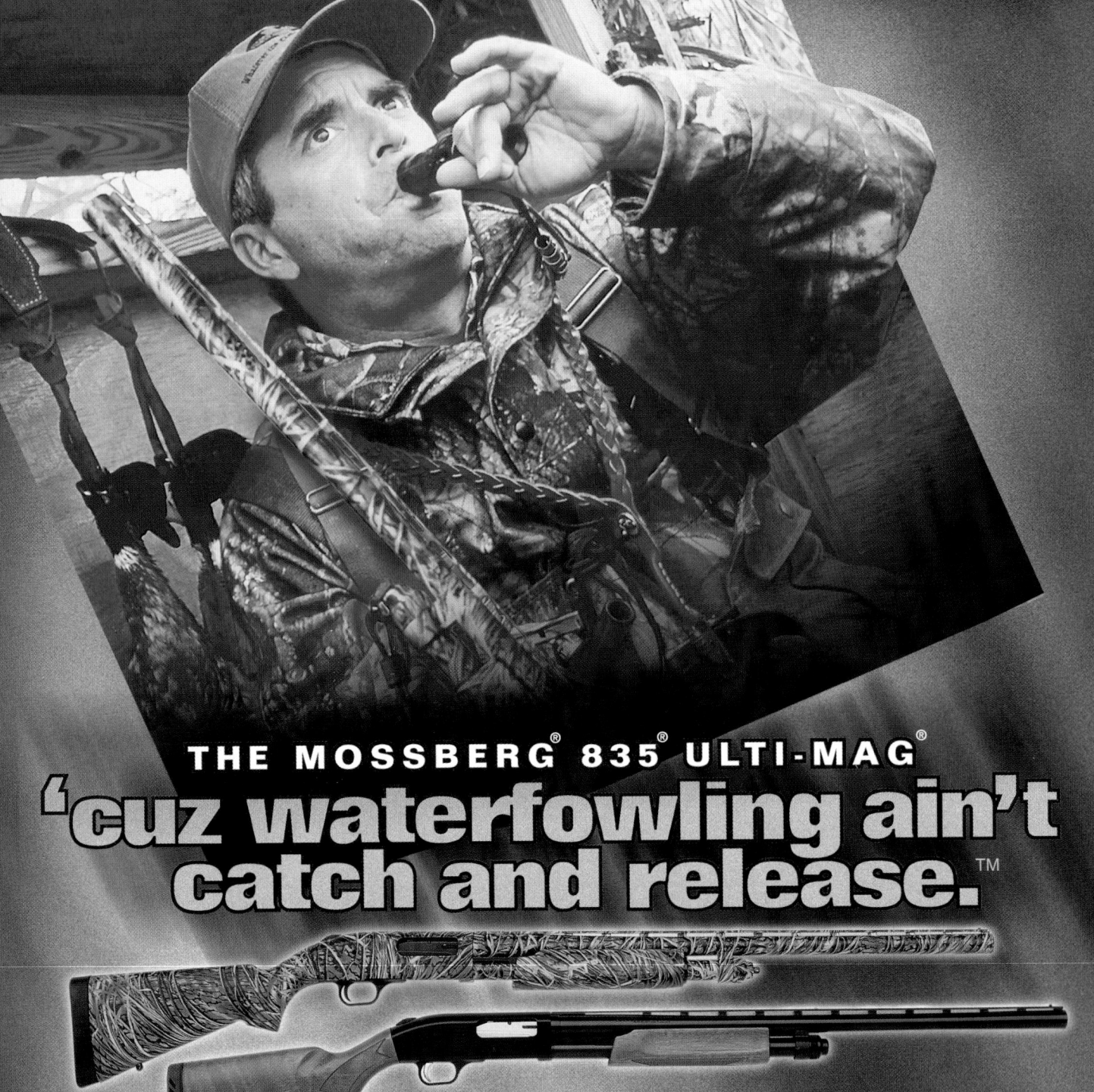

THE MOSSBERG® 835® ULTI-MAG®

'cuz waterfowling ain't catch and release.™

▲ TOP: 835® ULTI-MAG® Mossy Oak® Shadow Grass®
◀ BOTTOM: 835® ULTI-MAG® Crown Grade®

Lousy weather. Cold feet. Wary birds. To a serious waterfowler, they're just part of the game. To a serious waterfowler, the game can only be played one way, and that's with a Mossberg® 835® Ulti-Mag®. Why? High-flying snows' or late season greenheads that *think* they're out of range quickly find out.

The smooth-swinging 3-1/2" Magnum 12 ga. packs the kind of long-range punch that hunters shooting standard 12's only dream about. Its 28" interchange-able barrel is both ported and over-bored, significantly reducing felt recoil and delivering consistently superior patterns. The top-tang safety insures positive control

even when gloved hands are cold and stiff.

Beyond the marsh, a host of options expand the 835's hunting horizons. From fully rifled interchange-able slug barrels and tight patterning Accu-Mag™ choke tubes, to the latest in high definition camo, Mossberg provides the versatility, value, and performance you demand - all backed by a 10-year limited warranty!

The Mossberg 835 Ulti-Mag - everything you'd expect from the original 3-1/2" Magnum, and then some. See your local Mossberg Dealer today or call 203-230-5300 for a free catalog.

Safety and safe firearms handling is everyone's responsibility.

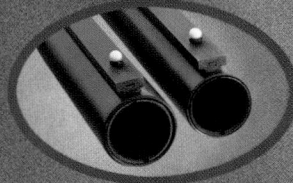
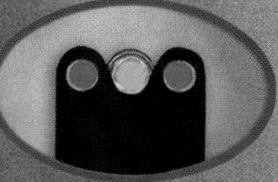
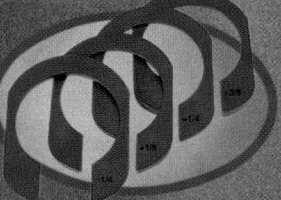

BENELLI

M1 FIELD
UP TO ANY CHALLENGE.
New for 2001, Benelli offers the work horse of its line in a 3" 20-gauge version. Available in either non-reflective matte-finish blue with a black synthetic stock or the new Advantage® Timber High Definition™ camouflage.

The reliable Benelli Inertia System™, four different barrel lengths, five choke tubes, a left-hand version, a rifled slug model, and now in 12- *and* 20-gauge.

When you need the right tool for the job, nothing beats the versatility of the Benelli M1 Field.

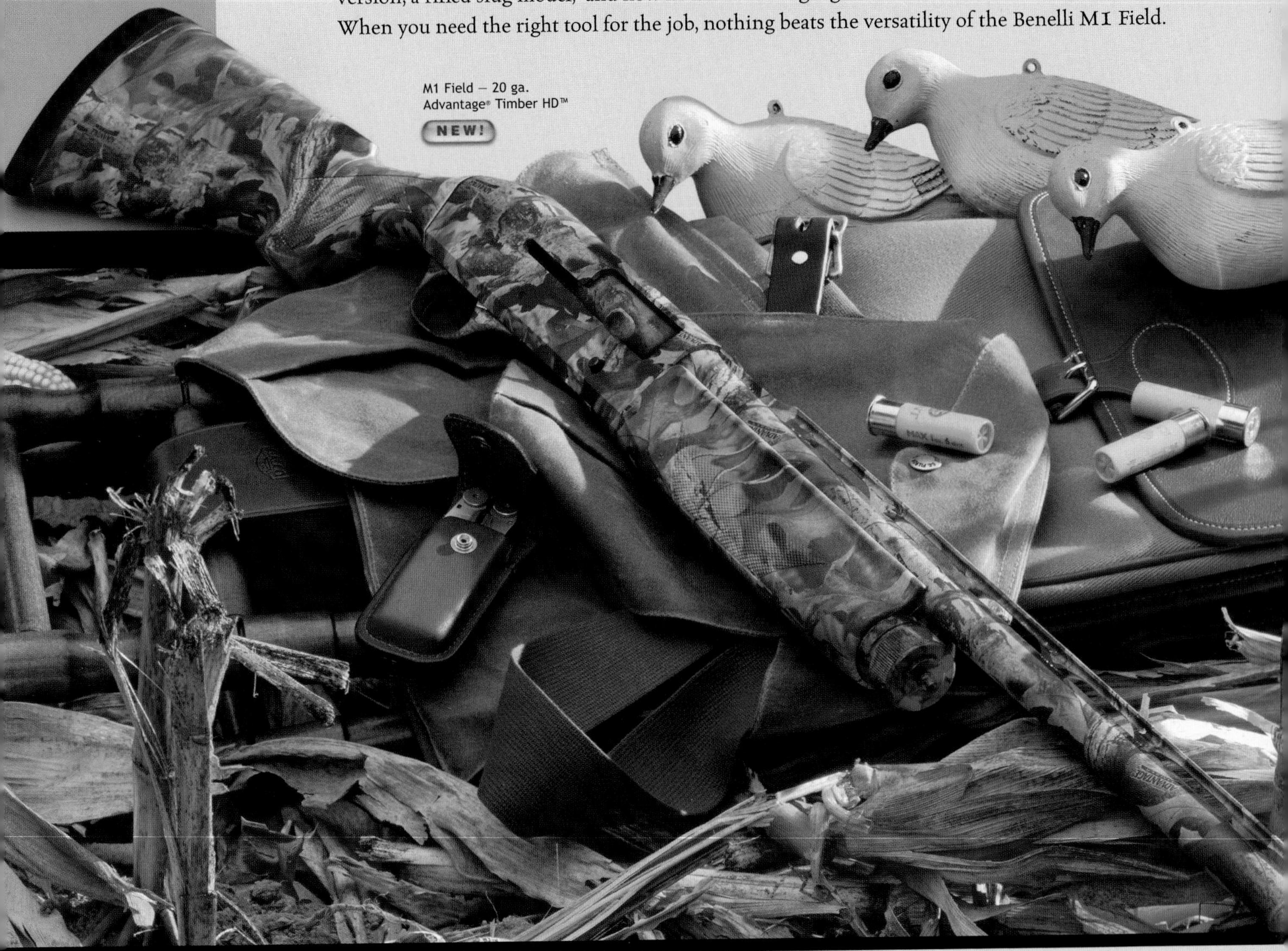

M1 Field — 20 ga.
Advantage® Timber HD™

NEW!

HIGH-TECH SIMPLICITY
Cycling is faster due to a reduced moving mass of parts
• No complicated linkages or o-rings to malfunction • Better gun balance without heavy weights and pistons in the forend • Rotating bolt head features oversized lugs for solid, steel-to-steel lock-up with the barrel extension • Stays cleaner due to the hard-chrome locking head which prevents powder residue build-up on the bolt assembly • Fouling and gases are expelled out the barrel, not through the operating system, therefore, the action remains cleaner and more reliable in wet and cold weather conditions.

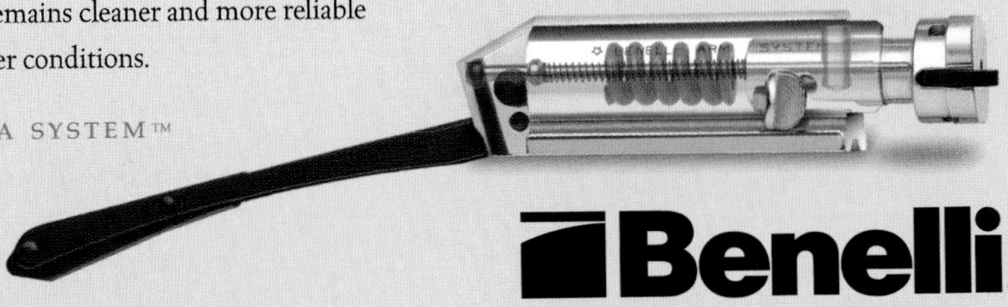

BENELLI INERTIA SYSTEM™

Benelli
Performance Worth the Price

WWW.BENELLIUSA.COM

Autoloading Shotguns

SP-10 MAGNUM SHOTGUN

Remington's **SP-10 MAGNUM** is the only gas-operated semi-automatic 10-gauge shotgun made today. This autoloader features a vented, noncorrosive, stainless-steel gas system, in which the cylinder moves—not the piston. This reduces felt recoil energy by spreading the recoil over a longer time. The receiver is machined from solid steel for integral strength. The SP-10 has a 3/8" vent rib with mid and front sights for a better sight plane. The American walnut stock and forend have a protective, low-gloss satin finish for reduced glare, and deep-cut checkering. The receiver and barrel have a matte finish, and the stainless-steel breech bolt features a non-reflective finish. The SP-10 also has a brown vented recoil pad and a padded camo sling of Cordura nylon. **Barrel lengths/choke:** 26" or 30"/REM Choke. **Overall length:** 51.5" (30" barrel) and 47.5" (26" barrel). **Weight:** 11 lbs. (30" barrel) and 10.75 lbs. (26" barrel). **Price:** w/23" barrel **$1,265.00**

Also available:
SP in Mossy Oak (Turkey) Camo
Price: **1,385.00**
 Synthetic **1,265.00**

MODEL 1100 LT-20
Price: (synthetic only) **$540.00**
Also Available:
MODEL 1100 LT-20 YOUTH (synthetic only) **540.00**
Also Available:
MODEL 1100 SYNTHETIC FR RS
 (fully rifled, rifle sights) **573.00**
MODEL 1100 SYNTHETIC FR CL
 (fully rifled, cantilever) **620.00**

MODEL 1100 SYNTHETIC 12 Gauge (not shown)
Price: **$540.00**

MODEL 1100 LT-20

The Remington **MODEL 1100** is a 5-shot gas-operated autoloader with a gas-metering system designed to reduce recoil. This design enables the shooter to use 2³/₄" standard velocity "Express" and 2³/₄" Magnum loads without gun adjustments. Barrels, within gauge and ver-sions, are interchangeable. All 12- and 20-gauge versions include REM™ Choke; interchangeable choke tubes in 26" and 28" (12 gauge only) barrels. American walnut stocks come with fine-line checkering and a scratch-resistant finish.

Over/Under Shotguns

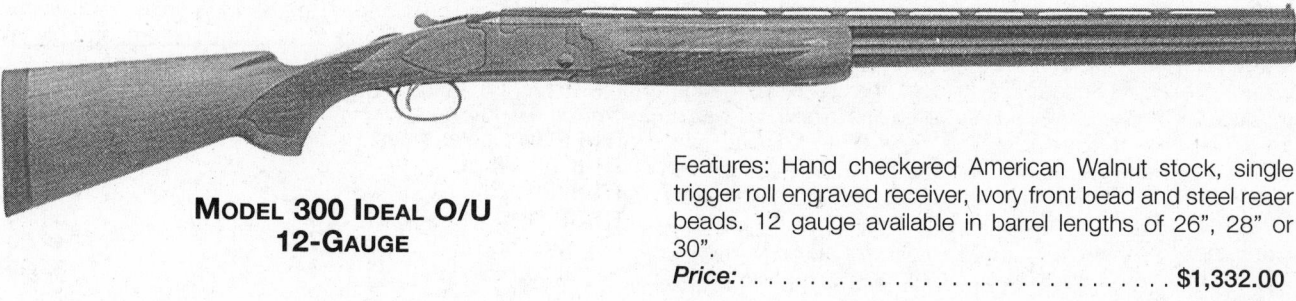

**MODEL 300 IDEAL O/U
12-GAUGE**

Features: Hand checkered American Walnut stock, single trigger roll engraved receiver, Ivory front bead and steel reaer beads. 12 gauge available in barrel lengths of 26", 28" or 30".
Price: **$1,332.00**

SHOTGUNS

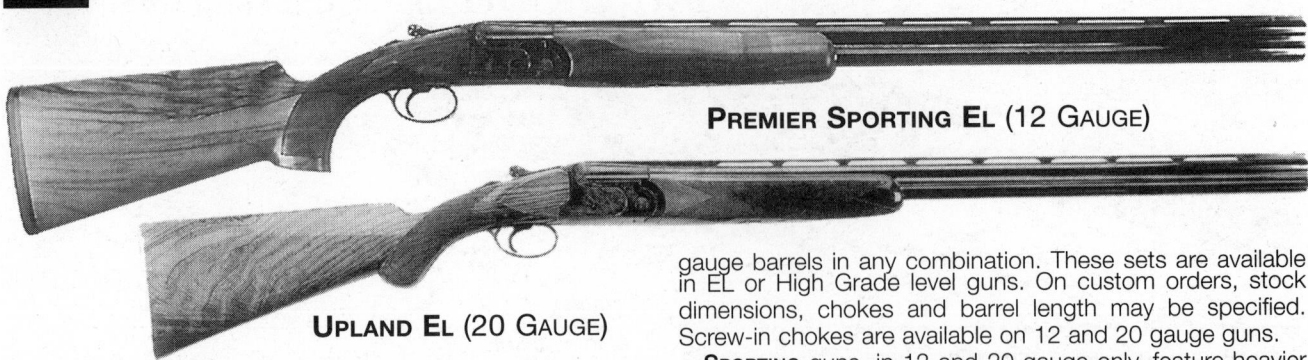

PREMIER SPORTING EL (12 GAUGE)

UPLAND EL (20 GAUGE)

Rizzini builds a well-finished boxlock ejector over/under that is available in all gauges and in many different configurations.

The **ARTEMIS** and **PREMIER** are production guns built to standard specifications. The EL models, which include the Upland EL, the Sporting EL and the High Grades feature higher grade wood, checkering and hand finishing.

FIELD guns are available with case-colored or coin-finish actions with straight grips or round knob semi-pistol grips. Also available are multi-gauge field sets with .410, 28 or 20 gauge barrels in any combination. These sets are available in EL or High Grade level guns. On custom orders, stock dimensions, chokes and barrel length may be specified. Screw-in chokes are available on 12 and 20 gauge guns.

SPORTING guns, in 12 and 20 gauge only, feature heavier weight and a target-style rib, stock and forearm. The Sporting models are available in three versions: Premier Sporting, Sporting EL and S790EL.

High Grade models, with or without sideplates, come in four engraving styles, including game scenes and gold inlays.

Prices: SPORTING EL (12 gauge). **$3,600.00**
UPLAND EL (20 gauge) 2,800.00
S790 EMEL HIGH GRADE. 7,800.00
ARTEMIS EL HIGH GRADE. 12,650.00

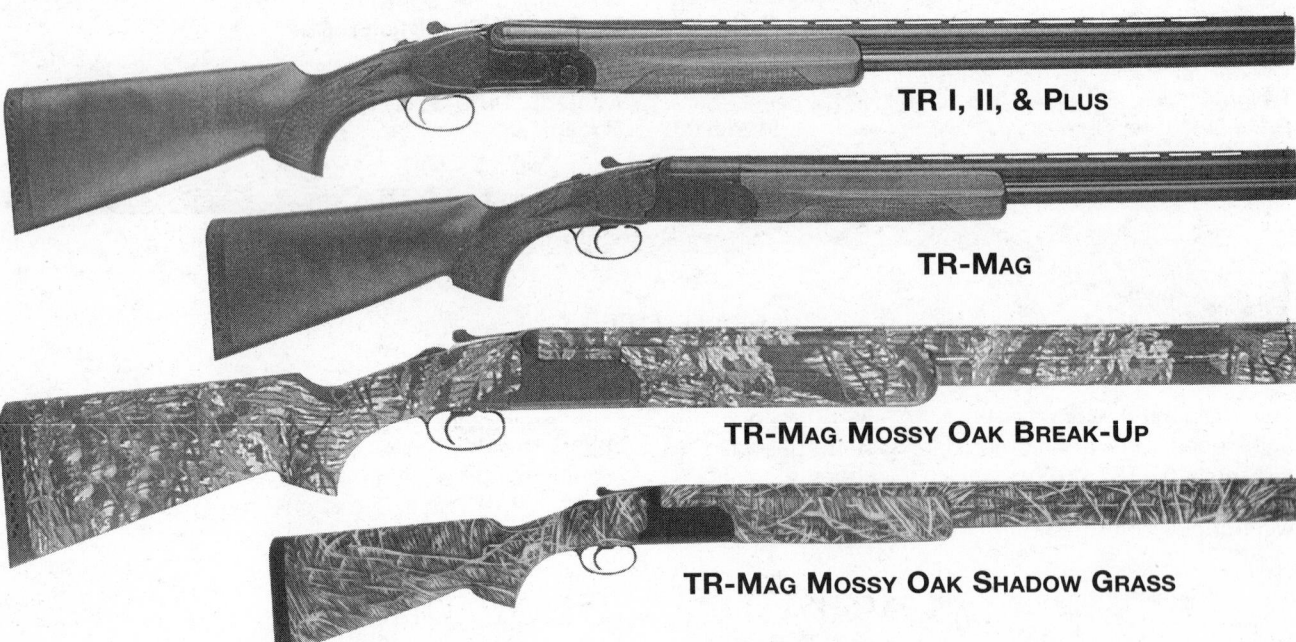

TR I, II, & PLUS

TR-MAG

TR-MAG MOSSY OAK BREAK-UP

TR-MAG MOSSY OAK SHADOW GRASS

EMILIO RIZZINI OVER/UNDERS

The TR-I, TR-I Plus, and TR-II Emilio Rizzini boxlocks have walnut stocks, 3" chambers (except the 28 & 16 gauge models: 2.75" chamber) and ventilated ribs. The TR-1 has a fixed choke and extractors, the new TR-I-Plus has two choke tubes and extractors, and the TR-II has three choke tubes (IC/M/F) and auto ejectors. The TR-MAG series provides powerful 3.5" magnum chambers, choke tubes, extractors (All 10GA, & 12GA.WF) or ejectors (12GA. MOB & 12 GA. MOS) and a ventilated 7mm top rib in three hand-some models: The standard matte blue finish with walnut stock, Mossy Oak Break-up camouflage pattern, and Mossy Oak Shadow Grass camouflage pattern. **Weight:** 6.75-7.5 lbs. (10 ga., 9.75 lbs.) **Barrel Length:** 24-28"

Prices: TR-I (fixed chokes). $687.00
TR-I PLUS (choke tubes). 748.00
TR-II 12, 16 ga.. . . . . 879.00
TR-II 20, 28, .410 . . . . 924.00
TR-MAG 12 ga. 764.00
12 ga. camo 942.00
10 ga. camo 1,132.00

ROSSI SHOTGUNS

YOUTH MODEL .410

FIELD GRADE 12 GAUGE

SINGLE BARREL SHOTGUNS

Rossi shotguns have the timeless single-shot break-open breech design updated with modern safety features. These shotguns feature spur hammer, transfer bar action and integral safety that prevents the action from opening or closing when the hammer is cocked, making them perfect for beginners. Available in 12, 20 and .410 that accept 2", 2.5" Magnum or 3" Magnum shells. Each gauge is offered in a lighter youth model scaled down to fit young shooters. Shotguns feature brass bead front sight, straight stock with pistol grip, oil finished hardwood and sling swivels.

All Rossi Shotguns Feature:
Brass Bead Front Sight
Satin, Oil Finished Exotic Hardwoods
Straight Stock with Pistol Grip
Modified Choke, Suitable for Steel Shot
Sling Swivels Installed
Ambidextrous Operation
Low Profile Serrated Hammer
Sure Grip Butt Plate
All Models Accept 2 inch, 2 1/2 inch Magnum
and 3 inch Magnum Shells

MATCHED PAIR

Rossi's Matched Pair is a single-shot break-open shotgun in a choice of .410, 20 gauge or 12 gauge, plus a completely interchangeable barrel chambered for .22 Long Rifle. The rifle barrel features fully adjustable sights. This makes the Matched Pair ideal (and economical) for the younger shooter.

Item #	Barrel Length	Finish	Weight	Length	Stocks/ Grips	Description	Price
FIELD GRADE SHOTGUNS							
S121280S	28'	blue	5.25 lbs.	43 1/4"	wood	S12 12 Gauge 28" Modified Choke	$99.00
S201280S	28"	blue	5.25 lbs.	43 1/4"	wood	S20 20 Gauge 28" Modified Choke	99.00
S411280S	28"	blue	4 lbs.	43 1/4"	wood	S41 .410 28" Modifiedl Choke	99.00
YOUTH MODEL SHOTGUNS							
S201220S	22"	blue	5 lbs.	35 1/2"	wood	S20 20 Gauge 22" Modified Choke Youth Model	$99.00
S411220S	22"	blue	3.75 lbs.	35 1/2"	wood	S41 .410 22" Modified Choke Youth Model	99.00
MATCHED PAIR COMBO GUNS							
S122280RS	28"/23"	blue	TBA	TBA	wood	Matched Pair 12 Gauge/.22 Mag., Adjustable Sights	$139.95
S121280RS	28"/23"	blue	TBA	TBA	wood	Matched Pair 12 Gauge/.22LR, Adjustable Sights	139.95
S201220RS	22"/18.5"	blue	TBA	TBA	wood	Matched Pair 20 Gauge/.22LR, Adjustable Sights	139.95
S411220RS	22"/18.5"	blue	TBA	TBA	wood	Matched Pair .410/.22LR, Adjustable Sights	139.95
S411229RS	22"/18.5"	stainless	TBA	TBA	wood	Matched Pair .410/.22LR, Adjustable Sights	169.95

SHOTGUNS

RUGER SHOTGUNS

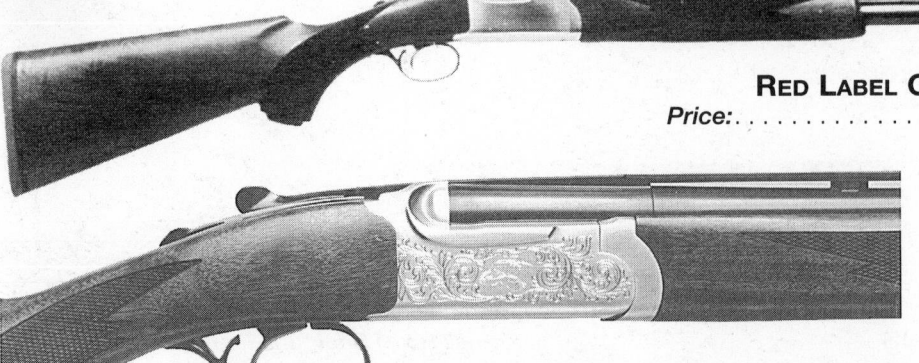

RED LABEL OVER/UNDER SHOTGUN
Price:. $1,399.00

SPORTING CLAYS
OVER/UNDER (not shown)
Price: w/Screw-in Chokes & 30"
Barrels $1,475.00

NEW FOR 2001, RUGER ENGRAVED RED LABEL SHOTGUNS

The Ruger Red Label is a solidly built boxlock gun with hammer-forged chrome-moly barrels silver-soldered to the monobloc. Back-boring is standard. A single selective trigger and automatic ejectors comple-ment a clearly profiled action with no exposed screws or pins.

Prices:
all-weather or walnut stock $1,575.00
w/30" barrel 1,650.00

SPECIFICATIONS RED LABEL AND SPORTING CLAYS OVER/UNDERS

CATALOG NUMBER	GAUGE	CHAMBER	CHOKE*	BARREL LENGTH	OVERALL LENGTH	LENGTH PULL	DROP COMB	DROP HEEL	SIGHTS**	APPROX. WT. (LBS.)	TYPE STOCK
KRL-1226 BR	12	3"	F,M,IC,S+	26"	43"	14 1/8"	1 1/2"	2 1/2"	GBF	7 3/4	Pistol Grip
KRL-1227 BR	12	3"	F,M.IC,S+	28"	45"	14 1/8"	1 1/2"	2 1/2"	GBF	8	Pistol Grip
KRLS-1226 BR	12	3"	F,M,IC,S+	26"	43"	14 1/8"	1 1/2"	2 1/2"	GBF	7 1/2	Straight
KRLS-1227 BR	12	3"	F,M.IC,S+	28"	45"	14 1/8"	1 1/2"	2 1/2"	GBF	7 3/4	Straight
KRL-1236 BR	12	3"	M,IC,S+	30"	47"	14 1/8"	1 1/2"	2 1/2"	GBF/GBM	7 3/4	Pistol Grip
KRL-2029 BR	20	3"	F,M,IC,S+	26"	43"	14 1/8"	1 1/2"	2 1/2"	GBF	7	Pistol Grip
KRL-2030 BR	20	3"	F,M,IC,S+	28"	45"	14 1/8"	1 1/2"	2 1/2"	GBF	7 1/4	Pistol Grip
KRLS-2029 BR	20	3"	F,M,IC,S+	26"	43"	14 1/8"	1 1/2"	2 1/2"	GBF	6 3/4	Straight
KRLS-2030 BR	20	3"	F,M,IC,S+	28"	45"	14 1/8"	1 1/2"	2 1/2"	GBF	7	Straight
KRL-2036 BR	20	3"	M,IC,S+	30"	47"	14 1/8"	1 1/2"	2 1/2"	GBF/GBM	7	Pistol Grip
KRLS-2826 BR	28	2 3/4"	F,M,IC,S+	26"	43"	14 1/8"	1 1/2"	2 1/2"	GBF	5 7/8	Straight
KRLS-2827 BR	28	2 3/4"	F,M,IC,S+	28"	45"	14 1/8"	1 1/2"	2 1/2"	GBF	6	Straight
KRL-2826 BR	28	2 3/4"	F,M,IC,S+	26"	43"	14 1/8"	1 1/2"	2 1/2"	GBF	6	Pistol Grip
KRL-2827 BR	28	2 3/4"	F,M,IC,S+	28"	45"	14 1/8"	1 1/2"	2 1/2"	GBF	6 1/8	Pistol Grip

*F-Full, M-Modified, IC-Improved Cylinder, S-Skeet. +Two skeet chokes standard with each shotgun. **GBF-Gold-Bead Front Sight, GBM-Gold-Bead Middle BR-Briley Ruger choke tube wrench included.*

WOODSIDE SPECIFICATIONS

CATALOG NUMBER	GAUGE	CHOKE*	BARREL LENGTH	OVERALL LENGTH	APPROX. WT.	STOCK
KWS-1226 BR	12	F,M,IC,S	26"	43"	7.75 lbs.	Pistol
KWS-1227 BR	12	F,M,IC,S	28"	45"	8 lbs.	Pistol
KWSS-1226 BR	12	F,M,IC,S	26"	43"	7.5 lbs.	Straight
KWSS-1227 BR	12	F,M,IC,S	28"	45"	7.75 lbs.	Straight
KWSS-1236 BR	12	F,M,IC,S	30"	47"	7.75 lbs.	Pistol

WOODSIDE OVER/UNDER SHOTGUN
(w/SCREW-IN CHOKES)
Price:. $1,889.00

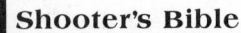

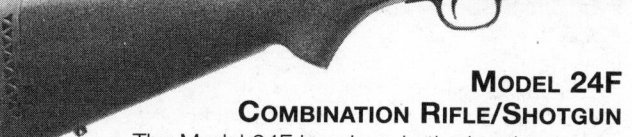

MODEL 24F
COMBINATION RIFLE/SHOTGUN

The Model 24F is unique in the hunting scene. Built as a true combination gun, it combines rifle and shotgun capabilities with a simple change of the barrel selector. Different caliber and gauge combinations are available. The various 24F combination rifle/shotguns outfit you for upland game, turkeys, waterfowl, small game and deer. This versatility has made the Savage 24F a favorite of hunters for generations.

Price: 24F-20 GA., .22 LR, .22 Hornet, .223 Rem, 30/30 Win. $460.00

24F-12 GA., .22 Hornet, .223 Rem, 30/30 Win. 486.00

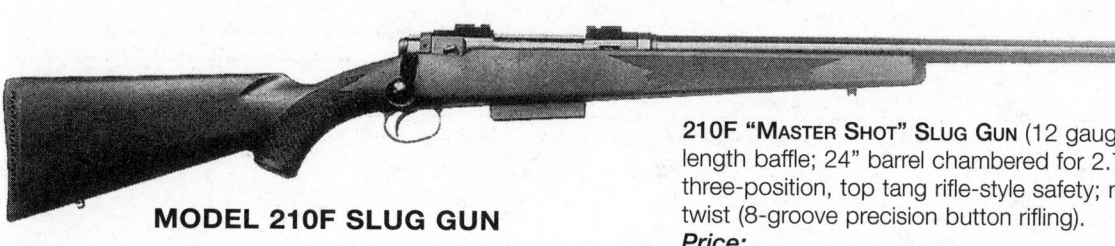

MODEL 210F SLUG GUN

210F "MASTER SHOT" SLUG GUN (12 gauge). Features full-length baffle; 24" barrel chambered for 2.75" or 3" shells; three-position, top tang rifle-style safety; no sights; 1 in 35" twist (8-groove precision button rifling).
Price: $402.00

SIG ARMS SHOTGUNS

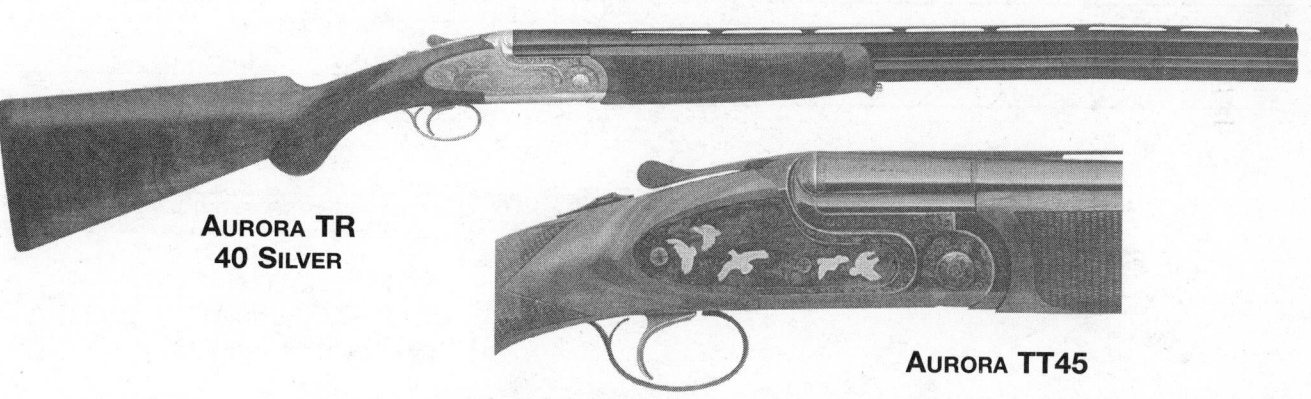

AURORA TR
40 SILVER

AURORA TT45

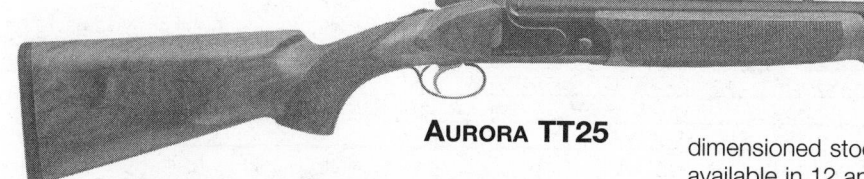

AURORA TT25

SIGARMS AURORA SHOTGUNS

The Aurora family of field and competition over-and-unders are available in a wide range of receiver styles. Competition TT25 models include Seminole choke tubes, specialty dimensioned stocks with palm swells and more. TT25s are available in 12 and 20 Gauge.

TR Series field guns feature polished blued barrels and Prince of Wales pistol grips on oiled select walnut stocks. TR field models are available in 12, 20 and 28 Gauge and .410.
Price: Aurora $1,865.00

SHOTGUNS

SKB Shotguns

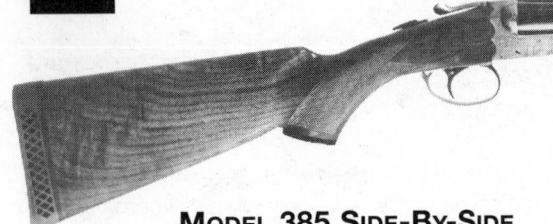

Model 385 Side-By-Side

The Model 385 features silver nitride receiver with engraved scroll and game scene design; solid boxlock action w/double locking lugs; single selective trigger; selective automatic ejectors; automatic safety; sculpted American walnut stock; pistol or English straight grip; semi-beavertail forend; stock and forend finished w/18-line fine checkering; standard series choke tube system; solid rib w/flat matte finish and metal front bead. For additional specifications, see table below.

Price:. **$2,049.00**
Field Set. **2,929.00**

Also available:
Model 485 Series. Features engraved upland game scene; semi-fancy American walnut stock and beavertail forend; raised vent rib with flat matte finish.

Price:. **$2,769.00**
Field Set. **3,949.00**

SPECIFICATIONS MODEL 385 & 485

FIELD MODELS

GAUGE	CHAMBER	BARREL LENGTH	OVERALL LENGTH	INTER CHOKE	SIGHTS✓	RIB WIDTH	STOCK	AVERAGE WEIGHT* 385	485
12	3"	28"	44 1/2"	STND-A	MFB	5/16"	PISTOL	7 lb. 3 oz.	7 lb. 1 oz.
12	3"	28"	44 1/2"	STND-A	MFB	5/16"	ENGLISH	7 lb. 1 oz.	7 lb. 5 oz.
12	3"	26"	42 1/2"	STND-A	MFB	5/16"	PISTOL	7 lb. 1 oz.	7 lb. 5 oz.
12	3"	26"	42 1/2"	STND-A	MFB	5/16"	ENGLISH	7 lb. 0 oz.	7 lb. 4 oz.
20	3"	26"	42 1/2"	STND-B	MFB	5/16"	PISTOL	6 lb. 10 oz.	6 lb. 14 oz.
20	3"	26"	42 1/2"	STND-B	MFB	5/16"	ENGLISH	6 lb. 10 oz.	6 lb. 14 oz.
28	2 3/4"	26"	42 1/2"	STND-B	MFB	5/16"	PISTOL	6 lb. 13 oz.	7 lb. 2 oz.
28	2 3/4"	26"	42 1/2"	STND-B	MFB	5/16"	ENGLISH	6 lb. 13 oz.	7 lb. 2 oz.

2 BARREL FIELD SETS

GAUGE	CHAMBER	BARREL LENGTH	OVERALL LENGTH	INTER CHOKE	SIGHTS✓	RIB WIDTH	STOCK	AVERAGE WEIGHT* 385	485
20	3"	26"	42 1/2"	STND-B	MFB	5/16"	PISTOL	6 lb. 10 oz.	
28	2 3/4"	26"	42 1/2"	STND-B	MFB	5/16"	PISTOL	6 lb. 13 oz.	
20	3"	26"	42 1/2"	STND-B	MFB	5/16"	ENGLISH	6 lb. 10 oz.	
28	2 3/4"	26"	42 1/2"	STND-B	MFB	5/16"	ENGLISH	6 lb. 13 oz.	

*Weights may vary due to wood density. Specifications may vary. *INTER-CHOKE SYSTEMS: COMP - Competition series includes Mod., Full, Imp. Cyl. STND-A - Standard series includes Mod., Full, Imp. Cyl. STND-B- Standard series includes Imp. Cyl., Mod. Skeet STOCK DIMENSIONS: Length of Pull - 14 1/8" Drop at Comb - 1 1/2" Drop at Heel - 2 3/4" ✓MFB-Metal Front Bead

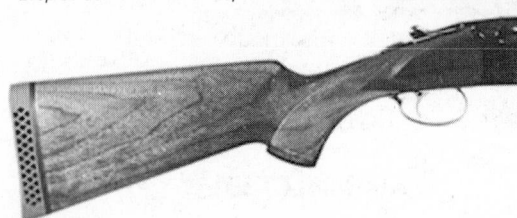

Model 505
$1,189.00 (Field)
$1,299.00 (Sporting Clays)

505 FIELD OVER AND UNDERS

GAUGE	CHAMBER	BARREL LENGTH	OVERALL LENGTH	INTER CHOKE	SIGHTS✓	RIB WIDTH	AVERAGE WEIGHT*
12	3"	28"	45 3/8"	STND-A	MFB	3/8"	7 lb. 12 oz.
12	3"	26"	45 3/8"	STND-B	MFB	3/8"	7 lb. 11 oz.
20	3"	26" or 28"	45 3/8"	STND-B	MFB	3/8"	6 lb. 10 oz. (6 lb. 11 oz.)

505 SPORTING CLAYS

GAUGE	CHAMBER	BARREL LENGTH	OVERALL LENGTH	INTER CHOKE	SIGHTS	RIB WIDTH	AVERAGE WEIGHT* 505
12	3"	30"	47 3/8"	STND-B	CP/WFB	15/32" CH/STP	8 lb. 5 oz.
12	3"	28"	45 3/8"	STND-B	CP/WFB	15/32" CH/STP	8 lb. 1 oz.

*Weights may vary due to wood density. Specifications may vary. *INTER-CHOKE SYSTEMS: STND-A-Standard series includes Full, Mod, Imp. Cyl. STND-B-Standard series includes Imp. Cyl., Mod, Skeet STOCK DIMENSIONS: Length of Pull-14 1/8" Drop at Comb-1 1/2" Drop at heel-2 3/16" **MFB-Metal Front Bead**

Model 585 and 785 Series

MODEL 785 OVER/UNDER

The SKB 785 Series features chrome-lined chambers and bores, lengthened forcing cones, chrome-plated ejectors and competition choke tube system.

MODEL 785   *Prices*
FIELD(12 & 20 ga.) $2,119.00
 28 or .410 ga. 2,199.00

TWO-BARREL FIELD SET (12 & 20 ga.) 3,079.00
 20/28 ga. or 28/.410 ga 3,179.00
SKEET (12 or 20 ga.) 2,199.00
 28 or .410 ga. 2,239.00
 2-Bbl. Set 4,439.00
SPORTING CLAYS (12 or 20 ga.) 2,269.00
 28 gauge 2,349.00
 2-Barrel Set (12 or 20 ga.) 3,249.00
TRAP (Monte Carlo or Std.) 2,199.00
 2-Barrel Trap Combo 3,079.00

GAUGE	BARREL√ LENGTH	OVERALL LENGTH	INTER CHOKE	SIGHTS√	785 RIB WIDTH	585 RIB WIDTH	AVERAGE WEIGHT* 785	585
TRAP MODELS – STANDARD OR MONTE CARLO								
12	30"	47 3/8"	COMP-A	CP/WFB	15/32" CH/STP	3/8" STP	8 lb. 15 oz.	8 lb. 7 oz.
12	32"	49 3/8:	COMP-A	CP/WFB	15/32" CH/STP	3/8" STP	9 lb. 1 oz.	8 lb. 10 oz.
TRAP COMBO'S – STANDARD OR MONTE CARLO								
12	O/U-30"	47 3/8"	COMP.	CP/WFB	15/32" CH/STP	3/8" STP	8 lb. 15 oz.	8 lb. 6 oz.
12	S/O-32"	49 3/8"	COMP.	CP/WFB	15/32" CH/STP	3/8" STP	9 lb. 0 oz.	8 lb. 6 oz.
12	O/U-30"	47 3/8"	COMP.	CP/WFB	15/32" CH/STP	3/8"STP	9 lb. 0 oz.	8 lb. 4 oz.
12	S/O-34"	51 3/8"	COMP.	CP/WFB	15/32" CH/STP	3/8"STP	9 lb. 1 oz.	8 lb. 6 oz.
12	O/U-32"	49 3/8"	COMP.	CP/WFB	15/32" CH/STP	3/8" STP	9 lb. 0 oz.	8 lb. 7 oz.
12	S/O-34"	51 3/8"	COMP.	CP/WFB	15/32" CH/STP	3/8" STP	9 lb. 1 oz.	8 lb. 8 oz.
YOUTH & LADIES								
12	28"	44 1/2"	COMP.	MFB	3/8"			7 lb. 11 oz.
12	26"	42 1/2"	COMP.	MFB	3/8"			7 lb. 9 oz.
20	26"	42 1/2"	STND-B	MFB	3/8"			6 lb. 7 oz.
SKEET MODELS								
12	30"	47 1/4"	COMP.	CP/WFB	3/8"		8 lb. 9 oz.	8 lb. 1 oz.
12	28"	45 1/4"	COMP.	CP/WFB	3/8"		8 lb. 6 oz.	7 lb. 12 oz.
20	28"	45 1/4"	STND.	CP/WFB	5/16"		7 lb. 2 oz.	6 lb. 15 oz.
28	28"	45 1/4"	STND.	CP/WFB	5/16"		7 lb. 5 oz.	6 lb. 15 oz.
410	28"	45 1/4"	SK/SK	CP/WFB	5/16"		7 lb. 5 oz.	7 lb. 0 oz.

*Weights may vary due to wood density. Specifications may vary. *INTER-CHOKE SYSTEMS: COMP. - Competition series includes 2 -SKI/SCI, 1-Mod/SCIV STND - Standard series includes Skeet, Skeet and Imp. Cyl. NOTE: 785's Are Equipped with Step-Up Style Ribs STOCK DIMENSIONS: Length of Pull - 14 1/8" Drop at Comb - 1 1/2" Drop at Heel - 2 3/16" √CP/WFB - Center Post/White Front Bead

585 UPLAND

MODEL 585 OVER/UNDER   *Prices*
FIELD (12 & 20 ga.) $1,499.00
 28 or .410 ga. 1,569.00
YOUTH/LADIES (12 & 20 ga.) 1,499.00
UPLAND (12 & 20 ga.) 1,499.00
 28 ga. 1,569.00

FIELD SET (12 & 20 ga.) 2,399.00
 20/28 + 28/410 . . . . .2,469.00
 (12 or 20 ga.) 2,199.00
SPORTING CLAYS (28" to 32" barrel)
 12 + 20 ga. 1,679.00
 28 ga. 1,729.00
 Sporting Clay Set .2,419.00
SKEET (12 + 20 ga.) .1,619.00
 28 + .410 ga. 1,679.00
 Skeet set 3,779.00
TRAP (12 + 20 ga.) .1,619.00
 Combo 2,419.00

SHOTGUNS

COACH GUN

ENGRAVED COACH GUN

The **STOEGER COACH GUN** sports a 20-inch barrel. Lightning fast, it is the perfect shotgun for hunting upland game in dense brush or close quarters. This endurance-tested workhorse of a gun is designed from the ground up to give you years of trouble-free service. Two massive underlugs provide a super-safe, vise-tight locking system for lasting strength and durability. The mechanical extraction of spent shells and double-trigger mechanism assures reliability. The automatic safety is actuated whenever the action is opened, whether or not the gun has been fired. The polish and blue is deep and rich, and the solid sighting rib is matte-finished for glare-free sighting. Chrome-moly steel barrels with micro-polished bores give dense, consistent patterns. Nickel finish is now available. The classic stock and forend are of durable hardwood...oil finished, hand-rubbed and hand-checkered. Improved Cylinder/Modified choking and its short barrel make the Coach gun the ideal choice for hunting in close quarters, security and police work. 3-inch chambers.
Prices: In 12 and 20 Gauge or .410 Bore.. . . . . . $310.00
Nickel 365.00

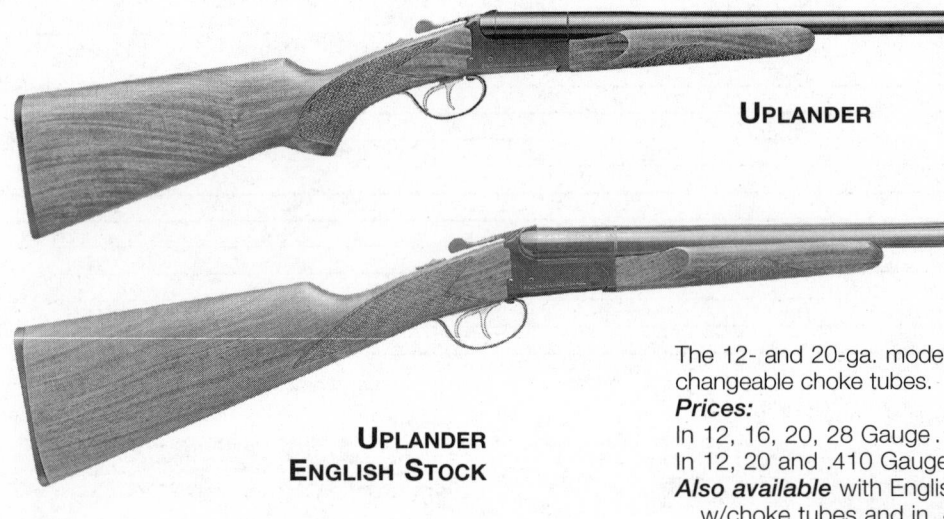

UPLANDER

UPLANDER
ENGLISH STOCK

The 12- and 20-ga. models are available with recessed interchangeable choke tubes.
Prices:
In 12, 16, 20, 28 Gauge. $325.00
In 12, 20 and .410 Gauge w/Choke Tubes 345.00
Also available with English stock and in 20 ga
   w/choke tubes and in .410 w/fixed modified
   chokes. 340.00

UPLANDER

American hunters have trusted the reliable side-by-side shotgun for more than 100 years, and the Stoeger Uplander carries on the tradition of sturdy double-trigger arms a hunter can count on. The safety is reset automatically anytime the gun is opened. Reliable mechanical extractors make it easy to keep empty shells. The Uplander is available in 12-, 16-, 20- and 28-ga. and in .410 bore. The 12- and 20-ga. and .410 guns all handle 3" ammunition, and barrels are proofed for steel shot.

UPLANDER SUPREME
The Supreme is a refinement of the Uplander, with a single selective trigger, automatic ejectors, interchangeable choke tubes and a cut checkered American walnut stock. Gold trigger, red front and middle beads and a soft rubber recoil pad round out the features of a gun that offers an unusual combination of features and low price. It is available only in 12- and 20-ga.
Price: $435.00

See table on page 349 for additional specifications

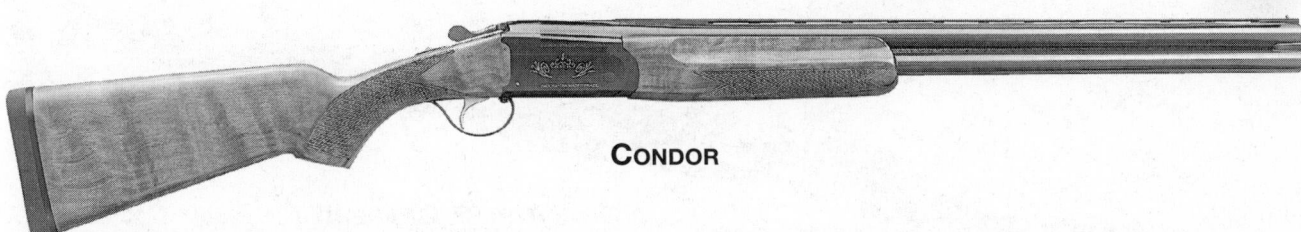

CONDOR

The **STOEGER CONDOR** brings the advantages of the over-under to the shotgunner on a budget. Features include a mechanical single trigger and mechanical extractors. Recessed choke tubes (improved cylinder and modified with 26" barrels, modified and full with 28") give the Condor flexibility. Both 12-ga. and 20-ga. versions handle 3" ammunition and steel shot. Stock and fore-end are made from Brazilian hardwood and have a hand-rubbed oil finish.

Price: $390.00

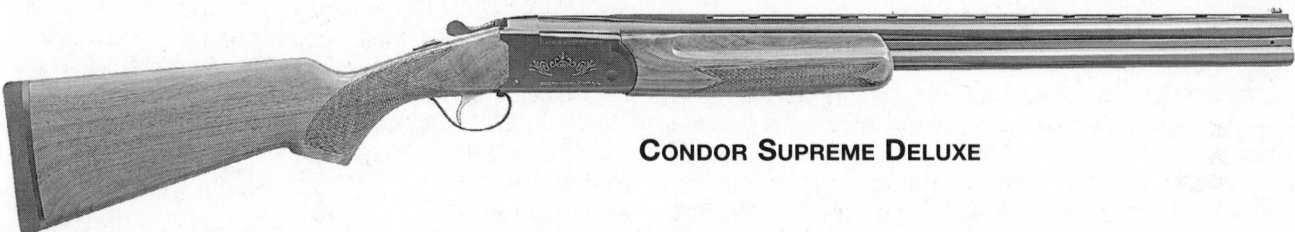

CONDOR SUPREME DELUXE

The **SUPREME DELUXE CONDOR** features a cut checkered American walnut stock with soft rubber recoil pad and high-luster bluing on the barrels. The stepped ventilated rib is fitted with red front and center beads. A single selective trigger and automatic ejectors distinguish this shotgun from the standard model.

Price: $490.00

MODEL 2000

MODEL 2000 DELUXE

The **STOEGER MODEL 2000** shotguns offer an unusual combination of efficient design and old-world craftsmanship to the American shotgunner.

The heart of the gun is an inertia-recoil operating system that offers great reliability with everything from light target ammunition to thumping turkey loads. There's no gas system to clean; the vital parts are all inside the receiver.

Both guns are fitted with ventilated ribs and eye-catching white bar front sights for fast target acquisition. Ventilated rubber recoil pads help dampen the already reduced recoil of the 2000 shotguns.

While the Model 2000 has a checkered American walnut stock and matte finished receiver, the Model 2000 Deluxe adds high grade American walnut to a floral-etched receiver with gold-colored trigger. A vent rib gives the 2000 Deluxe an immediately recognizable profile.

The Model 2000 is available in 12 gauge with 2.75" and 3" screw in chokes. **Barrel length:** 26", 28", 30"

Price: $490.00
　　Deluxe (26" or 28" barrel only) 620.00

See table on page 349 for additional specifications

SHOTGUNS

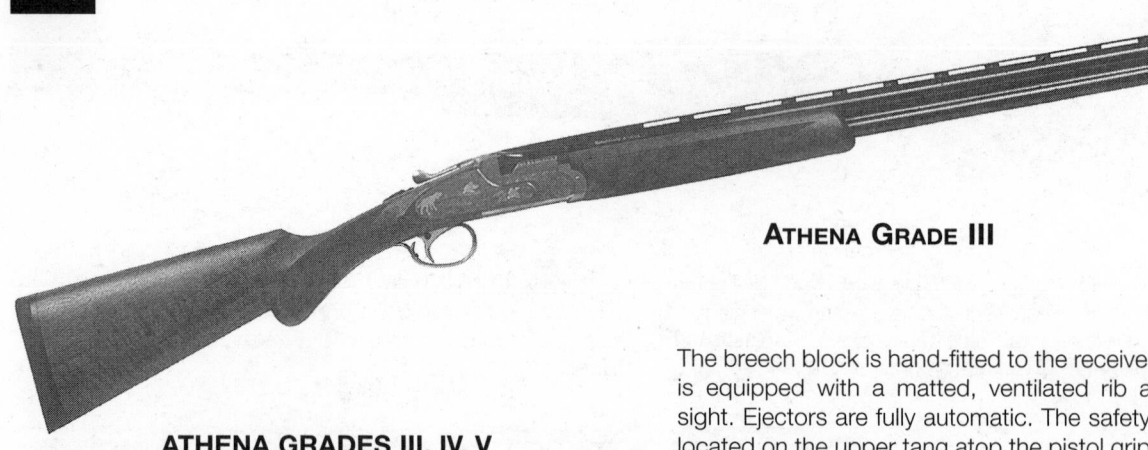

ATHENA GRADE III

ATHENA GRADES III, IV, V

The Athena features a boxlock action and sidelock-type plates with fine floral engraving. The hinge pivots are made of high-strength steel alloy. The locking system employs the Greener crossbolt design. The single selective trigger is mechanically operated, allowing the second barrel to be fired on a subsequent trigger pull, even after a misfire. The selector lever enables you to fire the lower barrel or upper barrel first.

The breech block is hand-fitted to the receiver. Every Athena is equipped with a matted, ventilated rib and bead front sight. Ejectors are fully automatic. The safety is a slide type located on the upper tang atop the pistol grip. Each stock is carved from Claro walnut, with fine-line hand-checkering and high-luster finish.

GRADE III, 12, 20, 28 ga.
GRADE IV + V, 12 or 20 ga.
Prices:

ATHENA GRADE III	$2.089.00
ATHENA GRADE IV	2,499.00
ATHENA GRADE V	2,919.00

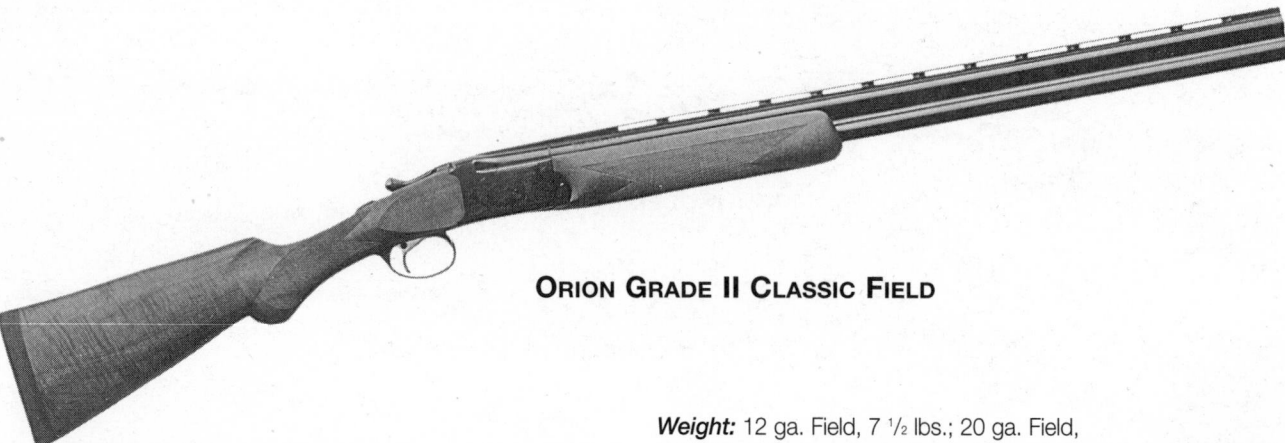

ORION GRADE II CLASSIC FIELD

ORION GRADES I, II & III OVER/UNDERS

For greater versatility, the Orion incorporates the integral multichoke (IMC) system. Available in Extra-full, Full, Modified, Improved Modified, Improved Cylinder and Skeet, the choke tubes fit flush with the muzzle. Three tubes are furnished with each gun. The precision hand-fitted monobloc and receiver are machined from high-strength steel with a highly polished finish. Pistol grip stock and fore-arm are carved of Claro walnut with hand-checkered diamond inlay pattern and high-gloss finish. Chrome-moly steel barrels and the receiver are deeply blued. The Orion also features selective automatic ejectors, single selective trigger, front bead sight and ventilated rib.

Weight: 12 ga. Field, 7 ½ lbs.; 20 ga. Field,
7 ½ lbs.; Trap, 8 lbs. **UPLAND** (12 or 20 ga.) . . . **$1,249.00**

Grade I (12 or 20 Gauge)	1,509.00
Grade II (12, 20, 28 ga.)	1,559.00
Fixed Choke, Field, .410 Gauge	1,559.00
Fixed Choke, Skeet, 12 or 20 Gauge	1,559.00
IMC Multi-Choke, Field, 12, 20 or 28 Gauge	1,559.00
IMC Multi-Choke, Trap, 12 Gauge	1,559.00
Sporting Clays (12 ga.)	
Sporting and Field Sporting	1,719.00
Super Sporting	1,979.00
Grade III	
IMC Multi-Choke, Field, 12 or 20 Gauge	1,876.00
Classic Field	1,876.00
English Field	1,959.00

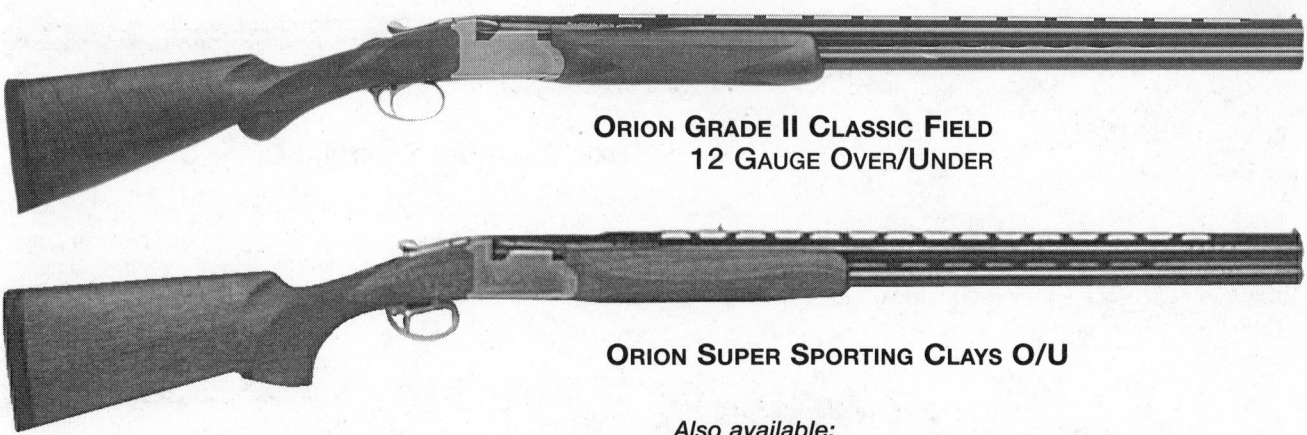

ORION GRADE II CLASSIC FIELD
12 GAUGE OVER/UNDER

ORION SUPER SPORTING CLAYS O/U

Also available:
ORION SUPER SPORTING CLAYS (SSC) O/U 12 Ga.
Barrel Length: 28", 30", 32". Features include Integral Multi-Choke (IMC) system, including five interchangeable screw-in stainless steel Briley choke tubes; Claro walnut stock w/Sporter style pistol grip. **Weight:** 8 lbs.
Price:. $1,979.00

Prices: ORION I. $1,509.00
ORION II CLASSIC FIELD. 1,559.00
ORION II SPORTING CLAYS, FIELD & CLASSIC FIELD . . . 1,719.00
ORION III FIELD & CLASSIC FIELD 1,879.00
ENGLISH FIELD 1,959.00

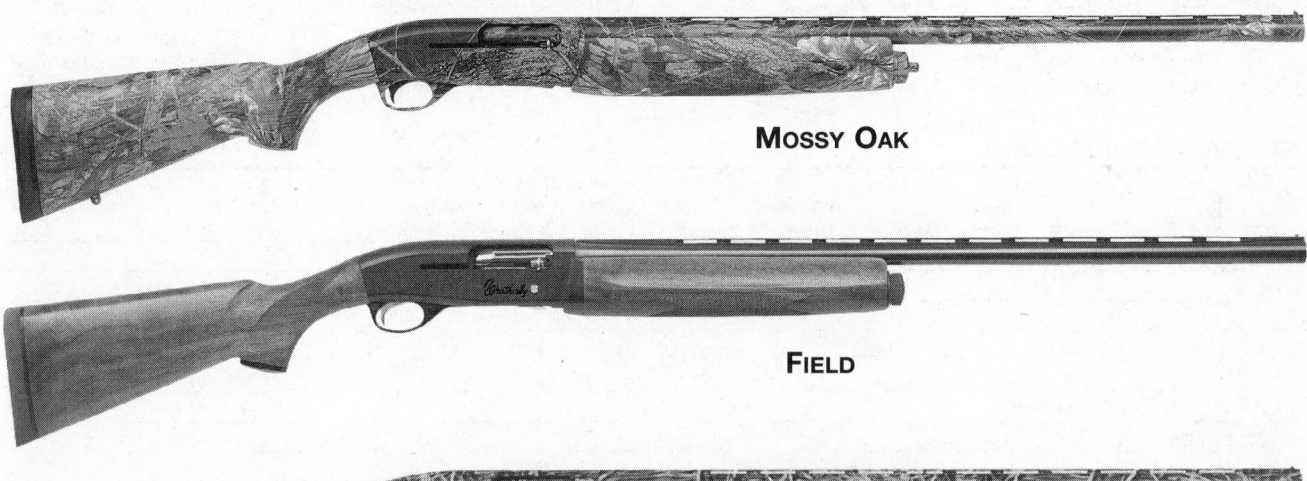

MOSSY OAK

FIELD

SHADOW GRASS

WEATHERBY SAS
SEMI-AUTOMATIC SHOTGUN

Weatherby's SAS autoloader is available in 12 gauge with 26- 28- and 30-inch vent rib barrels, and in 20-gauge with 26- and 28-inch barrels. To allow a wide range of shot patterns, it comes with the Weatherby Integral Multi-Choke (IMC) system, including five interchangeable Briley stainless steel screw-in choke tubes: skeet, improved cylinder, modified, improved modified and full. The self-compensating gas mechanism accommodates light and heavy loads, including 3" magnums. A magazine cutoff makes load changes a snap. The Claro walnut stock is carefully checkered and satin-finished. Synthetic stocks come in black, "Mossy Oak Break-Up" and "Shadow Grass" (12-gauge only). **Weight:** 6.8 to 7.8 lbs.

Price: Field $949.00
Synthetic 979.00
Camo patterns 1,115.00

SHOTGUNS

WINCHESTER SHOTGUNS

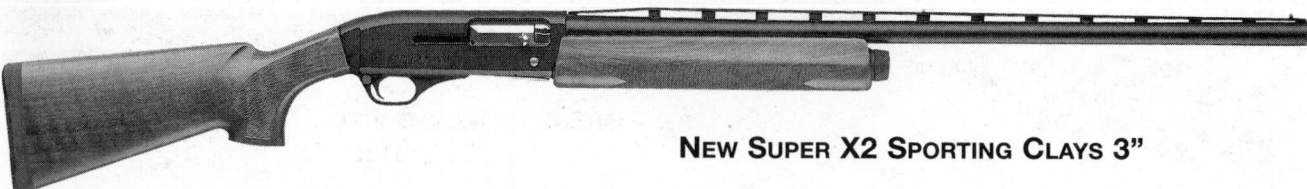

NEW SUPER X2 SPORTING CLAYS 3"

The SX2 Sporting is a hard-working, specialized shotgun with the extra features competitors need: like a specially designed adjustable sporting buttstock and a full selection of sporting choke tubes. Its two supplied gas pistons cover the full range of factory sporting ammo at its extremes with exceptional reliability.

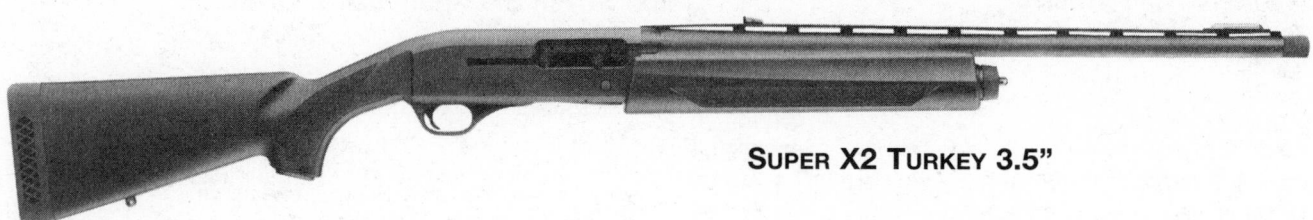

SUPER X2 TURKEY 3.5"

Nothing in turkey hunting is more important than shot placement and pattern density. The Super X2 Magnum 3 1/2" Turkey version has all the handling advantages of the Super X2 design. Like a 24" barrel combined with the short receiver. Center balance holds with greater steadiness and less fatigue.

The back-bored barrel fitted with an extra-full extended choke tube offers extreme pattern density. And the standard 3-dot TRUGLO® fiber optic sights offer an advantage, with more precise shot placement in early morning low-light conditions. And the gas-operated action reduces the kick of recoil.

SUPER X2 SHOTGUNS

Item Number	Gauge	Barrel Length & Type	Chamber	Shotshell Capacity	Choke(s)	Overall Length	Nominal Length Of Pull	Nominal Drop At Comb	Nominal Drop At Heel	Nominal Weight (Lbs.)	Features	Suggested Retail
SUPER X2 SHOTGUNS												
3-1/2" MODELS												
3-1/2" Magnum (Black Synthetic Stock)												
511-001250	12	26	3-1/2 Mag.	5	Invector(3)	47"	14-1/4	1-3/4	2	7-3/4	Studs, VR	$936
511-001246	12	28	3-1/2 Mag.	5	Invector(3)	49"	14-1/4	1-3/4	2	8	Studs, VR	936
3-1/2" NWTF Turkey (Black Synthetic Stock)												
511-022257 NEW	12	24"	3-1/2" Mag.	5	Invector XF	45"	14-1/4"	1-3/4"	2"	7-1/2	Studs, VR, TRUGLO®	997
3-1/2" NWTF Turkey (Mossy Oak Break-Up Camo)												
511-021257 NEW	12	24"	3-1/2" Mag.	5	Invector XF	45"	14-1/4"	1-3/4"	2"	7-1/2	Studs, VR, TRUGLO®	1080
3-1/2" Camo Waterfowl (Mossy Oak Shadow Grass)												
511-003246	12	28"	3-1/2" Mag	5	Invector(3)	49"	14-1/4"	1-3/4"	2"	8	Studs, VR	1080
3" MODELS												
3" Sporting Clays												
511-006446 NEW	12	28"	3" Mag.	5	Invector(SC)	49"	14-3/8"	1-1/2"	2-3/8"	8	VR	$1,206
511-006445 NEW	12	30	3 Mag.	5	Invector(SC)	51	14-3/8	1-1/2	2-3/8	8-1/8	VR	1,206
3" Magnum Field (Walnut Stock)												
511-004350	12	26"	3" Mag.	5	Invector(3)	47"	14-1/4	1-3/4	2"	7-1/4	VR	819
511-004346	12	28	3 Mag.	5	Invector(3)	49	14-1/4	1-3/4	2	7-3/8	VR	819
3" Magnum (Black Synthetic Stock)												
511-001350	12	26"	3" Mag.	5	Invector(3)	47"	14-1/4"	1-3/4"	2"	7-3/4	Studs, VR	819
511-001346	12	28	3 Mag.	5	Invector(3)	49	14-1/4	1-3/4	2	8	Studs, VR	819

WINCHESTER SHOTGUNS

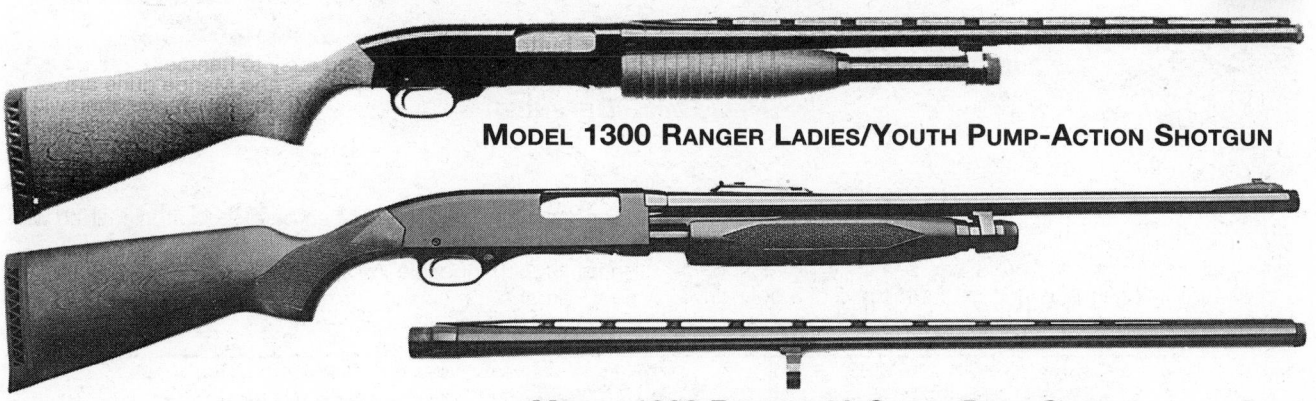

MODEL 1300 RANGER LADIES/YOUTH PUMP-ACTION SHOTGUN

MODEL 1300 RANGER 12 GAUGE DEER COMBO
22" Rifled w/Sights & 28" Vent-Rib Barrels

MODEL 1300 SHOTGUNS

ITEM NUMBER	GA.	BARREL LENGTH & TYPE	CHAMBER	SHOTSHELL CAPACITY	CHOKES	OVERALL LENGTH	NOMINAL LENGTH OF PULL	NOMINAL DROP AT COMB	NOMINAL DROP AT HEEL	NOMINAL WEIGHT (LBS)	U.S. SUGG. RETAIL
FIELD MODELS											
UPLAND											
512-050352	12	24"VR	3" Mag.	5	W3	45"	14"	1-1/2"	2-1/2"	6-3/4	$396
512-050641	20	24"VR	3" Mag.	5	W3	45	14	1-1/2	2-1/2	6-3/4	396
WALNUT FIELD											
512-034329	12	28 VR	3 Mag	5	W3	49	14	1-1/2	2-1/2	7-3/8	396
512-034330	12	26 VR	3 Mag	5	W3	47	14	1-1/2	2-1/2	7-1/8	396
BLACK SHADOW											
512-041303	12	28 VR	3"Mag	5	W1M	49	14	1-1/2	2-1/2	7-1/4	335
512-041307	12	26 VR	3" Mag	5	W1M	47	14	1-1/2	2-1/2	7	335
512-041607	20	26 VR	3" Mag	5	W1M	47	14	1-1/2	2-1/2	6-7/8	335
RANGER MODELS											
RANGER											
512-035239	12	28VR	3"Mag	5	W3	49"	14"	1-1/2"	2-1/2"	7-3/8	349
512-035629	20	28VR	3"Mag	5	W3	49	14	1-1/2	2-1/2	7-1/8	349
RANGER COMPACT											
512-036631	20	22VR	3"Mag	5	W3	42	13	1-1/2	2-3/8	6-5/8	348
512-036532	12	24VR	3"Mag	5	W3	44	13	1-1/2	2-3/8	7	348
TURKEY MODELS											
NWTF BLACK SHADOW TURKEY											
512-013333 *NEW*	12	22"VR	3"Mag	5	WXF	43"	14"	1-1/2"	2-1/2"	6-3/4	346
NWTF TURKEY SUPERFLAUGE											
512-014353 *NEW*	12	22"VR	3"Mag	5	HDXF	43	14	1-1/2	2-1/2	6-3/4	522
NWTF BUCK & TOM SUPERFLAUGE											
512-015334 *NEW*	12	22 Smooth	3"Mag	5	RS/HDXF	43	14	1-1/2	2-1/2	6-3/4	499
DEER MODELS											
DEER BLACK SHADOW											
512-040320	12	22 Smooth	3"Mag	5	W1C	43"	14"	1-1/2"	2-1/2"	6-3/4	334
512-040315	12	22 Rifled	3"Mag	5	Rifled Barrel	42-3/4	14	1-1/2	2-1/2	6-3/4	359
512-040615	20	22 Rifled	3"Mag	5	Rifled Barrel	42-3/4	14	1-1/2	2-1/2	6-1/2	359
DEER BLACK SHADOW WITH CANTILEVER SCOPE MOUNT											
512-040340	12	22 Rifled	3"Mag	5	Rifled Barrel	42-3/4	14	1-1/8	2-3/4***	7	400
DEER BLACK SHADOW COMBO											
512-042326	12	22 Rifled	3"Mag	5	Rifled Barrel	42-3/4	14	1-1/2	2-1/2	6-3/4	433
(includes)	12	28 VR	3"Mag	5	W3	49	14	1-1/2	2-1/	7-3/8	
DEER RANGER COMPACT											
512-036615	20	22 Rifled	3"Mag	5	Rifled Barrel	42-3/4	13	1-1/2	2-3/8	6-5/8	371

Includes one shotshell in chamber. For Model 1300 Feature & Choke and Barrel Abbreviations see following page.

SHOTGUNS

NEW CAMP DEFENDER

MODEL 1300 NEW CAMP DEFENDER

The new Camp Defender is a multi-purpose camp gun for the occasional grouse around camp, family protection, or even as a quick handling slug gun at the end of a deer drive.

Features a rugged, dark-stained hardwood stock. Fitted with fully adjustable open sights. Eight shot total capacity 22" barrel. Interchangeable WinChoke system for versatile buckshot, birdshot or slug performance.

SPECIFICATIONS MODEL 1300 DEFENDER

SUGGESTED RETAIL	GAUGE	BARREL LENGTH & TYPE	CHAMBER	SHOTSHELL CAPACITY*	CHOKE	OVERALL LENGTH	NOMINAL LENGTH OF PULL	NOMINAL DROP AT COMB	NOMINAL DROP AT HEEL	NOMINAL WEIGHT (LBS.)	FEATURES
SYNTHETIC PISTOL GRIP, 8 SHOT											
$326	12	18	3" Mag.	8	Cyl.	29-1/8	—	—	—	5-1/2	Studs, MBF
SYNTHETIC STOCK, 8 SHOT											
$326	12	18	3" MAG.	8	Cyl..	39-1/2	14	1-1/2	2-1/2	6-3/8	Studs, Truglo
326	20	18	3" MAG.	8	Cyl.	39-1/2	14	1-1/2	2-1/2	6-1/4	Studs, Truglo
STAINLESS MARINE SYNTHETIC STOCK											
$518	12	18	3" Mag.	7	Cyl.	39-1/2	14	1-1/2	2-1/2	6-3/8	Studs, MBF
CAMP DEFENDER											
$373	12	22	3" Mag.	8	W/C.	42-3/4	14	1-1/2	2-1/2	6-7/8	Studs, Rifle Sights

Model 1300 Feature Abbreviations: *MBF=Metal bead front, Rifle=Rifle type front and rear sights. Rifle sights=Adjustable rear sight and ramp style front sight.*
SB=Scope Bases Included. B&R=Scope, Bases and Rings included. D&T=Drilled and tapped to accept scope bases. Studs=Buttstock and magazine cap sling studs provided
VR=Ventilated rib. W3W=WinChoke, Extra Full, Full and Modified Tubes. W3=WinChoke, Full, Modified and Improved Cylinder Tubes.
Cyl.=Non-WinChoke, choked Cylinder Bore. WIM=Modified Tube. WIC=Cylinder Choke Tube. WF=Full Choke Tube. WXF=Extra Full Choke Tube. Smooth=Non-Rifled Bore.

NEW MODEL 9410 SHOTGUN

LEVER ACTION NEW MODEL 9410 SHOTGUN

At first glance it looks like a Model 94 rifle. But it's a shotgun inside: fitted with a smoothbore 24" barrel and chambered to handle all current factory 2-1/2" .410 bore shotgun loads, including Foster-type rifled slugs. With a variety of shotshells and slugs available today, the Model 9410 may be the most versatile combination gun ever. The unique sight system features an easy-to-

align TRUGLO front sight combined with a modified shallow "V" adjustable rear sight. The rear sight offers a clearer field of view for fast, shotgun-style shooting. The walnut straight-grip stock and traditional forearm ensures fast handling and pointability. The tubular magazine provides 9 shots at the ready.
Price: $531.00

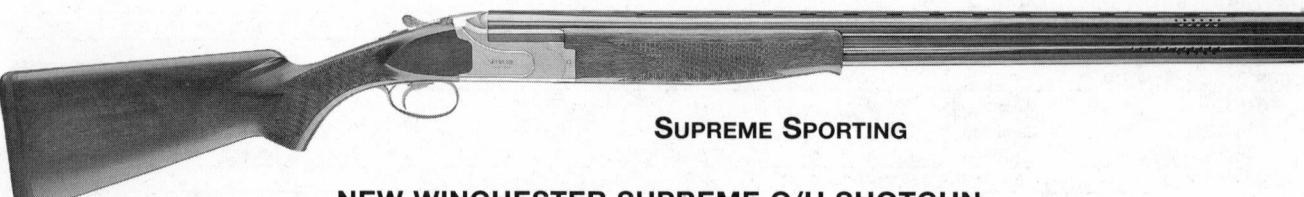

SUPREME SPORTING

NEW WINCHESTER SUPREME O/U SHOTGUN

Tapered locking lugs between the barrels reduce the bulk of this over/under without sacrificing strength. Back-bored barrels with Invector Plus chokes ensure uniform patterns. Chromed chambers, vent rib, checkered walnut stock are standard. Choose from Field or Sporting Models, both with

barrel selector on the safety. Field Model is bored for 3" shells; sporting model has a competition trigger, ported barrels.
Prices:
FIELD $1,383.00
SPORTING 1,551.00

Handguns

FIREARMS DISASSEMBLY WITH EXPLODED VIEWS

by John A. Karns & John E. Traister

A comprehensive reference guide to the disassembly of selected handguns, rifles and shotguns. General specifications, trouble shooting charts and special considerations unique to each firearm assure the reader a properly reassembled firearm.

*For addresses and phone/fax numbers of manufacturers and distributors included in this section, please turn to **DIRECTORY OF MANUFACTURERS AND SUPPLIERS** on page 557.*

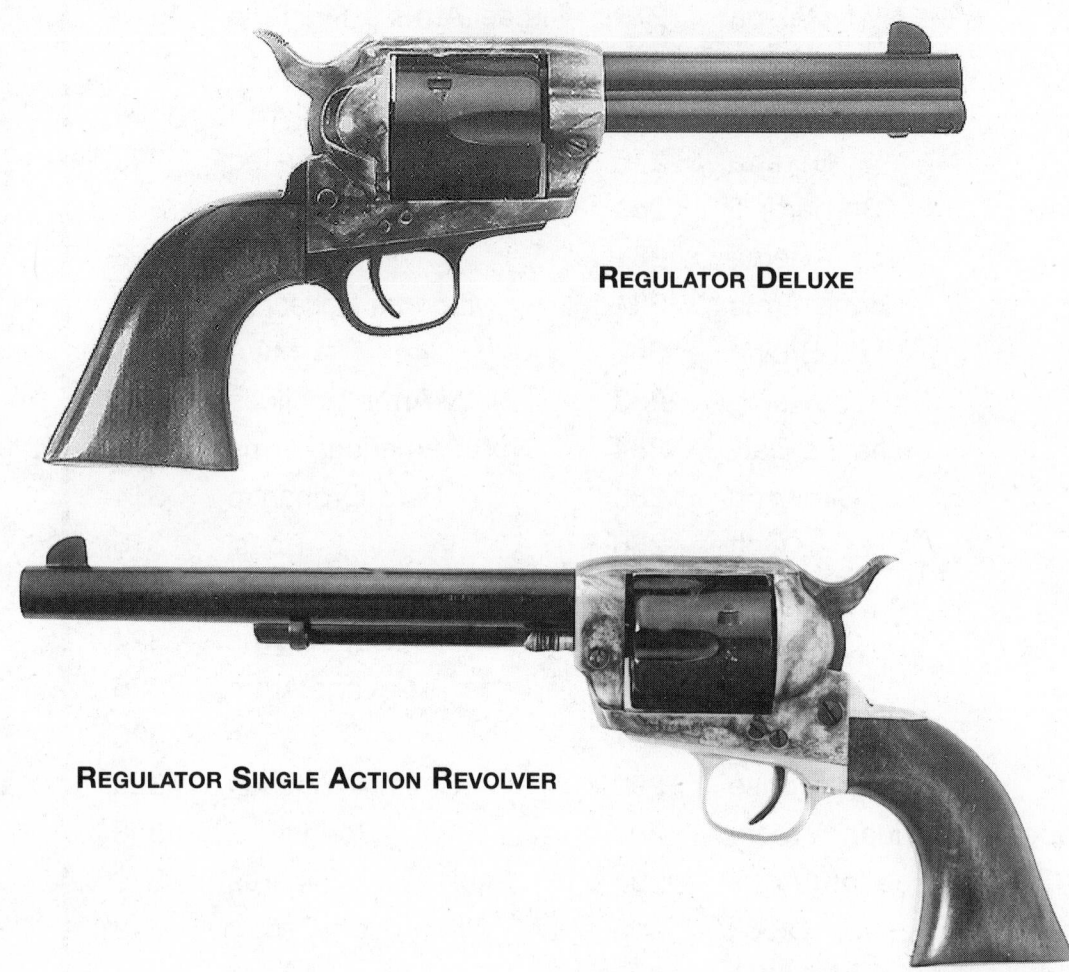

REGULATOR DELUXE

REGULATOR SINGLE ACTION REVOLVER

REGULATOR DELUXE

SPECIFICATIONS

Caliber: 45LC *Barrel Length:* 4.25" or 5.5"
Features: Blued steel backstrap and trigger guard; hammer block safety;
Price: $365.00

REGULATOR SINGLE ACTION

SPECIFICATIONS

Calibers: 45 Long Colt, 357 Mag.
Barrel Length: 4.75", 5.5" and 7.5"
Overall Length: 8 1/16"
Weight: 2 lb. 3 oz. (4.75" barrel)
Sights: Fixed
Safety: Hammer block
Features: Brass trigger guard and backstrap
Price: $320.00

MATEBA AUTO REVOLVER (not shown)

This firearm incorporates the fast function of a semi-auto pistol with the reliability of a revolver. When fired, the cylinder and slide assembly move back and the recoil causes the cylinder to rotate. The speed of firing is comparable to a semi-auto pistol. Low recoil allows the shooter to stay "on target." May be fired single action or double action.

SPECIFICATIONS

Caliber: 357
Capacity: 6 rounds
Overall Length: 8.77"
Barrel Length: 4"
Weight: 2.75 lbs.
Features: The mateba has an all blue finish, solid steel alloy frame and walnut grips
Price: $1,295.00
6" barrel 1,349.00
8" barrel 1,380.00

AMERICAN DERRINGER PISTOLS

MODEL 4

MODEL 4 STAINLESS STEEL DOUBLE DERRINGER

SPECIFICATIONS
Calibers: 45 Colt and 3" .410 **Capacity:** 2 shots
Barrel Length: 4.1" **Overall Length:** 6" **Weight:** 16.5 oz.
Finish: Satin or high-polish stainless steel
Price: $425.00
Also available:
In 357 Mag.. .... 410.00
   357 Maximum 415.00
In 45-70, both barrels 560.00
In 44 Mag. w/oversized grips 515.00
   45 Colt 410.00
   45 Automatic 415.00
MODEL M-4 ALASKAN SURVIVAL
   in 45-70/45-.410, 45-70/45 Colt 475.00
LADY DERRINGER (Stainless Steel Double)
38 Special 360.00
32 Mag. 375.00
357 Mag. 405.00
45 Colt, 45/410 .... 435.00

AMT/GALENA INDUSTRIES, INC.

Autoloading Pistols

22 AUTOMAG II RIMFIRE MAGNUM

The only production semiautomatic handgun in this caliber, the Automag II is ideal for the small-game hunter or shooting enthusiast who wants more power and accuracy in a light, trim handgun. The pistol features a bold open-slide design and employs a unique gas-channeling system for smooth, trouble-free action.

SPECIFICATIONS
Caliber: 22 Rimfire Magnum **Barrel lengths:** 3 3/8", 4.5" or 6" **Magazine capacity:** 9 shots (4.5" & 6"), 7 shots (3 3/8")
Weight: 32 oz. (6"), 30 oz. (4.5"), 24 oz. (3 3/8") **Sights:** Adjustable 3-dot **Finish:** Stainless steel **Features:** Squared trigger guard; grooved carbon fiber grips; gas channeling system
Price: $375.00

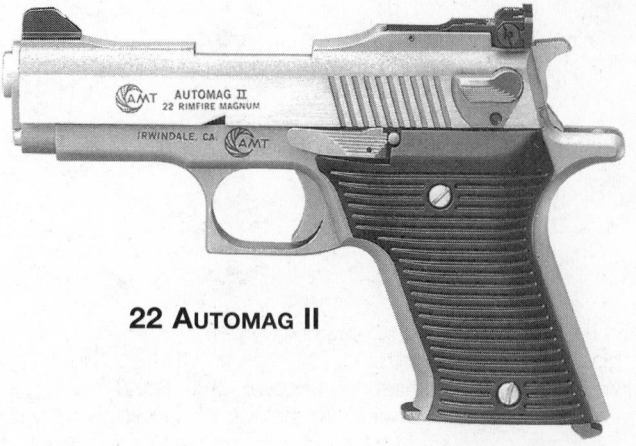

22 AUTOMAG II

AUTOMAG IV

A long-barreled, stainless-steel, single-action autoloader with more power than the familiar 1911 .45 ACP. The Automag IV is built to maintain a high level of accuracy during tough use.

SPECIFICATIONS
Caliber: 45 Win. Mag. **Capacity:** 7 shots
Barrel length: 6.5" **Overall length:** 10.5"
Weight: 46 oz. **Sights:** Adjustable
Grips: Carbon fiber **Finish:** Stainless steel
Price: $648.00

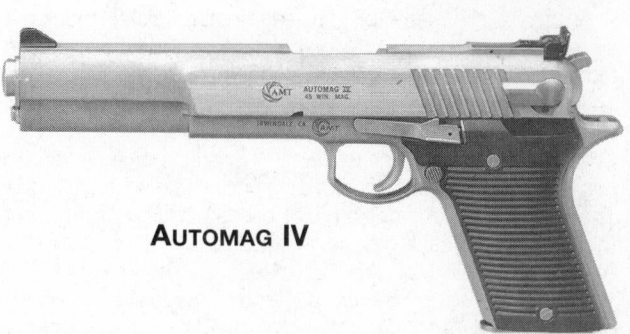

AUTOMAG IV

HANDGUNS

Handguns

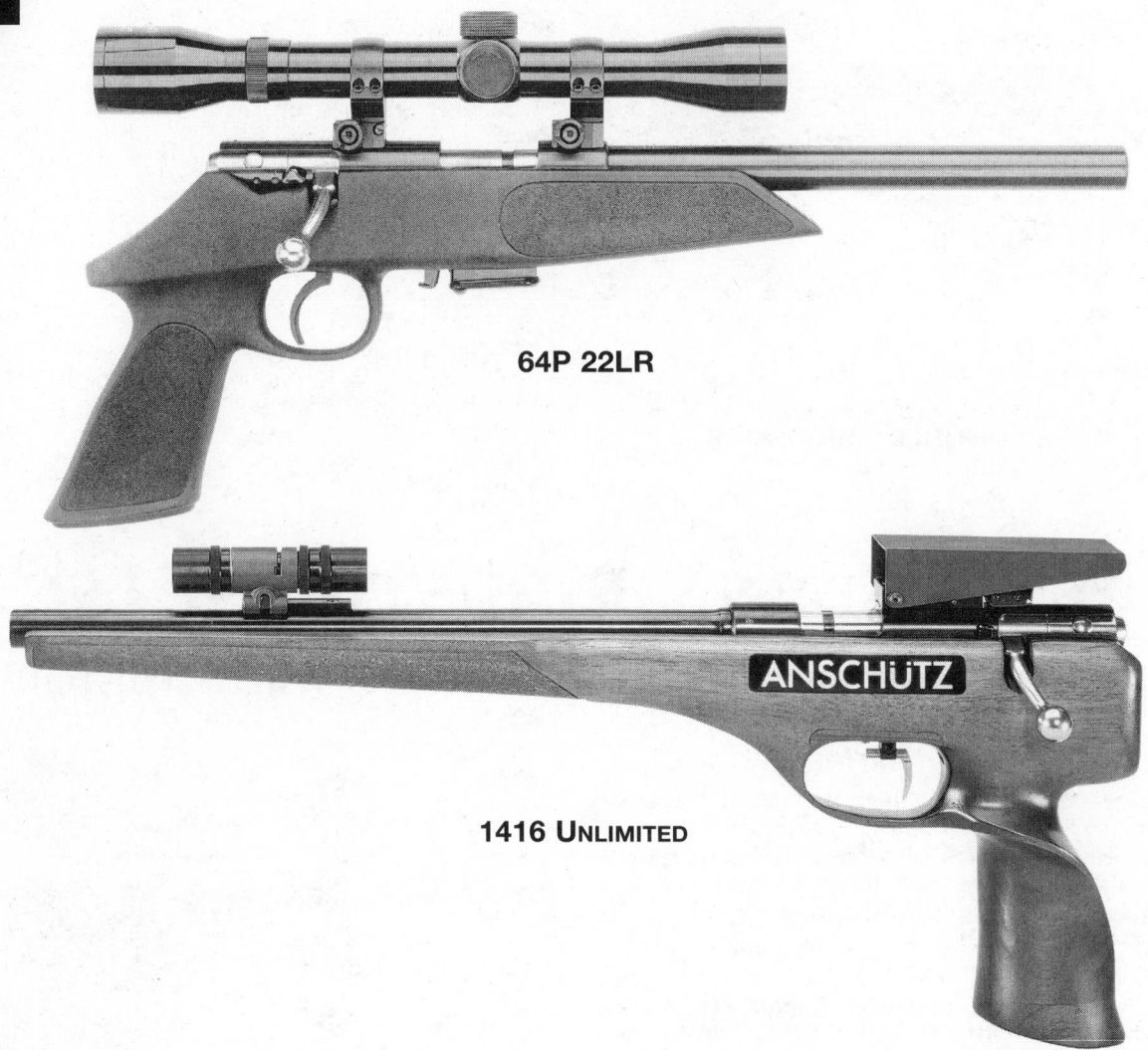

64P 22LR

1416 UNLIMITED

J.G. Anschutz began as a company in 1856, making pistols, rifles and shotguns. Since its rebirth following World War II, the firm has been best known for its fine rimfire target rifles. But there is also a line of bolt-action target pistols with the same features that have put Anschutz rifles in the winner's circle more often than any other rimfires in recent times.

Anschutz silhouette pistols feature a precisely machined single-shot action with left-side bolt handle and fully adjustable trigger (the blade can be moved longitudinally too). The Model 1416 MSP E "Unlimited" has a 14.1-inch barrel and full stock with wide thumb rest and stippling for a better hold in the Creedmoor position. The available Anschutz rear sight (#6836) has click adjustments of .035mm and a folding sight cover. The available front sight (#6523) has an anti-glare tube and three interchangeable inserts. Pistol weight: 14.1 pounds.

A shorter version of the "Unlimited" is the 1416 MSP E "Production" with 9.8-inch barrel that accelerates match-grade .22 bullets to just under the speed of sound. Avoiding the sound barrier helps ensure the greatest bullet stability and best accuracy. *Pistol weight:* 3.7 pounds.

The centerfire Anschutz Model 1730 MSP E Field is like the 1416 models in that its trigger is directly below the loading platform, for fine balance. The receiver is grooved, drilled and tapped for scope mounts. The adjustable trigger and grip of this pistol are like those of the 1416s. With its 9.4-inch barrel, the Model 1730 weighs 3.9 pounds.

Prices:
1416 MSP E Unlimited **$1,095.00**
1416 MSP E Production **1,095.00**
1730 MSP E Field (not shown). **1,140.00**
Anschutz also offers bolt-action repeating pistols on a 64-type action with a right-hand bolt and 9.8-inch barrels. Both the .22 Long Rifle and .22 Magnum versions are grooved, drilled and tapped for scopes. *Pistol weights:* 3.5 pounds.
Prices: 64 P .22 LR. **$375.00**
64 P .22 WMR. **395.00**

AUTO-ORDNANCE 1911A1 "WWII PARKERIZED"

SPECIFICATIONS
MODEL 1911PKZ
Caliber: .45 ACP
Barrel: 5"
Length: 8.5" overall
Weight: 39 oz.
Sights: Blade front, rear drift adj. for windage
Grip: Brown checkered plastic
Mag. Capacity: 7-shot
Price: $462.00

1911PKZ

AUTO-ORDNANCE 1911A1 "STANDARD"

SPECIFICATIONS
MODEL T1911
Caliber: .45 ACP
Barrel: 5"
Length: 8.5" overall
Weight: 39 oz.
Sights: Blade front, rear drift adj. for windage
Grip: Brown checkered plastic with medallion
Mag. Capacity: 7-shot
Price: $447.00

T1911

AUTO-ORDNANCE 1911A1 "DELUXE"

SPECIFICATIONS
MODEL 1911WGS
Caliber: .45 ACP
Barrel: 5"
Length: 8.5" overall
Weight: 39 oz.
Sights: Hi-profile 3 white dot system
Grip: Black textured, rubber wrap-around with medallion
Mag. Capacity: 7-shot
Prices: $455.00

1911WGS

• *All models have a one year warranty*

HANDGUNS

Compact Frame Cougar Pistols

MODEL 8000 (9mm) MODEL 8040 (40 CAL.) MODEL 8045 (45 ACP)

Beretta's 8000/8040/8045 Cougar Series semiautomatics use a proven locked-breech system with a rotating barrel. This design makes the pistol compact and easy to conceal and operate with today's high-powered 9mm, 40 cal. and 45 ACP cal. ammunition. When the pistol is fired, the initial thrust of recoil energy is partially absorbed as it pushes slide and barrel back, with the barrel rotating by cam action against a tooth on the rigid central block. When the barrel has turned 30 degrees, the locking lugs on the barrel clear the locking recesses, freeing the slide to continue rearward. The recoil spring absorbs the remaining recoil energy as the slide extracts and ejects the spent casing, rotates the hammer, and then reverses direction to chamber the next round. The Cougar reduces felt recoil by channeling part of the recoil energy into barrel rotation and by partially absorbing the barrel and slide recoil shock through the central block before it is transferred to the frame.

SPECIFICATIONS
Calibers: 9mm, 40 S&W, 45 ACP
Capacity: 10 rounds (8 rounds in 45 ACP)
Action: Double/Single or Double Action only
Barrel length: 3.6"
Overall length: 7"
Weight: 32.6 oz.
Overall height: 5.5"
Sight radius: 5.2"
Sights: Front and rear sights dovetailed to slide
Finish: Bruniton/Plastic
Features: Firing-pin block; chrome-lined barrel; short recoil, rotating barrel; anodized aluminum alloy frame
Prices:
Double or Single action (9mm and 40 cal.) $709.00
Double action only (45 ACP) 739.00
Double or Single action (45 ACP) 764.00
Also Available:
  8357 Cougar F,
  357 Sig Double or Single Action 709.00

**MODEL 8000/8040
COUGAR**

**MODEL 8040
MINI-COUGAR**

MODEL 8000/8040/8045 MINI-COUGAR
SPECIFICATIONS
Caliber: 9mm and 40 S&W, 45 ACP
Capacity: 8 rounds
Action: Double/Single
or Double Action only
Barrel length: 3.6"
Weight: 27.6 oz. (9mm); 27.4 oz. (40 S&W)
Features: One inch shorter in the grip than the standard Cougar
Prices:
Double or Single actions (9mm & 40 cal.) $709.00
Double action only (45 ACP) 739.00
Double or single action (45 ACP) 739.00

92G, 96G ELITE

BERETTA ELITE PISTOLS

The new Elite pistols were developed to meet the specific requirements of action shooting, personal defense, and law enforcement agencies. Elite pistols feature the recontoured slide and removable front sight of the Brigadier. The barrel is stainless steel, and slightly shorter (4.7") for compactness. The beveled magazine well facilitates rapid reloading while the rubber magazine base protects the magazine if it is dropped. Front and rear side serrations provide a sure grip for fast, easy racking of the slide, and the skeletonized hammer reduces lock time. The lanyard loop has no ring. Beretta Elite models are available only in the G configuration. The G models differ from FS models in that the hammer drop lever does not function as a traditional safety. When the lever is released, after having been activated to lower

the hammer, it automatically returns to the ready-to-fire position. The Elite II has stainless slide and barrel, front and backstrap checkering, low profile Novak sights.

Prices: 92G Elite (9mm) **$776.00**
96G Elite (40 S+W) **776.00**
92G Elite II (9mm) **874.00**
96G Elite II (40 S+W) **874.00**

9000S TYPE F

BERETTA 9000S SERIES

The new compact Beretta 9000S pistols are distinguished by their light weight and potent calibers (9mm and .40 S & W), making them comfortable and practical carry guns. The high magazine capacity (12 rounds in 9 mm, 10 rounds in .40 S & W) makes the 9000S pistols ideally suited for personal defense and the law enforcement profession.

The frame is manufactured with a fiberglass reinforced technopolymer incorporating two special steel alloy rail inserts that guarantee perfect slide-to-frame fit and the optimal tilt barrel movement during the locking and unlocking phases. The innovative locking system consists of a unique tilt-barrel, open-slide design. The two strong barrel locking lugs engage the slide directly.

The grips are made of a high-tech soft polymer, overmolded onto the frame. This durable and wear-resistant material absorbs vibrations and ensures a firm grip even in adverse weather conditions.

All 9000S models feature an automatic firing pin block that prevents the gun from firing in case of inadvertent drops or strikes against hard surfaces. It is de-activated only when the trigger is pulled back.

The type F models come in double or single action, while the type D is only available in double action.

Prices:
9000S Type D, 9mm or 40 S&W **$551.00**
9000S Type F, 9mm or 40 S&W **551.00**

HANDGUNS

Small Frame Pistols

MODEL 3032 TOMCAT

SPECIFICATIONS
Caliber: 32 Auto
Capacity: 7-shot magazine
Barrel length: 2.45"
Overall length: 4.9"
Weight: 14 1/2 oz.
Sights: Blade front, drift-adjustable rear
Features: Double or single action, thumb safety, tip-up barrel for direct loading/unloading, blued or matte finish
Prices:
Matte/Plastic $340.00
Blued/Plastic 370.00
Stainless/Plastic 418.00
Titanium/Plastic 572.00

MODEL 3032 TOMCAT

MODEL 21 BOBCAT DA SEMIAUTOMATIC

A safe, dependable, accurate small-bore pistol in 22 LR or 25 Auto. Easy to load with its unique barrel tip-up system.

SPECIFICATIONS
Caliber: 22 LR or 25 ACP
Magazine capacity: 7 rounds
(22 LR); 8 rounds (25 ACP)
Overall length: 4.9"
Barrel length: 2.4"
Weight: 11.5 oz. (25 ACP); 11.8 oz. (22 LR)
Sights: Blade front: V-notch rear
Safety: Thumb operated
Grips: Plastic or Walnut
Frame: Forged aluminum
Prices:
Matte/Plastic $252.00
Blued/Plastic 285.00
Stainless/Plastic 307.00

MODEL 21 BOBCAT

MODEL 950 JETFIRE
SINGLE-ACTION SEMIAUTOMATIC

SPECIFICATIONS
Calibers: 25 ACP
Barrel length: 2.4"
Overall length: 4.7"
Overall height: 3.4"
Safety: External, thumb-operated
Magazine capacity: 8 rounds
Sights: Blade front; V-notch rear
Weight: 9.9 oz.
Frame: Forged aluminum.
Prices:
Matte/Plastic $226.00
Stainless/Plastic 267.00

MODEL 950 JETFIRE

MODEL 84 CHEETAH

This pistol is pocket size with a large magazine capacity. The first shot (with hammer down, chamber loaded) can be fired by a double-action pull on the trigger without cocking the hammer manually.

The pistol also features a positive thumb safety (designed for both right- and left-handed operation), quick take-down (by means of special takedown button) and a conveniently located magazine release. Black plastic grips. Wood grips extra.

SPECIFICATIONS

Caliber: 380 Auto (9mm Short).
Magazine capacity: 10 rounds.
Barrel length: 3.8". (approx.)
Overall length: 6.8". (approx.)
Weight: 23.3 oz. (approx.).
Sights: Fixed front; rear dovetailed to slide.
Height overall: 4.85" (approx.).
Prices: Bruniton/Plastic $576.00
Nickel/Wood 652.00

MODEL 84 CHEETAH

MODEL 85 CHEETAH (not shown)

Some basic specifications as the model 84 Cheetah, except has a single line 8-round magazine, ambidextrous safety.
Prices: Bruniton/Plastic $545.00
Nickel/Wood 609.00
Also available:
MODEL 87 in 22 LR.
Capacity: 7 rounds. Straight blow-back open slide design.
Width: 1.3". *Barrel length:* 3.8"
Overall length: 6.8". *Overall height:* 4.7"
Weight: 20.1 oz. *Finish:* Blued with wood
Price: $576.00

MODEL 86 CHEETAH

SPECIFICATIONS

Caliber: 380 Auto (9mm Short).
Barrel length: 4.4". *Overall length:* 7.3"
Capacity: 8 rounds. *Weight:* 23.3 oz.
Sight radius: 4.9". *Overall height:* 4.8"
Overall width: 1.4". *Grip:* Walnut
Features: Same as other Medium Frame, straight blow-back models, plus the safety and convenience of a tip-up barrel (rounds can be loaded directly into chamber without operating the slide).
Price: Bruniton/Wood Grips $578.00

MODEL 86 CHEETAH

MODEL 87 TARGET

SPECIFICATIONS

Caliber: 22 LR. *Capacity:* 10 rounds.
Barrel length: 5.9" *Overall length:* 8.9"
Weight: 40.9 oz. *Finish:* Blued with plastic
Price: $669.00

MODEL 87 TARGET

HANDGUNS

Large Frame 92/96 Series Pistols

**MODELS 92FS (9mm)
& 96 (40 Cal.)**

MODEL 92FS COMPACT

MODELS 92FS (9MM) & 96 (40 CAL.)
SPECIFICATIONS
Calibers: 9mm and 40 cal.
Capacity: 10 rounds   *Action:* Double/Single
Barrel length: 4.9"   *Overall length:* 8.5"
Weight: 34.4 oz.   *Overall height:* 5.4"
Overall width: 1.5"   *Sights:* Integral front; windage
adjustable rear; 3-dot or tritium night sights
Grips: Wood or plastic
Finish: Bruniton (also available in blued, stainless,
silver or gold)
Features: Chrome-lined bore; visible firing-pin block; open
slide design; safety drop catch (half-cock); combat trigger
guard; external hammer; reversible magazine release
MODEL BRIGADIER (9mm and 40 cal.). Same as above but
with a heavier slide.*Barrel length:* 4.3". *Overall length:*
7.8". *Weight:* 35.3 oz.
MODEL 92 COMPACT L TYPE M (9mm)
Barrel length: 4.3" *Overall length:* 7.8" *Weight:* 30.9 oz.

MODEL 96 COMBAT
SPECIFICATIONS
Calibers: 40 S&W   *Capacity:* 11 rounds
Action: Single action only (Combat); single/double (Stock)
Barrel length: 5.9"   *Overall length:* 9.5"
Weight: 40 oz.   *Sights:* 3 interchageable front sights (Stock)
Features: Rubber magazine bumpers; replaceable accuriz-
ing barrel bushings; checkered grips; machine-checkered
front and backstraps; fitted ABS cases; Brigadier slide;
extended frame-mounted safety; competition-tuned trigger
and adjustable rear target set and tool set
Prices:
MODEL 96 COMBAT (single action only) $1,735.00
MODEL 96 BRIGADIER (heavy slide and removable
   front sight, 35 oz.) 716.00
MODEL 96 BRIGADIE STAINLESS 771.00
MODEL 96 COMPACT (32 oz.) 669.00
MODEL 96 COMPACT STAINLESS 734.00

MODEL 92FS COMPACT
AND COMPACT TYPE M
SPECIFICATIONS
Same features as the proven 92FS but in a more compact
overall size and weight. *Overall length:* 7.8" *Barrel
length:* 4.3" *Overall width:* 1.4" *Overall height:* 5.3"
Sight radius: 5.8" *Weight:* 32.0 oz. Compact, 30.9 oz.
Type M (unloaded). A special contoured magazine bottom
improves hand support and control. The Compact 92FS
features a double column magazine, while the Compact
Type M features a single column magazine for thinner grip
(1.28" instead of 1.39") and reduced weight.
Prices: MODEL 92 COMPACT $669.00
MODEL 92 COMPACT STAINLESS 734.00
MODEL 92FS PLASTIC w/3-Dot sights 669.00
MODEL 92FS Stainless w/3-dot sights 734.00
MODEL 96 w/3-dot sights 669.00
MODEL 96 STAINLESS 734.00
MODEL 92FS BRIGADIER 716.00
MODEL 92FS BRIGADIER STAINLESS 771.00
MODEL 92 TYPE M .669.00
MODEL 92 TYPE M STAINLESS 721.00
MODEL 92FS LIMITED EDITION 2,082.00
   (1 of 470, polished stainless, walnut grips, chrome-
   plated magazine)

MODEL 96 COMBAT

BERNARDELLI PISTOLS

MODEL P.010
TARGET

MODEL P.010 TARGET PISTOL

SPECIFICATIONS
Caliber: 22 LR *Capacity:* 5 or 10 rounds *Barrel length:* 5.9" *Weight:* 40 oz. *Sights:* Interchangeable front sight; rear sight adjustable for windage and elevation *Sight radius:* 7.5" *Features:* All steel construction; external hammer with safety notch; external slide catch for hold-open device; inertia safe firing pin; oil-finished walnut grips for right- and left-hand shooters; matte black or chrome finish; pivoted trigger with adjustable weight and take-ups
Price: $899.00

BERSA PISTOLS

THUNDER 380

THUNDER 380

SPECIFICATIONS
Caliber: 380 ACP
Capacity: 7 rounds
Barrel length:
3.5" *Overall length:* 6 $\frac{5}{8}$"
Weight: 23 oz.
Sights: Notched-bar dovetailed rear; blade integral with slide front
Safety: Manual firing pin
Grips: Black polymer
Finish: Blue, satin nickel.
Prices: Matte $248.95
Satin Nickel 264.95
9-Shot Deluxe 291.95

BOND ARMS

**450 BOND
SUPER DEFENDER**

450 BOND SUPER DEFENDER

SPECIFICATIONS
Barrel Length: 3" *Weight:* 21 oz. *Length:* 5"
Features: Custom grip, crossbolt safety, interchangeable barrels, retracting firing pin, rebounding hammer, stainless steel, blade front sight
Prices:
SUPER DEFENDER $349.00
CENTURY 2000 DEFENDER 369.00
TEXAS DEFENDER 349.00
COWBOY DEFENDER 349.00
ADDITIONAL BARRELS 119.00

HANDGUNS

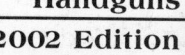

CLASS A LIMITED

CLASSIC CUSTOM

ED BROWN CLASS A LIMITED

The Class A Limited is highly customizable, with nearly limitless combinations of options and calibers. You can virtually build whatever you want. This gun is the perfect all-round companion for carry use, tactical use, or for practical competition. You can order a 4.25" Commander Bobtail which is great for concealed carry, a no-nonsense "FBI type" practical pistol for IDPA competitions or self-defense, a full race 40 S&W USPSA Limited competition gun with a bull barrel, or even a hunting handgun with 6" slide. The slide has square cut finger serrations in the rear only, is polished to a 400 grit finish, and has a rounded, coarse glass bead finished top sighting surface to eliminate glare.

Standard equipment includes all Ed Brown premium components including Ambidextrous safety, Memory Groove Beavertail grip safety, cross dovetail front sight, 30 LPI checkered forestrap and mainspring housing, 40 LPI checkered magazine catch, Commander style slotted hammer, Ed Brown premium match grade barrel, 7-round magazine, Novak LMC fixed rear sight buried deep into the slide, and Hogue exotic checkered wood grips with Ed Brown Products logo. All Ed Brown Hardcore parts are used where applicable. All parts are completely hand-fitted to a custom made, exclusive Ed Brown slide and frame, utilizing all Ed Brown custom internal components.

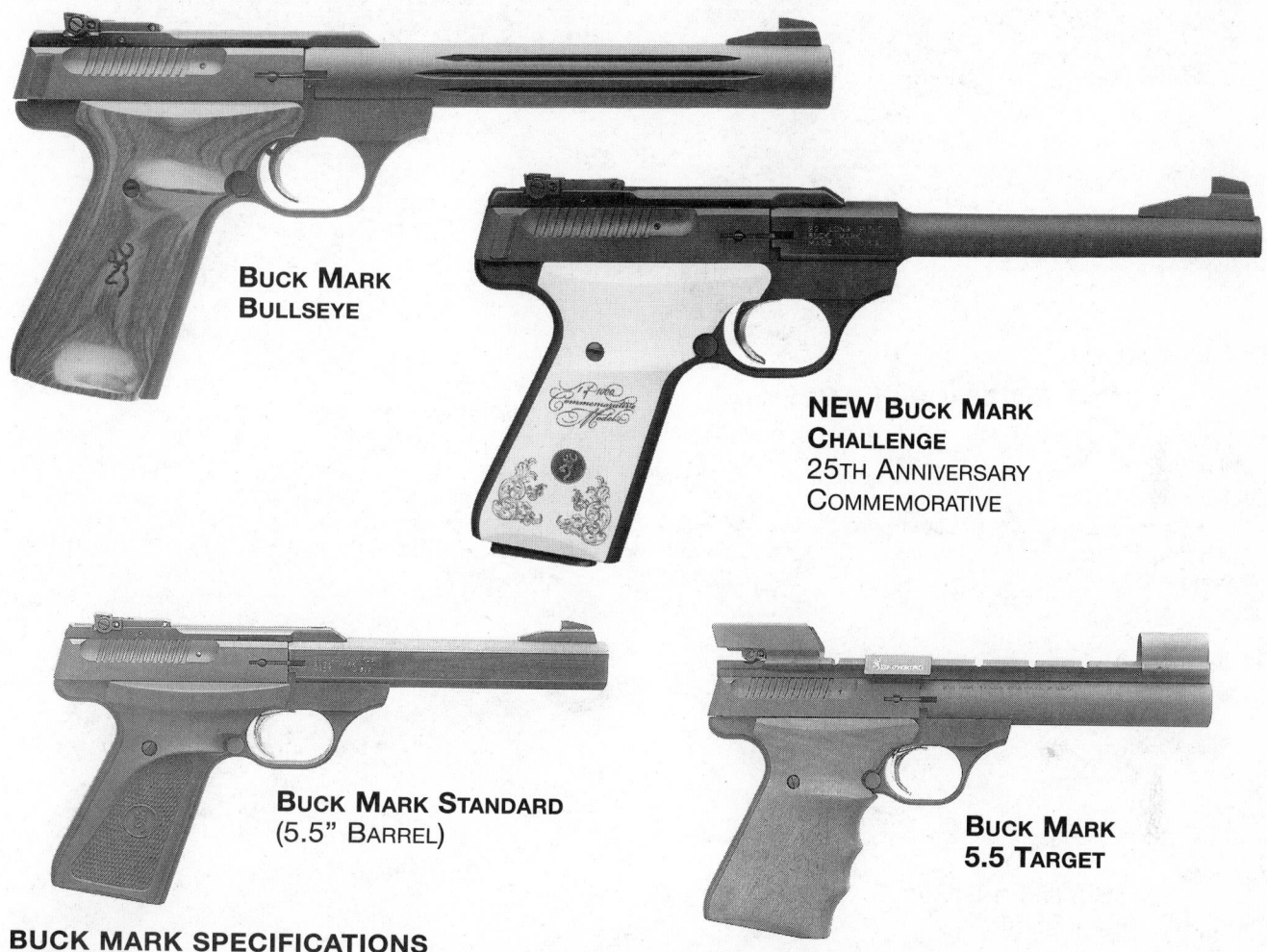

BUCK MARK BULLSEYE

NEW BUCK MARK CHALLENGE 25TH ANNIVERSARY COMMEMORATIVE

BUCK MARK STANDARD (5.5" BARREL)

BUCK MARK 5.5 TARGET

BUCK MARK SPECIFICATIONS

BUCK MARK MODELS	MAG. CAP.	BARREL LENGTH	OVERALL LENGTH	WEIGHT	OVERALL HEIGHT	SIGHT RADIUS	GRIPS	PRICE
Standard	10	5.5"	9.5"	36 oz.	5 3/8"	8"	Molded Composite, Ambidextrous	$286.00
Micro Standard	10	4"	8"	32 oz.	5 3/8"	9 9/16"	Molded Composite, Ambidextrous	286.00
Nickel	10	5.5"	9.5"	36 oz.	5 3/8"	8"	Molded Composite, Ambidextrous	338.00
Micro Nickel	10	4"	8"	32 oz.	5 3/8"	9 9/16"	Molded Composite, Ambidextrous	338.00
Plus Nickel	10	5.5"	9.5"	36 oz.	5 3/8"	8"	Laminated Hardwood	383.00
Plus	10	5.5"	9.5"	36 oz.	5 3/8"	8"	Laminated Hardwood	350.00
Micro Plus	10	4"	8"	32 oz.	5 3/8"	9 9/16"	Laminated Hardwood	350.00
Camper	10	5.5"	9.5"	34 oz.	5 3/8"	8"	Composite	258.00
Challenge	10	5.5"	9.5"	25 oz.	5 3/8"	8"	Walnut	320.00
NEW Commemorative Challenge	10	6.75"	10.75"	30.5 oz.	—	—	Etched Bonded Ivory, Ambidex	437.00
Bullseye, Standard	10	7.25"	11 5/16"	36 oz.	5 3/8"	9 7/8"	Molded Composite, Ambidextrous	420.00
Bullseye, Target	10	7.25"	11 5/16"	36 oz.	5 3/8"	9 7/8"	Contoured Rosewood or Wraparound fingergroove	541.00
5.5 Field	10	5.5"	9 5/8"	35.5 oz.	5 5/16"	8.25"	Contoured Walnut or Wraparound fingergroove	459.00
5.5 Target	10	5.5"	9 5/8"	35.5 oz.	5 5/16"	8.25"	Contoured Walnut or Wraparound fingergroove	459.00
Extra Magazine								26.00

Micro 4"-barrel models available for all standard Buck Marks and Challenge. Same price as 5.5".
Finishes are matte blue w/polished barrel flats or nickel plated slide and barrel. Pro Target rear sight and 1/8" wide front sight standard.

HANDGUNS

EMPIRE GRADE

FIELD GRADE

1911 A-1 45ACP PISTOLS

All pistols based on the M1911 Colt, a proven design that's still hugely popular.

Prices:

FIELD GRADE - 3.5", 4", or 5" barrel $499.00
TARGET - 5" barrel 599.00
TARGET - 5.75" barrel 679.00

EMPIRE GRADE - stainless steel
   3.5", 4", or 5" barrel 599.00
TARGET - stainless 699.00
SUPERIOR GRADE – Two-Tone, 5" barrel 549.00
CARRY COMP (not shown)
   Blue, 3.5" or 4" barrel 619.00
   Stainless steel 719.00

SUPERIOR GRADE

FIELD TARGET

DALY DOUBLE ACTION

Utilizing a 1911 type magazine, the DDA 10-45 and 10-40 feature 10+1 capacity. Available in compact or full-size.

Prices:

Compact in 45 or 40 S+W $519.00
Two-tone (45 only) 559.00
OD green or yellow/blue (45 only) 529.00
Fuchsia/Chrome (45 only). 549.00
Full size. 519.00
2-Tone (45 only) 559.00

DDA CS YELLOW

The Cimarron Firearms Co. has an impressive line of 19th-century replica revolvers and rifles. They are high-quality firearms, faithfully crafted to show the form, fit and function of the originals. They are ideal for Cowboy Action shooting. Take a look if you want the feel of another century between your hands.

1872 OPEN TOP

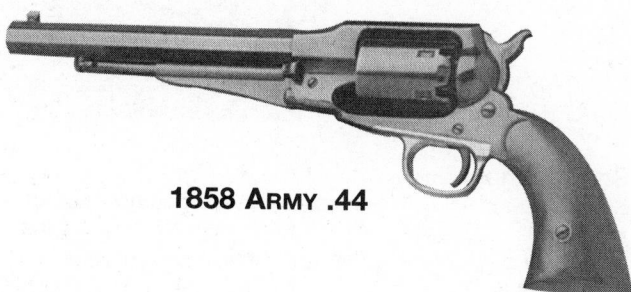

1858 ARMY .44

1872 OPEN TOP

The 1872 Open Top was the first cartridge firing six shooter manufactured by Colt and the forerunner of the famous 1873 Colt Model 'P' or Peacemaker. The Colt 1872 Open Top was manufactured at the same time as the percussion conversion models. The Cimarron Firearms Co. Open Top revolver is manufactured from the ground up, utilizing high quality modern gun steel. It is made much stronger than the original and other Open Top replicas made from percussion parts.

Barrels: 5 1/2" & 7 1/2"
Calibers: .38 Colt & S&W Special, .44 Colt & Russian, .45 S&W Schofield
Grips: Walnut, Early Navy style brass or Later steel Army style.
Finish: Blue, charcoal blue, nickel, or original finish
Retail $469.00
Also Available: 1858 ARMY .44 . . . . .249.00

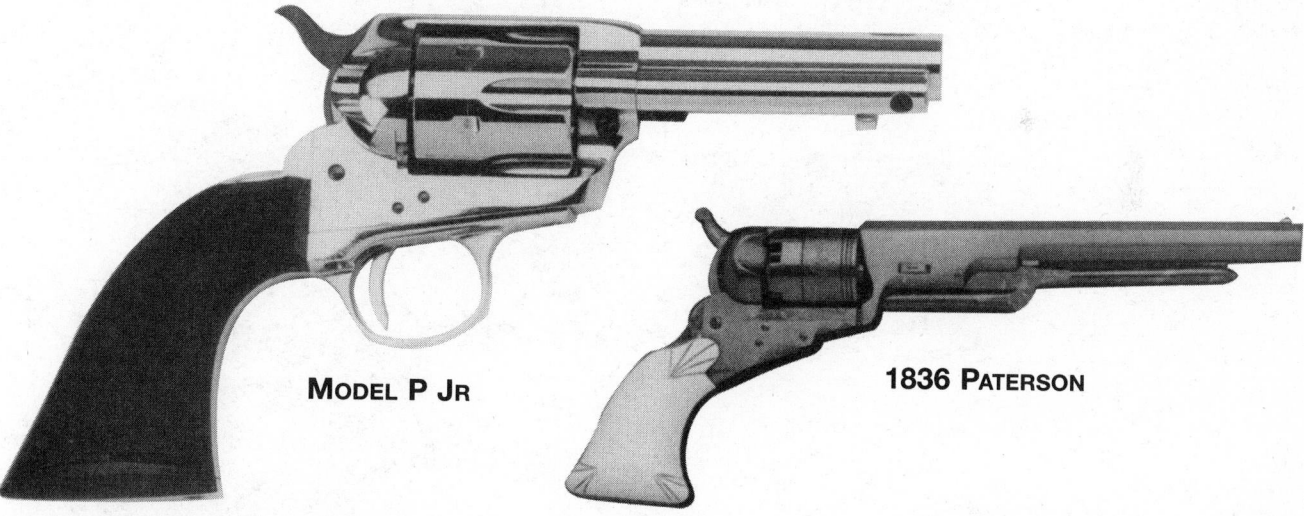

MODEL P JR

1836 PATERSON

1836 PATERSON

The 1836 Paterson in 36-caliber, was produced shortly before the factory shut down in 1942.
Price: $399.00

MODEL 'P' JR

The Cimarron Model 'P' Jr. (MPJ) is styled after–but 20% smaller than–the famous 1873 Colt Peacemaker. The MPJ features a down-sized traditional style Colt grip instead of the bird's head grip found on the Cimarron Lightning SA model. The MPJ features Cimarron's exclusive Cowboy Comp action and is manufactured to Cimarron's superior level of fit, finish and function. Shoulder rigs and holsters now available for the Lightning SA and Model 'P' Jr.
Barrels: 3 1/2" & 4 3/4"
Calibers: .38 Special
Finish: Blue with case hardened frame
Price:
Retail: $389.00

HANDGUNS

COLT M1911 PISTOLS

Model O Series 1991 and XSE

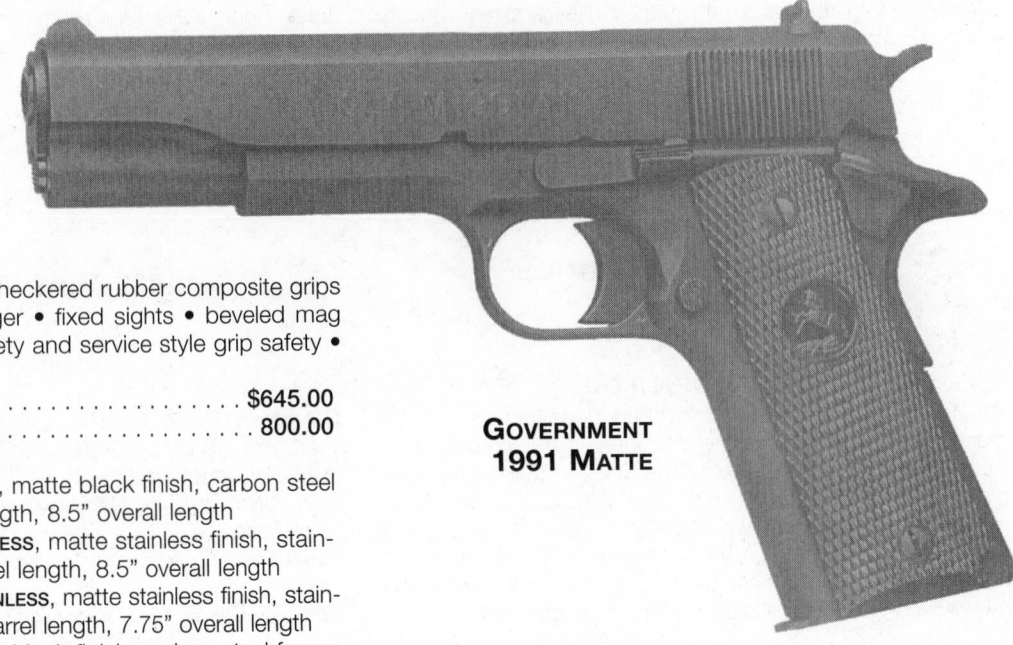

SPECIFICATIONS
Single-action, .45 ACP • checkered rubber composite grips • smooth, composite trigger • fixed sights • beveled mag well • standard thumb safety and service style grip safety • 7+1 capacity

Price: Blue $645.00
Stainless 800.00

Also available:
O1991/GOV'T 1991 MATTE, matte black finish, carbon steel frame & slide, 5" barrel length, 8.5" overall length
O1091/GOV'T 1991 STAINLESS, matte stainless finish, stainless frame & slide, 5" barrel length, 8.5" overall length
O4091U/COMMANDER STAINLESS, matte stainless finish, stainless frame & slide, 4.25" barrel length, 7.75" overall length
O4691/COMMANDER, matte black finish, carbon steel frame & slide, 4.25" barrel length, 7.75" overall length

**GOVERNMENT
1991 MATTE**

COMMANDER

SPECIFICATIONS
Single-action, .45 ACP • stainless brushed finish • front and rear slide serrations • checkered, double diamond, rosewood grips • extended ambidextrous thumb safeties • upswept beavertail with palm swell • three dot dovetail front and rear sights • adjustable 2-cut aluminum trigger • elongated slot hammer

Price: $950.00

Also available:
O1070XSE/GOVERNMENT, 5" barrel length, 8+1 capacity
O4012XSE/COMMANDER, 4.25" barrel length, 8+1 capacity
O4860XSE/LIGHTWEIGHT COMMANDER, 4.25" barrel length, 8+1 capacity

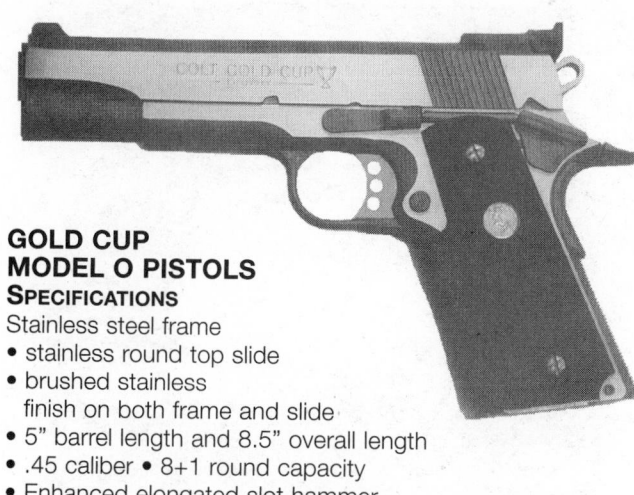

GOLD CUP
MODEL O PISTOLS
SPECIFICATIONS
Stainless steel frame
• stainless round top slide
• brushed stainless
 finish on both frame and slide
• 5" barrel length and 8.5" overall length
• .45 caliber • 8+1 round capacity
• Enhanced elongated slot hammer
• adjustable aluminum trigger • dovetail front sight
• bomar-style rear sight • black wrap around grips
• 39 ounce overall weight • single action
Price:
GOLD CUP SS $1,116.00
GOLD CUP BLUE 1,050.00

DEFENDER
MODEL O PISTOL
SPECIFICATIONS
Brushed stainless finish • wrap
around rubber finger groove grips
• skeletonized composite trigger
• single action • three dot dovetail
front and rear sights • .45 caliber • 3" barrel length, 6.75"
overall length • 7+1 capacity • beveled mag well • extended thumb safety and upswept beavertail with palm swell •
lightweight • enhanced tolerances
Price: MODEL O7000D $773.00

COWBOY SINGLE ACTION REVOLVER
SPECIFICATIONS
Blue color case finish • first generation grips • .45 Colt caliber • 5.5" barrel length, 11" overall length • 6 round capacity • transfer bar safety • enhanced tolerances
Price: MODEL CB1850 . . . . $670.00

Also available: TRADITIONAL SINGLE ACTION ARMY REVOLVERS
P1840, blue color case finish, .45 Colt, 4.75" barrel length,
10.25" overall length
P1841, nickel finish, .45 Colt, 4.75" barrel length, 10.25"
overall length
P1850, blue color case finish, .45 Colt, 5.5" barrel length,
11" overall length
P1856, nickel finish, .45 Colt, 5.5" barrel length, 11" overall
length
P1940, blue color case finish, .44-.40 caliber, 4.75" barrel
length, 10.25" overall length
P1941, nickel finish, .44-.40 caliber, 4.75" barrel length,
10.25" overall length
P1950, blue color case finish, .44-.40 caliber, 5.5" barrel
length, 11" overall length
P1956, nickel finish, .44-.40 caliber, 5.5" barrel length, 11"
overall length
Price: $1,938.00

HANDGUNS

CZ 75

The CZ 75 pistol is a product of Ceska Zbrojovka, Uhersky Brod. The CZ 75 B is the basis of the all-steel, semi-automatic, double action pistols of the CZ 75 pistol family.

CZ 75 B

The characteristic features of all CZ75 versions are the following: large capacity double-column magazine; comfortable grip in either hand; good results at instinctive shooting (without aiming); low trigger pull weight; high accuracy of fire; long service life; high reliability even with various brands of ammunition; the slide stays open after the last cartridge has been fired; the sights are outfitted with a three-dot illuminating system for better aiming in poor visibility conditions; suitable for competitive combat action shooting.

Versions differ in the caliber, size, weight, magazine capacity, trigger mechanism operation, safety elements, surface finish, grip panel types.

Caliber: 9 mm Luger, .40 S&W *Magazine capacity:* 10 cartridges *Overall length:* 8.1" *Barrel length:* 4.7" *Height:* 5.4" *Weight:* 2.2 lbs. *Trigger mechanism:* SA/DA *Safety elements:* Manual safety, safety stop on the hammer, firing pin safety

Price: 9mm $472.00
40 S&W 486.00

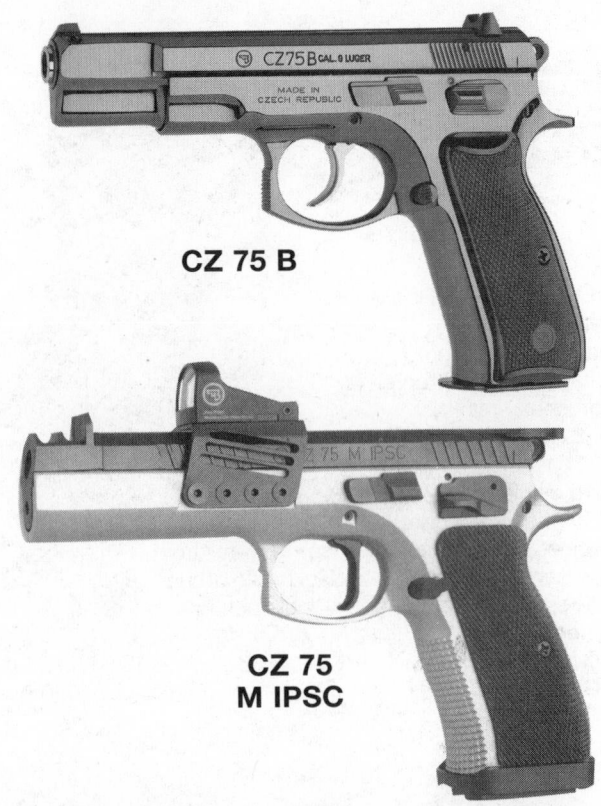

CZ 75 B

**CZ 75
M IPSC**

**CZ 75
STANDARD IPSC**

**CZ 75
CHAMPION**

CZ 75 CHAMPION

Caliber/Magazine capacity: 9 mm Luger / 10, 40 S&W / 10 *Length:* 9.5" *Barrel Length:* 4.5" *Height:* 5.6" *Weight:* 2.2 lbs. *Mode of operation:* SA *Safety elements:* Manual safety, safety stop on the hammer

Price: $1,484.00

CZ 75 STANDARD IPSC

Caliber/Magazine capacity: .40 S&W/10 *Length:* 8.9" *Barrel Length:* 5.4" *Height:* 5.9" *Weight:* 2.8 lbs. *Mode of operation:* SA *Safety elements:* Manual safety, safety stop on the hammer *Price:* $1,038.00

**CZ 75
COMPACT**

CZ 75 COMPACT

Frame: Steel *Caliber:* 9mm Luger *Magazine Capacity:* 10 cartridges *Overall Length:* 7.3" *Barrel Length:* 3.9" *Height:* 5.0" *Weight:* 2.0 lbs. *Trigger Mechanism:* SA/DA *Safety elements:* Manual safety, safety stop on the hammer, firing pin safety

Price: $499.00
Also available: CZ 75 BD Compact in 40 S&W

CZ 75 M IPSC

Caliber: .40 S&W *Magazine Capacity:* 10 cartridges *Overall Length:* 8.3" *Barrel Length:* 3.9" *Height (including Fire Point):* 6.3" *Weight:* 2.8 lbs. *Trigger Mechanism:* SA *Safety elements:* Ambidexrous thumb safety, safety notch on hammer *Sights:* Red-Dot-Reflex

Price: $1,498.00

CZ KADET PISTOL .22 CAL.

Caliber: .22 LR *Barrel length:* 4.9" *Magazine capacity:*
10 cartridges *Weight:* 2.4 lbs *Overall Length:* 8.1" *Barrel
Length:* 4.9"
Price: $485.00

CZ KADET .22 CAL. CONVERSION KIT (not shown)

The CZ 75 Kadet conversion kit is a separate accessory for
the CZ 75/85 pistol series, allowing the use of .22 LR calibre
cartridges. The Kadet adapter has its own sights, adjustable
for elevation and windage, so there's no loss of zero when
slides are switched.
Caliber: .22 LR *Magazine capacity:* 10 cartridges *Overall
length:* 8.1" *Barrel length:* 4.9" *Weight:* 1.1 lbs. *Empty
magazine weight:* 0.3 lbs.
Price: Adapter Kit $270.00

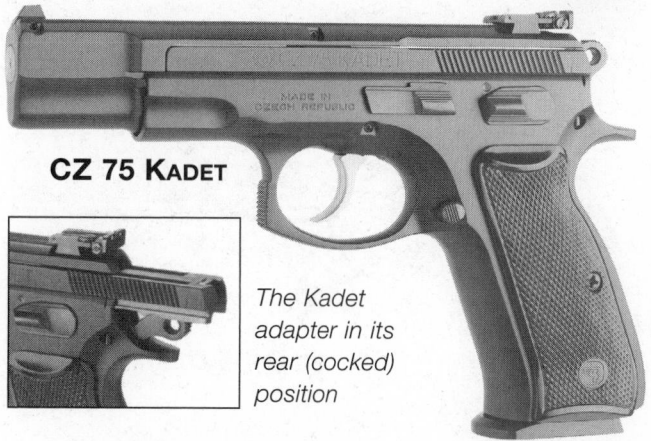

CZ 75 KADET

*The Kadet
adapter in its
rear (cocked)
position*

CZ 85 COMBAT

Caliber: 9mm Luger
Magazine Capacity: 10 cartridges
Overall Length: 8.1" *Barrel Length:* 4.7"
Height: 5.4" *Weight:* 2.2 lbs.
Trigger Mechanism: SA/DA
Safety elements: Manual safety,
safety stop on the hammer
Price: $562.00

CZ 97 B

*Caliber/Magazine
capacity:* .45 Auto / 10
Length: 8.3" *Barrel Length:* 4.8"
Height: 5.9" *Weight:* 2.6 lbs.
Mode of operation: SA/DA
Safety elements: Manual safety,
safety stop on the hammer, firing pin
safety, loaded chamber indicator
Price: $613.00

CZ 83

Caliber: 7,65 mm Browning;
9mm Makarov, 9mm Browning
Magazine Capacity: 10 *Length:*
6.8"; 6.8" *Barrel Length:* 3.8"; 3.8"
Height: 5.0"; 5.0" *Weight:* 1.7 lbs.;
1.8 lbs. *Mode of operation:* SA/DA;
SA/DA *Safety elements:* Manual safety, automatic safety
Price: $378.00

CZ 100

Caliber/Magazine capacity: 9mm
Luger/10; .40 S&W/10 *Length:* 180 mm
(7.1") *Barrel Length:* 98 mm (3.9")
Height: 130 mm (5.1") *Weight:* 665 g
1.5 lbs.) *Mode of operation:* SA/DA
Safety elements: firing pin block, loaded chamber indicator,
cocking indication button, decocking lever
Price: $405.00

HANDGUNS

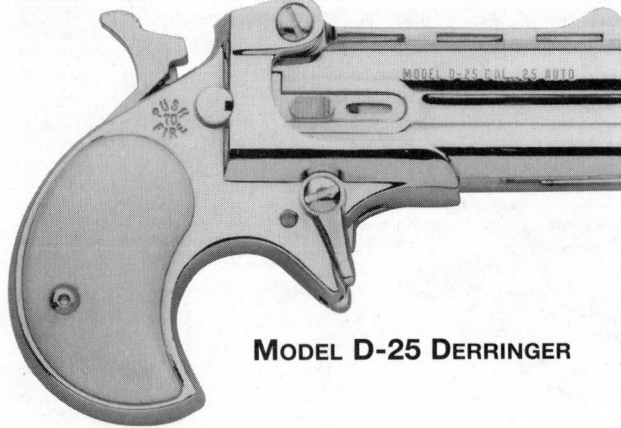

MODEL D-25 DERRINGER

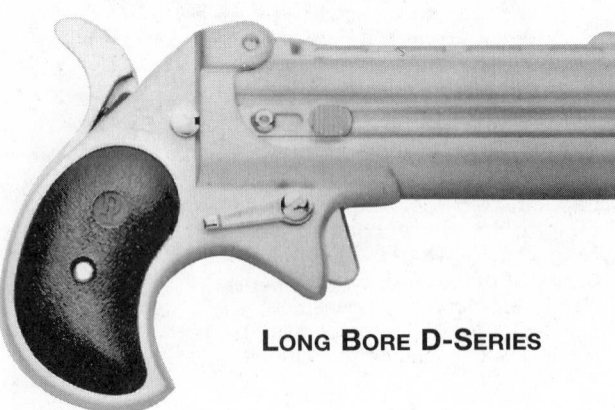

LONG BORE D-SERIES

D-SERIES DERRINGERS

SPECIFICATIONS
Calibers: 22 LR, 22 Mag., 25 Auto, 32 Auto
Capacity: 2 shot *Barrel Length:* 2.4"
Overall Length: 4" *Height:* 2.8" *Weight:* 9.5 oz.
Grips: Laminated wood *Finish:* Black teflon or chrome
Price: $75.00

LONG BORE D-SERIES

SPECIFICATIONS
Calibers: 22 Mag., 9mm, 32 H&R Mag., 38 Special
Capacity: 2 rounds *Barrel Length:* 3.5"
Overall Length: 5.4" *Height:* 3.31" *Weight:* 16 oz.
Price: $104.00
    9mm only 110.00
Also available:
BIG BORE D-SERIES.
Calibers: 22 WMR, 9mm, 32 H&R Mag., 38 Special.
Barrel Length: 2.75" *Overall Length:* 4.65"
Weight: 14 oz.
Price: $98.00
    9mm only 104.00

MODEL P-32

SPECIFICATIONS
Caliber: 32 Auto *Magazine Capacity:* 6 rounds
Barrel Length: 2.8" *Overall Length:* 5.4"
Weight: 22 oz. *Height:* 4"
Grips: Laminated wood *Finish:* Black teflon or chrome
Price: $87.50

MODEL P-380

SPECIFICATIONS
Caliber: 380 Auto *Magazine Capacity:* 5 rounds
Barrel Length: 2.8" *Overall Length:* 5.4"
Height: 4" *Weight:* 22 oz.
Price: $98.00

MODEL P-32

MODEL P-380

MODEL WSP
"WORLD'S SMALLEST PISTOL"

SPECIFICATIONS
Action: Single-shot double-action only
Caliber: 45 ACP, 357 Mag.
Barrel length: 2.1", tip-up barrel
Overall length: 3.25"
Weight: 11 oz. **Height:** 2.25" **Width:** 0.9"
Materials: Stainless steel; CNC machined from
solid bar stock
Price: $429.00

"WORLD'S
SMALLEST
PISTOL"

EMF/DAKOTA REVOLVERS

E.M.F. Hartford Single-Action Revolvers

1st and 2nd generations models available. Parts are interchangeable with the original Colts. Forged steel frames, case hardened, steel backstrap & trigger guard. Original blue finish, walnut grips. Barrel lengths: 4.75", 5.5", 7.5", 12" buntline.

MODEL 1875 REMINGTON SINGLE ACTION REVOLVER
Engraved; case hardened frame
Price: Blued $575.00
Nickel. 740.00

MODEL 1890 REMINGTON POLICE
SPECIFICATIONS – Calibers:
44-40, 45 Long Colt and 357 Magnum. **Barrel length:** 5.75". **Finish:** Blued or nickel
Features: Original design (1891-1894) with lanyard ring in buttstock; case hardened frame; walnut grips
Price: $610.00
Nickel 775.00

1873 HARTFORD "BUNTLINE"
SPECIFICATIONS – Caliber: 45 LC **Barrel Length:** 12" **Features:** Steel backstrap & trigger
Price: $670.00

HARTFORD PINKERTON
SPECIFICATIONS
Caliber: 45 LC, 357 Magnum
Barrel length: 4". Bird's-head grip with ejector tube.
Price: $570.00

1873 DAKOTA SINGLE ACTION
WITH 5.5" BARREL

1873 DAKOTA SINGLE ACTION
SPECIFICATIONS
Calibers: 357 Mag., 44-40, 45 Long Colt. **Barrel lengths:** 4.75", 5.5" and 7.5". **Finish:** Blued, case hardened frame. **Grips:** One-piece walnut. **Features:** Classic Colt design, set screw for cylinder pin release; black nickel backstrap and trigger design
Price: $400.00
Buntline (.45 L.C., 12") 670.00

HANDGUNS

TACTICAL P325 PLUS

SPECIFICATIONS

Caliber: .45 ACP, 10 round magazine.
Barrel: 3.25". *Weight:* 37 oz. *Length:* 7.25" overall.
Stocks: Black Ergo Ultra Slim, double diamond checkered grip panels. *Sights:* Tactical2 Ghost Ring sight or Novak Lo-mount sight. *Features:* Same as the Elite series plus extended ambidextrous thumb safety, front & rear cocking serrations, full length guide rod, barrel throated & frame ramp polished, tuned match extractor, fitted barrel & bushing, stainless steel firing pin, serrated ramp front sight, slide lapped to frame, dehorned and trigger set at a crisp 4.5 pounds.

Price: $979.00
  P425 (4.25" barrel) 979.00
  P500 (5" barrel) 979.00

TACTICAL P325 PLUS

ELITE P425 (and P500, P325)

SPECIFICATIONS

Caliber: .45 ACP, 10 round magazine.
Barrel: 4.25" (5" P500, 3.25" P325) *Weight:* 38 oz. (40 oz. P500, 36 oz. P325) *Length:* 7.75" overall
Stocks: Black Ergo Ultra Slim, double diamond checkered grip panels.
Sights: 3-dot fixed sights (dovetail cut front sight).
Features: Reinforced dustcover, lowered & flared ejection port, squared trigger guard, adjustable match trigger, bolstered front strap, high grip cut, hardened steel magazine release, high ride beavertail grip safety, steel flat mainspring housing (checkered 20 LPI), checkered slide release, extended thumb lock, EDM skeletonized match hammer & sear, match grade disconnector with polished contact points and Wolff springs throughout.

Price: $699.90

ELITE P425

BOXER P500

SPECIFICATIONS

Caliber: .45 ACP, .40 Cal. *Barrel:* 5". *Weight:* 40 oz.
Length: 8.5" overall. *Stocks:* Black Ergo Ultra Slim, double diamond checkered grip panels. *Sights:* Adjustable rear sight with dovetail patridge front sight. *Features:* Same as the Elite model plus machined slide parallel rails with polished breech face & barrel channel, front & rear cocking serrations, lowered & flared ejection port, full length stainless steel one piece guide rod with plug, National match barrel 5" Government length, match bushing, stainless steel firing pin, match extractor, oversized firing pin stop, fitted barrel & bushing, slide lapped to frame, barrel throated & ramp polished, extractor tuned and trigger set at a crisp 4.5 pounds.

Prices:
45ACP $1,399.00
40 Cal. 1,499.00

BOXER P500

EUROPEAN AMERICAN ARMORY

WITNESS DOUBLE-ACTION PISTOLS

SPECIFICATIONS
Calibers: 9mm, 38 Super, 40 S&W, 10mm, and 45 ACP
Capacity: 10 rounds, (45 ACP) *Barrel length:* 4.5"
Overall length: 8.1" *Weight:* 33 oz. *Finish:* Blued
or Wonder Finish *Sights:* 3-dot; windage adj. rear
Grips: Black rubber
Prices: Blue $439.00
Wonder Finish 459.00
Also available with decocking feature.

WITNESS

WITNESS COMPACT

SPECIFICATIONS
Calibers: 9mm, 40 S&W, 38 Super, 10mm, 45 ACP
Capacity: 10 rounds; (45 ACP)
Barrel length: 3 5/8"
Overall length: 7.3"
Weight: 29 oz.
Finish: Hard chrome
Prices:
Steel/Blue $439.00
  Wonder 459.00
Polymer/Blue..............................429.00
  Wonder 439.00

WITNESS COMPACT

WINDICATOR REVOLVER

SPECIFICATIONS
Calibers: 38 Special, 357 Mag. *Capacity:* 6 rounds
Action: Single/Double action *Barrel length:* 2" or 4"
Sights: Fixed (No-Snag) or windage adj. *Finish:* Blued only
Features: Swing-out cylinder; black rubber grips; hammer
block safety
Prices: 38 SPECIAL w/2" barrel $239.00
38 SPECIAL w/4" barrel....................269.00
357 MAGNUM w/2" barrel 269.00
357 MAGNUM w/4" barrel 279.00

WINDICATOR REVOLVER

BIG BORE BOUNTY HUNTER SINGLE ACTION

SPECIFICATIONS
Calibers: 357 Mag., 45 Long Colt and 44 Mag.
Capacity: 6 rounds *Barrel length:* 4.5" or 7.5"
Sights: Fixed *Weight:* 37 oz. (4.5") and 42 oz. (7.5")
Finish: Blued, color casehardened or nickel
Features: Transfer-bar safety, 3 position hammer; hammer-
forged barrel; walnut grips (polymer grips optional)
Prices: Blued or color casehardened receiver ... $379.00
Nickel 399.00
Also available: In 22 LR/WMR
  (4.75" or 6.75" barrel) w/blue finish 269.00
Nickel 299.00

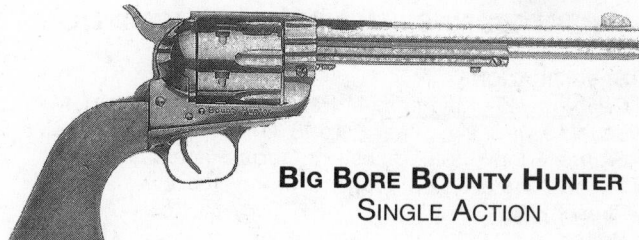

BIG BORE BOUNTY HUNTER
SINGLE ACTION

HANDGUNS

MODEL 83 RIMFIRE
SILHOUETTE CLASS 10" BARREL

MODEL 83
454 CASULL FIELD GRADE

MODEL 83
PREMIER
GRADE (50 AE)

SPECIFICATIONS
Caliber: 22 LR (optional 22 Magnum cylinder)
Barrel Lengths: 5.13", 7.5" (Varmint Class)
and 10" (Silhouette Class)
Sights: Silhouette competition sights
Silhouette Class); adjustable rear express sight;
removable front express blade; front sight hood
Grips: Black micarta (Silhouette Class);
black and green laminated hardwood (Varmint Class)
Finish: Stainless steel
Features: Dual
firing pin; lightened hammer; pre-set trigger stop; accepts
all sights and/or scope mounts
Prices:
SILHOUETTE CLASS (10" barrel). $1,765.00
VARMINT CLASS (5.13" & 7.5" barrels) 1,714.00

MODEL 97
PREMIER GRADE

MODEL 97 PREMIER GRADE
ADJUSTABLE SIGHT. 1,576.00

SPECIFICATIONS
Caliber: 357 Magnum, 45 Colt, 41 Magnum
Capacity: 6 shots (357) 5 shots (45 and 41)
Action: Single Action
Barrel Lengths: 4.25", 5.5" and 7.5"
Sights: Removable front blade; adjustable rear
Grips: Impregnated hardwood or optional black micanta

MODEL 83 SILHOUETTE/COMPETITION
(not shown)

SPECIFICATIONS
Calibers: 357 Magnum, 41 Rem. Mag. and 44 Rem. Mag.
Barrel Lengths: 9" (357 Mag.) and 10" (41 Rem. Mag., 44 Rem. Mag.)
Sights: Silhouette competition   *Grips:* Pachmayr
Trigger: Pre-set stop; trigger over travel screw
Finish: Field Grade
Price:. $1,549.85

MODEL 83 PREMIER & FIELD GRADES

SPECIFICATIONS
Calibers: 454 Casull, 41 Rem. Mag.,
44 Rem. Mag., .475 Linebaugh, 50 AE, 357 Mag.
Action: Single action
Capacity: 5 rounds
Barrel Lengths: 4.75", 6", 7.5", 10"
Overall Length: 14" (w/7.5" barrel)
Weight: 3 lbs. 2 oz. (w/7.5" barrel)
Safety: Patented sliding bar
Sights: Notched rear; blade front (optional adjustable rear
and replaceable front blade)
Grips: Impregnated hardwood (Premier Grade) or rubber
Pachmayr (Field Grade)
Finish: Brushed stainless (Premier Grade); Matte Finish (Field)
Features: ISGW silhouette, Millett competition and express
sights are optional; SSK T'SOB 3-ring or 2-ring Leupold
scope mount optional; optional cylinder in 454 Casull, 45
ACP, 45 Win. Mag. **($343.00)**
Prices:
MODEL 83 PREMIER GRADE
W/adjustable sights
 (50A, 475L, 454C) $1,958.00
357, 41 and 44
 Magnums w/adjustable sights 1,882.00
MODEL 83 FIELD GRADE
.454C, 475L, 50 AE, adj. sights 1,519.00
.357, 41, 44 adj. sights 1,442.00

FULL SIZE

MODEL G17
SPECIFICATIONS
Barrel Length: 4.49 in. *Weight:* 22.04 oz.
Mag Cap: 10/17 *Overall Height:* 5.43"
Overall Length: 7.32"

MODEL G22
SPECIFICATIONS
Barrel Length: 4.49 in. *Weight:* 22.92 oz.
Mag Cap: 10/15 *Overall Height:* 5.43"
Overall Length: 7.32"

MODEL G31
SPECIFICATIONS
Barrel Length: 4.49 in. *Weight:* 22.28 oz.
Mag Cap: 10/15 *Overall Height:* 5.43"
Overall Length: 7.32"

MODEL G20
SPECIFICATIONS
Barrel Length: 4.60 in. *Weight:* 26.28 oz.
Mag Cap: 10/13 *Overall Height:* 5.47"
Overall Length: 7.59"

MODEL G21
SPECIFICATIONS
Barrel Length: 4.60 in. *Weight:* 26.28 oz.
Mag Cap: 10/13 *Overall Height:* 5.47"
Overall Length: 7.59"

COMPACT

MODEL G19
SPECIFICATIONS
Barrel Length: 4.02 in. *Weight:* 20.99 oz.
Mag Cap: 10/15 *Overall Height:* 5.00"
Overall Length: 6.85" *Caliber:* 9x19

MODEL G23
SPECIFICATIONS
Barrel Length: 4.02in. *Weight:* 21.16 oz.
Mag Cap: 10/13 *Overall Height:* 5.00"
Overall Length: 6.85" *Caliber:* .40

9X19

.40

MODEL G17

MODEL G22

.357

MODEL G31

10MM

MODEL G20

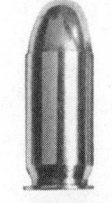

9X19

MODEL G17

MODEL G23

MODEL G19

Ported Barrel

Prices on request.

COMPACT

MODEL G32
SPECIFICATIONS
Barrel Length: 4.02 in. *Weight:* 21.16 oz.
Mag Cap: 10/13 *Overall Height:* 5.00"
Overall Length: 6.85" *Caliber:* 357

MODEL G29
SPECIFICATIONS
Barrel Length: 3.78 in. *Weight:* 24.69 oz.
Mag Cap: 10 *Overall Height:* 4.45"
Overall Length: 6.77" *Caliber:* 10mm

MODEL G309
SPECIFICATIONS
Barrel Length: 3.78 in. *Weight:* 23.99 oz.
Mag Cap: 10(9) *Overall Height:* 4.76"
Overall Length: 6.77" *Caliber:* 45 Auto

SUB COMPACT

MODEL G26
SPECIFICATIONS
Barrel Length: 3.46 in. *Weight:* 19.75 oz.
Mag Cap: 10 *Overall Height:* 4.17"
Overall Length: 6.29" *Caliber:* .40

MODEL G27
SPECIFICATIONS
Barrel Length: 3.46 in. *Weight:* 19.75 oz.
Mag Cap: 9 *Overall Height:* 4.17"
Overall Length: 6.29" *Caliber:* .40

MODEL G33
SPECIFICATIONS
Barrel Length: 3.46 in. *Weight:* 19.75 oz.
Mag Cap: 9 *Overall Height:* 4.17"
Overall Length: 6.29" *Caliber:* 357

MODEL G34
SPECIFICATIONS
Barrel Length: 5.32 in. *Weight:* 22.92 oz.
Mag Cap: 10/17 *Overall Height:* 5.43"
Overall Length: 8.15" *Caliber:* 9x19

MODEL G35
SPECIFICATIONS
Barrel Length: 5.32 in. *Weight:* 24.52 oz.
Mag Cap: 10/15 *Overall Height:* 5.43"
Overall Length: 8.15" *Caliber:* 40

Ported Barrel MODEL G32

MODEL G29

MODEL G30

MODEL G26

MODEL G27

MODEL G33

MODEL G34

9X19

MODEL G35

.40

Prices on request.

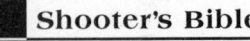

HÄMMERLI U.S.A. PISTOLS

MODEL 160 FREE PISTOL
$2,189.00 w/electronic trigger $2,410.00

SPECIFICATIONS
Caliber: 22 LR
Barrel Length: 11.3"
Overall Length: 17.5"
Height: 5.7" *Weight:* 45 oz.
Trigger Action: Infinitely variable set trigger weight; cocking lever located on left of receiver; trigger length variable along weapon axis
Locking Action: Martini-type locking action w/side-mounted locking lever *Barrel:* Free floating, cold swaged precision barrel w/low axis relative to the hand *Ignition:* Horizontal firing pin (hammerless) in line w/barrel axis; firing pin travel 0.15" *Grips:* Selected walnut w/adj. hand rest for direct arm to barrel extension

MODEL FP10 FREE PISTOL
Price on request

The Hammerli model FP 10 Free Pistol is designed for advanced competitors who know how to take advantage of this advanced pistol's many adjustments and very high level of accuracy. *Features:* Trigger tongue adjustable for length and rotates around its own vertical axis. Rear sight adjusts for width of notch; interchangeable front sight posts; integrated compensator in front ramp.

MODEL 160
FREE PISTOL

MODEL FP10
FREE PISTOL

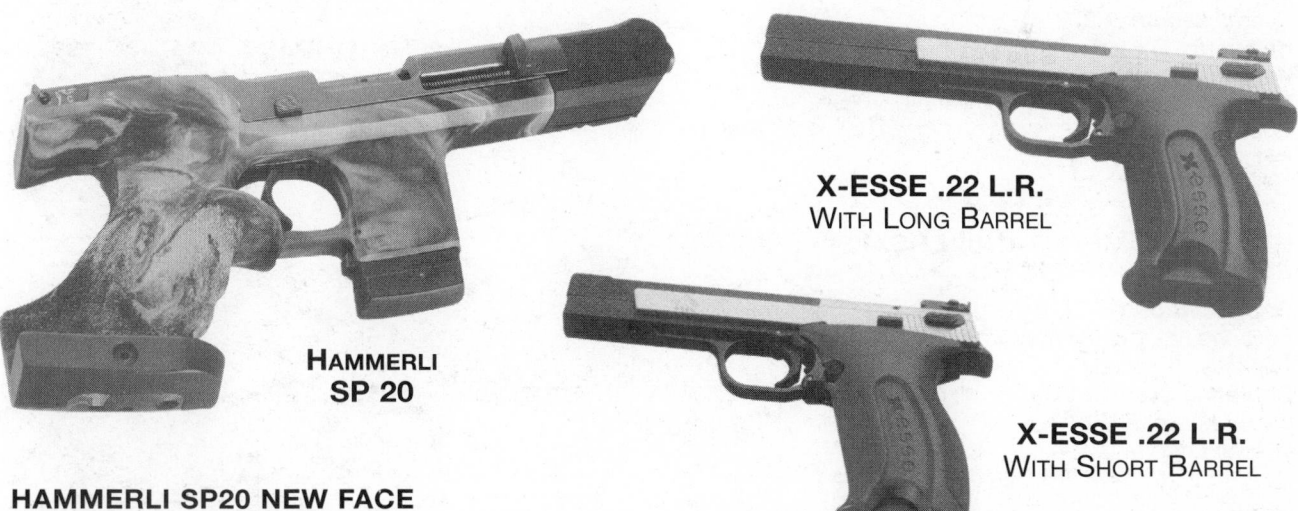

HAMMERLI
SP 20

X-ESSE .22 L.R.
WITH LONG BARREL

X-ESSE .22 L.R.
WITH SHORT BARREL

HAMMERLI SP20 NEW FACE

The HAMMERLI SP 20 target pistol has a front-end magazine, match trigger and synthetic stock.
SPECIFICATIONS
Caliber: 22 LR/.32 S&W LWC
Barrel Length: 4.58"
Magazine Capacity: 5/6 (22LR/32S&W)
Sights: Integral front sight with 3 different widths.
Available in blue, anthracite or black.

X-ESSE SPORT PISTOL

The all-steel, high precision 22LR pistol comes equipped with a "Hi-Grip" in a new anatomical shape and an adjustable support.
SPECIFICATIONS
Sights: Integral front sight with 3 widths *Magazine:* 10 round *Grips:* Available in red, black or yellow

HANDGUNS

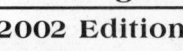

MODEL HK USP 9 &40 UNIVERSAL SELF-LOADING PISTOL

SPECIFICATIONS
Calibers: 9mm and 40 S&W
Capacity: 10 + 1
Operating System: Short recoil, modified Browning action
Barrel Length: 4.25"
Overall Length: 7.64"
Weight: 28 oz. (40 S&W); 26 oz. (9mm)
Height: 5.35"
Sights: Adjustable 3-dot
Grips: Polymer receiver and integral grips
Prices:
9mm & 40 S&W. $739.00
Also available:
HK USP45 TACTICAL PISTOL
   w/cleaning kit & case. **1,069.00**

MODEL HK USP45
TACTICAL PISTOL

MODEL USP45 UNIVERSAL SELF-LOADING PISTOL

SPECIFICATIONS
Caliber: 45 ACP
Capacity: 10 rounds
Action: DA/SA or DAO
Barrel Length: 4.41"
Overall Length: 7.87"
Height: 5.55"
Weight: 30 oz.
Grips: Polymer frame & integral grips
Prices: $799.00

MODEL HK USP45
UNIVERSAL SELF-
LOADING PISTOL

HK USP COMPACT UNIVERSAL SELF-LOADING PISTOL

SPECIFICATIONS
Calibers: 9mm, 40 S&W, .357 Sig and 45 ACP
Capacity: 10 rounds
Operating System: Short recoil, modified Browning action
Barrel Length: 3.58"
Overall Length: 6.81"
Weight: 28 oz. (40 S&W); 26 oz. (9mm)
Height: 5"
Sights: Adjustable 3-dot
Grips: Polymer frame and integral grips
Prices:
9mm, 40 S+W, and .357 Sig $759.00
Also available:
Stainless (9mm and 40 S+W) 849.00
45 ACP. 829.00
45 ACP, stainless. 879.00

HK USP45 COMPACT
UNIVERSAL SELF-
LOADING PISTOL

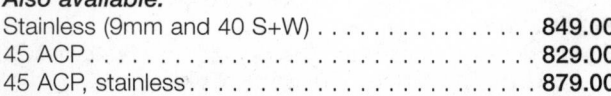

HK USP45 EXPERT

SPECIFICATIONS
Caliber: 45 ACP or 40 S+W
Capacity: 10 rounds
Operating System: Short recoil, modified Browning action
Barrel Length: 6.02"
Overall Length: 9.45"
Weight: 39 oz.
Height: 5.90"
Sights: Adjustable 3-dot
Grips & Stock: Polymer frame and integral grips
Prices:
Blued **$1,449.00**

HK USP EXPERT

MARK 23 SPECIAL OPERATIONS PISTOL (SOCOM)

SPECIFICATIONS
Caliber: 45 ACP
Capacity: 10 rounds
Operating System: Short recoil, modified Browning action
Barrel Length: 5.87"
Overall Length: 9.65"
Height: 5.9"
Weight: 42 oz.
Sights: 3-dot
Grips: Polymer frame & integral grips
Price: **$2,289.00**

MARK 23 SPECIAL OPERATIONS PISTOL (SOCOM)

MODEL P7M8

MODEL P7M8

SPECIFICATIONS
Caliber: 9mmX19 (Luger)
Capacity: 8 rounds
Barrel Length: 4.13"
Overall Length: 6.73"
Weight: 28 oz.
Sight Radius: 5.83"
Sights: Adjustable rear
Grips: Plastic *Finish:* Blue or nickel
Operating System: Recoil-operated; retarded inertia slide
Price: **$1,369.00**

HANDGUNS

HERITAGE MANUFACTURING

ROUGH RIDER
3.5" NICKEL w/BIRD'S
HEAD GRIP

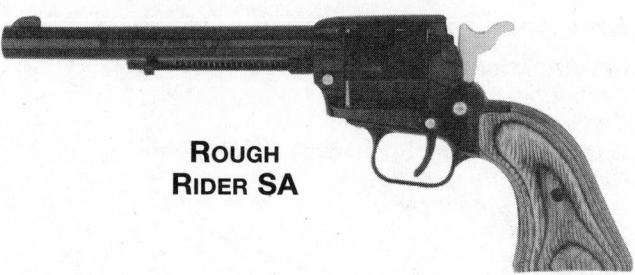

**ROUGH
RIDER SA**

These single-action revolvers are patterned after the Colt Single-Action Army.

SPECIFICATIONS
Caliber: 22 LR or 22 LR/22 WMR
Capacity: 6 rounds
Weight: 31 to 38 oz.
Barrel Lengths: 4.5", 6.5", 9" (regular grip); 2.5", 3.5", 4.75" (Bird's-Head grip)
Sights: Blade front, adjustable sight or Red Dot reflex
Grips: Exotic hardwood
Finish: Blue or nickel
Features: Rotating hammer block safety; brass accent screws
Prices:
22 LR (4.5", 6.5" bbl.) blued, regular grip **$133.95**

22 LR/22 WMR
W/blued finish, regular grip: 4.5" & 6.5" barrels **$149.95**
   9" barrel. **149.95**
W/nickel finish, regular grip: 4.5" & 6.5" barrels **184.95**
   9" barrel. **184.95**
W/blued finish, bird's-head grip:
   3.5" & 4.5" barrels **149.95**
W/nickel finish: bird's-head grip:
   3.5" & 4.5" barrels **179.95**
W/blued finish, adjustable sights (4.75",
   6.5", 9" barrels **179.95**
W/steel frame/blue
   (3.5", 4.5", 6.5" barrels) **184.95**
W/steel frame/nickel (6.5" barrel) **199.95**
W/steel frame/blue (9" barrel) **189.95**
W/steel frame/blue/adj. sights
   (4.75", 6.5", 9" barrel) **199.95**

HIGH STANDARD PISTOLS

**OLYMPIC
RAPID FIRE**

OLYMPIC RAPID FIRE

SPECIFICATIONS
Caliber: 22 Short   *Capacity:* 5 rounds
Barrel length: 4"   *Overall length:* 11.5"   *Weight:* 46 oz.
Sights: Click-adjustable for windage and elevations (rear); mounted on vent aluminum rib
Grips: Special International   *Finish:* Matte blue
Features: Push-button barrel takedown system; trigger adj. for weight of pull and travel; gold-plated trigger, slide stop, safety and magazine release
Price: **$1,995.00**

SUPERMATIC CITATION

SPECIFICATIONS
Caliber: 22 LR *Capacity:* 10 rounds
Barrel length: 5.5" *Overall length:* 9.5"
Weight: 44 oz. *Finish:* Blued or Parkerized
Features: Optional Universal Mount to replace open-sight rib (deduct $30.00)
Price: $462.00
Also available:
SUPERMATIC CITATION MS. Similar to Citation above, except 10" barrel (14" overall), 54 oz. weight, checkered right-hand thumbrest and matte blue finish $657.00
TROPHY/CITATION 22 SHORT CONVERSION KIT
(incl. barrel w/sight, slide, 2 magazines) $299.00

OLYMPIC MILITARY

SPECIFICATIONS
Caliber: 22 LR *Capacity:* 10 rounds
Barrel length: 5.5" *Overall length:* 9.5"
Weight: 44 oz. *Finish:* Matte frame
Features: Fully adjustable rear sight; non-adjustable trigger
Price: $590.00

SUPERMATIC TROPHY

SPECIFICATIONS
Caliber: 22 LR *Capacity:* 10 rounds
Actions: Recoil-operated semiautomatic
Barrel length: 5.5" bull or 7.25" fluted
Overall length: 9.5 (w/5.5" bbl.) and 11.25" (w/7.25" bbl.)
Weight: 44 oz. (w/5.5" bbl.) and 46 oz. (w/7.25" bbl.)
Sights: Click-adjustable rear for windage/elevation; undercut ramp front *Grips:* Checkered American walnut with right-hand thumbrest (left-hand optional)
Features: Gold-plated trigger; slide lock lever; push-button takedown system; magazine release
Prices: 5.5" BARREL $569.00
7.25" BARREL 650.00

VICTOR 22 LR

SPECIFICATIONS
Caliber: 22 LR
Capacity: 10 rounds
Barrel lengths: 4.5" and 5.5"
Overall length: 8.5" and 9.5"
Weight: 45 oz. (w/4.5" bbl.); 46 oz. (w/5.5" bbl.)
Finish: Blued or Parkerized frame
Features: Optional steel rib; click-adjustable sights for windage and elevation; optional barrel weights and Universal Mount (to replace open-sight rib)
Prices: $532.00
 w/5.5" barrel 591.00
Also available:
22 SHORT CONVERSION KIT 5.5" barrel w/vent rib, slide, two magazines $299.00

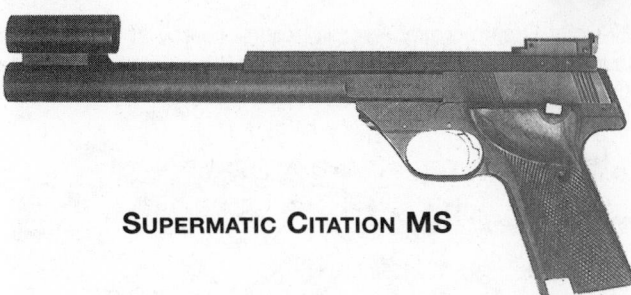
SUPERMATIC CITATION MS

OLYMPIC

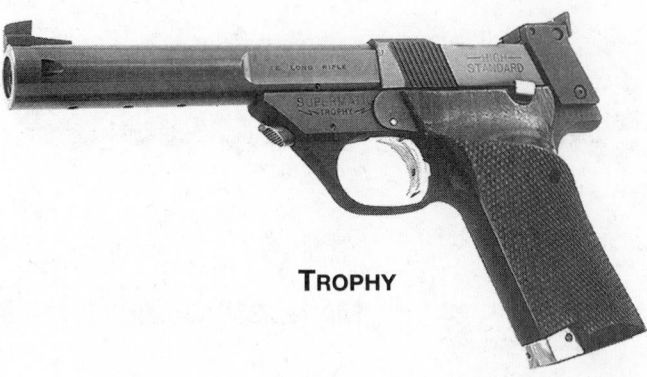
TROPHY

VICTOR 22 LR

HANDGUNS

HI-POINT FIREARMS

Semi-Automatic Handguns

Hi-Point Firearms offer reliability and accuracy at an affordable price. Hi-Point handguns are sized to feel good in your hand and provide exceptional recoil control. All models feature sleek lines and a scratch-resistant, non-glare military black finish with high-impact grips. New 3-dot sights.

9MM COMPACT POLYMER

SPECIFICATIONS
Caliber: 9mm parabellum
Capacity: 8 shot mag
Action: Single action
Barrel Length: 3.5" alloy steel barrel
Sights: Low-profile 3 dot adj. sights
Safety: Quick on-off thumb safety
Overall Length: 6.75"
Frame: Polymer frame
Price: $137.00

9MM COMP GUN

SPECIFICATIONS
Hi-Point Firearms has introduced a 9mm Comp Gun featuring a 4" barrel, adjustable sights, magazine disconnect safety, muzzle compensator, last round hold-open feature. 10 rounds. Also available with a laser sight mounted to the compensator
Prices: $159.00
   With laser and mount .209.00

MODEL 380 COMP

380 POLYMER

MODEL 380 COMP

SPECIFICATIONS
Hi-Point Firearms' 380 Comp Gun features a 4" barrel, adjustable sights, 2 magazines (10 round and 8 round). The 380 Comp Pistol is also available with a Laser Sight mounted to the compensator.
Price: $125.00
  w/laser sights 190.00

MODEL 380 POLYMER

Model 380 Polymer similar to 9mm but with 3.5" alloy steel barrel, 29 oz.
Price: $99.00
Also available:
Caliber: .45 ACP *Action:* semi-automatic *Capacity:* 7 shot *Barrel length:* 4.5" *Sights:* 3 dot adjustable sights
Price: $159.00
Caliber: 40 S&W *Action:* semi-automatic *Capacity:* 8 shot *Barrel length:* 4.5" *Sights:* 3 dot adjustable sights
Price: $159.00

H-S PRECISION PISTOLS

H-S SILHOUETTE PISTOL

H-S PRECISION

H-S Precision single-shot pistols employ a right-handle bolt, with handle engineered so the bolt head is over the well of the grip for good balance. As on the Series 2000 rifles, triggers are fully adjustable and can be set from 2.5 to 3.5 pounds pull. These super-accurate pistols are held to the same accuracy standards as Pro-Series rifles. They're available in many chamberings, in both varmint and silhouette versions. The silhouette pistol has a titanium safety shroud and a lighter barrel that is drilled and tapped for sights. It meets IHMSA competition weight requirements.

Price: (either version) **$1,250.00**

PRO-SERIES 2000 VP, SP (VARMINT, SILHOUETTE PISTOLS)

SPECIFICATIONS
- ***Pro-Series 2000*** stainless steel pistol action, single shot
- ***Pro-Series 10X*** match grade stainless steel barrel
  - Fluted (except 35 Rem, Silhouette style)
  - Sporter contour, silhouette model
  - Heavy contour, varmint model
- ***Pro-Series*** synthetic stock, center grip with bedding block chassis system
  - Choice of color
  - Metal finish – Teflon® or Pro-Series PFTE Matte Black
  - Weight
    - 4.5 pounds, silhouette
    - 5.25 - 5.50 pounds, varmint
  - Calibers – 17 Rem, 6mm PPC, 223 Rem, 22-250 Rem, 243 Win, 257 Roberts, 260 Rem, 35 Rem, 308 Winc, 7mm-08 Rem, 7mm BR

ISRAEL ARMS & FIREARMS INT'L

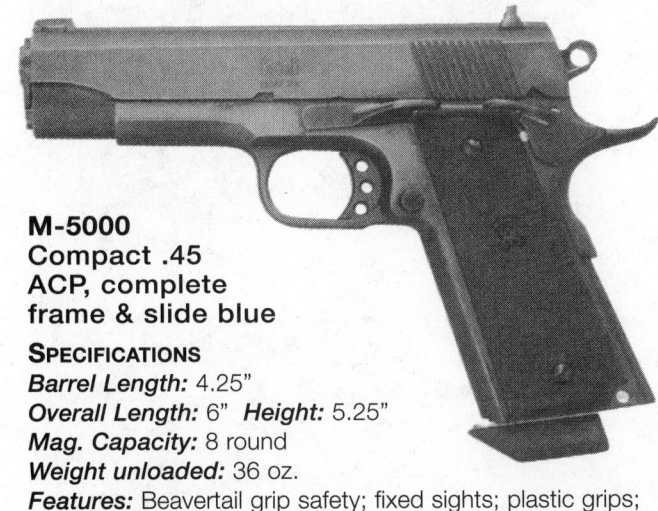

M-5000
Compact .45
ACP, complete
frame & slide blue

SPECIFICATIONS
Barrel Length: 4.25"
Overall Length: 6" ***Height:*** 5.25"
Mag. Capacity: 8 round
Weight unloaded: 36 oz.
Features: Beavertail grip safety; fixed sights; plastic grips; extended slide stop, safety magazine release; beveled feed ramp barrel; combat-style hammer; beveled magazine well; ambidextrous safety
Price: **$447.40**

M-6000
1911 Gov. .45
ACP, Complete Frame & Slide, 4140 Steel, Blue

SPECIFICATIONS
Barrel Length: 5"
Overall Length: 8.5" ***Height:*** 5.25"
Capacity: 8 ***Weight unloaded:*** 36 oz.
Features: Beveled feed ramp barrel; beavertail grip safety; beveled magazine well; extended slide stop, safety and magazine release; fixed sights; plastic grips; combat style hammer, ambidextrous safety
Price: **$447.40**
Also Available: M-3000 9mm Compact **373.70**
M-4000 .40 Compact **373.70**

HANDGUNS

P40

SPECIFICATIONS
Caliber: .40 S&W
Capacity: 6+1
Barrel: 3.5", 1-16 RH twist
Overall length: 6.1"
Height: 4.5" *Weight:* 18.7 oz.
Prices:
P40 . . . .$580.00
K40 . . . . .580.00
K40, Stainless .580.00
KS40, Stainless covert 594.00
K40 Wilson custom 1,310.00
K40 Elite 631.00

P9

SPECIFICATIONS
Caliber: 9x19
Capacity: 7+1
Barrel: 3.5", 1-10 RH twist
Overall length: 6.0"
Height: 4.5"
Weight: 17.7 oz.
Prices:
P9 (black or stainless) $580.00
K9 (black or stainless) 580.00
K9, Wilson custom 1,310.00
K9 Elite 631.00
MK9 Elite 98 . . . . .631.00
MK9 Elite 2000 . . . . .631.00
MK9 . . . . .580.00

KBI PISTOLS

FEG SMC AUTO PISTOL

SPECIFICATIONS
Calibers: 380 ACP *Capacity:* 6 rounds
Barrel Length: 3.5" *Overall Length:* 6 1/8"
Weight: 18.5 oz.
Stock: Checkered composition w/thumbrest
Sights: Blade front; rear adjustable for windage
Features: Alloy frame; steel slide; double action; blue
finish; two magazines and cleaning rod standard
Price: $239.00
Also Available: PMK-380 .380 ACP
   7 shot, 7" S/Auto and D/A 239.00

FEG SMC

FEG MODEL PJK-9HP (HI-POWER)

SPECIFICATIONS
Caliber: 9mm Luger Parabellum
Magazine capacity: 10 rounds
Action: Single *Barrel Length:* 4.75"
Overall Length: 8" *Weight:* 21 oz.
Grips: Hand-checkered walnut
Safety: Thumb safety
Sights: 3-dot system *Finish:* Blue
Features: One 10-round magazine, cleaning rod
Price: $279.00

**FEG MODEL
PJK-9HP**

P-32 CALIBER .32 AUTO

The P-32 is designed for maximum concealability. It is lighter and flatter than any other self-loading gun. This has been achieved by using a locked breech combined with the composite structure of the successful P-11 and P-40 pistols. The firing mechanism is slide assisted double action only, employing an internal hammer block. Trigger pull is 6 lbs. The P-32 can shoot any configuration, including hot European or emerging +P cartridges. All edges are rounded, sights are integrated, and the slide stop internal for a snag-free deployment.

SPECIFICATIONS
Caliber: .32 AUTO, 7.65x17 *Weight unloaded:* 6.6 oz., 186 g *Loaded magazine:* 2.8 oz., 81g *Length:* 5.07", 129mm *Height:* 3.52", 89mm *Width:* .75", 19 mm *Barrel length:* 2.68", 68mm *Muzzle energy:* 200 ftlbs, 270 J *Capacity:* 7+1 rounds
Prices: P-32 (not shown), 6.6 oz, 7+1 round capacity
blue $300.00
Parkerized 340.00
Chromed 355.00

P-40 CALIBER .40 S&W (NOT SHOWN)

The P-40 is developed from the highly successful P-11 pistol in 9 mm. Only 5/32 longer than the P-11 and slightly heavier, it is by a large margin the lightest .40 S&W available today. Still, it is designed so the recoil from the powerful .40 cartridge is managable. Optional 10-rd. magazine extension is available.

The P-40 is produced in blue, parkerized and hard chrome finishes. As with other Kel-Tec guns many accessories are available.

SPECIFICATIONS
Caliber: .40 S&W *Weight unloaded:* 15.8 oz., 448 g *Loaded magazine:* 7 oz., 180 g *Length:* 6.0", 152mm *Height:* 4.3", 109mm *Width:* 1.05", 26mm *Barrel length:* 3.3", 83 mm *Muzzle energy ftlbs:* 400 ftlbs, 540 J *Capacity:* 9+1+1 rounds *Trigger pull:* 9 lbs., 40N
Prices: P40, blue $330.00
Parkerized 371.00
Chromed 388.00

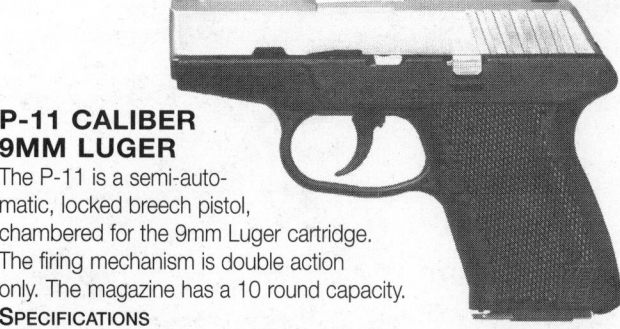

P-11 CALIBER 9MM LUGER

The P-11 is a semi-automatic, locked breech pistol, chambered for the 9mm Luger cartridge. The firing mechanism is double action only. The magazine has a 10 round capacity.

SPECIFICATIONS
Caliber: 9mm Luger, 9x19 *Weight unloaded:* 14.4 oz., 408g *Loaded magazine:* 5.6 oz., 159g *Length:* 5.85", 148mm *Height:* 4.3", 109mm *Width:* 1.05", 26 mm *Barrel length:* 3.1", 79mm *Muzzle energy ftlbs:* 400 ftlbs, 540 J *Capacity:* 10+1 rounds *Trigger Pull:* 9 lbs, 40N
Prices: P11, blue $314.00
Parkerized 355.00
Chromed 368.00

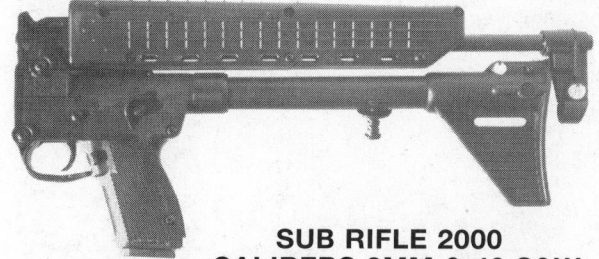

SUB RIFLE 2000 CALIBERS 9MM & 40 S&W

The SUB RIFLE 2000 is a self-loading carbine for pistol cartridges. Different veersions of the SUB-2000 will accept most modern handgun magazines, e.g. S&W, Glock or Beretta. By rotating the barrel upwards and back, the SUB-2000 can be reduced to a size of 16" x 7" to facilitate secure storage. The SUB-2000 also features an internal keyed deployment lock.

SPECIFICATIONS
Weight unloaded: 4 lbs., 1.8 kg *Length open:* 30", 762mm *Length closed:* 16", 406mm *Barrel length:* 16.1", 409 mm *Practical range:* 150 yd, 150 m *Safeties:* recessed push-bolt. Lock-back operating handle, keyed deployment lock.
Price: Sub-Rifle 2000 . . . . $383.00

HANDGUNS

SUB RIFLE 2000
(READY TO FIRE)

KIMBER PISTOLS

STAINLESS GOLD MATCH

CUSTOM & CUSTOM TARGET

The 1911 has been one of America's favorite pistols for nearly a century. Today it is still the best choice for action shooting, concealed carry or defense. Kimber has perfected the 1911 using state of the art technology. The custom Kimber has a 5" barrel, weighs 38 oz. and is 8.7" overall length, in 45 caliber.

Prices: Custom $730.00
Custom stainless 832.00
Custom stainless in 40 S&W 870.00
Royal (Rosewood grips) 886.00
Custom Target (not shown) 837.00
Stainless Target 944.00
Stainless Target in 40 S&W 974.00

GOLD MATCH

Features: Hand-fitted match grade barrel, match grade trigger, hand checkered rosewood grips.
Barrel length: 5"
Weight: 38 oz.
Overall length: 8.7"
Caliber: 45 ACP
Prices:
Gold Match $1,169.00
Stainless 1,315.00
Stainless in 40 S&W 1,345.00

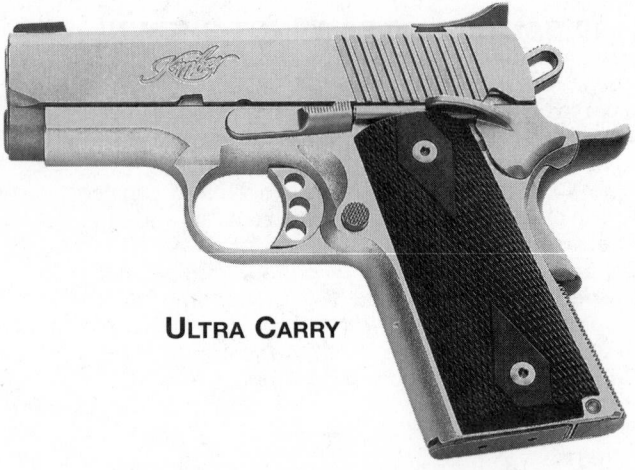

ULTRA CARRY

COMPACT & PRO CARRY

These compact pistols are good choices for concealed carry and defense.
Barrel: 4" **Overall length:** 7.7"
Weight: 34 oz. (compact) and 28 oz. (pro carry) **Caliber:** 45 ACP or 40 S&W

Prices:
Compact (45 ACP only) $764.00
Stainless 871.00
Stainless in 40 S&W 902.00
Aluminum stainless .837.00
in 40 S&W 873.00
Pro Carry (not shown) (45 ACP) 773.00
in 40 S&W 808.00
Stainless (45 ACP) .845.00
Stainless in 40 S&W 881.00
Pro Carry HD 879.00

STAINLESS ULTRA CARRY

Caliber: 45 ACP and 40 S&W
Barrel: 3"
Weight: 25 oz.
Overall length: 6.8"
Prices:
Ultra Carry 45 ACP $808.00
Stainless 886.00
Ultra Carry 40 S&W .847.00
Stainless 931.00

ULTRA TEN II

GOLD COMBAT

ULTRA TEN II

The new Ultra Ten II combines the features of the Ultra Carry with a shorter, lighter version of the Polymer Series frame.

SPECIFICATIONS
Caliber: 45 ACP
Barrel length: 3"
Weight: 24 oz.
Overall Length: 6.8"
Price: $896.00

CUSTOM SHOP PISTOLS

The **GOLD COMBAT** has most of the features of the Gold Match and includes many Custom Shop features like a stainless steel match grade barrel and chamber, 30 LPI front strap checkering, extended beveled magazine well, stainless steel match grade barrel bushing, special bordered and hand-checkered double diamond rosewood grips, extended ambidextrous thumb safety, match grade Premium Aluminum Trigger, Meprolight Tritium three dot (green) night sights and special Custom Shop markings.

Caliber: 45 ACP *Barrel length:* 5"
Weight: 38 oz. *Overall length:* 8.7"
Prices: Gold Combat....................$1,682.00
Stainless 1,623.00
Also Available: Super Match 1,927.00

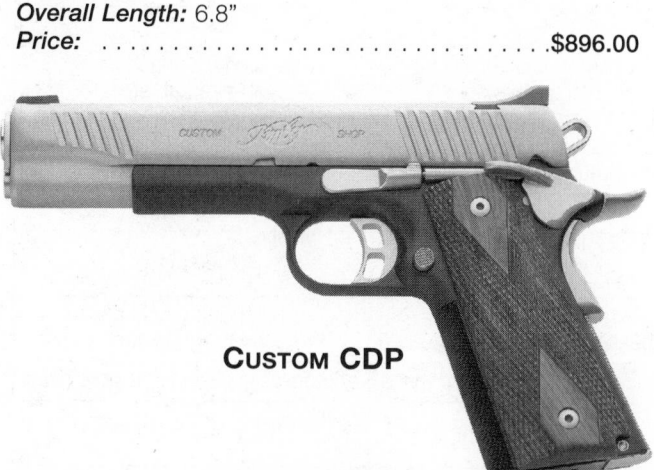

CUSTOM CDP

POLYMER CUSTOM

CDP SERIES

The Custom Defense Package pistols feature a lightweight aluminum frame and stainless steel slide. Edges and corners have been rounded and grips are checkered rosewood.

SPECIFICATIONS
Caliber: 45 ACP
Weight: 25-38 oz.
Overall length: 6.8-8.7"
Prices:
Ultra CDP (3" barrel) $1,142.00
Compact CDP (4" barrel) 1,142.00
Custom CDP (5" barrel) 1,142.00

POLYMER SERIES

Kimber Polymer pistols have the same features as other Kimbers, but with a lighter Polymer frame which holds 10 rounds. All in 45 ACP.

Prices:
Polymer Custom $795.00
  Stainless 856.00
Polymer Pro Carry 814.00
  Stainless 874.00
Polymer Gold Match 1,041.00
  Stainless 1,177.00

LLAMA PISTOLS

GOVERNMENT MODEL

MINI-MAX 45

LLAMA CLASSIC AUTOMATIC PISTOL SPECIFICATIONS

SPECIFICATIONS:	MICRO-MAX	MINI-MAX	GOVERNMENT MODEL
CALIBERS:	.32/.380 ACP	45 Auto	45 Auto
FRAME:	Precision machined from high-strength steel	Precision machined from high-strength steel	Precision machined from high-strength steel
TRIGGER:	Serrated	Serrated	Serrated
HAMMER:	External; wide spur, serrated	External; military style	External; military style
OPERATION:	Straight blow-back	Locked breech	Locked breech
LOADED CHAMBER INDICATOR:	Yes	Yes	Yes
SAFETIES:	Extended manual & grip safeties	Extended manual & beavertail grip safeties	Extended manual & beavertail grip safeties
GRIPS:	Matte black polymer	Anatomically designed rubber grips	Anatomically designed rubber grips
SIGHTS:	Patridge-type front; square-notch rear	3-dot combat sight	3-dot combat sights
SIGHT RADIUS:	4 $^1/_4$"	6 $^1/_4$"	6 $^1/_4$"
MAGAZINE CAPACITY:	8 shots/7 shots	6 shots	7 shots
WEIGHT:	23 oz.	34 oz.	36 oz.
BARREL LENGTH:	3 $^{11}/_{16}$"	3 $^1/_2$"	5 $^1/_8$"
OVERALL LENGTH:	6 $^1/_2$"	7 $^1/_3$"	8 $^1/_2$"
HEIGHT:	4 $^3/_8$"	5"	5 $^5/_{16}$"
FINISH:	Standard; Non-glare combat matte. Deluxe: Satin chrome	Matte	Non-glare combat matte
PRICES:	$281.95	$316.95	$298.95

MARK XIX COMPONENT SYSTEM

The Mark XIX Component system allows for three caliber changes in two different barrel lengths.

The Desert Eagle Pistol Mark XIX Component System is based on a single platform that transforms into six different pistols–three Magnum calibers, each with a 6-inch or 10-inch barrel. Changing calibers is a simple matter of switching barrels and magazines. (Converting to or from .357 Magnum also involves changing the bolt.)

All six barrels, including the optional 10-inch barrels, have a ⁷/₈" dovetailed design with cross slots to accommodate scope rings; no other scope mounts are required. The .50 A.E.'s new 10-inch barrel will fit existing .50s, as well as the new Mark XIX platform.

The pistol's gas operation, polygonal rifling, low recoil and safety features remain the same, as do the Mark VII adjustable trigger, slide release and safety levers.

SPECIFICATIONS

Calibers: 357 Magnum, 44 Magnum and 50 A.E. **Capacity:** 9 rounds (357 Mag.); 8 rounds (44 Mag.); 7 rounds (50 A.E.) **Barrel Lengths:** 6" and 10" **Overall Length:** 10.74" (w/6" bbl.); 14.75" (w/10" bbl.) **Weight:** 4 lbs. 6.5 oz. (w/6" bbl.); 4 lbs. 15 oz. (w/10" bbl.) (empty) **Height:** 6.25" **Width:** 1.25" **Finish:** Standard black and new Titanium nitride
Prices:

357 MAG. w/6" barrel	$1199.00
357 MAG. w/10" barrel	1299.00
44 MAG. w/6" barrel	1199.00
44 MAG. w/10" barrel	1299.00
50 A.E. MAG. w/6" barrel	1199.00
50 A.E. w/10" barrel	1299.00

(add $500 for Titanium finish, all models)

LONE EAGLE

LONE EAGLE SINGLE SHOT

This specialty pistol is designed for hunters, silhouette enthusiasts and long-range target shooters. Available w/interchangeable 14-inch barreled actions. Calibers: 22 Hornet, 22-250, 223 Rem., 243 Win., 30-06, 30-30, 308 Win., 35 Rem., 358 Win., 44 Mag., 444 Marlin, 7mm-08, 7mm Bench Rest., 7.62x39, 260 Rem., 440 Cor-Bon. Features ambidextrous grip, new cocking indicator and lever.

Also available:

Barreled action w/muzzle brake	$418.00
Barreled action w/chrome finish	$359.00
Barreled action w/chrome finish, muzzle brake	$469.00
Ambidextrous grip assembly	$119.00

HANDGUNS

DESERT EAGLE PISTOL MARK XIX .50 MAGNUM TITANIUM FINISH

DESERT EAGLE MARK VII 357 MAG.

The Desert Eagle Pistol is available in 357 Mag., 44 Mag. and 50 AE, in 6" and 10" barrels
Prices: with 6" barrel. **$1,199.00**

with 10" barrel **1,299.00**
Titanium finish, 6" **1,699.00**
Titanium finish, 10" **1,799.00**

BABY EAGLE RS

BABY EAGLE

The Baby Eagle RS in 9mm offers a frame-mounted safety and a shorter barrel than the standard Baby Eagle Pistol. The RS is available in standard black, matte hard chrome or brushed hard chrome (as shown).

A polymer-frame version is also available. These autoloading pistols are available in 9mm, .40 S+W and .45 ACP.
Price:
Baby Eagle **$499.00**

MAGNUM RESEARCH HANDGUNS

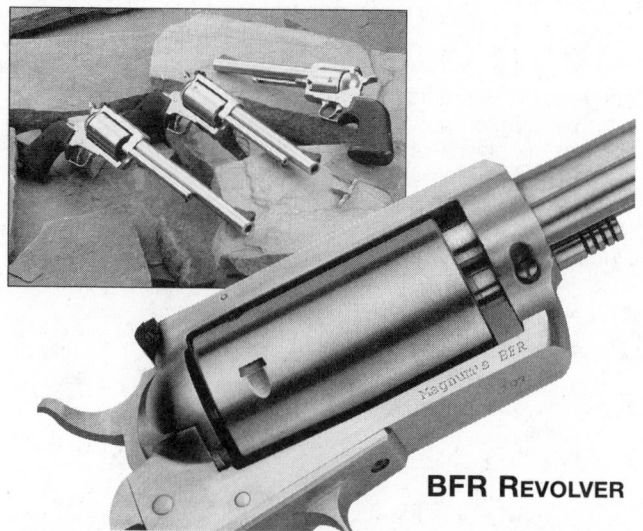

BFR REVOLVER

"SINGLE-ACTION HUNTING REVOLVER"

Magnum Research, Inc., creator of the legendary Desert Eagle Pistol, also offers a revolver. Magnum's BFR (Biggest Finest Revolver) is a single-action hunting revolver manufactured in the United States.

It is available in two models, both built to close tolerances entirely of stainless steel. The long-cylindered model fires big-bore calibers .45/70, .444 Marlin, and .45 Long Colt/.410. The short cylinder model is available in .454 Casull, .45 Long Colt + P, and .22 Hornet.

Barrel length options of 6.5, 7.5, and 10 inches depending on chambering.

Price: $999.00

ACCESSORIES

Hogue Rubber Finger Groove Grips	$34.95
Hogue Wood Grips Pau Ferro	74.95
Hogue Wood Grips Goncalo Alves	74.95
Full Choke Tube (0 marks)	17.00
Modified Choke Tube (2 marks)	17.00
Scatter Choke Tube (1 mark)	17.00
Choke Tube Wrench	5.00
Millett sights, rear adjustable, white outline	39.95

Standard equipment sights have fixed orange front ramp and rear sight adjustable for windage and elevation.

MOA MAXIMUM PISTOLS

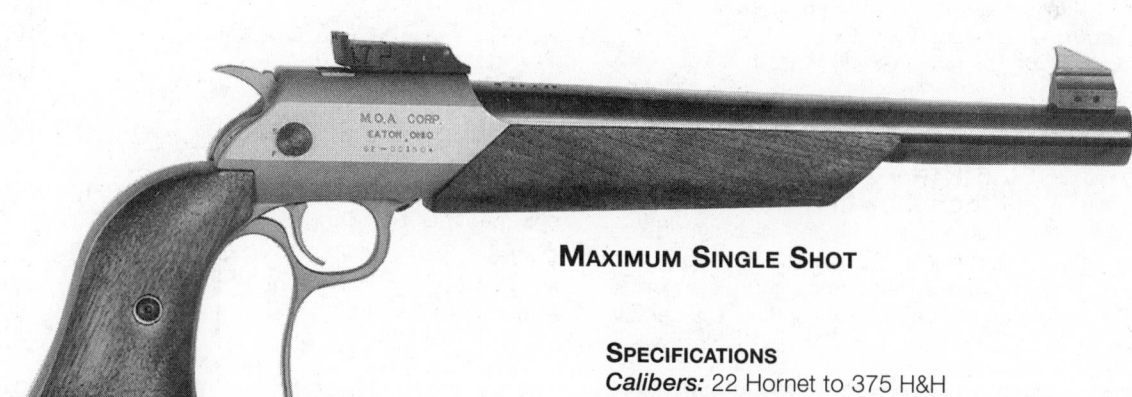

MAXIMUM SINGLE SHOT

MAXIMUM

This single-shot pistol with its unique falling-block action performs like a finely tuned rifle. The single-piece receiver of stainless steel is mated to a Douglas barrel for optimum accuracy and strength.

SPECIFICATIONS
Calibers: 22 Hornet to 375 H&H
Barrel Lengths: 8.5", 10.5" and 14"
Weight: 3 lbs. 8 oz. (8.5" bbl.); 3 lbs. 13 oz. (10.5" bbl.); 4 lbs. 3 oz. (14" bbl.)
Prices:
Stainless receiver, blued barrel $799.00
Stainless receiver and barrel. 883.00
Extra barrels (blue). 254.00
Stainless 317.00
Muzzle brake. 125.00

HANDGUNS

1873 SINGLE ACTION ARMY REVOLVER

1873 SINGLE ACTION ARMY REVOLVER

The quintessential sidearm of the American West. Superb replica of the Colt Single Action Army features color case hardened frame and hammer, and a blued steel barrel, cylinder, trigger guard and backstrap. One of the most popular revolvers of all time, manufactured from 1873-1940. Available in the same barrel lengths as the originals: 4-3/4", 5-1/2", 7-1/2". Chambered for .45 Colt, .44-40 and .357 Magnum
Price: **$395.00**

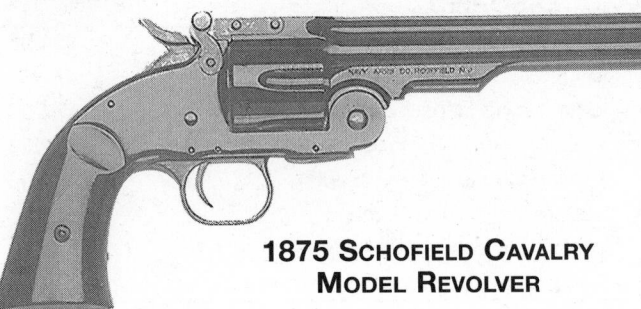

1875 SCHOFIELD CAVALRY MODEL REVOLVER

1875 SCHOFIELD REVOLVER

A favorite side arm of Jesse James, the hinged-breech 1875 Schofield revolver was one of the legendary handguns of the Old West.

Caliber: 44-40, 45 LC *Barrel Lengths:* 3.5" (Hide Out Model), 5" (Wells Fargo Model) or 7" (U.S. Cavalry Model) *Overall Length:* 9.5", 10.75" or 12.75" *Weight:* 2 lbs. 5 oz. *Sights:* Blade front; notch rear *Features:* Top-break, automatic ejector single action
Price: **$695.00**

NAVY ARMS NEW MODEL RUSSIAN REVOLVER

A replica of the Smith and Wesson Model 3 Russian Third Model top break revolver that was carried by Western Lawman Pat Garrett.

Caliber: .44 Russian *Barrel Lengths:* 6.5" *Overall Length:* 12" *Weight:* 2 lbs. 8 oz. *Sights:* Blade front; notch rear *Grips:* Walnut
Price: **$745.00**

NEW MODEL RUSSIAN REVOLVER

BISLEY MODEL SINGLE ACTION REVOLVER (not shown)

Introduced in 1894, Colt's "Bisley Model" was named after the Bisley shooting range in England. Most of these revolvers were sold in the United States and were popular sidearms in the American West at the turn of the century.

This replica features the unique Bisley grip style, low-profile spur hammer, blued barrel and color casehardened frame.

Calibers: 44-40 or 45 Long Colt *Barrel Lengths:* 4.75", 5.5" and 7.5" *Sights:* Blade front, notch rear *Grips:* Walnut
Price: **$415.00**

1873 U.S. CAVALRY MODEL (not shown)

An exact replica of the original U.S. Government issue Colt Single-Action Army, complete with Arsenal stampings and inspector's cartouche.

Caliber: 45 Long Colt
Barrel Length: 7.5"
Overall Length: 13.25" *Weight:* 2 lbs. 7 oz.
Sights: Blade front; notch rear *Grips:* Walnut
Price: **$465.00**

"FLAT TOP" TARGET MODEL SA REVOLVER (not shown)

A fine replica of Colt's rare "Flat Top" Single Action Army revolver used for target shooting.

Caliber: 45 Long Colt *Barrel Length:* 7.5"
Overall Length: 12.75" *Weight:* 2 lbs. 7 oz.
Sights: Spring-loaded German silver Patridge front, adjustable notch ear. *Grips:* Walnut. *Finish:* Blue
Price: **$435.00**

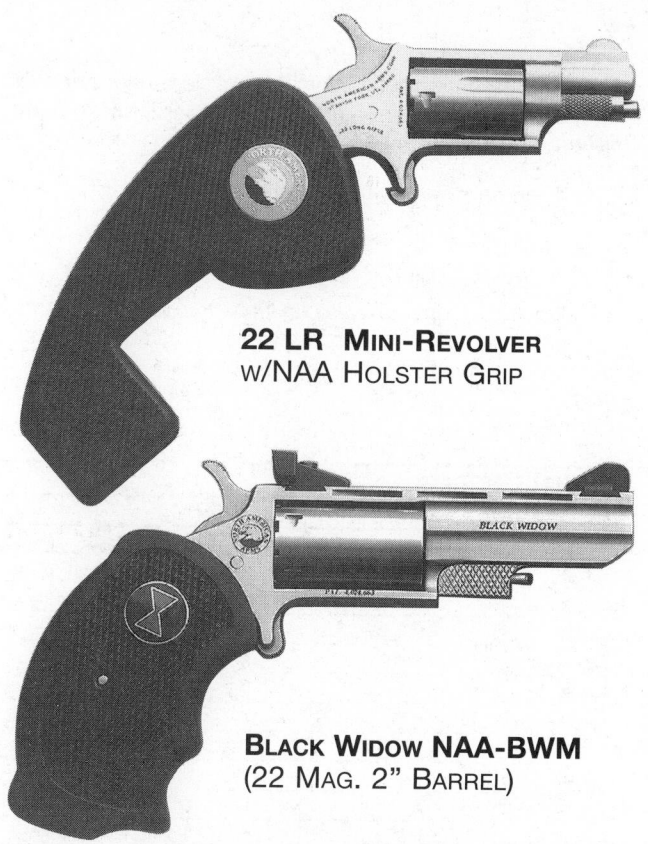

22 LR MINI-REVOLVER
w/NAA HOLSTER GRIP

BLACK WIDOW NAA-BWM
(22 MAG. 2" BARREL)

MINI-MASTER SERIES

Calibers: 22 LR and 22 Magnum *Rifling:* 8 land and grooves, 1:12 R.H. twist *Grips:* Oversized black rubber
Sights: Front integral with barrel; rear Millett adjustable white outlined (elelvation only) or low-profile fixed
Prices: MINI-MASTER NAA-MMT-M. $304.00
    w/Fixed sight 286.00
MINI-MASTER NAA BLACK WIDOW
    Adjustable sight $274.00
    Fixed sight 256.00

MINI-REVOLVERS

SPECIFICATIONS (See also table below)
Calibers: 22 Short (1 1/8" bbl. only), 22 LR and 22 Magnum
Capacity: 5-shot cylinder
Grips: Laminated rosewood
Safety: Half-cock safety
Sights: Blade front (integral w/barrel); fixed, notched rear
Material: Stainless steel
Finish: Matte with brushed sides

GUARDIAN 32

Stainless steel autoloading pistol; double action; fixed sights; 6-shot magazine in .32 ACP
Price: $408.00
Also available:
NAA GUARDIAN .380
.380/9mm Kurz *Features:* 6 shot, fixed sights
Barrel length: 2.5" *Height:* 3.5" *Total length:* 4.75"
Price: $449.00

SPECIFICATIONS: MINI-REVOLVERS & MINI-MASTER SERIES

MODEL	WEIGHT	BARREL LENGTH	OVERALL LENGTH	OVERALL HEIGHT	OVERALL WIDTH	PRICE
NAA-MMT-M	10.7 oz.	4"	7 3/4"	3 7/8"	7/8"	$304.00
NAA-MMT-L	10.7 oz.	4"	7 3/4"	3 7/8"	7/8"	304.00
*NAA-BW-M	8.8 oz.	2"	5 7/8"	3 7/8"	7/8"	256.00
*NAA-BW-L	8.8 oz.	2"	5 7/8"	3 7/8"	7/8"	256.00
NAA-22LR**	4.5 oz.	1 1/8"	4 1/4"	2 3/8"	13/16"	186.00
NAA-22LLR**	4.6 oz.	1 5/8"	4 3/4"	2 3/8"	13/16"	186.00
*NAA-22MS	5.9 oz.	1 1/8"	5"	2 7/8"	7/8"	205.00
*NAA-22M	6.2 oz.	1 5/8"	5 3/8"	2 7/8"	7/8"	205.00
NAA-22S	4 oz.	1 1/8"	3 5/8"	2 3/8"	13/16"	205.00

*Available with Conversion Cylinder chambered for 22 Long Rifle (**$245.00**) **Available with holster grip (**$240.00**)

HANDGUNS

Built on the proven M1911-A1 single-action autoloading pistol, the Para-Ordnance P-series was developed begin-ning in 1988. The P14.45 appeared in 1990 as one of the first high-capacity autoloaders of this type. Uninterrupted slide rails, beefier slide stop, contoured feed ramp and ejection port, combat hammer, 3-dot sights, beveled magazine well and polymer magazine are all standard. *Magazine Capacity:* 10+1 in compact models to 18+1 in full-size.

P-SERIES
Price: $750.00 *Stainless:* $799.00

MODEL P10•45ER
(BLACK)

MODEL P12•45 ACP
(3.5" BARREL, STAINLESS)

**MODEL
P10•45 LIMITED**

PARA-ORDNANCE "LIMITED"

Para-Ordnance "Limited" pistols feature adjustable sights, competition hammer, front slide serrations, match-grade barrel, ambidextrous safety, full-length recoil guide.
Price:. $875.00
   Stainless. 899.00

P-SERIES 2001
New P-Series Millennium 2001 Pistols

MODEL	CALIBER	ROUNDS	BARREL	WEIGHT	LENGTH	HEIGHT	RECEIVER	FINISH
P14-45ER	.45 ACP	*14+1	5"	40 oz.	8.5"	5.75"	Steel	Black
P14-45RR	.45 ACP	*14+1	5"	31 oz.	8.5"	5.75"	Alloy	Black
P14-45SR	.45 ACP	*14+1	5"	40 oz.	8.5"	5.75"	Stainless	Stainless
P16-40ER	.40 S&W	*16+1	5"	40 oz.	8.5"	5.75"	Steel	Black
P16-40SR	.40 S&W	*16+1	5"	40 oz.	8.5"	5.75"	Stainless	Stainless
P18-9SR	9mm	*18+1	5"	40 oz.	8.5"	5.75"	Stainless	Stainless
P13-45ER	.45 ACP	*13+1	4.25"	36 oz.	7.75"	5.25"	Steel	Black
P13-45RR	.45 ACP	*13+1	4.25"	28 oz.	7.75"	5.25"	Alloy	Black
P13-45SR	.45 ACP	*13+1	4.25"	36 oz.	7.75"	5.25"	Stainless	Stainless
P12-45ER	.45 ACP	*12+1	3.5"	34 oz.	7.13"	5"	Steel	Black
P12-45RR	.45 ACP	*12+1	3.5"	26 oz.	7.13"	5"	Alloy	Black
P12-45SR	.45 ACP	*12+1	3.5"	34 oz.	7.13"	5"	Stainless	Stainless
P10-45ER	.45 ACP	*10+1	3"	31 oz.	8.5"	5.75"	Steel	Black
P10-45RR	.45 ACP	*10+1	3"	24 oz.	8.5"	5.75"	Alloy	Black
P10-45SR	.45 ACP	*10+1	3"	31 oz.	8.5"	5.75"	Stainless	Stainless
P10-40ER	.40 S&W	*10+1	3"	31 oz.	8.5"	5.75"	Steel	Black
P10-40RR	.40 S&W	*10+1	3"	24 oz.	8.5"	5.75"	Alloy	Stainless
P10-40SR	.40 S&W	*10+1	3"	31 oz.	8.5"	5.75"	Stainless	Stainless
P10-9RR	9mm	*10+1	3"	24 oz.	8.5"	5.75"	Alloy	Black

LIMITED P-SERIES
P-Series Limited Pistols

MODEL	CALIBER	ROUNDS	BARREL	WEIGHT	LENGTH	HEIGHT	RECEIVER	FINISH
S14-45ER	.45 ACP	*14+1	5"	40 oz.	8.5"	5.75"	Steel	Black
S14-45SR	.45 ACP	*14+1	5"	40 oz.	8.5"	5.75"	Stainless	Stainless
S16-40ER	.40 S&W	*16+1	5"	40 oz.	8.5"	5.75"	Steel	Black
S16-40SR	.40 S&W	*16+1	5"	40 oz.	8.5"	5.75"	Stainless	Stainless
S13-45ER	.45 ACP	*13+1	4.25"	36 oz.	7.75"	5.25"	Steel	Black
S13-45RR	.45 ACP	*13+1	4.25"	28 oz.	7.75"	5.25"	Alloy	Black
S13-45SR	.45 ACP	*13+1	4.25"	36 oz.	7.75"	5.25"	Stainless	Stainless
S12-45ER	.45 ACP	*12+1	3.5"	34 oz.	7.13"	5"	Steel	Black
S12-45RR	.45 ACP	*12+1	3.5"	26 oz.	7.13"	5"	Alloy	Black
S12-45SR	.45 ACP	*12+1	3.5"	34 oz.	7.13"	5"	Stainless	Stainless
S10-45ER	.45 ACP	*10+1	3"	31 oz.	6.5"	4.5"	Steel	Black
S10-45RR	.45 ACP	*10+1	3"	24 oz.	6.5"	4.5"	Alloy	Black
S10-45SR	.45 ACP	*10+1	3"	31 oz.	6.5"	4.5"	Stainless	Stainless

PARA-ORDNANCE PISTOLS

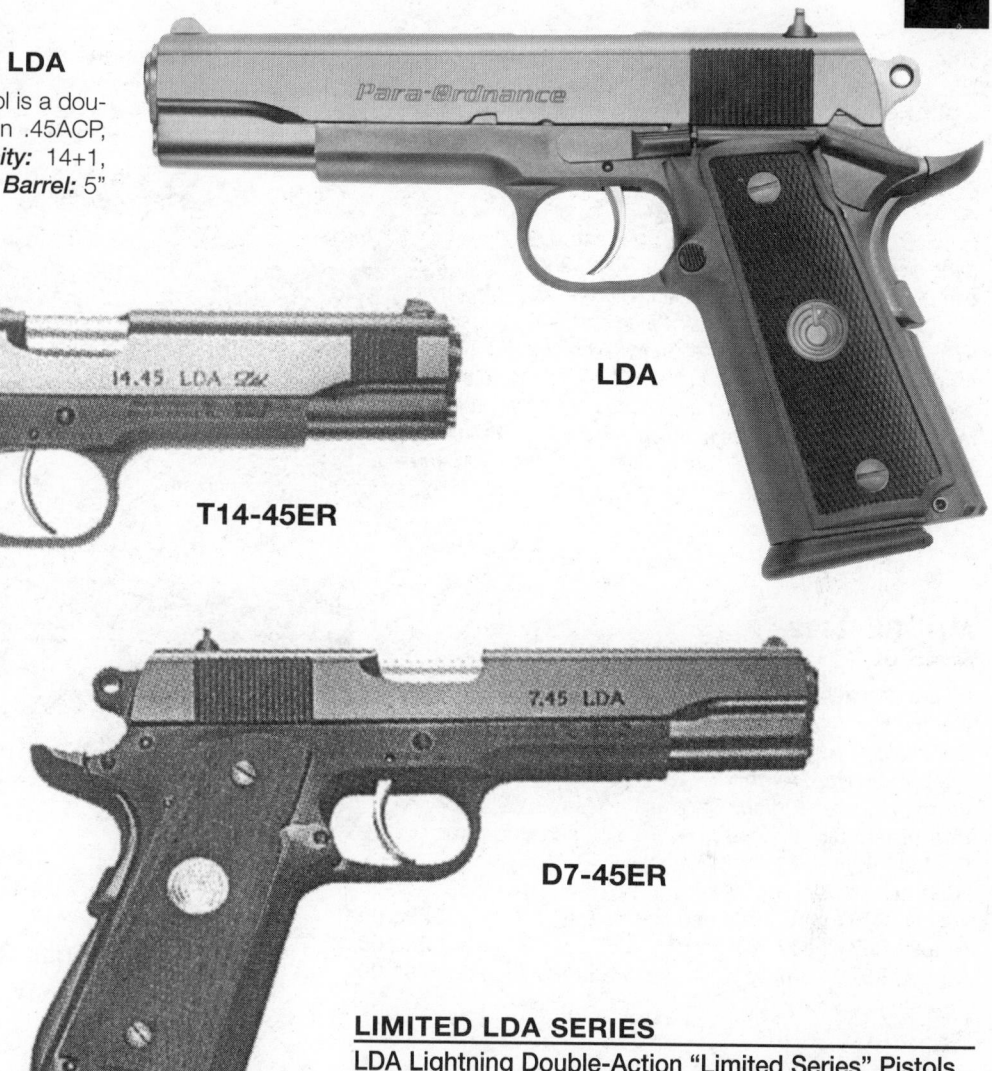

PARA-ORDNANCE LDA

The Para-Ordnance LDA pistol is a double-action carbon-steel gun in .45ACP, .40 S+W and 9mm. *Capacity:* 14+1, 16+1, and 18+1, respectively *Barrel:* 5" *Weight:* 40 oz.

LDA

T14-45ER

D7-45ER

LDA SERIES
LDA Lightning Double-Action Pistols

MODEL	CALIBER	ROUNDS	BARREL	WEIGHT	LENGTH	HEIGHT	RECEIVER	FINISH
D14-45ER	.45 ACP	*14+1	5"	40 oz.	8.5"	5.75"	Steel	Black
D14-45SR	.45 ACP	*14+1	5"	40 oz.	8.5"	5.75"	Stainless	Stainless
D16-40ER	.40 S&W	*16+1	5"	40 oz.	8.5"	5.75"	Steel	Black
D16-40SR	.40 S&W	*16+1	5"	40 oz.	8.5"	5.75"	Stainless	Stainless
D18-9ER	9mm	*18+1	5"	40 oz.	8.5"	5.75"	Steel	Black
D18-9SR	9mm	*18+1	5"	40 oz.	8.5"	5.75"	Stainless	Stainless
L12-45ER	.45 ACP	*12+1	3.5"	34 oz.	7.13"	5"	Steel	Black
L12-45SR	.45 ACP	*12+1	3.5"	34 oz.	7.13"	5"	Stainless	Stainless
L14-40ER	.40 S&W	*14+1	3.5"	34 oz.	7.13"	5"	Steel	Black
L14-40SR	.40 S&W	*14+1	3.5"	34 oz.	7.13"	5"	Stainless	Stainless

LIMITED LDA SERIES
LDA Lightning Double-Action "Limited Series" Pistols

MODEL	CALIBER	ROUNDS	BARREL	WEIGHT	LENGTH	HEIGHT	RECEIVER	FINISH
T14-45ER	.45 ACP	*14+1	5"	40 oz.	8.5"	5.75"	Steel	Black
T14-45SR	.45 ACP	*14+1	5"	40 oz.	8.5"	5.75"	Stainless	Stainless
T16-40ER	.40 S&W	*16+1	5"	40 oz.	8.5"	5.75"	Steel	Black
T16-40SR	.40 S&W	*16+1	5"	40 oz.	8.5"	5.75"	Stainless	Stainless
T18-9ER	9mm	*18+1	5"	40 oz.	8.5"	5.75"	Steel	Black
T18-9SR	9mm	*18+1	5"	40 oz.	8.5"	5.75"	Stainless	Stainless

LDA SINGLE STACK SERIES
LDA Single-Stack Series Pistols

MODEL	CALIBER	ROUNDS	BARREL	WEIGHT	LENGTH	HEIGHT	RECEIVER	FINISH
D7-45ER	.45 ACP	7+1	5"	39 oz.	8.5"	5.75"	Steel	Black
D7-45SR	.45 ACP	7+1	5"	39 oz.	8.5"	5.75"	Stainless	Stainless
L6-40SR	.45 ACP	7+1	3"	32 oz.	6.5"	5"	Stainless	Stainless
LL6-45SR	.45 ACP	7+1	3"	32 oz.	6.5"	5"	Stainless	Stainless

HANDGUNS

ROSSI REVOLVERS

For 2001, Rossi introduces new revolvers with longer barrels. These three new handguns are of the same quality and reliability that has been part of the Rossi name for the last century. In .357 Magnum, Rossi has two offerings - **Model 971**, with 4-inch chrome-moly barrel and **Model 972**, featuring a stainless steel 6 inch barrel model. There is also the **Model 851**, a .38 Special in blue steel with a 4 inch barrel and 6 round capacity. Like their shorter barreled companions, these revolvers are rated for factory new +P ammunition and have the lifetime repair policy, as well as the patented Taurus Security System. All three feature adjustable rear sights and red inserts on the front sight for easier aim.

**MODEL R972
.357 MAGNUM
6-SHOT**

MODEL R462
$345.00

SPECIFICATIONS
Caliber: 357 Magnum *Capacity:* 6 rounds
Barrel Length: 2" heavy *Overall Length:* 6.5"
Weight: 26 oz. *Height:* 5"
Grips: Rubber *Finish:* Stainless
Features: Fully enclosed ejector rod; serrated ramp front sight
Also available:
MODEL R461 w/matte blued finish $298.00
MODEL R971 (.357 w/4" barrel) 345.00
MODEL R972 (.357 w/6" stainless barrel) 391.00

MODEL R461

MODEL R352

SPECIFICATIONS
Caliber: 38 Special
Capacity: 5 rounds, swing-out cylinder
Barrel Lengths: 2"
Overall Length: 6.5" (2" barrel)
Weight: 24 oz. (2")
Sights: Ramp front, square-notched rear adjustable for windage
Grips: Rubber (2" barrel only)
Finish: Stainless steel
Price: $345.00
Also available:
MODEL R351 (not shown) w/matte blue finish 298.00
MODEL R851 (.38 Special w/4" barrel) 298.00

MODEL R352

REDHAWK REVOLVER

STAINLESS REDHAWK
MODEL KRH-44

STAINLESS REDHAWK
W/SCOPE (KRH-44R)

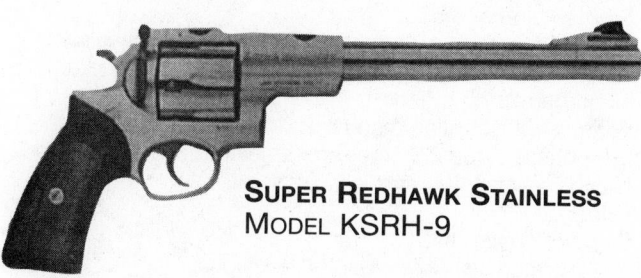

SUPER REDHAWK STAINLESS
MODEL KSRH-9

BLUED STEEL REDHAWK REVOLVER

The popular Ruger Redhawk® double-action revolver is available in an alloy steel model with blued finish or high-gloss standard steel in 44 Magnum caliber. Constructed of hardened chrome-moly and other alloy steels, this Redhawk is satin polished to a high luster and finished in a rich blue.

SPECIFICATIONS

Capacity: 6 rounds

CATALOG NUMBER	CALIBER	BARREL LENGTH	OVERALL LENGTH	APPROX. WEIGHT (OUNCES)	PRICE
RUGER BLUED REDHAWK REVOLVER					
RH-445	44 Mag.	5.5"	11"	49	$560.00
RH-44	44 Mag.	7.5"	13"	54	560.00
RH-44R*	44 Mag.	7.5"	13"	54	598.00

*Scope model, with Integral Scope Mounts, 1" Ruger Scope rings.

STAINLESS REDHAWK DOUBLE-ACTION REVOLVER

CATALOG NUMBER	CALIBER	BARREL LENGTH	OVERALL LENGTH	APPROX. WEIGHT (OUNCES)	PRICE
RUGER STAINLESS REDHAWK REVOLVER					
KRH-445	44 Mag.	5.5"	11"	49	$615.00
KRH-44	44 Mag.	7.5"	13"	54	615.00
KRH-44R*	44 Mag.	7.5"	13"	54	650.00
KRH-455	45 LC	5.5"	11"	49	615.00
KRH-45	45 LC	7.5"	13"	54	615.00
KRH-45R*	45 LC	7.5"	13"	54	650.00

*Scope model, with Integral Scope Mounts, 1" Stainless Steel Ruger Scope rings.

SUPER REDHAWK STAINLESS DOUBLE-ACTION REVOLVER

The Super Redhawk double-action revolver in stainless steel features a heavy extended frame with 7.5" and 9.5" barrels. Cushioned grip panels w/wood inserts provide comfortable, nonslip hold. Comes with case and lock, integral scope mounts and 1" stainless steel Ruger scope rings.

SPECIFICATIONS

Caliber: 44 Magnum, 454 Casull, 480 Ruger   *Barrel Lengths:* 7.5" and 9.5"   *Overall Length:* 13" w/7.5" bbl.; 15" w/9.5" bbl. *Weight (empty):* 53 oz. (7.5" bbl.); 58 oz. (9.5" bbl.) *Sight radius:* 9.5" (7.5" bbl.); 11.25" (9.5" bbl.) *Finish:* Stainless steell Casull has Target gray finish; satin polished

Prices: **KSRH-7** (7.5" barrel) $650.00
KSRH-9 (9.5" barrel)) 650.00
KSRH-7454 (7.5" barrel) .454 Casull. 745.00
KSRH-9454 (9.5" barrel) .454 Casull. 745.00
KSRH-7480 (7.5" barrel) 480 Ruger 745.00
KSRH-9480 (9.5" barrel) 480 Ruger 745.00

All Ruger revolvers come with transfer-bar mechanism for safety, plus a lockable box and padlock.

HANDGUNS

**VAQUERO SINGLE ACTION
$510.00 (ALL MODELS)**

BISLEY-VAQUERO

Ruger's Vaquero single-action revolver is a sturdier rendition of the classic Colt SAA. The original Bisley single-action design was developed in the 1890s for England's famous target shooting matches held at Bisley Common. Modification and repositioning of the grip to a nearly vertical position reduced a tendency of some standard-frame single-action grips to "ride-up" in the shooter's hand during recoil. The Bisley hammer is lower and has a wide spur. This enables a shooter to cock the hammer with a minimum amount of disturbance to the hand and revolver position. It combines the latest Ruger single-action mechanism with the classic appearance of Colt revolvers of a century ago. The design of the Bisley-Vaquero has captured renewed interest among serious single-action target shooters and Cowboy Action Shooters alike. As with the Vaquero, the new Ruger Bisley-Vaquero is based on the Ruger New Model Blackhawk, single-action revolver, in production since 1973.

**NEW! RUGER VAQUERO WITH
"BIRD'S HEAD" GRIP**

VAQUERO SINGLE-ACTION REVOLVER

SPECIFICATIONS
Calibers: .44 Magnum, .45 Long Colt, 44-40, and .357 Magnum
Capacity: 6 rounds
Barrel Length: 4 5/8"-7.5"
Safety: Transfer bar and loading gate interlock
Sights: Blade front; notch rear; fixed
Sights Radius: 6.5"
Grips: Smooth rosewood with inletted Ruger medallion
Finish: Blued: "color case finish" on frame; polished and blued barrel and cylinder
Features: Instruction manual, lockable plastic case with lock; heat treated Chrome-moly steel frame, barrel and grip (blued version); 400 stainless steel
Price: $510.00
BISLEY W/STAINLESS. 529.00
   (Simulated ivory grips $36.00 additional)

RUGER PISTOLS AND REVOLVERS

NEW MODEL BLACKHAWK REVOLVER

NEW MODEL BLACKHAWK REVOLVER STAINLESS STEEL

The Blackhawk has long been the workhorse of Ruger's single-action line. Extremely strong, it easily handles loads that would have jeopardized revolvers a century ago. Adjustable sights make it accurate. In .30 Carbine, .357, .41 and .44 Magnum stainless or blued. Transfer bar safety, barrels 4.5" to 7.5".

Price: . . . . **$415.00 to $505.00**

MODEL P-4 22/45

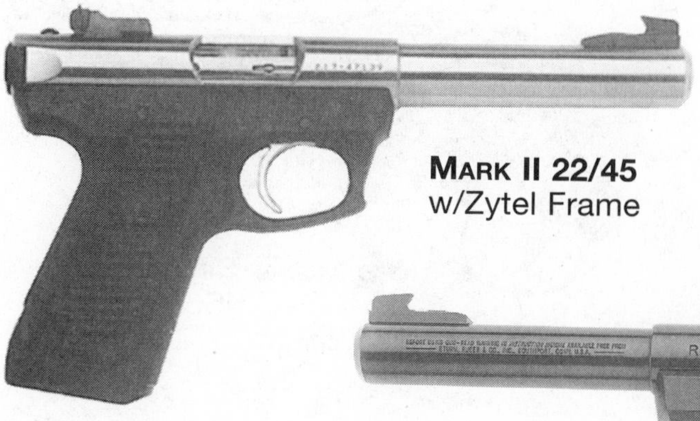

MARK II 22/45
w/Zytel Frame

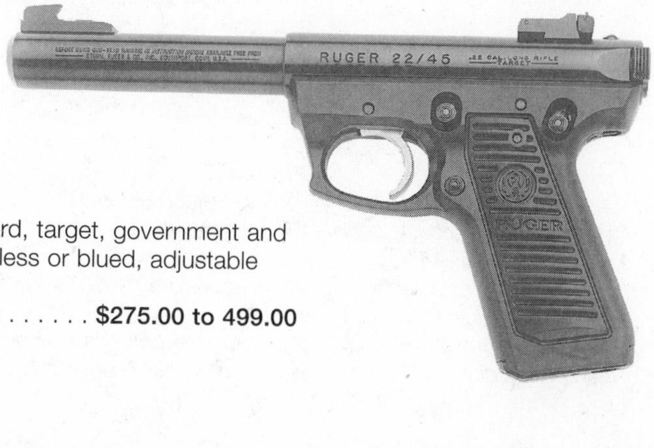

Blowback .22 pistols in standard, target, government and bull-barrel configurations, stainless or blued, adjustable sights.
Price: . . . . **$275.00 to 499.00**

22/45 TARGET MODEL P-512

HANDGUNS

NEW SUPER MODEL BLACKHAWK
SINGLE-ACTION REVOLVER

NEW MODEL SUPER BLACKHAWK SINGLE-ACTION REVOLVER

SPECIFICATIONS

Caliber: 44 Magnum; interchangeable with 44 Special
Barrel Lengths: 4 ⁵/₈", 5.5", 7.5", 10.5" *Overall Length:* 13 ³/₈"
(7.5" barrel) *Weight:* 45 oz. (4 ⁵/₈" bbl.), 46 oz. (5.5" bbl.), 48 oz.
(7.5" bbl.) and 51 oz. (10.5" bbl.) *Frame:* Chrome molybdenum
steel or stainless steel *Springs:* Music wire springs throughout
Sights: Patridge style, ramp front matted blade 18" wide; rear
sight click-adjustable for windage and elevation *Grip Frame:*
Chrome molybdenum or stainless steel, enlarged and contoured
to minimize recoil effect *Trigger:* Wide spur, low contour, sharply
serrated for convenient cocking with minimum disturbance of
grip *Finish:* Polished and blued or brushed satin stainless steel

Features: Case and lock included
Prices: **KS45N**
    5.5" bbl., brushed or satin stainless steel **$510.00**
KS458N
    4 ⁵/₈" bbl., brushed or high-gloss stainless **510.00**
KS47N
    7.5" bbl., brushed or high-gloss stainless **510.00**
KS411N 10.5" bull bbl., stainless steel **519.00**
S45N 5.5" bbl., blued **489.00**
S458N 4 ⁵/₈" bbl., blued **489.00**
S47N 7.5" bbl., blued **489.00**
S411N 10.5" bull bbl., blued. **499.00**

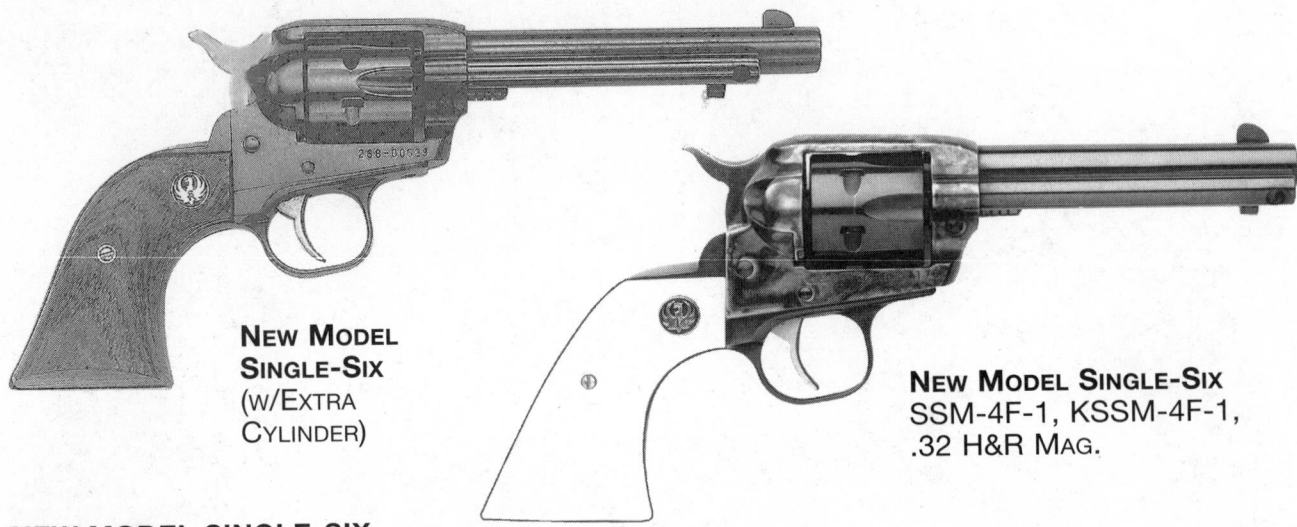

NEW MODEL SINGLE-SIX
(W/EXTRA CYLINDER)

NEW MODEL SINGLE-SIX
SSM-4F-1, KSSM-4F-1, .32 H&R MAG.

NEW MODEL SINGLE-SIX

SPECIFICATIONS

Caliber: 22 LR (fitted with 22 WMR cylinder) *Barrel Lengths:* 4 ⁵/₈",
5.5", 6.5", 9.5"; stainless steel model in 5.5" and 6.5" lengths only
Weight (approx.): 33 oz. (with 5.5" barrel); 38 oz. (with 9.5" barrel)
Sights: Patridge-type ramp front sight; rear sight click adjustable for
elevation and windage; protected by integral frame ribs. Adjustable
sight model available with 4 5/8", 5.5", 6.5", or 9.5" barrel. *Finish:*
Blue or stainless steel *Features:* Case and lock incl.

Prices: Blue Fixed sight $359.00
    Blue adjustable sight. 369.00
Stainless steel
    (convertible 5.5" and 6.5" barrels only) **449.00**
Also available: New Model Single six in 32 H&R Mag.
Price: 549.00
All Ruger revolvers come with transfer-bar mechanism for safety, plus a lockable box and padlock.

RUGER REVOLVERS

MODEL SP101
SPURLESS DA
$458.00

GP-100 357 MAGNUM
6" HEAVY BARREL

GP-100 & SP101 DOUBLE-ACTION REVOLVERS

In 1971 Ruger announced the Security Six, Police Service Six and Speed Six double-action revolvers that allowed quick dismantling without tools and handled the most powerful factory loads available. The improved G-P 100 followed in 1985, the SP101 in 1988. Cushioned grips soak up recoil and maintain hand position. Oversize frames bottle high-pressure loads. The cylinder is locked into firing position front and rear to ensure proper alignment.

SPECIFICATIONS SP101 REVOLVERS

CATALOG NUMBER	CALIBER	CAP.*	SIGHTS	BARREL LENGTH	APPROX WT. (Oz.)
KSP-241X	22 LR	6	A	4"	34
KSP-3231X	32 Mag.	6	A	3 1/16"	30
KSP-3241X	32 Mag.	6	A	4"	33
KSP-821X	38+P	5	F	2.25"	25
KSP-831X	38+P	5	F	3 1/16"	27
KSP-321X**	357 Mag.	5	F	2.25"	25
KSP-321XL**	357 Mag.	5	F	2.25"	25
KSP-331X**	357 Mag.	5	F	3 1/16"	27

*Indicates cylinder capacity **Revolvers chambered for 357 Magnum also accept 38 Special cartridges.
All Ruger revolvers come with transfer-bar mechanism for safety, plus a lockable box and padlock.

SPECIFICATIONS

CATALOG NUMBER	FINISH	SIGHTS+	SHROUD++	BARREL LENGTH	WT. (Oz.)	PRICE
GP-141	B	A	F	4"	41	$475.00
GP-160	B	A	S	6"	43	475.00
GP-161	B	A	F	6"	46	475.00
GPF-331	B	F	F	3"	36	465.00
GPF-340	B	F	S	4"	37	465.00
GPF-341	B	F	F	4"	38	465.00
KGP-141	SS	A	F	4"	41	515.00
KGP-160	SS	A	S	6"	43	515.00
KGP-161	SS	A	F	6"	46	515.00
KGPF-330	SS	F	S	3"	35	499.00
KGPF-331	SS	F	F	3"	36	499.00
KGPF-340	SS	F	S	4"	37	499.00
KGPF-341	SS	F	F	4"	38	499.00
KGPF-840*	SS	F	S	4"	37	499.00

*38 Special only. B = blued; SS = stainless; A = adjustable; F = fixed. ++ F = full; S = short.

HANDGUNS

RUGER REVOLVERS

BISLEY SINGLE-ACTION TARGET GUN

BISLEY SINGLE-ACTION TARGET GUN

The Bisley single-action was originally used at the British National Rifle Association matches held in Bisley, England, in the 1890s. Today's Ruger Bisleys are offered in two frame sizes, chambered from 22 LR to 45 Long Colt. These revolvers are the target-model versions of the Ruger single-action line.

Special Features: Unfluted cylinder roll-marked with classic foliate engraving pattern; hammer is low with smoothly curved, deeply checkered wide spur positioned for easy cocking.

Prices:
22 LR $402.00
357 Mag., 44 Mag., 45 Long Colt 510.00

BISLEY SPECIFICATIONS

Catalog Number	Caliber	Barrel Length	Overall Length	Sights	Approx. Wt. (Oz.)
RB22AW	22 LR	6.5"	11.5"	Adj.	41
RB35W	357 Mag.	7.5"	13"	Adj.	48
RB44W	44 Mag.	7.5"	13"	Adj.	48
RB45W	45 LC	7.5"	13"	Adj.	48

Dovetail rear sight adjustable for windage only.

OLD ARMY CAP-AND-BALL REVOLVER (not shown)

Reminiscent of pre-cartridge days and faithful to the elegant good look of its predecessors, this Ruger has modern-day strength and can be disassembled without tools. Available in .45 caliber, blued or stainless steel, with fixed or adjustable sights. All Old Armys have 7.5" barrels, rosewood grips, coil springs.

Price:
Stainless $510.00
Blued. 478.00
(see also Black Powder Section)

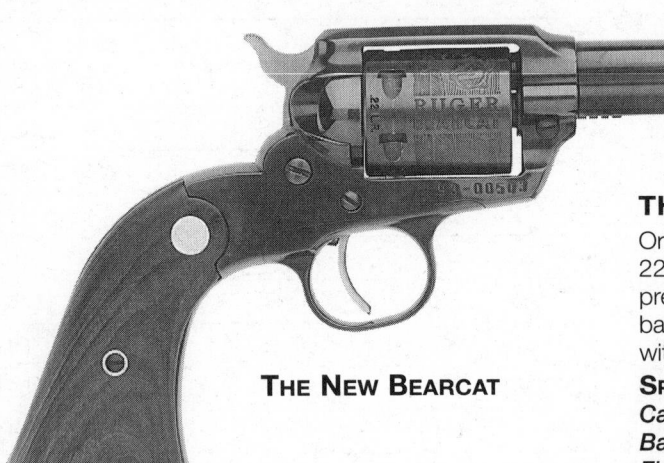

THE NEW BEARCAT

THE SBC-4 NEW BEARCAT

Originally manufactured between 1958 and 1973, the 22-rimfire single-action Bearcat features an all-steel precision investment-cast frame and patented transfer-bar mechanism. The New Bearcat also has walnut grips with the Ruger medallion.

SPECIFICATIONS
Caliber: 22 LR **Capacity:** 6 shots
Barrel Length: 4" **Grips:** Rosewood
Finish: Blued chrome-moly steel
Price:
Blued. $359.00
All Ruger revolvers come with transfer-bar mechanism for safety, plus a lockable box and padlock.

RUGER P-SERIES PISTOLS

MODEL P95

Ruger's first centerfire pistols were introduced in 1985. Now available in a wide range of models in 9mm and .45 ACP, the P-series pistols feature 3-dot sights and grips that hug the hand. Polymer-frame models offer a 4-oz. weight savings. Decock-Only pistols can be fired after decocking with a double-action pull of the trigger. Double-Action-Only models feature a spurless hammer. Ambidextrous grip, safety and decocking lever make the P-series pistols suitable for quick firing from either hand. An integral firing pin block prevents discharge unless the trigger is pulled and held rearward. P-series pistols come with a lockable case, spare magazine and magazine loading tool.

Weight: 31 to 34 oz., depending on model (95 is 27 oz.)

MODEL KP95D

MODEL KP94 9mm
(4.5" Barrel)

SPECIFICATIONS P SERIES PISTOLS

Cat. Number	Model	Finish	Caliber	Mag. Cap.	Price
P89	Manual Safety	Blued	9mm	10	$452.00
KP89	Manual Safety	Stainless	9mm	10	499.00
P89D	Decock Only	Blued	9mm	10	452.00
KP89D	Decock Only	Stainless	9mm	10	499.00
KP89DAO	Double-Action Only	Stainless	9mm	10	499.00
P90	Manual Safety	Blued	45 ACP	7	499.00
KP90*	Manual Safety	Stainless	45 ACP	7	539.00
KP90D	Decock Only	Stainless	45 ACP	7	539.00
P93D	Decock-Only	Blued	9mm	10	467.00
KP93D**	Decock Only	Stainless	9mm	10	546.00
KP93DAO	Double-Action Only	Stainless	9mm	10	546.00
P944	Manual Safety	Blued	40 Auto	10	467.00
KP944	Manual Safety	Stainless	40 Auto	10	546.00
KP944D	Decock Only	Stainless	40 Auto	10	546.00
KP944DAO	Double-Action Only	Stainless	40 Auto	10	546.00
KP95D	Decock Only	Stainless	9mm	10	453.00
KP95DAO	Double-Action Only	Stainless	9mm	10	453.00
P95D	Decock Only	Blued	9mm	10	407.00
P95DAO	Double-Action Only	Blued	9mm	10	407.00
P95	Manual Safety	Blued	9mm	10	407.00
KP95	Manual Safety	Stainless	9mm	10	453.00
KP97D	Decock-Only	Stainless	9mm	8	483.00
KP97DAO	Double-Action Only	Stainless	.45 ACP	8	483.00

*Available w/ambidextrous safety, blued ($476.00) Model P90.   **Available w/ambidextrous decocker, blued ($445.00) Model P93D.
****Available w/ambidextrous safety, blued ($445.00) Model P94. **All Ruger handguns come with a lockable box and lock.***

MATCHMASTER

SPECIFICATIONS
Caliber: 45 ACP
Capacity: 7 rounds
Barrel length: 5" or 6"
Overall length: 8.75" or 9.75"
Weight: 40.3 oz. (44 oz. for 6" barrel)
Finish: Stainless steel or black Parkerized carbon steel
Features: Extended safety & slide stop; wide beavertail grip safety; LPA fully adjustable rear sight; full-length recoil spring guide; squared trigger guide & finger-groove front strap frame; laser-etched walnut grips
Prices:
5" Barrel **$595.00**
6" Barrel 645.00

ENFORCER

ENFORCER

SPECIFICATIONS
Caliber: 45 ACP
Capacity: 6 rounds
Barrel length: 4" conical
Overall length: 7.3"
Height: 4 $^7/_8$"
Weight: 36 oz.
Sight radius: 5.75"
Finish: Stainless steel or matte black Parkerized carbon steel
Features: Beavertail grip safety; extended thumb safety and slide release; smooth walnut stock w/laser-etched Black Widow logo
Price: $625.00

COHORT

SPECIFICATIONS
Caliber: 45 ACP
Capacity: 7 rounds
Barrel length: 4" conical
Overall length: 7.3"
Height: 5.5"
Weight: 38 oz.
Sights: Ramped blade front, LPA adjustable rear
Finish: Stainless steel or black Parkerized carbon steel
Features: Beavertail grip safety; extended thumb safety and slide release; rounded trigger guard, checkered nut stock
Price: $649.00

COHORT

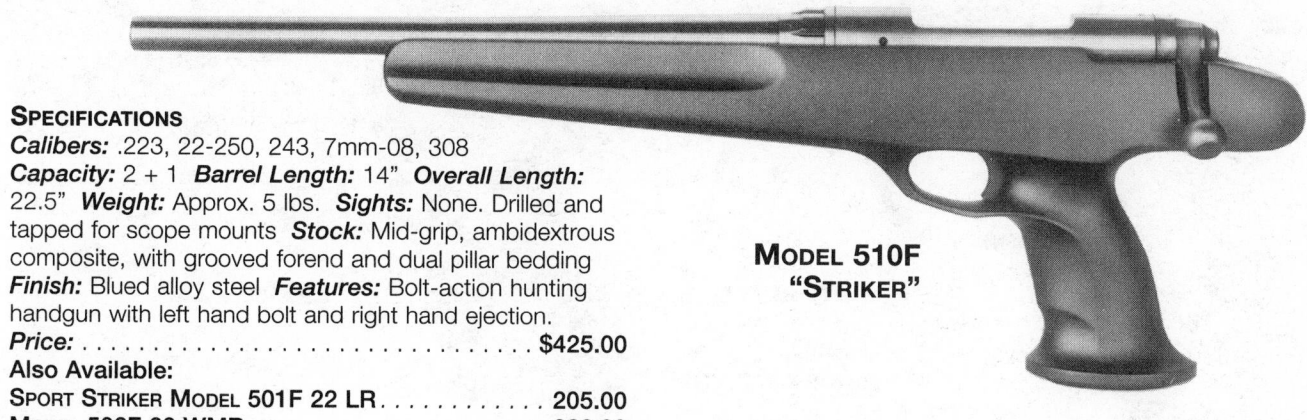

SPECIFICATIONS
Calibers: .223, 22-250, 243, 7mm-08, 308
Capacity: 2 + 1 *Barrel Length:* 14" *Overall Length:*
22.5" *Weight:* Approx. 5 lbs. *Sights:* None. Drilled and
tapped for scope mounts *Stock:* Mid-grip, ambidextrous
composite, with grooved forend and dual pillar bedding
Finish: Blued alloy steel *Features:* Bolt-action hunting
handgun with left hand bolt and right hand ejection.
Price: $425.00
Also Available:
SPORT STRIKER MODEL 501F 22 LR 205.00
MODEL 502F 22 WMR 226.00

**MODEL 510F
"STRIKER"**

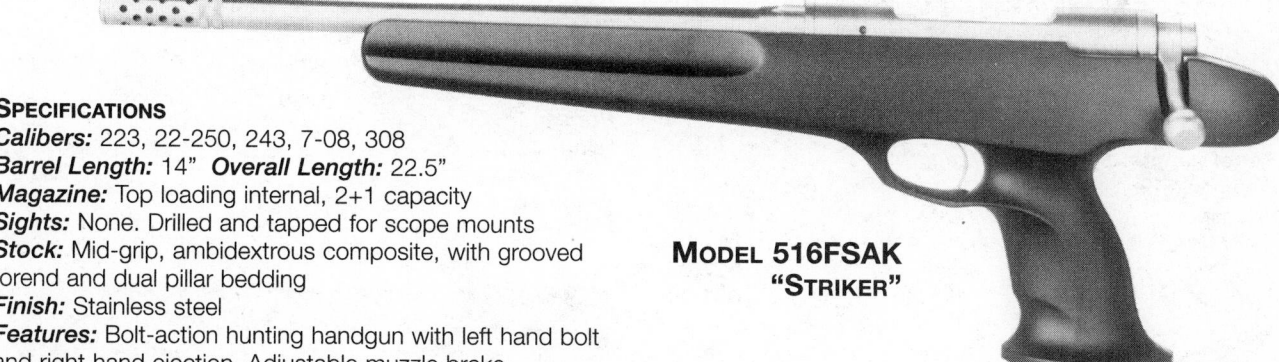

SPECIFICATIONS
Calibers: 223, 22-250, 243, 7-08, 308
Barrel Length: 14" *Overall Length:* 22.5"
Magazine: Top loading internal, 2+1 capacity
Sights: None. Drilled and tapped for scope mounts
Stock: Mid-grip, ambidextrous composite, with grooved
forend and dual pillar bedding
Finish: Stainless steel
Features: Bolt-action hunting handgun with left hand bolt
and right hand ejection. Adjustable muzzle brake.
Price: $512.00

**MODEL 516FSAK
"STRIKER"**

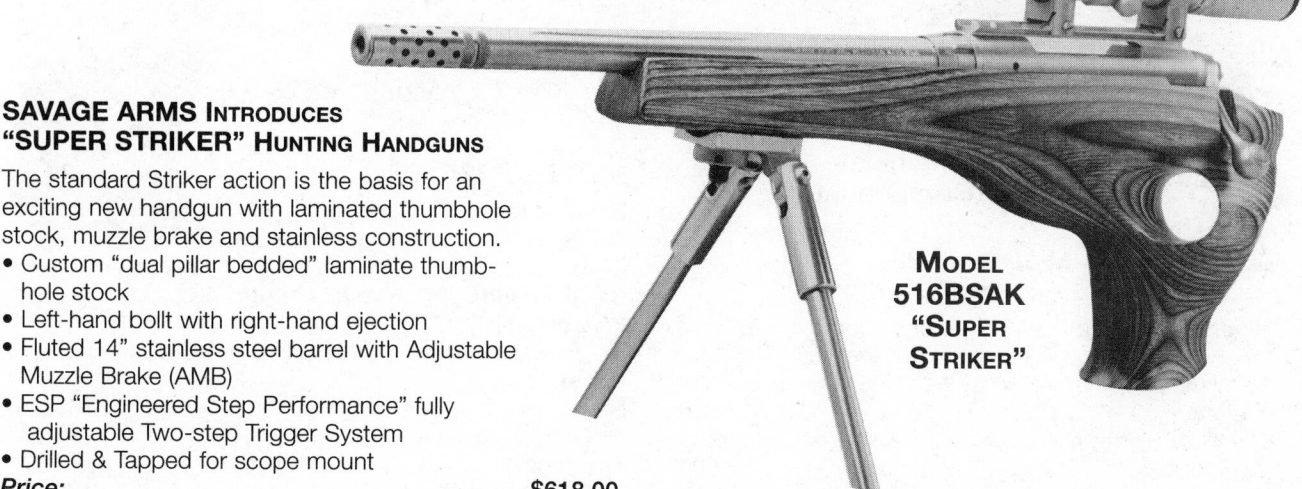

**SAVAGE ARMS INTRODUCES
"SUPER STRIKER" HUNTING HANDGUNS**

The standard Striker action is the basis for an
exciting new handgun with laminated thumbhole
stock, muzzle brake and stainless construction.
• Custom "dual pillar bedded" laminate thumb-
  hole stock
• Left-hand bollt with right-hand ejection
• Fluted 14" stainless steel barrel with Adjustable
  Muzzle Brake (AMB)
• ESP "Engineered Step Performance" fully
  adjustable Two-step Trigger System
• Drilled & Tapped for scope mount
Price: $618.00

**MODEL
516BSAK
"SUPER
STRIKER"**

HANDGUNS

SIG ARMS PISTOLS

SIG PRO PISTOLS

The Sig Pro is among the most advanced of polymer-frame pistols, with a slide machined from solid stainless steel, integral fire control unit for easy conversion from SA/DA to double-action-only, integral accessory rail to mount a tactical light or laser sight, and Sig Pro's unique four-point safety system. The lightweight, maintenance-free, virtually indestructible polymer frame is engineered for quick pointing.

SPECIFICATIONS
Calibers: 9mm, .357 SIG, 40 S&W **Capacity:** 10 rounds
Barrel Length: 3.9" **Overall Length:** 7.4"
Weight: 28-30 oz. **Finishes:** Nitron or Two Tone
Prices: $602.00
  w/"Siglite" night sights 661.00
Two Tone 627.00
  w/"Siglite" night sights 681.00

MODEL P229
Stainless
w/Compensator

MODEL P229
SPECIFICATIONS
Caliber: 357 SIG, 40 S&W **Capacity:** 10 rounds **Action:**
DA/SA **Barrel Length:** 3.9" **Overall Length:** 7.1" **Height:**
5.4" **Width:** 1.5" **Finish:** Nitron
Price: Nitron $851.00
  Nitron w/"Siglite" night sights. 953.00
  Two-Tone. 897.00
  Two-Tone w/"Siglite" night sights 994.00

MODEL P239

SPECIFICATIONS
Calibers: 357 SIG, 9mm, 40 S&W
Capacity: 7 rounds (8 in 9mm) **Barrel Length:** 3.6"
Overall Length: 6.6" **Height:** 5.2"
Width: 1.2" **Weight (empty):** 27.4 oz.
Finish: Nitron Stainless Steel, Two Tone
Prices:
Nitron $636.00
  w/"Siglite" night sights 738.00
Two Tone 682.00
  "Siglite" night sights 784.00

MODEL P226

MODEL P226
SPECIFICATIONS
Calibers: 357 SIG, 9mm and 40 S&W
Capacity: 10 rounds **Action:** DA/SA or DA only
Barrel Length: 4.4" **Overall Length:** 7.7"
Weight (empty): 26.5 oz.; 30.1 oz. in 357 SIG
Height: 5.5" **Finish:** Nitron or Two-tone
Prices:
Nitron $851.00
  w/"Siglite" night sight 953.00
Two-Tone 897.00
  w/"Siglite" night sights 994.00

SIG ARMS PISTOLS

MODEL P232

SPECIFICATIONS

Calibers: 9mm Short (380 ACP)
Action: DA/SA or DAO
Capacity: 7 rounds (380 ACP)
Barrel Length: 3.6" **Overall
Length:** 6.6" **Weight (empty):**
16.2 oz. **Height:** 4.7" **Width:** 1.2"
Safety: Automatic firing-pin lock **Finish:** Blued or stainless steel

Prices: Blued finish	$518.00
Stainless steel	559.00
Stainless w/"Siglite" night sight	600.00
Blued w/"Siglite" night sight	559.00

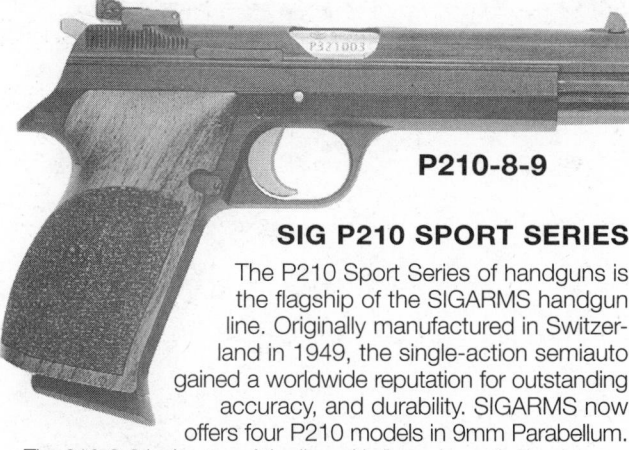

P210-8-9

SIG P210 SPORT SERIES

The P210 Sport Series of handguns is the flagship of the SIGARMS handgun line. Originally manufactured in Switzerland in 1949, the single-action semiauto gained a worldwide reputation for outstanding accuracy, and durability. SIGARMS now offers four P210 models in 9mm Parabellum.

- The 210-8-9 is the top of the line with figured wood grip plates, adjustable target sights and a lateral magazine catch.
- The 210-6-9 also offers adjustable target sights, wood grip plates and a target grade trigger action.
- The 210-5-9 has a target trigger, wood grip plates, adjustable target sights and extended barrel of 5.85" with compensator.
- The 210-2-9 is the 9mm Parabellum Swiss Army Service model now with wood grip plates and standard sights.
- All 210 models are built on an alloy heavy frame.
- All models come with one 8 round magazine and a magazine loader.

Price: .... TBD

TECHNICAL SPECIFICATIONS

	P210-8	P210-6	P210-5	P210-2
Caliber	9mm	9mm	9mm	9mm
Length, overall	8.5"	8.5"	9.6"	8.5"
Height, overall	5.4"	5.4"	5.4"	5.4"
Width, overall	1.3"	1.3"	1.3"	1.3"
Barrel Length	4.8"	4.8"	5.9"	4.8"

MODEL P229

SPECIFICATIONS

Calibers: 9mm, 357 and 40 S&W
Capacity: 10 rounds **Action:** DA/SA or DA only **Barrel Length:** 3.8"
Overall Length: 7.1" **Weight (empty):** 27.5 oz. **Height:** 5.4" **Width:** 1.5"
Finish: Blackened stainless steel
Features: Stainless steel slide; automatic firing-pin lock; wood grips (optional); aluminum alloy frame

Prices: Model P229	$830.00
w/"Siglite" night sight	930.00
w/Nickel slide	875.00
w/Nickel slide/"Siglite" night sight	970.00

**TRAILSIDE
COMPETITION**

SIG TRAILSIDE PL 22 PISTOL

With an integral frame and barrel, and Hammerli engineering, the new SIG Trailside pistol might be more at home on the target range, punching out the X-ring. But the standard models with 4.5" and 6" barrels are slim and easy to pack. At 28 and 30 ounces, they're nearly half a pound lighter than the Competition model, which features a hand-filling adjustable grip, modular counterweights and adjustable target sights. All guns feature an adjustable trigger and a top rail for scope mounts. The PL 22 Target model has target sights but a slender profile. Its laminated grips differ from the rubber composite grips of the trail model. The proven blow-back action feeds cartridges from a 10-round magazine.

Prices: Standard 4.5" barrel	$449.00
Target 4.5" barrel	529.00
Target 6" barrel	549.00
Competition 6" barrel	699.00

HANDGUNS

Full-Size Double-Action Pistols

MODEL 5900 SERIES

SPECIFICATIONS
Caliber: 9mm Parabellum *Capacity:* 15 rounds
Barrel Length: 4" *Overall Length:* 7.5"
Weight (empty): 29 oz. (Models 5903, 5943); 38.3 oz.
(Model 5906, 5946); 38 oz. (Model 5906 w/adj. sight)
Sights: Front, post w/white dot; fixed rear, adj. for windage only
w/2 white dots. Adjustable sights and night sights available.
Finish: satin stainless (Models 5903 and 5943 have stain-
less/alloy construction)
Prices: MODEL 5903 . . . . $841.00
MODEL 5906 Satin stainless 904.00
  With fixed sights 863.00
  With Tritium night sight 995.00
MODEL 5946 Double action only 863.00
MODEL 5943 Double action only 844.00

MODEL 5906 DA
STAINLESS

MODEL 410, 910, 457

SPECIFICATIONS
Caliber: 40 S&W, 9mm Parabellum, .45 ACP
Capacity: 10 rounds+1 (7+1, .45)
Barrel Length: 4" (3.75", 45 ACP) *Overall Length:* 7.5"
Weight: 28.5 oz. *Sights:* 3-dot sights
Grips: Straight backstrap *Features:* Right-hand slide-
mounted manual safety; decocking lever; aluminum alloy
frame; blue carbon steel slide; nonreflective matte blued
finish; beveled edge slide
Price: 410, 457 . . . . $591.00
910 . . . . 535.00

MODEL 410

MODEL 4000, 4500 SERIES

SPECIFICATIONS
Caliber: 40 S&W, 45 ACP
Capacity: 10 rounds, +1 (8 rounds + 1, .45)
Barrel Length: 4" (4.25", .45)
Overall Length: 7.5"
Weight: 28.5 oz. (.40 alloy), 30.5 oz. (.45 alloy), 37.8 oz.
(.40 stainless), 39.1 oz. (.45 stainless)
Sights: Post w/white dot front; fixed w/white 2-dot rear,
adjustable and night sights available
Grips: Straight backstrap
Finish: Stainless steel
Prices:
MODEL 4006 w/fixed sights $907.00
  Same as above w/adj. sights 944.00
  w/fixed night sight 1,040.00
MODEL 4043 DA only (28 oz.) 886.00
MODEL 4046 Fixed sights, DA only (39.5 oz.) 907.00
  Double action only, fixed Tritium night sight . . . 1,040.00
MODEL 4566 w/4.25" bbl., fixed sights 942.00
MODEL 4586 DA only, 4.25" bbl., 39.5 oz.,
  fixed 2-dot rear sight, white dot front 942.00

MODEL 4046

Compact And Sigma Series Double-Action Pistols

MODEL 3913 LADYSMITH

SPECIFICATIONS
Caliber: 9mm Parabellum (traditional double-action)
Capacity: 8 rounds **Barrel Length:** 3.5"
Overall Length: 6 7/8" *Weight (empty):* 24.8 oz.
Sights: Front sight: white dot, Rear sight: Novak Lo Mount
Carry 2-Dot
Finish: Satin stainless
Price: $782.00

MODEL 3913
LADYSMITH

Smith & Wesson's Polymer-frame Sigma Series pistols combine traditional craftmanship and the latest technology to allow the guns to be assembled without the usual "fitting" process required for other handguns.

MODEL SW99

**SIGMA SERIES
MODEL SW9VE**
FULL SIZE DA

SW99

SPECIFICATIONS
Calibers: 9mm, 40 S+W *Capacity:* 6 rounds *Barrel
Length:* 4", 4 1/8" *Overall Length:* 7 1/8", 7 1/4"
Weight: 25 oz. *Sights:* adjustable rear *Finish:* Blue
Features: Lightweight polymer frame, stainless slide + barrel
Price: $810.00
w/night sights. 925.00

SIGMA SERIES SW40E & VE

MODEL	SW9P	SW9VE	SW40E	SW40VE	SW40P
Caliber	9mm	9mm	.40 S&W	.40 S&W	.40 S&W
Mag. Capacity**	10 (16)**	10 (16)**	10 (14)**	10 (14)**	10 (14)**
Barrel Length	4 inches	4 inches	4 inches	4 inches	4 inches
Front Sight	White Dot	White Dot	Tritium Dot	White Dot	White Dot
Rear Sight	Fixed 2-Dot	Fixed 2-Dot	Tritium 2-Dot	Fixed 2-Dot	Fixed 2-Dot
Material, Mechanism	Polymer Frame/Stainless Slide & Barrel, Double Action Only				
Finish	Melonite Slide & Barrel	Stainless Slide & Barrel	Melonite Slide & Barrel	Stainless Steel & Barrel	Melonite Slide & Barrel
Weight Empty	24.7 oz.	24.7 oz.	24.4 oz.	24.4 oz.	24.4 oz.
Length	7.25"	7.25"	7.25"	7.25"	7.25"

Prices: SW40E $657.00
SW40VE, SW9VE 447.00
SW9P, SW40P 494.00

** High Capacity magazines available for law enforcement or export orders only

HANDGUNS

SMITH & WESSON PISTOLS

Rimfire Single-Action Pistols

MODEL No. 41

MODEL NO. 41

SPECIFICATIONS
Caliber: 22 LR
Magazine Capacity: 12 rounds *Barrel Lengths:* 5.5" and 7"
Weight: 41 oz. (5.5" barrel) *Overall Length:* 10.5" (7" bbl.)
Sights: Front, 1/8" Patridge undercut; rear, S&W micrometer
click sight adjustable for windage and elevation
Grips: Hardwood target *Finish:* S&W Bright blue
Trigger: .365" width; S&W grooving, adj. trigger stop
Features: Carbon steel slide and frame
Price: $958.00

MODEL 22A SPORT

SPECIFICATIONS
Caliber: 22 LR *Capacity:* 10 rounds
Action: Single *Barrel Lengths:* 4", 5.5"
(standard or bull barrel and 7")
Overall Length: 8" (4"), 9.5" (5.5"), 11" (7")
Grips: Two-piece polymer (4"); 2-piece Soft Touch (5.5" and 7")
Weight: 28 oz. (4"), 32 oz. (5.5"), 33 oz. (7")
Sights: Patridge front, adjustable rear *Finish:* Blue
Features: Single slide external safety
Prices:

4"	$264.00
5.5"	292.00
5.5" Bull Barrel	367.00
5.5" Bull/Synthetic, HiViz sights	387.00
7"	331.00

Also available: in stainless steel (5.5" and 7" only)

Prices:

5.5" Standard	$358.00
5.5" Bull Barrel	434.00
7" Standard	395.00
5.5" Bull/Synthetic, HiViz sights	453.00

MODEL 3913TSW (double action)
MODEL 3953TSW (double action only)

SPECIFICATIONS
Frame: Compact
Caliber: 9mm
Capacity: 8 Rounds + 1
Barrel Length: 3.5"
Front Sight: White Dot
Rear Sight: Novak Lo Mount Carry 2-Dot
Grips: Straight Backstrap
Weight: 24.8 oz.
Overall Length: 6 3/4"
Material: Aluminum Alloy/Stainless Steel
Finish: Satin Stainless
Price: $760.00

MODEL 3953TSW
DOUBLE ACTION

MODEL 4013TSW (double action)
MODEL 4053TSW (double action only)

SPECIFICATIONS
Frame: Compact *Caliber:* .40 S&W
Capacity: 9 rounds + 1 *Barrel Length:* 3.5"
Front Sight: White Dot
Rear Sight: Novak Lo Mount Carry 2-Dot
External Safety: Ambidextrous
Grips: Curbed Backstrap
Weight: 26.8 oz. *Overall Length:* 6 3/4"
Material: Aluminum Alloy/Stainless Steel
Finish: Satin Stainless
Price: $886.00

MODEL 4013TSW
TRADITIONAL DA

TRADITIONAL DA MODEL 4513TSW (double action)
TRADITIONAL DA MODEL 4553TSW (double action only)

SPECIFICATIONS
Frame: Compact *Caliber:* .45 ACP
Capacity: 7 Rounds + 1 *Barrel Length:* 3.75"
Front Sight: White Dot
Rear Sight: Novak Lo Mount Carry 2-Dot
Grips: Straight Backstrap *Weight:* 28.6 oz.
Overall Length: 7 3/4"
Material: Aluminum Alloy/Stainless Steel
Finish: Satin Stainless
Price: $924.00
　　Model 4553 . . . . **924.00**
Also available: Full-size TSW pistols with 4" barrels (4.25", .45)
Capacity: 10+1 (9mm and .40), 8+1 (.45)
Length: 7.5" (9mm and 40), 7 7/8" (.45)
Weight: 28.5 oz. (9mm and .40), 30.5 oz. (.45)
Sights: Same as compact series, but adjustable and night sights available.

MODEL 4513TSW
TRADITIONAL DA

HANDGUNS

Handguns

MODEL 60LS LADYSMITH
38 S&W Special

MODEL 37
CHIEFS SPECIAL AIRWEIGHT
38 S&W Special

MODEL 60
38 CHIEFS SPECIAL
Stainless

LADYSMITH HANDGUNS
MODEL 36-LS AND MODEL 60-LS

SPECIFICATIONS

Calibers: 38 S&W Special (357 Magnum 60-LS)
Capacity: 5 shots *Barrel Lengths:* 1 ⁷/₈" (2 ¹/₈", 3")
Overall Length: 6 ⁵/₁₆" (6 ⁹/₁₆", 7.5") *Weight:* 20 oz.
(22.5 oz., 24 oz.) *Sights:* Serrated ramp front (black
pinned ramp in 357 Mag.); fixed notch rear
Grips: Contoured laminated rosewood, round butt
Finish: Glossy deep blue (36) or stainless (60)
Features: Both models come with soft-side LadySmith
carry case
Prices:
MODEL 36-LS $502.00
MODEL 60-LS 566.00

MODEL 37
CHIEFS SPECIAL AIRWEIGHT

SPECIFICATIONS

Caliber: 38 S&W Special *Capacity:* 5 shots
Barrel Length: 1 ⁷/₈" *Overall Length:* 6 ⁵/₁₆"
Weight: 11.9 oz.
Sights: Serrated ramp front; fixed, square-notch rear
Grips: Uncle Mike's Boot
Finish: S&W blued carbon steel
Features: .312" smooth combat-style trigger; .240" service
hammer
Prices:
MODEL 37 CHIEFS SPECIAL AIRWEIGHT:
   Same as Model 36, except finish is blue or
   nickel aluminum alloy. $507.00
MODEL 637 CHIEFS SPECIAL AIRWEIGHT:
   Stainless finish., *Weight:* 13.5 oz. 526.00

MODEL 60
38 CHIEFS SPECIAL, STAINLESS

SPECIFICATIONS

Calibers: .357 Mag. *Capacity:* 5 shots
Barrel Lengths: 2 1/8" (357 Mag.); 3" full lug (38 S&W Spec.)
Overall Length: 6 ⁵/₁₆" (2 ¹/₈" bbl.)); 7.5" (3" bbl.)
Weight: 23.5 oz. (2 1/8" barrel); 24 oz. (3" full lug barrel)
Sights: Micrometer click rear, adj. for windage and eleva-
tion; pinned black front (3" full lug model only); standard
sights as on Model 36
Grips: Uncle Mike's Combat *Finish:* Satin stainless
Features: .312" smooth combat-style trigger
Prices:
2 ¹/₈" Barrel. $530.00
3" Barrel. 562.00

Small Frame

MODEL 317 AIRLITE

MODEL 442
38 SPECIAL

MODEL 640

MODEL 649
BODYGUARD

MODEL 317 AIRLITE

SPECIFICATIONS
Caliber: 22 LR *Action:* Single or double action *Capacity:*
8 rounds *Barrel Length:* 1 ⁷/₈" and 3" *Overall Length:* 6
³/₁₆" *Weight:* 9.9 oz. (10.5 oz. w/rubber grip) *Finish:* Clear
Cote *Sights:* Serrated ramp front; fixed notch rear
Prices: 1 ⁷/₈" barrel w/synthetic grips $533.00
3" barrel w/HiViz front sight 582.00

MODEL 317 LADYSMITH

SPECIFICATIONS
Same as **MODEL 317 AIRLITE** with round butt grip, fixed
sights and Dymondwood grip.
Price: $596.00

38 CENTENNIAL "AIRWEIGHT"
MODEL 442

SPECIFICATIONS
Caliber: 38 S&W Special *Capacity:* 5 rounds *Barrel
Length:* 1 ⁷/₈" *Overall Length:* 6 ⁵/₁₆" *Weight:* 15 oz.
Sights: Serrated ramp front; fixed, square-notch rear
Finish: Matte blue
Price: $526.00
Also available: **MODEL 642 CENTENNIAL AIRWEIGHT**
Stainless steel, synthetic round butt grip,
double-action only. 543.00
LADYSMITH MODEL (satin stainless). 579.00

MODEL 640 CENTENNIAL

SPECIFICATIONS
Calibers: 357 Magnum and 38 S&W Special
Action: Double action only *Capacity:* 5 rounds
Barrel Length: 2 ¹/₈" *Overall Length:* 6 ³/₄"
Sights: Pinned black ramp front; fixed, square-notch rear
Features: Fully concealed hammer; smooth hardwood
service stock; satin stainless steel finish; round-butt
synthetic grips
Price: $576.00

MODEL 649 BODYGUARD

SPECIFICATIONS
Caliber: 38 S&W Special/357 S&W Mag.
Capacity: 5 rounds
Barrel Length: 2 ¹/₈"
Overall Length: 6 ⁵/₁₆"
Weight: 20 oz.
Sights: Black pinned ramp front; fixed, square-notch rear
Grips: Uncle Mike's Combat
Finish: Satin stainless
Price: $576.00

HANDGUNS

Small Frame

**MODEL 386
MOUNTAIN LITE**

**MODEL 360
AIR LITE SC**

**MODEL 360
KIT GUN**

**MODEL 340 PD
.357 MAG**

MODEL 386 MOUNTAIN LITE AIRLITE SC
SPECIFICATIONS
Calibers: 357 Mag., .38 S+W Special
Action: SA/DA
Barrel Length: 3 ¹/₈"
Front Sight: Hi-Viz Green Dot
Rear Sight: adjustable V-Notch
Weight: 18.5 oz.
Overall Length: 8 ¹/₈"
Features: Scandium alloy frame, titanium cylinder, matte grey stainless finish, Hogue Bantam grips
Price: $830.00
Also Available:
MODEL 386PD, 2.5" barrel, blue,
    red ramp front sight 794.00

MODEL 360 AIRLITE SC
SPECIFICATIONS
Calibers: 357 Mag., .38 S+W Special
Action: DA/SA
Barrel Length: 1 ⁷/₈"
Front Sight: Black, serrated ramp
Rear Sight: fixed notch
Weight: 12 oz.
Overall Length: 6 ⁵/₁₆"
Features: Scandium alloy frame, titanium cylinder, matte grey stainless + Hogue grips
Price: $745.00
Also Available:
MODEL 360 KIT GUN, w/3 ¹/₈" barrel, HiViz
    orange dot sight 876.00

MODEL 340 AIRLITE SC
SPECIFICATIONS
Calibers: 357 Mag., .38 S+W Special
Action: SA/DA
Barrel Length: 1 ⁷/₈"
Front Sight: Black, serrated ramp
Rear Sight: fixed notch
Weight: 12 oz.
Overall Length: 6 ⁵/₁₆"
Features: Scandium alloy frame, titanium cylinder, matte grey stainless finish, Hogue grips
Price: $763.00
Also Available:
MODEL 340PD, Personal Defense w/red
    front ramp 785.00

MODEL 617 (6-shot, 6" barrel shown)

MODEL 10
HEAVY BARREL

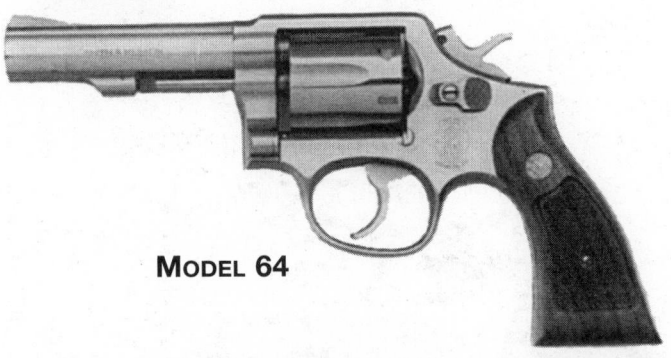

MODEL 64

MODEL 65

MODEL 617

SPECIFICATIONS
Caliber: 22 Long Rifle *Capacity:* 10 shots
Barrel Length: 4", 6" or 8 ³/₈" *Overall Length:* 9 ¹/₈" (4" barrel); 11 ¹/₈" (6" barrel); 13.5" (8 ³/₈" barrel)
Weight (loaded): 42 oz. with 4" barrel; 48 oz. with 6" barrel; 54 oz. with 8 ³/₈" barrel *Sights:* Front pinned Patridge; rear, S&W micrometer click sight adjustable for windage and elevation *Grips:* Hogue rubber, square butt
Finish: Satin stainless *Features:* Target hammer and trigger; drilled and tapped for scope
Prices: 4" Barrel $613.00
    6" Bbl. 600.00
    8 3/8" Barrel 662.00
Also available: 10-shot w/6" barrel 649.00

MODEL 10, 38 MILITARY & POLICE

SPECIFICATIONS
Caliber: 38 S&W Special *Capacity:* 6 shots
Barrel Length: 4" heavy barrel *Overall Length:* 9.25"
Weight: 33.5 oz.
Sights: Front, fixed ¹/₈" serrated ramp; square-notch rear
Grips: Uncle Mike's Combat *Finish:* S&W blue
Price: $481.00

MODEL 64, 38 MILITARY & POLICE STAINLESS

SPECIFICATIONS
Caliber: 38 S&W Special *Capacity:* 6 shots
Barrel Length: 4" heavy barrel, square butt;
2" regular barrel, round butt *Overall Length:* 9.25" w/4" bbl., 6 ⁷/₈" w/2" barrel *Weight:* 28 oz. w/2" barrel; 33.5 oz. w/4" barrel *Sights:* Fixed, ¹/₈" serrated ramp front; square-notch rear *Grips:* Uncle Mike's Combat *Finish:* Satin stainless
Prices: 2" Bbl. $511.00
    4" Bbl. 521.00

MODEL 65 (HEAVY BARREL) 357 MILITARY & POLICE

SPECIFICATIONS
K-frame .357 Magnum or 38 S+W Special with stainless steel frame and 4" barrel; 6 shots; fixed sights.
Price: $526.00
Also available: MODEL 65 LADYSMITH
Same specifications as MODEL 65 but with 3" barrel only (weighs 32 oz.) and rosewood laminate stock; satin stainless finish, smooth combat wood grips.
Price: $566.00

HANDGUNS

Medium Frame

MODEL 686

MODEL 686 PLUS

SPECIFICATIONS

Calibers: 357 Mag, 38 S+W Special *Capacity:* 6 shots
Barrel Lengths: 2.5", 4", 6", 8 3/8"
All models have stainless steel finish, combat or target stock
and/or trigger; adjustable sights optional.
Prices: 2.5" Barrel $590.00
    4" Barrel 602.00
    6" Barrel 607.00
    8 3/8" Barrel 631.00
Also Available: MODEL 686 POWERPORT, 6" barrel 647.00

MODEL 686 PLUS DISTINGUISHED COMBAT MAGNUM

Capacity: 7 rounds *Barrel Lengths:* 2.5", 4" or 6" full lug.
Overall Length: 7.5" – 11 15/16" *Weight:* 34.5 oz. – 45 oz.
Prices:
    2.5" bbl. $612.00
    4" Barrel 621.00
    6" Barrel 631.00

MODEL 66

MODEL 696

MODEL 66
357 COMBAT MAGNUM

SPECIFICATIONS

Caliber: 357 Magnum, 38 S+W Special *Capacity:* 6 shots
Barrel Lengths: 4" or 6" with square butt; 2.5" with round butt
Overall Length: 7.5" w/2.5" bbl.; 9.5" w/4" bbl.; 11 3/8"
w/6" bbl. *Weight:* 30.5 oz. w/2.5" bbl.; 36 oz. w/4" bbl.; 39
oz. w/6" bbl. *Sights:* Front, 1/8"; rear, S&W Red Ramp on
ramp base, S&W Micrometer Click, adjustable for windage
and elevation *Grips:* Uncle Mike's Combat *Trigger:* .312"
Smooth Combat *Finish:* Satin stainless
Prices: 2.5" Bbl. $572.00
    4" or 6" Bbl. 579.00

MODEL 696

SPECIFICATIONS

Caliber: 44 S&W Special *Capacity:* 5 rounds *Action:*
Single or double action *Barrel Length:* 3" *Overall
Length:* 8 3/16" *Weight:* 48 oz. *Sights:* Red ramp front;
adjustable white outline rear *Grips:* Hogue rubber *Finish:*
Satin stainless *Features:* .500" target hammer; .400"
smooth combat trigger
Price: $602.00

Large Frame Stainless

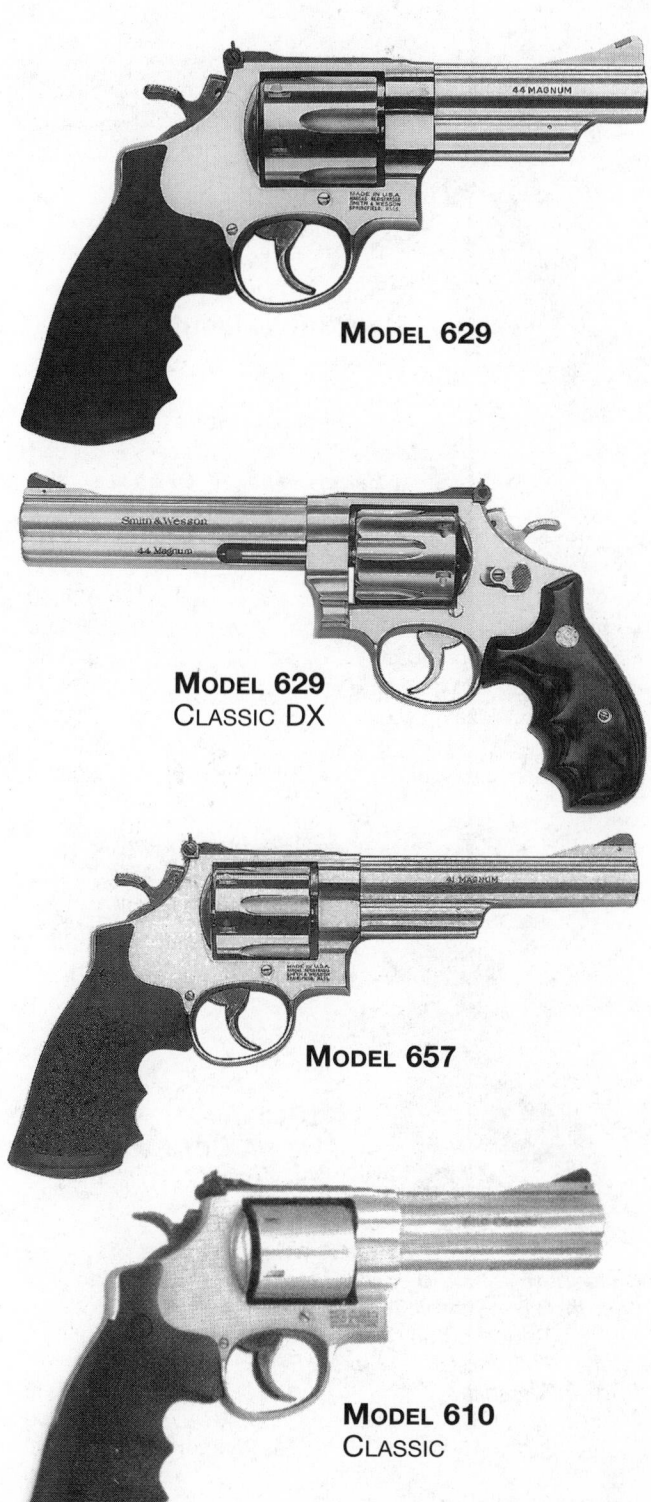

MODEL 629

MODEL 629
CLASSIC DX

MODEL 657

MODEL 610
CLASSIC

MODEL 629
SPECIFICATIONS
Calibers: 44 Magnum, 44 S&W Special *Capacity:* 6 shots
Barrel Lengths: 4", 6", 8 ³/₈" *Overall Length:* 9 ⁵/₈", 11 ³/₈", 13 ⁷/₈"
Weight (empty): 44 oz. (4" bbl.); 47 oz. (6" bbl.); 54 oz. (8 ³/₈" bbl.)
Sights: S&W Red Ramp front; white outline rear w/S&W
Micrometer Click, adjustable for windage and elevation;
drilled and tapped *Grips:* Hogue rubber *Finish:* Satin
stainless steel *Features:* Combat trigger, target hammer
Prices: 4" Bbl............................ $717.00
      6" Bbl............................ 724.00
      8 ³/₈" Bbl......................... 740.00

MODEL 629 CLASSIC
SPECIFICATIONS
Calibers: 44 Magnum, 44 S&W Special *Capacity:* 6 rounds
Barrel Lengths: 5", 6.5", 8 ³/₈" (all full lug) *Overall Length:* 10.5",
12", 13 ⁷/₈" *Weight:* 51 oz. (5" bbl.); 52 oz. (6.5" bbl.); 54 oz. (8
³/₈" bbl.) *Grips:* Hogue rubber
Prices: 5" & 6.5" Bbl................... $768.00
      8 ³/₈" Bbl......................... 793.00
Also available: MODEL 629 CLASSIC DX. Same features
as the MODEL 629 CLASSIC above, plus interchangeable
front sights, wood grips. With 6.5" barrel. $986.00
      With 8 ³/₈" barrel 1,018.00
MODEL 629 POWERPORT w/6.5" barrel (12" overall
length), weighs 52 oz. Patridge front sight, adjustable black
blade rear sight. *Price:*. $768.00

MODEL 625
SPECIFICATIONS
Caliber: 45 ACP *Capacity:* 6 shots *Barrel Length:* 5" full
lug barrel *Overall Length:* 10 ³/₈" *Weight (empty):* 45 oz.
Sights: Front, Patridge on ramp base; S&W Micrometer
Click rear, adjustable for windage and elevation *Grips:*
Hogue rubber, round butt *Finish:* Satin stainless
Price: $730.00

MODEL 657
SPECIFICATIONS
Calibers: 41 Magnum *Capacity:* 6 shots *Barrel Length:*
7.5" *Overall Length:* 11 ³/₈" *Weight (empty):* 52 oz. *Sights:*
Front, pinned ramp on ramp base; black blade rear,
adjustable for windage and elevation; drilled and tapped
Grips: Hogue rubber *Finish:* Satin stainless steel
Price: $672.00

MODEL 610 CLASSIC
SPECIFICATIONS
Calibers: 10mm *Frame:* N-Large *Capacity:* 6 rounds
Barrel Length: 4" *Overall Length:* 10.5" *Weight:* 50 oz.
Sights: Interchangeable front; micrometer click adj. black
blade *Grips:* Hogue rubber *Finish:* Stainless steel
Feature: Unfluted cylinder
Price: $785.00

HANDGUNS

SPRINGFIELD PISTOLS

Model 1911-A1 Pistols

**MODEL 1911-A1
CHAMPION 4-INCH**

SPECIFICATIONS
Calibers: 45 ACP *Capacity:* 7 rounds (45 ACP)
Barrel Length: 4" *Overall Length:* 7 ⁵/₈"
Trigger Pull: 5-6.5 lbs. *Sight Radius:* 5.25"
Weight: 34 oz. *Finish:* Parkerized, Blued, Stainless
Prices: Parkerized w/night sights **$817.00**
Stainless w/night sights **870.00**
Lightweight (26 oz.) matte w/night sights. **867.00**
Lightweight stainless w/night sights. **900.00**
Lightweight matte w/night sights. **826.00**
Also available: compact 4" 45ACP

**MODEL 1911-A1
STANDARD & LIGHTWEIGHT**

SPECIFICATIONS
Calibers: 45 ACP/9mm *Capacity:* 8 rounds
(45 ACP), 9 rounds/ 9mm *Barrel Length:* 5" *Overall Length:* 8
⁵/₈" *Weight:* 38.5 oz. (31.5 oz. Lightweight) *Features:* Walnut
grips; Bo-Mar-type sights optional
Prices: 45 ACP Blued **$770.00**
45 ACP Stainless. **828.00**
45 ACP Stainless Steel V-12 (ported) **878.00**
45 ACP Lightweight Matte **832.00**
45 Parkerized w/night sights. **796.00**
40 S&W, stainless steel **812.00**
9mm Stainless. **837.00**
High-capacity (10 rounds, 45 ACP) Parkerized. . . . **807.00**

**MODEL 1911-A1
TROPHY MATCH**

SPECIFICATIONS
Calibers: 45 ACP or 40S&W *Capacity:* 7 rounds *Barrel
Length:* 5" *Overall Length:* 8 ⁵/₈" *Weight:* 40 oz. *Trigger Pull:*
4-5.5 lbs. *Sights:* Fully adjustable target sights *Sight Radius:*
6.75" *Finish:* Blued, Bi-tone or stainless *Features:* Match grade
barrel; Videcki speed trigger; serrated front strap & top of slide
Prices: Blued 45 ACP. **$1,115.00**
Stainless 45 ACP **1,199.00**
40 S&W, Armory Kote **1,225.00**

**1911-A1
ULTRA COMPACT
BI-TONE V-10**

SPECIFICATIONS
Caliber: 45 ACP and 9mm *Capacity:* 7 rounds *Barrel
Length:* 3.5" *Overall Length:* 7.75" *Weight:* 34.8 oz.
Sights: 3-dot fixed combat sights *Sight Radius:* 5.25"
Trigger Pull: 5-6.5 lbs. *Finish:* Bi-Tone or Parkerized
Prices: Parkerized **$817.00**
Bi-Tone V-10 (Ported). **853.00**
High-capacity (10 rounds, 45 ACP), Parkerized . . . **870.00**
Stainless **884.00**
9mm, lightweight, stainless. **853.00**
45, lightweight, matte. **867.00**

MODEL PT 22

SPECIFICATIONS

Caliber: 22 LR *Action:* Semiautomatic (DA only)
Capacity: 8 shots *Barrel Length:* 2.75" *Overall Length:*
5.25" *Weight:* 12.3 oz. *Sights:* Fixed *Safety:* Manual
Grips: Rosewood grip panels or wood grips *Finish:* Blue,
nickel, duotone or gold trimmed
Prices:

Blue, Nickel or DuoTone w/rosewood $215.00
w/wood grips **190.00**
Gold Trim **230.00**

MODEL PT 22

MODEL PT-25

SPECIFICATIONS

Caliber: 25 ACP *Capacity:* 9 rounds *Action:* Double action
semiauto *Barrel Length:* 2.75" *Overall Length:* 5.25"
Weight: 12.3 oz. *Finish:* Blue, stainless steel, duotone or
gold trimmed *Sights:* Fixed *Features:* Rosewood or wood
grip panels; tip-up barrel; push button magazine release
Prices:

Blue, Nickel or DuoTone $215.00
w/wood grips **190.00**
Blue w/Gold Trim **230.00**

MODEL PT-938 COMPACT (not shown)

SPECIFICATIONS

Caliber: 380 ACP *Capacity:* 10 rounds
Action: Double action semiauto
Barrel Length: 3" *Overall Length:* 6.75"
Weight: 27 oz. *Finish:* Blue or stainless steel
Sights: Fixed *Grips:* Checkered rubber grips
Prices:

Blue $500.00
Stainless **530.00**

MODEL PT-25

PT 911 COMPACT (not shown)

SPECIFICATIONS

Caliber: 9mm *Capacity:* 10 rounds
Action: Double action semiauto *Barrel Length:* 4"
Overall Length: 7" *Weight:* 28.2 oz.
Safeties: Manual, ambidextrous hammer drop; intercept
notch; firing pin block; chamber load indicator
Grips: Santoprene II *Sights:* Fixed 3-dot combat
Finish: Blue or stainless *Features:* Floating firing pin
Prices:

Blue $505.00
Stainless **525.00**
Also available:
PT-111 9MM MILLENNIUM. *Barrel Length:* 3 ⅛" *Sights:* Fixed
3-dot *Capacity:* 10 rounds, polymer frame **$425.00**
Stainless **435.00**

MODEL PT 111
MILLENNIUM

HANDGUNS

TAURUS PISTOLS
Medium & Large Frame

MODEL PT-92

SPECIFICATIONS
Caliber: 9mm Parabellum *Action:* Semiautomatic double action *Capacity:* 15 + 1 *Hammer:* Exposed *Barrel Length:* 5" *Overall Length:* 8.5" *Height:* 5.39" *Width:* 1.45" *Weight:* 34 oz. *Rifling:* R.H., 6 grooves *Sights:* Front, fixed; rear adjustable *Finish:* Blue or stainless steel
Prices:
Blue $575.00
Stainless 595.00
Also available: MODEL PT-99 Same specifications as Model PT 92, but has micrometer click-adjustable rear sight.
Blue $595.00
Stainless 610.00

MODEL PT-92

MODEL PT-945

**MODEL PT 99
STAINLESS**

MODEL PT-945

SPECIFICATIONS
Caliber: 45 ACP *Capacity:* 8 shots *Action:* Semiautomatic double *Barrel Length:* 4.25" *Overall Length:* 7.48" *Weight:* 29.5 oz. *Sights:* Drift-adjustable front and rear; 3-dot combat *Grips:* Checkered rubber or rosewood *Finish:* Blue or stainless
Prices: Blue $560.00
Blue & gold w/rosewood 610.00
Stainless 580.00
Stainless & gold w/rosewood 625.00
w/factory porting (blue) 600.00
w/factory porting (stainless) 620.00

PT-145

MODEL PT-940 (not shown)

SPECIFICATIONS
Caliber: 40 S&W *Action:* Semiautomatic double *Capacity:* 10 rounds *Barrel Length:* 4" *Overall Length:* 7" *Weight:* 28.2 oz. *Grips:* Rubber, rosewood, or mother of pearl *Sights:* Low-profile 3-dot combat *Finish:* Blue or stainless *Features:* Factory porting standard
Prices: Blue w/rubber grips $525.00
Stainless w/rubber grips 535.00

MODEL PT-145

The Taurus Millennium PT-145 is available in .45 ACP caliber, carries a full 10+1 rounds in a double-stack magazine and features a manual safety. The PT-145 is also available with night sights.
Prices: Blue $490.00
Stainless 500.00
Blue w/night sights 560.00
Stainless w/night sights 575.00

TAURUS REVOLVERS

MODEL 44

SPECIFICATIONS
Caliber: 44 Mag. **Capacity:** 6 rounds
Barrel Lengths: 4" (solid rib ported); 6.5" and
8 ³/₈" (vent. rib) **Weight:** 44 oz. (4"); 52 oz.
(6.5"); 57 oz. (8 ³/₈") **Sights:** adjustable **Grips:**
Rubber **Finish:** Blue or stainless steel
Prices: 4" barrel blue, ported solid rib $500.00
    stainless steel, ported solid rib. 565.00
    6.5" and 8 ³/₈" blue, ported vent. rib 525.00
    stainless steel, ported vent. rib 575.00

MODEL 82

SPECIFICATIONS
Caliber: 38 Special
Capacity: 6 shot
Action: Double **Barrel Length:**
4" heavy barrel **Weight:** 34 oz. (4" barrel)
Sights: Notched rear; serrated ramp front
Grips: rubber **Finish:** Blue or stainless
Prices: Blue $325.00
Stainless 375.00

TITANIUM TRACKER

The Tracker family is
designed for handgun
hunting and personal protection.
Now available in Total TitaniumTM, the
Tracker features a Ribber GripTM and
extended ejector rod. The Tracker family is
available in 4 inch 5-shot .41 Magnum and
4 and 6 inch 7-shot .357 Magnums. All have fully
adjustable sights and come in lockable hard plastic cases.
Prices: .357 4" or 6" $690.00
.41 Mag 4" 690.00

MODEL 454 CASULL "RAGING BULL" DA

SPECIFICATIONS
Caliber: 454 Casull
Capacity: 5 rounds
Barrel Length: 6.5" or 8.375" w/integral
vent rib **Overall Length:** 12" (6.5" barrel); 14"
(8.375" barrel) **Weight:** 53 oz. (6.5" barrel); 62.75 oz.
(8.375" barrel) **Sights:** adjustable
Finish: Polished stainless steel or bright blue steel
Grips: Soft black rubber
Features: Ported barrel
Prices:
Blue ported $785.00
Stainless 855.00

MODEL 85

SPECIFICATIONS
Caliber: 38 Special & 32 H&R Mag.
Capacity: 5 shot **Action:** Double **Barrel Length:**
2" and 3" **Weight:** 21 oz. (2" barrel) **Sights:** Fixed sights
Grips: Rubber, rosewood, or mother of pearl **Finish:** Blue
or stainless steel
Prices: Blue w/rubber $345.00
Stainless w/rubber 395.00
Also available:
MODEL 85CH. Same as Model 85, except has concealed
hammer and 2" barrel only.
MODEL 85UL w/2" barrel only and optional porting . . . 375.00
Stainless 425.00
MODELS 85CHB2C/85B2C w/2" barrel, blue finish,
    ported barrels 360.00
Stainless 405.00

HANDGUNS

TAURUS REVOLVERS

MODEL 941

MODEL 94
SPECIFICATIONS
Caliber: 22 LR *Number*
Of Shots: 9 *Action:* Double *Barrel Lengths:*
2", 4", and 5" heavy, solid rib *Weight:* 25 oz
(w/4" barrel) *Sights:* Serrated ramp front; rear
micro-meter click adjustable for windage and eleva-
tion *Grips:* Brazilian hardwood (4", 5") *Finish:* Blue
or stainless steel
Prices: Blue **$325.00**
Stainless Steel **375.00**
Also available: MODEL 941 in 22 Magnum, 8-shot capacity;
2", 4", 5" barrel lengths available; ejector shroud.
In blue **$345.00**
In stainless steel **395.00**

**MODEL
445SS2**

MODEL 445
Bright Blue Steel
2" Barrel, Ported

MODEL 445
DOUBLE ACTION
SPECIFICATIONS
Caliber: 44 Special *Capacity:* 5 shots
Barrel Length: 2" *Weight:* 28.25 oz. *Grips:* rubber
Sights: Serrated ramp front; notched rear *Finish:* Blue or
stainless *Features:* Optional porting; heavy solid rib barrel
Prices: Blue **$345.00**
Stainless **395.00**
Also available: MODEL 445CH. Same specifications as Model
445 but features concealed hammer

MODEL 608
DOUBLE ACTION
SPECIFICATIONS
Caliber: 357 Magnum *Capacity:* 8
shots *Barrel Lengths:* 4" (heavy solid rib);
6.5" and 8 ³/₈" (ejector shroud) *Weight:*
51.5 oz. (6.5" barrel) *Grips:* Santoprene I
Sights: Serrated ramp front w/red insert; micrometer
click adjustable *Finish:* Blue or stainless
Features: Compensated barrel; transfer bar safety;
concealed hammer
Prices:
4" Blue **$445.00**
4" Stainless **510.00**
6.5", 8 ³/₈" Blue **465.00**
6.5", 8 ³/₈" Stainless **525.00**

MODEL 605

SPECIFICATIONS
Caliber: 357 Magnum
Capacity: 5 shot
Barrel Length: 2.25"
Weight: 24.5 oz.
Sights: Notched rear; serrated ramp front
Grips: Rubber
Safety: Transfer bar
Finish: Blue or stainless
Features: Optional porting (**$19.00** add'l.)
Prices:
Blue **$345.00**
Stainless **395.00**
Also available:
MODEL 605CH w/concealed hammer and ported barrel

ENCORE HUNTER PACKAGE

CONTENDER SUPER "14" BULL BARREL MODELS

ENCORE PISTOL

SPECIFICATIONS

Calibers: 22 Hornet, 22-250 Rem., 223 Rem., 243 Win., 25/06 Rem., 270 Win., 7mm-08 Rem., 308 Win., 30-06 Spfd. 44 Rem. Mag., 454 Casull, 45-70 Gov't, 45 Colt/.410 ga. *Action:* Single break-open
Barrel lengths: 12" and 15"
Overall length: 16.5" (12" bbl.); 19.5" (15" bbl.)
Weight: 4.25, 12"; 4.5 lbs. (15" bbl.)
Trigger: Adjustable
Safety: Automatic hammerblock w/bolt interlock
Grips: Ambidextrous walnut pistol grip w/finger grooves and butt cap; composite grips as accessory.
Sights: Adjustable rear; ramp front sight blade
Features: Interchangeable barrels (12"- **$245.49-268.51**; 15"- **$253.09-285.99** Blued, **$278.30** SST); drilled and tapped for T/C scope mounts
Prices:

12" Blued	$543.66-566.28
15" barrel Blued	551.02-583.60
SST	603.64

Also available: ENCORE HUNTER PACKAGE in 22-250 Rem., 270 Win., 308 Win. *Barrel length:* 15" *Features:* Weaver-style base and rings, 2.5-7X Recoil Proof pistol scope; blued frame and barrel; black composite grip and forend; soft carry case; no iron sights **$817.48**

THOMPSON/CENTER CONTENDER SHOOTER'S PACKAGE

Calibers: 7-30 Waters, 223 Rem., 30-30 Win., 22 LR Match *Barrel length:* 14" (10" 22 LR Match)
Overall length: 16" (10" 22 LR Match) *Weight:* 4 lbs.
Features: Mounted T/C Recoil Proof 2.5 X 7 scope plus carrying case
Price: Blued steel **$754.39**

CONTENDER SUPER "16" (Not Shown)

Calibers: 223 Rem., 45-70 (bull barrel); 45 Colt/.410 ga.
Prices:

Blued (223 Rem.)	$525.95
45-70 Gov't. w/Muzzle Tamer	531.52
45 Colt/.410 ga.	559.70

Calibers: 22 LR Match Grade Chamber, 22 Hornet, 223 Rem., 7-30 Waters, 30-30 Win., and 44 Mag. (Blued version also available in 22 Hornet, 222 Rem., 357 Rem. Max.). *See pg. 13 Catalog* *Barrel length:* 14" bull barrel.
Features: Fully adjustable target rear sight and Patridge-style ramped front sight with 13.5-inch sight radius.
Overall length: 18.25" *Weight:* 3.5 lbs.
Prices:

Blued	$520.24
Match Grade Chamber	531.50
Stainless	578.40
Vent Rib Model (14") in 45 Colt/.410, blue	556.74
Stainless	613.94
22 LR Match SST	590.79

CONTENDER BULL BARREL MODELS

These pistols with 10-inch barrel feature fully adjustable Patridge-style iron sights. All stainless steel models (including the Super "14" and Super "16") are equipped with Rynite finger-groove grip with rubber recoil cushion and matching Rynite forend, plus Cougar etching on the steel frame.
Standard calibers available: 22 WMR, 22 Hornet, 22 LR Match, 223 Rem., 30-30 Win., 357 Mag., 44 Mag. and 45 Colt/.410. Custom calibers also available.

Prices:

Bull Barrel Blue	$509.03-520.29
Bull Barrel Stainless	578.40-566.59
In 45/.410 - 10 inch SST	590.44
Vent Rib Model Stainless - 14 inch	613.94
Match Grade Barrel (22 LR only, stainless)	
10-inch	578.40
14-inch	590.79

HANDGUNS

1871 ROLLING BLOCK TARGET PISTOL

SPECIFICATIONS
Calibers: 22 LR, 22 Magnum, 22 Hornet and 357 Mag.
Capacity: Single shot **Barrel Length:** 9.5" (half-octagon/half-round or full round Navy Style)
Overall Length: 14" **Weight:** 2.75 lbs.
Sights: Fully adjustable rear; ramp front or open sight on Navy Style barrel
Grip and forend: Walnut **Trigger guard:** Brass
Frame: Color case hardened steel
Price: $410.00

1871 ROLLING BLOCK TARGET PISTOL

DRAGOON REVOLVERS (not shown)

Calibers: .44 *Capcity:* 6 shots **Barrel Length:** 7.5"
Frame: color-case **Grips:** walnut **Weight:** 4 lbs.
Price: First Model $315.00
Second Model 315.00
Third Model 315.00

1873 CATTLEMAN S.A.

SPECIFICATIONS
Calibers: 357 Magnum, 38/40, 44 Sp., 44-40, 45 L.C. **Capacity:** 6 shots
Barrel Lengths: 4.75", 5.5", 7.5" round, tapered; 18" (Buntline)
Overall Length: 10.75" w/5.5" barrel
Weight: 2.42 lbs. **Grip:** One-piece walnut
Frame: Color case hardened steel; also available in charcoal blue or nickel
Price: $410.00-435.00
Also available:
45 L.C./45 ACP Convertible $485.00

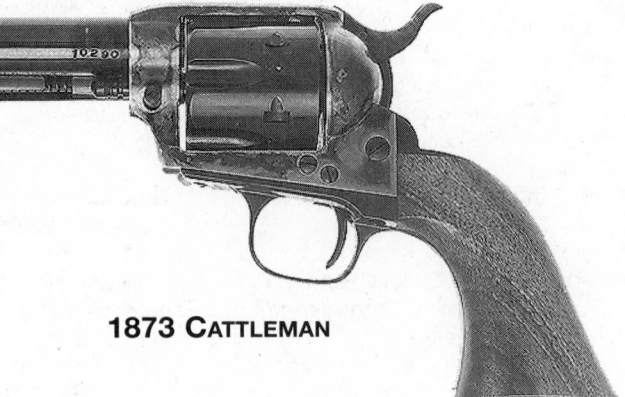

1873 CATTLEMAN

WALKER REVOLVER (not shown)

Calibers: .44 *Capcity:* 6 shots **Barrel Length:** 9" **Frame:** color-case **Grips:** walnut **Weight:** 4.4 lbs. This is the most massive revolver of the "Old West" era; named after a Texas Ranger who carried it.
Price: $330.00

1875 "OUTLAW"

SPECIFICATIONS
Calibers: 357 Magnum, 44-40, 45 ACP, 45 Long Colt **Capacity:** 6 shots
Barrel Lengths: 5.5", 7.5" round, tapered
Overall Length: 13.75" **Weight:** 2.75 lbs.
Grips: Two-piece walnut **Finish:** Color case hardened steel
Price: $483.00
45 L.C./45 ACP "Outlaw" Convertible 499.00
1890 Police (not shown) 483.00
45 L.C./45 ACP Police Convertible 499.00

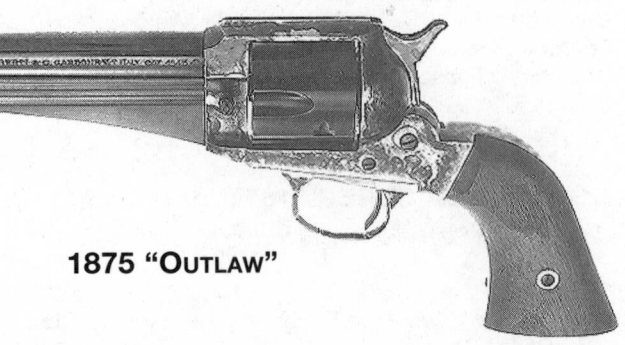

1875 "OUTLAW"

WALTHER PISTOLS

Models PPK and PPK/S double-action pistols differ only in the overalll length of the barrel and slide. Both models offer the same features, including live round indicator pin to signal a loaded chamber. An automatic internal safety blocks the hammer to prevent accidental striking of the firing pin, except with a deliberate pull of the trigger.

MODEL PPK & PPK/S

SPECIFICATIONS
Caliber: 380 ACP and 32 ACP
Capacity: 6 rounds (PPK), 7 rounds (PPK/S), 8 rounds (PPK/S in 32 ACP only)
Barrel Length: 3.35"
Overall Length: 6.25"
Weight: 21 oz. (PPK); 23 oz. (PPK/S)
Finish: Walther blue or stainless steel
Price: **$471.00**
   PPKS **475.00**

MODEL PPK/S

MODEL P 99 COMPACT

SPECIFICATIONS
Caliber: 9mm Parabellum, 40 S&W
Capacity: 10 rounds
Barrel Length: 4"
Overall Length: 7"
Weight: 25 oz.
Height: 5.37"
Width: 1.2"
Sights: Windage-adjustable micrometer rear; three inter-changeable front blades included; optional modular laser sight and halogen flashlight for installation on front rails
Features: Polymer frame; blued slide; customized back-strap; three automatic safeties; cocking and loaded chamber indicator; ambidextrous magazine release levers
Price: **$645.00**

MODEL P 99

GSP EXPERT

Walther's new target pistol is available in 22, 22 LR & 32 S+W. It features an ergonomic grip in three sizes, target sights and a newly developed recoil absorber.
Prices: .22 LR **$1,240.00**
   .32 S+W **1,420.00**

GSP EXPERT .32

HANDGUNS

SILHOUETTE PISTOL (Right-Hand Rear Grip)

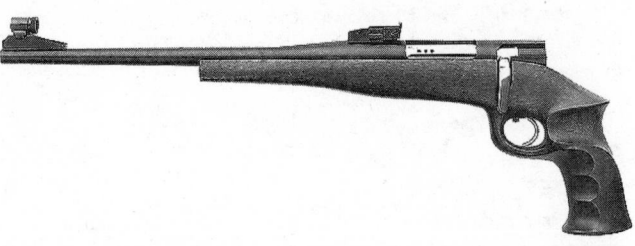

SPECIFICATIONS
Calibers: 308 Win. F.L., 7mm IHMSA and 7mmX308
Barrel length: 14 $^{15}/_{16}$" **Weight:** 4.5 lbs. **Action:** Single-shot bolt action **Sights:** Wichita Multi-Range Sight System **Grips:** Right-hand center walnut grip or right-hand rear walnut grip **Features:** Glass bedded; bolt ground to precision fit; adjustable Wichita trigger
Price:. $1,800.00
Also available:
WICHITA CLASSIC SILHOUETTE PISTOL. **Barrel:** 11.25".
Weight: 3 lbs. 15 oz. **Grips:** AAA grade walnut,
   glass bedded $3450.50
ENGRAVED MODEL 4850.00

INTERNATIONAL PISTOL

SPECIFICATIONS
Calibers: 7-30 Waters, 7mm Super Mag., 7R (30-30 Win. necked to 7mm), 30-30 Win., 357 Mag., 357 Super Mag., 32 H&H Mag., 22-RFM, 22 LR **Barrel lengths:** 10" and 14" (10.5" for centerfire calibers) **Weight:** 3 lbs. 2 oz. (10" barrel); 4 lbs. 7 oz. (14" barrel) **Action:** Top-break, single-shot, single action only **Sights:** Patridge front sight; rear sight adjustable for windage and elevation **Grips and Forend:** Walnut **Safety:** Crossbolt
Price: 10" Barrel $775.00
14" Barrel 875.00

WILDEY PISTOLS

These gas-operated pistols are designed to meet the needs of hunters who want to use handguns for big game. The Wildey pistol includes such features as: •Ventilated rib •Reduced recoil •Double-action trigger mechanism •Patented hammer and trigger blocks and rebounding fire pin •Sights adjustable for windage and elevation •Stainless construction •Fixed barrel for increased accuracy •Increased action strength (with 3-lug and exposed face rotary bolt) •Selective single or autoloading capability •Ability to handle high-pressure loads

SPECIFICATIONS
Calibers: 45 & 475 Wildey Magnums and 45 Win. Mag.
Capacity: 7 shots **Barrel lengths:** 5", 6", 7", 8", 10", 12", 14"
Overall length: 11" with 7" barrel **Weight:** 64 oz. with 5" barrel
Height: 6"

SURVIVOR AND GUARDSMAN in 45 Win. Mag. **Prices**
5", 6" or 7" barrels $1385.60
8" or 10" barrels 1408.50
12" barrel 1492.60
14" barrel 1895.00
SURVIVOR MODEL in Wildey Mags.
8" or 10" barrels $1408.50
12" barrel 1492.60
14" barrel 1895.00

HUNTER MODEL in 45 Win. Mag.
5", 6" or 7" barrels $1618.90
8" or 10" barrels 1642.50
12" barrel 1728.10
14" barrel 2115.00
HUNTER MODEL in Wildey Mags.
8" or 10" barrels 1642.50
12" barrel 1728.10
14" barrel 2115.00
Also available:
Interchangeable barrel extension assemblies
12" barrel 694.40
14" barrel 1148.00

Blackpowder

TAXIDERMY GUIDE
New Revised 3rd Edition

by Russel Tinsley

The new *Taxidermy Guide*, 3rd Edition, with its easy step-by-step instructions and updated information, enables the hobbyist to work on trophys and take pride in showing off the lifelike finished product.

ADVANCED BLACK POWDER HUNTING

by Toby Bridges

Advanced Black Powder Hunting is the first modern day publication to be filled from cover to cover with guns, loads, projectiles, accessories and the techniques to get the most from today's front loading guns.

*For addresses and phone/fax numbers of manufacturers and distributors included in this section, please turn to **DIRECTORY OF MANUFACTURERS AND SUPPLIERS** on page 557.*

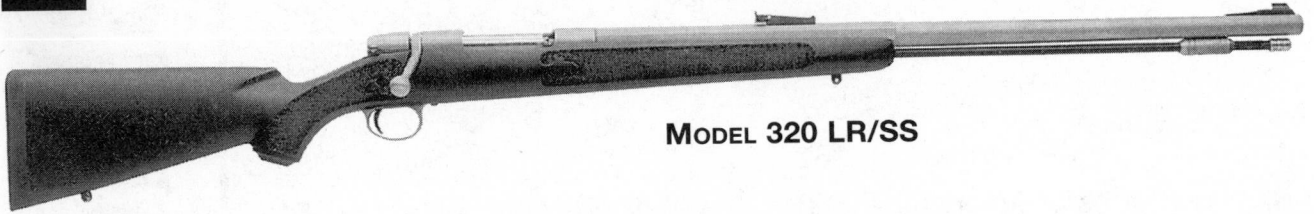

MODEL 320 LR/SS

MODEL 420 LR CLASSIC

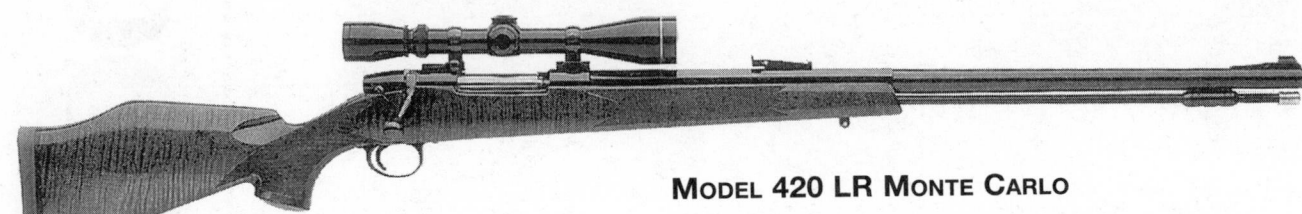

MODEL 420 LR MONTE CARLO

SPECIFICATIONS

Caliber: 50
Action: In-line percussion (removable weather shroud)
Barrel Length: 26" (1:28"); 8 lands & grooves;
octagon to .75" tapered round
Overall length: 47.5" *Weight:* 7 7/8 lbs.
Length of pull: 13.5" *Stock:* Select grade tiger-striped curly
maple (Classic model has filled-grain luster finish w/pistol grip
cap; Monte Carlo has filled-grain high-gloss finish)
Features: Match grade target triggers w/trigger block safety;
1" recoil pad; scope not included

Prices:

MODEL 420 LR MONTE CARLO & CLASSIC STANDARD	**$459.00**
Stainless Steel Standard	549.00
Fancy Stainless Steel	619.00
Hand Select	775.00
Hand Select Stainless Steel	876.00
Exhibition Grade	1,322.00
Exhibition Grade Stainless Steel	1,422.00
MODEL 320 LR BLU w/SYNTHETIC STOCK	380.00
MODEL 320 LR S/S	447.00

MOUNTAIN RIFLE

MOUNTAIN RIFLE

SPECIFICATIONS

Caliber: 50 percussion or flintlock
Barrel length: 32" (1:66 roundball or 1:28 bullet twist);
1" octagonal; rust brown finish
Overall length: 49" *Weight:* 7.5 lbs.
Stock: Select grade tiger-striped curly maple; filled-grain
luster finish

Sights: Fixed buckhorn rear; silver blade brass bead front
Features: Double throw adjustable set triggers

Price: Std. percussion	**$504.00**
Hand Select percussion	660.00
Fancy Percussion	592.00
Std. flint	559.00
Hand select flint	687.00
Fancy flint	618.00

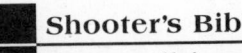

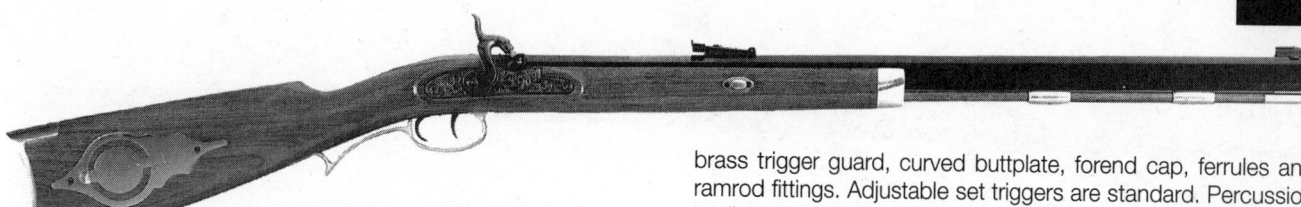

TRADITIONAL HAWKEN RIFLE

Cabela's Traditional Hawken is available in 50 or 54 caliber. It features fully adjustable sights, top-grade walnut stock with

brass trigger guard, curved buttplate, forend cap, ferrules and ramrod fittings. Adjustable set triggers are standard. Percussion available in right- or left-hand versions. Barrel: 24" octagon with 1-in-48 twist. *Weight:* 9 lbs.

Prices: Percussion, right-hand **$189.99**
  Percussion, left-hand **199.99**
  Flintlock, right-hand **224.99**

PINE RIDGE LR RIFLE

This long-range in-line Thompson Center rifle handles up to 150 grains of blackpowder for magnum velocities. Features include synthetic stock, an adjustable trigger and

the No. 209 flame-thrower nipple ignition system. *Barrel:* 26", blued or stainless. An optional scope kit includes a 2.5-7x32 scope, rings and bases.

Price: **$229.99**
  Stainless **269.99**
  w/Scope **279.99**
  Stainless w/scope **319.99**

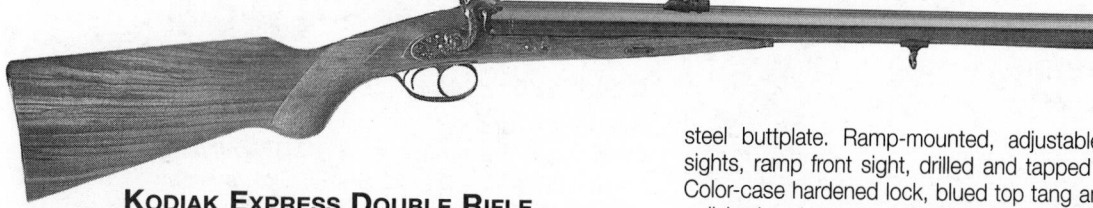

BLUE RIDGE RIFLE

From the era of the American long rifle (1760-1840) comes the design for this faithful reproduction. The so-called "squirrel rifle" was renowned for hitting small, often distant targets and Cabela's Blue Ridge rifles live up to that tradition. Precision-rifled 39" browned octagonal barrels with 1-in-48" twist deliver exceptional precision with patched round balls and will handle conical bullets surprisingly well. 8 lands and grooves. Percussion models have drum and bolster

system. Flintlocks have large, sure-spark frizzen and ample priming pan. Locks are color case-hardened. Adjustable double-set, double-phase triggers. Buttplate and trigger guard are polished brass.

ORDER NO. PERCUSSION	CAL.	OVERALL LENGTH	BARREL LENGTH	WT. LBS.	GROOVE & LANDS	GUN ONLY PRICE	KIT PRICE
HJ-21-0007-036	.36 Cal	55"	39"	7 3/4	7	$379.99	$419.99
HJ-21-0007-050	.50 Cal	55"	39"	7 1/4	8	$379.99	$419.99
FLINTLOCK							
HJ-21-0008-036	.36 Cal	55"	39"	7 3/4	7	$399.99	$439.99
HJ-21-0008-045	.45 Cal	55"	39"	7 1/4	8	$399.99	$439.99
HJ-21-0008-050	.50 Cal	55"	39"	7 1/4	8	$399.99	$439.99

KODIAK EXPRESS DOUBLE RIFLE

Early explorers of Africa and Asia had to rely on large-bore "express" rifles like this handsome sidelock replica featuring oil-finished, hand-checkered European walnut stock with case hardened

steel buttplate. Ramp-mounted, adjustable folding double rear sights, ramp front sight, drilled and tapped for folding tang sight. Color-case hardened lock, blued top tang and trigger guard are all polished and engraved. *Calibers:* 50, 54, 58, 72 *Barrels:* 28" with 1:48" twist (regulated at 75 yards); blued. *Overall Length:* 45.25" *Weight:* 9.3 lbs.

Price: . . . . **$649.99 to 679.99**

COLT BLACKPOWDER ARMS

Signature Series

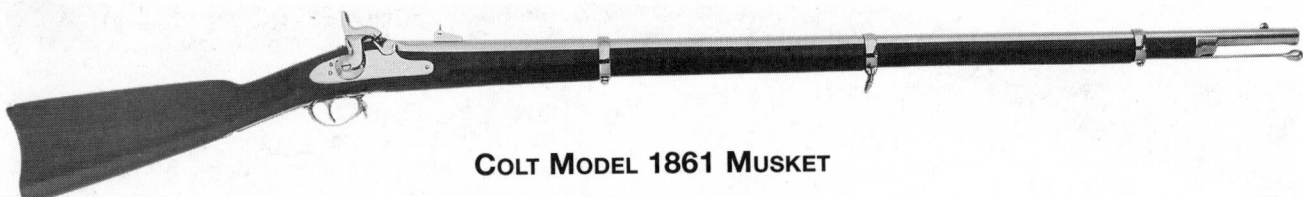

COLT MODEL 1861 MUSKET

Manufactured to original specifications using modern steels, this re-issue has the authentic Colt markings of its Civil War predecessor. Plus triangular bayonet.

SPECIFICATIONS
Caliber: .58
Barrel length: 40"
Overall length: 56"

Weight: 9 lbs. 3 oz. (empty)
Sights: Folding leaf rear; steel blade front
Sight Radius: 36"
Stock: One piece
Finish: Bright steel lockplate, hammer, buttplate, bands, ramrod and nipple; blued rear sight
Price: $799.95

COLT THIRD MODEL DRAGOON

SPECIFICATIONS
Caliber: 44 percussion
Barrel length: 7.5"
Overall length: 13.75"
Weight: 66 oz. (empty)
Sight: Fixed blade front
Sight radius: 10.75"
Stock: One-piece walnut
Finish: Colt blue with color case hardened frame; hammer, lever and plunger
Price: $499.95

COLT WALKER 150TH ANNIVERSARY MODEL

SPECIFICATIONS - *Caliber:* 44 *Weight:*
4 lbs. 9 oz. *Barrel length:* 9" *Cylinder length:*
2 7/16" *Finish:* Color case hardened frame and hammer; smooth wooden grips *Features:* Colt's Signature Series 150th anniversary re-issue carries the identical markings as the original 1847 Walker. "U.S. 1847" appears above the barrel wedge, exactly as on the Walkers produced for service in the Mexican War. The cylinder has a battle scene depicting 15 Texas Rangers defeating a Comanche war party using the first revolver invented by Sam Colt. This Limited Edition features original A Company No. 1 markings embellished in gold. Serial numbers begin with #221, a continuation of A Company numbers.
Price: $699.95
    Standard 1847 Walker 499.95

COLT 1849 POCKET REVOLVER

SPECIFICATIONS
Caliber: 31 *Barrel length:* 4"
Overall length: 9.5"
Weight: 24 oz. (empty)
Stock: One-piece
walnut *Finish:* Colt blue and color case hardened frame
Price: $429.95

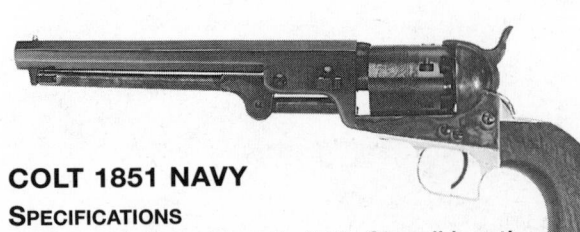

COLT 1851 NAVY

SPECIFICATIONS
Caliber: 36 *Barrel length:* 7.5" *Overall length:*
13 1/8" *Weight:* 40.5 oz. (empty) *Sights:* Fixed blade front *Sight radius:* 10" *Stock:* Oiled American walnut *Finish:* Colt blue and color case hardened frame
Price: $449.95

COLT BLACKPOWDER ARMS

Signature Series

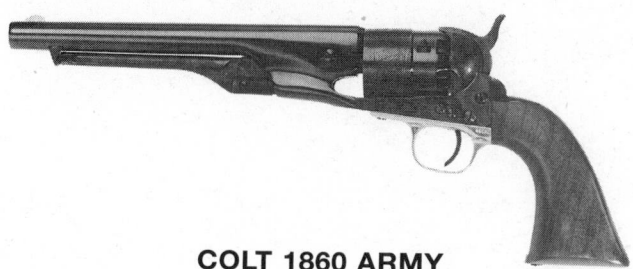

COLT 1860 ARMY

A continuation in production of the famous cap-and-ball revolver used by the U.S. Cavalry with color case hardened frame, hammer and loading lever. Blued backstrap and brass trigger guard, roll-engraved cylinder and one-piece walnut grips

SPECIFICATIONS
Caliber: 44 *Barrel length:* 8" *Overall length:* 13.75"
Weight: 42 oz. (empty) *Sights:* Fixed blade front
Sight radius: 10.5" *Stock:* One-piece walnut
Finish: Colt blue with color case hardened frame; hammer, lever and plunger
Price: $449.95

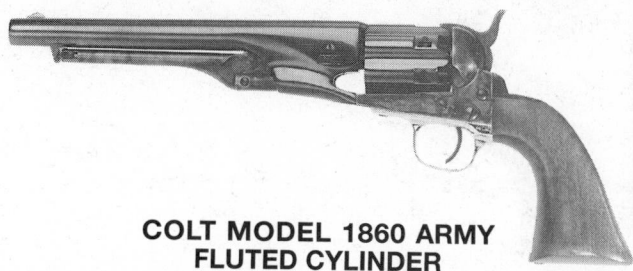

COLT MODEL 1860 ARMY FLUTED CYLINDER

The first Army revolvers shipped from Hartford were known as the "Cavalry Model"—with fluted cylinder, color case hardened frame, hammer, loading lever and plunger. Features blued barrel, backstrap and cylinder; brass trigger guard, fluted cylinder, one-piece walnut grip and a 4-screw frame (cut for optional shoulder stock)

SPECIFICATIONS
Caliber: 44 percussion *Barrel length:* 8"
Overall length: 13.75" *Weight:* 42 oz. (empty)
Sight: Fixed blade front *Sight radius:* 10.5"
Stock: One piece walnut *Finish:* Colt blue with color casehardened frame; hammer, lever and plunger
Price: $449.95

COLT 1861 NAVY

A personal favorite of George Armstrong Custer, who carried a pair of them during the Civil War. Loading lever and plunger; blued barrel, cylinder backstrap and trigger guard; roll-engraved cylinder; one-piece walnut grip.

SPECIFICATIONS
Caliber: 36 percussion *Barrel length:* 7.5"
Overall length: 13 1/8" *Weight:* 42 oz. (empty)
Sight: Fixed blade front *Sight radius:* 10"
Stock: One-piece walnut *Finish:* Colt blue with color case hardened frame; hammer, lever and plunger
Price: $449.95

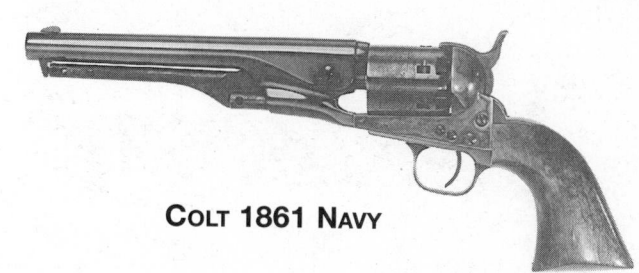

COLT 1861 NAVY

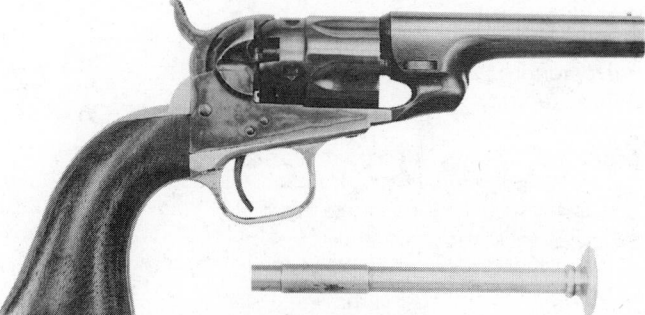

TRAPPER MODEL 1862 POCKET POLICE

TRAPPER MODEL 1862 POCKET POLICE

The first re-issue of the rare and highly desirable Pocket Police "Trapper Model." The Trapper's 3.5" barrel without attached loading lever makes it an ideal backup gun, as well as a welcome addition to any gun collection. Color case-hardened frame and hammer; silver-plated backstrap and trigger guard; blued semi-fluted cylinder and barrel; one-piece walnut grip. Separate 4 5/8" brass ramrod.

SPECIFICATIONS
Caliber: 36 *Barrel length:* 3.5" *Overall length:* 8.5"
Weight: 20 oz. (empty) *Sight:* Fixed blade front
Sight radius: 6" *Stock:* One-piece walnut
Finish: Colt blue with color casehardened frame and hammer
Price: $429.95

1851 NAVY REVOLVER BRASS FRAME

SPECIFICATIONS
Caliber: 44
Barrel length: 7.5" octagonal; hinged-style loading lever
Overall length: 13"
Weight: 44 oz.
Cylinder: 6-shot, engraved
Sights: Post front; hammer notch rear
Grip: One-piece walnut
Finish: Solid brass frame, trigger guard and backstrap; blued barrel and cylinder; color case hardened loading lever and hammer
Price: $143.95

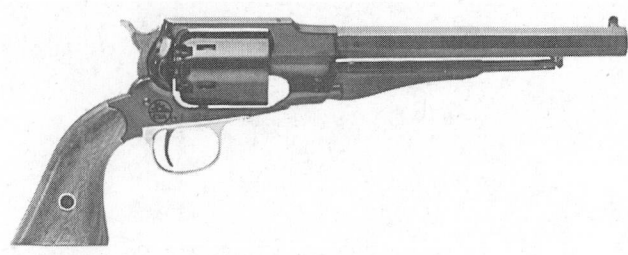

1858 REMINGTON

SPECIFICATIONS
Caliber: 44
Cylinder: 6-shot, engraved
Barrel length: 7.5" octagonal
Overall length: 13"
Weight: 38 oz.
Sights: Blade front; adjustable target
Grip: Two-piece walnut
Price:
Brass Frame $159.95

KENTUCKY PISTOL

SPECIFICATIONS
Caliber: 50 percussion
Barrel: 9.75", rifled, octagonal
Overall length: 15.5"   *Weight:* 40 oz.
Finish: Blued barrel, brass hardware
Sights: Brass blade front; fixed open rear
Stock: Select hardwood
Ignition: Engraved, color case hardened percussion lock, screw adjustable sear engagement
Accessories: Brass-tipped, hardwood ramrod; stainless-steel nipple or flash hole liner
Prices:
Finished. $167.95
Percussion Kit 119.95

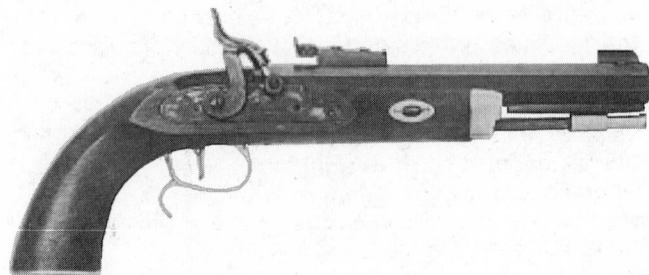

HAWKEN PISTOL

SPECIFICATIONS
Caliber: 50 percussion
Barrel length: 9.75", octagonal
Overall length: 16.5"
Weight: 50 oz.
Trigger: Early-style brass
Sights: Beaded steel blade front; fully adjustable rear (click adj. screw settings lock into position)
Stock: Select hardwood
Finish: Solid brass wedge plate, nose cap, ramrod thimbles, trigger guard and grip cap
Prices:
Finished. $167.95
Kit. 127.95

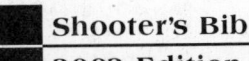

YOUTH HUNTER PR4104

The **YOUTH HUNTER** rifle was custom made for the smaller shooter. It has a 24" octagonal barrel and a shortened hardwood stock. CVA's patented breech plug/bolster system ensures consistent ignition. A 1:48" twist deep-groove rifled barrel, ensures accuracy with round ball or conical bullets. This rifle is also great for the petite lady. Fully equipped with a Williams adjustable rear sight, oversized trigger guard and synthetic ramrod. All Youth Hunter rifles are backed by CVA's lifetime mechanical warranty and include complete shooting instructions.

SPECIFICATIONS
Calibers: .50 *Barrel:* 24" Blued *Twist:* 1:48
Stock: Hardwood *Weight:* 5 lbs. *Length:* 38"
Price: $135.95

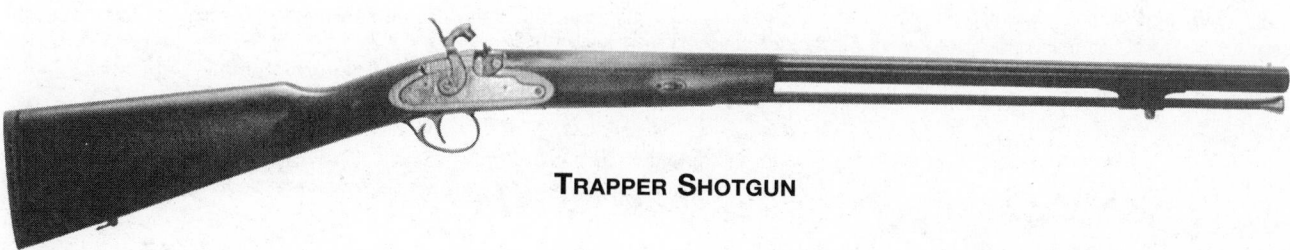

TRAPPER SHOTGUN

The new chrome lined barrel of the **TRAPPER** gives the shooter the option to shoot either lead or steel shot. The light weight English style hardwood stock allows for quick target pick up and follow through. The engraved color case hardened lock contains an authentic V-type main spring. The barrel has a brass bead front sight, hook style breech and snail type bolster for convenient and easy cleaning. Includes CVA's lifetime mechanical warranty and complete instructions.

SPECIFICATIONS: MODEL PS419M
Gauge: 12 *Barrel:* 28" Blued *Choke:* Fixed Modified
Ramrod: Synthetic *Weight:* 6 lbs.
Price: $287.95

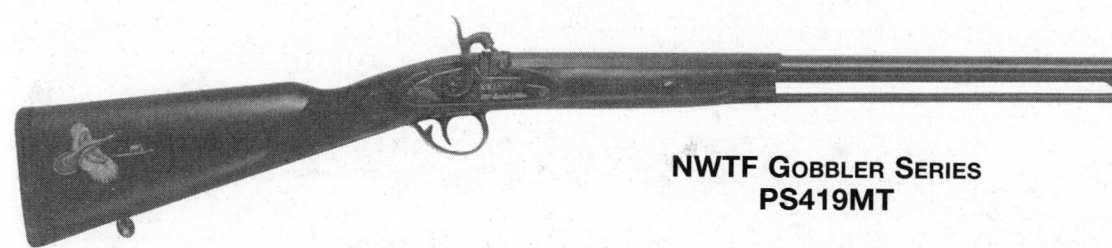

NWTF GOBBLER SERIES
PS419MT

The 2001 Gobbler Series shotgun features a hardwood stock with a laser engraved, full color tom flying down from the roost. The case hardened lock plate engraving displays the official seal of the NWTF and comes numbered in sequence. It is a collection piece that is also lethal in the woods! As with all NWTF endorsed products, a portion of the sales of all Gobbler series smokepoles goes directly to the NWTF, supporting their efforts to promote the conservation and wise management of the North American wild turkey.

Price:
12 GAUGE GOBBLER SERIES SHOTGUN
 PS419MT $367.95

CVA Rifles

PR4434N Firebolt Break-Up Camo

PR4433N Firebolt

FIREBOLT 209 ULTRAMAG RIFLE

Totally redesigned for 2001, the FireBolt 209 UltraMag is designed with the magnum shooter in mind. The matted blued 26" one-piece MonoBlock barrel ensures a complete powder burn. Six precision machined flutes increase barrel stability while reducing weight. The recoil reducing resin filled stock in a DuraGrip finish completes this perfectly balanced rifle. Like all the rifles in the FireBolt series, this gun is equipped with a stainless steel quick-release bolt, #209 ignition (installed), and a Bullet Guiding Muzzle. Other important features include Illuminator fiber optic sights, SureGrip rubber-coated stock, ventilated recoil pad, and sling swivel studs. The receiver is factory drilled and tapped for easy scope installation. Includes synthetic ramrod, cleaning jag, breech plug/nipple wrench, and #209 capper/decapper. Limited lifetime warranty. Now available in .45 Caliber.

PR4451 Hunterbolt 209
Magnum Break-Up Camo

HUNTERBOLT 209 MAGNUM RIFLE

The Hunterbolt 209 Magnum is equipped with the same stainless steel quick-release bolt design found on the FireBolt series. The #209 ignition provides unsurpassed reliability, even in the toughest hunting conditions, while the 24" one-piece MonoBlock barrel offers legendary accuracy. "Bullet Guiding Muzzle," Illuminator fiber optic sights, ventilated recoil pad synthetic stock, sling swivel studs, and trigger blocking safety complete this performance-oriented muzzleloader. The receiver is factory drilled and tapped for easy scope installation. Includes synthetic ramrod, cleaning jag breech plug/nipple wrench, and #209 capper/decapper. Limited lifetime warranty. Now available in .45 caliber.

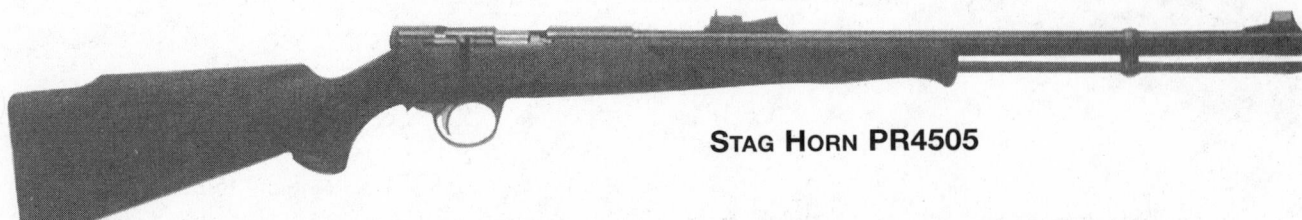

Stag Horn PR4505

STAG HORN 209 MAGNUM RIFLE

The Stag Horn 209 Magnum has a one-piece MonoBlock barrel design. The Stag Horn will now handle a 3-pellet load (150 grain equivalent). It features the reliable #209 ignition, Illuminator Solar Sights, ventilated recoil pad, manual notch safety, stainless steel bolt, oversized trigger guard, and synthetic stock. Standard accessories include: breech plug/nipple wrench, cleaning jag, allen wrench, and complete instructions. Lifetime mechanical warranty.

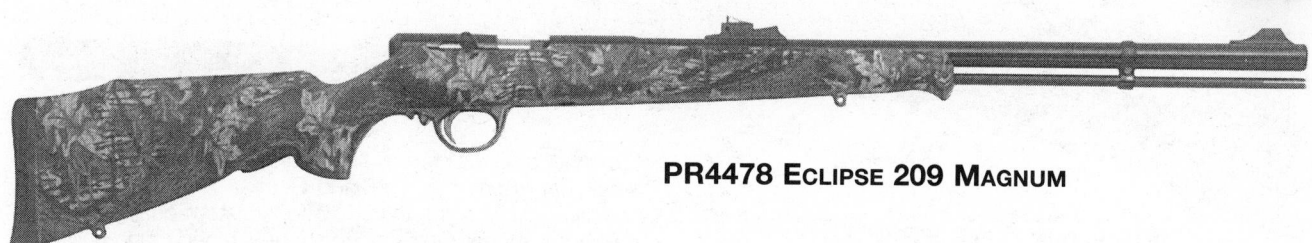

PR4478 ECLIPSE 209 MAGNUM

ECLIPSE 209 MAGNUM RIFLE

Long one of CVA's most popular rifle models, the 2001 Eclipse 209 Magnum now features a one-piece barrel design enabling the gun to handle a 3-pellet Magnum load (150 grain equivalent). Combine this with #209 primer ignition as standard equipment for an extremely reliable muzzleloader (#11 and musket cap nipples also included). Other standard features include ventilated recoil pad, Illuminator Fiber Optic sights, stainless steel bolt, automatic safety, oversized trigger guard, and deluxe cocking handle. The one-piece MonoBlock barrel design features a 1:32" twist for superior accuracy with PowerBelt Bullets. Factory drilled and tapped receiver allows for easy scope installation. Synthetic ramrod, cleaning jag, sling swivel studs, and breech plug/nipple wrench are also included with every gun. Limited Lifetime warranty. Also available in mossy oak break-up camo.

FIREBOLT

MODEL	CALIBER	BARREL	TWIST	STOCK	WEIGHT	LENGTH	RETAIL PRICE
PR4433N	.50	26" Nickel	1:32	Fiber grip	7 lbs.	44"	$279.95
PR4434N	.50	26" Nickel	1:32	Break-up	7 lbs.	44"	319.95
PR4433	.50	26" Blue	1:32	Fiber grip	7 lbs.	44"	259.95
PR4434	.50	26" Blue	1:32	Break-up	7 lbs.	44"	299.95
PR448N	.45	26" Nickel	1:22	Fiber grip	7 lbs.	44"	289.95
PR4449N	.45	26" Nickel	1:22	Break-up	7 lbs.	44"	329.95
PR4448	.45	26" Blue	1:22	Fibergrip	7 lbs.	44"	269.95
PR4449	.45	26" Blue	1:22	Break-up	7 lbs.	44"	309.95

HUNTERBOLT

MODEL	CALIBER	BARREL	TWIST	STOCK	WEIGHT	LENGTH	RETAIL PRICE
PR4451N	.50	24" Nickel	1:32	Syn.Break-up	6 lbs.	42"	$249.95
PR4461N	.45	24" Nickel	1:22	Syn. Break-up	6 lbs.	42"	239.95
PR4490N	.50	24" Nickel	1:32	Syn. Black	6 lbs.	42"	219.95
PR4451	.50	24" Blue	1:32	Syn. Break-up	6 lbs.	42"	229.95
PR4461	.45	24" Blue	1:22	Syn. Break-up	6 lbs.	42"	224.95
PR4490	.50	24" Blue	1:32	Syn. Black	6 lbs.	42"	199.95
PR4459N	.45	24" Nickel	1:22	Syn. Black	6 lbs.	42"	224.95
PR4459	.45	24" Blue	1:22	Syn. Black	6 lbs.	42"	209.95

ECLIPSE

MODEL	CALIBER	BARREL	RIFLING	STOCK	WEIGHT	LENGTH	RETAIL PRICE
PR4429	.50	24" Blue	1:32	Black	6 lbs.	42"	$159.95
PR4478	.50	24" Blue	1:32	Mossy-Oak Breakup	6 lbs.	42"	189.95

STAG HORN

MODEL	CALIBER	BARREL	RIFLING	STOCK	WEIGHT	LENGTH	RETAIL PRICE
PR4505	.50	24" Blue	1:32	Syn. Black	7 lbs.	42"	$129.95

CVA RIFLES

Caplock Rifles

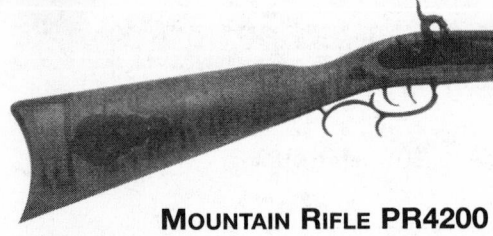

MOUNTAIN RIFLE PR4200

The **CVA MOUNTAIN RIFLE** helped launch the rebirth of black-powder hunting and shooting in the early 1970's. This gun authentically replicates the no-nonsense rifles of the mountain men who first explored the American West. Featuring all browned steel hardware, fine figured American hard maple stock, buckhorn rear sight and German silver wedge plates and blade front sight, this rifle offers custom quality and true traditional appeal. Designed to shoot patched round balls, the 32" browned steel barrel has 1 in 66" rifling and is extremely accurate. Made in the USA and limited to a production run of only 500 guns, the CVA Mountain Rifle is intended for the collector as well as the hunter.

ST. LOUIS HAWKEN PR454, PR463, PR464

The **ST. LOUIS HAWKEN** features CVA's patented breech plug/bolster system for reliable caplock ignition. Double set triggers allow for sensitive preset trigger pull for greater accuracy. This rifle is accented with brass buttplate, patchbox, trigger guard, wedge plates, nose cap, and thimbles. Left hand model available.

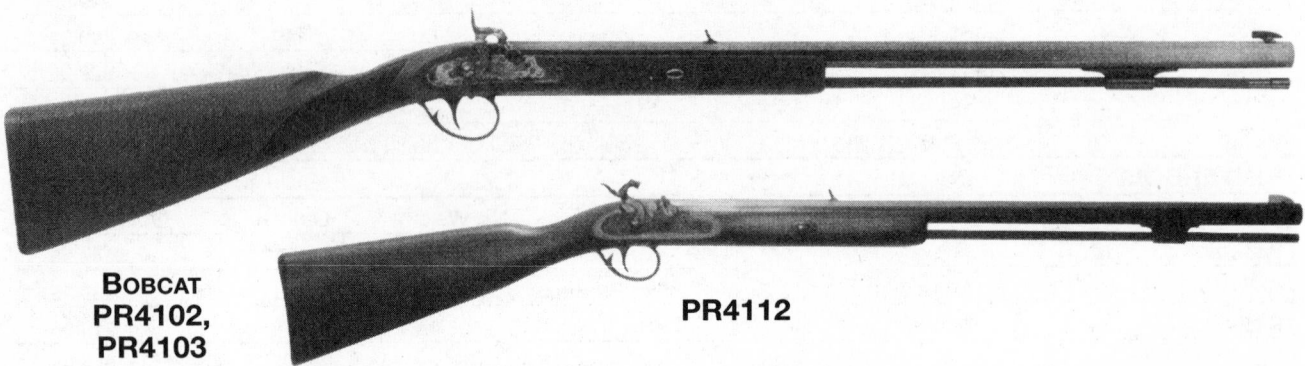

BOBCAT PR4102, PR4103

PR4112

The **BOBCAT RIFLE** is a basic muzzleloader that delivers value without compromising performance, now with a choice of hardwood or synthetic stock. The blued octagonal barrel is the same barrel used on CVA's top of the line hunting rifles. Accuracy with sabots, conical bullets, and round balls is assured by CVA's deep groove rifling. The rifle has fixed sights and a wooden ramrod.

SPECIFICATIONS

MODEL	CALIBER	SIGHTS	BARREL	RIFLING	STOCK	WEIGHT	LENGTH	RETAIL PRICE
PR4200	.50	Fixed	32" Browned	1:66	Am. Maple	8.5 lbs.	48"	$399.95
PR454	.50 L.H.	Adj.	28" Blue	1:48	Wood	8 lbs.	44"	264.95
PR463	.50	Adj.	28" Blue	1:48	Wood	8 lbs.	44"	207.95
PR464	.54	Adj.	28" Blue	1:48	Wood	8 lbs.	44"	207.95
PR4102	.50	Fixed	26" Blue	1:48	Syn. Black	6 lbs.	42"	104.95
PR4103	.54	Fixed	26" Blue	1:48	Syn. Black	6 lbs.	42"	104.95
PR4112	.50	Fixed	26" Blue	1:48	Wood	6 lbs.	42"	127.95

QUEEN ANNE PISTOL

QUEEN ANNE PISTOL

Named for the Queen of England (1702-1714), this flintlock pistol has a 7 1/2" barrel that tapers from rear to front with a cannon-shaped muzzle. The brass trigger guard is fluted and the brass butt on the walnut stock features a grotesque mask worked into it. *Overall length:* 13". *Weight:* 2.25 lbs.
Price: $225.00
KIT 175.00

**CHARLES MOORE
ENGLISH DUELING PISTOL**

CHARLES MOORE ENGLISH DUELING PISTOL

This reproduction of an English percussion dueling pistol, created by Charles Moore of London, features a European walnut halfstock with oil finish and checkered grip. The 45-caliber octagonal barrel is 11" with 12 grooves and a twist of 1 in 15". Nose cap and thimble are silver; barrel is blued; lock and trigger guard are color casehardened.
Price: FLINT $385.00
PERCUSSION 323.95

**MANG IN GRAZ
TARGET PISTOL**

MANG TARGET PISTOL

Designed specifically for the precision target shooter, this 38-caliber pistol has a 10 7/16" octagonal barrel with 7 lands and grooves. Twist is 1 in 15". Sights: Blade front dovetailed into barrel; rear mounted on breechplug tang, adjustable for windage. *Overall length:* 17 1/4". *Weight:* 2 .5 lbs.
Price: $786.00

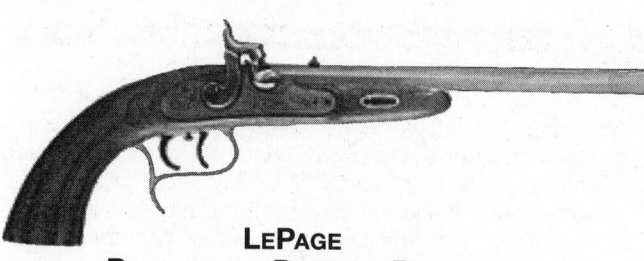

**LEPAGE
PERCUSSION DUELING PISTOL**

LePAGE PERCUSSION DUELING PISTOL

This 45-caliber percussion pistol features a blued 10" octagonal barrel with 12 lands and grooves; a brass-bladed front sight with open rear sight dovetailed into the barrel; polished silver-plated trigger guard and butt cap. Right side of barrel is stamped "LePage á Paris." Double-set riggers are single screw adjustable. *Overall length:* 16". *Weight:* 2.5 lbs.
Price: $275.00

SCREW BARREL PISTOL

SCREW BARREL (FOLDING TRIGGER) PISTOL

This little gun, only 6 1/2" overall, has a unique loading system that eliminates the need for a ramrod. The barrel is loosened with a barrel key, then unscrewed from the frame by hand. A .445 round ball is seated atop 10 grains FFFg and the barrel is then screwed back into place. The .245X32 nipple uses #11 percussion caps. The pistol also features a sheath trigger that folds into the frame, then drops down for firing when the hammer is cocked. Color case hardened frame, trigger and center-mounted hammer.
Price: $126.95
KIT 95.00

 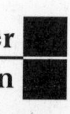

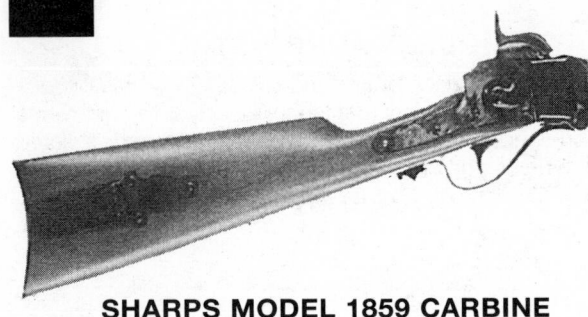

SHARPS MODEL 1859 CARBINE

About 115,000 Sharps New Model 1859 carbines and its variants were made during the Civil War. Characterized by durability and accuracy, they became a favorite of cavalry-men on both sides. Made in Italy by David Pedersoli & Co.

SPECIFICATIONS
Caliber: 54 *Barrel length:* 22" (1 in 48" twist); blued, round barrel has 7-groove rifling
Overall length: 37 1/2" *Weight:* 7 3/4 lbs.
Sights: Blade front; adjustable rear
Stock: Oil-finished walnut *Features:* Barrel band, hammer, receiver, saddle bar and ring all color casehardened
Price: **$775.00**

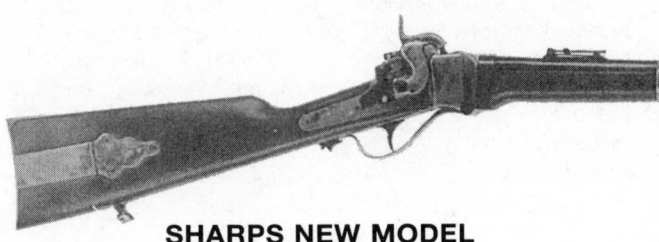

SHARPS NEW MODEL 1859 MILITARY RIFLE

Initially used by the First Connecticut Volunteers, this rifle is associated mostly with the 1st U.S. (Berdan's) Sharpshooters. There were 6,689 made with most going to the Sharpshooters (2,000) and the U.S. Navy (2,780). Made in Italy by David Pedersoli & Co.

SPECIFICATIONS
Caliber: 54 *Barrel length:* 30" (1 in 48" twist)
Overall length: 45 1/2" *Weight:* 9 lbs.
Sights: Blade front; rear sight adjustable for elevations and windage
Features: Buttstock and forend of straight-grained oil fin-ished walnut; three barrel bands, receiver, hammer, nose cap, lever, patchbox cover and butt are all color case hard-ened; sling swivels attached to middle band and butt
Price: **$895.00**

1874 SHARPS LIGHTWEIGHT HUNTER RIFLE

This Sharps rifle in 45-70 Government caliber has a 30" octagon barrel with blued matte finish (1:18" twist). It also features an adjustable ladder rear sight and blade front, making it ideal for blackpowder hunters. The tang is drilled and threaded for tang sights. The oil-finished military-style buttstock has a blued metal buttplate. Double-set triggers. Color case hardened receiver and hammer. *Overall length:* 49 1/2". *Weight:* 10 lbs.
Price: **$995.00**

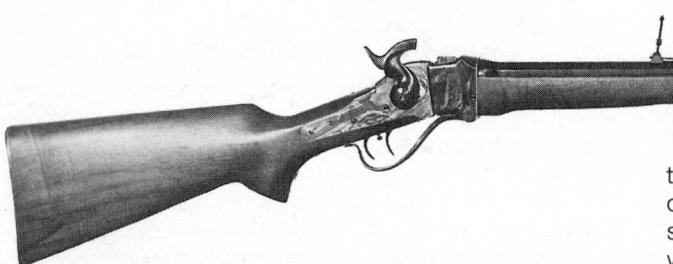

1874 SHARPS SILHOUETTE MODEL

This rifle in .40-65 and .45-70 caliber has a shotgun-style buttstock with pistol grip and metal buttplate. The 30-inch tapered octagon barrel is blued and has a 1 in 18" twist. The receiver, hammer, lever and buttplate are color case hardened. Ladder-type hunting rear and blade front sights are standard. Four screw holes are in the tang (two with 10 x 28 threads, two with metric threads) for attaching tang sights. Double set triggers are standard. *Weight* is 10 lbs. 3 oz. without target sights. *Overall length:* 47 1/2". Also available in 45-70
Price: **$995.00**

DIXIE TENNESSEE MOUNTAIN RIFLE

This 50-caliber rifle features double-set triggers with adjustable set screw, bore rifled with 6 lands and grooves, barrel of 15/16 inch across the flats, brown finish and cherry stock.
Overall length: 41 1/2 inches. Left-hand versions available.
Prices:
PERCUSSION OR FLINTLOCK $575.00
KIT 495.00

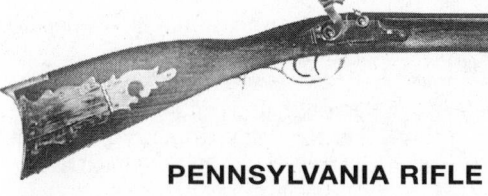

PENNSYLVANIA RIFLE

A lightweight at just 8 pounds, the 41 1/2" blued rifle barrel is fitted with an open buckhorn rear sight and front blade. The walnut one-piece stock is stained to contrast with the polished brass buttplate, toe plate, patch-box, sideplate, trigger guard, thimbles and nose cap. Featuring double-set triggers, the rifle can be fired by pulling only the front trigger, which has a normal trigger pull of 4 to 5 pounds; or the rear trigger can first be pulled to set a spring-loaded mechanism that greatly reduces the amount of pull needed for the front trigger to release the lock. Land diameter is .450; recommended ball size is .445.
Overall length: 51 1/2".
Prices: PERCUSSION OR FLINTLOCK $472.00
KIT (Flint or Perc.) 415.00

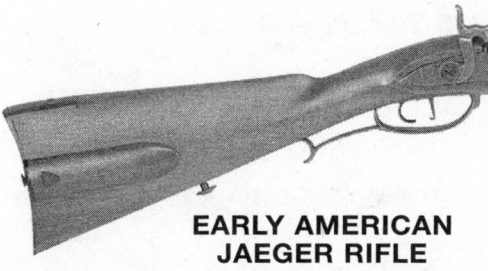

EARLY AMERICAN JAEGER RIFLE

This rifle is patterned after the original Jaeger which was popular in central Europe at the end of the 17th century. The .54 caliber has a browned octagon barrel, full stock with sliding wooden patchbox on the butt. Sights are fixed blade front and notch rear.
Overall length: 43 1/2" *Weight:* 8.25 lbs.
Prices:
FLINT $695.00
PERCUSSION 695.00

HAWKEN RIFLE (Not Shown)

The favorite of American frontiersman in the mid-1800s. This replica has a blued barrel 15/16" across the flats and 30" in length with a twist of 1 in 64". Stock is of walnut with a steel crescent buttplate, halfstock with brass nosecap. Double-set triggers, front-action lock and adjustable rear sight. Ramrod is equipped with jag. *Overall length:* 46 1/2". *Weight:* about 8 lbs., depending on the caliber; shipping weight is 10 lbs. Available in either finished gun or kit. *Calibers:* 45, 50 and 54.
Price: $250.00
KIT 205.00

WAADTLANDER RIFLE (Not Shown)

This authentic re-creation of a Swiss muzzloading target rifle features a heavy octagonal barrel (31") that has 7 lands and grooves. *Caliber:* 45. Rate of twist is 1 turn in 48". Double-set triggers are multi-lever type and are easily removable for adjustment. Sights are fitted post front and tang-mounted Swiss-type diopter rear. Walnut stock, color case hardened hardware, classic buttplate and curved trigger guard complete this reproduction. The original was made between 1839 and 1860 by Marc Bristlen, Morges, Switzerland.
Price: $1,412.00

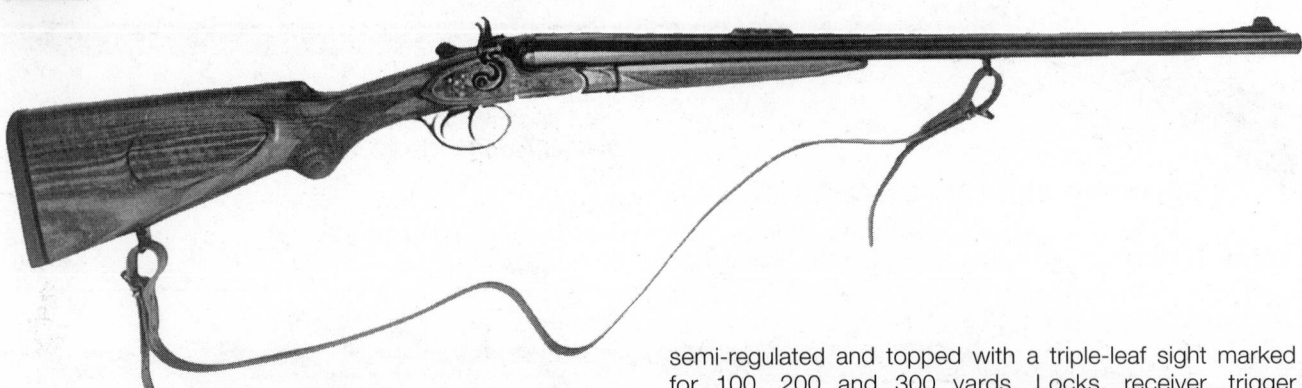

KODIAK MARK IV .45-70 DOUBLE BARREL RIFLE

Patterned after a classic, limited edition 19th century Colt double rifle, the Kodiak Mark IV has been designed for hunters and collectors. The 24-inch browned barrels are semi-regulated and topped with a triple-leaf sight marked for 100, 200 and 300 yards. Locks, receiver, trigger guard and hammers are case-hardened. The two-piece stock is European walnut; forearm and pistol grip are checkered. The buttstock has a cheekpiece and a solid, red rubber pad. Sling swivels are standard. *Weight:* 10 lbs. *Overall length:* 40"
Price:. **$2,295.00**

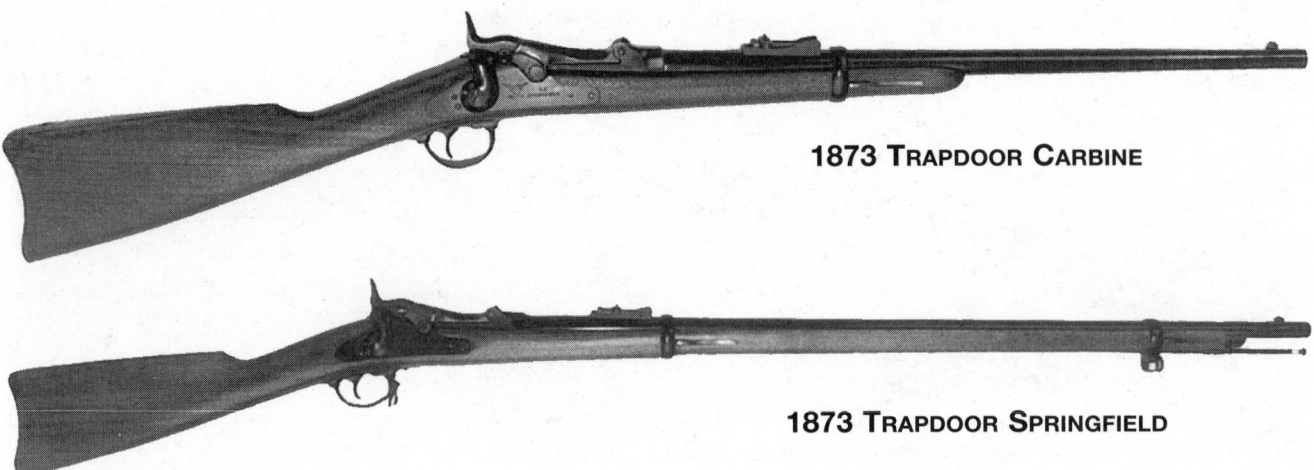

1873 TRAPDOOR CARBINE

1873 TRAPDOOR SPRINGFIELD

1873 SPRINGFIELD RIFLE AND CARBINE

Developed from the Allin Conversion of Springfield muskets from the Civil War, 1873 Springfield "Trapdoors" finished the "winning of the West." Adopted in 1873 and immediately issued to troops on the frontier, the Trapdoor was the last single-shot, blackpowder rifle of the U.S. military, later supplanted by the .30-.40 Krag-Jorgensen bolt rifle.

RIFLE
Caliber: 45-70
Barrel length: 32.5" round. 1-22 twist; 3 groove rifling; all furniture blued; sling swivels; open sights; ladder style elevation rear adjustable to 500 yards
Overall length: 52" *Weight:* 8.5 lbs. Walnut stock
Price:. $895.00

CARBINE
Caliber: 45-70. *Barrel length:* 22" round. 1-22 twist; 3 groove rifling; all furniture blued; saddle bar and ring; open sights; ladder-style elevation rear adjustable to 400 yards. *Overall length:* 41" *Weight:* 8.5 lbs. Walnut stock.
Price:. **$895.00**

OFFICER'S MODEL
Caliber: 45-70. *Barrel length:* 26" round. 1-18 twist; 6 groove rifling; pewter ramrod tip and nosecap; case-hardened hammer and lock; walnut stock; checkered wrist and forearm; single set trigger; fully adjustable tang sight. *Overall length:* 45" *Weight:* 8 lbs.
Price:. **$995.00**

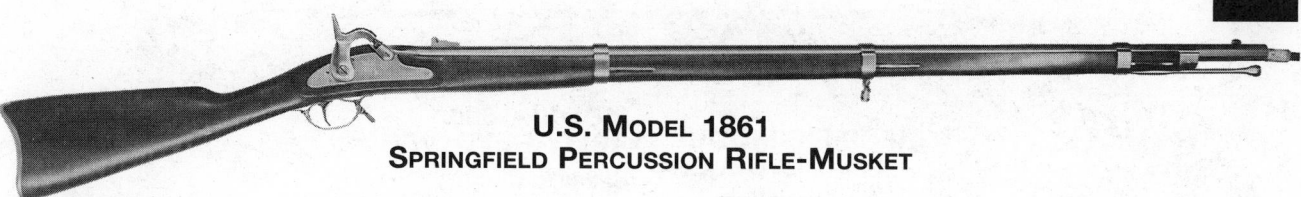

U.S. MODEL 1861
SPRINGFIELD PERCUSSION RIFLE-MUSKET

An exact re-creation of an original rifle produced by Springfield National Armory, Dixie's Model 1861 Springfield 58-caliber rifle features a 40" round, tapered barrel with three barrel bands. Sling swivels are attached to the trigger guard bow and middle barrel band. The ramrod has a trumpet-shaped head with swell; sights are standard military rear and bayonet-attachment lug front. The percussion lock is marked "1861" on the rear of the lockplate with an eagle motif and "U.S. Springfield" in front of the hammer. "U.S." is stamped on top of buttplate. All furniture is "National Armory Bright."
Overall length: 55 13/16". ***Weight:*** 8 lbs.
Prices: **$595.00**
KIT 525.00

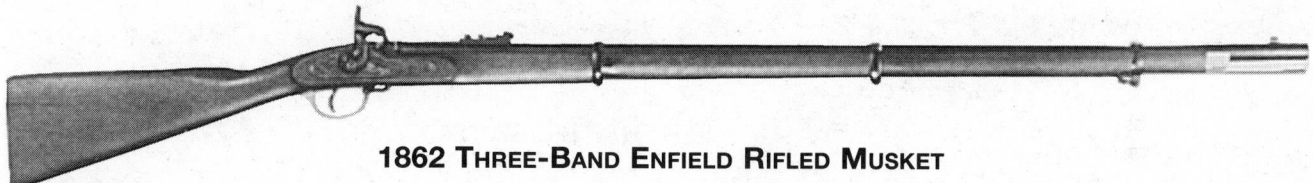

1862 THREE-BAND ENFIELD RIFLED MUSKET

The 1861 Enfield was widely used during the Civil War in its original version. This rifle follows the lines of the original almost exactly. The 58-caliber musket features a 39-inch barrel and walnut stock. Three steel barrel bands and the barrel itself are blued; the lockplate and hammer are case colored, and the remainder of the furniture is highly polished brass. The lock is marked, "London Armory Co." ***Weight:*** 10.5 lbs. ***Overall length:*** 55".
Prices: **$495.00**
KIT 425.00

U.S. MODEL 1816 FLINTLOCK MUSKET

The U.S. Model 1816 Flintlock Musket was made by Harpers Ferry and Springfield Arsenal from 1816 until 1864. It had the highest production of any U.S. flintlock musket and after conversion to percussion saw service in the Civil War. It has a 69-caliber, 42" smoothbore barrel held by three barrel bands with springs. All metal parts are finished in "National Armory Bright." The lockplate has a brass pan and is marked "Harpers Ferry" vertically behind the hammer, with an American eagle placed in front of the hammer. The bayonet lug is on top of the barrel and the steel ramrod has a button-shaped head. Sling swivels are mounted on trigger guard and middle barrel band.
Overall length: 56.5"
Weight: 9.75 lbs.
Price: **$699.95**

1858 TWO-BAND ENFIELD RIFLE

This 33-inch barrel version of the British Enfield is an exact copy of similar rifles used during the Civil War. The 58-caliber rifle sports a European walnut stock, deep blue-black finish on the barrel, bands, breech-plug tang and bayonet mount. The percussion lock is casehardened, and the rest of the furniture is brightly polished brass.
Price: **$475.00**

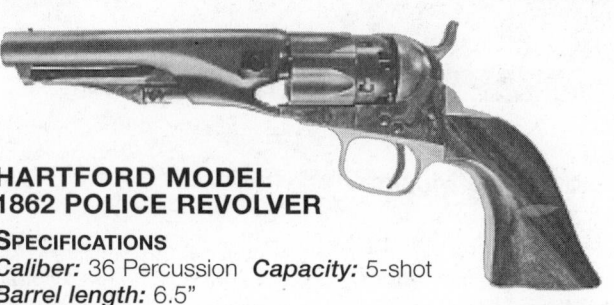

SHERIFF'S MODEL 1851 REVOLVER

SPECIFICATIONS

Caliber: 44 Percussion *Ball diameter:* .376 round or conical, pure lead *Barrel length:* 5" *Overall length:* 10.5" *Weight:* 39 oz. *Sights:* V-notch groove in hammer (rear); truncated cone in front *Percussion cap size:* #11

Prices:Brass $150.00
Steel 200.00

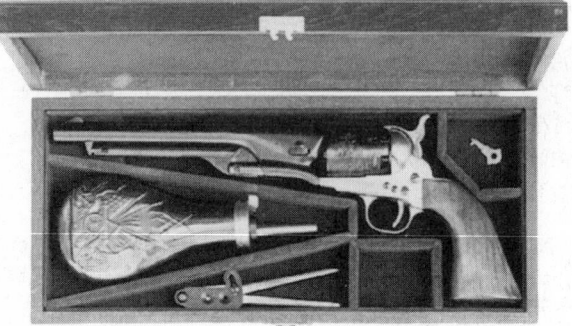

HARTFORD MODEL 1862 POLICE REVOLVER

SPECIFICATIONS

Caliber: 36 Percussion *Capacity:* 5-shot *Barrel length:* 6.5"
Prices: Steel $250.00
Brass 170.00

1860 ARMY BRASS FRAME CASED SET
Price: $315.00

MODEL 1860 ARMY REVOLVER

SPECIFICATIONS

Caliber: 44 Percussion *Barrel length:* 8"
Overall length: 13 5/8" *Weight:* 41 oz. *Frame:* Case hardened *Finish:* High-luster blue with walnut grips
Price: Brass Frame $165.00
Also available: CASED SET with steel frame, wood case, flask and mould $380.00
Engraved cased set 480.00

HARTFORD 1863 TEXAS DRAGOON

SPECIFICATIONS

Caliber: 44 *Barrel length:* 7" (round) *Overall length:* 14" *Weight:* 4 lbs. *Finish:* Steel case-hardened frame
Price: $330.00

1851 NAVY
(36 or 44 Cal.) – $305.00
Brass frame .44 - **150.00**

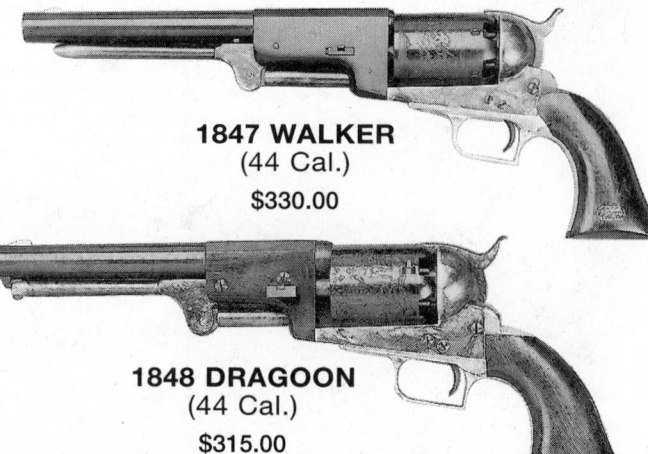

1847 WALKER
(44 Cal.)
$330.00

1849 BABY DRAGOON
(31 Cal., Brass Frame)
$150.00

1848 DRAGOON
(44 Cal.)
$315.00

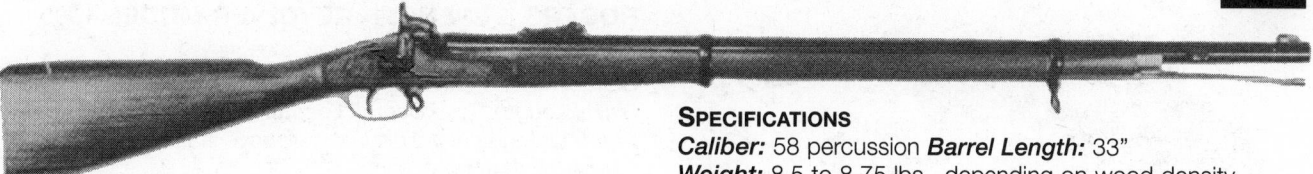

LONDON ARMORY COMPANY ENFIELD P-1858 2-BAND RIFLE MUSKET MODEL 2270

SPECIFICATIONS
Caliber: 58 percussion *Barrel Length:* 33"
Weight: 8.5 to 8.75 lbs., depending on wood density
Stock: One-piece walnut; polished "bright" brass buttplate, trigger guard and nose cap; blued barrel and bands
Sights: Inverted 'V' front sight; Enfield folding ladder rear
Ramrod: Steel
Price: $470.00

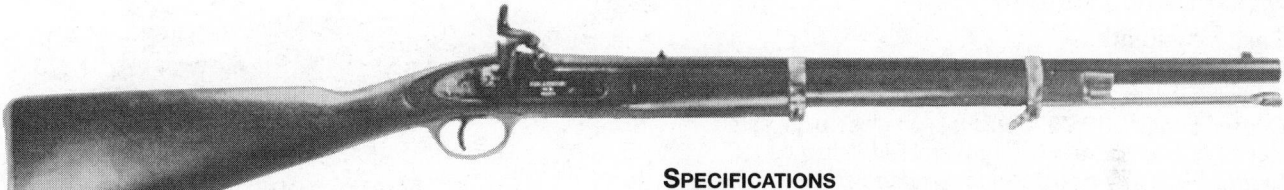

COOK & BROTHER CONFEDERATE CARBINE MODEL 2300

Classic re-creation of the rare 1861, New Orleans-made Artillery Carbine.

SPECIFICATIONS
Caliber: 58 percussion *Barrel Length:* 24"
Sights: Fixed blade front and adjustable dovetailed rear
Ramrod: Steel *Finish:* Barrel is antique brown; buttplate, trigger guard, barrel bands, sling swivels and nose cap are polished brass; stock is walnut *Recommended ball sizes:* .575 r.b., .577 Minie and .580 maxi; uses musket caps
Price: $447.00
Also available: MODEL 2301 COOK & BROTHER FIELD with 33" barrel 480.00

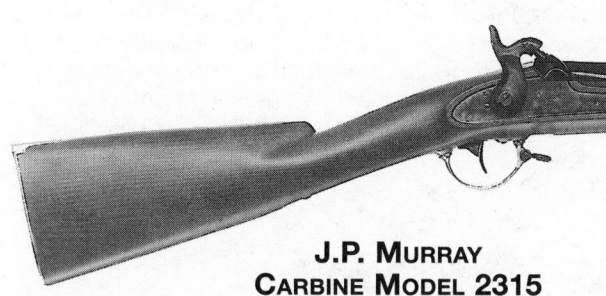

J.P. MURRAY CARBINE MODEL 2315

Replica of an extremely rare CSA Cavalry Carbine based on an 1841 design of parts and lock.

SPECIFICATIONS
Caliber: 58 percussion *Barrel Length:* 23"
Features: Brass barrel bands and buttplate; oversized trigger guard; sling swivels
Price: $453.00

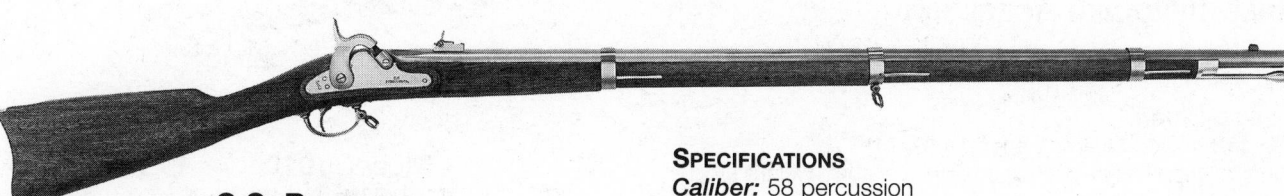

C.S. RICHMOND MUSKET MODEL 2370

SPECIFICATIONS
Caliber: 58 percussion
Barrel Length: 40"
Price: $530.00

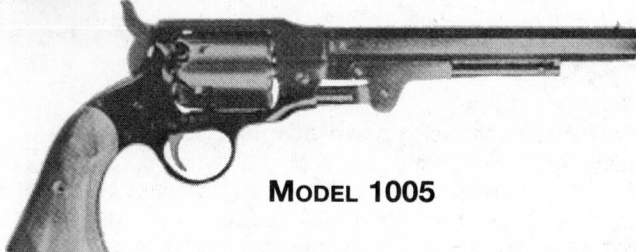

MODEL 1005

ROGERS & SPENCER REVOLVER MODEL 1005

SPECIFICATIONS
Caliber: 44 Percussion; #11 percussion cap
Barrel Length: 7.5" *Overall Length:* 13.75" *Weight:* 47 oz.
Sights: Integral rear sight notch groove in frame; brass truncated cone front sight
Finish: High gloss blue; flared walnut grip; solid frame design; precision-rifled barrel *Recommended ball diameter:* .451 round or conical, pure lead
Price: $227.00

ROGERS & SPENCER ARMY REVOLVER MODEL 1006 (Target)

SPECIFICATIONS
Caliber: 44; takes .451 round or conical balls; #11 percussion cap *Weight:* 47 oz. *Barrel Length:* 7.5"
Overall Length: 13.75" *Finish:* High gloss blue; flared walnut grip; solid frame design; precision-rifled barrel
Sights: Rear fully adjustable for windage and elevation; ramp front sight
Price: $239.00

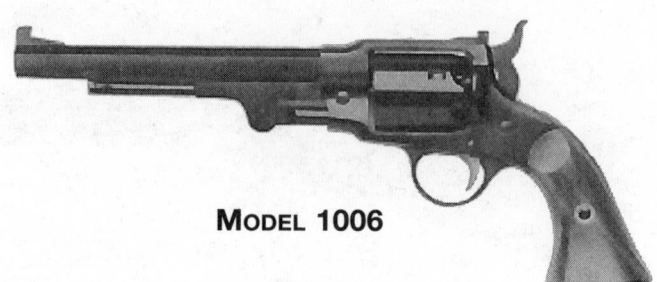

MODEL 1006

ROGERS & SPENCER REVOLVER LONDON GRAY MODEL 1007 (Not Shown)

Revolver is the same as Model 1005, except for London Gray finish, which is heat treated and buffed for rust resistance; .451 balls, #11 percussion caps

Price: $245.00
Also available: MODEL 1120 COLT 1851 NAVY Steel or brass frame. 36 cal. *Barrel Length:* 7.5" octagonal.
Overall Length: 13" *Weight:* 42 oz.
Price: 156.00
MODEL 1210 COLT 1860 ARMY Steel frame. 44 percussion
Overall Length: 10 5/8" or 13 5/8" *Weight:* 41 oz.
Price: 177.00

REMINGTON 1858 NEW MODEL ARMY ENGRAVED MODEL 1040 (Not Shown)

Classical 19th-century style scroll engraving on this 1858 Remington New Model revolver.

SPECIFICATIONS
Caliber: 44 Percussion; #11 cap *Barrel Length:* 8"
Overall Length: 14.75" *Weight:* 41 oz. *Sights:* Integral rear sight notch groove in frame; blade front sight
Recommended ball diameter: .451 round or conical, pure lead
Price: $275.00

REMINGTON 1858 NEW MODEL ARMY REVOLVER MODEL 1020

This model features blued steel frame, brass trigger guard and 8" 44-caliber barrel

SPECIFICATIONS
Weight: 40 oz. *Overall Length:* 14.75"
Finish: Deep luster blue rifled barrel; polished walnut stock; brass trigger guard.
Price: $200.00
Also available: MODEL 1010 Same as Model 1020, except w/6.5" barrel and in 36 caliber: $200.00

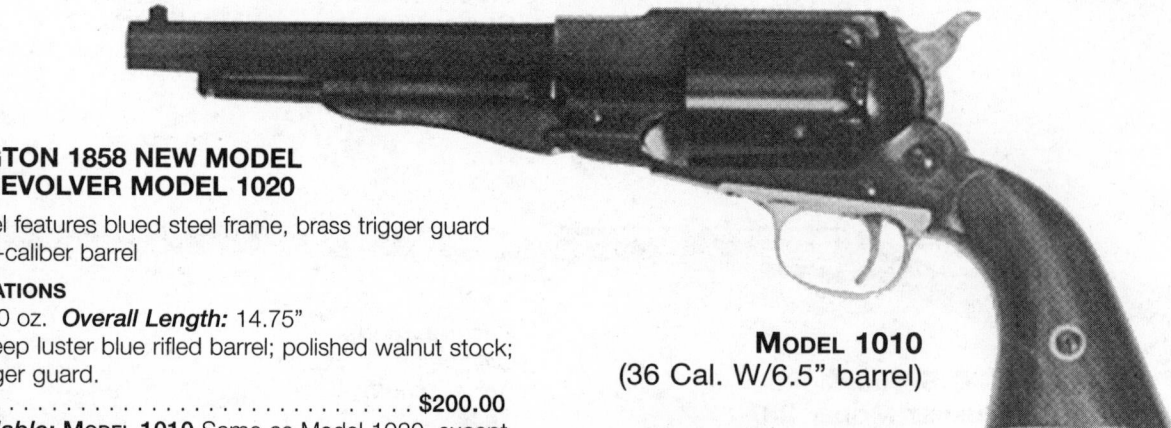

MODEL 1010
(36 Cal. W/6.5" barrel)

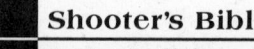

Model 93 Rifle Series

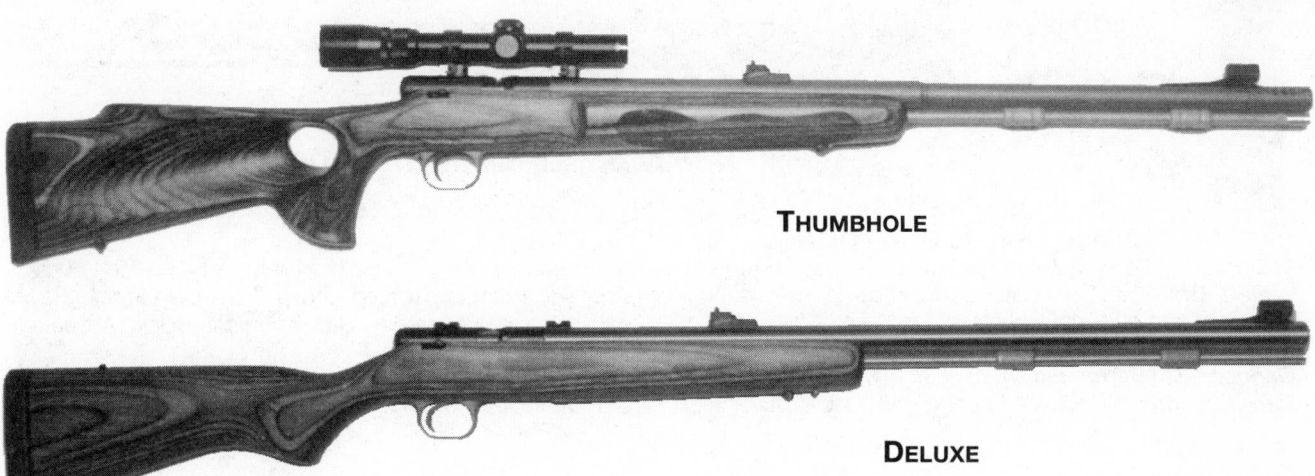

THUMBHOLE

DELUXE

MODEL 93 RIFLE

SPECIFICATIONS
Caliber: 45 or 50 Magnum
Barrel Length: 26" 4140 chrome-moly blued satin or 416 stainless steel w/matte finish; 1-in-24" twist
Length Of Pull: 14"
Trigger: Single, adjustable w/side safety
Weight: 6.5 to 7 lbs.
Sights: Open or peep sights, fully adjustable for windage and elevation; ramp front w/gold bead and protector hood

Stock: Walnut or laminated (left or right hand)
Features: Unbreakable ram rod; classic cheekpiece; three-point pillar bedding system; 1" decelerator recoil pad; sling swivel studs; E-Z-Load Muzzle System w/muzzle break
Price:. **$2,132.00**
Also Available:
MODEL 93 THUMBHOLE RIFLE w/same specification and features as above, but w/thumbhole Monte Carlo rollover cheekpiece, beavertail forend and palm swell grip
Price:. **$2,625.00**
  Stainless (50 mag. only) 2,625.00

STANDARD

Gonic Arm's blackpowder rifle has a unique loading system that produces better consistency and utilizes the full powder charge of the specially designed penetrator bullet (2,650 foot-pounds at 1,600 fps w/465-grain .500 bullet).

SPECIFICATIONS
Caliber: 45 or 50 Magnum
Barrel Lengths: 26"
Overall Length: 43"
Weight: 6 to 6.5 lbs.
Sights: Open hunting sights (adjustable)

Features: Walnut-stained hardwood stock; adjustable trigger; nipple wrench; drilled and tapped for scope bases; ballistics and instruction manual

Prices: Open Sights. **$720.00**
Stainless w/Open Sights (50 mag. only) 782.00
Also Available:
MODEL 93 DELUXE w/grey laminated stock or walnut
  Weaver scope base; open sights; E-Z-Load
  Muzzle System. 902.00
  Stainless w/open sights (50 mag. only) 964.00

TK2000 MUZZLELOADING SHOTGUN, NOW AVAILABLE IN ADVANTAGE TIMBER HD

KNIGHT TK2000 SHOTGUN

The Knight TK2000 achieves 85% shot density at 40 yards in a 30" circle with developed loads. In-line percussion ignition is favored by serious hunters.

SPECIFICATIONS

Gauge: 12 *Barrel Finish:* Blued, Advantage Timer HD *Barrel Length:* 26" *Overall Length:* 45" *Weight:* 7 lbs., 9 oz. *Sight:* Fully adjustable metallic Tru-Glo Fiber Optics *Trigger:* Adjustable (Creep and pull weight) *Stock:* Recoil pad, sling swivel studs *Stock Finish:* Black, Advantage Timber HD

Prices: Blue/Black Composite $349.95
Camo Stock/Barrel 399.95

BIGHORN, STAINLESS, MOSSY OAK BREAK-UP

KNIGHT BIGHORN RIFLE

The Knight Bighorn Rifle is a classic magnum. With its standard three ignition choices, 150-grain capability, and dependable ignition system combined with Knight's Red Hot nipple and a musket cap, the Bighorn has game stopping power. The Bighorn has a full stock, complete with deluxe rubber recoil pad and sling swivel studs. It comes in a 22" or 26" Green Mountain Barrel, blued or stainless steel finish. And for the left-handed shooter, Knight is offering the Bighorn in a left-handed stock with the trigger safely positioned for easy thumb access.

As a bonus, every Bighorn includes a #209 conversion kit and two Red Hot nipples: musket (pre-installed) and a #11.

SPECIFICATIONS

Caliber: .50 *Barrel Finish:* Blued or stainless *Barrel Length:* 22"/26" *Overall Length:* 41"/45" *Weight:* 7 lbs., 7 lbs., 5 oz. *Sight:* Fully adjustable metallic Tru-Glo Fiber Optics *Trigger:* Adjustable (Creep and pull weight) *Stock:* Checkered, recoil pad, sling swivel studs; thumbhole available (14.25" length of pull) *Stock Finish:* Advantage Timber HD, Mossy Oak Break-Up, Black

Prices:

BIGHORN

Blue/Black Composite $349.95
   Left hand 349.95
Blue/camo. 399.95
Stainless/camo 459.95

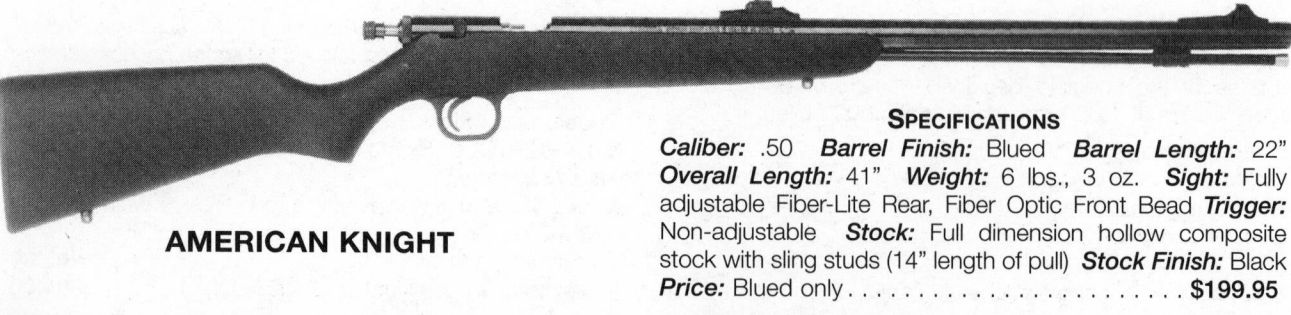

AMERICAN KNIGHT

SPECIFICATIONS

Caliber: .50 *Barrel Finish:* Blued *Barrel Length:* 22" *Overall Length:* 41" *Weight:* 6 lbs., 3 oz. *Sight:* Fully adjustable Fiber-Lite Rear, Fiber Optic Front Bead *Trigger:* Non-adjustable *Stock:* Full dimension hollow composite stock with sling studs (14" length of pull) *Stock Finish:* Black

Price: Blued only $199.95

KNIGHT MUZZLELOADERS

THUMBHOLE WOLVERINE w/MOSSY OAK CAMO

MODEL LK-93 WOLVERINE II

SPECIFICATIONS

Calibers: 50 and 54 *Barrel length:* 22"; blued or stainless (1:28" twist) *Overall length:* 41" *Weight:* 6.5 lbs. *Sights:* adjustable TRUGLO fiber-optic *Stock:* Checkered lightweight synthetic molded stock with choice of black or camo finishes *Features:* Patented double-safety system; adjustable trigger; removable breechplug; stainless-steel hammer. Also available in youth version.

Prices:

Blued	$269.95
Stainless	329.95
Blued Advantage or Break-Up	319.95
Stainless Advantage or Break-up	379.95

Also Available: THUMBHOLE WOLVERINE

Blued w/Black Stock	$309.95
Blued w/Camo Stock.	359.95
Stainless Steel w/Black Stock.	369.95
Stainless Steel w/Camo Stock	419.95

.45 SUPER DISC, STAINLESS, MOSSYOAK BREAK-UP

KNIGHT .45 SUPER DISC

The .45 caliber Super Disc is Knight's latest in-line muzzleloader. It features a precisely-rifled Green Mountain Barrel air-gauged to exact tolerances with a 1:20" twist. The Knight .45 Super DISC outperforms other muzzloaders as it: 1. Launches bullets up to 2,600 feet per second. 2. Connects at 100 yards with a whopping 1,353 foot pounds of energy. 3. At 200 yards, the bullet drops only 7.29 inches! As on all Knight Rifles, the .45 Super DISC includes a patented double-safety system.

SPECIFICATIONS

Caliber: .45 *Barrel Finish:* Blued or stainless *Barrel Length:* 26" *Overall Length:* 45" *Weight:* 8 lbs., 3 oz. *Sight:* Fully adjustable metallic Tru-Glo Fiber Optics *Trigger:* Adjustable (Creep and pull weight) *Stock:* Checkered, recoil pad, sling swivel studs; thumbhole available (14.5" length of pull) *Stock Finish:* Advantage Timber HD, Mossy Oak break-up, black

Price: $549.95

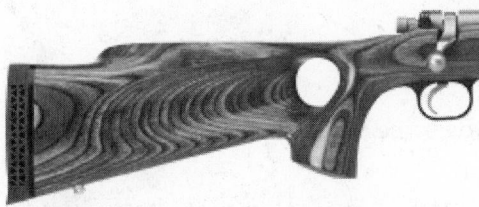

.50 CALIBER MASTER HUNTER II DISC, STAINLESS, LAMINATED

MASTER HUNTER II DISC MUZZLELOADER

The Master Hunter II DISC is built with only the highest grade stainless steel Green Mountain 26" barrel and comes in a brushed satin finish. The fluting is precise and elegant, and is engineered to reduce overall weight. Accuracy is key, so the rifling in the barrel is air-gauged to exact tolerances with a 1:28" rifling ratio, providing the optimum projectile spin for highest accuracy. Two stocks are included with this premium model. A two-tone laminated stock with a comfortable thumbhole grip is complemented by a second stock made from a black, solid composite in the same thumbhole grip design.

SPECIFICATIONS

Caliber: .50 *Barrel Finish:* Fluted stainless *Barrel Length:* 26" *Overall Length:* 45" *Weight:* 7 lbs., 7 oz. *Sight:* Fully adjustable metallic Tru-Glo Fiber Optics *Trigger:* Adjustable for creep and letoff *Stock Finish:* Laminated thumbhole w/recoil pad, sling swivel studs (14.5" length of pull); black composite shipped with rifle

Price: $1,099.95

Also Available:
KNIGHT .50 DISC

Price: Blue/Black composite	459.95
Blue/camo.	509.95
Stainless/Black composite	529.95
Stainless/camo	579.95

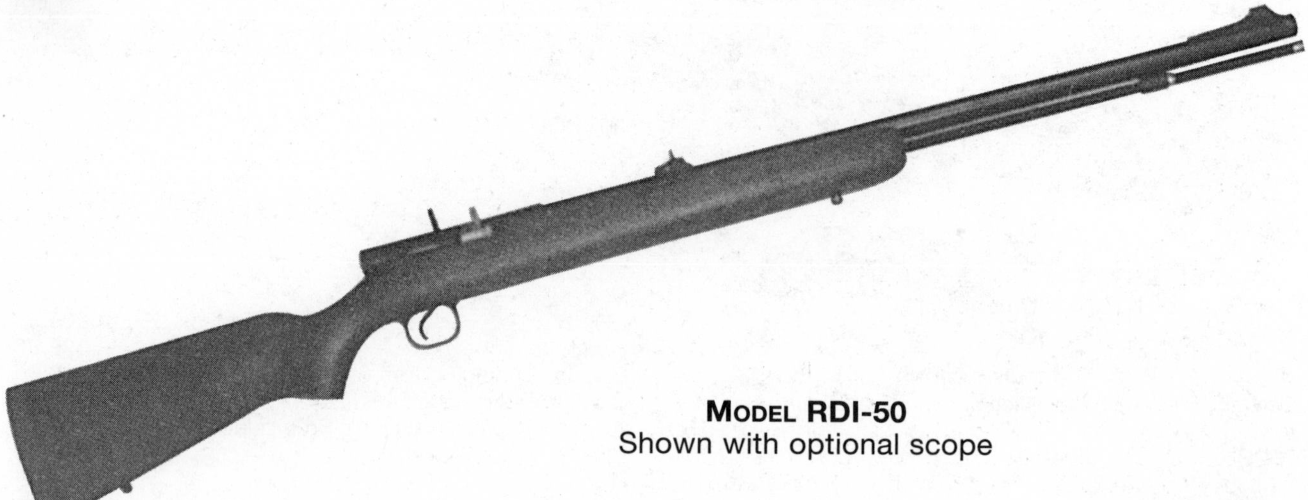

MODEL RDI-50
Shown with optional scope

RDI-50

The Rdi-50 is a new 50-caliber muzzleloader by Lenartz Muzzleloading Inc. The Rdi-50 features a Radial Drop Ignition System (Rdi), which allows the shooter to drop a 209 shot shell primer into the Rdi Nipple cradle, close the cover and shoot. To remove the 209 shot shell primers, open the Rdi cover and the printer drops into your hand. Uses a 209 Shot Shell Primer and 3-50 grain Pyrodex Pellets with Black Beauty Sabots and a 300 gr. Jacketed Bullet at over 1900 ft/sec.

SPECIFICATIONS
Manufacturer: Lenartz Muzzleloading Inc., 8001 Whitneyville Rd, Alto, MI 49302

Mechanism type: Inline Muzzleloader using 209 Shot Shell Primers
Caliber: .50
Stock: Walnut (with or without Comb.)
Barrel: 26.5 inches with a 1-turn-in-28 inch rifling.
Trigger: Adjustable made by Bold.
Sights: Williams gun sights, with receiver drilled and tapped for scope mounts.

LMI CONVERSION KIT

The Percussion Cap Bolt converts the Rdi-50 Muzzleloader to primitive ignition and #11 Percussion Cap. Simply place percussion cap on Slave Nipple then drop in Radial Cover and secure by rolling the cover down.

LYMAN TRADE RIFLE

The **LYMAN TRADE RIFLE** features a 28-inch octagonal barrel, rifled 1 turn at 48 inches, designed to fire both patched round balls and the popular conical bullets. Polished brass furniture with blued finish on steel parts; walnut stock; hook breech; single spring-loaded trigger; coil-spring percussion lock; fixed steel sights; adjustable rear sight for elevation also included. Steel barrel rib and ramrod ferrule.
Caliber: 50 and 54 percussion and flint.
Overall Length: 45"
Price:
Percussion $309.95
Flintlock 334.95

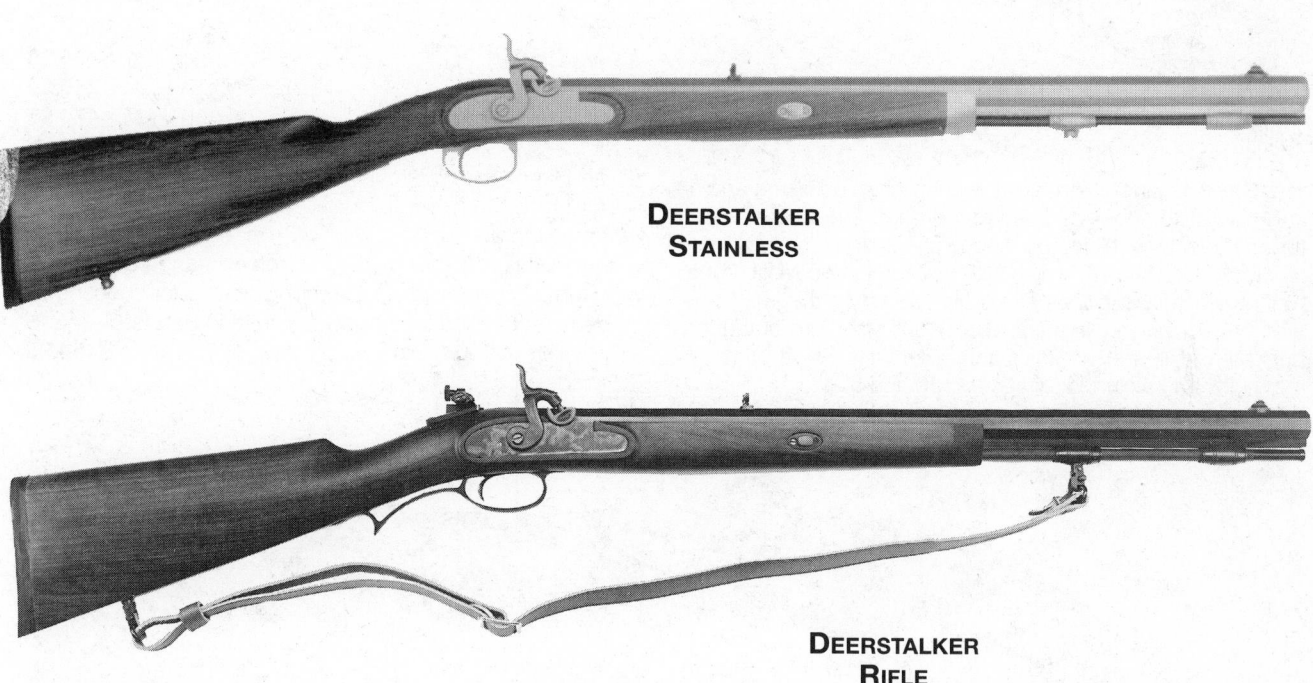

DEERSTALKER STAINLESS

DEERSTALKER RIFLE

LYMAN'S DEERSTALKER rifle incorporates • high comb for quick sighting • nonglare hardware • 24" octagonal barrel • case hardened sideplate • Q.D. sling swivels • Lyman sight package (37MA beaded front, fully adjustable fold-down 16A rear) • walnut stock with black recoil pad • single trigger. Left-hand models available (same price). **Calibers:** 50 and 54, flintlock or percussion. **Weight:** 7.5 lbs.

Price: Percussion $304.95
Left-Hand 324.95
Flintlock 344.95
Left Hand 359.95
DEERSTALKER STAINLESS. Features all stainless steel parts, plus walnut stock, recoil pad, Delrin ramrod, Lyman front and rear hunting sights.
Price: $394.95

GREAT PLAINS RIFLE

GREAT PLAINS HUNTER

The **GREAT PLAINS** has a 32-inch deep-grooved barrel and 1 in 66" twist to shoot patched round balls. Blued steel furniture including the thick steel wedge plates and toe plate; correct lock and hammer styling with coil spring dependability; a walnut stock w/o patchbox. A Hawken-style trigger guard protects double-set triggers. Steel front sight and authentic buckhorn styling in an adjustable rear sight. Fixed primitive rear sight also included. **Calibers:** 50 and 54.

Price:
Percussion $454.95
Kit 349.95
Flintlock 474.95
Kit 374.95
Left-Hand Model Percussion 459.95
Left-Hand Model Flintlock 489.95
Also available:
GREAT PLAINS HUNTER. Same features as standard rifle but with 1 in 32" twist and shallow rifling groove for shooting modern sabots and black powder hunting bullets.
Price: Percussion $454.95
Flintlock 474.95

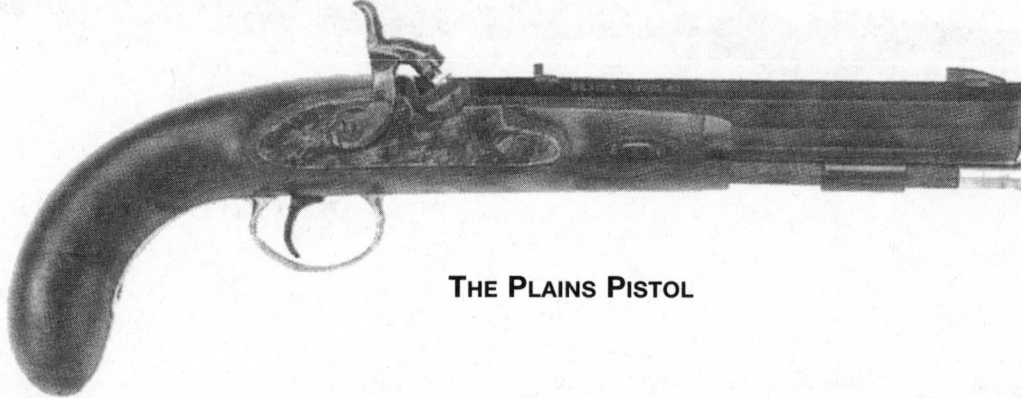

THE PLAINS PISTOL

LYMAN PLAINS PISTOL recreates the trapper's pistol of the mid-1800's while incorporating the best of modern steels and technology.
The stained walnut stock complements blackened iron furniture, polished brass trigger guard and ramrod tips. The hooked patent breech takes down quickly and easily for cleaning. Just like the originals, the thimble is recessed into the rib and a detachable belt hook provides an alternative to a holster. A spring-loaded trigger and fast 1 in 30" twist make it accurate.
Caliber: 50, 54
Price: $195.00

MARKESBERY MUZZLE LOADERS

Markesbery's Black Bear, Grizzly Bear and Brown Bear rifles are made of eight cast, polished molded parts, coupled with an all-cast receiver and trigger guard. Pillow mount system with interchangeable barrels in 36, 45, .50 and 54 calibers. All rifles are constructed with Markesbery's **MAGNUM HAMMER IN-LINE IGNITION SYSTEM**, the 400 SRP (small rifle primer) system or optional No. 11 cap and nipple. This system, along with a 1-26" twist button precision 24" rifle barrel, is available in either 4140 or stainless steel models. All models have a double safety system with half cock and cross bolt hammer safeties. Marble adjustable sights with double adjustment features, hammer thumb rest and rubber recoil pad are standard.

The Black Bear features a two-piece, handcrafted hardwood walnut, black laminate and green laminate pistol grip stock. **Weight:** 6.5 lbs. **Overall Length:** 38.5". The Brown and Grizzly Bear models offer custom-checkered Monte Carlo (Grizzly Bear two-piece or Brown Bear one-piece) thumbhole stocks. **Overall Length:** 38.5" **Weight:** 6.5 lbs. (Brown Bear is 6.75 lbs.). Both models are available in black composite, crotch walnut, Mossy Oak Break-up, XTRA-Grey and Real Tree Advantage camo stock patterns. **Metal finishes:** blued, matte and stainless steel. All models have a solid aluminum ram rod with brass jag and bullet starter.
Price: **BLACK BEAR** (two-piece pistol grip stock)
(depending on stock). **$536.63-573.73**

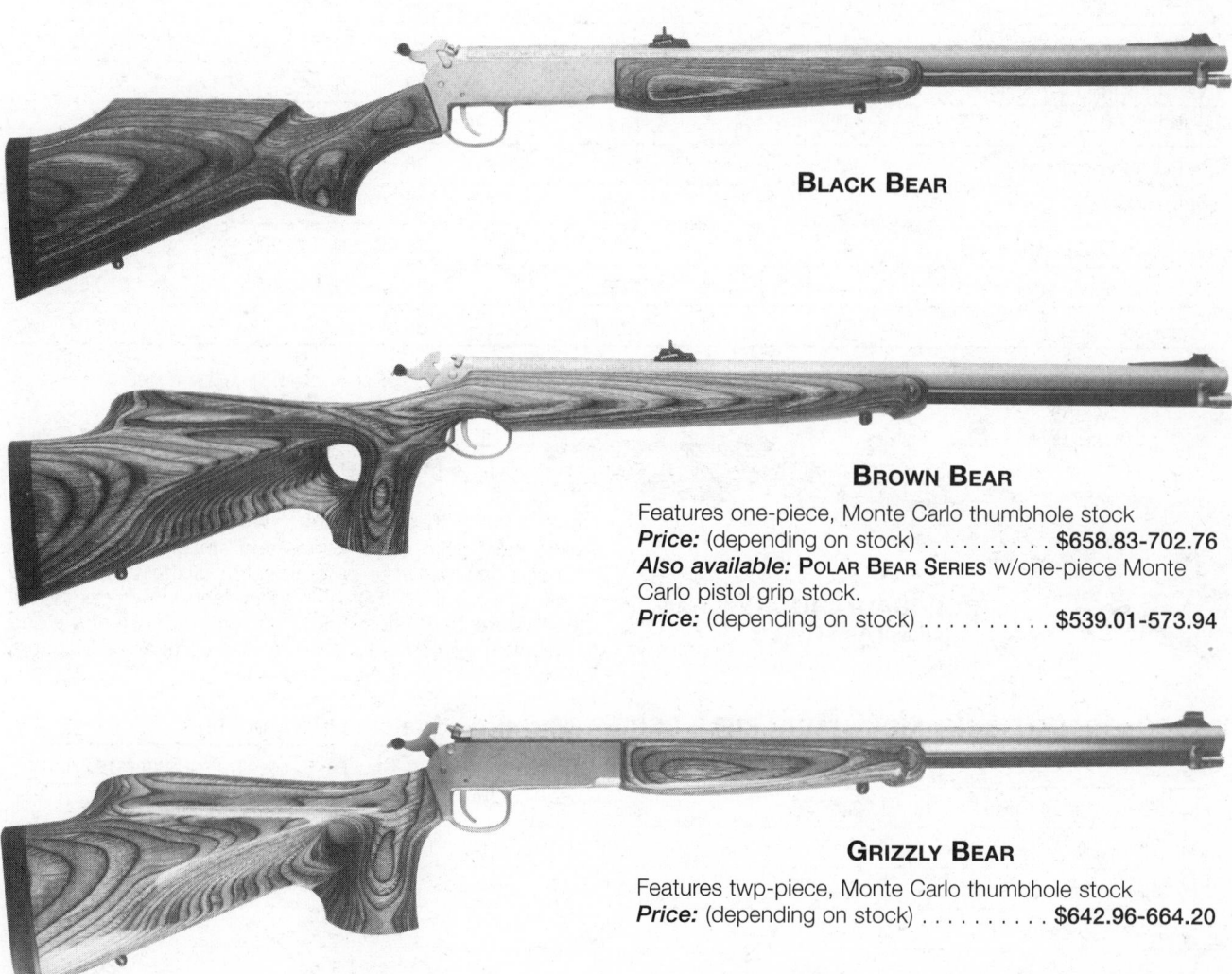

BLACK BEAR

BROWN BEAR
Features one-piece, Monte Carlo thumbhole stock
Price: (depending on stock) **$658.83-702.76**
Also available: POLAR BEAR SERIES w/one-piece Monte Carlo pistol grip stock.
Price: (depending on stock) **$539.01-573.94**

GRIZZLY BEAR
Features twp-piece, Monte Carlo thumbhole stock
Price: (depending on stock) **$642.96-664.20**

POLAR BEAR

The Polar Bear has Markesbery's standard features plus a one-piece pistol-grip stock of solid hardwood or laminated wood construction in black or green.

KM POLAR BEAR™ RIFLE SERIES (One piece Monte Carlo pistol grip stock)

MODEL	BARREL LENGTH	TWIST	CALIBER	SUGGESTED RETAIL
KMPB-B-Walnut Finish	24"	1-26"	36, 45, 50, 54	$539.01
KMPB-B-Black	24"	1-26"	36, 45, 50, 54	536.63
KMPB-B-Black Laminate	24"	1-26"	36, 45, 50, 54	541.17
KMPB-B-Green Laminate	24"	1-26"	36, 45, 50, 54	541.17
KMPB-B-Camo	24"	1-26"	36, 45, 50, 54	560.43
KMPB-SS-Walnut	24"	1-26"	36, 45, 50, 54	556.27
KMPB-SS-Black	24"	1-26"	36, 45, 50, 54	556.04
KMPB-SS-Black Laminate	24"	1-26"	36, 45, 50, 54	570.56
KMPB-SS-Green Laminate	24"	1-26"	36, 45, 50, 54	570.56
KMPB-SS-Camo	24"	1-26"	36, 45, 50, 54	573.94

COLORADO ROCKY MOUNTAIN RIFLE

New for 2001, this traditional-style muzzleloader features a walnut stock with barrel bands and straight grip. The pronounced hammer spur is reminiscent of the style used by frontiersmen in the 1800s. The same rear-hammer design of other Markesbery rifles has been retained. A No. 11 cap mechanism comes standard, but the company's Magnum Ignition System can be installed.

KM COLORADO ROCKY MOUNTAIN™ RIFLE SERIES (One piece Straight Grip stock)

MODEL	BARREL LENGTH	TWIST	CALIBER	SUGGESTED RETAIL
KM-CRM-B-Walnut Finish	24"	1-26"	36, 45, 50, 54	$545.92
KM-CRM-B-Black Laminate	24"	1-26"	36, 45, 50, 54	548.30
KM-CRM-B-Green Laminate	24"	1-26"	36, 45, 50, 54	548.30
KM-CRM-SS-Walnut Finish	24"	1-26"	36, 45, 50, 54	563.17
KM-CRM-SS-Black Laminate	24"	1-26"	36, 45, 50, 54	566.34
KM-CRM-SS-Green Laminate	24"	1-26"	36, 45, 50, 54	566.34

COLT 1847 WALKER

COLT 1847 WALKER

The 1847 Walker replica comes in 44 caliber with a 9-inch barrel. Weight: 4 lbs. 8 oz. Features include: rolled cylinder scene blued and case hardened finish and brass guard. Proof tested.

COLT 1847 WALKER $275.00

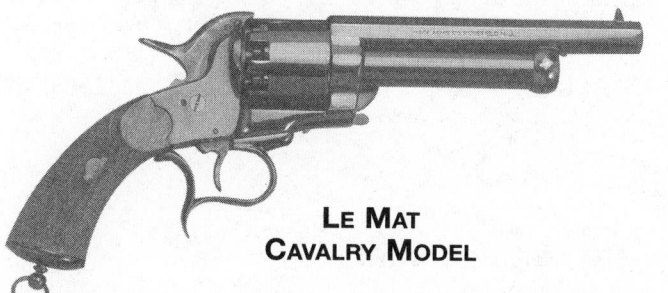

LE MAT CAVALRY MODEL

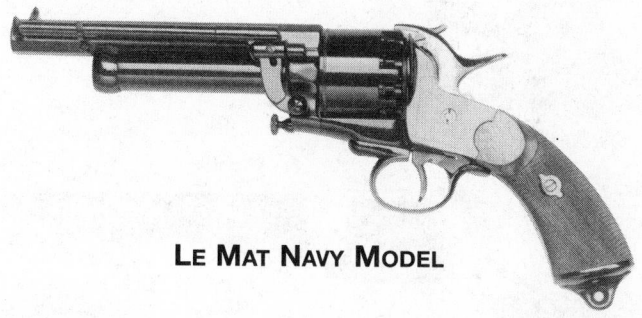

LE MAT NAVY MODEL

LE MAT REVOLVERS

Once the official sidearm of many Confederate cavalry officers, this 9-shot .44-caliber revolver with a central single-shot barrel of 65 caliber gave the cavalry man great firepower.

Barrel Length: 7 ⅝" *Overall Length:* 14" *Weight:* 3 lbs. 7 oz.
CAVALRY MODEL $665.00
NAVY MODEL 665.00
ARMY MODEL 665.00

1862 NEW MODEL POLICE

ROGERS & SPENCER REVOLVER

1862 NEW MODEL POLICE

This is the last gun manufactured b y the Colt plant in the percussion era. It encompassed all the modifications of each gun, starting from the early Paterson to the 1861 Navy. It was favored by the New York Police Dept. for many years. Fluted and rebated cylinder, 36 cal., 5 shot. This replica features brass trigger guard and backstrap. Case hardened frame, loading lever and hammer. *Barrel Length:* 5.5"

1862 POLICE $315.00

ROGERS & SPENCER REVOLVER

This revolver features a six-shot cylinder, octagonal barrel, hinged-type loading lever assembly, two-piece walnut grips, blued finish and case hardened hammer and lever. *Caliber:* 44 *Barrel Length:* 7.5" *Overall Length:* 13.75" *Weight:* 3 lbs.

Price: ROGERS & SPENCER $260.00

1851 NAVY "YANK"

A favorite of "Wild Bill" Hickok, the 1851 Navy was originally manufactured by Colt from 1850 through 1876. This model was the most popular of the Union revolvers, mostly because it was lighter and easier to handle than the Dragoon. *Barrel Length:* 7.5" *Overall Length:* 14" *Weight:* 2 lbs. *Rec. Ball Diam.:* .375 R.B. (.451 in 44 cal) *Calibers:* 36 and 44 *Capacity:* 6 shot *Features:* Steel frame, octagonal barrel, cylinder roll-engraved with naval battle scene; backstrap and trigger guard are polished brass.

Price:
1851 NAVY "YANK" $165.00

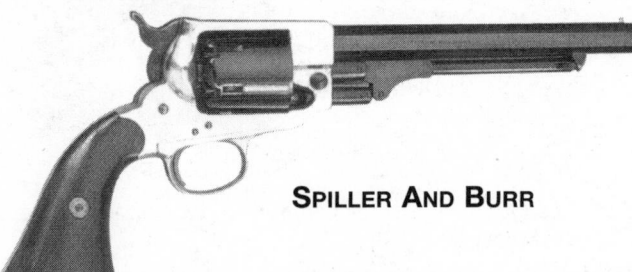

SPILLER AND BURR

SPILLER AND BURR
To ensure production, the Confederate government purchased the company that made this important Civil War revolver. This faithful replica has highly polished brass frame, blued cylinder and octagonal barrel.
Price: $155.00

REB MODEL 1860

1860 ARMY

A modern replica of the confederate Griswold & Gunnison percussion Army revolver. Rendered with a polished brass frame and a rifled steel barrel finished in a high-luster blue with genuine walnut grips. All Army Model 60s are completely proof-tested by the Italian government to the most exacting standards. *Calibers:* 36 and 44. *Barrel Length:* 7.25" *Overall Length:* 13" *Weight:* 2 lbs. 10 oz.- 11 oz. *Features:* Brass frame, backstrap and trigger guard, round barrel.

Price:
REB MODEL 1860 . . . . $120.00

The 1860 Army satisfied the Union Army's need for a more powerful .44-caliber revolver. The cylinder on this replica is roll engraved with a polished brass trigger guard and steel strap cut for shoulder stock. The frame, loading level and hammer are finished in high-luster color case hardening. Walnut grips. *Weight:* 2 lbs. 9 oz. *Barrel Length:* 8" *Overall Length:* 13 5/8" *Caliber:* 44. *Finish:* Brass trigger guard, steel backstrap, round barrel, creeping lever, rebated cylinder, engraved Navy scene.

Price:
1860 ARMY $185.00

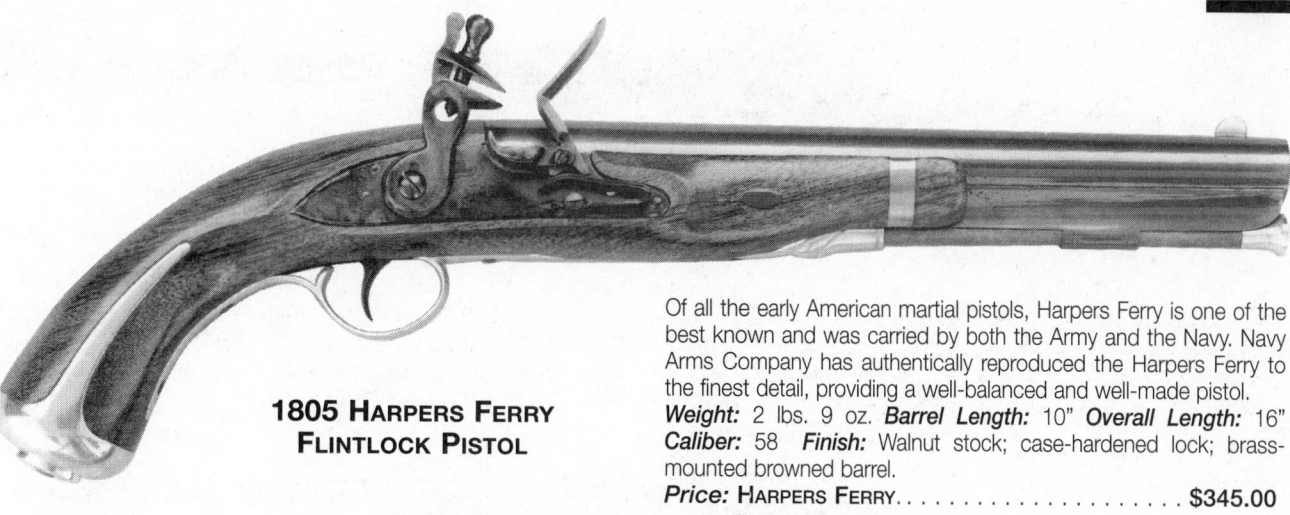

1805 HARPERS FERRY FLINTLOCK PISTOL

Of all the early American martial pistols, Harpers Ferry is one of the best known and was carried by both the Army and the Navy. Navy Arms Company has authentically reproduced the Harpers Ferry to the finest detail, providing a well-balanced and well-made pistol. *Weight:* 2 lbs. 9 oz. *Barrel Length:* 10" *Overall Length:* 16" *Caliber:* 58 *Finish:* Walnut stock; case-hardened lock; brass-mounted browned barrel.
Price: HARPERS FERRY $345.00

REB 60 SHERIFF'S MODEL

1858 NEW MODEL ARMY

REB 60 SHERIFF'S MODEL

A compact version of the Reb Model 60 Revolver. The Sheriff's model version became popular because the shortened barrel was fast out of the leather. This is actually the original snub nose, the predecessor of the detective specials or "belly" guns designed for quick-draw use.
Calibers: 36 and 44
Price:
REB 60 SHERIFF'S MODEL $120.00

1858 NEW MODEL ARMY REMINGTON-STYLE REVOLVER

This rugged, dependable, battle-proven veteran with its top strap and rugged frame was considered the Magnum of Civil War revolvers, ideally suited for heavy 44 charges. Blued finish.
Caliber: 44. *Barrel Length:* 8" *Overall Length:* 14.25"
Weight: 2 lbs. 8 oz.
NEW MODEL ARMY REVOLVER $180.00
Also available: BRASS FRAME 135.00

Black Powder
2002 Edition

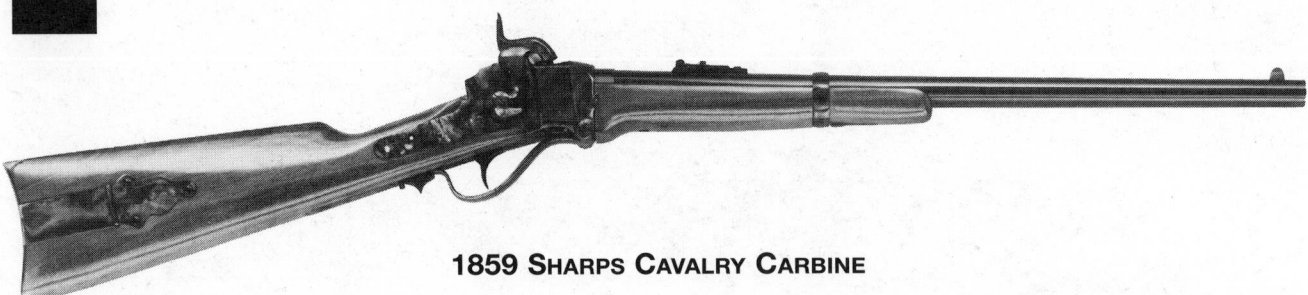

1859 SHARPS CAVALRY CARBINE

This percussion version of the Sharps is a copy of the popular breechloading Cavalry Carbine of the Civil War. It features a patchbox and bar and saddle ring on left side of the stock. *Caliber:* 54 *Barrel Length:* 22" *Overall Length:* 39" *Weight:*

7.75 lbs. *Sights:* Blade front; military ladder rear. *Stock:* Walnut
SHARPS CAVALRY CARBINE $1,000.00
Also available:
1859 SHARPS INFANTRY RIFLE (54 cal.) 1,100.00

SMITH CARBINE

The Smith Carbine was considered one of the finest breechloading carbines of the Civil War period. The hinged breech action allowed fast reloading for cavalry units. Available in either the Cavalry Model (with saddle ring and bar) or

Artillery Model (with sling swivels). *Caliber:* 50 *Barrel Length:* 21.5" *Overall Length:* 39" *Weight:* 7.75 lbs. *Sights:* Blass blade front; folding ladder rear *Stock:* American walnut
SMITH CARBINE. $635.00

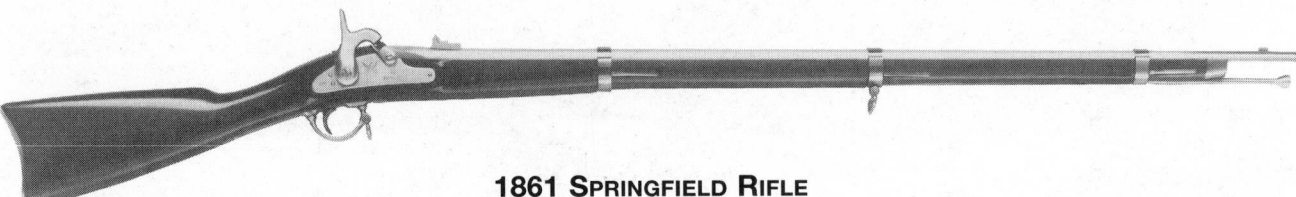

1861 SPRINGFIELD RIFLE

One of the most popular Union rifles of the Civil War, the 1861 model featured the 1855-style hammer. The lockplate on this replica is marked "1861, U.S. Springfield." *Caliber:* 58

Barrel Length: 40" *Overall Length:* 56" *Weight:* 10 lbs. *Finish:* Walnut stock with polished metal lock and stock fitting.
1861 SPRINGFIELD RIFLE $590.00

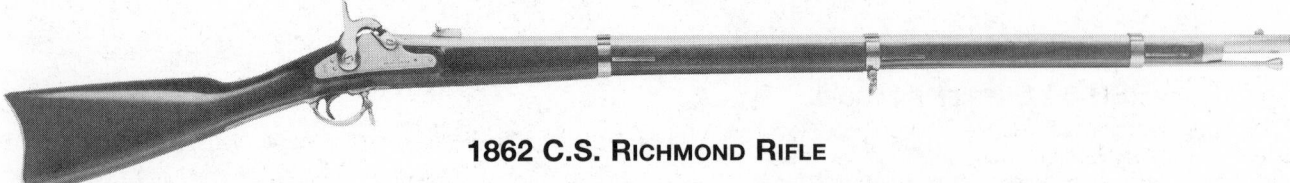

1862 C.S. RICHMOND RIFLE

This model was manufactured by the Confederacy at the Richmond Armory utilizing 1855 Rifle Musket parts captured from the Harpers Ferry Arsenal. This replica features the unusual 1855 lockplate, stamped "1862 C.S. Richmond, V.A."

Caliber: 58 *Barrel Length:* 40" *Overall Length:* 56" *Weight:* 10 lbs. *Finish:* Walnut stock with polished metal lock and stock fittings.
1863 C.S. RICHMOND RIFLE $590.00

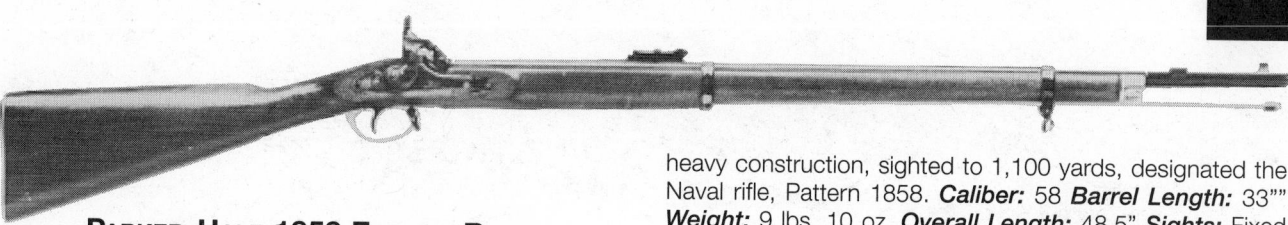

PARKER-HALE 1858 ENFIELD RIFLE

In the late 1850s the British Admiralty, after extensive experiments, settled on a pattern rifle with a 5-groove barrel of heavy construction, sighted to 1,100 yards, designated the Naval rifle, Pattern 1858. *Caliber:* 58 *Barrel Length:* 33"" *Weight:* 9 lbs. 10 oz. *Overall Length:* 48.5" *Sights:* Fixed front; graduated rear. *Stock:* Seasoned walnut w/solid brass furniture.
PH1858 ENFIELD RIFLE $600.00

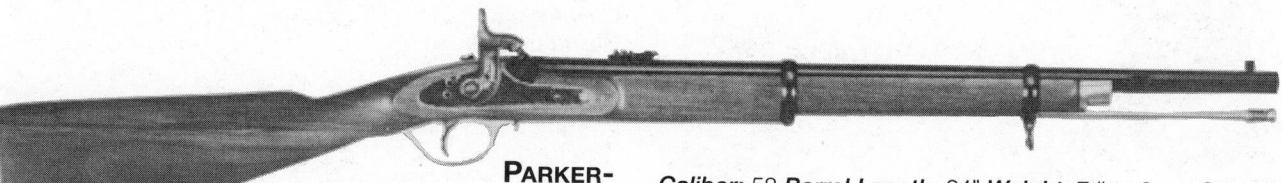

PARKER-HALE 1861 MUSKETOON

The 1861 Enfield Musketoon was the favorite long arm of the Confederate Cavalry. *Caliber:* 58 *Barrel Length:* 24" *Weight:* 7 lbs. 8 oz. *Overall Length:* 40.25" *Sights:* Fixed front; graduated rear. *Stock:* Seasoned walnut with solid brass furniture.
PH1861 MUSKETOON $515.00

BROWN BESS MUSKET

Used extensively in the French and Indian War, the Brown Bess Musket proved itself in the American Revolution as well. This fine replica of the "Second Model" is marked "Grice" on the lockplate. *Caliber:* 75 *Barrel Length:* 42" *Overall Length:* 59" *Weight:* 9.5 lbs. *Sights:* Lug front *Stock:* Walnut
BROWN BESS MUSKET. $895.00
Also available:
BROWN BESS CARBINE *Caliber:* 75 *Barrel Length:* 30" *Overall Length:* 47" *Weight:* 7.75 lbs. $895.00

1803 HARPERS FERRY RIFLE

This 1803 Harpers Ferry rifle was carried by Lewis and Clark on their expedition to explore the Northwest territory. This replica of the first rifled U.S. Martial flintlock features a browned barrel, case hardened lock and a brass patchbox. *Caliber:* 54 *Barrel Length:* 35" *Overall Length:* 50.5" *Weight:* 8.5 lbs.
1803 HARPERS FERRY RIFLE $675.00

"BERDAN" 1859 SHARPS RIFLE

A replica of the Union sniper rifle used by Col. Hiram Berdan's First and Second U.S. Sharpshooters Regiments during the Civil War. *Caliber:* 54 *Barrel Length:* 30" *Overall Length:* 46.75" *Weight:* 8 lbs. 8 oz. *Sights:* Military-style ladder rear; blade front *Stock:* Walnut *Features:* Double-set trigger, case hardened receiver; patchbox and furniture.
"BERDAN" 1859 SHARPS RIFLE $1,165.00
Also available:
SINGLE TRIGGER INFANTRY MODEL 1,100.00

PISTOL LE PAGE

PEDERSOLI "PISTOL LE PAGE" .45 INTERNATIONAL FLINTLOCK TARGET PISTOL

SPECIFICATIONS
Caliber: .45
Barrel Length: 10.5"
Twist: 1-in-18" twist
Trigger: Single set
Weight: 2.5 lbs. (also in .44 smoothbore)
Stock: Walnut
Prices: $710.00
 Percussion model in 36, 38 or 44 caliber **575.00**

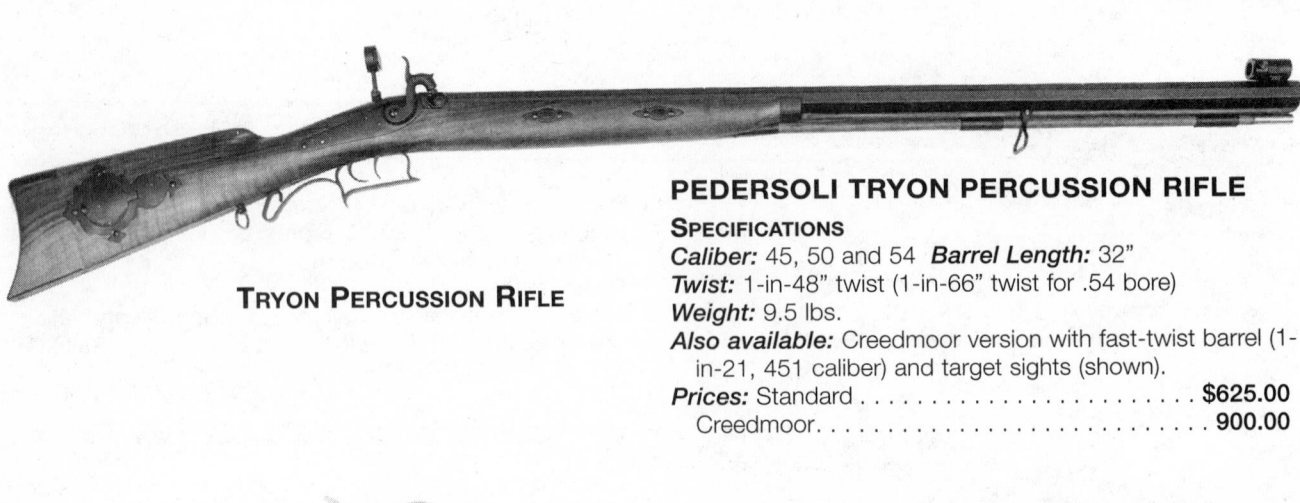

TRYON PERCUSSION RIFLE

PEDERSOLI TRYON PERCUSSION RIFLE

SPECIFICATIONS
Caliber: 45, 50 and 54 *Barrel Length:* 32"
Twist: 1-in-48" twist (1-in-66" twist for .54 bore)
Weight: 9.5 lbs.
Also available: Creedmoor version with fast-twist barrel (1-in-21, 451 caliber) and target sights (shown).
Prices: Standard $625.00
 Creedmoor. **900.00**

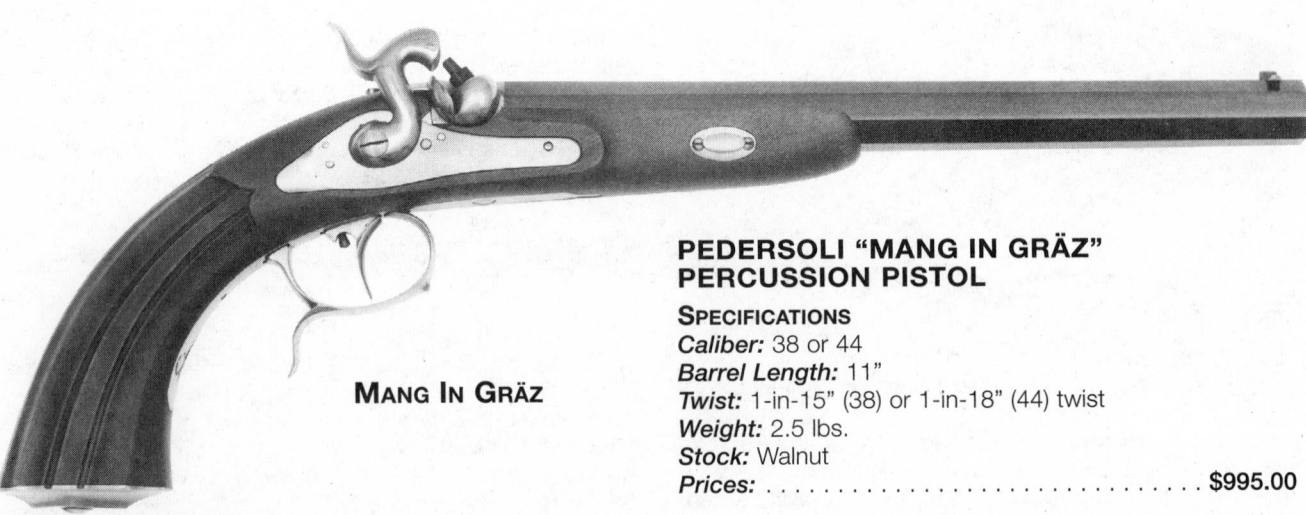

MANG IN GRÄZ

PEDERSOLI "MANG IN GRÄZ" PERCUSSION PISTOL

SPECIFICATIONS
Caliber: 38 or 44
Barrel Length: 11"
Twist: 1-in-15" (38) or 1-in-18" (44) twist
Weight: 2.5 lbs.
Stock: Walnut
Prices: $995.00

MODEL 700 ML

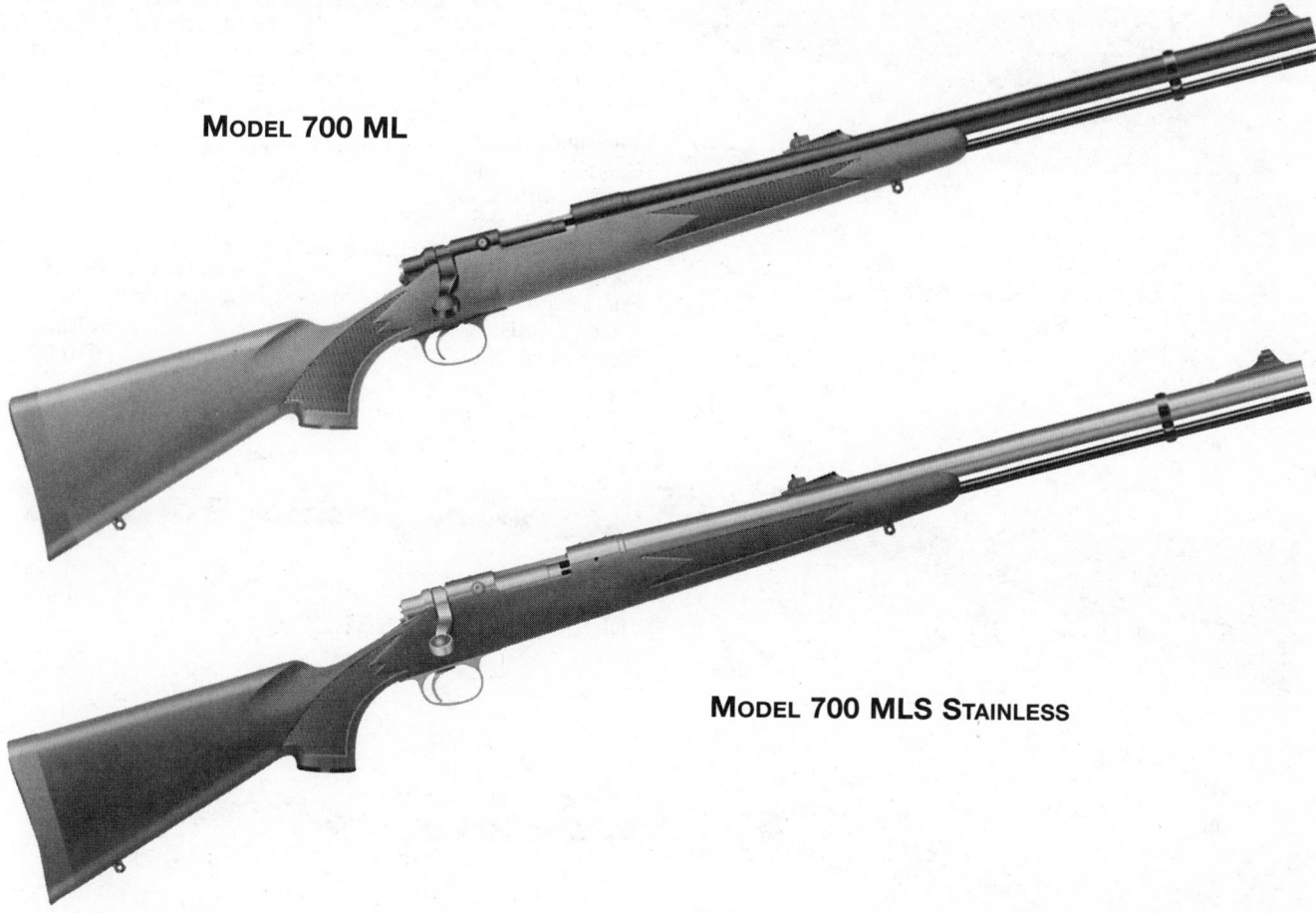

MODEL 700 MLS STAINLESS

MODEL 700 ML AND MLS IN-LINE MUZZLELOADING RIFLES

Remington began building flintlock muzzleloaders in 1816. These two in-line muzzleloading rifles have the same cocking action and trigger mechanism as the original versions. The difference comes from a modified bolt and ignition system. The Model 700 ML has a traditionally blued carbon-steel barreled action. On the Model 700 MLS the barrel, receiver and bolt are made of 416 stainless steel with a non-reflective, satin finish. Each is set in a fiberglass-reinforced synthetic stock fitted with a Magnum-style recoil pad. One end of the solid aluminum ramrod is recessed into the forend and the outer end is secured by a barrel band. Instead of an open chamber, the breech is closed by a stainless-steel plug and nipple. In the internal structure of the modified bolt, the firing pin is replaced by a cylindrical rod that is cocked by normal bolt lift. It is released by pulling the trigger to strike a

#11 percussion cap seated on the nipple. Lock time is 3.0 milli-seconds. Barrels are rifled with a 1 in 28" twist. The barrels are fitted with standard adjustable iron sights; receivers are drilled and tapped for short-action scope mount.

SPECIFICATIONS:
Barrel length: 24"
Twist: 1-28"
Overall Length: 44.5"
Weight: 7.75 lbs.
Length Of Pull: 13 3/8"
Drop At Comb: .5" *Drop At Heel:* 3/8"
Prices:
MODEL ML (.50 cal.) $407.00
MODEL MLS STAINLESS (.50 + .54 cal.) 507.00
Also available:
w/Mossy Oak Break-up camo stock $449.00
Stainless Steel 543.00

OLD ARMY CAP AND BALL
FIXED SIGHT

OLD ARMY CAP AND BALL

This Old Army cap-and-ball revolver is reminiscent of the Civil War era martial revolvers and those used by the early frontiersmen in the 1800s. This Ruger model comes in both blued and stainless-steel finishes and features modern materials, technology and design throughout, including steel music-wire coil springs. Fixed or adjustable sights.

SPECIFICATIONS
Caliber: 45 (.443" bore; .45" groove)
Barrel Length: 7.5"
Weight: 2 7/8 lbs.
Rifling: 6 grooves, R.H. twist (1:16")
Sights: Fixed, ramp front; topstrap channel rear
Percussion cap nipples: Stainless steel (#10 or #11)
Price: Blued $478.00
Stainless Steel 510.00

MODEL K77/50 RSBBZ

MODEL 77/50 RS

MODEL K77/50 RSBBZ STAINLESS STEEL BLACK LAMINATED STOCK BLACK POWDER RIFLE

SPECIFICATIONS
Caliber: .50 *Action:* Bolt action In-line muzzle loader
Finish: Non-glare matte stainless steel finish
Barrel Length: 22" 400 series stainless steel
Overall Length: 41.5"
Rifling: 8 grooves, right hand twist (1-turn-in-28")
Safety: Three-position wing safety
Sights: Single folding leaf rear; gold bead front; rear receiver drilled and tapped for peep sights
Stock: Black/gray laminated American hardwood w/rubber buttpad; studs for sling swivels
Length Of Pull: 13.75" *Drop At Comb:* 11/16"

Drop At heel: 15/16" *Weight (approx.):* 6.5 lbs. (unloaded) *Features:* Operator's manual, set of 1" stainless steel scope range; standard breech plug wrench; bolt disassemble tool; cleaning tube; right hand 90° turn bolt
Price: $601.00
Also available:
MODEL 77/50 RS. Same specifications as above, except finish is matte blue and stock is American Hardwood w/rubber buttpad. 434.00
MODEL 77/50 RSO. Same specifications as above, except for following: *Drop at Comb:* 25/32 *Drop At Heel:* 29/32
Stock: Straight gripped, checkered American black walnut stock, w/curved buttplate. 555.00
K77/50 RSP All-weather, stainless, synthetic stock. . . . 580.00

THOMPSON/CENTER RIFLES

BLACK MOUNTAIN MAGNUM

The .50 caliber Black Mountain Magnum™ is designed to handle magnum loads of up to 150 grains of FFg black powder or the Pyrodex equivalent volume (up to three 50-grain Pyrodex pellets). Shooting a Mag Express Sabot with 240-grain XTP bullet, a 150-grain load produces a muzzle velocity of 2203 feed per second. The Black Mountain Magnum™ has a musket cap nipple, the hottest ignition available in a traditional-style muzzleloader. Standard nipples with #11 or #11 Magnum percussion caps can also be used.

The blued, 26-inch barrel is button rifled with a 1-in-28-inch twist to maximize performance with conical projectiles. It is equipped with Thompson/Center's exclusive QLA™ muzzle system for easy loading, even without a short starter. Tru-Glo™ fiber optic sights allow hunters to take advantage of productive dawn and dusk hunting time. Hunters who prefer to use a riflescope will appreciate that the rifle is drilled and tapped for easy scope mounting. The sidelock rifle is stocked with a tough, durable Rynite® stock.

Price: **$360.59**
Also Available: with walnut stock **406.50**
 .54 with walnut stock **406.50**
 12-gauge Turkey caplock w/camo stock **431.40**

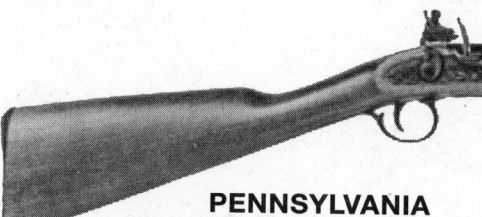

PENNSYLVANIA HUNTER FLINTLOCK RIFLE

The 28" barrel on this model is cut rifled (.010" deep) with 1 turn in 66" twist. Its outer contour is octagonal. Sights are fully adjustable for both windage and elevation. Stocked with select American black walnut; metal hardware is blued steel. Features a hooked breech system and coilspring lock, plus T/C's QLA™ Muzzle System for improved accuracy and easier reloading. **Caliber:** 50. **Overall length:** 45". **Weight:** Approx. 7.50 lbs.
Price: PENNSYLVANIA HUNTER FLINTLOCK **$451.15**

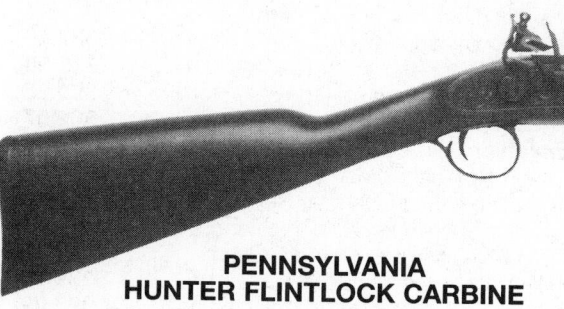

PENNSYLVANIA HUNTER FLINTLOCK CARBINE

Thompson/Center's Pennsylvania Hunter Flintlock Carbine is 50-caliber with 1:66" twist and cut-rifling. It was designed specifically for the hunter who uses patched round balls only and hunts in thick cover or brush. The 21" barrel is octagonal. Features T/C's QLA™ Muzzle System. **Overall length:** 38". **Weight:** 6.5 lbs. **Sights:** Fully adjustable open hunting-style rear with bead front. **Stock:** Select American walnut. **Trigger:** Single hunting-style trigger. **Lock:** Color cased, coil spring, with floral design.
Price: PENNSYLVANIA HUNTER FLINTLOCK CARBINE . **$451.15**

FIRE STORM

Designed for Pyrodex pellets, the Fire Storm's removable breech plug is conical, directing flame to the pellet's center for efficient ignition. Available with caplock or flintlock mechanism. **Caliber:** 50 **Barrel Length:** 26"-with QLA™ Muzzle System built in **Rifling Twist:** 1 in 48" for use with Round Balls & Conicals **Overall Length:** 41.75" **Weight:** 7 lbs. (approximate) **Rifle Sights:** Competition click adjustable steel rear sight and ramp style front sights are fitted with Tru-Glo™ Fiber Optics **Stock:** Black Composite **Trigger:** Single trigger with large trigger guard bow. **Extra Features:** Aluminum ramrod is standard **Loading:** The Fire Storm™ can accept magnum charges of up to 150 grains of FFG Black Powder or Pyrodex® equivalent (or 3 Pyrodex 50 caliber, 50 grain Pellets). **Price:** **$398.97**
 Stainless steel **438.05**

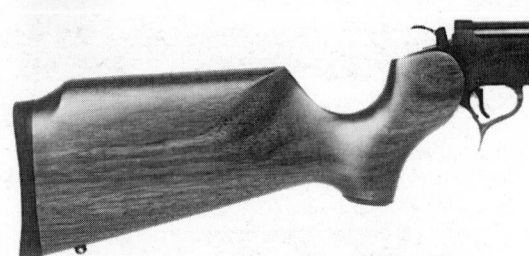

ENCORE 209 X 50
MAGNUM MUZZLELOADING RIFLE

SPECIFICATIONS
Caliber: .50 *Action:* Break-open action muzzleloader
Ignition: 209 shotgun primer *Barrel Length:* 26" with
QLA Muzzle System *Twist:* 1 in 28" *Overall Length:* 40.5"
Weight: 7 lbs. *Sights:* Tru-Glo adjustable rear fiber optic

sight; ramp-style fiber optic front sight *Safety:* Automatic
hammerblock w/ bolt interlock *Finish:* Blued *Stock:*
American walnut with schnabel forend and Monte Carlo
buttstock *Features:* Barrel interchangeable with Encore
rifles; equipped with sling swivel studs; accepts magnum
charges of up to 150 grains of black powder or Pyrodex
equivalent (or three 50-grain Pyrodex Pellets).
Price: Blued/Walnut $610.18
Blued with hardwood camo stock 634.27
Stainless/composite accessory barrel
   only-blued 264.28
Accessory barrel only-SST 301.62

BLACK DIAMOND
MUZZLELOADING RIFLE

SPECIFICATIONS
Caliber: .50 *Ignition:* In-line ignition using Flame Thrower
musket cap nipple or No. 11 nipple *Barrel:* Free-floated,
22.5" barrel with QLA *Twist:* 1 in 18" *Overall Length:*
41.5" *Weight:* 6 lbs. 9 oz. *Safety:* Patented sliding thumb
safety *Sights:* Tru-Glo Fiber Optic adjustable rear sight;
Fiber Optic ramp-style front sight *Stock:* Black Rynite
stock with molded-in checkering and pistol grip cap
Loading: Accepts magnum charges of up to 150 grains of
black powder or Pyrodex equivalent, or three 50-grain

Pyrodex Pellets *Features:* Removable universal breech
plug; Aluminum ram rod; sling swivel studs; rubber recoil
pad; musket nipple wrench, 5-pack or T/C Mag Express
Sabots, and No. 11 nipple standard
Prices: Blued w/walnut stock $367.45
Blued w/Rynite Stock. 316.00
Blued with hardwoods camo stock 360.25
Stainless 362.57
Also Available: BLACK DIAMOND PREMIUM PACK (includes T-
Handle Short Starter, 10 Mag Express Sabots, rifle powder
measure, In-line U-View Capper, Super Jag, ball and bullet
puller, 2 Quick Shots, breech plug wrench, Hunter's Field
Pouch, Lube-N-Clean Kit, Gorilla Grease).
Prices: Blued $339.16
Stainless 397.96

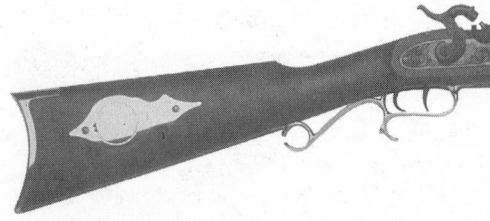

THE HAWKEN 50 AND 54 CALIBER

Similar to the famous Rocky Mountain rifles made during the
early 1800s, the Hawken has an octagon barrel. Button-
rifled for ultimate precision, the Hawken is available in 45-,
50- or 54-caliber percussion or 50- caliber flintlock. It features a hooked breech, double-set triggers, first-grade

American walnut stock, adjustable hunting sights, solid
brass trim and color casehardened lock. Beautifully deco-
rated; comes equipped with T/C's QLA™ Muzzle System.
Weight: Approx. 8.5 lbs.
Prices:
HAWKEN CAPLOCK 50 or 54 caliber $504.03
HAWKEN FLINTLOCK 50 caliber 526.19
Also Available: CLELAND MATCH HAWKEN CAPLOCK,
  40 caliber, blued, walnut stock 700.58

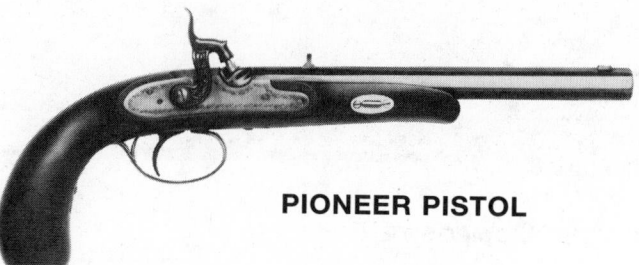

PIONEER PISTOL

SPECIFICATIONS
Caliber: 45 percussion *Barrel length:* 9 ⁵/₈" octagonal with tenon; ¹³/₁₆" across flats, rifled 1 in 16", fixed tang breech *Overall length:* 15" *Weight:* 1lb. 15 oz. *Sights:* Blade front; fixed rear *Trigger:* Single *Stock:* Beech, rounded *Lock:* V-type mainspring *Features:* German silver furniture; blackened hardware
Price: $139.00
Kit. 119.00

WILLIAM PARKER PISTOL

SPECIFICATIONS
Caliber: 50 percussion (1:20") *Barrel length:* 10 ³/₈" octagonal (15/16" across flats) *Overall length:* 17.5" *Weight:* 2 lbs. 5 oz. *Sights:* Brass blade front; fixed rear *Stock:* Walnut, checkered at wrist *Triggers:* Double set; will fire set and unset *Lock:* Adjustable sear engagement with fly and bridle; V-type mainspring *Features:* Brass percussion cap guard; polished hardware, brass inlays and separate ramrod
Price: $269.00

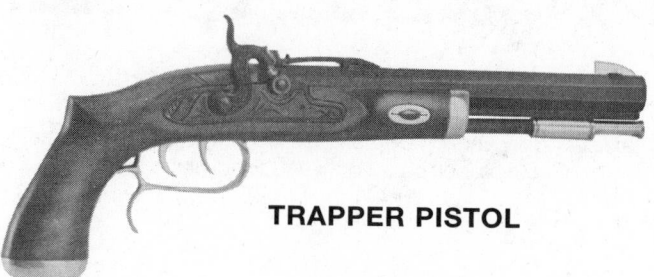

TRAPPER PISTOL

SPECIFICATIONS
Caliber: 50 percussion or flintlock (1:20") *Barrel length:* 9 ³/₄"; octagonal (7/8" across flats) with tenon *Overall length:* 15.5" *Weight:* 2 lbs. 14 oz. *Stock:* Beech *Lock:* Adjustable sear engagement with fly and bridle *Triggers:* Double set, will fire set and unset *Sights:* Primitive-style adjustable rear; brass blade front *Furniture:* Solid brass; blued steel on assembled pistol
Price: Percussion $189.00
Percussion Kit. 149.00
Flintlock. 209.00

BUCKHUNTER PRO ALL-WEATHER

BUCKHUNTER PRO-IN-LINE PISTOLS
SPECIFICATIONS
Calibers: 50 Percussion *Barrel length:* 9.5" or 12.5" *Overall length:* 14.25" (17.75") *Weight:* 3.2 oz. (3.4 oz.) *Trigger:* Single *Sights:* Fold-down adjustable rear; beaded blade front *Stock:* Walnut or All-Weather *Features:* Blued or C-Nickel furniture; PVC ramrod; drilled and tapped for scop mounting; coil mainspring; thumb safety
Price: $229.00
w/All-Weather Stock. 239.00
14.75" fluted nickel w/muzzle brake. 284.00

KENTUCKY PISTOL

SPECIFICATIONS
Caliber: 50 Percussion (1:20") *Barrel length:* 10" octagon (7/8" flats) *Overall length:* 15" *Weight:* 2 lbs. 8 oz. *Trigger:* Single *Sights:* Fixed rear; blade front *Stock:* Beechwood *Features:* Brass furniture; wood ramrod; kit available
Price: $138.00
Kit 109.00

Deerhunter Rifles

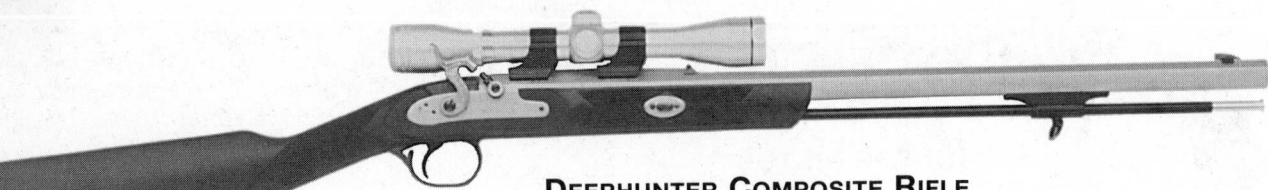

DEERHUNTER COMPOSITE RIFLE

SPECIFICATIONS

Calibers: 32, 50 and 54 percussion
Barrel length: 24" octagonal **Rifling twist:** 1:48"
(percussion only); 1:66" (flint or percussion)
Overall length: 40"
Weight: 6 lbs. (6 lbs. 3 oz. in Small Game rifle)
Trigger: Single **Sights:** Fixed rear; blade front

Features: PVC ramrod; blackened furniture; inletted wedge plates
Prices:

Percussion w/blued barrel $149.00
Percussion w/nickel barrel 159.00
Flintlock w/nickel barrel 189.00
Flintlock w/select hardwood stock 189.00
PANTHER (50 cal.) w/All-Weather composite stock,
   fixed blade sights 119.00

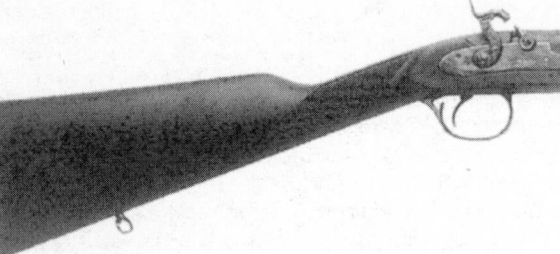

PANTHER RIFLE
All-Weather Composite Stock

An economy version of the Deerhunter, the Panther comes with 24" 50-caliber barrel only and fixed blade sights.
Price: $119.00

TRACKER 209 IN-LINE RIFLE

SPECIFICATIONS

Features: 209 Primer Ignition system gives hot, reliable powder ignition; adjustable lite optic sights. **Caliber:** 50
Barrel: 22" blued or nickel (1-in-28" twist) **Length:** 41"
Stock: synthetic with checkering or camo
Prices: Synthetic w/blued stock $119.00
Synthetic w/nickel stock. 129.00
Camo w/nickel stock 179.00

E-BOLT 209 RIFLE

SPECIFICATIONS

Caliber: 50 **Barrel:** 22" blued or nickel (1-in-28" twist)
Length: 41" **Stock:** synthetic with checkering or camo
Sights: Light optic
Prices: Synthetic w/blued barrel $169.00
Synthetic w/nickel barrel. 179.00
Camo w/nickel barrel 229.00

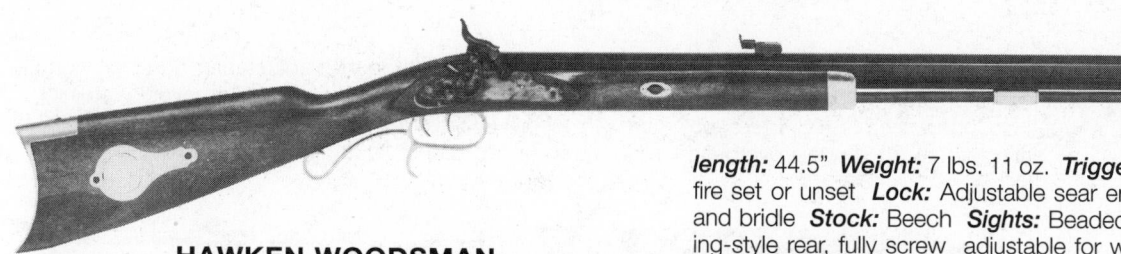

HAWKEN WOODSMAN

SPECIFICATIONS
Calibers: 50 and 54 percussion or flint (50 caliber only)
Barrel length: 28" (octagonal); hooked breech; rifled 1 turn in 48" (1 turn in 66" in 50 caliber also available) **Overall**

length: 44.5" **Weight:** 7 lbs. 11 oz. **Triggers:** Double set; will fire set or unset **Lock:** Adjustable sear engagement with fly and bridle **Stock:** Beech **Sights:** Beaded blade front; hunting-style rear, fully screw adjustable for windage and elevation **Furniture:** Solid brass, blued steel or blackened (50 cal. only); unbreakable ramrod
Prices: Percussion. $229.00
Flint. 249.00
Percussion, left-hand 239.00

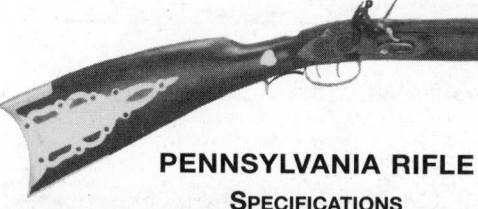

PENNSYLVANIA RIFLE

SPECIFICATIONS
Caliber: 50 **Barrel length:** 401/4"; octagonal (7/8" across flats) with 3 pins; rifled 1 turn in 66" **Overall length:** 57" **Weight:** 8

lbs. 8 oz. **Lock:** Adjustable sear engagement with fly and bridle **Stock:** Walnut, beavertail style **Triggers:** Double set; will fire set and unset **Sights:** Primitive-style adjustable rear; brass blade front **Furniture:** Solid brass, blued steel
Prices: Percussion. $469.00
Flintlock 479.00

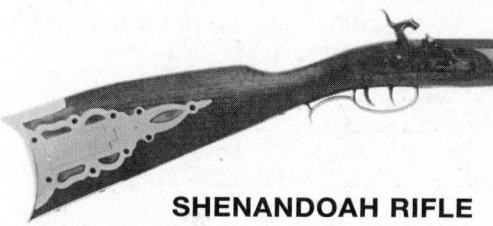

SHENANDOAH RIFLE

The Shenandoah Rifle captures the frontier styling and steady performance of Tradition's Pennsylvania Rifle in slightly shorter length and more affordable price. Choice of engraved and color case hardened flintlock or percussion V-type mainspring lock with double-set triggers. The full-length

stock in walnut finish is accented by a solid brass curved buttplate, inletted patch box, nose cap, thimbles, trigger guard and decorative furniture.

SPECIFICATIONS
Caliber: 50 (1:66") flint or percussion **Barrel length:** 33.5" octagon **Overall length:** 49.5" **Weight:** 7 lbs. 3 oz.
Sights: Buckhorn rear, blade front **Stock:** Beech
Prices: Percussion. $349.00
Flintlock 369.00

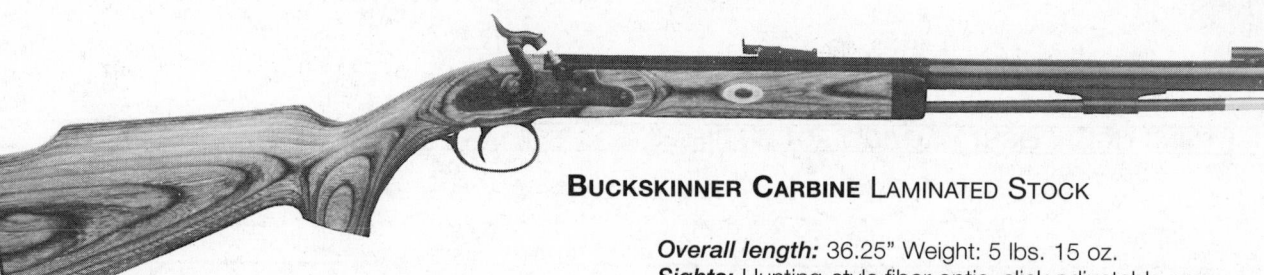

BUCKSKINNER CARBINE LAMINATED STOCK

Overall length: 36.25" Weight: 5 lbs. 15 oz.
Sights: Hunting-style fiber optic, click adjustable rear; beaded blade front **Trigger:** Single
Features: Blackened furniture: German silver ornamentation; sling swivels; unbreakable ramrod
Prices:
Flintlock $219.00
Laminated Stock, Flintlock. 299.00

BUCKSKINNER CARBINE

SPECIFICATIONS
Caliber: 50 percussion or flintlock
Barrel length: 21": octagonal-to-round with tenon; 15/16" across flats; 1:66" twist (flintlock) and 1:20" (percussion)

TRADITIONS RIFLES

Lightning Bolt-Action Rifles

Traditions' Lightning Bolt rifles include models with blued, chemical-nickel and stainless steel. Stock finishes include Advantage Timber (All-Weather Composite), Camo, Break-up and Spider Web. All models come with rugged synthetic ramrods, adjustable triggers, adjustable hunting sights, drilled and tapped barrels and field-removable stainless breech plugs. LFS (lightning fire system) allows use of #11 cap, musket cap on provided nipples.

LIGHTNING w/CHECKERED COMPOSITE STOCK
Fluted Stainless Steel Barrel w/Muzzle Break

LIGHTNING w/ALL-WEATHER COMPOSITE STOCK

LIGHTNING w/ADVANTAGE™, (OR BREAK UP™ OR SHADOW BRANCH™ OR HARDWOOD™) CAMO COMPOSITE STOCK

LIGHTNING MAG BOLT-ACTION RIFLES

MODEL NUMBER	STOCK	CALIBER	BARREL	SIGHTS	RAMROD	OVERALL LENGTH	WEIGHT	RETAIL
R610029	AW Synthetic	.50p	24" Blued	Adj. Fiber Optic	Aluminum	43"	7 lb. 2 oz.	$199
R6100209	AW Synthetic	.50p	24" Blued/Muzzle Brake	Adj. Fiber Optic	Aluminum	45"	7 lb. 4 oz.	229
R61003954	High Definition Advantage Timber	.50p	24" Blued	Adj. Fiber Optic	Aluminum	43"	7 lb. 2 oz.	229
R6100295	Break-Up/AW Synthetic	.50p	24" Blued	Adj. Fiber Optic	Aluminum	43"	7 lb. 2 oz.	229
R610489	AW Synthetic	.54p	24" Blued	Adj. Fiber Optic	Aluminum	43"	7 lb. 9 oz.	199
R611029	AW Synthetic	.50p	24" C-Nickel	Adj. Fiber Optic	Aluminum	43"	7 lb. 10 oz.	219
R617029	AW Synthetic	.50p	24" Fluted Stainless/Muzzle Brake	Adj. Fiber Optic	Aluminum	45"	7 lb. 10 oz.	329
R6170295	Break Up/AW Synthetic	.50p	24" Fluted Stainless/Muzzle Brake	Adj. Fiber Optic	Aluminum	45"	7 lb. 10 oz.	359
R618029	AW Synthetic	.50p	24" Stainless	Adj. Fiber Optic	Aluminum	43"	7 lb. 10 oz.	279
R6180295	Break Up/AW Synthetic	.50p	24" Stainless	Adj. Fiber Optic	Aluminum	43"	7 lb. 10 oz.	309
R618489	AW Synthetic	.54p	24" Stainless	Adj. Fiber Optic	Aluminum	43"	6 lb. 8 oz.	279

LIGHTNING LIGHTWEIGHT MAG BOLT-ACTION RIFLES *with the "Lightning Fire Magnum System" and Fiber Optic Sights*

MODEL NUMBER	STOCK	CALIBER	BARREL	SIGHTS	RAMROD	OVERALL LENGTH	WEIGHT	RETAIL
R630023	AW Synthetic/Spider Web	.50p	21" Fluted Blued	Adj. Fiber Optic	Aluminum	40"	6 lb. 5 oz.	$239
R631023	AW Synthetic/Spider Web	.50p	21" Fluted C-Nickel	Adj. Fiber Optic	Aluminum	40"	6 lb. 5 oz.	249
R637023	AW Synthetic/Spider Web	.50p	21" Fluted Stainless	Adj. Fiber Optic	Aluminum	40"	6 lb. 5 oz.	279
R63103955	AW Synthetic/Spider Web	.50p	21" Fluted C-Nickel	Adj. Fiber Optic	Aluminum	40"	6 lb. 5 oz.	289

LIGHTNING 45 LD BOLT-ACTION RIFLES

MODEL NUMBER	STOCK	CALIBER	BARREL	RATE OF TWIST	SIGHTS	RAMROD	OVERALL LENGTH	WEIGHT	RETAIL
R65050950	AW Synthetic/Check	.45p	26" Fluted Blued	1 in 20"	Adj. Fiber Optic	Aluminum	45"	7 lb. 0 oz.	$229
R65150950	AW Synthetic/Check	.45p	26" Fluted C-Nickel	1 in 20"	Adj. Fiber Optic	Aluminium	45"	7 lb. 2 oz.	239
R65150954	High Definition Advantage Timber	.45p	26" Fluted C-Nickel	1 in 20"	Adj. Fiber Optic	Aluminum	45"	7 lb. 2 oz.	289

All composite stocks are checkered. All Lightning 45 LD Bolt-Action Rifles are Drilled & Tapped for scope mounting. All Lightning Bolt-Action Rifles have Cheek-pieces. AW-All Weather

Buckhunter Pro™ In-Line Rifles

BUCKHUNTER PRO™ IN-LINE RIFLE
w/Walnut-Stained Stock

BUCKHUNTER PRO™ IN-LINE RIFLE
w/Black Composite Stock, Stainless Barrel, Optional Scope

Traditions has upgraded its Buckhunter In-line ignition rifles and shotguns with the Buckhunter Pro series. The guns feature an adjustable trigger, thumb safety and a choice of Ultracoat Teflon, C-Nickel, blued or stainless steel barrels. Slimmed-down matte black composite stocks are available as are two camouflage patterns, laminated, thumbhole or walnut-stained stocks. All Buckhunter Pros have field-removable stainless steel breech plugs and improved adjustable hunting sights. The Buckhunter Pro rifles are available in 50 caliber (1:32") or 54 caliber (1:48") for use with conical and saboted bullets.
Prices: . . . . **$169.00 - $219.00**

BUCKHUNTER IN-LINE COMPOSITE RIFLE
SPECIFICATIONS
Calibers: 50 (1:32") and 54 (2:48") percussion *Barrel*

length: Blued 24" round *Overall length:* 42" *Weight:* 7 lbs. 6 oz. *Stock:* All-Weather Composite (matte black) *Sights:* Beaded blade front; fully adjustable rear *Features:* Blackened furniture; PVC ramrod; stainless steel removable breech plug; optional Redi-Pak (includes composite powder flask with valve dispenser, powder measure, two universal fast loaders, 5-in-1 loader, cleaning jag and patches, ball puller, 20 conical bullets, in-line nipple wrench
Price: . . . . **$149.00 - $159.00**

BUCKHUNTER PRO™ IN-LINE RIFLES WITH FIBER OPTIC SIGHTS

MODEL NUMBER	STOCK	CALIBER	BARREL	RATE OF TWIST	SIGHTS	OVERALL LENGTH	WEIGHT
R50102	AW Composite	.50p	24" c-Nickel	1:32	Adj. Fiber Optic	43"	7 lb. 4 oz.
R51102	AW Composite	.50p	24" Blued	1:32	Adj. Fiber Optic	43"	7 lb. 2 oz.
R501025	AW Comp./Break-Up	.50p	24" c-Nickel	1:32	Adj. Fiber Optic	43"	7 lb. 4 oz.

Replacement drop-in black and composite stocks available FCS50101   *All composite stocks are checkered*

BUCKHUNTER™ IN - LINE RIFLES

MODEL NUMBER	STOCK	CALIBER	BARREL	RATE OF TWIST	SIGHTS	OVERALL LENGTH	WEIGHT
R42102	AW Composite	.50p	24" Blued	1:32	Adj/BB	43"	7 lb.
R42148	AW Composite	.54p	24" Blued	1:48	Adj/BB	43"	6 lb. 14 oz.
R42302	AW Composite	.50p	24" c-Nickel	1:32	Adj/BB	43"	7 lb. 2 oz.

PATERSON REVOLVER

Manufactured at Paterson, New Jersey, by the Patent Arms Manufacturing Company from 1836 to 1842, these were the first revolving pistols designed by Samuel Colt. All early Patersons featured a five-shot cylinder, roll-engraved with one or two scenes, octagon barrel and folding trigger that extends when the hammer is cocked.

SPECIFICATIONS
Caliber: 36 *Capacity:* 5 shots (engraved cylinder)
Barrel Length: 7.5" octagonal
Overall Length: 11.5"
Weight: 2.552 lbs.
Frame: Color casehardened steel
Grip: One-piece walnut
Price: $375.00
w/Lever 415.00

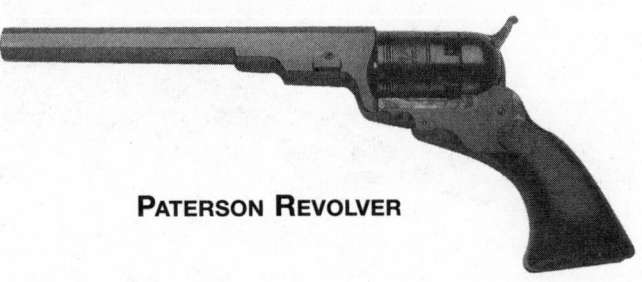

PATERSON REVOLVER

1858 REMINGTON NEW ARMY 44 REVOLVER

Prices: 8" barrel, open sights $260.00
With stainless steel and open sights 350.00
TARGET MODEL w/black finish 295.00
TARGET MODEL w/stainless steel 389.00

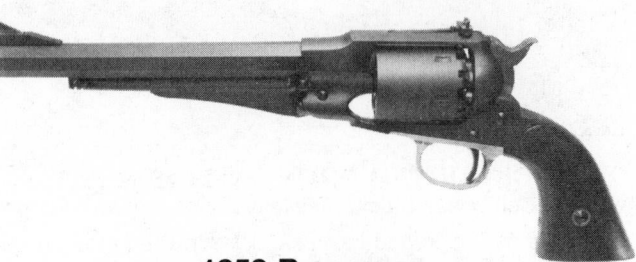

1858 REMINGTON NEW ARMY TARGET MODEL

1860 ARMY REVOLVER

SPECIFICATIONS
Caliber: 44
Barrel length: 8" (round, tapered)
Overall length: 13 3/4"
Weight: 2.65 lbs.
Frame: One-piece, color case hardened steel
Trigger guard: Brass
Cylinder: 6 shots (engraved)
Grip: One-piece walnut
Price: $265.00
Also available:
1860 ARMY FLUTED 270.00

1860 ARMY REVOLVER

1861 NAVY REVOLVER

SPECIFICATIONS
Caliber: 36
Capacity: 6 shots
Barrel length: 7 1/2"
Overall length: 13"
Weight: 2.75 lbs.
Grip: One-piece walnut
Frame: Color case hardened steel
Prices: 1861 NAVY CIVIC $250.00
MODEL 1851 (not shown) 250.00

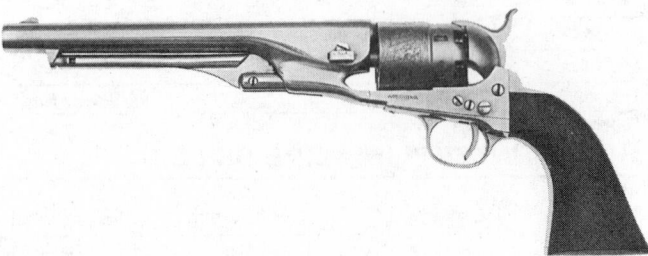

1861 NAVY REVOLVER

Sights & Scopes

HUNTING AND SHOOTING WITH THE MODERN BOW
by Roger Maynard

Expert bowhunter Roger Maynard gives an in-depth look at what it takes to be successful in the hunt for game. Maynard explains it all based on his vast experience and from the advice of bowhunters and bow makers he has met over his 30-plus years of hunting.

FISH & SHELLFISH CARE & COOKERY
by Ken Oberrecht

For those who harvest their own fish and shellfish or buy from seafood markets. More than three hundred easy-to-follow, kitchen-tested recipes covering every method of fish and shellfish preparation.

*For addresses and phone/fax numbers of manufacturers and distributors included in this section, please turn to **DIRECTORY OF MANUFACTURERS AND SUPPLIERS** on page 557.*

AIMPOINT 7000S SIGHT

SPECIFICATIONS
System: Parallax free *Optical:* Anti-reflex coated lenses
Adjustment: 1 click = 1/2 inch at 100 yards
Length: 6.3" *Weight:* 7.4 oz. *Objective diameter:* 36mm
Mounting system: 30mm rings *Magnification:* 1X
Material: Anodized aluminum; black finish
Diameter of dot: Red dot, 4 MOA
Price: $297.00
Also Available:
7000L (*length:* 7.9") 297.00
7000S 2X (fixed 2X) 388.00
7000L 2X (fixed2X) 388.00

SERIES 3000 UNIVERSAL

SPECIFICATIONS
System: 100% parallax free
Weight: 6 oz.
Length: 6.25"
Magnification: 1X
Scope attachment: 3X
Eye relief: Unlimited
Battery choices: 2X Mercury SP 675 1X Lithium or DL 1/3N
Material: Anodized aluminum, black finish
Mounting: 1" Rings (Medium or High)
Price: Black $232.00

COMP M2 AND
COMP ML2

AIMPOINT COMP C2X

SPECIFICATIONS
System: Parallax free *Optical:* Anti-reflex coated lens
Adjustment: 1 click = 1/2" at 100 yards *Length:* 4.7"
Weight: 6.5 oz.
Objective diameter: 36 mm
Diameter of dot: 2 MOA
Mounting system: 30mm ring
Magnification: 2X fixed
Material: Anodized aluminum; black finish
Price: $445.00
  Comp M2 2X, gray 555.00
  Comp ML2 2X, gray 520.00

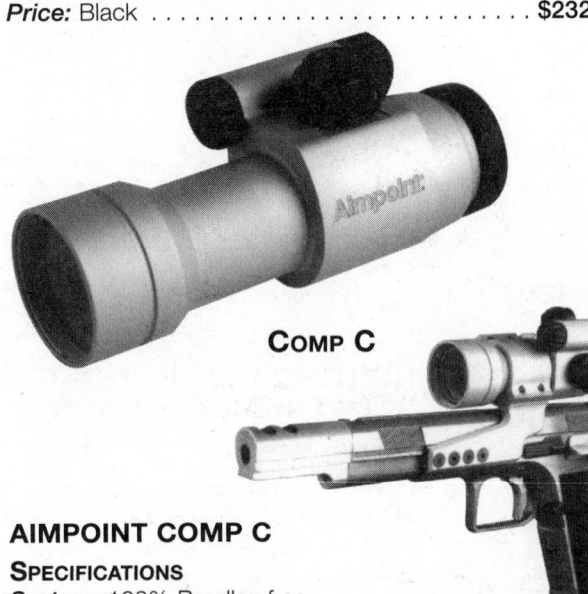

COMP C

AIMPOINT COMP C

SPECIFICATIONS
System: 100% Parallax free
Optics: Anti-reflex coated lenses
Eye relief: Unlimited *Batteries:* 3V Lithium
Adjustment: 1 click = 1/2-inch at 100 yards
Length: 4 3/4" *Weight:* 6.5 oz.
Objective diameter: 36mm
Dot diameter: 4 MOA
Mounting system: 30mm ring
Magnification: 1X
Material: Black or stainless finish
Price: $331.00
Also Available: heavy-duty, hard anodized, graphite
  gray, submersible to 80'
  Comp M2 . . . . 409.00
  Comp ML2 . . . . 375.00

AO SIGHT SYSTEMS

SMLE SCOUT SCOPE MOUNT

GUIDE GUN

Front Post

Rear Ghost Ring

MOUNT INSTALLATION

AO SIGHT SYSTEMS GHOST-RING SIGHTS & NEW LEVER SCOUT MOUNTS

• Scout Scope Mount with 8" long Weaver style rail and cross slots on 1/2" Centers • Scope mounts 1/8" lower than previously possible on Marlin Lever Guns • Drop-in installation, no gunsmithing required • Installs using existing rear dovetail & front two screw holes on receiver • Allows fast target acquisition with both eyes open—better peripheral vision • Affords use of Ghost-Ring Sights with Scope dismounted • Recoil tested for even the stoutes 45/70 and .450 Loads • Available for Marlin Lever Models: 1895 Guide Series, new .450, .444P, the 336, and 1894.

Prices:
28-2141A-095-1 AO Lever Scout Mount for Marlin 1895
    for .45-70, .450, .444 . . . . **$50.00**
28-2169B-092-2 AO Lever Scout Mount for Marlin 336
    for 30-30 Win, 35 Rem 50.00
28-2169C-092-1 AO Lever Scout Mount for
    Marlin 1894 . . . . 50.00

AO GHOST-RING HUNTING SIGHTS

• Fully adjustable for windage & elevation • Available for most rifles including blackpowder • Minimum gunsmithing for most installations; matches most existing mounting holes • Compact design, CNC machined from steel and heat treated • Perfect for low light hunting conditions and brush/timer hunting, offers minimal target obstruction.

Price: **AO GHOST-RING HUNTING SIGHT SET** **$90.00**

NEW FOR 2001 SMLE SCOUT SCOPE MOUNTS

• Offers Scout Scope Mount with 7" long Weaver style rail
• Requires no machining of barrel to fit—no drilling or tapping
• Tapered counter bore for snug fit of SMLE Barrels
• Circular Mount is final filled with Brownells Acraglass

Prices:
28-2154A-115-1 SMLE Scout Scope Mounts for
    No. 1 MkIII, No. 2A, No. 2A1 and No. 7
28-2154A-124-1 SMLE Scout Scope Mount for
    No. 4 Mk1, No. 4 Mk1/2, No. 4 Mk2, No. 5 Mk1,
    and Quest Extreme
SMLE SCOUT MOUNT **$60.00**

BERETTA ALLEYCAT

KIMBER ULTRA CARRY

GLOCK 36 w/PRO EXPRESS BIG DOT TRITIUM

COLT COMMANDER w/ADJUSTABLE PRO EXPRESS SIGHTS

BIG DOT TRITIUM w/TRITIUM REAR

AO EXPRESS SIGHTS

Extremely Fast Front Sight using proven Express Sight Principles. Low profile Shallow V Express rear with white vertical line, front white dot available with or without Tritium. Machined steel sights in matte black finish. Rear sight available in different heights. Made for most pistols, and limited styles of revolvers. Rear available in double set-screw for most installations. From AO Sight Systems (formerly Ashley Outdoors).

Prices: STANDARD DOT SET $60.00
BIG DOT SET 60.00
BIG DOT TRITIUM SET 90.00
STANDARD DOT TRITIUM SET 90.00

AO PRO EXPRESS SIGHTS

Uses proven Express Sight Principle with Big Dot Tritium or Standard Dot Tritium Front Sight incorporating a vertical Tritium Bar within the Rear Express Sight. Enhanced low light sight acquisition with speed of Express Sight Principle. Rear sights available in double set-screw style for easier installation. From AO Sight Systems (formerly Ashley Outdoors).

Prices: PRO EXPRESS BIG DOT TRITIUM $120.00
PRO EXPRESS STANDARD DOT TRITIUM 120.00

AO ADJUSTABLE EXPRESS SIGHT SETS

Incorporates Adjustable Rear Express Sight with a white stripe rear, or Pro Express Rear with a Vertical Tritium Bar, fits Bomar style cut, LPA style cut, or a Kimber Target cut rear sight. Affords same Express Sight principles as fixed sight models. From AO Sight Systems (formerly Ashley Outdoors).

Prices:
Adjustable Express w/White Stripe Rear and
   Big Dot Front or Standard Dot Front $90.00
Adjustable Express w/White Stripe Rear and
   Big Dot Tritium or Standard Dot Tritium Front . . . 150.00
Adjustable Pro Express w/Tritium Rear and Big
   Dot Tritium or Standard Dot Tritium Front 150.00

AO SIGHT SYSTEMS

Sights And Accessories

ASHLEY EXPRESS SIGHT SYSTEM

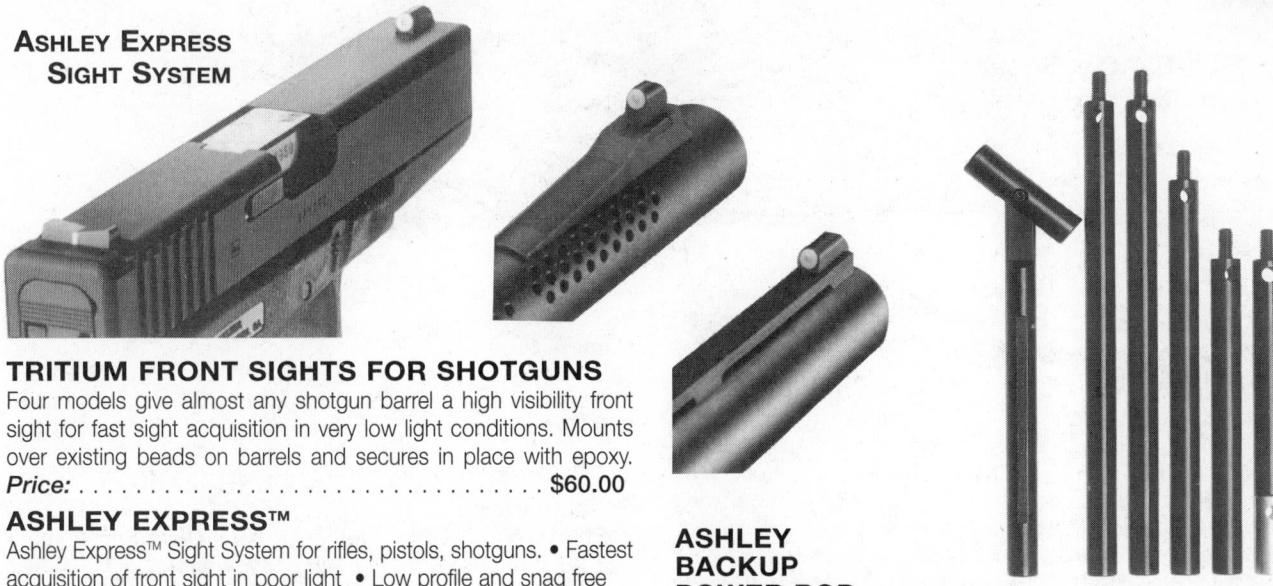

TRITIUM FRONT SIGHTS FOR SHOTGUNS
Four models give almost any shotgun barrel a high visibility front sight for fast sight acquisition in very low light conditions. Mounts over existing beads on barrels and secures in place with epoxy.
Price: $60.00

ASHLEY EXPRESS™
Ashley Express™ Sight System for rifles, pistols, shotguns. • Fastest acquisition of front sight in poor light • Low profile and snag free
Price: Ashley Big Dot Tritium Sight set $90.00

LEVER SCOPE MOUNTS
8" long Weaver-style rail, drop-in installation, for Marlin Lever actions.
Price: $50.00

ASHLEY BACKUP POWER ROD FOR MUZZLELOADERS
Price: $30.00

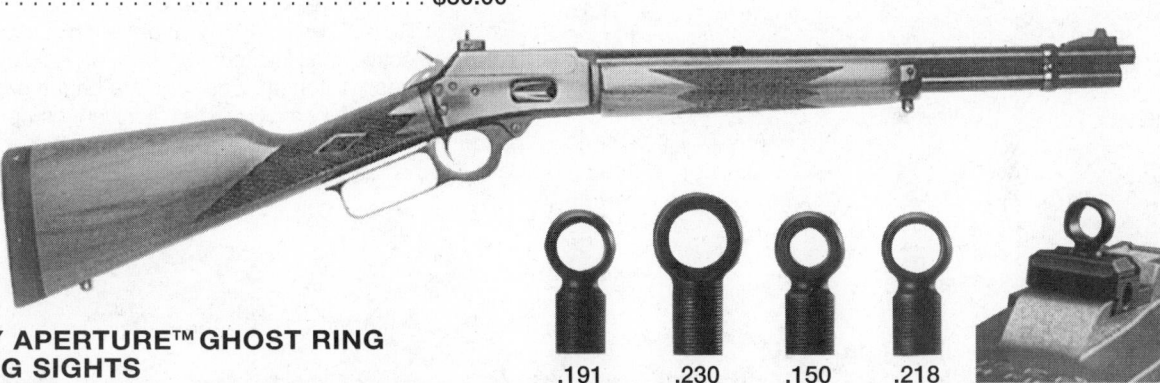

ASHLEY APERTURE™ GHOST RING HUNTING SIGHTS
• Fully adjustable for windage and elevation • Available for most rifles including blackpowder • Minimum gunsmithing for most installations; matches most existing mounting holes • Compact design, CNC machined from steel and heat treated • Perfect for low light conditions and offers minimal target obstruction
Price: Ashley Aperture Ghost Ring Hunting Sight Set . . . $90.00
Available for most rifles including blackpowder

.191   .230   .150   .218

GHOST RING SIGHTS FOR RIFLES AND CARBINES
Price: rear. $60.00
front 30.00

ASHLEY UTILITY SCOUT RIFLE KIT FOR MAUSER 98 & OTHERS
Price: $325.00

Big Cat Scope BC 4.5-14x52

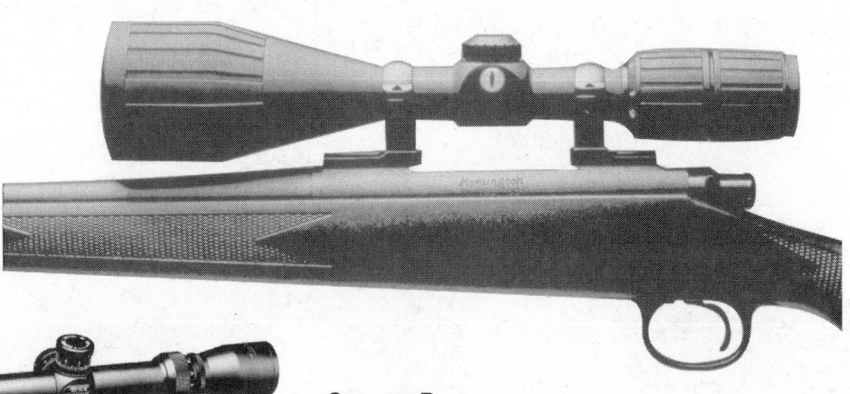

6-24x50

The BSA name once reserved for superior rifles and motorcycles is now appearing on rifle scopes. The Catseye line, with multi-coated objective and ocular lenses and a European-style reticle for shooting in dim light, includes two new looks for 2001. The PowerBright has the features of a BSA Catseye plus a PowerBright reticle that lights up bright red against dark backgrounds. The Big Cat has all the features wanted in a hunting scope: long eye relief, fully multicoated, very bright three piece objective lens.

Prices: CATSEYE

1.5-4x32	$91.95
3-10x44	151.95
3.5-10x50	171.95
4-16x50 AO	191.95
6-24x50 AO	222.95

BIGCAT

2-7x42	$189.95
3.5-10x42	219.95
4.5-14x52 AO	249.95
1.5-4.5x42	219.95
3-9x42	249.95
3.5-10x42	269.95

CATSEYE PLUS

1.5-4.5x32	$121.95
3-10x44	171.95
3.5-10x50	191.95

BSA CATSEYE CE 6-24X50

SPECIFICATIONS
Magnification: 6x-24x *Objective Lens Diameter:* 50mm
Exit Pupil Range: 8.3-2.0 *Field of View at 100 yd:* 16'-3'
Optimum Eye Relief: 4.5" *Length/Weight:* 16"/23 oz.
Price: $222.95

BIG CAT SCOPE BC 4.5-14X52

The Big Cat is an all new scope design. A longer eye relief. Finger adjustable windage and elevation knobs. A three piece objective lens system for sharper resolution, better color, and less distortion. And for extra brightness, the lenses are 14-layer, fully multi-coated. It is very compact and finished in Shadow Black. There are six BigCat models, 3 with large 30mm tubes.

BIG WHEEL SCOPE

BSA PLATINUM TARGET SCOPES

BSA Platinum target scopes are fitted with finger-adjustable windage and elevation dials that move point of impact in 1/8-minute clicks. New for 2001 are BSA's Big Wheel. The Big Wheel is for long distance shooting where parallax adjustments are extremely critical. It has a convenient sidewheel for extra-sensitive focusing. Actually the side wheel is two wheels in one. The larger outer wheel is best for off-hand or prone shooting, and the smaller wheel for benchrest. You just snap off the outer wheel to use the smaller focusing wheel. These new scopes are more compact than older models and have three-piece objective lens systems for sharper resolution, better color and less distortion.

SPECIFICATIONS
For PT 6.5-26x52 • *Magnification:* 6.5x-26x *Objective lens Diameter:* 52mm *F.O.V. @ 100 yds:* 15'-3.5' *Eye Relief:* 4" *Weight:* 30 oz. *Tube:* 1"

Prices: PT 6-24x44 AO $221.95

PT 8-32x44 AO	241.95
PT 6.5-26x42 AO	299.95
PT 8.5-34x42 AO	329.95
PT 6.5-26x52 AO	329.95
PT 8.5-34x52 AO	399.95

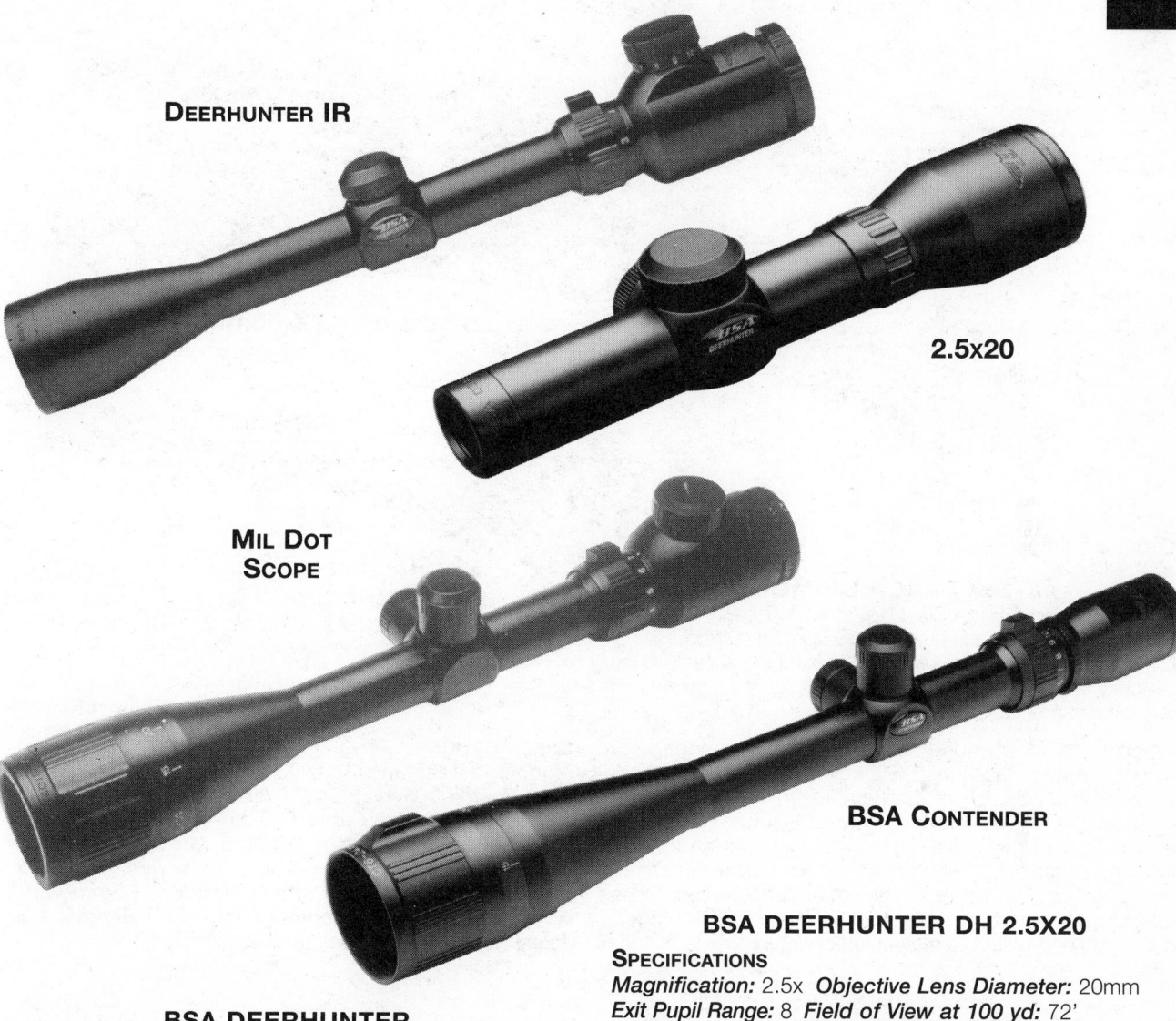

DEERHUNTER IR

2.5x20

MIL DOT SCOPE

BSA CONTENDER

BSA DEERHUNTER 3-9X40 ILLUMINATED RETICLE

SPECIFICATIONS
Magnification: 3x-9x *Objective Lens Diameter:* 40mm
Exit Pupil Range: 13.3-4.4 *Field of View at 100 yd:* 26'
Eye Relief: 4.5" *Weight:* 13 oz.
Price: $129.95

BSA Deer Hunter scopes, from a 2.5x20 (shown) to a 3-9x50 offer value for the big game hunter on a budget.
Prices: from . . . . $59.95 to 129.95

NEW: MIL DOT SCOPE AVAILABLE

Prices: MD 4-16x40 . . . . $149.95
MD 4-16x40 illuminated reticle 179.95
MD 6-24x40 illuminated reticle 199.95

BSA DEERHUNTER DH 2.5X20

SPECIFICATIONS
Magnification: 2.5x *Objective Lens Diameter:* 20mm
Exit Pupil Range: 8 *Field of View at 100 yd:* 72'
Optimum Eye Relief: 6" *Length/Weight:* 7.5"/7.5 oz.
Price: $59.95

BSA CONTENDER CT 6-24X40 TS

SPECIFICATIONS
Magnification: 6x-24x *Objective Lens Diameter:* 40mm
Exit Pupil Range: 6.7-1.7 *Field of View at 100 yd:* 16'-4'
Optimum Eye Relief: 3" *Length/Weight:* 15.5"/20 oz.
Price: $149.95
Also Available: 3-12x40 . . . . 212.95
4-16x40 . . . . 131.95
8-32x40 . . . . 171.95
3-12x50 . . . . 131.95
4-16x50 . . . . 151.95
6-24x50 . . . . 171.95
8-32x50 . . . . 191.95

BURRIS SCOPES

Black Diamond Riflescopes

BURRIS DUAL-BIAS SPRING

BURRIS POSI-LOCK

MODEL 3X-12X-50mm

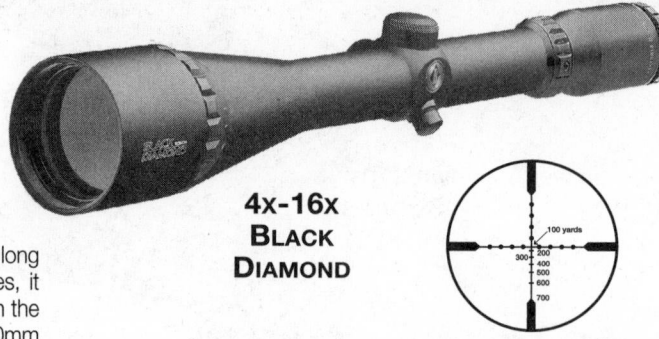

4x-16x BLACK DIAMOND

BALLISTIC MIL-DOT

4X-16X BLACK DIAMOND

New for 2002 is the 4x-16x Burris Black Diamond. Designed for long range big game rifles and dual-purpose big game/varmint rifles, it has a 50mm objective and Burris' best optics. It is available with the trajectory compensating Ballistic Mil-Dot reticle. The heavy 30mm tube is notable for its ruggedness.

Burris's Black Diamond line includes five models of a 30mm main tube 3-12X50mm with various finishes, reticles, and adjustment knobs. These riflescopes have easy-to-grip rubber-armored parallax-adjust rings, an adjustable and resettable adjustment dial, and an internal focusing eyepiece. Other features include fully multi-coated lens surfaces, 110 inches of internal adjustment, four times magnification range, and 3.5" to 4" of eye relief. Alll models come in a non-reflective matte black finish.

SPECIFICATIONS
Models: 3-12X50mm/4-16x50/6-24x50/8-32x50 *Field of View (feet @ 100yds.):* 34'-12'/18-6 *Optimum eye relief:* 3.5"-4.0"/3.5-4 *Exit Pupil:* 13.7mm-4.2mm/7.6-2.1 *Click adjust value (@ 100 yds.):* .25"/.125 *Max. internal adj. (@ 100 yds.):* 100"/52 *Clear objective diameter:* 50mm/50mm *Ocular end diameter:* 42mm/42mm *Weight:* 25 oz./25 oz. *Length:* 13.8"/16.2" *Reticles available:* Plex, Mil-Dot, Ballistic MDot, and Fine Plex

1X XER SCOUT

2.75X SCOUT

BURRIS SPEEDDOT 135

SCOUT SCOPES

...for hunters who need a 7- to 14-inch eye relief for mounting in front of the ejection port, allows you to shoot with both eyes open. The 15-foot field of view and 2.75X magnification are ideal for brush guns and shotgunners. Rugged, reliable and fog proof.

BURRIS SPEEDDOT 135

1x35mm pistol and shotgun sight. Electronic red dot reticle, 3 moa or 11 moa

2.5X-10X TITANIUM GRAY

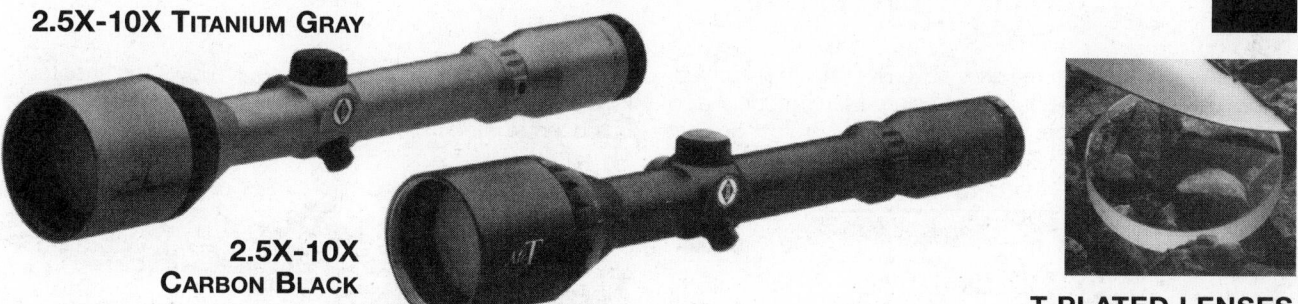

2.5X-10X CARBON BLACK

BURRIS "MR T"
• TITANIUM BLACK • DIAMOND SCOPES

Substantially stronger than aluminum, and much lighter than steel, Mr. T is one scope worthy of the description 'tough'. Beyond the whole scope tube and eyepiece being made of solid titanium, each scope is coated with a nitride harder than carbide or hard chrome—such as titanium nitride, aluminum titanium nitride, or chrome nitride, depending on the color. These nitrides are molecularly bonded to the titanium through high intensity physical vapor deposition for maximum adhesion that will not blister, flake, or chip. The result is an ultra-hard (up to 85 Rockwell C), abrasion resistant surface. *Also available* in Autumn Gold.

T-PLATED LENSES

The toughness of this scope doesn't end with the metal work. The scratch-proof T-Plate coating applied to the objective and eyepiece lenses is remarkable. These lenses do not come with the warning of other "scratch-resistant" coatings about removing all dust before cleaning. T-plated lenses do not require a "soft clean lens cloth". Just knock the mud off the lens and wipe it clean with a dirty shirt tail. Ordinary dirt, dust, and grit won't touch it. This coating technology is prohibitively expensive for ordinary scopes. Mr. T is a premium - quality sight for discriminating hunters.

SIGHTS & SCOPES

4.5X-14X

1.75X-5X

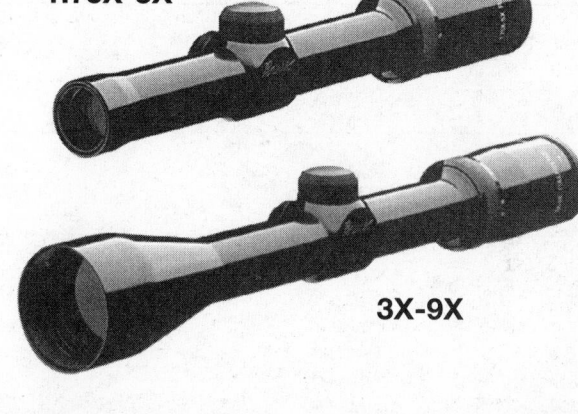

3X-9X

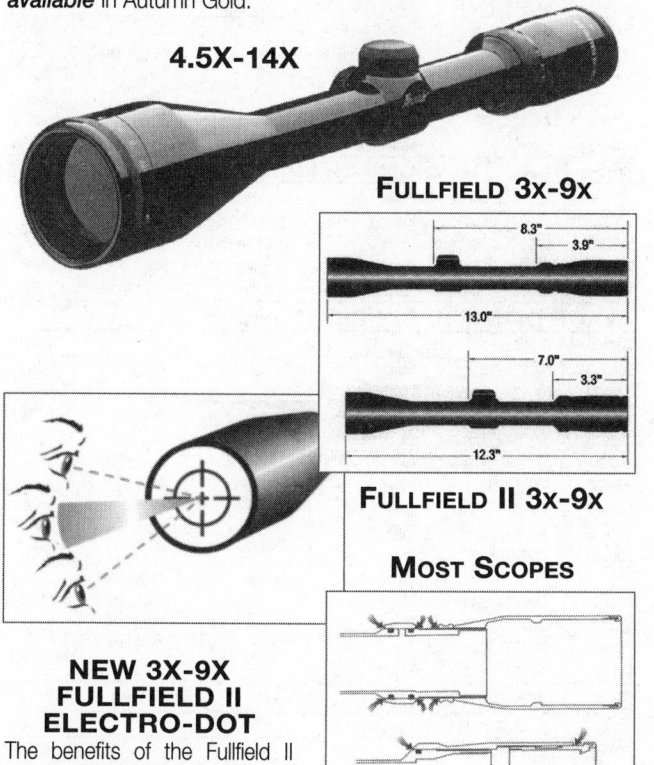

FULLFIELD 3x-9x

8.3" 3.9"
13.0"
7.0" 3.3"
12.3"

FULLFIELD II 3x-9x

MOST SCOPES

FULLFIELD II 3x-9x

NEW 3X-9X FULLFIELD II ELECTRO-DOT

The benefits of the Fullfield II design in a lighter, more compact, package now has the low light capabilities of the Electro-Dot. A simple turn of the rotary switch pin-point-lights the center of the crosshair.

BURRIS FULLFIELD II VARIABLE SCOPES

The Fullfield II is now much more forgiving for eye positioning both fore and aft, and left and right. Burris has shaved roughly four ounces of weight on each model without effecting durability or optical performance. In fact, several areas are even stronger and more precisely fitted than before. Overall, the Fullfield is about one inch shorter than its predecessor for a more compact look and feel. Like the Fullfield, and unlike other scopes, Fullfield II eyepieces are sealed with special quad seals rather than old-tech O-rings. And the eyepiece is now part of the power ring. To change magnification, simply turn the entire eyepiece. A European-style adjustable eyepiece is easy to use and requires no locking mechanism. Relocation of the turret on Fullfield II scopes, combined with a shorter eyepiece, allows more room for scope rings.
Also available: 3.5-10x50 and 6.5-20x50

BURRIS SCOPES

Signature Series

All models in the Signature Series have **HI-LUME** (multi-coated) lenses for maximum light transmission. Many models also feature **POSI-LOCK** to prevent recoil shift and protect against loss of zero from rough hunting use. It allows the shooter to lock the internal optics of the scope in position after the rifle has been sighted in.

8X-32X SIGNATURE

MR. T 2.5X-10X TITANIUM GRAY

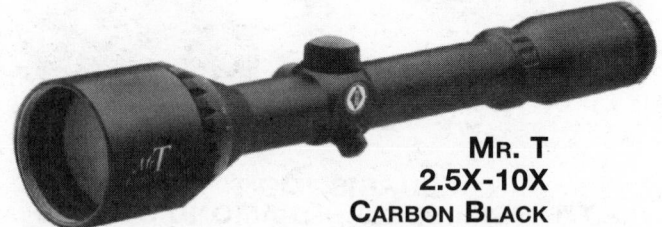

MR. T 2.5X-10X CARBON BLACK

SIGNATURE SERIES SCOPES

Item	Model	Reticle	Finish	Features	List
200510	6X	Plex	blk		$442
200511	6X	Plex	mat		462
200700	1.5X-6X	Plex	blk		518
200701	1.5X-6X	Plex	mat		538
200706	1.5X-6X	Plex	mat	Posi-Lock	588
200711	1.5X-6X	Electro-Dot	mat		647
200712	1.5X-6X	Electro-Dot	mat	Posi-Lock	697
200550	2X-8X	Plex	blk		580
200551	2X-8X	Plex	mat		600
200553	2X-8X	Plex	blk	Posi-Lock	629
200554	2X-8X	Plex	mat	Posi-Lock	648
200600	3X-9X	Plex	blk		611
200601	3X-9X	Plex	mat		631
200597	3X-9X	Plex	blk	Posi-Lock	660
200598	3X-9X	Plexmat		Posi-Lock	680
200580	3X-9X	Electro-Dot	blk		721
200581	3X-9X	Electro-Dot	mat		741
200590	3X-9X	Electro-Dot	blk	Posi-Lock	771
200591	3X-9X	Electro-Dot	mat	Posi-Lock	791
200574	3X-9X-50mm	Plex	blk		645
200607	2.5X-10X	Plex	blk	PA	647
200608	2.5X-10X	Plex	mat	PA	665
200631	2.5X-10X	Plex	mat	Posi-Lock/PA	728
200633	2.5X-10X	Plex	nic	Posi-Lock/PA	738
200610	3X-12X	Plex	blk	PA	705
200611	3X-12X	Plex	mat	PA	723
200614	3X-12X	Plex	blk	Posi-Lock/PA	755
200615	3X-12X	Plex	mat	Posi-Lock/PA	774
200750	4X-16X	Plex	blk	PA	738
200751	4X-16X	Plex	mat	PA	757
200763	4X-16X	Fine Plex	mat	Target/PA	795
200767	4X-16X	Ballistic MDot	mat	PA	887
200756	4X-16X	Plex	mat	Posi-Lock/PA	810
200765	4X-16X	Electro-Dot	mat	PA	861
200766	4X-16X	Electro-Dot	mat	Posi-Lock/PA	914
200800	6X-24X	Plex	blk	PA	757
200804	6X-24X	Plex	mat	PA	776

Item	Model	Reticle	Finish	Features	List
200803	6X-24X	Fine Plex	blk	Target/PA	$795
200806	6X-24X	Fine Plex	mat	Target/PA	814
200811	6X-24X	Fine Plex	nic	Target/PA	823
200816	6X-24X	Ballistic MDot	mat	Target/PA	947
200815	6X-24X	1"-.25" Dot	mat	Target/PA	852
200812	6X-24X	Plex	blk	Posi-Lock/PA	812
200813	6X-24X	Plex	mat	Posi-Lock/PA	831
200821	6X-24X	Electro-Dot	mat	PA	880
200850	8X-32X	Fine Plex	blk	Target/PA	814
200860	8X-32X	Fine Plex	mat	Target/PA	833
200866	8X-32X	Fine Plex	nic	Target/PA	842
200854	8X-32X	Mil-Dot	mat	Target/PA	965
200861	8X-32X	Ballistic MDot	mat	Target/PA	965
200855	8X-32X	Fine Plex	blk	Posi-Lock/PA	871

Mr. T BLACK DIAMOND TITANIUM SCOPES (30mm)

Item	Model	Reticle	Finish	Features	List
200920	2.5X-10X-50mm	Plex	titanium gray		$2129
200921	2.5X-10X-50mm	Plex	carbon black		2129
200922	2.5X-10X-50mm	Mil-Dot	carbon black	Target	2272
200923	2.5X-10X-50mm	Plex	carbon black	Posi-Lock	2191
200924	2.5X-10X-50mm	Plex	autumn gold		2129

BLACK DIAMOND SCOPES (30mm)

Item	Model	Reticle	Finish	Features	List
200906	6X-50mm	Plex	mat		$745
200900	3X-12X-50mm	Plex	mat	PA	960
200901	3X-12X-50mm	Plex	mat	Posi-Lock/PA	1,031
200904	3X-12X-50mm	Mil-Dot	mat	Posi-Lock/PA	1,139
200910	3X-12X-50mm	Plex	mat	Target/PA	1001
200911	3X-12X-50mm	Mil-Dot	mat	Target/PA	1123
200950	4X-16X-50mm	Plex	mat	PA	933
200951	4X-16X-50mm	Ballistic Dot	mat	PA	1084
200952	4X-16X-50mm	Plex	mat	Posi-Lock/PA	1000
200953	4X-16X-50mm	Ballistic Dot	mat	Posi-Lock/PA	1155
200930	6X-24X-50mm	Fine Plex	mat	Target/PA	1,041
200931	6X-24X-50mm	Mil-Dot	mat	Target/PA	1,202
200932	6X-24X-50mm	Ballistic MDot	mat	Target/PA	1,202
200940	8X-32X-50mm	Fine Plex	mat	Target/PA	1,091
200941	8X-32X-50mm	Ballistic MDot	mat	Target/PA	1,272

ELECTRO-DOT SCOPES

Item	Model	Reticle	Finish	Features	List
200167	3X-9X Fullfield II	Electro-Dot	mat		$506
200711	1.5X-6X Signature	Electro-Dot	mat		647
200712	1.5X-6X Signature	Electro-Dot	mat	Posi-Lock	697
200581	3X-9X Signature	Electro-Dot	mat		741
200590	3X-9X Signature	Electro-Dot	blk	Posi-Lock	771
200591	3X-9X Signature	Electro-Dot	mat	Posi-Lock	791
200765	4X-16X Signature	Electro-Dot	mat	PA	861
200766	4X-16X Signature	Electro-Dot	mat	Posi-Lock/PA	914
200821	6X-24X Signature	Electro-Dot	mat	PA	880

FULLFIELD SCOPES
FIXED POWER WITH HI-LUME LENSES

3X-9X GLOSS ELECTRO-DOT

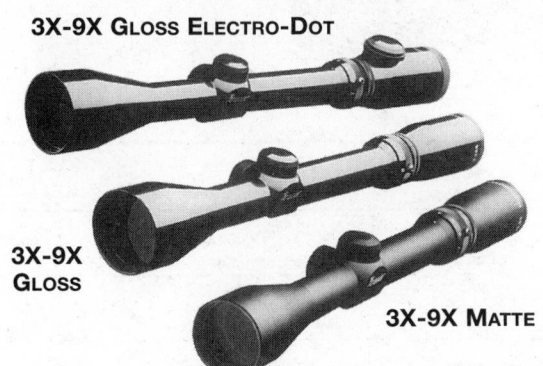

3X-9X GLOSS

3X-9X MATTE

2.5X SHOTGUN SCOPE

FULLFIELD II SCOPES

ITEM	MODEL	RETICLE	FINISH	FEATURES	LIST
200086	1.75-5X	Plex	blk		$392
200087	1.75-5X	Plex	mat		412
200160	3X-9X-40mm	Plex	blk		392
200161	3X-9X-40mm	Plex	mat		392
200162	3X-9X-40mm	Ballistic Plex	mat		401
200163	3X-9X-40mm	Plex	nic		422
200167	3X-9X-40mm	Electro-Dot	mat		506
200170	3.5X-10X-50mm	Plex	blk		531
200171	3.5X-10X-50mm	Plex	mat		550
200172	3.5X-10X-50mm	Ballistic Plex	mat		559
200180	4.5X-14X	Plex	blk	PA	572
200181	4.5X-14X	Plex	mat	PA	572
200182	4.5X-14X	Fine Plex	mat	PA	591
200183	4.5X-14X-42mm	Ballistic Plex	mat	PA	591
200190	6.5X-20X-50mm	Fine Plex	blk	PA	644
200191	6.5X-20X-50mm	Fine Plex	mat	PA	661
200192	6.5X-20X-50mm	Fine Plex	mat	Target/PA	701
200193	6.5X-20X-50mm	Ballistic MDot	mat	PA	792

FULLFIELD SCOPES

ITEM	MODEL	RETICLE	FINISH	FEATURES	LIST
200413	2.5X shotgun	Plex	mat		$308
200010	4X	Plex	blk		329
200014	4X	Plex	mat		348
200050	6X	Plex	blk		360
200054	6X	Plex	mat		379
200020	2X-7X	Plex	blk		399
200024	2X-7X	Plex	mat		418
200150	3X-9X-50mm	Plex	blk		436
200151	3X-9X-50mm	Plex	mat		454
200103	6X-18X	Fine Plex	blk	PA	543
200109	6X-18X	Fine Plex	mat	PA	562
200104	6X-18X	Fine Plex	blk	Target/PA	580
200108	6X-18X	Peep Plex	mat	PA	580

COMPACT SCOPES

ITEM	MODEL	RETICLE	FINISH	FEATURES	LIST
200424	1X XER	Plex	mat		$319
200432	1X-4X XER	Plex	mat		396
200310	4X	Plex	blk		298
200311	4X	Plex	mat		319
200350	6X	Plex	blk		317

ITEM	MODEL	RETICLE	FINISH	FEATURES	LIST
200352	6X	Plex	blk	PA	359
200356	6X Magnum	Plex	mat	PA	416
200357	6X HBR	Fine Plex	blk	Target/PA	487
200358	6X HBR	.375" Dot	blk	Target/PA	528
200375	2X-7X	Plex	blk		404
200376	2X-7X	Plex	mat		424
200378	2X-7X	Plex	nic		434
200385	3X-9X	Plex	blk		414
200387	3X-9X	Plex	mat		434
200388	3X-9X	Plex	nic		445
200384	3X-9X	Plex	mat	PA	443
200383	3X-9X	Plex	nic	PA	453
200390	4X-12X	Plex	blk	PA	520
200395	4X-12X	Plex	mat	PA	527
200393	4X-12X	Fine Plex	blk	Target/PA	559
200394	4X-12X	Fine Plex	mat	Target/PA	578

RIMFIRE/AIRGUN SCOPES

ITEM	MODEL	RETICLE	FINISH	FEATURES	LIST
200313	4X	Plex	blk	PA	$341
200352	6X	Plex	blk	PA	359
200384	3X-9X	Plex	mat	PA	443
200383	3X-9X	Plex	nic	PA	453
200390	4X-12X	Plex	blk	PA	520
200395	4X-12X	Plex	mat	PA	527
200393	4X-12X	Fine Plex	blk	Target/PA	559
200394	4X-12X	Fine Plex	mat	Target/PA	578
200858	8X-32X	Plex	blk	Target/PA	835
200859	8X-32X	Fine Plex	mat	Target/PA	854

HANDGUN SCOPES

ITEM	MODEL	RETICLE	FINISH	FEATURES	LIST
200424	1X XER	Plex	mat		$319
200220	2X	Plex	blk		281
200218	2X	Plex	mat		275
200229	2X	Plex	nic		301
200222	2X	Plex	blk	Posi-Lock	320
200228	2X	Plex	mat	Posi-Lock	330
200227	2X	Plex	nic	Posi-Lock	340
200235	4X	Plex	blk		333
200237	4X	Plex	nic		354
200263	10X Target/PA	Plex	blk	Target	507
200210	1.5X-4X	Plex	blk		385
200214	1.5X-4X	Plex	nic		404
200208	1.5X-4X	Plex	blk	Posi-Lock	424
200207	1.5X-4X	Plex	mat	Posi-Lock	442
200213	1.5X-4X	Plex	nic	Posi-Lock	443
200290	2X-7X	Plex	blk		451
200291	2X-7X	Plex	mat		461
200293	2X-7X	Plex	blk	PA	499
200298	2X-7X	Plex	nic		472
200294	2X-7X	Plex	blk	Posi-Lock	492
200297	2X-7X	Plex	nic	Posi-Lock	513
200288	3X-9X	Plex	blk	Posi-Lock/PA	540
200306	3X-12X	Plex	blk	PA	550
200307	3X-12X	Plex	mat	PA	560
200308	3X-12X	Plex	blk	PA	569
200305	3X-12X	Fine Plex	blk	Target/PA	561
200303	3X-12X	Plex	mat	Posi-Lock	599

SPEEDDOT 135 SIGHTS

ITEM	MODEL	RETICLE	FINISH	FEATURES	LIST
300200	1X-35mm	3 MOA Dot	mat		$291
300201	1X-35mm	11 MOA Dot	mat		291

SCOUT SCOPES

ITEM	MODEL	RETICLE	FINISH	FEATURES	LIST
200424	1X XER	Plex	mat		$319
200269	2.75X	Heavy Plex	mat		342

SIGHTS & SCOPES

BUSHNELL RIFLESCOPES

ELITE 3200 — 5X-15X

ELITE™ 3200 RIFLESCOPES WITH RAINGUARD™

Model	Special Feature	Actual Magni-fication	Obj. Lens Aperature (mm)	Field of View @ 100yds (ft.)	Weight (oz)	Length	Eye Relief (in.)	Exit Pupil (mm)	Click Value @ 100yds (in.)	Adjust Range @ 100yds (in.)	Selection	Suggested Retail
32-2632M	Handgun (30-2632S Silver Finish)	2x-6x	32	10-4	10	9	20	16-5.3	.25	50	Constant 20" eye relief At all powers w/max. recoil resistance	$444.95
32-2732M	Matte Finish	2x-7x	32	44.6-12.7	12	11.6	3	12.2-4.6	.25	50	Compact variable for close-in brush ormed. range shooting. Excellent for shotguns	$342.95
32-3940G	(32-3940M Matte Finish, 32-3940S Silver Finish)	3x-9x	40	33.8-11.5	13	12.6	3	13.3-4.4	.25	50	For the full range of hunting. From varmint to big game. Tops in versatility.	$351.95
32-3943	Matte, 3-2-1 low light reticle	3x-9x	40	33.8-11.5	13	12.6	3	13.3-4.4	.25	50	All types of hunting	$351.95
32-3950G	(32-3950M Matte Finish)	3x-9x	50	31.5-10-5	19	15.7	3	16-5.6	.25	50	All purpose variable with extra brightness.	$428.95
32-3955E	European Reticle Matte Finish	3x-9x	50	31.5-10.5	22	15.6	3	16-5.6	.36	70	Large exit pupil and 30mm tube for max. brightness.	$640.95
32-3953	Matte, 3-2-1 low light reticle	3x-9x	50	31.5-10.5	19	15.7	3	16-5.6	.25	50	All purpose, extra bright	$428.95
32-4124A	Adjustable Objective	4x-12x	40	26.9-9	15	13.2	3	10-3.33	.25	50	Medium to long-range variable makes a superb choice for varmint or big game	$469.95
32-5154M	Matte adj. objective sunshade	5x-15x	40	21-7	19	14.5	4-3.5	9-2.7	.25	50	Long range, big game	$501.95
32-5155M	Adjustable Objective	5x-15x	50	21-7	24	15.9	3	10-3.3	.25	40	Large objective for brightness	$528.95

ELITE 4200 — 2.5-10X40

ELITE 4200

ELITE™ 4200 RIFLESCOPES WITH RAINGUARD™

Model	Special Feature	Actual Magni-fication	Obj. Lens Aperature (mm)	Field of View @ 100yds (ft.)	Weight (oz)	Length	Eye Relief (in.)	Exit Pupil (mm)	Click Value @ 100yds (in.)	Adjust Range @ 100yds (in.)	Selection	Suggested Retail
42-1636M	Matte Finish	1.5x-6x	36	61.8-16.1	15.4	12.8	3	14.6-6	.25	60	Compact wide angle for close-in & brush hunting. Max. brightness. Execel. for shotguns	$608.95
42-2104G	(40-2104M Matte Finish, 40-2104S Silver Finish)	2.5x-10x	40	41.5-10.8	16	13.5	3	15.6-4	.25	50	All purpose hunting scope w/4x zoom range for close-in brush & long range shooting	$642.95
42-2105M	Matte Finish	2.5x-10x	50	40-10.8	18	14.3	3.5	15-2.5	.25	50	Ideal hunting and all purpose	$763.95
42-3640A	Adjustable Objective	36x	40	3	17.6	15	3.2	1.1	.125	30	Ideal benchrest scope.	$955.95
42-4165M	Matte Finish	4x-16x	50	26-7.2	22	15.6	3	12.5-3.1	.25	50	The ultimate varmint, airgun and precision shooting scope. Parallax focus from 10 meter to infinity.	$834.95
42-6244A	Adjustable Objective, Sunshade (42-6244M Matte Finish)	6x-24x	40	18-4.5	20.2	16.9	3	6.7-1.7	.125	26	Varmint, target & silhouette long range shooting and airgun. Parallax focus adjust. for pinpoint accuracy. Parallax focus from 10 meter to infinity.	$729.95
42-6243A	Adjustable Objective and 1/4" MOA dot reticle	6-24x	40	18-4.5	20.2	16.9	3	6.7-1.7	.125	26	Varmint, target and silhouette long range shooting and airgun. Parallax focus adjust for pinpoint accuracy. Parallax focus from 10 meter to infinity.	$729.95
42-6242M	Matte w/Mil Dot	6x-24x	40	18-6	20.2	16.9	3	6.7-1.7	.125	26	Long range varmint or target	$608.95
42-8324M	Matte finish, adj. objective sunshade	8x-32x	40	14-3.75	22	18	4-3.5	5-1.25	.125	20	Long range varmint, bench	$802.95

4-12x40MM

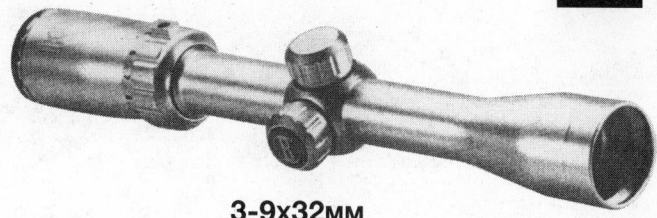

3-9x32MM

SPORTSMAN RIFLESCOPES

Introducing Sportsman Riflescopes with multi-coated optics. A long list of standard features include a fast-focus eyepiece for superior clarity and 1/4 M.O.A. fingertip windage and elevation adjustments. The easy-grip power change ring makes chang-ing magnifications fast and easy. The rigid one-piece 1" tube is waterproof, fogproof and shockproof.

3-9x32MM: *Gloss*, 72-1393; *Silver*, 72-1393S; *Matte*, 72-1398
4-12x40MM: *Gloss*, 72-0412

BUSHNELL SPORTVIEW® RIFLESCOPES

Model	Finish	Features/Selection	Actual Magnification	Obj. Lens Aperture (mm)	Field of View Ft@100 yds	Weight (oz)	Length (in)	Eye Relief (in)	Exit Pupil (mm)	Click Value In@100yds	Adj. Range In@100yds	Price
72-0004	G	Adjustable Objective. Rings. General Purpose for Air Rifle and Rimfire Range Focus and Target Adjustments. 10yd-Infinity.	4x	32	29.5	13.7	11.9	3	8	.25	90	$98.95
72-0039	G	Adjustable Objective. Rings. Air Rifle, Rimfire with Range Focus Adjustments 10yd-Infinity.	3x-9x	32	13.1	163	12.2	3	3.6-11	.25	100	116.95
72-0130	M	Red Dot Sight. 6 M.O.A. Dot. Ideal for Hand-gun, Shotgun and Competitive Shooting.	1x	23	60	4.9	5.5	Unlimited	2.3@1x	.5	50	84.95
720-412	G	Adjustable Objective. Long Range.	4x-12x	40	8.5 25.8	14.6	13.75	3	10-3.3	.25	90	141.95
72-1393 72-1393S 72-1398	G S M	All-Purpose Variable	3x-9x	32	14 41	13.5	12	3	10-3.6	.25	100	68.95
72-1403	M	General Purpose	4x	32	29	11	11.7	3	8	.25	110	57.95
72-1416	G	3/4"Tube with Rings. Airgun/ .22 Scope. Coated Optics	4x	15	17	3.6	10.7	3.5	3.8	Friction	60	11.95
72-1545	M	Shotgun/Muzzle Loader. Low Power Variable Ideal for Close-In or Medium-Range Shooting.	1.5x-4.5x	21	24 69	11.7	10.1	3	10-3.6	.25	210	86.95
72-1548	M	Circle-X Reticle. Turkey Hunting Shotgun Slugs and Muzzle Loading.	1.5x-4.5x	32	19.3 46.2	13.5	11.7	3	7.1-123	.25	100	104.95
72-3720	G	3/4" Tube with Rings. Airgun/ .22 Scope. Coated Optics	3x-7x	20	11 23	5.7	11.3	2.6	6.7-2.9	Friction	50	36.95
72-3940 72-3940M	G M	Excellent for Use at Any Range.	3x-9x	40	12 37	15	13	3.5	13-4.4	.25	100	95.95
72-3943	M	3-2-1 Low-Light Reticle. Improved Crosshair Visibility for Low-Light Shooting.	3x-9x	40	12 37	15	13	3.5	13-4.4	.25	100	95.95
72-3960	M	Extra-Large Objective for Enhanced	3x-9x	60	13 37	20	13.3	3	13-6.7	.25	90	271.95

BUSHNELL RIFLESCOPES

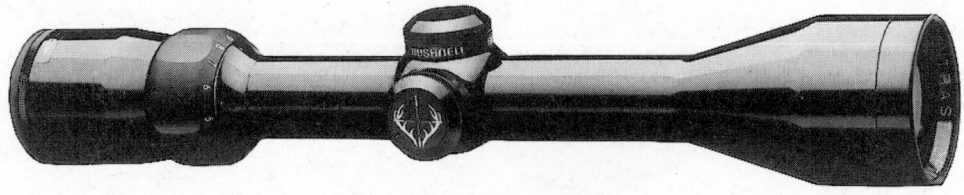

3X-9X (40MM) TROPHY®
WIDE ANGLE RIFLESCOPE

BUSHNELL TROPHY® RIFLESCOPES

Model	Special Feature	Actual Magnification	Obj. Lens Aperature (mm)	Field of View @ 100yds (ft.)	Weight (oz)	Length	Eye Relief (in.)	Exit Pupil (mm)	Click Value @ 100yds (in.)	Adjust Range @ 100yds (in.)	Selection	Suggested Retail
73-0131	Red Dot Sight G.M.O.A. Dot	1x	28	68	6	5.5	-	28	.5	50	Ideal for handgun, shotgun, competitive	$102.95
73-1500	Wide Angle	1.75x-5x	32	68-23	12.3	10.8	3.5	18.3-1.75x	.25	120	Shotgun, black powder or centerfire. Close-in brush hunting.	$177.95
73-3940	Wide angle (73-3940S Silver)	3x-9x	40	42/14-14/5	13.2	11.7	3	13.3-4.44	.25	60	All purpose variable, excellent for use from close to long range. Circular view provides a definite advantage over "TV screen" type scopes for running game-uphill or down.	$159.95
73-3942	Long mounting length designed for long-action rifles	3x-9x	42	42-14	13.8	12	3	14-4.7	.25	40	7" mounting length.	$164.95
73-3949	Wide angle with Circle-x™ Reticle	3x-9x	40	42-14	13.2	11.7	3	13.3-4.4	.25	60	Matte finish, Ideal low light reticle.	$170.95
73-3948	Matte finish Wide Angle	3x-9x	40	42-14	13.2	11.7	3	13.3-4.4	.25	60	Ideal for game running uphill or down	$159.95
73-4124	Wide angle, adjustable objective (73-4124M Matte)	4x-12x	40	32-11	16.1	12.6	3	10-3.3	.25	60	Medium to long range variable for varmint and big game. Range focus adjustment. Excellent air riflescope.	$300.95
73-6184	Semi-turret target adjustments, adjustable objective	6x-18x	40	17.3-6	17.9	14.8	3	6.6-2.2	.125	40	Long-range varmint centerfire or short range air rifle target precision accuracy.	$378.95
TROPHY® HANDGUN SCOPES												
73-0232S	(73-0232S Silver)	2x	32	20	7.7	8.7	9	16	.25	90	Designed for target and short to med. range hunting. Magnum recoil resistant.	$218.95
73-2632	(73-2632S Silver)	2x-6x	32	11-4	10.9	9.1	18	16-5.3	.25	50	18 inches of eye relief at all powers	$287.95
TROPHY® SHOTGUN/HANDGUN SCOPES												
73-1421	Brush Scope/Turkey with Circle-x™ Reticle	1.75x-4x	32	73-30	10.9	10.8	3.5	18-8	.25	120	Ideal for turkey hunting, slug guns or blackpowder guns. Matte finish.	$171.95
TROPHY® AIR RIFLESCOPES												
73-4124	Wide angle, adjustable objective (73-4124M Matte)	4x-12x	40	32-11	16.1	12.6	3	10-3.3	.25	60	Medium to long range variable for varmint and big game. Range focus adjustment. Excellent air riflescope.	$300.95
73-6184	Semi-turret target adjustments, adjustable objective	6x-18x	40	17-6	17.9	14.8	3	6.6-2.2	.125	40	Long-range varmint centerfire or short range air rifle target precision accuracy.	$378.95

BUSHNELL®
HOLOSIGHT®

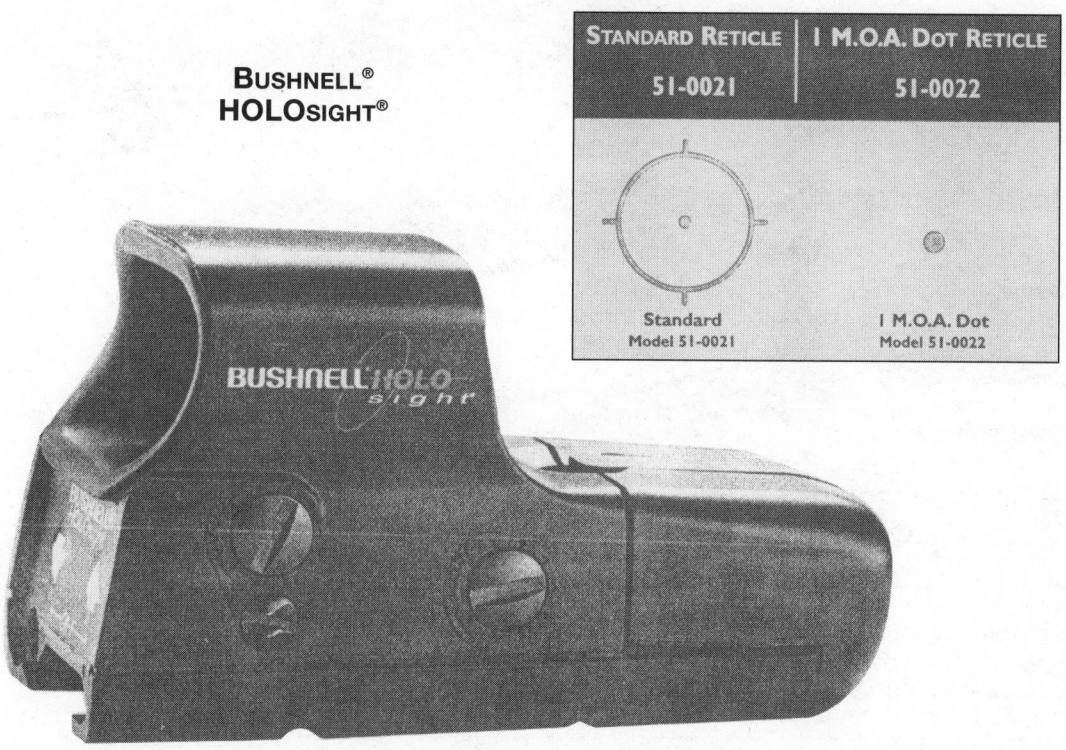

STANDARD RETICLE	1 M.O.A. DOT RETICLE
51-0021	51-0022

Standard
Model 51-0021

1 M.O.A. Dot
Model 51-0022

BUSHNELL® HOLOSIGHT®

The BUSHNELL® HOLOsight® delivers instant target acquisition, improved accuracy, and can be tailored to virtually any shooting discipline. How does it work? A hologram of a reticle pattern is recorded on a heads-up display window. When illuminated by laser (coherent) light, a holographic image becomes visible at the target plane - where it remains in focus with the target. Critical eye alignment is not required and multi-plane focusing error is eliminated. With the BUSHNELL® HOLOsight®, you simply look through the window, place the reticle image on the target and shoot. The use of holographic technology allows the creation of virtually any image as a reticle pattern, in either two or three dimensions. Shooters have the flexibility to design reticles in any geometric shape, size and in any dimension to enhance a specific shooting discipline. Since no light is cast on the target, use of the BUSHNELL® HOLOsight® is legal in most hunting, target and competition areas.

BUSHNELL HOLOSIGHT® SPECIFICATIONS

OPTICS	MAGNI- FICATION @ 100 YDS	FIELD OF VIEW FT @ 100 YDS	WEIGHT (OZ/G)	LENGTH (IN/MM)	EYE RELIEF (IN/MM)	BATTERIES	WINDAGE CLICK VALUE IN @100 YDS MM@ 100M	ELEVATION CLICK VALUE IN @100 YDS MM@ 100M	BRIGHTNESS ADJUSTMENT SETTINGS
Holographic	1x	Unlimited	6.4/181	4.125/104.8	1/2" to 10 ft. 13 to 3045 mm	2 Type N 1.5 Volt	.25 M.O.A./ 7mm @100m	.5 M.O.A./ 14mm@100m	20 levels

MODEL	RETICLE	DESCRIPTION	USES	
HOLOsight®				
50-0021	Standard	2-Dimensional 65 M.O.A. ring with one M.O.A. dot and tick marks.	General all-purpose handguns, rifles, slug guns, and wing shooting	$444.95
50-0122	Dot	1 M.O.A. Dot	Precision rifle, handgun, and slug gun shooting.	$444.95

BUSHNELL RIFLESCOPES

SCOPECHIEF

BANNER

70-4145A

SCOPECHIEF

Incredibly bright optics provide startlingly clear resolution. All lenses are fully multi-coated and feature an aspheric design for edge-to-edge clarity. A 3.5" long eye relief provides an extra magrin of comfort.

The wide field of view makes tracking game and moving targets easy. An all-weather, rotating power change eyepiece with fast focus makes changing mangnification effortless. Also features fingertip audible and resettable 1/4 M.O.A. click windage and elevation adjustments. Single-piece tube construction is fully waterproof, fogproof and shockproof.

BANNER

Banner Dusk & Dawn riflescopes feature DDB multi-coated lenses to maximize dusk and dawn brightness for clarity in low and full light. A fast-focus eyepiece and wide-angle field of veiw focus on and follow game easily. One-piece tube for durability under all conditions. Features 1/4" M.O.A. fingertip resettable windage and elevation adjustments. An easy-grip power change ring allows fast and easy zoom changes. Fully water-proof, fogproof and shockproof.

BUSHNELL SCOPECHIEF® RIFLESCOPES

Model	Special Feature	Actual Magni-fication	Obj. Lens Aperature (mm)	Field of View ft @ 100yds/m	Weight (oz/g)	Length (in/mm)	Eye Relief (in/mm)	Exit Pupil (mm)	Click Value in @ 100yds mm @ 100m	Adjust Range in @ 100yds m @ 100m	Selection	Suggested Retail
70-3104M	Matte Finish	3.5x-10x	42	43/14.3@3.5x 15/5.0@10x	17/482	13/330	3.5/89	12@3.5x 4.2@10x	.25/7	50/1.4	6 inch mounting length	$266.95
70-4145A	Matte Finish, Adj. Objective, Sunshade	4x-14x	50	31/103@4x 9/3.0@14x	23/652	14.1/358	3.5/89	12.5@4x 3.6@14x	.25/7	50/1.4	Higher magnification with longer objective for enhanced brightness at longer ranges.	$342.95

BUSHNELL BANNER RIFLESCOPES

Model	Special Feature											
71-0432	Shotgun/.22 scope Circle-x reticle, matte finish	4x	32	31.5	11.1	11.3	3.5	8	.25	50	Ideal for .22S/shotgun	$102.95
71-1432	Circle-x reticle Matte finish	1x-4x	32	78.5-24.9	12.2	10.5	3.8	16.9	.25	50	Ideal for .22S/shotgun	$123.95
71-1545	Wide Angle	1.5x-4.5x	32	67-23	10.5	10.5	3.5	17-7	.25	60	Ideal Shotgun and median to short range scope.	$116.95
71-3944	Black powder scope w/extended eye relief and Circle-x@ reticle	3x-9x	40	36-13	12.5	11.5	4	13-4.4	.25	60	Specifically designed for black powder and shotguns	$125.95
71-3948	Ideal scope for multi purpose guns	3x-9x	40	40-74	13	12	3	13.3-4.4	.25	60	General purpose.	$120.95
71-3950	Large objective for extra brightness in low light	3x-9x	50	31-10	19	16	3	16-5.6	.25	50	Low light conditions	$186.95
71-3951	Matte finish low light reticle	3x-9x	50	26-12	19	16	3.5	16-5.6	.25	50	Good for low-light	$186.95
71-4124	Adjustable objective	4x-12x	40	29-11	15	12	3	10-3.3	.25	60	Ideal scope for long-range shooting.	$157.95
71-6185	Adjustable objective	6x-18x	50	17-6	18	16	3	8.3-2.8	.25	40	Long range varmint and target scope.	$209.95

Docter Optic is a well-known name in European optics that has been marketed with varying success in the U.S. B.C. Outdoors of Boulder City, Nevada, is handling Docter Optic's expanded line of rifle scopes and binoculars. It includes these four models, designed expressly for the American shooter.

MAGNIFICATION X OBJ. DIA.	FIELD OF VIEW (FT., 100 YDS)	DIA./LENGTH (IN.)	WEIGHT (OZ.)	PRICE
3-9x40	31-13	1/12.5	17	$378.00
3-10x40	34-12	1/13	18.5	626.00
4.5-14x40	23-8	1/13.5	21.5	652.00
8-25x50	13-4	1/16	26.5	901.00

Some of Docter Optic 30mm scopes feature aspherical lenses, as do the company's binoculars. All Docter scopes offer these advantages:

RIFLE SCOPE SPECIFICATIONS

• *High strength, one-piece tube construction of aircraft-grade aluminum eliminates weak screw-together joints that can leak or break, won't rust or corrode in adverse weather.*
• *Precise click-stop adjustments of 1/4" at 100 yards for windage and elevation. Wide range of adjustment (50") makes it easier to compensate for mounting errors. Excellent repeatability.*
• *Advanced lens technology and high grade multi-coating provides unparalled light transmission and image resolution for crisp, clear sighting picture - especially advantageous during low light conditions at dawn and dusk when most animal movement occurs.*
• *Every DOCTER scope is subjected to stringent leak and shock testing before it leaves the factory.*
• *Every joint where a leak may possibly occur is sealed with statically and dynamically loaded ring gaskets.*
• *Diopter focusing adapts the focus to your particular needs.*
• *Eye relief of over 3 inches, plus a wide rubber ring on the eye-piece protects the shooter from half-moon cuts, even with heavy calibers.*

A red dot sight is now available from Docter Optic. Weighing just one ounce, it is not much bulkier than a standard rear sight, yet it offers the advantage of a single sighting plane. A red dot appears to project itself on the target—there's nothing to line up. You can shoot more quickly than with any other type of sight. Coated, high-quality lenses ensure a clear sight picture. There is no battery switch; batteries last up to five years without rest.

ONE-INCH TUBE SCOPES

DESCRIPTION	MAGNIFICATION	OBJECTIVE LENS DIA.	COLOR	RETICLE
3-9 x 40 Variable	3x to 9x	40 mm	Matte Black	Plex
3-9 x 40 Variable	3x to 9x	40 mm	Matte Black	German #4
3-10 x 40 Variable	3x to 10x	40 mm	Matte Black	Plex
3-10 x 40 Variable	3x to 10x	40 mm	Matte Black	German #4
4.5-14 x 40 Variable	4.5x to 14x	40 mm	Matte Black	Plex
4.5-14 x 40 Variable	4.5x to 14x	40 mm	Matte Black	Dot
8-25 x 50 Variable	8x to 25x	50 mm	Matte Black	Dot
8-25 x 50 Variable	8x to 25x	50 mm	Matte Black	Plex

30 mm TUBE SCOPES

DESCRIPTION	MAGNIFICATION	OBJECTIVE LENS DIA.	COLOR	RETICLE
4 x 32 Fixed	4x	32 mm	Matte Black	Plex
4 x 32 Fixed	4x	32 mm	Matte Black	German #4
6 x 42 Fixed	6x	42 mm	Matte Black	Plex
6 x 42 Fixed	6x	42 mm	Matte Black	German #4
6 x 42 Fixed, Aspherical Lens	6x	42 mm	Matte Black	Plex
6 x 42 Fixed, Aspherical Lens	6x	42 mm	Matte Black	German #4
1.5-6 x 42 Variable	1.5x to 6x	42 mm	Matte Black	Plex
1.5-6 x 42 Variable	1.5x to 6x	42 mm	Matte Black	German #4
1.5-6 x 42 Var., Aspherical Lens	1.5x to 6x	42 mm	Matte Black	Plex
1.5-6 x 42 Var., Aspherical Lens	1.5x to 6x	42 mm	Matte Black	German #4
2.5-10 x 48 Variable	2.5x to 10x	48 mm	Matte Black	Plex
2.5-10 x 48 Variable	2.5x to 10x	48 mm	Matte Black	German #4
2.5-10 x 48 Var., Aspherical Lens	2.5x to 10x	48 mm	Matte Black	Plex
2.5-10 x 48 Var., Aspherical Lens	2.5x to 10x	48 mm	Matte Black	German #4
3-12 x 56 Variable	3x to 12x	56 mm	Matte Black	Plex
3-12 x 56 Variable	3x to 12x	56 mm	Matte Black	German #4
3-12 x 56 Var., Aspherical Lens	3x to 12x	56 mm	Matte Black	Plex
3-12 x 56 Var., Aspherical Lens	3x to 12x	56 mm	Matte Black	German #4

SIGHTS & SCOPES

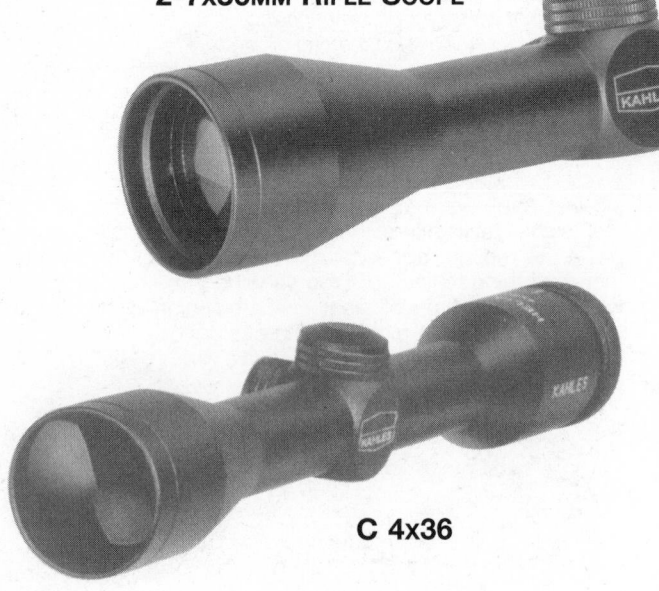

2-7x36mm RIFLE SCOPE

C 4x36

C 1,1-4x24

4A

7A

Plex

TDS

4 NK

Plex N

AMERICAN HUNTER

Kahles rifle scopes with a 1" main tube are compact and light-weight with excellent optical performance. One piece construction, generous eye relief, hard anodized, scratch resistent finish, shockproof and fogproof.

The AH's reticle is mounted in the second image focal plane thus ensuring that the reticle's size in high magnification is minimized. Accurate aiming is enhanced at long distances.

Prices:

AH 2-7x36 (7A)	$532.22
AH 2-7x36 (Plex)	532.22
AH 3-9x42 (4A)	621.00
AH 3-9x42 (Plex)	621.00
AH 3-9x42 (TDS)	665.00

COMPACT

Kahles AMV-multi-coatings transmit up to 99.5% per air-to-glass surface. This ensures optimum use of incident light, especially in lowlight level conditions or at twilight.

Kahles rifle scopes are rugged, shockproof, waterproof and fogproof. Nitrogen purged several times to assure the absolute elimination of any moisture. 30mm tube.

Prices:

C 1.1-4x24 (4A or 7A)	$722.00
C 1.5-6x42 (4A or 7A)	832.00
C 2.5-10x50 (7A or Plex)	999.00
C 3-12x56 (7A or Plex)	1,110.00
C 4x36 (1" tube, 4A or 7A)	555.00
C 6x42 (1" tube, 4A or 7A)	694.00
C 8x50 (1" tube, 4A or 7A)	749.00

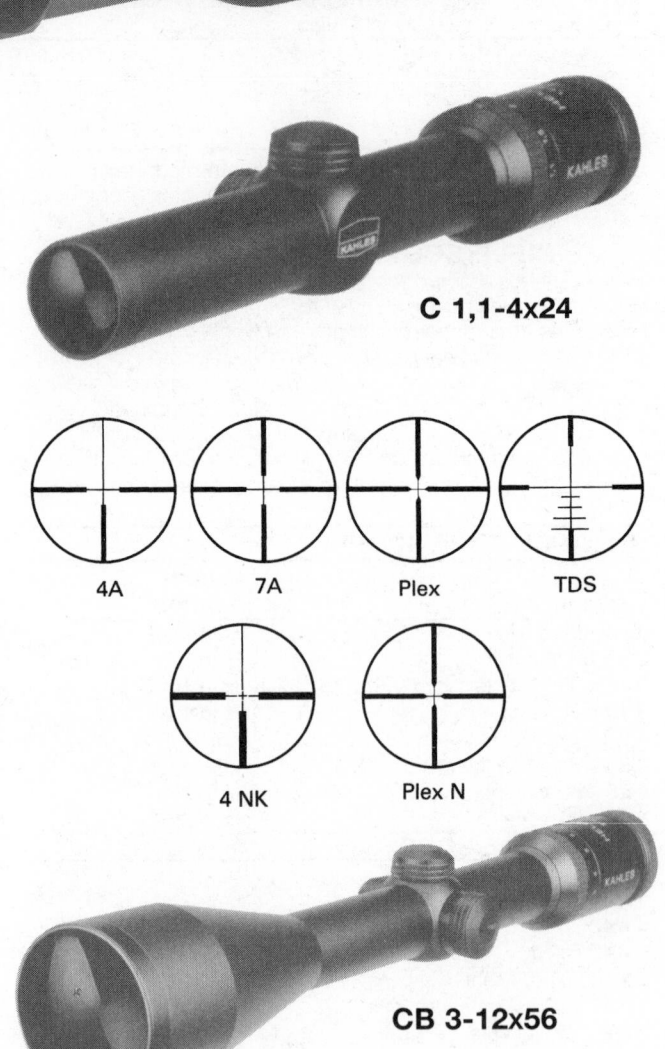

CB 3-12x56

ILLUMINATED

Bright reticle is adjustable for illumination, 30mm tube (1" tube on 8x50). Optimum illumination. Minimized straylight. Battery life - 110 hours.

Prices:

CB 1.5-6x42 (4N or PlexN)	$1,249.00
CB 2.5-10x50 (4N or PlexN)	1,353.00
CB 3-12x56 (4N, PlexN, or 4NK)	1,471.00
K 8x50 (4N or PlexN)	1,110.00

LASERAIM TECHNOLOGIES INC.

AL1B LASER SIGHT

The **AL1B** sight mounts quickly and easily to most pistols and revolvers and producies a 2" dot at 100 yds. Four button cell batteries power the water and shock-resistant sight up to one hour continuous use. Windage and elevation are accomplished with the 3 pin windage and elevation system, giving precise adjustments and yielding 9 ft. of travel at 25 yards. Adaptable to rifles, shotguns, muzzleloaders, and bows. Available in black. *Universal mount included.* **Length:** 2.75" **Diameter:** 5/8" **Weight (approx.):** 2 oz. Made in U.S.A.
Price: **$99.00**

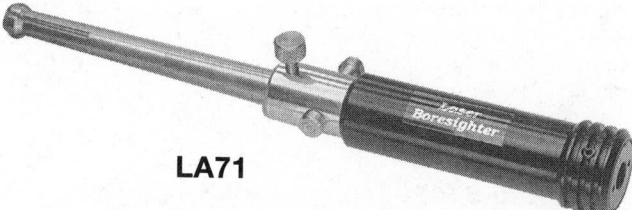

LA71

LA71 SHOTLESS LASER BORE SIGHTER™
The **LA71 SHOTLESS LASER BORE SIGHTER**™ makes sighting in easier and quicker. To check the center of the bore, simply rotate the laser on axis of the gun bore. The LA71 is equipped with a rotational **LASERAIM**™ with constant ON switch and six arbors fitting calibers 22 thru 45, 12-gauge shotguns and muzzleloaders (50 and 54 cal.). **Length:** 8" (w/laser and arbor).
Price: **$169.00**

AR15 CUSTOM LASER SIGHT
(not shown)
The **AR15** laser sight is custom designed to fit all AR15/M16 rifles equipped with triangular front sight post. Laser provides three hours of continuous battery life with convenient replaceable battery. Machined from aircraft grade aluminum. **Weight:** 3 oz. **Length:** 2"
Price: **$199.00**

AL6 HOTDOG LASER SIGHT
Ten times brighter than many other laser sights, this laser produces a 2-inch dot at 100 yards. The remote pressure switch provides operation for up to 2 hours of continuous power. The laser features LASERAIM's unique 3-way micro-lock windage and elevation adjustment. Fits LASERAIM mounts with no gunsmithing required and is suitable for handguns, rifles, shotguns, muzzle loaders, and bows. Uses convenient replaceable watch batteries.
Price: AL6 Hotdot laser sight **$99.00**

Model LA5XB

MODEL LA5XB HOTDOT MIGHTY SIGHT
Up to 10 times brighter than other laser sights, Laseraim's Hotdot Lasersights include a rechargeable NICad battery and in-field charger. Produce a 2" dot at 100 yards with a 500-yard range. **Length:** 2". **Diameter:** .75". Can be used with handguns, rifles, shotguns and bows. Fit all Laseraim mounts. Available in black or satin.
Price: **$139.00**

Vari-X III Line

The Vari-X III scopes feature a power-changing system that is similar to the sophisticated lens systems in today's finest cameras. Improvements include an extremely accurate internal control system and a sharp sight picture. All lenses are coated with Multicoat 4. Reticles are the same apparent size throughout the power range and stay centered during elevation/windage adjustments. Eyepieces are adjustable and fog-free. Reticles are also available in German #1, German #1 European, German #4, Post and Duplex, and Leupold Dot.

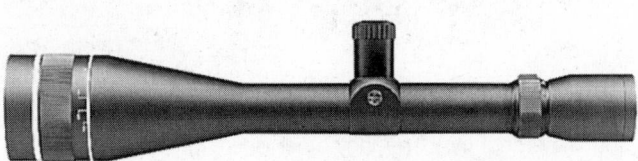

VARI-X III 6.5-20X50mm Varmint

VARI-X III 1.5-5X20mm
This selection of hunting powers is for ranges varying from very short to those at which big game is normally taken. The field at 1.5X lets you get on a fast-moving animal quickly. With magnification at 5X, medium and big game can be hunted around the world at all but the longest ranges.
Duplex or Heavy Duplex	$664.00
In black matte finish	689.00
Dot, Post + Duplex, or German #1 or #4 (gloss)	718.00
German #1 or #4 (matte)	743.00

Also available:
VARI-X III 1.75-6X32mm. Matte finish	714.00
German Reticles	768.00

VARI-X III 2.5-8X36mm
This is an excellent range of powers for almost any kind of big game hunting. The top magnification provides enough resolution for varmint shooting.
Duplex	$709.00
In matte or silver finish	734.00
Mil Dot (Matte)	868.00
Dot, CPC, Post + Duplex, or German #4	780.00

VARI-X III 3.5-10X40mm
The extra power range makes these scopes the optimum choice for year-around big game and varmint hunting. The adjustable objective model, with its precise focusing at any range beyond 50 yards, also is an excellent choice for some forms of target shooting.
Duplex	$730.00
With matte or silver finish	755.00
Dot, Post + Duplex, German #1 or #4	784.00
German #4 or #1 (matte)	809.00

VARI-X III 3.5-10X50mm
The hunting scope is designed specifically for low-light situations. The 3.5X10-50mm scope, featuring lenses coated with Multicoat 4, is ideal for twilight hunting because of its efficient light transmission. The new scope

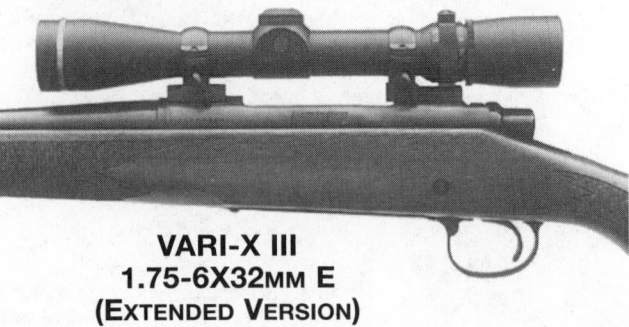

VARI-X III 1.75-6X32mm E (Extended Version)

delivers an exit pupil that transmits all the light the human eye can handle in typical low-light circumstances, even at the highest magnification.
Duplex or Heavy Duplex	$829.00
With matte or silver finish	854.00
Dot, CPC, Post, or German (gloss)	882.00
Matte	907.00

VARI-X III 4.5-14X40mm (Adj. Objective)
This model has enough range to double as a hunting scope and as a varmint scope.
Duplex or Heavy Duplex	$816.00
With matte finish	841.00
German #1 or #4	870.00
Matte	895.00
Same as above with 50mm adj. obj., Duplex or Heavy Duplex; matte finish only	939.00

VARI-X III 6.5-20X40mm (Adj. Objective)
This scope has a wide range of power settings, and can be used for any kind of big-game hunting where higher magnifications are useful. Side-focus adjustment allows shooters to eliminate parallax while in shooting position without taking their eyes off the target.
Gloss finish (duplex)	$861.00
CPC, dot, or Post	914.00
With matte or silver finish	886.00

Also available:
6.5-20X50mm Adj. Obj. w/duplex matte finish	984.00
6.5-20X50mm Adj. Obj. w/Mil Dot matte finish	1,118.00

VARI-X III 6.5-20X40MM E.F.R. TARGET
For those situations, such as air rifle or rimfire silhouette, where normal adjustable objective ranges are simply too distant, Leupold offers the EFR (Extended Focus Rifle) model of the 6.5-20. With this model, parallax distances as close as 10 meters can be set.
Fine Duplex (matte)	$957.00
Target Dot (matte)	1,064.00

The Vari-X II line offers magnesium fluoride-coated lenses for improved light transmission, continuous tension adjustment dials with increments as fine as 1/2 minute of angle, a locking eyepiece for reliable ocular adjustment, and a sealed, nitrogen-filled interior for fog-free reliability. Many models are available with Dot, CPC, German #1, German #4, and Post & Duplex reticles in addition to Duplex.

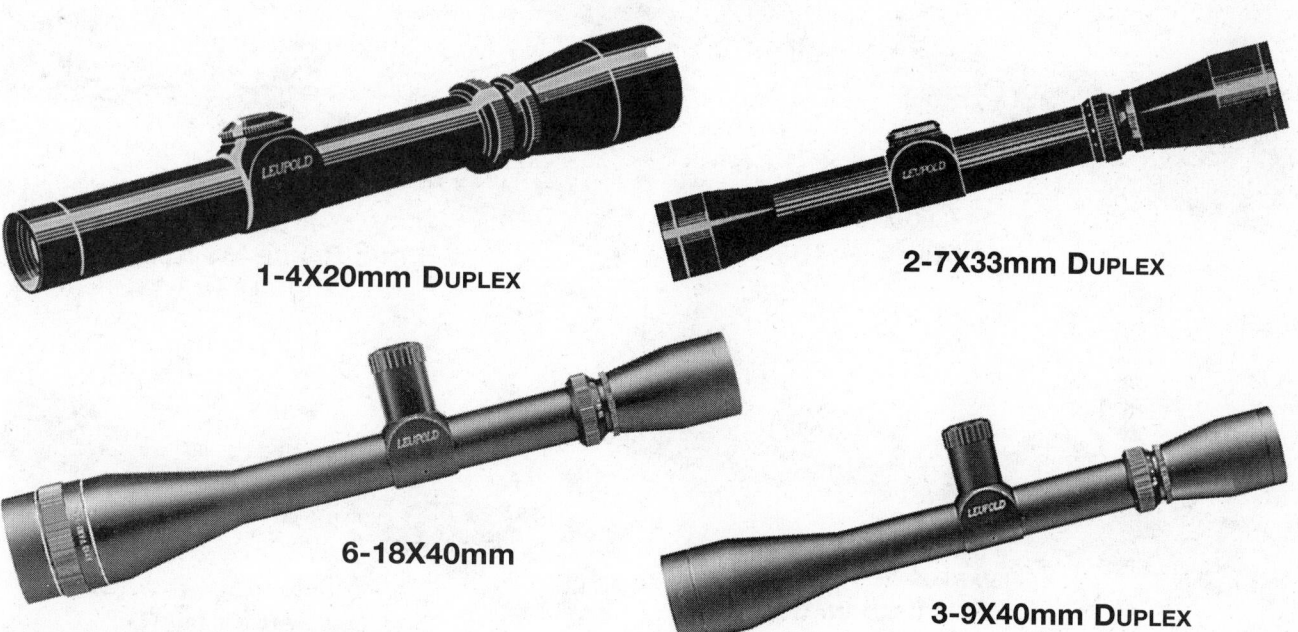

1-4X20mm DUPLEX

2-7X33mm DUPLEX

6-18X40mm

3-9X40mm DUPLEX

VARI-X II 1-4X20mm DUPLEX

This scope, the smallest of Leupold's VARI-X II line, is noted for its large field of view: 70 feet at 100 yards.

Gloss finish only	**$414.00**
CPC, Dot, or Post and Duplex	468.00

VARI-X II 2-7X33mm DUPLEX

A compact scope, no larger than the Leupold M8-4X, offering a wide range of power. It can be set at 2X for close ranges in heavy cover or zoomed to maximum power for shooting or identifying game at longer ranges.

VARI-X II 2-7x 33 SHOTGUN (heavy Duplex) matte	**$448.00**
CPC, Dot, or Post + Duplex	502.00

VARI-X II 3-9X50mm

This LOV scope delivers a 5.5mm exit pupil for low-light visibility:

Gloss	**$532.00**
Matte finish	557.00
CPC, Post + Duplex, or German reticles (matte)	611.00

VARI-X II 3-9X40mm DUPLEX

A wide selection of powers offers the right combination of field of view and magnification to fit most hunting conditions. Many hunters use the 3X or 4X setting most of the time, cranking up to 9X for positive identification of game or for extremely long shots. The adjustable objective eliminates parallax and permits precise focusing on any object from less than 50 yards to infinity for extra-sharp definition.

Gloss finish	**$432.00**
In matte, silver	457.00
Tactical (Mil Dot, matte)	457.00

VARI-X II 4-12X40mm (Adj. Objective)

The ideal answer for big game and varmint hunters alike. At 12.25 inches, the 4X12 is virtually the same length as Vari-X II 3X9. New fixed objective has same long eye relief and is factory-set to be free of parallax at 150 yds.

Gloss finish	**$619.00**
Matte or silver finish	645.00
3/4 Mil. Dot (gloss)	754.00
3/4 Mil. Dot (matte)	779.00
CPC, German #1 or #4 or Dot (gloss)	673.00
CPC, German #1 or #4 or Dot (matte)	698.00

VARI-X II 6-18X40mm Adj. Obj. Target

Features target-style click adjustments, fully coated lenses, adj. objective for parallax-free shooting from 50 yards to infinity.

In matte or silver	**$689.00**
Target Dot Model	743.00
Target Dot w/Target knobs	796.00
Duplex w/Target knobs	743.00

LEUPOLD SCOPES

Illuminated Reticle

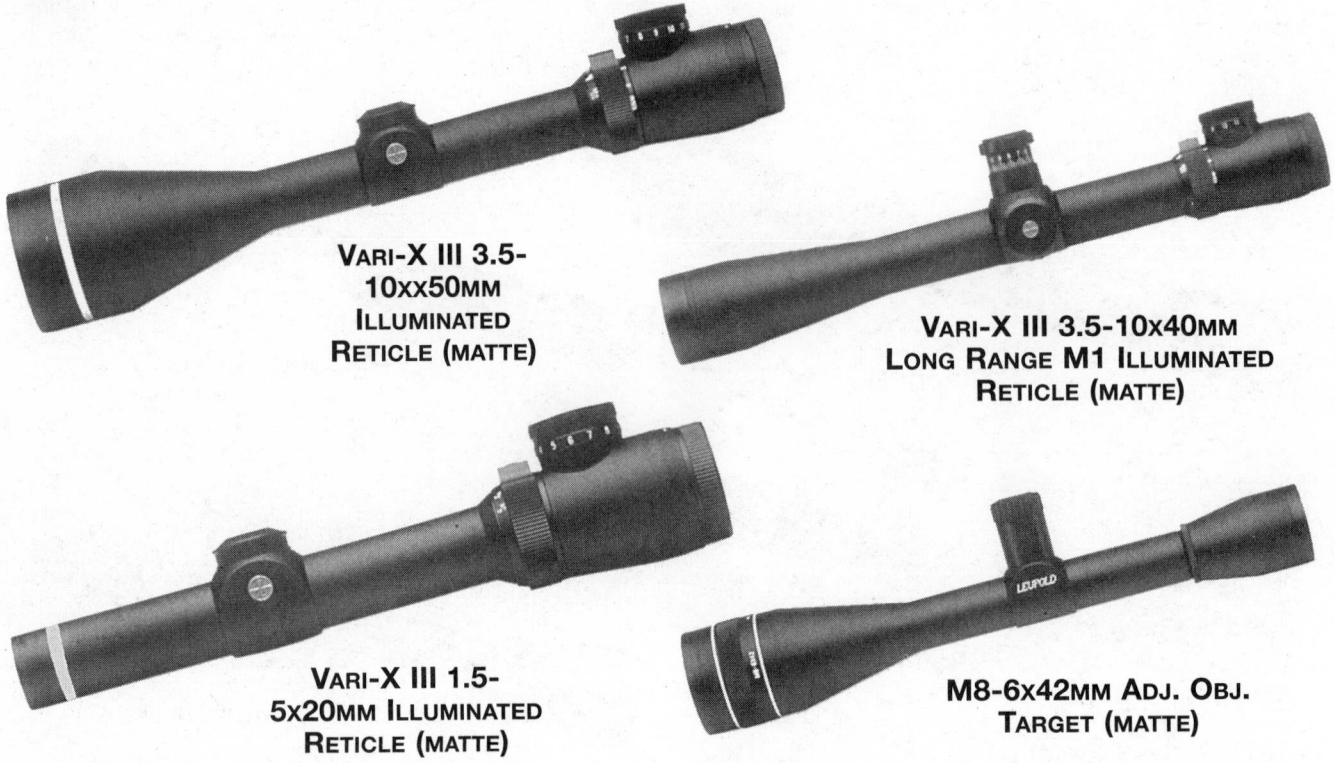

VARI-X III 3.5-10XX50MM ILLUMINATED RETICLE (MATTE)

VARI-X III 3.5-10X40MM LONG RANGE M1 ILLUMINATED RETICLE (MATTE)

VARI-X III 1.5-5X20MM ILLUMINATED RETICLE (MATTE)

M8-6X42MM ADJ. OBJ. TARGET (MATTE)

Leupold's Illuminated Reticle Scope helps hunters and target shooters take aim in poor light.

All Leupold Illuminated Reticle Scopes feature the world renowned Vari-X III system with Multicoat 4 lenses, and audible and tactile click adjustments. They are waterproof and fog proof. An 11-position intensity setting dial allows reticle brightness to be adjusted for dim and bright conditions. A 3-volt lithium cell supplies the power to keep the reticle evenly and constantly lit.

For big game hunters, the Leupold Vari-X III 1.5-5x20mm Illuminated Reticle Scope, with either an Illuminated Duplex or Illuminated German #4 reticle, makes the aiming point leap right to the eye and offers lightning fast target acquisition. For more general hunting and sporting applications, the Vari-X III 4.5-14x50mm Adjustable Objective and the new Vari-X III 3.5-10x50 models offer extra-big objective lenses for conditions when you must use high magnification in low light. Both models are available in a matte finish with a choice of Illuminated Duplex, Illuminated German #4, or Illuminated Mil. Dot reticles.

Tactical shooters will welcome the Leupold Vari-X III 3.5-10x40mm Long Range M1 Illuminated Reticle and Vari-X III 3.5-10x40mm Long Range M3 Illuminated Reticle models. Both are outstanding choices for military,

law enforcement, and other tactical applications. Both models are available in a matte finish and feature side focus parallax adjusment dials and a 30mm maintube design to enhance long range capability. Each model can be had with either the Illuminated Duplex or Illuminated Mil. Dot reticle.

LEUPOLD 6 X 42 AO TARGET SCOPE

The Leupold M8 6x42mm Adjustable Objective Target Scope offers all the features needed by hunters and benchrest shooters. Both the elevation and windage dials of this scope feature 1/4 minute of angle, target-style click adjustments. An adjustable objective dial offers the ability to correct parallax from a distance of 50 yards to infinity.

The lenses of the M8 6x42mm Adjustable Objective Target Scope are coated with Multicoat 4, the same anti-reflective coating found on the Leupold Vari-X III scopes, for increased light transmission. This combined with superior system design and a very large exit pupil makes the scope one of the brightest Leupold scopes available. The large exit pupil also reduces eye strain. The Leupold M8 6x42mm Adjustable Objective Target Scope is not just for target shooting. Durable and rugged, it's an ideal scope for low-light hunting conditions.

Leupold Premier Scopes (LPS)

The Leupold Premiere Scope (LPS) line features 30mm tubes, fast-focus eyepieces, armored power selector dials that can be read from the shooting position, a 4-inch constant eye relief, Diamondcoat lenses for increased light transmission scratch resistance, and finger adjustable, low-profile elevation and windage adjustments.

LPS 1.5-6x42mm
A wide field of view and a generous magnification range make this scope an outstanding choice for all big game hunting. Available in a satin finish.

Duplex (satin)	**$1,248.00**
German #1 or German #4 (satin)	**1,302.00**

LPS 2.5-10x45
Big game hunters in particluar will enjoy the mid-range magnification of the new LPS 2.5-10x45mm. It's unusually bright sight picture is due in part to 99.65% light transmission per lens surface; constant, non-critical eye relief; scratch resistant DiamondCoat anti-reflective lens coating on all interior and exterior lenses; the fast-focus eyepiece; and all the other features common to every Leupold Premier Scope.

Prices: 2.5-10x45 Duplex (satin)	**$1,427.00**
German #1 or #4 (satin)	**1,480.00**

LPS 3.5-14x50
The new LPS 3.5-14x50mm has a turret-mounted side-focus parallax adjustment so you can change parallax settings easily, even from the shooting position. The 50mm objective lens produces a bright sight picture, in dim light. Finally, the long maintube allows generous ring mount space for rifles with long actions.

Prices: Duplex (satin)	**$1,570.00**
Target Dot, German #1 or #4 (satin)	**1,623.00**
Mil Dot (satin)	**1,704.00**

LPS 3.5-14x50MM SIDE FOCUS (SATIN FINISH)

SHOTGUN & MUZZLELOADER SCOPES (not shown)

Leupold shotgun scopes are parallax-adjusted to deliver precise focusing at 75 yards. Each scope features a special Heavy Duplex reticle that is more effective against heavy, brushy backgrounds. All scopes have matte finish.

Prices:

VARI-X II 1-4X20mm MODEL HEAVY DUPLEX	**$438.00**
M8-4X33mm HEAVY DUPLEX	**429.00**
VARI-X II 2-7X33MM HEAVY DUPLEX	**473.00**

Compact Scopes

M8 2.5-20MM COMPACT
This small scope presents the shooter with an enormous field of view for fast target acquisition. It also features generous elevation and windage adjustment. Standard models are parallax adjusted to 100 yards. The Turkey Ranger model, with a special Post & Duplex reticle designed to subtend 9 inches from the post to crosswire at 40 yards, is parallax adjusted to 40 yards. Offered in a matte finish.

Duplex or Heavy Duplex (matte)	**$330.00**
Turkey Ranger (matte)	**384.00**

M8 4x28MM COMPACT RIMFIRE SPECIAL
Fine Duplex (gloss)	**400.00**

VARI-X 2-7x28MM COMPACT
Duplex (gloss)	**500.00**

VARI-X 2-7x28MM COMPACT RIMFIRE SPECIAL
Fine Duplex (gloss)	**500.00**

VARI-X 3-9x33MM COMPACT Duplex
(matte, silver)	**543.00**

VARI-X 3-9X33MM COMPACT E.F.R.
With an adjustable objective capable of correcting parallax as close as 10 meters, this scope is perfectly suited to .22 rimfire silhouette and air rifle shooting.

Duplex (gloss)	**$573.00**

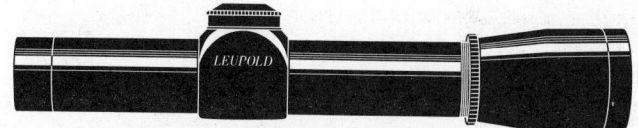

M8 - 2.5x20MM COMPACT

M8 4x28 COMPACT RF SPECIAL

VARI-X 2-7x28 & RF SPECIAL

VARI-X 3-9x33 COMPACT SILVER

SIGHTS & SCOPES

LEUPOLD SCOPES

Tactical Models

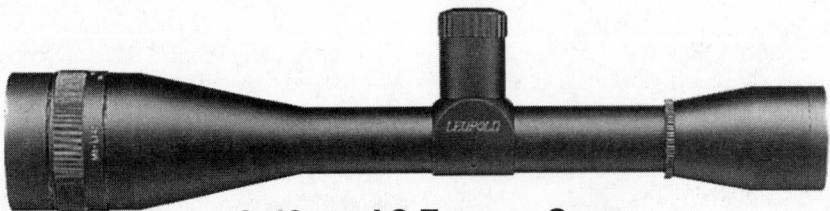

6x42mm AO TACTICAL SCOPE

The Leupold 6x42mm features 1/4-minute target-style adjustments for precise corrections in the field. Adjustment travel for windage or elevation is 76 inches. The exact 6X magnification, and adjustable objective make it an excellent choice for Hunter Benchrest Competitions. Leupold's exclusive Multicoat 4 lens coating is applied to all air-to-glass surfaces to provide the 6X42mm maximum light transmission.
Length: 12"
Weight: 11.5 ounces
Two reticles styles: classic Duplex or a 3/4-minute Military Dot. Black matte finish.
Matte finish $650.00
With 3/4-minute Military Dot 784.00

MARK 4 MI 10x40 (MATTE)/MARK 4 MI 16x40 (MATTE)
MARK 4 MI 10x40 (MATTE) • M3 10x40 WITH BDC
  Duplex $1,888.00
  Mil Dot 2,021.00
VARI-X II 3-9x40 (MATTE)
  Duplex 561.00
  Mil Dot 695.00
VARI-X III 3.5-10x40 (MATTE)
  Duplex 834.00
  Mil Dot 968.00
VARI-X III 4.5-14x40 AO (MATTE)
  Duplex 920.00
  Mil Dot 1,054.00

Fixed Power Scopes

M8-2.5X28mm
For all the shooters wirldwide who are rediscovering the classic lever-action rifle, the M8-2.5x28mm IER Scout is the ideal choice. Designed specifically for lever-action and scout-style rifles, it offers 9 to 17 inches of eye relief (IER stands for "Intermediate Eye Relief"). The Scout is mounted on the barrel, in front of the receiver.
Matte finish or silver (duplex) $427.00
Matte or silver (German #1) 480.00

M8-4X
The 4X delivers a widely used magnification and a generous field of view $404.00
In black matte finish 429.00

M8-6X
The 6X extends the range for big-game hunting and doubles in some cases as a varmint scope $429.00

M8-6X42mm
Large 42mm objective lens features a 7mm exit pupil for increased light-gathering capability. Recommended for varmint shooting at night.
Duplex or Heavy Duplex $534.00
In matte finish 559.00

M8-12X40MM STANDARD (Adj. Obj.)
Outstanding optical qualities, resolution and magnification make the 12X a natural for the varmint shooter. Adjustable objective is standard for parallax-free focusing.
Duplex $596.00
With CPC reticle or Dot 650.00

M8-2.5x28MM IER SCOUT

M8-4X33

M8-6X36

M8-6X42mm

M8-12X40mm STANDARD

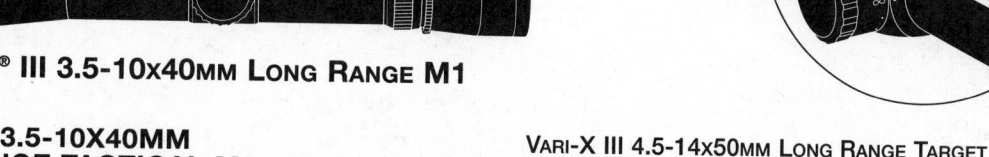

1/4 Minute Click M1 Style Adjustments with Side Focus Parallax

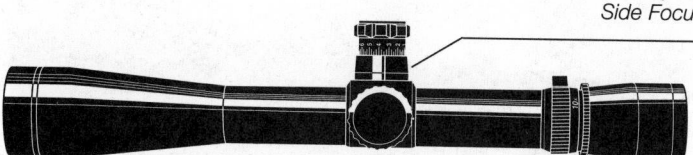

VARI-X® III 3.5-10x40MM LONG RANGE M1

VARI-X III 3.5-10X40MM LONG RANGE TACTICAL M1

This scope combines the bold 1/4 minute of angle target dial design of the Leupold Mark 4 M1 scopes with the 30 mm maintube and side parallax dial of a long range scope to produce a low-profile, close-mounted tactical scope of remarkable versatility for hunters as well as snipers. Available in an all matte (including the Leupold Golden Ring) finish.

Duplex (matte). $1,209.00
Target Dot (matte) 1,263.00
3/4 Min. Mil. Dot (matte) 1,343.00

VARI-X III 4.5-14X50MM LONG RANGE TACTICAL

With the increasing popularity of long range shooting, special scopes have been developed to accommodate the additional adjustment necessary to success in this discipline. The 4.5-14x50mm Long Range models with their 30mm maintubes, target style adjustment knobs, and side mounted parallax dials offer the shooter everything necessary to achieve success at great distances.

VARI-X III 4.5-14x50MM LONG RANGE TARGET Duplex or
   Fine Duplex (matte) $1,130.00

VARI-X III 4.5-14x50MM LONG RANGE TARGET
   Target Dot (matte) 1,184.00
VARI-X III 4.5-14x50MM LONG RANGE TACTICAL
   3/4 Min. Mil. Dot (matte) 1,264.00

VARI-X III 6.5-20X50MM LONG RANGE TARGET

Designed with a 30mm maintube to provide additional elevation and windage adjustment, and featuring target style adjustment dials and a side-mounted parallax dial, this scope offers the long range shooter impressive magnification and convenient adjustment mechanisms.

Fine Duplex (matte, silver) $1,218.00
Target Dot (matte, silver) 1,271.00
3/4 Min. Mil. Dot (matte) 1,352.00

VARI-X III 8.5-25X50MM LONG RANGE TARGET

With a 30mm maintube to provide additional elevation and windage adjustment, target style adjustment dials, and a side mounted parallax dial, this scope offers the long range shooter impressive magnification and convenient adjustment mechanisms.

Fine Duplex (matte) $1,316.00
Target Dot (matte) 1,370.00

LG-35, 35MM RED DOT SIGHT

LEUPOLD GILMORE RED DOT SIGHTS

The Leupold Gilmore Red Dot Sights feature a compact frame that is easily mounted on any type of firearm, from shotguns and muzzleloaders to rifles and pistols. You get 11 brightness settings a choice of three dot sizes—plus, unlimited eye relief, and 1/3 minute of angle elevation and windage adjustments.

LG-1
2-Minute Dot (matte and silver two tone) $278.60

LG-35
Offered in either solid matte black or a two-tone matte and silver finish.
4-Minute Dot (matte, matte and silver two tone) $421.40

NIKON MONARCH SCOPES

6.5-20X44 AO

2-7X32

5.5-16x44AO

1.5-4x20

TITANIUM SCOPE
3.3-10x44 ($899.95)
5.5-16.5x44 ($938.95)

RIFLESCOPES

MODEL **6500** 4x40 Lustre $330.95
MODEL **6505** 4x40 Matte 350.95
MODEL **6510** 2-7x32 Lustre 426.95
MODEL **6515** 2-7x32 Matte 446.95
MODEL **6520** 3-9x40 Lustre 430.95
MODEL **6525** 3-9x40 Matte 450.95
MODEL **6528** 3-9x40 Silver Matte 470.95
MODEL **6530** 3.5-10x50 Lustre 644.95
MODEL **6535** 3.5-10x50 Matte 664.95
MODEL **6540** 4-12x40 AO Lustre 552.95
MODEL **6545** 4-12x40 AO Matte 572.95
MODEL **6580** 5.5-16.5x44 AO Black Lustre 602.95

MODEL **6585** 5.5-16.5x44 AO Black Matte 622.95
MODEL **6550** 6.5-20x44 AO Lustre 684.95
MODEL **6555** 6.5-20x44 AO Matte 704.95
MODEL **6570** 6.5-20x44 HV 684.95
MODEL **6575** 6.5-20x44 HV 704.95
MODEL **6630** 3.3-10x44 AO 898.95
MODEL **6680** 5.5-16.5x44 AO 938.95

HANDGUN AND SHOTGUN SCOPES

MODEL **6560** 2x20 EER Black Lustre $248.95
MODEL **6565** 2x20 EER Silver 268.95
MODEL **6590** 1.5-4.5x20 Shotgun Black Matte 364.95
MODEL **6595** 1.5-4.5x20 Sabot/Slug Black Matte . . . 370.95

MONARCH™ UCC RIFLESCOPE SPECIFICATIONS

Model	4x40	1.5-4.5x20	2-7x32	3-9x40	3.5-10x50	4-12x40AO	5.5-16.5x44AO	6.5-20x44AO	2x20EER
Lustre	6500	N/A	6510	6520	6530	6540	6580	6550	6560
Matte	6505	6595	6515	6525	6535	6545	6585	6555	N/A
Silver	N/A	N/A	N/A	6528	N/A	N/A	N/A	N/A	6565
Actual Magnification	4x	1.5x-4.5x	2x-7x	3x-9x	3.5x-10x	4x-12x	5.5x-16.5x	6.5x-19.46x	1.75x
Objective Diameter	40mm	20mm	32mm	40mm	50mm	40mm	44mm	44mm	20mm
Exit Pupil (mm)	10	13.3-4.4	16-4.6	13.3-4.4	14.3-5	10-3.3	8-2.7	6.7-2.2	11.4
Eye Relief (in)	3.5	3.7-3.5	3.9-3.6	3.6-3.5	3.9-3.8	3.6-3.4	3.2-3.0	3.5-3.1	26.4-10.5
FOV @ 100 yds (ft)	26.9	50.3-16.7*	44.5-12.7	33.8-11.3	25.5-8.9	25.6-8.5	19.1-6.4	16.1-5.4	22
Tube Diameter	1 in.	1 in.	1 in.	1 in.	1 in.	1 in.	1 in.	1 in.	1 in.
Objective Tube(mm/in)	47.3-1.86	25.4/1	39.3-1.5	47.3-1.86	57.3-2.2	53.1-2.09	54-2.13	54-2.13	25, 4/1
Eyepiece O.D. (mm)	38	38	38	38	38	38	38	38	38
Length (in)	11.7	10	11.1	12.3	13.7	13.7	13.4	14.6	8.1
Weight (oz)	11.2	9.3	11.2	12.6	15.5	16.9	18.4	20.1	6.6
Adjustment Gradation	1/4 MOA	1/4 MOA	1/4 MOA	1/4 MOA	1/4 MOA	1/4 MOA	1/4 MOA	1/8 MOA	1/4 MOA
Max Internal Adjustment	120 MOA	120 MOA	70 MOA	55 MOA	45 MOA	45 MOA	40 MOA	38 MOA	120 MOA
Parallax Setting (yds)	100	75	100	100	100	50 to ∞	50 to ∞	50 to ∞	100

*FOV @ 75 yds (ft)   *FOV @ 50 yds (ft)

SPECIAL LIMITED EDITION 3-9x40

4.5-14

Nikon has teamed with Buckmasters to produce a limited edition riflescope line. Built to withstand the toughest hunting conditions, the scopes integrate shockproof, fogproof and waterproof construction, plus numerous other features seldom found on riflescopes in this price range. Nikon's Brightvue™ anti-reflective system of high-quality, multicoated lenses provides over 93% anti-reflection capability for high levels of light transmission and optical clarity required for dawn-to-dusk big game hunting. These riflescopes are parallax-adjusted at 100 yards and have durable matte finishes that reduce glare while afield. They also feature positive steel-to-brass, quarter-minute-click windage and elevation adjustments for instant, repeatable accuracy and a Nikoplex® reticle for quick target acquisition.

Prices:

MODEL 6465 1x20	$240.95
MODEL 6405 4x40	244.95
MODEL 6425 3-9x40 BLACK MATTE	302.95
MODEL 6415 3-9x40 SILVER	324.95
MODEL 6435 3-9x50	452.95
MODEL 6450 4.5-14x40 AO BLCK MATTE	416.95
MODEL 6455 4.5-14x40 AO SILVER	436.95

BUCKMASTERS SCOPES

Model	4x40	3-9x40	3-9x50	4.5-14x40AO
Matte	6405	6425	6435	6450
Silver	N/A	6415	N/A	6455
Actual Magnification	4x	3.3-8.5x	3.3-8.5x	4.5-13.5x
Objective Diameter	40mm	40mm	50mm	40mm
Exit Pupil (mm)	10	12.1-4.7	15.1-5.9	8.9-2.9
Eye Relief (in)	3.5	3.5-3.4	3.5-3.4	3.6-3.4
FOV @ 100 yds (ft)	30.6	33.9-12.9	33.9-12.9	22.5-7.5
Tube Diameter	1 in.	1 in.	1 in.	1 in.
Objective Tube (mm/in)	47.3/1.86	47.3/1.86	58.7/2.3	53/2.1
Eyepiece O.D. (mm)	42.5	42.5	42.5	38
Length (in)	12.7	12.7	12.9	14.8
Weight (oz)	11.8	13.4	18.2	18.7
Adjustment Gradation	1/4: 1 click	1/4: 1 click	1/4: 1 click	1/4: 1 click
Max Internal Adjustment	80	80	70	40
Parallax Setting (yds)	100	100	100	50 to ∞

PENTAX SCOPES

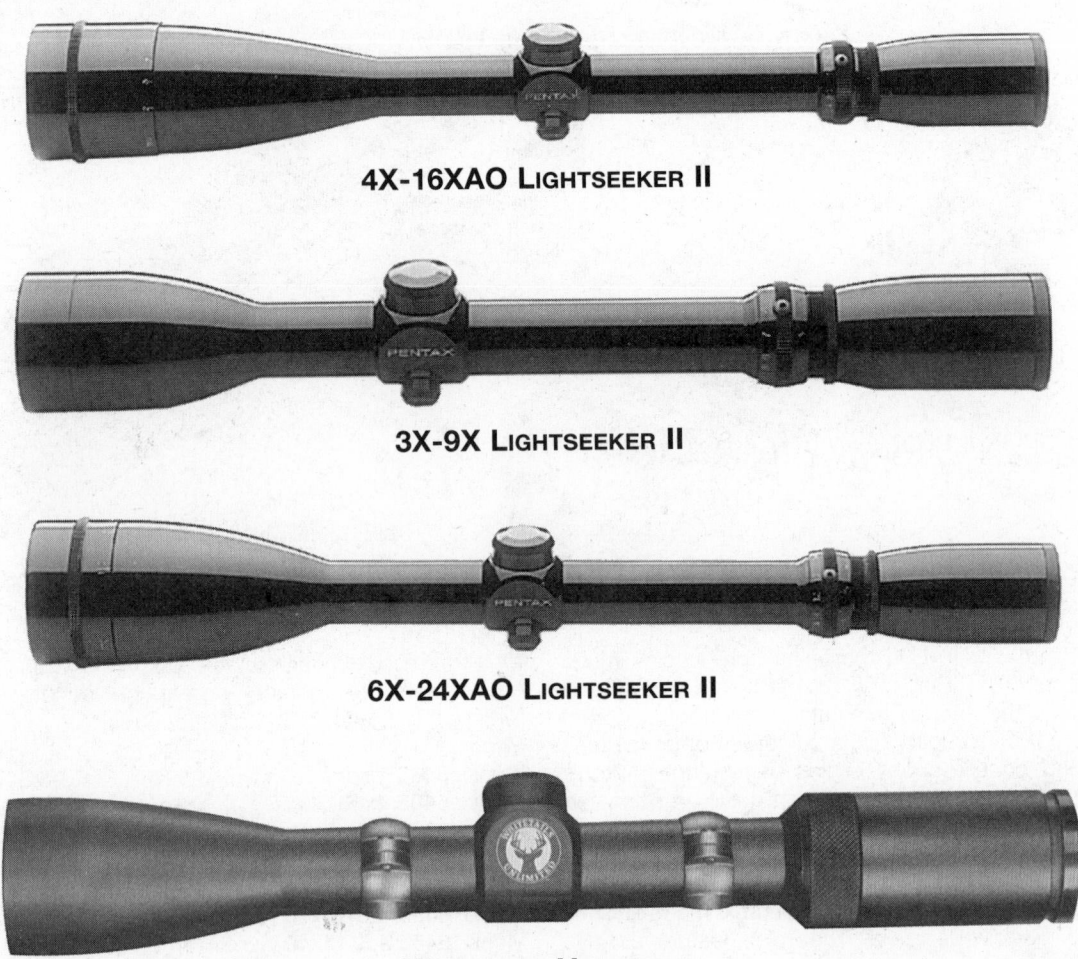

4X-16XAO LIGHTSEEKER **II**

3X-9X LIGHTSEEKER **II**

6X-24XAO LIGHTSEEKER **II**

WHITETAILS UNLIMITED

Features:

- **Scratch-resistant outer tube.** Under ordinary wear and tear, the outer tube is almost impossible to scratch.
- **High Quality cam zoom tube.** No plastics are used. The tube is made of a bearing-type brass with precision machined cam slots. The zoom control screws are precision-ground to 1/2 of one thousandth tolerance.
- **Leak Prevention.** The power rings are sealed on a separate precision-machined seal tube. The scopes are then filled with nitrogen and double-sealed with heavy-duty "O" rings, making them leak-proof and fog-proof.
- **Excellent eyepieces.** The eyepiece lenses have a greater depth of field than most others. Thus, a more focused target at 100, 200 or 500 yards is attainable. Most Pentax Riflescopes are available in High Gloss, Matte or Satin Chrome finish.

The **LIGHTSEEKER-30** has the same features as the Lightseeker II, but with a 30mm tube.

The purchase of every Pentax Whitetails Unlimited rifle or shotgun scope includes a free one-year membership in Whitetails Unlimited, and a portion of the purchase price goes to the organization to support its conversation efforts.

PENTAX CORPORATION expands its extensive line of scopes by adding a Mil-Dot reticle option to three of its current models. The Mil-Dot reticle helps you estimate range up to 1,000 yards. Mil-Dot reticles are available on the 3X-9X Lightseeker and 4X-16X, 6X-24X, and 8.5X-32X AO Lightseeker 30 scopes.

The Mil-Dot reticle looks like a standard crosshair, with the addition of four oval dots radiating in each direction from the center. The distance from each dot to the next is one mil, or one yard at one thousand yards. If the shooter knows the height or width of the target or other nearby object, the range to the target can be estimated accurately by making a simple calculation or referring to a Mil-Dot chart.

2.5 LIGHTSEEKER SG PLUS
MOSSY OAK® BREAK-UP SCOPE

LIGHTSEEKER-30 6-24xAO

SIGHTS & SCOPES

LIGHTSEEKER RIFLESCOPE AND WHITETAILS UNLIMITED

	TUBE DIAMETER (IN)	OBJECTIVE DIAMETER (MM)	EYEPIECE DIAMETER (MM)	EXIT PUPIL (MM)	EYE RELIEF (IN)	FIELD OF VIEW (FT@100 YD)	ADJUSTMENT GRADUATION (IN@100 YD)	MAXIMUM ADJUSTMENT (IN@100 YD)	LENGTH (IN)	WEIGHT (OZ)	RETICLE	PRICE
RIFLE SCOPES												
Lightseeker 1.75X - 6X	1	35	39	15.3-5	3.5-4.0	71-20	1/2	110	10.75	13	P, TW	$526-546
Lightseeker 2X - 8X	1	39	39	11.0-4.0	3.5-4.0	53-17	1/3	80	11.7	14	P	594
Lightseeker 3X - 9X	1	43	39	12.0-5.0	3.5-4.0	36-14	1/4	50	12.7	15	P, MD	594-798
Lightseeker 3X - 9X	1	50	39	16.1-5.6	3.5-4.0	35-12	1/4	50	13.0	19	TW	844
Lightseeker 2.5X - 10X	1	50	39	16.3-4.6	4.2-4.7	35-10	1/4	100	14.1	23	TW	964
Lightseeker Zero-X/V SG Plus	1	27	39	19.5-5.5	3.5-7	53.8-15	1/2	129	8.9	10.3	CP	476
Lightseeker 2.5X SG Plus	1	25	39	7.0	3.5-4.0	55	1/2	60	10.0	9	DW	350-364
Lightseeker II 3X - 9X	1	43	39	12.0-5.0	3.5-4.0	36-14	1/4	50	12.7	15	P	660
Lightseeker II 4X - 16X AO	1	44	39	10.4-2.8	3.5-4.0	33-9	1/4	35	15.4	22.7	P	844
Lightseeker II 6X - 24X AO	1	44	39	6.9-2.3	3.5-4.0	18-5.5	1/8	26	16.0	23.7	FP	878
LIGHTSEEKER-30												
4X-16X AO	30mm	50	42	12-3.1	3.3-3.8	27-7.5	1/4	74	15.2	23	TW, MD	$998-1120
6X-24X AO	30mm	50	42	7.6-2.1	3.2-3.7	18-5	1/8	52	16.9	27	MD, FP	1076-1196
8.5X-32X AO	30mm	50	42	6.2-1.7	3.0-3.5	14-4	1/8	39	18.0	27	MD, FP	1116-1250
WHITETAILS UNLIMITED												
2X-5X WTU	1	20	39	11.1-4.2	3.1-3.8	65-23	1/2	70	10.7	10	TW	$398
3X-9X WTU	1	40	39	12.9-4.7	3.1-3.8	31-13	1/4	50	12.4	13	TW	398-418
3.7X-11X WTU	1	42	39	13-5.1	3.1-3.8	28-11	1/4	50	13.1	15	TW	558
4.5X-14X WTU	1	50	39	9.1-3.1	3.1-3.8	25-9	1/4	40	14.1	15	TW	698

Scopes are available in high gloss black, matte black, or camouflage, depending on model.
P=Penta-Plex, FP=Fine-Plex, DW=Deepwoods Plex, MD=Mil-Dot, CP=Comp-Plex, TW=Twilight Plex

REDFIELD SCOPES

A couple of years ago the famous Redfield scope company in Colorado shut its doors. But the time-honored name didn't die. Blount has resurrected the Redfield name - and its products. These scopes may well earn the allegiance of hunters just as their forebears did!

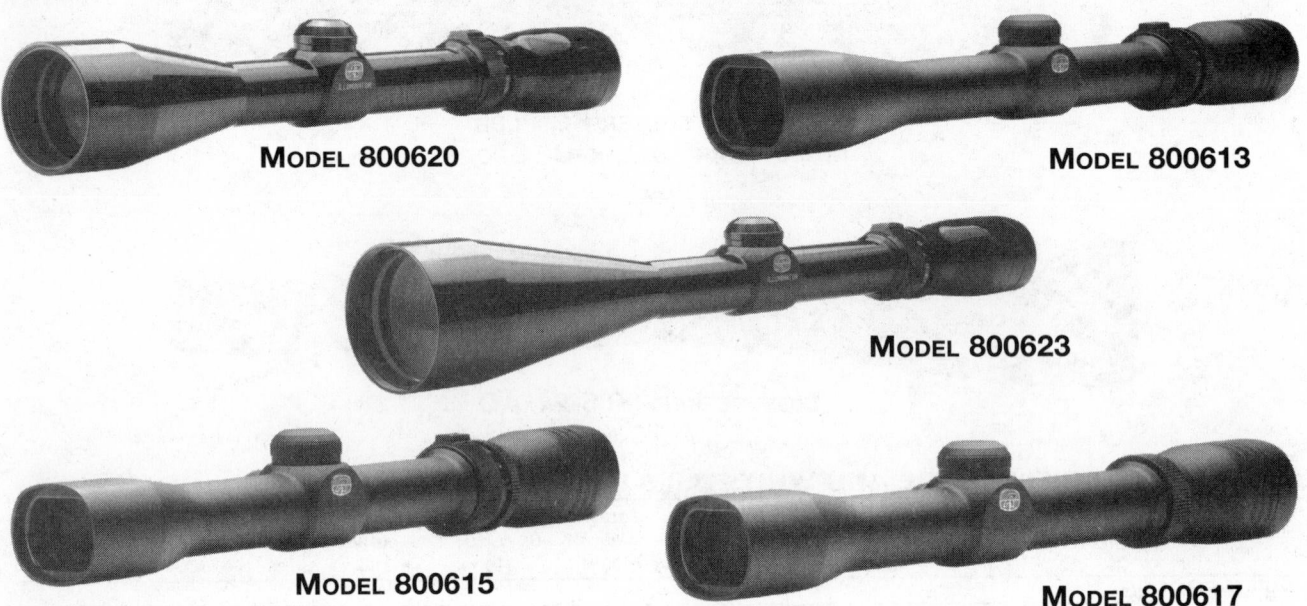

MODEL 800620

MODEL 800613

MODEL 800623

MODEL 800615

MODEL 800617

ILLUMINATOR

Illuminator is Redfield's best scope - made for the hardest of the hardcore hunters. Its large objective lens transmits maximum contrast and target definittion to the eye, giving an edge in the uncertain light of dawn and dust. Crank up the magnification and Illuminator holds zero. The 3-9 variable with a 42mm objective lens comes in gloss, matte or brushed silver finish. The 3-10 variable with 50mm objective lens is available in gloss or matte black.

WIDEFIELD

Widefield's field of view is 30% wider than that of conventional scopes - over 40 feet at 100 yards on two models. It helps scan more area to detect the flick of an ear, or to pick the best shooting lane on running game. It's also designed to mount low on the receiver, a quicker sight picture when mounting the rifle. Choose a 2-7 power, 3-9 power or a fixed 4 power, in gloss or matte finish.

REDFIELD ILLUMINATOR

MODEL	MAGNIFICATION OBJECT LENS DIA-MM	FINISH	EXIT PUPIL RANGE IN VARIABLE MM	FIELD OF VIEW IN FEET @ 100 YDS	OPTIMUM EYE RELIEF INCHES	OVERALL LENGTH INCHES	WEIGHT OUNCES	RETICLE	PRICE
800619	3-9x42	Black matte	13-4.6	31x24-12.1x9.6	3.25-3.13	12.63	14.9	Truplex TV	$649.95
800620	3-9x42	Black polished	13-4.6	31x24-12.1x9.6	3.25-3.13	12.63	14.9	Truplex TV	649.95
800621	3-9x42	Silver matte	13-4.6	31x24-12.1x9.6	3.25-3.13	12.63	14.9	Truplex TV	654.95
800622	3-10x50	Black matte	12-5	34.5x24.5-11.3x8.7	3.125-3	14.75	1 lb 2.1 oz.	Truplex TV	719.95
800623	3-10x50	Black polished	12-5	34.5x24.5-11.3x8.7	3.125-3	14.75	1 lb 2.1 oz.	Truplex TV	719.95

REDFIELD WIDEFIELD

MODEL	MAGNIFICATION OBJECT LENS DIA-MM	FINISH	EXIT PUPIL RANGE IN VARIABLE MM	FIELD OF VIEW IN FEET @ 100 YDS	OPTIMUM EYE RELIEF INCHES	OVERALL LENGTH INCHES	WEIGHT OUNCES	RETICLE	PRICE
800612	3-9x27x36	Black gloss	12x10-4x3	42.5x33-14.3x10.9	3.25-3	12.38	15	Truplex TV Oval	$429.95
800613	3-9x27x36	Black matte	12x10-4x3	42.5x33-14.3x10.9	3.25-3	12.38	15	Truplex TV Oval	429.95
800614	2-7x22x30	Black gloss	9x75x11.75-3.1x4	43.27x57.78-13.53x18.34	3.75-2.88	11.5	13.7	Truplex TV Oval	399.95
800615	2-7x22x30	Black matte	9x75x11.75-3.1x4	43.27x57.78-13.53x18.34	3.75-2.88	11.5	13.7	Truplex TV Oval	399.95
800616	4x22x30	Black gloss	5.3x7.4	29.75x35.95	2.88	11.38	12.4	Truplex TV Oval	349.95
800617	4x22x30	Black matte	5.3x7.4	29.75x35.95	2.88	11.38	12.4	Truplex TV Oval	349.95

MODEL 800604

MODEL 800607

MODEL 800608

MODEL 800610

MODEL 800618

GOLDEN FIVE STAR

The Golden Five Star is purely practical. Its fully multi-coated optics give bright, clear sight pictures. The 3-9 power comes with 40 or 50mm objective lenses. A 40mm objective is standard on the 4-12 and 6-18 power.

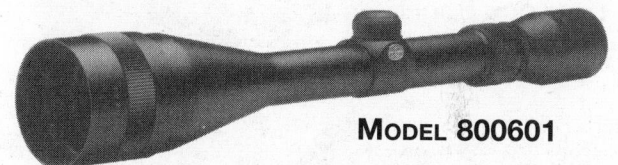

MODEL 800601

TRACKER

The Tracker is designed for the value-conscious hunter who wants a rugged Redfield scope at a modest price. Each Tracker is built from strong, lightweight aircraft aluminum and fine optical glass for maximum performance and clear bright images. The popular 3-9 power gives you a choice of 40 or 50m objective lens. There's also a 3-12x44 and a 4-16x44 with adjustable objective. Each scope has a black matte finish and is covered by the Redfield limited lifetime warranty.

REDFIELD GOLDEN FIVE STAR

Model	Magnification Object Lens Dia-mm	Finish	Exit Pupil Range In Variable MM	Field of View in Feet @ 100 yds	Optimum Eye Relief Inches	Overall Length Inches	Weight Ounces	Reticle	Price
800602	3-9x40	Black matte	13.3-4.4	34-11.3	3-2.88	12.75	13.5	Truplex	$299.95
800603	3-9x40	Black gloss	13.3-4.4	34-11.3	3-2.88	12.75	13.5	Truplex	299.95
800604	3-9x40	Silver matte	13.3-4.4	34-11.3	3-2.88	12.75	13.5	Truplex	309.95
800605	3-9x50	Black matte	11.85-5.1	36.7-12.66	3.63-3.38	13.13	1 lb. 2.7 oz.	Truplex	369.95
800606	3-9x50	Black gloss	11.85-5.1	36.7-12.66	3.63-3.38	13.13	1 lb. 2.7 oz.	Truplex	369.95
800607	3-9x50	Silver matte	11.85-5.1	36.7-12.66	3.63-3.38	13.13	1 lb. 2.7 oz.	Truplex	374.95
800608	4-12x40	Black matte	10.3-3.3	27-9.1	3-2.88	12.63	16	Truplex	429.95
800609	4-12x40	Black gloss	10.3-3.3	27-9.1	3-2.88	12.63	16	Truplex	429.95
800610	6-18x40	Black matte	6.6-2.22	17.8-6.1	3-2.88	13.5	16.3	Truplex	469.95
800611	6-18x40	Black gloss	6.6-2.22	17.8-6.1	3-2.88	13.5	16.3	Truplex	469.95

REDFIELD TRACKER

Model	Magnification Object Lens Dia-mm	Finish	Exit Pupil Range In Variable MM	Field of View in Feet @ 100 yds	Optimum Eye Relief Inches	Overall Length Inches	Weight Ounces	Reticle	Price
800631	3-9x40	Black matte	13.3-4.5	35-11.3	3.25-3.13	12.75	13.5	Truplex	$209.95
800632	3-9x40	Black matte	15.8-6.3	35-11.75	3.25-3	13	1 lb. 2.5 oz.	Truplex	229.95
800618	3-12x44	Black matte	5.5-3.0	33-8.7	3-2.75	12.38	13.5	Truplex	259.95
800601	3-12x44	Black matte	5.5-2.7	26.2-7.42	3-2.625	14.375	16	Truplex	289.95

SAKO SCOPE MOUNTS

OPTILOCK SCOPE MOUNTS

OPTILOCK SCOPE MOUNTS

SAKO Optilock™ mount keeps the scope centered in all conditions. The scope rests in a tight but gentle grip of the evolutionary ball-bearing type ring. The clasping force is distributed evenly along the scope shaft, not spotlike as in conventional mounts, ensuring your valuable optics won't become twisted or scratched. The mounting of the scope is easier and the point of impact stays intact if the scope and mounts are removed as a unit. Available in 1"/25, 4 mm and 30 mm diameters and 3 heights, also in stainless, to fit any scope.

Prices:

1" LOW, MEDIUM & HIGH
(Short, Medium & Long Action) **$99.00**

30mm LOW, MEDIUM & HIGH
(Short, Medium & Long Action) **122.00**

1" LOW & MEDIUM STAINLESS **122.00**

30MM MEDIUM STAINLESS **142.00**

FINNFIRE RINGMOUNTS (for 3/8"-11mm Rail) **50.00**

Scope tube diameter ø	Mount height	mm	Scope lens. end max ø
1. Quickmount for Sako TRG			
1"	Low	30,5	58
1"	Medium	35,5	68
1"	High	40,5	78
30 mm	Low	32,5	62
30 mm	Medium	36,5	70
30 mm	High	40,5	78
2. Steel base mount for Sako 75.			
Extended version also available.			
1"	Low	30,5	55...63
1"	Medium	35,5	65...73
1"	High	40,5	75...83
30 mm	Low	32,5	59...67
30 mm	Medium	36,5	67...75
30 mm	High	40,5	75...83
3. Stainless base mount for Sako 75			
1"	Low	30,5	55...63
1"	Medium	35,5	65...73
30 mm	Low	32,5	59...67
30 mm	Medium	36,5	67...75
4. Steel ring mount for Sako 75			
1"	Low	27	48...56
30 mm	Low	29	52...60

Special aluminum scope mount for 11 mm rail for Sako Finnfire

1"	Low	27	48...56

Standard rings without inner Optilock fastening ring.

Indicated maximum outer diameter of objective end shows values both for heavy barrel (smaller) and standard barrel.

1.

3.

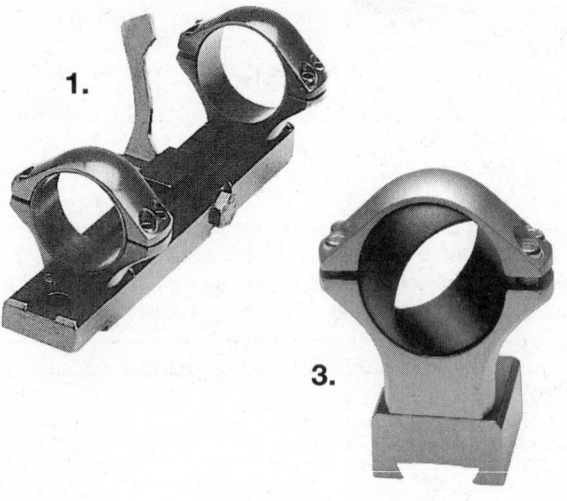

2.

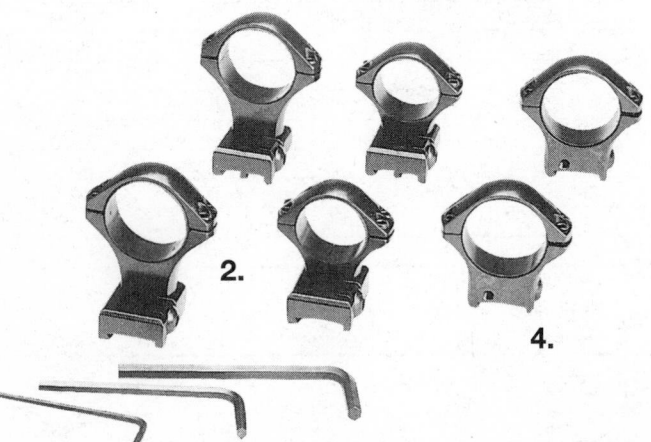

4.

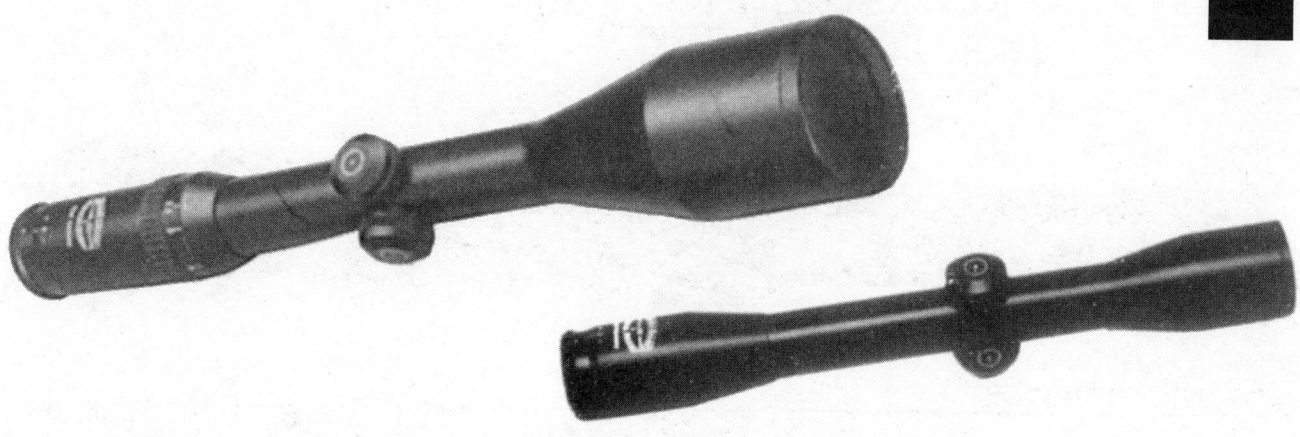

L.E.R. 2.5-10X56 VARIABLE POWER SCOPE $1390.00

Also available: 1.25-4X20 VARIABLE POWER SCOPE . . . $995.00
1.5-6X42 VARIABLE POWER SCOPE 1125.00
3-12X42 VARIABLE POWER SCOPE. 1290.00
3-12X50 VARIABLE POWER SCOPE. 1360.00
4-16X50 VARIABLE POWER SCOPE. 1525.00

Note: All variable power scopes have glass reticles and aluminum tubes.

Also available:
4X36 FIXED POWER SCOPE
1" Steel Tube w/o Mounting Rail $760.00
6X42 FIXED POWER SCOPE
Steel Tube w/o Mounting Rail 835.00
8X56 FIXED POWER SCOPE
Steel Tube w/o Mounting Rail 960.00
10X42 FIXED POWER SCOPE
Steel Tube w/o Mounting Rail 955.00

ILLUMINATED SCOPES

This 1.25-4x is designed for use on magnum rifles and for quick shots at dangerous game. Long eye relief, and a wide field of view (31.5 yards at 200 yards) speed your aim. The new Flash Dot reticle shows up bright against the target at the center of the crosswire.

Magnification: 1.25-4X
Objective lens diameter: 12.7-20mm
Field of view at 100m: 32m-10m; at 100 yards: 96'-16'
Objective housing diameter: 30mm
Scope tube diameter: 30mm
Twilight factor: 3,7-8,9 *Lenses:* hard multi-coating
Click value 1 click @100 meters: 15mm; @100 yards: .540"
Price: $1480.00
Also available:
ILLUMINATED RETICLES
1.5-6x42 . . . . 1525.00
3-12x50 . . . . 1640.00
2.5-10x56 . . . . 1725.00

VARMINT

Designed for long-range target shooters and varmint hunters, Schmidt & Bender 4-16X50 "Varmint" riflescope features a precise parallax adjustment located in a third turret on the left side of the scope, making setting adjustments quick and convenient. The fine crosshairs of Reticle No. 6 and 8 cover only 1.5mm at 100 meters (.053" at 100 yards) throughout the entire magnification range.

Magnification: 4-16X
Objective lens diameter: 50mm
Field of view at 100m: 7.5-2.5m; at 100 yards: 22.5'-7.5'
Objective housing diameter: 57mm
Scope tube diameter: 30mm
Twilight factor: 14-28
Lenses: Hard multi-coating
Click value 1 click @100 meters: 10mm; @100 yards: .360"
Price: $1,595.00

SCHMIDT & BENDER

Police/Marksman II

PM II

SPECIFICATIONS

	10 x 42	3-12 x 50	3-12 x 50 W/PARALLAX ADJ.	3-12 x 50 ILLLUMINATED	4-16 x 50 W/PARALLAX ADJ.
Magnification	10x	3-12x	3-12x	3-12x	4-16x
Field of View	4m	11.1-4.2m	11.1-4.2m	11.1-4.2m	7.5-2.5m
(100m/100yd)	12'	33.3-12.6'	33.3-12.6'	33.3-12.6'	22.5-7.5'
Objective Diameter	42mm	50mm	50mm	50mm	5mm
Exit Pupil	4.2mm	14.3-4.3mm	14.3-4.3mm	14.3-4.3mm	12.5-3.1mm
(mm/inches)	.165"	.563-.169"	.563-.169"	.563-.169"	.492"-.122"
Twilight Factor	20.5	11.4-24.5	11.4-24.5	11.4-24.5	14-28
Eye Relief	95mm	995mm	95mm	95mm	95mm
(mm/inches)	3.74"	3.74"	3.74"	3.74"	3.74"
Middle Tube Diameter	30mm	34mm	34mm	34mm	34mm
Weight	520g	7600g	810g	780g	880g
(gram/lb., oz.)	1 lb. 2 oz.	1 lb. 2.5 oz.	1 lb. 12.5 oz.	1 lb. 11.5 oz.	1 lb. 15 oz.
Adj. Range @	*270 cm/97"	200 cm/72"	200 cm/72"	200 cm/72"	185 cm/67"
(100m/100 yd)	**250 cm/990"	180 cm/64.8"	180 cm/64.8"	180 cm/64.8"	170 cm/61.2"
	***130 cm/46.8"	130 cm/46.8"	130 cm/46.8"	130 cm/46.8"	130 cm/46.8"

*Using the very ends of the elevation adjustment will reduce the windage adjustment range **Sighting-in adjustment range without restriction of windage
***With adjustment knob locked in place

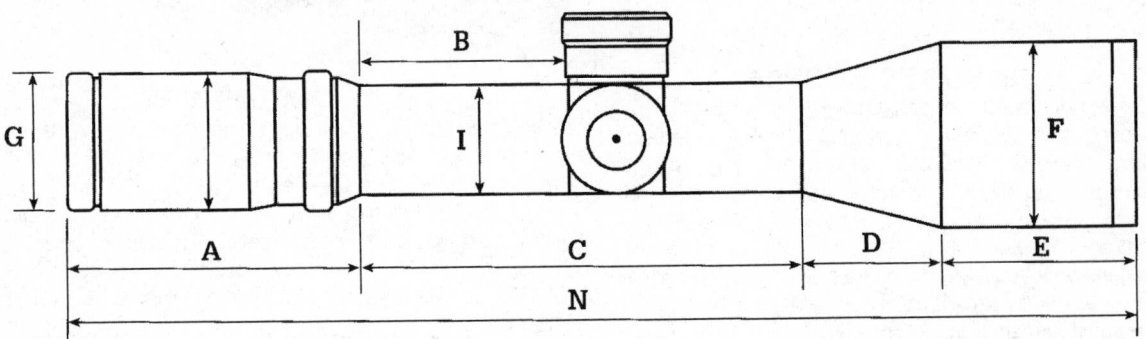

DIMENSIONS

MODEL	A	B	C	D	E	F	G	I	N
10x42	98mm	56mm	139mm	55mm	54mm	50mm	43mm	30mm	346mm
	3.858"	2,204"	5.472"	2.165"	2.126"	1.969"	1.693"		13.622"
3-12x50	101.3mm	68.3mm	145.4mm	43.5mm	64.8mm	57mm	43mm	34mm	355mm
	3.988"	2.689"	6.076"	1.713"	3.354"	2.244"	1.693"		13.976"
4-16x50	101.3mm	68.3mm	145.4mm	85.2mm	75.5mm	57mm	43mm	34mm	405.7mm
	3.988"	2.689"	6.076"	1.713"	3.354"	2.244"	1.693"		15.972"

Scopes For Long Range Shooting

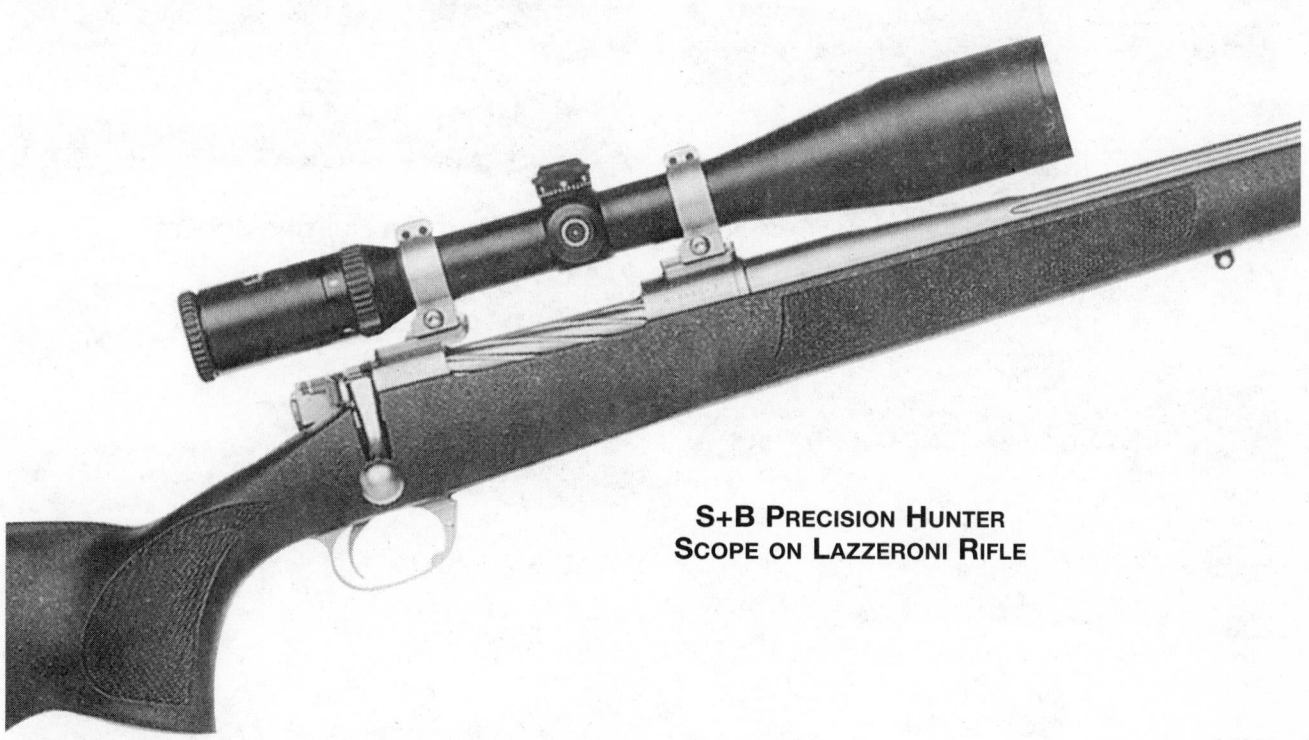

**S+B Precision Hunter
Scope on Lazzeroni Rifle**

PRECISION HUNTER

Very accurate rifles, high-speed cartridges and modern bullets make it possible to shoot accurately at long distances...with the right scope. Scope must let shooter see the target clearly. It must help determine the distance, bullet drop, and wind drift, and it must do it quickly and precisely.

PRECISION HUNTER scopes combine the optical quality of S&B hunting scopes, the most appropriate magnification ranges, and a sophisticated mil-dot reticle (developed by the U.S. Marine Corps) with a bullet drop compensator to give shooters the ability and confidence to place an accurate shot at up to 500 yards. Three different models are available:

4-16 X 50 PRECISION HUNTER SCOPE WITH PARALLAX ADJUSTMENT

Set on 4 power, the mil-dot reticle with fine crosshairs and four posts allows quick target acquisition.

Turned up to 16 power, the mil-dots become visible and can be used for range, trajectory and windage calculations. The top-mounted bullet drop compensator has 5mm (1/5") clicks, permitting quick adjustments up to 500 yards.

The windage adjustment also has 5mm (1/5") clicks, allowing for precise sighting in.

The standard elevation adjustment knob has graduations and numbers for creating a meaningful distance chart for preferred caliber. A blank elevation knob can be special-ordered with markings to be specified after sighting in rifle. A parallax adjustment is conveniently located in a third turret on the left side. This allows shooter to make necessary adjustments with the rifle shouldered, ready to shoot.
Price:. **$1,555.00**

3-12 X 50 PRECISION HUNTER

Identical to the 4-16 x 50 with mil-dot reticle but 1cm (2/5") clicks and no parallax adjustment. It is factory-adjusted to be parallax free at 200 meters.
Price:. **$1,285.00**

2.5-10 X 56 PRECISION HUNTER

Identical to the 3-12 x 50, but with 1 cm (2/5") clicks for windage and elevation adjustment and with our Reticle No. 9, which makes it suitable for dangerous game.
Price:. **$1,325.00**

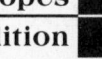

SIGHTRON SHOTGUN SCOPES

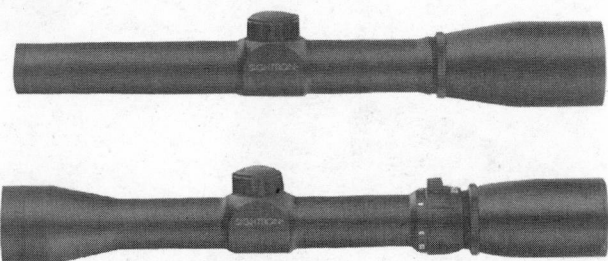

SIGHTRON PISTOL SCOPES

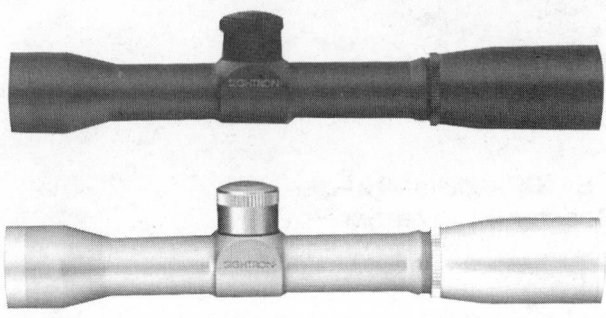

SIGHTRON SERIES III 3.5-10x44
WITH SIDE-MOUNTED ("SADDLE")
PARALLAX ADJUSTMENT

Sightron's scope line offers nearly 40 models in fixed and variable power at modest prices. The SII series features 1-inch alloy tubes; the SIII series has 30 mm magnesium tubes, multicoated lenses, aspherical eyepiece glass and "saddle" mounted parallax adjustments. Most target and competition scopes feature 1/8-minute clicks. Sightron offers stainless finish and a broad choice of reticles including the mil dot.

Prices:

SIII 10x42 mil dot	$625.95
SIII 3.5-10x44 mil dot	696.95
SIII 1.5-6x50 plex	579.95
SII shotgun 2.5-7x32	242.95
SII shotgun 2.5x20	194.95
SII pistol 1x28	212.95
SII pistol 2x28	212.95

SII hunting scopes:

3-9x42	274.95
3-9x42 dot	323.95
3-9x50	339.95
1.5-6x42	287.95

SIGHTRON BENCHREST SCOPES

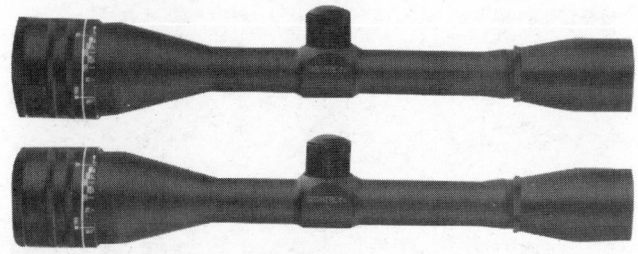

SIGHTRON HUNTING SCOPES

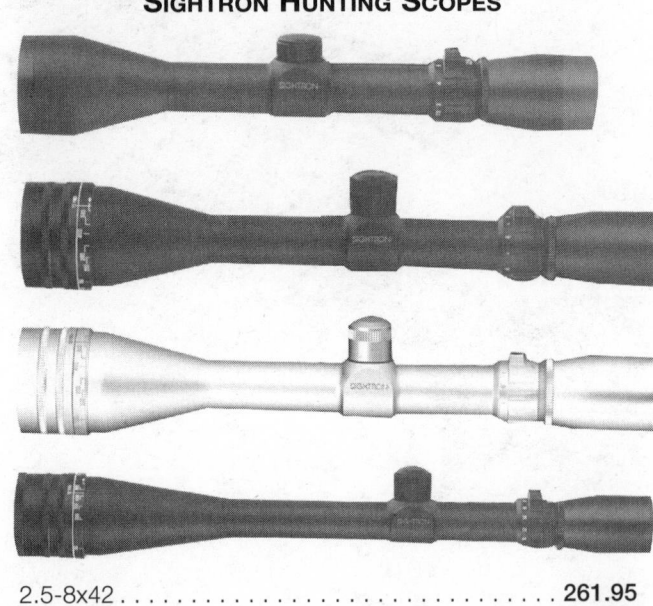

2.5-8x42	261.95
3-12x42	311.95
3-12x50	342.95
3.5-10x42	324.95
3.5-10x50	341.95
4.5-14x42	371.95
4.5-14x50	365.95
6.5-25x50	509.95

SII target scopes:

4-16x42	371.95
4-16x42 dot	411.95
6-24x42	393.95
6-24x42 dot	434.95

SII competition scopes:

3-9x42 mil dot	323.95
3-12x42 mil dot	330.95
4-16x42 mil dot	438.95
6-24x42 mil dot	462.95
24x42 AO	341.95
6x42 AO	341.95

SII compact scopes:

4x32	205.95
2.5-10x32	260.95
2.5-7x32	242.95
6x42	224.95

EXACTRACK

Conventional scopes have a curved surface against a flat surface. This contact is only complete at zero adjustment. As the adjustments press the erector tube in any direction, the contact becomes imperfect, causing the reticle to drift from the optical center. In many cases, since the point of contact is less than what is required to hold the erector tube in position, point of impact can shift. Sightron has developed a new erector tube with an integral ring. ExacTrack will keep constant and perfect point-of-impact, at or off zero. This constant pressure point will ensure the accuracy of all Sightron scopes under heavy recoil and severe use afield.

SIGHTRON COMPACT SCOPES

RETICLE DIMENSION REFERENCES

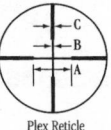 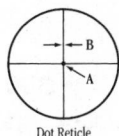 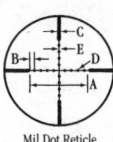 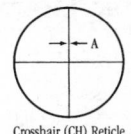 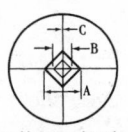 

Plex Reticle   Dot Reticle   Mil Dot Reticle   Crosshair (CH) Reticle   Double Diamond Reticle

Item Number	Magnification	Objective Dia. (mm)	Field of View (ft @ 100 yds)	Eye Relief (in.)	Reticle Type	Reticle Subtensions (in. @ 100 yds) Min. Power A/B/C/D/E	Max. Power A/B/C/D/E	Click Value	Windage/ Elevation Travel (in.)	Tube (Dia.)	Weight (oz.)	Finish
SIII SERIES RIFLE SCOPES												
30mm Side Saddle Rifle Scopes												
SIII10X42MD	10X	42	9.2	3.5	Mil-Dot	36/3.6/1.15/.8/23		1/4 MOA	100	30mm	23.60	Satin Black
SIII3.510X44MD	3.5-10X	44	28-9.2	3.5	Mil-Dot	102.6/10.26/3.25/2.2/.69	36/3.6/1.15/.8/.23	1/4 MOA	100	30mm	24.60	Satin Black
SIII1.56X50MD	1.5-6X	50	64-17	4.3-3.7	Plex	79.0/1.33/5.32	19.8/.33/1.32	1/4 MOA	*	30mm	15.90	Satin Black
SII SERIES RIFLE SCOPES												
Variable Power Rifle Scopes												
SII1.56X42	1.5-6X	42	50-15	4.0-3.8	Plex	79.0/1.33/5.32	19.8/.33/1.32	1/4 MOA	70	1.0 in.	14.00	Satin Black
SII2.58X42	2.5-8X	42	36-12	3.6-4.2	Plex	48.0/.80/3.20	15.0/.25/1.0	1/4 MOA	90	1.0 in.	12.82	Satin Black
SII39X42	3-9X	42	34-12	3.6-4.2	Plex	39.9/.66/2.66	13.2/.22/.88	1/4 MOA	95	1.0 in.	13.22	Satin Black
SII39X42ST	3-9X	42	34-12	3.6-4.2	Plex	39.9/.66/2.66	13.2/.22/.88	1/4 MOA	95	1.0 in.	13.22	Stainless
SII39X42D	3-9X	42	34-12	3.6-4.2	Dot	4/.66	1.3/.22	1/4 MOA	95	1.0 in.	13.22	Satin Black
SII312X42	3-12X	42	32-9	3.6-4.2	Plex	39.9/.66/2.66	9.9/.16/.66	1/4 MOA	80	1.0 in.	12.99	Satin Black
SII3.510X42	3.5-10X	42	32-11	3.6	Plex	34.2/.57/2.28	12.0/.20/.80	1/4 MOA	60	1.0 in.	13.80	Satin Black
SII4.514X42	4.5-14X	42	22-7.9	3.6	Plex	26.4/.44/1.76	8.5/.14/.56	1/4 MOA	50	1.0 in.	16.07	Satin Black
SII39X50	3-9X	50	34-12	4.2-3.6	Plex	39.9/.66/2.66	13.2/.22/.88	1/4 MOA	*	1.0 in.	15.40	Satin Black
SII312X50	3-12X	50	34-8.5	4.5-3.7	Plex	39.9/.66/2.66	9.9/.16/.66	1/4 MOA	*	1.0 in.	16.30	Satin Black
SII3.510X50	3.5-10X	50	30-10	4.0-3.4	Plex	34.2/.57/2.28	12.0/.20/.80	1/4 MOA	50	1.0 in.	15.10	Satin Black
SII4.514X50	4.5-14X	50	23-8	3.9-3.25	Plex	26.4/.44/1.76	8.4/.14/.56	1/4 MOA	60	1.0 in.	15.20	Satin Black
SII6.525X50	6.5-25X	50	15-4.2	3.8-3.3	Plex	18.5/.3/1.2	4.8/0.1/.3	1/4 MOA	40	1.0 in.	20.70	Satin Black
Variable Power Target Scopes												
SII416X42	4-16X	42	26-7	3.6	Plex	30/.50/2.0	7.5/.125/.50	1/8 MOA	56	1.0 in.	16.00	Satin Black
SII416X42ST	4-16X	42	26-7	3.6	Plex	30/.50/2.0	7.5/.125/.50	1/8 MOA	56	1.0 in.	16.00	Stainles
SII416X42D	4-16X	42	26-7	3.6	Dot	1.7/.10	.425/.025	1/8 MOA	56	1.0 in.	16.00	Satin Black
SII416X42DST	4-16X	42	26-7	3.6	Dot	1.7/.10	.425/.025	1/8 MOA	56	1.0 in.	16.00	Stainless
SII624X42	6-24X	42	15.7-4.4	3.6	Plex	19.8/.33/1.32	4.8/.08/.32	1/8 MOA	40	1.0 in.	18.70	Satin Black
SII624X42ST	6-24X	42	15.7-4.4	3.6	Plex	19.8/.33/1.32	4.8/.08/.32	1/8 MOA	40	1.0 in.	18.70	Stainless
SII624X42D	6-24X	42	15.7-4.4	3.6	Dot	1.12/.066	.27/.016	1/8 MOA	40	1.0 in.	18.70	Satin Black
SII624X42DST	6-24X	42	15.7-4.4	3.6	Dot	1.12/.066	.27/.016	1/8 MOA	40	1.0 in.	18.70	Stainless
Competition/Tactical Scopes												
SII39X42MD	3-9X	42	34-14	3.6-4.2	Mil-Dot	150/15/10/4/1	50/5/3.3/1.3/.3	1/4 MOA	95	1.0 in.	13.22	Satin Black
SII312X42MD	3-12X	42	32-9	3.6-4.2	Mil-Dot	144/14/4.7/3.1/.7	36/3.6/1.2/.79/.1	1/4 MOA	80	1.0 in.	12.99	Satin Black
SII416X42MD	4-16X	42	26-7	3.6	Mil-Dot	144/14/4.7/3.1/.6	36/3.6/1.2/.79/.1	1/8 MOA	56	1.0 in.	16.00	Satin Black
SII416X42MDST	4-16X	42	26-7	3.6	Mil-Dot	144/14/4.7/3.1/.6	36/3.6/1.2/.79/.1	1/8 MOA	56	1.0 in.	16.00	Stainless
SII624X42MD	6-24X	42	15.7-4.4	3.6	Mil-Dot	144/14/4.7/3.1/.4	36/3.6/1.2/.79/.1	1/8 MOA	40	1.0 in.	18.70	Satin Black
SII624X42MDST	6-24X	42	15.7-4.4	3.6	Mil-Dot	144/14/4.7/3.1/.4	36/3.6/1.2/.79/.1	1/8 MOA	40	1.0 in.	18.70	Stainless
SII24X44D	24X	44	4.4	4.33	Dot	.27/.016		1/8 MOA	60	1.0 in.	15.87	Satin Black
SII6X42HBRD	6X	42	20	4.00	Dot	.375/.070		1/8 MOA	100	1.0 in.	16.00	Satin Black
SII6X42HBR	6X	42	20	4.00	CH	.33		1/8 MOA	100	1.0 in.	16.00	Satin Black
Compact Rifle Scopes												
SII4X32	4X	32	25	4.52	Plex	30/.50/2.0		1/4 MOA	120	1.0 in.	9.80	Satin Black
SII2.57X32	2.5-7X	32	41-11.8	3.8-3.2	Plex	48/.80/3.20	17.2/.29/1.2	1/4 MOA	120	1.0 in.	11.60	Satin Black
SII2.510X32	2.5-10X	32	41-10.5	3.8-3.5	Plex	48/.80/3.20	12/.20/.80	1/4 MOA	120	1.0 in.	10.93	Satin Black
SII6X42	6X	42	20	3.60	Plex	19.8/.33/1.32		1/4 MOA	100	1.0 in.	12.69	Satin Black
Shotgun Scopes												
SII2.5X20SG	2.5X	20	41	4.33	Plex	48.0/.80/3.20		1/4 MOA	160	1.0 in.	9.00	Satin Black
SII2.57X32SG	2.5-7X	32	41-11.8	3.8-3.2	DD	48/24/.60	17/8.5/.26	1/4 MOA	120	1.0 in.	11.60	Satin Black
Pistol Scopes												
SII1X28P	1X	28	30	9-24	Plex	120.0/2.0/8.0		1/8 MOA	60	1.0 in.	9.30	Satin Black
SII1X28PST	1X	28	30	9-24	Plex	120.0/2.0/8.0		1/8 MOA	60	1.0 in.	9.30	Stainless
SII2X28P	2X	28	15	9-24	Plex	60.0/1.0/4.0		1/8 MOA	60	1.0 in.	9.30	Satin Black

*Specifications not available at press time

SIGHTS & SCOPES

SIMMONS SCOPES

Aetec

AETEC MODEL 800865

MODELS 2100/2101/2102
2.8-10X44 WA *Field of view:* 44'-14' *Eye relief:* 5"
Length: 11.9" *Weight:* 15.5 oz. *Reticle:* Truplex
Price: **$209.99**
  Model 2104 3.8-12x44mm AO **229.99**

MODELS 800865/800866
Illuminated Reticle, black matte
Prices: Model 800865 (2.8-10x44) **$229.99**
  Model 800866 (3.8-12x44) **259.99**

44 Mag Riflescopes

MODEL M1044 (Black Matte)
3-10X44mm
Field of view: 34'-10.5' *Eye relief:* 3"
Length: 12.75" *Weight:* 15.5 oz.
Price: **$159.99**

MODEL M1050DM
44 DIAMOND MAG (Black Matte)
RANGE-CALCULATING SMART RETICLE
(Black Matte)
3.8-12X44mm
Field of view: 26'-9' *Eye relief:* 3"
Length: 13.08" *Weight:* 16.75 oz.
Price: **$219.99**

MODEL M1050DM

MODEL M1047 (Black Matte)
6.5-20X44mm
Field of view: 14'-5'
Eye relief: 2.6"-3.4"
Length: 12.8"
Weight: 19.5 oz.
Price: **$199.99**
Also available:
MODEL M1048
6.5-20X44 Target Turrets Black Matte ($^{1}/_{8}$" MOA) . **$229.99**
  Sunshade for M1047/M1048 . . . . **11.99**

MODEL M1045 (Black Matte)
4-12X44mm
Field of view: 29.5'-9.5' *Eye relief:* 3"
Length: 13.2" *Weight:* 18.25 oz.
Price: **$189.99**

Prohunter and Pro 50 Riflescopes

PRO 50 MODEL 8800

MODEL 7710
3-9X40mm Wide Angle Riflescope
Field of view: 36'-13' *Eye relief:* 3" *Length:* 12.6"
Weight: 13.5 oz. *Features:* Truplex reticle; silver matte finish
Price: **$129.99**
(Same in black matte or black polish, Models 7711 and 7712)
Also available:
MODEL 7700 2-7X32 Black Matte **109.99**
MODEL 7716 4-12X40 Black Matte AO **149.99**

MODEL 7721 6-18X40 AO Black Matte **159.99**
MODEL 7740 6X40 Black Matte. **109.99**

MODEL PRO50
Pro 50's have all the features of the Prohunter models, only with a 50mm lens.
Prices: MODEL 8800 4-12x50mm, AO Black Matte . . **$132.99**
MODEL 8810 6-18x50mm, AO Black Matte **145.99**
MODEL 8825 3.5-10x50mm, Black Matte **174.99**
MODEL 8830 2.5-10x50mm, Black Matte **169.99**

1022T RIMFIRE TARGET SCOPE

Magnification: 3-9X32mm WA/AO
Finish: Black matte
Features: Adjustable for windage and elevation; adjustable objective lens, target knobs
Price: $149.99
Also available:
1022 4X32 black matte w/22 rings $64.99
1031 4X28 22 Mag Mini black matte w/22 rings . . . 69.99
1032 4X28 22 Mag Mini silver matte w/22 rings . . . 72.99
1033 4X32 silver matte w/22 rings 64.99
1037 3-9X32 silver matte w/22 rings. 74.99
1039 3-9X32 black matte w/22 rings 72.99

1022T RIMFIRE TARGET SCOPE

Black Powder Scopes

MODEL BP2732M

MODEL BP2732M

Magnification: 2-7X32 *Finish:* Black matte
Field of view: 57.7'-16.6' 100 yards *Eye relief:* 3"
Reticle: Truplex *Length:* 11.6" *Weight:* 12.4 oz.
Price: $119.99

Also available: MODELS BP400M/400S
4X20 Black Matte or Silver Matte, Long Body
Field of view: 28' *Eye relief:* 5.0"
Length: 10.25" *Weight:* 8.7 oz. *Reticle:* Truplex
Price: $44.99

Shotgun Scopes

MODEL 7790D

MODELS 21004/7790D

Magnification: 4X32
Finish: Black matte
Field of view: 16' (Model 21004); 17' (Model 7790D)
Eye relief: 5.5"
Reticle: Truplex (Model 21004); ProDiamond (Model 7790D)
Length: 8.5" (8.8" Model 21004)
Weight: 8.75 oz. (9.1 oz. Model 7790D)

Prices:
MODEL 21004 . . . . $74.99
MODEL 7790D 109.99
Also available:
MODEL 21005 2.5X20 Black matte (Truplex reticle) 54.99
MODEL 7789D 2X32 Black matte
(ProDiamond reticle) 94.99
MODEL 7791D 1.5-5X20 WA Black matte
(ProDiamond reticle) 124.99

Sights & Scopes

SIGHTS & SCOPES

SIMMONS SCOPES

8-Point

The Simmons 8-Point series is aimed at the entry level or budget-minded shooter who needs a reliable scope at an affordable price. The 8-Point family includes seven scopes in popular configurations: 3-9x32mm, 3-9x40mm, 3-9x50mm, 4x32mm, 4-12x40mm AO, and 4x32 mm shotgun. All versions are offered in black matte finish, and the 3-9x40mm is also available in silver. Fully coated lenses enhance light transmission for low-light viewing and reduce reflections. Simmons' popular Truplex reticle is standard. Windage and elevation are adjusted in 1/4-MOA increments. The new 8-Point scopes are shockproof, waterproof, and fogproof.

**SIMMONS 8 POINT
3-9x40 BLACK**

8-POINT SCOPE
4-12X40MM AO

Magnification: 4-12X
Field of View: 29 - 10 ft. at 100 yards
Eye Relief: 3 inches at 4X and 2 7/8 inches at 12X
Length: 13.5 inches
Weight: 15.75 oz.
Reticle: Duplex
Finish: Black Matte
Price: $89.99

8-POINT SCOPE
4X32MM

Magnification: 4X
Field of View: 28.75 ft. at 100 yards
Eye Relief: 3 inches
Length: 11.625 inches
Weight: 14.25 oz.
Reticle: Duplex
Finish: Black Matte
Price: $29.99

8-POINT SCOPE
3-9X32 MM

Magnification: 3-9X
Field of View: 37.5 - 13 ft. at 100 yards
Eye Relief: 3 inches at 3X and 2 7/8 inches at 9X

Length: 11.875 inches
Weight: 11.5 oz.
Reticle: Duplex
Finish: Black Matte
Price: $39.99

8-POINT SCOPE
3-9X40MM

Magnification: 3-9X
Field of View: 37 - 13 ft. at 100 yards
Eye Relief: 3 inches at 3X and 2 7/8 inches at 9X
Length: 12.25 inches
Weight: 12.25 oz.
Reticle: Duplex
Finish: Black Matte or Silver
*Price:*Black Matte $44.99
Silver 49.99

8-POINT SCOPE
3-9X50MM

Magnification: 3-9X
Field of View: 32 - 11.75 ft. at 100 yards
Eye Relief:: 3 inches at 3X and 2 7/8 inches at 9X
Length: 13 inches
Weight: 15.25 oz.
Reticle: Duplex
Finish: Black Matte
Price: $64.99

Whitetail Expedition

Simmons introduced aspherical lenses to shooters with the AETEC series of riflescopes. Now, Simmons offers aspherical lenses in the Whitetail Expedition series. Because aspherical lenses eliminate minor aberrations found in regular spherical lens systems, these scopes produce a sharp, crisp view all the way to the edges of the lens. Field of view is 30% greater than that of other scopes of comparable magnification and objective lens size. All lens surfaces of the new Whitetail Expedition scopes, inside and out, are fully-multicoated for maximum edge-to-edge brightness and reflection reduction. The scopes have a Truplex reticle, the most versatile and popular in the marketplace, and are shockproof, waterproof, and fogproof. Configurations available in the Whitetail Expedition series are: 1.5-6x32mm WA, 3-9x42mm WA, 4-12x42mm WA, and 6-18x42mm WA. The two higher-range scopes have adjustable objective lenses for precision shooting at any range. Adjustments for windage and elevation are 1/4-MOA increments.

**SIMMONS 3-9x42MM
WHITETAIL EXPEDITION SCOPE**

WHITETAIL EXPEDITION 1.5-6X32MM

Magnification: 1.5-6X *Field of View:* 72 - 19 ft. at 100 yards *Eye Relief:* 3 inches *Length:* 11.16 inches *Weight:* 15 oz. *Reticle:* Duplex *Finish:* Black Matte
Price: $259.99

WHITETAIL EXPEDITION 3-9X42MM

Magnification: 3-9X *Field of View:* 40 - 13.5 ft. at 100 yards *Eye Relief:* 3 inches *Length:* 13.2 inches *Weight:* 17.5 oz. *Reticle:* Duplex *Finish:* Black Matte
Price: $269.99

WHITETAIL EXPEDITION 4-12X42MM

Magnification: 4-12X *Field of View:* 29 - 9.6 ft. at 100 yards *Eye Relief:* 3 inches *Length:* 13.46 inches *Weight:* 21.25 oz. *Reticle:* Duplex *Finish:* Black Matte
Price: $299.99

WHITETAIL EXPEDITION 6-18X42MM

Magnification: 6-18X *Field of View:* 18.3 - 6.5 ft. at 100 yards *Eye Relief:* 3 inches *Length:* 15.35 inches *Weight:* 22.5 oz. *Reticle:* Duplex *Finish:* Black Matte
Price: $319.99

Prohunter Handgun Scopes

MODEL 7738 (4X)

MODEL 7732 (2X)

MODEL #7732/7733 (Silver Matte)
SPECIFICATIONS
Magnification: 2X *Field Of View:* 22' *Eye Relief:* 9-17"
Length: 8.75" *Weight:* 7 oz. *Reticle:* Truplex
Finish: Black matte
Price: $124.99

MODEL #7738/7739 (Silver Matte)
SPECIFICATIONS
Magnification: 4X *Field Of View:* 15' *Eye Relief:* 11.8-17.6" *Length:* 9" *Weight:* 8 oz. *Reticle:* Truplex
Finish: Black matte
Price: $134.99

SIGHTS & SCOPES

SWAROVSKI SCOPES

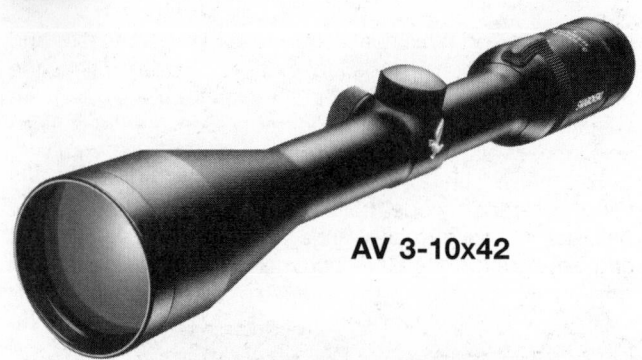

AV 3-10x42

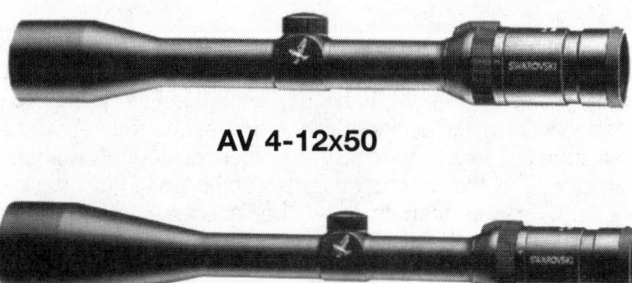

AV 4-12x50

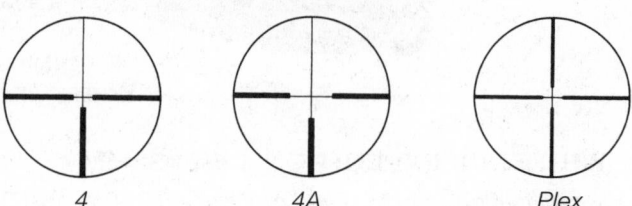

AV 3-9x36

SWAROVSKI AV-SERIES LIGHTWEIGHT 1-INCH SCOPES

Developed for American hunters, the AV scopes feature constant-size reticles, lightweight alloy tubes and satin finish. Totally waterproof even with caps removed, these scopes have fully multi-coated lenses and the quality that has made Swarovski famous.

Prices:
AV 3-10 x 42 (4A, Plex) $821.11
AV 4-12 x 50 (4A, Plex) 843.33
AV 3-9 x 36 (4A, Plex) 743.33
AV 6-18x50P (4A, Plex) 887.78

AV RETICLES AVAILABLE:

4   4A   Plex

AV 6-18X50 NEW

Swarovski's new 6-18x50 incorporates a parallex adjustment ring that insures parallex free accuracy from 50 yds to beyond 500. The objective bell, 1" tube, turret housing and ocular bell are machined out of one solid piece of alloy bar stock for strength, weight and waterproof integrity.

Price: $887.78

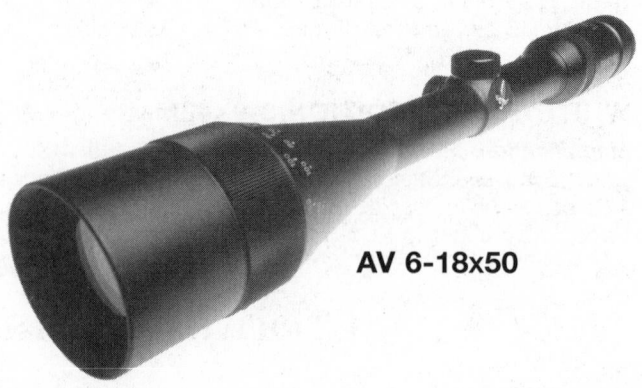

AV 6-18x50

	AV 3-9x36	AV 3-10x42	AV 4-12x50	AV 6-18x50
Magnification	3-9x	3.3-10x	4-12x	6-18x
Objective lens diameter: mm	36	42	50	50
in	1.42	1.55	1.97	1.97
Exit pupil, diameter: mm	12-4	12.6-4.2	12.5-4.2	8.3-2.8
Eye relief: in	3.5	3.5	3.5	3.5
Field of view, real: m/100m	13-4.5	11-3.9	9.7-3.3	17.4-6.5
ft/100yds	39-13.5	33-11.7	29.1-9.9	17.4-6.5
Diopter compensation (dpt)	± 2.6	±2.5	±2.5	±2.5
Transission (%)	94	94	94	92
Twilight factor (DIN 58388)	9-18	9-21	11-25	17-30
Impact Point correction per click: in/100yds	0.25	0.25	0.25	0.25
Max. elevation/windage adjustment range: ft/100yds	4.8	4.2	3.6	3.9
Length, approx: in	11.8	12.44	13.5	14.85
Weight, approx (oz.): L	11.6	12.7	13.9	20.3
LS	–	13.6	15.2	–

L=light alloy • LS=light alloy with rail

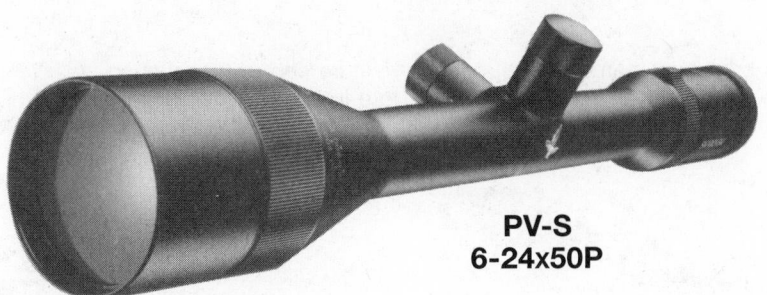

**PV-S
6-24x50P**

Swarovski's 6-24X50mm "PH" riflescope was developed for long-range target, big-game and varmint shooting. Its waterproof parallax adjustment system should be popular with whitetail "Bean Field Shooters" and long-range varmint hunters looking for a choice of higher powers in a premium rifle scope and still deliver accuracy. The scope will also appeal to many bench rest shooters who compete in certain classes where power and adjustment are limited. A non-magnifying, fine plex reticle and an all-new fine crosshair reticle with 1/8" MOA dot are available in the 6-24X50mm scope. Reticle adjustment clicks are 1/6" (minute) by external, waterproof target knobs. The internal optical system features a patented coil spring suspension system for dependablle accuracy and positive reticle adjustment. The objective bell, 30mm middle tube, turret housing and ocular bell are machined from one solid bar of aluminum.

Price: $1,687.78

PRICES PH SERIES RIFLESCOPES

PF 6x42 (4A, 7A) **$987.78**
PF 8x50 (4A, 7A). **1,010.00**
PF 8x56 (4A, 7A). **1,054.44**
PH 1.25-4x24 (4A) **1,087.78**
PH 1.25-4x24 (#24). **1,110.00**
PH 1.25-4x24 (Ill. ret. #24N) **1,354.44**
PH 1.5-6x42 (4A, 7A) **1,221.11**
PH 1.5-6x42 (#24) **1,243.33**
PH 2.5-10x42 (4A, 7A, PLEX) **1,376.67**
  illum reticle (4NK) **1,665.56**

PH 2.5-10x56 (4A, 7A) **1,410.00**
  w/illum reticle (4NK, PLEXN). **1,754.44**
PH 3-12x50 (4A, 7A, PLEX) **1,421.11**
  TDS reticle **1,532.22**
  w/illum reticle (4NK, PLEXN). **1,754.44**
PH 6-24x50 (4A, PLEX) with low turret **1,610.00**
PH 6-24x50 (low turrets, TDS). **1,665.55**
PH 4-16x50 (4A, PLEX) **1,476.67**
PH 4-16x50 (TDS). **1,532.22**

PF& PV

	PF 6x42	PF/PF-N 8x50	PF/PF-N 8x56	PV/PV-1 1.25-4x24	PV 1.5-6x42	PV/PV-N 2.5-10x42	PV/PV-N 2.5-10x56	PV/PV-N 3-12x50	PV 4-16x50P	PV 6-24x50P	PV-S 6-24x50P
Magnification	6x	8x	8x	1.25-4x	1.5-6x	2.5-10x	2.5-10x	3-12x	4-16x	6-24x	6-24x
Objective lens diameter: mm	42	50	56	17-24	20-42	33-42	33-56	39-50	50	50	50
in	1.65	1.97	2.20	0.67-0.94	0.79-1.65	1.3-1.65	1.3-2.20	1.54-1.97	1.97	1.97	1.97
Exit pupil, diameter: mm	7	6.25	7	12.5-6	13.1-7	13.1-4.2	13.1-5.6	13.1-4.2	12.5-3.1	8.3-2.1	8.3-2.1
Eye relief: in	3.15	3.15	3.15	3.15	3.15	3.15	3.15	3.15	3.15	3.15	3.15
Field of view, real: m/100m	7	5.2	5	32.8-10.4	21.8-7	13.2-4.2	13.2-4.1	11-3.5	9.1-2.6	6.2-1.8	6.2-1.8
ft/100yds	21	15.6	15.6	98.4-31.2	65.4-21	39.6-12.6	39.6-12.3	33-10.5	27.3-7.8	18.6-5.4	18.6-5.4
Diopter compensation (dpt)	+2. -3	+2. -3	+2. -3	+2. -3	+2. -3	+2. -3	+2. -3	+2. -3	+2. -3	+2. -3	+2. -3
Transission (%)	94	94/92	93/91	93/91	93	94/92	93/91	94/92	90	90	90
Twilight factor (DIN 58388)	16	20	21	4-10	4-16	7-21	7-24	9-25	11-28	17-35	17-35
Impact Point correction per click: in/100yds	0.36	0.36	0.36	0.54	0.36	0.36	0.36	0.36	0.18	0.18	0.17
Max. elevation/windage adjustment range: ft/100yds	3.9	3.3	3.9	9.9	6.6	3.9	3.9	3.3	E:5.4/W:3	E:3.6/W:2.1	E:3.6/W:2.1
Length, approx: in	12.83	13.94	13.27	10.63	12.99	13.23	13.62	14.33	14.21	15.43	15.43
Weight, approx (oz.): L	12.0	14.8	15.9	12.7	16.2	15.2	18.0	16.9	22.2	23.6	24.5
LS	13.4	15.9	16.9	13.8	17.5	16.4	19.0	18.3	—	—	—

L=light alloy • LS=light alloy with rail

Swift Instruments, Inc., a prominent name in the optics industry since 1926, has four new scopes in its line: 3 rifle scopes that offer faster focusing with the Swift Speed Focus feature and one new shock resistant pistol scope. All four are waterproof, shock-tested and have multi-coated lenses for a bright image from dawn to dusk without glare.

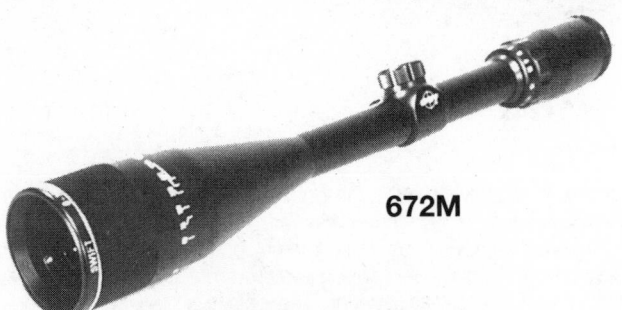

672M

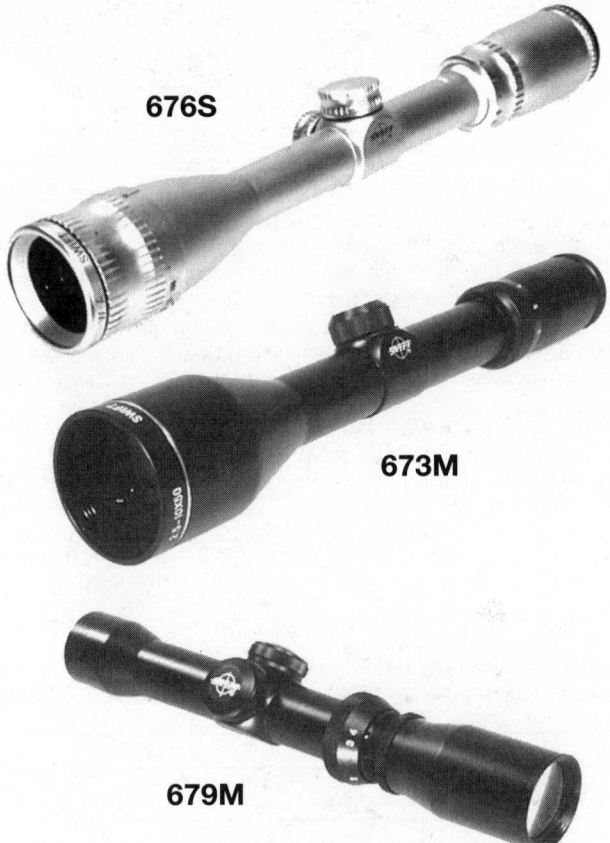

676S

673M

679M

MODEL 672M
SWIFT PREMIER RIFLE SCOPE
6-18X, 50MM - WA - MULTI-COATED - WATERPROOF - SPEED FOCUS

A great scope for varmint, silhouette and target shooters. The Speed Focus feature presents optimum focusing ability at any power setting. Multi-coated lenses with an adjustable objective to correct parallax. New longer tube body allows more eye relief adjustment in long action firearms. Black matte finish.

Price: **$260.00**

MODEL 673M
SWIFT PREMIER RIFLE SCOPE
FEATURING A 30MM TUBE FOR A BRIGHTER IMAGE AT DAWN OR DUSK 2.5-10X, 50 - WIDE ANGLE - WATERPROOF - MULTI-COATED - SPEED FOCUS

This scope with a 30mm tube and a 50mm objective is brighter than other scopes under poor light condition. It has an extremely wide field. The objective adjustment allows accurate shooting from close up to distant ranges. Elevation and windage adjustments, full saddle hard anodized 30mm tube.

Price: **$295.00**

MODEL 676S
SWIFT PREMIER RIFLE SCOPE
4-12X, 40 - WA - WATERPROOF - MULTI-COATED - SPEED FOCUS

With a parallax adjustment from 10 yards to infinity, this scope is highly adaptable and excellent for use as a varmint scope or on gas powered air rifles. Elevation and windage adjustments are mounted full saddle on the hard anodized 1-inch tube. Speed Focus adjustment brings shooters on target easily. The objectives are multi-coated; Quadraplex reticle is standard. Available in regular (676), matte (676M), and silver finish (676S).

Price: **$190.00**
Gloss **180.00**
Matte **185.00**

MODEL 679M
SWIFT PISTOL SCOPE
1.25-4X, 28MM - 8.2 OZ.

An extremely versatile full saddle scope with excellent eye relief of 23 inches at 1.25x, 15 inches at 4x. This ruggedly made scope is shock resistant and waterproof. It has 7 magenta coated lens elements and weighs only 8.2 ounces. Matte finished.

Price: **$250.00**

Swift offers a broad range of scopes, including:

SHOTGUN	THE PREMIER LINE FEATURES
1x20	4x32
4x32	4x40
1.5-4.5x21	6x40
3-9x40	2-7x40
3-9x50	3-9x32
2.5-10x50	3.9x40
6-18x44	3.5-10x44
6-18x50	4-12x50

New for 2001

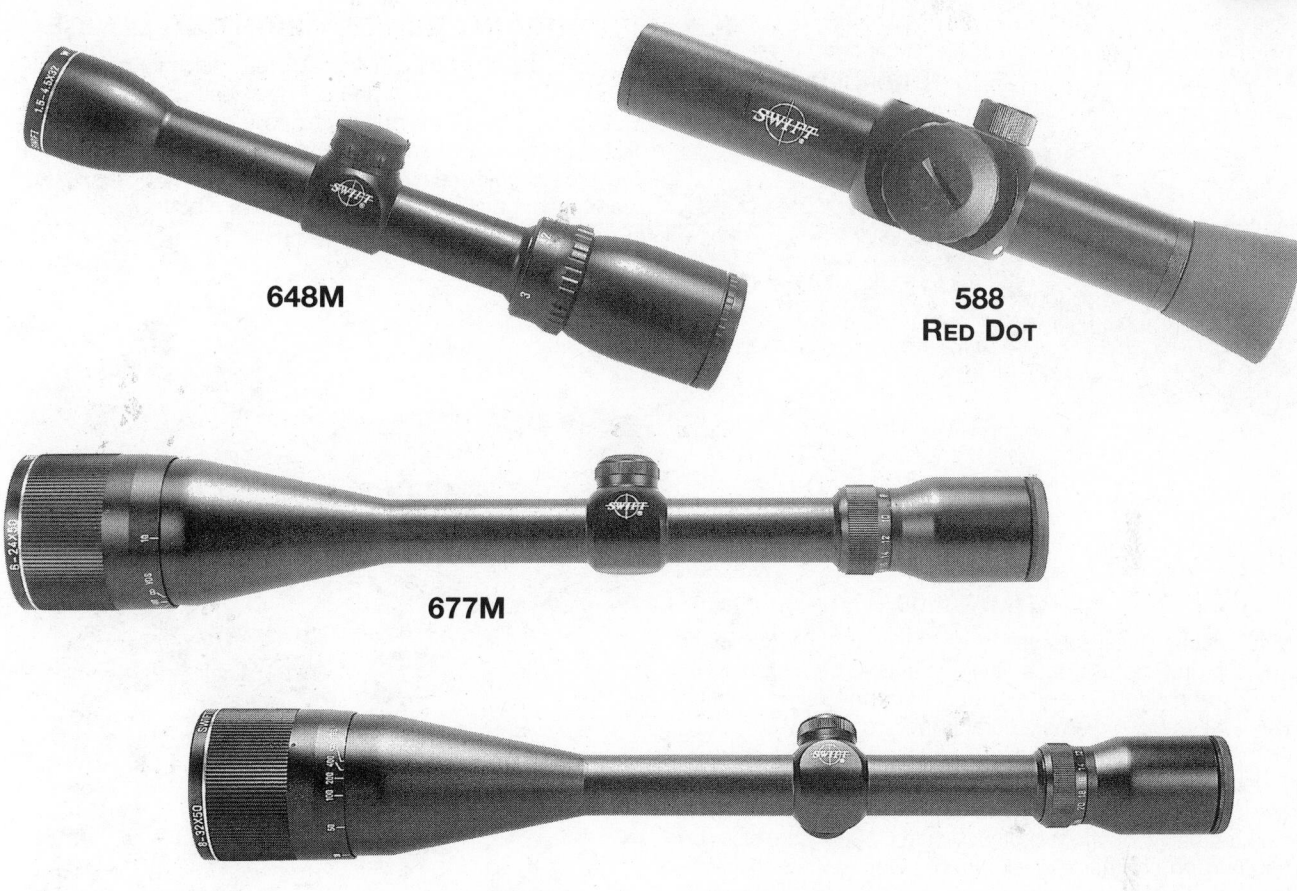

648M

588
RED DOT

677M

678M

MODEL 648M SWIFT PREMIER
1.5-4.5x, 32mm - WA-Waterproof-Multi-coated-SPEED FOCUS

Considered to be the most versatile scope in the Premier line, the 1.5-45x is ideal on shotguns and black powder rifles. Eye relief ranges from 3.05 to 3.27. Crosshair and circle reticle make this riflescope easy to focus on target, and ideal for turkey hunting. Black matte finish.

MODEL 677M SWIFT PREMIER
6-24x, 50mm - WA - Waterproof - Multi-coated - SPEED FOCUS

With a magnification range of 6 to 24 power and a 50mm objective lens with sunshade, this scope is the one to use when you're after really tight groups. Elevation and windage adjustments are mounted full saddle on the hand anodized 1-inch tube. The objective may be adjusted for parallax. This is a fine scope for long-range big game hunting and varminting.

MODEL 678M SWIFT PREMIER
8-32x, 50mm - Waterproof - Multi-Coated - SPEED FOCUS

With an ample field of view of 13 feet at 100 yards and eye relief of 3.13 inches, this scope can be used for bench rest shooting and long range hunting. It is very effective on prairie dogs. Its parallax adjustment adds versatility. Elevation and windage adjustments are mounted full saddle on the hard anodized 1-inch tube. Equipped with sunshade.

MODEL 588 RED DOT SCOPE
1x, 21mm - Fog-proof - Fully coated

Under any light conditions this Aerolite red dot electronic sight can be rapidly aligned for pinpoint accuracy. It has a field of view of 39 feet at 100 yards and unlimited eye relief. It is free of parallax from 5 meters to infinity. Body length is 6 1/4" to 7 1/8" with the rubber eyecup. Weighs only 5 ounces. These characteristics make it especially suitable for handgun shooting, shotguns and bows. CR-2032: 3-volt button battery is included.

PROPOINT 1x25

PROPOINT RED DOT SIGHTING DEVICE

Propoint Red Dot Sights have been the choice for competitive shooters, turkey hunters and slug gun enthusiasts for years. Built to last, the Propoint features solid construction, flawless tracking and a rheostat-controlled illuminated red dot. Included accessories: rings to fit standard 5/8" bases, extension tubes, polarizing filter and one lithium battery.

OPTIMA 2000 SIGHT

OPTIMA 2000

What makes this ProPoint so revolutionary is that, unlike previous ProPoints, it does not have a tube. It's smaller (only 1 1/2") and lighter (only 1/2 oz.) than any other sighting device. It's also extremely durable and rugged. After thousands of test rounds it held its point of aim and its one-piece, dovetailed-style slide mount remained immovable. Its red dot was always on, with no time lost turning it on. While used primarily on pistols, the Optima 2000 can also be mounted on shotguns or slug guns. Optima 2000 is available with a bright, in-focus 3.5 or 7 M.O.A. dot on the same plane as iron sights for fast target acquisition.
Price: **$475.33**

PROPOINT SCOPES

Model	Power	Objective Diameter	Finish	Reticle	Field of View @ 100 Yds.	Eye Relief	Tube Diam.	Scope Length	Scope Weight	Prices
PDP2	1X	25mm	Black Matte	5 M.O.A. Dot	40'	Unlimited	30mm	5"	5.5 oz.	$267.37
PDP2ST	1X	25mm	Stainless	5 M.O.A. Dot	40'	Unlimited	30mm	5"	5.5 oz.	267.37
PDP3	1X	25mm	Black Matte	5 M.O.A. Dot	52'	Unlimited	30mm	5"	5.5 oz.	320.85
PDP3ST	1X	25mm	Stainless	10 M.O.A. Dot	52'	Unlimited	30mm	5"	5.5 oz.	320.85
PDP3CMP	1X	30mm	Black Matte	10 M.O.A. Dot	68'	Unlimited	33mm	4.75"	5.4 oz.	373.47
PDP5CMP	1X	45mm	Black Matte	4,8,12,16 M.O.A. Dot	82'	Unlimited	47mm	4"	8 oz.	427.80
PDP6CMP	1X	30mm	Black Matte	10 M.O.A. Dot	72'	Unlimited	38mm	3"	5.8 oz.	409.97
PDP5VR	1X	28mm	Black Matte		14.9'	Unlimited	30mm			669.70

PISTOL SCOPES

Model	Power	Objective Diameter	Finish	Reticle	Field of View @ 100 Yds.	Eye Relief	Tube Diam.	Scope Length	Scope Weight	Prices
P2X20	2X	20mm	Black Gloss	30/30	21'	10"-23"	1"	8"	6.5 oz.	126.47
P2X20ST	2X	20mm	Stainless	30/30	21'	10"-23"	1"	8"	6.5 oz.	126.47
P1.254X28	1.25X-4X	28mm	Black Gloss	30/30	23'-9'	15"-23"	1"	9.25"	8.2 oz.	194.38
P1.254X28ST	1.25X-4X	28mm	Stainless	30/30	23'-9'	15"-23"	1"	9.25"	8.2 oz.	194.38

World Class Plus Riflescopes

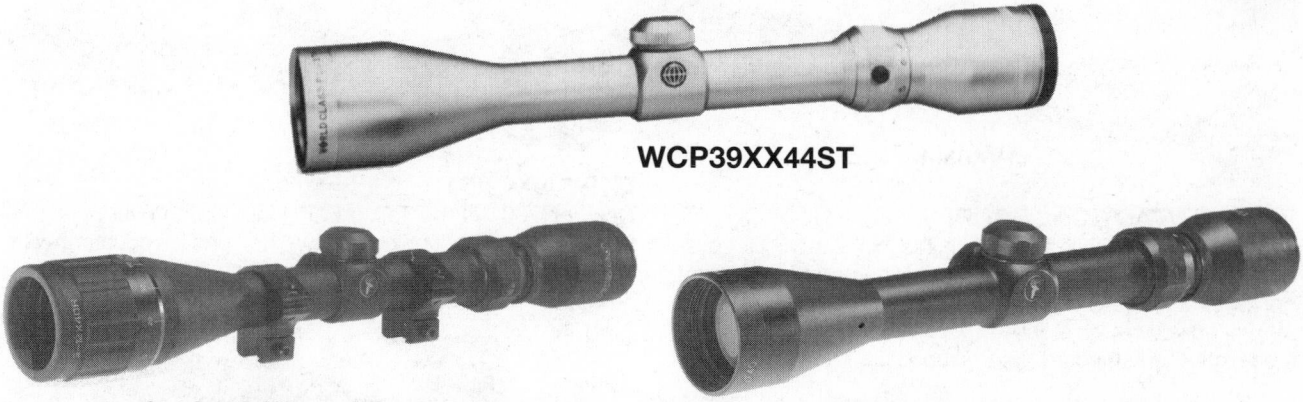

WCP39XX44ST

3-12x40 WORLD CLASS .22

3-9x40 WORLD CLASS 40

WORLD CLASS RIFLESCOPES

Long a favorite with sportsmen, wide-angle World Class Riflescopes now have 1" Advanced Monotube Construction to make them even stronger and more shock resistant. SuperCon multi-layered coating on the objective and ocular lenses and fully-coated optics throughout increase light transmission. World Class Riflescopes are waterproof, fogproof and shockproof.

Model	Power	Objective Diameter	Finish	Reticle	F.O.V. @ 100 Yd.s	Eye Relief	Tube Diameter	Length	Weight	Prices
WORLD CLASS PLUS RIFLESCOPES										
WCP39X44	3X-9X	44mm	Black Gloss	30/30	39'-14'	3.5"	1"	12.75"	15.8 oz.	305.57
DWCP39X44	3X-9X	44mm	Black Matte	30/30	39'-14'	3.5"	1"	12.75"	15.8 oz.	305.57
WCP39X44ST	3X-9X	44mm	Stainless Steel	30/30	39'-14'	3.5"	1"	12.75"	15.8 oz.	305.57
WCP3.510X50	3.5X-10X	50mm	Black Gloss	30/30	30'-10.5'	3.75"	1"	13"	17.1 oz.	322.54
DWCP3.510X50	3.5X-10X	50mm	Black Matte	30/30	30'-10.5'	3.75"	1"	13"	17.1 oz.	322.54
DWCP416X44	4X-16X	44mm	Black Matte	30/30	27'-8'	3"	1"	14.75"	20 oz.	322.54
DWCP416X40TR	4X-16X	40mm	Black Matte	stadia	26'-7'	2.75"	1"	14.5"	16.4 oz.	322.54
DWCP624X50	6X-24X	50mm	Black Matte	30/30	17'-5.5'	3"	1"	16"	24 oz.	322.54
DWCP624X40TR	6X-24X	40mm	Black Matte	stadia	17'-4'	3"	1"	15.5"	17.2 oz.	322.54
WORLD CLASS RIFLESCOPES										
DWCP39X40N	3x-9x	40mm	Black matte	30/30	41'-15'	3"	1"	12.75"	13 oz.	
DWCP39X40TV	3x-9x	40mm	Black matte	30/30 TV	41'-15'	3"	1"	12.75"	13 oz.	
WA39X40N	3x-9x	40mm	Black gloss	30/30	41'-15'	3"	1"	12.75"	13 oz.	
WA39X40STN	3x-9x	40mm	Stainless	30/30	41'-15'	3"	1"	12.75"	13 oz.	
DWC39X40IR	3x-9x	40mm	Black matte	30/30 electronic	36'-13'	3"	1"	13"	15.3 oz.	
DWC4X40	4x	40mm	Black matte	30/30	28.3'	3"	1"	12"	12.5 oz.	
WORLD CLASS 50										
DWC39X50N	3x-9x	50mm	Black matte	30/30	41'-13'	3"	1"	12.5"	15.8 oz.	
DWC416X50	4x-16x	50mm	Black matte	30/30	28'-7'	3"	1"	16"	20.5 oz.	
DWC520X50	5x-20x	50mm	Black matte	30/30	16'-3'	3"	1"	16"	20 oz.	
DWC624X50	6x-24x	50mm	Black matte	30/30	16'-3'	3"	1"	16.5"	20 oz.	
WORLD CLASS COMPACT										
DWC28X32	2x-8x	32mm	AWF/Black matte	30/30	50'-17'	4"	1"	10.5"	12.5 oz.	
DWC4X32IR	4x	32mm	AWF/Black matte	30/30 electronic	20'	6"	1"	10.25"	12.6 oz.	
DWC4X32	4x	32mm	AWF/Black matte	30/30	25'	5"	1"	10"	10.5 oz.	
WORLD CLASS BLACK POWDER										
BP1X32	1x	32mm	Black matte	30/30	59'	3"	1"	10.75"	11.5 oz.	
BP1755X20	1.75x-5x	20mm	Black matte	30/30	63'-21'	3"	1"	10.75"	10.7 oz.	
BP27X32	2x-7x	32mm	Black matte	30/30	56'-17'	3.25"	1"	11.5"	10 oz.	
BP39X32	3x-9x	32mm	Black matte	30/30	41'-14'	3"	1"	11.75"	11.9 oz.	
WORLD CLASS .22										
DWC28X32R	2x-8x	32mm	AWF/Black matte	30/30	55'-14'	2.75"	1"	10.5"	12.5 oz.	
DWC312X40R	3x-12x	40mm	AWF/Black matte	30/30	26'-7'	3"	1"	13.75"	17.5 oz.	

SIGHTS & SCOPES

TASCO RIFLESCOPES

VARMINT 2.5-10x42

VARMINT/TACTICAL SCOPES

Long range shooting is easier with Tasco's True Mil-Dot system. SuperCon multi-layered lens coatings and fully coated optics throughout provide clear resolution. With extra large 42mm objectives, this line of Varmint riflescopes transmit more light than standard 40mm scopes.

EXP 3-9X42/54

New for 2001 is the Tasco EXP featuring an oval objective lens. This new technology allows low profile mounting with standard or low rings without sacrificing light transmission.

3-12x40

MAG IV RIFLESCOPES

The large 40mm objective of MAG IV riflescopes delivers a full four times magnification with more zooming range than most variable scopes. In addition, a focusing objective provides valuable parallax correction. MAG IV scopes feature 1/4-minute windage/elevation click stops and black matte finish. The result is a line of scopes that provide superior light transmission and clarity even at high magnifications. Waterproof, fogproof and shockproof.

Model No.	Power	Objective Diameter	Finish	Reticle	F.O.V. @100 Yds.	Eye Relief	Tube Diameter	Length	Weight	Price
NEW VARMINT/TACTICAL										
VAR2.510X42M	2.5X-10X	42mm	Black Matte	30/30	35'-9'	3"	1"	14"	19.1 oz.	
VAR624X42M	6X-24X	42mm	Black Matte	30/30	13'-3.7'	2.75"	1"	16"	19.6 oz.	
EXP										
H1.55X32/44	1.5X-5X	oval 32/44mm	AWF/Black Matte	30/30 wide view oval	62'-22'	5"	1"	13"	17 oz.	
H39X42/54	3X-9X	oval 42/54mm	AWF/Black Matte	30/30 wide view oval	41'-15'	3"	1"	13.5"	19.3 oz.	
MAG IV RIFLESCOPES										
MAG312X40	3X-12X	40mm	Black Matte	30/30	35'-9'	3"	1"	13.75"	17.3 oz.	
MAG624X40	6X-24X	40mm	Black Matte	30/30	17'-4'	3"	1"	16"	19.1 oz.	
MAG416X40	4X-16X	40mm	Black Matte	30/30	26'-7'	3"	1"	15.25"	18.6 oz.	
MAG416X40ST	4X-16X	40mm	Stainless	30/30	26'-7'	3"	1"	15.25"	18.6 oz.	
PRONGHORN										
PH4X32	4X	32mm	Black Gloss	30/30	32'	3"	1"	12"	12.5 oz.	$61.11
PHG39X32	3X-9X	32mm	Black Gloss	30/30	39'-13'	3"	1"	12"	11 oz.	
PH39X32	3X-9X	32mm	Black Gloss	30/30	39'-13'	3"	1"	12"	11 oz.	83.18
PH39X40	3X-9X	40mm	Black Gloss	30/30	39'-13'	3"	1"	13"	12.1 oz.	110.34
TACTICAL SCOPES										
TAC10X42	10X	42mm	Black Matte	30/30	13'	3.75"	30mm	14.25"	26 oz.	
TAC840X56	8X-40X	56mm	Black Matte	30/30	13'-2.6'	3"	30mm	18.5"	32 oz.	
RIMFIRE										
RF4X15*	4X	15mm	Black Gloss	Crosshair	22.5'	2.5"	3/4"	11"	4 oz.	16.13
RF4X20WA*	4X	20mm	Black Matte	30/30	23'	2.5"	3/4"	10.5"	3.8 oz.	23.77
RF37X20*	3X-7X	20mm	Black Gloss	30/30TV	24'-11'	2.5"	3/4"	11.5"	5.7 oz.	40.74
E201*	1X	20mm	Black Matte	Red Dot	35'	Unlimited	1"	4.75"	2.5 oz.	
NEW RIMFIRE MAG										
MAG4X32	4X	32mm	Black Matte	30/30	27'	3"	1"	12.25"	12.1 oz.	
MAG4X32ST	4X	32mm	Stainless	30/30	27'	3"	1"	12.25"	12.1 oz.	
MAG39X32	3X-9X	32mm	Black Matte	30/30	35.5'-11.5'	3"	1"	12.75"	11.3 oz.	
MAG39X32ST	3X-9X	32mm	Stainless	30/30	35.5'-11.5	3"	1"	12.75"	11.3 oz.	

*Includes rings

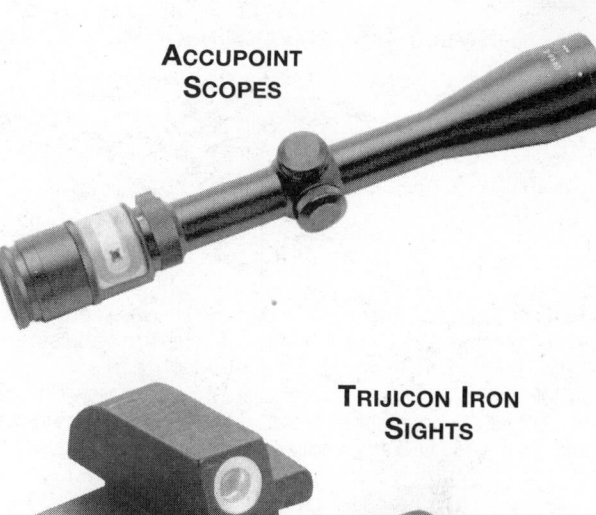

ACCUPOINT SCOPES

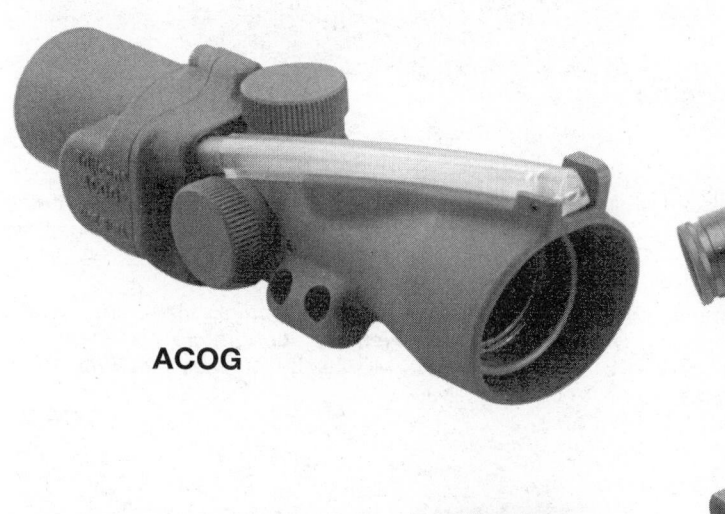

ACOG

TRIJICON IRON SIGHTS

REFLEX SIGHTS

SIGHTS & SCOPES

ACOG

The ACOGs are internally-adjustable, compact telescopic sights with tritium illuminated reticle patterns for use in low light or at night. Many models are dual-illuminated, featuring fiber optics which collect ambient light for maximum brightness in day-time shooting. The ACOGs combine traditional, precise distance marksmanship with close-in aiming speed.

Prices: . . . . $895.00 to $1,367.00
  Compact ACOG 795.00

ACCUPOINT SCOPES

AccuPoint's dual-illuminated aiming point offers a major advancement over crosshairs that can disappear due to lack of contrast when aiming at a dark animal, or in low-light conditions. Reticle illumination is supplied by advanced fiber optics or, in low-light conditions, by a self-contained tritium lamp.

Prices: 3-9x40, red or amber triangle $699.00
  1.2-4x24, red or amber triangle 599.00

REFLEX SIGHTS

The dual-illuminated, Trijicon Reflex sight gives shooters next-generation technology for super-fast, any-light aiming-without batteries.

Developed for the military for use in both-eyes-open Close Quarters Battle (CQB) situations, the Reflex sight features an amber aiming dot that is illuminated both by light from the target area and from a tritium lamp.

Price: . . . . $329.00 to 528.00

TRIJICON IRON SIGHTS

Trijicon self-luminous iron sights are proven to give shooters greater night fire accuracy-with the same speed as instinctive shooting. That's why, along with their 12-year limited warranty, Trijicon Bright & Tough night sights are the first choice of major handgun manufacturers and standard issue with hundreds of municipal and county departments, numerous state and police departments and several Federal agencies.

T-Series

T-SERIES TARGET/VARMINT T-36

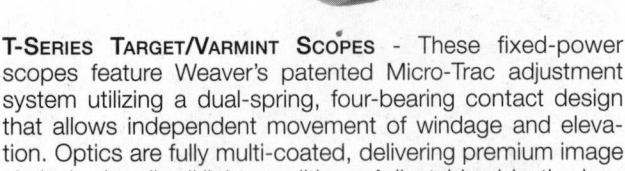

T-SERIES TARGET/VARMINT SCOPES - These fixed-power scopes feature Weaver's patented Micro-Trac adjustment system utilizing a dual-spring, four-bearing contact design that allows independent movement of windage and elevation. Optics are fully multi-coated, delivering premium image clarity in virtually all light conditions. Adjustable objective lens allows for zero parallax from 50' to infinity. Choice of fine cross hair or dot reticles. Scopes come with sunshade, extra pair of oversize benchrest adjustment knobs, and screw-in metal lens caps.

Model: T-36 **Magnification/Objective:** 36X40mm **Field Of View:** 3.0' **Eye Relief:** 3.0" **Length:** 15.1" **Weight:** 16.7 oz. **Reticle:** 1/8 MOA Dot, Fine Crosshair **Finish:** Matte black or silver

Price: $714.99

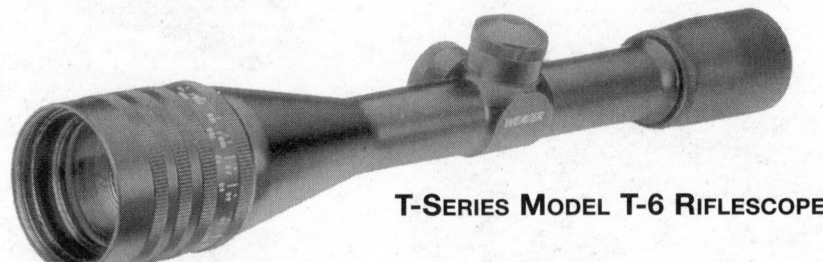

T-SERIES MODEL T-6 RIFLESCOPE

Weaver's T-6 competition 6x scope is only 12.7 inches long and weighs less than 15 ounces. All optical surfaces are fully multi-coated for maximum clarity and light transmission. The T-6 features Weaver's Micro-Trac precision adjustments in 1/8-minute clicks to ensure parallel tracking. The protected target-style turrets are a low-profile configuration combining ease of adjustment with weight reduction. A 40mm adjustable objective permits parallax correction from 50 feet to infinity without shifting the point of impact. A special AO lock ring eliminates bell vibration or shift. The T-6 comes with screw-in metal lens caps and features a competition matte black finish.

Reticles: dot, Fine Crosshair

Price: 6x40 Satin Black $382.99

WEAVER TACTICAL SCOPES (not shown)

These tactical scopes have a first-plane reticle, meaning the crosshair measurement maintains the same relativity to the size of the target at any power. The range-calculating reticle of the Tactical scope is etched into the glass in front of the adjustment housing.

At the center of the reticle is a small diamond that covers one inch outside. Marks beyond the diamond on the cross-pieces can be used to bracket a target and determine range. Tactical scopes have 1/8-minute-of-angle windage and elevation adjustments with target-style knobs. The knobs also offer a "guaranteed zero" feature that allows the shooter to move the reticle for a specific shooting need, then return the scope to zero without sighting in again. An adjustable objective lens is also included on the 4.5-14x44mm scope for precise parallax-free adjustments.

All air-to-glass lens surfaces are fully multi-coated, and the scopes are waterproof to 10,000 feet and to 120 degrees with 100% humidity. Weaver's Tactical scopes are offered in black matte finish.

Price: $694.99

SPECIFICATIONS

Magnification X Obj. Diam. (mm)	Exit Pupil (mm)	FOV (Ft. @ 100 Yds.)	Eye Relief (In.)	Overall Length (In.)	Weight (Oz.)	Reticle
3-9x40	13.3-4.4	33-14.5	4.17-3.02	12.5	17.0	Diamond
4.5-14x44	10-3	22-9.4	4.1-2.8	15.2	20.6	Diamond

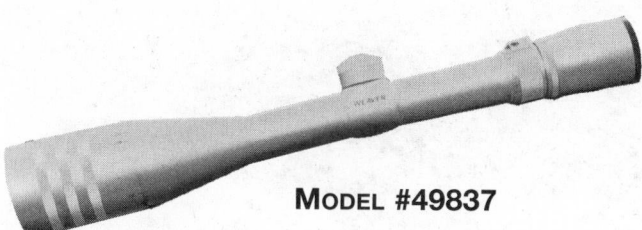

MODEL #49837

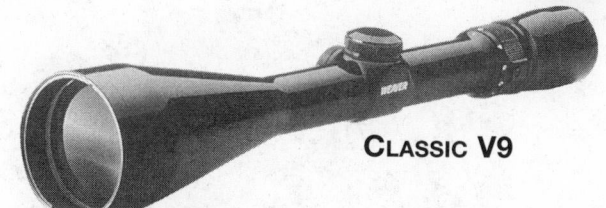

CLASSIC V9

V16 RIFLESCOPES - The V16 is popular for a variety of shooting applications, from close shots that require a wide field of view to long-range varmint or benchrest shooting. Adjustable objective allows a parallax-free view from 30 feet to infinity. Features one-piece tube for strength and moisture resistance and multicoated lenses for clear, crisp images. Two finishes and three reticle options.
Magnification/Objective: 4-16X42mm *Field Of View:* 26.8'-6.8' *Eye Relief:* 3.1" *Length:* 13.9" *Weight:* 16.5 oz. *Reticle:* Choice of Dual-X, 1/4 MOA Dot, or Fine Crosshair *Finish:* Matte black
Price: $389.99
V24 6-24x42 (not shown) black matte......... 454.99

OTHER V-SERIES RIFLESCOPES (not shown)- With broad magnification ranges, these versatile scopes come in a choice of finishes, with dual X-reticle.

V10 (not shown)
Magnification/Objective: 2-10X38mm *Field Of View:* 38.5-9.5 *Eye Relief:* 3.5" *Length:* 12.2" *Weight:* 11.2 oz. *Reticle:* Dual-X *Finish:* Matte black, silver
Price: Matte black..................... $232.99
Silver...............................237.99
In gloss black 232.99

V9
Magnification/Objective: 3.9x38
Field Of View: 34-11' *Eye Relief:* 3.5" *Length:* 12" *Weight:* 11 oz. *Finish:* Matte black, gloss
Price: Matte black..................... $209.99
Gloss 209.99

V3 (not shown)
Magnification/Objective: 1-3x20
Field Of View: 100x34 *Eye Relief:* 3.5" *Length:* 9"
Weight: 9 oz. *Finish:* Matte black
Price: Matte black..................... $208.99

SIGHTS & SCOPES

CLASSIC HANDGUN 1.5-4x20

CLASSIC RIMFIRE RV7

WEAVER CLASSIC HANDGUN SCOPES
Fixed-power scopes include 2x28 and 4x28 scopes in gloss black or silver. Variables in 1.5-4x20 and 2.5-8x28 come with a gloss black finish. The 2.5-8x28 is also available in black matte. One-piece tubes, fully multi-coated lenses and generous eye relief (4-29") make these scopes top performers on hunting handguns.
Prices: 2x28.............. $191.99 (202.99 in silver)
4x28................. 207.99 (212.99 in silver)
1.5-4x20 ....255.99
2.5-8x28 ....267.99
2.5-8x28 matte 271.99

CLASSIC RIMFIRE RV7
Lenses are multi-coated for bright, clear low-light performance and the one-piece tube design is shockproof and waterproof.
Prices:
2.5-7x28 Rimfire Matte.................. $166.99
2.5-7x28 Rimfire Silver 168.99
RIMFIRE SCOPE RV4 (not shown)
Fixed 4x scope is ideal for a variety of shooting applications. It's durable, light-weight and waterproof.
Prices:
Rimfire Matte Black 4x28 .... $143.99

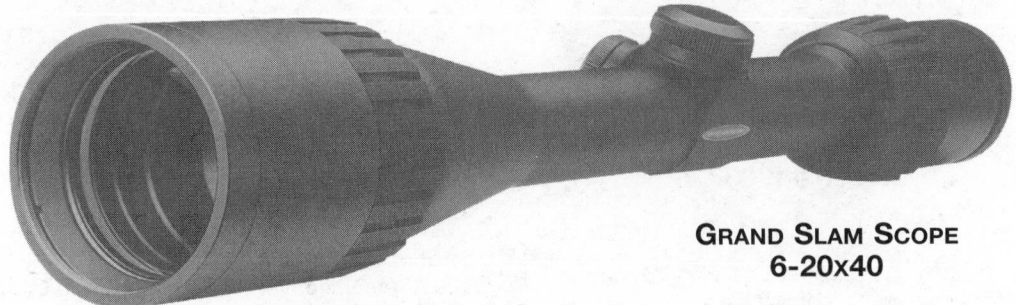

**GRAND SLAM SCOPE
6-20x40**

WEAVER GRAND SLAM SCOPES

Among the advanced features of the Grand Slam series are a "sure-grip" power ring and AO adjustment that let you easily adjust the variable scopes, even while wearing heavy gloves, and an offset parallax indicator so you can remain in shooting position while adjusting the scope. Grand Slam scopes feature camera-quality, fully multi-coated lenses that ensure sharp, bright viewing. For quick focusing, the eyepiece has a fast-focus adjustment ring. Simply rotate the ring until the reticle becomes sharp.

Grand Slam scopes' solid, one-piece construction makes them not only rugged and reliable, but resistant to moisture and humidity. Configurations include: 4.75x40mm, a fixed-power scope with sufficient magnification for longer shots, yet a wide field of view for finding running game close in; 1.5-5x32mm, the ideal scope for short-range rifles and fast target acquisition in brushy country; 3.5-10x40mm, the traditional choice of big-game hunters for short- or long-range shooting; 3.5-10x50mm, which provides the brightest view in low-light situations; 4.5-14x40mm AO, possibly the most versatile Grand Slam scope, with a low range suitable for

stand hunting and high enough magnification for target shooting or varmint hunting; and 6-20x40mm AO, two target/varminter models.

Windage and elevation knobs have target-type finger adjustments so 1/4-MOA adjustments can be made by gripping the rim of the knob between the thumb and index finger. The Grand Slam scopes are also equipped with Micro-Trac, Weaver's patented four-point adjustment system.

All Grand Slam scopes are offered with a plex reticle (except the 6-20x model, which is offered with a choice of Weaver's Varminter reticle or fine crosshairs with a dot). The scopes have a non-glare black matte finish, featuring the new green and gold oval Weaver logo medallion on the scope saddle and green ring inside the objective lens hood.

Price: 6-20x40 AO $452.99
4.5-14x40 AO 442.99
3.5-10x50 . . . . 408.99
3-10x40 . . . . 336.99
1.5-5x32 . . . . 382.99
4.75x40 . . . . 324.99

**CLASSIC 2.5
2.5x20MM**

WEAVER CLASSIC K SERIES

The K2.5, K4 and K6 have a long history in America's game fields. New logos distinguish these versatile hunting scopes at a glance. Reasonably priced and great values, K scopes–including the target model, KT-15–have one-piece tubes and bright optics.

Prices:
KT-15 (15x40 gloss) $334.99
K6 (black matte or gloss) 176.99
K4 (black matte or gloss) 165.99
K2.5 (2.5x20 gloss) 157.99

FP Series

Internal micrometer adjustments have positive internal locks. The FP is strong, rugged, dependable. The alloy used to manufacture this sight has a tensile strength of 85,000 pounds. Yet, the FP is light and compact, weighing only 1-1/2 ounces. Target knobs are available on all models of the FP receiver sight if desired.

Prices:

For most models $63.85
Target knobs 75.50
Mini 14 w/sub-base 71.20

FP-KNIGHT-TK
SILVER on MK-85

FP-GR-TK
on Remingto 581

FP-AG-TK
on Beeman
Air Rifle

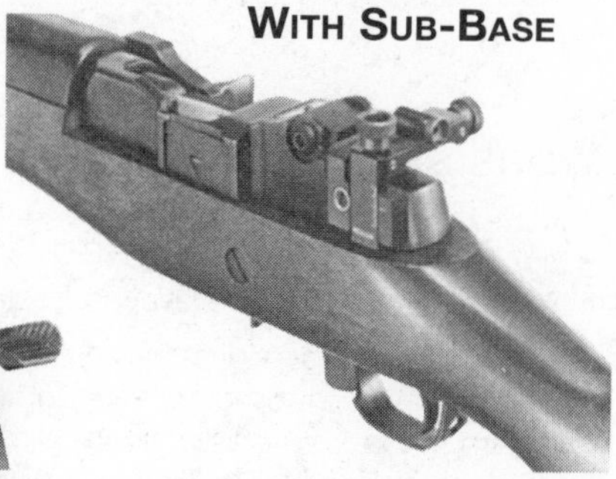

FP-94 SE shown
on Winchester
94 Side Eject

FP MINI-14-TK
WITH SUB-BASE

SIGHTS & SCOPES

FP RECEIVER SIGHT OPTIONS

STANDARD | **TARGET KNOBS (TK)** | **SHOTGUN/BIG GAME APERTURE** | **BLADE**

Open Sights

WGOS SERIES

• Made from high tensile strength Aluminum.
  Will not rust.
• All parts milled - no stampings.
• Streamlined and lightweight with tough anodized
  finish.
• Dovetailed windage and elevation - Easy to adjust,
  positive locks.
• Interchangeable blades available in four heights and
  four styles.
Price: $17.35-24.06

Blades are sold separately, except "U" blades are available
installed on WGOS octagon T/C and CVA.
Price: $6.70

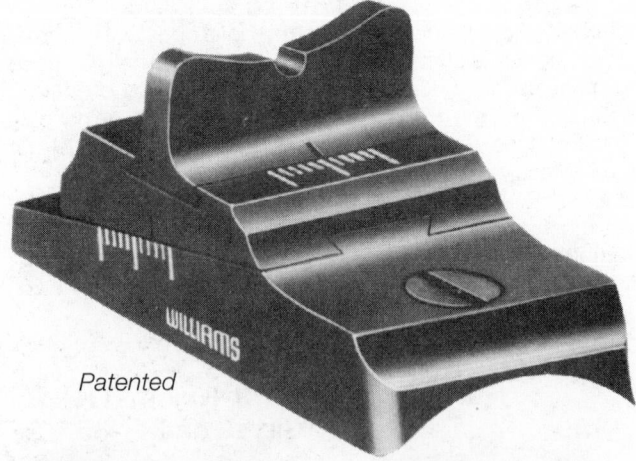

Patented

"SQ"

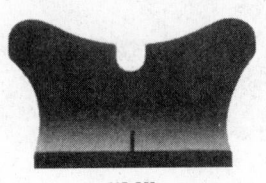

"U"

"V"

"B"

Receiver Sights

WGRS SERIES

• Compact Low Profile
• Lightweight, Strong, Rustproof
• Positive Windage and Elevation Locks

In most cases these sights utilize dovetail or
existing screws on top of receiver for installation.
They are made from an aluminum alloy that is stronger
than many steels. Light. Rustproof. Williams quality
throughout.
Price: most models $31.80

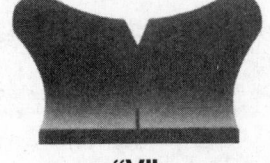

*WGRS-CVA on
CVA Apolllo*

"GHOST RING"
Shotgun aperture available
For WGRS receiver sights.
Sold separately.

FIRE SIGHTS

Williams has introduced new "Fire Sights". These sights are
machined from aircraft-strength aluminum + steel. This sight
is lightweight, durable and brightens in low-light situations.
Prices:
Pistol Fire Sight Sets $41.95
Shotgun Fire Sight Sets . . . . 25.95 to 36.95
Muzzleloader Fire Sight Sets. . . . . 25.95 to 49.95
Rifle Fire Sight Sets . . . . 25.95 to 35.95
Peep Sets . . . . 39.95 to 75.95
Rifle Beads 14.95

*Fire
Sights*

SIGHTS & SCOPES

5D SERIES

- *For Big Game Rifles, 22's, Shotguns*
- *Positive Windage and Elevation Locks*
- *Lightweight, Strong, Accurate*
- *Williams Quality Throughout - Rustproof*

The inexpensive, quality-made 5D sight is available for most of the more popular rifles and shotguns. These sights have the same strength, lightweight, and neat appearance, but without the micrometer adjustments. Designed for rugged hunting use, the 5D sights are dependable and accurate. Positive locks. Clear unobstructed vision. No knobs or side plates to blot out shooter's field of vision. Wherever possible, the manufacturers' mounting screw holes in the receivers of the guns have been utilized for easy installation. The upper staff of the Williams 5D sight is readily detachable. It is only necessary to loosen one screw so that the upper staff slides easily in the close-fitting dovetail. The angular bushing locks this upper staff in a positive manner. A set screw is provided as a stop screw so that the sight will return to absolute zero upon detaching and reattaching. The material used in the manufacture of the Williams 5D sight is one of the highest grade alloys obtainable. Laboratory tests show that the material used has a tensile strength approximately 25% greater than mild steels.

Price: Most 5D models. $33.50

Target FP Series

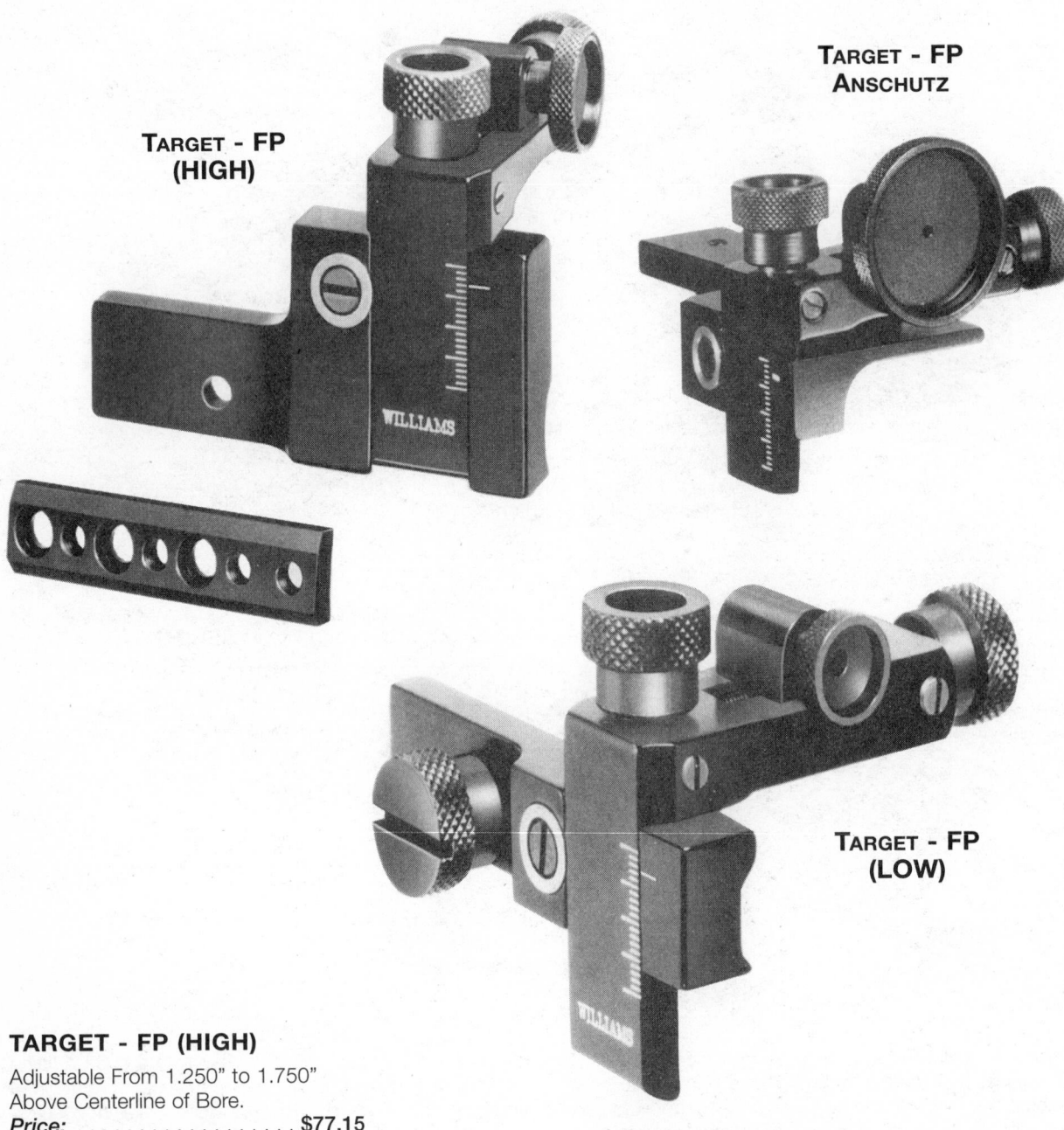

TARGET - FP
(HIGH)

TARGET - FP
ANSCHUTZ

TARGET - FP
(LOW)

TARGET - FP (HIGH)

Adjustable From 1.250" to 1.750"
Above Centerline of Bore.
Price: $77.15

TARGET FP-ANSCHUTZ

Designed to fit many of the Anschutz Lightweight .22
Cal. Target and Sporter Models. No Drilling and Tapping
required.
Price: $73.90

TARGET - FP (LOW)

Adjustable From .750" to 1.250"
Above Centerline of Bore.
Price: $77.15

CONQUEST 3-9x40

CONQUEST 3.5-10x44
Stainless steel finish

NEW! ZEISS CONQUEST SERIES RIFLESCOPES

The Conquest series has Zeiss' proprietary MC anti-reflective coating and is backed by a Lifetime Transferable Warranty. Couple this with Zeiss' world renowned low-light performance, new arsenic/lead free glass technology, precision engineering, quick focus and constant eye relief design and you have one of the world's highest performance riflescope series.

Price: 3-9x40 MC $499.00
Stainless 529.00

CONQUEST 3-9X40

The 3-9x40 Conquest is the most versatile scope in the series, featuring a 4-inch eye-relief with unique European quick focus and advanced internal design, enabling the widest windage/elevation adjustment to 64 inches. All this combined with a solid one-piece alloy body manufactured to German standards makes the 3-9x40 Conquest a practical hunting sight.

CONQUEST 3-9X40S (NOT SHOWN)

The 3-9x40S Conquest is designed to support sportsman who demands a shotgun, airgun, or muzzleloader scope with heavy reticle. The 3-9x40S has the same glass and coating as the 3-9, with a safe 4-inch eye relief, etched glass reticle and one-piece alloy tube.

Price: 3-9x40S $499.00
w/turkey reticle 499.00

CONQUEST 3.5-10X44

The 3.5-10x44 Conquest, designed to replace Zeiss' Diavari C 3-9x36, is superior in design and has all the standard Conquest features. Additionally, the 3.5-10x44 Conquest offers a 22-percent larger objective and a 66-inch windage/elevation adjustment. Combine these features with a weight of just 14 oz., the 3.5-10x44 Conquest makes it suitable for general big game hunting.

Price: 3.5-10x44 MC $599.00
Stainless 629.00
Target 699.00

CONQUEST 4.5-14X44 (NOT SHOWN)

The 4.5-14x44 Conquest offers the first turret-mounted parallax adjustment from Zeiss. The 64-inch windage/elevation adjustment coupled with the 25-foot to 8.3-foot field of view made the 4.5-14x44 Conquest the selection of choice. Precise magnification is obtained through the mechanical erector system, which reduces stray light caused by oily lubricants. The objective clarity and light transmission exceeds most models that have larger objectives and provides for perfect balance without adding weight or requiring raised mounts.

Conquest riflescopes are water- and fog-proof, are free of lead and arsenic, and are backed by Zeiss' lifetime transferable warranty.

Price: 4.5-14x44 AO $749.00
w/crosshair reticle 749.00
Stainless 769.00
Target 849.00

SIGHTS & SCOPES

SPECIFICATIONS	ZEISS CONQUEST 3-9x40	ZEISS CONQUEST 3-9x40S	ZEISS CONQUEST 3.5-10x44	ZEISS CONQUEST 4.5-14x44
Magnification	3-9x	3-9x	3.5-10x	4.5-14
Objective	40	40	44	44
Tube diameter	1"	1"	1"	1"
Field of View(ft.@100yards)	11.01'-34'	11.01'-34'	11.61'-35.1'	8.31'-24.99'
Parallax (yards)	100	50	100	30-Infinity
Reticle Image Plane(Magnifying)	2nd (No)	2nd (No)	2nd (No)	2nd (No)
Exit Pupil (mm)	13.3-4.4	13.3-4.4	12.57-4.4	9.7-3.14
Eye Relief	4"	4"	3.5"	3.5"
Length	13.15"	13.15"	12.7"	13.86"
Weight	15 oz.	15 oz.	15.8 oz.	17.5 oz.
MOA	1/4	1/4	1/4	1/4
Windage/Elevation Adj.	64"	64"	66"	43"
Diopter Adj.	+2/-3	+2/-3	+2/-3	+2/-3

ZEISS SCOPES

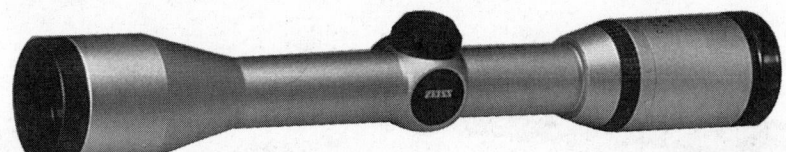

1.5-6x42 ZM/Z STAINLESS

ZM/Z SERIES RIFLESCOPE SPECIFICATIONS

MODEL	DIATAL-ZM/Z 6X42T	DIAVARI-ZM/Z 1.5-6x42 T	DIAVARI-ZM/Z 3-12x56 T	DIATAL-ZM/Z 8x56 T	DIAVARI-ZM/Z 2.5-10x48 T	DIAVARI-ZM/Z 1.25-4x24
Magnification	6X	1.5 X 6X	3X 12X	8X	2.5X-10X	1.25-4X
Effective obj. diam.	42mm/1.7"	19.5/0.8" 42/1.7"	38/1.5" 56/2.2"	56mm/2.2"	33/1.30" 48/1.89"	NA
Diameter of exit pupil	7mm	13mm 7mm	12.7mm 4.7mm	7mm	13.2mm 4.8mm	12.6mm 6.3mm
Twilight factor	15.9	4.2 15.9	8.5 25.9	21.2	7.1 21.9	3.54 9.6
Field of view at 100 m/ ft. at 100 yds.	6.7m/20.1'	18/54.0' 6.5/19.5'	9.2/27.6' 3.3/9.9'	5m/15.0'	11.0/33.0 3.9/11.7	32 10
Approx. eye relief	8cm/3.2"	8cm/3.2"	8cm/3.2"	8cm/3.2"	8cm/3.2"	8cm/3.2"
Max adj. (elv./wind.) at 100m (cm) (1 click=1cm)	187	190	95	138	110/39.6	300
Center tube dia.	25.4mm/1"	30mm/1.18"	30mm/1.18"	25.4mm/1"	30mm/1.18"	30mm/1.18"
Objective bell dia.	48mm/1.9"	48mm/1.9"	62mm/2.44"	62mm/2.44"	54mm/2.13"	NA
Ocular bell dia.	40mm/1.57"	40mm/1.57"	40mm/1.57"	40mm/1.57"	40mm/1.57"	NA
Length	324mm/12.8"	320mm/12.6"	388mm/15.3"	369mm/14.5"	370mm/14.57"	290mm/11.46"
Approx. weight: ZM	350g/15.3 oz.	586g/20.7 oz.	765g/27.0 oz.	550g/19.4 oz.	715g/25.2 oz.	490g/17.3 oz.
Z	400g/14.1 oz.	562g/19.8	731g/25.8 oz.	520g/18.3 oz.	680g/24 oz.	NA
PRICES:						
Black Matte	$749.00	$899.00	$1,099.00	$829.00	$1,029.00	$779.00
Stainless		939.00	1,149.00		1,069.00	
Illum. Reticle			1,499.00		1,449.00	

Zeiss Reticles

			AVAILABLE RETICLES							
VM/V MODELS	1	2	4	6	7	8	11	20	21	42
Diavari VM/V 1.5-6x42 T*	•		•	•	•		•			
Diavari VM/V 2.5-100x50 T*	•		•	•		•	•			•
Diavari VM/V 3-12x56 T*	•		•		•		•			
Diavari VM/V 3-9x42 T*		•	•	•			•	•	•	
Diavari VM/V 5-15x42 T*		•	•		•			•	•	•
Diavari C 3-9x36 MC			•		•			•	•	•

Reticle 1

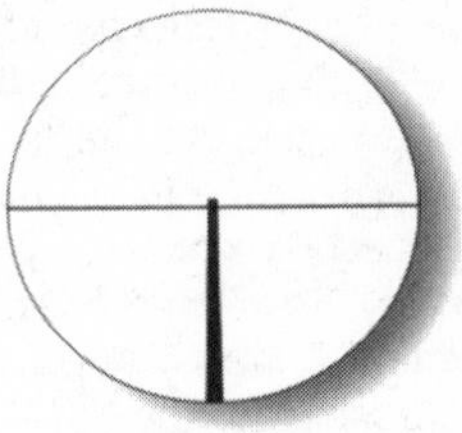

Reticle 2

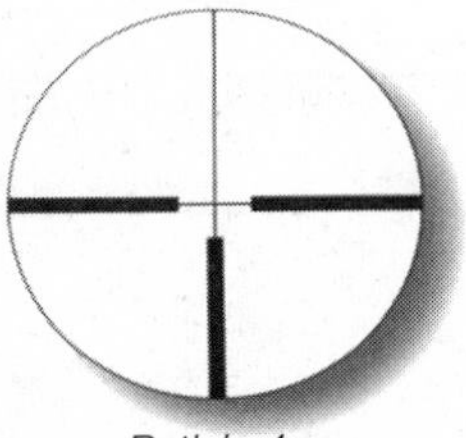

Reticle 4

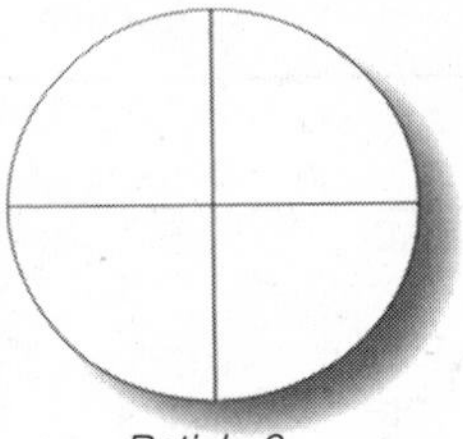

Reticle 6

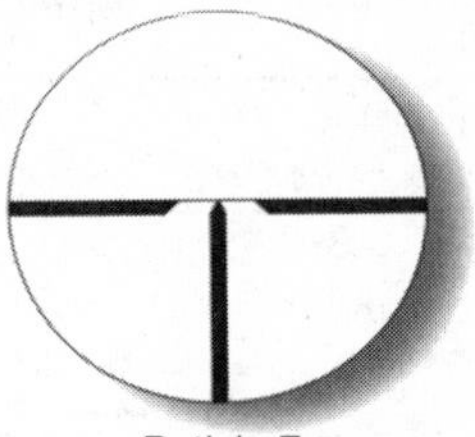

Reticle 7

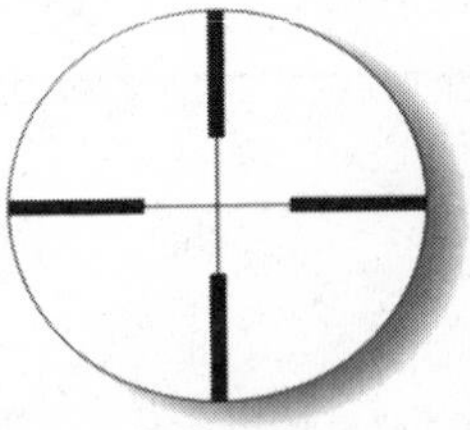

Reticle 8

Reticle 11

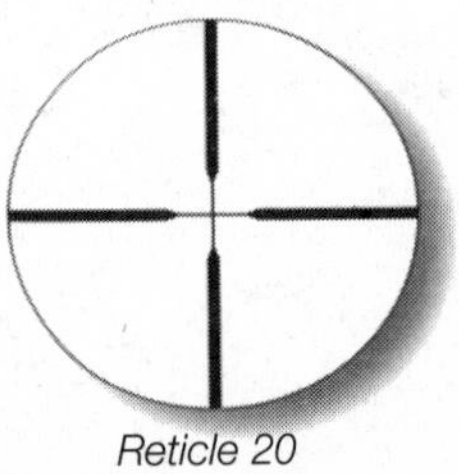

Reticle 20

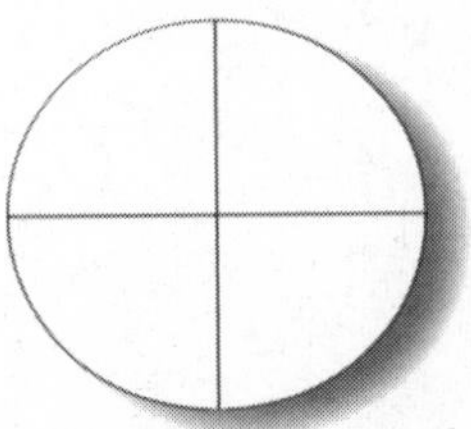

Reticle 21

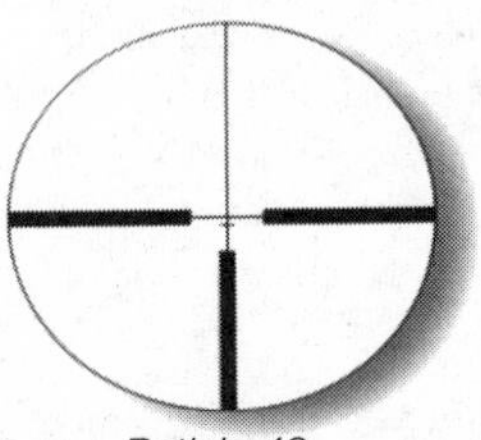

Reticle 42

Diavari VM/V 3-9x42 T*

Over the years, the 3-9x power range has proven its staying power. It is still the favorite power range of North American hunters. The 42 mm objective, coupled with the Zeiss T* coating, extends the hunting day. Whether the quarry is elk, Dall sheep or Boone and Crockett white-tail, the VM/V Diavari 3-9 x 42T* offers top quality and the right magnification.

POWER	3-9x	EYE RELIEF (inch)	3.74
EFFECTIVE OBJECTIVE DIAMETER (mm)	30-42	CENTER TUBE DIAMETER (inch)	1
EXIT PUPIL DIAMETER (mm)	10-4.7	OBJECTIVE BELL DIAMETER (inch)	1.89
TWILIGHT FACTOR	8.5-18.4	LENGTH (inch)	13.3
FIELD OF VIEW AT 100 YARDS (feet)	39.6-13.2	WEIGHT (ounces)	14.8-14
MINIMUM SQUARE ADJUSTMENT RANGE		PARALLAX FREE (yards)	109.4
AT 100 YARDS (inch)	49.7	*Price:* $1,249.95

Diavari VM/V 5-15x42 T*

Precise windage and elevation adjustments make the Diavari VM/V 5 - 15 x 42 T* the perfect companion for a target or varmint rifle. The rugged adjustment system provides fast, accurate and repeatable adjustments. By aligning the optical and mechanical axes, Zeiss ensures full range of adjustment.

POWER	5-15x	EYE RELIEF (inch)	3.74
EFFECTIVE OBJECTIVE DIAMETER (mm)	42-42	CENTER TUBE DIAMETER (inch)	1
EXIT PUPIL DIAMETER (mm)	8.4-2.8	OBJECTIVE BELL DIAMETER (inch)	1.89
TWILIGHT FACTOR	14.1-25.1	LENGTH (inch)	13.3
FIELD OF VIEW AT 100 YARDS (feet)	23.7-7.8	WEIGHT (ounces)	14.9-14
MINIMUM SQUARE ADJUSTMENT RANGE		PARALLAX FREE (yards)	109.4
AT 100 YARDS (inch)	30	*Price:* $1,499.95

Diavari VM/V 3-12x56 T*

In the quiet haze of dawn or the fleeting light of sunset, a riflescope is put to the ultimate test. Under these conditions, the Diavari VM/V 3-12x56 T* excels. The patented Zeiss T* anti-reflection coating is designed to transmit the optimum percentage of light throughout the spectral range to take full advantage of your eye's sensitivity. Weighing in at 13.5 ounces, the VM/V 3-12x56 T* won't slow you down.

POWER	3-12x	EYE RELIEF (inch)	3.54
EFFECTIVE OBJECTIVE DIAMETER (mm)	44.0-56	CENTER TUBE DIAMETER (inch)	1.18
EXIT PUPIL DIAMETER (mm)	14.7-4.7	OBJECTIVE BELL DIAMETER (inch)	2.44
TWILIGHT FACTOR	8.5-25.9	LENGTH (inch)	13.54
FIELD OF VIEW AT 100 YARDS (feet)	37.5-10.4	WEIGHT (ounces)	17.8/16.8
MINIMUM SQUARE		PARALLAX FREE (yards)	109.4
ADJUSTMENT RANGE		*Price:* $1,599.95
AT 100 YARDS (inch)	36.7	w/illuminated reticle 2,049.95

SIGHTS & SCOPES

ZEISS SCOPES

Zeiss–Premium Sports Optics

1.1-4 x 24 T*

DIAVARI 1.1-4 X 24 T* VM/V

- Compact riflescope with 108 ft. field of view at 1.1 power
- Extremely lightweight - ideal for safari rifles
- With illuminated varipoint reticle for fast target acquisition clearly visible also in critical lighting conditions
- Especially designed for running shots and hunting in heavy brush • Available with bullet drop compensator
- Eye relief: 3.74 in.

Price:. **$1,799.95**

1.5-6 x 42 T*

DIAVARI 1.5-6 X 42 T* VM/V

- Excellent choice for white-tail or moose hunter
- Compact and easy to handle
- Lightest scope of its class
- 72 ft. field of view - largest field of view in premium class
- Easy-grip adjustment knob
- Available with bullet drop compensator
- Eye relief: 3.54 in.

Price:. **$1,349.95**
w/Varipoint, reticle **1,849.95**
w/Varipoint 54 reticle **1,899.95**

2.5-10 x 50 T*

DIAVARI 2.5-10 X 50 T* VM/V

- High powered riflescope with superior twilight performance
- Light, compact with a wide field of view
- Available with an illuminated reticle
- Easy-grip adjustment knob
- Excellent choice for world-wide all-round hunting
- Available with bullet drop compensator
- Eye relief: 3.54 in.

Price:. **$1,549.95**
w/illuminated reticle **1,999.95**

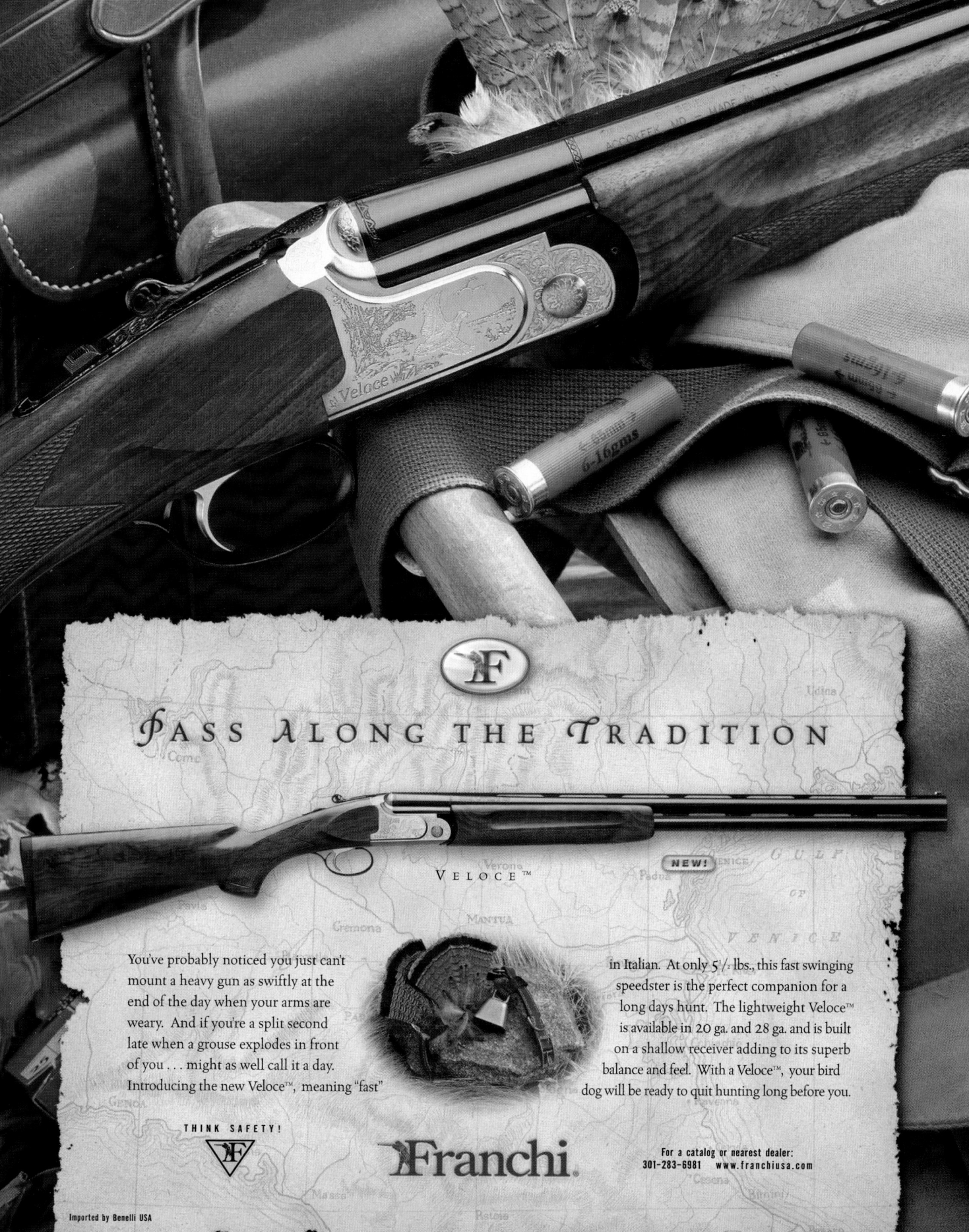

Ammunition

*For addresses and phone/fax numbers of manufacturers and distributors included in this section, please turn to **DIRECTORY OF MANUFACTURERS AND SUPPLIERS** on page 557.*

Black Hills, aptly named for its South Dakota base of operations, offers an expanding line of factory-new and remanufactured ammunition, for handguns and rifles. The Cowboy Action Line includes loads for the .32 H+R, .357 Magnum, .38-40, .44-40, .45 Colt, .32-20, .44 Colt, .44 Spt., .45 Schofield, .38 Spl, .38 Long Colt, .44 Russian, .45-70. Modern handgun ammunition, from .40 S+W to .44 Magnum, features a variety of bullet types. Black Hills rifle cartridges include the popular .223, .308, 6.5-284, .300 Win. Mag, and the potent long-range tactical round, the .338 Lapua. There's also specialty ammo, with frangible or moly-coated bullets.

Federal's 2001 line-up includes ammunition and components for big game and wildfowl hunters and personal defense. Some examples:

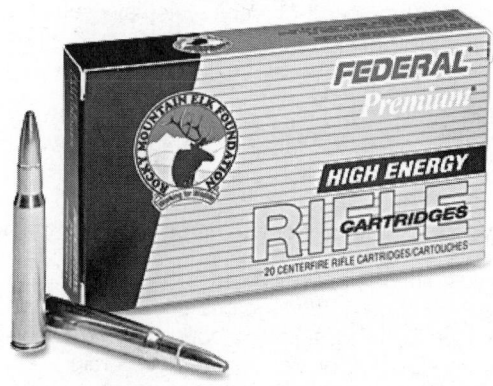

PREMIUM RIFLE –
TROPHY BONDED BEAR CLAW

The new .338 Rem. Ultra Mag. Cartridge features a 250 grain Trophy Bonded Bear Claw bullet at 2860 FPS. This new load is ideal for hunting heavy big game. The Trophy Bonded bullet's jacket and core are 100% fusion-bonded to create the most reliable bullet expansion from 25 yards to extreme ranges. The bullet retains 95% of its weight assuring deep penetration. The bullet jacket features a hard, copper base tapering to a soft, copper nose section for controlled expansion.

PREMIUM HANDGUN – PREMIUM
EXPANDING FULL METAL JACKET

This revolutionary barrier-penetrating design combines a scored full metal nose over an internal rubber tip that collapses on impact. It never fills with barrier material and assures expansion on every shot. A base lead core assures weight retention. It's an ideal choice for agencies that don't permit hollow point ammunition.

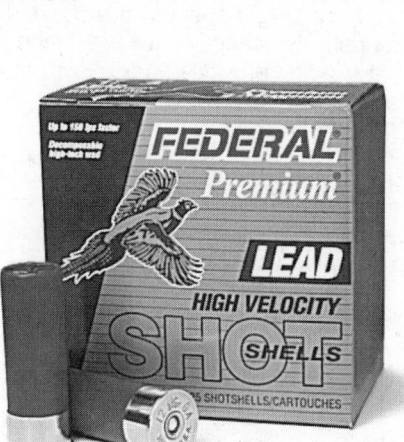

PREMIUM SHOTSHELL
LOADS – PREMIUM LEAD

This new Premium High Velocity load features 1 3/8 oz. of hard copper plated shot at 1400 FPS. This 2 3/4" load is available in No. 4, 5, and 6 shot. The increased velocity provides higher downrange energy. The hard copper plated pellets ensure tight dense patterns and enhanced penetration.

PREMIUM SHOTSHELL –
PREMIUM TUNGSTEN IRON & STEEL

Our Power Pattern System (PPS) stacks a layer of steel over a layer of Tungsten-Iron. At 40 yards, each shotshell delivers up to 85% of the pellets within a 30 inch circle. It's also buffered to keep the pattern uniform at longer ranges. Available in 12 gauge 3", 3 1/2" and 10 gauge shells.

AMMUNITION

Premium Load Bullet Selection

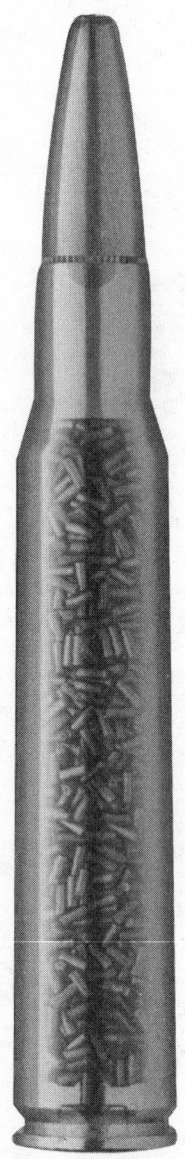

Round for round, Federal Premium Centerfire Rifle ranks among the best cartridges available. We start with the world's most technologically advanced bullets, Federal's are made with world-class brass, precision powders and legendary primers. The result is a cartridge that outperforms handloads.

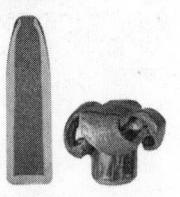
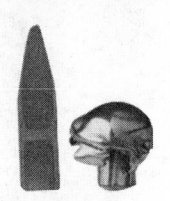

PREMIUM CENTERFIRE RIFLE

Combining one of the world's best brand-name bullet designs with advanced delivery systems, Federal Premium performs better than handloads, right out of the box.

TROPHY BONDED BEAR CLAW®

Excellent for small to heavy game.
Only Federal offers this famous Jack Carter design in a factory load. The jacket and core are 100% fusion bonded. Superb accuracy, 95% weight retention, deep penetration and reliable expansion from 25 yards to extreme ranges.

TROPHY BONDED SLEDGEHAMMER®

Excellent for large and dangerous game.
Also a Jack Carter design, this bonded bronze solid delivers maximum stopping power. The flat nose minimizes deflection for a straight, deep wound cavity.

BARNES XLC COATED-X BULLET™

Superb stopping power for small to large game.
This hard-hitting design features a 100% copper bullet, four petal expansion and hollow cavity 1/3 the bullet length for deep penetration and 100% weight retention. Heat cured dry film lubricant prevents copper fouling, reduces bore friction and won't rub off on hands.

WOODLEIGH® WELDCORE

Smaller calibers are excellent for medium to large game. Larger calibers are favored for very large or dangerous game.
Safari hunters have long respected this bonded Australian bullet for its superb accuracy and excellent stopping power. Its special heavy jacket provides 80-85% weight retention.

NOSLER® PARTITION®

A proven favorite for medium to large game.
The tapered H-shaped brass jacket of the Nosler Partition allows the front half of the bullet to mushroom on impact while the rear core remains intact, providing additional penetration and stopping power.

SIERRA GAMEKING® BOAT-TAIL

Long-range choice for varmints to big game.
The tapered design of the Sierra GameKing Boat-Tail provides extremely flat trajectories while offering higher retained velocity and downrange energy for excellent stopping power. Reduced wind drift makes it a good choice for long-range shots.

NOSLER BALLISTIC TIP®

Especially for long-range shots at varmints, predators and small to medium game.
Proven fast, flat-shooting, wind-defying performance. Color-coded polycarbonate tip provides easy identification, prevents deformation in the magazine and drives back on impact for explosive expansion and immediate energy transfer.

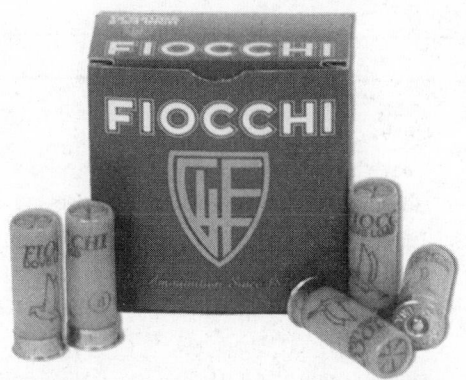

Known for its shotshells and .22 rimfire ammunition, Fiocchi also markets centerfire pistol and rifle cartridges. This Italian firm has been in business since 1876.

Fiocchi Target Loads offer you many choices to suit the shell to your game: Standard 1 1/8-ounce loads for everything from registered trap and skeet to sporting clays. One-ounce loads that deliver superior performance with less recoil than a comparable 1 1/8-ounce load. Also, a 7/8-ounce training load for new or recoil sensitive shooters. Fiocchi lilac-colored hulls are fully reloadable.

Stock #		Gauge	Shell Length	Dram. Equiv.	Muzzle Velocity	Shot Oz.	Shot Sizes	Rds./Box	Shot Type
STEEL (WATERFOWL LOADS)									
1235ST	Speed Steel	12	3 1/2"	Max.	1460	1 3/8	T BBB BB 1	25	Treated Steel
1235SH	Heavy Steel	12	3 1/2"	Max.	1300	1 9/16	T BBB BB 1	25	Treated Steel
123ST	Speed Steel	12	3"	Max.	1475	1 1/8	BBB BB 1 2 3 4	25	Treated Steel
123S	Steel	12	3"	Max.	1320	1 1/4	T BBB BB 1 2 3 4	25	Treated Steel
123SH	Heavy Steel	12	3"	Max.	1350	1 3/8	BB 1 2 3 4	25	Treated Steel
12S78	Training Load	12	2 3/4"	Max.	1440	7/8	7	25	Treated Steel
12S1OZ	Upland Steel	12	2 3/4"	Max.	1400	1	4 6 7	25	Treated Steel
12S118	Steel	12	2 3/4"	Max.	1375	1 1/8	BB 1 2 3 4 6 2 5		Treated Steel
12S114	Heavy Steel	12	2 3/4"	Max.	1275	1 1/4	BB 1 2 3 4	25	Treated Steel
20S	Upland Steel	20	2 3/4"	Max.	1470	3/4	3 4 6 7	25	Treated Steel
203ST	Speed Steel	20	3"	Max.	1500	7/8	2 3 4	25	Treated Steel
FIELD LOADS (UPLAND GAME LOADS)									
12HF	Heavy Field	12	2 3/4"	3 1/4	1225	1 1/4	6 7-12/ 8 9	25	Lead
12FLD	Field Load	12	2 3/4"	3 1/4	1255	1 1/8	6 7-1/2 8 9	25	Lead
16FLD	Field Load	16	2 3/4"	2 3/4	1185	1 1/8	6 7-12 8	25	Lead
20FLD	Field Load	20	2 3/4"	2 1/2	1165	1	6 7-1/2 8 9	25	Lead
DOVE LOADS									
12MS3	Multi Sport	12	2 3/4"	3	1250	1	7-1/2 8 9	25	Lead
12GT1	Game & Target	12	2 3/4"	3 1/4	1290	1	6 7-1/2 8 9	25	Lead
12GT118	Game & Target	12	2 3/4"	3	1200	1 1/8	7-1/2 8	25	Lead
16GT	Game & Target	16	2 3/4"	2 1/2	1165	1	6 7-1/2 8 9	25	Lead
20GT	Game & Target	20	2 3/4"	2 1/2	1210	7/8	6 7-1/2 8 9	25	Lead
28GT	Game & Target	28	2 3/4"	2	1200	3/4	8 9	25	Lead
410GT	Game & Target	410	2 1/2"	Max	1200	1/2	8 9	25	Lead
TARGET LOADS									
12TL	Target Light	12	2 3/4"	2 3/4	1150	1	7-1/2 8 8-1/2 9	25	Hi-Antimony Lead
12TH	Target Heavy	12	2 3/4"	3	1200	1	7-1/2 8 8-1/2	25	Hi-Antimony Lead
12TX	Little Rino	12	2 3/4"	HDCP	1250	1	7-1/2 8 8-1/2	25	Hi-Antimony Lead
12CRSR	Crusher	12	2 3/4"	Max	1300	1	7-1/2 8 8-1/2 9	25	Hi-Antimony Lead
12LITE	Lite	12	2 3/4"	2 7/8	1165	1 1/8	7-1/2 8 9	25	Hi-Antimony Lead
12VIPL	VIP Light	12	2 3/4"	2 3/4	1150	1 1/8	7-1/2 8 9	25	Hi-Antimony Lead
12VIPH	VIP Heavy	12	2 3/4"	3	1200	1 1/8	7-1/2 8 9	25	Hi-Antimony Lead
12WRNO	White Rino	12	2 3/4"	HDCP	1250	1 1/8	7-1/2 8 8-1/2 9	25	Hi-Antimony Lead
1278OZ	Training Load	12	2 3/4"	3	1200	7/8	7-1/2 8	25	Hi-Antimony Lead
12IN24	International	12	2 3/4"	Max	1350	24 grams	7-1/2 8 8-1/2	25	Hi-Antimony Lead
SUB-GAUGE									
20VIP	VIP	20	2 3/4"	2 1/2	1200	7/8	7-1/2 8 9	25	Hi-Antimony Lead
28GT	Game & Target	28	2 3/4"	2	1200	3/4	8 9	25	Lead
28HV	High Velocity	28	2 3/4"	2 1/4	1285	3/4	6 7-1/2 8 9	25	Lead
410GT	Game & Target	410	2 1/2"	Max	1200	1/2	8 9	25	Lead
HIGH VELOCITY									
12HV	High Velocity	12	2 3/4"	3 3/4	1330	1 1/4	4 5 6 7-1/2 8 9	25	Lead
16HV	High Velocity	16	2 3/4"	3 1/8	1300	1 1/8	4 6 7-1/2 8	25	Lead
20HV	High Velocity	20	2 3/4"	2 3/4	1220	1	4 5 6 7-1/2 8 9	25	Lead
28HV	High Velocity	28	2 3/4"	2 1/4	1285	3/4	6 7-1/2 8 9	25	Lead
410HV	High Velocity	410	3"	Max	1140	11/16	6 7-1/2 8 9	25	Lead

AMMUNITION

SHOTSHELL APPLICATION GUIDE

Game	Lead Shot Size	Steel Shot Size	Recommended Loads
Geese	NA	T-BBB-BB-1	Heavy Steel, Speed Steel
Ducks	NA	BB-1-2-3-4-6	Heavy Steel, Speed Steel, Upland Steel
Pheasant	4-5-6	3-4-5-6	Golden Pheasant, HV, Speed Steel, Upland Steel, HVN
Turkey	4-5-6	4-5	Turkey Tunder, HV, HVN
Grouse/Partridge	5-6-7 1/2-8	4-6-7	Field Loads, Upland Steel, HV, HVN, HFN
Quail	7 1/2-8-9	7	Field Loads, HV, Upland Steel, HVN, HFN
Dove/Pigeon	6-7 1/2-8-9	6-7	Field Loads, GT, Dove, HV, HFN, HVN
Rabbit/Squirrel	4-5-6-7 1/2	6-7	Field Loads, HV, GT, Upland Steel, HFN, HVN
Deer/Boar	00-Slug	NA	12HV00BK, 12 Gauge Slug, 20 Gauge Slug
Trap	7 1/2-8-8 1/2	6-7	TL, TH, TX, VIP, LITE, WRNO, MS, TRAPH, TRAPL
Skeet	8-8 1/2-9	7	TL, TH, TX, VIP, LITE, WRNO, MS
Sporting Clays	7 1/2-8-8 1/2-9	7	TL, TH, TX, TIP, LITE, WRNO, MS
Steel Target			Upland Steel, Training Load

SHOT PELLET SIZES

Size #	9	8-1/2	8	7-1/2	6	5	4	3	2	1	BB	BBB	T	#4	00
Dia.In.	.08	.085	.09	.095	.11	.12	.13	.14	.15	.16	.18	.19	.20	.24	.33
Dia.MM	2.03	2.16	2.29	2.41	279	3.05	3.30	3.56	3.81	4.06	4.57	4.83	5.08	6.10	8.38

NUMBER OF LEAD PELLETS IN VARIOUS LOADS

Lead Pellets	9	8-1/2	8	7-1/2	6	5	4
1 oz.	585	480	409	345	232	172	136
1 1/8 oz. 658	540	460	388	251	194	153	
1 1/4 oz. 731	600	511	431	276	215	170	
1 3/8 oz. 804	660	562	474	307	237	187	
1 3/4 oz. -	-	-	-	395	304	239	

NUMBER OF STEEL PELLETS IN VARIOUS LOADS

Steel Pellets	7	6	4	3	2	1	BB	BBB	T
3/4 oz.	315	237	143	115	-	-	-	-	-
7/8 oz.	365	-	167	134	109	-	-	-	-
1 oz.	420	316	191	-	-	-	-	-	-
1 1/8 oz. -		355	215	172	140	115	81	68	-
1 1/4 oz. -		-	239	191	151	128	90	-	-
1 3/8 oz. -		-	262	210	171	141	99	84	73
1 9/16 oz.-		-	-	-	-	161	113	95	83

Note: *When comparing steel shot to lead shot, increase shot size by two to get similar downrange results (i.e. Lead #4 to Steel #2). Check your shotgun and choke manufacturer for steel shot compatibility.*

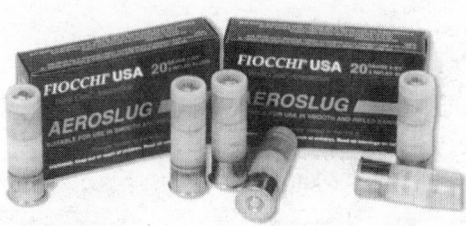

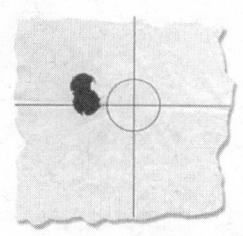

SLUGS

Fiocchi's Slugs in both 12 and 20 gauge feature an attached wad profiled to provide in-flight stability and increased accuracy. Three shot group measures .450 inches. Group fired at 50 yds. from a bench rest with a Mossberg 500 Crown Grade 24" fully rifled barrel and 4 power scope.

Stock #		Gauge	Shell Length	Dram. Equiv.	Muzzle Velocity	Pellet Ct.	Shot Sizes	Rds. Box	Shot Type
BUCKSHOT									
12HV4BKBuckshot		12	2 3/4"	Max	1325	27 pell.	4 Buck	10	Hi-Antimony Nickel Plated
12HV00BK Buckshot		12	2 3/4"	Max	1300	9 pell.	00 Buck	10	Hi-Antimonay Nickel Plated
12LE00BK Reduced Recoil*		12	2 3/4"	Max	1150	9 pell.	00 Buck	10	Hi-Antimony Nickel Plated

Stock #		Gauge	Shell Length	MM	Dram. Equiv.	Muzzle Velocity	Shot Oz.	Shot Sizes	Rds. Box	Shot Type
SLUGS										
12TS1	Trophy Slug	12	2 3/4"	70	Max	1560	1	Rifled Slug	5	Lead w/attached Wad
20TS78	Trophy Slug	20	2/34"	70	Max	1650	7/8	Rifled Slug	5	Lead w/attached Wad

Stock #		Gauge	Shell Length	Dram. Equiv.	Muzzle Velocity	Shot Oz.	Shot Sizes	Rds. Box	Shot Type
NICKEL PLATED HUNTING LOADS									
12HFN Live Bird Pigeon		12	2 3/4"	3 1/4	1225	1 1/4	7-1/2 8	25	Nickel Plated Lead
12HVN High Velocity Nickel		12	2 3/4"	3 3/4	1330	1 1/4	4 5 6 7-1/2 8 9	25	Nickel Plated Lead
12GP Golden Pheasant		12	2 3/4"	Max	1250	1 3/8	4 5 6	25	Nickel Plated Lead
203GP Golden Pheasant 20		20	3"	Max	1200	1 1/4	4 5 6	25	Nickel Plated Lead
12TT Turkey Thunder		12	2 3/4"	Max	1250	1 3/8	4 5 6	10	Nickel Plated Lead
123TT Turkey Thunder		12	3	Max	1150	1 3/4	4 5 6	10	Nickel Plated Lead
FITASC									
12HFN Live Bird Pigeon/FITASC		12	2 3/4"	3 1/4	1225	1 1/4	7-1/2 8	25	Nickel Plated Lead
12HFN Heavy Field		12	2 3/4"	3 1/4	1225	1 1/4	7-1/2 8	25	Lead
INTERCEPTOR SPREADER									
12CPTR Interceptor		12	2 3/4"	Max	1300	1	7-1/2 8 8-1/2 9	25	Lead
SPORTING CLAYS POWER SPREADERS									
12SSCH Power Spreader		12	2 3/4"	3	1200	1 1/8	7-1/2 8 8-1/2 9	25	Lead
12SSCX Power Spreader		12	2 3/4"	Max	1250	1 1/8	8 8-1/2 9	25	Lead
STEEL TARGET LOAD									
12S78 Steel Target Load		12	2 3/4"	Max	1440	7/8	7	25	Steel
12S1OZ Steel Target Load		12	2 3/4"	Max	1400	1	6 7	25	Steel
20S Steel Target Load		20	2 3/4"	Max	1490	3/4	6 7	25	Steel
ULTRA LOW RECOIL LOADS									
1278OZ Trainer		12	2 3/4"	Lite	1200	7/8	7-1/2 8	25	Hi-Antimony Lead
MULTI-SPORT LOADS-GAME & TARGET									
12MS3 Multi Sport		12	2 3/4"	3	1250	1	7-1/2 8 9	25	Lead
12GT Game & Target		12	2 3/4"	3 1/4	1290	1	6 7-1/2 8 9	25	Lead
12GT118 Game & Target		12	2 3/4"	3	1200	1 1/8	7-1/2 8	25	Lead
LOW RECOIL TRAP LOADS									
12TRAPL Low Recoil Trap Light		12	2 3/4"	2 3/4	1140	1 1/8	7-1/2 8	25	Hi Antimony Lead
12TRAPH Low Recoil Trap Heavy		12	2 3/4"	3	1185	1 1/8	7-1/2 8	25	Hi Antimony Lead

AMMUNITION

THE NEW .480 RUGER cartridge for the .480 Ruger Super Redhawk is the first cartridge to bear the Ruger name. Currently available only in Hornady Custom pistol ammunition, this cartridge is loaded with high-quality Hornady brass, so reloading is a practical option.

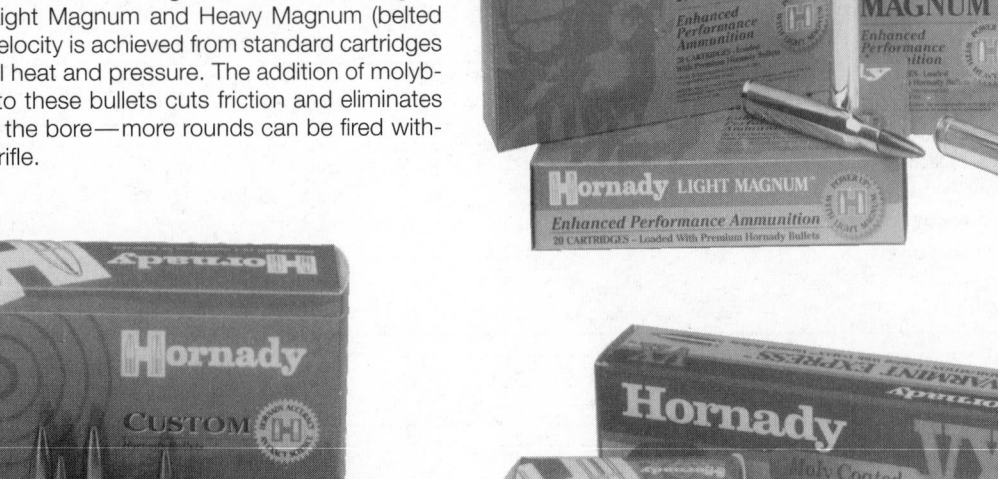

Hornady's moly-coated LIGHT MAGNUM ammo achieves more energy, flatter trajectory and velocities up to 200 feet per second faster than standard ammo. That same performance is available in .280 Remington and 7mm Remington Magnum. With Light Magnum and Heavy Magnum (belted rounds) greater velocity is achieved from standard cartridges with no additional heat and pressure. The addition of molybdenum disulfide to these bullets cuts friction and eliminates copper fouling in the bore—more rounds can be fired without cleaning the rifle.

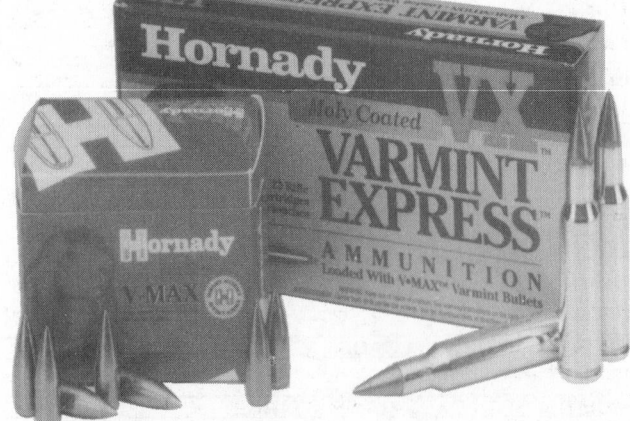

The effectiveness of Hornady's factory-loaded rifle match ammunition is assured by hand-selection and matching for premium uniformity. Cases, powder and primer are all loaded so as to guarantee superb ignition and pinpoint accuracy. These match cartridges are loaded with either Hornady A-MAX or BTHP match bullets and are available with high-performance moly-coating that reduces barrel wear and increases speed.

Hornady's VARMINT EXPRESS ammunition now features moly-coated V-MAX bullets, which offer faster speeds in most calibers. Other features include high quality brass cases, hand-inspection, individually selected primers and powders.

FOR SPORTING RIFLES

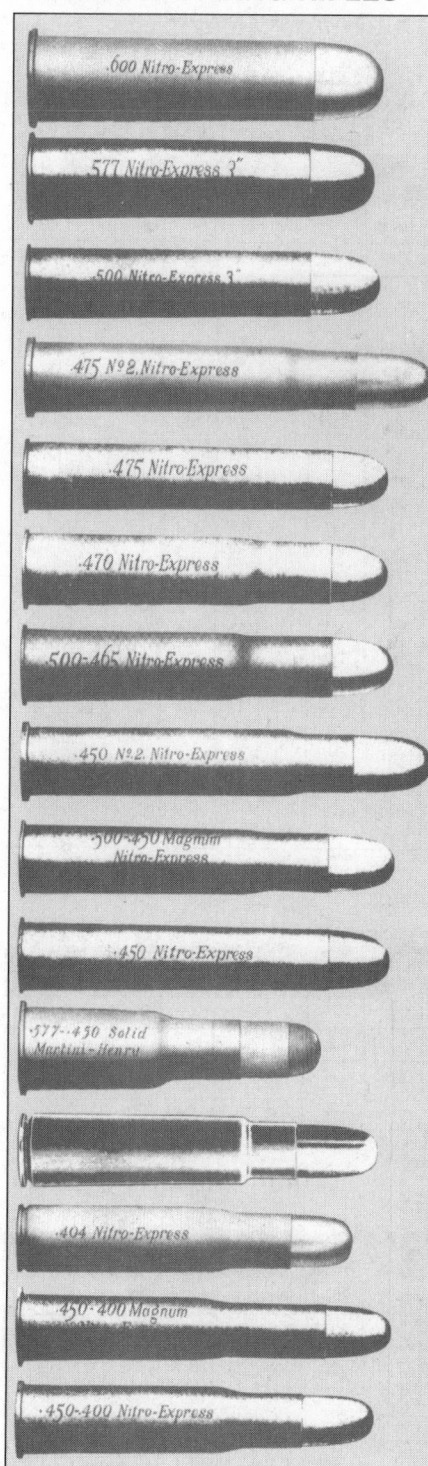

.600 NE
900 gr Solid or SN

.577 NE 3"
750 gr Solid or SN

.500 NE 3"
570 gr Solid or SN

.475 No. 2 NE
480 gr Solid or SN
for Jeffery Rifles:
500 gr Solid or SN

.475 NE
480 gr Solid or SN

.470 NE
500 gr Solid or SN

.500/.465 NE
480 gr Solid or SN

.450 No. 2 NE
480 gr Solid or SN

.500/.450
Magnum NE
480 gr Solid or SN

.450 NE
480 gr Solid or SN

.577/.450 MH
480 gr Solid Lead

.416 Rigby
410 gr Solid or SN

.404 Rimless NE
400 gr Solid or SN

.450/.400
Magnum NE
400 gr Solid or SN

.450/.440 NE
400 gr Solid or SN

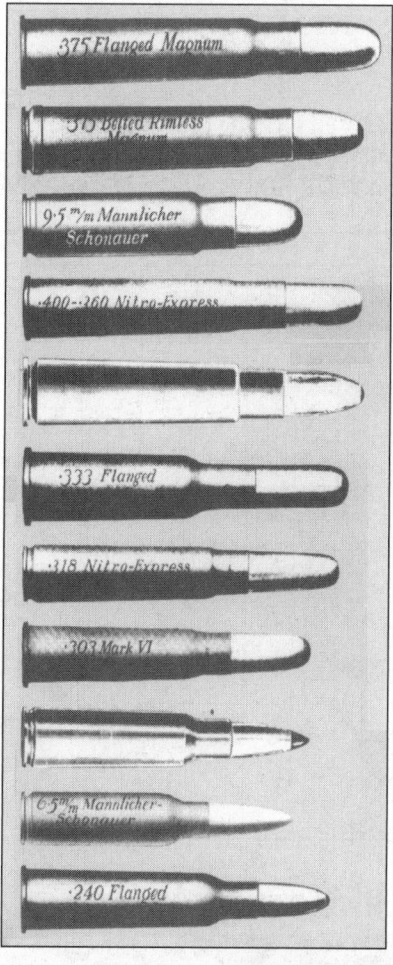

.375 Flanged Magnum
300, 270 or 235 gr
Solid or SN

.375 Belted Magnum
300, 270 or 235 gr
Solid or SN

9.5 mm Mannlicher
Schonauer 270 gr Solid or SN

.400/.360 NE for Purdey
Rifles: 300 gr for Westley
Richards: 314 gr. Solid or SN

.350 Rigby Magnum 225 gr
or 250 gr, Solid or SN

.333 Jeffrey Flanged NE
300 gr Solid or SN

.318 Rimless NE
250 gr Solid or SN
180 gr SN

.303 British
215 gr Solid or SN

.275 Rigby Rimless
140 gr SN

6.5 m/m Mannlicher
Schonauer
160 gr SN

.240 H&H Flanged
100 gr SN

AMMUNITION

ADDITIONAL PROPRIETARY CALIBERS AVAILABLE:

.700 NE
1000 gr Solid

.500 Jeffery
535 gr Solid
or SN

.450 Rigby Rimless
Magnum
480 gr Solid
or SN

.400 - 3" Purdey
230 gr SN

.505 Gibbs Magnum
525 gr Solid
or SN

.425 Westley Richards
Magnum
410 gr Solid
or SN

.300 H&H Flanged
Magnum
220 gr Solid
or SN

MAGTECH AMMUNITION

Magtech Ammunition Co. imports and distributes high-quality rifle and pistol cartridges manufactured by Companhia Brasileira de Cartuchos (CBC). This firm, in business since 1926, has a modern factory in Sao Paulo, Brazil. Before 1976 it was owned and managed by Remington Arms and ICI - the UK's Imperial Chemical Company.

MAGTECH REVOLVER CARTRIGES

Symbol	Caliber	Bullet			Velocity						Energy						Mid-Range Trajectory				Test Barrel Length	
		Style	Weight		Muzzle		50m		50 yd	100m	100 yd	Muzzle		50m		50 yd	100m	100 yd	50m	50 yd	100 m	100 yd	
			g	gr	m/s	fps	m/s	fps	m/s	fps	J	ft/lbs	J	ft/lbs	J	ft lbs	cm	inch	cm	inch	cm	inch
32SWA	.32 S&W	LRN	5.50	85	207	680	195	645	187	610	118	87	105	78	96	70	7.6	2.5	36.8	10.5	7.6	3
32SWLA	.32 S&W Long	LRN	6.35	98	215	705	202	670	192	635	147	108	130	98	117	88	7.0	2.3	32.0	10.5	10.2-V	4-V
32SWLB	.32 S&W Long	LWC	6.35	98	208	682	174	579	145	491	137	102	96	73	67	52	7.0	2.3	38.5	12.6	10.2-V	4-V
32SWLC	.32 S&W Long	SJHP	6.35	98	250	820	226	744	214	709	198	145	163	120	147	109	5.5	1.9	105.4	33.9	10.2-V	4-V
38SWA	.38 S&W	LRN	9.45	146	209	686	199	655	190	267	207	152	188	139	170	127	6.9	2.3	134.8	43.6	10.2-V	4-V
38A	.38 SPL	LRN	10.24	158	230	755	218	728	209	693	271	200	243	183	224	168	6.2	2.0	24.9	8.3	10.2-V	4-V
38B	.38 SPL	LWC	9.59	148	216	710	190	634	170	566	224	166	173	132	139	105	7.4	2.4	33.7	10.8	10.2-V	4-V
38C	.38 SPL	SJSP	10.24	158	246	807	237	779	228	753	310	230	287	213	266	199	4.0	1.3	20.4	6.7	10.2-V	4-V
38D	.38 SPL+P	SJSP	8.10	125	286	938	270	891	257	851	331	245	295	220	267	200	4.0	1.3	16.5	5.1	10.2-V	4-V
38E	.38 SPL	SJHP	10.24	158	246	807	237	779	228	753	310	230	287	213	266	199	4.0	1.3	20.4	6.7	10.2-V	4-V
38F	.38 SPL+P	SJHP	8.10	125	286	938	270	891	257	851	331	245	295	220	267	200	4.0	1.3	16.5	5.4	10.2-V	4-V
38G	.38 SPL-Short	LRN	8.10	125	209	686	199	649	189	628	177	130	160	120	145	109	6.2	2.0	29.6	9.7	10.2-V	4-V
38H	.38 SPL+P	SJHP	10.24	158	270	890	235	774	226	746	376	278	283	210	261	196	4.3	1.4	20.2	30.4	10.2-V	4-V
38J	.38 SPL	LSWC	10.24	158	230	755	217	721	207	689	271	200	243	182	224	167	6.1	2.0	25.6	8.4	10.2-V	4-V
38P	.38 SPL	FMC-Flat	10.24	158	246	807	237	779	228	753	310	230	287	213	266	199	4.0	1.3	20.4	6.7	10.2-V	4-V
357A	.357 MAG	SJSP	10.24	158	376	1235	333	1104	305	1015	724	535	568	428	476	361	2.4	0.8	10.7	3.5	10.2-V	4-V
357B	.357 MAG	SJHP	10.24	158	376	1235	333	1104	305	1015	724	535	568	428	476	361	2.4	0.8	10.7	3.5	10.2-V	4-V
357C	.357 MAG	LSWC	10.24	158	376	1235	333	1104	305	1015	724	535	568	428	476	361	2.4	0.8	10.7	3.5	10.2-V	4-V
357D	.357 MAG	FMC-Flat	10.24	158	376	1235	340	1125	314	1045	724	535	592	444	507	383	2.4	0.8	8.7	2.7	10.2-V	4-V
357E	.357 MAG	SJSP	10.24	158	376	1235	333	1104	305	1015	724	535	868	428	476	361	2.4	0.5	10.7	3.6	10.2-V	4-V
44A	.44 REM MAG	SJSP	15.55	240	360	1180	326	1081	304	1010	1010	741	828	632	720	623	2.8	0.9	11.4	3.7	10.2-V	4-V
454A	.454 CASULL	SJSP	16.85	260	548	1800	475	1577	412	1383	2540	1871	1903	1437	1429	1104	1.2	0.4	5.5	1.8	19V	7.5-V

V~VENTED TEST BARREL

MAGTECH RIFLE CARTRIGES

Symbol	Caliber	Bullet			Velocity						Energy						Mid-Range Trajectory				Test Barrel Length	
		Style	Weight		Muzzle		50m		50 yd	100m	100 yd	Muzzle		50m		50 yd	100m	100 yd	50m	50 yd	100 m	100 yd	
			g	gr	m/s	fps	m/s	fps	m/s	fps	J	ft/lbs	J	ft/lbs	J	ft lbs	cm	inch	cm	inch	cm	inch
30A	30 Carbine	FMC	7.13	110	607	1990	549	1817	495	1654	1313	967	1075	806	875	668	2.2	0.6	18.4	5.7	50.8	20

MAGTECH COWBOY ACTION CARTRIGES

Symbol	Caliber	Bullet			Velocity						Energy						Mid-Range Trajectory				Test Barrel Length	
		Style	Weight		Muzzle		50m		50 yd	100m	100 yd	Muzzle		50m		50 yd	100m	100 yd	50m	50 yd	100 m	100 yd	
			g	gr	m/s	fps	m/s	fps	m/s	fps	J	ft/lbs	J	ft/lbs	J	ft lbs	cm	inch	cm	inch	cm	inch
4440B	.44-40 WIN	LFN	14.58	225	221	725	214	703	206	681	356	281	333	247	311	232	6.5	2.1	26.9	8.8	10.2	4
44B	.44 SPL	LFN	15.55	240	229	750	220	722	211	696	408	300	376	278	347	258	6.1	2.0	25.4	8.3	10.2	4
45D	.45 Colt	LFN	16.20	250	229	750	221	726	213	702	425	312	395	293	367	274	6.0	2.0	25.2	8.2	10.2	4
38L	.38 SPL	LFN	10.24	158	244*	800*	236	776	228	753	305	225	285	211	267	199	5.3	1.8	22.0	7.2	10.2-V	4-V

Velocity obtained from 10.2 cm (4") vented test barrel. Abbreviation: LFN LEAD FLAT NOSE

MAGTECH GOLD™ CARTRIDGES

Symbol	Caliber	Bullet			Velocity						Energy						Mid-Range Trajectory				Test Barrel Length	
		Style	Weight		Muzzle		50m	50 yd	100m	100 yd	Muzzle		50m	50 yd	100m	100 yd	50m	50 yd	100 m	100 yd		
			g	gr	m/s	fps	m/s	fps	m/s	fps	J	ft/lbs	J	ft/lbs	J	ft lbs	cm	inch	cm	inch	cm	inch
380C	.380 Auto+P	JHP	5.5	85	330	1,082	303	999	282	936	300	221	252	188	219	166	3.1	1.0	13.3	4.3	9.5	3-3/4
40E	.40 S&W	JHP	10.0	155	367	1,025	338	1,118	317	1,052	677	500	596	430	523	381	2.5	0.8	10.9	3.5	10.2	4
45E	.45 Auto+P	JHP	12.0	185	350	1,148	323	1,066	303	1,005	735	540	626	467	551	415	2.7	0.9	11.8	3.8	12.7	5
38M	.38 SPL+P	JHP	8.10	125	310*	1,017*	295	971	282	931	389	287	352	262	322	241	3.4	1.1	14.3	4.6	10.2	4
9M	9mm Luger+P	JHP	7.45	115	380	1,246	344	1,137	318	1,056	538	397	441	330	377	285	2.4	0.8	10.5	3.4	10.2	4

*Velocity obtained from 10.2 cm (4") vented test barrel.   Abbreviation: JHP JACKETED HOLLOW POINT

MAGTECH PISTOL CARTRIDGES

Symbol	Caliber	Bullet			Velocity						Energy						Mid-Range Trajectory				Test Barrel Length	
		Style	Weight		Muzzle		50m	50 yd	100m	100 yd	Muzzle		50m	50 yd	100m	100 yd	50m	50 yd	100 m	100 yd		
			g	gr	m/s	fps	m/s	fps	m/s	fps	J	ft/lbs	J	ft/lbs	J	ft lbs	cm	inch	cm	inch	cm	inch
25A	.25 Auto	FMC	3.24	50	232	760	214	707	199	659	87	64	74	56	64	48	6.1	2.0	26.2	8.7	5.1	2
32A	.32 Auto	FMC	4.60	71	276	905	259	855	245	810	175	129	154	115	138	103	4.3	1.4	18.5	5.8	10.2	4
32B	.32 Auto	JHP	4.60	71	276	905	259	855	245	810	175	129	154	115	138	103	4.3	1.4	18.5	5.8	10.2	4
380A	.380 Auto	FMC	6.15	95	290	951	261	861	236	781	259	190	209	156	171	128	4.3	1.4	18.0	5.9	9.5	3-3/4"
380B	.380 Auto	JHP	6.15	95	290	951	261	861	236	781	259	190	209	156	171	128	4.3	1.4	18.0	5.9	9.5	3-3/4"
9A	9mm Luger	FMC	7.45	115	346	1135	310	1027	290	961	446	330	358	270	313	235	2.7	0.9	12.2	4.0	10.2	4
9B	9mm Luger	FMC	8.03	124	338	1109	308	1030	290	971	459	339	381	292	338	259	3.1	1.0	12.5	4.1	10.2	4
9C	9mm Luger	JHP	7.45	115	352	1155	316	1047	293	971	462	340	372	280	320	240	2.7	0.9	12.2	3.9	10.2	4
9D	9mm Luger	JSP Flat	6.15	95	410	1345	356	1185	317	1055	517	380	390	295	309	235	2.4	0.8	12.4	3.4	10.2	4
9E	9mm Luger	LRN	8.03	124	334	1109	308	1030	290	971	459	339	381	292	338	259	3.1	1.0	12.5	4.1	10.2	4
9F	9mm Luger	JSP Flat*	6.15	95	410	1345	356	1185	317	1085	817	380	390	295	309	238	2.4	0.8	10.4	3.4	10.2	4
9G	9mm Luger (sub-sonic)	FMC Flat	9.52	147	302	990	286	945	274	907	434	320	389	292	357	268	3.7	1.2	14.6	4.8	10.2	4
9H	9mm Luger+P+	JHP	7.45	115	380	1246	347	1145	322	1069	538	397	448	335	387	292	1.0	0.3	8.8	2.9	10.2	4
40A	.40 S&W	JHP	11.66	180	302	990	282	933	268	886	532	390	464	348	419	314	3.7	1.2	14.6	5.0	10.2	4
40B	.40 S&W	FMC	11.66	180	302	990	282	933	268	886	532	390	464	348	419	314	3.7	1.2	14.6	5.0	10.2	4
40C	.40 S&W	LSWC	10.37	160	355	1165	325	1076	297	984	653	484	548	411	457	343	2.7	0.9	11.9	3.9	10.2	4
40D	.40 S&W	JHP	10.05	155	367	1205	330	1018	307	1096	677	500	547	414	474	357	2.4	0.8	11.0	3.6	10.2	4
45A	.45 Auto	FMC	14.90	230	255	837	242	800	232	767	484	356	436	326	401	300	4.9	1.6	20.7	6.8	12.7	5
45B	.45 Auto	FMC-SWC	14.90	230	238	780	218	720	199	660	422	310	354	265	295	222	5.5	1.8	23.8	7.8	12.7	5
45C	.45 Auto	LSWC	12.96	200	290	950	277	910	265	874	545	401	496	368	455	339	2.4	0.8	11.0	4.8	12.7	5

• Bullet without grooves * Available early 2000

MAGTECH CLEAN RANGE CARTRIDGES

Symbol	Caliber	Bullet			Velocity						Energy						Mid-Range Trajectory				Test Barrel Length	
		Style	Weight		Muzzle		50m	50 yd	100m	100 yd	Muzzle		50m	50 yd	100m	100 yd	50m	50 yd	100 m	100 yd		
			g	gr	m/s	fps	m/s	fps	m/s	fps	J	ft/lbs	J	ft/lbs	J	ft lbs	cm	inch	cm	inch	cm	inch
9J	9mm Luger	TMJ	8.03	124	338	1109	308	1030	290	971	459	339	381	292	338	259	3.1	1.0	12.5	4.1	10.2	4
9K	9mm Luger	JSP Flat	6.15	95	410	1345	356	1185	317	1055	517	380	390	295	309	235	2.4	0.8	10.4	3.4	10.2	4
38K	.38 SPL	TMJ	10.24	158	230	755	218	723	209	693	271	200	243	183	224	168	6.2	2.0	24.9	8.3	10.2	4V

Magtech ammunition is manufactured according to SAAMI and CIP technical specifications and carefully tested in fully equipped Ballistics Laboratories in order to meet prescribed values for primer sensitivity, bullet velocities, maximum, mean and port pressures, accuracy, etc. Safety, accuracy and quality are always the prime concern at Magtech.

AMMUNITION

PMC (Precision Made Cartridges) is the same firm as Eldorado Cartridge Company. It is a fast-growing enterprise whose product line continues to expand. The firm offers more than 50 handgun loads, from .25 Auto to .44 Magnum, including five specifically for Cowboy Action shooting. The centerfire rifle stable includes cowboy action loads in .30-30 and .45-70, plus a wide variety of hunting and match ammunition from .222 Remington to .375 H&H Magnum. The selection of .22 rimfire rounds features hunting, plinking and match loads.

PMC offers a broad choice of bullet styles. In pistol ammo, there's the quick-opening Starfire hollowpoint, a traditional jacketed hollowpoint, a jacketed softpoint and a full-metal-jacket (hardball) bullet — plus lead wadcutter, semi-wadcutter and round-nose options. Rifle bullets include the Barnes X-Bullet, .30-30 Starfire hollowpoint, Sierra boat-tail hollowpoint, Sierra boat-tail softpoint, pointed softpoint, softpoint, flat-nose softpoint and full metal jacket.

PMC also manufactures shotshells, from light dove and quail and target loads to heavy steel-shot loads for geese. PMC also has a rural Nevada plant that offers test-firing opportunities out the back door.

PMC has entered the popular Cowboy Action game with an assortment of low-recoil ammunition that speeds recovery for a second shot. The Lite Clay Target shotshell works at this game as well as at hand-thrown clay targets. The firm offers Cowboy Action pistol and rifle rounds in .38 Special, .357 Magnum, .44 Special, .44-40 Winchester, .45 Colt, .30-30 and .45-70 Government.

PMC rifle cartridges include hunting loads for heavy-hitters like the .338 Winchester and .375 H&H magnums as well as for varmint rounds like the .222 and .223. There are match loads for cartridges commonly used in competition. Bullet choices for big game hunters include a wide variety of softpoint and hollowpoint designs — for example, the Barnes X-Bullet and Sierra boat-tails.

PMC handgun ammunition is loaded for target, hunting and personal defense. The firm's own Starfire bullet dumps energy right away with quick, violent expansion. It is available in nine pistol cartridges, from .380 Auto to .44 magnum. Target rounds include a new 180-grain FMJ .40 S&W. There's also a low-cost practice load for the .357 SIG; it features a 124-grain FMJ bullet.

NEW PMC PRODUCTS FOR 2001

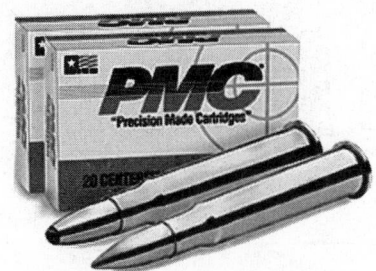

BRONZE LINE RIFLE

SILVER LINE RIFLE

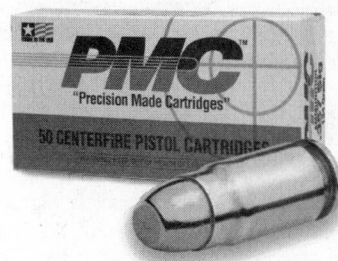

BRONZE LINE PISTOL

SILVER LINE PISTOL

SHOT SHELLS - HEAVY FIELD

SHOT SHELLS - STEEL SHOT

ITEM NUMBER	DESCRIPTION
BRONZE LINE RIFLE	
25-06B	.25-06 Rem., 117gr, PSP
7mm-08A	7mm-08 Rem., 140gr, PSP
30B	.30, Carbine, 110gr, RNSP
SILVER LINE RIFLE	
223SMB	.223 Rem., 69gr, HPBT, MatchKing
375HA	375, H&H Mag., 270gr, PSP
45-70HA	45-70 Govt., 350gr, FNSP, Interlock
BRONZE LINE PISTOL	
45LB	45 Long Colt, 250gr, FN-FMJ
SILVER LINE PISTOL	
45HA	45 Long Colt, 300gr, JSP
SHOT SHELLS	
Heavy Field	
HF206 (7.5&8)	20GA, 2 3/4", 1-oz., (6,7.5,8), 2 3/4, Dram
Steel Shot (3 1/2")	
SSG12T (BB&2)	12GA, 3 1/2", 1 3/8 oz., (T, BB, 2), Max Dram

AMMUNITION

Premier Ultra Mag Rifle Ammunition

Headspacing on the shoulder of the case, rather than the use of a belt, promotes better accuracy due to precise bore alignment. A "non-belted magnum" with a larger case diameter also allows for increased powder capacity. The Remington Ultra Mag line now has more bullet options and two new calibers.

7MM REMINGTON ULTRA MAG

All-new for 2001: the flattest-shooting big game cartridge on the planet. Flatter than 7mm STW. Even flatter than a .22-250 varmint load. In fact, it delivers a flatter trajectory with a 140-grain bullet than a .22-250 does with a 55-grain bullet. Also produces 24% greater energy than standard 7mm Remington and 12% greater energy than 7mm STW at 300 yards. Best for long-range antelope, deer and sheep.

.300 REMINGTON ULTRA MAG

The cartridge that launched the Ultra Mag line and set the standard for big game from deer to elk to caribou. The .300 Remington Ultra Mag delivers a a muzzle velocity of 3300 feet-per-second and 2145 foot-pounds of retained energy at 500 yards. Even more impressive is how it fares against the competition. At 200 yards, it delivers up to 18% greater retained energy than the 300 Wby. Mag and up to 27% greater retained energy than the 300 Win. Mag.

.338 REMINGTON ULTRA MAG

The .338 Remington Ultra Mag is one of the most powerful .338-caliber rounds available. The figures speak for themselves. It delivers 25% greater muzzle energy than .338 Win Mag and retains a flatter trajectory all the way out to 500 yards. Loaded with reliable 250-grain Swift A-Frame or Core-Lokt Pointed Soft Point bullets. Excellent for bear, elk and moose.

.375 REMINGTON ULTRA MAG

New this year. Has 23% more energy at the muzzle than .375 H&H. Also delivers more energy at 200 yards than .375 H&H at 100 yards - and with the same flat-shooting trajectory as a 150-grain .270 Win. load.

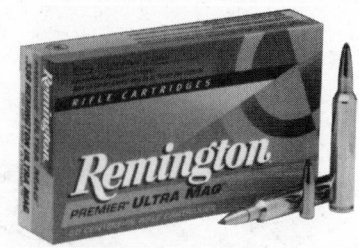

PREMIER ULTRA MAG

Caliber	Index/EDI No.	Bullet Wt. (grs)	Bullet Type
* 7mm Rem. Ultra Mag	PR7UM1	140	PSP, Core-Lokt
* 7mm Rem. Ultra Mag.	PR7UM2	140	Nosler Partition
* .300 Rem. Ultra Mag.	PR300UM5	150	Swift Scirocco
.300 Rem. Ultra Mag	PR300UM1	180	Nosler Partition
.300 Rem. Ultra Mag	PR300UM3	180	Swift Scirocco
* .300 Rem. Ultra Mag.	PR300UM4	180	Core-Lokt PSP
.300 Rem. Ultra Mag.	PR300UM2	200	Nosler Partition
.338 Rem. Ultra Mag.	PR338UM1	250	Swift A-Frame PSP
* .338 Rem. Ultra Mag.	PR338UM2	250	PSP, Core-Lokt
* .375 Rem. Ultra Mag.	PR375UM2	270	Soft Point
* .375 Rem. Ultra Mag.	PR375UM3	300	Swift A-Frame

New for 2001

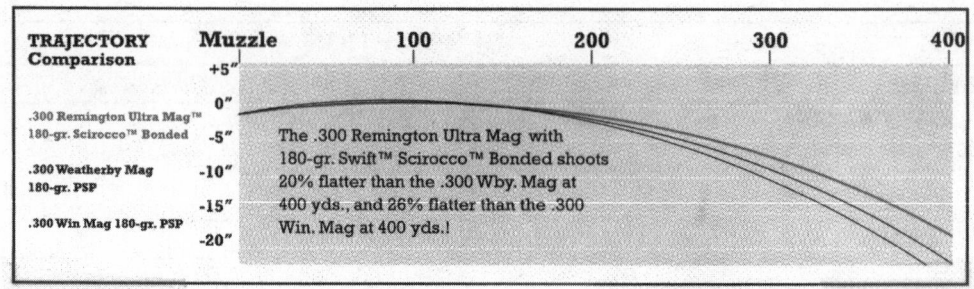

TRAJECTORY Comparison

.300 Remington Ultra Mag™ 180-gr. Scirocco™ Bonded

.300 Weatherby Mag 180-gr. PSP

.300 Win Mag 180-gr. PSP

The .300 Remington Ultra Mag with 180-gr. Swift™ Scirocco™ Bonded shoots 20% flatter than the .300 Wby. Mag at 400 yds., and 26% flatter than the .300 Win. Mag at 400 yds.!

SWIFT SCIROCCO

Precision-shaped polymer top for reduced frontal air resistance

Jacket and core locked together with proven Swift banding technology

Long bearing surface for improved rotational stability

NOSLER PARTITION

Semi-protected exposed lead tip for initial expansion

Special crimp at jacket base locks in the rear core to resist firing deformation

SWIFT A-FRAME

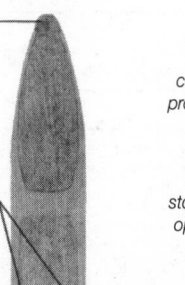

Pure lead core is bonded to pure copper jacket with proprietary process

Swift A-Frame cross-member stops expansion at optimum diameter of 2x caliber

CORE-LOKT PSP

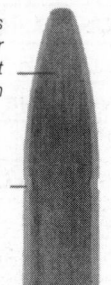

Soft point provides broad frontal area for high energy impact and rapid expansion

Jacket "locked" to the core to prevent separation on breakup

REMINGTON ULTRA MAG BULLET CHOICES:

ETRONX AMMUNITION

To complement its EtronX rifles, Remington has developed a line of EtronX centerfire ammunition. EtronX ammunition includes three, flat-shooting centerfire loadings: Premier Varmint .22-250 Remington, .220 Swift with 50-grain V-Max polymer-tip bullets, and Premier Ballistic Tip .243 Win. with a 90-grain Nosler Ballistic Tip bullet. The design and construction of these cartridges is identical to standard centerfire ammunition with one significant exception. They utilize new electrically ignited EtronX primers, which contain a patent-ed electrically conductive primer mix specially formulated to ignite reliably and evenly from the electrical pulse.

Because the EtronX primer is carefully calibrated to duplicate the performance of the standard primer, cartridges can be loaded with the same amount and type of powder as they would for a mechanical firing system, with virtually no change in pressure levels or velocities.

Premier Varmint and Premier Ballistic Tip cartridges, combined with the near-zero lock time of the Model 700 EtronX rifle, promise even tighter accuracy performance than previously obtainable from over-the-counter rifles and ammunition. And for those who reload their centerfire ammunition, EtronX primers will also be available as components. They have identical ignition characteristics and external dimensions as standard large-rifle percussion primers. Shooters will be able to reload EtronX ammunition by following the same published loading data they have been using for cartridges of the same caliber and bullet weight.

Head of EtronX cartridge showing electrically responsive primer

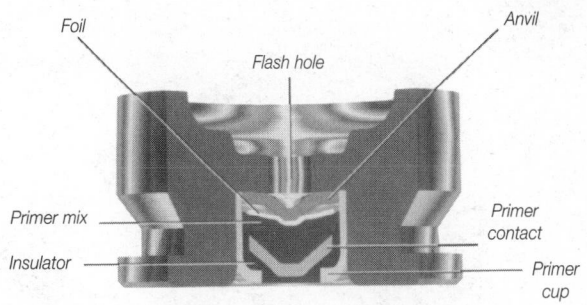

Foil — Anvil
Flash hole
Primer mix — Primer contact
Insulator — Primer cup

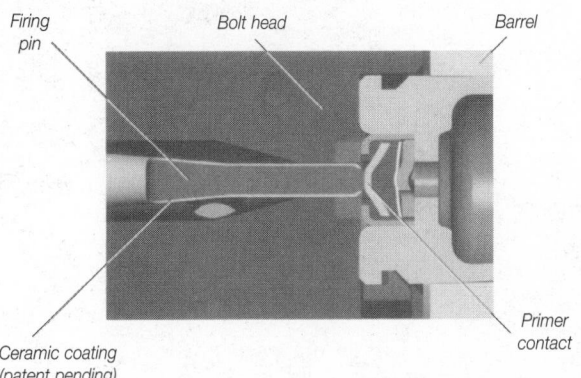

Firing pin — Bolt head — Barrel
Ceramic coating (patent pending) — Primer contact

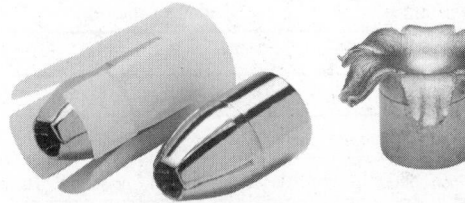

IMPROVED COPPER SOLID™ SABOT SLUGS

REMINGTON® IMPROVES DESIGN AND PERFORMANCE 12-GAUGE COPPER SOLID™ SABOT SLUGS

Already accurate and effective, Remington's 12-gauge Copper Solid™ slug has been designed to provide more reliable and uniform expansion and even higher weight retention. The hollow point cavity is now formed by six, separate petals in an inwardly-curved, spiral design. Upon impact, these petals mushroom open quickly to twice the diameter of the 58-caliber slug body. However, they remain intact, with no separation for deep, reliable penetration. Groups from rifled barrels stay within 3 inches at 100 yards.

These improved 12-gauge Copper Solid™ sabot slugs weigh one ounce. They are loaded in 12-gauge, 2 3/4-inch shells at a muzzle velocity of 1450 feet per second, and in three-inch shells, at 1550 feet per second.

UMC LEADLESS HANDGUN CARTRIDGES

New for 2001. The perfect solution for virtually eliminating lead exposure at the firing line. A must-have for shooters that frequent indoor ranges. New, specially designed Flat Nose Enclosed Base (FNEB) bullet actually prevents the vaporizing of lead from the bullet's base upon firing. Also features a lead-free primer. Standard bullet weights duplicate the ballistics of conventional loads. As always, economical UMC pricing is ideal for high-volume shooting.

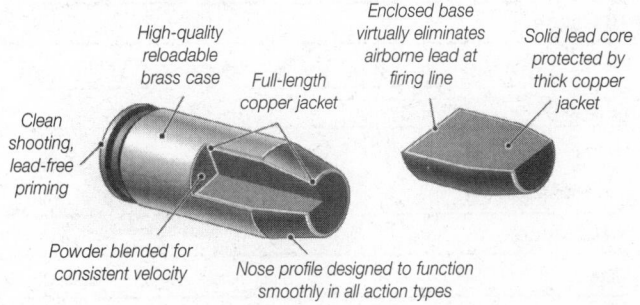

High-quality reloadable brass case
Full-length copper jacket
Enclosed base virtually eliminates airborne lead at firing line
Solid lead core protected by thick copper jacket
Clean shooting, lead-free priming
Powder blended for consistent velocity
Nose profile designed to function smoothly in all action types

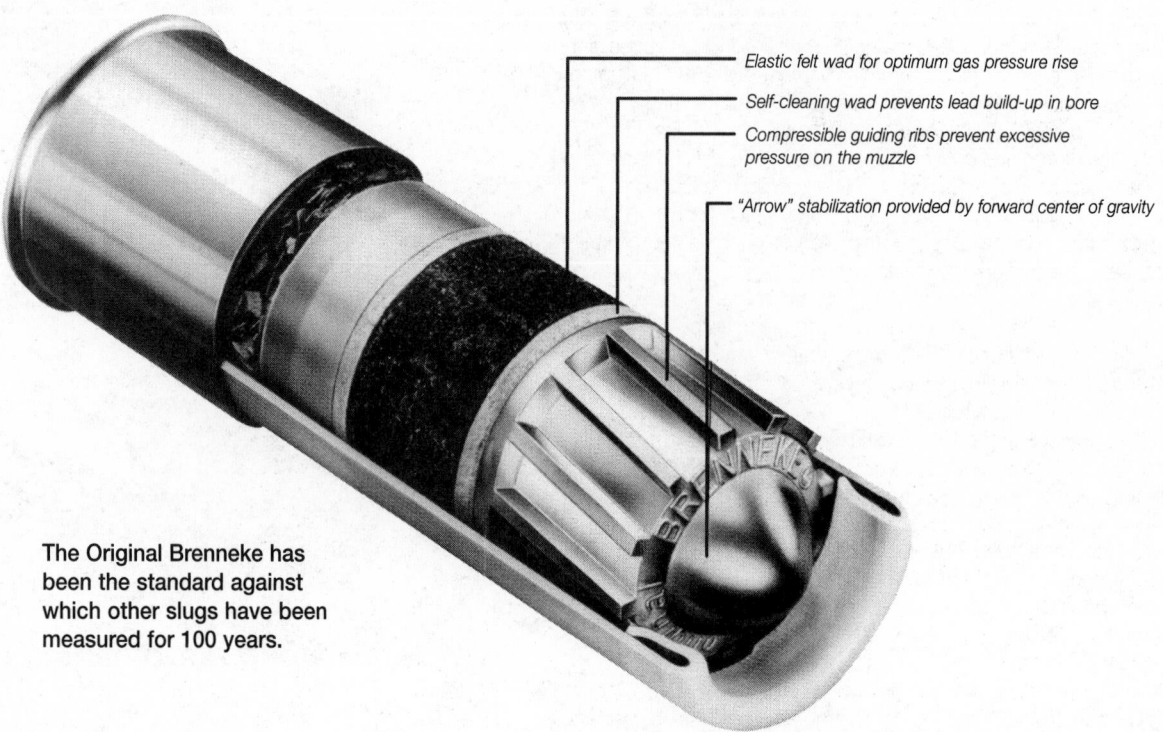

- Elastic felt wad for optimum gas pressure rise
- Self-cleaning wad prevents lead build-up in bore
- Compressible guiding ribs prevent excessive pressure on the muzzle
- "Arrow" stabilization provided by forward center of gravity

The Original Brenneke has been the standard against which other slugs have been measured for 100 years.

SPECIFICATIONS

BRENNEKE LOAD	SIZE	BARREL	SLUG WEIGHT	VELOCITY (FT./SEC.)	ENERGY (FT./LBS.)
12 Gauge					
Super Magnum	3"	Rifled only	1-3/8 oz.	*Muzzle:* 1476, *50 y:* 1200, *100 y:* 1025	*Muzzle:* 2902, *50 y:* 1915, *100 y:* 1410
Magnum	3"	Rifled or smooth	1-3/8 oz.	*Muzzle:* 1476, *50 y:* 1200, *100 y:* 1025	*Muzzle:* 2902, *50 y:* 1915, *100 y:* 1410
Heavy Field Short Magnum	2-3/4"	Rifled or smooth	1-1/4 oz.	*Muzzle:* 1476, *50 y:* 1200, *100 y:* 1030	*Muzzle:* 2540, *50 y:* 1675, *100 y:* 1235
Field Short Magnum	2-3/4"	Smooth only	1-1/8 oz.	*Muzzle:* 1510, *50 y:* 1220, *100 y:* 1040	*Muzzle:* 2480, *50 y:* 1625, *100 y:* 1181
High Velocity	2-3/4"	Smooth only	1 oz.	*Muzzle:* 1560, *50 y:* 1255, *100 y:* 1060	*Muzzle:* 2375, *50 y:* 1545, *100 y:* 1100
Low Recoil	2-3/4"	Smooth only	1 oz.	*Muzzle:* 1150, *50 y:* 1000, *100 y:* 905	*Muzzle:* 1290, *50 y:* 980, *100 y:* 805
Buckshot	2-3/4"	Smooth	1 oz. (9 pellets)	–	–
16 Gauge					
Field Short Magnum	2-3/4"	Smooth only	1 oz.	*Muzzle:* 1510, *50 y:* 1220, *100 y:* 1040	*Muzzle:* 2100, *50 y:* 1375, *100 y:* 1000
20 Gauge					
Magnum	3"	Rifled or smooth	1 oz.	*Muzzle:* 1476, *50 y:* 1200, *100 y:* 1025	*Muzzle:* 2130, *50 y:* 1400, *100 y:* 1035
Field Short Magnum	2-3/4"	Smooth only	7/8 oz.	*Muzzle:* 1510, *50 y:* 1220, *100 y:* 1040	*Muzzle:* 1870, *50 y:* 1225, *100 y:* 890
.410 Gauge					
Magnum	3"	Smooth only	1/4 oz.	*Muzzle:* 1510, *50 y:* 1220, *100 y:* 1040	*Muzzle:* 556, *50 y:* 365, *100 y:* 265

Bullets And Ballistics For Norma

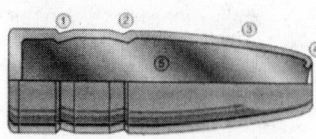

VULKAN

Vulkan bullets are strengthened by the folded jacket at the front. The folds protect the tip from deformation. The bullet penetrates before expansion starts. Subsequently, mushrooming to double the original diameter follows rapidly. *1. Reinforced rear jacket with lead core lock. 2. Crimping groove for secure seating in the case. 3. Thin forward jacket with internal notches. 4. Jacket folded into the lead core. 5. Antimony hardened lead core.*

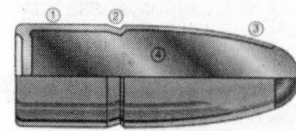

SOFT POINT

Soft Point bullets have optimum ballistic shape. They offer good penetration and mushroom well even on smaller game. The Soft Point is an excellent all-around bullet particularly suitable for small and medium game. *1. Reinforced rear jacket. 2. Crimping groove for secure seating in the case. 3. Thin forward jacket. 4. Antimony hardened lead core.*

The design of the DK bullet is the result of Dynamit Nobel's extensive ballistics research.

Manufactured at considerable expense, DK bullets barely splinter, mushroom in a controlled manner, have a residue body of over 50 percent, and usually produce an exit hole. A true twin core that separates to perform two separate functions upon impact, penetration and a high degree of impact force, combine to give the DK a clear advantage over traditional bullets, especially for large game with heavy bones and muscles.

The RWS cone point bullet was designed and developed after exhaustive studies in the laboratory as well as in the field.

A carefully engineered matching of casing and core material and an aerodynamically favorable bullet shape have been paired to produce a controlled mushrooming to almost twice caliber size. The rear groove, which joins the lead core and casing, controls mushrooming and preserves effective residual body to give it killing power.

Due to external shape, the RWS cone point performs well in light brush, with minimal deflection.

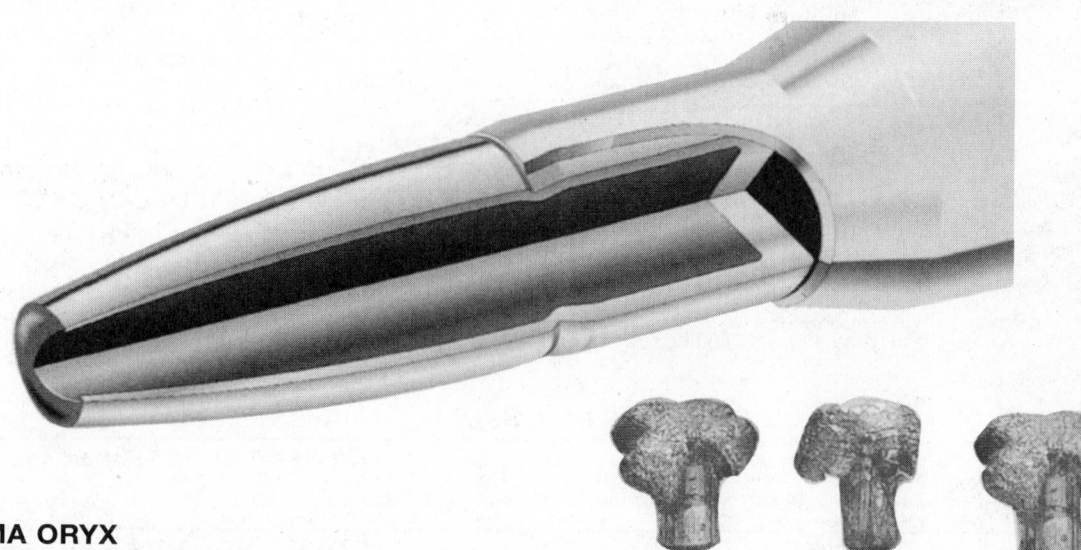

NORMA ORYX

This bullet is designed to penetrate deep. The jacket and core are bonded together through a chemical process. This ensures a very high residual weight, even in tough targets. Despite the solid construction, mushrooming starts early. The Oryx bullet delivers excellent deep energy transfer and is suitable for big and medium sized game.

Price: box of 20 cartridges . . . . . . **From $27.25 to 57.75**

- *Bonded bullet-lead core soldered into copper jacket*
- *Good penetration*
- *Exceptional expansion, combined with bonding, results in deep wound channel and minimal meat damage*
- *Very high weight retention*

AMMUNITION

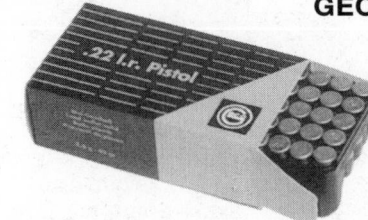

GECO .22 L.R. RIFLE

Combining quality and cost effectiveness this rimfire ammunition is made in the RWS Nuremberg factory to exacting standards. Perfect for informal target shooting and entry level competition.

GECO .22 L.R. PISTOL

The same quality and affordability as the rifle version but with a reduced velocity. For the pistol shooter looking for muzzle control. *Price:* **$2.85/box**

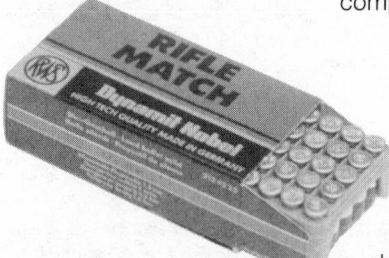

RWS .22 L.R. RIFLE MATCH

Perfect for the club level target competitor. Accurate and affordable. *Price:* **$2.85/box**

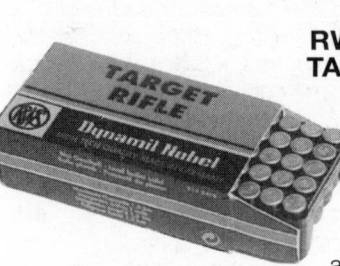

RWS .22 L.R. TARGET RIFLE

An ideal training and field cartridge, the .22 Long Rifle Target also excels in informal competitions. The target .22 provides the casual shooter with accuracy at an economical price. *Price:* **$3.40/box**

RWS .22 L.R. SUBSONIC HOLLOW POINT

Subsonic ammunition is a favorite ammunition of shooters whose shooting range is limited to where the noise of a conventional cartridge would be a problem. *Price:* **$4.50/box**

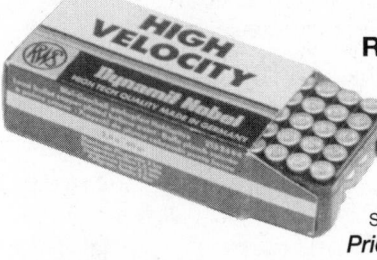

RWS .22 L.R. HV HOLLOW POINT

A higher velocity hollow point offers the shooter greater shocking power in game, suitable for both small game and vermin. *Price:* **$5.75/box**

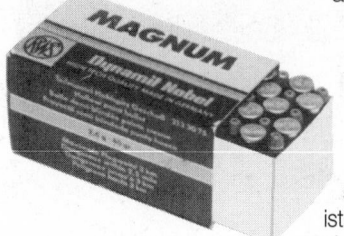

RWS .22 MAGNUM HOLLOW POINT

The soft point allows good expansion on impact while preserving the penetration characteristics necessary for larger vermin and game. *Price:* **$23.00/box**

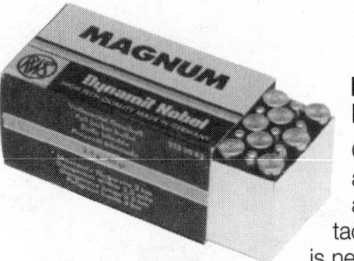

RWS .22 MAGNUM FULL JACKET

Outstanding penetration characteristics of this cartridge allow the shooter to easily tackle game where penetration is necessary. *Price:* **$23.00/box**

TECHNICAL DATA

Cartridges	Bullet Style	Bullet Weight (Grains)	Max. Chamber Pressure (psi)	Velocity (Ft./Sec.) Muzzle	50Y	100Y	Energy (Ft./Lbs.) Muzzle	50Y	100Y	Open Sight At	Scope Sighted 25 Yds	50 Yds	75 Yds	100Yds	In At	25 Yds	50 Yds	75 Yds	100 Yds
.22 L.R. R 50	Lead	40	25.600	1.070	970	890	100	80	70	--	--	--	--	--	--	--	--	--	--
.22 Short R 25	Lead	28	18.500	560	490	---	20	15	--	--	--	--	--	--	--	--	--	--	--
.22 L.R. Geco Rifle	Lead	40	25.600	1.080	990	900	100	8/5	70	50 yds.	+0.6		-3.1	-8.7	50 yds	+0.1		-2.5	-7.5
.22 L.R. Rifle Match	Lead	40	25.600	1.035	945	860	95	80	65	50 yds.	+0.7		-3.2	-9.0	50 yds	+0.1		-2.6	-7.8
.22 L.R. Target Rifle	Lead	40	25.600	1.080	990	900	100	85	70	50 yds.	+0.6		-3.1	-8.7	50 yds	+0.1		-2.5	-7.5
.22 L.R. Subsonic	Hollow Point	40	25.600	1.000	915	835	90	75	60	50 yds.	+0.8		-3.4	-4.7	50 yds	+0.2		+2.8	-8.5
.22 L.R. HV Hollow point	Lead coppered	40	25.600	1.310	1.120	990	150	110	85		--	--	--	--	--	--	--	--	--
.22 Magnum	Soft Point	40	25.600	2.020	1.710	1.430	360	260	180	100 yds.	+0.6	+1.3	+1.1	0	100 yds	-0.3	+0.7	+0.8	0
.22 Magnum	Full Jacket	40	25.600	2.020	1.710	1.430	360	260	180	100 yds.	+0.6	+1.3	+1.1	0	100 yds	-0.3	+0.7	+0.8	0

(Trajectory inches above (+) or below (-) line of sight)

INTRODUCING
THE 300 WINCHESTER
SHORT MAGNUM (300 WSM)

It's the first new, jointly-developed commercial Rifle Cartridge from Winchester Ammunition in almost 20 years. The new 300 WSM cartridge is designed to deliver 300 Winchester Magnum energy and velocity performace in a short action cartridge and lighter weight rifle!

This beltless magnum cartridge delivers the same precise head spacing and high accuracy as cartridges designed for bench rest shooting. Its "short & fat" cartridge shape delivers a highly efficient powder burn and quicker cycle time via a shorter and lighter rifle action with a standard magnum bolt face.

Browning A-Bolt and Winchester 70 Featherweight rifles are now chambered in .300 WSM.

SUPREME PARTITION
GOLD HIGH VELOCITY SLUG

This 50-caliber, 385 gr. Partition Gold slug develops a muzzle velocity of 1,900 fps - and a muzzle energy of 3,085 ft-lbs. Plus, the Partition Slug retains a greater energy level at 100 yards than competitive slug offerings develop at the muzzle—and 50% greater in-target penetration!

The Supreme Partition Gold's proprietary one piece, 4-petal sabot design ensures proper projectile launch and release. And the proven Partition projectile design ensures dependable upset performance and integrity at all ranges. Specially selected propellants offer maximum velocity and flat trajectory.

NEW FOR 2001
WESTERN TARGET & FIELD LOADS

Western Target & Field loads feature hard shot, eight-segment crimp, clean-burning propellants and Winchester primers for consistent ignition and performance. These loads are ideal for all informal target shooting, Sporting Clays events and upland game hunting.

AMMUNITION

Custom Dies And Ammunition

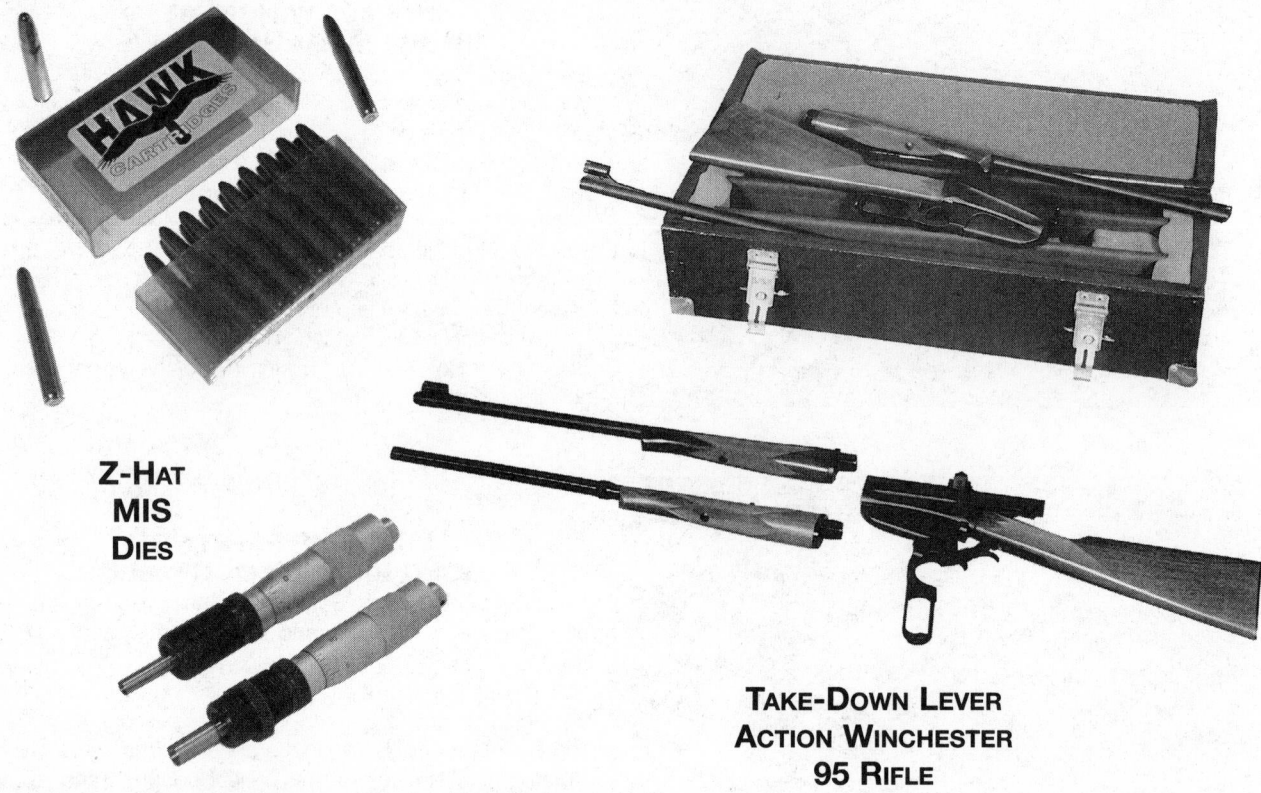

**Z-HAT
MIS
DIES**

**TAKE-DOWN LEVER
ACTION WINCHESTER
95 RIFLE**

Fred Zeglin's work with Hawk wildcat cartridges, and his experience as a gunsmith, have resulted in a business that includes building and servicing rifles, developing loads and marketing premium-quality brass for Hawk cartridges and supplying shooters with match-grade loading dies. The Z-Hat Micrometer Inline Seating (MIS) die is a universal in line bullet seater, similar to a "Vickerman" die. The universal seater comprises one die body and caliber sleeves for any caliber. It works with wildcats and obsolete rounds, as well as standard cartridges.

The MIS indexes on the datum line of the case shoulder and on the give of the bullet. This allows use of the MIS die with any caliber, .22 through .378 Wby. and 411 Hawk. 17 caliber is available on special order.

The Z-Hat takedown rifle conversion is a full thread system based on the 100-year-old Thomas Bland design. Simplicity of design insures longevity. This takedown involves the installation of a heavy contact plate on the barrel assembly, so that the barrel will always index to the same point. The 95 Winchester or Browning actions are fitted to the plate/barrel assembly, and a simple lock screw holds the assembly tightly aligned. Mutliple barrels are possible, each with it's own complete forearm assembly, making it easy to switch barrels and calibers. The original factory barrel can be converted, as can any new barrel. This system, like the ability to use various calibers, has sight systems setup on one gun. For instance, Express sights on one barrel and a Scout Scope on the other. Zeglin is developing a version of this takedown design for the Winchester Model 70 bolt action.

Takedowns are normally shipped in a high-quality aluminum travel case. Charcoal is standard; other colors are available. These custom cases, designed specifically for takedown rifles, hold the rifle snugly in transit. At the same time they look more like tool boxes than gun cases, so are less likely to attract unwanted attention from baggage handlers. More conventional shotgun style cases are available too.

HAWK CARTRIDGES:

240 Hawk • 257 Hawk • 264 Hawk • 270 Hawk • 284 Hawk • 300 Hawk • 8mm Hawk • 338 Hawk • 358 Hawk • 9.3 Hawk • 375 Hawk • 411 Hawk

Z-Hat offers formed brass for all 12 Hawk cartridges, at $29.95 per 20. Loaded rounds are available at $69.95 per box, in .338, .358 and .375 Hawk. Custom loads for your rifle can be developed at Z-Hat (Rifle.Builder @ Z-Hat.com or phone 307-577-7443).

Fred also offers custom sizing dies with Z-Hat custom rifles, and he builds a ring die that can size standard bullets to fit obsolete bore diameters.

Prices:

In-Line Seater set up for one cartridge **$99.00**
Caliber inserts **16.00**
Extra micrometer heads **58.00**

Ballistics

THE ULTIMATE IN RIFLE ACCURACY
by Glen Newick

The Ultimate in Rifle Accuracy contains the information needed to extract the best performance from your rifle. It is an up-to-date picture of what goes on in creating and shooting the ultimate in accurate rifles.

GUNSMITHING AT HOME
LOCK STOCK AND BARREL
by John Traister

A comprehensive guide to setting up shop for all types of repairs, refinishing and customizing. Easy to follow instructions, plus step-by-step illustrations lead the novice or veteran through successful trouble shooting and correcting of common firearms problems.

MODERN SPORTING RIFLE CARTRIDGES
by Wayne van Zwoll

Wayne van Zwoll, author of America's Great Gunmakers and hundreds of magazine articles on all aspects of hunting, offers his new book on the history and makeup of sporting cartridges. Illustrated with hundreds of photos and dozens of tables and schematic drawings with descriptions and loads for virtually every American-made cartridge. Features a full set of ballistics tables.

FEDERAL HANDGUN BALLISTICS

Federal offers what may be the industry's most comprehensive lineup of handgun ammunition. A wide assortment of bullet profiles and weights, in a broad range of calibers, assures that there is a Classic load for every situation, from self-defense to hunting to target shooting.

CLASSIC BULLET STYLES

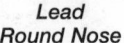

Lead Round Nose	Full Metal Jacket	Hi-Shok Jacketed Soft Point	Lead Semi-Wadcutter	Hi-Shok Jacketed Hollow Point	Semi-Wadcutter Hollow Point

CLASSIC® AUTOMATIC PISTOL

Usage	Federal Load No.	Caliber	Bullet Wgt. In Grains	Bullet Wgt. In Grams	Bullet Style*	Factory Primer No.	Velocity Muzzle	25Yds	50Yds	75Yds	100Yds	Energy Muzzle	25Yds	50Yds	75Yds	100Yds	Mid-Range 25Yds	50Yds	75Yds	100Yds	Test Barrel Length Inches
5,6	C25AP	25 Auto (6.35mm Browning)	50	3.24	Full Metal Jacket	200	760	750	730	720	700	65	60	60	55	55	0.5	1.9	4.5	8.1	2
5,6	C32AP	32 Auto (7.65mm Browning)	71	4.60	Full Metal Jacket	100	910	880	860	830	810	130	120	115	110	105	0.3	1.4	3.2	5.9	4
5,6	C380AP	380 Auto (9x17mm Short)	95	6.15	Full Metal Jacket	100	960	910	870	830	790	190	175	160	145	130	0.3	1.3	3.1	5.8	3¾
6	C380BP	380 Auto (9x17mm Short)	90	5.83	Hi-Shok JHP	100	1000	940	890	840	800	200	175	160	140	130	0.3	1.2	2.9	5.5	3¾
6	C9MKB	9mm Makarov (9x18 Makarov)	90	5.83	Hi-Shok JHP	100	990	950	910	880	850	195	180	165	155	145	0.3	1.2	2.9	5.3	3¾
5,6	C9AP	9mm Luger (9x19mm Parabellum)	124	8.03	Full Metal Jacket	100	1120	1070	1030	990	960	345	315	290	270	255	0.2	0.9	2.2	4.1	4
6	C9BP	9mm Luger (9x19mm Parabellum)	115	7.45	Hi-Shok JHP	100	1160	1100	1060	1020	990	345	310	285	270	250	0.2	0.9	2.1	3.8	4
6	C9MS	9mm Luger (9x19mm Parabellum)	147	9.52	Hi-Shok JHP	100	980	950	930	900	880	310	295	285	265	255	0.3	1.2	2.8	5.1	4
6	C357S2	357 Sig	125	8.10	Full Metal Jacket	100	1350	1270	1190	1130	1080	510	445	395	355	325	0.2	0.7	1.6	3.1	4
6	C40SWA	40 S&W	180	11.66	Hi-Shok JHP	100	990	960	930	910	890	390	365	345	330	315	0.3	1.2	2.8	5.0	4
6	C40SWB	40 S&W	155	10.04	Hi-Shok JHP	100	1140	1080	1030	990	950	445	400	365	335	315	0.2	0.9	2.2	4.1	4
6	C10C	10mm Auto	180	11.66	Hi-Shok JHP	150	1030	1000	970	950	920	425	400	375	355	340	0.3	1.1	2.5	4.7	5
6	C10E	10mm Auto	155	10.04	Hi-Shok JHP	150	1330	1230	1140	1080	1030	605	515	450	400	360	0.2	0.7	1.8	3.3	5
6	C45A	45 Auto	230	14.90	Full Metal Jacket	150	850	830	810	790	770	370	350	335	320	305	0.4	1.6	3.6	6.6	5
6	C45C	45 Auto	185	11.99	Hi-Shok JHP	150	950	920	900	880	860	370	350	335	315	300	0.3	1.3	2.9	5.3	5
6	C45D	45 Auto	230	14.90	Hi-Shok JHP	150	850	830	810	790	770	370	350	335	320	300	0.4	1.6	3.7	6.7	5

*JHP = Jacketed Hollow Point

CLASSIC® REVOLVER

Usage	Federal Load No.	Caliber	Bullet Wgt. In Grains	Bullet Wgt. In Grams	Bullet Style*	Factory Primer No.	Velocity Muzzle	25Yds	50Yds	75Yds	100Yds	Energy Muzzle	25Yds	50 Yds	75Yds	100Yds	Mid-Range 25Yds	50Yds	75Yds	100Yds	Test Barrel Length Inches
5	C32LA	32 S&W Long	98	6.35	Lead Wadcutter	100	780	700	630	560	500	130	105	85	70	55	0.5	2.2	5.6	11.1	4
5	C32LB	32 S&W Long	98	6.35	Lead Round Nose	100	710	690	670	650	640	115	105	100	95	90	0.6	2.3	5.3	9.6	4
6	C32HRA	32 H&R Magnum	95	6.15	Lead Semi-Wadcutter	100	1030	1000	940	930	900	225	210	195	185	170	0.3	1.1	2.5	4.7	4½
6	C32HRB	32 H&R Magnum	85	5.50	Hi-Shok JHP	100	1100	1050	1020	970	930	230	210	195	175	165	0.2	1.0	2.3	4.3	4½
5	C38B	38 Special	158	10.23	Lead Round Nose	100	760	740	720	710	690	200	190	185	175	170	0.5	2.0	4.6	8.3	4-V
5,6	C38C	38 Special	158	10.23	Lead Semi-Wadcutter	100	760	740	720	710	690	200	190	185	175	170	0.5	2.0	4.6	8.3	4-V
1,6	C38E	38 Special (High-Velocity+P)	125	8.10	Hi-Shok JHP	100	950	920	900	880	860	250	235	225	215	205	0.3	1.3	2.9	5.4	4-V
1,6	C38F	38 Special (High-Velocity+P)	110	7.13	Hi-Shok JHP	100	1000	960	930	900	870	240	225	210	195	185	0.3	1.2	2.7	5.0	4-V
1,6	C38G	38 Special (High-Velocity+P)	158	10.23	Semi-Wadcutter HP	100	890	870	860	840	820	280	265	260	245	235	0.3	1.4	3.3	5.9	4-V
5,6	C38H	38 Special (High-Velocity+P)	158	10.23	Lead Semi-Wadcutter	100	890	870	860	840	820	270	265	260	245	235	0.3	1.4	3.3	5.9	4-V
1,6	C38J	38 Special (High-Velocity+P)	125	8.10	Hi-Shok JSP	100	950	920	900	880	860	250	235	225	215	205	0.3	1.3	2.9	5.4	4-V
2,6	C357A	357 Magnum	158	10.23	Hi-Shok JSP	100	1240	1160	1100	1060	1020	535	475	430	395	385	0.2	0.8	1.9	3.5	4-V
1,6	C357B	357 Magnum	125	8.10	Hi-Shok JHP	100	1450	1350	1240	1160	1100	580	495	430	370	335	0.1	0.6	1.5	2.8	4-V
5	C357C	357 Magnum	158	10.23	Lead Semi-Wadcutter	100	1240	1160	1100	1060	1020	535	475	430	395	365	0.2	0.8	1.9	3.5	4-V
1,6	C357D	357 Magnum	110	7.13	Hi-Shok JHP	100	1300	1180	1090	1040	990	410	340	290	260	235	0.2	0.8	1.9	3.5	4-V
2,6	C357E	357 Magnum	158	10.23	Hi-Shok JHP	100	1240	1160	1100	1060	1020	535	475	430	395	365	0.2	0.8	1.9	3.5	4-V
2	C357G	357 Magnum	180	11.66	Hi-Shok JHP	100	1090	1030	980	930	890	475	425	385	350	320	0.2	1.0	2.4	4.5	4-V
1,6	C41A	41 Rem. Magnum	210	13.60	Hi-Shok JHP	150	1300	1210	1130	1070	1030	790	680	595	540	495	0.2	0.7	1.8	3.3	4-V
1,6	C44SA	44 S&W Special	200	12.96	Semi-Wadcutter HP	150	900	860	830	800	770	360	330	305	285	260	0.3	1.4	3.4	6.3	6½-V
2,6	C44A	44 Rem. Magnum	240	15.55	Hi-Shok JHP	150	1180	1130	1080	1050	1010	740	675	625	580	550	0.2	0.9	2.0	3.7	6½-V
1,2	C44B	44 Rem. Magnum	180	11.66	Hi-Shok JHP	150	1610	1480	1370	1270	1180	1035	875	750	640	555	0.1	0.5	1.2	2.3	6½-V
1,6	C45LCA	45 Colt	225	14.58	Semi-Wadcutter HP	150	900	880	860	840	820	405	385	370	355	340	0.3	1.4	3.2	5.8	5½

+P ammunition is loaded to a higher pressure. Use only in firearms recommended by the gun manufacturer. "V" indicates vented barrel to simulate service conditions.
**JHP = Jacketed Hollow Point HP = Hollow Point JSP = Jacketed Soft Point
Usage Key: 1 = Varmints, predators, small game 2 = Medium game 3 = Large, heavy game 4 = Dangerous game 5 = Target shooting, training, practice 6 = Self Defense

PREMIUM HANDGUN

Premium Handgun ammunition increasingly has become the choice of law enforcement personnel, and of knowledgeable shooters buying ammunition for personal defense or handgun hunting. Power, accuracy, reliability – these are the hallmarks of Premium Handgun cartridges.

PREMIUM BULLET STYLES

Hydra-Shok

Premium Personal Defense

Premium Expanding Full Metal Jacket

Premium Nyclad

Usage	Federal Load No.	Caliber	Bullet Wgt. in Grains	Grams	Bullet Style*	Factory Primer No.	Muzzle	25 Yds.	50 Yds.	75 yds.	100 Yds.	Muzzle	25 Yds.	50 Yds.	75 Yds.	100 Yds.	25 Yds.	50 yds.	75 Yds.	100 Yds.	Test Barrel Length Inches
							Velocity In Feet Per Second (To Nearest 10 FPS)					Energy In Foot-Pounds (To Nearest 5 Foot-Pounds)					Mid-Range Trajectory				
PREMIUM HYDRA-SHOK																					
6	P32HS1	32 Auto (7.65mm Browning)	65	4.21	Hydra-Shok JHP	100	950	920	890	860	830	130	120	115	105	100	0.3	1.3	3.0	5.6	4
6	P9HS1	9mm Luger (9x19mm Parabellum)	124	8.03	Hydra-Shok JHP	200	1120	1070	1030	990	960	345	315	290	270	255	0.2	0.9	2.2	4.1	4
6	P9HS2	9mm Luger (9x19mm Parabellum)	147	9.52	Hydra-Shok JHP	200	1000	960	920	890	860	325	300	275	260	240	0.3	1.2	2.8	5.1	4
6	P38HS1	38 Special (High Velocity + P)	129	8.36	Hydra-Shok JHP	100	950	930	910	890	870	255	245	235	225	215	0.3	1.3	2.9	5.3	4-V
6	P357S1	357 Sig	125	8.10	Jacketed Hollow Point	200	1350	1270	1190	1130	1080	510	445	395	355	325	0.2	0.7	1.6	3.1	4
6	P357S3	357 Sig	150	9.72	Jacketed Hollow Point	200	1130	1080	1030	1000	970	420	385	355	330	310	0.2	0.9	2.1	4.0	4
6	P357HS1	357 Magnum	158	10.23	Hydra-Shok JHP	100	1240	1160	1100	1060	1020	535	475	430	395	365	0.2	0.8	1.9	3.5	4-V
6	P40HS1	40 S&W	180	11.66	Hydra-Shok JHP	100	990	960	930	910	890	390	365	345	330	315	0.3	1.2	2.8	5.0	4
6	P40HS2	40 S&W	155	10.04	Hydra-Shok JHP	100	1140	1080	1030	990	950	445	400	365	335	315	0.2	0.9	2.2	4.1	4
6	P40HS3	40 S&W	165	10.66	Hydra-Shok JHP	100	980	950	930	910	890	350	330	315	300	290	0.3	1.2	2.7	5.1	4
6	P10HS1	10 mm Auto	180	11.66	Hydra-Shok JHP	150	1030	1000	970	950	920	425	400	375	355	340	0.3	1.1	2.5	4.7	5
6	P45HS1	45 Auto	230	14.90	Hydra-Shok JHP	150	850	830	810	790	770	370	350	335	320	305	0.4	1.6	3.6	6.6	5
6	P44HS1	44 Rem. Magnum	240	15.55	Hydra-Shok JHP	150	1180	1130	1080	1050	1010	740	675	625	580	550	0.2	0.9	2.0	3.7	6.5-V
PREMIUM PERSONAL DEFENSE																					
6	PD38HS3	38 Special	110	7.10	Hydra-Shok JHP	100	1000	970	930	910	880	245	225	215	200	190	0.3	1.2	2.7	5.0	4-V
6	PD357HS2	357 Magnum	130	8.42	Hydra-Shok JHP	100	1300	1210	1130	1070	1020	490	420	370	330	300	0.2	0.7	1.8	3.4	4-V
6	PD380HS1	380 Auto (9x17mm Short)	90	5.83	Hydra-Shok JHP	100	1000	940	890	840	800	200	175	160	140	130	0.3	1.2	2.9	5.5	3.75
6	PD9HS5	9mm Luger (9x19mm Parabellum)	135	8.75	Hydra-Shok JHP	100	1050	1030	1010	980	970	330	315	300	290	280	0.4	1.2	2.4	4.3	4
6	PD40HS4	40 S&W	135	8.75	Hydra-Shok JHP	100	1190	1050	970	900	850	420	330	280	245	215	0.2	1.0	2.4	4.6	4
6	PD45HS3	45 Auto	165	10.66	Hydra-Shok JHP	150	1060	1020	980	950	920	410	375	350	330	310	0.2	1.1	2.5	4.5	5
PREMIUM EXPANDING FULL METAL JACKET																					
6 New	P9CSP1	9mm+P	124	8.03	Full Metal Jacket	200	1120	1070	1030	990	960	345	315	290	270	255	0.2	0.9	2.2	4.1	4
6 New	P40CSP1	40 S&W	165	10.667	Full Metal Jacket	100	1050	1020	990	960	935	405	380	355	335	320	0.3	1.2	2.7	4.8	4
PREMIUM NYCLAD																					
6	P9BP	9mm Luger (9x19mm Parabellum)	124	8.03	Nyclad Hollow Point	200	1120	1070	1030	990	960	345	315	290	270	255	0.2	0.9	2.2	4.1	4
5	P38B	38 Special	158	10.23	Nyclad Round Nose	100	760	740	720	710	690	200	190	185	175	170	0.5	2.0	4.6	8.3	4-V
1,6	P38G	38 Special (High Velocity +P)	158	10.23	Nyclad SWC-HP	100	890	870	860	840	820	270	265	260	245	235	0.3	1.4	3.3	5.9	4-V
6	P38M	38 Special	125	8.10	Nyclad Hollow Point	100	830	780	730	690	650	190	170	150	130	115	0.4	1.8	4.3	8.1	2-V
1,6	P38N	38 Special (High Velocity +P)	125	8.10	Nyclad Hollow Point	100	950	920	900	880	860	250	235	225	215	205	0.3	1.3	2.9	5.4	4-V
PREMIUM HANDGUN HUNTING																					
2	P357J	357 Magnum	180	11.66	CastCore	100	1250	1200	1160	1120	1080	625	575	535	495	465	0.5	1.1	0.0	-2.8	7.5-V
2	P41B	41 Rem. Magnum	250	16.20	CastCore	150	1250	1200	1150	1110	1080	865	795	735	685	645	0.6	1.1	0.0	-2.9	7.5-V
2	P44E	44 Rem. Magnum	300	19.44	CastCore	150	1250	1200	1160	1120	1080	1040	960	885	825	775	0.5	1.1	0.0	-2.8	7.5-V
2	P454T1	454 Casull	300	19.44	Trophy Bonded Bear Claw	205	1630	1540	1450	1380	1300	1760	1570	1405	1260	1130	0.0	0.5	0.0	-1.7	7.5-V

+ P ammunition is loaded to a higher pressure. Use only in firearms recommended by the gun manufacturer. • JHP = Jacketed Hollow Point • V = Indicated vented barrel to simulate service conditions • SWC = Semi-wadcutter • HP = Hollow Point • TMF = Toxic-Metal Free • **Usage Key:** 1=Varmints, predators, small game • 2=Medium game • 3=Large, heavy game • 4=Dangerous game • 5=Target shooting, training, practice • 6=Self defense
These trajectory tables were calculated by computer using the best available data for each load. Trajectories are representative of the nominal behavior of each load at standard conditions (59 F temperature; barometric pressure at 29.53 inches; altitude at sea level) Shooters are cautioned that actual trajectories may differ due to variations in altitude, atmospheric conditions, guns, sights and ammunition.

BALLISTICS

AMERICAN EAGLE HANDGUN

Usage	Federal Load No.	Caliber	Bullet Wgt. in Grains	Grams	Bullet Style*	Factory Primer No.	Velocity In Feet Per Second (To Nearest 10 FPS) Muzzle	25 Yds.	50 Yds.	75 yds.	100 Yds.	Energy In Foot-Pounds (To Nearest 5 Foot-Pounds) Muzzle	25 Yds.	50 Yds.	75 Yds.	100 Yds.	Mid-Range Trajectory 25 Yds.	50 yds.	75 Yds.	100 Yds.	Test Barrel Length Inches
REVOLVLER																					
5	AE38B	38 Special	158	10.23	Lead Round Nose	100	760	740	720	710	690	200	190	185	175	170	0.5	2.0	4.6	8.3	4-V
5	AE38K	38 Special	130	8.43	Full Metal Jacket	100	950	920	890	870	840	260	245	230	215	205	0.3	1.3	3.0	5.5	4-V
2, 6	AE357A	357 Magnum	158	10.23	Jacketed Soft Point	100	1240	1160	1100	1060	1020	535	475	430	395	365	0.2	0.8	1.0	3.5	4-V
2, 6	AE44A	44 Rem. Magnum	240	15.55	Jacketed Hollow Point	150	1180	1130	1080	1050	1010	740	675	625	580	550	0.2	0.9	2.0	3.7	6.5-V
PISTOL																					
5	AE25A	25 Auto (6.35mm Browning)	50	3.24	Full Metal Jacket	200	760	750	730	720	700	65	60	60	60	55	0.5	1.9	4.5	8.1	2
5	AE32AP	32 Auto (7.65mm Browning)	71	4.60	Full Metal Jacket	100	910	880	860	830	810	130	120	115	110	105	0.3	1.4	3.2	5.9	4
5	AE380AP	380 Auto (9x17mm Short)	95	6.15	Full Metal Jacket	100	960	910	870	830	790	190	175	160	145	130	0.3	1.3	3.1	5.8	3.75
5	AE9AP	9mm Luger (9x19mm Parabellum)	124	8.03	Full Metal Jacket	200	1120	1070	1030	990	960	345	315	290	270	255	0.2	0.9	2.2	4.1	4
5	AE9DP	9mm Luger (9x19mm Parabellum)	115	7.45	Full Metal Jacket	200	1160	1100	1060	1020	990	345	310	285	270	250	0.2	0.9	2.1	3.9	4
5	AE9FP	9mm Luger (9x19mm Parabellum)	147	9.52	Full Metal Jacket Flat Pt.	200	960	930	910	890	870	295	280	270	260	250	0.3	1.3	2.9	5.3	4
5	AE9N1	9mm Luger (9x19mm Parabellum)	124	8.04	TMJ TMF Primer*	205TMF	1120	1070	1030	990	960	345	315	290	270	255	0.2	1.0	2.2	4.1	—
5	AE9N2	9mm Luger (9x19mm Parabellum)	147	9.53	TMJ TMF Primer*	205TMF	960	940	910	890	870	300	285	270	260	245	0.3	1.3	2.9	5.3	—
5	AE9MK	9mm Makarov (9 x 18 Makarov)	95	6.15	Full Metal Jacket	100	990	960	920	900	870	205	190	180	170	160	0.3	1.2	2.8	5.1	3.75
5	AE38S1	38 Super High Velocity +P	130	8.42	Full Metal Jacket	200	1200	1140	1100	1050	1020	415	380	350	320	300	0.2	0.8	1.9	3.6	5
5	AE40	40 S&W	180	11.66	High Antimony Lead	100	990	960	930	910	890	390	365	345	330	315	0.3	1.2	2.8	5.0	4
5	AE40N1	40 S&W	180	11.66	TMJ TMF Primer*	205TMF	990	960	940	910	890	390	370	350	330	315	0.3	1.2	2.7	5.0	—
5	AE40R1	40 S&W	180	11.66	Full Metal Jacket Ball	200	990	960	940	910	890	390	370	350	330	315	0.3	1.2	2.7	5.0	4
5	AE40R2	40 S&W	155	10.04	Full Metal Jacket Ball	200	1140	1080	1030	990	960	445	400	365	335	315	0.2	0.9	2.2	4.1	4
5	AE40R3	40 S&W	165	10.66	Full Metal Jacket Ball	200	980	950	920	900	880	350	330	310	295	280	0.3	1.2	2.8	5.1	4
5	AE10	10mm Auto	180	11.66	High Antimony Lead	150	1030	1000	970	950	920	425	400	375	355	340	0.3	1.1	2.5	4.7	5
5	AE45A	45 Auto	230	14.90	Full Metal Jacket	150	850	830	810	790	770	370	350	335	320	305	0.4	1.6	3.6	6.6	5
5	AE45N1	45 Auto	230	14.90	TMJ TMF Primer*	205TMF	850	830	810	790	770	370	350	335	315	305	0.4	1.6	3.7	6.7	—

+ P ammunition is loaded to a higher pressure. Use only in firearms recommended by the gun manufacturer. • *Total Metal Jacket, Toxic "Metal Free" Primer • V = Indicated vented barrel to simulate service conditions

Usage Key: 1=Varmints, predators, small game • 2=Medium game • 3=Large, heavy game • 4=Dangerous game • 5=Target shooting, training, practice • 6=Self defense

These trajectory tables were calculated by computer using the best available data for each load. Trajectories are representative of the nominal behavior of each load at standard conditions

(59 F temperature; barometric pressure at 29.53 inches; altitude at sea level)

Shooters are cautioned that actual trajectories may differ due to variations in altitude, atmospheric conditions, guns, sights and ammunition.

REMINGTON HANDGUN BALLISTICS

Golden Saber™ = GS **Core-Lokt® Hunting = RH** **Disintegrator™ Frangible = LF**

Caliber	Order No.	Primer No.	Weight (grs.)	Bullet Style	Velocity (ft./sec.) Muzzle	50 yds.	100 yds.	Energy (ft.-lbs.) Muzzle	50 yds.	100 yds.	Mid-range Trajectory 50 yds.	100 yds.	B.L.
.25 (6.35mm) Auto. Pistol	R25AP	1½	50	Metal Case	760	707	659	64	56	48	2.0"	8.7"	2"
.32 S&W	R32SW	1½	88	Lead	680	645	610	90	81	73	2.5"	10.5"	3"
.32 S&W Long	R32SWL	1½	98	Lead	705	670	635	115	98	88	2.3"	10.5"	4"
.32 (7.65mm) Auto. Pistol	R32AP	1½	71	Metal Case	905	855	810	129	115	97	1.4"	5.8"	4"
.357 Mag. (Vented Barrel Ballistics)	R357M7	5½	110	Semi-Jacketed Hollow Point	1295	1094	975	410	292	232	0.8"	3.5"	4"
	R357M1	5½	125	Semi-Jacketed Hollow Point	1450	1240	1090	583	427	330	0.6"	2.8"	4"
	GS357MA	5½	125	Brass-Jacketed Hollow Point	1220	1095	1009	413	333	283	0.8"	3.5"	4"
	RH357MA	5½	165	JHP Core-Lokt®	1290	1189	1108	610	518	450	0.7"	3.1"	8³/₈"
	R357M2	5½	158	Semi-Jacketed Hollow Point	1235	1104	1015	535	428	361	0.8"	3.5"	4"
	R357M3	5½	158	Soft Point	1235	1104	1015	535	428	361	0.8"	3.5"	4"
	R357M5	5½	158	Semi-Wadcutter	1235	1104	1015	535	428	361	0.8"	3.5"	4"
	R357M10	5½	180	Semi-Jacketed Hollow Point	1145	1053	985	524	443	388	0.9"	3.9"	8³/₈"
9mm Luger Auto. Pistol	R9MM1	1½	115	Jacketed Hollow Point	1155	1047	971	341	280	241	0.9"	3.9"	4"
	R9MM10	1½	124	Jacketed Hollow Point	1120	1028	960	346	291	254	1.0"	4.1"	4"
	R9MM2	1½	124	Metal Case	1110	1030	971	339	292	259	1.0"	4.1"	4"
	R9MM3	1½	115	Metal Case	1135	1041	973	329	277	242	0.9"	4.0"	4"
	R9MM6	1½	115	Jacketed Hollow Point (+P)‡	1250	1113	1019	399	316	265	0.8"	3.5"	4"
	R9MM8	1½	147	Jacketed Hollow Point (Subsonic)	990	941	900	320	289	264	1.1"	4.9"	4"
	R9MM9	1½	147	Metal Case (Match)	990	941	900	320	289	264	1.1"	4.9"	4"
	LF9MMA	1½	101	Disintegrator™ Plated Frangible	1220	1092	1004	334	267	226	0.9"	3.6"	4"
	GS9MMB	1½	124	Brass-Jacketed Hollow Point	1125	1031	963	349	293	255	1.0"	4.0"	4"
	GS9MMC	1½	147	Brass-Jacketed Hollow Point	990	941	900	320	289	264	1.1"	4.9"	4"
	GS9MMD	1½	124	Brass-Jacketed Hollow Point (+P)‡	1180	1089	1021	384	327	287	0.8"	3.8"	4"
.380 Auto. Pistol	R380AP	1½	95	Metal Case	955	865	785	190	160	130	1.4"	5.9"	4"
	R380A1	1½	88	Jacketed Hollow Point	990	920	868	191	165	146	1.2"	5.1"	4"
	GS380B	1½	102	Brass-Jacketed Hollow Point	940	901	866	200	184	170	1.2"	5.1"	4"
.38 S&W	R38SW	1½	146	Lead	685	650	620	150	135	125	2.4"	10.0"	4"
.38 Special (Vented Barrel Ballistics)	R38S10	1½	110	Semi-Jacketed Hollow Point (+P)‡	995	926	871	242	210	185	1.2"	5.1"	4"
	R38S16	1½	110	Semi-Jacketed Hollow Point	950	890	840	220	194	172	1.4"	5.4"	4"
	R38S2	1½	125	Semi-Jacketed Hollow Point (+P)‡	945	898	858	248	224	204	1.3"	5.4"	4"
	GS38SB	1½	125	Brass-Jacketed Hollow Point (+P)‡	975	929	885	264	238	218	1.0"	5.2"	4"
	R38S3	1½	148	Targetmaster® Lead WC Match	710	634	566	166	132	105	2.4"	10.8"	4"
	R38S5	1½	158	Lead (Round Nose)	755	723	692	200	183	168	2.0"	8.3"	4"
	R38S14	1½	158	Semi-Wadcutter (+P)‡	890	855	823	278	257	238	1.4"	6.0"	4"
	R38S6	1½	158	Semi-Wadcutter	755	723	692	200	183	168	2.0"	8.3"	4"
	R38S12	1½	158	Lead Hollow Point (+P)‡	890	855	823	278	257	238	1.4"	6.0"	4"
.38 Short Colt	R38SC	1½	125	Lead	730	685	645	150	130	115	2.2"	9.4"	6"
.357 Sig.	R357S1	5½	125	Jacketed Hollow Point	1350	1157	1032	506	372	296	0.7"	3.2"	4"
	LF357 SA	5½	104	Lead-Free Frangible	1400	1223	1094	453	345	276	0.6"	2.9"	—
.40 S&W	R40SW1	5½	155	Jacketed Hollow Point	1205	1095	1017	499	413	356	0.8"	3.6"	4"
	R40SW2	5½	180	Jacketed Hollow Point	1015	960	914	412	368	334	1.3"	4.5"	4"
	LF40SWA	5½	141	Disintegrator™ Plated Frangible	1135	1056	996	403	349	311	0.9"	3.9"	4"
	GS40SWA	5½	165	Brass-Jacketed Hollow Point	1150	1040	964	485	396	340	1.0"	4.0"	4"
	GS40SWB	5½	180	Brass-Jacketed Hollow Point	1015	960	914	412	368	334	1.3"	4.5"	4"
.41 Rem. Mag. (Vented BBL Ballistics)	R41MG1	2½	210	Soft Point	1300	1162	1062	788	630	526	0.7"	3.2"	4"
.44 Rem. Mag. (Vented BBL Ballistics)	R44MG5	2½	180	Semi-Jacketed Hollow Point	1610	1365	1175	1036	745	551	0.5"	2.3"	4"
	R44MG2	2½	240	Soft Point	1180	1081	1010	741	623	543	0.9"	3.7"	4"
	R44MG3	2½	240	Semi-Jacketed Hollow Point	1180	1081	1010	741	623	543	0.9"	3.7"	4"
	RH44MGA	2½	275	JHP Core-Lokt®	1235	1142	1070	931	797	699	0.8"	3.3"	6¹/₂"
.44 S&W Special	R44SW	2½	246	Lead	755	725	695	310	285	265	2.0"	8.3"	6"
.45 Colt	R45C	2½	250	Lead	860	820	780	410	375	340	1.6"	6.6"	5"
	R45C1	2½	225	Semi-Wadcutter (Keith)	960	890	832	460	395	346	1.3"	5.5"	5"
.45 Auto	R45AP2	2½	185	Jacketed Hollow Point	1000	939	889	411	362	324	1.1"	4.9"	5"
	R45AP4	2½	230	Metal Case	835	800	767	356	326	300	1.6"	6.8"	5"
	R45AP7	2½	230	Jacketed Hollow Point (Subsonic)	835	800	767	356	326	300	1.6"	6.8"	5"
	LF45APA	2½	175	Disintegrator™ Plated Frangible	1020	923	851	404	331	281	1.2"	5.1"	5"
	GS45APA	2½	185	Brass-Jacketed Hollow Point	1015	951	899	423	372	332	1.1"	4.5"	5"
	GS45APB	2½	230	Brass-Jacketed Hollow Point	875	833	795	391	355	323	1.5"	6.1"	5"
	GS45APC	2½	185	Brass-Jacketed Hollow Point (+P)‡	1140	1042	971	534	446	388	1.0"	4.0"	5"

‡Ammunition with (+P) on the case headstamp is loaded to higher pressure. Use only in firearms designated for this cartridge and so recommended by the gun manufacturer.

BALLISTICS

WINCHESTER HANDGUN BALLISTICS

SUPREME

Cartridge	Symbol	Bullet Wt. Grs.	Type	User Guide	Velocity (FPS) Muzzle	50 Yds.	100 Yds.	Energy (Ft.Lbs.) Muzzle	50 Yds.	100 Yds.	Mid Range Traj. (In.) 50 Yds.	100 Yds.	Barrel Length In.
380 Automatic SXT	S380	95	SXT	PP	955	889	835	192	167	147	1.3	5.5	3-3/4
38 Special + P # SXT	S38SP	130	SXT	PP	925	887	852	247	227	210	1.3	5.5	4V
9mm Luger SXT	S9	147	SXT	PP	990	947	909	320	293	270	1.2	4.8	4
40 Smith & Wesson SXT	S401	165	SXT	PP	1130	1041	977	468	397	349	0.9	4.0	4
40 Smith & Wesson SXT	S40	180	SXT	PP	1010	954	909	408	364	330	1.1	4.8	4
45 Automatic SXT	S45	230	SXT	PP	880	846	816	396	366	340	1.5	6.1	5
357 Magnum	S357P	180	PartitionGold	H	1180	1088	1020	557	473	416	0.8	3.6	8V
44 Magnum	S44MP	250	PartitionGold	H	1230	1132	1057	840	711	620	0.8	2.9	6.5V
45 Winchester Magnum #	SPG45WM	260	PartitionGold	H	1200	1105	1033	832	705	617	0.8	3.5	5
454 Casull #	SPG454	260	PartitionGold	H	1800	1605	1427	1871	1485	1176	0.4	1.7	7.5V

SUPER X

Cartridge	Symbol	Bullet Wt. Grs.	Type	User Guide	Velocity (FPS) Muzzle	50 Yds.	100 Yds.	Energy (Ft.Lbs.) Muzzle	50 Yds.	100 Yds.	Mid Range Traj. (In.) 50 Yds.	100 Yds.	Barrel Length In.
25 Automatic	X25AXP	45	Expanding Point**	PP	815	729	655	66	53	42	1.8	7.7	2
30 Luger (7.65 mm)	X30LP	93	Full Metal Jacket	T	1220	1110	1040	305	255	225	0.9	3.5	4-1/2
30 Carbine #	X30M1	110	Hollow Soft Point	H	1790	1601	1430	783	626	500	0.4	1.7	10
32 Smith & Wesson	32BL2P	Blk.Pwd.	Blank										
32 Smith & Wesson	X32SWP	85	Lead-Round Nose	T	680	645	610	90	81	73	2.5	10.5	3
32 Smith & Wesson Long	X32SWLP	98	Lead-Round Nose	T	705	670	635	115	98	88	2.3	10.5	4
32 Short Colt	X32SCP	80	Lead-Round Nose	T	745	665	590	100	79	62	2.2	9.9	4
32 Automatic	X32ASHP	60	Silvertip Hollow Point	PP	970	895	835	125	107	93	1.3	5.4	4
38 Smith & Wesson	X38SWP	145	Lead-Round Nose	T	685	650	620	150	135	125	2.4	10.0	4
380 Automatic	X380ASHP	85	Silvertip Hollow Point	PP	1000	921	860	189	160	140	1.2	5.1	3-3/4
38 Special	38SBLP	Smokeless	Blank										
38 Special	X38S9HP	110	Silvertip Hollow Point	PP	945	894	850	218	195	176	1.3	5.4	4V
38 Special Super Match	X38SMRP	148	Lead-Wad Cutter	T	710	634	566	166	132	105	2.4	10.8	4V
38 Special	X38S1P	158	Lead-Round Nose	T	755	723	693	200	183	168	2.0	8.3	4V
38 Special	X38WCPSV	158	Lead-Semi Wad Cutter	T	755	721	689	200	182	167	2.0	8.4	4V
38 Special + P #	X38S7PH	125	Jacketed Hollow Point	PP	945	898	858	248	224	204	1.3	5.4	4V
38 Special + P #	X38S8HP	125	Silvertip Hollow Point	PP	945	898	858	248	224	204	1.3	5.4	4V
38 Special + P	X38SPD	158	Lead-Semi Wad Cutter Hollow Point	PP	890	855	823	278	257	238	1.4	6.0	4V
9mm Luger	X9MMSHP	115	Silvertip Hollow Point	PP	1225	1095	1007	383	306	259	0.8	3.6	4
9mm Luger	X9MMST147	147	Silvertip Hollow Point	PP	1010	962	921	333	302	277	1.1	4.7	4
38 Super Automatic +P*	X38ASHP	125	Silvertip Hollow Point	T/PP	1240	1130	1050	427	354	306	0.8	3.4	5
9 x 23 Winchester	X923W	125	Silvertip Hollow Point	T/PP	1450	1249	1103	583	433	338	0.6	2.8	5
357 Magnum	X357SHP	145	Silvertip Hollow Point	PP	1290	1155	1060	535	428	361	0.8	3.5	4V
357 Magnum #	X3574P	158	Jacketed Hollow Point	H/PP	1235	1104	1015	535	428	361	0.8	3.5	4V
357 Magnum #	X3575P	158	Jacketed Soft Point	H/PP	1235	1104	1015	535	428	361	0.8	3.5	4V
40 Smith & Wesson	X40SWSTHP	155	Silvertip Hollow Point	PP	1205	1096	1018	500	414	357	0.8	3.6	4
10 mm Automatic	X10MMSTHP	175	Silvertip Hollow Point	PP	1290	1141	1037	649	506	418	0.7	3.3	5-1/2
41 Remington Magnum #	X41MSTHP2	175	Silvertip Hollow Point	H/PP	1250	1120	1029	607	488	412	0.8	3.4	4V
44 Smith & Wesson Special #	X44STHPS2	200	Silvertip Hollow Point	PP	900	860	822	360	328	300	1.4	5.9	6-1/2
44 Smith & Wesson Special	X44SP	246	Lead-Round Nose	T	755	725	695	310	285	265	2.0	8.3	6-1/2
44 Remington Magnum #	X44MS	210	Silvertip Hollow Point	H/PP	1250	1106	1010	729	570	475	0.8	3.5	4V
44 Remington Magnum #	X44MHSP2	240	Hollow Soft Point	H	1180	1081	1010	741	623	543	0.9	3.7	4V
45 Automatic	X45ASHP2	185	Silvertip Hollow Point	PP	1000	938	888	411	362	324	1.2	4.9	5
45 Automatic Subsonic	XSUB45A	230	Jacketed Hollow Point	PP	880	842	808	396	363	334	1.5	6.1	5
45 Colt #	X45CSHP2	225	Silvertip Hollow Point	PP	920	877	839	423	384	352	1.4	5.6	5-1/2
45 Colt	X45CP2	255	Lead-Round Nose	T	860	820	780	420	380	345	1.5	6.1	5-1/2
45 Winchester Magnum #	X45WMA	260	Jacketed Hollow Point	H	1200	1099	1026	831	698	607	0.8	3.6	5
454 Casull #	X454C3	250	Jacketed Hollow Point	H	1300	1151	1047	938	735	608	0.7	3.2	7.5V
454 Casull #	X454C22	300	Jacketed Flat Point	H	1625	1451	1308	1759	1413	1141	0.5	2.0	7.5V

SUPER CLEAN NT (TIN)

Cartridge	Symbol	Bullet Wt. Grs.	Type	User Guide	Velocity (FPS) Muzzle	50 Yds.	100 Yds.	Energy (Ft.Lbs.) Muzzle	50 Yds.	100 Yds.	Mid Range Traj. (In.) 50 Yds.	100 Yds.	Barrel Length In.
38 Special	SC38NT	110	Jacketed Soft Point	T	975	906	849	222	191	168	0.2	3.7	4V
9 mm Luger	SC9NT	105	Jacketed Soft Point	T	1200	1074	989	336	269	228	0.8	3.7	4
357 Magnum	SC357NT	110	Jacketed Soft Point	T	1275	1105	998	397	298	243	0.8	3.5	4V
357 SIG	SC357SNT	105	Jacketed Soft Point	T	1370	1179	1050	438	324	257	0.7	3.1	4
40 Smith & Wesson	SC40NT	140	Jacketed Soft Point	T	1155	1039	960	415	336	286	1.2	5.3	4
45 Automatic	SC45NT	170	Jacketed Soft Point	T	1050	982	928	416	364	325	0.9	0.4	4

WinClean CENTERFIRE HANDGUN AMMUNITION

Cartridge	Symbol	Bullet Wt. Grs.	Type	User Guide	Velocity (FPS) Muzzle	50 Yds.	100 Yds.	Energy (Ft.Lbs.) Muzzle	50 Yds.	100 Yds.	Mid Range Traj. (In.) 50 Yds.	100 Yds.	Barrel Length In.
380 Automatic	WC3801	95 gr.	Brass Enclosed Base	T		TBA							
38 Special WinClean	WC381	125 gr.	Jacketed Soft Point	T	775	742		167	153				
9mm Luger WinClean	WC91	115 gr.	Brass Enclosed Base	T	1190	1088		362	302				
9mm Luger	WC92	124 gr.	Brass Enclosed Base	T									
9mm Luger	WC93	147 gr.	Brass Enclosed Base	T									
357 SIG	WC357SIG	125 gr	Brass Enclosed Base	T									
357 Magnum	WC3571	125 gr	Jacketed Soft Point	T		TBA							
40 Smith & Wesson WinClean	WC401	165 gr.	Brass Enclosed Base	T	1130	1054		468	407				
40 Smith & Wesson WinClean	WC402	180 gr.	Brass Enclosed Base	T	990	943		392	286				
45 Automatic WinClean	WC451	185 gr.	Brass Enclosed Base	T	910	835		340	286				
45 Automatic WinClean	WC452	230 gr.	Brass Enclosed Base	T	835	802		356	329				

COWBOY LOADS

Cartridge	Symbol	Bullet Wt. Grs.	Type	User Guide	Velocity (FPS) Muzzle	50 Yds.	100 Yds.	Energy (Ft.Lbs.) Muzzle	50 Yds.	100 Yds.	Mid Range Traj. (In.) 50 Yds.	100 Yds.	Barrel Length In.
38 Special	CB38SP	158	Lead	T	800	761	725	225	203	185	1.8	7.5	4
44-40 Winchester	CB4440W	225	Lead	T	750	723	695	281	261	242	2.0	8.3	4
44 Special	CB44SP	240	Lead	T	750	719	690	300	275	253	2.0	8.4	4
45 Colt	CB45C	250	Lead	T	750	720	692	312	288	266	2.0	8.4	5

T-training **PP**-Personal Protection **H**-Hunting

Comprehensive Ballistics Tables For
Currently Manufactured Sporting Rifle Cartridges

No more collecting catalogs and peering at microscopic print to find out what ammunition is offered for a cartridge, and how it performs relative to other factory loads! Shooter's Bible has assembled the data for you, in easy-to-read tables, by cartridge. Of course, this section will be updated every year to bring you the latest information.

NOTES: Data is taken from manufacturers' charts; your chronograph readings may vary. Listings are current as of February the year Shooter's Bible appears (not the cover year). Listings are not intended as recommendations. For example, the data for the .44 Magnum at 400 yards shows its effective range is much shorter. The lack of data for a 285-grain .375 H&H bullet beyond 300 yards does not mean the bullet has no authority farther out. Besides ammunition, the rifle, sights, conditions and shooter ability all must be considered when contemplating a long shot. Accuracy and bullet energy both matter when big game is in the offing. Barrel length affects velocity, and at various rates depending on the load. As a rule, figure 50 fps per inch of barrel, plus or minus, if your barrel is longer or shorter than 22 inches. Bullets are given by make, weight (in grains) and type.

MOST TYPE ABBREVIATIONS ARE SELF-EXPLANATORY: BT=Boat-Tail, **FMJ**=Full Metal Jacket, **HP**=Hollow Point, **SP**=Soft Point, except in Hornady listings, where SP is the firm's Spire Point. **TNT** and **TXP** are trademarked designations of Speer and Norma. **XLC** identifies a coated Barnes X bullet. **HE** indicates a Federal High Energy load, similar to the Hornady **LM** (Light Magnum) and **HM** (Heavy Magnum) cartridges. **Arc** (trajectory) is based on a zero range published by the manufacturer, from 100 to 300 yards. If a zero does not fall in a yardage column, it lies halfway between - at 150 yards, for example, if the bullet's strike is "+" at 100 yards and "-" at 200.

.17 Remington to .222 Remington

CARTRIDGE BULLET	RANGE, YARDS:	0	100	200	300	400
.17 Remington						
Rem. 25 HP Power-Lokt	velocity, fps:	4040	3284	2644	2086	1606
	energy, ft-lb:	906	599	388	242	143
	arc, inches:		+1.8	0	-3.3	-16.6
.218 Bee						
Win. 46 Hollow Point	velocity, fps:	2760	2102	1550	1155	961
	energy, ft-lb:	778	451	245	136	94
	arc, inches:		0	-7.2	-29.4	
.22 Hornet						
Hornady 35 V-Max	velocity, fps:	3100	2278	1601	1135	929
	energy, ft-lb:	747	403	199	100	67
	arc, inches:		+2.8	0	-16.9	-60.4
Rem. 45 Pointed Soft Point	velocity, fps:	2690	2042	1502	1128	948
	energy, ft-lb:	723	417	225	127	90
	arc, inches:		0	-7.1	-30.0	
Rem. 45 Hollow Point	velocity, fps:	2690	2042	1502	1128	948
	energy, ft-lb:	723	417	225	127	90
	arc, inches:		0	-7.1	-30.0	
Win. 34 Jacketed HP	velocity, fps:	3050	2132	1415	1017	852
	energy, ft-lb:	700	343	151	78	55
	arc, inches:		0	-6.6	-29.9	
Win. 45 Soft Point	velocity, fps:	2690	2042	1502	1128	948
	energy, ft-lb:	723	417	225	127	90
	arc, inches:		0	-7.7	-31.3	
Win. 46 Hollow Point	velocity, fps:	2690	2042	1502	1128	948
	energy, ft-lb:	739	426	230	130	92
	arc, inches:		0	-7.7	-31.3	

CARTRIDGE BULLET	RANGE, YARDS:	0	100	200	300	400
.222 Remington						
Federal 50 Hi-Shok	velocity, fps:	3140	2600	2120	1700	1350
	energy, ft-lb:	1095	750	500	320	200
	arc, inches:		+1.9	0	-9.7	-31.6
Federal 55 FMJ boat-tail	velocity, fps:	3020	2740	2480	2230	1990
	energy, ft-lb:	1115	915	750	610	484
	arc, inches:		+1.6	0	-7.3	-21.5
Hornady 40 V-Max	velocity, fps:	3600	3117	2673	2269	1911
	energy, ft-lb:	1151	863	634	457	324
	arc, inches:		+1.1	0	-6.1	-18.9
Hornady 50 V-Max	velocity, fps:	3140	2729	2352	2008	1710
	energy, ft-lb:	1094	827	614	448	325
	arc, inches:		+1.7	0	-7.9	-24.4
Norma 50 Soft Point	velocity, fps:	3199	2667	2193	1771	
	energy, ft-lb:	1136	790	534	348	
	arc, inches:		+1.7	0	-9.1	
Norma 50 FMJ	velocity, fps:	2789	2326	1910	1547	
	energy, ft-lb:	864	601	405	266	
	arc, inches:		+2.5	0	-12.2	
Norma 62 Soft Point	velocity, fps:	2887	2457	2067	1716	
	energy, ft-lb:	1148	831	588	405	
	arc, inches:		+2.1	0	-10.4	
PMC 50 Pointed Soft Point	velocity, fps:	3044	2727	2354	2012	1651
	energy, ft-lb:	1131	908	677	494	333
	arc, inches:		+1.6	0	-7.9	-24.5
Rem. 50 Pointed Soft Point	velocity, fps:	3140	2602	2123	1700	1350
	energy, ft-lb:	1094	752	500	321	202
	arc, inches:		+1.9	0	-9.7	-31.7
Rem. 50 HP Power-Lokt	velocity, fps:	3140	2635	2182	1777	1432
	energy, ft-lb:	1094	771	529	351	228
	arc, inches:		+1.8	0	-9.2	-29.6

BALLISTICS

Cartridge Bullet	Range, Yards:	0	100	200	300	400
Rem. 50 V-Max boat-tail	velocity, fps:	3140	2744	2380	2045	1740
	energy, ft-lb:	1094	836	629	464	336
	arc, inches:		+1.6	0	-7.8	-23.9
Win. 40 Ballistic Silvertip	velocity, fps:	3370	2915	2503	2127	1786
	energy, ft-lb:	1009	755	556	402	283
	arc, inches:		+1.3	0	-6.9	-21.5
Win. 50 Pointed Soft Point	velocity, fps:	3140	2602	2123	1700	1350
	energy, ft-lb:	1094	752	500	321	202
	arc, inches:		+2.2	0	-10.0	-32.3

.223 Remington

Cartridge Bullet	Range, Yards:	0	100	200	300	400
Federal 50 Jacketed HP	velocity, fps:	3400	2910	2460	2060	1700
	energy, ft-lb:	1285	940	675	470	320
	arc, inches:		+1.3	0	-7.1	-22.7
Federal 50 Speer TNT HP	velocity, fps:	3300	2860	2450	2080	1750
	energy, ft-lb:	1210	905	670	480	340
	arc, inches:		+1.4	0	-7.3	-22.6
Federal 52 Sierra Match-King BTHP	velocity, fps:	3300	2860	2460	2090	1760
	energy, ft-lb:	1255	945	700	505	360
	arc, inches:		+1.4	0	-7.2	-22.4
Federal 55 Hi-Shok	velocity, fps:	3240	2750	2300	1910	1550
	energy, ft-lb:	1280	920	650	445	295
	arc, inches:		+1.6	0	-8.2	-26.1
Federal 55 FMJ boat-tail	velocity, fps:	3240	2950	2670	2410	2170
	energy, ft-lb:	1280	1060	875	710	575
	arc, inches:		+1.3	0	-6.1	-18.3
Federal 55 Sierra Game-King BTHP	velocity, fps:	3240	2770	2340	1950	1610
	energy, ft-lb:	1280	935	670	465	315
	arc, inches:		+1.5	0	-8.0	-25.3
Federal 55 Trophy Bonded	velocity, fps:	3100	2630	2210	1830	1500
	energy, ft-lb:	1175	845	595	410	275
	arc, inches:		+1.8	0	-8.9	-28.7
Federal 55 Nosler Bal. Tip	velocity, fps:	3240	2870	2530	2220	1920
	energy, ft-lb:	1280	1005	780	600	450
	arc, inches:		+1.4	0	-6.8	-20.8
Federal 55 Sierra BlitzKing	velocity, fps:	3240	2870	2520	2200	1910
	energy, ft-lb:	1280	1005	775	590	445
	arc, inches:		+-1.4	0	-6.9	-20.9
Federal 62 FMJ	velocity, fps:	3020	2650	2310	2000	1710
	energy, ft-lb:	1225	970	735	550	405
	arc, inches:		+1.7	0	-8.4	-25.5
Federal 69 Sierra Match-King BTHP	velocity, fps:	3000	2720	2460	2210	1980
	energy, ft-lb:	1380	1135	925	750	600
	arc, inches:		+1.6	0	-7.4	-21.9
Hornady 40 V-Max	velocity, fps:	3800	3305	2845	2424	2044
	energy, ft-lb:	1282	970	719	522	371
	arc, inches:		+0.8	0	-5.3	-16.6
Hornady 53 Hollow Point	velocity, fps:	3330	2882	2477	2106	1710
	energy, ft-lb:	1305	978	722	522	369
	arc, inches:		+1.7	0	-7.4	-22.7
Hornady 55 V-Max	velocity, fps:	3240	2859	2507	2181	1891
	energy, ft-lb:	1282	998	767	581	437
	arc, inches:		+1.4	0	-7.1	-21.4
Hornady 55 Urban Tactical	velocity, fps:	2970	2626	2307	2011	1739
	energy, ft-lb:	1077	842	650	494	369
	arc, inches:		+1.5	0	-8.1	-24.9
Hornady 60 Soft Point	velocity, fps:	3150	2782	2442	2127	1837
	energy, ft-lb:	1322	1031	795	603	450
	arc, inches:		+1.6	0	-7.5	-22.5

Cartridge Bullet	Range, Yards:	0	100	200	300	400
Hornady 60 Urban Tactical	velocity, fps:	2950	2619	2312	2025	1762
	energy, ft-lb:	1160	914	712	546	413
	arc, inches:		+1.6	0	-8.1	-24.7
Hornady 75 BTHP Match	velocity, fps:	2790	2554	2330	2119	1926
	energy, ft-lb:	1296	1086	904	747	617
	arc, inches:		+2.4	0	--8.8	-25.1
Hornady 75 BTHP Tactical	velocity, fps:	2630	2409	2199	2000	1814
	energy, ft-lb:	1152	966	805	666	548
	arc, inches:		-2.0	0	-9.2	-25.9
PMC 55 HP boat-tail	velocity, fps:	3240	2717	2250	1832	1473
	energy, ft-lb:	1282	901	618	410	265
	arc, inches:		+1.6	0	-8.6	-27.7
PMC 55 FMJ boat-tail	velocity, fps:	3195	2882	2525	2169	1843
	energy, ft-lb:	1246	1014	779	574	415
	arc, inches:		+1.4	0	-6.8	-21.1
PMC 55 Pointed Soft Point	velocity, fps:	3112	2767	2421	2100	1806
	energy, ft-lb:	1182	935	715	539	398
	arc, inches:		+1.5	0	-7.5	-22.9
PMC 64 Pointed Soft Point	velocity, fps:	2775	2511	2261	2026	1806
	energy, ft-lb:	1094	896	726	583	464
	arc, inches:		+2.0	0	-8.8	-26.1
PMC 69 BTHP Match	velocity, fps:	2900	2591	2304	2038	1791
	energy, ft-lb:	1288	1029	813	636	492
	arc, inches:		+1.6	0	-8.6	-27.7
Rem. 50 V-Max, boat-tail	velocity, fps:	3300	2889	2514	2168	1851
	energy, ft-lb:	1209	927	701	522	380
	arc, inches:		+1.4	0	-6.9	-21.2
Rem. 55 Pointed Soft Point	velocity, fps:	3240	2747	2304	1905	1554
	energy, ft-lb:	1282	921	648	443	295
	arc, inches:		+1.6	0	-8.2	-26.2
Rem. 55 HP Power-Lokt	velocity, fps:	3240	2773	2352	1969	1627
	energy, ft-lb:	1282	939	675	473	323
	arc, inches:		+1.5	0	-7.9	-24.8
Rem. 55 Metal Case	velocity, fps:	3240	2759	2326	1933	1587
	energy, ft-lb:	1282	929	660	456	307
	arc, inches:		+1.6	0	-8.1	-25.5
Rem. 62 HP Match	velocity, fps:	3025	2572	2162	1792	1471
	energy, ft-lb:	1260	911	643	442	298
	arc, inches:		+1.9	0	-9.4	-29.9
Win. 40 Ballistic Silvertip	velocity, fps:	3700	3166	2693	2265	1879
	energy, ft-lb:	1216	891	644	456	314
	arc, inches:		+1.0	0	-5.8	-18.4
Win. 50 Ballistic Silvertip	velocity, fps:	3410	2982	2593	2235	1907
	energy, ft-lb:	1291	987	746	555	404
	arc, inches:		+1.2	0	-6.4	-19.8
Win. 53 Hollow Point	velocity, fps:	3330	2882	2477	2106	1770
	energy, ft-lb:	1305	978	722	522	369
	arc, inches:		+1.7	0	-7.4	-22.7
Win. 55 Pointed Soft Point	velocity, fps:	3240	2747	2304	1905	1554
	energy, ft-lb:	1282	921	648	443	295
	arc, inches:		+1.9	0	-8.5	-26.7
Win. 55 Super Clean NT	velocity, fps:	3150	2520	1970	1505	1165
	energy, ft-lb:	1212	776	474	277	166
	arc, inches:		+2.8	0	-11.9	-38.9
Win. 64 Power-Point	velocity, fps:	3020	2656	2320	2009	1724
	energy, ft-lb:	1296	1003	765	574	423
	arc, inches:		+1.7	0	-8.2	-25.1

.223 Remington to .220 Swift

Left Column

Cartridge Bullet	Range, Yards:	0	100	200	300	400
Win. 64 Power-Point Plus	velocity, fps:	3090	2684	2312	1971	1664
	energy, ft-lb:	1357	1024	760	552	393
	arc, inches:		+1.7	0	-8.2	-25.4

.5.6 x 52 R

Cartridge Bullet	Range, Yards:	0	100	200	300	400
Norma 71 Soft Point	velocity, fps:	2789	2446	2128	1835	
	energy, ft-lb:	1227	944	714	531	
	arc, inches:		+2.1	0	-9.9	

.22 PPC

Cartridge Bullet	Range, Yards:	0	100	200	300	400
A-Square 52 Berger	velocity, fps:	3300	2952	2629	2329	2049
	energy, ft-lb:	1257	1006	798	626	485
	arc, inches:		+1.3	0	-6.3	-19.1
.225 Winchester Win. 55 Pointed Soft Point	velocity, fps:	3570	3066	2616	2208	1838
	energy, ft-lb:	1556	1148	836	595	412
	arc, inches:		+2.4	+2.0	-3.5	-16.3

.224 Weatherby Magnum

Cartridge Bullet	Range, Yards:	0	100	200	300	400
Wby. 55 Pointed Expanding	velocity, fps:	3650	3192	2780	2403	2056
	energy, ft-lb:	1627	1244	944	705	516
	arc, inches:		+2.8	+3.7	0	-9.8

.22-250 Remington

Cartridge Bullet	Range, Yards:	0	100	200	300	400
Federal 40 Sierra Varminter	velocity, fps:	4000	3320	2720	2200	1740
	energy, ft-lb:	1420	980	660	430	265
	arc, inches:		+0.8	0	-5.6	-18.4
Federal 55 Hi-Shok	velocity, fps:	3680	3140	2660	2220	1830
	energy, ft-lb:	1655	1200	860	605	410
	arc, inches:		+1.0	0	-6.0	-19.1
Federal 55 Sierra BlitzKing	velocity, fps:	3680	3270	2890	2540	2220
	energy, ft-lb:	1655	1300	1020	790	605
	arc, inches:		+0.9	0	-5.1	-15.6
Federal 55 Sierra Game-King BTHP	velocity, fps:	3680	3280	2920	2590	2280
	energy, ft-lb:	1655	1315	1040	815	630
	arc, inches:		+0.9	0	-5.0	-15.1
Federal 55 Trophy Bonded	velocity, fps:	3600	3080	2610	2190	1810
	energy, ft-lb:	1585	1155	835	590	400
	arc, inches:		+1.1	0	-6.2	-19.8
Hornady 40 V-Max	velocity, fps:	4150	3631	3147	2699	2293
	energy, ft-lb:	1529	1171	879	647	467
	arc, inches:		+0.5	0	-4.2	-13.3
Hornady 50 V-Max	velocity, fps:	3800	3349	2925	2535	2178
	energy, ft-lb:	1603	1245	950	713	527
	arc, inches:		+0.8	0	-5.0	-15.6
Hornady 53 Hollow Point	velocity, fps:	3680	3185	2743	2341	1974
	energy, ft-lb:	1594	1194	886	645	459
	arc, inches:		+1.0	0	-5.7	-17.8
Hornady 55 V-Max	velocity, fps:	3680	3265	2876	2517	2183
	energy, ft-lb:	1654	1302	1010	772	582
	arc, inches:		+0.9	0	-5.3	-16.1
Hornady 60 Soft Point	velocity, fps:	3600	3195	2826	2485	2169
	energy, ft-lb:	1727	1360	1064	823	627
	arc, inches:		+1.0	0	-5.4	-16.3
Norma 53 Soft Point	velocity, fps:	3707	3234	2809	1716	
	energy, ft-lb:	1618	1231	928	690	
	arc, inches:		+0.9	0	-5.3	
PMC 55 HP boat-tail	velocity, fps:	3680	3104	2596	2141	1737
	energy, ft-lb:	1654	1176	823	560	368
	arc, inches:		+1.1	0	-6.3	-20.2

Right Column

Cartridge Bullet	Range, Yards:	0	100	200	300	400
PMC 55 Pointed Soft Point	velocity, fps:	3586	3203	2852	2505	2178
	energy, ft-lb:	1570	1253	993	766	579
	arc, inches:		+1.0	0	-5.2	-16.0
Rem. 50 V-Max boat-tail (also in EtronX)	velocity, fps:	3725	3272	2864	2491	2147
	energy, ft-lb:	1540	1188	910	689	512
	arc, inches:		+1.7	+1.6	-2.8	-12.8
Rem. 55 Pointed Soft Point	velocity, fps:	3680	3137	2656	2222	1832
	energy, ft-lb:	1654	1201	861	603	410
	arc, inches:		+1.9	+1.8	-3.3	-15.5
Rem. 55 HP Power-Lokt	velocity, fps:	3680	3209	2785	2400	2046
	energy, ft-lb:	1654	1257	947	703	511
	arc, inches:		+1.8	+1.7	-3.0	-13.7
Rem. 60 Nosler Partition (also in EtronX)	velocity, fps:	3500	3045	2634	2258	1914
	energy, ft-lb:	1632	1235	924	679	488
	arc, inches:		+2.1	+1.9	-3.4	-15.5
Win. 40 Ballistic Silvertip	velocity, fps:	4150	3591	3099	2658	2257
	energy, ft-lb:	1530	1146	853	628	453
	arc, inches:		+0.6	0	-4.2	-13.4
Win. 50 Ballistic Silvertip	velocity, fps:	3810	3341	2919	2536	2182
	energy, ft-lb:	1611	1239	946	714	529
	arc, inches:		+0.8	0	-4.9	-15.2
Win. 55 Pointed Soft Point	velocity, fps:	3680	3137	2656	2222	1832
	energy, ft-lb:	1654	1201	861	603	410
	arc, inches:		+2.3	+1.9	-3.4	-15.9

.220 Swift

Cartridge Bullet	Range, Yards:	0	100	200	300	400
Federal 52 Sierra Match-King BTHP	velocity, fps:	3830	3370	2960	2600	2230
	energy, ft-lb:	1690	1310	1010	770	575
	arc, inches:		+0.8	0	-4.8	-14.9
Federal 55 Sierra BlitzKing	velocity, fps:	3800	3370	2990	2630	2310
	energy, ft-lb:	1765	1390	1090	850	650
	arc, inches:		+0.8	0	-4.7	-14.4
Federal 55 Trophy Bonded	velocity, fps:	3700	3170	2690	2270	1880
	energy, ft-lb:	1670	1225	885	625	430
	arc, inches:		+1.0	0	-5.8	-18.5
Hornady 40 V-Max	velocity, fps:	4200	3678	3190	2739	2329
	energy, ft-lb:	1566	1201	904	666	482
	arc, inches:		+0.5	0	-4.0	-12.9
Hornady 50 V-Max	velocity, fps:	3850	3396	2970	2576	2215
	energy, ft-lb:	1645	1280	979	736	545
	arc, inches:		+0.7	0	-4.8	-15.1
Hornady 50 SP	velocity, fps:	3850	3327	2862	2442	2060
	energy, ft-lb:	1645	1228	909	662	471
	arc, inches:		+0.8	0	-5.1	-16.1
Hornady 55 V-Max	velocity, fps:	3680	3265	2876	2517	2183
	energy, ft-lb:	1654	1302	1010	772	582
	arc, inches:		+0.9	0	-5.3	-16.1
Hornady 60 Hollow Point	velocity, fps:	3600	3199	2824	2475	2156
	energy, ft-lb:	1727	1364	1063	816	619
	arc, inches:		+1.0	0	-5.4	-16.3
Norma 50 Soft Point	velocity, fps:	4019	3380	2826	2335	
	energy, ft-lb:	1794	1268	887	605	
	arc, inches:		+0.7	0	-5.1	
Rem. 50 Pointed Soft Point	velocity, fps:	3780	3158	2617	2135	1710
	energy, ft-lb:	1586	1107	760	506	325
	arc, inches:		+0.3	-1.4	-8.2	
Rem. 50 V-Max boat-tail (also in EtronX)	velocity, fps:	3780	3321	2908	2532	2185
	energy, ft-lb:	1586	1224	939	711	530
	arc, inches:		+0.8	0	-5.0	-15.4

Cartridge Bullet	Range, Yards:	0	100	200	300	400
Win. 40 Ballistic Silvertip	velocity, fps:	4050	3518	3048	2624	2238
	energy, ft-lb:	1457	1099	825	611	445
	arc, inches:		+0.7	0	-4.4	-13.9
Win. 50 Pointed Soft Point	velocity, fps:	3870	3310	2816	2373	1972
	energy, ft-lb:	1663	1226	881	625	432
	arc, inches:		+0.8	0	-5.2	-16.7

6mm PPC

Cartridge Bullet	Range, Yards:	0	100	200	300	400
A-Square 68 Berger	velocity, fps:	3100	2751	2428	2128	1850
	energy, ft-lb:	1451	1143	890	684	516
	arc, inches:		+1.5	0	-7.5	-22.6

.243 Winchester

Cartridge Bullet	Range, Yards:	0	100	200	300	400
Federal 70 Nosler Bal. Tip	velocity, fps:	3400	3070	2760	2470	2200
	energy, ft-lb:	1795	1465	1185	950	755
	arc, inches:		+1.1	0	-5.7	-17.1
Federal 70 Speer TNT HP	velocity, fps:	3400	3040	2700	2390	2100
	energy, ft-lb:	1795	1435	1135	890	685
	arc, inches:		+1.1	0	-5.9	-18.0
Federal 80 Sierra Pro-Hunter	velocity, fps:	3350	2960	2590	2260	1950
	energy, ft-lb:	1995	1550	1195	905	675
	arc, inches:		+1.3	0	-6.4	-19.7
Federal 85 Sierra Game-King BTHP	velocity, fps:	3320	3070	2830	2600	2380
	energy, ft-lb:	2080	1770	1510	1280	1070
	arc, inches:		+1.1	0	-5.5	-16.1
Federal 90 Trophy Bonded	velocity, fps:	3100	2850	2610	2380	2160
	energy, ft-lb:	1920	1620	1360	1130	935
	arc, inches:		+1.4	0	-6.1	-19.2
Federal 100 Hi-Shok	velocity, fps:	2960	2700	2450	2220	1990
	energy, ft-lb:	1945	1615	1330	1090	880
	arc, inches:		+1.6	0	-7.5	-22.0
Federal 100 Sierra Game-King BTSP	velocity, fps:	2960	2760	2570	2380	2210
	energy, ft-lb:	1950	1690	1460	1260	1080
	arc, inches:		+1.5	0	-6.8	-19.8
Federal 100 Nosler Partition	velocity, fps:	2960	2730	2510	2300	2100
	energy, ft-lb:	1945	1650	1395	1170	975
	arc, inches:		+1.6	0	-7.1	-20.9
Hornady 58 V-Max	velocity, fps:	3750	3319	2913	2539	2195
	energy, ft-lb:	1811	1418	1093	830	620
	arc, inches:		+1.2	0	-5.5	-16.4
Hornady 75 Hollow Point	velocity, fps:	3400	2970	2578	2219	1890
	energy, ft-lb:	1926	1469	1107	820	595
	arc, inches:		+1.2	0	-6.5	-20.3
Hornady 100 BTSP	velocity, fps:	2960	2728	2508	2299	2099
	energy, ft-lb:	1945	1653	1397	1174	979
	arc, inches:		+1.6	0	-7.2	-21.0
Hornady 100 BTSP LM	velocity, fps:	3100	2839	2592	2358	2138
	energy, ft-lb:	2133	1790	1491	1235	1014
	arc, inches:		+1.5	0	-6.8	-19.8
Norma 100 FMJ	velocity, fps:	3018	2747	2493	2252	
	energy, ft-lb:	2023	1677	1380	1126	
	arc, inches:		+1.5	0	-7.1	
Norma 100 Soft Point	velocity, fps:	3018	2748	2493	2252	
	energy, ft-lb:	2023	1677	1380	1126	
	arc, inches:		+1.5	0	-7.1	
PMC 80 Pointed Soft Point	velocity, fps:	2940	2684	2444	2215	1999
	energy, ft-lb:	1535	1280	1060	871	709
	arc, inches:		+1.7	0	-7.5	-22.1

Cartridge Bullet	Range, Yards:	0	100	200	300	400
PMC 85 HP boat-tail	velocity, fps:	3275	2922	2596	2292	2009
	energy, ft-lb:	2024	1611	1272	991	761
	arc, inches:		+1.3	0	-6.5	-19.7
PMC 100 Pointed Soft Point	velocity, fps:	2743	2507	2283	2070	1869
	energy, ft-lb:	1670	1395	1157	951	776
	arc, inches:		+2.0	0	-8.7	-25.5
PMC 100 SP boat-tail	velocity, fps:	2960	2742	2534	2335	2144
	energy, ft-lb:	1945	1669	1425	1210	1021
	arc, inches:		+1.6	0	-7.0	-20.5
Rem. 75 V-Max boat-tail	velocity, fps:	3375	3065	2775	2504	2248
	energy, ft-lb:	1897	1564	1282	1044	842
	arc, inches:		+2.0	+1.8	-3.0	-13.3
Rem. 80 Pointed Soft Point	velocity, fps:	3350	2955	2593	2259	1951
	energy, ft-lb:	1993	1551	1194	906	676
	arc, inches:		+2.2	+2.0	-3.5	-15.8
Rem. 80 HP Power-Lokt	velocity, fps:	3350	2955	2593	2259	1951
	energy, ft-lb:	1993	1551	1194	906	676
	arc, inches:		+2.2	+2.0	-3.5	-15.8
Rem. 90 Nosler Bal. Tip (also in EtronX)	velocity, fps:	3120	2871	2635	2411	2199
	energy, ft-lb:	1946	1647	1388	1162	966
	arc, inches:		+1.4	0	-6.4	-18.8
Rem. 100 PSP Core-Lokt (also in EtronX)	velocity, fps:	2960	2697	2449	2215	1993
	energy, ft-lb:	1945	1615	1332	1089	882
	arc, inches:		+1.6	0	-7.5	-22.1
Rem. 100 PSP boat-tail	velocity, fps:	2960	2720	2492	2275	2069
	energy, ft-lb:	1945	1642	1378	1149	950
	arc, inches:		+2.8	+2.3	-3.8	-16.6
Speer 100 Grand Slam	velocity, fps:	2950	2684	2434	2197	
	energy, ft-lb:	1932	1600	1315	1072	
	arc, inches:		+1.7	0	-7.6	-22.4
Win. 55 Ballistic Silvertip	velocity, fps:	4025	3597	3209	2853	2525
	energy, ft-lb:	1978	1579	1257	994	779
	arc, inches:		+0.6	0	-4.0	-12.2
Win. 80 Pointed Soft Point	velocity, fps:	3350	2955	2593	2259	1951
	energy, ft-lb:	1993	1551	1194	906	676
	arc, inches:		+2.6	+2.1	-3.6	-16.2
Win. 95 Ballistic Silvertip	velocity, fps:	3100	2854	2626	2410	2203
	energy, ft-lb:	2021	1719	1455	1225	1024
	arc, inches:		+1.4	0	-6.4	-18.9
Win. 100 Power-Point	velocity, fps:	2960	2697	2449	2215	1993
	energy, ft-lb:	1945	1615	1332	1089	882
	arc, inches:		+1.9	0	-7.8	-22.6
Win. 100 Power-Point Plus	velocity, fps:	3090	2818	2562	2321	2092
	energy, ft-lb:	2121	1764	1458	1196	972
	arc, inches:		+1.4	0	-6.7	-20.0

6mm Remington

Cartridge Bullet	Range, Yards:	0	100	200	300	400
Federal 80 Sierra Pro-Hunter	velocity, fps:	3470	3060	2690	2350	2040
	energy, ft-lb:	2140	1665	1290	980	735
	arc, inches:		+1.1	0	-5.9	-18.2
Federal 100 Hi-Shok	velocity, fps:	3100	2830	2570	2330	2100
	energy, ft-lb:	2135	1775	1470	1205	985
	arc, inches:		+1.4	0	-6.7	-19.8
Federal 100 Nosler Partition	velocity, fps:	3100	2860	2640	2420	2220
	energy, ft-lb:	2135	1820	1545	1300	1090
	arc, inches:		+1.4	0	-6.3	-18.7
Hornady 100 SP boat-tail	velocity, fps:	3100	2861	2634	2419	2231
	energy, ft-lb:	2134	1818	1541	1300	1088
	arc, inches:		+1.3	0	-6.5	-18.9

CARTRIDGE BULLET	RANGE, YARDS:	0	100	200	300	400
Hornady 100 SPBT LM	velocity, fps:	3250	2997	2756	2528	2311
	energy, ft-lb:	2345	1995	1687	1418	1186
	arc, inches:		+1.6	0	-6.3	-18.2
Rem. 75 V-Max boat-tail	velocity, fps:	3400	3088	2797	2524	2267
	energy, ft-lb:	1925	1587	1303	1061	856
	arc, inches:		+1.9	+1.7	-3.0	-13.1
Rem. 100 PSP Core-Lokt	velocity, fps:	3100	2829	2573	2332	2104
	energy, ft-lb:	2133	1777	1470	1207	983
	arc, inches:		+1.4	0	-6.7	-19.8
Rem. 100 PSP boat-tail	velocity, fps:	3100	2852	2617	2394	2183
	energy, ft-lb:	2134	1806	1521	1273	1058
	arc, inches:		+1.4	0	-6.5	-19.1
Win. 100 Power-Point	velocity, fps:	3100	2829	2573	2332	2104
	energy, ft-lb:	2133	1777	1470	1207	983
	arc, inches:		+1.7	0	-7.0	-20.4

.240 Weatherby Magnum

CARTRIDGE BULLET	RANGE, YARDS:	0	100	200	300	400
Wby. 87 Pointed Expanding	velocity, fps:	3523	3199	2898	2617	2352
	energy, ft-lb:	2397	1977	1622	1323	1069
	arc, inches:		+2.7	+3.4	0	-8.4
Wby. 90 Barnes-X	velocity, fps:	3500	3222	2962	2717	2484
	energy, ft-lb:	2448	2075	1753	1475	1233
	arc, inches:		+2.6	+3.3	0	-8.0
Wby. 95 Nosler Bal. Tip	velocity, fps:	3420	3146	2888	2645	2414
	energy, ft-lb:	2467	2087	1759	1475	1229
	arc, inches:		+2.7	+3.5	0	-8.4
Wby. 100 Pointed Expanding	velocity, fps:	3406	3134	2878	2637	2408
	energy, ft-lb:	2576	2180	1839	1544	1287
	arc, inches:		+2.8	+3.5	0	-8.4
Wby. 100 Partition	velocity, fps:	3406	3136	2882	2642	2415
	energy, ft-lb:	2576	2183	1844	1550	1294
	arc, inches:		+2.8	+3.5	0	-8.4

.25-20 Winchester

CARTRIDGE BULLET	RANGE, YARDS:	0	100	200	300	400
Rem. 86 Soft Point	velocity, fps:	1460	1194	1030	931	858
	energy, ft-lb:	407	272	203	165	141
	arc, inches:		0	-22.9	-78.9	-173.0
Win. 86 Soft Point	velocity, fps:	1460	1194	1030	931	858
	energy, ft-lb:	407	272	203	165	141
	arc, inches:		0	-23.5	-79.6	-175.9

.25-35 Winchester

CARTRIDGE BULLET	RANGE, YARDS:	0	100	200	300	400
Win. 117 Soft Point	velocity, fps:	2230	1866	1545	1282	1097
	energy, ft-lb:	1292	904	620	427	313
	arc, inches:		+2.1	-5.1	-27.0	-70.1

.250 Savage

CARTRIDGE BULLET	RANGE, YARDS:	0	100	200	300	400
Rem. 100 Pointed SP	velocity, fps:	2820	2504	2210	1936	1684
	energy, ft-lb:	1765	1392	1084	832	630
	arc, inches:		+2.0	0	-9.2	-27.7
Win. 100 Silvertip	velocity, fps:	2820	2467	2140	1839	1569
	energy, ft-lb:	1765	1351	1017	751	547
	arc, inches:		+2.4	0	-10.1	-30.5

.257 Roberts

CARTRIDGE BULLET	RANGE, YARDS:	0	100	200	300	400
Federal 120 Nosler Partition	velocity, fps:	2780	2560	2360	2160	1970
	energy, ft-lb:	2060	1750	1480	1240	1030
	arc, inches:		+1.9	0	-8.2	-24.0
Hornady 117 SP boat-tail	velocity, fps:	2780	2550	2331	2122	1925
	energy, ft-lb:	2007	1689	1411	1170	963
	arc, inches:		+1.9	0	-8.3	-24.4

CARTRIDGE BULLET	RANGE, YARDS:	0	100	200	300	400
Hornady 117 SP boat-tail LM	velocity, fps:	2940	2694	2460	2240	2031
	energy, ft-lb:	2245	1885	1572	1303	1071
	arc, inches:		+1.7	0	-7.6	-21.8
Rem. 117 SP Core-Lokt	velocity, fps:	2650	2291	1961	1663	1404
	energy, ft-lb:	1824	1363	999	718	512
	arc, inches:		+2.6	0	-11.7	-36.1
Win. 117 Power-Point	velocity, fps:	2780	2411	2071	1761	1488
	energy, ft-lb:	2009	1511	1115	806	576
	arc, inches:		+2.6	0	-10.8	-33.0

.25-06 Remington

CARTRIDGE BULLET	RANGE, YARDS:	0	100	200	300	400
Federal 90 Sierra Varminter	velocity, fps:	3440	3040	2680	2340	2030
	energy, ft-lb:	2365	1850	1435	1100	825
	arc, inches:		+1.1	0	-6.0	-18.3
Federal 100 Barnes XLC	velocity, fps:	3210	2970	2750	2540	2330
	energy, ft-lb:	2290	1965	1680	1430	1205
	arc, inches:		+1.2	0	-5.8	-17.0
Federal 100 Nosler Bal. Tip	velocity, fps:	3210	2960	2720	2490	2280
	energy, ft-lb:	2290	1940	1640	1380	1150
	arc, inches:		+1.2	0	-6.0	-17.5
Federal 115 Nosler Partition	velocity, fps:	2990	2750	2520	2300	2100
	energy, ft-lb:	2285	1930	1620	1350	1120
	arc, inches:		+1.6	0	-7.0	-20.8
Federal 115 Trophy Bonded	velocity, fps:	2990	2740	2500	2270	2050
	energy, ft-lb:	2285	1910	1590	1310	1075
	arc, inches:		+1.6	0	-7.2	-21.1
Federal 117 Sierra Pro Hunt.	velocity, fps:	2990	2730	2480	2250	2030
	energy, ft-lb:	2320	1985	1645	1350	1100
	arc, inches:		+1.6	0	-7.2	-21.4
Federal 117 Sierra Game-King BTSP	velocity, fps:	2990	2770	2570	2370	2190
	energy, ft-lb:	2320	2000	1715	1465	1240
	arc, inches:		+1.5	0	-6.8	-19.9
Hornady 117 SP boat-tail	velocity, fps:	2990	2749	2520	2302	2096
	energy, ft-lb:	2322	1962	1649	1377	1141
	arc, inches:		+1.6	0	-7.0	-20.7
Hornady 117 SP boat-tail LM	velocity, fps:	3110	2855	2613	2384	2168
	energy, ft-lb:	2512	2117	1774	1476	1220
	arc, inches:		+1.8	0	-7.1	-20.3
PMC 117 PSP	velocity, fps:	2950	2706	2472	2253	2047
	energy, ft-lb:	2261	1900	1588	1319	1088
	arc, inches:		+1.6	0	-7.3	-21.6
Rem. 100 PSP Core-Lokt	velocity, fps:	3230	2893	2580	2287	2014
	energy, ft-lb:	2316	1858	1478	1161	901
	arc, inches:		+1.3	0	-6.6	-19.8
Rem. 120 PSP Core-Lokt	velocity, fps:	2990	2730	2484	2252	2032
	energy, ft-lb:	2382	1985	1644	1351	1100
	arc, inches:		+1.6	0	-7.2	-21.4
Speer 120 Grand Slam	velocity, fps:	3130	2835	2558	2298	
	energy, ft-lb:	2610	2141	1743	1407	
	arc, inches:		+1.4	0	-6.8	-20.1
Win. 90 Pos. Exp. Point	velocity, fps:	3440	3043	2680	2344	2034
	energy, ft-lb:	2364	1850	1435	1098	827
	arc, inches:		+2.4	0	-3.4	-15.0
Win. 115 Ballistic Silvertip	velocity, fps:	3060	2825	2603	2390	2188
	energy, ft-lb:	2391	2038	1729	1459	1223
	arc, inches:		+1.4	0	-6.6	-19.2

BALLISTICS

CARTRIDGE BULLET	RANGE, YARDS:	0	100	200	300	400

.257 Weatherby Magnum

CARTRIDGE BULLET		0	100	200	300	400
Federal 115 Nosler Partition	velocity, fps:	3150	2900	2660	2440	2220
	energy, ft-lb:	2535	2145	1810	1515	1260
	arc, inches:		+1.3	0	-6.2	-18.4
Federal 115 Trophy Bonded	velocity, fps:	3150	2890	2640	2400	2180
	energy, ft-lb:	2535	2125	1775	1470	1210
	arc, inches:		+1.4	0	-6.3	-18.8
Wby. 87 Pointed Expanding	velocity, fps:	3825	3472	3147	2845	2563
	energy, ft-lb:	2826	2328	1913	1563	1269
	arc, inches:		+2.1	+2.8	0	-7.1
Wby. 100 Pointed Expanding	velocity, fps:	3602	3298	3016	2750	2500
	energy, ft-lb:	2881	2416	2019	1680	1388
	arc, inches:		+2.4	+3.1	0	-7.7
Wby. 115 Nosler Bal. Tip	velocity, fps:	3400	3170	2952	2745	2547
	energy, ft-lb:	2952	2566	2226	1924	1656
	arc, inches:		+3.0	+3.5	0	-7.9
Wby. 115 Barnes X	velocity, fps:	3400	3158	2929	2711	2504
	energy, ft-lb:	2952	2546	2190	1877	1601
	arc, inches:		+2.7	+3.4	0	-8.1
Wby. 117 RN Expanding	velocity, fps:	3402	2984	2595	2240	1921
	energy, ft-lb:	3007	2320	1742	1302	956
	arc, inches:		+3.4	+4.31	0	-11.1
Wby. 120 Nosler Partition	velocity, fps:	3305	3046	2801	2570	2350
	energy, ft-lb:	2910	2472	2091	1760	1471
	arc, inches:		+3.0	+3.7	0	-8.9
6.53 (.257) Scramjet Lazzeroni Bal. Tip	velocity, fps:	3960	3652	3365	3096	2844
	energy, ft-lb:	2961	2517	2137	1810	1526
	arc, inches:		+1.7	+2.4	0	-6.0
Lazzeroni 100 Nosler Part.	velocity, fps:	3740	3465	3208	2965	2735
	energy, ft-lb:	3106	2667	2285	1953	1661
	arc, inches:		+2.1	+2.7	0	-6.7

6.5x50 Japanese

		0	100	200	300	400
Norma 156 Alaska	velocity, fps:	2067	1832	1615	1423	
	energy, ft-lb:	1480	1162	904	701	
	arc, inches:		+4.4	0	-17.8	
6.5x52 Carcano Norma 156 Alaska	velocity, fps:	2428	2169	1926	1702	
	energy, ft-lb:	2043	1630	1286	1004	
	arc, inches:		+2.9	0	-12.3	

6.5x55 Swedish

		0	100	200	300	400
Federal 140 Hi-Shok	velocity, fps:	2600	2400	2220	2040	1860
	energy, ft-lb:	2100	1795	1525	1285	1080
	arc, inches:		+2.3	0	-9.4	-27.2
Federal 140 Trophy Bonded	velocity, fps:	2550	2350	2160	1980	1810
	energy, ft-lb:	2020	1720	1450	1220	1015
	arc, inches:		+2.4	0	-9.8	-28.4
Federal 140 Sierra MatchKing BTHP	velocity, fps:	2630	2460	2300	2140	2000
	energy, ft-lb:	2140	1880	1640	1430	1235
	arc, inches:		+16.4	+28.8	+33.9	+31.8
Hornady 129 SP LM	velocity, fps:	2770	2561	2361	2171	1994
	energy, ft-lb:	2197	1878	1597	1350	1138
	arc, inches:		+2.0	0	-8.2	-23.2
Hornady 140 SP LM	velocity, fps:	2740	2541	2351	2169	1999
	energy, ft-lb:	2333	2006	1717	1463	1242
	arc, inches:		+2.4	0	-8.7	-24.0

CARTRIDGE BULLET	RANGE, YARDS:	0	100	200	300	400
Norma 139 Vulkan	velocity, fps:	2854	2569	2302	2051	
	energy, ft-lb:	2515	2038	1636	1298	
	arc, inches:		+1.8	0	-8.4	
Norma 140 Nosler Partition	velocity, fps:	2789	2592	2403	2223	
	energy, ft-lb:	2419	2089	1796	1536	
	arc, inches:		+1.8	0	-7.8	
Norma 156 TXP Swift A-Fr.	velocity, fps:	2526	2276	2040	1818	
	energy, ft-lb:	2196	1782	1432	1138	
	arc, inches:		+2.6	0	-10.9	
Norma 156 Alaska	velocity, fps:	2559	2245	1953	1687	
	energy, ft-lb:	2269	1746	1322	986	
	arc, inches:		+2.7	0	-11.9	
Norma 156 Vulkan	velocity, fps:	2644	2395	2159	1937	
	energy, ft-lb:	2422	1987	1616	1301	
	arc, inches:		+2.2	0	-9.7	
Norma 156 Oryx	velocity, fps:	2559	2308	2070	1848	
	energy, ft-lb:	2269	1845	1485	1183	
	arc, inches:		+2.5	0	-10.6	
PMC 139 Pointed Soft Point	velocity, fps:	2850	2560	2290	2030	1790
	energy, ft-lb:	2515	2025	1615	1270	985
	arc, inches:		+2.2	0	-8.9	-26.3
PMC 140 HP boat-tail	velocity, fps:	2560	2398	2243	2093	1949
	energy, ft-lb:	2037	1788	1563	1361	1181
	arc, inches:		+2.3	0	-9.2	-26.4
PMC 140 SP boat-tail	velocity, fps:	2560	2386	2218	2057	1903
	energy, ft-lb:	2037	1769	1529	1315	1126
	arc, inches:		+2.3	0	-9.4	-27.1
PMC 144 FMJ	velocity, fps:	2650	2370	2110	1870	1650
	energy, ft-lb:	2425	1950	1550	1215	945
	arc, inches:		+2.7	0	-10.5	-30.9
Rem. 140 PSP Core-Lokt	velocity, fps:	2550	2353	2164	1984	1814
	energy, ft-lb:	2021	1720	1456	1224	1023
	arc, inches:		+2.4	0	-9.8	-27.0
Speer 140 Grand Slam	velocity, fps:	2550	2318	2099	1892	
	energy, ft-lb:	2021	1670	1369	1112	
	arc, inches:		+2.5	0	-10.4	-30.6
Win. 140 Soft Point	velocity, fps:	2550	2359	2176	2002	1836
	energy, ft-lb:	2022	1731	1473	1246	1048
	arc, inches:		+2.4	0	-9.7	-28.1

.260 Remington

		0	100	200	300	400
Federal 140 Sierra GameKing BTSP	velocity, fps:	2750	2570	2390	2220	2060
	energy, ft-lb:	2350	2045	1775	1535	1315
	arc, inches:		+1.9	0	-8.0	-23.1
Federal 140 Trophy Bonded	velocity, fps:	2750	2540	2340	2150	1970
	energy, ft-lb:	2350	2010	1705	1440	1210
	arc, inches:		+1.9	0	-8.4	-24.1
Rem. 120 Nosler Bal. Tip	velocity, fps:	2890	2688	2494	2309	2131
	energy, ft-lb:	2226	1924	1657	1420	1210
	arc, inches:		+1.7	0	-7.3	-21.1
Rem. 125 Nosler Partition	velocity, fps:	2875	2669	2473	2285	2105
	energy, ft-lb:	2294	1977	1697	1449	1230
	arc, inches:		+1.71	0	-7.4	-21.4
Rem. 140 PSP Core-Lokt	velocity, fps:	2750	2544	2347	2158	1979
	energy, ft-lb:	2351	2011	1712	1448	1217
	arc, inches:		+1.9	0	-8.3	-24.0
Speer 140 Grand Slam	velocity, fps:	2750	2518	2297	2087	
	energy, ft-lb:	2351	1970	1640	1354	
	arc, inches:		+2.3	0	-8.9	-25.8

.264 Winchester Magnum

Cartridge Bullet	Range, Yards:	0	100	200	300	400
Rem. 140 PSP Core-Lokt	velocity, fps:	3030	2782	2548	2326	2114
	energy, ft-lb:	2854	2406	2018	1682	1389
	arc, inches:		+1.5	0	-6.9	-20.2
Win. 140 Power-Point	velocity, fps:	3030	2782	2548	2326	2114
	energy, ft-lb:	2854	2406	2018	1682	1389
	arc, inches:		+1.8	0	-7.2	-20.8

.270 Winchester

Cartridge Bullet	Range, Yards:	0	100	200	300	400
Federal 130 Hi-Shok	velocity, fps:	3060	2800	2560	2330	2110
	energy, ft-lb:	2700	2265	1890	1565	1285
	arc, inches:		+1.5	0	-6.8	-20.0
Federal 130 Sierra Pro-Hunt.	velocity, fps:	3060	2830	2600	2390	2190
	energy, ft-lb:	2705	2305	1960	1655	1390
	arc, inches:		+1.4	0	-6.4	-19.0
Federal 130 Sierra GameKing	velocity, fps:	3060	2830	2620	2410	2220
	energy, ft-lb:	2700	2320	1980	1680	1420
	arc, inches:		+1.4	0	-6.5	-19.0
Federal 130 Nosler Bal. Tip	velocity, fps:	3060	2840	2630	2430	2230
	energy, ft-lb:	2700	2325	1990	1700	1440
	arc, inches:		+1.4	0	-6.5	-18.8
Federal 130 Barnes XLC	velocity, fps:	3060	2840	2620	2420	2220
	energy, ft-lb:	2705	2320	1985	1690	1425
	arc, inches:		+1.4	0	-6.4	-18.9
Federal 130 Trophy Bonded	velocity, fps:	3060	2810	2570	2340	2130
	energy, ft-lb:	2705	2275	1905	1585	1310
	arc, inches:		+1.5	0	-6.7	-19.8
Federal 140 Trophy Bonded	velocity, fps:	2940	2700	2480	2260	2060
	energy, ft-lb:	2685	2270	1905	1590	1315
	arc, inches:		+1.6	0	-7.3	-21.5
Federal 140 Trophy Bonded HE	velocity, fps:	3100	2860	2620	2400	2200
	energy, ft-lb:	2990	2535	2140	1795	1500
	arc, inches:		+1.4	0	-6.4	-18.9
Federal 150 Hi-Shok RN	velocity, fps:	2850	2500	2180	1890	1620
	energy, ft-lb:	2705	2085	1585	1185	870
	arc, inches:		+2.0	0	-9.4	-28.6
Federal 150 Sierra GameKing	velocity, fps:	2850	2660	2480	2300	2130
	energy, ft-lb:	2705	2355	2040	1760	1510
	arc, inches:		+1.7	0	-7.4	-21.4
Federal 150 Sierra GameKing HE	velocity, fps:	3000	2800	2620	2430	2260
	energy, ft-lb:	2995	2615	2275	1975	1700
	arc, inches:		+1.5	0	-6.5	-18.9
Federal 150 Nosler Partition	velocity, fps:	2850	2590	2340	2100	1880
	energy, ft-lb:	2705	2225	1815	1470	1175
	arc, inches:		+1.9	0	-8.3	-24.4
Hornady 130 SP	velocity, fps:	3060	2800	2560	2330	2110
	energy, ft-lb:	2700	2265	1890	1565	1285
	arc, inches:		+1.8	0	-7.1	-20.6
Hornady 130 SST LM	velocity, fps:	3215	2998	2790	2590	2400
	energy, ft-lb:	2983	2594	2246	1936	1662
	arc, inches:		+1.2	0	-5.8	-17.0
Hornady 140 SP boat-tail	velocity, fps:	2940	2747	2562	2385	2214
	energy, ft-lb:	2688	2346	2041	1769	1524
	arc, inches:		+1.6	0	-7.0	-20.2
Hornady 140 SP boat-tail LM	velocity, fps:	3100	2894	2697	2508	2327
	energy, ft-lb:	2987	2604	2261	1955	1684
	arc, inches:		+1.4	0	6.3	-18.3
Hornady 150 SP	velocity, fps:	2800	2684	2478	2284	2100
	energy, ft-lb:	2802	2400	2046	1737	1469
	arc, inches:		+1.7	0	-7.4	-21.6
Norma 130 SP	velocity, fps:	3140	2862	2601	2354	
	energy, ft-lb:	2847	2365	1953	1600	
	arc, inches:	0	+1.3	0	-6.5	
Norma 150 SP	velocity, fps:	2799	2555	2323	2104	
	energy, ft-lb:	2610	2175	1798	1475	
	arc, inches:	0	+1.9	0	-8.3	
PMC 130 Barnes X	velocity, fps:	2910	2717	2533	2356	2186
	energy, ft-lb:	2444	2131	1852	1602	1379
	arc, inches:		+1.6	0	-7.1	-20.4
PMC 130 SP boat-tail	velocity, fps:	3050	2830	2620	2421	2229
	energy, ft-lb:	2685	2312	1982	1691	1435
	arc, inches:		+1.5	0	-6.5	-19.0
PMC 130 Pointed Soft Point	velocity, fps:	2816	2593	2381	2179	1987
	energy, ft-lb:	2288	1941	1636	1370	1139
	arc, inches:		+1.8	0	-8.0	-23.2
PMC 150 Barnes X	velocity, fps:	2700	2541	2387	2238	2095
	energy, ft-lb:	2428	2150	1897	1668	1461
	arc, inches:		+2.0	0	-8.1	-23.1
PMC 150 SP boat-tail	velocity, fps:	2850	2660	2477	2302	2134
	energy, ft-lb:	2705	2355	2043	1765	1516
	arc, inches:		+1.7	0	-7.4	-21.4
PMC 150 Pointed Soft Point	velocity, fps:	2547	2368	2197	2032	1875
	energy, ft-lb:	2160	1868	1607	1375	1171
	arc, inches:		+2.4	0	-9.5	-27.5
Rem. 100 Pointed Soft Point	velocity, fps:	3320	2924	2561	2225	1916
	energy, ft-lb:	2448	1898	1456	1099	815
	arc, inches:		+2.3	+2.0	-3.6	-16.2
Rem. 130 PSP Core-Lokt	velocity, fps:	3060	2776	2510	2259	2022
	energy, ft-lb:	2702	2225	1818	1472	1180
	arc, inches:		+1.5	0	-7.0	-20.9
Rem. 130 Bronze Point	velocity, fps:	3060	2802	2559	2329	2110
	energy, ft-lb:	2702	2267	1890	1565	1285
	arc, inches:		+1.5	0	-6.8	-20.0
Rem. 130 Swift Scirocco	velocity, fps:	3060	2838	2677	2425	2232
	energy, ft-lb:	2702	2325	1991	1697	1438
	arc, inches:		+1.4	0	-6.5	-18.8
Rem. 140 Swift A-Frame	velocity, fps:	2925	2652	2394	2152	1923
	energy, ft-lb:	2659	2186	1782	1439	1150
	arc, inches:		+1.7	0	-7.8	-23.2
Rem. 140 PSP boat-tail	velocity, fps:	2960	2749	2548	2355	2171
	energy, ft-lb:	2723	2349	2018	1724	1465
	arc, inches:		+1.6	0	-6.9	-20.1
Rem. 140 Nosler Bal. Tip	velocity, fps:	2960	2754	2557	2366	2187
	energy, ft-lb:	2724	2358	2032	1743	1487
	arc, inches:		+1.6	0	-6.9	-20.0
Rem. 150 SP Core-Lokt	velocity, fps:	2850	2504	2183	1886	1618
	energy, ft-lb:	2705	2087	1587	1185	872
	arc, inches:		+2.0	0	-9.4	-28.6
Rem. 150 Nosler Partition	velocity, fps:	2850	2652	2463	2282	2108
	energy, ft-lb:	2705	2343	2021	1734	1480
	arc, inches:		+1.7	0	-7.5	-21.6
Speer 130 Grand Slam	velocity, fps:	3050	2774	2514	2269	
	energy, ft-lb:	2685	2221	1824	1485	
	arc, inches:		+1.5	0	-7.0	-20.9

BALLISTICS

Cartridge Bullet	Range, Yards:	0	100	200	300	400
Speer 150 Grand Slam	velocity, fps:	2830	2594	2369	2156	
	energy, ft-lb:	2667	2240	1869	1548	
	arc, inches:		+1.8	0	-8.1	-23.6
Win. 130 Power-Point	velocity, fps:	3060	2802	2559	2329	2110
	energy, ft-lb:	2702	2267	1890	1565	1285
	arc, inches:		+1.8	0	-7.1	-20.6
Win. 130 Power-Point Plus	velocity, fps:	3150	2881	2628	2388	2161
	energy, ft-lb:	2865	2396	1993	1646	1348
	arc, inches:		+1.3	0	-6.4	-18.9
Win. 130 Silvertip	velocity, fps:	3060	2776	2510	2259	2022
	energy, ft-lb:	2702	2225	1818	1472	1180
	arc, inches:		+1.8	0	-7.4	-21.6
Win. 130 Ballistic Silvertip	velocity, fps:	3050	2828	2618	2416	2224
	energy, ft-lb:	2685	2309	1978	1685	1428
	arc, inches:		+1.4	0	-6.5	-18.9
Win. 140 Fail Safe	velocity, fps:	2920	2671	2435	2211	1999
	energy, ft-lb:	2651	2218	1843	1519	1242
	arc, inches:		+1.7	0	-7.6	-22.3
Win. 150 Power-Point	velocity, fps:	2850	2585	2336	2100	1879
	energy, ft-lb:	2705	2226	1817	1468	1175
	arc, inches:		+2.2	0	-8.6	-25.0
Win. 150 Power-Point Plus	velocity, fps:	2950	2679	2425	2184	1957
	energy, ft-lb:	2900	2391	1959	1589	1276
	arc, inches:		+1.7	0	-7.6	-22.6
Win. 150 Partition Gold	velocity, fps:	2930	2693	2468	2254	2051
	energy, ft-lb:	2860	2416	2030	1693	1402
	arc, inches:		+1.7	0	-7.4	-21.6

.270 Weatherby Magnum

Cartridge Bullet	Range, Yards:	0	100	200	300	400
Federal 130 Nosler Partition	velocity, fps:	3200	2960	2740	2520	2320
	energy, ft-lb:	2955	2530	2160	1835	1550
	arc, inches:		+1.2	0	-5.9	-17.3
Federal 130 Sierra GameKing BTSP	velocity, fps:	3200	2980	2780	2580	2400
	energy, ft-lb:	2955	2570	2230	1925	1655
	arc, inches:		+1.2	0	-5.7	-16.6
Federal 140 Trophy Bonded	velocity, fps:	3100	2840	2600	2370	2150
	energy, ft-lb:	2990	2510	2100	1745	1440
	arc, inches:		+1.4	0	-6.6	-19.3
Wby. 100 Pointed Expanding	velocity, fps:	3760	3396	3061	2751	2462
	energy, ft-lb:	3139	2560	2081	1681	1346
	arc, inches:		+2.3	+3.0	0	-7.6
Wby. 130 Pointed Expanding	velocity, fps:	3375	3123	2885	2659	2444
	energy, ft-lb:	3288	2815	2402	2041	1724
	arc, inches:		+2.8	+3.5	0	-8.4
Wby. 130 Nosler Partition	velocity, fps:	3375	3127	2892	2670	2458
	energy, ft-lb:	3288	2822	2415	2058	1744
	arc, inches:		+2.8	+3.5	0	-8.3
Wby. 140 Nosler Bal. Tip	velocity, fps:	3300	3077	2865	2663	2470
	energy, ft-lb:	3385	2943	2551	2204	1896
	arc, inches:		+2.9	+3.6	0	-8.4
Wby. 140 Barnes X	velocity, fps:	3250	3032	2825	2628	2438
	energy, ft-lb:	3283	2858	2481	2146	1848
	arc, inches:		+3.0	+3.7	0	-8.7
Wby. 150 Pointed Expanding	velocity, fps:	3245	3028	2821	2623	2434
	energy, ft-lb:	3507	3053	2650	2292	1973
	arc, inches:		+3.0	+3.7	0	-8.7
Wby. 150 Nosler Partition	velocity, fps:	3245	3029	2823	2627	2439
	energy, ft-lb:	3507	3055	2655	2298	1981
	arc, inches:		+3.0	+3.7	0	-8.

Cartridge Bullet	Range, Yards:	0	100	200	300	400

7-30 Waters

Cartridge Bullet	Range, Yards:	0	100	200	300	400
Federal 120 Sierra GameKing BTSP	velocity, fps:	2700	2300	1930	1600	1330
	energy, ft-lb:	1940	1405	990	685	470
	arc, inches:		+2.6	0	-12.0	-37.6

7mm Mauser (7x57)

Cartridge Bullet	Range, Yards:	0	100	200	300	400
Federal 140 Sierra Pro-Hunt.	velocity, fps:	2660	2450	2260	2070	1890
	energy, ft-lb:	2200	1865	1585	1330	1110
	arc, inches:		+2.1	0	-9.0	-26.1
Federal 140 Nosler Partition	velocity, fps:	2660	2450	2260	2070	1890
	energy, ft-lb:	2200	1865	1585	1330	1110
	arc, inches:		+2.1	0	-9.0	-26.1
Federal 175 Hi-Shok RN	velocity, fps:	2440	2140	1860	1600	1380
	energy, ft-lb:	2315	1775	1340	1000	740
	arc, inches:		+3.1	0	-13.3	-40.1
Hornady 139 SP boat-tail	velocity, fps:	2700	2504	2316	2137	1965
	energy, ft-lb:	2251	1936	1656	1410	1192
	arc, inches:		+2.0	0	-8.5	-24.9
Hornady 139 SP boat-tail LM	velocity, fps:	2830	2620	2450	2250	2070
	energy, ft-lb:	2475	2135	1835	1565	1330
	arc, inches:		+1.8	0	-7.6	-22.1
Hornady 139 SP LM	velocity, fps:	2950	2736	2532	2337	2152
	energy, ft-lb:	2686	2310	1978	1686	1429
	arc, inches:		+2.0	0	-7.6	-21.5
Norma 150 Soft Point	velocity, fps:	2690	2479	2278	2087	
	energy, ft-lb:	2411	2048	1729	1450	
	arc, inches:		+2.0	0	-8.8	
PMC 140 Pointed Soft Point	velocity, fps:	2660	2450	2260	2070	1890
	energy, ft-lb:	2200	1865	1585	1330	1110
	arc, inches:		+2.4	0	-9.6	-27.3
PMC 175 Soft Point	velocity, fps:	2440	2140	1860	1600	1380
	energy, ft-lb:	2315	1775	1340	1000	740
	arc, inches:		+1.5	-3.6	-18.6	-46.8
Rem. 140 PSP Core-Lokt	velocity, fps:	2660	2435	2221	2018	1827
	energy, ft-lb:	2199	1843	1533	1266	1037
	arc, inches:		+2.2	0	-9.2	-27.4
Win. 145 Power-Point	velocity, fps:	2660	2413	2180	1959	1754
	energy, ft-lb:	2279	1875	1530	1236	990
	arc, inches:		+1.1	-2.8	-14.1	-34.4

7x57 R

Cartridge Bullet	Range, Yards:	0	100	200	300	400
Norma 150 FMJ	velocity, fps:	2690	2489	2296	2112	
	energy, ft-lb:	2411	2063	1756	1486	
	arc, inches:		+2.0	0	-8.6	
Norma 154 Soft Point	velocity, fps:	2625	2417	2219	2030	
	energy, ft-lb:	2357	1999	1684	1410	
	arc, inches:		+2.2	0	-9.3	

7mm-08 Remington

Cartridge Bullet	Range, Yards:	0	100	200	300	400
Federal 140 Nosler Partition	velocity, fps:	2800	2590	2390	2200	2020
	energy, ft-lb:	2435	2085	1775	1500	1265
	arc, inches:		+1.8	0	-8.0	-23.1
Federal 140 Nosler Bal. Tip	velocity, fps:	2800	2610	2430	2260	2100
	energy, ft-lb:	2440	2135	1840	1590	1360
	arc, inches:		+1.8	0	-7.7	-22.3
Federal 140 Trophy Bonded HE	velocity, fps:	2950	2660	2390	2140	1900
	energy, ft-lb:	2705	2205	1780	1420	1120
	arc, inches:		+1.7	0	-7.9	-23.2

CARTRIDGE Bullet	RANGE, YARDS:	0	100	200	300	400
Federal 150 Sierra Pro-Hunt.	velocity, fps:	2650	2440	2230	2040	1860
	energy, ft-lb:	2340	1980	1660	1390	1150
	arc, inches:		+2.2	0	-9.2	-26.7
Hornady 139 SP boat-tail LM	velocity, fps:	3000	2790	2590	2399	2216
	energy, ft-lb:	2777	2403	2071	1776	1515
	arc, inches:		+1.5	0	-6.7	-19.4
PMC 140 PSP	velocity, fps:	2850	2610	2384	2170	1969
	energy, ft-lb:	2507	2103	1754	1454	1197
	arc, inches:		+1.8	0	-7.9	-23.8
Rem. 120 Hollow Point	velocity, fps:	3000	2725	2467	2223	1992
	energy, ft-lb:	2398	1979	1621	1316	1058
	arc, inches:		+1.6	0	-7.3	-21.7
Rem. 140 PSP Core-Lokt	velocity, fps:	2860	2625	2402	2189	1988
	energy, ft-lb:	2542	2142	1793	1490	1228
	arc, inches:		+1.8	0	-7.8	-22.9
Rem. 140 PSP boat-tail	velocity, fps:	2860	2656	2460	2273	2094
	energy, ft-lb:	2542	2192	1881	1606	1363
	arc, inches:		+1.7	0	-7.5	-21.7
Rem. 140 Nosler Bal. Tip	velocity, fps:	2860	2670	2488	2313	2145
	energy, ft-lb:	2543	2217	1925	1663	1431
	arc, inches:		+1.7	0	-7.3	-21.2
Rem. 140 Nosler Partition	velocity, fps:	2860	2648	2446	2253	2068
	energy, ft-lb:	2542	2180	1860	1577	1330
	arc, inches:		+1.7	0	-7.6	-22.0
Speer 145 Grand Slam	velocity, fps:	2845	2567	2305	2059	
	energy, ft-lb:	2606	2121	1711	1365	
	arc, inches:		+1.9	0	-8.4	-25.5
Win. 140 Power-Point	velocity, fps:	2800	2523	2268	2027	1802
	energy, ft-lb:	2429	1980	1599	1277	1010
	arc, inches:		+2.0	0	-8.8	-26.0
Win. 140 Power-Point Plus	velocity, fps:	2875	2597	2336	2090	1859
	energy, ft-lb:	2570	1997	1697	1358	1075
	arc, inches:		+2.0	0	-8.8	26.0
Win. 140 Fail Safe	velocity, fps:	2760	2506	2271	2048	1839
	energy, ft-lb:	2360	1953	1603	1304	1051
	arc, inches:		+2.0	0	-8.8	-25.9
Win. 140 Ballistic Silvertip	velocity, fps:	2770	2572	2382	2200	2026
	energy, ft-lb:	2386	2056	1764	1504	1276
	arc, inches:		+1.9	0	-8.0	-23.8

7x64 Brenneke

CARTRIDGE Bullet	RANGE, YARDS:	0	100	200	300	400
Federal 160 Nosler Partition	velocity, fps:	2650	2480	2310	2150	2000
	energy, ft-lb:	2495	2180	1895	1640	1415
	arc, inches:		+2.1	0	-8.7	-24.9
Norma 154 Soft Point	velocity, fps:	2821	2605	2399	2203	
	energy, ft-lb:	2722	2321	1969	1660	
	arc, inches:		+1.8	0	-7.8	
Norma 170 Vulkan	velocity, fps:	2756	2501	2259	2031	
	energy, ft-lb:	2868	2361	1927	1558	
	arc, inches:		+2.0	0	-8.8	
Norma 170 Oryx	velocity, fps:	2756	2481	2222	1979	
	energy, ft-lb:	2868	2324	1864	1478	
	arc, inches:		+2.1	0	-9.2	
Norma 170 Plastic Point	velocity, fps:	2756	2519	2294	2081	
	energy, ft-lb:	2868	2396	1987	1635	
	arc, inches:		+2.0	0	-8.6	
Rem. 175 PSP Core-Lokt	velocity, fps:	2650	2445	2248	2061	1883
	energy, ft-lb:	2728	2322	1964	1650	1378
	arc, inches:		+2.2	0	-9.1	-26.4

CARTRIDGE Bullet	RANGE, YARDS:	0	100	200	300	400
Speer 160 Grand Slam	velocity, fps:	2600	2376	2164	1962	
	energy, ft-lb:	2401	2006	1663	1368	
	arc, inches:		+2.3	0	-9.8	-28.6
Speer 175 Grand Slam	velocity, fps:	2650	2461	2280	2106	
	energy, ft-lb:	2728	2353	2019	1723	
	arc, inches:		+2.4	0	-9.2	-26.2

7x65 R

Norma 170 Plastic Point	velocity, fps:	2625	2390	2167	1956	
	energy, ft-lb:	2602	2157	1773	1445	
	arc, inches:		+2.3	0	-9.7	
Norma 170 Vulkan	velocity, fps:	2657	2392	2143	1909	
	energy, ft-lb:	2666	2161	1734	1377	
	arc, inches:		+2.3	0	-9.9	
Norma 170 Oryx	velocity, fps:	2657	2378	2115	1871	
	energy, ft-lb:	2666	2135	1690	1321	
	arc, inches:		+2.3	0	-10.1	

.284 Winchester

Win. 150 Power-Point	velocity, fps:	2860	2595	2344	2108	1886
	energy, ft-lb:	2724	2243	1830	1480	1185
	arc, inches:		+2.1	0	-8.5	-24.8

.280 Remington

Federal 140 Sierra Pro-Hunt.	velocity, fps:	2990	2740	2500	2270	2060
	energy, ft-lb:	2770	2325	1940	1605	1320
	arc, inches:		+1.6	0	-7.0	-20.8
Federal 140 Trophy Bonded	velocity, fps:	2990	2630	2310	2040	1730
	energy, ft-lb:	2770	2155	1655	1250	925
	arc, inches:		+1.6	0	-8.4	-25.4
Federal 140 Tr. Bonded HE	velocity, fps:	3150	2850	2570	2300	2050
	energy, ft-lb:	3085	2520	2050	1650	1310
	arc, inches:		+1.4	0	-6.7	-20.0
Federal 150 Hi-Shok	velocity, fps:	2890	2670	2460	2260	2060
	energy, ft-lb:	2780	2370	2015	1695	1420
	arc, inches:		+1.7	0	-7.5	-21.8
Federal 150 Nosler Partition	velocity, fps:	2890	2690	2490	2310	2130
	energy, ft-lb:	2780	2405	2070	1770	1510
	arc, inches:		+1.7	0	-7.2	-21.1
Federal 160 Trophy Bonded	velocity, fps:	2800	2570	2350	2140	1940
	energy, ft-lb:	2785	2345	1960	1625	1340
	arc, inches:		+1.9	0	-8.3	-24.0
Hornady 139 SPBT LMmoly	velocity, fps:	3110	2888	2675	2473	2280
	energy, ft-lb:	2985	2573	2209	1887	1604
	arc, inches:		+1.4	0	-6.5	-18.6
Norma 170 Vulkan	velocity, fps:	2592	2346	2113	1894	
	energy, ft-lb:	2537	2078	1686	1354	
	arc, inches:		+2.4	0	-10.2	
Norma 170 Oryx	velocity, fps:	2690	2416	2159	1918	
	energy, ft-lb:	2732	2204	1760	1389	
	arc, inches:		+2.2	0	-9.7	
Norma 170 Plastic Point	velocity, fps:	2707	2468	2241	2026	
	energy, ft-lb:	2767	2299	1896	1550	
	arc, inches:		+2.1	0	-9.1	
Rem. 140 PSP Core-Lokt	velocity, fps:	3000	2758	2528	2309	2102
	energy, ft-lb:	2797	2363	1986	1657	1373
	arc, inches:		+1.5	0	-7.0	-20.5

BALLISTICS

CARTRIDGE BULLET	RANGE, YARDS:	0	100	200	300	400
Rem. 140 PSP boat-tail	velocity, fps:	2860	2656	2460	2273	2094
	energy, ft-lb:	2542	2192	1881	1606	1363
	arc, inches:		+1.7	0	-7.5	-21.7
Rem. 140 Nosler Bal. Tip	velocity, fps:	3000	2804	2616	2436	2263
	energy, ft-lb:	2799	2445	2128	1848	1593
	arc, inches:		+1.5	0	-6.8	-19.0
Rem. 150 PSP Core-Lokt	velocity, fps:	2890	2624	2373	2135	1912
	energy, ft-lb:	2781	2293	1875	1518	1217
	arc, inches:		+1.8	0	-8.0	-23.6
Rem. 165 SP Core-Lokt	velocity, fps:	2820	2510	2220	1950	1701
	energy, ft-lb:	2913	2308	1805	1393	1060
	arc, inches:		+2.0	0	-9.1	-27.4
Speer 145 Grand Slam	velocity, fps:	2900	2619	2354	2105	
	energy, ft-lb:	2707	2207	1784	1426	
	arc, inches:		+2.1	0	-8.4	-24.7
Speer 160 Grand Slam	velocity, fps:	2890	2652	2425	2210	
	energy, ft-lb:	2967	2497	2089	1735	
	arc, inches:		+1.7	0	-7.7	-22.4
Win. 140 Fail Safe	velocity, fps:	3050	2756	2480	2221	1977
	energy, ft-lb:	2893	2362	1913	1533	1216
	arc, inches:		+1.5	0	-7.2	-21.5
Win. 140 Ballistic Silvertip	velocity, fps:	3040	2842	2653	2471	2297
	energy, ft-lb:	2872	2511	2187	1898	1640
	arc, inches:		+1.4	0	-6.3	-18.4

7mm Remington Magnum

CARTRIDGE BULLET	RANGE, YARDS:	0	100	200	300	400
A-Square 175 Monolithic Solid	velocity, fps:	2860	2557	2273	2008	1771
	energy, ft-lb:	3178	2540	2008	1567	1219
	arc, inches:		+1.92	0	-8.7	-25.9
Federal 140 Nosler Partition	velocity, fps:	3150	2930	2710	2510	2320
	energy, ft-lb:	3085	2660	2290	1960	1670
	arc, inches:		+1.3	0	-6.0	-17.5
Federal 140 Trophy Bonded	velocity, fps:	3150	2910	2680	2460	2250
	energy, ft-lb:	3085	2630	2230	1880	1575
	arc, inches:		+1.3	0	-6.1	-18.1
Federal 150 Hi-Shok	velocity, fps:	3110	2830	2570	2320	2090
	energy, ft-lb:	3220	2670	2200	1790	1450
	arc, inches:		+1.4	0	-6.7	-19.9
Federal 150 Sierra GameKing BTSP	velocity, fps:	3110	2920	2750	2580	2410
	energy, ft-lb:	3220	2850	2510	2210	1930
	arc, inches:		+1.3	0	-5.9	-17.0
Federal 150 Nosler Bal. Tip	velocity, fps:	3110	2910	2720	2540	2370
	energy, ft-lb:	3220	2825	2470	2150	1865
	arc, inches:		+1.3	0	-6.0	-17.4
Federal 160 Barnes XLC	velocity, fps:	2940	2760	2580	2410	2240
	energy, ft-lb:	3070	2695	2360	2060	1785
	arc, inches:		+1.5	0	-6.8	-19.6
Federal 160 Sierra Pro-Hunt	velocity, fps:	2940	2730	2520	2320	2140
	energy, ft-lb:	3070	2640	2260	1920	1620
	arc, inches:		+1.6	0	-7.1	-20.6
Federal 160 Nosler Partition	velocity, fps:	2950	2770	2590	2420	2250
	energy, ft-lb:	3090	2715	2375	2075	1800
	arc, inches:		+1.5	0	-6.7	-19.4
Federal 160 Trophy Bonded	velocity, fps:	2940	2660	2390	2140	1900
	energy, ft-lb:	3070	2505	2025	1620	1280
	arc, inches:		+1.7	0	-7.9	-23.3
Federal 165 Sierra GameKing BTSP	velocity, fps:	2950	2800	2650	2510	2370
	energy, ft-lb:	3190	2865	2570	2300	2050
	arc, inches:		+1.5	0	-6.4	-18.4

CARTRIDGE BULLET	RANGE, YARDS:	0	100	200	300	400
Federal 175 Hi-Shok	velocity, fps:	2860	2650	2440	2240	2060
	energy, ft-lb:	3180	2720	2310	1960	1640
	arc, inches:		+1.7	0	-7.6	-22.1
Federal 175 Trophy Bonded	velocity, fps:	2860	2600	2350	2120	1900
	energy, ft-lb:	3180	2625	2150	1745	1400
	arc, inches:		+1.8	0	-8.2	-24.0
Hornady 139 SPBT	velocity, fps:	3150	2933	2727	2530	2341
	energy, ft-lb:	3063	2656	2296	1976	1692
	arc, inches:		+1.2	0	-6.1	-17.7
Hornady 139 SPBT HMmoly	velocity, fps:	3250	3041	2822	2613	2413
	energy, ft-lb:	3300	2854	2458	2106	1797
	arc, inches:		+1.1	0	-5.7	-16.6
Hornady 154 Soft Point	velocity, fps:	3035	2814	2604	2404	2212
	energy, ft-lb:	3151	2708	2319	1977	1674
	arc, inches:		+1.3	0	-6.7	-19.3
Hornady 162 SP boat-tail	velocity, fps:	2940	2757	2582	2413	2251
	energy, ft-lb:	3110	2735	2399	2095	1823
	arc, inches:		+1.6	0	-6.7	-19.7
Hornady 175 SP	velocity, fps:	2860	2650	2440	2240	2060
	energy, ft-lb:	3180	2720	2310	1960	1640
	arc, inches:		+2.0	0	-7.9	-22.7
Norma 170 Vulkan	velocity, fps:	3018	2747	2493	2252	
	energy, ft-lb:	3439	2850	2346	1914	
	arc, inches:		+1.5	0	-2.8	
Norma 170 Oryx	velocity, fps:	2887	2601	2333	2080	
	energy, ft-lb:	3147	2555	2055	1634	
	arc, inches:		+1.8	0	-8.2	
Norma 170 Plastic Point	velocity, fps:	3018	2762	2519	2290	
	energy, ft-lb:	3439	2880	2394	1980	
	arc, inches:		+1.5	0	-7.0	
PMC 140 Barnes X	velocity, fps:	3000	2808	2624	2448	2279
	energy, ft-lb:	2797	2451	2141	1863	1614
	arc, inches:		+1.5	0	-6.6	18.9
PMC 140 Pointed Soft Point	velocity, fps:	3099	2878	2668	2469	2279
	energy, ft-lb:	2984	2574	2212	1895	1614
	arc, inches:		+1.4	0	-6.2	-18.1
PMC 140 SP boat-tail	velocity, fps:	3125	2891	2669	2457	2255
	energy, ft-lb:	3035	2597	2213	1877	1580
	arc, inches:		+1.4	0	-6.3	-18.4
PMC 160 Barnes X	velocity, fps:	2800	2639	2484	2334	2189
	energy, ft-lb:	2785	2474	2192	1935	1703
	arc, inches:		+1.8	0	-7.4	-21.2
PMC 160 Pointed Soft Point	velocity, fps:	2914	2748	2586	2428	2276
	energy, ft-lb:	3016	2682	2375	2095	1840
	arc, inches:		+1.6	0	-6.7	-19.4
PMC 160 SP boat-tail	velocity, fps:	2900	2696	2501	2314	2135
	energy, ft-lb:	2987	2582	2222	1903	1620
	arc, inches:		+1.7	0	-7.2	-21.0
PMC 175 Pointed Soft Point	velocity, fps:	2860	2645	2442	2244	2957
	energy, ft-lb:	3178	2718	2313	1956	1644
	arc, inches:		+2.0	0	-7.9	-22.7
Rem. 140 PSP Core-Lokt	velocity, fps:	3175	2923	2684	2458	2243
	energy, ft-lb:	3133	2655	2240	1878	1564
	arc, inches:		+2.2	+1.9	-3.2	-14.2
Rem. 140 PSP boat-tail	velocity, fps:	3175	2956	2747	2547	2356
	energy, ft-lb:	3133	2715	2345	2017	1726
	arc, inches:		+2.2	+1.6	-3.1	-13.4

Cartridge Bullet	Range, Yards:	0	100	200	300	400
Rem. 150 PSP Core-Lokt	velocity, fps:	3110	2830	2568	2320	2085
	energy, ft-lb:	3221	2667	2196	1792	1448
	arc, inches:		+1.3	0	-6.6	-20.2
Rem. 150 Nosler Bal. Tip	velocity, fps:	3110	2912	2723	2542	2367
	energy, ft-lb:	3222	2825	2470	2152	1867
	arc, inches:		+1.2	0	-5.9	-17.3
Rem. 150 Swift Scirocco	velocity, fps:	3110	2927	2751	2582	2419
	energy, ft-lb:	3221	2852	2520	2220	1948
	arc, inches:		+1.3	0	-5.9	-17.0
Rem. 160 Swift A-Frame	velocity, fps:	2900	2659	2430	2212	2006
	energy, ft-lb:	2987	2511	2097	1739	1430
	arc, inches:		+1.7	0	-7.6	-22.4
Rem. 160 Nosler Partition	velocity, fps:	2950	2752	2563	2381	2207
	energy, ft-lb:	3091	2690	2333	2014	1730
	arc, inches:		+0.6	-1.9	-9.6	-23.6
Rem. 175 PSP Core-Lokt	velocity, fps:	2860	2645	2440	2244	2057
	energy, ft-lb:	3178	2718	2313	1956	1644
	arc, inches:		+1.7	0	-7.6	-22.1
Speer 145 Grand Slam	velocity, fps:	3140	2843	2565	2304	
	energy, ft-lb:	3174	2602	2118	1708	
	arc, inches:		+1.4	0	-6.7	
Speer 175 Grand Slam	velocity, fps:	2850	2653	2463	2282	
	energy, ft-lb:	3156	2734	2358	2023	
	arc, inches:		+1.7	0	-7.5	-21.7
Win. 140 Fail Safe	velocity, fps:	3150	2861	2589	2333	2092
	energy, ft-lb:	3085	2544	2085	1693	1361
	arc, inches:		+1.4	0	-6.6	-19.5
Win. 140 Ballistic Silvertip	velocity, fps:	3100	2889	2687	2494	2310
	energy, ft-lb:	2988	2595	2245	1934	1659
	arc, inches:		+1.3	0	-6.2	-17.9
Win. 150 Power-Point	velocity, fps:	3090	2812	2551	2304	2071
	energy, ft-lb:	3181	2634	2167	1768	1429
	arc, inches:		+1.5	0	-6.8	-20.2
Win. 150 Power-Point Plus	velocity, fps:	3130	2849	2586	2337	2102
	energy, ft-lb:	3264	2705	2227	1819	1472
	arc, inches:		+1.4	0	-6.6	-19.6
Win. 150 Ballistic Silvertip	velocity, fps:	3100	2903	2714	2533	2359
	energy, ft-lb:	3200	2806	2453	2136	1853
	arc, inches:		+1.3	0	-6.0	-17.5
Win. 160 Partition Gold	velocity, fps:	2950	2743	2546	2357	2176
	energy, ft-lb:	3093	2674	2303	1974	1682
	arc, inches:		+1.6	0	-6.9	-20.1
Win. 160 Fail Safe	velocity, fps:	2920	2678	2449	2331	2025
	energy, ft-lb:	3030	2549	2131	1769	1457
	arc, inches:		+1.7	0	-7.5	-22.0
Win. 175 Power-Point	velocity, fps:	2860	2645	2440	2244	2057
	energy, ft-lb:	3178	2718	2313	1956	1644
	arc, inches:		+2.0	0	-7.9	-22.7

7mm Weatherby Magnum

Cartridge Bullet	Range, Yards:	0	100	200	300	400
Federal 160 Nosler Partition	velocity, fps:	3050	2850	2650	2470	2290
	energy, ft-lb:	3305	2880	2505	2165	1865
	arc, inches:		+1.4	0	-6.3	-18.4
Federal 160 Sierra GameKing BTSP	velocity, fps:	3050	2880	2710	2560	2400
	energy, ft-lb:	3305	2945	2615	2320	2050
	arc, inches:		+1.4	0	-6.1	-17.4
Federal 160 Trophy Bonded	velocity, fps:	3050	2730	2420	2140	1880
	energy, ft-lb:	3305	2640	2085	1630	1255
	arc, inches:		+1.6	0	-7.6	-22.7

Cartridge Bullet	Range, Yards:	0	100	200	300	400
Hornady 154 Soft Point	velocity, fps:	3200	2971	2753	2546	2348
	energy, ft-lb:	3501	3017	2592	2216	1885
	arc, inches:		+1.2	0	-5.8	-17.0
Hornady 175 Soft Point	velocity, fps:	2910	2709	2516	2331	2154
	energy, ft-lb:	3290	2850	2459	2111	1803
	arc, inches:		+1.6	0	-7.1	-20.6
Wby. 139 Pointed Expanding	velocity, fps:	3340	3079	2834	2601	2380
	energy, ft-lb:	3443	2926	2478	2088	1748
	arc, inches:		+2.9	+3.6	0	-8.7
Wby. 140 Nosler Partition	velocity, fps:	3303	3069	2847	2636	2434
	energy, ft-lb:	3391	2927	2519	2159	1841
	arc, inches:		+2.9	+3.6	0	-8.5
Wby. 150 Nosler Bal. Tip	velocity, fps:	3300	3093	2896	2708	2527
	energy, ft-lb:	3627	3187	2793	2442	2127
	arc, inches:		+2.8	+3.5	0	-8.2
Wby. 150 Barnes X	veloctiy, fps:	3100	2901	2710	2527	2352
	energy, ft-lb:	3200	2802	2446	2127	1842
	arc, inches:		+3.3	+4.0	0	-9.4
Wby. 154 Pointed Expanding	velocity, fps:	3260	3028	2807	2597	2397
	energy, ft-lb:	3634	3134	2694	2307	1964
	arc, inches:		+3.0	+3.7	0	-8.8
Wby. 160 Nosler Partition	velocity, fps:	3200	2991	2791	2600	2417
	energy, ft-lb:	3638	3177	2767	2401	2075
	arc, inches:		+3.1	+3.8	0	-8.9
Wby. 175 Pointed Expanding	velocity, fps:	3070	2861	2662	2471	2288
	energy, ft-lb:	3662	3181	2753	2373	2034
	arc, inches:		+3.5	+4.2	0	-9.9

7mm Dakota

Cartridge Bullet	Range, Yards:	0	100	200	300	400
Dakota 140 Barnes X	velocity, fps:	3500	3253	3019	2798	2587
	energy, ft-lb:	3807	3288	2833	2433	2081
	arc, inches:		+2.0	+2.1	-1.5	-9.6
Dakota 160 Barnes X	velocity, fps:	3200	3001	2811	2630	2455
	energy, ft-lb:	3637	3200	2808	2456	2140
	arc, inches:		+2.1	+1.9	-2.8	-12.5

7mm STW

Cartridge Bullet	Range, Yards:	0	100	200	300	400
A-Square 140 Nos. Bal. Tip	velocity, fps:	3450	3254	3067	2888	2715
	energy, ft-lb:	3700	3291	2924	2592	2292
	arc, inches:		+2.2	+3.0	0	-7.3
A-Square 160 Nosler Part.	velocity, fps:	3250	3071	2900	2735	2576
	energy, ft-lb:	3752	3351	2987	2657	2357
	arc, inches:		+2.8	+3.5	0	-8.2
A-Square 160 SP boat-tail	velocity, fps:	3250	3087	2930	2778	2631
	energy, ft-lb:	3752	3385	3049	2741	2460
	arc, inches:		+2.8	+3.4	0	-8.0
Federal 140 Trophy Bonded	velocity, fps:	3330	3080	2850	2630	2420
	energy, ft-lb:	3435	2950	2520	2145	1815
	arc, inches:		+1.1	0	-5.4	-15.8
Federal 150 Trophy Bonded	velocity, fps:	3250	3010	2770	2560	2350
	energy, ft-lb:	3520	3010	2565	2175	1830
	arc, inches:		+1.2	0	-5.7	-16.7
Federal 160 Sierra GameKing BTSP	velocity, fps:	3200	3020	2850	2670	2530
	energy, ft-lb:	3640	3245	2890	2570	2275
	arc, inches:		+1.1	0	-5.5	-15.7
Rem. 140 PSP Core-Lokt	velocity, fps:	3325	3064	2818	2585	2364
	energy, ft-lb:	3436	2918	2468	2077	1737
	arc, inches:		+2.0	+1.7	-2.9	-12.8

BALLISTICS

7mm STW to .30-30 Winchester

Cartridge Bullet	Range, Yards:	0	100	200	300	400
Rem. 140 Swift A-Frame	velocity, fps:	3325	3020	2735	2467	2215
	energy, ft-lb:	3436	2834	2324	1892	1525
	arc, inches:		+2.1	+1.8	-3.1	-13.8
Speer 145 Grand Slam	velocity, fps:	3300	2992	2075	2435	
	energy, ft-lb:	3506	2882	2355	1909	
	arc, inches:		+1.2	0	-6.0	-17.8
Win. 140 Ballistic Silvertip	velocity, fps:	3320	3100	2890	2690	2499
	energy, ft-lb:	3427	2982	2597	2250	1941
	arc, inches:		+1.1	0	-5.2	-15.2
Win. 150 Power-Point	velocity, fps:	3250	2957	2683	2424	2181
	energy, ft-lb:	3519	2913	2398	1958	1584
	arc, inches:		+1.2	0	-6.1	-18.1
Win. 160 Fail Safe	velocity, fps:	3150	2894	2652	2422	2204
	energy, ft-lb:	3526	2976	2499	2085	1727
	arc, inches:		+1.3	0	-6.3	-18.5

7mm Remington Ultra Mag

Cartridge Bullet	Range, Yards:	0	100	200	300	400
Rem. 140 PSP Core-Lokt	velocity, fps:	3425	3158	2907	2669	2444
	energy, ft-lb:	3646	3099	2626	2214	1856
	arc, inches:		+1.8	+1.6	-2.7	-11.9
Rem. 140 Nosler Partition	velocity, fps:	3425	3184	2956	2740	2534
	energy, fps:	3646	3151	2715	2333	1995
	arc, inches:		+1.7	+1.6	-2.6	-11.4

7.21 (.284) Firehawk

Cartridge Bullet	Range, Yards:	0	100	200	300	400
Lazzeroni 140 Nosler Part.	velocity, fps:	3580	3349	3130	2923	2724
	energy, ft-lb:	3985	3488	3048	2656	2308
	arc, inches:		+2.2	+2.9	0	-7.0
Lazzeroni 160 Swift A-Frame	velocity, fps:	3385	3167	2961	2763	2574
	energy, ft-lb:	4072	3565	3115	2713	2354
	arc, inches:		+2.6	+3.3	0	-7.8

7.5x55 Swiss

Cartridge Bullet	Range, Yards:	0	100	200	300	400
Norma 180 Soft Point	velocity, fps:	2651	2432	2223	2025	
	energy, ft-lb:	2810	2364	1976	1639	
	arc, inches:		+2.2	0	-9.3	

7.62x39 Russian

Cartridge Bullet	Range, Yards:	0	100	200	300	400
Federal 123 Hi-Shok	velocity, fps:	2300	2030	1780	1550	1350
	energy, ft-lb:	1445	1125	860	655	500
	arc, inches:		0	-7.0	-25.1	
Federal 124 FMJ	velocity, fps:	2300	2030	1780	1560	1360
	energy, ft-lb:	1455	1135	875	670	510
	arc, inches:		+3.5	0	-14.6	-43.5
Norma 150 Soft Point	velocity, fps:	2953	2622	2314	2028	
	energy, ft-lb:	2905	2291	1784	1370	
	arc, inches:		+1.8	0	-8.3	
Norma 180 Soft Point	velocity, fps:	2575	2360	2154	1960	
	energy, ft-lb:	2651	2226	1856	1536	
	arc, inches:		+2.4	0	-9.9	
PMC 123 FMJ	velocity, fps:	2350	2072	1817	1583	1368
	energy, ft-lb:	1495	1162	894	678	507
	arc, inches:		0	-5.0	-26.4	-67.8
PMC 125 Pointed Soft Point	velocity, fps:	2320	2046	1794	1563	1350
	energy, ft-lb:	1493	1161	893	678	505
	arc, inches:		0	-5.2	-27.5	-70.6
Rem. 125 Pointed Soft Point	velocity, fps:	2365	2062	1783	1533	1320
	energy, ft-lb:	1552	1180	882	652	483
	arc, inches:		0	-6.7	-24.5	
Win. 123 Soft Point	velocity, fps:	2365	2033	1731	1465	1248
	energy, ft-lb:	1527	1129	818	586	425
	arc, inches:		+3.8	0	-15.4	-46.3

.30 Carbine

Cartridge Bullet	Range, Yards:	0	100	200	300	400
Federal 110 Hi-Shok RN	velocity, fps:	1990	1570	1240	1040	920
	energy, ft-lb:	965	600	375	260	210
	arc, inches:		0	-12.8	-46.9	
Federal 110 FMJ	velocity, fps:	1990	1570	1240	1040	920
	energy, ft-lb:	965	600	375	260	210
	arc, inches:		0	-12.8	-46.9	
PMC 110 FMJ	velocity, fps:	1927	1548	1248		
	energy, ft-lb:	906	585	380		
	arc, inches:		0	-14.2		
PMC 110 RNSP	velocity, fps:	1927	1548	1248		
	energy, ft-lb:	906	585	380		
	arc, inches:		0	-14.2		
Rem. 110 Soft Point	velocity, fps:	1990	1567	1236	1035	923
	energy, ft-lb:	967	600	373	262	208
	arc, inches:		0	-12.9	-48.6	
Win. 110 Hollow Soft Point	velocity, fps:	1990	1567	1236	1035	923
	energy, ft-lb:	967	600	373	262	208
	arc, inches:		0	-13.5	-49.9	

.30-30 Winchester

Cartridge Bullet	Range, Yards:	0	100	200	300	400
Federal 125 Hi-Shok HP	velocity, fps:	2570	2090	1660	1320	1080
	energy, ft-lb:	1830	1210	770	480	320
	arc, inches:		+3.3	0	-16.0	-50.9
Federal 150 Hi-Shok FN	velocity, fps:	2390	2020	1680	1400	1180
	energy, ft-lb:	1900	1355	945	650	460
	arc, inches:		+3.6	0	-15.9	-49.1
Federal 170 Hi-Shok RN	velocity, fps:	2200	1900	1620	1380	1190
	energy, ft-lb:	1830	1355	990	720	535
	arc, inches:		+4.1	0	-17.4	-52.4
Federal 170 Sierra Pro-Hunt.	velocity, fps:	2200	1820	1500	1240	1060
	energy, ft-lb:	1830	1255	845	575	425
	arc, inches:		+4.5	0	-20.0	-63.5
Federal 170 Nosler Partition	velocity, fps:	2200	1900	1620	1380	1190
	energy, ft-lb:	1830	1355	990	720	535
	arc, inches:		+4.1	0	-17.4	-52.4
Hornady 150 Round Nose	velocity, fps:	2390	1973	1605	1303	1095
	energy, ft-lb:	1902	1296	858	565	399
	arc, inches:		0	-8.2	-30.0	
Hornady 170 Flat Point	velocity, fps:	2200	1895	1619	1381	1191
	energy, ft-lb:	1827	1355	989	720	535
	arc, inches:		0	-8.9	-31.1	
Norma 150 Soft Point	velocity, fps:	2329	2008	1716	1459	
	energy, ft-lb:	1807	1344	981	709	
	arc, inches:		+3.6	0	-15.5	
PMC 150 Starfire HP	velocity, fps:	2100	1769	1478		
	energy, ft-lb:	1469	1042	728		
	arc, inches:		0	-10.8		
PMC 150 Flat Nose	velocity, fps:	2159	1819	1554		
	energy, ft-lb:	1552	1102	804		
	arc, inches:		0	-9.0		
PMC 170 Flat Nose	velocity, fps:	1965	1680	1480		
	energy, ft-lb:	1457	1065	827		
	arc, inches:		0	-10.7		

CARTRIDGE BULLET	RANGE, YARDS:	0	100	200	300	400
Rem. 55 PSP (sabot) "Accelerator"	velocity, fps:	3400	2693	2085	1570	1187
	energy, ft-lb:	1412	886	521	301	172
	arc, inches:		+1.7	0	-9.9	-34.3
Rem. 150 SP Core-Lokt	velocity, fps:	2390	1973	1605	1303	1095
	energy, ft-lb:	1902	1296	858	565	399
	arc, inches:		0	-7.6	-28.8	
Rem. 170 SP Core-Lokt	velocity, fps:	2200	1895	1619	1381	1191
	energy, ft-lb:	1827	1355	989	720	535
	arc, inches:		0	-8.3	-29.9	
Rem. 170 HP Core-Lokt	velocity, fps:	2200	1895	1619	1381	1191
	energy, ft-lb:	1827	1355	989	720	535
	arc, inches:		0	-8.3	-29.9	
Speer 150 Flat Nose	velocity, fps:	2370	2067	1788	1538	
	energy, ft-lb:	1870	1423	1065	788	
	arc, inches:		+3.3	0	-14.4	-43.7
Win. 150 Hollow Point	velocity, fps:	2390	2018	1684	1398	1177
	energy, ft-lb:	1902	1356	944	651	461
	arc, inches:		0	-7.7	-27.9	
Win. 150 Power-Point	velocity, fps:	2390	2018	1684	1398	1177
	energy, ft-lb:	1902	1356	944	651	461
	arc, inches:		0	-7.7	-27.9	
Win. 150 Silvertip	velocity,fps:	2390	2018	1684	1398	1177
	energy, ft-lb:	1902	1356	944	651	461
	arc, inches:		0	-7.7	-27.9	
Win. 150 Power-Point Plus	velocity, fps:	2480	2095	1747	1446	1209
	energy, ft-lb:	2049	1462	1017	697	487
	arc, inches:		0	-6.5	-24.5	
Win. 170 Power-Point	velocity, fps:	2200	1895	1619	1381	1191
	energy, ft-lb:	1827	1355	989	720	535
	arc, inches:		0	-8.9	-31.1	
Win. 170 Silvertip	velocity, fps:	2200	1895	1619	1381	1191
	energy, ft-lb:	1827	1355	989	720	535
	arc, inches:		0	-8.9	-31.1	

.300 Savage

CARTRIDGE BULLET	RANGE, YARDS:	0	100	200	300	400
Federal 150 Hi-Shok	velocity, fps:	2630	2350	2100	1850	1630
	energy, ft-lb:	2305	1845	1460	1145	885
	arc, inches:		+2.4	0	-10.4	-30.9
Federal 180 Hi-Shok	velocity, fps:	2350	2140	1940	1750	1570
	energy, ft-lb:	2205	1825	1495	1215	985
	arc, inches:		+3.1	0	-12.4	-36.1
Rem. 150 PSP Core-Lokt	velocity, fps:	2630	2354	2095	1853	1631
	energy, ft-lb:	2303	1845	1462	1143	806
	arc, inches:		+2.4	0	-10.4	-30.9
Rem. 180 SP Core-Lokt	velocity, fps:	2350	2025	1728	1467	1252
	energy, ft-lb:	2207	1639	1193	860	626
	arc, inches:		0	-7.1	-25.9	
Win. 150 Power-Point	velocity, fps:	2630	2311	2015	1743	1500
	energy, ft-lb:	2303	1779	1352	1012	749
	arc, inches:		+2.8	0	-11.5	-34.4

.307 Winchester

CARTRIDGE BULLET	RANGE, YARDS:	0	100	200	300	400
Win. 180 Power-Point	velocity, fps:	2510	2179	1874	1599	1362
	energy, ft-lb:	2519	1898	1404	1022	742
	arc, inches:		+1.5	-3.6	-18.6	-47.1

.30-40 Krag

CARTRIDGE BULLET	RANGE, YARDS:	0	100	200	300	400
180 PSP Core-Lokt Rem.	velocity, fps:	2430	2213	2007	1813	1632
	energy, ft-lb:	2360	1957	1610	1314	1064
	arc, inches, s:		0	-5.6	-18.6	
Win. 180 Power-Point	velocity, fps:	2430	2099	1795	1525	1298
	energy, ft-lb:	2360	1761	1288	929	673
	arc, inches, s:		0	-7.1	-25.0	

.308 Winchester

CARTRIDGE BULLET	RANGE, YARDS:	0	100	200	300	400
Federal 150 Hi-Shok	velocity, fps:	2820	2530	2260	2010	1770
	energy, ft-lb:	2650	2140	1705	1345	1050
	arc, inches:		+2.0	0	-8.8	-26.3
Federal 150 Nosler Bal. Tip.	velocity, fps:	2820	2610	2410	2220	2040
	energy, ft-lb:	2650	2270	1935	1640	1380
	arc, inches:		+1.8	0	-7.8	-22.7
Federal 150 FMJ boat-tail	velocity, fps:	2820	2620	2430	2250	2070
	energy, ft-lb:	2650	2285	1965	1680	1430
	arc, inches:		+1.8	0	-7.7	-22.4
Federal 150 Barnes XLC	velocity, fps:	2820	2610	2400	2210	2030
	energy, ft-lb:	2650	2265	1925	1630	1370
	arc, inches:		+1.8	0	-7.8	-22.9
Federal 155 Sierra MatchKing BTHP	velocity, fps:	2950	2740	2540	2350	2170
	energy, ft-lb:	2995	2585	2225	1905	1620
	arc, inches:		+13.2	+23.3	+28.1	+26.5
Federal 165 Sierra GameKing BTSP	velocity, fps:	2700	2520	2330	2160	1990
	energy, ft-lb:	2670	2310	1990	1700	1450
	arc, inches:		+2.0	0	-8.4	-24.3
Federal 165 Trophy Bonded	velocity, fps:	2700	2440	2200	1970	1760
	energy, ft-lb:	2670	2185	1775	1425	1135
	arc, inches:		+2.2	0	-9.4	-27.7
Federal 165 Trophy Bonded HE	velocity, fps:	2870	2600	2350	2120	1890
	energy, ft-lb:	3020	2485	2030	1640	1310
	arc, inches:		+1.8	0	-8.2	-24.0
Federal 168 Sierra MatchKg. BTHP	velocity, fps:	2600	2410	2230	2060	1890
	energy, ft-lb:	2520	2170	1855	1580	1340
	arc, inches:		+17.7	+31.0	+37.2	+35.4
Federal 180 Hi-Shok	velocity, fps:	2620	2390	2180	1970	1780
	energy, ft-lb:	2745	2290	1895	1555	1270
	arc, inches:		+2.3	0	-9.7	-28.3
Federal 180 Sierra Pro-Hunt.	velocity, fps:	2620	2410	2200	2010	1820
	energy, ft-lb:	2745	2315	1940	1610	1330
	arc, inches:		+2.3	0	-9.3	-27.1
Federal 180 Nosler Partition	velocity, fps:	2620	2430	2240	2060	1890
	energy, ft-lb:	2745	2355	2005	1700	1430
	arc, inches:		+2.2	0	-9.2	-26.5
Federal 180 Nosler Part. HE	velocity, fps:	2740	2550	2370	2200	2030
	energy, ft-lb:	3000	2600	2245	1925	1645
	arc, inches:		+1.9	0	-8.2	-23.5
Hornady 110 Urban Tactical	velocity, fps:	3170	2825	2504	2206	1937
	energy, ft-lb:	2454	1950	1532	1189	916
	arc, inches:		+1.5	0	-7.2	-21.2
Hornady 150 SP boat-tail	velocity, fps:	2820	2560	2315	2084	1866
	energy, ft-lb:	2648	2183	1785	1447	1160
	arc, inches:		+2.0	0	-8.5	-25.2
Hornady 150 SP LM	velocity, fps:	2980	2703	2442	2195	1964
	energy, ft-lb:	2959	2433	1986	1606	1285
	arc, inches:		+1.6	0	-7.5	-22.2

BALLISTICS

CENTERFIRE RIFLE BALLISTICS

.308 Winchester

Cartridge Bullet	Range, Yards:	0	100	200	300	400
Hornady 155 A-Max	velocity, fps:	2815	2610	2415	2229	2051
	energy, ft-lb:	2727	2345	2007	1709	1448
	arc, inches:		+1.9	0	-7.9	-22.6
Hornady 165 SP boat-tail	velocity, fps:	2700	2496	2301	2115	1937
	energy, ft-lb:	2670	2283	1940	1639	1375
	arc, inches:		+2.0	0	-8.7	-25.2
Hornady 165 SPBT LM	velocity, fps:	2870	2658	2456	2283	2078
	energy, ft-lb:	3019	2589	2211	1877	1583
	arc, inches:		+1.7	0	-7.5	-21.8
Hornady 168 BTHP Match	velocity, fps:	2700	2524	2354	2191	2035
	energy, ft-lb:	2720	2377	2068	1791	1545
	arc, inches:		+2.0	0	-8.4	-23.9
Hornady 168 BTHP Match LM	velocity, fps:	2640	2630	2429	2238	2056
	energy, ft-lb:	3008	2579	2201	1868	1577
	arc, inches:		+1.8	0	-7.8	-22.4
Hornady 168 A-Max Match	velocity, fps:	2620	2446	2280	2120	1972
	energy, ft-lb:	2560	2232	1939	1677	1450
	arc, inches:		+2.6	0	-9.2	-25.6
Hornady 168 A-Max	velocity, fps:	2700	2491	2292	2102	1921
	energy, ft-lb:	2719	2315	1959	1648	1377
	arc, inches:		+2.4	0	-9.0	-25.9
Hornady 178 A-Max	velocity, fps:	2965	2778	2598	2425	2259
	energy, ft-lb:	3474	3049	2666	2323	2017
	arc, inches:		+1.6	0	-6.9	-19.8
Hornady 180 A-Max Match	velocity, fps:	2550	2397	2249	2106	1974
	energy, ft-lb:	2598	2295	2021	1773	1557
	arc, inches:		+2.7	0	-9.5	-26.2
Norma 150 Soft Point	velocity, fps:	2861	2537	2235	1954	
	energy, ft-lb:	2727	2144	1664	1272	
	arc, inches:		+2.0	0	-9.0	
Norma 165 TXP Swift A-Fr.	velocity, fps:	2700	2459	2231	2015	
	energy, ft-lb:	2672	2216	1824	1488	
	arc, inches:		+2.1	0	-9.1	
Norma 180 Plastic Point	velocity, fps:	2612	2365	2131	1911	
	energy, ft-lb:	2728	2235	1815	1460	
	arc, inches:		+2.4	0	-10.1	
Norma 180 Nosler Partition	velocity, fps:	2612	2414	2225	2044	
	energy, ft-lb:	2728	2330	1979	1670	
	arc, inches:		+2.2	0	-9.3	
Norma 180 Alaska	velocity, fps:	2612	2269	1953	1667	
	energy, ft-lb:	2728	2059	1526	1111	
	arc, inches:		+2.7	0	-11.9	
Norma 180 Vulkan	velocity, fps:	2612	2325	2056	1806	
	energy, ft-lb:	2728	2161	1690	1304	
	arc, inches:		+2.5	0	-10.8	
Norma 180 Oryx	velocity, fps:	2612	2305	2019	1755	
	energy, ft-lb:	2728	2124	1629	1232	
	arc, inches:		+2.5	0	-11.1	
Norma 200 Vulkan	velocity, fps:	2461	2215	1983	1767	
	energy, ft-lb:	2690	2179	1747	1387	
	arc, inches:		+2.8	0	-11.7	
PMC 147 FMJ boat-tail	velocity, fps:	2751	2473	2257	2052	1859
	energy, ft-lb:	2428	2037	1697	1403	1150
	arc, inches:		+2.3	0	-9.3	-27.3
PMC 150 Barnes X	velocity, fps:	2700	2504	2316	2135	1964
	energy, ft-lb:	2428	2087	1786	1518	1284
	arc, inches:		+2.0	0	-8.6	-24.7

Cartridge Bullet	Range, Yards:	0	100	200	300	400
PMC 150 Pointed Soft Point	velocity, fps:	2643	2417	2203	1999	1807
	energy, ft-lb:	2326	1946	1615	1331	1088
	arc, inches:		+2.2	0	-9.4	-27.5
PMC 150 SP boat-tail	velocity, fps:	2820	2581	2354	2139	1935
	energy, ft-lb:	2648	2218	1846	1523	1247
	arc, inches:		+1.9	0	-8.2	-24.0
PMC 165 Barnes X	velocity, fps:	2600	2425	2256	2095	1940
	energy, ft-lb:	2476	2154	1865	1608	1379
	arc, inches:		+2.2	0	-9.0	-26.0
PMC 168 HP boat-tail	velocity, fps:	2650	2460	2278	2103	1936
	energy, ft-lb:	2619	2257	1935	1649	1399
	arc, inches:		+2.1	0	--8.8	-25.6
PMC 180 Pointed Soft Point	velocity, fps:	2410	2223	2044	1874	1714
	energy, ft-lb:	2320	1975	1670	1404	1174
	arc, inches:		+2.8	0	-11.1	-32.0
PMC 180 SP boat-tail	velocity, fps:	2620	2446	2278	2117	1962
	energy, ft-lb:	2743	2391	2074	1790	1538
	arc, inches:		+2.2	0	-8.9	-25.4
Rem. 150 PSP Core-Lokt	velocity, fps:	2820	2533	2263	2009	1774
	energy, ft-lb:	2648	2137	1705	1344	1048
	arc, inches:		+2.0	0	-8.8	-26.2
Rem. 150 Swift Scirocco	velocity, fps:	2820	2611	2410	2219	2037
	energy, ft-lb:	2648	2269	1935	1640	1381
	arc, inches:		+1.8	0	-7.8	-22.7
Rem. 165 PSP boat-tail	velocity, fps:	2700	2497	2303	2117	1941
	energy, ft-lb:	2670	2284	1942	1642	1379
	arc, inches:		+2.0	0	-8.6	-25.0
Rem. 165 Nosler Bal. Tip	velocity, fps:	2700	2613	2333	2161	1996
	energy, ft-lb:	2672	2314	1995	1711	1460
	arc, inches:		+2.0	0	-8.4	-24.3
Rem. 165 Swift Scirocco	velocity, fps:	2700	2513	2233	2161	1996
	energy, fps:	2670	2313	1994	1711	1459
	arc, inches:		+2.0	0	-8.4	-24.3
Rem. 168 HPBT Match	velocity, fps:	2680	2493	2314	2143	1979
	energy, ft-lb:	2678	2318	1998	1713	1460
	arc, inches:		+2.1	0	-8.6	-24.7
Rem. 180 SP Core-Lokt	velocity, fps:	2620	2274	1955	1666	1414
	energy, ft-lb:	2743	2066	1527	1109	799
	arc, inches:		+2.6	0	-11.8	-36.3
Rem. 180 PSP Core-Lokt	velocity, fps:	2620	2393	2178	1974	1782
	energy, ft-lb:	2743	2288	1896	1557	1269
	arc, inches:		+2.3	0	-9.7	-28.3
Rem. 180 Nosler Partition	velocity, fps:	2620	2436	2259	2089	1927
	energy, ft-lb:	2743	2371	2039	1774	1485
	arc, inches:		+2.2	0	-9.0	-26.0
Speer 150 Grand Slam	velocity, fps:	2900	2599	2317	2053	
	energy, ft-lb:	2800	2249	1788	1404	
	arc, inches:		+2.1	0	-8.6	-24.8
Speer 165 Grand Slam	velocity, fps:	2700	2475	2261	2057	
	energy, ft-lb:	2670	2243	1872	1550	
	arc, inches:		+2.1	0	-8.9	-25.9
Speer 180 Grand Slam	velocity, fps:	2620	2420	2229	2046	
	energy, ft-lb:	2743	2340	1985	1674	
	arc, inches:		+2.2	0	-9.2	-26.6
Win. 150 Power-Point	velocity, fps:	2820	2488	2179	1893	1633
	energy, ft-lb:	2648	2061	1581	1193	888
	arc, inches:		+2.4	0	-9.8	-29.3

CARTRIDGE BULLET	RANGE, YARDS:	0	100	200	300	400
Win. 150 Power-Point Plus	velocity, fps:	2900	2558	2241	1946	1678
	energy, ft-lb:	2802	2180	1672	1262	938
	arc, inches:		+1.9	0	-8.9	-27.0
Win. 150 Partition Gold	velocity, fps:	2900	2645	2405	2177	1962
	energy, ft-lb:	2802	2332	1927	1579	1282
	arc, inches:		+1.7	0	-7.8	-22.9
Win. 150 Ballistic Silvertip	velocity, fps:	2810	2601	2401	2211	2028
	energy, ft-lb:	2629	2253	1920	1627	1370
	arc, inches:		+1.8	0	-7.8	-22.8
Win. 150 Fail Safe	velocity, fps:	2820	2533	2263	2010	1775
	energy, ft-lb:	2649	2137	1706	1346	1049
	arc, inches:		+2.0	0	-8.8	-26.2
Win. 168 Ballistic Silvertip	velocity, fps:	2670	2484	2306	2134	1971
	energy, ft-lb:	2659	2301	1983	1699	1449
	arc, inches:		+2.1	0	-8.6	-24.8
Win. 168 HP boat-tail Match	velocity, fps:	2680	2485	2297	2118	1948
	energy, ft-lb:	2680	2303	1970	1674	1415
	arc, inches:		+2.1	0	-8.7	-25.1
Win. 180 Power-Point	velocity, fps:	2620	2274	1955	1666	1414
	energy, ft-lb:	2743	2066	1527	1109	799
	arc, inches:		+2.9	0	-12.1	-36.9
Win. 180 Silvertip	velocity, fps:	2620	2393	2178	1974	1782
	energy, ft-lb:	2743	2288	1896	1557	1269
	arc, inches:		+2.6	0	-9.9	-28.9

.30-06 Springfield

CARTRIDGE BULLET	RANGE, YARDS:	0	100	200	300	400
A-Square 180 M & D-T	velocity, fps:	2700	2365	2054	1769	1524
	energy, ft-lb:	2913	2235	1687	1251	928
	arc, inches:		+2.4	0	-10.6	-32.4
A-Square 220 Monolythic Solid	velocity, fps:	2380	2108	1854	1623	1424
	energy, ft-lb:	2767	2171	1679	1287	990
	arc, inches:		+3.1	0	-13.6	-39.9
Federal 125 Sierra Pro-Hunt.	velocity, fps:	3140	2780	2450	2140	1850
	energy, ft-lb:	2735	2145	1660	1270	955
	arc, inches:		+1.5	0	-7.3	-22.3
Federal 150 Hi-Shok	velocity, fps:	2910	2620	2340	2080	1840
	energy, ft-lb:	2820	2280	1825	1445	1130
	arc, inches:		+1.8	0	-8.2	-24.4
Federal 150 Sierra Pro-Hunt.	velocity, fps:	2910	2640	2380	2130	1900
	energy, ft-lb:	2820	2315	1880	1515	1205
	arc, inches:		+1.7	0	-7.9	-23.3
Federal 150 Sierra GameKing BTSP	velocity, fps:	2910	2690	2480	2270	2070
	energy, ft-lb:	2820	2420	2040	1710	1430
	arc, inches:		+1.7	0	-7.4	-21.5
Federal 150 Nosler Bal. Tip	velocity, fps:	2910	2700	2490	2300	2110
	energy, ft-lb:	2820	2420	2070	1760	1485
	arc, inches:		+1.6	0	-7.3	-21.1
Federal 150 FMJ boat-tail	velocity, fps:	2910	2710	2510	2320	2150
	energy, ft-lb:	2820	2440	2100	1800	1535
	arc, inches:		+1.6	0	-7.1	-20.8
Federal 165 Sierra Pro-Hunt.	velocity, fps:	2800	2560	2340	2130	1920
	energy, ft-lb:	2875	2410	2005	1655	1360
	arc, inches:		+1.9	0	-8.3	-24.3
Federal 165 Sierra GameKing BTSP	velocity, fps:	2800	2610	2420	2240	2070
	energy, ft-lb:	2870	2490	2150	1840	1580
	arc, inches:		+1.8	0	-7.8	-22.4
Federal 165 Sierra GameKing HE	velocity, fps:	3140	2900	2670	2450	2240
	energy, ft-lb:	3610	3075	2610	2200	1845
	arc, inches:		+1.5	0	-6.9	-20.4

CARTRIDGE BULLET	RANGE, YARDS:	0	100	200	300	400
Federal 165 Nosler Bal. Tip	velocity, fps:	2800	2610	2430	2250	2080
	energy, ft-lb:	2870	2495	2155	1855	1585
	arc, inches:		+1.8	0	-7.7	-22.3
Federal 165 Trophy Bonded	velocity, fps:	2800	2540	2290	2050	1830
	energy, ft-lb:	2870	2360	1915	1545	1230
	arc, inches:		+2.0	0	-8.7	-25.4
Federal 165 Trophy Bonded HE	velocity, fps:	3140	2860	2590	2340	2100
	energy, ft-lb:	3610	2990	2460	2010	1625
	arc, inches:		+1.6	0	-7.4	-21.9
Federal 168 Sierra MatchKg. BTHP	velocity, fps:	2700	2510	2320	2150	1980
	energy, ft-lb:	2720	2350	2010	1720	1460
	arc, inches:		+16.2	+28.4	+34.1	+32.3
Federal 180 Hi-Shok	velocity, fps:	2700	2470	2250	2040	1850
	energy, ft-lb:	2915	2435	2025	1665	1360
	arc, inches:		+2.1	0	-9.0	-26.4
Federal 180 Sierra Pro-Hunt RN	velocity, fps:	2700	2350	2020	1730	1470
	energy, ft-lb:	2915	2200	1630	1190	860
	arc, inches:		+2.4	0	-11.0	-33.6
Federal 180 Nosler Partition	velocity, fps:	2700	2500	2320	2140	1970
	energy, ft-lb:	2915	2510	2150	1830	1550
	arc, inches:		+2.0	0	-8.6	-24.6
Federal 180 Nosler Part. HE	velocity, fps:	2880	2690	2500	2320	2150
	energy, ft-lb:	3315	2880	2495	2150	1845
	arc, inches:		+1.7	0	-7.2	-21.0
Federal 180 Sierra GameKing BTSP	velocity, fps:	2700	2540	2380	2220	2080
	energy, ft-lb:	2915	2570	2260	1975	1720
	arc, inches:		+1.9	0	-8.1	-23.1
Federal 180 Barnes XLC	velocity, fps:	2700	2530	2360	2200	2040
	energy, ft-lb:	2915	2550	2220	1930	1670
	arc, inches:		+2.0	0	-8.3	-23.8
Federal 180 Trophy Bonded	velocity, fps:	2700	2460	2220	2000	1800
	energy, ft-lb:	2915	2410	1975	1605	1290
	arc, inches:		+2.2	0	-9.2	-27.0
Federal 180 Trophy Bonded HE	velocity, fps:	2880	2630	2380	2160	1940
	energy, ft-lb:	3315	2755	2270	1855	1505
	arc, inches:		+1.8	0	-8.0	-23.3
Federal 220 Sierra Pro-Hunt. RN	velocity, fps:	2410	2130	1870	1630	1420
	energy, ft-lb:	2835	2215	1705	1300	985
	arc, inches:		+3.1	0	-13.1	-39.3
Hornady 150 SP	velocity, fps:	2910	2617	2342	2083	1843
	energy, ft-lb:	2820	2281	1827	1445	1131
	arc, inches:		+2.1	0	-8.5	-25.0
Hornady 150 SP LM	velocity, fps:	3100	2815	2548	2295	2058
	energy, ft-lb:	3200	2639	2161	1755	1410
	arc, inches:		+1.4	0	-6.8	-20.3
Hornady 150 SP boat-tail	velocity, fps:	2910	2683	2467	2262	2066
	energy, ft-lb:	2820	2397	2027	1706	1421
	arc, inches:		+2.0	0	-7.7	-22.2
Hornady 165 SP boat-tail	velocity, fps:	2800	2591	2392	2202	2020
	energy, ft-lb:	2873	2460	2097	1777	1495
	arc, inches:		+1.8	0	-8.0	-23.3
Hornady 165 SPBT LM	velocity, fps:	3015	2790	2575	2370	2176
	energy, ft-lb:	3330	2850	2428	2058	1734
	arc, inches:		+1.6	0	-7.0	-20.1
Hornady 168 HPBT Match	velocity, fps:	2790	2620	2447	2280	2120
	energy, ft-lb:	2925	2561	2234	1940	1677
	arc, inches:		+1.7	0	-7.7	-22.2

BALLISTICS

Cartridge Bullet	Range, Yards:	0	100	200	300	400
Hornady 180 SP	velocity, fps:	2700	2469	2258	2042	1846
	energy, ft-lb:	2913	2436	2023	1666	1362
	arc, inches:		+2.4	0	-9.3	-27.0
Hornady 180 SPBT LM	velocity, fps:	2880	2676	2480	2293	2114
	energy, ft-lb:	3316	2862	2459	2102	1786
	arc, inches:		+1.7	0	-7.3	-21.3
Norma 150 Soft Point	velocity, fps:	2972	2640	2331	2043	
	energy, ft-lb:	2943	2321	1810	1390	
	arc, inches:		+1.8	0	-8.2	
Norma 180 Alaska	velocity, fps:	2700	2351	2028	1734	
	energy, ft-lb:	2914	2209	1645	1202	
	arc, inches:		+2.4	0	-11.0	
Norma 180 Nosler Partition	velocity, fps:	2700	2494	2297	2108	
	energy, ft-lb:	2914	2486	2108	1777	
	arc, inches:		+2.1	0	-8.7	
Norma 180 Plastic Point	velocity, fps:	2700	2455	2222	2003	
	energy, ft-lb:	2914	2409	1974	1603	
	arc, inches:		+2.1	0	-9.2	
Norma 180 Vulkan	velocity, fps:	2700	2416	2150	1901	
	energy, ft-lb:	2914	2334	1848	1445	
	arc, inches:		+2.2	0	-9.8	
Norma 180 Oryx	velocity, fps:	2700	2387	2095	1825	
	energy, ft-lb:	2914	2278	1755	1332	
	arc, inches:		+2.3	0	-10.2	
Norma 180 TXP Swift A-Frame	velocity, fps:	2700	2479	2268	2067	
	energy, ft-lb:	2914	2456	2056	1708	
	arc, inches:		+2.0	0	-8.8	
Norma 200 Vulkan	velocity, fps:	2641	2385	2143	1916	
	energy, ft-lb:	3098	2527	2040	1631	
	arc, inches:		+2.3	0	-9.9	
Norma 200 Oryx	velocity, fps:	2625	2362	2115	1883	
	energy, ft-lb:	3061	2479	1987	1575	
	arc, inches:		+2.3	0	-10.1	
PMC 150 X-Bullet	velocity, fps:	2750	2552	2361	2179	2005
	energy, ft-lb:	2518	2168	1857	1582	1339
	arc, inches:		+2.0	0	-8.2	-23.7
PMC 150 Pointed Soft Point	velocity, fps:	2773	2542	2322	2113	1916
	energy, ft-lb:	2560	2152	1796	1487	1222
	arc, inches:		+1.9	0	-8.4	-24.6
PMC 150 SP boat-tail	velocity, fps:	2900	2657	2427	2208	2000
	energy, ft-lb:	2801	2351	1961	1623	1332
	arc, inches:		+1.7	0	-7.7	-22.5
PMC 150 FMJ	velocity, fps:	2773	2542	2322	2113	1916
	energy, ft-lb:	2560	2152	1796	1487	1222
	arc, inches:		+1.9	0	-8.4	-24.6
PMC 165 Barnes X	velocity, fps:	2750	2569	2395	2228	2067
	energy, ft-lb:	2770	2418	2101	1818	1565
	arc, inches:		+1.9	0	-8.0	-23.0
PMC 180 Barnes X	velocity, fps:	2650	2487	2331	2179	2034
	energy, ft-lb:	2806	2472	2171	1898	1652
	arc, inches:		+2.1	0	-8.5	-24.3
PMC 180 Pointed Soft Point	velocity, fps:	2550	2357	2172	1996	1829
	energy, ft-lb:	2598	2220	1886	1592	1336
	arc, inches:		+2.4	0	-9.7	-28.2
PMC 180 SP boat-tail	velocity, fps:	2700	2523	2352	2188	2030
	energy, ft-lb:	2913	2543	2210	1913	1646
	arc, inches:		+2.0	0	-8.3	-23.9

Cartridge Bullet	Range, Yards:	0	100	200	300	400
Rem. 55 PSP (sabot) "Accelerator"	velocity, fps:	4080	3484	2964	2499	2080
	energy, ft-lb:	2033	1482	1073	763	528
	arc, inches:		+1.4	+1.4	-2.6	-12.2
Rem. 125 Pointed Soft Point	velocity, fps:	3140	2780	2447	2138	1853
	energy, ft-lb:	2736	2145	1662	1269	953
	arc, inches:		+1.5	0	-7.4	-22.4
Rem. 150 PSP Core-Lokt	velocity, fps:	2910	2617	2342	2083	1843
	energy, ft-lb:	2820	2281	1827	1445	1131
	arc, inches:		+1.8	0	-8.2	-24.4
Rem. 150 Bronze Point	velocity, fps:	2910	2656	2416	2189	1974
	energy, ft-lb:	2820	2349	1944	1596	1298
	arc, inches:		+1.7	0	-7.7	-22.7
Rem. 150 Nosler Bal. Tip	velocity, fps:	2910	2696	2492	2298	2112
	energy, ft-lb:	2821	2422	2070	1769	1485
	arc, inches:		+1.6	0	-7.3	-21.1
Rem. 150 Swift Scirocco	velocity, fps:	2910	2696	2492	2298	2111
	energy, ft-lb:	2820	2421	2069	1758	1485
	arc, inches:		+1.6	0	-7.3	-21.1
Rem. 165 PSP Core-Lokt	velocity, fps:	2800	2534	2283	2047	1825
	energy, ft-lb:	2872	2352	1909	1534	1220
	arc, inches:		+2.0	0	-8.7	-25.9
Rem. 165 PSP boat-tail	velocity, fps:	2800	2592	2394	2204	2023
	energy, ft-lb:	2872	2462	2100	1780	1500
	arc, inches:		+1.8	0	-7.9	-23.0
Rem. 165 Nosler Bal. Tip	velocity, fps:	2800	2609	2426	2249	2080
	energy, ft-lb:	2873	2494	2155	1854	1588
	arc, inches:		+1.8	0	-7.7	-22.3
Rem. 180 SP Core-Lokt	velocity, fps:	2700	2348	2023	1727	1466
	energy, ft-lb:	2913	2203	1635	1192	859
	arc, inches:		+2.4	0	-11.0	-33.8
Rem. 180 PSP Core-Lokt	velocity, fps:	2700	2469	2250	2042	1846
	energy, ft-lb:	2913	2436	2023	1666	1362
	arc, inches:		+2.1	0	-9.0	-26.3
Rem. 180 Bronze Point	velocity, fps:	2700	2485	2280	2084	1899
	energy, ft-lb:	2913	2468	2077	1736	1441
	arc, inches:		+2.1	0	-8.8	-25.5
Rem. 180 Swift A-Frame	velocity, fps:	2700	2465	2243	2032	1833
	energy, ft-lb:	2913	2429	2010	1650	1343
	arc, inches:		+2.1	0	-9.1	-26.6
Rem. 180 Nosler Partition	velocity, fps:	2700	2512	2332	2160	1995
	energy, ft-lb:	2913	2522	2174	1864	1590
	arc, inches:		+2.0	0	-8.4	-24.3
Rem. 220 SP Core-Lokt	velocity, fps:	2410	2130	1870	1632	1422
	energy, ft-lb:	2837	2216	1708	1301	988
	arc, inches, s:		0	-6.2	-22.4	
Speer 150 Grand Slam	velocity, fps:	2975	2669	2383	2114	
	energy, ft-lb:	2947	2372	1891	1489	
	arc, inches:		+2.0	0	-8.1	-24.1
Speer 165 Grand Slam	velocity, fps:	2790	2560	2342	2134	
	energy, ft-lb:	2851	2401	2009	1669	
	arc, inches:		+1.9	0	-8.3	-24.1
Speer 180 Grand Slam	velocity, fps:	2690	2487	2293	2108	
	energy, ft-lb:	2892	2472	2101	1775	
	arc, inches:		+2.1	0	-8.8	-25.1
Win. 125 Pointed Soft Point	velocity, fps:	3140	2780	2447	2138	1853
	energy, ft-lb:	2736	2145	1662	1269	953
	arc, inches:		+1.8	0	-7.7	-23.0

CARTRIDGE BULLET	RANGE, YARDS:	0	100	200	300	400
Win. 150 Power-Point	velocity, fps:	2920	2580	2265	1972	1704
	energy, ft-lb:	2839	2217	1708	1295	967
	arc, inches:		+2.2	0	-9.0	-27.0
Win. 150 Power-Point Plus	velocity, fps:	3050	2685	2352	2043	1760
	energy, ft-lb:	3089	2402	1843	1391	1032
	arc, inches:		+1.7	0	-8.0	-24.3
Win. 150 Silvertip	velocity, fps:	2910	2617	2342	2083	1843
	energy, ft-lb:	2820	2281	1827	1445	1131
	arc, inches:		+2.1	0	-8.5	-25.0
Win. 150 Partition Gold	velocity, fps:	2960	2705	2464	2235	2019
	energy, ft-lb:	2919	2437	2022	1664	1358
	arc, inches:		+1.6	0	-7.4	-21.7
Win. 150 Ballistic Silvertip	velocity, fps:	2900	2687	2483	2289	2103
	energy, ft-lb:	2801	2404	2054	1745	1473
	arc, inches:		+1.7	0	-7.3	-21.2
Win. 150 Fail Safe	velocity, fps:	2920	2625	2349	2089	1848
	energy, ft-lb:	2841	2296	1838	1455	1137
	arc, inches:		+1.8	0	-8.1	-24.3
Win. 165 Pointed Soft Point	velocity, fps:	2800	2573	2357	2151	1956
	energy, ft-lb:	2873	2426	2036	1696	1402
	arc, inches:		+2.2	0	-8.4	-24.4
Win. 165 Fail Safe	velocity, fps:	2800	2540	2295	2063	1846
	energy, ft-lb:	2873	2365	1930	1560	1249
	arc, inches:		+2.0	0	-8.6	-25.3
Win. 168 Ballistic Silvertip	velocity, fps:	2790	2599	2416	2240	2072
	energy, ft-lb:	2903	2520	2177	1872	1601
	arc, inches:		+1.8	0	-7.8	-22.5
Win. 180 Power-Point	velocity, fps:	2700	2348	2023	1727	1466
	energy, ft-lb:	2913	2203	1635	1192	859
	arc, inches:		+2.7	0	-11.3	-34.4
Win. 180 Power-Point Plus	velocity, fps:	2770	2563	2366	2177	1997
	energy, ft-lb:	3068	2627	2237	1894	1594
	arc, inches:		+1.9	0	-8.1	-23.6
Win. 180 Silvertip	velocity, fps:	2700	2469	2250	2042	1846
	energy, ft-lb:	2913	2436	2023	1666	1362
	arc, inches:		+2.4	0	-9.3	-27.0
Win. 180 Partition Gold	velocity, fps:	2790	2581	2382	2192	2010
	energy, ft-lb:	3112	2664	2269	1920	1615
	arc, inches:		+1.9	0	-8.0	-23.2
Win. 180 Fail Safe	velocity, fps:	2700	2486	2283	2089	1904
	energy, ft-lb:	2914	2472	2083	1744	1450
	arc, inches:		+2.1	0	-8.7	-25.5

.300 H&H Magnum

CARTRIDGE BULLET	RANGE, YARDS:	0	100	200	300	400
Federal 180 Nosler Partition	velocity, fps:	2880	2620	2380	2150	1930
	energy, ft-lb:	3315	2750	2260	1840	1480
	arc, inches:		+1.8	0	-8.0	-23.4
Win. 180 Fail Safe	velocity, fps:	2880	2628	2390	2165	1952
	energy, ft-lb:	3316	2762	2284	1873	1523
	arc, inches:		+1.8	0	-7.9	-23.2

.308 Norma Magnum

CARTRIDGE BULLET	RANGE, YARDS:	0	100	200	300	400
Norma 200 Vulkan	velocity, fps:	2903	2624	2361	2114	
	energy, ft-lb:	3744	3058	2476	1985	
	arc, inches:	0	+1.8	0	-8.0	

.300 Winchester Magnum

CARTRIDGE BULLET	RANGE, YARDS:	0	100	200	300	400
A-Square 180 Dead Tough	velocity, fps:	3120	2756	2420	2108	1820
	energy, ft-lb:	3890	3035	2340	1776	1324
	arc, inches:		+1.6	0	-7.6	-22.9

CARTRIDGE BULLET	RANGE, YARDS:	0	100	200	300	400
Federal 150 Sierra Pro Hunt.	velocity, fps:	3280	3030	2800	2570	2360
	energy, ft-lb:	3570	3055	2600	2205	1860
	arc, inches:		+1.1	0	-5.6	-16.4
Federal 150 Trophy Bonded	velocity, fps:	3280	2980	2700	2430	2190
	energy, ft-lb:	3570	2450	2420	1970	1590
	arc, inches:		+1.2	0	-6.0	-17.9
Federal 180 Sierra Pro Hunt.	velocity, fps:	2960	2750	2540	2340	2160
	energy, ft-lb:	3500	3010	2580	2195	1860
	arc, inches:		+1.6	0	-7.0	-20.3
Federal 180 Barnes XLC	velocity, fps:	2960	2780	2600	2430	2260
	energy, ft-lb:	3500	3080	2700	2355	2050
	arc, inches:		+1.5	0	-6.6	-19.2
Federal 180 Trophy Bonded	velocity, fps:	2960	2700	2460	2220	2000
	energy, ft-lb:	3500	2915	2410	1975	1605
	arc, inches:		+1.6	0	-7.4	-21.9
Federal 180 Trophy Bonded HE	velocity, fps:	3100	2830	2580	2340	2110
	energy, ft-lb:	3840	3205	2660	2190	1790
	arc, inches:		+1.4	0	-6.6	-19.7
Federal 180 Nosler Partition	velocity, fps:	2960	2700	2450	2210	1990
	energy, ft-lb:	3500	2905	2395	1955	1585
	arc, inches:		+1.6	0	-7.5	-22.1
Federal 190 Sierra MatchKing BTHP	velocity, fps:	2900	2730	2560	2400	2240
	energy, ft-lb:	3550	3135	2760	2420	2115
	arc, inches:		+12.9	+22.5	+26.9	+25.1
Federal 200 Sierra GameKing BTSP	velocity, fps:	2830	2680	2530	2380	2240
	energy, ft-lb:	3560	3180	2830	2520	2230
	arc, inches:		+1.7	0	-7.1	-20.4
Federal 200 Nosler Part. HE	velocity, fps:	2930	2740	2550	2370	2200
	energy, ft-lb:	3810	3325	2885	2495	2145
	arc, inches:		+1.6	0	-6.9	-20.1
Federal 200 Trophy Bonded	velocity, fps:	2800	2570	2350	2150	1950
	energy, ft-lb:	3480	2935	2460	2050	1690
	arc, inches:		+1.9	0	-8.2	-23.9
Hornady 150 SP boat-tail	velocity, fps:	3275	2988	2718	2464	2224
	energy, ft-lb:	3573	2974	2461	2023	1648
	arc, inches:		+1.2	0	-6.0	-17.8
Hornady 165 SP boat-tail	velocity, fps:	3100	2877	2665	2462	2269
	energy, ft-lb:	3522	3033	2603	2221	1887
	arc, inches:		+1.3	0	-6.5	-18.5
Hornady 180 SP boat-tail	velocity, fps:	2960	2745	2540	2344	2157
	energy, ft-lb:	3501	3011	2578	2196	1859
	arc, inches:		+1.9	0	-7.3	-20.9
Hornady 180 SPBT HM	velocity, fps:	3100	2879	2668	2467	2275
	energy, ft-lb:	3840	3313	2845	2431	2068
	arc, inches:		+1.4	0	-6.4	-18.7
Hornady 190 SP boat-tail	velocity, fps:	2900	2711	2529	2355	2187
	energy, ft-lb:	3549	3101	2699	2340	2018
	arc, inches:		+1.6	0	-7.1	-20.4
Norma 180 Soft Point	velocity, fps:	3018	2780	2555	2341	
	energy, ft-lb:	3641	3091	2610	2190	
	arc, inches:		+1.5	0	-7.0	
Norma 180 Plastic Point	velocity, fps:	3018	2755	2506	2271	
	energy, ft-lb:	3641	3034	2512	2062	
	arc, inches:		+1.6	0	-7.1	
Norma 180 TXP Swift A-Frame	velocity, fps:	2920	2688	2467	2256	
	energy, ft-lb:	3409	2888	2432	2035	
	arc, inches:		+1.7	0	-7.4	

BALLISTICS

Cartridge Bullet	Range, Yards:	0	100	200	300	400
Norma 200 Vulkan	velocity, fps:	2887	2609	2347	2100	
	energy, ft-lb:	3702	3023	2447	1960	
	arc, inches:		+1.8	0	-8.2	
Norma 200 Oryx	velocity, fps:	3018	2755	2506	2271	
	energy, ft-lb:	4046	3371	2791	2292	
	arc, inches:		+1.5	0	-7.0	
PMC 150 Barnes X	velocity, fps:	3135	2918	2712	2515	2327
	energy, ft-lb:	3273	2836	2449	2107	1803
	arc, inches:		+1.3	0	-6.1	-17.7
PMC 150 Pointed Soft Point	velocity, fps:	3150	2902	2665	2438	2222
	energy, ft-lb:	3304	2804	2364	1979	1644
	arc, inches:		+1.3	0	-6.2	-18.3
PMC 150 SP boat-tail	velocity, fps:	3250	2987	2739	2504	2281
	energy, ft-lb:	3517	2970	2498	2088	1733
	arc, inches:		+1.2	0	-6.0	-17.4
PMC 180 Barnes X	velocity, fps:	2910	2738	2572	2412	2258
	energy, ft-lb:	3384	2995	2644	2325	2037
	arc, inches:		+1.6	0	-6.9	-19.8
PMC 180 PSP	velocity, fps:	2853	2643	2446	2258	2077
	energy, ft-lb:	3252	2792	2391	2037	1724
	arc, inches:		+1.7	0	-7.5	-21.9
PMC 180 SP boat-tail	velocity, fps:	2900	2714	2536	2365	2200
	energy, ft-lb:	3361	2944	2571	2235	1935
	arc, inches:		+1.6	0	-7.1	-20.3
Rem. 150 PSP Core-Lokt	velocity, fps:	3290	2951	2636	2342	2068
	energy, ft-lb:	3605	2900	2314	1827	1859
	arc, inches:		+1.6	0	-7.0	-20.2
Rem. 180 PSP Core-Lokt	velocity, fps:	2960	2745	2540	2344	2157
	energy, ft-lb:	3501	3011	2578	2196	1424
	arc, inches:		+2.2	+1.9	-3.4	-15.0
Rem. 180 Nosler Partition	velocity, fps:	2960	2725	2503	2291	2089
	energy, ft-lb:	3501	2968	2503	2087	1744
	arc, inches:		+1.6	0	-7.2	-20.9
Rem. 180 Nosler Bal. Tip	velocity, fps:	2960	2774	2595	2424	2259
	energy, ft-lb:	3501	3075	2692	2348	2039
	arc, inches:		+1.5	0	-6.7	-19.3
Rem. 190 PSP boat-tail	velocity, fps:	2885	2691	2506	2327	2156
	energy, ft-lb:	3511	3055	2648	2285	1961
	arc, inches:		+1.6	0	-7.2	-20.8
Rem. 200 Swift A-Frame	velocity, fps:	2825	2595	2376	2167	1970
	energy, ft-lb:	3544	2989	2506	2086	1722
	arc, inches:		+1.8	0	-8.0	-23.5
Speeer 180 Grand Slam	velocity, fps:	2950	2735	2530	2334	
	energy, ft-lb:	3478	2989	2558	2176	
	arc, inches:		+1.6	0	-7.0	-20.5
Speer 200 Grand Slam	velocity, fps:	2800	2597	2404	2218	
	energy, ft-lb:	3481	2996	2565	2185	
	arc, inches:		+1.8	0	-7.9	-22.9
Win. 150 Power-Point	velocity, fps:	3290	2951	2636	2342	2068
	energy, ft-lb:	3605	2900	2314	1827	1424
	arc, inches:		+2.6	+2.1	-3.5	-15.4
Win. 150 Fail Safe	velocity, fps:	3260	2943	2647	2370	2110
	energy, ft-lb:	3539	2884	2334	1871	1483
	arc, inches:		+1.3	0	-6.2	-18.7
Win. 165 Fail Safe	velocity, fps:	3120	2807	2515	2242	1985
	energy, ft-lb:	3567	2888	2319	1842	1445
	arc, inches:		+1.5	0	-7.0	-20.0

Cartridge Bullet	Range, Yards:	0	100	200	300	400
Win. 180 Power-Point	velocity, fps:	2960	2745	2540	2344	2157
	energy, ft-lb:	3501	3011	2578	2196	1859
	arc, inches:		+1.9	0	-7.3	-20.9
Win. 180 Power-Point Plus	velocity, fps:	3070	2846	2633	2430	2236
	energy, ft-lb:	3768	3239	2772	2361	1999
	arc, inches:		+1.4	0	-6.4	-18.7
Win. 180 Ballistic Silvertip	velocity, fps:	2950	2764	2586	2415	2250
	energy, ft-lb:	3478	3054	2673	2331	2023
	arc, inches:		+1.5	0	-6.7	-19.4
Win. 180 Fail Safe	velocity, fps:	2960	2732	2514	2307	2110
	energy, ft-lb:	3503	2983	2528	2129	1780
	arc, inches:		+1.6	0	-7.1	-20.7
Win. 180 Partition Gold	velocity, fps:	3070	2859	2657	2464	2280
	energy, ft-lb:	3768	3267	2823	2428	2078
	arc, inches:		+1.4	0	-6.3	-18.3

.300 Winchester Short Magnum

Cartridge Bullet	Range, Yards:	0	100	200	300	400
Win. 150 Bal. Silvertip	velocity, fps:	3300	3061	2834	2619	2414
	energy, ft-lb:	3628	3121	2676	2285	1941
	arc, inches:		+1.1	0	-5.4	-15.9
Win. 180 Fail Safe	velocity, fps:	2970	2741	2524	2317	2120
	energy, ft-lb:	3526	3005	2547	2147	1797
	arc, inches:		+1.6	0	-7.0	-20.5
Win. 180 Power Point	velocity, fps:	2970	2755	2549	2353	2166
	energy, ft-lb:	3526	3034	2598	2214	1875
	arc, inches:		+1.5	0	-6.9	-20.1

.300 Weatherby Magnum

Cartridge Bullet	Range, Yards:	0	100	200	300	400
A-Square 180 Dead Tough	velocity, fps:	3180	2811	2471	2155	1863
	energy, ft-lb:	4041	3158	2440	1856	1387
	arc, inches:		+1.5	0	-7.2	-21.8
A-Square 220 Monolythic Solid	velocity, fps:	2700	2407	2133	1877	1653
	energy, ft-lb:	3561	2830	2223	1721	1334
	arc, inches:		+2.3	0	-9.8	-29.7
Federal 180 Sierra GameKing BTSP	velocity, fps:	3190	3010	2830	2660	2490
	energy, ft-lb:	4065	3610	3195	2820	2480
	arc, inches:		+1.2	0	-5.6	-16.0
Federal 180 Trophy Bonded	velocity, fps:	3190	2950	2720	2500	2290
	energy, ft-lb:	4065	3475	2955	2500	2105
	arc, inches:		+1.3	0	-5.9	-17.5
Federal 180 Trophy Bonded HE	velocity, fps:	3330	3080	2850	2750	2410
	energy, ft-lb:	4430	3795	3235	2750	2320
	arc, inches:		+1.1	0	-5.4	-15.8
Federal 180 Nosler Partition	velocity, fps:	3190	2980	2780	2590	2400
	energy, ft-lb:	4055	3540	3080	2670	2305
	arc, inches:		+1.2	0	-5.7	-16.7
Federal 180 Nosler Partition HE	velocity, fps:	3330	3110	2810	2710	2520
	energy, ft-lb:	4430	3875	3375	2935	2540
	arc, inches:		+1.0	0	-5.2	-15.1
Federal 200 Trophy Bonded	velocity, fps:	2900	2670	2440	2230	2030
	energy, ft-lb:	3735	3150	2645	2200	1820
	arc, inches:		+1.7	0	-7.6	-22.2
Hornady 180 SP	velocity, fps:	3120	2891	2673	2466	2268
	energy, ft-lb:	3890	3340	2856	2430	2055
	arc, inches:		+1.3	0	-6.2	-18.1
Rem. 180 PSP Core-Lokt	velocity, fps:	3120	2866	2627	2400	2184
	energy, ft-lb:	3890	3284	2758	2301	1905
	arc, inches:		+2.4	+2.0	-3.4	-14.9

Cartridge Bullet	Range, Yards:	0	100	200	300	400
Rem. 190 PSP boat-tail	velocity, fps:	3030	2830	2638	2455	2279
	energy, ft-lb:	3873	3378	2936	2542	2190
	arc, inches:		+1.4	0	-6.4	-18.6
Rem. 200 Swift A-Frame	velocity, fps:	2925	2690	2467	2254	2052
	energy, ft-lb:	3799	3213	2701	2256	1870
	arc, inches:		+2.8	+2.3	-3.9	-17.0
Speer 180 Grand Slam	velocity, fps:	3185	2948	2722	2508	
	energy, ft-lb:	4054	3472	2962	2514	
	arc, inches:		+1.3	0	-5.9	-17.4
Wby. 150 Pointed Expanding	velocity, fps:	3540	3225	2932	2657	2399
	energy, ft-lb:	4173	3462	2862	2351	1916
	arc, inches:		+2.6	+3.3	0	-8.2
Wby. 150 Nosler Partition	velocity, fps:	3540	3263	3004	2759	2528
	energy, ft-lb:	4173	3547	3005	2536	2128
	arc, inches:		+2.5	+3.2	0	-7.7
Wby. 165 Pointed Expanding	velocity, fps:	3390	3123	2872	2634	2409
	energy, ft-lb:	4210	3573	3021	2542	2126
	arc, inches:		+2.8	+3.5	0	-8.5
Wby. 165 Nosler Bal. Tip	velocity, fps:	3350	3133	2927	2730	2542
	energy, ft-lb:	4111	3596	3138	2730	2367
	arc, inches:		+2.7	+3.4	0	-8.1
Wby. 180 Pointed Expanding	velocity, fps:	3240	3004	2781	2569	2366
	energy, ft-lb:	4195	3607	3091	2637	2237
	arc, inches:		+3.1	+3.8	0	-9.0
Wby. 180 Barnes X	velocity, fps:	3190	2995	2809	2631	2459
	energy, ft-lb:	4067	3586	3154	2766	2417
	arc, inches:		+3.1	+3.8	0	-8.7
Wby. 180 Nosler Partition	velocity, fps:	3240	3028	2826	2634	2449
	energy, ft-lb:	4195	3665	3193	2772	2396
	arc, inches:		+3.0	+3.7	0	-8.6
Wby. 200 Nosler Partition	velocity, fps:	3060	2860	2668	2485	2308
	energy, ft-lb:	4158	3631	3161	2741	2366
	arc, inches:		+3.5	+4.2	0	-9.8
Wby. 220 RN Expanding	velocity, fps:	2845	2543	2260	1996	1751
	energy, ft-lb:	3954	3158	2495	1946	1497
	arc, inches:		+4.9	+5.9	0	-14.6

.300 Dakota

Cartridge Bullet	Range, Yards:	0	100	200	300	400
Dakota 165 Barnes X	velocity, fps:	3200	2979	2769	2569	2377
	energy, ft-lb:	3751	3251	2809	2417	2070
	arc, inches:		+2.1	+1.8	-3.0	-13.2
Dakota 200 Barnes X	velocity, fps:	3000	2824	2656	2493	2336
	energy, ft-lb:	3996	3542	3131	2760	2423
	arc, inches:		+2.2	+1.5	-4.0	-15.2

.300 Pegasus

Cartridge Bullet	Range, Yards:	0	100	200	300	400
A-Square 180 SP boat-tail	velocity, fps:	3500	3319	3145	2978	2817
	energy, ft-lb:	4896	4401	3953	3544	3172
	arc, inches:		+2.3	+2.9	0	-6.8
A-Square 180 Nosler Part.	velocity, fps:	3500	3295	3100	2913	2734
	energy, ft-lb:	4896	4339	3840	3392	2988
	arc, inches:		+2.3	+3.0	0	-7.1
A-Square 180 Dead Tough	velocity, fps:	3500	3103	2740	2405	2095
	energy, ft-lb:	4896	3848	3001	2312	1753
	arc, inches:		+1.1	0	-5.7	-17.5

.300 Remington Ultra Mag

Cartridge Bullet	Range, Yards:	0	100	200	300	400
Federal 180 Trophy Bonded	velocity, fps:	3250	3000	2770	2550	2340
	energy, ft-lb:	4220	3605	3065	2590	2180
	arc, inches:		+1.2	0	-5.7	-16.8
Rem. 150 Swift Scirocco	velocity, fps:	3450	3208	2980	2762	2556
	energy, ft-lb:	3964	3427	2956	2541	2175
	arc, inches:		+1.7	+1.5	-2.6	-11.2
Rem. 180 Nosler Partition	velocity, fps:	3250	3037	2834	2640	2454
	energy, ft-lb:	4221	3686	3201	2786	2407
	arc, inches:		+2.4	+1.8	-3.0	-12.7
Rem. 180 Swift Scirocco	velocity, fps:	3250	3048	2856	2672	2495
	energy, ft-lb:	4221	3714	3260	2853	2487
	arc, inches:		+2.0	+1.7	-2.8	-12.3
Rem. 180 PSP Core-Lokt	velocity, fps:	3250	2988	2742	2508	2287
	energy, ft-lb:	3517	2974	2503	2095	1741
	arc, inches:		+2.1	+1.8	-3.1	-13.6
Rem. 200 Nosler Partition	velocity, fps:	3025	2826	2636	2454	2279
	energy, ft-lb:	4063	3547	3086	2673	2308
	arc, inches:		+2.4	+2.0	-3.4	-14.6

.30-378 Weatherby Magnum

Cartridge Bullet	Range, Yards:	0	100	200	300	400
Wby. 165 Nosler Bal. Tip	velocity, fps:	3500	3275	3062	2859	2665
	energy, ft-lb:	4488	3930	3435	2995	2603
	arc, inches:		+2.4	+3.0	0	-7.4
Wby. 180 Barnes X	velocity, fps:	3450	3243	3046	2858	2678
	energy, ft-lb:	4757	4204	3709	3264	2865
	arc, inches:		+2.4	+3.1	0	-7.4
Wby. 200 Nosler Partition	velocity, fps:	3160	2955	2759	2572	2392
	energy, ft-lb:	4434	3877	3381	2938	2541
	arc, inches:		+3.2	+3.9	0	-9.1

7.82 (.308) Warbird

Cartridge Bullet	Range, Yards:	0	100	200	300	400
Lazzeroni 150 Nosler Part.	velocity, fps:	3680	3432	3197	2975	2764
	energy, ft-lb:	4512	3923	3406	2949	2546
	arc, inches:		+2.1	+2.7	0	-6.6
Lazzeroni 180 Nosler Partition	velocity, fps:	3425	3220	3026	2839	2661
	energy, ft-lb:	4689	4147	3661	3224	2831
	arc, inches:		+2.5	+3.2	0	-7.5
Lazzeroni 200 Swift A-frame	velocity, fps:	3290	3105	2928	2758	2594
	energy, ft-lb:	4808	4283	3808	3378	2988
	arc, inches:		+2.7	+3.4	0	-7.9

7.65x53 Argentine

Cartridge Bullet	Range, Yards:	0	100	200	300	400
Norma 180 Soft Point	velocity, fps:	2592	2386	2189	2002	
	energy, ft-lb:	2686	2276	1916	1602	
	arc, inches:		+2.3	0	-9.6	

.303 British

Cartridge Bullet	Range, Yards:	0	100	200	300	400
Federal 150 Hi-Shok	velocity, fps:	2690	2440	2210	1980	1780
	energy, ft-lb:	2400	1980	1620	1310	1055
	arc, inches:		+2.2	0	-9.4	-27.6
Federal 180 Sierra Pro-Hunt.	velocity, fps:	2460	2230	2020	1820	1630
	energy, ft-lb:	2420	1995	1625	1315	1060
	arc, inches:		+2.8	0	-11.3	-33.2
Federal 180 Tr. Bonded HE	velocity, fps:	2590	2350	2120	1900	1700
	energy, ft-lb:	2680	2205	1795	1445	1160
	arc, inches:		+2.4	0	-10.0	-30.0

BALLISTICS

CENTERFIRE RIFLE BALLISTICS

.303 British to .338 Winchester Magnum

CARTRIDGE BULLET	RANGE, YARDS:	0	100	200	300	400
Hornady 150 Soft Point	velocity, fps:	2685	2441	2210	1992	1787
	energy, ft-lb:	2401	1984	1627	1321	1064
	arc, inches:		+2.2	0	-9.3	-27.4
Hornady 150 SP LM	velocity, fps:	2830	2570	2325	2094	1884
	energy, ft-lb:	2667	2199	1800	1461	1185
	arc, inches:		+2.0	0	-8.4	-24.6
Norma 150 Soft Point	velocity, fps:	2723	2438	2170	1920	
	energy, ft-lb:	2470	1980	1569	1228	
	arc, inches:		+2.2	0	-9.6	
PMC 180 SP boat-tail	velocity, fps:	2450	2276	2110	1951	1799
	energy, ft-lb:	2399	2071	1779	1521	1294
	arc, inches:		+2.6	0	-10.4	-30.1
Rem. 180 SP Core-Lokt	velocity, fps:	2460	2124	1817	1542	1311
	energy, ft-lb:	2418	1803	1319	950	687
	arc, inches, s:	0	-5.8	-23.3		
Win. 180 Power-Point	velocity, fps:	2460	2233	2018	1816	1629
	energy, ft-lb:	2418	1993	1627	1318	1060
	arc, inches, s:	0	-6.1	-20.8		

7.7x58 Japanese Arisaka

CARTRIDGE BULLET	RANGE, YARDS:	0	100	200	300	400
Norma 180 Soft Point	velocity, fps:	2493	2291	2099	1916	
	energy, ft-lb:	2485	2099	1761	1468	
	arc, inches:		+2.6	0	-10.5	

.32-20 Winchester

CARTRIDGE BULLET	RANGE, YARDS:	0	100	200	300	400
Rem. 100 Lead	velocity, fps:	1210	1021	913	834	769
	energy, ft-lb:	325	231	185	154	131
	arc, inches:		0	-31.6	-104.7	
Win. 100 Lead	velocity, fps:	1210	1021	913	834	769
	energy, ft-lb:	325	231	185	154	131
	arc, inches:		0	-32.3	-106.3	

.32 Winchester Special

CARTRIDGE BULLET	RANGE, YARDS:	0	100	200	300	400
Federal 170 Hi-Shok	velocity, fps:	2250	1920	1630	1370	1180
	energy, ft-lb:	1910	1395	1000	710	520
	arc, inches:		0	-8.0	-29.2	
Rem. 170 SP Core-Lokt	velocity, fps:	2250	1921	1626	1372	1175
	energy, ft-lb:	1911	1393	998	710	521
	arc, inches:		0	-8.0	-29.3	
Win. 170 Power-Point	velocity, fps:	2250	1870	1537	1267	1082
	energy, ft-lb:	1911	1320	892	606	442
	arc, inches:		0	-9.2	-33.2	

8mm Mauser (8x57)

CARTRIDGE BULLET	RANGE, YARDS:	0	100	200	300	400
Federal 170 Hi-Shok	velocity, fps:	2360	1970	1620	1330	1120
	energy, ft-lb:	2100	1465	995	670	475
	arc, inches:		0	-7.6	-28.5	
Norma 196 Alaska	velocity, fps:	2395	2112	1850	1611	
	energy, ft-lb:	2714	2190	1754	1399	
	Arc, inches:		0	-6.3	-22.9	
Norma 196 Soft Point (JS)	velocity, fps:	2526	2244	1981	1737	
	energy, ft-lb:	2778	2192	1708	1314	
	arc, inches:		+2.7	0	-11.6	
Norma 196 Vulkan (JS)	velocity, fps:	2526	2276	2041	1821	
	energy, ft-lb:	2778	2256	1813	1443	
	arc, inches:		+2.6	0	-11.0	
PMC 170 Pointed Soft Point	velocity, fps:	2360	1969	1622	1333	1123
	energy, ft-lb:	2102	1463	993	671	476
	arc, inches:		+1.8	-4.5	-24.3	-63.8

CARTRIDGE BULLET	RANGE, YARDS:	0	100	200	300	400
Rem. 170 SP Core-Lokt	velocity, fps:	2360	1969	1622	1333	1123
	energy, ft-lb:	2102	1463	993	671	476
	arc, inches:		0	-7.6	-28.6	
Win. 170 Power-Point	velocity, fps:	2360	1969	1622	1333	1123
	energy, ft-lb:	2102	1463	993	671	476
	arc, inches:		0	-8.2	-29.8	

8mm Remington Magnum

CARTRIDGE BULLET	RANGE, YARDS:	0	100	200	300	400
A-Square 220 Monolithic Solid	velocity, fps:	2800	2501	2221	1959	1718
	energy, ft-lb:	3829	3055	2409	1875	1442
	arc, inches:		+2.1	0	-9.1	-27.6
Rem. 200 Swift A-Frame	velocity, fps:	2900	2623	2361	2115	1885
	energy, ft-lb:	3734	3054	2476	1987	1577
	arc, inches:		+1.8	0	-8.0	-23.9

.338-06

CARTRIDGE BULLET	RANGE, YARDS:	0	100	200	300	400
A-Square 200 Nos. Bal. Tip	velocity, fps:	2750	2553	2364	2184	2011
	energy, ft-lb:	3358	2894	2482	2118	1796
	arc, inches:		+1.9	0	-8.2	-23.6
A-Square 250 SP boat-tail	velocity, fps:	2500	2374	2252	2134	2019
	energy, ft-lb:	3496	3129	2816	2528	2263
	arc, inches:		+2.4	0	-9.3	-26.0
A-Square 250 Dead Tough	velocity, fps:	2500	2222	1963	1724	1507
	energy, ft-lb:	3496	2742	2139	1649	1261
	arc, inches:		+2.8	0	-11.9	-35.5

.338 Winchester Magnum

CARTRIDGE BULLET	RANGE, YARDS:	0	100	200	300	400
A-Square 250 SP boat-tail	velocity, fps:	2700	2568	2439	2314	2193
	energy, ft-lb:	4046	3659	3302	2972	2669
	arc, inches:		+4.4	+5.2	0	-11.7
A-Square 250 Triad	velocity, fps:	2700	2407	2133	1877	1653
	energy, ft-lb:	4046	3216	2526	1956	1516
	arc, inches:		+2.3	0	-9.8	-29.8
Federal 210 Nosler Partition	velocity, fps:	2830	2600	2390	2180	1980
	energy, ft-lb:	3735	3160	2655	2215	1835
	arc, inches:		+1.8	0	-8.0	-23.3
Federal 225 Sierra Pro-Hunt.	velocity, fps:	2780	2570	2360	2170	1980
	energy, ft-lb:	3860	3290	2780	2340	1960
	arc, inches:		+1.9	0	-8.2	-23.7
Federal 225 Trophy Bonded	velocity, fps:	2800	2560	2330	2110	1900
	energy, ft-lb:	3915	3265	2700	2220	1800
	arc, inches:		+1.9	0	-8.4	-24.5
Federal 225 Trophy Bonded HE	velocity, fps:	2940	2690	2450	2230	2010
	energy, ft-lb:	4320	3610	3000	2475	2025
	arc, inches:		+1.7	0	-7.5	-22.0
Federal 225 Barnes XLC	velocity, fps:	2800	2610	2430	2260	2090
	energy, ft-lb:	3915	3405	2950	2545	2190
	arc, inches:		+1.8	0	-7.7	-22.2
Federal 250 Nosler Partition	velocity, fps:	2660	2470	2300	2120	1960
	energy, ft-lb:	3925	3395	2925	2505	2130
	arc, inches:		+2.1	0	-8.8	-25.1
Federal 250 Nosler Part HE	velocity, fps:	2800	2610	2420	2230	2080
	energy, ft-lb:	4350	3775	3260	2805	2395
	arc, inches:		+1.8	0	-7.8	-22.5
Hornady 225 Soft Point HM	velocity, fps:	2920	2678	2449	2232	2027
	energy, ft-lb:	4259	3583	2996	2489	2053
	arc, inches:		+1.8	0	-7.6	-22.0
Norma 250 Nosler Partition	velocity, fps:	2657	2470	2290	2118	
	energy, ft-lb:	3920	3387	2912	2490	
	arc, inches:		+2.1	0	-8.7	

CARTRIDGE BULLET	RANGE, YARDS:	0	100	200	300	400
PMC 225 Barnes X	velocity, fps:	2780	2619	2464	2313	2168
	energy, ft-lb:	3860	3426	3032	2673	2348
	arc, inches:		+1.8	0	-7.6	-21.6
Rem. 200 Nosler Bal. Tip	velocity, fps:	2950	2724	2509	2303	2108
	energy, ft-lb:	3866	3295	2795	2357	1973
	arc, inches:		+1.6	0	-7.1	-20.8
Rem. 210 Nosler Partition	velocity, fps:	2830	2602	2385	2179	1983
	energy, ft-lb:	3734	3157	2653	2214	1834
	arc, inches:		+1.8	0	-7.9	-23.2
Rem. 225 PSP Core-Lokt	velocity, fps:	2780	2572	2374	2184	2003
	energy, ft-lb:	3860	3305	2815	2383	2004
	arc, inches:		+1.9	0	-8.1	-23.4
Rem. 225 Swift A-Frame	velocity, fps:	2785	2517	2266	2029	1808
	energy, ft-lb:	3871	3165	2565	2057	1633
	arc, inches:		+2.0	0	-8.8	-25.2
Rem. 250 PSP Core-Lokt	velocity, fps:	2660	2456	2261	2075	1898
	energy, ft-lb:	3927	3348	2837	2389	1999
	arc, inches:		+2.1	0	-8.9	-26.0
Speer 250 Grand Slam	velocity, fps:	2645	2442	2247	2062	
	energy, ft-lb:	3883	3309	2803	2360	
	arc, inches:		+2.2	0	-9.1	-26.2
Win. 200 Power-Point	velocity, fps:	2960	2658	2375	2110	1862
	energy, ft-lb:	3890	3137	2505	1977	1539
	arc, inches:		+2.0	0	-8.2	-24.3
Win. 200 Ballistic Silvertip	velocity, fps:	2950	2724	2509	2303	2108
	energy, ft-lb:	3864	3294	2794	2355	1972
	arc, inches:		+1.6	0	-7.1	-20.8
Win. 230 Fail Safe	velocity, fps:	2780	2573	2375	2186	2005
	energy, ft-lb:	3948	3382	2881	2441	2054
	arc, inches:		+1.9	0	-8.1	-23.4
Win. 250 Partition Gold	velocity, fps:	2650	2467	2291	2122	1960
	energy, ft-lb:	3899	3378	2914	2520	2134
	arc, inches:		+2.1	0	-8.7	-25.2

.340 Weatherby Magnum

CARTRIDGE BULLET	RANGE, YARDS:	0	100	200	300	400
A-Square 250 SP boat-tail	velocity, fps:	2820	2684	2552	2424	2299
	energy, ft-lb:	4414	3999	3615	3261	2935
	arc, inches:		+4.0	+4.6	0	-10.6
A-Square 250 Triad	velocity, fps:	2820	2520	2238	1976	1741
	energy, ft-lb:	4414	3524	2781	2166	1683
	arc, inches:		+2.0	0	-9.0	-26.8
Federal 225 Trophy Bonded	velocity, fps:	3100	2840	2600	2370	2150
	energy, ft-lb:	4800	4035	3375	2800	2310
	arc, inches:		+1.4	0	-6.5	-19.4
Wby. 200 Pointed Expanding	velocity, fps:	3221	2946	2688	2444	2213
	energy, ft-lb:	4607	3854	3208	2652	2174
	arc, inches:		+3.3	+4.0	0	-9.9
Wby. 200 Nosler Bal. Tip	velocity, fps:	3221	2980	2753	2536	2329
	energy, ft-lb:	4607	3944	3364	2856	2409
	arc, inches:		+3.1	+3.9	0	-9.2
Wby. 210 Nosler Partition	velocity, fps:	3211	2963	2728	2505	2293
	energy, ft-lb:	4807	4093	3470	2927	2452
	arc, inches:		+3.2	+3.9	0	-9.5
Wby. 225 Pointed Expanding	velocity, fps:	3066	2824	2595	2377	2170
	energy, ft-lb:	4696	3984	3364	2822	2352
	arc, inches:		+3.6	+4.4	0	-10.7
Wby. 225 Barnes X	velocity, fps:	3001	2804	2615	2434	2260
	energy, ft-lb:	4499	3927	3416	2959	2551
	arc, inches:		+3.6	+4.3	0	-10.3

CARTRIDGE BULLET	RANGE, YARDS:	0	100	200	300	400
Wby. 250 Pointed Expanding	velocity, fps:	2963	2745	2537	2338	2149
	energy, ft-lb:	4873	4182	3572	3035	2563
	arc, inches:		+3.9	+4.6	0	-11.1
Wby. 250 Nosler Partition	velocity, fps:	2941	2743	2553	2371	2197
	energy, ft-lb:	4801	4176	3618	3120	2678
	arc, inches:		+3.9	+4.6	0	-10.9

.330 Dakota

CARTRIDGE BULLET	RANGE, YARDS:	0	100	200	300	400
Dakota 200 Barnes X	velocity, fps:	3200	2971	2754	2548	2350
	energy, ft-lb:	4547	3920	3369	2882	2452
	arc, inches:		+2.1	+1.8	-3.1	-13.4
Dakota 250 Barnes X	velocity, fps:	2900	2719	2545	2378	2217
	energy, ft-lb:	4668	4103	3595	3138	2727
	arc, inches:		+2.3	+1.3	-5.0	-17.5

.338 Remington Ultra Mag

CARTRIDGE BULLET	RANGE, YARDS:	0	100	200	300	400
Federal 250 Trophy Bonded	velocity, fps:	2860	2630	2420	2210	2020
	energy, ft-lb:	4540	3850	3245	2715	2260
	arc, inches:		+0.8	0	-7.7	-22.6
Rem. 250 Swift A-Frame	velocity, fps:	2860	2645	2440	2244	2057
	energy, ft-lb:	4540	3882	3303	2794	2347
	arc, inches:		+1.7	0	-7.6	-22.1
Rem. 250 PSP Core-Lokt	velocity, fps:	2860	2647	2443	2249	2064
	energy, ft-lb:	4540	3888	3314	2807	2363
	arc, inches:		+1.7	0	-7.6	-22.0

.338-378 Weatherby Magnum

CARTRIDGE BULLET	RANGE, YARDS:	0	100	200	300	400
Mag. Wby. 200 Nosler Bal. Tip	velocity, fps:	3350	3102	2868	2646	2434
	energy, ft-lb:	4983	4273	3652	3109	2631
	arc, inches:	0	+2.8	+3.5	0	-8.4
Wby. 225 Barnes X	velocity, fps:	3180	2974	2778	2591	2410
	energy, ft-lb:	5052	4420	3856	3353	2902
	arc, inches:	0	+3.1	+3.8	0	-8.9
Wby. 250 Nosler Partition	velocity, fps:	3060	2856	2662	2475	2297
	energy, ft-lb:	5197	4528	3933	3401	2927
	arc, inches:	0	+3.5	+4.2	0	-9.8

8.59 (.338) Titan

CARTRIDGE BULLET	RANGE, YARDS:	0	100	200	300	400
Lazzeroni 200 Nos. Bal. Tip	velocity, fps:	3430	3211	3002	2803	2613
	energy, ft-lb:	5226	4579	4004	3491	3033
	arc, inches:		+2.5	+3.2	0	-7.6
Lazzeroni 225 Nos. Partition	velocity, fps:	3235	3031	2836	2650	2471
	energy, ft-lb:	5229	4591	4021	3510	3052
	arc, inches:		+3.0	+3.6	0	-8.6
Lazzeroni 250 Swift A-Frame	velocity, fps:	3100	2908	2725	2549	2379
	energy, ft-lb:	5336	4697	4123	3607	3143
	arc, inches:		+3.3	+4.0	0	-9.3

.338 A-Square

CARTRIDGE BULLET	RANGE, YARDS:	0	100	200	300	400
A-Square 200 Nos. Bal. Tip	velocity, fps:	3500	3266	3045	2835	2634
	energy, ft-lb:	5440	4737	4117	3568	3081
	arc, inches:		+2.4	+3.1	0	-7.5
A-Square 250 SP boat-tail	velocity, fps:	3120	2974	2834	2697	2565
	energy, ft-lb:	5403	4911	4457	4038	3652
	arc, inches:		+3.1	+3.7	0	-8.5
A-Square 250 Triad	velocity, fps:	3120	2799	2500	2220	1958
	energy, ft-lb:	5403	4348	3469	2736	2128
	arc, inches:		+1.5	0	-7.1	-20.4

BALLISTICS

.338 Excaliber

CARTRIDGE BULLET	RANGE, YARDS:	0	100	200	300	400
A-Square 200 Nos. Bal. Tip	velocity, fps:	3600	3361	3134	2920	2715
	energy, ft-lb:	5755	5015	4363	3785	3274
	arc, inches:		+2.2	+2.9	0	-6.7
A-Square 250 SP boat-tail	velocity, fps:	3250	3101	2958	2684	2553
	energy, ft-lb:	5863	5339	4855	4410	3998
	arc, inches:		+2.7	+3.4	0	-7.8
A-Square 250 Triad	velocity, fps:	3250	2922	2618	2333	2066
	energy, ft-lb:	5863	4740	3804	3021	2370
	arc, inches:		+1.3	0	-6.4	-19.2

.348 Winchester

CARTRIDGE BULLET	RANGE, YARDS:	0	100	200	300	400
Win. 200 Silvertip	velocity, fps:	2520	2215	1931	1672	1443
	energy, ft-lb:	2820	2178	1656	1241	925
	arc, inches:		0	-6.2	-21.9	

.357 Magnum

CARTRIDGE BULLET	RANGE, YARDS:	0	100	200	300	400
Federal 180 Hi-Shok HP Hollow Point	velocity, fps:	1550	1160	980	860	770
	energy, ft-lb:	960	535	385	295	235
	arc, inches:		0	-22.8	-77.9	-173.8
Win. 158 Jacketed SP	velocity, fps:	1830	1427	1138	980	883
	energy, ft-lb:	1175	715	454	337	274
	arc, inches:		0	-16.2	-57.0	-128.3

.35 Remington

CARTRIDGE BULLET	RANGE, YARDS:	0	100	200	300	400
Federal 200 Hi-Shok	velocity, fps:	2080	1700	1380	1140	1000
	energy, ft-lb:	1920	1280	840	575	445
	arc, inches:		0	-10.7	-39.3	
Rem. 150 PSP Core-Lokt	velocity, fps:	2300	1874	1506	1218	1039
	energy, ft-lb:	1762	1169	755	494	359
	arc, inches:		0	-8.6	-32.6	
Rem. 200 SP Core-Lokt	velocity, fps:	2080	1698	1376	1140	1001
	energy, ft-lb:	1921	1280	841	577	445
	arc, inches:		0	-10.7	-40.1	
Win. 200 Power-Point	velocity, fps:	2020	1646	1335	1114	985
	energy, ft-lb:	1812	1203	791	551	431
	arc, inches:		0	-12.1	-43.9	

.356 Winchester

CARTRIDGE BULLET	RANGE, YARDS:	0	100	200	300	400
Win. 200 Power-Point	velocity, fps:	2460	2114	1797	1517	1284
	energy, ft-lb:	2688	1985	1434	1022	732
	arc, inches:		+1.6	-3.8	-20.1	-51.2

.358 Winchester

CARTRIDGE BULLET	RANGE, YARDS:	0	100	200	300	400
Win. 200 Silvertip	velocity, fps:	2490	2171	1876	1610	1379
	energy, ft-lb:	2753	2093	1563	1151	844
	arc, inches:		+1.5	-3.6	-18.6	-47.2

.35 Whelen

CARTRIDGE BULLET	RANGE, YARDS:	0	100	200	300	400
Federal 225 Trophy Bonded	velocity, fps:	2600	2400	2200	2020	1840
	energy, ft-lb:	3375	2865	2520	2030	1690
	arc, inches:		+2.3	0	-9.4	-27.3
Rem. 200 Pointed Soft Point	velocity, fps:	2675	2378	2100	1842	1606
	energy, ft-lb:	3177	2510	1958	1506	1145
	arc, inches:		+2.3	0	-10.3	-30.8
Rem. 250 Pointed Soft Point	velocity, fps:	2400	2197	2005	1823	1652
	energy, ft-lb:	3197	2680	2230	1844	1515
	arc, inches:		+1.3	-3.2	-16.6	-40.0

.358 Norma Magnum

CARTRIDGE BULLET	RANGE, YARDS:	0	100	200	300	400
A-Square 275 Triad	velocity, fps:	2700	2394	2108	1842	1653
	energy, ft-lb:	4451	3498	2713	2072	1668
	arc, inches:		+2.3	0	-10.1	-29.8
Norma 250 Woodleigh	velocity, fps:	2799	2442	2112	1810	
	energy, ft-lb:	4350	3312	2478	1819	
	arc, inches:		+2.2	0	-10.0	

.358 STA

CARTRIDGE BULLET	RANGE, YARDS:	0	100	200	300	400
A-Square 275 Triad	velocity, fps:	2850	2562	2292	2039	1764
	energy, ft-lb:	4959	4009	3208	2539	1899
	arc, inches:		+1.9	0	-8.6	-26.1

9.3x57

CARTRIDGE BULLET	RANGE, YARDS:	0	100	200	300	400
Norma 232 Vulkan	velocity, fps:	2329	2031	1757	1512	
	energy, ft-lb:	2795	2126	1591	1178	
	arc, inches:		+3.5	0	-14.9	
Norma 286 Alaska	velocity, fps:	2067	1857	1662	1484	
	energy, ft-lb:	2714	2190	1754	1399	
	arc, inches:		+4.3	0	-17.0	

9.3x62

CARTRIDGE BULLET	RANGE, YARDS:	0	100	200	300	400
A-Square 286 Triad	velocity, fps:	2360	2089	1844	1623	1369
	energy, ft-lb:	3538	2771	2157	1670	1189
	arc, inches:		+3.0	0	-13.1	-42.2
Norma 232 Vulkan	velocity, fps:	2625	2327	2049	1792	
	energy, ft-lb:	3551	2791	2164	1655	
	arc, inches:		+2.5	0	-10.8	
Norma 232 Oryx	velocity, fps:	2625	2294	1988	1708	
	energy, ft-lb:	3535	2700	2028	1497	
	arc, inches:		+2.5	0	-11.4	
Norma 286 Plastic Point	velocity, fps:	2362	2141	1931	1736	
	energy, ft-lb:	3544	2911	2370	1914	
	arc, inches:		+3.1	0	-12.4	
Norma 286 Alaska	velocity, fps:	2362	2135	1920	1720	
	energy, ft-lb:	3544	2894	2342	1879	
	arc, inches:		+3.1	0	-12.5	

9.3x64

CARTRIDGE BULLET	RANGE, YARDS:	0	100	200	300	400
A-Square 286 Triad	velocity, fps:	2700	2391	2103	1835	1602
	energy, ft-lb:	4629	3630	2808	2139	1631
	arc, inches:		+2.3	0	-10.1	-30.8

9.3x74 R

CARTRIDGE BULLET	RANGE, YARDS:	0	100	200	300	400
A-Square 286 Triad	velocity, fps:	2360	2089	1844	1623	
	energy, ft-lb:	3538	2771	2157	1670	
	arc, inches:		+3.6	0	-14.0	
Norma 232 Vulkan	velocity, fps:	2625	2327	2049	1792	
	energy, ft-lb:	3551	2791	2164	1655	
	arc, inches:		+2.5	0	-10.8	
Norma 232 Oryx	velocity, fps:	2526	2191	1883	1605	
	energy, ft-lb:	3274	2463	1819	1322	
	arc, inches:		+2.9	0	-12.8	
Norma 286 Alaska	velocity, fps:	2362	2135	1920	1720	
	energy, ft-lb:	3544	2894	2342	1879	
	arc, inches:		+3.1	0	-12.5	
Norma 286 Plastic Point	velocity, fps:	2362	2135	1920	1720	
	energy, ft-lb:	3544	2894	2342	1879	
	arc, inches:		+3.1	0	-12.5	

.375 Winchester

Cartridge / Bullet		0	100	200	300	400
Win. 200 Power-Point	velocity, fps:	2200	1841	1526	1268	1089
	energy, ft-lb:	2150	1506	1034	714	
	arc, inches:		0	-9.5	-33.8	

.375 H&H Magnum

Cartridge / Bullet		0	100	200	300	400
A-Square 300 SP boat-tail	velocity, fps:	2550	2415	2284	2157	2034
	energy, ft-lb:	4331	3884	3474	3098	2755
	arc, inches:		+5.2	+6.0	0	-13.3
A-Square 300 Triad	velocity, fps:	2550	2251	1973	1717	1496
	energy, ft-lb:	4331	3375	2592	1964	1491
	arc, inches:		+2.7	0	-11.7	-35.1
Federal 250 Trophy Bonded	velocity, fps:	2670	2360	2080	1820	1580
	energy, ft-lb:	3955	3100	2400	1830	1380
	arc, inches:		+2.4	0	-10.4	-31.7
Federal 270 Hi-Shok	velocity, fps:	2690	2420	2170	1920	1700
	energy, ft-lb:	4340	3510	2810	2220	1740
	arc, inches:		+2.4	0	-10.9	-33.3
Federal 300 Hi-Shok	velocity, fps:	2530	2270	2020	1790	1580
	energy, ft-lb:	4265	3425	2720	2135	1665
	arc, inches:		+2.6	0	-11.2	-33.3
Federal 300 Nosler Partition	velocity, fps:	2530	2320	2120	1930	1750
	energy, ft-lb:	4265	3585	2995	2475	2040
	arc, inches:		+2.5	0	-10.3	-29.9
Federal 300 Trophy Bonded	velocity, fps:	2530	2280	2040	1810	1610
	energy, ft-lb:	4265	3450	2765	2190	1725
	arc, inches:		+2.6	0	-10.9	-32.8
Federal 300 Trophy Bonded HE	velocity, fps:	2700	2440	2190	1960	1740
	energy, ft-lb:	4855	3960	3195	2550	2020
	arc, inches:		+2.2	0	-9.4	-28.0
Fed. 300 Trophy Bonded Sledgehammer Solid	velocity, fps:	2530	2160	1820	1520	1280
	energy, ft-lb:	4265	3105	2210	1550	1090
	arc, inches, s:		0	-6.0	-22.7	-54.6
Hornady 270 SP HM	velocity, fps:	2870	2620	2385	2162	1957
	energy, ft-lb:	4937	4116	3408	2802	2296
	arc, inches:		+2.2	0	-8.4	-23.9
Hornady 300 FMJ RN HM	velocity, fps:	2705	2376	2072	1804	1560
	energy, ft-lb:	4873	3760	2861	2167	1621
	arc, inches:		+2.7	0	-10.8	-32.1
Norma 300 Soft Point	velocity, fps:	2549	2211	1900	1619	
	energy, ft-lb:	4329	3258	2406	1747	
	arc, inches:		+2.8	0	-12.6	
Norma 300 TXP Swift A-Frame	velocity, fps:	2559	2296	2049	1818	
	energy, ft-lb:	4363	3513	2798	2203	
	arc, inches:		+2.6	0	-10.9	
PMC 270 PSP	velocity, fps:	2650	2414	2192	1984	1788
	energy, ft-lb:	4210	3495	2882	2359	1917
	arc, inches:		+2.2	0	-9.5	-27.9
PMC 270 Barnes X	velocity, fps:	2690	2528	2372	2221	2076
	energy, ft-lb:	4337	3831	3371	2957	2582
	arc, inches:		+2.0	0	-8.2	-23.4
PMC 300 Barnes X	velocity, fps:	2530	2389	2252	2120	1993
	energy, ft-lb:	4263	3801	3378	2994	2644
	arc, inches:		+2.3	0	-9.2	-26.1
Rem. 270 Soft Point	velocity, fps:	2690	2420	2166	1928	1707
	energy, ft-lb:	4337	3510	2812	2228	1747
	arc, inches:		+2.2	0	-9.7	-28.7

(continued)

Cartridge / Bullet		0	100	200	300	400
Rem. 300 Swift A-Frame	velocity, fps:	2530	2245	1979	1733	1512
	energy, ft-lb:	4262	3357	2608	2001	1523
	arc, inches:		+2.7	0	-11.7	-35.0
Speer 285 Grand Slam	velocity, fps:	2610	2365	2134	1916	
	energy, ft-lb:	4310	3540	2883	2323	
	arc, inches:		+2.4	0	-9.9	
Speer 300 African GS Tungsten Solid	velocity, fps:	2609	2277	1970	1690	
	energy, ft-lb:	4534	3453	2585	1903	
	arc, inches:		+2.6	0	-11.7	-35.6
Win. 270 Fail Safe	velocity, fps:	2670	2447	2234	2033	1842
	energy, ft-lb:	4275	3590	2994	2478	2035
	arc, inches:		+2.2	0	-9.1	-28.7
Win. 300 Fail Safe	velocity, fps:	2530	2336	2151	1974	1806
	energy, ft-lb:	4265	3636	3082	2596	2173
	arc, inches:		+2.4	0	-10.0	-26.9

.375 Dakota

Cartridge / Bullet		0	100	200	300	400
Dakota 270 Barnes X	velocity, fps:	2800	2617	2441	2272	2109
	energy, ft-lb:	4699	4104	3571	3093	2666
	arc, inches:		+2.3	+1.0	-6.1	-19.9
Dakota 300 Barnes X	velocity, fps:	2600	2316	2051	1804	1579
	energy, ft-lb:	4502	3573	2800	2167	1661
	arc, inches:		+2.4	-0.1	-11.0	-32.7

.375 Weatherby Magnum

Cartridge / Bullet		0	100	200	300	400
A-Square 300 SP boat-tail	velocity, fps:	2700	2560	2425	2293	2166
	energy, ft-lb:	4856	4366	3916	3503	3125
	arc, inches:		+4.5	+5.2	0	-11.9
A-Square 300 Triad	velocity, fps:	2700	2391	2103	1835	1602
	energy, ft-lb:	4856	3808	2946	2243	1710
	arc, inches:		+2.3	0	-10.1	-30.8

.375 JRS

Cartridge / Bullet		0	100	200	300	400
A-Square 300 SP boat-tail	velocity, fps:	2700	2560	2425	2293	2166
	energy, ft-lb:	4856	4366	3916	3503	3125
	arc, inches:		+4.5	+5.2	0	-11.9
A-Square 300 Triad	velocity, fps:	2700	2391	2103	1835	1602
	energy, ft-lb:	4856	3808	2946	2243	1710
	arc, inches:		+2.3	0	-10.1	-30.8

.375 Remington Ultra Mag

Cartridge / Bullet		0	100	200	300	400
Rem. 270 Soft Point	velocity, fps:	2900	2558	2241	1947	1678
	energy, fps:	5041	3922	3010	2272	1689
	arc, inches:		+1.9	0	-9.2	-27.7
Rem. 300 Swift A-Frame	velocity, fps:	2760	2505	2263	2035	1822
	energy, fps:	5073	4178	3412	2759	2210
	arc, inches:		+2.0	0	-8.8	-26.1

.375 A-Square

Cartridge / Bullet		0	100	200	300	400
A-Square 300 SP boat-tail	velocity, fps:	2920	2773	2631	2494	2360
	energy, ft-lb:	5679	5123	4611	4142	3710
	arc, inches:		+3.7	+4.4	0	-9.8
A-Square 300 Triad	velocity, fps:	2920	2596	2294	2012	1762
	energy, ft-lb:	5679	4488	3505	2698	2068
	arc, inches:		+1.8	0	-8.5	-25.5

BALLISTICS

CARTRIDGE BULLET	RANGE, YARDS:	0	100	200	300	400
.378 Weatherby Magnum						
A-Square 300 SP boat-tail	velocity, fps:	2900	2754	2612	2475	2342
	energy, ft-lb:	5602	5051	4546	4081	3655
	arc, inches:		+3.8	+4.4	0	-10.0
A-Square 300 Triad	velocity, fps:	2900	2577	2276	1997	1747
	energy, ft-lb:	5602	4424	3452	2656	2034
	arc, inches:		+1.9	0	-8.7	-25.9
Wby. 270 Pointed Expanding	velocity, fps:	3180	2921	2677	2445	2225
	energy, ft-lb:	6062	5115	4295	3583	2968
	arc, inches:		+1.3	0	-6.1	-18.1
Wby. 270 Barnes X	velocity, fps:	3150	2954	2767	2587	2415
	energy, ft-lb:	5948	5232	4589	4013	3495
	arc, inches:		+1.2	0	-5.8	-16.7
Wby. 300 RN Expanding	velocity, fps:	2925	2558	2220	1908	1627
	energy, ft-lb:	5699	4360	3283	2424	1764
	arc, inches:		+1.9	0	-9.0	-27.8
Wby. 300 FMJ	velocity, fps:	2925	2591	2280	1991	1725
	energy, ft-lb:	5699	4470	3461	2640	1983
	arc, inches:		+1.8	0	-8.6	-26.1
.38-40 Winchester						
Win. 180 Soft Point	velocity, fps:	1160	999	901	827	
	energy, ft-lb:	538	399	324	273	
	arc, inches:		0	-23.4	-75.2	
.38-55 Winchester						
Win. 255 Soft Point	velocity, fps:	1320	1190	1091	1018	
	energy, ft-lb:	987	802	674	587	
	arc, inches:		0	-33.9	-110.6	
.450/.400 (3")						
A-Square 400 Triad	velocity, fps:	2150	1910	1690	1490	
	energy, ft-lb:	4105	3241	2537	1972	
	arc, inches:		+4.4	0	-16.5	
.450/.400 (3 1/4")						
A-Square 400 Triad	velocity, fps:	2150	1910	1690	1490	
	energy, ft-lb:	4105	3241	2537	1972	
	arc, inches:		+4.4	0	-16.5	
.404 Jeffery						
A-Square 400 Triad	velocity, fps:	2150	1901	1674	1468	1299
	energy, ft-lb:	4105	3211	2489	1915	1499
	arc, inches:		+4.1	0	-16.4	-49.1
.416 Taylor						
A-Square 400 Triad	velocity, fps:	2350	2093	1853	1634	1443
	energy, ft-lb:	4905	3892	3049	2371	1849
	arc, inches:		+3.2	0	-13.6	-39.8
.416 Hoffman						
A-Square 400 Triad	velocity, fps:	2380	2122	1879	1658	1464
	energy, ft-lb:	5031	3998	3136	2440	1903
	arc, inches:		+3.1	0	-13.1	-38.7

CARTRIDGE BULLET	RANGE, YARDS:	0	100	200	300	400
.416 Remington Magnum						
A-Square 400 Triad	velocity, fps:	2380	2122	1879	1658	1464
	energy, ft-lb:	5031	3998	3136	2440	1903
	arc, inches:		+3.1	0	-13.2	-38.7
Fed. 400 Trophy Bonded Sledgehammer Solid	velocity, fps:	2400	2150	1920	1700	1500
	energy, ft-lb:	5115	4110	3260	2565	2005
	arc, inches:		0	-6.0	-21.6	-49.2
Federal 400 Trophy Bonded	velocity, fps:	2400	2180	1970	1770	1590
	energy, ft-lb:	5115	4215	3440	2785	2245
	arc, inches:		0	-5.8	-20.6	-46.9
Rem. 400 Swift A-Frame	velocity, fps:	2400	2175	1962	1763	1579
	energy, ft-lb:	5115	4201	3419	2760	2214
	arc, inches:		0	-5.9	-20.8	
.416 Rigby						
A-Square 400 Triad	velocity, fps:	2400	2140	1897	1673	1478
	energy, ft-lb:	5115	4069	3194	2487	1940
	arc, inches:		+3.0	0	-12.9	-38.0
Federal 400 Trophy Bonded	velocity, fps:	2370	2150	1940	1750	1570
	energy, ft-lb:	4990	4110	3350	2715	2190
	arc, inches:		0	-6.0	-21.3	-48.1
Fed. 400 Trophy Bonded Sledgehammer Solid	velocity, fps:	2370	2120	1890	1660	1460
	energy, ft-lb:	4990	3975	3130	2440	1895
	arc, inches:		0	-6.3	-22.5	-51.5
Federal 410 Woodleigh Weldcore	velocity, fps:	2370	2110	1870	1640	1440
	energy, ft-lb:	5115	4050	3165	2455	1895
	arc, inches:		0	-7.4	-24.8	-55.0
Federal 410 Solid	velocity, fps:	2370	2110	2870	1640	1440
	energy, ft-lb:	5115	4050	3165	2455	1895
	arc, inches:		0	-7.4	-24.8	-55.0
Norma 400 TXP Swift A-Frame	velocity, fps:	2350	2127	1917	1721	
	energy, ft-lb:	4906	4021	3266	2632	
	arc, inches:		+3.1	0	-12.5	
.416 Rimmed						
A-Square 400 Triad	velocity, fps:	2400	2140	1897	1673	
	energy, ft-lb:	5115	4069	3194	2487	
	arc, inches:		+3.3	0	-13.2	
.416 Dakota						
Dakota 400 Barnes X	velocity, fps:	2450	2294	2143	1998	1859
	energy, ft-lb:	5330	4671	4077	3544	3068
	arc, inches:		+2.5	-0.2	-10.5	-29.4
.416 Weatherby Magnum						
A-Square 400 Triad	velocity, fps:	2600	2328	2073	1834	1624
	energy, ft-lb:	6004	4813	3816	2986	2343
	arc, inches:		+2.5	0	-10.5	-31.6
Wby. 350 Barnes X	velocity, fps:	2850	2673	2503	2340	2182
	energy, ft-lb:	6312	5553	4870	4253	3700
	arc, inches:		+1.7	0	-7.2	-20.9
Wby. 400 Swift A-Frame	velocity, fps:	2650	2426	2213	2011	1820
	energy, ft-lb:	6237	5227	4350	3592	2941
	arc, inches:		+2.2	0	-9.3	-27.1
Wby. 400 RN Expanding	velocity, fps:	2700	2417	2152	1903	1676
	energy, ft-lb:	6474	5189	4113	3216	2493
	arc, inches:		+2.3	0	-9.7	-29.3

Cartridge Bullet	Range, Yards:	0	100	200	300	400
Wby. 400 Monolithic Solid	velocity, fps:	2700	2411	2140	1887	1656
	energy, ft-lb:	6474	5162	4068	3161	2435
	arc, inches:		+2.3	0	-9.8	-29.7

10.57 (.416) Meteor

Cartridge Bullet	Range, Yards:	0	100	200	300	400
Lazzeroni 400 Swift A-Frame	velocity, fps:	2730	2532	2342	2161	1987
	energy, ft-lb:	6621	5695	4874	4147	3508
	arc, inches:		+1.9	0	-8.3	-24.0

.425 Express

Cartridge Bullet	Range, Yards:	0	100	200	300	400
A-Square 400 Triad	velocity, fps:	2400	2136	1888	1662	1465
	energy, ft-lb:	5115	4052	3167	2454	1906
	arc, inches:		+3.0	0	-13.1	-38.3

.44-40 Winchester

Cartridge Bullet	Range, Yards:	0	100	200	300	400
Rem. 200 Soft Point	velocity, fps:	1190	1006	900	822	756
	energy, ft-lb:	629	449	360	300	254
	arc, inches:		0	-33.1	-108.7	-235.2
Win. 200 Soft Point	velocity, fps:	1190	1006	900	822	756
	energy, ft-lb:	629	449	360	300	254
	arc, inches:		0	-33.3	-109.5	-237.4

.44 Remington Magnum

Cartridge Bullet	Range, Yards:	0	100	200	300	400
Federal 240 Hi-Shok HP	velocity, fps:	1760	1380	1090	950	860
	energy, ft-lb:	1650	1015	640	485	395
	arc, inches:		0	-17.4	-60.7	-136.0
Rem. 210 Semi-Jacketed HP	velocity, fps:	1920	1477	1155	982	880
	energy, ft-lb:	1719	1017	622	450	361
	arc, inches:		0	-14.7	-55.5	-131.3
Rem. 240 Soft Point	velocity, fps:	1760	1380	1114	970	878
	energy, ft-lb:	1650	1015	661	501	411
	arc, inches:		0	-17.0	-61.4	-143.0
Rem. 240 Semi-Jacketed Hollow Point	velocity, fps:	1760	1380	1114	970	878
	energy, ft-lb:	1650	1015	661	501	411
	arc, inches:		0	-17.0	-61.4	-143.0
Rem. 275 JHP Core-Lokt	velocity, fps:	1580	1293	1093	976	896
	energy, ft-lb:	1524	1020	730	582	490
	arc, inches:		0	-19.4	-67.5	-210.8
Win. 210 Silvertip HP	velocity, fps:	1580	1198	993	879	795
	energy, ft-lb:	1164	670	460	361	295
	arc, inches:		0	-22.4	-76.1	-168.0
Win. 240 Hollow Soft Point	velocity, fps:	1760	1362	1094	953	861
	energy, ft-lb:	1650	988	638	484	395
	arc, inches:		0	-18.1	-65.1	-150.3

.444 Marlin

Cartridge Bullet	Range, Yards:	0	100	200	300	400
Rem. 240 Soft Point	velocity, fps:	2350	1815	1377	1087	941
	energy, ft-lb:	2942	1755	1010	630	472
	arc, inches:		+2.2	-5.4	-31.4	-86.7

.45-70 Government

Cartridge Bullet	Range, Yards:	0	100	200	300	400
Federal 300 Sierra Pro-Hunt. HP FN	velocity, fps:	1880	1650	1430	1240	1110
	energy, ft-lb:	2355	1815	1355	1015	810
	arc, inches:		0	-11.5	-39.7	-89.1
PMC 350 FNSP	velocity, fps:	2025	1678	1390		
	energy, ft-lb:	3167	2187	1502		
	arc, inches:		0	-12.0		

Cartridge Bullet	Range, Yards:	0	100	200	300	400
Rem. 300 Jacketed HP	velocity, fps:	1810	1497	1244	1073	969
	energy, ft-lb:	2182	1492	1031	767	625
	arc, inches:		0	-13.8	-50.1	-115.7
Rem. 405 Soft Point	velocity, fps:	1330	1168	1055	977	918
	energy, ft-lb:	1590	1227	1001	858	758
	arc, inches:		0	-24.0	-78.6	-169.4
Win. 300 Jacketed HP	velocity, fps:	1880	1650	1425	1235	1105
	energy, ft-lb:	2355	1815	1355	1015	810
	arc, inches:		0	-12.8	-44.3	-95.5
Win. 300 Partition Gold	velocity, fps:	1880	1558	1292	1103	988
	energy, ft-lb:	2355	1616	1112	811	651
	arc, inches:		0	-12.9	-46.0	-104.9

.450 Nitro Express (3 1/4")

Cartridge Bullet	Range, Yards:	0	100	200	300	400
A-Square 465 Triad	velocity, fps:	2190	1970	1765	1577	
	energy, ft-lb:	4952	4009	3216	2567	
	arc, inches:		+4.3	0	-15.4	

.450 #2

Cartridge Bullet	Range, Yards:	0	100	200	300	400
A-Square 465 Triad	velocity, fps:	2190	1970	1765	1577	
	energy, ft-lb:	4952	4009	3216	2567	
	arc, inches:		+4.3	0	-15.4	

.458 Winchester Magnum

Cartridge Bullet	Range, Yards:	0	100	200	300	400
A-Square 465 Triad	velocity, fps:	2220	1999	1791	1601	1433
	energy, ft-lb:	5088	4127	3312	2646	2121
	arc, inches:		+3.6	0	-14.7	-42.5
Federal 350 Soft Point	velocity, fps:	2470	1990	1570	1250	1060
	energy, ft-lb:	4740	3065	1915	1205	870
	arc, inches:		0	-7.5	-29.1	-71.1
Federal 400 Trophy Bonded	velocity, fps:	2380	2170	1960	1770	1590
	energy, ft-lb:	5030	4165	3415	2785	2255
	arc, inches:		0	-5.9	-20.9	-47.1
Federal 500 Solid	velocity, fps:	2090	1870	1670	1480	1320
	energy, ft-lb:	4850	3880	3085	2440	1945
	arc, inches:		0	-8.5	-29.5	-66.2
Federal 500 Trophy Bonded	velocity, fps:	2090	1870	1660	1480	1310
	energy, ft-lb:	4850	3870	3065	2420	1915
	arc, inches:		0	-8.5	-29.7	-66.8
Fed. 500 Trophy Bonded Sledgehammer Solid	velocity, fps:	2090	1860	1650	1460	1300
	energy, ft-lb:	4850	3845	3025	2365	1865
	arc, inches:		0	-8.6	-30.0	-67.8
Federal 510 Soft Point	velocity, fps:	2090	1820	1570	1360	1190
	energy, ft-lb:	4945	3730	2790	2080	1605
	arc, inches:		0	-9.1	-32.3	-73.9
Hornady 500 FMJ-RN HM	velocity, fps:	2260	1984	1735	1512	
	energy, ft-lb:	5670	4368	3341	2538	
	arc, inches:		0	-7.4	-26.4	
Norma 500 TXP Swift A-Frame	velocity, fps:	2116	1903	1705	1524	
	energy, ft-lb:	4972	4023	3228	2578	
	arc, inches:		+4.1	0	-16.1	
Rem. 450 Swift A-Frame PSP	velocity, fps:	2150	1901	1671	1465	1289
	energy, ft-lb:	4618	3609	2789	2144	1659
	arc, inches:		0	-8.2	-28.9	
Speer 500 African GS Tungsten Solid	velocity, fps:	2120	1845	1596	1379	
	energy, ft-lb:	4989	3780	2828	2111	
	arc, inches:		0	-8.8	-31.3	

BALLISTICS

CENTERFIRE RIFLE BALLISTICS

.458 Weatherby Magnum to .700 Nitro Express

CARTRIDGE BULLET	RANGE, YARDS:	0	100	200	300	400
Speer African Grand Slam	velocity, fps:	2120	1853	1609	1396	
	energy, ft-lb:	4989	3810	2875	2163	
	arc, inches:		0	-8.7	-30.8	
Win. 510 Soft Point	velocity, fps:	2040	1770	1527	1319	1157
	energy, ft-lb:	4712	3547	2640	1970	1516
	arc, inches:		0	-10.3	-35.6	

.458 Lott

		0	100	200	300	400
A-Square 465 Triad	velocity, fps:	2380	2150	1932	1730	1551
	energy, ft-lb:	5848	4773	3855	3091	2485
	arc, inches:	+3.0	0	-12.5	-36.4	

.450 Ackley

		0	100	200	300	400
A-Square 465 Triad	velocity, fps:	2400	2169	1950	1747	1567
	energy, ft-lb:	5947	4857	3927	3150	2534
	arc, inches:	+2.9	0	-12.2	-35.8	

.460 Short A-Square

		0	100	200	300	400
A-Square 500 Triad	velocity, fps:	2420	2198	1987	1789	1613
	energy, ft-lb:	6501	5362	4385	3553	2890
	arc, inches:	+2.9	0	-11.6	-34.2	

.450 Dakota

		0	100	200	300	400
Dakota 500 Barnes Solid	velocity, fps:	2450	2235	2030	1838	1658
	energy, ft-lb:	6663	5544	4576	3748	3051
	arc, inches:	+2.5	-0.6	-12.0	-33.8	

.460 Weatherby Magnum

		0	100	200	300	400
A-Square 500 Triad	velocity, fps:	2580	2349	2131	1923	1737
	energy, ft-lb:	7389	6126	5040	4107	3351
	arc, inches:	+2.4	0	-10.0	-29.4	
Wby. 450 Barnes X	velocity, fps:	2700	2518	2343	2175	2013
	energy, ft-lb:	7284	6333	5482	4725	4050
	arc, inches:	+2.0	0	-8.4	-24.1	
Wby. 500 RN Expanding	velocity, fps:	2600	2301	2022	1764	1533
	energy, ft-lb:	7504	5877	4539	3456	2608
	arc, inches:	+2.6	0	-11.1	-33.5	
Wby. 500 FMJ	velocity, fps:	2600	2309	2037	1784	1557
	energy, ft-lb:	7504	5917	4605	3534	2690
	arc, inches:	+2.5	0	-10.9	-33.0	

.500/.465

		0	100	200	300	400
A-Square 480 Triad	velocity, fps:	2150	1928	1722	1533	
	energy, ft-lb:	4926	3960	3160	2505	
	arc, inches:	+4.3	0	-16.0		

.470 Nitro Express

		0	100	200	300	400
A-Square 500 Triad	velocity, fps:	2150	1912	1693	1494	
	energy, ft-lb:	5132	4058	3182	2478	
	arc, inches:	+4.4	0	-16.5		
Federal 500 Woodleigh Weldcore	velocity, fps:	2150	1890	1650	1440	1270
	energy, ft-lb:	5130	3965	3040	2310	1790
	arc, inches:		0	-9.3	-31.3	-69.7
Federal 500 Woodleigh Weldcore Solid	velocity, fps:	2150	1890	1650	1440	1270
	energy, ft-lb:	5130	3965	3040	2310	1790
	arc, inches:		0	-9.3	-31.3	-69.7
Federal 500 Trophy Bonded	velocity, fps:	2150	1940	1740	1560	1400
	energy, ft-lb:	5130	4170	3360	2695	2160
	arc, inches:		0	-7.8	-27.1	-60.8

CARTRIDGE BULLET	RANGE, YARDS:	0	100	200	300	400
Fed. 500 Trophy Bonded Sledgehammer Solid	velocity, fps:	2150	1940	1740	1560	1400
	energy, ft-lb:	5130	4170	3360	2695	2160
	arc, inches:		0	-7.8	-27.1	-60.8

.470 Capstick

		0	100	200	300	400
A-Square 500 Triad	velocity, fps:	2400	2172	1958	1761	1553
	energy, ft-lb:	6394	5236	4255	3445	2678
	arc, inches:	+2.9	0	-11.9	-36.1	

.475 #2

		0	100	200	300	400
A-Square 480 Triad	velocity, fps:	2200	1964	1744	1544	
	energy, ft-lb:	5158	4109	3240	2539	
	arc, inches:	+4.1	0	-15.6		

.475 #2 Jeffery

		0	100	200	300	400
A-Square 500 Triad	velocity, fps:	2200	1966	1748	1550	
	energy, ft-lb:	5373	4291	3392	2666	
	arc, inches:	+4.1	0	-15.6		

.495 A-Square

		0	100	200	300	400
A-Square 570 Triad	velocity, fps:	2350	2117	1896	1693	1513
	energy, ft-lb:	6989	5671	4552	3629	2899
	arc, inches:	+3.1	0	-13.0	-37.8	

.500 Nitro Express (3")

		0	100	200	300	400
A-Square 570 Triad	velocity, fps:	2150	1928	1722	1533	
	energy, ft-lb:	5850	4703	3752	2975	
	arc, inches:	+4.3	0	-16.1		

.500 A-Square

		0	100	200	300	400
A-Square 600 Triad	velocity, fps:	2470	2235	2013	1804	1620
	energy, ft-lb:	8127	6654	5397	4336	3495
	arc, inches:	+2.7	0	-11.3	-33.5	

.505 Gibbs

		0	100	200	300	400
A-Square 525 Triad	velocity, fps:	2300	2063	1840	1637	
	energy, ft-lb:	6166	4962	3948	3122	
	arc, inches:	+3.6	0	-14.2		

.577 Nitro Express

		0	100	200	300	400
A-Square 750 Triad	velocity, fps:	2050	1811	1595	1401	
	energy, ft-lb:	6998	5463	4234	3267	
	arc, inches:	+4.9	0	-18.5		

.577 Tyrannosaur

		0	100	200	300	400
A-Square 750 Triad	velocity, fps:	2460	2197	1950	1723	1516
	energy, ft-lb:	10077	8039	6335	4941	3825
	arc, inches:	+2.8	0	-12.1	-36.0	

.600 Nitro Express

		0	100	200	300	400
A-Square 900 Triad	velocity, fps:	1950	1680	1452	1336	
	energy, ft-lb:	7596	5634	4212	3564	
	arc, inches:	+5.6	0	-20.7		

.700 Nitro Express

		0	100	200	300	400
A-Square 1000 Monolithic Solid	velocity, fps:	1900	1669	1461	1288	
	energy, ft-lb:	8015	6188	4740	3685	
	arc, inches:	+5.8	0	-22.2		

SAKO RIFLE BALLISTICS

501

CALIBER	BULLET GRS	WEIGHT/TYPE TYPE	VELOCITY IN FEET PER SECOND MUZZLE	100Y	200Y	300Y	400Y	500Y
22 Hornet	45	SPEEDHEAD FMJ	2300	1724	1291	1069	944	861
	45	SOFT POINT RN	2300	1724	1291	1069	944	861
	42	HOLLOW PIONT	2700	2193	1764	1419	1161	1011
22 PPC USA	52	HPBT MATCH	3400	2990	2613	2255	1920	1616
222 Remington 222	50	SPEEDHEAD FMJ	3200	2663	2182	1776	1447	1192
	50	SOFT POINT P	3200	2663	2182	1776	1447	1192
	55	SOFT POINT P	3280	2800	2372	1978	1637	1350
	52	HPBT MATCH	3035	2613	2235	1894	1589	1333
222 Remington	50	SPEEDHEAD FJM	3230	2690	2207	1798	1466	1207
	50	SOFT POINT P	3230	2690	2207	1798	1466	1207
	55	SOFT POINT P	3330	2848	2414	2016	1671	1378
223 Remington	50	SPEEDHEAD FJM	3230	2690	2207	1798	1466	1207
	50	SOFT POINT P	3230	2690	2207	1798	1466	1207
	55	SOFT POINT P	3330	2848	2414	2016	1671	1378
22-250 Remington	50	SPEEDHEAD FMJ	3770	3168	2639	2168	1751	1396
	50	SOFT POINT P	3770	3168	2639	2168	1751	1396
	55	SOFT POINT P	3660	3146	2681	2255	1871	1533
6PPC USA	70	HPBT MATCH	3200	2740	2407	2090	1793	1527
243 Winchester	90	SPEEDHEAD FJM	2855	2587	2340	2110	1895	1693
	90	SOFT POINT P	3130	2850	2587	2343	2114	1898
6.5X55 Swedish	100	SPEEDHEAD FJM	2625	2270	1946	1651	1397	1196
	139	HPBT MATCH	2790	2648	2512	2381	2252	2129
	156	SOFT POINT RN	2625	23843	2156	1941	1740	1554
270 Wlinchester	130	SPEEDHEAD FMJ	2820	2506	2212	1938	1687	1463
	156	HAMMERHEAD	2755	2470	2208	1967	1743	1538
7x33 Sako	78	SPEEDHEAD FJM	2430	1920	1500	1190	1013	906
	78	SOFT POINT SP	2430	1920	1500	1190	1013	906
7mm Mauser(7x57)	78	SPEEDHEAD FMJ	2950	2324	783	1362	1090	950
	170	SOFT POINT SP	2495	2283	2086	1901	1728	1567
7x64	120	SOFT POINT P	3100	2816	2545	2296	2069	1856
	170	HAMMERHEAD	2790	2563	2351	2154	1967	1791
7x65R	170	HAMMERHEAD	2625	2409	2208	2019	1839	1670
7mm Remington Mag	170	HAMMERHEAD	2970	2734	2512	2303	2108	1924
7.62x39 Russian	123	SPEEDHEAD FMJ	2345	2096	1863	1651	1466	1305
	123	SPEEDHEAD FMJ	2345	2096	1863	1651	1466	1305
	123	SOFT POINT P	2345	2096	1863	1651	1466	1305
30-30 Winchester	93	SPEEDHEAD FMJ	2970	2354	1818	1400	1126	976
	150	SOFT POINT FP	2310	1982	1681	1439	1240	1096
308 Winchester	93	SPEEDHEAD FMJ	2970	2354	1818	1400	1126	976
	123	SPEEDHEAD FMJ	2920	2622	2347	2097	1868	1654
	123	SOFT POINT P	3035	2734	2455	2194	1958	1738
	156	S-HAMMERHEAD	2790	2563	2353	2158	1973	1800
	180	HAMERMHEAD	2610	2382	2169	1971	1786	1612
	180	S-HAMMERHEAD	2610	2400	2204	2017	1839	1672
	200	HAMMERHEAD	2445	2210	1990	1782	1588	1415
	123	RANGE	2950	2652	2378	2126	1895	1679
	102	SUPER RANGE	3120	2712	2342	2003	1695	1428
	168	HPBT MATCH	2690	2500	2321	2159	2004	1857
	190	HPBT MATCH	2525	2372	2224	2080	1940	1806
7.62x53R	93	SPEEDHEAD FMJ	2970	2354	1818	1400	1126	976
	123	SPEEDHEAD FMJ	2920	2622	2347	2097	1868	1654
	156	S-HAMMERHEAD	2790	2563	2353	2158	1973	1800
	180	S-HAMMERHEAD	2610	2400	2204	2017	1839	1672
	200	HAMMERHEAD	2445	2210	1990	1782	1588	1415
	123	RANGE	2950	2652	2378	2126	1895	1679
30-06 Springfield	123	SPEEDHEAD FMJ	2920	2622	2347	2097	1868	1654
	123	SOFT POINT P	3120	2800	2510	2250	2010	1786
	156	S-HAMMERHEAD	2900	2670	2454	2255	2070	1893
	180	HAMMERHEAD	2700	2465	2242	2042	1857	1682
	180	S-HAMMERHEAD	2700	2500	2295	2100	1920	1750
	220	HAMMERHEAD	2410	2200	2000	1826	1664	1517
	123	RANGE	2950	2652	2378	2126	1895	1679
300 Winchester Mag	156	S-HAMMERHEAD	3150	2905	2673	2453	2243	2044
	180	HAMMERHEAD	2950	2700	2467	2243	2031	1833
	180	S-HAMMERHEAD	2950	2730	2517	2314	2121	1938
	168	HPBT MATCH	3020	2816	2622	2438	2260	2090
8.2x57JRS	200	HAMMERHEAD	2395	2093	1815	1563	1347	1176
338 Winchester Mag	250	HAMMERHEAD	2676	2413	2169	1946	1742	1554
9.3x53R Finnish	256	SOFT POINT RN	2330	2000	1695	1439	1236	1091
9.3x62	250	POWERHEAD BARNES	2360	2170	1988	1815	1652	1503
375 H&H Mag	270	POWERHEAD BARNES	2720	2535	2354	2181	2015	1857

SPEEDHEAD=FMJ-Full Metal Jacket • HAMMERHEAD=Soft Point Bonded Core • HPBT=Hollow Point Boat Tail, Precision • SP P=Soft Point Pointed • HP = Hollow Point, Varmint, Precision • RANGE=Full Metal Jacket

(Continued on following page)

BALLISTICS

www.StoegerIndustries.com

Ballistics
2002 Edition

SAKO RIFLE BALLISTICS

Cartridge	ENERGY IN FOOT-POUNDS						TRAJECTORY INCHES/YARDS						BOX
	MUZZLE	100Y	200Y	300Y	400Y	500Y	MUZZLE	100Y	200Y	300Y	400Y	500Y	PCS
22 Hornet	524	295	165	114	89	74	-1.5	0	-14.3	-47.1	-108.9	-203.5	20
	524	295	165	114	89	74	-1.5	0	-14.3	-47.1	-108.9	-203.5	20
	652	428	277	179	120	91	-1.5	0	-6.6	-24.5	-60.1	-120.9	20
22 PPC USA	1342	1040	795	592	429	304	-1.5	1.2	0	-6.0	-19.1	-41.8	20
222 Remington 222	1135	786	528	350	232	158	-1.5	1.2	0	-10.3	-31.1	-67.3	20
	1135	786	528	350	232	158	-1.5	1.7	0	-10.3	-31.1	-67.3	20
	1312	958	686	477	326	222	-1.5	1.4	0	-8.0	-24.8	-54.5	20
	1072	795	581	417	294	207	-1.5	1.8	0	-9.0	-27.9	-60.7	20
222 Remington	1159	803	540	359	238	161	-1.5	1.6	0	-10.0	-30.3	-67.0	20
	1159	803	540	359	238	161	-1.5	1.6	0	-10.0	-30.3	-67.0	20
	1352	989	710	495	340	231	-1.5	1.4	0	-7.7	-23.8	-51.9	20
223 Remington	1159	803	540	359	238	161	-1.5	1.6	0	-10.0	-30.3	-67.0	20
	1159	803	540	359	238	161	-1.5	1.6	0	-10.0	-30.3	-67.0	20
	1352	989	710	495	340	231	-1.5	1.4	0	-7.7	-23.8	-51.9	20
22-250 Remington	1579	1113	773	522	340	216	-1.5	1.0	0	-6.0	-19.5	-44.0	20
	1579	1113	7773	522	340	216	-1.5	1.0	0	-6.0	-19.5	-44.0	20
	1631	1206	876	620	426	286	-1.5	1.0	0	-5.9	-18.7	-41.3	20
6PPC USA	1481	1156	892	673	495	359	-1.5	1.5	0	-7.2	-22.8	-49.2	20
243 Winchester	1618	1329	1087	884	713	569	-1.5	1.9	0	-8.2	-24.3	-49.9	20
	1949	1612	1329	1090	887	715	-1.5	1.5	0	-6.5	-19.5	-40.2	20
6.5X55 Swedish	1533	1147	842	606	434	319	-1.5	2.6	0	-11.9	-36.0	-76.8	20
	2396	2161	1945	1746	1563	1396	-1.5	1.7	0	-7.2	-20.5	-40.7	20
	2382	1966	1607	1303	1047	835	-1.5	2.3	0	-9.8	-28.9	-59.7	20
270 Wlinchester	2290	1805	1407	1080	818	616	-1.5	2.0	0	-9.2	-27.5	-58.3	20
	2625	2111	1685	1338	1051	818	-1.5	2.2	0	-9.3	-27.6	-57.5	20
7x33 Sako	1029	643	392	247	179	143	-1.5	0	-8.5	-31.0	-78.8	-158.0	50
	1029	643	392	247	179	243	-1.5	0	-8.5	-31.0	-78.8	-158.0	50
7mm Mauser(7x57)	1522	943	555	324	208	158	-1.5	2.6	0	-14.9	-50.4	-112.2	20
	2324	1962	1638	1361	1125	925	-1.5	2.6	0	-10.8	-31.1	-63.3	20
7x64	2567	2117	1730	1408	1143	920	-1.5	1.4	0	-7.3	-20.9	-42.6	20
	2929	2473	2081	1747	1458	1208	-1.5	1.9	0	-8.2	-23.9	-48.6	20
7x65R	2594	2186	1836	1535	1274	1050	-1.5	2.3	0	-9.4	-27.4	-55.6	20
7mm Remington Mag	3320	2814	2376	1996	1674	1394	-1.5	1.6	0	-7.2	-21.0	-42.5	20
7.62x39 Russian	1507	1203	951	747	589	466	-1.5	0	-6.5	-23.6	-53.2	-98.5	30
	1507	1203	951	747	589	466	-1.5	0	-6.5	-23.6	-53.2	-98.5	250
	1507	1203	951	747	589	466	-1.5	0	-6.5	-23.6	-53.2	-98.5	30
30-30 Winchester	1811	1138	679	403	260	196	-1.5	0	-4.9	-21.8	-57.7	-117.3	20
	1777	1304	938	688	510	400	-1.5	0	-8.1	-28.3	-65.6	-125.6	20
308 Winchester	1811	1138	679	403	260	196	-1.5	0	-4.9	-21.8	-56.7	-117.3	20
	2335	1883	1509	1205	955	749	-1.5	1.8	0	-8.4	-24.5	-50.7	20
	2523	2047	1650	1318	1050	827	-1.5	1.6	0	-7.6	-22.4	-46.2	20
	2689	2271	1914	1610	1346	1120	-1.5	2.0	0	-8.2	-23.9	-48.9	20
	2725	2273	1885	1556	1277	1041	-1.5	2.4	0	-9.9	-28.6	-58.1	20
	2725	2310	1946	1629	1355	1119	-1.5	2.3	0	-9.5	-27.5	-55.8	20
	2660	2172	1762	1414	1122	891	-1.5	2.8	0	-11.3	-33.7	-70.1	20
	2388	1927	1549	1238	983	772	-1.5	1.8	0	-8.0	-23.7	-49.0	50
	2195	1662	1240	907	649	461	-1.5	1.6	0	-8.0	-24.7	-53.7	50
	2701	2328	2010	1739	1499	1286	-1.5	2.3	0	-8.5	-24.5	-49.1	20
	2688	2369	2082	1822	1585	1373	-1.5	2.4	0	-9.0	-26.3	-52.9	20
7.62x53R	1811	1138	679	403	260	196	-1.5	0	-4.9	-21.8	-56.7	-117.3	20
	2335	1883	1509	1205	955	749	-1.5	1.8	0	-8.4	-24.5	-50.7	20
	2689	2271	1914	1610	1346	1120	-1.5	2.0	0	-8.2	-23.9	-48.9	20
	2725	2310	1946	1629	1355	1119	-1.5	2.3	0	-9.5	-27.5	-55.8	20
	2660	2172	1762	1414	1122	891	-1.5	2.8	0	-11.3	-33.7	-70.1	20
	2388	1927	1549	1238	983	772	-1.5	1.8	0	-8.0	-23.7	-49.0	50
30-06 Springfield	2335	1883	1509	1205	955	749	-1.5	1.8	0	-8.4	-24.5	-50.7	20
	2661	2148	1726	1385	1106	873	-1.5	1.6	0	-7.3	-21.3	-43.9	20
	2915	2466	2083	1759	1481	1240	-1.5	1.8	0	-7.8	-22.2	-44.7	20
	2935	2433	2013	1670	1381	1133	-1.5	2.3	0	-9.4	-27.0	-54.5	20
	2935	2495	2105	1768	1475	1223	-1.5	2.1	0	-8.7	-25.3	-51.3	20
	2847	2369	1963	1632	1356	1126	-1.5	3.3	0	-12.4	-34.7	-69.6	20
	2388	1927	1549	1238	983	772	-1.5	1.8	0	-8.0	-23.7	-49.0	50
300 Winchester Mag	3430	2918	2470	2080	1740	1445	-1.5	1.3	0	-6.1	-18.1	-37.0	20
	3493	2926	2438	2015	1653	1345	-1.5	1.6	0	-7.4	-21.7	-44.4	20
	3493	2983	2537	2144	1801	1504	-1.5	1.6	0	-7.1	-20.7	-42.0	20
	3400	2959	2566	2217	1905	1630	-1.5	1.5	0	-6.5	-18.8	-38.0	20
8.2x57JRS	2553	1949	1465	1087	807	616	-1.5	3.3	0	-13.9	-42.0	-89.7	20
338 Winchester Mag	3966	3229	2608	21012	1683	1339	-1.5	2.3	0	-10.0	-29.1	-59.7	20
9.3x53R Finnish	3010	2211	1593	1148	847	660	-1.5	3.6	0	-16.9	-50.3	-107.0	20
9.3x62	3095	2612	2192	1828	1514	1253	-1.5	3.0	0	-11.8	-34.2	-69.4	10
375 H&H Mag	4440	3848	3319	2848	2432	2066	-1.5	1.9	0	-8.3	-23.8	-48.0	10

S-HAMMERHEAD=SUPER HAMMERHEAD=Hollow Point Bonded Core • SP SP = Soft Point Semi Pointed • SP FP = Soft Point Flat Point • POWERHEAD BARNES = Hollow Piont Solid Copper • SUPER RANGE = HPBT, Varmint, Precision • SP RN = Soft Point Round Nose

Reloading

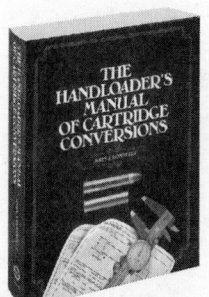

HANDLOADER'S MANUAL OF CARTRIDGE CONVERSIONS
by John J. Donnelly

All the physical data, how-to details, drawings, and tools needed to convert over 900 obsolete cartridge cases into shootable centerfire ammo.

COMPLETE RELOADING GUIDE
by John Traister & Bob Traister

Combining over fifty years of reloading knowledge to introduce the reader to reloading, metallic cartridge cases, types of gunpowder, primers, loading tools, bullets and ballistics—valuable information for all levels of skill and a must for every reloader's library.

*For addresses and phone/fax numbers of manufacturers and distributors included in this section, please turn to **DIRECTORY OF MANUFACTURERS AND SUPPLIERS** on page 557.*

BARNES BULLETS

In 1989 Barnes introduced the **X-Bullet**. It has since supplanted the company's lead-core softpoints (still made) as a premier big game bullet. Now the **X-Bullet** is also available for handguns, muzzleloaders and shotguns, and for rifles with a special blue dry-film lubricant–the **XLC**. The **XLC** promises higher velocities at modest pressures.

308 Cal. 180 GR. XBT
recovered from a Moose
98% Wgt. Retention.

X-Bullets
PISTOL

	Dia.	Bullet Weight	Desr.	Sect. Dens.	Ballist. Coeff.	Cat. #
44 Mag	.429"	200 GR	"X" PB	.155	.172	42920
	.429"	225 GR	"X" PB	.175	.195	42922
45	451"	250 GR	"X" PB	.176	188	45123
50 AE	.500"	275 GR	"X" PB	.157	.183	50025

Expander MZ
MUZZLELOADER

	Dia.	Bullet Weight	Desr.	Sect. Dens.	Ballist. Coeff.	Cat. #
50 Cal	.451"	250 GR	MZ	.176	.189	45125
	.451"	300 GR	MZ	.211	.207	45130
54 Cal	.500"	275 GR	MZ	.157	.184	50027
	.500"	325 GR	MZ	.186	.204	50032

Expander SGS
SHOTGUN

	Dia.	Bullet Weight	Desr.	Sect. Dens.	Ballist. Coeff.	Cat. #
	.575"	438 GR	SGS	.189	.214	57500

COATED X-BULLETS
RIFLE

Cal.	Dia.	Bullet Weight	Desr.	Sect. Dens.	Ballist. Coeff.	Cat. #
22	.224"	45 GR	"XLC" BT	.128	.203	22452
	.224"	50 GR	"XLC" S	.142	.220	22454
	.224"	53 GR	"XLC" S	.151	.231	22455
6mm	.243"	85 GR	"XLC" BT	.206	.401	24352
25	.257"	100 GR	"XLC" BT	.216	.420	25754
6.5	.264"	120 GR	"XLC" S	.246	.441	26451
	.264"	140 GR	"XLC" S	.287	.522	26453
270	.277"	130 GR	"XLC" BT	.242	.466	27754
7mm	.284"	140 GR	"XLC" BT	.248	.477	28455
	.284"	160 GR	"XLC" S	.283	.508	28458
30	.308"	130 GR	"XLC" BT	.196	.374	30851
	.308"	150 GR	"XLC" BT	.226	.428	30854
	.308"	165 GR	"XLC" BT	.247	.505	30857
	.308"	180 GR	"XLC" S	.271	.511	30858
	.308"	180 GR	"XLC" BT	.271	.552	30859
338	.338"	185 GR	"XLC" BT	.231	.437	33854
	.338"	210 GR	"XLC" BT	.263	.471	33856
	.338"	225 GR	"XLC" S	.281	.482	33855
375	.375"	235 GR	"XLC" S	.239	.400	37553
	.375"	270 GR	"XLC" S	.275	.503	37557
416	.416"	400 GR	"XLC" S	.330	.546	41658
470 NIT	.474"	500 GR	"XLC" S	.326	.318	47550
500 NIT	.509"	570 GR	"XLC" S	.335	.316	50957

X-BULLETS
RIFLE

Dia.	Bullet Weight	Desr.	Sect. Dens.	Ballist. Coeff.	Cat. #
.224"	50 GR	"X" S	.142	.220	22450
.224"	53 GR	"X" S	.151	.231	22453
.243"	85 GR	"X" BT	.206	.401	24310
.243"	90 GR	"X" S	.218	.382	24315
.243"	95 GR	"X" S	.230	.398	24320
.257"	90 GR	"X" BT	.195	.343	25710
.257"	100 GR	"X" S	.216	.401	25715
.257"	100 GR	"X" BT	.216	.420	25717
.257"	115 GR	"X" S	.249	.429	25722
.264"	120 GR	"X" S	.246	.441	26402
.264"	130 GR	"X" S	.266	.479	26403
.264"	140 GR	"X" S	.287	.522	26405
.277"	120 GR	"X" BT	.223	.423	27713
.277"	130 GR	"X" S	.242	.428	27715
.277"	130 GR	"X" BT	.242	.466	27717
.277"	140 GR	"X" S	.261	.462	27725
.277"	140 GR	"X" BT	.261	.497	27727
.277"	150 GR	"X" S	.279	.491	27735
.284"	120 GR	"X" BT	.213	.411	28417
.284"	130 GR	"X" BT	.230	.444	28420
.284"	140 GR	"X" S	.248	.436	28425
.284"	140 GR	"X" BT	.248	.477	28426
.284"	150 GR	"X" S	.266	.488	28427
.284"	150 GR	"X" BT	.266	.529	28428
.284"	160 GR	"X" S	.283	.508	28435
.284"	175 GR	"X" S	.310	.530	28445
.308"	110 GR	"X" S	.166	.322	30800
.308"	130 GR	"X" BT	.196	.374	30808
.308"	140 GR	"X" BT	.211	.398	30810
.308"	150 GR	"X" S	.226	.386	30815
.308"	150 GR	"X" BT	.226	.428	30817
.308"	165 GR	"X" S	.247	.456	30825
.308"	165 GR	"X" BT	.247	.505	30827
.308"	180 GR	"X" S	.271	.511	30835
.308"	180 GR	"X" BT	.271	.552	30840
.308"	200 GR	"X" S	.301	.550	30845
.308"	150 GR	"X" FN	.226	.269	30819
.323"	180 GR	"X" S	.246	.382	32305
.323"	200 GR	"X" S	.274	.429	32310
.323"	220 GR	"X" S	.301	.462	32315
.338"	160 GR	"X" S	.200	.337	33878
.338"	175 GR	"X" S	.218	.392	33880

BARNES BULLETS

X-BULLETS
RIFLE

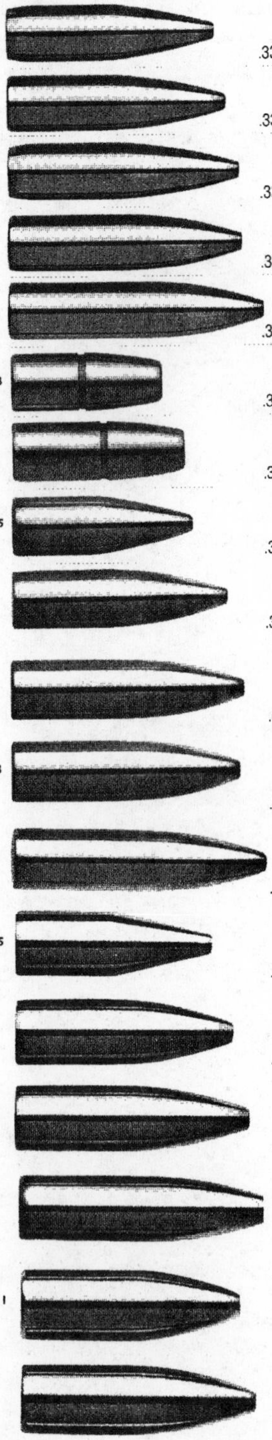

Dia.	Bullet Weight	Desr.	Sect. Dens.	Ballist. Coeff.	Cat. #
.338"	185 GR	"X" BT	.231	.437	33881
.338"	200 GR	"X" S	.250	.440	33882
.338"	210 GR	"X" BT	.263	.471	33883
.338"	225 GR	"X" S	.281	.482	33885
.338"	250 GR	"X" S	.313	.521	33890
.348"	200 GR	"X" FN	.234	.291	34800
.348"	220GR	"X" FN	.260	.315	34802
.358"	180 GR	"X" S	.201	.298	35810
.358"	225 GR	"X" S	.250	.405	35825
.358"	250 GR	"X" S	.279	.458	35835
.366"	250 GR	"X" S	.267	.428	36605
.366"	286 GR	"X" S	.305	.468	36615
.375"	210 GR	"X" S	.213	.341	37575
.375"	250 GR	"X" S	.254	.450	37582
.375"	270 GR	"X" S	.275	.503	37585
.375"	300 GR	"X" S	.305	.555	37590
.411"	300 GR	"X" S	.254	.401	41180
.411"	325 GR	"X" S	.275	.478	41182

X-BULLETS
RIFLE

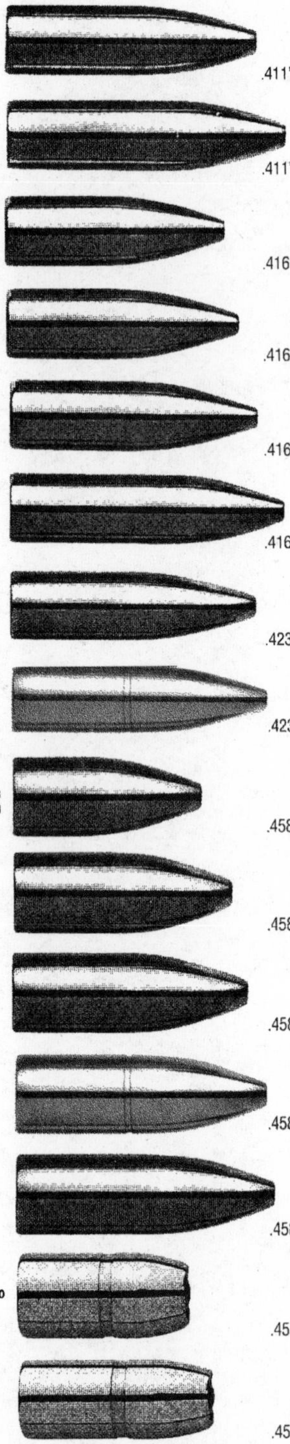

Dia.	Bullet Weight	Desr.	Sect. Dens.	Ballist. Coeff.	Cat. #
.411"	350 GR	"X" S	.296	.536	41185
.411"	400 GR	"X" S	.338	.562	41190
.416"	300 GR	"X" S	.247	.394	41680
.416"	325 GR	"X" S	.268	.467	41682
.416"	350 GR	"X" S	.289	.521	41685
.416"	400 GR	"X" S	.330	.546	41690
.423"	350 GR	"X" S	.279	.481	42382
.423"	400 GR	"X" S	.319	.537	42385
.458"	300 GR	"X" S	.204	.340	45802
.458"	350 GR	"X" S	.283	.402	45805
.458"	400 GR	"X" S	.272	.457	45815
.458"	450 GR	"X" S	.306	.488	45818
.458"	500 GR	"X" S	.341	.526	45822
.458"	250 GR	"X" FN	.170	.172	45831
.458"	300 GR	"X" FN	.206	.204	45832

Section labels (left column): 348, 35, 9.3, 375, 411

Section labels (right column): 416, 404 JEFF EXP 425, 458 Mag, 45/70

SOLIDS RIFLE

Dia.	Bullet Weight	Desr.	Sect. Dens.	Ballist. Coeff.	Cat. #
.224"	45 GR	Solid	.128	.212	22401
.224"	50 GR	Solid	.142	.235	22402
.243"	75 GR	Solid	.181	.330	24301
.243"	85 GR	Solid	.206	.353	24302
.257"	75 GR	Solid	.162	.297	25718
.257"	90 GR	Solid	.195	.324	25720
.264"	100 GR	Solid	.205	.395	26410
.264"	120 GR	Solid	.246	.453	26411
.264"	130 GR	Solid	.266	.461	26412
.277"	100 GR	Solid	.186	.370	27700
.277"	120 GR	Solid	.223	.418	27702
.277"	130 GR	Solid	.242	.448	27720
.277"	150 GR	Solid	.279	.307	27722
.284"	100 GR	Solid	.177	.343	28401
.284"	120 GR	Solid	.213	.399	28403
.284"	140 GR	Solid	.248	.448	28431
.284"	160 GR	Solid	.283	.522	28432
.284"	175 GR	Solid	.310	.321	28433
.308"	110 GR	Solid	.166	.337	30811
.308"	125 GR	Solid	.188	.372	30812
.308"	165 GR	Solid	.248	.481	30822
.308"	220 GR	Solid	.331	.305	30842
.323"	220 GR	Solid	.301	.294	32332
.338"	200 GR	Solid	.250	.465	33818
.338"	210 GR	Solid	.263	.480	33820

SOLIDS RIFLE

Dia.	Bullet Weight	Desr.	Sect. Dens.	Ballist. Coeff.	Cat. #
.338"	225 GR	Solid	.281	.506	33821
.338"	250 GR	Solid	.313	.326	33825
.358"	250 GR	Solid	.285	.313	35822
.366"	286 GR	Solid	.305	.342	36612
.375"	235 GR	Solid	.239	.442	37503
.375"	250 GR	Solid	.313	.551	37505
.375"	270 GR	Solid	.275	.284	37512
.375"	300 GR	Solid	.305	.307	37525
.411"	350 GR	Solid	.296	.374	41128
.411"	400 GR	Solid	.338	.406	41160
.416"	350 GR	Solid	.289	.364	41628
.416"	400 GR	Solid	.330	.388	41660
.423"	350 GR	Solid	.279	.347	42308
.423"	400 GR	Solid	.319	.361	42330
.430"	240 GR	Solid	.186	.182	43011
.435"	410 GR	Solid	.310	.390	43520
.458"	400 GR	Solid	.272	.321	45825
.458"	450 GR	Solid	.306	.362	45840
.458"	500 GR	Solid	.341	.394	45855

BARNES BULLETS

SOLIDS
RIFLE

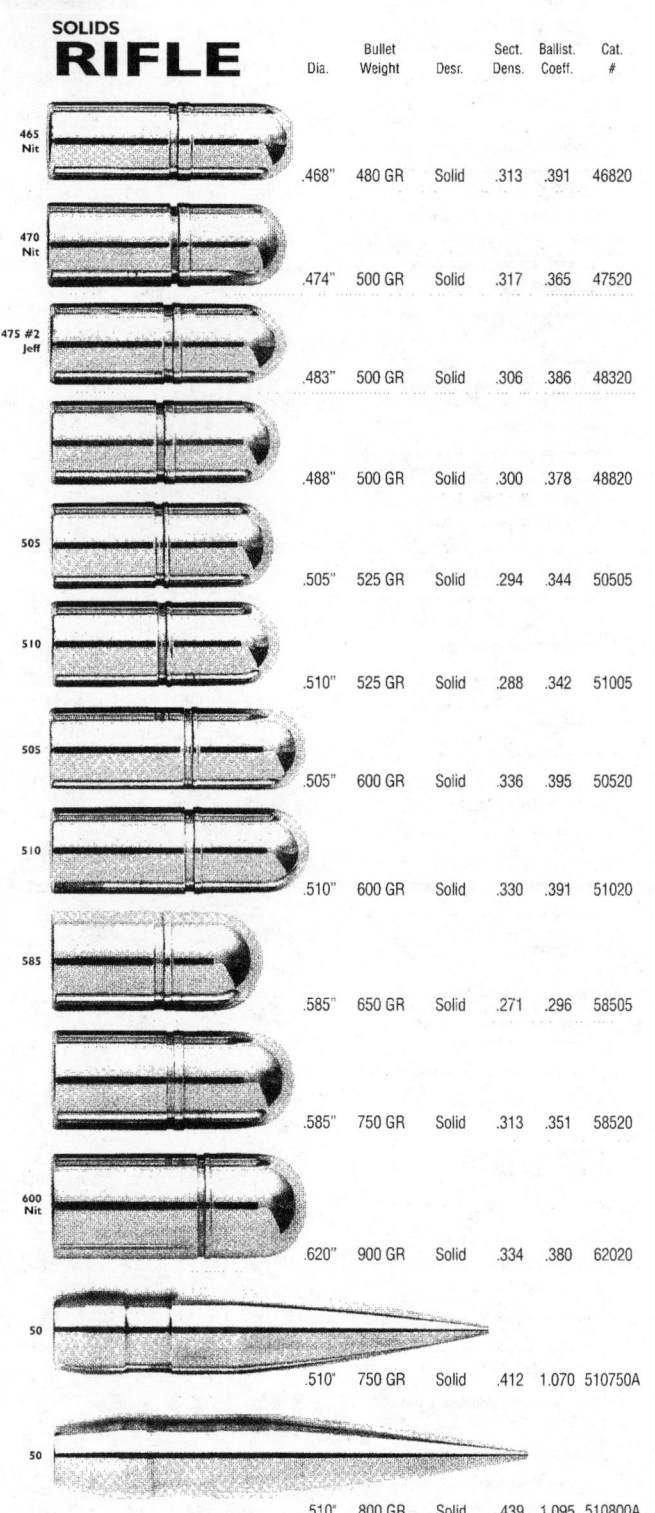

	Dia.	Bullet Weight	Desr.	Sect. Dens.	Ballist. Coeff.	Cat. #
465 Nit	.468"	480 GR	Solid	.313	.391	46820
470 Nit	.474"	500 GR	Solid	.317	.365	47520
475 #2 Jeff	.483"	500 GR	Solid	.306	.386	48320
	.488"	500 GR	Solid	.300	.378	48820
505	.505"	525 GR	Solid	.294	.344	50505
510	.510"	525 GR	Solid	.288	.342	51005
505	.505"	600 GR	Solid	.336	.395	50520
510	.510"	600 GR	Solid	.330	.391	51020
585	.585"	650 GR	Solid	.271	.296	58505
	.585"	750 GR	Solid	.313	.351	58520
600 Nit	.620"	900 GR	Solid	.334	.380	62020
50	.510"	750 GR	Solid	.412	1.070	510750A
50	.510"	800 GR	Solid	.439	1.095	510800A

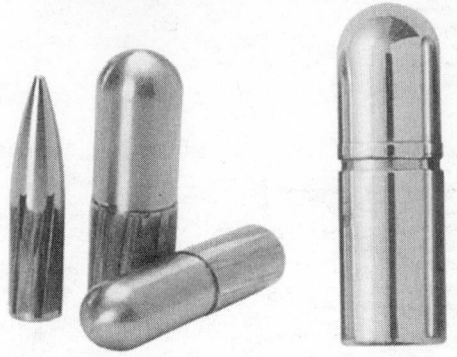

BARNES SOLIDS-UNBEATABLE STOPPING POWER FOR HUNTING DANGEROUS GAME

Barnes Round Nose Solids, made of copper/zinc alloy, do not disintegrate or deflect when striking heavy bone. Rather, they plow on through to the vitals. Designed for stopping large, dangerous game, Barnes Solids are also availble in Spitzer shape in some calibers for hunting furbearing animals. They do minimal damage to valuable pelts.

BARNES ORIGINALS—THE PREFERRED BULLET OF DISCRIMINATING HUNTERS FOR MORE THAN 65 YEARS

Designed by Fred Barnes in 1932 for his own use on big game, this bullet quickly gained favor among serious hunters. Made by pressure-forming a thick copper jacket around a pure lead core, the Original typically expands to more than 200 percent of its original diameter and retains 70-90 percent of its original bullet weight.

ORIGINALS RIFLE

	Dia.	Bullet Weight	Desr.	Jacket Thick.	Sect. Dens.	Ballist. Coeff.	Cat. #
6mm	.243"	115 GR	R.N.S.P.	.030"	.290	.322	24330
270	.277"	180 GR	R.N.S.P.	.032"	.335	.372	27750
7mm	.284"	195 GR	S.S.P.	.032"	.345	.570	28450
30	.308"	250 GR	R.N.S.P.	.032"	.376	.417	30860
348 Win	.348"	220 GR	F.N.S.P.	.032"	.260	.301	34805
	.348"	250 GR	F.N.S.P.	.032"	.295	.327	34810
375 Win	.375"	220 GR	F.N.S.P.	.032"	.223	.246	375W10
	.375"	255 GR	F.N.S.P.	.032"	.259	.290	375W20
38/55	.375"	255 GR	F.N.S.P.	.032"	.259	.290	38/5510
	.377"	255 GR	F.N.S.P.	.032"	.256	.290	38/5520
401 Win	.406"	250 GR	R.N.S.P.	.032"	.217	.241	40610
425	.435"	410 GR	R.N.S.P.	.049"	.310	.344	43510
	.458"	300 GR	S.S.P.	.032"	.204	.291	457010
45/70	.458"	300 GR	F.N.S.P.	.032"	.204	.227	457020
	.458"	400 GR	S.S.P.	.032"	.272	.389	457030

ORIGINALS RIFLE

	Dia.	Bullet Weight	Desr.	Jacket Thick.	Sect. Dens.	Ballist. Coeff.	Cat. #
	.458"	400 GR	F.N.S.P	.032"	.272	.302	457040
458 Mag	.458"	600 GR	R.N.S.P.	.049"	.409	.454	45860
465 Nit	.468"	480 GR	R.N.S.P.	.049"	.318	.362	46810
470 Nit	.475"	500 GR	R.N.S.P.	.049"	.317	.352	47510
	.475"	600 GR	R.N.S.P.	.049"	.380	.422	47530
475 #2 JEFF	.488"	500 GR	R.N.S.P.	.049"	.300	.333	48810
50/110 Win	.510"	300 GR	F.N.S.P.	.032"	.165	.183	5011010
	.510"	450 GR	F.N.S.P.	.032"	.247	.274	5011020
50	.510"	600 GR	R.N.S.P.	.049"	.336	.365	51010
	.510"	700 GR	R.N.S.P.	.049"	.392	.436	51030
577 Nit	.585"	750 GR	R.N.S.P.	.049"	.313	.346	58510
600 Nit	.620"	900 GR	R.N.S.P.	.049"	.334	.371	62010

BERGER BULLETS

Berger's match bullets are well-known for their superior performance in benchrest matches. Now Berger offers a variety of bullets from .17 to .30. All feature J4 jackets with wall concentricity tolerance of .0003. Lead cores are 99.9% pure and swaged in dies to within .0001 of round. Berger's line includes several profiles: Low Drag, Very Low Drag, Length Tolerant, Maximum-Expansion, besides standard flat-base and standard boat-tail.

ITEM	WEIGHT	TWIST
.172 17 Cal.	15 Gr. MEF	12
.172 17 Cal.	18 Gr. MEF	12
.172 17 Cal.	20 Gr.	12
.172 17 Cal.	22 Gr.	11
.172 17 Cal.	25 Gr.	10
.172 17 Cal.	30 Gr.	9
.172 17 Cal.	37 Gr. VLD	6
.204 20 Cal.	36 Gr. MEF	12
.224 22 Cal.	30 Gr MEF	15
.224 22 Cal.	35 Gr. MEF	15
.224 22 Cal.	40 Gr. MEF	15
.224 22 Cal.	45 Gr.	15
.224 22 Cal.	50 Gr.	14
.224 22 Cal.	52 Gr.	14
.224 22 Cal.	55 Gr.	14
.224 22 Cal.	60 Gr.	12
.224 22 Cal.	62 Gr.	12
.224 22 Cal.	64 Gr.	12
.224 22 Cal.	70 Gr. VLD	9
.224 22 Cal.	70 Gr. LTB	10
.224 22 Cal.	73 Gr. LTB	9
.224 22 Cal.	75 Gr. VLD	9
.224 22 Cal.	80 Gr. VLD	8
.243 (6mm) Cal.	60 Gr.	14
.243 (6mm) Cal.	62 Gr	14
.243 (6mm) Cal.	65 Gr	13
.243 (6mm) Cal.	65 Gr. Short	14
.243 (6mm) Cal.	65 Gr. BT	13
.243 (6mm) Cal.	66 Gr. LD	13
.243 (6mm) Cal.	68 Gr.	13
.243 (6mm) Cal.	69 Gr. LD	12
.243 (6mm) Cal.	70 Gr.	13
.243 (6mm) Cal.	71 Gr. BT	12
.243 (6mm) Cal.	74 Gr.	13
.243 (6mm) Cal.	80 Gr.	12
.243 (6mm) Cal.	88 Gr. LD	10
.243 (6mm) Cal.	90 Gr. BT	10
.243 (6mm) Cal.	95 Gr. VLD	9
.243 (6mm) Cal.	105 Gr. LTB	9
.243 (6mm) Cal.	105 Gr. VLD	8
.243 (6mm) Cal.	115 Gr. VLD	7
.257 25 Cal.	72 Gr.	15
.257 25 Cal.	78 Gr.	13
.257 25 Cal.	82 Gr.	14
.257 25 Cal.	87 Gr.	13
.257 25 Cal.	95 Gr.	12
.257 25 Cal.	110 Gr.	12
.257 25 Cal.	115 Gr. VLD	10
.264 (6.5mm) Cal.	140 Gr. VLD	9
.284 (7mm) Cal.	168 Gr. VLD	10
.284 (7mm) Cal.	180 Gr. VLD	9
.308 30 Cal.	110 Gr.	19
.308 30 Cal.	125 Gr.	19
.308 30 Cal.	135 Gr.	16
.308 30 Cal.	150 Gr.	15
.308 30 Cal.	155 Gr. LTB	14
.308 30 Cal.	155 Gr. VLD	14
.308 30 Cal.	168 Gr. LTB	13
.308 30 Cal.	168 Gr. VLD	13
.308 30 Cal.	175 Gr. VLD	13
.308 30 Cal.	185 Gr. VLD	12
.308 30 Cal.	190 Gr. VLD	12
.308 30 Cal.	210 Gr. VLD	11

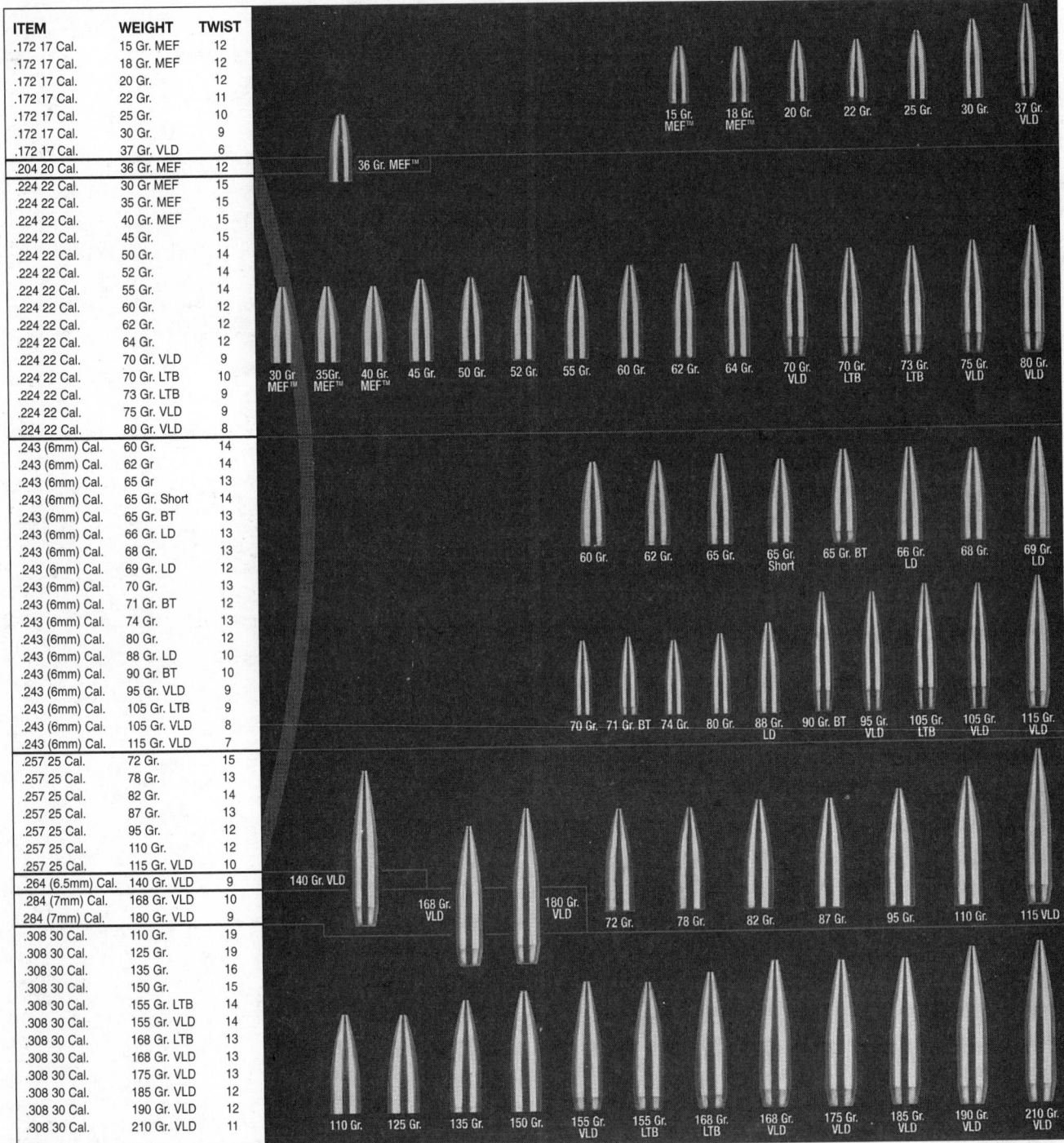

CLASSIC CENTERFIRE RIFLE

Federal Classic Rifle ammunition is still the choice of many serious hunters who know what it takes to succeed in the field. Whether choosing the Sierra Pro-Hunter®, the most widely reloaded bullet in America, or Federal's renowned Hi-Shok® bullet, dependable, consistent performance with deadly accuracy and double-caliber expansion are ensured.

SIERRA PRO-HUNTER BULLETS

The Pro-Hunter makes the reliable Classic Rifle cartridges even better. Sierra's copper jackets are extremely uniform and their tolerances tighter than are found in standard jackets. Sierra's core has a weight tolerance of just three-tenths of a grain for consistent performance from shot to shot. Pro-Hunters are made under the eye of trained inspectors and each production run is tested before it hits the shelf. Combine Pro-Hunter's quality with Federal's dedication to reliable powders, primers and brass, and the result is deadly hunting ammo.

HI-SHOK BULLETS

Federal Hi-Shok bullets hit hard and expand reliably for effective game-getting performance. The tapered jacket is designed to provide good initial penetration plus controlled expansion. Rigid manufacturing controls ensure consistency. Generations of hunters swear by their reliability.

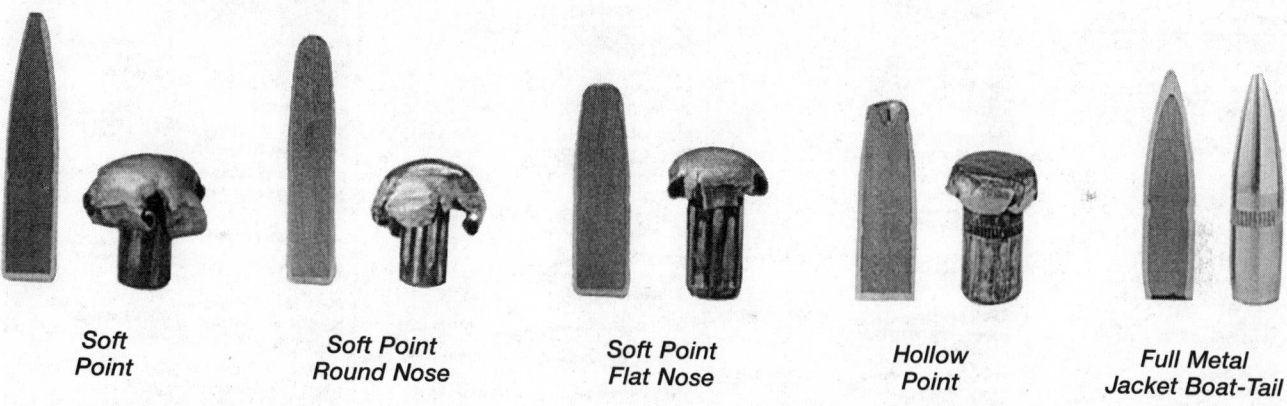

Soft Point — *Soft Point Round Nose* — *Soft Point Flat Nose* — *Hollow Point* — *Full Metal Jacket Boat-Tail*

SOFT POINT
Excellent for small game and thin-skinned medium game.
The aerodynamic tip provides flat shooting, and the exposed soft point expands rapidly, even at reduced velocities found at longer ranges.

SOFT POINT ROUND NOSE
A traditional choice for deer and bear in the brush.
A large exposed tip, extra weight, and specially tapered jacket provide controlled expansion, good weight retention, and deep penetration.

SOFT POINT FLAT NOSE
A good choice for light to medium game, even in brush.
Especially designed for rifles with tubular magazines, the flat nose prevents accidental discharge. It also expands reliably and offers deep penetration.

HOLLOW POINT
A great mid-distance load for medium game.
Available in 30-30 Win., 357 Mag., 44 Rem. Mag., and 45-70 Govt., the hollow-point provides hard-hitting accuracy and dramatic expansion.

FULL METAL JACKET BOAT-TAIL
Excellent for fur-bearing animals and target shooting.
The jacket prevents point deformation for smooth, reliable feeding in semi-automatics. The non-expanding bullet leaves a small exit hole for minimal pelt damage.

HORNADY RIFLE BULLETS

RIFLE BULLETS

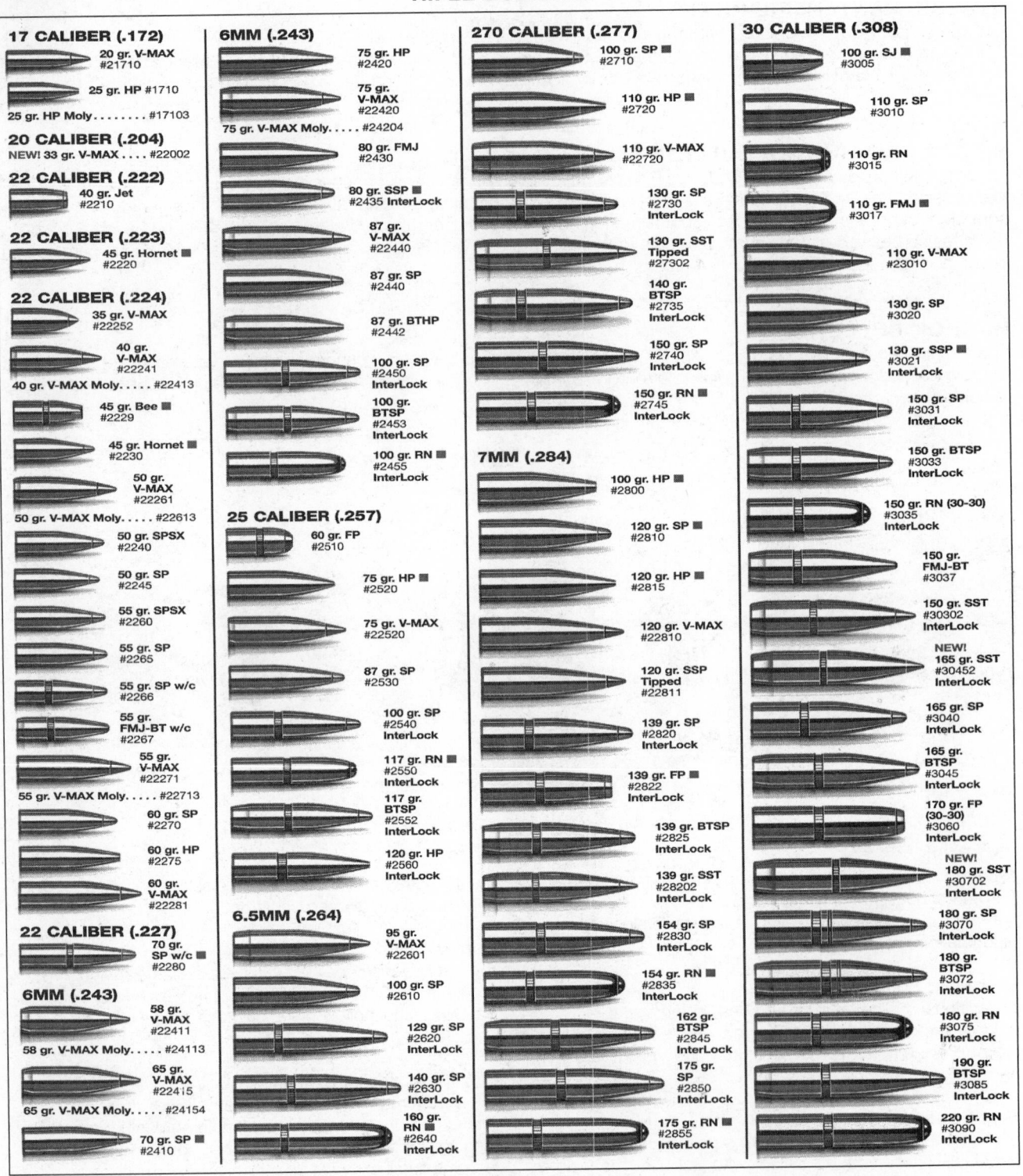

17 CALIBER (.172)
- 20 gr. V-MAX #21710
- 25 gr. HP #1710
- 25 gr. HP Moly . . . . #17103

20 CALIBER (.204)
- NEW! 33 gr. V-MAX . . . . #22002

22 CALIBER (.222)
- 40 gr. Jet #2210

22 CALIBER (.223)
- 45 gr. Hornet #2220

22 CALIBER (.224)
- 35 gr. V-MAX #22252
- 40 gr. V-MAX #22241
- 40 gr. V-MAX Moly . . . . . #22413
- 45 gr. Bee #2229
- 45 gr. Hornet #2230
- 50 gr. V-MAX #22261
- 50 gr. V-MAX Moly . . . . . #22613
- 50 gr. SPSX #2240
- 50 gr. SP #2245
- 55 gr. SPSX #2260
- 55 gr. SP #2265
- 55 gr. SP w/c #2266
- 55 gr. FMJ-BT w/c #2267
- 55 gr. V-MAX #22271
- 55 gr. V-MAX Moly . . . . . #22713
- 60 gr. SP #2270
- 60 gr. HP #2275
- 60 gr. V-MAX #22281

22 CALIBER (.227)
- 70 gr. SP w/c #2280

6MM (.243)
- 58 gr. V-MAX #22411
- 58 gr. V-MAX Moly . . . . . #24113
- 65 gr. V-MAX #22415
- 65 gr. V-MAX Moly . . . . . #24154
- 70 gr. SP #2410

6MM (.243)
- 75 gr. HP #2420
- 75 gr. V-MAX #22420
- 75 gr. V-MAX Moly . . . . . #24204
- 80 gr. FMJ #2430
- 80 gr. SSP #2435 InterLock
- 87 gr. V-MAX #22440
- 87 gr. SP #2440
- 87 gr. BTHP #2442
- 100 gr. SP #2450 InterLock
- 100 gr. BTSP #2453 InterLock
- 100 gr. RN #2455 InterLock

25 CALIBER (.257)
- 60 gr. FP #2510
- 75 gr. HP #2520
- 75 gr. V-MAX #22520
- 87 gr. SP #2530
- 100 gr. SP #2540 InterLock
- 117 gr. RN #2550 InterLock
- 117 gr. BTSP #2552 InterLock
- 120 gr. HP #2560 InterLock

6.5MM (.264)
- 95 gr. V-MAX #22601
- 100 gr. SP #2610
- 129 gr. SP #2620 InterLock
- 140 gr. SP #2630 InterLock
- 160 gr. RN #2640 InterLock

270 CALIBER (.277)
- 100 gr. SP #2710
- 110 gr. HP #2720
- 110 gr. V-MAX #22720
- 130 gr. SP #2730 InterLock
- 130 gr. SST Tipped #27302
- 140 gr. BTSP #2735 InterLock
- 150 gr. SP #2740 InterLock
- 150 gr. RN #2745 InterLock

7MM (.284)
- 100 gr. HP #2800
- 120 gr. SP #2810
- 120 gr. HP #2815
- 120 gr. V-MAX #22810
- 120 gr. SSP Tipped #22811
- 139 gr. SP #2820 InterLock
- 139 gr. FP #2822 InterLock
- 139 gr. BTSP #2825 InterLock
- 139 gr. SST #28202 InterLock
- 154 gr. SP #2830 InterLock
- 154 gr. RN #2835 InterLock
- 162 gr. BTSP #2845 InterLock
- 175 gr. SP #2850 InterLock
- 175 gr. RN #2855 InterLock

30 CALIBER (.308)
- 100 gr. SJ #3005
- 110 gr. SP #3010
- 110 gr. RN #3015
- 110 gr. FMJ #3017
- 110 gr. V-MAX #23010
- 130 gr. SP #3020
- 130 gr. SSP #3021 InterLock
- 150 gr. SP #3031 InterLock
- 150 gr. BTSP #3033 InterLock
- 150 gr. RN (30-30) #3035 InterLock
- 150 gr. FMJ-BT #3037
- 150 gr. SST #30302 InterLock
- NEW! 165 gr. SST #30452 InterLock
- 165 gr. SP #3040 InterLock
- 165 gr. BTSP #3045 InterLock
- 170 gr. FP (30-30) #3060 InterLock
- NEW! 180 gr. SST #30702 InterLock
- 180 gr. SP #3070 InterLock
- 180 gr. BTSP #3072 InterLock
- 180 gr. RN #3075 InterLock
- 190 gr. BTSP #3085 InterLock
- 220 gr. RN #3090 InterLock

HORNADY RIFLE BULLETS

RIFLE BULLETS (continued)

MATCH BULLETS

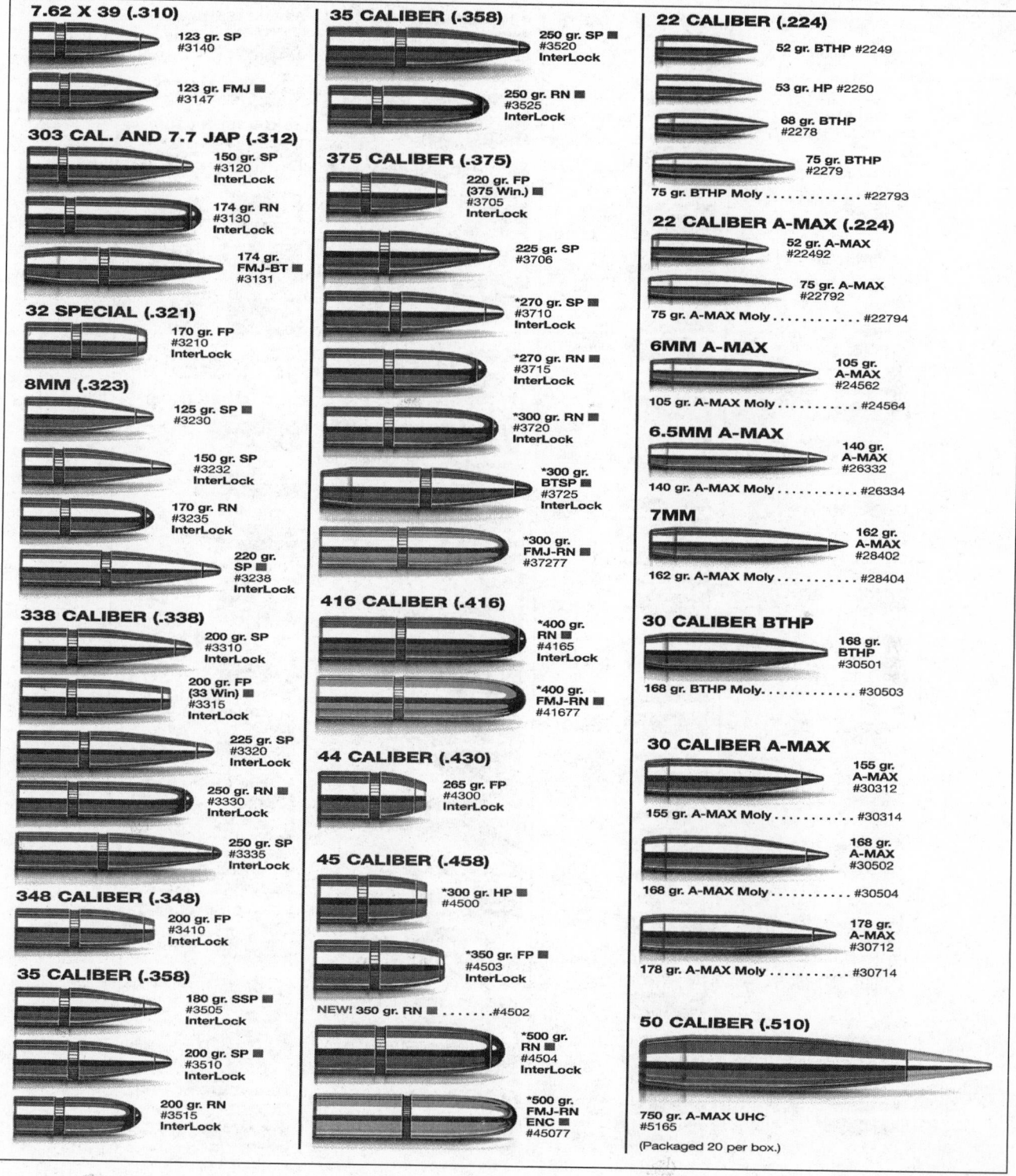

7.62 X 39 (.310)

123 gr. SP
#3140

123 gr. FMJ ■
#3147

303 CAL. AND 7.7 JAP (.312)

150 gr. SP
#3120
InterLock

174 gr. RN
#3130
InterLock

174 gr.
FMJ-BT ■
#3131

32 SPECIAL (.321)

170 gr. FP
#3210
InterLock

8MM (.323)

125 gr. SP ■
#3230

150 gr. SP
#3232
InterLock

170 gr. RN
#3235
InterLock

220 gr.
SP ■
#3238
InterLock

338 CALIBER (.338)

200 gr. SP
#3310
InterLock

200 gr. FP
(33 Win) ■
#3315
InterLock

225 gr. SP
#3320
InterLock

250 gr. RN ■
#3330
InterLock

250 gr. SP
#3335
InterLock

348 CALIBER (.348)

200 gr. FP
#3410
InterLock

35 CALIBER (.358)

180 gr. SSP ■
#3505
InterLock

200 gr. SP ■
#3510
InterLock

200 gr. RN
#3515
InterLock

35 CALIBER (.358)

250 gr. SP ■
#3520
InterLock

250 gr. RN ■
#3525
InterLock

375 CALIBER (.375)

220 gr. FP
(375 Win.) ■
#3705
InterLock

225 gr. SP
#3706

*270 gr. SP ■
#3710
InterLock

*270 gr. RN ■
#3715
InterLock

*300 gr. RN ■
#3720
InterLock

*300 gr.
BTSP ■
#3725
InterLock

*300 gr.
FMJ-RN ■
#37277

416 CALIBER (.416)

*400 gr.
RN ■
#4165
InterLock

*400 gr.
FMJ-RN ■
#41677

44 CALIBER (.430)

265 gr. FP ■
#4300
InterLock

45 CALIBER (.458)

*300 gr. HP ■
#4500

*350 gr. FP ■
#4503
InterLock

NEW! 350 gr. RN ■ . . . .#4502

*500 gr.
RN ■
#4504
InterLock

*500 gr.
FMJ-RN
ENC ■
#45077

22 CALIBER (.224)

52 gr. BTHP #2249

53 gr. HP #2250

68 gr. BTHP
#2278

75 gr. BTHP
#2279

75 gr. BTHP Moly . . . . #22793

22 CALIBER A-MAX (.224)

52 gr. A-MAX
#22492

75 gr. A-MAX
#22792

75 gr. A-MAX Moly . . . . #22794

6MM A-MAX

105 gr.
A-MAX
#24562

105 gr. A-MAX Moly . . . . #24564

6.5MM A-MAX

140 gr.
A-MAX
#26332

140 gr. A-MAX Moly . . . . #26334

7MM

162 gr.
A-MAX
#28402

162 gr. A-MAX Moly . . . . #28404

30 CALIBER BTHP

168 gr.
BTHP
#30501

168 gr. BTHP Moly . . . . #30503

30 CALIBER A-MAX

155 gr.
A-MAX
#30312

155 gr. A-MAX Moly . . . . #30314

168 gr.
A-MAX
#30502

168 gr. A-MAX Moly . . . . #30504

178 gr.
A-MAX
#30712

178 gr. A-MAX Moly . . . . #30714

50 CALIBER (.510)

750 gr. A-MAX UHC
#5165

(Packaged 20 per box.)

HORNADY PISTOL BULLETS

PISTOL BULLETS

LEAD PISTOL BULLETS

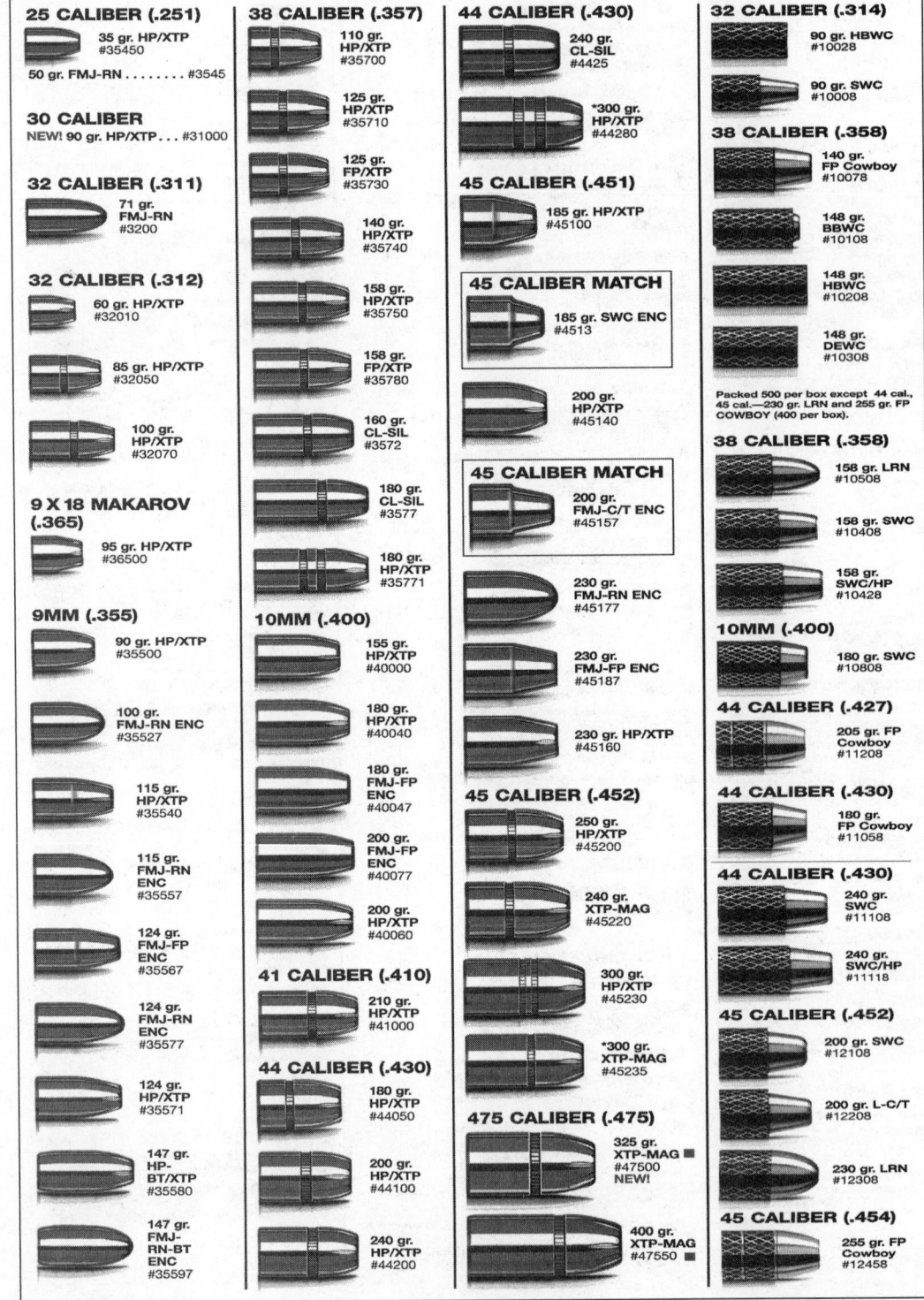

25 CALIBER (.251)
35 gr. HP/XTP #35450
50 gr. FMJ-RN . . . . #3545

30 CALIBER
NEW! 90 gr. HP/XTP . . . #31000

32 CALIBER (.311)
71 gr. FMJ-RN #3200

32 CALIBER (.312)
60 gr. HP/XTP #32010
85 gr. HP/XTP #32050
100 gr. HP/XTP #32070

9 X 18 MAKAROV (.365)
95 gr. HP/XTP #36500

9MM (.355)
90 gr. HP/XTP #35500
100 gr. FMJ-RN ENC #35527
115 gr. HP/XTP #35540
115 gr. FMJ-RN ENC #35557
124 gr. FMJ-FP ENC #35567
124 gr. FMJ-RN ENC #35577
124 gr. HP/XTP #35571
147 gr. HP-BT/XTP #35580
147 gr. FMJ-RN-BT ENC #35597

38 CALIBER (.357)
110 gr. HP/XTP #35700
125 gr. HP/XTP #35710
125 gr. FP/XTP #35730
140 gr. HP/XTP #35740
158 gr. HP/XTP #35750
158 gr. FP/XTP #35780
160 gr. CL-SIL #3572
180 gr. CL-SIL #3577
180 gr. HP/XTP #35771

10MM (.400)
155 gr. HP/XTP #40000
180 gr. HP/XTP #40040
180 gr. FMJ-FP ENC #40047
200 gr. FMJ-FP ENC #40077
200 gr. HP/XTP #40060

41 CALIBER (.410)
210 gr. HP/XTP #41000

44 CALIBER (.430)
180 gr. HP/XTP #44050
200 gr. HP/XTP #44100
240 gr. HP/XTP #44200

44 CALIBER (.430)
240 gr. CL-SIL #4425
*300 gr. HP/XTP #44280

45 CALIBER (.451)
185 gr. HP/XTP #45100

45 CALIBER MATCH
185 gr. SWC ENC #4513

200 gr. HP/XTP #45140

45 CALIBER MATCH
200 gr. FMJ-C/T ENC #45157

230 gr. FMJ-RN ENC #45177
230 gr. FMJ-FP ENC #45187
230 gr. HP/XTP #45160

45 CALIBER (.452)
250 gr. HP/XTP #45200
240 gr. XTP-MAG #45220
300 gr. HP/XTP #45230
*300 gr. XTP-MAG #45235

475 CALIBER (.475)
325 gr. XTP-MAG #47500 NEW!
400 gr. XTP-MAG #47550 ■

32 CALIBER (.314)
90 gr. HBWC #10028
90 gr. SWC #10008

38 CALIBER (.358)
140 gr. FP Cowboy #10078
148 gr. BBWC #10108
148 gr. HBWC #10208
148 gr. DEWC #10308

Packed 500 per box except 44 cal., 45 cal.—230 gr. LRN and 255 gr. FP COWBOY (400 per box).

38 CALIBER (.358)
158 gr. LRN #10508
158 gr. SWC #10408
158 gr. SWC/HP #10428

10MM (.400)
180 gr. SWC #10808

44 CALIBER (.427)
205 gr. FP Cowboy #11208

44 CALIBER (.430)
180 gr. FP Cowboy #11058

44 CALIBER (.430)
240 gr. SWC #11108
240 gr. SWC/HP #11118

45 CALIBER (.452)
200 gr. SWC #12108
200 gr. L-C/T #12208
230 gr. LRN #12308

45 CALIBER (.454)
255 gr. FP Cowboy #12458

NOSLER BULLETS

NOSLER J4 COMPETITION

Nosler has blended the renowned accuracy of J4 bullet jacket with its own ultra-precise lead alloy cores to create a new performance standard for the popular .30 caliber match bullets.

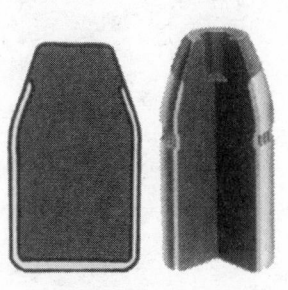

Bullets for Pistols

Cal. Dia.		BULLET WEIGHT AND STYLE	SECT. DENS.	BAL. COEF.	PART#
30 .308"		155 GR. HPBT 250 QUANTITY BULK PACK	.233	.450	53155 53169
		168 GR. HPBT 250 QUANTITY BULK PACK	.253	.462	53164 53168
9mm .355"		115 GR. HOLLOW POINT 250 QUANTITY BULK PACK	.130	.110	44848
38 .357"		115 GR. HOLLOW POINT PRACTICAL PISTOL™ 250 QUANTITY BULK PACK	.129	.110	44835
		135 GR. PRACTICAL PISTOL™ 250 QUANTITY BULK PACK	.151	.149	44836
10mm .400"		135 GR. HOLLOW POINT 250 QUANTITY BULK PACK	.121	.093	44852
		150 GR. HOLLOW POINT 250 QUANTITY BULK PACK	.134	.106	44860
45 .451"		185 GR. HOLLOW POINT 250 QUANTITY BULK PACK	.130	.142	44847
		230 GR. FULL METAL JACKET	.162	.183	42064

Bullets for Revolvers

Cal. Dia.		BULLET WEIGHT AND STYLE	SECT. DENS.	BAL. COEF.	PART#
38 .357"		125 GR. HOLLOW POINT 250 QUANTITY BULK PACK	.140	.143	44840
		158 GR. HOLLOW POINT 250 QUANTITY BULK PACK	.177	.182	44841
		180 GR. SILHOUETTE 250 QUANTITY BULK PACK	.202	.210	44851
41 .410"		210 GR. HOLLOW POINT	.178	.170	43012
		200 GR. HOLLOW POINT 250 QUANTITY BULK PACK	.155	.151	44846
44 .429"		240 GR. HOLLOW POINT 250 QUANTITY BULK PACK	.186	.173	44842
		240 GR. SOFT POINT 250 QUANTITY BULK PACK	.186	.177	44868
		300 GR. HOLLOW POINT	.233	.206	42069
45 Colt .451"		250 GR. HOLLOW POINT	.176	.177	43013

Partition-HG™

50 cal/250 GR. JHP	.429"	50441
50 cal/260 GR. JHP	.451"	50260
54 cal/260 GR. JHP	.451"	54261
50 cal/300 GR. JPP	.451"	50281
54 cal/300 GR. JPP	.451"	54281

S.H.O.T.S.™

50 cal/250 grain JHP	.451"	50251
50 cal/300 grain JHP	.429"	50301
54 cal/250 grain JHP	.451"	54251

High volume shooters can now get Nosler's specially designed plastic muzzleloading sabots in 50-count Bulk Packs:

50 cal. sabots for 44 cal. bullets	50095
50 cal. sabots for 45 cal. bullets	50096
54 cal. sabots for 45 cal. bullets	50097

NOSLER BULLETS

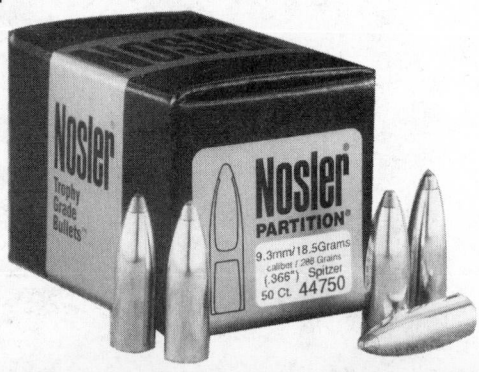

NOSLER PARTITION® BULLETS

The Nosler Partition® bullet earned its reputation among professional guides and serious hunters for one reason: it doesn't fail. The patented Partition® design offers a dual core that is unequalled in mushrooming, weight retention and hydrostatic shock.

Cal. Dia.	BULLET WEIGHT AND STYLE	SECT. DENS.	BAL. COEF.	PART#
22 .224"	60 GR. SPITZER	.171	.228	16316
6mm .243"	85 GR. SPITZER	.206	.315	16314
	95 GR. SPITZER	.230	.365	16315
	100 GR. SPITZER	.242	.384	35642
25 .257"	100 GR. SPITZER	.216	.377	16317
	115 GR. SPITZER	.249	.389	16318
	120 GR. SPITZER	.260	.391	35643
6.5mm .264"	100 GR. SPITZER	.205	.326	16319
	125 GR. SPITZER	.256	.449	16320
	140 GR. SPITZER	.287	.490	16321
270 .277"	130 GR. SPITZER	.242	.416	16322
	150 GR. SPITZER	.279	.465	16323
	160 GR. SEMI SPITZER	.298	.434	16324
7mm .284"	140 GR. SPITZER	.248	.434	16325
	150 GR. SPITZER	.266	.456	16326
	160 GR. SPITZER	.283	.475	16327
	175 GR. SPITZER	.310	.519	35645
30 .308"	150 GR. SPITZER	.226	.387	16329
	165 GR. SPITZER	.248	.410	16330
	170 GR. ROUND NOSE	.256	.252	16333
	180 GR. PROTECTED POINT	.271	.361	25396

Cal. Dia.	BULLET WEIGHT AND STYLE	SECT. DENS.	BAL. COEF.	PART#
	180 GR. SPITZER	.271	.474	16331
	200 GR. SPITZER	.301	.481	35626
	220 GR. SEMI SPITZER	.331	.351	16332
8mm .323"	200 GR. SPITZER	.274	.426	35277
	210 GR. SPITZER	.263	.400	16337
338 .338"	225 GR. SPITZER	.281	.454	16336
	250 GR. SPITZER	.313	.473	35644
35 .358"	225 GR. SPITZER	.251	.430	44800
	250 GR. SPITZER	.279	.446	44801
9.3mm .366"	286 GR. SPITZER (18.5 GRAM)	.307	.482	44750
375 .375"	260 GR. SPITZER	.264	.314	44850
	300 GR. SPITZER	.305	.398	44845
416 .416"	400 GR. SPITZER	.330	.390	45200
45-70 .458"	300 GR. PROTECTED POINT	.204	.199	45325
PARTITION-HG™ 38 .357"	180 GR. HOLLOW POINT	.202	.201	35180
44 .429"	250 GR. HOLLOW POINT	.194	.200	44250
	260 GR. HOLLOW POINT	.182	.174	45260
45 .451"	300 GR. PROTECTED POINT	.211	.199	45350

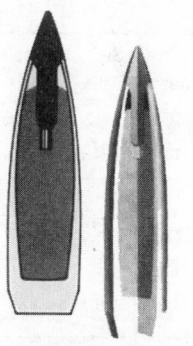

NOSLER BALLISTIC TIP® HUNTING BULLETS

Nosler has replaced the familiar lead point of the Spitzer with a tough polycarbonate tip. The purpose of this new Ballistic Tip® is to resist deforming in the magazine and feed ramp of many rifles. The Solid Base® design produces controlled expansion for excellent mushrooming and exceptional accuracy.

Varmint Bullets

Cal. Dia.	BULLET WEIGHT AND STYLE		SECT. DENS.	BAL. COEF.	PART#
22 .224"		40 GR. SPITZER (ORANGE TIP) 250 CT. VARMINT PAK™	.114	.221	39510 / 39555
		45 GR. HORNET (SOFT LEAD TIP)	.128	.144	35487
		50 GR. SPITZER (ORANGE TIP) 250 CT. VARMINT PAK™	.142	.238	39522 / 39557
		55 GR. SPITZER (ORANGE TIP) 250 CT. VARMINT PAK™	.157	.267	39526 / 39560
6mm .243"		55 GR. SPITZER (PURPLE TIP) 250 CT. VARMINT PAK™	.133	.276	24055 / 39565
		70 GR. SPITZER (PURPLE TIP) 250 CT. VARMINT PAK™	.169	.310	39532 / 39570
		80 GR. SPITZER (PURPLE TIP)	.194	.339	24080
25 .257"		85 GR. SPITZER (BLUE TIP)	.183	.331	43004

Hunting Bullets

Cal. Dia.	BULLET WEIGHT AND STYLE		SECT. DENS.	BAL. COEF.	PART#
6mm .243"		90 GR. SPITZER (PURPLE TIP)	.218	.365	24090
		95 GR. SPITZER (PURPLE TIP)	.230	.379	24095
25 .257"		100 GR. SPITZER (BLUE TIP)	.216	.393	25100
		115 GR. SPITZER (BLUE TIP)	.249	.453	25115
6.5mm .264"		100 GR. SPITZER (BROWN TIP)	.205	.350	26100
		120 GR. SPITZER (BROWN TIP)	.246	.458	26120

Cal. Dia.	BULLET WEIGHT AND STYLE		SECT. DENS.	BAL. COEF.	PART#
270 .277"		130 GR. SPITZER (YELLOW TIP)	.242	.433	27130
		140 GR. SPITZER (YELLOW TIP)	.261	.456	27140
		150 GR. SPITZER (YELLOW TIP)	.279	.496	27150
7mm .284"		120 GR. FLAT POINT (SOFT LEAD TIP)	.213	.195	28121
		120 GR. SPITZER (RED TIP)	.213	.417	28120
		140 GR. SPITZER (RED TIP)	.248	.485	28140
		150 GR. SPITZER (RED TIP)	.266	.493	28150
30 .308"		125 GR. SPITZER (GREEN TIP)	.188	.366	30125
		150 GR. SPITZER (GREEN TIP)	.226	.435	30150
		165 GR. SPITZER (GREEN TIP)	.248	.475	30165
		180 GR. SPITZER (GREEN TIP)	.271	.507	30180
8mm .323"		180 GR. SPITZER (GUNMETAL TIP)	.247	.394	32180
338 .338"		180 GR. SPITZER (MAROON TIP)	.225	.372	33180
		200 GR. SPITZER (MAROON TIP)	.250	.414	33200
35 .358"		225 GR. WHELEN (BUCKSKIN TIP)	.251	.421	35225
9.3mm .366"		250 GR. SPITZER (OLIVE TIP) *Available Mid-year*	.267	.494	36250

NOSLER BULLETS

BALLISTIC SILVER TIP

CAL.	DIA.	BULLET WEIGHT	SECT. DENS.	BAL. COEF.	PART #	CAL.	DIA.	BULLET WEIGHT	SECT. DENS.	BAL. COEF.	PART #
22	.224"	40 grain	.114	.221	51005	270	.277"	130 grain	.242	.433	51075
22	.224"	50 grain	.142	.238	51010	7mm	.284"	140 grain	.248	.485	51105
22	.224"	55 grain	.157	.267	51031	7mm	.284"	150 grain	.266	.493	51110
6mm	.243"	55 grain	.133	.276	51030	30	.308"	150 grain	.226	.435	51150
6mm	.243"	95 grain	.230	.379	51040	30	.308"	168 grain	.253	.490	51160
25	.257"	85 grain	.183	.331	51045	30	.308"	180 grain	.271	.507	51170
25	.257"	115 grain	.249	.453	51050	338	.338"	200 grain	.250	.414	51200

FAIL SAFE

CAL.	DIA.	BULLET WEIGHT	SECT. DENS.	BAL. COEF.	PART #
270	.277"	140 grain	.261	.322	53140
7mm	.284"	140 grain	.248	.323	53150
7mm	.284"	160 grain	.283	.382	53160
30	.308"	150 grain	.226	.308	53170
30	.308"	165 grain	.248	.314	53175
30	.308"	180 grain	.271	.391	53180
338	.338"	230 grain	.288	.436	53230
375	.375"	270 grain	.274	.393	53350
375	.375"	300 grain	.305	.441	53360

Ballistic Silvertip, Fail Safe and Partition Gold bullets are made by Nosler for loading in Winchester ammunition in a project known as Combined Technology.

PARTITION GOLD

CAL.	DIA.	BULLET WEIGHT	SECT. DENS.	BAL. COEF.	PART #
270	.277"	150 grain	.279	.465	52100
7mm	.284"	160 grain	.283	.475	52150
30	.308"	150 grain	.226	.387	52200
30	.308"	180 grain	.271	.474	52230
338	.338"	250 grain	.313	.473	52280

PARTITION GOLD MOLY-FREE

CAL.	DIA.	BULLET WEIGHT	SECT. DENS.	BAL. COEF.	PART #
270	.277"	150 grain	.279	.465	52101
7mm	.284"	160 grain	.283	.475	52151
30	.308"	150 grain	.226	.387	52201
30	.308"	180 grain	.271	.474	52231
338	.338"	250 grain	.313	.473	52281

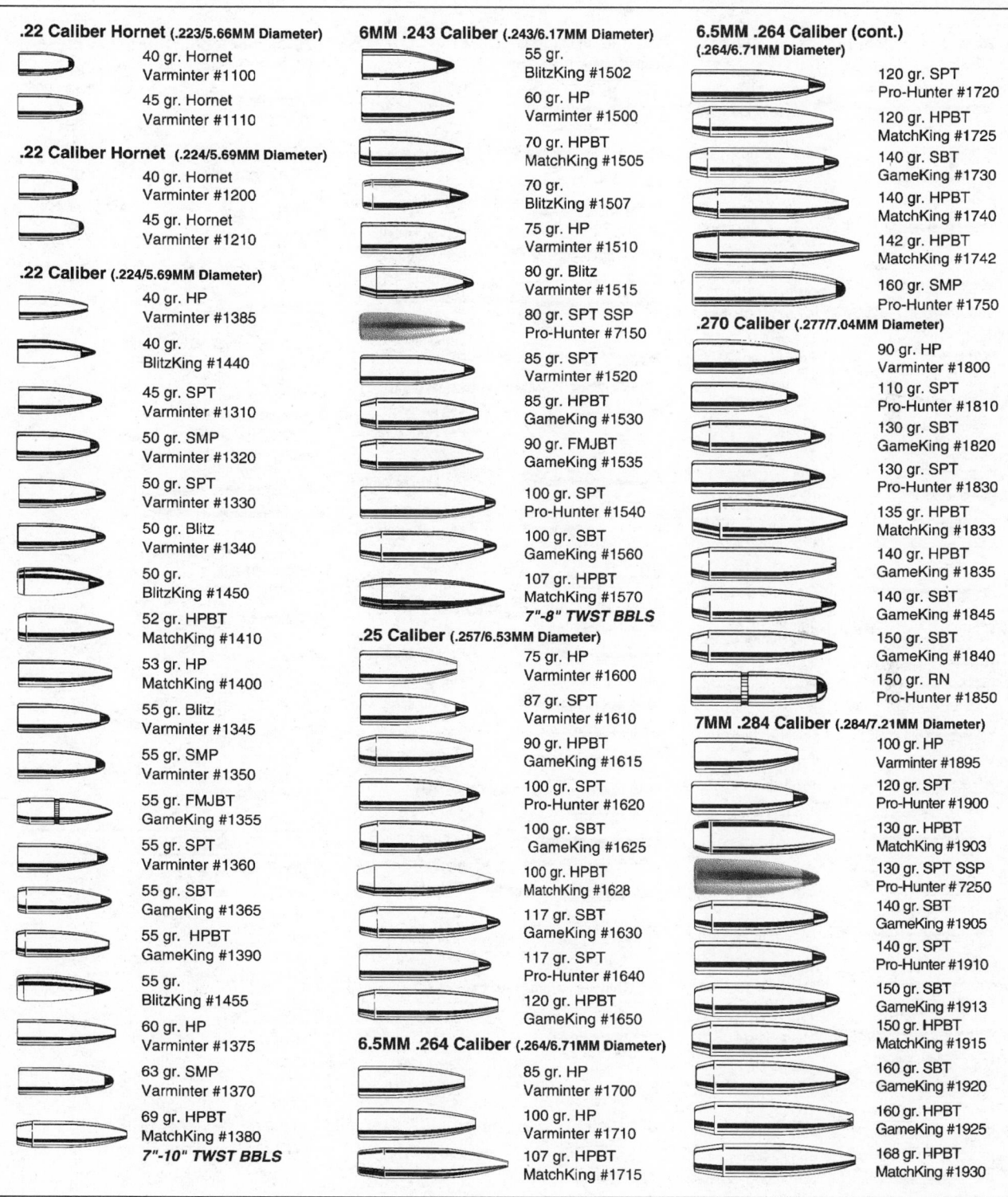

.22 Caliber Hornet (.223/5.66MM Diameter)

40 gr. Hornet
Varminter #1100

45 gr. Hornet
Varminter #1110

.22 Caliber Hornet (.224/5.69MM Diameter)

40 gr. Hornet
Varminter #1200

45 gr. Hornet
Varminter #1210

.22 Caliber (.224/5.69MM Diameter)

40 gr. HP
Varminter #1385

40 gr.
BlitzKing #1440

45 gr. SPT
Varminter #1310

50 gr. SMP
Varminter #1320

50 gr. SPT
Varminter #1330

50 gr. Blitz
Varminter #1340

50 gr.
BlitzKing #1450

52 gr. HPBT
MatchKing #1410

53 gr. HP
MatchKing #1400

55 gr. Blitz
Varminter #1345

55 gr. SMP
Varminter #1350

55 gr. FMJBT
GameKing #1355

55 gr. SPT
Varminter #1360

55 gr. SBT
GameKing #1365

55 gr. HPBT
GameKing #1390

55 gr.
BlitzKing #1455

60 gr. HP
Varminter #1375

63 gr. SMP
Varminter #1370

69 gr. HPBT
MatchKing #1380
7"-10" TWST BBLS

6MM .243 Caliber (.243/6.17MM Diameter)

55 gr.
BlitzKing #1502

60 gr. HP
Varminter #1500

70 gr. HPBT
MatchKing #1505

70 gr.
BlitzKing #1507

75 gr. HP
Varminter #1510

80 gr. Blitz
Varminter #1515

80 gr. SPT SSP
Pro-Hunter #7150

85 gr. SPT
Varminter #1520

85 gr. HPBT
GameKing #1530

90 gr. FMJBT
GameKing #1535

100 gr. SPT
Pro-Hunter #1540

100 gr. SBT
GameKing #1560

107 gr. HPBT
MatchKing #1570
7"-8" TWST BBLS

.25 Caliber (.257/6.53MM Diameter)

75 gr. HP
Varminter #1600

87 gr. SPT
Varminter #1610

90 gr. HPBT
GameKing #1615

100 gr. SPT
Pro-Hunter #1620

100 gr. SBT
GameKing #1625

100 gr. HPBT
MatchKing #1628

117 gr. SBT
GameKing #1630

117 gr. SPT
Pro-Hunter #1640

120 gr. HPBT
GameKing #1650

6.5MM .264 Caliber (.264/6.71MM Diameter)

85 gr. HP
Varminter #1700

100 gr. HP
Varminter #1710

107 gr. HPBT
MatchKing #1715

6.5MM .264 Caliber (cont.)
(.264/6.71MM Diameter)

120 gr. SPT
Pro-Hunter #1720

120 gr. HPBT
MatchKing #1725

140 gr. SBT
GameKing #1730

140 gr. HPBT
MatchKing #1740

142 gr. HPBT
MatchKing #1742

160 gr. SMP
Pro-Hunter #1750

.270 Caliber (.277/7.04MM Diameter)

90 gr. HP
Varminter #1800

110 gr. SPT
Pro-Hunter #1810

130 gr. SBT
GameKing #1820

130 gr. SPT
Pro-Hunter #1830

135 gr. HPBT
MatchKing #1833

140 gr. HPBT
GameKing #1835

140 gr. SBT
GameKing #1845

150 gr. SBT
GameKing #1840

150 gr. RN
Pro-Hunter #1850

7MM .284 Caliber (.284/7.21MM Diameter)

100 gr. HP
Varminter #1895

120 gr. SPT
Pro-Hunter #1900

130 gr. HPBT
MatchKing #1903

130 gr. SPT SSP
Pro-Hunter #7250

140 gr. SBT
GameKing #1905

140 gr. SPT
Pro-Hunter #1910

150 gr. SBT
GameKing #1913

150 gr. HPBT
MatchKing #1915

160 gr. SBT
GameKing #1920

160 gr. HPBT
GameKing #1925

168 gr. HPBT
MatchKing #1930

SIERRA BULLETS

Rifle Bullets

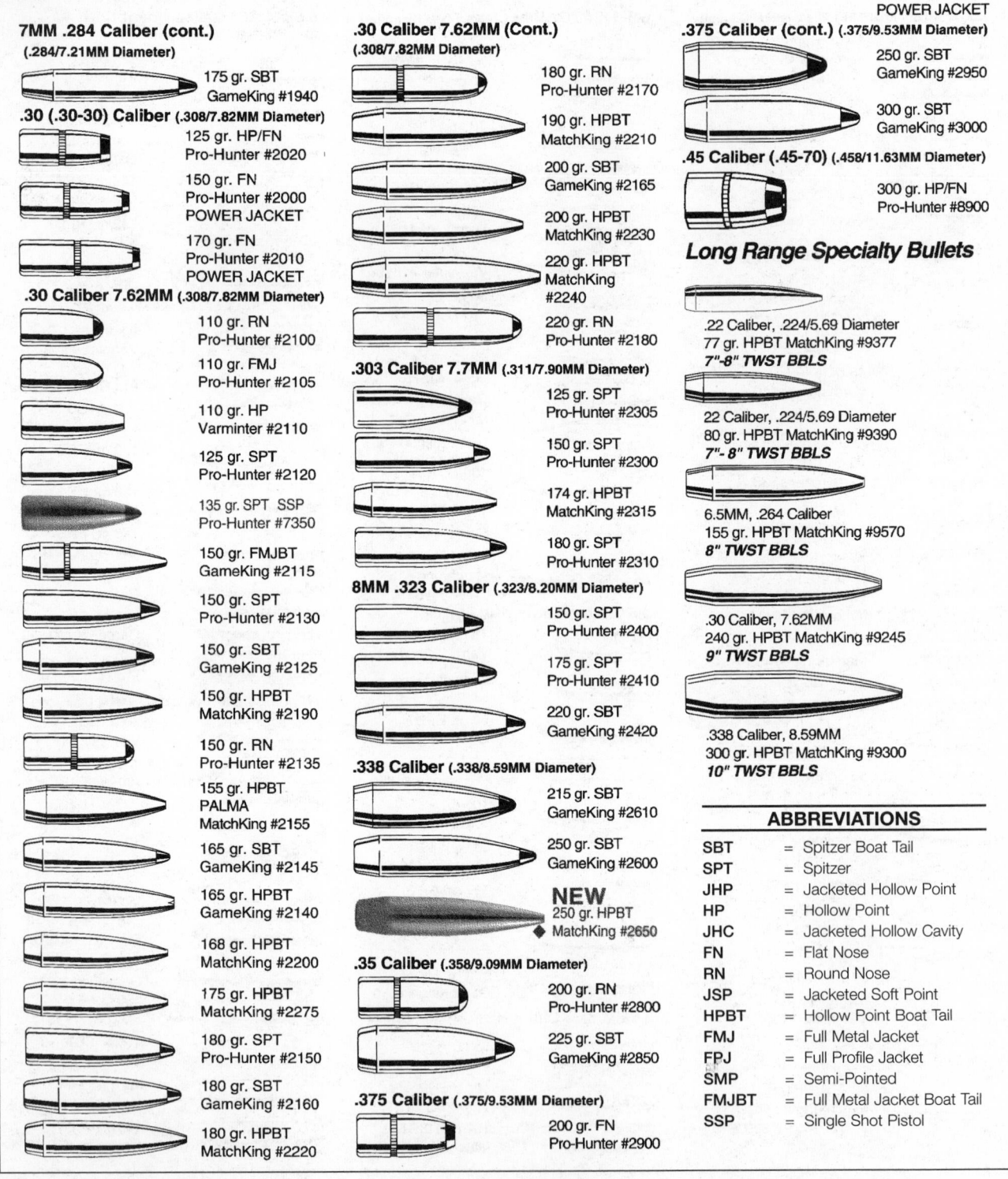

7MM .284 Caliber (cont.)
(.284/7.21MM Diameter)

175 gr. SBT
GameKing #1940

.30 (.30-30) Caliber (.308/7.82MM Diameter)

125 gr. HP/FN
Pro-Hunter #2020

150 gr. FN
Pro-Hunter #2000
POWER JACKET

170 gr. FN
Pro-Hunter #2010
POWER JACKET

.30 Caliber 7.62MM (.308/7.82MM Diameter)

110 gr. RN
Pro-Hunter #2100

110 gr. FMJ
Pro-Hunter #2105

110 gr. HP
Varminter #2110

125 gr. SPT
Pro-Hunter #2120

135 gr. SPT SSP
Pro-Hunter #7350

150 gr. FMJBT
GameKing #2115

150 gr. SPT
Pro-Hunter #2130

150 gr. SBT
GameKing #2125

150 gr. HPBT
MatchKing #2190

150 gr. RN
Pro-Hunter #2135

155 gr. HPBT
PALMA
MatchKing #2155

165 gr. SBT
GameKing #2145

165 gr. HPBT
GameKing #2140

168 gr. HPBT
MatchKing #2200

175 gr. HPBT
MatchKing #2275

180 gr. SPT
Pro-Hunter #2150

180 gr. SBT
GameKing #2160

180 gr. HPBT
MatchKing #2220

.30 Caliber 7.62MM (Cont.)
(.308/7.82MM Diameter)

180 gr. RN
Pro-Hunter #2170

190 gr. HPBT
MatchKing #2210

200 gr. SBT
GameKing #2165

200 gr. HPBT
MatchKing #2230

220 gr. HPBT
MatchKing #2240

220 gr. RN
Pro-Hunter #2180

.303 Caliber 7.7MM (.311/7.90MM Diameter)

125 gr. SPT
Pro-Hunter #2305

150 gr. SPT
Pro-Hunter #2300

174 gr. HPBT
MatchKing #2315

180 gr. SPT
Pro-Hunter #2310

8MM .323 Caliber (.323/8.20MM Diameter)

150 gr. SPT
Pro-Hunter #2400

175 gr. SPT
Pro-Hunter #2410

220 gr. SBT
GameKing #2420

.338 Caliber (.338/8.59MM Diameter)

215 gr. SBT
GameKing #2610

250 gr. SBT
GameKing #2600

NEW
250 gr. HPBT
◆ MatchKing #2650

.35 Caliber (.358/9.09MM Diameter)

200 gr. RN
Pro-Hunter #2800

225 gr. SBT
GameKing #2850

.375 Caliber (.375/9.53MM Diameter)

200 gr. FN
Pro-Hunter #2900

POWER JACKET

.375 Caliber (cont.) (.375/9.53MM Diameter)

250 gr. SBT
GameKing #2950

300 gr. SBT
GameKing #3000

.45 Caliber (.45-70) (.458/11.63MM Diameter)

300 gr. HP/FN
Pro-Hunter #8900

Long Range Specialty Bullets

.22 Caliber, .224/5.69 Diameter
77 gr. HPBT MatchKing #9377
7"-8" TWST BBLS

22 Caliber, .224/5.69 Diameter
80 gr. HPBT MatchKing #9390
7"-8" TWST BBLS

6.5MM, .264 Caliber
155 gr. HPBT MatchKing #9570
8" TWST BBLS

.30 Caliber, 7.62MM
240 gr. HPBT MatchKing #9245
9" TWST BBLS

.338 Caliber, 8.59MM
300 gr. HPBT MatchKing #9300
10" TWST BBLS

ABBREVIATIONS	
SBT	= Spitzer Boat Tail
SPT	= Spitzer
JHP	= Jacketed Hollow Point
HP	= Hollow Point
JHC	= Jacketed Hollow Cavity
FN	= Flat Nose
RN	= Round Nose
JSP	= Jacketed Soft Point
HPBT	= Hollow Point Boat Tail
FMJ	= Full Metal Jacket
FPJ	= Full Profile Jacket
SMP	= Semi-Pointed
FMJBT	= Full Metal Jacket Boat Tail
SSP	= Single Shot Pistol

.25 Caliber (.251/6.38MM Diameter)
50 gr. FMJ
Tournament Master #8000

.30 Caliber (.308/7.82MM Diameter)
85 gr. RN
Sports Master #8005

.32 Caliber 7.65MM (.312/7.92MM Diameter)
71 gr. FMJ
Tournament Master #8010

.32 Mag. (.312/7.92MM Diameter)
90 gr. JHC
Sports Master #8030
POWER JACKET

9MM .355 Caliber (.355/9.02MM Diameter)
90 gr. JHP
Sports Master #8100
POWER JACKET

95 gr. FMJ
Tournament Master #8105

115 gr. JHP
Sports Master #8110
POWER JACKET

115 gr. FMJ
Tournament Master #8115

125 gr. JHP Sports Master
#8125 POWER JACKET

125 gr. FMJ
Tournament Master #8120

130 gr. FMJ
Tournament Master #8345

.38 Super (.356/9.04MM Diameter)
150 gr. FPJ Match
Tournament Master #8250

.38 Caliber (.357/9.07MM Diameter)
110 gr. JHC Blitz
Sports Master #8300
POWER JACKET

125 gr. JSP
Sports Master #8310

125 gr. JHC
Sports Master #8320
POWER JACKET

.38 Caliber (cont.) (.357/9.07MM Diameter)
140 gr. JHC
Sports Master #8325
POWER JACKET

158 gr. JSP
Sports Master #8340

158 gr. JHC
Sports Master #8360
POWER JACKET

170 gr. JHC
Sports Master #8365
POWER JACKET

170 gr. FMJ Match
Tournament Master #8350

180 gr. FPJ Match
Tournament Master #8370

9MM Makarov (.363/9.22MM Diameter)
95 gr. JHP
Sports Master #8200
POWER JACKET

100 gr. FPJ
Tournament Master #8210

10MM .400 Caliber (.400/10.16MM Diameter)
135 gr. JHP
Sports Master #8425
POWER JACKET

150 gr. JHP
Sports Master #8430
POWER JACKET

165 gr. JHP
Sports Master #8445
POWER JACKET

180 gr. JHP
Sports Master #8460
POWER JACKET

190 gr. FPJ
Tournament Master #8480

.41 Caliber (.410/10.41MM Diameter)
170 gr. JHC
Sports Master #8500
POWER JACKET

210 gr. JHC
Sports Master #8520
POWER JACKET

.44 Caliber (.4295/10.91MM Diameter)
180 gr. JHC
Sports Master #8600
POWER JACKET

.44 Caliber (cont.) (.4295/10.91MM Diameter)
210 gr. JHC
Sports Master #8620
POWER JACKET

220 gr. FPJ Match
Tournament Master #8605

240 gr. JHC
Sports Master #8610
POWER JACKET

250 gr. FPJ Match
Tournament Master #8615

300 gr. JSP
Sports Master #8630

.45 Caliber (.4515/11.47MM Diameter)
185 gr. JHP
Sports Master #8800
POWER JACKET

185 gr. FPJ Match
Tournament Master #8810

200 gr. FPJ Match
Tournament Master #8825

230 gr. JHP
Sports Master #8805
POWER JACKET

230 gr. FMJ Match
Tournament Master #8815

240 gr. JHC
Sports Master #8820
POWER JACKET

300 gr. JSP
Sports Master #8830

ABBREVIATIONS
SBT	= Spitzer Boat Tail
SPT	= Spitzer
JHP	= Jacketed Hollow Point
HP	= Hollow Point
JHC	= Jacketed Hollow Cavity
FN	= Flat Nose
RN	= Round Nose
JSP	= Jacketed Soft Point
HPBT	= Hollow Point Boat Tail
FMJ	= Full Metal Jacket
FPJ	= Full Profile Jacket
SMP	= Semi-Pointed
FMJBT	= Full Metal Jacket Boat Tail
SSP	= Single Shot Pistol

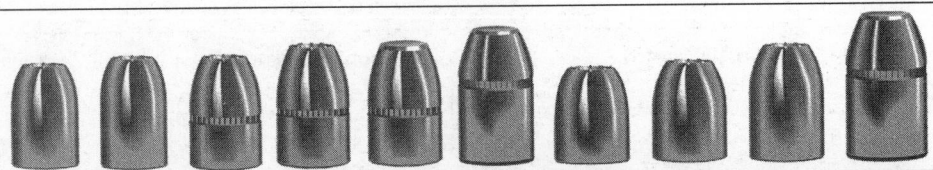

GOLD DOT HANDGUN BULLETS

Caliber & Type	40/10mm Gold Dot HP	40/10mm Gold Dot HP	44 Special Gold Dot HP	44 Mag Gold Dot HP	44 Mag Gold Dot SP	44 Mag Gold Dot SP	45 Gold Dot HP	45 Gold Dot HP	45 Gold Dot HP	475 Linebaugh Gold Dot SP
Diameter	.400"	.400"	.429"	.429"	.429"	.429"	.451"	.451"	.451"	.475"
Weight (grs.)	165	180	200	240	240	270	185	200	230	400
Ballist. Coef.	0.138	0.143	0.145	0.175	0.175	0.193	0.109	0.138	0.143	0.178
Part Number	4397	4406	4427	4455	4456	4461	4470	4478	4483	3976
Box Count	100	100	100	100	100	50	100	100	100	50

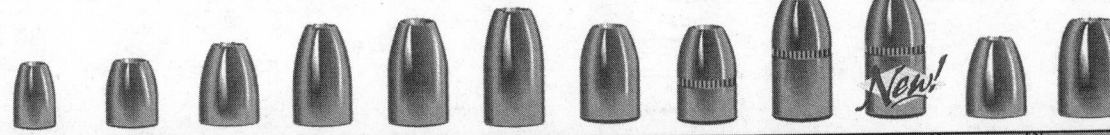

Caliber & Type	25 Auto Gold Dot HP	32 Auto Gold Dot HP	380 Auto Gold Dot HP	9mm Gold Dot HP	9mm Gold Dot HP	9mm Gold Dot HP	357 SIG 38 Super Gold Dot HP	38/357 Gold Dot HP	38/357 Gold Dot HP	357 Mag Gold Dot SP	9x18mm Makarov Gold Dot HP	40/10mm Gold Dot HP
Diameter	.251"	.312"	.355"	.355"	.355"	.355"	.355"	.357"	.357"	.357"	.364"	.400"
Weight (grs.)	35	60	90	115	124	147	125	125	158	170	90	155
Ballist. Coef.	0.091	0.118	0.101	0.125	0.134	0.164	0.141	0.140	0.168	0.185	0.107	0.123
Part Number	3985	3986	3992	3994	3998	4002	4360	4012	4215	4230	3999	4400
Box Count	100	100	100	100	100	100	100	100	100	100	100	100

UNI-COR HANDGUN BULLETS

Caliber &Type	25 Auto TMJ	380 Auto TMJ	9mm TMJ	9mm SP	9mm TMJ	9mm TMJ	357 SIG 38 Super TMJ	38/357 TMJ
Diameter	.251"	.355"	.355"	.355"	.355"	.355"	.355"	.357"
Weight	50	95	115	124	130	147	125	125
Ballist. Coef.	0.110	0.131	0.177	0.115	0.165	0.208	0.147	0.146
Part Number	3982	4001	3995	3997	4010	4006	4362	4015
Box Count	100	100	100	100	100	100	100	100

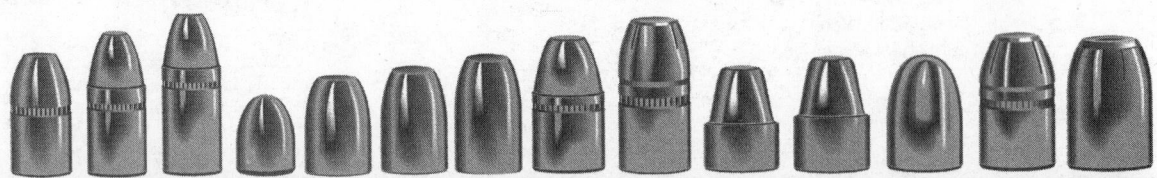

Caliber &Type	38/357 TMJ	357 Mag Sil. Match TMJ	357 Mag Sil. Match TMJ	9x18mm Makarov TMJ	40/10mm TMJ	40/10mm TMJ	40/10mm TMJ	44 Mag Sil. Match TMJ	44 Mag SP	45 Match TMJ	45 Match TMJ	45 Auto TMJ	45 Colt 454 Casull SP	50 Action Express HP
Diameter	.357"	.357"	.357"	.364"	.400"	.400"	.400"	.429"	.429"	.451"	.451"	.451"	.451"	.500"
Weight	158	180	200	95	155	165	180	240	300	185	200	230	300	325
Ballist. Coef.	0.173	0.230	0.236	0.127	0.125	0.135	0.143	0.206	0.213	0.090	0.128	0.153	0.199	0.149
Part Number	4207	4229	4231	4375	4399	4410	4402	4459	4463	4473	4475	4480	4485	4495
Box Count	100	100	100	100	100	100	100	100	50	100	100	100	50	50

SPEER HANDGUN BULLETS

JACKETED HANDGUN BULLETS

Caliber &Type	32 JHP	32 JHP	38/357 JHP	38/357 JSP	38/357 JHP	38/357 JHP	38/357 JHP-SWC	38/357 JHP
Diameter	.312"	.312"	.357"	.357"	.357"	.357"	.357"	.357"
Weight	85	100	110	125	125	140	146	158
Ballist. Coef.	0.121	0.167	0.122	0.140	0.135	0.152	0.159	0.158
Part Number	3987	3981	4007	4011	4013	4203	4205	4211
Box Count	100	100	100	100	100	100	100	100

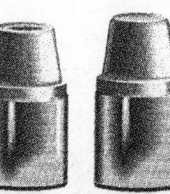

Caliber &Type	38/357 JSP	41 Mag JHP-SWC	41 Mag JSP-SWC	44 Mag JHP	44 Mag JHP-SWC	44 Mag JSP-SWC	44 Mag JHP	44 Mag JSP	45 JHP	45 JHP
Diameter	.357"	.410"	.410"	.429"	.429"	.429"	.429"	.429"	.451"	.451"
Weight	158	200	220	200	225	240	240	240	225	260
Ballist. Coef.	0.158	0.113	0.137	0.122	0.146	0.157	0.165	0.164	0.169	0.183
Part Number	4217	4405	4417	4425	4435	4447	4453	4457	4479	4481
Box Count	100	100	100	100	100	100	100	100	100	100

LEAD HANDGUN BULLETS

Want to shoot more for less money? Speer lead handgun bullets give you an economical alternative to jacketed bullets. Swaged, not cast, construction means you get the same quality–box after box. No worries about voids or slag that can cause flyers with cast bullets. Each Speer lead handgun bullet is coated with a clean lubricant to reduce fouling. Available in a variety of styles in calibers from 32 to 45.

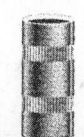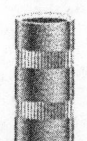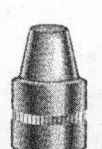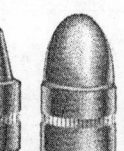

LEAD HANDGUN BULLETS

Caliber & Type	32 HB-WC	9mm RN	38 BB-WC	38 DE-WC	38 HB-WC	38 SWC	38 HP-SWC	38 RN	44 SWC	45 SWC	45 RN	45 SWC
Diameter	.314"	.356"	.358"	.358"	.358"	.358"	.358"	.358"	.430"	.452"	.452"	.452"
Weight (grs.)	98	125	148	148	148	158	158	158	240	200	230	250
Part Number	--	4601	4605	--	4617	4623	4627	4647	4660	4677	4690	4683
Bulk Part No.	4600	4602	4606	4611	4618	4624	4628	4648	4661	4678	4691	4684

SPEER RIFLE BULLETS

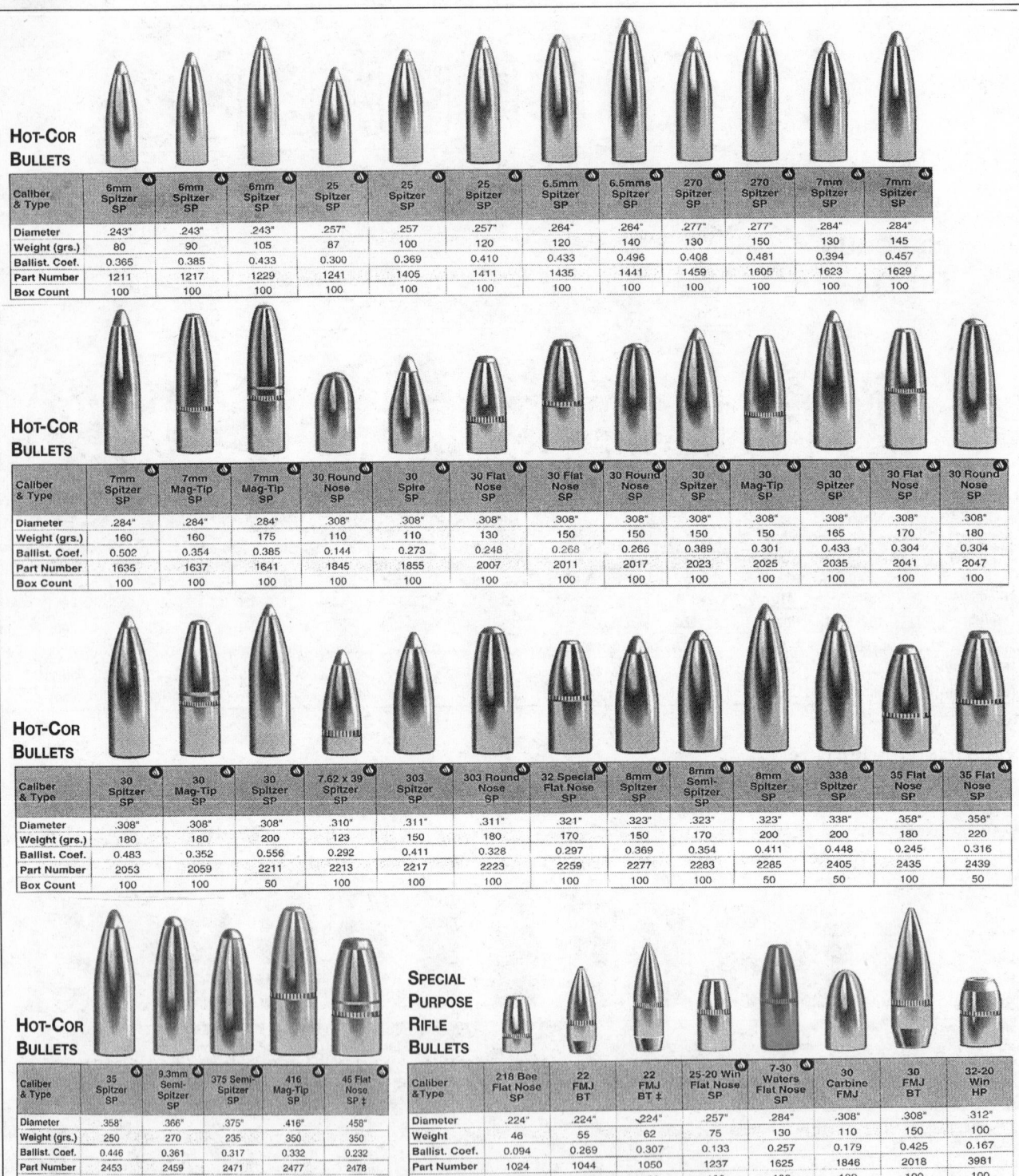

HOT-COR BULLETS

Caliber & Type	6mm Spitzer SP	6mm Spitzer SP	6mm Spitzer SP	25 Spitzer SP	25 Spitzer SP	25 Spitzer SP	6.5mm Spitzer SP	6.5mm Spitzer SP	270 Spitzer SP	270 Spitzer SP	7mm Spitzer SP	7mm Spitzer SP
Diameter	.243"	.243"	.243"	.257"	.257	.257"	.264"	.264"	.277"	.277"	.284"	.284"
Weight (grs.)	80	90	105	87	100	120	120	140	130	150	130	145
Ballist. Coef.	0.365	0.385	0.433	0.300	0.369	0.410	0.433	0.496	0.408	0.481	0.394	0.457
Part Number	1211	1217	1229	1241	1405	1411	1435	1441	1459	1605	1623	1629
Box Count	100	100	100	100	100	100	100	100	100	100	100	100

HOT-COR BULLETS

Caliber & Type	7mm Spitzer SP	7mm Mag-Tip SP	7mm Mag-Tip SP	30 Round Nose SP	30 Spire SP	30 Flat Nose SP	30 Flat Nose SP	30 Round Nose SP	30 Spitzer SP	30 Mag-Tip SP	30 Spitzer SP	30 Flat Nose SP	30 Round Nose SP
Diameter	.284"	.284"	.284"	.308"	.308"	.308"	.308"	.308"	.308"	.308"	.308"	.308"	.308"
Weight (grs.)	160	160	175	110	110	130	150	150	150	150	165	170	180
Ballist. Coef.	0.502	0.354	0.385	0.144	0.273	0.248	0.268	0.266	0.389	0.301	0.433	0.304	0.304
Part Number	1635	1637	1641	1845	1855	2007	2011	2017	2023	2025	2035	2041	2047
Box Count	100	100	100	100	100	100	100	100	100	100	100	100	100

HOT-COR BULLETS

Caliber & Type	30 Spitzer SP	30 Mag-Tip SP	30 Spitzer SP	7.62 x 39 Spitzer SP	303 Spitzer SP	303 Round Nose SP	32 Special Flat Nose SP	8mm Spitzer SP	8mm Semi-Spitzer SP	8mm Spitzer SP	338 Spitzer SP	35 Flat Nose SP	35 Flat Nose SP
Diameter	.308"	.308"	.308"	.310"	.311"	.311"	.321"	.323"	.323"	.323"	.338"	.358"	.358"
Weight (grs.)	180	180	200	123	150	180	170	150	170	200	200	180	220
Ballist. Coef.	0.483	0.352	0.556	0.292	0.411	0.328	0.297	0.369	0.354	0.411	0.448	0.245	0.316
Part Number	2053	2059	2211	2213	2217	2223	2259	2277	2283	2285	2405	2435	2439
Box Count	100	100	50	100	100	100	100	100	100	50	50	100	50

HOT-COR BULLETS

Caliber & Type	35 Spitzer SP	9.3mm Semi-Spitzer SP	375 Semi-Spitzer SP	416 Mag-Tip SP	45 Flat Nose SP ‡
Diameter	.358"	.366"	.375"	.416"	.458"
Weight (grs.)	250	270	235	350	350
Ballist. Coef.	0.446	0.361	0.317	0.332	0.232
Part Number	2453	2459	2471	2477	2478
Box Count	50	50	50	50	50

‡ Not recommended for lever-action rifles.

SPECIAL PURPOSE RIFLE BULLETS

Caliber & Type	218 Bee Flat Nose SP	22 FMJ BT	22 FMJ BT ‡	25-20 Win Flat Nose SP	7-30 Waters Flat Nose SP	30 Carbine FMJ	30 FMJ BT	32-20 Win HP
Diameter	.224"	.224"	.224"	.257"	.284"	.308"	.308"	.312"
Weight	46	55	62	75	130	110	150	100
Ballist. Coef.	0.094	0.269	0.307	0.133	0.257	0.179	0.425	0.167
Part Number	1024	1044	1050	1237	1625	1846	2018	3981
Box Count	100	100	100	100	100	100	100	100

‡ Recommended for twist rates of 1 in 10" or faster.

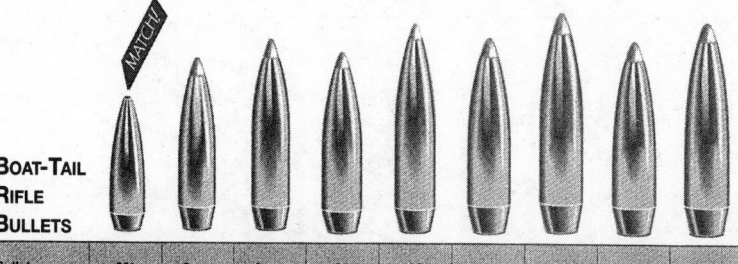

BOAT-TAIL RIFLE BULLETS

Bullet Caliber & Type	22" Match HPBT	6mm Spitzer SPBT	6mm Spitzer SPBT	25 Spitzer SPBT	25 Spitzer SPBT	270 Spitzer SPBT	270 Spitzer SPBT	7mm Spitzer SPBT	7mm Spitzer SPBT
Diameter	.224"	.243"	.243"	.257"	.257"	.277"	.277"	.284"	.284"
Weight (grs.)	52	85	100	100	120	130	150	130	145
Ballist. Coef.	0.253	0.404	0.430	0.393	0.435	0.449	0.496	0.411	0.502
Part Number	1036	1213	1220	1408	1410	1458	1604	1624	1628
Box Count	100	100	100	100	100	100	100	100	100

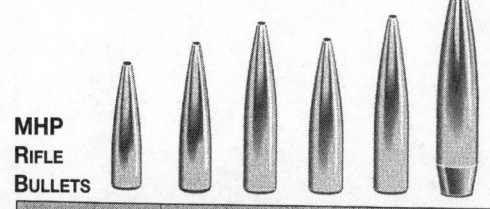

MHP RIFLE BULLETS

Caliber & Type	22 MHP HP	6mm MHP HP	25 MHP HP	270 MHP HP	7mm MHP HP	30 MHP Match HPBT
Diameter	.224"	.243"	.257"	.277"	.284"	.308"
Weight	50	70	87	90	110	168
Ballist. Coef.	0.234	0.296	0.325	0.289	0.355	0.504
Part Number	1031	1207	1247	1457	1615	2039
Box Count	100	100	100	100	100	100

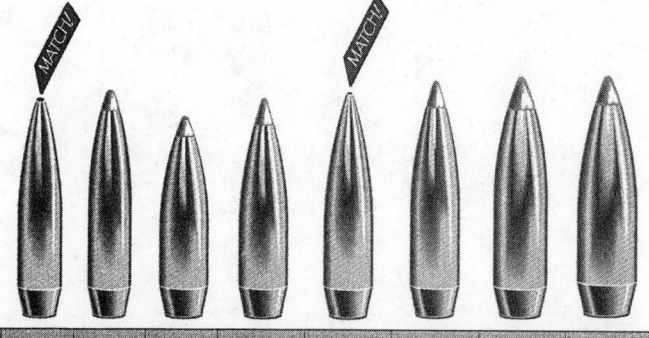

BOAT-TAIL RIFLE BULLETS

Bullet Caliber & Type	7mm* Match HPBT	7mm Spitzer SPBT	30 Spitzer SPBT	30 Spitzer SPBT	30* Match HPBT	30 Spitzer SPBT	338 Spitzer SPBT	375 Spitzer SPBT
Diameter	.284"	.284"	.308"	.308"	.308"	.308"	.338"	.375"
Weight (grs.)	145	160	150	165	168	180	225	270
Ballist. Coef.	0.465	0.556	0.423	0.477	0.480	0.540	0.484	0.429
Part Number	1631	1634	2022	2034	2040	2052	2406	2472
Box Count	100	100	100	100	100	100	50	50

*Match bullets are not recommended for use on game animals.

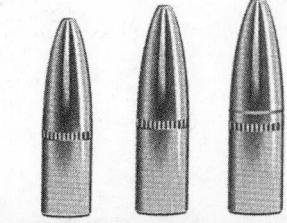

GRAND SLAM

Bullet Caliber & Type	6mm GS SP	25 GS SP	6.5mm GS SP
Diameter	.243"	.257"	.264"
Weight (grs.)	100	120	140
Ballist. Coef.	0.351	0.328	0.385
Part Number	1222	1415	1444
Box Count	50	50	50

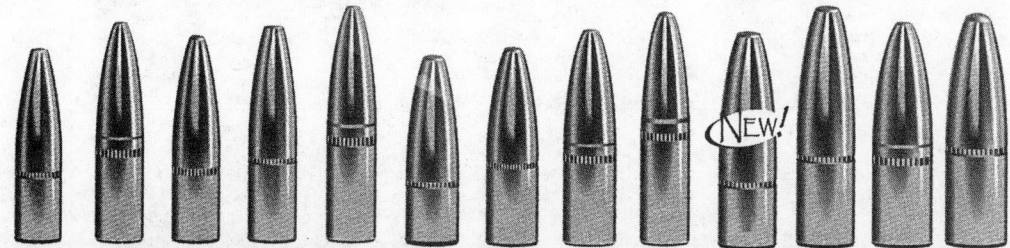

GRAND SLAM

Bullet Caliber & Type	270 Grand Slam SP	270 Grand Slam SP	7mm Grand Slam SP	7mm Grand Slam SP	7mm Grand Slam SP	30 Grand Slam SP	30 Grand Slam SP	30 Grand Slam SP	30 Grand Slam SP	338 Grand Slam SP	338 Grand Slam SP	35 Grand Slam SP	375 Grand Slam SP
Diameter	.277"	.277"	.284"	.284"	.284"	.308"	.308"	.308"	.308"	.338"	.338"	.358"	.375"
Weight (grs.)	130	150	145	160	175	150	165	180	200	225	250	250	285
Ballist. Coef.	0.345	0.385	0.327	0.387	0.465	0.305	0.393	0.416	0.448	.0382	0.431	0.335	0.354
Part Number	1465	1608	1632	1638	1643	2026	2038	2063	2212	2407	2408	2455	2473
Box Count	50	50	50	50	50	50	50	50	50	50	50	50	50

SPEER RIFLE BULLETS

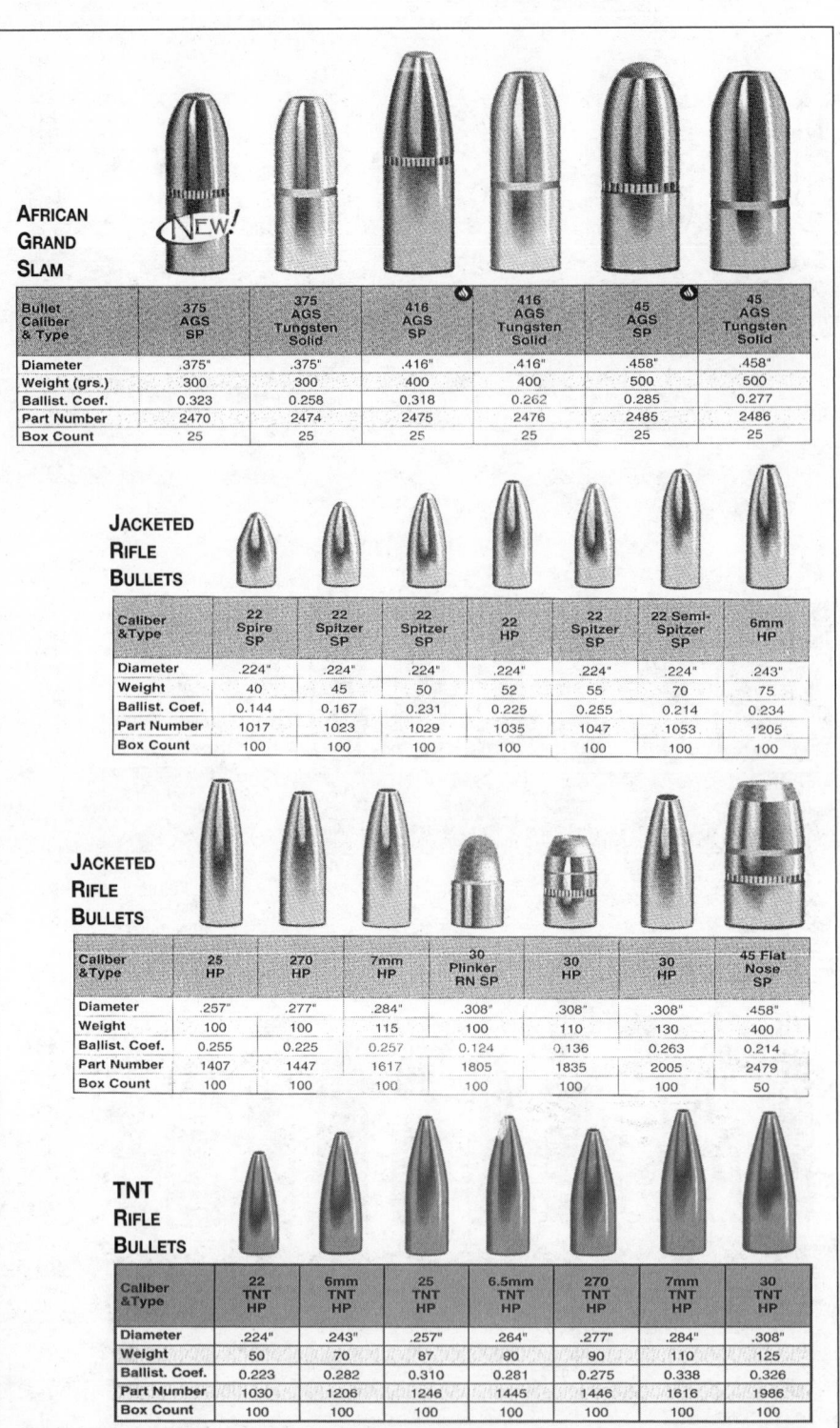

AFRICAN GRAND SLAM

NEW!

Bullet Caliber & Type	375 AGS SP	375 AGS Tungsten Solid	416 AGS SP	416 AGS Tungsten Solid	45 AGS SP	45 AGS Tungsten Solid
Diameter	.375"	.375"	.416"	.416"	.458"	.458"
Weight (grs.)	300	300	400	400	500	500
Ballist. Coef.	0.323	0.258	0.318	0.262	0.285	0.277
Part Number	2470	2474	2475	2476	2485	2486
Box Count	25	25	25	25	25	25

JACKETED RIFLE BULLETS

Caliber & Type	22 Spire SP	22 Spitzer SP	22 Spitzer SP	22 HP	22 Spitzer SP	22 Semi-Spitzer SP	6mm HP
Diameter	.224"	.224"	.224"	.224"	.224"	.224"	.243"
Weight	40	45	50	52	55	70	75
Ballist. Coef.	0.144	0.167	0.231	0.225	0.255	0.214	0.234
Part Number	1017	1023	1029	1035	1047	1053	1205
Box Count	100	100	100	100	100	100	100

JACKETED RIFLE BULLETS

Caliber & Type	25 HP	270 HP	7mm HP	30 Plinker RN SP	30 HP	30 HP	45 Flat Nose SP
Diameter	.257"	.277"	.284"	.308"	.308"	.308"	.458"
Weight	100	100	115	100	110	130	400
Ballist. Coef.	0.255	0.225	0.257	0.124	0.136	0.263	0.214
Part Number	1407	1447	1617	1805	1835	2005	2479
Box Count	100	100	100	100	100	100	50

TNT RIFLE BULLETS

Caliber & Type	22 TNT HP	6mm TNT HP	25 TNT HP	6.5mm TNT HP	270 TNT HP	7mm TNT HP	30 TNT HP
Diameter	.224"	.243"	.257"	.264"	.277"	.284"	.308"
Weight	50	70	87	90	90	110	125
Ballist. Coef.	0.223	0.282	0.310	0.281	0.275	0.338	0.326
Part Number	1030	1206	1246	1445	1446	1616	1986
Box Count	100	100	100	100	100	100	100

Swift Scirocco® Polymer-Tipped Bullet Combines Accuracy, Reliable Expansion and Integrity On Virtually All Game At All Velocities

**SWIFT
SCIROCCO™ BONDED
30 cal. (.308") 180-gr.
Polymer Tip/Boat Tail Spitzer**

Tapered jacket and proprietary bonding process produce controlled mushrooming with high weight retention. Ideally suited to fast, flat-shooting calibers.

**SWIFT BULLETS
30 cal. (.308")
200-gr.**

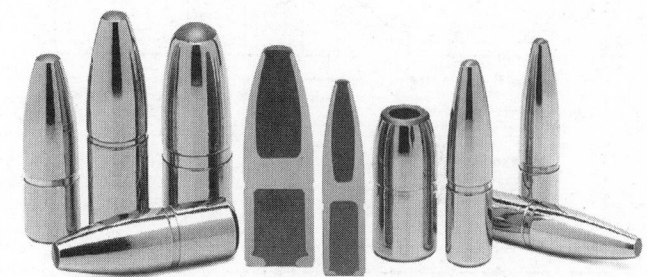

The SWIFT A-FRAME, noted for deep penetration in tough game, is loaded in Remington Premier ammunition.

The Swift Bullet Company has two types of big game bullets.

The **Scirocco** design starts with a tough, pointed, polymer tip that reduces air resistance, prevents tip deformation, and blends symmetrically into the curved radius of its secant ogive nose section. A moderate 15-degree boat tail base reduces drag and eases seating. The thick base prevents bullet deformation during launch. **Scirocco's** shape creates two other significant advantages. One is an extremely high ballistic coefficient. The other, derived from the secant ogive nose, is a comparatively long bearing surface for a sharply pointed bullet, a feature that improves rotational stability.

Inside, the **Scirocco** has a bonded-core construction with a pure lead core encased in a tapered, progressively thickening jacket of pure copper. Pure copper was selected because it is more malleable and less brittle than less expensive gilding metal. Both jacket and core are bonded together by Swift's proprietary bonding process so that the bullet expands without break-up as if the two parts were the same metal. In tests, the new bullet mushroomed effectively at velocities as low as 1440 fps, yet stayed together at velocities in excess of 3,000 fps, with over 70 percent weight retention.

Swift's A-Frame bullet, with its mid-section wall of copper, is still earning praise for its deep-driving dependability in tough game. Less aerodynamic than the Scirocco, it produces a broad mushroom while carrying almost all its weight through muscle and bone. Available in a wide range of weights and diameters, it is also a bonded-core bullet.

1. 1440 FPS   2. 1730 FPS   3. 2245 FPS   4. 2700+ FPS

Swift Scirocco™ Expands dependably over a wide range of velocities, and maintains high jacket/core integrity.

SWIFT

A-Frame Rifle Bullet Specifications

Cal.	A-Frame™ Bullet	Dia.	Wt. (gr.)	Profile	Sect. Den.	Ball. Coef.
.25		.257"	100	AF/SS	.216	.318
		.257"	120	AF/SS	.260	.382
6.5 mm		.264"	120	AF/SS	.246	.344
		.264"	140	AF/SS	.287	.401
.270		.277"	130	AF/SS	.242	.323
		.277"	140	AF/SS	.261	.414
		.277"	150	AF/SS	.279	.444
7mm		.284"	140	AF/SS	.248	.335
		.284"	160	AF/SS	.283	.450
		.284"	175	AF/SS	.310	.493
.30		.308"	165	AF/SS	.249	.367
		.308"	180	AF/SS	.271	.400
		.308"	200	AF/SS	.301	.444
8mm		.323"	200	AF/SS	.274	.357
		.323"	220	AF/SS	.301	.393
.338		.338"	225	AF/SS	.281	.384
		.338"	250	AF/SS	.313	.427
		.338"	275	AF/SS	.344	.469
.35		.358"	225	AF/SS	.251	.312
		.358"	250	AF/SS	.279	.347
		.358"	280	AF/SS	.312	.388

Cal.	A-Frame™ Bullet	Dia.	Wt. (gr.)	Profile	Sect. Den.	Ball. Coef.
9.3 mm		.366"	250	AF/SS	.267	.285
		.366"	300	AF/SS	.320	.342
.375		.375"	250	AF/SS	.254	.271
		.375"	270	AF		
		.375"	300	AF/SS	.305	.325
.416		.416"	350	AF/SS	.289	.321
		.416"	400	AF/SS	.330	.367
.458		.458"	400	AF/FN	.272	.258
		.458"	450	AF/SS	.307	.325
		.458"	500	AF/SS	.341	.361
.470		.475"	500	AF/RN	.329	.364

HANDGUN BULLET SPECIFICATIONS

Cal.	A-Frame™ Bullet	Dia.	Wt. (gr.)	Profile	Sect. Den.	Ball. Coef.
.44		.430"	240	AF/HP	.185	.119
		.430"	280	AF/HP	.216	.139
		.430"	300	AF/HP	.232	.147
.45		.452"	265	AF	.210	.135
		.452"	300	AF/HP	.210	.135
		.452"	325	AF	.210	.135

AF/SS = A-Frame Semi-Spitzer • **AF/FN** = A-Frame Flat Nose • **AF/RN** = A-Frame Round Nose • **AF/HP** = A-Frame Hollow Point

WOODLEIGH PREMIUM BULLETS

WELDCORE SOFT NOSE

Woodleigh Weldcore Soft Nose bullets are made from 90/100 gilding metal (90% copper: 10% zinc) 1.6 mm thick. Maximum retained weight is obtained by fusing the pure lead to the gilding metal jacket, hence the name "Weldcore."

FULL METAL JACKET

Made from gilding metal-clad steel 2mm thick, jackets on fmj bullets are heavy at the nose for extra impact resistance. The jacket then tapers towards the base to assist rifling engraving.

Calibre Diameter	Type	Weight Grain	SD	BC
700 Nitro .700"	SN	1000	.292	.340
	FMJ	1000	.292	.340
600 Nitro .620"	SN	900	.334	.371
	FMJ	900	.334	.334
577 Nitro .585"	SN	750	.313	.346
	FMJ	750	.313	.351
	SN	650	.271	.292
	FMJ	650	.271	.292
577 B.P. .585"	SN	650	.271	.320
500 Nitro .510"	SN	570	.313	.474
	FMJ	570	.313	.434
500 B.P. .510"	SN	440	.242	.336
500 Jeffery .510"	PP	535	.304	.460
	SN	535	.304	.460
	FMJ	535	.304	.422
500 Gibbs .505"	PP	600	.336	.450
	SN	525	.294	.445
	FMJ	525	.294	.408
475 No2 Jeffery .488"	SN	500	.300	.420
	FMJ	500	.300	.416
475 No2 .483"	SN	480	.303	.400
	FMJ	480	.303	.410
476 W.R. .476"	SN	520	.328	.420
	FMJ	520	.328	.455
475 Nitro .476"	SN	480	.227	.307
	FMJ	80	.227	.257
470 Nitro .474"	SN	500	.318	.411
	FMJ	500	.318	.410
465 Nitro .468"	SN	480	.318	.410
	FMJ	480	.318	.407
450 Nitro .458"	SN	480	.327	.419
	FMJ	480	.327	.410
458 Mag. .458"	SN	500	.341	.430
	SN	550	.375	.480
	FMJ	500	.341	.405
	FMJ	550	.375	.426
	PP	400	.272	.420
	RN	350	.238	.305
45/70 .458"	FN	405	.276	.250
11.3x62 Schuler .440"	SN	401	.296	.411
425 W.R. .435"	SN	410	.310	.344
	FMJ	410	.310	.336
404 Jeffery .423"	SN	400	.319	.354
	FMJ	400	.319	.358
	SN	350	.279	.357
10.75x68mm .423"	SN	347	.277	.355
	FMJ	347	.277	.307
416 Rigby .416"	SN	410	.338	.375
	FMJ	410	.338	.341
	PP	340	.281	.425

Calibre Diameter	Type	Weight Grain	SD	BC
450/400 Nitro .411" or .408"	SN	400	.338	.384
	FMJ	400	.338	.433
375 Mag. .375"	PP	235	.239	.331
	RN	270	.275	.305
	SP	270	.275	.380
	PP	270	.275	.352
	RN	300	.305	.340
	SP	300	.305	.425
	PP	300	.305	.420
	FMJ	300	.305	.307
405 Win., .411"	SN	300	.254	.194
9.3mm .366"	SN	286	.305	.331
	FMJ	286	.305	.324
	SN	250	.267	.296
360 No2 .366"	SN	320	.341	.378
	FMJ	320	.341	.362
358 Cal .358"	SN	225	.250	.277
	FMJ	225	.250	.298
	SN	250	.285	.365
	SN	310	.346	.400
	FMJ	310	.346	.378
338 Mag .338"	PP	225	.281	.425
	SN	250	.313	.332
	PP	250	.313	.470
	FMJ	250	.313	.326
	SN	300	.375	.416
	FMJ	300	.375	.398
333 Jeffery .333"	SN	250	.328	.400
	SN	300	.386	.428
	FMJ	300	.386	.419
318 W.R. .330"	SN	250	.328	.420
	FMJ	250	.328	.364
8mm .323"	SN	196	.268	.370
	SN	220	.302	.363
	SN	250	.343	.389
303 British .312	SN	174	.257	.342
	PP	215	.316	.359
308 Cal .308"	FMJ	220	.331	.359
	RN	220	.331	.367
	PP	180	.273	.376
	PP	165	.250	.320
	PP	150	.226	.301
Win. Mag.	PP	180	.273	.435
	PP	200	.301	.450
275 H&H .287"	PP	160	.275	.474
	PP	175	.301	.518
7mm .284"	PP	140	.247	.436
	PP	160	.282	.486
	PP	175	.312	.530
270 Win .277"	PP	130	.241	.409
	PP	150	.278	.463

SP = Semi-point • PP = Protected Point • FN = Flat Nose
• RN = Round Nose • FMJ = Full Metal Jacket
All PP, FN, RN, SP, SN bullets are Weldcore Softnose

98% & 95% retained weight 300 Win Mag 180gr PP

458 x 500gn SN recovered from buffalo

270 Win 150gn PP 86% retained weight

94% retained weight 300 Win Mag 180gr PP

500/465 recovered from buffalo

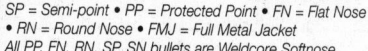

ACCURATE POWDER

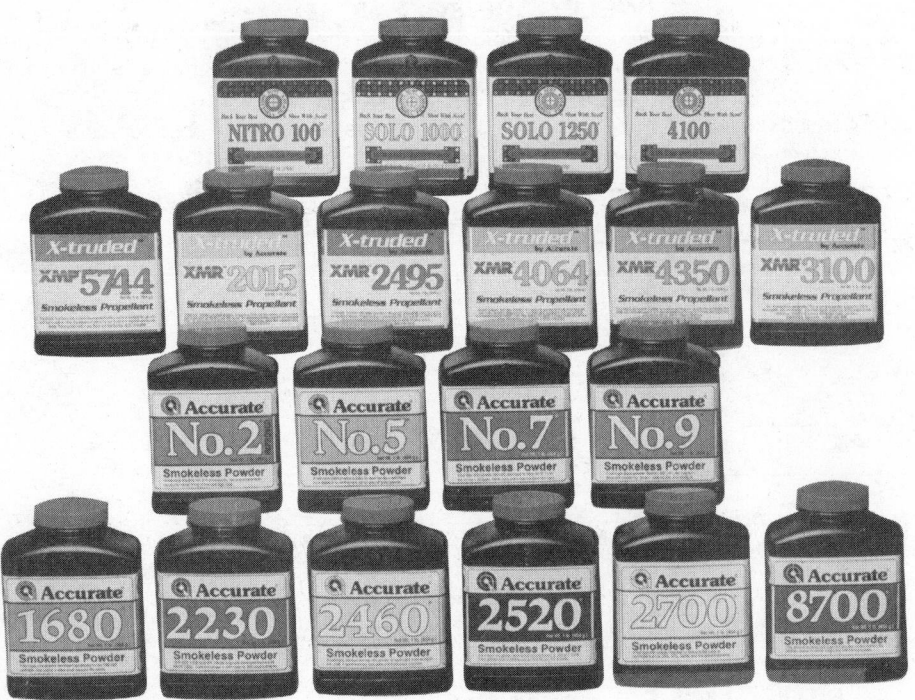

ACCURATE POWDER SPECIFICATIONS

	NG*	AVG. LENGTH	AVG. GRAIN DIAMETER	BULK DENSITY**	COMPARATIVE POWDERS***
BALL PROPELLANTS					
No. 2 Imp.	14.0%	N/A	0.018	0.670	Bullseye, HP38,231
No. 5	17.0%	N/A	0.027	0.950	Unique, 540, 800X
No. 7	10.5%	N/A	0.012	0.985	Blue Dot, HS7, 630
No. 9	10.0%	N/A	0.015	0.975	2400, H110, 296
1680	10.0%	N/A	0.014	0.950	680, 4227, 4198
2230	10.0%	N/A	0.022	1.000	H335, BL-C2, 3031, 748
2460	10.0%	N/A	0.022	0.990	748, H335, BL-C2, 3031
2520	10.0%	N/A	0.022	0.970	4895
2700	10.0%	N/A	0.022	0.960	4350, 760, 4320
8700	10.0%	N/A	0.030	0.960	870, 5010
X-TRUDED PROPELLANTS					
XMP-5744	20.0%	0.048	0.033	0.880	Beyond Comparision
XMR-2015	-	0.039	0.031	0.880	H322, N201, 3031
XMR-2495	-	0.068	0.029	0.900	4895
XMR-4064	-	0.050	0.035	0.900	IMR-4064, 748, BL-C2
XMR-4350	-	0.083	0.038	0.920	IMR-4350
XMR-3100	-	0.083	0.038	0.920	4831, 785
SHOTSHELL PROPELLANTS					
Nitro 100	21.0%	0.010	0.058	0.505	700X, Red Dot
Solo 1000	-	0.010	0.052	0.510	Green Dot
Solo 1250	-	0.010	0.051	0.550	PB
Solo 4100	10.0%	-	0.011	0.960	No. 9, 2400, 296

*NG-Nitroglycerin (glyceryl trinitrate) **glcc ***For comparison only, not a loading recommendation

Alliant Rifle, Shotgun and Pistol Powders

Powder	Relative Quickness	Principal Purpose	Secondary Uses
Bullseye®	100%	Handgun Loads	12 ga. Light Target Loads
Red Dot®	94.1%	Light & Standard 12 & 16 ga. Target Loads	Handgun Loads
American Select®	81.0%	12 ga. Target Loads	Cowboy Action Handgun Loads
Green Dot®	77.9%	Handicap Trap Loads	20 & 28 ga. Target Loads
Unique®	61.6%	All-around Shotshell Powder, 12, 16 & 20 ga.	Handgun Loads
Power Pistol®	58.6%	High Performance 9mm, .40 S&W & 10mm	Moderate Pistol Cartridges
Herco®	56.1%	Heavy Shotshell Loads 10, 12 16, 20 & 28 ga.	Heavy Handgun Loads
Blue Dot®	37.8%	Magnum Shotshell Loads 10, 12, 16, 20 & 28 ga.	Magnum Handgun Loads
Steel™	34.0%	Non-Toxic Hunting Shotshell	2 oz. Turkey Loads
2400®	27.00%	Magnum Handgun Loads	.22 Hornet & 218 Bee
Reloader® 7	19.4%	Light Rifle	45-70 Gov't
Reloader® 15	13.7%	Medium Rifle	Silhouette Rifle
Reloader® 19	11.3%	Standard Rifle	Light Magnum Rifle
Reloader® 22	11.1%	Magnum Rifle	Heavy Bullet Stand Rifle
Reloader® 25	10.5%	Heavy Magnum Rifle	Magnum Rifle

PYRODEX PELLETS
Both rifle and pistol pellets eliminate powder measures, speeds shooting for black powder enthusiasts.

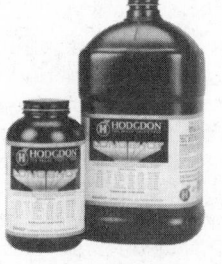

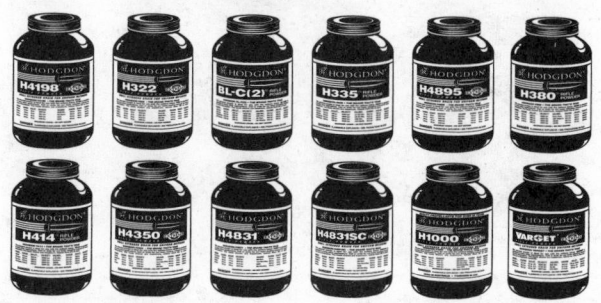

EXTREME H4198
H4198 was developed especially for small and medium capacity cartridges.

EXTREME H322
This powder fills the gap between H4198 and BL-C9(2). Performs best in small to medium capacity cases.

Extreme Benchmark
A fine choice for small rifle cases like the .223 Rem and PPC competition rounds. Appropriate also for the 300-30 and 7x57.

SPHERICAL BL-C2
Best performance is in the 222, .308 other cases smaller than 30/06.

SPHERICAL H335®
Similar to BL-C(2), H335 is popular for its performance in medium capacity cases, especially in 222 and 308 Winchester.

EXTREME VARGET
Features small extruded grain powder for uniform metering, plus higher velocities/normal pressures in such calibers as .223, 22-250, 306, 30-06, 375 H&H

EXTREME H4895®
4895 gives desirable performance in almost all cases from 222 Rem. to 458 Win. Reduced loads, to as low as 3/5 maximum, still give target accuracy.

SPHERICAL H380®
This number fills a gap between 4320 and 4350. It is excellent in 22/250, 220 Swift, the 6mm's, 257 and 30/06.

SPHERICAL H414®
In many popular medium to medium-large calibers, pressure velocity relationship is better.

EXTREME H4350
This powder gives superb accuracy at optimum velocity for many large capacity metallic rifle cartridges.

EXTREME H4831®
Outstanding performance with medium and heavy bullets in the 6mm's, 25/06, 270 and Magnum calibers. Also available with shortened grains (H4831SC) for easy metering.

EXTREME H1000 EXTRUDED POWDER
Fills the gap between H4831 and H870. Works especially well in overbore capacity cartridges (1,000-yard shooters take note).

EXTREME H50 BMG
Designed for the 50 Browning Machine Gun cartridge. Highly insensitive to extreme temperature changes.

CLAYS
Tailored for use in 12 ga., 7/8, 1-oz. and 1 1/8-oz. loads. Also performs well in many handgun applications, including .38 Special, .40 S&W and 45 ACP. Perfect for 1 1/8 and 1 oz. loads.

Universal Clays
Loads nearly all of the straight-wall pistol cartridges as well as 12 ga. 1.25 oz. thru 28 ga. 3/4 oz. target loads.

International Clays
Ideal for 12 and 20 ga. autoloaders who want reduced recoil.

Titewad
This 12 ga. flattened spherical shotgun powder is ideal for 7/8, 1 and 1 1/8 oz. loads, with minimum recoil and mild muzzle report.

HS-6 AND HS-7
HS-6 and HS-7 for Magnum field loads are unsurpassed, since they do not pack in the measure. They deliver uniform charges and are dense to allow sufficient wad column for best patterns.

Longshot
A new spherical powder for heavy shotgun loads.

HP38
A fast pistol powder for most pistol loading. Especially recommended for mid-range 38 specials.

Titegroup
Excellent for most straight-walled pistol cartridges, incl. 38 Spec., 44 Spec., 45 ACP. Low charge weights, clean burning; position insensitive and flawless ignition.

H110
A spherical powder made especially for the 30 M1 carbine. H110 also does very well in 357, 44 spec., 44 Mag. or .410 ga. shotshell. Magnum primers are recommended for consistent ignition.

H4227
An extruded powder similar to H110, it is the fastest burning in Hodgdon's line. Recommended for the 22 Hornet and some specialized loading in the 45-70 caliber. Also excellent in magnum pistol and .410 shotgun.

LIL' GUN
This powder was developed specifically for the .410 shotgun but works very well in rifle cartridges like the .22 Hornet and in the .44 magnum.

RAMSHOT POWDERS

WESTERN POWDERS, INC. recently introduced a line of nine spherical powders for shooters. They are all double-base propellants, meaning they contain nitrocellulose and nitroglycerine. While some spherical or ball powders are known for leaving plenty of residue in barrels, Ramshots people say these new fuels burn very clean. They meter easily, as do all ball powders. Plastic cannisters are designed for spill-proof use and include basic loading data on the labels. More extensive loading information is being prepared.

RAMSHOT COMPETITION is for the clay target shooter. A fast-burning powder comparable to 700-X or Red Dot it performs well in a variety of 12-gauge target loads, offering low recoil, consistent pressures and clean combustion.

RAMSHOT TRUE BLUE was designed for small to medium-size handgun cartridges. Similar to Winchester 231 and Hodgdon HP-38, it has enough bulk to nearly fill most cases, thereby better positioning the powder for ignition.

RAMSHOT ZIP, a fast-burning target powder for cartridges like the .38 Special and .45 ACP, gives competitors uniform velocities.

RAMSHOT SILHOUETTE is ideal for the 9mm handgun cartridge, from light to heavy loads. It also works well in the .40 Smith & Wesson and combat loads for the .45 Auto.

RAMSHOT ENFORCER a match for high-performance handgun hulls like the .40 Smith & Wesson. It is designed for full-power loading and high velocities.

Ramshot X-Terminator, a fast-burning rifle powder, excels in small-caliber, medium-capacity cartridges. It has the versatility to serve in both target and high-performance varmint loads.

RAMSHOT TAC was formulated for tactical rifle cartridges, specifically the .223 and .308. It has produced exceptional accuracy with a variety of bullets and charge weights.

RAMSHOT BIG GAME is a versatile propellant for cartridges as diverse as the .30-06 and the .338 Winchester, and for light-bullet loads in small-bore magnums.

RAMSHOT BIG BOY is the slowest powder of the Western line, and does its best work in cartridges with lots of case volume and small to medium bullet diameter. It is the powder of choice in 7mm and .30 Magnums.

DILLON PRECISION RELOADERS

Dillon Precision is a leader in the shotgun shooting sports market with its SL 900 progressive shotshell reloader. Based on Dillon's proven XL 650 O-frame design, it incorporates the same powerful compound linkage. The automatic case insert system, fed by an electric case collator, ranks high among the new features of this reloader. Adjustable shot and powder bars come as standard equipment. Both the powder and shot bars are case-activated, so no powder or shot can spill when no shell is at that station. Should the operator forget to insert a wad during the reloading process, the SL 900 will not dispense shot into the powder-charged hull. Both powder and shot systems are based on Dillon's adjustable powder bar design, which is accurate to within a few tenths of a grain. These systems also eliminate the need for fixed-volume bushings. Simply adjust the measures to dispense the exact charges required.

The Dillon SL 900 is the first progressive shotshell loader on which it is practical to change gauges. An interchangeable tool-head makes it quick and easy to change from one gauge to another. The SL 900 also has an extra large, remote shot hopper that holds an entire 25-pound bag of shot, making it easy to fill with a funnel. The unique shot reservoir/dispenser helps ensure that a consistent volume of shot is delivered to each shell.

For shotgunners who shoot and load for multiple gauges or different kinds of shooting, the SL 900's interchangeable toolhead feature makes quick work of changing from one gauge to another. It uses a collet-type sizing die that re-forms the base of the shot-shell to factory specifications—a feature that ensures reliable feeding in all shotguns. The heat-treated steel crimp die forms and folds the hull before the final taper crimp die radiuses and blends the end of the hull and locks the crimp into place.

MODEL RL550B PROGRESSIVE LOADER

- Accommodates over 120 calibers
- Interchangeable toolhead assembly
- Auto/Powder priming systems
- Uses standard 7/8" by 14 dies
- Loading rate: 500-600 rounds per hour

Price: $325.95

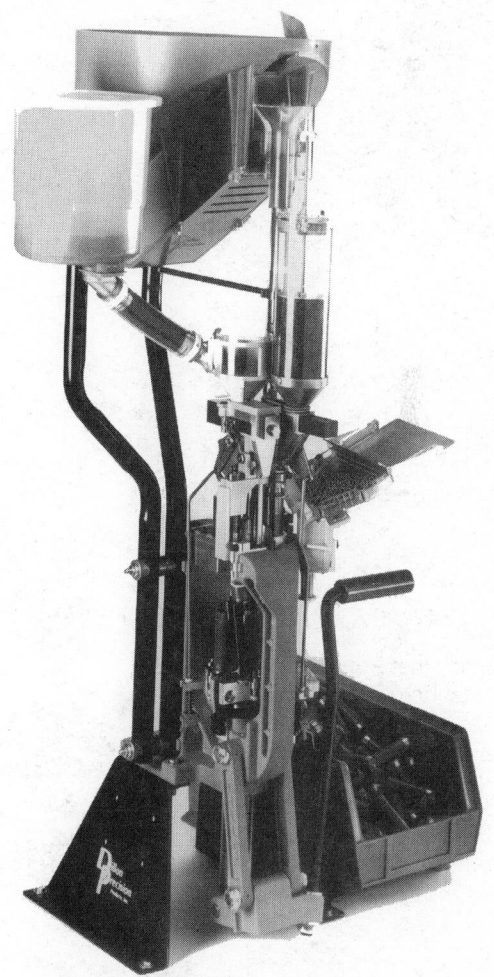

MODEL SL900
$819.95

MODEL SQUARE DEAL B

- Automatic Indexing
- Auto Powder/Priming Systems
- Available in 14 handgun calibers
- Loading rate: 400-500 rounds per hour
- Loading dies standard
- Factory adjusted, ready-to-use

Price: $252.95

MODEL RL 1050

- Automatic indexing
- Auto powder/priming systems
- Automatic casefeeder
- Commercial grade machine
- Swages military primer pockets
- Loading rate: 1000-1200 rounds per hour
- Weighs 54 lbs.
- Eight station

Price: $1,299.95

MODEL XL 650

- Rotary indexing plate for primers
- Automatic indexing
- Uses standard 7/8" x 14 dies
- Loading rate: 800-1000 rounds per hour
- Five station interchangeable toolhead

Price: $443.95

MODEL AT-500

- Loads over 40 calibers
- Uses standard 7/8" by 14 dies
- Upgradeable to Model RL 550B
- Interchangeable toolhead
- Switch from one caliber to another in 30 seconds
- Universal shellplate

Price: $193.95

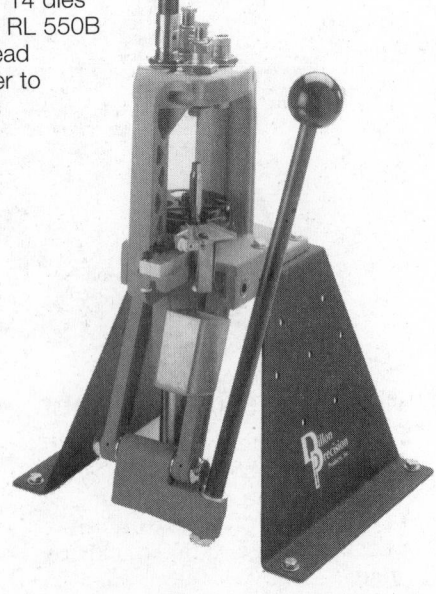

CO-AX® BENCH REST® RIFLE DIES

Bench Rest Rifle Dies are glass hard and polished mirror smooth with special attention given to headspace, tapers and diameters. Sizing die has an elevated expander button to ensure better alignment of case and neck.

BENCH REST® DIE SET	$72.00
ULTRA BENCH REST DIE SET	94.98
FULL LENGTH SIZER	32.98
BENCH REST SEATING DIE	39.98

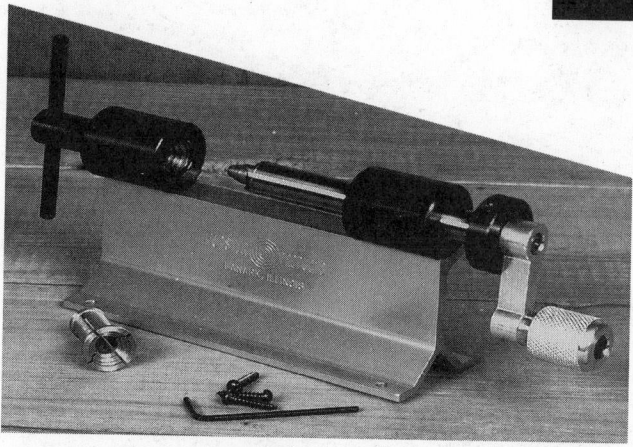

PRIMER SEATER

CO-AX® CARTRIDGE INSPECTOR

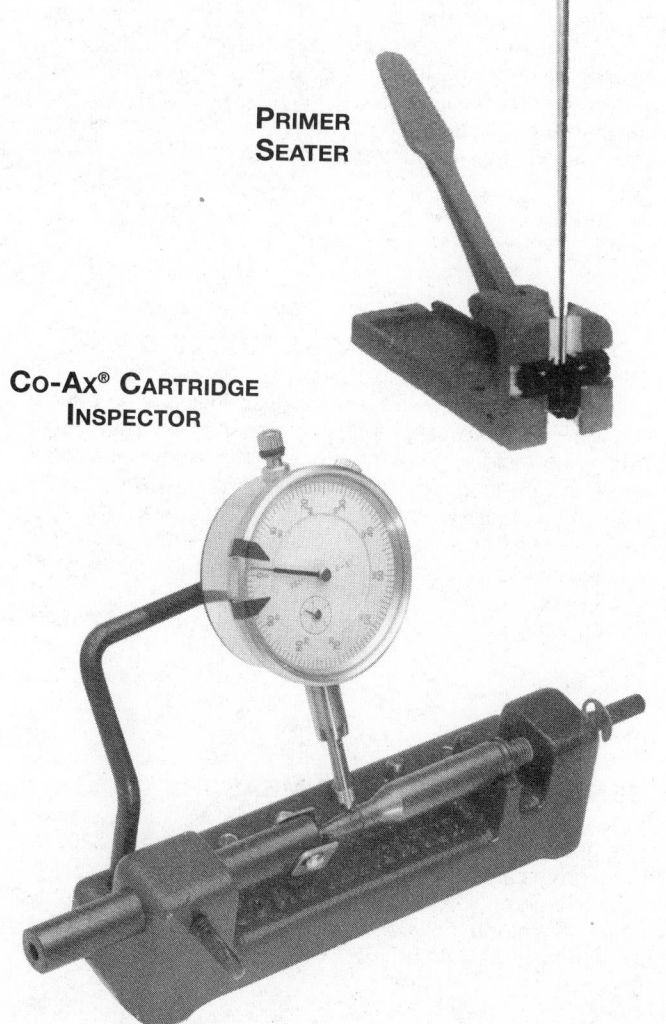

HAND CASE TRIMMER

Shell holder is a Brown & Sharpe-type collet. Case and cartridge conditioning accessories include inside neck reamer, outside neck turner, deburring tool, hollow pointer and primer pocket cleaners. The case trimmer trims all cases, ranging from 17 to 458 Winchester caliber.

Price: $59.00

PRIMER SEATER
With "E-Z-Just" Shellholder

The Bonanza Primer Seater is designed so that primers are seated Co-Axially (primer in line with primer pocket). Mechanical leverage allows primers to be seated fully without crushing. With the addition of one extra set of Disc Shell Holders and one extra Primer Unit, all modern cases, rim or rimless, from 222 up to 458 Magnum, can be primed. Shell holders are easily adjusted to any case by rotating to contact rim or cannelure of the case.

PRIMER SEATER	$70.40
PRIMER POCKET CLEANER	7.20

"CLASSIC 50" CASE TRIMMER (not shown)

Handles more than 100 different big bore calibers–500 Nitro Express, 416 Rigby, 50 Sharps, 475 H&H, etc. *Also available:* .50 BMG Case Trimmer, designed specifically for reloading needs of .50 Cal. BMG shooters.

Price: "CLASSIC 50" CASE TRIMMER	$85.00
.50 BMG CASE TRIMMER	91.00

CO-AX® CASE AND CARTRIDGE INSPECTOR

One tool to perform three vital measurements. Accurate performance from ammunition is absolutely dependent on uniformity of both the bullet and the case. Achieving that uniformity is not possible without an accurate, reliable measuring device. Forster's exclusive Co-Ax® Case & Cartridge Inspector provides the ability to ensure uniformity by measuring three critical dimensions: • Neck wall thickness • Case neck concentricity • Bullet runout.

Measurements are in increments of one-thousandth of an inch. The Inspector is unique because it checks both the bullet and case alignment in relation to the centerline (axis) of the entire cartridge or case.

Price: $81.50

CO-AX LOADING PRESS B-2

BENCH REST POWDER MEASURE

ULTRA BULLET SEATER DIE

Forster's new Ultra Die is available in 56 calibers, more than any other brand of micrometer-style seater. Adjustment is identical to that of a precision micrometer—the head is graduated to .001" increments with .025" bullet movement per revolution. The cartridge case, bullet and seating stem are completely supported and perfectly aligned in a close-fitting chamber before and during the bullet seating operation.
Price: $62.98

UNIVERSAL SIGHT MOUNTING FIXTURE

This product fills the exacting requirements needed for drilling and tapping holes for the mounting of scopes, receiver sights, shotgun beads, etc. The fixture handles any single-barrel gun—bolt-action, lever-action or pump-action—as long as the barrel can be laid into the "V" blocks of the fixture. Rifles with tube magazines are drilled in the same manner by removing the magazine tube. The fixture's main body is made of aluminum casting. The two "V" blocks are adjustable for height and are made of hardened steel ground accurately on the "V" as well as the shaft.
Price: $368.00

CO-AX® LOADING PRESS MODEL B-2

Designed to make reloading easier and more accurate, this press offers the following features: Snap-in and snap-out die change • Positive spent primer catcher • Automatic self-acting shell holder • Floating guide rods • Working room for right- or left-hand operators • Top priming device seats primers to factory specifications • Uses any standard 7/8"X14 dies • No torque on the head • Perfect alignment of die and case • Three times the mechanical advantage of a "C" press
Price: $298.00

BENCH REST POWDER MEASURE

When operated uniformly, this measure will throw uniform charges from 2 1/2 grains Bullseye to 95 grains #4320. No extra drums are needed. Powder is metered from the charge arm, allowing a flow of powder without extremes in variation while minimizing powder shearing. Powder flows through its own built-in baffle so that powder enters the charge arm uniformly.
Price: $109.98

LOCK-N-LOAD CLASSIC PRESS

Lock-N-Load is available on Hornady's single stage and progressive reloader models. This bushing system locks the die into the press like a rifle bolt. Instead of threading dies in and out of the press, you simply lock and unlock them with a slight twist. Dies are held firmly in a die bushing that stays with the die and retains the die setting. The Lock-N-Load Classic Press features an easy-grip handle, an O-style frame made of high-strength alloy, and a positive priming system that feeds, aligns and seats the primer smoothly and automatically.

Prices:
LOCK-N-LOAD CLASSIC PRESS KIT $259.95
Also Available*: LOCK-N-LOAD*
  50 BMG PRESS KIT 471.92

LOCK-N-LOAD AUTO PROGRESSIVE PRESS

The Lock-N-Load Automatic Progressive reloading press featuring the Lock-N-Load bushing system offers the flexibility to add a roll or taper crimp die. Dies and powder measure are inserted into Lock-N-Load die bushings, which lock securely into the press. The bushings remain with the die and powder measure and can be removed in seconds. They also fit on other presses. Other features include: deluxe powder measure, automatic indexing, off-set handle, power-pac linkage, case ejector.

LOCK-N-LOAD AUTO PROGRESSIVE PRESS (includes five die bushings, shellplate, primer catcher, Positive Priming System, powder drop, Deluxe Powder Measure, automatic primer feed) $367.65

MODEL 366 AUTO SHOTSHELL RELOADER

The 366 Auto features full-length resizing with each stroke, automatic primer feed, swing-out wad guide, three-state crimping featuring Taper-Loc for factory tapered crimp, automatic advance to the next station and automatic ejection. The turntable holds 8 shells for 8 operations with each stroke. Automatic charge bar loads shot and powder, dies and crimp starters for 6 point, 8 point and paper crimps.

MODEL 366 AUTO SHOTSHELL RELOADER:
12, 20, 28 gauge or .410 bore $434.95

CUSTOM GRADE RELOADING DIES

Features an Elliptical Expander that minimizes friction and reduces case neck stretch, plus the need for a tapered expander for "necking up" to the next larger caliber. Other recent design changes include a hardened steel decap pin that will not break, bend or crack even when depriming stubborn military cases. A bullet seater alignment sleeve guides the bullet and case neck into the die for in-line benchrest alignment. All New Dimension Reloading Dies include: collar and collar lock to center expander precisely; one-piece expander spindle with tapered bottom for easy cartridge insertion; wrench flats on die body, Sure-Loc™ lock rings and collar lock for easy tightening; and built-in crimper.

NEW DIMENSION CUSTOM GRADE RELOADING DIES:
SERIES I TWO-DIE RIFLE SET $28.97
SERIES II THREE-DIE RIFLE SET 30.60
SERIES II THREE-DIE PISTOL SET (w/Titanium Nitride) 40.49
50 CALIBER BMG DIES (TWO-DIE SET) 243.00

LOCK-N-LOAD CLASSIC RELOADING PRESS

LOCK-N-LOAD

MODEL 366

MODEL 1200 CLASSIC TURBO TUMBLER

This sturdy case tumbler features a redesigned base and drive system, plus a stronger suspension system and built-in exciters for better tumbling action and faster cleaning

MODEL 1200 CLASSIC	.$79.95
MODEL 1200 AUTO-FLO	.99.95

Also available:

MODEL 600	.69.95
MODEL 2200	.116.50
MODEL 2200 AUTO-FLO	.125.00
MODEL 3200	.164.95
MODEL 3200 AUTO-FLO	.184.95

"INSIDE/OUTSIDE" DEBURRING TOOL

This tool features an adjustable cutting blade that adapts easily to the mouth of any rifle or pistol case from 22 caliber to 45 caliber with a simple hex wrench adjustment. Inside deburring is completed by a conical internal section with slotted cutting edges, thus providing uniform inside and outside deburring in one simple operation. The deburring tool is mounted on an anodized aluminum handle that is machine-knurled for a sure grip.

DEBURRING TOOL	.$13.50

TURBO TWIN TUMBLER

The Twin features Lyman 1200 Pro Tumbler with an extra, 600 bowl system. Reloaders may use each bowl interchangeably for small or large capacity loads. 1200 Pro Bowl System has a built-in sifter lid for easy sifting of cases and media at the end of the polishing cycle. The Twin Tumbler features the Lyman Hi-Profile base design with built-in exciters and anti-rotation pads for faster, more consistent tumbling action.

TURBO TWIN TUMBLER 110V	.$79.95

MASTER CASTING KIT

Designed especially to meet the needs of blackpowder shooters, this kit features Lyman's combination round ball and maxi ball mould blocks. It also contains a combination double cavity mould, mould handle, mini-mag furnace, lead dipper, bullet lube, a user's manual and a cast bullet guide. Kits are available in 45, 50 and 54 caliber.

MASTER CASTING KIT	.$164.95

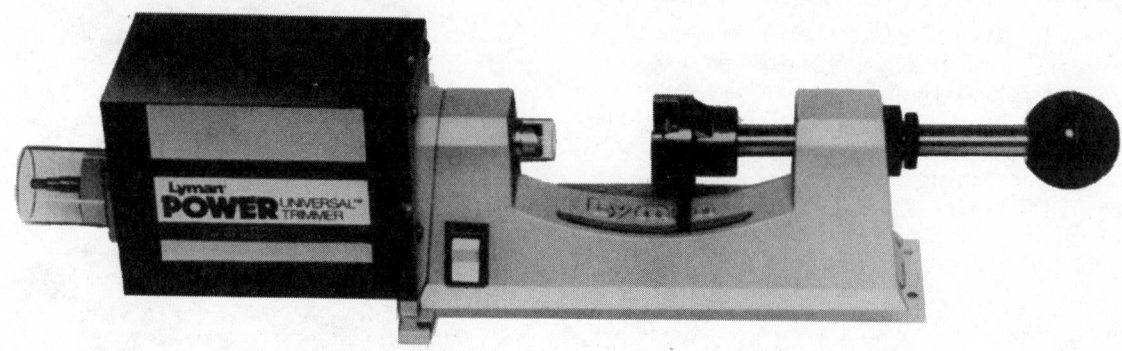

POWER CASE TRIMMER

The Lyman Power Trimmer is powered by a fan-cooled electric motor designed to withstand the severe demands of case trimming. The unit, which features the Universal™ Chuckhead, allows cases to be positioned for trimming or removed with fingertip ease. The Power Trimmer package includes Nine-Pilot Multi-Pack. In addition to two cutter heads, a pair of wire end brushes for cleaning primer pockets are included. Other features include safety guards, on-off rocker switch, heavy cast base with receptacles for nine pilots, and bolt holes for mounting on a work bench. Available for 110 V or 220 V systems.

Prices: 110 V Model $194.95
220 V Model 194.95

ACCULINE OUTSIDE NECK TURNER
(not shown)

To obtain perfectly concentric case necks, Lyman's Outside Neck Turner assures reloaders of uniform neck wall thickness and outside neck diameter. The unit fits Lyman's Universal Trimmer and AccuTrimmer. In use, each case is run over a mandrel, which centers the case for the turning operation. The cutter is carefully adjusted to remove a minimum amount of brass. Rate of feed is adjustable and a mechanical stop controls length of cut. Mandrels are available for calibers from .17 to .375; cutter blade can be adjusted for any diameter from .195" to .405".

OUTSIDE NECK TURNER w/extra blade, 6 mandrels . .$28.95
INDIVIDUAL MANDRELS 4.00

CRUSHER II PRO KIT

Includes press, loading block, case lube kit, primer tray, Model 500 Pro scale, powder funnel and *Lyman Reloading Handbook*.
STARTER KIT $159.95

LYMAN CRUSHER II RELOADING PRESS

The only press for rifle or pistol cartridges that offers the advantage of powerful compound leverage combined with a true Magnum press opening. A unique handle design transfers power easily to the center of the ram. A 4 1/2-inch press opening accommodates even the largest cartridges.

CRUSHER II PRESS
With Priming Arm and Catcher $114.95

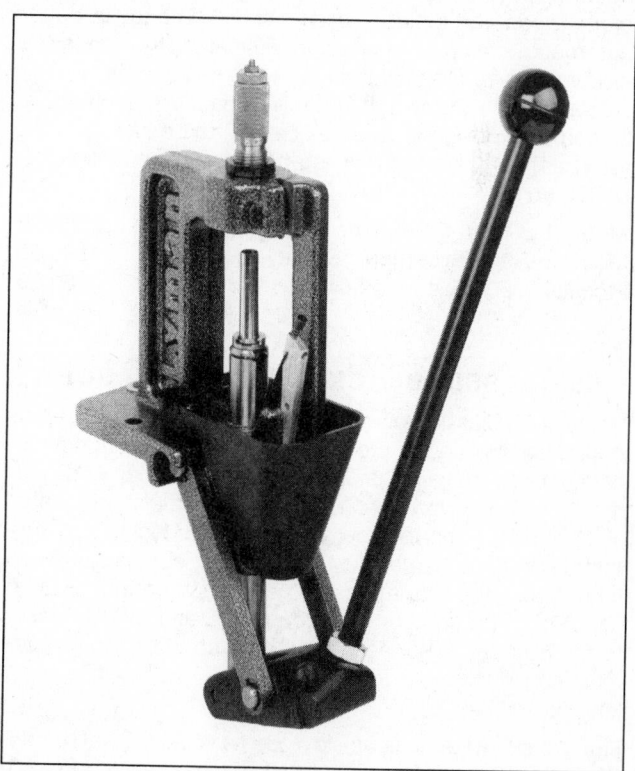

CRUSHER II

T-MAG II TURRET RELOADING PRESS

With the T-Mag II up to six different reloading dies can be mounted on one turret. This means all dies can be set up, precisely mounted, locked in and ready to reload at all times. The T-Mag works with all 7/8 x 14 dies. The T-Mag II turret with its quick-disconnect release system is held in rock-solid alignment by a 3/4-inch steel stud.

Also featured is Lyman's Crusher II compound leverage system. It has a longer handle with a ball-type knob that mounts easily for right- or left-handed operation.

T-MAG II PRESS w/Priming Arm & Catcher $159.95
  Extra Turret Head 36.00
Also available:
EXPERT KIT that includes T-MAG II Press, Universal Case Trimmer and pilot Multi-Pak, Model 500 powder scale and Model 50 powder measure, plus accessories and Reloading Manual. Available in calibers 9mm Luger, 38/357, 44 Mag., 45 ACP and 30-06 . . . .$359.95

ELECTRONIC SCALE MODEL LE-1000

Accurate to 1/10 grain, Lyman's LE: 1000 measures up to 1000 grains of powder and easily converts to the gram mode for metric measurements. The push-button automatic calibration feature eliminates the need for calibrating with a screwdriver. The scale works off a single 9V battery or AC power adapter (included with each scale). Its compact design allows the LE-1000 to be carried to the field easily. A sculpted carrying case is optional. 110 Volt or 220 Volt.

MODEL LE-1000 ELECTRONIC SCALE $259.95
MODEL LE-300 ELECTRONIC SCALE 166.50
MODEL LE-500 ELECTRIC SCALE 183.25

MODEL LE-500 ELECTRONIC SCALE

55 CLASSIC BLACK POWDER MEASURE

Lyman's 55 Classic Powder Measure is ideal for the Cowboy Action Competition or the growing number of black powder cartridge shooters. The large, one-pound capacity aluminum reservoir, along with brass powder meter, eliminates static. The internal powder baffel assures highly accurate and consistent charges. The 24" powder compacting drop tube allows the maximum charge in each cartridge. Drop tube works on calibers .38 through .50, and mounts easily to the bottom of the measure. Clamp on back allows easy mounting of the measure at a convenient height, when using long drop tubes.

55 CLASSIC POWDER MEASURE (std model-no tubes) $104.95
55 CLASSIC POWDER MEASURE (with drop tubes) 122.50
POWDER DROP TUBES ONLY 24.95

ELECTRONIC DIGITAL MICROMETER $94.95

BLACK POWDER MEASURE

LYMAN RELOADING TOOLS

DRILL PRESS CASE TRIMMER

Intended for competitive shooters, varmint hunters, and other sportsmen who use large amounts of reloaded ammunition, this drill press case trimmer consists of the Universal™ Chuckhead, a cutter shaft adapted for use in a drill press, and two quick-change cutter heads. Its two major advantages are speed and accuracy. An experienced operator can trim several hundred cases in an hour, and each will be trimmed to a precise length.

DRILL PRESS CASE TRIMMER $48.50

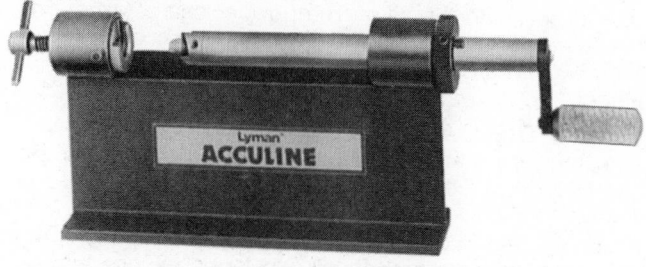

ACCU-TRIMMER

Lyman's Accu Trimmer can be used for all rifle and pistol cases from 22 to 458 Winchester Magnum. Standard shell-holders are used to position the case, and the trimmer incorporates standard Lyman cutter heads and pilots. Mounting options include bolting to a bench, C-clamp or vise.

ACCU TRIMMER w/9-pilot multi-pak $43.00

UNIVERSAL TRIMMER
WITH NINE PILOT MULTI-PACK

This trimmer with patented chuckhead accepts all metallic rifle or pistol cases, regardless of rim thickness. To change calibers, simply change the case head pilot. Other features include coarse and fine cutter adjustments, an oil-impregnated bronze bearing, and a rugged cast base to assure precision alignment and years of service. Optional carbide cutter available. Trimmer Stop Ring includes 20 indicators as reference marks.

REPLACEMENT CARBIDE CUTTER $42.00
TRIMMER MULTI-PACK (incl. 9 pilots: 22, 24, 27,
   28/7mm, 30, 9mm, 35, 44 and 4A 66.00
NINE PILOT MULTI-PACK 11.25
POWER PACK TRIMMER 76.50
UNIVERSAL TRIMMER POWER ADAPTER 18.50

UNIVERSAL TRIMMER POWER ADAPTER

ELECTRONIC DIGITAL CALIPER
(not shown)

Lyman's 6" electronic caliper gives a direct digital readout for both inches and millimeters and can perform both inside and outside depth measurements. Its zeroing function allows the user to select zeroing dimensions and sort parts or cases by their plus or minus variation. The caliper works on a single, standard 1.5 volt silver oxide battery and comes with a fitted wooden storage case.

ELECTRONIC CALIPER $99.95
Also Available:
  4" Pocket Electronic Caliper 83.25

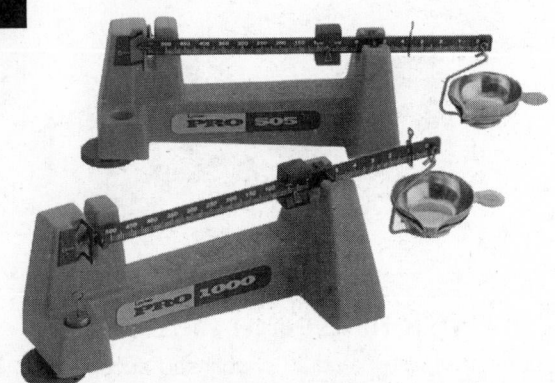

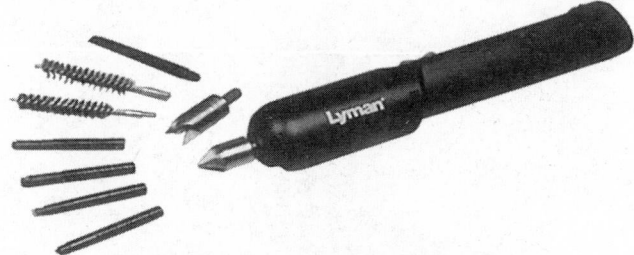

PRO 1000 & 505 RELOADING SCALES

Features include improved platform system; hi-tech base design of high-impact styrene; extra-large, smooth leveling wheel; dual agate bearings; larger damper for fast zeroing; built-in counter weight compartment; easy-to-read beam

PRO 1000 SCALE $59.95
PRO 500 SCALE 43.95

PREMIUM 4-DIE SET WITH TAPER CRIMP AND POWDER CHARGE EXPANDING DIE

PISTOL DIES FEATURE ONE PIECE HARDENED STEEL DECAPPING ROD

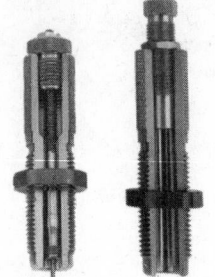

RIFLE DIE SETS

Lyman precision rifle dies are manufactured on computer controlled equipment ensuring that each die is chambered perfectly and has a smooth finish. Each sizing die for bottle-necked rifle cartridges is then carefully vented. This vent hole is precisely placed to prevent air traps that can damage cartridge cases. Each sizing die is polished, then heat treated for toughness. It receives a final hand polish for extra smoothness. Fine adjustment threads on the bullet seating stem allow for precision adjustments of bullet seating depth. Lyman dies fit all popular presses using industry standard 7/8 x 14 threads, including RCBS, Lee, Hornady, Dillon, Redding and others.

POWER DEBURRING KIT

Features a high torque, rechargeable power driver plus a complete set of accessories, including inside and outside deburr tools, large and small reamers and cleaners and case neck brushes. No threading or chucking required. Set also includes battery recharger and standard flat and phillips driver bits.
POWER DEBURRING KIT $54.95

RIFLE 2-DIE SETS

Set consists of a full length resizing die with decapping stem and neck expanding button and a bullet seating die for loading jacketed bullets in bottlenecked rifle cases. For those who load cast bullets, use a neck expanding die, available separately.
Price: $28.95

RIFLE 3-DIE SETS

Straight wall rifle cases require these three die sets consisting of a full length resizing die with decapping stem, a two step neck expanding (M) die and a bullet seating die. These sets are ideal for loading cast bullets due to the inclusion of the neck expanding die.
Price: $38.95
Classic Calibers 47.50

PREMIUM CARBIDE 4-DIE SETS FOR PISTOLS

Lyman 4-Die Sets feature a separate taper crimp die and powder charge/expanding die. The powder charge/expand die has a special hollow 2-step neck expanding plug which allows powder to flow through the die from a powder measure directly into the case. The powder charge/expanding die has a standard 7/8 x 14 thread and will accept Lyman's 55 Powder Measure, or most other powder measures.
Price: $54.00

3-DIE CARBIDE PISTOL DIE SETS

Lyman originated the Tungsten Carbide (T-C) sizing die and the addition of extra seating screws for pistol die sets and the two step neck expanding die. Multi-Deluxe Die sets offer these features; a one-piece hardened steel decapping rod and extra seating screws for all popular bullet nose shapes; all-steel construction.
Price: $40.95

STANDARD PISTOL DIE SETS

These 3-die pistol sets are designed for bottleneck pistol cases. The full length sizing die is precision machined from solid steel. 3-Die sets also feature Lyman's two step neck expanding die.
Price: $29.95

MEC SHOTSHELL RELOADERS

MODEL 600 JR. MARK V

This single-stage reloader features a cam-action crimp die to ensure that each shell returns to its original condition. MEC's 600 Jr. Mark 5 can load 6 to 8 boxes per hour and can be updated with the 285 CA primer feed. Press is adjustable for 3" shells.

MODEL 600 . . . .$105.20

MODEL 650

This reloader works on 6 shells at once. A reloaded shell is completed with every stroke. The MEC 650 does not resize except as a separate operation. Automatic Primer feed is standard. Simply fill it with a full box of primers and it will do the rest. Reloader has 3 crimping stations: the first one starts the crimp, the second closes the crimp, and the third places a taper on the shell. Available in 12, 16, 20 and 28 gauge and .410 bore. No die sets are available.

Price: $206.88

MODEL 8567 GRABBER

This reloader features 12 different operations at all 6 stations, producing finished shells with each stroke of the handle. It includes a fully automatic primer feed and Auto-Cycle charging, plus MEC's exclusive 3-stage crimp. The "Power Ring" resizer ensures consistent, accurately sized shells without interrupting the reloading sequence. Simply put in the wads and shell casings, then remove the loaded shells with each pull of the handle. Optional kits to load 3" shells and steel shot make this reloader tops in its field. Resizes high and low base shells. Available in 12, 16, 20, 28 gauge and .410 bore. No die sets are available.

Price: $297.51

MODEL 8120 SIZEMASTER

Sizemaster's "Power Ring" collet resizer returns each base to factory specifications. This generation resizing station handles brass or steel heads, both high and low base. An 8-fingered collet squeezes the base back to original dimensions, then opens up to release the shell easily. The E-Z Prime auto primer feed is standard equipment (not offered in .410 bore). Press is adjustable for 3" shells and is available in 10, 12, 16, 20, 28 gauge and .410 bore. Die sets are available at: $88.67 ($104.06 in 10 ga.)

Price:

MODEL 8120 . . . .$158.52

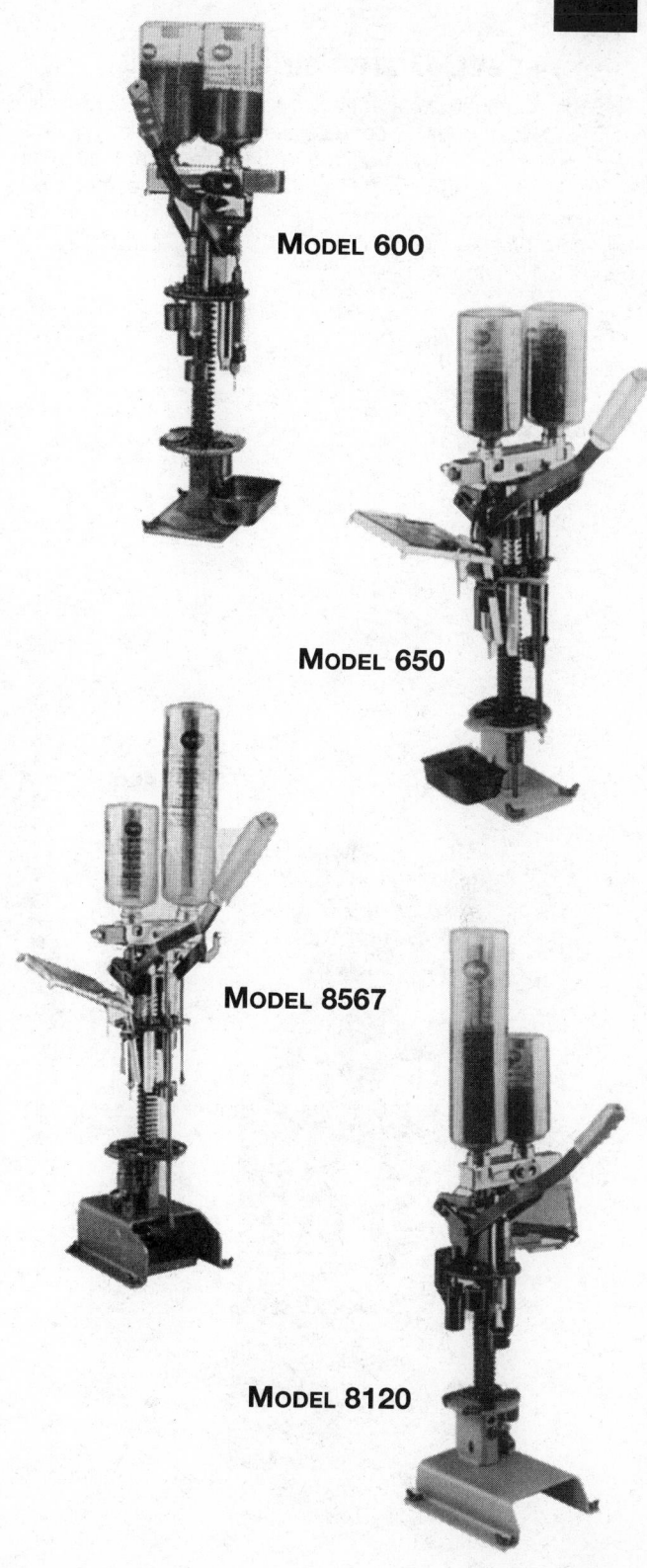

MODEL 600

MODEL 650

MODEL 8567

MODEL 8120

STEELMASTER SINGLE STATE

The only shotshell reloader equipped to load steel shotshells as well as lead ones. Every base is resized to factory specs by a precision "power ring" collet. Handles brass or steel heads in high or low base. The E-Z prime auto primer feed dispenses primers automatically and is standard equipment. Separate presses are available for 12 gauge 2 3/4", 3", 12 gauge 3 1/2" and 10 gauge.

STEELMASTER $171.37
In 12 ga. 3 1/2" only 192.13

STEEL MASTER

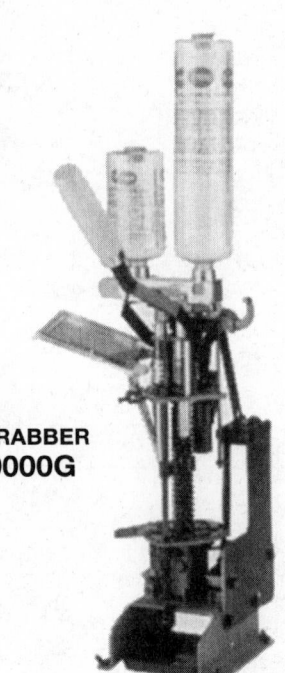

GRABBER 9000G

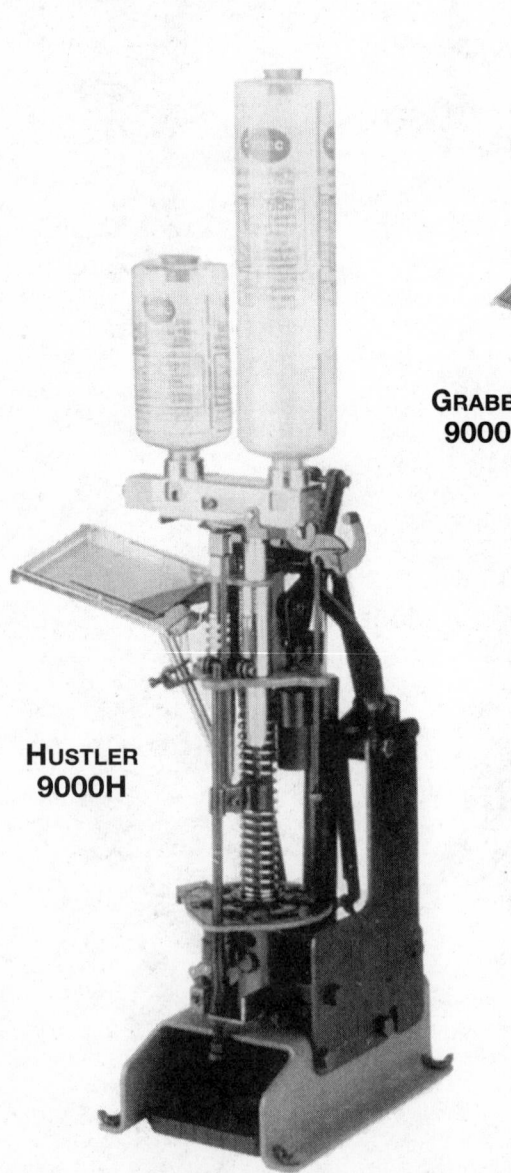

HUSTLER 9000H

MEC 9000 SERIES SHOTSHELL RELOADER

MEC's 9000 Series features automatic indexing and finished shell ejection for quicker and easier reloading. The factory set speed provides uniform movement through every reloading stage. Dropping the primer into the reprime station no longer requires operator "feel." The reloader requires only a minimal adjustment from low to high brass domestic shells, any one of which can be removed for inspection from any station. Can be set up for automatic or manual indexing. Available in 12, 16, 20 and 28 gauge and .410 bore. No die sets are available.

MEC 9000H $870.54
MEC 9000H without pump 470.78
MEC 9000G SERIES 360.34
Also Available: MEC SUPER SIZER
Resize shotgun shells back to factory specs!
Price: 59.02

RELOADING

Loading And Range Accessories

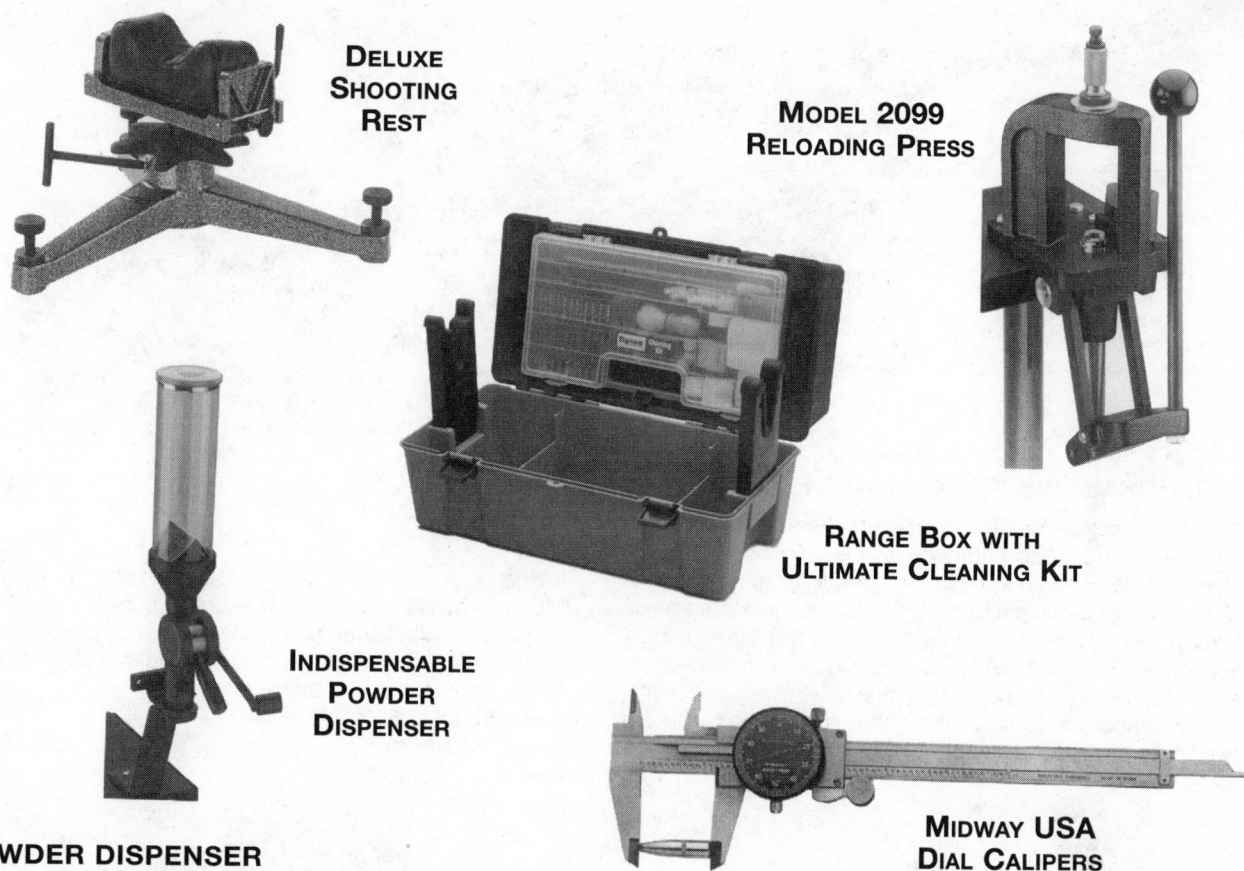

DELUXE SHOOTING REST

MODEL 2099 RELOADING PRESS

RANGE BOX WITH ULTIMATE CLEANING KIT

INDISPENSABLE POWDER DISPENSER

MIDWAY USA DIAL CALIPERS

POWDER DISPENSER

Precision metering and quick-change caliber-specific drop tubes are hallmarks of this powder dispenser. Shelf bracket is included with both rifle and pistol versions. A master kit is also available, with the dispenser, bench mount and shelf mount brackets, a powder funnel and clear drop tube. The dispenser is equipped for loading both rifle and pistol cases.
Price: $89.99
Master Kit 114.99

STAINLESS STEEL DIAL CALIPERS

Accuracy at the range starts with accuracy at the loading bench. This useful tool is a must for serious handloaders.
Price: $18.49

RELOADING PRESS

The Midway USA Model 2099 reloading press incorporates state-of-the-industry advances in tool design and metallurgy. The 2099 is manufactured to the strictest tolerances and has the strength to handle tough tasks like case forming. Its huge clearance enables you to load cartridges as big as the 3 3/4-inch Sharps, plus British Express cartridges.
Price: $89.99

RANGE BOX

Once in a while an accessory comes along that makes so much sense you wonder why someone didn't come up with it earlier. The Midway range box is essentially a portable shop, which can be used to hold firearms for repair or cleaning. It's many compartments hold tools and cleaning supplies. A complete cleaning kit comes with each box. The cradle can be used as an impromptu shooting rest.
Price
rifle $99.99
shotgun 79.99

DELUXE SHOOTING REST

The Gibraltar Deluxe Shooting Rest is among the finest on the market, with a wide, heavy-duty base to ensure stability and adjustable feet to give exactly the right angle of support. The cradle is adjustable for height. Made of steel and aluminum for years of dependable performance, the Gibraltar Rest weighs 5.5 pounds.
Price: $74.99

GUNSMITH'S MAINTENANCE CENTER

MTM's Gunsmiths Maintenance Center (RMC-5) is designed for mounting scopes and swivels, bedding actions or for cleaning rifles and shotguns. Multi-positional forks allow for eight holding combinations, making it possible to service firearm level, upright or upside down. The large middle section keeps tools and cleaning supplies in one area. Individual solvent compartments help to eliminate accidental spills. Cleaning rods stay where they are needed with the two built-in holders provided. Both forks (covered with a soft molded-on rubber pad) grip and protect the firearm. The RMC-5 is made of engineering- grade plastic for years of rugged use. *Not Shown:* Extensive line of plastic ammo boxes, reloading trays, pistol cases, target holders, clay target throwers, arrow and tackle boxes.
Dimensions: 29.5" X 9.5"
MODEL RMC-5-30 . . . .$30.77

PISTOL REST MODEL PR-30

MTM's PR-30 Pistol Rest will accommodate any size handgun, from a Derringer to a 14" Contender. A locking front support leg adjusts up or down, allowing 20 different positions. Rubber padding molded to the tough polypropylene fork protects firearms from scratches. Fork clips into the base when not in use for compact storage.
Dimensions: 6" x 11" x 2.5
PISTOL REST MODEL PR-30 . . . .$16.40

CASE-GARD IN WILD CAMO

The CASE-GARD SF-100 holds 100 shotshells in two removable trays. Designed primarily for hunters, this dust and moisture resistant carrier features a heavy-duty latch, fold-down handle, integral hinge and textured finish.
Price:
SF-100 12 or 20 ga.
WILD CAMO SHOTSHELL BOX $16.44

RCBS RELOADING TOOLS

ROCK CHUCKER PRESS

With its easy operation, outstanding strength and versatility, a Rock Chucker press serves beginner and pro alike. It can also be upgraded to a progressive press with an optional Piggyback conversion unit.

- Heavy-duty cast iron for easy case-resizing
- 1" ram held in place by 12.5 sq. in. of rambearing surface
- Toggle blocks of ductile iron
- Compound leverage system
- 7/8"-14 thread for all standard reloading dies and accessories
- Milled slot and set screws accept optional RCBS automatic primer feed

Price: $141.95

ROCK CHUCKER MASTER RELOADING KIT

The Rock Chucker Master Reloading Kit includes all the tools and accessories needed to start handloading: • Rock Chucker Press • RCBS 505 Reloading Scale • Speer TrimPro Manual #12 • Uniflow Powder Measure • RCBS Rotary Case Trimmer-2 • deburring tool • case loading block • Primer Tray-2 • Automatic Primer Feed Combo • powder funnel • case lube pad • case neck brushes • fold-up hex key set • Trim Pro Manual Case Trimmer Kit

Price: $399.95

.50 BMG PACK

Shooters who favor the .50 BMG have all they need in the .50 BMG Pack from RCBS®. The Pack includes the press, dies, and accessory items needed, all in one box. The press is the powerful Ammo Master® Single Stage rigged for 1.5-inch dies. It has a massive 1.5-inch solid steel ram and plenty of height for the big .50. The kit also has a set of RCBS .50 BMG, 1.5-inch reloading dies, including both full-length sizer and seater. Other items are a shell holder, ram priming unit, and a trim die.

Price: $547.95

AMMOMASTER SINGLE STAGE

AMMOMASTER RELOADING SYSTEM

The AmmoMaster offers any handloader the freedom to configure a press to his particular needs and preferences. It covers the complete spectrum of reloading, from single stage through fully automatic progressive reloading, from .25 Auto to .50 caliber. The AmmoMaster Auto has all the features of a five-station press.

SINGLE STAGE $206.95

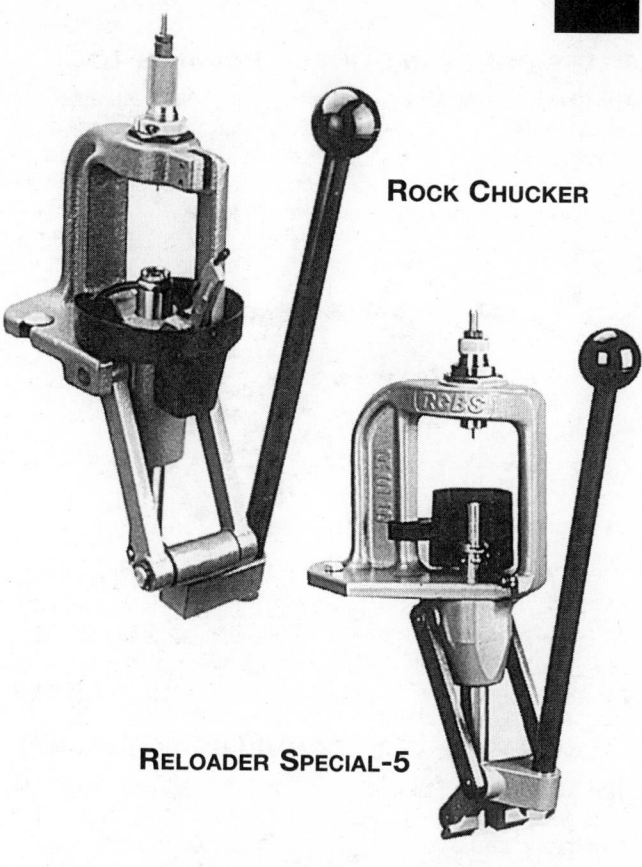

ROCK CHUCKER

RELOADER SPECIAL-5

RELOADER SPECIAL-5

The Reloader Special press features a comfortable ball handle and a primer arm so that cases can be primed and resized at the same time.

- Compound leverage system
- Solid aluminum black "O" frame offset for unobstructed access
- Corrosion-resistant baked-powder finish
- Can be upgraded to progressive reloading with an optional Piggyback II conversion unit
- 7/8" - 14 thread for all standard reloading dies and accessories

Price: $112.95

PIGGYBACK III CONVERSION KIT
(not shown)

- The Piggyback III conversion unit moves from single-stage reloading to 5-station, manual-indexing, progressive reloading in one step
- Increases output from 50 rounds an hour to well over 400

The Piggyback III will work with the RCBS Rock Chucker, Reloader Special-3, and Reloader Special-5.

Price: . . . . .TBD

APS BENCH-MOUNTED PRIMING TOOL

The APS Bench-Mounted Priming Tool was created for reloaders who prefer a separate, specialized tool dedicated to priming only. The handle of the bench-mounted tool is designed to provide hours of comfortable loading. Handle position can be adjusted for bench height.
Price: $92.95

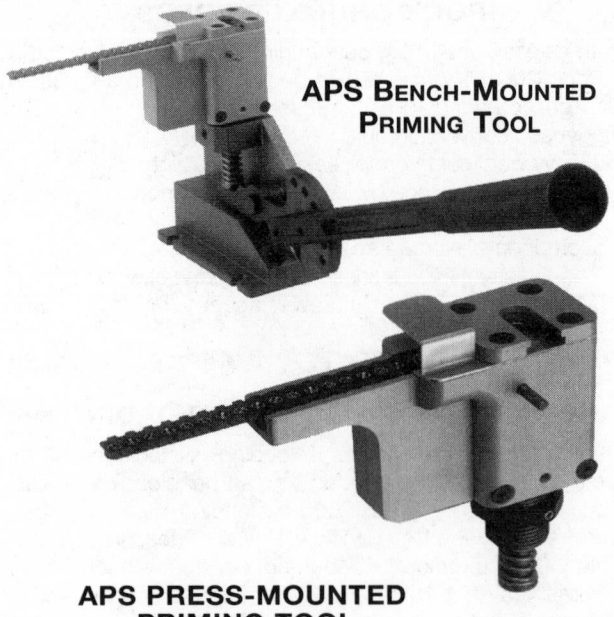

APS BENCH-MOUNTED PRIMING TOOL

APS PRIMER STRIP LOADER

For those who keep a supply of CCI primers in conventional packaging, the APS primer strip loader allows quick filling of empty strips. Each push of the handle seats 25 primers.
Price: $25.95

POW'R PULL BULLET PULLER (not shown)

The RCBS Pow'r Pull bullet puller features a three-jaw chuck that grips the case rim—just rap it on any solid surface like a hammer, and powder and bullet drop into the main chamber for re-use. A soft cushion protects bullets from damage. Works with most centerfire cartridges from .22 to .45 (not for use with rimfire cartridges).
Price: $27.95

APS PRESS-MOUNTED PRIMING TOOL

This APS press-mounted priming tool provides the same features as the bench-mounted tool except it attaches to any single-stage press that accepts standard 7/8" x 14 dies.
Price: $58.95

RELOADING SCALE MODEL 5-0-5

This 511-grain capacity scale has a three-poise system with widely spaced, deep beam notches to keep them in place. Two smaller poises on right side adjust from 0.1 to 10 grains, larger one on left side adjusts in full 10-grain steps. The first scale to use magnetic dampening to eliminate beam oscillation, the 5-0-5 also has a sturdy die-cast base with large leveling legs for stability. Self-aligning agate bearings support the hardened steel beam pivots for a guaranteed sensitivity to 0.1 grains.
Price: $84.95

TRIM PRO™ CASE TRIMMER

Cartridge cases are trimmed quickly and easily with a few turns of the RCBS Trim Pro case trimmer. The lever-type handle is more accurate to use than draw collet systems. A flat plate shell holder keeps cases locked in place and aligned. A micrometer fine adjustment bushing offers trimming accuracy to within .001". Made of die-cast metal with hardened cutting blades. The power model is like having a personal lathe, delivering plenty of torque. Positive locking handle and in-line power switch make it simple and safe.
Price: Power 110 Vac Kit $228.95
Manual $72.95
Also available:
TRIM PRO CASE TRIMMER STAND $16.95
CASE HOLDER ACCESSORY .37.95

RCBS RELOADING TOOLS

POWDER PRO™ DIGITAL SCALE

The RCBS Powder Pro Digital Scale has a 1500-grain capacity. Powder, bullets, even cases can be weighed with accuracy of 0.1 grain. Includes infra-red data port for transferring information to the Powdermaster Electronic Powder Dispenser and electronic powder trickler. *Price:* 110 VAC $227.95

POWDERMASTER ELECTRONIC POWDER DISPENSER

Works in combination with the RCBS Powder Pro Digital Scale and with all types of smokeless powder. Can be used as a power trickler as well as a powder dispenser. Accurate to one-tenth of a grain.
Price: $244.95

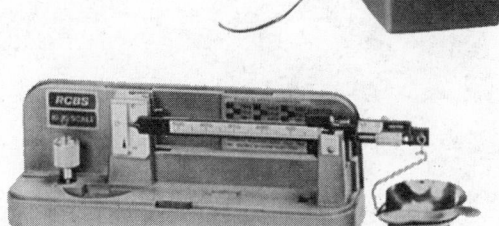

RELOADING SCALE MODEL 10-10
Up to 1010 Grain Capacity

Normal capacity is 510 grains, which can be increased without loss of sensitivity by attaching the included extra weight. Features include micrometer poise for quick, precise weighing, special approach-to-weight indicator, easy-to-read graduation, magnetic dampener, agate bearings, anti-tip pan, and dustproof lid snaps on to cover scale for storage. Sensitivity is guaranteed to 0.1 grains.
Price: $136.95

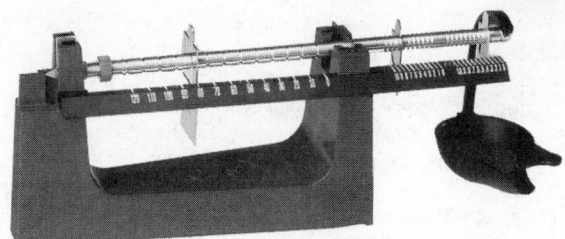

RC-130 MECHANICAL SCALE

The RC130 features a 130 grain capacity and maintenance-free movement, plus a magnetic dampening system for fast readings. A 3-poise design incorporates easy adjustments with a beam that is graduated in increments of 10 grains and one grain. A micrometer poise measures in 0.1 grain increments with acuracy to ±0.1 grain.
Price: $37.95

POWDER CHECKER (not shown)

Operates on a free-moving rod for simple, mechanical operation with nothing to break. Standard 7/8x14 die body can be used in any progressive loader.
Price: $26.95

ELECTRONIC DIGITAL MICROMETER

• Instant reading • Large, easy to read numbers for error reduction with instant inch/millimeter conversion • Zero adjust at any position • thimble lock for measuring like objects • replaceable silver oxide cell – 1.55 Volt • auto off after 5 minutes for longer battery life • adjustment wrench included • fitted wooden storage cases
Price: $99.95

PARTNER ELECTRONIC POWDER SCALE

Accurate for +/- one-tenth of a grain up to 350 grains and +/- two-tenths from 350 to 750 grains. Large LCD display is angled for easy reading over a wide range of positions. Powered by 9-volt battery.
Price: $163.95

RCBS TURRET PRESS

Handloaders who want to speed up the loading process without giving up the level of control offered by a single-stage press can boost their output fourfold with the RCBS Turret Press. With preset dies in the six-station turret head, the Turret Press can increase production from 50 to 200 rounds per hour with a simple manual operation.

The frame, links, and toggle block of the press are constructed of strong, reliable, cast iron. The handle offers compound leverage for full-length sizing of any caliber from .25 ACP to .460 Weatherby Magnum. Priming is accomplished with a reliable tube feed priming system.

Six stations allow the handloader to customize his set-up with the options of using a lube die in station one and seating and crimping bullets in separate operations. The quick-change turret head makes caliber changes fast and easy. Dies can be left in the turret head to eliminate set-up and tear-down time. This press accepts all standard 7/8 - 14 dies and shell holders and comes with the RCBS no-questions-asked lifetime warranty.

Price: RCBS TURRET PRESS $195.95
TURRET DELUXE RELOADING KIT 371.95

RCBS PRO 2000 PROGRESSIVE PRESS

Constructed of strong and reliable cast iron, the Pro 2000 features five reloading stations. It can be set up with a lube die in station one, sizing dies in station two and three, a Powder Checker or Lock Out Die in station four and seating die in station five. Bullet seating and crimping can also be done in separate operations in station four and five.

The Die Plate removes and installs in seconds. The Powder Measure remains on the press when changing calibers. Primer plug changeover is quick and easy, as is changing the Shell Plate with the removal of one bolt.

The case-actuated powder measure assures repeatability of dispensing powder and eliminates spillage caused from dropping a powder charge when no case is in the powder charge station. A Micrometer Adjustment Screw allows precise return to previously recorded powder charges. The Powder Measure easily adjusts to various case lengths and works perfectly with all powders. It is easily removed for cleaning and/or removing excess powder. All dies are standard 7/8-14, including the Expander Die.

The press incorporates RCBS's exclusive APS Priming System. Using preloaded plastic priming strips, it eliminates handling of primers and loading tube priming. An alternate tube primer is available as an optional purchase. A primer seating depth adjustment screw allows for precise setting of primer seating, and spent primers are contained in a clear, easy-to-empty catcher.

Compound leverage in the press allows effortless full-length sizing in any caliber, from .32 Auto to the .460 Weatherby Magnum. Manual indexing eliminates a complicated automatic advancing mechanism and gives the user total control and "feel" when cases are indexed.

Other features of the Pro 2000 include a Shell Plate Holder machined to remove extraneous powder from the Shell Plate and

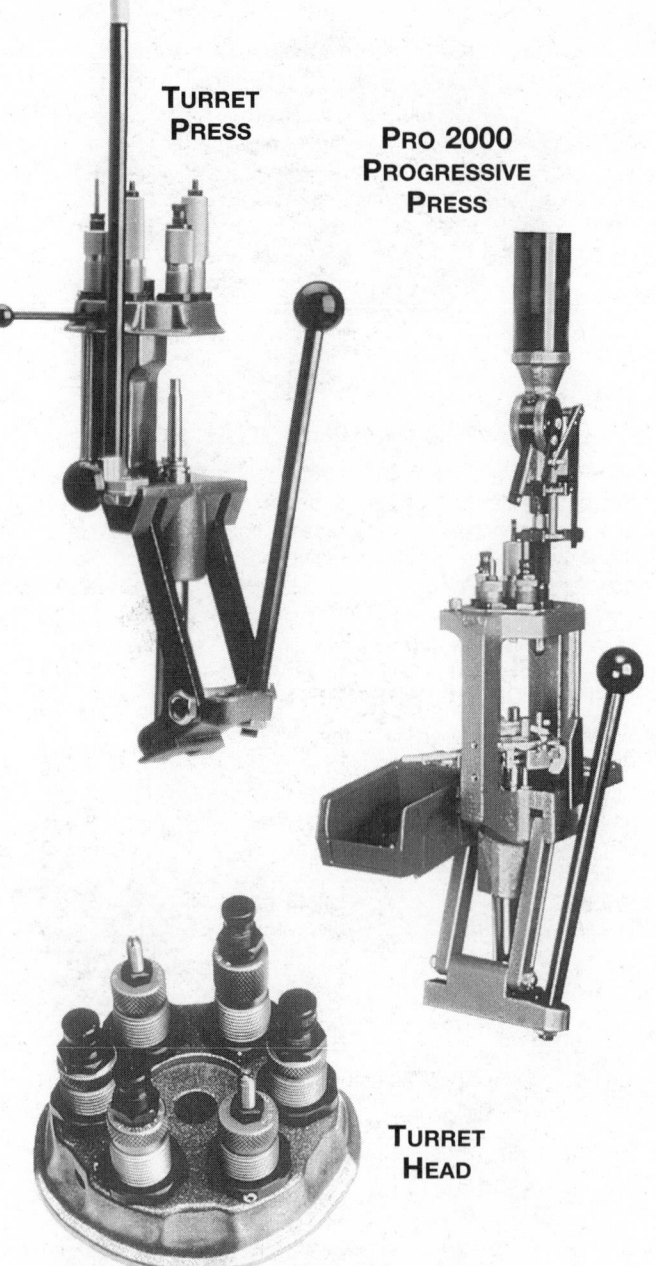

TURRET PRESS

PRO 2000 PROGRESSIVE PRESS

TURRET HEAD

provide smooth, positive indexing; a larger working window for greater visibility and easy access to all stations; a Universal Case Retention System for simple, one-step removal and installation/insertion of cases at any station with no screws to loosen or buttons to remove; and the inclusion of a bullet tray, empty case box, and loaded cartridge box.

The press is covered by the RCBS Lifetime Warranty.

Prices:
RCBS PRO 2000 PROGRESSIVE PRESS $468.95
PRO 2000 DELUXE RELOADING KIT 803.95

MODEL 721 "THE BOSS" PRESS

This "O" type reloading press features a rigid cast iron frame whose 36° offset provides the best visibility and access of comparable presses. Its "Smart" primer arm moves in and out of position automatically with ram travel. The priming arm is positioned at the bottom of ram travel for lowest leverage and best feel. Model 721 accepts all standard 7/8-14 threaded dies and universal shell holders.

MODEL 721 "THE BOSS" $135.00
  With Shellholder and 10A Dies 172.00
Also available:
BOSS PRO-PAK RELOADING KIT. Includes Boss Reloading Press, #2 Powder and Bullet Scale, Powder Trickler, Reloading Dies $354.00
  w/o dies and shellholder 309.00
BOSS DELUXE RELOADING KIT. Includes all items in the Pro-Pak plus: Match-Grade Model 3BR Powder Measure and Model 1400 case trimmer 511.50

ULTRAMAG MODEL 7000

Unlike other reloading presses that connect the linkage to the lower half of the press, the Ultramag's compound leverage system is connected at the top of the press frame. This allows the reloader to develop tons of pressure without the usual concern about press frame deflection. Huge frame opening will handle 50 x 3 1/4-inch Sharps with ease.

NO. 700 PRESS, complete $298.50
NO. 700K KIT, includes shell holder and
  one set of dies 336.00

METALLIC TURRET RELOADING PRESS MODEL 25000

Extremely rugged, ideal for production reloading. No need to move shell, just rotate turret head to positive alignment. Ram accepts any standard snap-in shell holder. Includes primer arm for seating both small and large primers.

NO. 25 PRESS, complete $298.50
NO. 25K KIT, includes press, shell holder, and one
  set of dies 336.00

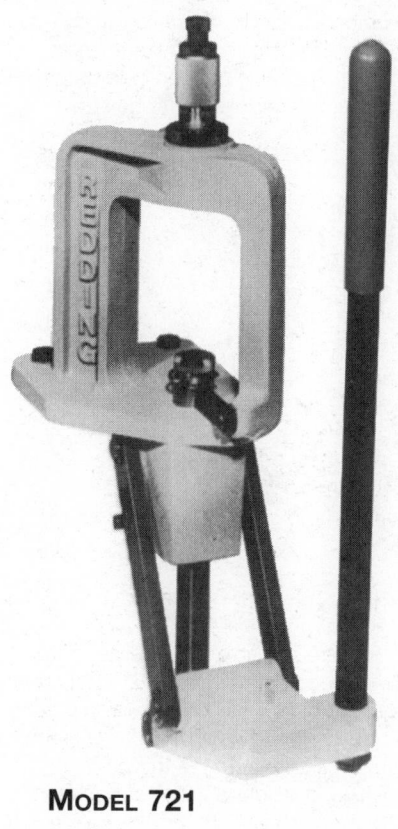

MODEL 721

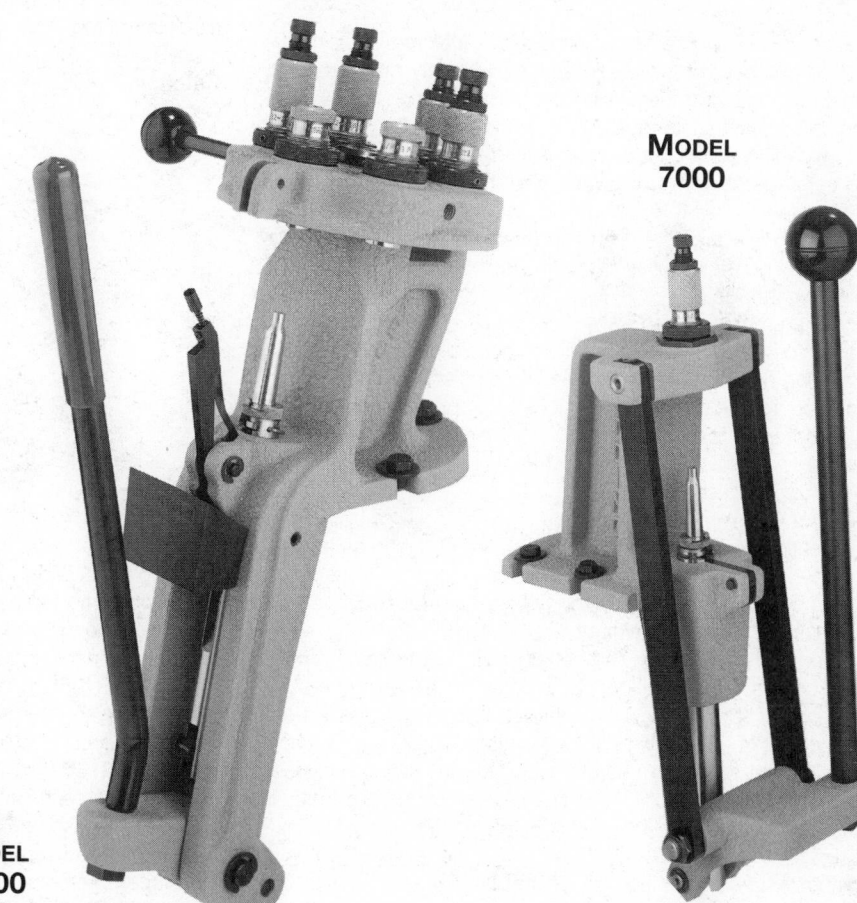

MODEL 7000

MODEL 25000

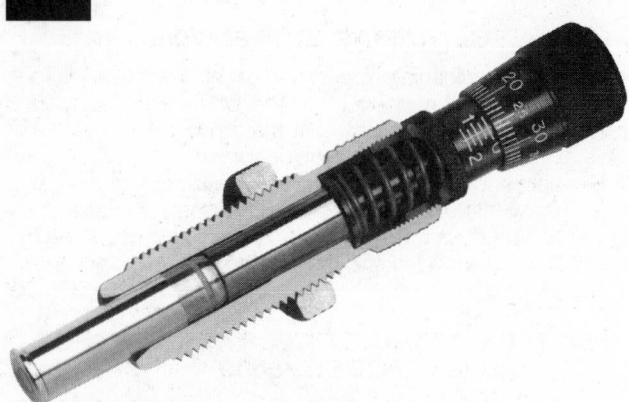

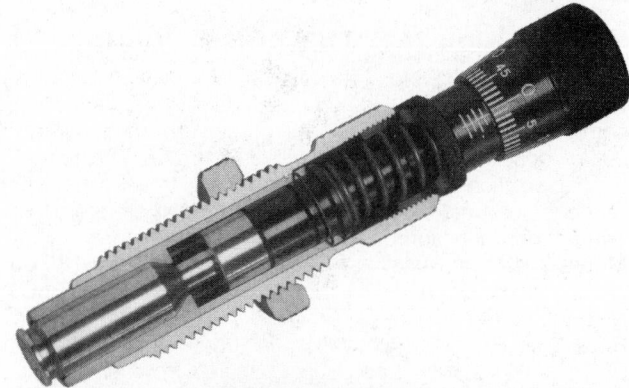

COMPETITION BULLET SEATING DIE FOR HANDGUN & STRAIGHT-WALL RIFLE CARTRIDGES

ADVANCED BULLET ALIGNMENT

Positive alignment between the bullet and cartridge case prior to bullet seating is essential to fine accuracy. Here is how this die works:

The precision fitting seating stem is allowed to move well down into the chamber of the die to accomplish early bullet contact. The spring loading of the seating stem provides the positive alignment bias between its tapered nose and the bullet ogive. Thus spring loading and bullet alignment are maintained as the bullet and cartridge case move upward until the actual seating of the bullet begins.

Redding's Advanced Bullet Alignment feature assures the straightest possible bullet alignment for handgun and straight-wall rifle cartridges.

MICROMETER ADJUSTMENT

The micrometer adjustment simplifies setting and recording bullet seating depth. By recording the micrometer setting of reloads can return to that same overall length by simply "dialing it in." The micrometer is calibrated in .001" increments, is infinitely adjustable and has a "zero" set feature that allows setting desired load to zero if desired.

SEPARATE CRIMP

Competition shooters generally prefer bullet crimping as a separate operation from bullet seating. A superior crimp will be acomplished by using a Redding "Profile Crimp" or "Taper Crimp" die.

PROGRESSIVE PRESS COMPATIBLE

The Competition Seating Die for straight-wall cartridges has been made compatible with all popular progressive reloading presses. The industry standard 7/8 x 14 threaded die bodies have been slightly extended to allow full thread engagement of the lock ring. An oversize bell-mouth chamfer with smooth radius has been added to the bottom of the die to ease case and bullet entry in progressive presses.

Price: $75.00
Competition bullet seating dies for bottleneck cases
   Category I 99.00
   Category II 120.00

COMPETITION BUSHING STYLE - NECK SIZING DIE

This die allows you to fit the neck of your case perfectly in the chamber. As in the Competition Seating Die, the cartridge case is completely supported and aligned with the sizing bushing and remains supported in the tightly chambered, sliding sleeve as it moves upward while the resizing bushing self-centers on the case neck. The micrometer adjustment of the bushing position delivers precise control to the desired amount of neck length to be sized. *All dies are supplied without bushings.*
Category I $99.00
Category II 120.00

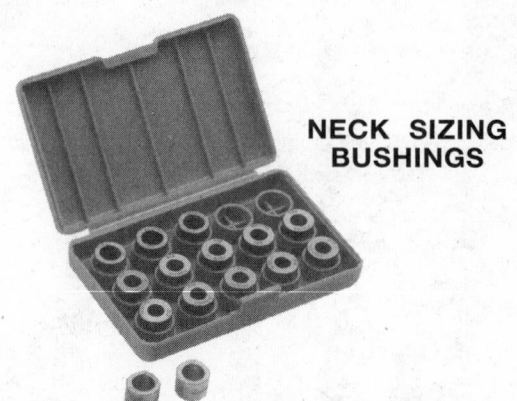

NECK SIZING BUSHINGS

Redding Neck Sizing Bushings are available in two styles. Both share the same external dimensions (1/2" O.D. x 3/8" long) and freely interchange in all Redding Bushing style Neck Sizing Dies. They are available in .001" size increments throughout the range of .185" thru .365", covering all calibers from .17 to .338.

By selecting the correct bushing, the right amount of neck tension is provided to properly hold the bullet.

Part No. 73185 thru 73365 . . . .$12.50
Heat treated steel. The sizing diameters are hand-polished with a surface hardness of Rc 60-62 to reduce sizing effort.

Part No. 76185 thru 76365 . . . . .19.50
Heat treated steel as above but with the addition of a *Titanium Nitride* surface treatment to further increase the effective surface hardness and reduce sizing friction.

MATCH-GRADE
POWDER MEASURE MODEL 3BR

Universal- or pistol-metering chambers interchange in seconds. Measures charges 100 grains. Unit is fitted with lock ring for fast dump with large "clear" plastic reservoir. "See-thru" drop tube accepts all calibers from 22 to 600. Precision-fitted rotating drum is critically honed to prevent powder escape. Knife-edged powder chamber shears coarse-grained powders with ease, ensuring accurate charges.

Prices:

MATCH GRADE 3BR measure $156.00
3BR KIT, with both Chambers 196.50
PISTOL METERING chamber (0-10 grains) 46.80

MASTER CASE TRIMMER MODEL 1400

This unit features a universal collet that accepts all rifle and pistol cases. The frame is cast iron with storage holes in the base for extra pilots. Coarse and fine adjustments are provided for case length.

- Six pilots (22, 6mm, 25, 270, 7mm and 30 cal.)
- Universal collet
- Two neck cleaning brushes (22 thru 30 cal.)
- Two primer pocket cleaners (large and small)
- Tin coated replaceable cutter
- Accessory power screwdriver adaptor

Prices:

No. 1400 MASTER CASE TRIMMER COMPLETE $93.00
No. 1500 PILOTS 3.90

COMPETITION MODEL BR-30
POWDER MEASURE (not shown)

This powder measure features a drum and micrometer that limit the overall charging range from a low of 10 grains to a maximum of approx. 50 grains. The diameter of Model 3BR's metering cavity has been reduced, and the metering plunger has a unique hemispherical shape, creating a powder cavity that resembles the bottom of a test tube. The result: irregular powder setting is alleviated and charge-to-charge uniformity is enhanced.

COMPETITION MODEL BR-30 POWDER MEASURE . . .$187.50

STANDARD POWDER
AND BULLET SCALE MODEL RS-1

For the beginner or veteran reloader. Only two counterpoises need to be moved to obtain the full capacity range of 1/10 grain to 380 grains.

MODEL NO. RS-1 . . . .$52.50

Also available:

MASTER POWDER & BULLET SCALE. Same as standard model, but includes a magnetic dampened beam swing for extra fast readings. 505-grain capacity $79.50

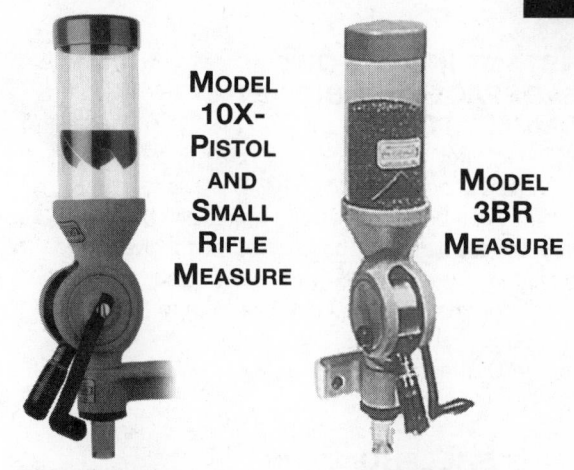

MODEL 10X-PISTOL AND SMALL RIFLE MEASURE

MODEL 3BR MEASURE

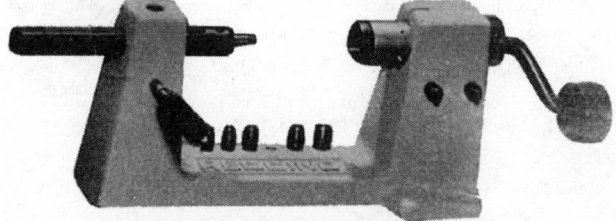

MODEL 1400 TRIMMER

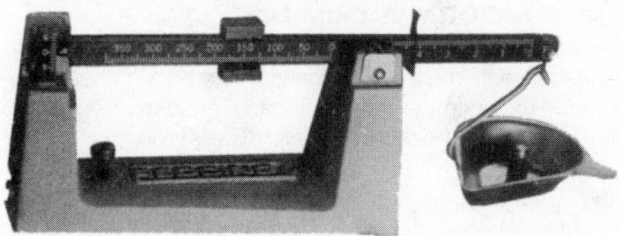

MODEL RS-1 SCALE

COMPETITION MODEL 10X-PISTOL AND
SMALL RIFLE POWDER MEASURE

This powder measure uses all of the special features of Competition Model BR-30 combined with new drum and metering unit designed to provide the most uniform metering of small charge weights. To achieve the best metering possible at the targeted charge weight of approximately 10 grains, the diameter of the metering cavity is reduced and the metering plunger is given a unique hemispherical shape. Charge range: 1 to 25 grains.

To provide increased versatility, the 10X-Pistol Powder Measure has a drum assembly that can be easily changed from right to left-handed operation. In addition to offering left-handed reloaders increased ease of operation, this feature adapts the 10X-Pistol Powder Measure to progressive reloading presses.

No. 03400 COMPETITION MODEL 10X-PISTOL
POWDER MEASURE $187.50

"INSTANT INDICATOR" HEADSPACE AND BULLET COMPARATOR

The Instant Indicator checks the headspace from the case shoulder to the base. Bullet seating depths can be compared and bullets can be sorted by checking the base of bullet to give dimension. Case length can be measured. Available for 28 cartridges from .222 Rem to .338 Win. Mag.

Price: w/Dial Indicator $99.00
  w/o Dial Indicator 69.00

SHELLHOLDERS

Redding shellholders are of a Universal "snap-in" design recommended for use with all Redding dies and presses, as well as all other popular brands. They are precision machined to very close tolerances and heat treated to fit cases and eliminate potential resizing problems. The outside knurling makes them easier to handle and change. For proper size, refer to die reference charts.

Price: $7.95

FORM & TRIM DIES

Redding trim dies file trim cases without unnecessary resizing because they are made to chamber dimensions. For case forming and necking brass down from another caliber, Redding trim dies can be the perfect intermediate step before full length resizing.

Prices:
Series A $27.00
Series B 36.00
Series C 42.00
Series D 49.50

NECK SIZING DIES

These dies size only the necks of bottleneck cases to prolong brass life and improve accuracy. These dies size only the neck and not the shoulder or body, fired cases should not be interchanged between rifles of the same caliber. Available individually or in Deluxe Die Sets.

Prices:
Series A $31.50
Series B 42.00
Series C 51.00
Series D 58.50

PISTOL TRIM DIES

Redding trim dies for pistol calibers allow trimming cases without excessive resizing. Pistol trim dies require extended shellholders.
Series A $27.00
Series B 36.00
Series C 42.00
Series D 49.50

PROFILE CRIMP DIES

For handgun cartridges which do not headspace on the case mouth. These dies were designed for those who want the best possible crimp. Profile crimp dies provide a tighter, more uniform roll type crimp, and require the bullet to be seated to the correct depth in a previous operation.
Series A $24.90
Series B 30.00
Series C 34.50
Series D 39.00

CARBIDE SIZE BUTTON KITS

Make inside neck sizing smoother and easier without lubrication. Now die sets can be upgraded with a carbide size button kit. Available for bottleneck cartridges 22 thru 338 cal. The carbide size button is free-floating on the decap rod allowing it to self-center in the case neck. Kits contain: carbide size button, retainer and spare decapping pin. These kits also fit all Type-S dies.

Price: $22.50

EXTENDED SHELL HOLDERS

Extended shellholders are required when trimming short cases under 1 1/2" O.A.L. They are machined to the same tolerances as standard shellholders except they're longer.
Price: $12.90

TAPER AND CRIMP DIES

Designed for handgun cartridges which headspace on the case mouth where conventional roll crimping is undesirable. Also available for some revolver cartridges, for those who prefer the uniformity of a taper crimp. Now available in the following *rifle* calibers: 223 Rem.. 7.62MM x 39, 30-30, 308 Win, 30-06, 300 Win Mag

Prices:
Series A $24.90
Series B 30.00
Series C 34.50
Series D 39.00

Reference

LEGENDARY SPORTING RIFLES
by Sam Fadala

Legendary Sporting rifles covers a vast span of time and
technology beginning with the Kentucky Longrifle—
the firearm of Colonial America—followed by other
early rifles such as the Plains Rifle, Hunt, Jennings and
Volcanic Rifles.

HOW TO BUY AND
SELL USED GUNS
by Gene Gangarosa Jr.

Gun control laws; how to make preliminary inspec-
tions; firearms identification; care and maintenance;
determining current market value and more.

AMERICA'S GREAT GUNMAKERS
by Wayne van Zwoll

This thoroughly illustrated book on arms making in
America mirrors the history of our nation. It details the
evolution of guns and ammunition in America and the
men who formed the companies that produced them.

The following manufacturers, suppliers and distributors of firearms, reloading equipment, sights, scopes, ammo and accessories all appear with their products in the "Specifications" and/or "Manufacturers' Showcase" sections of this edition of SHOOTER'S BIBLE.

ACCURATE ARMS CO., INC.
(gunpowder, reloading)
5891 Hwy. 230 W
McEwen, Tennessee 37101
Tel: 931-729-4207; 800-416-3006
Fax: 931-729-4211
Web Site: www.accuratepowder.com

AIMPOINT (sights, scopes, mounts)
7702 Leesburg Pike
Falls Church, Virginia 22043
Tel: 703-749-2320; 877-246-7646
Fax: 703-749-2323
Web Site: www.aimpoint.com
E-mail: sales@aimpoint.com

ALLIANT POWDER (gunpowder)
Route 114, P.O. Box 6 Bldg. 229
Radford, Virginia 24141-0096
Tel: 540-639-7805; 800-276-9337
Fax: 540-639-8496
E-mail: peter_jackson@atk.com
Web site: www.alliant_powder.com

AMERICAN ARMS
(handguns, shotguns)
2604 N.E. Industrial Dr. #290
N. Kansas City, Missouri 64117
Tel: 816-474-3161 Fax: 816-474-1225
Web site: www.americanarms.com

AMERICAN DERRINGER CORP.
(handguns)
127 North Lacy Drive
Waco, Texas 76705
Tel: 817-799-9111 Fax: 817-799-7935
Web site: www.amderringer.com

AMERICAN HUNTING RIFLES, INC.
(AHR rifles)
P.O. Box 300
Hamilton, MT 59840
Tel: 406-961-1410

AMERICAN SECURITY PRODUCTS
(AMSEC) (safes)
11925 Pacific Avenue
Fontana, California 92337
Tel: 800-423-1881 Fax: 909-681-9056
(see p. 76 in Manufacturer's Showcase)

AMT/GALENA INDUSTRIES
(AMT handguns, rifles)
3551 Mayer Ave.
Sturgis, South Dakota 57785
Tel: 605-423-4105

A.G. ANSCHUTZ GmbH
(rifles, pistols)
Postfach 1128
D-89001 Ulm, Germany
Tel: (001) 731-40120
Fax: (001) 731-4012700
E-mail: JGAinfo@anschuetz-sport.com

AO SIGHT SYSTEMS
(formerly Ashley Outdoors)
2401 Ludelle St.
Forth Worth, Texas 76105
Tel: 817-536-0136; 888-744-4880
Fax: 800-734-7939
Web site: www.aosights.com
(see also p. 78 in Manufacturer's Showcase)

ARMES DE CHASSE
(Francotte rifles, shotguns)
P.O. Box 86
Hertford, North Carolina 27944
Tel: 919-426-2245 Fax: 919-426-1557

ARMSPORT, INC.
(Bernardelli handguns, shotguns)
P.O. Box 523066
Miami, Florida 33152-3066
Tel: 305-635-7850 Fax: 305-633-2877

ARNOLD ARMS (rifles)
P.O. Box 1011
Arlington, Washington 98223
Tel: 800-371-1011 Fax: 360-435-7304
Web site: www.arnoldarms.com

ASHLEY OUTDOORS
(See AO Sight Systems)

AUSTIN & HALLECK
(blackpowder rifles)
1099 Welt
Weston, Missouri 64098
Tel: 816-386-2176 Fax: 816-386-2177

AUTO-ORDNANCE CORP.
(handguns, rifles)
Williams Lane
West Hurley, New York 12491
Tel: 914-679-7225 Fax: 914-679-2698

AYA (shotguns)
Available through New England Custom
Gun Service

BARNES BULLETS
P.O. Box 215
750 N. 2600 W.
American Fork, Utah 84003
Lindon, Utah 84042
Tel: 385-756-4222; 800-574-9200
Fax: 385-756-2465
E-mail: email@barnesbullets.com
Web site: www.barnesbullets.com

BENELLI U.S.A. CORP.
(shotguns)
17603 Indian Head Hwy
Accokeek, Maryland 20607-2501
Tel: 301-283-6981 Fax: 301-283-6988
Web site: www.benelliusa.com
E-mail benusa1@aol.com

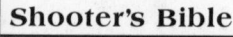

BERETTA U.S.A. CORP.
(handguns, rifles, shotguns)
17601 Beretta Drive
Accokeek, Maryland 20607
Tel: 301-283-2191 Fax: 301-283-0189
Web site: www.berettausa.com
E-mail: cwilliams@berettausa.com

BERGER BULLETS, LTD.
5342 West Camelback,Suite 200
Glendale, AZ 85301
Tel: 602-842-4001 Fax: 602-934-9083
Web site: www.bergerbullets.com

BERNARDELLI
(handguns, shotguns)
Available through Armsport

BERSA (handguns)
Available through Eagle Imports Inc.

ROGER BIESEN (custom guns)
w. 5021 Rosewood
Spokane, Washington 92008
Tel: 509-328-9340

BLACK HILLS AMMUNITION
P.O. Box 3090
3050 Eglin
Rapid City, South Dakota 57709
Tel: 605-348-5150 Fax: 605-348-9827
Web site www.black-hills.com
E-mail: black-hills.com

BLASER USA, INC. (rifles)
Available through Sig Arms

BLUE BOOK PUBLICATIONS, INC.
(books)
8009 34th Ave. South, Suite 175
Minneapolis, Minnesota 55425
Tel: 952-854-5229; 800-877-4867
Fax: 952-853-1486
Web site: www.bluebookinc.com
E-mail: bluebook@bluebookinc.com
(see P. 79 in Manufacturer's Showcase)

BONANZA (reloading tools)
See Forster Products

BOND ARMS INC. (handguns)
204 Alpha Lane
P.O. Box 1296
Granbury, Texas 76048
Tel: 817-573-4445 Fax: 817-573-5636
(see p. 77 in Manufacturers' Showcase)

KENT BOWERLY (custom guns)
710 Golden Pheasant Drive
Redmond, Oregon 97756
Tel: 541-923-3501

BRENNEKE OF AMERICA LTD.
(Rottweil ammunition)
81 Eades Drive
Irvine, Kentucky 40336-9463
Tel: 606-723-1045 Fax: 606-723-3253

ED BROWN PRODUCTS, INC.
(custom gunmaker)
43825 Muldrow Trail
Perry, Missouri 63462
Tel: 573-565-3261 Fax: 573-565-2791
Web site: www.edbrown.com

BROWNING (handguns, rifles,
shotguns, blackpowder guns)
One Browning Place
Morgan, Utah 84050
Tel: 801-876-2711 Fax: 801-876-3331
Web site: www.browning.com

BROWN PRECISION, INC.
(custom rifles)
7786 Molinos Avenue P.O. Box 270 W.
Los Molinos, California 96055
Tel: 530-384-2506 Fax: 530-384-1638

BSA OPTICS, INC.
3911 SW 47th Ave., Ste 914
Ft. Lauderdale, Florida 33314
Tel: 954-581-2144 Fax: 954-581-3165
Web site: www.bsa.optic.com
E-mail: bsaoptic@bellsouth.net

BURRIS COMPANY, INC. (scopes)
331 East Eighth Street P.O. Box 1747
Greeley, Colorado 80631-9559
Tel: 970-356-1670; 888-228-7747
Fax: 970-356-8702
Web site: www.burrisoptics.com

BUSHNELL (scopes)
Performance Optics
9200 Cody
Overland Park, Kansas 66214
Tel: 913-752-3400 Fax: 913-752-3550
Web site: www.bushnell.com

CABELA'S INC. (blackpowder rifles)
812 13th Ave.
Sidney, Nebraska 69160
Tel: 308-254-5505 Fax: 308-254-6669

CCI/SPEER-BLOUNT, INC.
(ammunition, bullets)
2299 Snake Rive Ave., P.O. Box 856
Lewiston, Idaho 83501
Tel: 208-746-2351 Fax: 208-746-3904
Web site: www.cci-ammunition.com
www.speer-bullets.com

CHRISTENSEN ARMS (rifles)
192 E. 100 N.
Fayette, Utah 84630
Tel: 801-528-7199
Web site: www.christensenarms.com

CIMARRON FIREARMS CO.
(revolvers, rifles)
P.O. Box 906
105 Winding Oaks Rd.
Fredericksburg, Texas 78624
Tel: 830-997-9090 Fax: 830-997-0802
Web site: www.cimarron-firearms.com
E-mail: cimarron@fbg.net

JIM COFFIN (custom guns)
1224 NW Fernwood Circle
Corvallis, Oregon 97330-2909
Tel: 541-754-7662 Fax: 541-754-0255

REFERENCE

COLT BLACKPOWDER ARMS CO.
   (handguns)
110 8th street
Brooklyn, New York 11215
Tel: 718-499-4678 Fax: 718-768-8056

COLT'S MANUFACTURING CO., INC.
   (handguns, rifles)
P.O. Box 1868
Hartford, Connecticut 06144-1868
Tel: 800-962-COLT Fax: 860-244-1467
Web site: www.colt.com

CONNECTICUT SHOTGUN MFG. CO.
   (A.H. Fox shotguns)
35 Woodland Street, P.O. Box 1692
New Britain, Connecticut 06051-1692
Tel: 860-225-6581 Fax: 860-832-8707

COOPER FIREARMS
P.O. Box 114
Stevensville, Montana 59870
Tel: 406-777-5534
Web site: www.cooperfirearms.com

CVA (blackpowder arms)
5988 Peachtree Corners East
Norcross, Georgia 30071
Tel: 800-320-8767 Fax: 770-242-8546
Web site: www.cva.com
E-mail: sales@cva.com

CZ-USA (pistols, rifles)
P.O. Box 171073
Kansas City, Kansas 66117-0073
Tel: 913-321-1811; 800-955-4486
Fax: 913-321-2251
Web site: www.cz-usa.com
E-mail: cz-usa@qvl.net

DAKOTA ARMS (rifles, shotguns)
HC 55, Box 326
Sturgis, South Dakota 57785
Tel: 605-347-4686 Fax: 605-347-4459;
508-302-4784
Web site: www.dakotarms.com
E-mail: dakarms@sturgis.com

CHARLES DALY (pistols, shotguns)
Available through K.B.I., Inc.

DAVIS INDUSTRIES (handguns)
15150 Sierra Bonita Ln.
Chino, California 91710
Tel: 909-597-4726 Fax: 909-393-9771
Web site: www.davisindguns.com

DESERT EAGLE (handguns)
Available through Magnum Research Inc.

DESERT MOUNTAIN MFG. (rifle rests)
44950 Elk Mountain Rd.
Banks, Oregon 97106
Tel: 800-477-0762 Fax: 406-387-5361
Web site: www.bench-master.com
(see p. 79 in Manufacturers' Showcase)

DGS, INC. (Dale A. Storey custom guns)
1117 E. 12th Street
Casper, Wyoming 82601
Tel: 307-237-2414

DILLON PRECISION PRODUCTS
(reloading equipment)
8009 East Dillon's Way
Scottsdale, Arizona 85260-1809
Tel: 800-223-4570; 602-948-8009
Fax: 602-998-2786
Web site: www.dillonprecision.com

DIXIE GUN WORKS
   (blackpowder guns)
Gunpowder Lane, P.O. Box 130
Union City, Tennessee 38281
Tel: 901-885-0561; 800-238-6785
Fax: 901-885-0440
Web site: www.dixiegunworks.com
E-mail: dixieguns@iswt.com

DOCTER OPTIC
B.C. Outdoors
P.O. box 61497
Boulder City, Nevada 89006
Tel: 702-294-3056

DOWNSIZER CORPORATION
   (handguns)
P.O. Box 710316
Santee, California 92072-0316
Tel: 619-448-5510 Fax: 619-448-5780
Web site: www.downsizer.com

DYNAMIT NOBEL/RWS
   (Rottweil shotguns and ammunition)
81 Ruckman Road
Closter, New Jersey 07624
Tel: 201-767-1995 Fax: 201-767-1589

EAGLE IMPORTS, INC.
   (Bersa handguns)
1750 Brielle Avenue, Unit 1B
Asbury Park, New Jersey 07712-3953
Tel: 732-493-0333 Fax: 732-493-0301

D'ARCY ECHOLS (custom rifles)
98 West 300 South, P.O. Box 421
Millville, Utah 84326
Tel: 435-755-6842

E.M.F. COMPANY, INC.
   (Dakota handguns; Uberti handguns,
   blackpower arms, rifles)
1900 East Warner Avnue 1-D
Santa Ana, California 92705
Tel: 714-261-6611
Fax: 714-756-0133
Web site: www.emf-company.com

ENTRÉPRISE ARMS (handguns)
15861 Busines Center Drive
Irwindale, California 91706-2062
Tel: 626-962-8712
Fax: 626-962-4692
Web site: www.entreprise.com

EUROARMS OF AMERICA INC.
(blackpowder arms)
P.O. Box 3277
Winchester, Virginia 22604
Tel: 540-662-1863

EUROPEAN AMERICAN ARMORY CORP. (E.A.A. handguns, rifles)
P.O. Box 1299
Sharpes, Florida 32959
Tel: 800-536-4442 Tel: 321-639-4942
Fax: 321-639-7006
Web site: www.eaacorp.com

FABARMS (shotguns)
Available through Heckler & Koch

FEDERAL CARTRIDGE CO.
(ammunition, ballistics)
900 Ehlen Drive
Anoka, Minnesota 55303-7503
Tel: 800-322-2342; 763-323-2300
Fax: 763-323-2506
Web site: www.federalcartridge.com

FIOCCHI U.S.A. (ammunition)
5030 Fremont Rd.
Ozark, Missouri 65721
Tel: 800-721-AMMO; 417-725-4118
Fax: 417-725-1039
Web Site: www.fiocchiusa.com

FLINTLOCKS, ETC.
(Pedersoli replica rifles)
160 Rossiter Road, P.O. Box 181
Richmond, Massachusetts 01254
Tel: 413-698-3822 Fax: 1-888-GUNCLIP
Web site: www.GUNMAGS.com

FORREST INC. (magazines)
P.O. Box 326
Lakeside, California 92040
Tel: 619-561-5800 Fax: 888-GUNCLIP
Web site: www.GUNCLIP.COM
(see p. 77 in Manufacturers' Showcase)

FORSTER PRODUCTS (reloading)
310 East Lanark Avenue
Lanark, Illinois 61046
Tel: 815-493-6360 Fax: 815-493-2371
Web site: forsterproducts.com
E-mail: infor@forsterproducts.com

A.H. FOX (shotguns)
Available through Connecticut Shotgun
Mfg. Co.

FRANCHI (shotguns)
Available through Beretta

FRANCOTTE (rifles)
Available through Armes de Chasse

FREEDOM ARMS (handguns)
314 Hyw. 239, P.O. Box 150
Freedom, Wyoming 83120-0150
Tel: 307-883-2468 Fax: 307-883-2005
Web site: www.freedomarms.com
E-mail: freedom@freedomarms.com

GIBBS RIFLE COMPANY
211 Lawn Street
Martinsburg, West Virginia 25401
Tel: 304-262-1651 Fax: 304-262-1658
E-mail: support@gibbsrifle.com

GLASER SAFETY SLUG, INC.
(ammunition, gun accessories)
P.O. Box 8223
Foster City, California 94404
Tel: 800-221-3489 Fax: 510-785-6685
(see p. 78 in Manufacturers' Showcase)

GLOCK, INC. (pistols)
6000 Highland Parkway
Smyrna, Georgia 30082
Tel: 770-432-1202 Fax: 770-433-8719

GONIC ARMS (blackpowder rifles)
134 Flagg Road
Gonic, New Hampshire 03839
Tel: 603-332-8456 Fax: 603-332-8457
Web site: www.gonic.com

CHARLES GRACE
(custom gunmaker)
1305 Arizona Avenue
Trinidad, Colorado 81081

GRIZZLY INDUSTRIAL, INC.
3 locations:
Bellingham, Washington
Williamsport, Pennsylvania
Springfield, Missouri
Tel: 800-523-4777 Fax: 800-438-5901
Web site: www.grizzly.com
(see p. 76, 77, 78, 79, 80 in Manufacturers' Showcase)

GSI (GUN SOUTH INC.)
(Mauser rifles; Merkel shotguns;
Steyr-Mannlicher rifles)
7661 Commerce Lane, P.O. Box 129
Trussville, Alabama 35173
Tel: 800-821-3021; 205-655-8299
Fax: 205-655-7078
Web site: www.gsifirearms.com
E-mail: infor@gsifirearms.com

H&R 1871 INC. (Harrington &
Richardson/Wesson & Harrington
or New England Firearms)
60 Industrial Rowe
Gardner, Massachusetts 01440
Tel: 978-632-9393 Fax: 978-632-2300

H-S PRECISION (rifles, pistols)
1301 Turbine Drive
Rapid City, South Dakota 57703
Tel: 605-341-3006 Fax: 605-342-8964
Web site: www.hsprecision.com

HÄMMERLI U.S.A. (handguns)
19296 Oak Grove Circle
Groveland, California 95321
Tel: 209-962-5311 Fax: 209-962-5931

HARRIS ENGINEERING, INC.
(bipods)
999 Broadway
Barlow, Kentucky 42024
Tel: 270-334-3633 Fax: 270-334-3000
Web site: www.cyberteldabs.com/
harris/main/htm
(see p. 76 in Manufacturers' Showcase)

HARRINGTON & RICHARDSON
(handguns, rifles, shotguns) Available
through H&R 1871 Inc.

HECKLER & KOCH (handguns, rifles;
and Fabarms shotguns)
21480 Pacific Blvd.
Sterling, Virginia 20166
Tel: 703-450-1900 Fax: 703-450-8160
Web site: www.hecklerkoch-usa.com

HENRY REPEATING ARMS CO. (rifles)
110 8th Street
Brooklyn, New York 11215
Tel: 718-499-5600 Fax: 718-768-8056
Web site: www.henryrepeatingcom

DARWIN HENSLEY (custom rifles)
63133 E. Barlow Trail Rd.
Brightwood, Oregon 97011
Tel: 503-622-5411

HERITAGE MANUFACTURING
(handguns)
4600 NW 135 St.
Opa Locka, Florida 33054
Tel: 305-685-5966 Fax: 305-687-6721
Web site: www.heritagemfg.com

HI-POINT FIREARMS (handguns)
MKS Supply, Inc.
5990 Philadelphia Drive
Dayton, Ohio 45415
Tel/Fax: 937-275-4991
Web site: www.hi-pointfirearms.com

HIGH STANDARD MFG CO. (handguns)
10606 Hempstead Highway #116
Houston, Texas 77092
Tel: 713-462-4200 Fax: 713-686-9699
Web site: www.highstandard.com

HILL COUNTRY RIFLE INC.
5726 Morningside Dr.
New Braunfels, Texas 78132
Tel: 830-609-3139
Web site: www.hillcountryrifle.com

BOB HISSERICH (custom gunmaker)
StockWorks Rifles
1843 S. Los Alamos
Mesa, Arizona 85204
Tel: 480-545-2994- Fax: 480-507-7560
Web site: www.stockworks.net

HODGDON POWDER CO., INC.
(gunpowder)
6231 Robinson, P.O. Box 2932
Shawnee Mission, Kansas 66201
Tel: 913-362-9455 Fax: 913-362-1307
Web site: www.hodgdon.com
E-mail: info@hodgdon.com

PATRICK HOLEHAN (custom rifles)
5758 E. 34th St.
Tucson, Arizona 85711
Tel: 520-745-0622
E-mail: plholehan@juno.com

HORNADY MFG. CO.
(ammunition, reloading)
P.O. Box 1848; 3625 Old Potash Hwy.
Grand Island, Nebraska 68803
Tel: 308-382-1390 Fax: 308-382-5761
Web site: www.hornady.com

HOWA (rifles)
Available through Interarms

STEVEN DODD HUGHES (custom rifles)
P.O. Box 545
Livingston, Montana 59047
Tel: 406-222-9377

INTERARMS (imported handguns
and rifles)
10 Prince Street
Alexandria Virginia 22314
Tel: 703-548-1400 Fax: 703-549-7826

ISRAEL ARMS INT'L, INC. (handguns)
5709 Hartsdale
Houston, Texas 77036
Tel: 713-789-0745 Fax: 713-789-7513

ITHACA GUN CO. (shotguns)
891 Route 34-B
Kings Ferry, New York 13081
Tel: 315-364-7171 Fax: 315-364-5134
Web site: www.ithacagun.com

JARRETT RIFLES INC.
(custom rifles)
383 Brown Road
Jackson, South Carolina 29831
Tel: 803-471-3616 Fax: 803-471-9246
Web site: www.jarrettrifles.com

JOHANNSEN (Express Rifle)
Available through New England
Custom Gun

KAHLES (scopes)
2 Slater Rd.
Cranston, Rhode Island 02920
Fax: 401-734-5888

KAHR ARMS (handguns)
630 Route 303
Blauvelt, New York 10913
Tel: 845-353-7770 Fax: 845-353-7833
Web site: www.kahr.com
E-mail: kahrhq@compuserve.com

K.B.I., INC. (rifles, handguns, shotguns;
Charles Daly rifles, shotguns; FEG
handguns)
P.O. box 6625
Harrisburg, Pennsylvania 17112-0625
Tel: 717-540-8518
Fax: 717-540-8567
Web site: www.kbi-inc.com or
www.charlesdaly.com
E-mail: sales @kbi-inc.com

KEL-TEC CNC IND. (handguns)
P.O. Box 3427
Cocoa, Florida 32924
Tel: 407-631-0068 Fax: 407-631-1169
Web site: www.kel-tec.com
E-mail: aimkeltec@aol.com

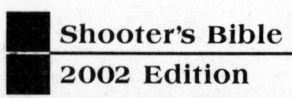

KIMBER MANUFACTURING, INC.
(handguns, rifles)
1 Lawton Street
Yonkers, New York 10705
Tel: 914-964-0771; 888-243-4522
E-mail: info@kimberamerica.com

KNIGHT RIFLES (blackpowder rifles)
P.O. Box 130, 21852 Hwy. J46
Centerville, Iowa 52544-0130
Tel: 515-856-2626 Fax: 515-856-2628
Web site: www.knightrifles.com
E-mail: knightrifles@lisco.net

KRIEGHOFF INTERNATIONAL INC.
(rifles, shotguns)
337A Route 611, P.O. Box 549
Ottsville, Pennsylvania 18942
Tel: 610-847-5173 Fax: 610-847-8691

KYNOCH AMMUNITION
Kynamco Limited - The Old Railway Station
Mildenhall, IP28 7DT England
Tel: +44 (0) 1638 711999
Fax: +44 (0) 1638 515251

L.A.R. MANUFACTURING, INC.
(Grizzly rifles)
4133 West Farm Rd.
West Jordan, Utah 84088-4997
Tel: 801-280-3505 Fax: 801-280-1972
Web site: www.largrizzly.com
E-mail: guns@largrizzly.com

LASERAIM TECHNOLOGIES INC.
(sights)
721 Main St., P.O. Box 3548
Little Rock, Arkansas 72203-3548
Tel: 501-375-2227 Fax: 501-372-1445

LAZZERONI ARMS CO. (rifles)
1415 South Cherry Ave.
Tucson, Arizona 85713
Tel: 520-624-4250; 888-4WARBIRD
Fax: 520-624-4250
Web site: www.lazzeroni.com
E-mail arms@lazzeroni.com
(see also p. 80 in Manufacturers' Showcase)

LENARTZ MUZZLOADING
(blackpowder guns)
8001 Whitneyville Rd.
Alto, Michigan 49302

LEUPOLD & STEVENS, INC.
(scopes, mounts)
14400 N.W. Greenbriar Parkway,
P.O. Box 688
Beaverton, Oregon 97006
Tel: 503-646-9171
Fax: 503-526-1475
Web site: www.leupold.com

LLAMA (handguns)
Available through SGS Importers Int'l

LONE STAR RIFLE CO., INC.
11231 Rose Road
Conroe, Texas 77303
Tel: 409-856-3363
Web site: www.lonstarrifle.com

LYMAN PRODUCTS CORP.
(blackpowder guns, reloading tools)
475 Smith Street
Middletown, Connecticut 06457
Tel: 800-225-9626; 860-632-2020
Fax: 860-632-1699
Web site: www.lymanproducts.com
E-mail: lymansales@cshore.com

MAGNUM RESEARCH INC.
(handguns, rifles)
7110 University Avenue N.E.
Minneapolis, Minnesota 55432
Tel: 612-574-1868 Fax: 612-574-0109
Web site: www.magnumresearch.com

MAGTECH AMMUNITION CO., INC.
837 Boston Post Road, #12
Madison, CT 06443
Tel: 800-466-7191; 203-245-8983
Fax: 203-245-2883
E-mail: rfinemtek@aol.com

MARKESBERY MUZZLELOADERS, INC. (blackpowder guns)
7785 Foundation Drive, Suite 6
Florence, Kentucky 4142
Tel: 606-342-5553
Fax: 606-342-2380
Web site: www.markesbery.com

MARLIN FIREARMS COMPANY
(rifles, shotguns, blackpowder)
100 Kenna Drive, P.O. Box 248
North Haven, Connecticut 06473
Tel: 203-239-5621 Fax: 203-234-7991
Web site: www.marlinfirearms.com

MAROCCHI (Conquista shotguns)
Available through Precision Sales Int'l.

MEC INC. (reloading tools)
c/o Mayville Engineering Co.
715 South Street
Mayville, Wisconsin 53050
Tel: 800-797-4MEC; 920-387-4500
Fax: 920-387-5802
Web site: www.mecreloaders.com
E-mail: reloaders@mayvl.com

MERKEL (shotguns, rifles)
Available through GSI (Gun South Inc.)
Web site: www.gsifirearms.com

MIDWAY USA (reloading equipment)
5875 West Van Horn Tavery Rd.
Columbia, Missouri 65203
Tel: 573-445-6363
Fax: 800-992-8312
Web site: www.midwayusa.com

DAVID MILLER (custom rifles)
3131 E. Greenlee Rd.
Tucson, AZ 85716

M.O.A. CORP. (handguns)
2451 Old Camden Pike
Eaton, Ohio 45302
Tel: 937-456-3669 Fax: 937-456-9331

REFERENCE

O.F. MOSSBERG & SONS, INC.
(shotguns, rifles)
7 Grasso Avenue, P.O. Box 497
North Haven, Connecticut 06473
Tel: 203-230-5300
Fax: 203-230-5420
Web site: www.mossberg.com

MTM CASE-GARD CO.
(cases, reloading accessories)
P.O. Box 13117
Dayton, Ohio 45413
Tel: 937-890-7461 Fax: 937-890-1747
(see also p. 80 in Manufacturers' showcase)

NAVY ARMS COMPANY, INC.
(handguns, rifles, blackpowder guns)
689 Bergen Blvd
Ridgefield, New Jersey 07657-14999
Tel: 201-945-2500 Fax: 201-945-6859
Web site: www.navyarms.com

NEW ENGLAND ARMS CORP./FAIR TECHNI MEC (Rizzini shotguns)
6 Lawrence Lane, P.O. Box 278
Kittery Point, Maine 03905
Tel: 207-439-0593 Fax: 207-439-6726

NEW ENGLAND CUSTOM GUN LTD.
(Johannsen Rifle)
428 Willow Brook Rd.
Plainfield, NH 03781
Tel: 603-469-3450 Fax 603-469-3471

NEW ENGLAND FIREARMS CO. INC.
(handguns, rifles, shotguns)
60 Industrial Rowe
Gardner, Massachusetts 01440
Tel: 978-632-9393 Fax: 978-632-2300

NEW ULTRA LIGHT ARMS, LLC
1024 Grafton Road
Morgantown, West Virginia 26508
Tel: 304-292-0600 Fax: 304-292-9662

NIKON INC. (scopes)
1300 Walt Whitman Road
Melville, New York 11747-3064
Tel: 631-547-4200 Fax: 631-547-4040
Web site: www.nikonusa.com

NORTH AMERICAN ARMS
(handguns)
2150 South 950 East
Provo, Utah 84606-6285
Tel: 800-821-5783; 801-374-9990
Fax: 801-374-9998
Web site: www.naaminis.com

NOSLER BULLETS, INC. (bullets)
P.O. Box 671, 107 SW Columbia
Bend, Oregon 97709
Tel: 541-382-3921 Fax: 541-388-4667
Web site: www.nosler.com

OLIN/WINCHESTER (ammunition, primers, cases)
427 No. Shamrock St.
East Alton, Illinois 62024-1174
Tel: 618-258-3692 Fax: 618-258-3609
Web site: www.winchester.com

PARA-ORDNANCE (handguns)
980 Tapscott Road
Scarborough, Ontario, Canada M1X 1C3
Tel: 416-297-7855 Fax: 416-297-1289
Web site: www.paraord.com
E-mail: info@paraord.com

PEDERSOLI, DAVIDE (replica arms)
Available through Flintlocks Etc.
Web site: www.davide-pedersoli.com

PENTAX (scopes)
P.O. Box 6509 (80155)
35 Inverness Drive East
Englewood, Colorado 80112
Tel: 303-799-8000 Fax: 303-790-1131
Web site: www.pentax.com

PERAZZI U.S.A. (shotguns)
1207 S. Shamrock Ave.
Monrovia, California 91016-4244
Tel: 626-334-1234 Fax: 626-334-0344

PMC CARTRIDGES
Eldorado Cartridge Corp.
P.O. Box 62508, 12801 US Hwy #95 S.
Boulder City, Nevada 89005
Tel: 702-294-0025 Fax: 702-294-0121
Web site: www.pmcammo.com
E-mail: pmcecc@aol.com

PRAIRIE GUN WORKS (rifles)
1-761 Marion St.
Winnipeg, Manitoba, Canada R2J0K6
Tel: 204-231-2976 Fax: 204-231-8566
Web site: www.prairiegunworks.com

PRECISION SALES INTERNATIONAL
(Marocchi shotguns)
P.O. Box 1776
Westfield, Massachusetts 01086
Tel: 413-562-5055 Fax: 413-562-5056
Web site: www.precision-sales.com

JAMES PURDEY & SONS (shotguns)
844 Madison Ave.
New York, New York 10021
Tel: 212-639-1500 Fax: 212-452-9675

J.C. RACK SYSTEMS
Available through Versatile Rack Co.

RAMSHOT PROPELLANT (gunpowder)
Western Powders, P.O. Box 158
Miles City, Montana 59301
Tel: 406-232-0422 Fax: 406-232-0430
Web site: www.westernpowders.com

RCBS-BLOUNT, INC.
(reloading equipment)
605 Oro Dam Blvd.
Oroville, California 95965
Tel: 916-533-5191 Fax: 916-533-1647
Web site: www.rcbs.com

REFERENCE

REDDING RELOADING EQUIPMENT
(reloading tools)
1089 Starr Road
Cortland, New York 13045
Tel: 607-753-3331 Fax: 607-756-8445
Web site: www.redding-reloading.com
E-mail: techline@redding-reloading.com

REDFIELD-BLOUNT, INC. (scopes)
P.O. Box 38
Onalaska, Wisconsin 54650
Tel: 608-781-5800
Fax: 608-781-0368
Web site: www.redfieldoptics.com

GARY REEDER CUSTOM GUNS
2710 N. Steves Blvd.
Flagstaff, Arizona 86044, Suite 22
Tel: 520-526-3313 Fax: 520-526-1287
Web site: www.reedercustomguns.com
(see p. 78, 80 in Manufacturers' Showcase)

REMINGTON ARMS COMPANY,
INC. (rifles, shotguns, blackpowder
arms, ammunition)
870 Remington Drive, P.O. Box 700
Madison, North Carolina 27025-0700
Tel: 800-243-9700 Fax: 336-548-7741
Web site: www.remington.com

RIFLES, INC. (rifles)
873 West 5400 North
Cedar City, Utah 84720
Tel: 435-586-5995 Fax: 435-586-5996

RIZZINI (shotguns)
Available through New England Arms
Web site: www.rizzini.it

ROSSI FIREARMS (handguns,
rifles, shotguns)
16175 NW 49th Ave.
Miami,Florida 33014
Tel: 305-624-1115 Fax: 305-623-7506

ROTTWEIL BRENNEKE (see Brenneke)

RUGER (handguns, rifles, shotguns,
blackpowder guns)
See Sturm, Ruger & Co., Inc.

RWS
Available through Dynamit Nobel

SAFARI ARMS (handguns)
c/o Olympic Arms, Inc.
620-626 Old Pacific Hwy SE
Olympia, Washington 98513
Tel: 360-459-7940 Fax: 360-491-3447
Web site: www.olyarms.com

SAKO (rifles, actions, scope mounts, ammo)
Available through Stoeger
Industries/Beretta U.S.A. Corp.

SAUER (rifles)
c/o Paul Company, Inc.
27385 Pressonville Road
Wellsville, Kansas 66092
Tel: 913-883-4444 Fax: 913-883-1515

SAVAGE ARMS (handguns, rifles,
shotguns)
100 Springdale Road
Westfield, Massachusetts 01085
Tel: 413-568-7001 Fax: 413-562-7764
Web site: www.savagearms.com

SCHMIDT AND BENDER INC. (scopes)
Schmidt & Bender U.S.A.
P.O. Box 134
Meriden, New Hampshire 03770
Tel: 800-468-3450 Fax: 603-469-3471
Web site: www.schmidt-bender.de

ANTHONY SCHUELKE (custom guns)
1606 N. Baxter Ave.
Glencoe, Minnesota 55336
Tel: 320-864-3905

SGS IMPORTERS INTERNATIONAL
INC. (Llama handguns)
1750 Brielle Avenue, Unit B1
Wanamassa, New Jersey 07712
Tel: 732-493-0302
Fax: 732-493-0301
E-mail: sgsparts@aol.com
Web site www.firestorm-sgs.com

SIERRA BULLETS (bullets)
P.O. Box 818
1400 West Henry Steet
Sedalia, Missouri 65301
Tel: 888-223-3006; 660-827-6300
Fax: 660-827-4999
Web site: www.sierrabullets.com
E-mail: sierra@sierrabullets.com

SIG ARMS INC. (Sig-Sauer shotguns,
handguns, Blaser rifles)
Corporate Park
Exeter, New Hampshire 03833
Tel: 603-772-2302 Fax: 603-772-1481
Web site: www.sigarms.com

SIGHTRON, INC.
(scopes, binoculars)
1672B Highway 96
Franklin, North Carolina 17525
Tel: 919-528-8783
Fax: 919-528-0995

GENE SIMILLION (custom guns)
220 S. Wisconsin'
Gunnison, Colorado 81230
Tel: 970-641-1126

SIMMONS-BLOUNT, INC. (scopes,
sporting equipments)
201 Plantation Oak Drive
Thomasville, GA 31792
Tel: 912-227-9053 Fax: 912-227-9054
Web site: www.simmonsoptics.com

SISK RIFLES (cusom rifles)
Charlie Sisk
16607 Port O'Call
Crosby, Texas 77532
Tel: 281-328-5458

SKB SHOTGUNS (shotguns)
4325 S. 120th Street
Omaha, Nebraska 68137-1253
Tel: 800-752-2767
Fax: 402-330-8040
Web site: www.skbshotguns.com
E-mail: SKB@radiks.net

SMITH & WESSON (handguns)
2100 Roosevelt Avenue, P.O. Box 2208
Springfield, Massachusetts 01104-1698
Tel: 413-781-8300; 800-331-0852
Fax: 413-747-3317
Web site: www.smith-wesson.com

SPEER (bullets)
Available through CCI/Speer-Blount, Inc.

SPRINGFIELD INC. (handguns, rifles,
  Aimpoint scopes, & sights)
420 West Main Street
Geneseo, Illinois 61254
Tel: 800-680-6866; 309-944-5631
Fax: 309-944-3676
Web site: www.springfield-armory.com

STEYR-MANNLICHER (rifles)
Available through GSI (Gun South Inc.)
Web site: www.gsifirearms.com

STOEGER INDUSTRIES (shotguns;
  Sako ammo, bullets, actions, mounts,
  rifles; Tikka rifles)
1760 Indian Head Hwy.
Accokeek, Maryland 20607
Tel: 301-283-6300
Fax: 301-283-6586
Web site: jtroiani@stoegerindustries.com

DALE STOREY (custom gunmaker)
  (See DGS, Inc.)

MARK STRATTON (custom gunmaker)
13704 Beverly Park Rd.
Lynnwood, Washington 98037
Tel: 425-745-8309
Web Site: www.gunmaker.net
E-mail: octbarrel@aol.com

STURM, RUGER AND COMPANY, INC.
  (Ruger handguns, rifles, shotguns,
  blackpower, revolvers)
200 Ruger Road
Prescott, Arizona 86301
Tel: 520-541-8820 Fax: 520-541-8850
Web site: www.ruger-firearms.com

**SWAROVSKI OPTIK NORTH
  AMERICA** (scopes)
2 Slater Road
Cranston, Rhode Island 02920
Tel: 800-426-3089; 401-734-1800
Fax: 401-734-5888; 877-287-8517
Web site: www.swarovskioptik.com

SWIFT BULLET CO. (bullets)
201 Main Street
P.O. Box 27
Quinter, Kansas 67752
Tel: 785-754-3959 Fax: 785-754-2359

SWIFT INSTRUMENTS, INC.
  (scopes, mounts)
952 Dorchester Avenue
Boston, Massachusetts 02125
Tel: 800-446-1116 Fax: 617-436-3232
Web site: www.swift-optics.com

SZECSEI & FUCHS (custom rifles)
450 Charles Street
Windsor, Ontario
N8X 371 Canada
Tel: 001 519 966 1234

TASCO WORLDWIDE, INC.
  (scopes, mounts)
2889 Commerce Parkway
Miramar, Florida 33025
Tel: 800-368-2726; 954-252-3600
Fax: 954-252-3705
Web site: www.tascosales.com
E-mail: dduquesne@tascosales.com

TAURUS INT'L, INC. (handguns)
16175 N.W. 49th Avenue
Miami, Florida 33014-6314
Tel: 800-327-3776; 305-624-1115
Fax: 305-623-7506
Web site: www.taurususa.com

TAYLOR'S & CO. INC.
  (rifles, carbines)
304 Lenoir Drive
Winchester, Virginia 22603
Tel: 540-722-2017
Fax: 540-722-2018
Web site: www.taylorsfirearms.com
E-mail: info@taylorsfirearms.com

THOMPSON & CAMPBELL
  (custom rifles)
  Cromarty – The Black Isle
Ross-Shire IV11 8YB Scotland
Tel: +44 (0) 1381 600 536
Fax: +44 (0) 1381 600 767

THOMPSON/CENTER ARMS
  (handguns, rifles, reloading,
  blackpowder arms)
Farmington Road, P.O. Box 5002
Rochester, New Hampshire 03867
Tel: 603-332-2394
Fax: 603-332-5133
Web site: www.tcarms.com

TIKKA (rifles, shotguns))
Available through Stoeger
Industries/Beretta U.S.A.

TRADITIONS PERFORMANCE FIREARMS (blackpowder arms)
1375 Boston Post Road
P.O. Box 776
Old Saybrook, Connecticut 06475-0776
Tel: 860-388-4656 Fax: 860-388-4657
Web site: www.traditionfirearms.com
E-mail: info@traditionsfirearms.com

TRIJICON (rifle scopes)
49385 Shafer Ave. P.O. Box 930059
Wixom, Michigan 48393
Tel: 248-960-7700; 800-338-0563
Fax: 248-960-7725
Web site: www.trijikon-inc.com

TRIUS PRODUCTS, INC.
(traps, targets)
221 South Miami Avenue, P.O. Box 25
Cleves, Ohio 45002
Tel: 513-941-5682 Fax: 513-941-7970
(see p. 77 in Manufacturers' Showcase)

UBERTI USA, INC. (handguns, rifles, blackpowder guns) See also American Arms, EMF, Navy Arms
362 Limerock Rd., P.O. Box 509
Lakeville, Connecticut 06039
Tel: 860-435-8068

U.S. REPEATING ARMS CO.
(Winchester rifles, shotguns)
275 Winchester Ave.
Morgan, Utah 84050-9326
Tel: 801-876-3440 Fax: 801-876-3737
Web site: www.winchesterguns.com

VERSATILE RACK CO.
5761 Anderson Street
Vernon, California 90058
Tel: 323-588-0137 Fax: 323-588-5067
Web site: www.versatilegunrack.com
E-mail: versatile@earthlink.net
(see p. 76 in Manufacturer'Showcase)

VOLQUARTSEN CUSTOM, LTD.
(pistols, rifles)
24276 240th Street
Carroll, Iowa 51401-8537
Tel: 712-792-4238 Fax: 712-792-2542
Web site: www.volquartsen.com
E-mail: vcl@netins.com
(see p. 79 in Manufacturers' Showcase)

WALTHER U.S.A. (handguns)
2100 Roosevelt Ave.
Springfield, Massachusetts 01104
Tel: 800-372-6454 Fax: 413-747-3592
Web site: www.walther-usa.com

WEATHERBY, INC. (rifles, shotguns, ammunition)
3100 El Camino Real
Atascadero, California 93422
Tel: 800-227-2016; 805-466-1767
Fax: 805-466-2527
Web Site: www.weatherby.com

WEAVER-BLOUNT, INC. (scopes)
201 Plantation Oak Drive
Thomasville, Georgia 31792
Tel: 912-227-9053 Fax: 912-227-9054
Wev site: www.weaveroptics.com

WICHITA ARMS (handguns)
P.O. Box 11371, 923 E. Gilbert
Wichita, Kansas 67211
Tel: 316-265-0661

WILDEY F.A. INC. (handguns)
Angevine Road
Warren, Connecticut 06754
Tel: 860-355-9000 Fax: 860-354-7759
Web site: www.wildeyguns.com

WILD WEST GUNS, INC. (Summit rifles)
7521 Old Seward Hwy., Unit A
Anchorage, Alaska 99518

Tel: 800-992-4570 Fax: 907-344-4005
Web site: www.wildwestguns.com
E-mail: wwguns@ak.net

WILLIAMS GUN SIGHT CO.
7389 Lapeer Road
P.O. Box 329
Davison, Michigan 48423
Tel: 800-530-9028; 810-653-2131
Fax: 810-658-2140
Web site: www.williamsgunsight.com

WINCHESTER (ammunition, primers, cases, ballistics)
Available through Olin/Winchester
Web site: www.winchester.com

WINCHESTER FIREARMS (rifles, shotguns)
Available through U.S. Repeating Arms Co.
Web site: www.winchester-guns.com

WOODLEIGH BULLETS
P.O. Box 15
Murrabit, Victoria, Australia
Tel: 011 61 3545 72266
Fax: 011 61 3545 72339
Web site: www.woodleigh-bullets.com.au
E-mail: zedfield@swanhill.net.au

ZEISS OPTICAL, INC. (scopes)
13017 N. Kingston Avenue
Chester, Virginia 23836
Tel: 804-530-5841
Web site: www.zeiss.com

Z-HAT CUSTOM DIES
(reloading)
4010A S. Poplar, Suite 72
Casper, Wyoming 82601
Tel: 307-577-7443
Web site: www.z-hat.com
E-mail: RifleBuilder@z-hat.com

REFERENCE

To help you find the model of your choice, the following index includes every firearm found in the *Shooter's Bible 2002*, listed by type of gun.

REFERENCE

THOMPSON/CENTER
Classic	196
Contender Carbines	196
Encore	196

RIMFIRE BOLT ACTION & SINGLE SHOT

ANSCHUTZ
Model 2013 Supermatch	97
Model 1907	98
Model 1808 "Running Target"	98
Model 1912 Sport	98
Model 54, 18 MSR Silhouette	99
Model 1827 "Fortner"	99
Model 1903	99
Model 1451	100
Model 1451R Sport Target	100
Model 2013 Benchrest	100

BLASER
Model K	95

CZ
Sniper	122

EUROPEAN AMERICAN ARMORY
HW660 Weihrauch Target	125

JARRETT
Rimfire Rifle	134

KBI/CHARLES DALY
Model CDGA Empire and Field Grades	136

KIMBER
Model 82C Series (Classic, SVT, Super-America, HS)	137

MARLIN
Model 81TS	144
Model 15YN "Little Buckaroo"	145
Models 25MN & 25N	144
Model 444P Outfitter	146
Model 922 Magnum	143
Model 2000L Target	149
Model 336 Series	146

REMINGTON
Models 40-XR	164

RUGER
77/22 Rimfire Series	171

SAKO
Finnfire (Scout, Hunter, Varmint)	176

SAVAGE
Mark I-G Single Shot	188
Model 93G Magnum, 93F Magnum, FVSS	187
Model 900TR	187
Mark II-FV Heavy Barrel, Mark II-FSS Mark II-LV	188

WINCHESTER
Model 52B	213

RIMFIRE LEVER ACTION

BROWNING
Model BL-22	110

HENRY REPEATING ARMS
Henry Rifle	129
U.S. Survival	129
Golden Boy	129

MARLIN
Golden 39AS	145
1897 Cowboy	145

WINCHESTER
Model 9422 Traditional	211
Model 9422, Legacy, Trapper	211

RIMFIRE SEMIAUTOMATIC & SLIDE ACTION

BROWNING
22 Semiauto Grades I & VI	110

BROWN PRECISION
Custom Team Challenger	114

HENRY
Pump Action .22	129

KBI/CHARLES DALY
Model CDGA Empire Grade	136
Model M-20P Standard	136

MARLIN
Models 60, 60SS	143
Models 7000	145
Model 70PSS "Papoose"	143

REMINGTON
Model 597 Series	165
Model 552 BDL Speedmaster	164
Model 572 BDL Fieldmaster	164

RUGER
Model 10/22 Series	167, 169

SPRINGFIELD
Model M-6 Scout Combo	189

THOMPSON/CENTER
Model T/C 22LR Classic	196

DOUBLE RIFLES, ACTIONS & DRILLINGS

BERETTA
Express Rifles (5506, 455)	104
Silver/Gold Sable II Over/Under	105

FRANCOTTE
Boxlocks/Sidelocks/Mountain	126

KRIEGHOFF
Classic Side-by-Side	138

MERKEL
Safari Double Rifles	149

PURDEY
Double Barrel Rifle .577 NITRO	157

SAKO
Actions	175

SZECSEI & FUCHS
Double Barrel Rifles	193

REPLICA RIFLES

CIMARRON FIREARMS
1885 High Wall	117
Billy Dixon 1874 Sharps Sporting Rifle	117
Quigley 1874 Sharps Sporting Rifle	117
Silhouette 1874 Sharps Sporting Rifle	117

EMF
1860 Henry	125
1866 Yellowboy Carbine/Rifle	125
1873 Sporting Rifle & Carbine	125

LONE STAR
Silhouette, Sporting, Cowboy Action	141

REFERENCE

REFERENCE

Four Ways NRA

You know all about what NRA does in the halls of Congress for gun owners. But did you know we also have 177 programs that serve gun owners on the shooting range, in the hunting fields and even in the defense of their homes and property? Four of our major programs are shown below; to find out more about these or any of the others, call (800) 672-3888, or log on to: www.nrahq.org.

1.

WOMEN ON TARGET
From the Women of the NRA™

Join *Women On Target™* and the women of the NRA at more than 100 ladies-only hunts, charity shoots, and instructional clinics nationwide this year.

Call **(800) 861-1166** for more information, or log on to **www.nrahq.org/ shooting/women**

2.

Personal Protection in the Home

If firearm ownership is part of your personal protection plan, *The Basics of Personal Protection in the Home,* available as a book or a video, will answer all your questions about using a handgun in a last-resort crisis. Topics cover everything from firearm selection and awareness levels to defensive shooting skills and legal issues. To order the book, cite item number ES 26828 ($19.95 plus shipping and tax if applicable); for the video, cite item number ES 26838 ($24.95 plus shipping and tax if applicable).

Call (800) 336-7402
and refer to offer # SHBIB001

Serves Gun Owners

National Police Shooting Championships

3.

Law enforcement and security officers must be proficient in a demanding and specialized form of shooting in order to protect and serve the public. Training for and competing in NRA's National Police Shooting Championships helps officers achieve the highest levels of skill and readiness possible to do their jobs.

www.nrahq.org/safety/law

N
R
A **NPSC**

40th Annual

1962   2001

NRA National Rifle and Pistol Matches

4.

The NRA National Matches at Camp Perry, Ohio, are one of the largest-participation athletic events in America. More than 4,200 shooters were there in 2001--the highest attendance since 1992. And entry-level shooters may compete alongside Olympic champions in this one-of-a-kind test of shooting skill.

www.nrahq.org/shooting/compete

Call toll free (800) 336-7402 to request a catalog

The NRA's Institute for Legislative Action (NRA-ILA), founded in 1975, is the lobbying arm of the NRA that works to defend the rights of law-abiding gun owners in Congress, state legislatures, and local government bodies across our great nation.

The NRA-ILA Grassroots Network is NRA-ILA's base of legislative and political volunteers working together to defend our Second Amendment rights. As a member of this _free_ program, you will receive:

NRA-ILA's _free_ weekly FAX Alert;

NRA-ILA's _free_ monthly political newsletter— "Freedom's Voice";

Invitations to NRA-ILA's _free_ Grassroots-Election Workshops and other meetings:

And much, much more!!!

To join NRA-ILA's _FREE_ Grassroots Network, call (800) 392-8683, and request an _NRA-ILA Volunteer Information Form_. Once we receive your completed form, you will enrolled in the Grassroots Network, and we can begin working together immediately to defend our freedom.

NRA-ILA Grassroots Division•11250 Waples Mill Road•Fairfax, VA 22030• (800) 392-8683•
Fax (703) 267-1172•www.NRAILA.org